THE DEATH OF THE MESSIAH

Volume Two

THE ANCHOR BIBLE REFERENCE LIBRARY is designed to be a third major component of the Anchor Bible group, which includes the Anchor Bible commentaries on the books of the Old Testament, the New Testament, and the Apocrypha, and the Anchor Bible Dictionary. While the Anchor Bible commentaries and the Anchor Bible Dictionary are structurally defined by their subject matter, the Anchor Bible Reference Library will serve as a supplement on the cutting edge of the most recent scholarship. The series is open-ended; its scope and reach are nothing less than the biblical world in its totality, and its methods and techniques the most up-to-date available or devisable. Separate volumes will deal with one or more of the following topics relating to the Bible: anthropology, archaeology, ecology, economy, geography, history, languages and literatures, philosophy, religion(s), theology.

As with the Anchor Bible commentaries and the Anchor Bible Dictionary, the philosophy underlying the Anchor Bible Reference Library finds expression in the following: the approach is scholarly, the perspective is balanced and fair-minded, the methods are scientific, and the goal is to inform and enlighten. Contributors are chosen on the basis of their scholarly skills and achievements, and they come from a variety of religious backgrounds and communities. The books in the Anchor Bible Reference Library are intended for the broadest possible readership, ranging from world-class scholars, whose qualifications match those of the authors, to general readers, who may not have special training or skill in studying the Bible but are as enthusiastic as any dedicated professional in expanding their knowledge of the Bible and its world.

David Noel Freedman
GENERAL EDITOR

THE ANCHOR BIBLE REFERENCE LIBRARY

THE DEATH

OF THE MESSIAH

From Gethsemane to the Grave

A COMMENTARY
ON THE PASSION NARRATIVES
IN THE FOUR GOSPELS

Volume Two

BY

Raymond E. Brown, S.S.

ABRL

Doubleday

NEW YORK   LONDON   TORONTO   SYDNEY   AUCKLAND

THE ANCHOR BIBLE REFERENCE LIBRARY
PUBLISHED BY DOUBLEDAY
a division of Bantam Doubleday Dell Publishing Group, Inc.
1540 Broadway, New York, New York 10036

THE ANCHOR BIBLE REFERENCE LIBRARY, DOUBLEDAY, and the portrayal
of an anchor with the letters ABRL are trademarks of Doubleday,
a division of Bantam Doubleday Dell Publishing Group, Inc.

The Library of Congress has cataloged
the Anchor Bible Reference Library hardcover edition as follows:
Brown, Raymond Edward.
The death of the Messiah : from Gethsemane to the grave : a commentary on the
Passion narratives in the four Gospels / Raymond E. Brown.—1st ed.
p. cm.—(The Anchor Bible reference library)
Includes bibliographical references and indexes.
1. Passion narratives (Gospels)   I. Title.   II. Series.
BS2555.3.B7633   1994
226'.07—dc20   93–9241
CIP

Nihil obstat
Myles M. Bourke, S.T.D., S.S.L.
Censor deputatus
Imprimatur
✠Patrick J. Sheridan, D.D.
Vicar General, Archdiocese of New York
April 30, 1993

The *nihil obstat* and *imprimatur* are official declarations that a book or pamphlet is free of doctrinal or moral error. No implication is contained therein that those who have granted the *nihil obstat* and *imprimatur* agree with the contents, opinions, or statements expressed.

ISBN 0-385-49449-1 (Volume 2)
ISBN 0-385-49448-3 (Volume 1)

CONTENTS OF VOLUME TWO

(Before each "Act" and "Scene" of the Commentary, a more detailed table will be given breaking the sections [marked by §] into subsections.)

COMMENTARY (in Four Acts)

ACT IV: JESUS IS CRUCIFIED AND DIES ON GOLGOTHA
HE IS BURIED NEARBY
(Mark 15:20b–47; Matt 27:31b–66; Luke 23:26–56; John 19:16b–42)

SCENE ONE: Jesus Is Crucified and Dies (Mark 15:20b–41;
Matt 27:31b–56; Luke 23:26–49; John 19:16b–37)

APPENDIXES

INDEXES

ILLUSTRATIVE TABLES

ABBREVIATIONS

AB	Anchor Bible
AER	*American Ecclesiastical Review*
AJBI	*Annual of the Japanese Biblical Institute*
AJEC	*Anti-Judaism in Early Christianity; Vol. 1: Paul and the Gospels,* ed. P. Richardson (Waterloo, Ont.: Canadian Corp. for Studies in Religion and Wilfred Laurier Univ., 1986)
AJINT	*Antijudaismus im Neuen Testament?* eds. W. P. Eckert et al. (Munich: Kaiser, 1967)
AJSL	*American Journal of Semitic Languages and Literature*
AJT	*American Journal of Theology*
AnBib	Analecta Biblica
AnGreg	Analecta Gregoriana
ANRW	Aufstieg und Niedergang der römischen Welt
Ant.	The *Antiquities* of Flavius Josephus
AP	*Apocrypha and Pseudepigrapha of the Old Testament,* ed. R. H. Charles (2 vols.; Oxford: Clarendon, 1913)
AsSeign	*Assemblées du Seigneur*
ASTI	*Annual of the Swedish Theological Institute*
ATANT	Abhandlungen zur Theologie des Alten und Neuen Testaments
ATR	*Anglican Theological Review*
A.U.C.	*anno urbis conditae* or *ab urbe condita* (a specified year from the founding of Rome)
AUSS	*Andrews University Seminary Studies*
BA	*Biblical Archaeologist*
BAA	M. Black, *An Aramaic Approach to the Gospels and Acts* (3d ed.; Oxford: Clarendon, 1967)
BAG	W. Bauer, W. F. Arndt, and F. W. Gingrich, *Greek-English Lexicon of the New Testament and Other Early Christian Literature* (Cambridge Univ., 1957)
BAGD	BAG revised by F. W. Danker (Univ. of Chicago, 1979)
BARev	*Biblical Archaeology Review*

BBM	R. E. Brown, *The Birth of the Messiah* (Garden City, NY: Doubleday, 1977; new ed., 1993)
BDF	F. Blass, A. Debrunner, and R. W. Funk, *A Greek Grammar of the New Testament* (Univ. of Chicago, 1961). Refs. to sections.
BEJ	R. E. Brown, *The Epistles of John* (AB 30; Garden City, NY: Doubleday, 1982)
BeO	*Bibbia e Oriente*
BETL	Bibliotheca Ephemeridum Theologicarum Lovaniensium
BExT	P. Benoit, *Exégèse et Théologie* (4 vols.; Paris: Cerf, 1961–82)
BGJ	R. E. Brown, *The Gospel According to John* (2 vols.; AB 29, 29A; Garden City, NY: Doubleday, 1966, 1970)
BHST	R. Bultmann, *History of the Synoptic Tradition* (New York: Harper & Row, 1963)
BibLeb	*Bibel und Leben*
BibLit	*Bibel und Liturgie*
BJG	P. Benoit, *Jesus and the Gospel* (2 vols.; New York: Herder, 1973)
BJRL	*Bulletin of the John Rylands Library of the University of Manchester*
BK	*Bibel und Kirche*
BR	*Biblical Research*
BS	Biblische Studien
BSac	*Bibliotheca Sacra*
BSSNT	K. Beyer, *Semitische Syntax im Neuen Testament* (Göttingen: Vandenhoeck & Ruprecht, 1962)
BT	*The Bible Translator*
BTB	*Biblical Theology Bulletin*
BU	Biblische Untersuchungen
BVC	*Bible et Vie Chrétienne*
BW	*Biblical World*
BWANT	Beiträge zur Wissenschaft vom Alten und Neuen Testament
ByF	*Biblia y Fe*
BZ	*Biblische Zeitschrift*
BZNW	Beihefte zur ZNW
CB	*Cultura Bíblica*
CBQ	*Catholic Biblical Quarterly*
CC	Corpus Christianorum (Series Latina)
CCat	*Civiltà Cattolica*
CCER	*Cahiers du Cercle Ernest Renan*

CD	Cairo (Genizah text of the) Damascus (Document)
CH	*Church History*
CKC	*Chronos, Kairos, Christos,* eds. J. Vardaman and E. M. Yamauchi (J. Finegan Festschrift; Winona Lake, IN: Eisenbrauns, 1989)
ColB	*Collationes Brugenses*
ConNT	*Coniectanea Neotestamentica*
CQR	*Church Quarterly Review*
CR	*Clergy Review*
CSA	*Chicago Studies* (Anniversary Volume) 25 (#1; 1986: Passion, Death, and Resurrection of Jesus)
CSEL	Corpus Scriptorum Ecclesiasticorum Latinorum
CT	*Christianity Today*
CTM	*Concordia Theological Monthly*
CTom	*Ciencia Tomista*
CurTM	*Currents in Theology and Mission*
DACL	*Dictionnaire d'Archéologie Chrétienne et de Liturgie*
DBG	M. Dibelius, *Botschaft und Geschichte* (2 vols.; Tübingen: Mohr, 1953, 1956)
DBS	H. Denzinger and C. Bannwart, *Enchiridion Symbolorum,* rev. by A. Schönmetzer (32d ed.; Freiburg: Herder, 1963). Refs. to sections.
DBSup	*Dictionnaire de la Bible, Supplément*
DJ	*The Digest of Justinian,* ed. T. Mommsen (4 vols.; Philadelphia: Univ. of Pennsylvania, 1985)
DJD	Discoveries in the Judaean Desert
DJS	A. Denaux, ed. *John and the Synoptics* (BETL 101; Leuven Univ., 1992). Analyzed by Denaux in ETL 67 (1991), 196–203.
DNTRJ	D. Daube, *The New Testament and Rabbinic Judaism* (London: Athlone, 1956)
DRev	*Downside Review*
DSNT	J.D.M. Derrett, *Studies in the New Testament* (4 vols.; Leiden: Brill, 1977–86)
DSS	The Dead Sea Scrolls
DSSW	G. Dalman, *Sacred Sites and Ways* (New York: Macmillan, 1935; German orig. 3d ed., 1924)
EBib	Études Bibliques
EH	Eusebius, *Ecclesiastical History*
EJMI	*Early Judaism and its Modern Interpreters,* eds. R. A. Kraft and G.W.E. Nickelsburg (Atlanta: Scholars, 1986)

EKKNT	Evangelisch-katholischer Kommentar zum Neuen Testament
EQ	*Evangelical Quarterly*
ErbAuf	*Erbe und Auftrage*
EspVie	*Esprit et Vie* (later *L'Ami du Clergé*)
EstBib	*Estudios Bíblicos*
EstEcl	*Estudios Eclesiásticos*
ETL	*Ephemerides Theologicae Lovanienses*
ETR	*Études Théologiques et Religieuses*
EvT	*Evangelische Theologie*
ExpTim	*Expository Times*
FANT	J. Finegan, *The Archaeology of the New Testament* (Princeton Univ., 1969)
FAWA	J. A. Fitzmyer, *A Wandering Aramean* (SBLMS 25; Missoula, MT: Scholars, 1979)
FB	Forschung zur Bibel
FESBNT	J. A. Fitzmyer, *Essays on the Semitic Background of the New Testament* (London: Chapman, 1971)
FGN	*The Four Gospels 1992,* eds. F. Van Segbroeck et al. (F. Neirynck Festschrift; BETL 100; 3 vols.; Leuven Univ., 1992)
FRLANT	Forschungen zur Religion und Literatur des Alten und Neuen Testaments
FTAG	J. A. Fitzmyer, *To Advance the Gospel* (New York: Crossroad, 1981)
FV	*Foi et Vie*
FZPT	*Freiburger Zeitschrift für Philosophie und Theologie*
GCS	Die Griechischen Christlichen Schriftsteller (Berlin)
GPet	*The Gospel of Peter* (see APPENDIX I)
GVMF	*Gottesverächter und Menschenfeinde? Juden zwischen Jesus und frühchristlicher Kirche,* ed. H. Goldstein (Düsseldorf: Patmos, 1979)
HeyJ	*Heythrop Journal*
HibJ	*Hibbert Journal*
HJPAJC	E. Schürer, *The History of the Jewish People in the Age of Jesus Christ* (rev. by G. Vermes et al.; 3 vols.; Edinburgh: Clark, 1973–87)
HPG	*The Holy Places of the Gospels* by C. Kopp (New York: Herder and Herder, 1963)
HSNTA	E. Hennecke and W. Schneemelcher, *New Testament Apocrypha*

	(2 vols.; Philadelphia: Westminster, 1963, 1965; rev. ed., vol. 1, 1991)
HTR	*Harvard Theological Review*
HUCA	*Hebrew Union College Annual*
IBS	*Irish Biblical Studies*
IEJ	*Israel Exploration Journal*
IER	*Irish Ecclesiastical Record*
ILS	*Inscriptiones Latinae Selectae,* ed. H. Dessau (3 vols.; Berlin: Weidmann, 1892–1916). Cited by inscription number.
ITQ	*Irish Theological Quarterly*
JAAR	*Journal of the American Academy of Religion*
JANT	M. R. James, *The Apocryphal New Testament* (2d ed.; Oxford: Clarendon, 1953)
JBap	John the Baptist
JBL	*Journal of Biblical Literature*
JBR	*Journal of Bible and Religion*
JE	*Jewish Encyclopedia*
JES	*Journal of Ecumenical Studies*
JETS	*Journal of the Evangelical Theological Society*
JEWJ	J. Jeremias, *The Eucharistic Words of Jesus* (2d ed.; New York: Scribners, 1966)
JJC	*Josephus, Judaism, and Christianity,* eds. L. H. Feldman and G. Hata (Leiden: Brill, 1987)
JJS	*Journal of Jewish Studies*
JJTJ	J. Jeremias, *Jerusalem in the Time of Jesus* (Philadelphia: Fortress, 1969)
JPFC	*The Jewish People in the First Century,* eds. S. Safrai and M. Stern (2 vols.; Philadelphia: Fortress, 1974)
JPHD	*Jesus and the Politics of His Day,* eds. E. Bammel and C.F.D. Moule (Cambridge Univ., 1984)
JQR	*Jewish Quarterly Review*
JRS	*Journal of Roman Studies*
JSJ	*Journal for the Study of Judaism in the Persian, Hellenistic and Roman Period*
JSNT	*Journal for the Study of the New Testament*
JSNTSup	Journal for the Study of the New Testament—Supplement Series
JTS	*Journal of Theological Studies*
KACG	H. Koester, *Ancient Christian Gospels* (Philadelphia: Trinity, 1990)

KBW   Katholisches Bibelwerk (Verlag, Stuttgart)

KJV   *King James Version* or *Authorized Version of the Bible*

KKS   W. H. Kelber, A. Kolenkow, and R. Scroggs, "Reflections on the
           Question: Was There a Pre-Markan Passion Narrative?" SBLSP
           (1971), 2.503–86.

Kyr   *Kyriakon,* eds. P. Granfield and J. A. Jungmann (J. Quasten Fest-
           schrift; 2 vols.; Münster: Aschendorff, 1970)

LB   *Linguistica Biblica*

LD   Lectio Divina

LFAE   *Light from the Ancient East* by A. Deissmann (rev. ed.; New York:
           Doran, 1927)

LKS   H. Lietzmann, *Kleine Schriften II* (TU 68; Berlin: Akademie,
           1958)

LS   *Louvain Studies*

LumVie   *Lumière et Vie*

LXX   (The) Septuagint Greek Translation of the OT

MACM   H. Musurillo, *The Acts of the Christian Martyrs* (Oxford:
           Clarendon, 1972)

MAPM   H. Musurillo, *The Acts of the Pagan Martyrs* (Oxford:
           Clarendon, 1954)

MGNTG   J. H. Moulton (and N. Turner), *Grammar of New Testament Greek*
           (4 vols.; Edinburgh: Clark, 1908–76)

MIBNTG   C.F.D. Moule, *An Idiom-Book of New Testament Greek* (Cam-
           bridge Univ., 1960)

MM   J. H. Moulton and G. Milligan, *The Vocabulary of the Greek New
           Testament Illustrated from the Papyri and Other Non-Literary
           Sources* (repr.; Grand Rapids: Eerdmans, 1963)

MNTS   *Die Mitte des Neuen Testaments,* eds. U. Luz and H. Weder
           (E. Schweizer Festschrift; Göttingen: Vandenhoeck & Ruprecht,
           1983)

ms., mss. manuscript(s)

MT   (The) Mas(s)oretic Text of the OT or standard Hebrew Bible

MTC   B. M. Metzger, *A Textual Commentary on the Greek New Testa-
           ment* (New York: United Bible Societies, 1971)

MTZ   *Münchener Theologische Zeitschrift*

NAB   *New American Bible* (1970; Revised NT 1986)

NDIEC   *New Documents Illustrating Early Christianity*

NEB   *New English Bible* (1961)

NEv   F. Neirynck, *Evangelica, Gospel Studies—Études d'Évangile* (2 vols.; Louvain: Peeters, 1982, 1991). Vol. 1 covers articles written in 1966–81; vol. 2, 1982–91.

NHL   *The Nag Hammadi Library,* ed. J. M. Robinson (3d ed.; New York: Harper & Row, 1988)

NICOT   New International Commentary on the Old Testament

NJBC   *New Jerome Biblical Commentary,* eds. R. E. Brown et al. (Englewood Cliffs, NJ: Prentice-Hall, 1990). Refs. to articles and sections.

NKZ   *Neue Kirchliche Zeitschrift*

NorTT   *Norsk Teologisk Tidsskrift*

NovT   *Novum Testamentum*

NovTSup   Novum Testamentum, Supplements

NRSV   *New Revised Standard Version of the Bible*

NRT   *Nouvelle Revue Théologique*

NS   new series (of a periodical)

NT   New Testament

NTA   *New Testament Abstracts*

NTAbh   Neutestamentliche Abhandlungen

NTS   *New Testament Studies*

NTT   *Nederlands Theologisch Tijdschrift*

OL   The Old Latin Version of the Bible

OS   The Old Syriac Version of the Bible

OS^cur   The Curetonian tradition of the OS

OS^sin   The Sinaitic tradition of the OS

OT   Old Testament

OTP   *The Old Testament Pseudepigrapha,* ed. J. H. Charlesworth (2 vols.; Garden City, NY: Doubleday, 1983–85)

par.   parallel(s) in one or both of the other Synoptic Gospels to the passage cited

PBI   The Pontifical Biblical Institute (Rome)

PEFQS   *Palestine Exploration Fund, Quarterly Statement*

PEQ   *Palestine Exploration Quarterly*

PG   Patrologia Graeca-Latina (Migne)

PGJK   *Der Prozess gegen Jesus,* ed. K. Kertelge (QD 112; Freiburg: Herder, 1988)

PIBA   Proceedings of the Irish Biblical Association

PILA   *Political Issues in Luke-Acts,* eds. R. J. Cassidy and P. J. Scharper (Maryknoll: Orbis, 1983)

PL   Patrologia Latina (Migne)

PMK	*The Passion in Mark. Studies on Mark 14–16,* ed. W. H. Kelber (Philadelphia: Fortress, 1976)
PN	Passion Narrative. Most often the Passion Narratives of the canonical Gospels that this book considers to be Mark 14:26–15:47; Matt 26:30–27:66; Luke 22:39–23:56; John 18:1–19:42.
PNT	*Peter in the New Testament,* eds. R. E. Brown et al. (New York: Paulist, 1973)
Q	*Quelle* or source for material shared by Matt and Luke but absent from Mark
QD	Quaestiones Disputatae
RA	*Revue Apologétique*
RArch	*Revue Archéologique*
RB	*Revue Biblique*
RBen	*Revue Bénédictine*
RDLJ	*Reimaging the Death of the Lukan Jesus,* ed. D. D. Sylva (Bonner Biblische Beiträge 73; Frankfurt: Hain, 1990)
REA	*Revue des Études Anciennes*
RechBib	Recherches Bibliques
RechSR	*Recherches de Science Religieuse*
REJ	*Revue des Études Juives*
RevExp	*Review and Expositor*
RevQ	*Revue de Qumran*
RevSR	*Revue des Sciences Religieuses*
RHPR	*Revue d'Histoire et de Philosophie Religieuses*
RHR	*Revue de l'Histoire des Religions*
RivB	*Rivista Biblica*
RQ	*Römische Quartalschrift für Christliche Altertumskunde und Kirchengeschichte*
RSJ	G. Richter, *Studien zum Johannesevangelium,* ed. J. Hainz (BU 13; Regensburg: Pustet, 1977)
RSV	*Revised Standard Version of the Bible*
RThom	*Revue Thomiste*
RTL	*Revue Théologique de Louvain*
RTP	*Revue de Théologie et de Philosophie*
RTPL	*Redaktion und Theologie des Passionsberichtes nach den Synoptikern,* ed. M. Limbeck (Wege der Forschung 481; Darmstadt: Wissenschaftliche Buch., 1981)
RV	*The Revised Version of the Bible*

SANT	Studien zum Alten und Neuen Testament
SB	Sources Bibliques
SBB	Stuttgarter Biblische Beiträge
SBE	Semana Bíblica Española
SBFLA	Studii Biblici Franciscani Liber Annuus
SBJ	*La Sainte Bible de Jérusalem*
SBLA	Society of Biblical Literature Abstracts
SBLDS	Society of Biblical Literature Dissertation Series
SBLMS	Society of Biblical Literature Monograph Series
SBLSBS	Society of Biblical Literature Sources for Biblical Studies
SBLSP	Society of Biblical Literature Seminar Papers
SBS	Stuttgarter Bibelstudien
SBT	Studies in Biblical Theology
SBU	Symbolae Biblicae Upsalienses
SC	Sources Chrétiennes
ScEsp	*Science et Esprit*
SEA	*Svensk Exegetisk Årsbok*
SGM	*Secret Gospel of Mark*
SJT	*Scottish Journal of Theology*
SNTSMS	Society for New Testament Studies Monograph Series
SO	Symbolae Osloenses
SPAW	*Sitzungsberichte der (königlichen) Preussischen Akademie der Wissenschaften*
SPNM	D. P. Senior, *The Passion Narrative According to Matthew* (BETL 39; Leuven Univ., 1975)
SRSTP	*Society and Religion in the Second Temple Period*, eds. M. Avi Yonah and Z. Baras (World History of the Jewish People 8; Jerusalem: Massada, 1977)
ST	*Studia Theologica*
St-B	H. L. Strack and P. Billerbeck, *Kommentar zum Neuen Testament aus Talmud und Midrasch* (6 vols.; Munich: Beck, 1926–61)
StEv	Studia Evangelica (I = TU 73 [1959]; II = TU 87 [1964]; III = TU 88 [1964]; IV = TU 102 [1968]; V = TU 103 [1968]; VI = TU 112 [1973]; VII = TU 126 [1982])
SuS	*Sein und Sendung*
SWJT	*Southwestern Journal of Theology*
TalBab	The Babylonian Talmud
TalJer	The Jerusalem Talmud

TBT	*The Bible Today*
TCSCD	*Theologia Crucis—Signum Crucis,* eds. C. Andresen and G. Klein (E. Dinkler Festschrift; Tübingen: Mohr, 1979)
TD	*Theology Digest*
TDNT	*Theological Dictionary of the New Testament,* eds. G. Kittel and G. Friedrich (10 vols.; Grand Rapids: Eerdmans, 1964–76; German orig. 1928–73)
TG	*Theologie und Glaube*
TJCSM	*The Trial of Jesus—Cambridge Studies in Honour of C.D.F. Moule,* ed. E. Bammel (SBT, 2d series 13; London: SCM, 1970)
TJT	*Toronto Journal of Theology*
TLOTC	*The Language of the Cross,* ed. A. Lacomara (Chicago: Franciscan Herald, 1977)
TLZ	*Theologische Literaturzeitung*
TNTSJ	*The New Testament and Structuralism,* ed. A. M. Johnson, Jr. (Pittsburgh Theol. Monograph 11; Pittsburgh: Pickwick, 1976)
TPNL	V. Taylor, *The Passion Narrative of St Luke* (Cambridge Univ., 1972)
TPQ	*Theologisch-Praktische Quartalschrift*
TQ	*Theologische Quartalschrift*
TS	*Theological Studies*
TSK	*Theologische Studien und Kritiken*
TTK	*Text and Testimony,* eds. T. Baarda et al. (A.F.J. Klijn Festschrift; Kampen: Kok, 1988)
TToday	*Theology Today*
TTZ	*Trierer Theologische Zeitschrift*
TU	Texte und Untersuchungen
TV	*Theologische Versuche,* eds. J. Rogge and G. Schille (Berlin: Evangelische Verlag). In this annual a Roman numeral distinguishing the volume is part of the title.
TZ	*Theologische Zeitschrift*
UBSGNT	*United Bible Societies Greek New Testament*
VC	*Vigiliae Christianae*
VCaro	*Verbum Caro*
VD	*Verbum Domini*
VInt	*Vie Intellectuelle*
VSpir	*Vie Spirituelle*
VT	*Vetus Testamentum*
WD	*Wort und Dienst*

WUNT	Wissenschaftliche Untersuchungen zum Neuen Testament
WW	*Wort und Wahrheit*
ZAGNT	M. Zerwick and M. Grosvenor, *An Analysis of the Greek New Testament* (2 vols.; Rome: PBI, 1974, 1979)
ZAW	*Zeitschrift für die Alttestamentliche Wissenschaft*
ZBG	M. Zerwick, *Biblical Greek* (Rome: PBI, 1963)
ZBTJ	*Zur Bedeutung des Todes Jesu,* ed. F. Viering (Gütersloh: Mohn, 1967)
ZDMG	*Zeitschrift der Deutschen Morgenländischen Gesellschaft*
ZDPV	*Zeitschrift des Deutschen Palästina-Vereins*
ZKT	*Zeitschrift für Katholische Theologie*
ZNW	*Zeitschrift für die Neutestamentliche Wissenschaft*
ZTK	*Zeitschrift für Theologie und Kirche*
ZWT	*Zeitschrift für Wissenschaftliche Theologie*

Standard abbreviations are used for the biblical books and the Dead Sea Scrolls. (For information about the major scrolls, see NJBC 67:82–95.) The OT in general and the psalms in particular are cited according to Hebrew chapter and verse numbers. This holds true even when the LXX is under discussion. It will help readers to know that in the psalms the LXX number is frequently one lower than the Hebrew number, e.g., Hebrew Ps 22 is LXX Ps 21. The KJV and RSV number of a psalm *verse* is frequently one number lower than the Hebrew, e.g., Hebrew Ps 22:2 is RSV Ps 22:1.

The names Mark, Matt, Luke, and John are used both for the writings and the writers. No supposition is made about the identity of the individual evangelists; thus when used for the writer, John means whoever was the principal writer of the Gospel according to John. Mark/Matt is used where Mark and Matt (Gospels or evangelists) are so close that they may be considered as presenting the same data or view.

An asterisk after the name of a ms. of the Bible indicates a reading in the hand of the original copyist as distinct from later additions or changes. Sections (= chapters) in this book are marked by the § sign plus a numeral from 1 to 48 (see list of Contents above). Cross-references within the book will employ that sign with the appropriate section number; see the running head at the top of pages for easy access to the section indicated.

COMMENTARY
ON ACT IV:

JESUS IS CRUCIFIED
AND DIES ON GOLGOTHA
HE IS BURIED NEARBY

(Mark 15:20b–47; Matt 27:31b–66; Luke 23:26–56;
John 19:16b–42)

The fourth Act of the Passion Narrative describes how Jesus, having been led out to Golgotha, was crucified between two others as "the King of the Jews." During the hours that he hung on the cross, there were reactions by various people who stood nearby, as well as words spoken by Jesus until he gave up/over his spirit. His death was greeted by wondrous events, and again reactions by various people. Finally Joseph from Arimathea took the body and buried it nearby, while the women looked on.

CONTENTS OF ACT IV, SCENE ONE

SCENE ONE: Jesus Is Crucified and Dies (Mark 15:20b–41; Matt 27:31b–56; Luke 23:26–49; John 19:16b–37)

COMMENT:

ANALYSIS:

§37. SECTIONAL BIBLIOGRAPHY
for Scene One of Act IV:
The Crucifixion of Jesus (§§38–44)

Discussions of the crucifixion of Jesus are particularly numerous. For this bibliography to be useful, a greater division into parts than usual seemed imperative. See the thirteen subdivisions outlined in the immediately preceding list of Contents.

Part 1: Transitional: Jesus Led from Pilate's Praetorium to the Site of Crucifixion (§39)

Bishop, E.F.F., "Simon and Lucius: Where did they come from?" ExpTim 51 (1939–40), 148–53.

Giblin, C. H., *The Destruction of Jerusalem According to Luke's Gospel* (AnBib 107; Rome: PBI, 1985), esp. 93–104 on Luke 23:26–32.

Käser, W., "Exegetische und theologische Erwägungen zur Seligpreisung der Kinderlosen, Lc 23,29b," ZNW 54 (1963), 240–54.

Kinsey, A. B., "Simon the Crucifer and Symeon the Prophet," ExpTim 35 (1923–24), 84–88.

Kudasciewicz, J., abstract of his Polish article on Luke 23:27–31, NTA 21 (1977), #427.

Lee, G. M., "Mark xv 21, 'The Father of Alexander and Rufus,'" NovT 17 (1975), 303.

Neyrey, J. H., "Jesus' Address to the Women of Jerusalem (Lk 23.27–31)—A prophetic judgment Oracle," NTS 29 (1983), 74–86.

Reinach, S., "Simon de Cyrène," *Cultes, Mythes et Religions* (5 vols.; Paris: Leroux, 1904–23), 4.181–88. Orig. in *Revue de l'Université de Bruxelles* 17 (1912), 721–28.

Rinaldi, B., "Beate le sterili (Lc. 23,29)," BeO 15 (1973), 61–64.

Soards, M. L., "Tradition, Composition, and Theology in Jesus' Speech to the 'Daughters of Jerusalem,' (Luke 23,26–32)," *Biblica* 68 (1987), 221–44.

Untergassmair, F. G., "Der Spruch vom 'grünen und dürren Holz' (Lk 23,31)," *Studien zum Neuen Testament und seiner Umwelt* 16 (1991), 55–87.

Part 2: Geography of the Crucifixion, Specifically the Site of Golgotha and Jesus' Sepulcher

Bahat, D., "Does the Holy Sepulchre Church Mark the Burial of Jesus?" BARev 12 (3; 1986), 26–45.

Barkay, G., "The Garden Tomb—Was Jesus Buried There?" BARev 12 (2; 1986), 40–57.

Benoit, P., "Les remparts de Jérusalem," BExT 4.292–310. Orig. in *Le Monde de la Bible* 1 (Nov. 1977), 21–35.

Bible et Terre Sainte 149 (1973). Whole issue on Golgotha.

Corbo, V. C., *Il Santo Sepulcro di Gerusalemme* (3 vols.; Jerusalem: Franciscan, 1981–82).

Coüasnon, C., *The Church of the Holy Sepulchre in Jerusalem* (London: Oxford, 1974).

Dalman, G., DSSW 346–81 on "Golgotha and the Sepulchre."

Evans, L.E.C., "The Holy Sepulchre," PEQ 100 (1968), 112–36.

Harvey, A. E., "Melito and Jerusalem," JTS NS 17 (1966), 401–4 (in ref. to Mark 15:20b).

Jeremias, J., *Golgotha* (Leipzig: Pfeiffer, 1926).

Kretschmar, G., "Kreuz und Auferstehung Jesu Christi. Das Zeugnis der Heiligen Stätten," ErbAuf 54 (1978), 423–31; 55 (1979), 12–26.

Lux (-Wagner), U., "Vorläufiger Bericht über die Ausgrabung unter der Erlöserkirche im Muristan in der Altstadt von Jerusalem in den Jahren 1970 und 1971," ZDPV 88 (1972), 185–201.

Martin, E. L., "The Place of the Crucifixion," *The Foundation Commentator* 10 (8; Sept. 1983), 1–13.

———, *Secrets of Golgotha* (Alahambra, CA: ASK, 1988). Updated information in his *A.S.K. Historical Report,* Jan. 1992.

Riesner, R., "Golgotha und die Archäologie," BK 40 (1985), 21–26.

Ross, J.-P. B., "The Evolution of a Church—Jerusalem's Holy Sepulchre," BARev 2 (3; 1976), 3–8, 11.

Schein, B. E., "The Second Wall of Jerusalem," BA 44 (1981), 21–26.

Smith, R. H., "The Tomb of Jesus," BA 30 (1967), 74–90.

Vincent, L.-H., "Garden Tomb: histoire d'un mythe," RB 34 (1925), 401–31.

Wilkinson, J., "The Church of the Holy Sepulchre," *Archaeology* 31 (4; 1978), 6–13.

———, "The Tomb of Christ: An Outline of its Structural History," *Levant* 4 (1972), 83–97.

Part 3: Overall: Ancient Crucifixion; Gospel Accounts of Jesus' Crucifixion (§40)

Bacon, B. W., "Exegetical Notes: John 19:17–20:20," BW NS 13 (1899), 423–25.

Bailey, K. E., "The Fall of Jerusalem and Mark's Account of the Cross," ExpTim 102 (1991), 102–5.

Bammel, E., "Crucifixion as a Punishment in Palestine," TJSCM 162–65.

Baumgarten, J. M., "Does *TLH* in the Temple Scroll Refer to Crucifixion?" JBL 91 (1972), 472–81.

Bible et Terre Sainte 133 (1971). Whole issue on crucifixion.

Brandenburger, E., "*Stauros,* Kreuzigung Jesu und Kreuzestheologie," WD 10 (1969), 17–43.

Cantinat, J., "Le crucifiement de Jésus," VSpir 84 (1951), 142–53.

Carroll, J. T., "Luke's Crucifixion Scene," RDLJ 108–24, 194–203.

Charlesworth, J. H., "Jesus and Jehohanan: An Archaeological Note on Crucifixion," ExpTim 84 (1972–73), 147–50.

Collins, J. J., "The Archaeology of the Crucifixion," CBQ 1 (1939), 154–59.

Diéz Merino, L., "La crucifixión en la antigua literatura judía (Período intertestamental)," EstEcl 51 (1976), 5–27.

Fitzmyer, J. A., "Crucifixion in Ancient Palestine, Qumran Literature, and the New Testament," CBQ 40 (1979), 493–513. Reprinted in FTAG 125–46.

Ford, J. M., "'Crucify Him, Crucify Him,' and the Temple Scroll," ExpTim 87 (1975–76), 275–78.

Guillet, P.-E., "Les 800 'crucifiés' d'Alexandre Jannée," CCER 25 (100; 1977), 11–16.

Haas, N., "Anthropological Observations on the Skeletal Remains from Givʿat ha-Mivtar," IEJ 20 (1970), 38–59, esp. 42, 49–59 on a crucified man.

Halperin, D. J., "Crucifixion, the Nahum Pesher, and the Rabbinic Penalty of Strangulation," JJS 32 (1981), 32–46.

Hengel, M., *Crucifixion in the Ancient World and the Folly of the Message of the Cross* (Philadelphia: Fortress, 1977).

Hewitt, J. W., "The Use of Nails in the Crucifixion," HTR 25 (1932), 29–45.

Holzmeister, U., "Crux Domini eiusque crucifixio ex Archaeologia Romana illustrantur," VD 14 (1934), 149–55; 216–20; 241–49; 257–63.

Jeremias, J., "Perikopen-Umstellungen bei Lukas?" NTS 4 (1957–58), 115–19 (on Luke 23:26–49).

Kreitzer, L., "The Seven Sayings of Jesus on the Cross," *New Blackfriars* 72 (1991), 239–44.

Kuhn, H.-W., "Zum Gekreuzigten von Givʿat ha-Mivtar. Korrektur eigenes Versehens in der Erstveröffentlichung," ZNW 69 (1978), 118–22.

———, "Der Gekreuzigte von Givʿat ha-Mivtar," TCSCD 303–34.

———, "Jesus als Gekreuzigter in der frühchristlichen Verkündigung bis zur Mitte des 2. Jahrhunderts," ZTK 72 (1975), 1–46.

———, "Der Kreuzesstrafe während der frühen Kaiserzeit," ANRW II/25.1 (1982), 648–793.

Leclercq, H., "Croix et Crucifix," DACL 3 (1914), 3045–3131, esp. 3045–71 on early centuries.

Møller-Christensen, V., "Skeletal Remains from Givʿat ha-Mivtar," IEJ 26 (1976), 35–38.

Naveh, J., "The Ossuary Inscriptions from Givʿat ha-Mivtar," IEJ 20 (1970), 33–37, esp. 35 pertaining to a crucified man.

Nestle, Eb., "The Seven Words from the Cross," ExpTim 11 (1899–1900), 423–24.

Osborne, G. R., "Redactional Trajectories in the Crucifixion Narrative," EQ 51 (1979), 80–96.

Paton, W. R., "Die Kreuzigung Jesu," ZNW 2 (1901), 339–41.

Robbins, V. K., "The Crucifixion and the Speech of Jesus," *Forum* 4 (#1; 1988), 33–46.

Rüdel, W., "Die letzten Worte Jesu," NKZ 21 (1910), 199–227.

Schreiber, J., *Der Kreuzigungsbericht der Markusevangeliums Mk 15, 20b–41* (BZNW 48; Berlin: de Gruyter, 1986).

Scroggs, R., "The Crucifixion," KKS 2.556–63.

Taylor, V., "The Narrative of the Crucifixion," NTS 8 (1961–62), 333–34 (on Luke 23:26–49).

Trilling, W., "Le Christ, roi crucifié. Lc 23,35–43," AsSeign 2d series, 65 (1973), 56–65.

Tzaferis, V., "Jewish Tombs at and near Giv'at ha-Mivtar, Jerusalem," IEJ 20 (1970), 18–32, on the tomb of a crucified man.

————, "Crucifixion—the Archaeological Evidence," BARev 11 (#1; Jan/Feb 1985), 44–53. See corrective in 11 (#6; Nov/Dec 1985), 20–21.

van Unnik, W. C., "Der Fluch der Gekreuzigten," TCSCD 483–99.

Wansbrough, H., "The Crucifixion of Jesus," CR 56 (1971), 251–61.

Weeden, T. J., "The Cross as Power in Weakness (Mark 15:20b–41)," in PMK 115–34.

Wilcox, M., "'Upon the Tree'—Deut 21:22–23 in the New Testament," JBL 96 (1977), 85–99.

Wilkinson, J., "The Seven Words from the Cross," SJT 17 (1964), 69–82.

Winandy, J., "Le témoignage du sang et de l'eau," BVC 31 (1960), 19–27, on John 19:17–37.

Yadin, Y., "Epigraphy and Crucifixion," IEJ 23 (1973), 19–22.

Young, B., "The Cross, Jesus and the Jewish People," *Immanuel* 24/25 (1990), 23–34.

Zias, J., and J. H. Charlesworth, "Crucifixion: Archaeology, Jesus, and the Dead Sea Scrolls," in *Jesus and the Dead Sea Scrolls,* ed. J. H. Charlesworth (New York: Doubleday, 1992), 273–89.

Zias, J., and E. Sekeles, "The Crucified Man from Giv'at ha-Mivtar—A Reappraisal," IEJ 35 (1985), 22–27; BA 48 (1985), 190–91.

Part 4: Setting: Title, Third Hour, Garments, First Drink, "Father, forgive them" (§40)

Aubineau, M., "La tunique sans couture du Christ. Exégèse patristique de Jean 19, 23–24," Kyr 1.100–27.

Bammel, E., "The *titulus,*" JPHD 353–64.

Braun, F.-M., "Quatre 'signes' johanniques de l'unité chrétienne," NTS 9 (1962–63), 147–55, esp. 150–52 on John 19:23–24.

Conybeare, F. C., "New Testament Notes: (2) The Seamless Coat," *Expositor* 4th Ser., 9 (1894), 458–60.

Cowling, C. C., "Mark's Use of *Hora,*" *Australian Biblical Review* 5 (1956), 153–60.

Dammers, A., "Studies in Texts: Luke xxiii,34a," *Theology* 52 (1949), 138–39.

Daube, D., "'For they know not what they do': Luke 23,34," *Studia Patristica* 4.2 (TU 79; Berlin: Akademie, 1961), 58–70.

Davies, J. G., "The Cup of Wrath and the Cup of Blessing," *Theology* 51 (1948), 178–80.

de la Potterie, I., "La tunique 'non divisée' de Jésus, symbole de l'unité messia-
      nique," in *The New Testament Age,* ed. W. C. Weinrich (Honor of B. Reicke; 2
      vols.; Macon, GA: Mercer, 1984), 1.127–38.
————, "La tunique sans couture, symbole du Christ grand prêtre?" *Biblica* 60
      (1979), 255–69.
Démann, P., "'Père, pardonnez-leur' (Lc 23,34)," *Cahiers Sioniens* 5 (1951),
      321–36.
de Waal, A., "Das Mora-Spiel auf den Darstellungen der Verlosung des Kleides
      Christi," RQ 8 (1894), 145–46.
Epp, E. J., "The 'Ignorance Motif' in Acts and the Antijudaic Tendencies in Codex
      Bezae," HTR 55 (1962), 51–62 (in ref. to Luke 23:34,41).
Flusser, D., "'Sie wissen nicht was sie tun'. Geschichte eines Herrenwortes," in *Kon-
      tinuität und Einheit,* eds. P.-G. Müller and W. Stenger (F. Mussner Festschrift;
      Freiburg: Herder, 1981), 393–410.
Fuller, R. C., "The Drink Offered to Christ at Calvary," *Scripture* 2 (1947),
      114–15.
Harris, J. R., "New Points of View in Textual Criticism," *Expositor* 8th Ser., 7
      (1914), 316–34, esp. 324–34 on Luke 23:34a.
Heppner, T., "Eine vormoderte Hypothese und—eine neue Apokryphe?" TG 18
      (1926), 657–71.
Karavidopoulos, J., "L'heure de la crucifixion de Jésus selon Jean et les synoptiques.
      Mc 15,25 par rapport à Jn 19,14–16," in DJS 608–13.
Kennedy, A.R.S., "The Soldiers' Portions (John xix. 23,24)," ExpTim 24 (1912–
      13), 90–91.
Ketter, P., "Ist Jesus auf Golgotha mit Galle und Essig getränkt worden?" *Pastor
      Bonus* 38 (1927), 183–94.
Lee, G. M., "The Inscription on the Cross," PEQ 100 (1968), 144.
Lipinski, E., abstract of his Polish article on the hour of the crucifixion, NTA 4
      (1959–60), #54.
Mahoney, A., "A New Look at 'The Third Hour' of Mk 15,25," CBQ 28 (1966),
      292–99.
Miller, J. V., "The Time of the Crucifixion," JETS 26 (1983), 157–66.
Moffatt, J., "Exegetica: Luke xxiii.34," *Expositor* 8th Ser., 7 (1914), 92–93.
Nestle, Eb., "The Coat without Seam," ExpTim 21 (1909–10), 521.
————, "Der ungenähte Rock Jesu und der bunte Rock Josefs," ZNW 3 (1902), 169.
————, "'Father, forgive them,'" ExpTim 14 (1902–3), 285–86.
O'Rahilly, A., "The Title on the Cross," IER 65 (1945), 289–97.
Primentas, N., abstract of his Modern Greek article on "The Tunic without Seam,"
      NTA 37 (1993), #810.
Regard, P.-F., "Le titre de la croix d'après les évangiles," RArch 28 (1928), 95–105.
Rodgers, P., "Mark 15:28," EQ 61 (1989), 81–84.
Rutherford, W. S., "The Seamless Coat," ExpTim 22 (1910–11), 44–45.
Saintyves, P., "Deux thèmes de la Passion et leur signification symbolique," RArch
      Ser. V, 6 (1917 B), 234–70, esp. 234–48 on John 19:23.
Wilcox, M., "The Text of the *Titulus* in John 19.19–20 as Found in Some Italian
      Renaissance Paintings," JSNT 27 (1986), 113–16.

Willcock, J., "'When he had tasted' (Matt. xxvii.34)," ExpTim 32 (1920–21), 426.

Part 5: Synoptic Accounts of Activities at the Cross; Luke's "Good Thief" (§41)

Altheim, F., and R. Stiehl, *Die Araber in der alten Welt* (5 vols.; Berlin: de Gruyter, 1964–69), 5/2.361–363 ("Aramäische Herrenworte" on Luke 23:42–43).

Aytoun, R. A., "'Himself He cannot save' (Ps. xxii 29 and Mark xv 31)," JTS 21 (1919–20), 245–48.

Bishop, E.F.F., "*oua*. Mark xv.29: A Suggestion," ExpTim 57 (1945–46), 112.

Blathwayt, T. B., "The Penitent Thief," ExpTim 18 (1906–7), 288.

Boulogne, C.-D., "La gratitude et la justice depuis Jésus Christ," VSpir 96 (1957), 142–56 (on Luke 23:43).

Crowe, J., "The *Laos* at the Cross: Luke's Crucifixion Scene," TLOTC 75–101.

de la Calle, F., "'Hoy estarás conmigo en el Paraíso.' ¿Visión inmediata de Dios o purificación en el 'más allá'?" ByF 3 (1977), 276–89.

Derrett, J.D.M., "The Two Malefactors (Lk. xxiii 33,39–43)," DSNT 3.200–14.

Donaldson, T. L., "The Mockers and the Son of God (Matthew 27.37–44): Two Characters in Matthew's Story of Jesus," JSNT 41 (1991), 3–18.

Fitzmyer, J. A., "'Today You Shall Be with Me in Paradise' (Luke 23:43)," *Luke the Theologian* (NY: Paulist, 1989), 203–33.

García Pérez, J. M., "El relato del Buen Ladrón (Lc 23,39–43)," EstBib 44 (1986), 263–304.

Grelot, P., "'Aujourd'hui tu seras avec moi dans le Paradis' (*Luc*, xxiii 43)," RB 74 (1967), 194–214.

Hope, L. P., "The King's Garden," ExpTim 48 (1936–37), 471–73 (on Luke 23:43).

Klein, G(ottlieb), "Zur Erläuterung der Evangelien aus Talmud und Midrasch," ZNW 5 (1904), 144–53, esp. 147–49 on Luke 23:42; John 19:23.

Leloir, L., "Hodie mecum eris in paradiso (Lc. xxiii,43)," *Revue Diocésaine de Namur* 13 (1959), 471–83. Slightly diff. Latin form of this French article in VD 28 (1950), 372–80.

Lewis, A. S., "A New Reading of Lk. xxiii.39," ExpTim 18 (1906–7), 94–95.

Macgregor, W. M., "The Penitent Thief (Lk. xxiii.39–43)," ExpTim 41 (1929–30), 151–54.

MacRae, G. W., "With Me in Paradise," *Worship* 35 (1960–61), 235–40.

Manrique, A., "El premio del 'más allá' en la enseñanza de Jesús," ByF 3 (1977), 162–77 (in ref. to Luke 23:43; Matt 27:53).

Martin, G. C., "A New Reading of Lk xxiii.39," ExpTim 18 (1906–7), 334–35.

Metzger, B. M., "Names for the Nameless in the New Testament," Kyr 1.79–99, esp. 89–95 on the two robbers of Mark 15:27.

Nestle, Eb., "Luke xxiii.43," ExpTim 11 (1899–1900), 429.

O'Neill, J. C., "The Six Amen Sayings in Luke," JTS NS 10 (1959), 1–9, esp. 8–9 on Luke 23:43.

Smith, R. H., "Paradise Today: Luke's Passion Narrative," CurTM 3 (1976), 323–36.

Trilling, W., "La promesse de Jésus au bon larron (Lc 23,33–43)," AsSeign 96 (1967), 31–39. Reprinted with minor changes as "Le Christ, roi crucifié" in AsSeign 2d Ser., 65 (1973), 56–65.

Weisengoff, J. F., "Paradise and St. Luke 23:43," AER 103 (1940), 163–67.

Part 6: Those Near the Cross (John 19:25–27); Identity of the Women (§41)

(Discussions of these verses where the dominant interest is primarily mariological are not included.)

Bishop, E.F.F., "Mary Clopas—John xix.25," ExpTim 65 (1953–54), 382–83.

———, "Mary (of) Clopas and Her Father," ExpTim 73 (1961–62), 339.

Boguslawski, S., "Jesus' Mother and the Bestowal of the Spirit," IBS 14 (1992), 106–29.

Buck, H. M., "The Fourth Gospel and the Mother of Jesus," in *Studies in New Testament and Early Christian Literature*, ed. D. E. Aune (Honor of A. P. Wikgren; NovTSup 33; Leiden: Brill, 1972), 170–80 (in ref. to John 19:25–27).

Chevallier, M.-A., "La fondation de 'l'Église' dans le quatrième Évangile: Jn 19/25–30," ETR 58 (1983), 343–53.

Dauer, A., "Das Wort des Gekreuzigten an seine Mutter und den 'Jünger den er liebte,'" BZ 11 NS (1967), 222–39; 12 NS (1968), 80–93.

de Goedt, M., "Un Schème de Révélation dans le Quatrième Évangile," NTS 8 (1961–62), 142–50, esp. 145ff. on 19:26–27.

de la Potterie, I., "La parole de Jésus 'Voici ta mère' et l'accueil du Disciple (Jn 19,27b)," *Marianum* 36 (1974), 1–39. Abridged German form in *Neues Testament und Kirche*, ed. J. Gnilka (R. Schnackenburg Festschrift; Freiburg: Herder, 1974), 191–219.

———, "'Et à partir de cette heure, le Disciple l'accueillit dans son intimité' (Jn 19, 27b)," *Marianum* 42 (1980), 84–125. Reaction to Neirynck, "*eis*."

Evans, G. E., "The Sister of the Mother of Jesus," RevExp 44 (1947), 475–85.

Feuillet, A., "Les adieux du Christ à sa Mère (Jn 19,25–27) et la maternité spirituelle de Marie," NRT 86 (1964), 469–89. Eng. summary in TD 15 (1967), 37–40.

———, "L'heure de la femme (Jn 16, 21) et l'heure de la Mère de Jésus (Jn 19,25–27)," *Biblica* 47 (1966), 169–84, 361–80, 557–73.

Klauck, H.-J., "Die dreifache Maria. Zur Rezeption von Joh 19,25 in EvPhil 32," FGN 3.2343–58.

Koehler, T., "Les principales interprétations traditionnelles de Jn. 19, 25–27, pendant les douze premiers siècles," *Études Mariales* 16 (1959), 119–55.

Langkammer, H., "Christ's 'Last Will and Testament' (Jn 19,26–27) in the Interpretations of the Fathers of the Church and the Scholastics," *Antonianum* 43 (1968), 99–109.

Neirynck, F., "*eis ta idia*: Jn 19,27 (et 16,32)," ETL 55 (1979), 357–65. Reprinted in NEv 1.456–64.

————, "La traduction d'un verset johannique: Jn 19,27b," ETL 57 (1981), 83–106. Reprinted in NEv 1.465–88. Response to de la Potterie, "Et à partir."

Preisker, H., "Joh 2,4 und 19,26," ZNW 42 (1949), 209–14.

Schürmann, H., "Jesu letzte Weisung. Jo. 19,26–27a," *Ursprung und Gestalt* (Düsseldorf: Patmos, 1970), 13–28. Orig. in *Sapientes ordinare*, eds. F. Hoffmann et al. (E. Kleineidam Festgabe; Leipzig: St. Benno, 1969), 105–23.

Zerwick, M., "The Hour of the Mother—John 19:25–27," TBT 18 (1965), 1187–94.

Part 7: Last Events and Words, Exclusive of the Death Cry in Mark/Matt (§42)

Abramowski, L., and A. E. Goodman, "Luke xxiii.46 *paratithenai* in a Rare Syriac Reading," NTS 13 (1966–67), 290–91.

Bampfylde, G., "John XIX 28, a Case for a Different Translation," NovT 11 (1969), 247–60.

Bergmeier, R., "TETELESTAI John 19:30," ZNW 79 (1988), 282–90.

Bertram, G., "Die Himmelfahrt Jesu vom Kreuz aus und der Glaube an seine Auferstehung," in *Festgabe für Adolf Deissmann* (Tübingen: Mohr, 1927), 187–217.

Clarke, W.K.L., "St. Luke and the Pseudepigrapha: Two Parallels," JTS 15 (1913–14), 597–99, esp. 597 on Luke 23:44–48.

Colin, J., "Il soldato della Matrona d'Efeso e l'aceto dei crocifissi (Petronio III)," *Rivista di Filologia e Istruzione Classica* NS 31 (1953), 97–128.

Driver, G. R., "Two Problems in the New Testament," JTS NS 16 (1965), 327–37, esp. 331–37 on Luke 23:44–45.

Galbiati, E., "Issopo e canna in Gv 19,29," in *Parola e Spirito*, ed. C. C. Marcheselli (Onore di S. Cipriani; 2 vols.; Brescia: Paideia, 1982), 1.393–400.

Garvie, A. E., "The Desolation of the Cross," *Expositor* 7th Ser., 3 (1907), 507–27 (the "seven last words" of the crucified Jesus).

Grández, R. M., "Las tinieblas en la muerte de Jesús. Historia de la exégesis de Lc 23,44–45a (Mt 27,45; Mc 15,33)," EstBib 47 (1989), 177–223.

Grayston, K., "The Darkness of the Cosmic Sea: A Study of the Symbolism in St Mark's Narrative of the Crucifixion," *Theology* 55 (1952), 122–27.

Holzmeister, U., "Die Finsternis beim Tode Jesu," *Biblica* 22 (1941), 404–11.

Killermann, S., "Die Finsternis beim Tode Jesu," TG 23 (1941), 165–66.

Milligan, W., "St. John's View of Jesus on the Cross," *Expositor* 1st Ser., 6 (1877), 17–36 (on 19:28–29); 129–42 (on 19:30–37).

Moretto, G., "Giov. 19,28: La sete di Cristo in croce," RivB 15 (1967), 249–74.

Nestle, Eb., "Die Sonnenfinsternis bei Jesu Tod," ZNW 3 (1902), 246–47.

————, "Zum Ysop bei Johannes, Josephus und Philo," ZNW 14 (1913), 263–65 (on John 19:29).

Powell, J. E., " 'Father, Into Thy Hands . . . ,' " JTS NS 40 (1989), 95–96.

Sawyer, J.F.A., "Why is a Solar Eclipse Mentioned in the Passion Narrative (Luke xxiii 44–45)?" JTS NS 23 (1972), 124–28.

Schwarz, G., "*Hyssōpō perithentes* (Johannes 19,29)," NTS 30 (1984), 625–26.

Spurrell, J. M., "An Interpretation of 'I Thirst,' " CQR 167 (1966), 12–18.

Veale, H. C., "'The Merciful Bystander,'" ExpTim 28 (1916–17), 324–25 (on Mark 15:36).

Witkamp, L. T., "Jesus' laatste woorden volgens Johannes 19:28–30," NTT 43 (1989), 11–20.

Part 8: Death Cry ("My God, my God . . .") in Mark/Matt, and Elijah (§42)

Baker, N. B., "The Cry of Dereliction," ExpTim 70 (1958–59), 54–55.

Bligh, J., "Christ's Death Cry," HeyJ 1 (1960), 142–46.

Boman, T., "Das letzte Wort Jesu," ST 17 (1963), 103–19.

Braumann, G., "Wozu (Mark 15, 34)," *Theokratia* 2 (1970–72 [K. H. Rengstorf Festgabe]), 155–65.

Brower, K., "Elijah in the Markan Passion Narrative," JSNT 18 (1983), 85–101, on Mark 15:33–39.

Buckler, F. W., "Eli, Eli, Lama Sabachthani?" AJSL 55 (1938), 378–91.

Burchard, C., "Markus 15,34," ZNW 74 (1983), 1–11.

Burkitt, F. C., "On St. Mark xv 34 in *Cod. Bobiensis*," JTS 1 (1899–1900), 278–79.

————, "Ubertino da Casale and a Variant Reading," JTS 23 (1921–22), 186–88 (on Matt 27:49).

Caza, L., "Le relief que Marc a donné au cri de la croix," ScEsp 39 (1987), 171–91.

Cohn-Sherbok, D., "Jesus' Cry on the Cross: An Alternative View," ExpTim 93 (1981–82), 215–17.

Danker, F. W., "The Demonic Secret in Mark: A Reexamination of the Cry of Dereliction (15,34)," ZNW 61 (1970), 48–69.

Eissfeldt, O., "'Mein Gott' im Alten Testament," ZAW 61 (1945–48), 3–16.

Floris, E., "L'abandon de Jésus et la mort de Dieu," ETR 42 (1967), 277–98.

Gnilka, J., "'Mein Gott, mein Gott, warum hast du mich verlassen' (Mk 15,34 Par.)," BZ NS 3 (1959), 294–97.

Guillaume, A., "Mt. xxvii,46 in the Light of the Dead Sea Scroll of Isaiah," PEQ 83 (1951), 78–80.

Hasenzahl, W., *Die Gottverlassenheit des Christus nach dem Kreuzeswort bei Matthäus und Markus und das christologische Verständnis des griechisches Psalters* (Beiträge zur Forderung christlicher Theologie 39; Gütersloh: Bertelsmann, 1938).

Holst, R., "The 'Cry of Dereliction'—Another Point of View," *Springfielder* 35 (1971–72), 286–89.

Johnson, S. L., Jr., "The Death of Christ," BS 125 (1968), 10–19 (on Matt 27:45–46).

Kenneally, W. J., "'Eli, Eli, Lamma Sabacthani,' (Mt. 27:46)," CBQ 8 (1946), 124–34.

Lacan, M.-F., "'Mon Dieu, mon Dieu, pourquoi?' (Matthieu, 27,46)," LumVie 13 (66; 1964), 33–53.

Lee, G. M., "Two Notes on St. Mark," NovT 18 (1976), 36 (on Mark 15:36).

Léon-Dufour, X., "Le dernier cri de Jésus," *Études* 348 (1978), 666–82.

Lofthouse, W. F., "The Cry of Dereliction," ExpTim 53 (1941–42), 188–92.

Nestle, Eb., "Mark xv.34," ExpTim 9 (1897–98), 521–22.

Pella, G., "'Pourquoi m'as-tu abandonné?' Marc 15,33–39," *Hokhma* 39 (1988), 3–24.

Pennells, S., "The Spear Thrust (Mt. 27.49b,v.l./Jn. 19.34)," JSNT 19 (1983), 99–115.

Read, D.H.C., "The Cry of Dereliction," ExpTim 68 (1956–57), 260–62.

Rehm, M., "Eli, Eli lamma sabacthani," BZ ns 2 (1958), 275–78.

Rogers, P., "The Desolation of Jesus in the Gospel of Mark," TLOTC 53–74.

Rossé, G., *The Cry of Jesus on the Cross* (New York: Paulist, 1987).

Sagne, J.-C., "The Cry of Jesus on the Cross," *Concilium* 169 (1983), 52–58.

Sahlin, H., "Zum Verständnis von drei Stellen des Markus-Evangeliums," *Biblica* 33 (1952), 53–66, esp. 62–66 on Mark 15:34.

Schützeichel, H., "Der Todesschrei Jesu. Bemerkungen zu einer Theologie des Kreuzes," TTZ 83 (1974), 1–16.

Sidersky, D., "La parole suprême de Jésus," RHR 103 (1931), 151–54 (on Mark 15:34).

———, "Un passage hébreu dans le Nouveau Testament," *Journal Asiatique* 11th Ser., 3 (1914), 232–33 (on Mark 15:34).

Skehan, P., "St. Patrick and Elijah," in *Mélanges Dóminique Barthélemy*, eds. P. Cassette et al. (Orbis Biblicus & Orientalis 38; Göttingen: Vandenhoeck & Ruprecht, 1981), 471–83 (on Mark 15:34–35).

Smith, F., "The Strangest 'Word' of Jesus," ExpTim 44 (1932–33), 259–61.

Trudinger, L. P., "'Eli, Eli, Lama Sabachthani?' A Cry of Dereliction? or Victory?" JETS 17 (1974), 235–38.

van Kasteren, J. P., "Der Lanzenstich bei Mt 27,49," BZ 12 (1914), 32–34.

Vogels, H. J., "Der Lanzenstich vor dem Tode Jesu," BZ 10 (1912), 396–405.

Zilonka, P., *Mark 15:34 in Catholic Exegesis and Theology 1911–1965* (S.T.D. Dissertation; Rome: Gregorian, 1984).

Zimmermann, F., "The Last Words of Jesus," JBL 66 (1947), 465–66.

Part 9: Reality of the Death of Jesus and Its Physiological Cause (§42)

Ball, R. O., and K. Leese, "Physical Cause of the Death of Jesus," ExpTim 83 (1971–72), 248.

Barbet, P., *A Doctor at Calvary* (New York: Kenedy, 1953).

Blinzler, J., "Ist Jesus am Kreuze gestorben?" *Glaube und Leben* 10 (1954), 562–76.

Bréhant, J., "What Was the Medical Cause of Christ's Death?" *Medical World News* (Oct. 27, 1966), 154–59.

Crawford, L., "Non, Jésus n'est pas mort sur le Golgotha!" CCER 33 (142; 1985), 17–29; 34 (143; 1986), 20–22; (144; 1986), 37–42.

Edwards, W. D., et al., "On the Physical Death of Jesus," *Journal of the American Medical Association* 255 (#11; March 21, 1986), 1455–63.

Gilly, R., *Passion de Jésus. Les conclusions d'un médicin* (Paris: Fayard, 1985).

Lossen, W., "Blut und Wasser aus der Seite Jesu," TG 33 (1941), 48–49.

Marcozzi, V., "Osservazioni medico-psicologiche sui fatti concernenti la risurrezione di. N. S.," *Gregorianum* 39 (1958), 440–62.

Merrins, E. M., "Did Jesus Die of a Broken Heart?" BSac 62 (1905), 38–53, 229–44.

Primrose, W. B., "A Surgeon Looks at the Crucifixion," HibJ 47 (1948–49), 382–88.

Sava, A. F., "The Wounds of Christ," CBQ 16 (1954), 438–43.

———, "The Wound in the Side of Christ," CBQ 19 (1957), 343–46. The basic thesis is repeated in "The Blood and Water from the Side of Christ," AER 138 (1958), 341–45.

Sharpe, N. W., "A Study of the Definitive Cause of Death of the Lord Jesus Christ," BSac 87 (1930), 423–52.

Simpson, A. R., "The Broken Heart of Jesus," *Expositor* 8th Ser., 2 (1911), 310–21.

Smith, D. E., "An Autopsy of an Autopsy: Biblical Illiteracy Among Medical Doctors," *Westar* 1 (#2; 1987), 3–6, 14–15.

Southerland, W., "The Cause of Christ's Death," BSac 88 (1931), 476–85. Response to Sharpe and Young.

Tröger, K.-W., "Jesus, the Koran, and Nag Hammadi," TD 38 (1991), 213–18 (on the Islamic view that Jesus did not die on the cross).

Wilkinson, J., "The Physical Cause of the Death of Christ," ExpTim 83 (1971–72), 104–7.

Young, G. L., "The Cause of Our Lord's Death," BSac 88 (1931), 197–206. Response to Sharpe.

Zugibe, F. T., "Two Questions About Crucifixion. Does the Victim Die of Asphyxiation? Would Nails in the Hand Hold the Weight of the Body?" *Bible Review* 5 (1989), 34–43.

Part 10: Rending of the Sanctuary Veil (§43)

Bonner, C., "Two Problems in Melito's Homily on the Passion," HTR 31 (1938), 175–90, esp. 182–90 on "The Angel and the Rending of the Temple Veil."

Brown, D., "The Veil of the Temple Rent in Twain from the Top to the Bottom," *Expositor* 5th Ser., 2 (1895), 158–60.

Celada, B., "El velo del Templo," CB 15 (1958), 109–12.

Chronis, H. L., "The Torn Veil: Cultus and Christology in Mark 15:37–39," JBL 101 (1982), 97–114.

Daube, D., "The Veil of the Temple," DNTRJ 23–26.

de Jonge, M., "De berichten over het scheuren van het voorhangsel bij Jesus' dood in de synoptische evangelien," NTT 21 (1966–67), 90–114.

———, "Het motief van het gescheurde voorhangsel van de tempel in een aantal vroegchristelijke geschriften," NTT 21 (1966–67), 257–76.

———, "Matthew 27:51 in Early Christian Exegesis," HTR 79 (1986), 67–79.

———, "Two Interesting Interpretations of the Rending of the Temple-veil in the Testaments of the Twelve Patriarchs," *Bijdragen* 46 (1985), 350–62.

Green, J. B., "The Death of Jesus and the Rending of the Temple Veil (Luke 23:44–49)," SBLSP 1991, 543–57.

Jackson, H. M., "The Death of Jesus in Mark and the Miracle from the Cross," NTS 33 (1987), 16–37.

Lamarche, P., "La mort du Christ et le voile du temple selon Marc," NRT 96 (1974), 583–99.

Légasse, S., "Les voiles du Temple de Jérusalem. Essai de parcours historique," RB 87 (1980), 560–89.

Lindeskog, G., "The Veil of the Temple," in *In honorem Antonii Fridrichsen sexagenarii* (ConNT 11; Lund: Gleerup, 1947), 132–37.

McCasland, S. V., "Portents in Josephus and the Gospels," JBL 51 (1932), 323–35 (in ref. to Mark 15:38; Matt 27:51–53).

Montefiore, H. W., "Josephus and the New Testament," NovT 4 (1960), 139–60, esp. 148–54 on "The Rending of the Temple Veil."

Motyer, S., "The Rending of the Veil: A Markan Pentecost?" NTS 33 (1987), 155–57.

Nestle, Eb., "Matt 27,51 und Parallelen," ZNW 3 (1902), 167–68.

Pelletier, A., "Le grand rideau du vestibule du Temple de Jérusalem," *Syria* 35 (1958), 218–26.

————, "La tradition synoptique du 'Voile déchiré' à la lumière des réalités archéologiques," RechSR 46 (1958), 161–80.

————, "Le 'Voile' du temple de Jérusalem est-il devenu la 'Portière' du temple d'Olympie?" *Syria* 32 (1955), 289–307.

Sylva, D. D., "The Temple Curtain and Jesus' Death in the Gospel of Luke," JBL 105 (1986), 239–50.

Ulansey, D., "The Heavenly Veil Torn: Mark's Cosmic *Inclusio*," JBL 110 (1991), 123–25.

Yates, J. E., "The *Velum Scissum:* Mark 15.38," *The Spirit and the Kingdom* (London: SPCK, 1963), 232–37.

Zahn, T., "Der zerrissene Tempelvorhang," NKZ 13 (1902), 729–56.

Part 11: Special Phenomena in Matt 27:51–53 (§43)

Aguirre, R., "El Reino de Dios y la muerte de Jesús en el evangelio de Mateo," EstEcl 54 (1979), 363–82 (on Matt 27:51–53). Eng. summary in TD 29 (1981), 149–53.

Aguirre Monasterio, R., *Exégesis de Mateo, 27,51b–53* (Institucion San Jeronimo 9; Vitoria: Eset, 1980).

Allison, D. C., *The End of the Ages Has Come* (Philadelphia: Fortress, 1985), 40–50 on the eschatological character of Matthew's death scene.

Bieder, W., *Die Vorstellung von der Höllenfahrt Jesu Christi* (ATANT 19; Zurich: Zwingli, 1949), esp. 49–56 on Matt 27:51b–53.

Blinzler, J., "Zur Erklärung von Mt 27,51b–53. Totenauferstehung am Karfreitag?" TG 35 (1943), 91–93.

Cerfaux, L., " 'Les Saintes' de Jérusalem," *Recueil Lucien Cerfaux* (3 vols.; Gembloux: Duculot, 1954–62), 2.389–413.

Essame, W. G., "Matthew xxvii.51–54 and John v.25–29," ExpTim 76 (1964–65), 103.

Fascher, E., *Das Weib des Pilatus* (Matthäus 27,19). *Die Auferweckung der Heiligen* (Matthäus 27,51–53) (Hallische Monographien 20; Halle: Niemeyer, 1951), respectively 5–31, 32–51.

Fuller, R. C., "The Bodies of the Saints, Mt 27,52–53," *Scripture* 3 (1948), 86–87.

Grassi, J. A., "Ezekiel 37,1–14 and the New Testament," NTS 11 (1964–65), 162–64.

Gschwind, K., *Die Niederfahrt Christi in die Unterwelt* (NTAbh 2.3–5; Münster: Aschendorf, 1911), esp. 185–99 on Matt 27:52–53.

Hill, D., "Matthew 27:51–53 in the Theology of the Evangelist," IBS 7 (1985), 76–87.

Hutton, D. D., "The Resurrection of the Holy Ones" (Th.D. Dissertation; Cambridge, MA: Harvard Univ., 1970).

Keane, W., "The Dead Arose [Matt 27:52–53]," *Australasian Catholic Record* 25 (1948), 279–89.

Lange, J., "Zur Ausgestaltung der Szene vom Sterben Jesu in den synoptischen Evangelien," in *Biblische Randbemerkungen*, eds. H. Merklein and J. Lange (R. Schnackenburg Schülerfestschrift; Würzburg: Echter, 1974), 40–55.

Maisch, I., "Die österliche Dimension des Todes Jesu. Zur Osterverkündigung in Mt 27,51–54," in *Auferstehung Jesus—Auferstehung der Christen*, ed. L. Oberlinner (QD 105; Freiburg: Herder, 1986), 96–123.

Riebl, M., *Auferstehung Jesu in der Stunde seines Todes? Zur Botschaft von Mt 27.51b–53* (SBB 8; Stuttgart: KBW, 1978).

———, "Jesu Tod und Auferstehung—Hoffnung für unser Sterben," BibLit 57 (1984), 208–13, on Matt 27:51b–53.

Schubert, U., "Eine Jüdische Vorlage für die Darstellung der Erschaffung des Menschen in des sogenannten Cotton-Genesis-Rezension?" *Kairos* 17 (1975), 1–10 (in ref. to Matt 27:51b–53).

Senior, D., "The Death of God's Son and the Beginning of the New Age (Matthew 27:51–54)," TLOTC 29–51.

———, "The Death of Jesus and the Resurrection of the Holy Ones (Mt 27:51–53)," CBQ 38 (1976), 312–29.

———, "Matthew's Special Material" (p. 101 above), 277–85.

Vittonatto, G., "La risurrezione dei morti (Mt. xxvii,52–53)," *Sapienza* 9 (1956), 131–50.

Wenham, J. W., "When were the Saints Raised? A Note on the Punctuation of Matthew xxvii.51–53," JTS NS 32 (1981), 150–52.

Winklhofer, A., "*Corpora Sanctorum*," TQ 133 (1953), 30–67, 210–17. Response to Zeller, "*Corpora.*"

Witherup, R. D., "The Death of Jesus and the Raising of the Saints: Matthew 27:51–54 in Context," SBLSP 1987, 574–85.

Zeller, H., "*Corpora sanctorum.* Eine Studie zu Mt 27,52–53," ZKT 71 (1949), 385–465.

Part 12: Synoptic Reactions to Death: Centurion's Confession; Galilean Women (§44: Mark 15:39–41; Matt 27:54–56; Luke 23:47–49)

Bauckham, R., "Salome the Sister of Jesus, Salome the Disciple of Jesus, and the Secret Gospel of Mark," NovT 33 (1991), 245–75.

Bligh, P. H., "A Note on *Huios Theou* in Mark 15:39," ExpTim 80 (1968–69), 51–53.

Bratcher, R. G., "A Note on *huios theou* (Mark xv.39)," ExpTim 68 (1956–57), 27–28.

———, "Mark xv.39: the Son of God," ExpTim 80 (1968–69), 286.

Crossan, J. D., "Mark and the Relatives of Jesus," NovT 15 (1973), 81–113, esp. 105–10 on Mark 15:40,47.

Davis, P. G., "Mark's Christological Paradox," JSNT 35 (1989), 3–18, on Mark 15:39.

Dechent, H., "Der 'Gerechte'—eine Bezeichnung für den Messias," TSK 100 (1927–28), 438–43 (in ref. to Luke 23:47).

Gerhardsson, B., "Mark and the Female Witnesses," in DUMU-E₂-DUB-BA-A, eds. H. Behrens et al. (Å. W. Sjöberg Festschrift; Philadelphia: University of Penn. Museum, 1989), 217–26.

Glasson, T. F., "Mark xv.39: the Son of God," ExpTim 80 (1968–69), 286.

Goodspeed, E. J., *Problems of New Testament Translation* (University of Chicago, 1945), esp. 90–91 on Luke 23:47.

Goodwin, D. R., *"Theou Huios,* Matt xxvii.54, and Mark xv.39," JBL 6 (June 1886), 129–31.

Guy, H. A., "Son of God in Mk 15:39," ExpTim 81 (1969–70), 151.

Hanson, R.P.C., "Does *dikaios* in Luke xxiii.47 Explode the Proto-Luke Hypothesis?" *Hermathena* 60 (1942), 74–78.

Harner, P. B., "Qualitative Anarthrous Predicate Nouns: Mark 15:39 and John 1:1," JBL 92 (1973), 75–87.

Harris, J. R., "The Origin of a Famous Lucan Gloss," ExpTim 35 (1923–24), 7–10 (on Luke 23:48).

Hengel, M., "Maria Magdalene und die Frauen als Zeugen," in *Abraham unser Vater*, eds. O. Betz et al. (O. Michel Festschrift; Leiden: Brill, 1963), 243–56 (in ref. to Mark 15:40–41,47 and par.).

Johnson, E. S., "Is Mark 15:39 the Key to Mark's Christology?" JSNT 31 (1987), 3–22.

Karris, R. J., "Luke 23:47 and the Lucan View of Jesus' Death," JBL 105 (1986), 65–74. Also RDLJ 68–78, 187–89.

Ketter, P., "Zur Ehrenrettung der Männer auf Golgotha," TPQ 84 (1931), 746–58 (in ref. to Luke 23:49).

Kilpatrick, G. D., "A Theme of the Lucan Passion Story and Luke xxiii,47," JTS 43 (1942), 34–36.

Manus, C. U., "The Centurion's Confession of Faith (Mk 15:39)," *Bulletin de Théologie Africaine/Bulletin of African Theology* 7 (1985), 261–78.

Michaels, J. R., "The Centurion's Confession and the Spear Thrust," CBQ 29 (1967), 102–9.

Pobee, J., "The Cry of the Centurion—a Cry of Defeat," TJCSM 91–102.

Ryan, R., "The Women from Galilee and Discipleship in Luke," BTB 15 (1985), 56–59.

Schneider, C., "Der Hauptmann am Kreuz. Zur Nationalisierung neutestamentlicher Nebenfiguren," ZNW 33 (1934), 1–17.

Schottroff, L., "Maria Magdalena und die Frauen am Grabe Jesu," EvT NS 42 (1982), 3–25.

Schweizer, E., "Scheidungsrecht der jüdischen Frau? Weibliche Jünger Jesu?" EvT
    NS 42 (1982), 294–300, esp. 297–300 on Mark 15:40ff.
Stock, K., "Das Bekenntnis des Centurio. Mk 15,39 im Rahmen des Markusevan-
    geliums," ZKT 100 (1978), 289–301.
Stockklausner, S. K., and C. A. Hole, "Mark 15:39 and 16:6–7; A Second Look,"
    McMaster Journal of Theology 1 (1990), 34–44.

Part 13: Johannine Reactions to Death: Pierced Side; Broken Bones
(§44: John 19:31–37)

(Purely physiological studies of the wound in the side and the flow of blood and
water as the cause of Jesus' death are listed in Part 9 above.)

Barton, G. A., "'A Bone of Him Shall Not Be Broken,' John 19:36," JBL 49
    (1930), 13–19.
Blass, F., "Über Ev. John. 19,35," TSK 75 (1902), 128–33.
Braun, F.-M., "L'eau et l'Esprit," RThom 49 (1949), 5–30, esp. 15–20 on John 19:34.
Chase, F. H., "Two Notes on St John's Gospel," JTS 26 (1925), 381, on John 19:35.
Culpepper, R. A., "The Death of Jesus: An Exegesis of John 19:28–37," *Faith and
    Mission* 5 (1988), 64–70.
Dechent, H., "Zur Auslegung der Stelle Joh 19,35," TSK 72 (1899), 446–67.
de la Potterie, I., "Le symbolisme du sang et de l'eau en Jn 19,34," *Didaskalia* 14
    (1984), 201–30.
————, "'Volgeranno lo sguardo a colui che hanno trafitto.' Sangue di Christo e
    oblatività," CCat 137 (3266; 1986), 105–18.
Dunlop, L., "The Pierced Side. Focal Point of Johannine Theology," TBT 86
    (1976), 960–65.
Ford, J. M., "'Mingled Blood' from the Side of Christ (John xix. 34)," NTS 15
    (1968–69), 337–38.
Haensler, B., "Zu Jo 19,35," BZ 11 (1913), 44–48.
Harder, G., "Die bleibenden Zeugen (1 Cor 15,6 . . . Jn 19,35)," *Theologia Viatorum*
    11 (1966–72), 83–90.
Harrison, S. J., "Cicero and 'Crurifragium,'" *Classical Quarterly* 33 (1983), 453–
    55, esp. 454.
Hemelsoet, B., "L'ensevelissement selon Saint Jean," in *Studies in John* (J. N. Sev-
    enster Festschrift; NovTSup 24; Leiden: Brill, 1970), 47–65 (on John
    19:31–42).
Henninger, J., "Neuere Forschungen zum Verbot des Knochenzerbrechens," in
    Studia Ethnographica et Folkloristica in honorem Béla Gunda, eds. J. Szabad-
    falvi et al. (Debrecen: Kossuth, 1971), 673–702.
Hultkvist, G., *What Does the Expression "Blood and Water" Mean in the Gospel of
    John 19,34?* (Vrigstad, Sweden, 1947).
Kempthorne, R., "'As God is my Witness!' John 19,34–35," StEv VI, 287–90.
Lavergne, C., "Le coup de lance au coeur de Jésus," *Sindon* 10 (#11; 1967), 7–14.
Lefèvre, A., "Die Seitenwunde Jesu," *Geist und Leben* 33 (1960), 86–96.
Leroy, H., "'Kein Bein wird ihm zerbrochen werden' (Jo 19,31–37)," in *Eschatolo-

gie, eds. R. Kilian et al. (E. Neuhäusler Festschrift; St. Ottilien: EOS, 1981), 73–81.

Malatesta, E., "Blood and Water from the Pierced Side of Christ," in *Segni e sacramenti nel Vangelo di Giovanni*, ed. P.-R. Tragan (Studia Anselmiana 66; Rome: Anselmiana, 1977), 165–81.

Menken, M.J.J., "The Old Testament Quotation in Jn 19,36. Sources, Redaction, Background," FGN 3.2101–18.

————, "The Textual Form and the Meaning of the Quotation from Zech 12:10 in John 19:37," CBQ 55 (1993), 494–511.

Meyer, E., "Sinn und Tendenz der Schlusszene am Kreuz in Johannesevangelium," SPAW (1924), 157–62.

Miguens, M., "'Salió sangre y agua' (Jn. 19,34)," SBFLA 14 (1963–64), 5–31.

Minear, P. S., "Diversity and Unity: A Johannine Case-Study," in MNTS 162–75 (on John 19:34–37).

Nestle, Eb., "John xix.37," ExpTim 24 (1912–13), 92. On *ekeinos* in 19:35 (despite title).

Richter, G., "Blut und Wasser aus der durchbohrten Seite Jesu (Joh 19,34b)," MTZ 21 (1970), 1–21. Reprinted in RSJ 120–42.

Seynaeve, J., "Les citations scripturaires en Jn., 19,36–37: une preuve en faveur de la typologie de l'Agneau pascal?" *Revue Africaine de Théologie* 1 (1977), 67–76.

Vellanickal, M., "Blood and Water," *Jeevadhara* 8 (1978), 218–30.

Venetz, H. J., "Zeuge des Erhöhten. Ein exegetischer Beitrag zu Joh 19, 31–37," FZPT 23 (1976), 81–111.

Wilkinson, J., "The Incident of the Blood and Water in John 19.34," SJT 28 (1975), 149–72.

§38. INTRODUCTION: STRUCTURE OF THE CRUCIFIXION AND BURIAL ACCOUNTS

We now come to the last of the four major divisions of the PN that I have called "Acts" in the drama. As previously, in commenting on these accounts I shall subdivide mostly along the lines of the Marcan sequence. I recognize, of course, that such partitioning does not do full justice to the sequence in the other Gospels to the extent that they vary from Mark. Yet as I comment on the respective scenes, I shall take care to alert the reader to the peculiarities in the other Gospel treatments of each scene and to the arrangements of material in those Gospels. This final "Act" of the PN has a variety of characters and locales, and the arrangement of this diverse material by each evangelist is unusually important for diagnosing the evangelist's thought. Therefore, I have thought it wise, even before commenting on individual sections, to give the reader an overall view of three different structures in the crucifixion and burial accounts (Mark/Matt, Luke, and John). Detection of those structures throws some light on how the individual Gospel accounts of the crucifixion and burial were composed; and so as I describe each structure, I shall make some general observations about composition. In part Luke is close to Mark/Matt; in part Luke has a different structure. To facilitate appreciation of both Lucan facets I shall include a comparative Lucan column in my presentation of the Mark/Matt structure and then devote a separate discussion to the Lucan structure taken alone.

A. *Structure of the Mark/Matt Account*

Table 6 on pp. 902–3 schematizes the main elements in Mark 15:20b–47 and Matt 27:31b—61[1] (and supplementarily in Luke 23:26–56). In this schema, after the introductory transition, the Marcan account consists of five component parts (four [§§40–44] concern Jesus crucified, with the burial as a fifth with its own subdivisions [§§45–46]). The centerpiece is the third part (§42) where Jesus, dying, speaks his only words. On either side, in the

---

[1]One could extend this to 27:66. Both the burial (27:57–61) and the guard at the tomb (27:62–66), while concluding the PN, function as part of a five-section narrative of the resurrection (p. 1302 below).

second and fourth parts, are activities that show the reactions to Jesus of those who are present at the cross. Besides this general artistry in arrangement, the storytelling pattern of three is present in the three mockeries of Jesus before he dies and in three notations of three-hour time periods (3d, 6th, 9th hours).[2] Matera thinks he detects a Marcan pattern of bracketing sections by putting the same kind of statement before and after, but the examples he offers are often strained.[3]

The contents of the Marcan narrative are to a great extent determined, both materially and verbally, by a desire to show fulfillment. The mockery of Jesus on the cross and what happens after his death continue and fulfill claims made in the Jewish trial about destroying the sanctuary and being the Messiah, the Son of God. More prominent still is the fulfillment of OT themes, e.g., the psalmist's portrayal of the suffering just one who is mocked and buffeted by his enemies; the charge recorded in Wisdom 2:17–20 that the just one is impotent to prevent a disgraceful death, despite his claim that God is on his side and he is God's son; the use of a psalm verse for Jesus' prayer as he dies on the cross. Such motifs in the crucifixion narrative are indisputable; less certain guiding motifs have also been proposed. For instance, Matera (*Kingship*) finds the king motif throughout Mark, even where it is not clearly visible.[4] Neither a particular theme nor the motif of fulfillment, however, explains all that Mark reports about the crucifixion. Especially in Part One (§40 below) there are items included that serve for Mark

[2]These are part of a larger three-hour time pattern that runs through the whole Marcan PN (p. 628 above) but are not helpful for subdividing the crucifixion account (e.g., the references to the 6th and 9th hour are found within one verse!).

[3]See his *Kingship* 57. He claims that the references to the 3d and 6th hour bracket traditional material, ignoring what I reported in n. 2. It is imaginative to call "They put purple on him" and "They undressed him of the purple" in 15:17,20a a bracketing repetition; these are simply correlative actions. I would say the same of "He is crying to Elijah" and "Let us see if Elijah comes to take him down" in 15:35,36. I would also find strained the division proposed by Robbins ("Reversed"), who would join in one unit (15:16–24) the Roman mockery of Jesus in the praetorium, Jesus' being led to crucifixion, some of the crucifixion preliminaries—all under the title "Mockery of Jesus as Royalty." How do Simon from Cyrene, the place name Golgotha, and the offering of wine mixed with myrrh fit together under that heading? Bailey ("Fall" 103) would cut off 15:40–46 and find an elaborate chiastic structure in 15:20–39. However, the chiasm involves too many implausibilities, e.g., making the central scene the mockeries by the passersby rather than Jesus' only words and his death, or making the Roman centurion who confesses Jesus parallel to Simon from Cyrene, when in Mark (unlike Luke) Simon is closer in story structure and background to Joseph from Arimathea.

[4]On pp. 62–63 he makes these suggestions. The criminals at Jesus' right and left (15:27) correspond to the seats at Jesus' right and left in glory, as requested by James and John (10:37,40)! The mockery of Jesus' cry of dereliction in 15:34–35 is the mockery of a cry by a false Messiah king (even though neither of the terms appears in these verses). That Pilate was amazed that Jesus had already died (15:44) echoes Pilate's amazement in 15:5 related to "the King of the Jews" (even though 15:5 relates the amazement to Jesus' refusal to answer other charges) and contributes to the atmosphere of a royal burial for Jesus! Matera observes that Pilate got his information about the death from the centurion "who proclaimed the King of the Jews to be the Son of God" (even though Mark does not associate the centurion with the title "the King of the Jews").

TABLE 6. COMPARING THE SYNOPTIC CRUCIFIXION AND BURIAL ACCOUNTS

§39. Transitional Episode: Jesus Led Out to Be Crucified[5]

Mark 15:20b–21	Matt 27:31b–32	Luke 23:26–32
• Leading him out	• same	• same
• Simon the Cyrenian	• same	• same
• Father of Alexander, Rufus		• Multitude and Daughters of Jerusalem followed and lamented; J. [= Jesus] spoke to them

§40. Jesus Crucified, Part One: The Setting

Mark 15:22–27	Matt 27:33–38	Luke 23:33–34
• Seven items (listed on p. 935 below)	• Six items in same order as Mark (Omits 3d hour; adds guard[6])	• Four items rearranged (centered on Jesus' saying "Father, forgive them")

§ 41. Jesus Crucified, Part Two: Activities at the Cross

Mark 15:28–32	Matt 27:39–44	Luke 23:35–43
• Three mocking groups	• same (2d group and mocking expanded)	• People standing, observing • Three mocking groups (partly different makeup from Mark) • "Penitent thief"

§42. Jesus Crucified, Part Three: Last Events, Death

Mark 15:33–37	Matt 27:45–50	Luke 23:44–46
• Darkness 6th to 9th hours	• same	• same (sun eclipsed)
• At 9th hour J. screamed to God cry of dereliction	•same	• Sanctuary veil rent
• Elijah interpretation	•same	• J. cried loud cry committing into Father's hands
• Offering vinegary wine; Elijah mockery	•same	
• Having cried aloud, J. expired	•Having shouted, J. let go the spirit	• Having said this, J. expired

§§43–44. Jesus Crucified, Part Four: Happenings after Jesus' Death

Mark 15:38-41	Matt 27:51-56	Luke 23:47-49
• Sanctuary veil rent	• same • earth shaken, rocks rent, tombs opened, holy ones raised, entered holy city	
• Centurion, having seen, confessed J. as Son of God	• same (others with centurion)	• Centurion, having seen, confessed J. as just man • Crowds returned striking beasts
• Four Galilean women observed from distance	• same	• Those known to J. and Galilean women standing from a distance saw

§§46–47. The Burial of Jesus, Parts One and Two: Joseph and Entombment

Mark 15:42-47	Matt 27:57-61	Luke 23:50-56a
• Evening, preparation day before Sabbath • Joseph asked Pilate for body • Pilate asked centurion if J. was dead[7] • Pilate granted corpse to Joseph	• Evening • same • same	• same (Joseph did not agree with decision vs. J.)
• Joseph tied up body and buried it • Two women observed tomb	• same • Two women sat opposite sepulcher	• same • Women looked at tomb • They returned, readied spices

§48. The Burial of Jesus, Part Three: On the Sabbath

Matt 27:62-66	Luke 27:56b
• After preparation day chief priests got guard from Pilate to watch sepulcher[8]	• Women rested

[5] This is not really a separate scene in Mark/Matt (or in John), but a transitional sentence. The Lucan expansion will force me to devote §39 to it.

[6] Mark 15:25, "Now it was the third hour, and they crucified him," is in the same place in the sequence as Matt 27:36, "And having sat, they were keeping (guard over) him there."

[7] In terms of Matt's departures from the Marcan outline, this is Matt's longest omission.

[8] Matt has two significant addenda to the Marcan outline: at the end, this scene; and, earlier, the reactions of the earth, the rocks, and the tombs to Jesus' death (see under §43).

no obvious dramatic or theological purpose. I think particularly of the place name Golgotha, the title "the King *of the Jews*," and the first offering of wine mixed *with myrrh*. These were probably ancient elements in a recounting of the event, and some of them have a claim to be historical.

COMPOSITION. The general observations just made about the structure of the Marcan crucifixion narrative have value no matter what precise theory of composition one espouses. Inevitably one encounters the same variety of composition theories that we have seen in relation to previous portions of the PN. For instance, many would detect *a preMarcan primitive core* (sometimes judged to be historical) that was edited or reedited by Mark. To that core Finegan would attribute 15:21,22a,24a,26,37,40–41, while Linnemann proposes 15:22a,24a,25a,33,34a,37,38, and Bultmann suggests 15:20b–24a,(27),37. Dormeyer thinks that 15:21,22a,23,24a,26,27,31a, 32c,34ab,37,38,40 stemmed from an early Jewish-Christian community. Another popular approach theorizes that Mark's narrative results from the *combination of two accounts*. Schreiber thinks of the first as historical and relates it to Simon of Cyrene (15:20b–22a,24,27) and of the second as apocalyptic, colored by OT reminiscences (15:25,26,29a,32c,33,34a,37,38). In reference to 15:22–33 Taylor would apportion 15:22–24,26,29,30 to Mark A, and 15:25,27,31,32,33 to Mark B. In both compositional theories the usual (fragile) criteria of wording, doublets, and theological interest are invoked to detect preMarcan stages. Where such criteria produce the most agreement is in reference to the items that I described at the end of the preceding paragraph as apparently unmotivated (chiefly in 15:22–27).[9]

To the contrary, if one judges that as far back as we can trace there were narrative features (pattern of three) and reflections on the OT, the method behind the exact analysis of preMarcan verses and half-verses becomes suspect. The discouraging lack of agreement among the results advocated by the various scholars (see also APPENDIX IX) makes the whole enterprise fragile. To these problems, if John is not dependent on Mark, one must add the Johannine issue. The agreement between the two Gospels is not only in details (place name, crucifixion between two criminals, charge posted against Jesus, mockery by chief priests, division of clothes, offering of sour wine (*oxos*), Mary Magdalene and another Mary) but also in patterns of three and echoes of psalms—in other words, Johannine agreement with Mark in aspects that most preMarcan analyses would regard as Marcan additions or characteristic of a second source. My judgment, then, is that here as elsewhere one may detect early traditions (shared independently by the

---

[9]Pesch (*Markus* 2.482) as usual argues that Mark as it stands reflects the primitive account, and thus he rejects fragmentation. He detects two subsections: 15:20b–24 and 15:25–32.

Gospels) but that we cannot reconstruct with serious probability a preMarcan narrative, even if we have good reason to think one existed.

B. *Structure of Luke's Account*

A look at the Lucan column in the Mark/Matt outline above shows the extent of the Lucan parallels with Mark. Especially striking is that the overall sequence of similar episodes is the same. Yet Taylor (*Passion* 92) makes the point that Luke 23:33–49 (my Parts One through Four of Jesus Crucified) has 265 words of which only 74 are found in the comparable material in Mark (thus only 28 percent).[10] The impressiveness of such statistics is somewhat lessened when we realize that Luke offers here some material found elsewhere in Mark, e.g., the Roman mockery of Jesus.

Many of the Lucan elements that are not identical with Mark echo themes common to Luke-Acts, e.g., forgiveness, being at peace with God, the sympathetic multitude contrasted with the rulers. Thus one encounters the usual disagreement as to whether Luke had a special source or reworked freely the Marcan material (possibly with the aid of isolated items of tradition not known to Mark). Here (as previously) I favor the latter position. Be all that as it may, one fact is certain: The final account in 23:26–56 was carefully written and shaped by Luke. Whatever he took over from Mark was fitted into a structure of even greater artistry than Mark's:

(a) 23:26–32 (§39: Jesus Led Out to be Crucified). Three parties favorable to Jesus: (i) Simon who brings the cross behind Jesus in the posture of a disciple; (ii) a large multitude of the people and the Daughters of Jerusalem who beat themselves and lament; (iii) two wrongdoers, one of whom will later sympathize with Jesus. See the parallel consisting of three sympathetic parties after the death of Jesus in (e).

(b) 23:33–34 (§40: Setting for the Crucifixion of Jesus). This consists of three subsections: (i) place name, fact of crucifixion, arrangement of the two wrongdoers—items taken from Mark; (ii) Jesus' prayer to the Father for forgiveness—peculiar to Luke; (iii) division of the clothes—item taken from Mark. The graciousness of the typically Lucan Jesus is heightened by the surrounding hostility.

(c) 23:35–43 (§41: Activities at the Cross). Five items in all: (i) People stand and observe—not hostile; (ii) rulers sneer; (iii) soldiers mock; (iv) one wrongdoer blasphemes; (v) one wrongdoer sympathizes and is rewarded. The three central hostile reactions resemble Mark with some shifting of per-

---

[10]Of the seventy-four parallel words nearly one-quarter are found in two verses (23:44–45).

sonnel from a scene elsewhere in Mark.[11] The first and the fifth, which frame the central three and are not hostile, are peculiar to Luke, and soften the negative impact of the scene.

(d) 23:44–46 (§42: Last Events, Death). Shorter than Mark, Luke has two elements: (i) *darkness* from the 6th till the 9th hour (while the sun's light is eclipsed) and the *rending* of the sanctuary veil—both from Mark where, however, the darkness precedes and the rending follows the death of Jesus; (ii) Jesus cries with a loud voice (from Mark) entrusting his spirit to the Father (almost the opposite of Mark where he feels forsaken by God). Luke has gathered the negative elements beforehand so that after Jesus' more resigned death, all can be positive.

(e) 23:47–49 (§44: Activities at the Cross after the Death). This is not antithetically parallel to §41 as in Mark (because there Luke has already neutralized the hostility of the three mockeries by his framework) but complementarily parallel to §39 with its three parties favorable to Jesus before the crucifixion. Here too are three parties favorable to Jesus: (i) the centurion who praises God and confesses that Jesus is a just man, comparable to Simon who carried the cross behind Jesus; (ii) the crowds who return home beating their breasts—matching the multitude of the people in §39; (iii) Jesus' acquaintances (masc.) and the women from Galilee who stand afar and watch—corresponding to the Daughters of Jerusalem in §39.

(f) 23:50–56 (§§46–48: Burial of Jesus and the Next Day). Joseph of Arimathea asks Pilate for the body of Jesus and buries it in a tomb where no one has been laid. This material parallels Mark, leaving out (as does Matt) Pilate's amazement that Jesus is already dead, increasing the emphasis on the righteousness of Joseph (who, although a member of the council [Sanhedrin], did not consent to their purpose), and (with an apologetic goal) avoiding the possibility that Jesus' body could have been confused with another body in the same tomb. To the Marcan report of the women who see where Jesus is laid, Luke adds the information that they prepared spices and ointments and rested on the Sabbath. The latter element I shall treat in a separate section, for it corresponds functionally to the much longer Matthean effort to fill in the day between the Friday of Jesus' death and the Sunday when his resurrection is revealed.

This analysis of the structure of the Lucan crucifixion account has been done in such a way as to suggest how an imaginative adaptation of Marcan material could account for many of the differences between the two Gospels.

---

[11]The passersby from Mark's negative triad of mockers become Luke's more positive people who observe. Since Luke also presents a negative triad of mockers, the (Roman) soldiers take the place therein of Mark's passersby. Mark presented Roman soldiers hostile to Jesus earlier (15:16–20a) in a scene after the Roman trial that Luke did not preserve in that sequence but has appropriated here.

Luke's more benevolent theology, both of the role of the human participants and of Jesus' exercise of mercy, lies behind that adaptation. Yet it should be recognized that Luke's artistry goes beyond an architectonic arrangement of items to serve his theology. The dramatic development of the role of the sympathetic wrongdoer ("the good thief") comes close to John's technique of choosing a few crucifixion incidents and highlighting their possibilities. His sovereign Jesus who can promise a share in paradise to the wrongdoer "this day" (23:43) resembles the Jesus who rules from the cross in John's account. It is to the structure of the latter we now turn.

C. *Structure of John's Account*

In Luke, unlike Mark/Matt, Jesus' being led out to the place of crucifixion constitutes a scene in itself, integral to the overall structure. In John, while not a separate scene, Jesus' exit to Golgotha is combined with other items pertinent to the setting of the crucifixion, so that it constitutes an introduction that may be joined to six episodes describing Jesus on the cross and his burial and thus yield a chiastic pattern (next page). This is partly similar to the more elaborate chiastic arrangement of seven episodes in the Pilate trial (p. 758 above); but in the absence of the outside/inside pattern that served there as a guide, the guidelines for divisions here are more disputable.[12]

The amount of parallelism in this chiasm is not even. The chief similarity between the Introduction and Episode 6 lies in the laconic way in which they list what happened, but Episode 6 is longer than the Introduction. There is good parallelism between Episode 1 and Episode 5. In each Jews hostile to Jesus go to Pilate with a request designed to reduce Jesus' importance or get him off the scene, but Pilate does not accede in the manner they wish. There is moderate parallelism between Episode 2 and Episode 4 in the theme of fulfillment. Granted that the overall theme in John's PN is Jesus' control of all and his victory on the cross, Episode 3 makes an excellent centerpiece of the crucifixion account. In it Jesus is surrounded by a believing community whom he makes into a family obedient to his will. He has preserved those whom the Father has given him, and so he can well follow this with the statement that all is now finished.

John is dealing with some of the same traditional items pertinent to cruci-

---

[12]For instance, Janssens de Varebeke ("Structure") would detect seven episodes in the crucifixion account even as in the Pilate trial. He joins what I call "Introduction" to my "Episode 1," while he splits up my "Episode 6" into two. Also one can debate whether my terminology "Episode 6" is appropriate, or should I speak of a Conclusion to match the Introduction? Neither designation does justice to the fact that stylistically 19:38–42 is more developed than 19:16b–18 but less developed dramatically and theologically than the other episodes.

TABLE 7. CHIASTIC STRUCTURE OF
JOHN'S ACCOUNT OF THE CRUCIFIXION AND BURIAL

Introduction (19:16b–18)
Jesus taken along; carries own cross; Golgotha; crucified with two others

Episode 6 (19:38–42)
Joseph asks Pilate for Jesus' body; Nicodemus brings myrrh; they bind it with cloths and spices, burying it in new garden tomb

Episode 1 (19:19–22)
Inscription dramatized in Pilate's trilingual proclamation of Jesus as king; chief priests ask Pilate to change, but he refuses

Episode 5 (19:31–37)
Day of Preparation; Jews ask Pilate to take away bodies; his soldiers break legs of others, stab Jesus' side; blood and water; two Scripture citations

Episode 2 (19:23–24)
Soldiers divide clothes in four parts; lots for seamless tunic; Scripture fulfilled

Episode 4 (19:28–30)
Aware of finishing all, Jesus says he is thirsty; vinegary wine sponge on hyssop; "It is finished";[13] gives over spirit

Episode 3 (19:25–27)
Women standing near cross; Jesus addresses mother and beloved disciple; disciple takes her to his own

fixion that Mark lists in his setting. Yet while John lists three of those in the Introduction (comparable to Mark's seven), two more (inscription, division of clothes) he makes into his Episodes 1 and 2, using them to dramatize theology. One is tempted to regard such development as entirely the work of the fourth evangelist until one realizes that John's Episodes 1, 2, and 3 present three reactions to Jesus on the cross similar to the grouping of three that Mark has in his activities at the cross (§41). Mark's three groups (passersby, chief priests, co-crucified) are all hostile. John has one truly hostile group (chief priests), one partially hostile (Roman soldiers), and one favorable (women, mother, disciple).[14] One can theorize that John is imaginatively adapting Mark, but it seems more plausible to me that the storytelling pattern of three was part of the crucifixion narrative as far back as we can trace and that each evangelist made his own adaptation. The same may be said of OT scriptural coloring. There is no doubt that John has shaped structurally, dramatically, and theologically material that came to him about the crucifixion; but I deem it less plausible that that material came from Mark.

[13]The crucified Jesus makes three statements in John and three in Luke; but there is no duplication between the two sets of statements (and each set is characteristic of the theology of the respective Gospel). Moreover, none of the six statements in Luke and John matches the one statement attributed to Jesus in Mark/Matt. The traditional "Seven Last Words of Jesus (on the Cross)" are highly composite.

[14]Of John's four (?) women who stand near the cross and Mark's three women who observe from afar, one is clearly identical (Mary Magdalene) and one other may be the same (a woman named Mary; see Table 8 on p. 1016 below).

Because I shall be treating John alongside the Synoptic accounts of the crucifixion and burial and therefore implicitly calling attention to similarities, it might be useful here to offer a list of details that appear in (all three or one of) the Synoptic accounts but are absent from John:

Simon of Cyrene (all three)
Lamenting women on the way to Calvary (Luke)
Initial offering of mixed wine (Mark/Matt)
Jesus' prayer for the forgiveness of his executioners (Luke)
Time indications, e.g., 9 A.M. (Mark); noon to 3 P.M. (all three)
Various mockeries (all three)
Repentance of the "good thief" (Luke)
Darkness over the land (all three)
The cry *"Elōi, Elōi, lama sabachthani"* (Mark/Matt)
The suggestion that he seek deliverance by Elijah (Mark/Matt)
Jesus' final loud cry (all three)
The words "Father, into your hands I place my spirit" (Luke)
The rending of the sanctuary veil (all three)
The earthquake and the opening of the tombs (Matt)
Reaction of the centurion (all three)
Repentance of the crowds returning home (Luke)
Pilate's investigation to affirm the death of Jesus (Mark)
The wrapping of the body in a linen shroud (all three)
The presence of the women at the tomb (all three)
Purchase of spices by the women (Luke)

(*Bibliography for this* INTRODUCTION *may be found in §37.*)

§39. TRANSITIONAL EPISODE: JESUS LED OUT TO BE CRUCIFIED

(Mark 15:20b–21; Matt 27:31b–32; Luke 23:26–32; John 19:16b–17a)

Translation

Mark 15:20b–21: [20b]And they lead him out in order that they might crucify him; [21]and they compel a certain passerby, Simon the Cyrenian, coming in from the field, the father of Alexander and Rufus, to take up his [Jesus'] cross.

Matt 27:31b–32: [31b]And they led him away to be crucified. [32]But coming out, they found a Cyrenian man by the name of Simon; this fellow they compelled to take up his [Jesus'] cross.

Luke 23:26–32: [26]And as they led him away, having taken hold of Simon, a certain Cyrenian coming in from the field, they put upon him the cross to bring behind Jesus. [27]Now there was following him [Jesus] a large multitude of the people and of women who were beating themselves and lamenting for him. [28]But having turned to them, Jesus said, "Daughters of Jerusalem, do not weep for me. Rather for yourselves weep, and for your children [29]because, behold, coming are days in which they will say, 'Blessed are the barren, and the wombs that have not borne, and the breasts that have not fed.' [30]Then they will begin to say to the mountains, 'Fall on us,' and to the hills, 'Cover us.' [31]Because if in the green wood they do such things, in the dry what will happen?" [32]But others also were being led off, two wrongdoers, with him to be put to death.

John 19:16b–17a: [16b]So they took Jesus along; [17a]and carrying the cross by himself, he came out. . . .

COMMENT

This is a transitional scene that moves Jesus from the place where Roman authority was centered in Jerusalem and where he had been tried and condemned to the place outside Jerusalem where executions took place. It consists of two basic elements: *First,* common to all the Gospels is a description of the leading out of Jesus and the carrying of the cross, either by Simon or by Jesus. *Second,* peculiar to Luke is a following of Jesus by the people and the women, i.e., the Daughters of Jerusalem to whom Jesus addresses a prophecy of woe. In two Gospels (Mark and Matt) the first element follows directly upon the mockery and abuse of Jesus by the Roman soldiers. Yet some scholars regard the Roman mockery in Mark 15:16–20a as a secondary addition and would argue that Mark 15:20b once came after 15:15 in the immediate implementation of the death sentence.

LEADING JESUS OUT; THE CARRYING OF THE CROSS; SIMON THE CYRENIAN

Leading Jesus Out. The four Gospels describe the same initial action whereby Jesus is led out/away/along toward the place of execution. In Mark 15:15 Pilate gave Jesus over "in order that he be crucified"; the leading out in 15:20b is described as the first step "in order that they might crucify him" (similarly Matt 27:26 and 27:31b). The "they" who lead/led Jesus out (Mark: *exagein*) or away (Matt: *apagein*) are Roman soldiers—the soldiers who shortly before had led him away (Mark 15:16: *apagein*) or taken him along (Matt 27:27: *paralambanein*) into the praetorium and then had proceeded with "the whole cohort" to mock and abuse him. Since in Luke and John that Roman mockery is absent after Pilate's giving Jesus over, there is ambiguity in those Gospels about the "they" who act upon Jesus: "they led him away" (Luke 23:26: *apagein*); "they took Jesus along" (John 19:16b: *paralambanein,* in the sense of taking Jesus into custody). The Johannine phraseology must have seemed abrupt to copyists; some textual witnesses reduce *paralambanein* to a participle (taking Jesus along) and add in imitation of the Synoptics either "they put upon him the cross" (Luke 23:26b) or "they led him away" (Luke 23:26a; Matt 27:31b). In both Luke and John on first impression the "they" would be the Jewish authorities and people present at the end of the Roman trial. On pp. 855–56 above I gave reasons for thinking that despite the vagueness of antecedent, the readers of John 19:16b would think that Roman soldiers were involved in taking Jesus to the cross, because earlier in the midst of the Roman trial (19:1–4) Pilate had turned Jesus over to such soldiers for scourging and mocking, and immediately after arrival at the place of crucifixion soldiers are present and active (19:23–24). Probably too the Lucan readers would have thought of Roman soldiers as those who led Jesus away in 23:26.[1] In any case neither evangelist writes in the overtly antiJewish spirit of *GPet* 3:5c–6, where explicitly the Jewish people drag Jesus along.

In the sequence of Mark/Matt the "out" or "away" expressed in the *ex* or *ab* prefixes of the verb "lead" (*agein*) logically means from inside the praetorium, although the evangelists may have had a wider presupposition. No Synoptic Gospel tells us precisely where the place of execution was in relation to the walled city of Jerusalem, but in various ways all three give the impression that the crucifixion took place outside the walls. The spot is pictured as near a road or path, for passersby speak to Jesus on the cross (Mark 15:29; Matt 27:39). Apparently the road leads into the city from the countryside, for Simon the Cyrenian is a passerby coming in from the field (Luke 23:26). Matt 27:32 has a second verb, "coming out" (*exerchesthai*), that may suggest coming out of the city, as does that same verb ("he came out") in John 19:17, since in that Gospel Jesus was already outside the praetorium when he was given over by Pilate (19:13,16a). Eventually John 19:20 is quite specific: "The place where he was crucified was near the city"; in it there was a garden and in this garden a tomb (19:41). The imagery in Heb 13:11–13 that Jesus died "outside the gate (or camp)" is part of what must have been the common picture.

All this fits with what we know of Jewish and Roman customs. Lev 24:14 specifies that the blasphemer was to be taken outside the camp and stoned by the whole community (also Num 15:35–36—both passages use *exagein,* the verb employed here only by Mark 15:20b). When Israel settled in the Promised Land, that directive was understood in terms of *outside the city;* that is where Naboth was led to be stoned for cursing God and king (I Kings 21:13) and where Stephen was dragged to be stoned for blasphemy against Moses and God (Acts 7:58; see 6:11). Quintilian (*Declamationes* 274) reports that whenever criminals were crucified very crowded roads were chosen so that the greatest number of people could see and be moved by fear. A fragment of Plautus (*Carbonaria* 2) states that the criminal carried the crossbeam (*patibulum*) through the city before he was affixed to the cross. In *Miles gloriosus* 2.4.6–7; #359–60 Plautus is more specific that the person who carried the crossbeam would perish outside the gate. The only discordant voice is that of Melito of Sardis, who three times in his *On the Pasch* (72, 93, 94; SC 100, 114, 116) says that Jesus died in the midst of the city.

---

[1]On pp. 856–59 above I argued at length that although Luke 23:24–25 used "their" vaguely to refer to the Jewish authorities and people (23:13), by the "they" of 23:26 he meant the Roman soldiers who are not mentioned until 23:36.

Shortly after Jesus died Herod Agrippa I built the "third wall" of Jerusalem considerably enlarging the city to the north, so that the place where Jesus died was incorporated into the city. When in the first half of the 2d cent. the Romans built Aelia Capitolina over the site of Jerusalem, the site of the crucifixion was within that city (also see the 6th cent. Madaba map, and indeed Jerusalem ever since). Melito visited that Roman city some decades later, and the site of the crucifixion that he was shown was in the midst of the city.[2]

Carrying the Cross; Simon the Cyrenian. Again all four Gospels describe the transportation of the cross: Mark/Matt use *airein* ("to take up, pick up"), Luke uses *pherein* ("to bear, bring"[3]), while John employs *bastazein* ("to carry"). The object of these verbs is always *stauros* ("cross"). Normally the vertical part of the cross (*stipes, staticulum* ["scaffold"]) stood implanted at the place of execution; and the condemned carried only the crossbeam (*patibulum,* i.e., a bar for closing a door; or *antenna,* a sail yardarm). Often it was carried behind the nape of the neck like a yoke, with the condemned's arms pulled back and hooked over it. By synecdoche "cross" could be used for the crossbeam (Seneca, *De vita beata* 19.3), even as "crossbeam" could be used for cross (Tacitus, *History* 4.3); and so, unlike later artists, 1st-cent. Gospel readers could have understood that only the crossbeam was involved as Jesus was led out.

The Synoptic Gospels have Simon the Cyrenian carry this. He appears in no other role in NT tradition. In part because Simon is absent from John and *GPet*, Denker (also Linnemann) holds that he was not part of the earliest preMarcan tradition; but the opposite view is more common (Bultmann, Dibelius, Finegan, J. Weiss). Indeed, some contend that his name was an important part of the eyewitness backing for the oldest crucifixion tradition (e.g., Gnilka, *Markus* 2.314—along with the named women at the burial end of the story). Complementary to that is the thesis that he became a Christian and was remembered for the service he did for the Lord. (A similar thesis will be proposed for the retention of the name of Joseph from Arimathea.) That thesis seems to be fortified by Mark's retaining the names of his sons, presumably known to Mark's Christian readers and/or where the tradition was shaped. Despite John's failure to mention him, Taylor (*Mark* 588) writes that Simon is undoubtedly a historical figure. On the other end of the spectrum Reinach ("Simon" 183–84) contends that Simon's role was invented to dramatize Mark 8:34 (= Luke 9:23; see 14:27): "If anyone wills to follow after [*opisō*] me, let him deny himself and take up [*airein*] his cross and

---

[2]See Harvey, "Melito."
[3]Mark will employ that verb in 15:22 for the soldiers bringing Jesus to Golgotha.

follow me."[4] Yet in Mark's description of Simon, beyond the use of "take up his cross," there is no reference to following Jesus. That appears (implicitly) only in Luke's "They put upon him the cross to bring [*pherein*] behind [*opisthen*] Jesus." Although like the majority of scholars,[5] I think that Luke had the saying about following in mind, he has added an echo of it to the tradition of Simon that he took over from Mark; and Reinach's thesis is unverifiable for Mark. In all three Synoptics one gets the impression that Simon was previously an *unknown* figure ("a certain") and was *coerced* into his role of taking up or bringing the crossbeam. Mark/Matt use *aggareuein*, a loanword in Greek from Persian where it had the connotation of forcing into government service; Luke describes Jesus' captors as taking hold (*epilambanesthai*) and putting on (*epitithenai*) Simon the cross.[6] If one were inventing the story to portray Simon as a disciple, one would scarcely have him as an unknown forced to serve Jesus. (Reinach imagines that forcing was not an original part of Simon's role when it was created by his sons who were aggrandizing their father; Mark added that to tone the story down!)

Two objections have been raised against the Simon story, both based on Roman practice. Plutarch (*De sera numinis vindicta* 9; #554AB) says, "Every wrongdoer who goes to execution carries out [to the execution site] his own cross [*stauros*]." In the *Oneirokritika* (2.56) of Artemidorus Daldianus we read: "The person who is nailed to the cross first carries it out [to the execution site]." Thus it would not have been normal for the Romans to allow someone else to carry Jesus' cross. Beyond that, would they have *forced* someone into service in this way (even if we leave aside for the moment whether they were forcing a Jew to work on Passover)? While some scholars (Blinzler, *Prozess* 363) state that this was typical Roman imperiousness in the provinces, Josephus (*Against Apion* 2.6; #73) admires the "magnanimity and moderation of the Romans since they do not force their subjects to transgress their national laws." If the Simon episode is historical, why would the Romans have been acting so unusually? That they were touched by pity for Jesus seems most unlikely in Mark/Matt where they have just mocked and abused him.[7] A more plausible suggestion is that Jesus had become so physically weak from the flogging that the soldiers were afraid that he would die

[4]On the historical level Brandenburger ("Stauros" 32–33) argues that this cross-carrying image was not Jewish and so the saying was formulated after Jesus' own crucifixion. That both the saying and Simon as its fulfillment were postcrucifixion creations of the community seems unlikely.

[5]Loisy, followed by Soards ("Tradition . . . Daughters" 227), doubts that even Luke has been influenced by Jesus' saying on discipleship.

[6]Luke-Acts accounts for a high percentage of the use of both of these verbs in the NT.

[7]Even were we to leave aside the issue of historicity, there remains the problem of the plausibility of the storyline.

before he got to the place of execution and the sentence of the governor could be carried out.[8] The theory of dangerous weakness on Jesus' part gains some support from the surprise shown over the swiftness of his death once he is crucified (Mark 15:44; John 19:33).

Certain details in the description of Simon need comment. He is identified as a Cyrenian, an unusual detail to invent if his role was not historical. Cyrene was the capital city of the North African district of Cyrenaica in the area of Libya. Josephus (*Against Apion* 2.4; #44) reports that Ptolemy I Soter (ca. 300 BC), in order to solidify Egyptian hold on the cities of Libya, sent in Jews to settle.[9] There was a Cyrenian synagogue in Jerusalem (Acts 6:9). Christian preachers from Cyrene appear in Acts 11:20; and Lucius the Cyrenian is mentioned alongside Simon Niger in Acts 13:1 as a Christian leader at Antioch. Thus there is no inherent implausibility that there could have been a Cyrenian Jew named Simon in Jerusalem at the time of Jesus' death and that he could have become a Christian.

Simon is said in Mark (and Luke) to have been coming in from the *agros,* "field, country." This has frequently been interpreted to mean that he was working out there, but that is not stated.[10] Even without the possible farming dimension, Simon is making a one-way trip into Jerusalem (or a round-trip if he set out from Jerusalem to go to his field or to the country that morning). Was such activity by a Jew permissible on Passover? In fact, we are never told Simon is a Jew; Simon is a Greek name, even if frequently it serves as the Greek equivalent for the Jewish name Simeon (as in the case of Simon Peter); and the names of Simon's two sons are Greco-Roman. Allowing the greater likelihood that Simon was a Cyrenian Jew, Jeremias (JEWJ 76–77) argues that the activity described could be allowed on Passover. I find that solution particularly dubious here because Matt's omission of "coming in from the field" may stem from his recognition that Mark was describing what was improper on a feast. As explained in APPENDIX II, B3 below, I approach the problem of the feast differently. Mark's account, which is fundamental to the Synoptic chronology, describes only the Last Supper in a Passover context, never giving any indication that the day following the Supper is Passover. A theological observation about the meal may have created

[8]Luke is a problem because Jesus has not been scourged or flogged in the story that has preceded. Perhaps as Luke shifted around and modified blocks of Marcan material, he did not notice that his new arrangement produced problems of logic. We have already seen that although the Lucan Jesus predicts he will be scourged, he never is.

[9]Jews became a favored one of the four groups in Cyrene; yet a Jewish revolt there is mentioned by Josephus in *Ant.* 14.7.2; #114–18.

[10]Very dubious support is offered by the imaginative contention of C. C. Torrey (*Our Translated Gospels* [New York: Harper, 1936], 131) that the name Cyrenian suggests farming.

a spurious dating; John is plausible in indicating that this is the day before Passover.[11]

As for the sons of Simon named by Mark, Alexander is a Greek name, while Rufus is a Roman name (common for slaves). Thinking Mark was written to people at Rome, some would identify Simon's son with the only other NT Rufus, "the chosen one in the Lord" mentioned with his mother in Rom 16:13. "Alexander" appears four other times in the NT as the name for one or more of the opponents of Paul.[12]

There has been much ancient and modern speculation about Simon and his sons; it seems as if imagination abounds about NT figures in inverse proportion to what the NT tells us about them. The two sons appear in stories in the Coptic *Assumption of the Virgin* and in *The Acts of Peter and Andrew* (JANT 194, 458). Bishop ("Simon") suggests that Simon came from Kyrenia on the north coast of Cyprus, and Paul met the mother of the family while he was there (Acts 13:4; Rom 16:13). Like Barnabas from Cyprus (Acts 4:36–37) Simon had a field in Judea. Lee ("Mark xv") contends that Mark was written in Jerusalem in AD 41 when Simon and his two sons were still there. Some would identify Simon with Symeon Niger listed next to Lucius of Cyrene at Antioch in Acts 13:1. Because of the association of Cyrenians with the Stephen story (Acts 6:9; 11:19–20) and because of the Greek-style names of Simon and Alexander, there have been frequent attempts to identify the father and his sons as Hellenist Christians (Acts 6:1–6).[13] Irenaeus (*Adv. haer.* 1.24.4) associates with Basilides (perhaps incorrectly) the gnostic idea that Jesus exchanged appearances with Simon and stood by laughing while Simon was crucified. That idea leads us to discuss John's silence about Simon.

The Absence of Simon in John. Attempts have been made to harmonize John's affirmation that Jesus carried his own cross with the role that the Synoptics allot to Simon. Taking advantage of Luke's wording ("They put upon him the cross to bring behind Jesus"), artists have portrayed Jesus carrying the front part of the cross and Simon carrying the rear half. In fact, however, Luke does not mean that Simon carried the back part; he carried the whole

---

[11]On Passover eve, work often did cease about noon (APPENDIX II, n. 19); and that could explain why Simon is coming in from the field. Yet John, which gives the Passover eve setting and noon as the time when the trial ended, does not mention Simon.

[12]N. Avigad (IEJ 21 [1962], 1–12) reports on an early-1st-cent. AD ossuary discovered in the SW Kidron valley near Jerusalem in 1941. It seems to have belonged to a diaspora Jewish family from Cyrenaica and has the name of Alexander, son of Simon. Inevitably some have speculated that this is the son mentioned in Mark (see Pesch, *Markus* 2.477).

[13]Further afield, Derrett ("Haggadah" 313) would connect Simon with the OT Symeon, one of Jacob's twelve sons who hated his brother Joseph and counseled the brothers to kill him. The idea that Simon carried Jesus' crossbeam gave rise to the designation *Kyrēnaios* from Hebrew *qôrâ* ("beam").

crossbeam as Jesus walked ahead of him, so that Jesus was free to turn and converse in 23:28. Responsible scholars (Blinzler, Taylor) would harmonize by having Jesus carry the cross himself for a while (John) and then, as Jesus grew weak, Simon being forced to carry it (Synoptics). However, there seems to be a deliberate quality in John 19:17a indicating that while John knew the Simon tradition (and thus implicitly testified to its antiquity), he rejected it for his own reasons.

In part this approach depends on the force of the dative *heautō* in 19:17a. Some would understand it as a dative of advantage, "for himself" (BDF 188²); but D. Tabachovitz (*Eranos* 44 [1946], 301–5) argues that it is an instrumental dative of person, equivalent to *di' heautou*, "by himself." A similar use of *heautō* is found in *Mart. Polycarp* 13:2, as the martyr takes off his clothes by himself. Why would John so firmly reject Simon's role in favor of Jesus' carrying his own cross? Some think that the above-mentioned gnostic view denounced by Irenaeus (in which Simon was the one crucified) was already in circulation and John was refuting it. Another highly speculative explanation is that John was introducing here the typology of Isaac, who carried the wood for his own sacrifice (Gen 22:6). Whether that symbolism is farfetched depends to some extent on whether when John wrote, there were already in circulation midrashic developments in which Isaac was portrayed as an adult who voluntarily accepted being put to death (the Suffering Servant motif). For that issue, see APPENDIX VI.

Less speculative and more probable is the observation that John's christology has no room for Jesus' needing or accepting help. The basic principle of John 10:17–18 comes into play: "I lay down my life . . . no one has taken it away from me; rather I lay it down of my own accord." We have seen previous Johannine touches in the PN to underline Jesus' sovereignty: Jesus forced the arresting party to move backward and fall to the ground in 18:6; he challenged the high priest about why he was being questioned in 18:21; he told Pilate, "You have no power over me at all" (19:11). That John's omission of Simon was to emphasize Jesus' control or authority even in the crucifixion may be hinted at in Justin's statement (*Apology* 1.35.2) that when Jesus was crucified, he applied his shoulders to the cross, a statement that he accompanies with a citation of Isa 9:5(6): "On his shoulders rests the authority/rule."

JESUS SPEAKS TO THE DAUGHTERS OF JERUSALEM (LUKE 23:27–31)

The Framework for This Scene. Mark 15:20b uses this sentence to preface the appearance of Simon the Cyrenian: "And they lead him out in order that they might crucify him." Luke 23:26 borrowed the first half of Mark's sentence also to preface Simon ("And as they led him away").[14] Luke will use the other half of Mark's sentence in 23:32 to conclude the present scene: "led off . . . to be put to death." Thus from Mark 15:20b Luke creates a framework into which he puts the material in vv. 27–31 that has no Marcan parallel. (See the ANALYSIS below as to whether Luke drew the material in vv. 27–31 from a preLucan source or from his own free composition.)

Luke also made changes in the material about Simon the Cyrenian that he borrowed from Mark, so that some changes visible in 23:26 lead into the new material of vv. 27–31.[15] From Mark's account one may assume that Simon became a Christian (because his name was preserved by Christian memory), but Luke by having Simon bring the cross "behind" (*opisthen*) Jesus allusively gives him the stance of a disciple (9:23). Some would deny that because even if Luke softens Mark's "compel," Simon still has the cross put upon him. Yet for Luke, contact with Jesus changes people unexpectedly and suddenly. Jesus goes ahead of Simon and shows the way to the cross.[16] The conversion of an involuntary follower and cross-bearer is no more difficult than the instant change of a penitent wrongdoer (the "good thief" of 23:40–43) or the proclamation of Jesus' innocence drawn from the Roman centurion who crucified him (23:47). The Lucan Simon, then, is a positive figure who helps the transition to the description of others not opposed to Jesus whom Luke will now introduce. Thus it would seem that in copying from Mark, Luke compensates by way of theological development for defects that he has created in the storyline (e.g., Jesus gets help carrying the cross even though he has not been flogged).

The Multitude and the Women (Luke 23:27). The same somewhat divided results for storyline and theology appear in the large Lucan insertion about others who followed Jesus to the place of execution. Luke last mentioned "the people" as participants in the PN in 23:13 in a context in which they were hostile to Jesus. He may have implicitly included them alongside the Jewish authorities in the final moments of the Roman trial when Pilate gave Jesus "over to their will" (23:25). What impression, then, do we get when we read in 23:27: "Now there was following him a large multitude

[14]The agreement of Luke and Matt here in employing *apagein* against Mark's *exagein* is not significant. *Apagein* has been used six times in the PN for moving Jesus, and independently Matt and Luke prefer to remain consistent with the previous usage rather than to follow Mark in introducing a new verb—a verb Mark used in imitation of the LXX directives about the death of blasphemers: Lev 24:14; Num 15:36.

[15]A minor change is the initial "And as" in v. 26 (*kai hōs*), which has been used elsewhere by Luke to indicate a change of place or time (2:39; 15:25; etc.; see Büchele, *Tod* 42).

[16]Acts 3:15; 5:31 describes Jesus as *archēgos,* a term difficult to translate but which has the sense of precedence; cf. Luke 19:28 (Talbert, *Reading* 219).

of the people"?[17] Although "following him" is not necessarily a posture of discipleship, there is no prima facie suggestion of hostility (pace Büchele, *Tod* 43). Indeed, Luke seems to assign a progressively favorable role to this portion of the Jerusalem populace. If in 23:27 the "large multitude of the people" is not itself said to mourn, it is associated with women who do mourn and are clearly sympathetic to Jesus. Later (23:35), as Jesus hangs on the cross, we shall be told that "the people were standing there observing." Although that description is noncommittal, the people are thus kept distinct from the three types of mockers whose description follows immediately. In a scene after Jesus dies on the cross (a scene that matches by inclusion the present scene before the crucifixion) Luke 23:48 reports that "all the crowds who were gathered together for the observation of this . . . returned striking their breasts." The total effect of this progression toward siding with Jesus is found in the apocryphal *Acts of Pilate* 4.5: "Now as the governor looked around on the multitudes of the Jews standing around, he saw many of the Jews weeping, and said, 'Not all the multitude wish that he should be put to death.'" This picture would not strike ancient readers as implausible: Lucian (*De morte Peregrini* 34) remarks cynically that "those being led off to the cross . . . have a large number of people at their heels."

In Luke's Greek "a large multitude," besides governing "of the people," also governs "and of women." It is dubious, however, that Luke means to emphasize the number of women; rather through the correlative *kai* ("and") he seems to be calling attention to a group of women *alongside* the general multitude of the people, somewhat as in Acts 17:4: "a large multitude of devout Greeks and not a few of the leading women." (A correlating *kai* will be found again in the parallel scene after the crucifixion in Luke 23:49: "all those known to him . . . and the women.") In any case the women are the ones "who were beating themselves and lamenting for him."[18]

Benoit, Lagrange, and Marshall are among those who think that this mourning for a person about to be executed was an act of religious piety, but others like Schneider doubt that lamentation for criminals on their way to die was permitted in public. Suetonius (*Tiberius* 61) reports, "The relatives [of those condemned in the aftermath of the fall of Sejanus—p. 693 above]

[17]In the NT a "multitude of the people" is peculiar to Luke (1:10; 6:17; Acts 21:36), with *poly* ("large") representing Luke's penchant for rhetorical exaggeration (Fitzmyer, *Luke* 1.324).

[18]Many scholars see here the influence of Zech 12:10: "They shall look on him whom they have pierced, and they shall beat themselves in mourning for him as for an only son, and grieve with grief as for a firstborn son." (The subsequent Zech verses attribute the mourning to the various families *and their wives*.) Part of this verse is cited by John 19:37 *after* Jesus dies on the cross; and it would seem more applicable to the crowds beating their breasts after Jesus has died (Luke 23:48) than to the present scene where no physical injury has yet been done to Jesus.

were forbidden to go into mourning." Whether or not that restriction was in effect earlier, it is dubious that such a rule would have been applied to every minor case in the provinces. Accordingly there is little to support the countersuggestion that instead of mourning, the women had come out to protest the execution and express their support for Jesus as king. Luke tends to double verbs of mourning (7:32; 8:52); and the combination of *koptesthai* and *thrēnein* that he uses here is found in Josephus (*Ant.* 6.14.8; #377) to describe the self-beating and lamenting for the death of Saul.

How does Luke understand these women? Because Jesus calls them "Daughters of Jerusalem" and addresses to them a negative prophecy about the fate of the city in which they will be embroiled, some like Neyrey (*Passion* 111) would identify them with that element in Israel that consistently rejected God's messengers (see also Untergassmair, *Kreuzweg* 144). That is surely wrong, as both Giblin (*Destruction* 97) and Soards ("Tradition . . . Daughters" 229) point out. These women are figures sympathetic to Jesus, and the tragedy is that even their sympathetic tears cannot save them from the fate of the city that kills the prophets. There is no reason, however, to go to the other extreme by describing them as disciples, for Jesus' female followers in the narrative are the women from Galilee (23:49,55). Also this is too early in the movement toward crucifixion for readers to think of the women who administered pain-killing drinks to the condemned (p. 941 below). Rather we are in the well-known context of women who lament for the dead by keening (as in the case of Saul just described; see John 11:31; *GPet* 12:52). The abandoned sorrow displayed by their smiting themselves is a dramatic touch, as is the use of them to portray an aspect of Jerusalem. Jesus entered Jerusalem in 19:37–40 amid the rejoicing of a whole multitude of the disciples and their singing the blessings of the king; he is now led away from the city followed by "a large multitude of the people" and the women who lament his death. It is interesting that at Jesus' entry into Jerusalem in Matt 21:5 and John 12:15 there is a personal address to "Daughter Zion"; Luke has saved his equivalent address till here, and it is to that we now turn.

The Fate of the Daughters of Jerusalem and Their Children (23:28). Neyrey (*Passion* 111) points out that the turning of Jesus to address someone is a characteristic Lucan feature; *strapheis* occurs seven times in Luke compared to five in the other three Gospels. Yet the nature of the address to follow, positive or negative, is not determined by that action.[19] While "daughters" can mean inhabitants, Luke follows here an OT pattern of ad-

---

[19]Sometimes when the Lucan Jesus turns, he says something positive to the party (7:9; 10:23), sometimes something negative (9:55; see 22:61), and sometimes something that fits neither category (7:44; 14:25).

dressing females as representatives of the nation or the city in oracles of joy
or woe: "Daughters of Israel" (II Sam 1:24); "Daughter Zion" (Zeph 3:14;
Zech 9:9); and "Daughters of Jerusalem" (Song [Canticle] 2:7). Calling the
women "Daughters of Jerusalem" is not pejorative,[20] but it identifies their
fate with that of the city.

The words "do not weep" have been addressed previously by Jesus to the
widow of Nain grieving for her son (Luke 7:13) and to those who mourned
the death of the ruler's daughter (8:52); and so they fit well the context of
mourning for one about to die. In the previous cases Jesus was about to
remove the cause for mourning by resuscitating the dead; here he is turning
away the grief from his own death toward the death of the city and its inhabitants. A *plēn* ("rather") sets up the contrast, which is enhanced by the chiastic
word order: "not weep for me . . . for yourselves weep" (see a somewhat
similar structure in 10:20). The atmosphere here is not far from that of Jer
9:16–19, where the Lord summons the women to lament over Jerusalem: "A
dirge is heard from Zion, 'How ruined are we and greatly ashamed.' . . .
Hear, you women. . . . Teach your daughters this dirge and each other this
lament." While the instruction of Jesus is directed to the women who follow
him, through them he speaks to the whole multitude of the people of Jerusalem who have not been hostile to him. The message is that now no amount
of lamenting for what is being done to him can save Jerusalem or its people
from the destruction to come. Jesus is not speaking words of compassion, as
Dalman thought, although that element is present; nor is he appealing to
reform (Grundmann, Danker), for it is too late; nor is he denouncing, since
those who follow are not doing evil. Like the prophets of old who uttered
oracles against the nations (so Neyrey, Giblin), Jesus is speaking to Jerusalem as representative of Israel—the last of a series of words of woe.

In Luke 11:49–50 Jesus warned that this generation would be held
accountable for the blood of all the prophets. In 13:34–35 Jesus spoke
directly to Jerusalem, warning that because she refused to listen, her house
(= Temple and the whole city) would be forsaken; "How often I would have
gathered *your children* together as a hen gathers her brood under her wings!"
In 19:41–44 Jesus himself *wept* over Jerusalem and spoke to her of *the coming days* of destruction by her enemies; "They will throw you to the ground,
you and your children within you." Finally in 21:20–24 he spoke of the devastation of Judea as having come near; "Let those who are in Judea flee to
the mountains. . . . And woe to those who have (children) in *the womb* and
to those who are *nursing* in those days." I have italicized words in these

[20]Here Luke uses the Hebraized form *Hierousalēm* for the city. In §33, n. 1, I mentioned the
thesis of de la Potterie that this spelling is used in positive contexts. In my judgment that thesis is
challenged here because a word of dire woe is about to be pronounced.

passages to show how in vocabulary and theme what Jesus says to the Daughters of Jerusalem in 23:28–31 is consistent with sayings of the Lucan Jesus to and about Jerusalem during the ministry. In particular, there had already been a warning that innocent women and children would perish.[21] Functionally (but without Jewish self-acceptance of responsibility) this passage is not far from Matt's scene in 27:25, "His blood on us and on our children." The punishment is to be visited not only on the generation living at the time of Jesus' death but also on their children in the generation of Jerusalem's fall in 70.

Jesus' Pronouncement in 23:29: "Behold, coming are days in which they will say, 'Blessed are the barren, and the wombs that have not borne, and the breasts that have not fed.'"[22] As one studies this verse, it is useful to keep distinct two sets of biblical words (and ideas) involving blessing, one that we may call "participial" and the other "adjectival":

PASSIVE PARTICIPLE: Hebrew *bārûk*, Greek *eulogētos* or *eulogēmenos*, Latin *benedictus*, English *blessed* (pronounced *blest*)—more properly addressed to God who is to be blessed by human beings.

ADJECTIVE: Hebrew *'ašrē*, Greek *makarios*, Latin *beatus*, English *blessed* (with the "ed" pronounced), meaning happy or fortunate—a macarism that does not confer or wish for a blessing but recognizes an existing state of good fortune among human beings, sometimes because of something God has done for them.

Although I shall use the undifferentiated term "blessing" to refer to this saying in 23:29, a macarism is meant.

In the ANALYSIS I shall discuss the overall composition of this section in Luke to which the present verse is a key, but even here some facts pertinent to the origin of the verse are important for understanding the commentary. Does Luke draw it from a special PN source; or does he draw it from a sayings source and adapt it to the present context; or does he simply compose it on the model of the LXX and Jesus' previous warnings about Jerusalem? With these questions in mind let us look at each phrase.

An initial *idou* ("behold") before an oracle of woe to Jerusalem is found in Luke 13:35. With slight variations the LXX uses "coming are days" in

---

[21]So Dupont, "Il n'en sera" 314–19; Rinaldi, "Beate" 62.

[22]This verse exhibits a number of scribal variants. P[75], Codex Bezae, OL, and OS omit "behold." Some variants represent efforts to improve the poetic balance of the objects affected by the woeful blessing, viz., changes that bring closer together "barren" and "wombs," so that only the two parts of the women's bodies are involved (wombs, breasts) rather than a tripartite arrangement with an overall reference to barren women, followed by the two organs related to bearing children. The latter arrangement (which I have followed) matches better, however, the reference to "you" and "your children" in v. 28.

the present tense in a number of prophecies of joy and of woe: Jer 7:32; 16:14; Amos 4:2; Mal 3:19 (4:1). Luke has used the phrase previously, e.g., in the Jerusalem warnings of 19:43 and 21:6, but always in the future tense. Does the present tense here in Luke indicate dependence on a source, or has Luke shifted to the present (imitating the LXX) to signal that with Jesus' death the days of final divine action are closer at hand? As for days "in which they will say," Taylor and Rehkopf see preLucan style and evidence for a PN source. Yet this clause is also LXX style (Isa 3:7; 12:1); and both in Jer 31:29,31 (= LXX 38:29,31) and in Luke 17:22–23 one finds in close proximity the phrases "coming days" and "they will say."

As for what will be said ("Blessed are the barren"), some like Käser ("Exegetische" 246) would have Luke drawing upon Isa 54:1: "Sing, O barren one, who did not bear." They point to Isa 54:10, which mentions mountains and hills even as does the next verse in Luke. Isa 54:1 was well known to early Christians, being cited in Gal 4:27; *II Clement* 2:1; Justin, *Apology* 1.53. Yet in all these citations the Isaian passage is taken as the prophet meant it: a message of joy that the barren one will now have children. That is not what Luke means.[23] Rather Luke is paradoxically saying that it is better to be childless when the harsh retribution will come; for children are not able to protect themselves in such times, and parents have the anguish of seeing those whom they brought into the world destroyed—if the parents try to save the children, both perish. Lam 4:4 provides a close analogy: In the horrible fall of Jerusalem to the Babylonians, the suckling babes cry for food, but there is none to feed them. This mournful theme was well known in Greco-Roman literature as well (Fitzmyer, *Luke* 2.1498). Thus if Luke was drawing on Isa 54:1, he had to change not only the format to a macarism but the basic meaning. It requires much less imagination to relate Luke 23:29 to passages that truly bless those without child, e.g., Wis 3:13: "Blessed is the undefiled barren one who did not know the transgression of the marriage bed." Pessimistically Qoh 4:2–3 praises the dead over the living, and better off than either is the person never born. Syriac *II Baruch* 10:5b–10, written within a few decades of Luke, uses that theme in a lamentation over Jerusalem destroyed by the Romans: "Blessed is he who was not born or he who, having been born, has died." Seemingly, then, Luke has drawn on a common theme appropriate to the catastrophe facing Jerusalem. Previously he has phrased that theme in reference to Jerusalem's destruction as a woe: "Woe to those who have (children) in the womb and to those who are nursing in those days" (21:23, drawn from Mark 13:17); here he phrases

---

[23]Käser ("Exegetische" 251) would try to bend v. 29 in that direction: The barren constitute a spiritual Israel trusting in God for children, replacing the Daughters of Jerusalem, who represent fleshly Israel.

it as a blessing (macarism). For Luke's phrasing of blessings and woes in antithetic parallelism, see 6:20–26.

All this suggests strongly that Luke did not draw 23:29 from a preLucan PN. But did Luke himself fashion entirely this blessing that is phrased in biblical language, and reflects a biblical theme that he has used elsewhere in relation to Jerusalem? Or did he draw it from a sayings tradition and re-fashion it? Logion 79 in *GThom* is important in this discussion:

> A woman from the crowd said to him, "Blessed are the womb that bore you and the breasts that nourished you." He said to [her], "Blessed are those who have heard the word of the Father and have kept it in truth. For there will be days when you will say, 'Blessed are the womb that has not conceived and the breasts that have not suckled.'"

In a careful analysis of this passage Soards ("Tradition . . . Daughters" 232–37) shows how difficult it is to decide whether *GThom* by using chain words had brought together Luke 11:27–28 and Luke 23:29, or whether vice versa Luke has split into two an original unity that *GThom* has preserved. He favors the latter, pointing to instances in the Lucan use of Mark where elements from a single Marcan piece appear in two different places in Luke. An example even closer to the splitting that is proposed here is offered by Luke 2:14 and 19:38, two verses that were originally part of a preLucan hymn (BBM 427). Thus it is not unlikely that the macarism in Luke 23:29 came from a collection of Jesus' sayings, where it may have been associated with the macarism in 11:27–28. (This saying would have had a partial Marcan counterpart in Mark 13:7 = Luke 21:23.) To introduce it here in the context of an oracle to the Daughters of Jerusalem, Luke would have employed familiar LXX language, so that *GThom*'s "there will be days" becomes "coming are days."

The Pronouncement Continued (23:30): "Then they will begin to say to the mountains, 'Fall on us,' and to the hills, 'Cover us.'" Luke uses the auxiliary "begin to" some twenty-nine times; and the sequence in 29:29–30 "will say . . . will begin to say" is found in an inverted order in Luke 13:26 and 14:9. In the covenant relationship between God and Israel, mountains and hills are appealed to as witnesses: They were there when the covenant was made and are still present to testify at crucial moments (Micah 6:1–2). Isa 54:10 is often cited as background: "Though the mountains depart and the hills be shaken, my love will not depart nor my covenant of peace be shaken." Yet that is very far from the import of this verse in Luke, even as Isa 54:1 was very far from the import of the previous verse in Luke. The clear antecedent is Hosea 10:8b which, in a context pertaining to the capital city Samaria (similar to Luke's use of Jerusalem), warns that under God's punishment Israel will cry out for release: "And they shall say to the mountains, 'Cover us,' and to the hills, 'Fall on us.'" (Notice that Luke has inverted the order of Hosea's imperatives found in the MT and the LXX Codex Vaticanus.[24]) The Hosea verse served in the arsenal of early Christian apocalyptic expectation; for Rev 6:16 echoes it to describe the plight of the powerful of the earth before the wrath of the Lamb, "And they will say to the mountains and the rocks, 'Fall on us and cover us'" (notice the same inversion of the imperatives as in Luke). If Luke reshaped a saying of Jesus to form v. 29, he has paralleled it with an OT warning of the same import in v. 30. God's Son and the prophets have the same message of violent doom for the disobedient.

The Pronouncement Terminated (23:31): "Because if in the green wood they do such things, in the dry what will happen [be done]?" The verb in the last clause (the apodosis) is future.[25] It concerns what will be done in the time of punishment, even as did vv. 29–30. There we heard what the inhabitants of Jerusalem would say; here we hear a question about what will be done *to them.* The protasis of the condition (*ei* plus the present indicative), however, describes something that is actually happening, and so the "they" has changed meaning from those who will react in the future to those who are doing something to Jesus. (Rather than admit there is a narrative logic in such a change, some would describe vv. 29–30 as an insertion, so that the "Because" of v. 31 would follow v. 28.) The thrust of the condition involves the well-known proverbial formula *a minore ad maius* (from the lesser to the greater), e.g., in the OT, Prov 11:31: "If the just person is punished on earth, how much more the wicked and the sinner"; in the NT, I Pet 4:17: "Judgment begins with God's house: if judgment is done first with us, what will be the end for those who disobey God's gospel"; in rabbinic literature, in reference to the crucified Jose ben Jo'ezer (*Midrash Rabbah* 65.22 on Gen 27:27): "If this happens to those who do the will of God, what will happen to those who offend Him?"

As for the imagery used in Luke's condition, in Ezek 17:24 a green (= fresh) tree and a dry one (*xylon chlōron, xylon xēron*) are a contrasted pair. In *Seder Elijah Rabbah* 14 (p. 65—9th cent. AD) without the use of "wood," we find, "When the moist catch fire, what will the dry do?" Luke is not specific as to what things are done in the green wood and the dry; but drawing on Ezek 21:3 (= RSV 20:47); 24:9–10; and Isa 10:17, Caird, Marshall and many others assume that burning is involved: If they can burn

---

[24]The LXX of Codex Alexandrinus has the Lucan order. Has that codex (5th cent. AD) been conformed to Luke, or did Luke use this other Greek form?

[25]That holds true whether we read the aorist subjunctive *genētai* used as an emphatic future in a deliberative question (BDF 366[1]), or the indicative future *genēsetai* (Codex Bezae).

green, wet wood, how much more will the dry wood be burned? However, with Leaney, Neyrey, and others, one could think that the focus of the comparison is time difference between the beginning life of the tree and its aged period, e.g., applied to the time difference between when Jesus is crucified and when Jerusalem will be destroyed. The latter could be supported by vv. 29–30, which refer to God's *future* punishment of Jerusalem and Israel. Fitzmyer (*Luke* 2.1498–99) mentions an additional possible comparison between the wood on which Jesus was crucified (Acts 5:30; 10:39; 13:29) that was not consumed by flames and the wood of Jerusalem consumed by flames—yet none of the Lucan prophetic descriptions of the destruction of Jerusalem mentions wood or flames.[26]

The vagueness of the subjects in the protasis and the apodosis and the lack of certainty about the precise import of the imagery have led to many interpretations of v. 31 (see Plummer, Fitzmyer). Let me group them under four headings:

(1) The Romans as the subject throughout, e.g., if the Romans so treat me whom they admit to be innocent, how will they treat those who revolt against them. Yet the Romans have *not* been formally identified in Luke as the agents who are taking Jesus off to crucify him.

(2) God as the subject throughout, e.g., if God has not spared the beloved Jesus, how much the more will an impenitent Judaism receive the impact of divine judgment (so Creed, Fitzmyer, Manson, J. Schneider [TDNT 5.38], G. Schneider, Zerwick). But does Luke think of crucifixion as what *God* is doing to Jesus?

(3) Human beings as the subject throughout, e.g., if people so behave before their cup of wickedness is filled, what will they do when it overflows. This interpretation does not do justice to the specificity of the Lucan context and the address to the Daughters of *Jerusalem;* Jesus is concerned with the fate of that city. *The first three suggestions do not posit a difference between the subjects of the two verbs in the condition:* "they do" and "will happen or be done" (passive).

(4) Jesus' opponents as subject of the protasis, and God as the subject of the apodosis. Which opponents? Luke has reported that Pilate gave Jesus over "to their will." Accordingly, although Lucan readers would probably recognize that Roman soldiers were taking Jesus out to crucify him, they would think of the primary opponents as "the chief priests and the rulers and the people" of 23:13 who wanted Jesus crucified. The mindset is illustrated

---

[26]Still less likely is an echo of the plotting of Jeremiah's opponents (Jer 11:19): "Come and we shall put wood in his bread" (LXX) or "Let us destroy the tree in its vigor" (MT).

by the texts of Luke-Acts that generalize in describing the Jews of Jerusalem or their leaders as those who crucified Jesus (see Blinzler, *Trial* 280–81). Thus the context certainly favors the Jewish opponents of Jesus as the subject of "they do" in the protasis. As for the apodosis, the immediately preceding verses have supposed a divine judgment coming on Jerusalem, and so the most obvious subject behind what will happen or will be done is God. The use of the passive to imply God's action is a well-attested phenomenon in biblical Greek, reflecting the Jewish avoidance of naming God too frequently (BDF 130[1], 313; C. Macholz, ZNW 81 [1990], 247–53). Thus the basic suggestion of Neyrey is the most plausible in my judgment: If they (the Jewish leaders and people) treat me like this in a favorable time (when they are not forced by the Romans), how much the worse will they be treated in an unfavorable time (when the Romans suppress them). In this interpretation green wood and dry wood are simply proverbially diverse periods of time, one more favorable than the other, and "wood" is not interpreted allegorically. As in the previous verses, reform is not a possibility; the fate of Jerusalem and its inhabitants has been sealed by what the adversaries of Jesus are now doing.

Two Wrongdoers with Jesus (23:32). The somewhat awkward word order attested in P[75] and Codices Sinaiticus and Vaticanus reads literally, "And there were led others wrongdoers two with him to be put to death"; the meaning is "others, who were wrongdoers, two of them." Presumably, however, to avoid the possibility of reading it in a way that would make Jesus himself a wrongdoer, the Koine tradition of mss. changed the word order to "others, two wrongdoers." In no way could the Lucan Jesus be a *kakourgos* (a "bad-doer"); for in 23:22 Pilate could find nothing "bad" (*kakos*) that Jesus had done, and after his death a Roman centurion would declare Jesus a "just [*dikaios*]" man (23:47).

The vocabulary of this verse consists of words that have a high percentage of Lucan use in the NT: *agein* ("to lead"), *de kai* ("But . . . also"), *heteros* ("other"), *kakourgos* ("wrongdoer"), *anairein* ("to put to death"). Yet Soards ("Tradition . . . Daughters" 239–40) is surely right in judging that this is simply a Lucan rewriting of Marcan material. Luke uses *agein* at the beginning of the verse to signal an inclusion with *apagein* ("to lead away") in 23:26. With references to Jesus being led (away) on both sides of it, the oracle to the Daughters of Jerusalem is neatly packaged—a static moment in the journey.[27] As already mentioned, Luke 23:26 used only the first half

---

[27]While Luke does not contain the stories of Veronica and the three falls of Jesus on the way to crucifixion, his scene with the women would contribute to the much later devotion of the "Stations of the Cross." A woman named Berenice (Latin: Veronica) appears at the trial of Jesus before Pilate

of Mark 15:20b (the part about leading Jesus out/away). He chose to delay use of the second part of the Marcan verse, "in order that they might crucify him" until here where he rephrases it as "to be put to death." That is the expression Luke (alone; 22:2) used for the plot of the chief priests hatched before Passover: "They were seeking to put him to death." By a larger inclusion Luke is telling us that what was plotted previously by the Jewish authorities is now about to take place.[28]

Mark (also Matt and John) waits until Jesus has arrived at the place of crucifixion to mention that two others (Mark: *lēstai*, "bandits") were crucified with him. Luke anticipates, assuming that these two must have been led out with him to the execution site. Some have thought that having two wrongdoers with Jesus on this journey is Luke's way of underlining the fulfillment of Jesus' prediction at the Last Supper (22:37): "And with outlaws [*anomoi*] was he reckoned," a citation of Isa 53:12. That is not clear: The vocabulary here ("wrongdoers," *kakourgoi*) is different, and the prophecy would have just as easily been fulfilled if Luke left the first mention of these two men where Mark had it, at the time of crucifixion. Rather Luke calls attention to these two men by anticipating their presence and separating it from the other crucifixion events because of the very important scene in which he plans to feature them while Jesus hangs on the cross. In 23:39–43, the longest and most important Lucan change in the crucifixion narrative, Luke will portray their different reactions to Jesus. He seems also to be quite deliberate about preferring "wrongdoers" to Mark's "bandits" (*lēstai*), probably because of the pejorative tone the latter had gained in the troubled 50s and 60s and the First Jewish Revolt. While Luke can describe Barabbas who was preferred to Jesus by the Jewish leaders and people as someone who had a role in a riot (23:18–19), he prefers to keep those who are crucified with Jesus free from any such seditious context. After all, one of them will be with Jesus in paradise this day (23:43).

ANALYSIS

Of the two elements in this scene where Jesus is being led/taken to the cross, the COMMENT has already discussed in detail various theories about the ori-

---

in the *Acts of Pilate* 7 and identifies herself as the woman who touched Jesus' garment and was healed of a flow of blood (Luke 8:44 and par.). Despite the meaning of her name ("*bearer* of the *image*"), there is no reference to a portrait of Jesus. In the Latin *Death of Pilate* (JANT 157–58), when Jesus met Veronica (but not on the way to Calvary), at her request he imprinted the features of his face on a linen cloth. See E. Kuryluk, *Veronica and Her Cloth* (Oxford: Blackwell, 1991).

[28]See also Acts 2:23; 10:39; 13:28 for the verb "put to death, kill" (*anairein*) used to describe the execution of Jesus by the will or complicity of the Jewish authorities and the Jerusalem populace.

gin of the first, i.e., the carrying of the cross. I rejected the theories that Simon the Cyrenian was invented as a person (he never existed) or as a role (he existed as the father of Alexander and Rufus but was fictionally aggrandized as having helped Jesus). The contention that this invention was in order to supply in the crucifixion narrative the example of a disciple who denied himself, took up the cross, and followed Jesus (Mark 8:34) is weak, since in no Gospel does Simon volunteer (= deny himself) or take up a cross of his own, and in Mark/Matt he does not follow behind Jesus. The contention that the invention was meant to supply an eyewitness for the crucifixion also falters, for Simon is never mentioned again in the NT, and so is not claimed to have been present and watching during the crucifixion (contrast Mark 15:40).[29] Paradoxically the anomaly of one person carrying another's cross increases the odds that Simon was a historical figure, remembered because he or his sons became Christians. John's (seemingly deliberate) omission of his role through the insistence that Jesus carried the cross by himself probably reflects Johannine christology wherein Jesus laid down his own life under no human duress and with no human help. The absence of the attractive figure of Simon from *GPet* may reflect the antiJewish thrust of that apocryphon.

Peculiar to Luke (23:27–31) is the second element in this scene, the heart of which involves the following of Jesus by the multitude of the people, the women beating themselves and lamenting, and Jesus' oracle to the Daughters of Jerusalem. As with all material peculiar to the Lucan PN there is a wide diversity of views about composition. It is widely recognized that Luke drew at least 23:26 from Mark 15:20b–21. I would agree with Büchele, Soards, and others that Luke also derived 23:32 from that source (+ Mark 15:27), rewriting it so as to form an inclusion with 23:26 and thus frame the inserted material about the people and the women. (Luke also wished to form an inclusion with 22:2, where the Jewish authorities sought to put Jesus to death; and he wanted to prepare for the insertion pertaining to the two wrongdoers in 23:39–43.)

The major disagreements are centered on the inserted material in 23:27–31. Since there is no close parallel in Mark, many (Fitzmyer, Rehkopf, Taylor, etc.) would think that here Luke drew from a special source or a special PN. Yet, as indicated in the COMMENT, most of the vocabulary is attested elsewhere in Luke-Acts, sometimes with notable frequency; and so the special-source thesis raises acutely the stylistic relationship between Luke and that putative source. Others think almost totally in terms of Lucan com-

---

[29]The idea that early Christians felt a pressing need to have eyewitnesses to back up the story of the crucifixion events is dubious (see Wansbrough, "Crucifixion" 258–59); even more dubious is the thesis that they freely invented characters to fill this need.

position of these verses, differing only as to whether and where Luke drew on earlier elements.[30] For instance, *as to vv. 27–28,* Bultmann, Dupont, and Soards would hold that Luke composed them himself, while Käser and Kudasciewicz would find here (along with v. 31) the old preLucan nucleus of the scene. *As to vv. 29–30,* Käser and Kudasciewicz would hold that Luke composed them himself out of OT (LXX) motifs, while Bultmann and Dupont would find here (along with v. 31) the old preLucan nucleus, perhaps existing in Aramaic.[31] Soards and Untergassmair would attribute v. 29 and v. 31 to preLucan (oral) tradition but think of v. 30 as adapted by Luke from the LXX (perhaps orally remembered). I report those views (without reproducing every nuance) to show how impossible it is to get any agreement.

I indicated in the COMMENT that there is good reason to think that Luke found the macarism in v. 29 in the Jesus' sayings tradition and has adapted it to the present context. V. 30 clearly echoes Hos 10:8b, while v. 31 is an obscure proverb: thus both prophecy and wisdom are used by Luke to confirm the oracle of Jesus. As to whether there was a preLucan tradition about women lamenting for Jesus as he went to die or Luke has used a common motif to supply context for the macarism in v. 29, I see no way of telling.

What is clear is that whether we have creative composition or adaptive reuse, Luke's hand and mind-set are apparent in almost every line. Why did Luke put all this material together? Those who emphasize the parenetic motif in Luke point out that only this Gospel's account of Simon highlights his bringing the cross *behind* Jesus. Others, however, like Dibelius (*From* 202–3), Surkau (*Martyrien* 96), and Aschermann ("Agoniegebet" 149), see a strong martyrological thrust in such Lucan elements as Jesus' being braver than the sympathetic onlookers, his insistence that his death will bring divine intervention affecting their fate, and that the times to come will be worse. Later Christian and Jewish martyr stories (*Martyrdom of Polycarp* 11:2; crucifixion of Jose ben Jo'ezer [p. 925 above]) are invoked as parallels. These suggestions are so allusive, however, as to be debatable (Untergassmair, *Kreuzweg* 162–63, challenges the martyr parallels).

Less problematic, in my judgment, are the structural parallels within the Lucan PN (see pp. 905–6 above). In the heart of the crucifixion account Mark 15:29–32 has three parties who mock Jesus, and Luke 23:35b–39 adopts and adapts that hostile triad. But Luke alone prefixes the crucifixion

---

[30]In the text above I mention views where Luke has preserved an earlier element. Some scholars (Finegan, Feldkämper) so emphasize Lucan composition that either little reference is made to earlier elements or those elements become a mere springboard for Lucan creation and are not really preserved.

[31]For Bultmann this is a pronouncement story consisting of a Christian prophecy placed in the mouth of Jesus, but not a genuine saying of Jesus. Fitzmyer (*Luke* 2.1495) thinks v. 28 may have come from Jesus but in a different context.

with three involved parties (Simon, the multitude of the people and of women, the two wrongdoers) and affixes sequentially to the death of Jesus another three involved parties (23:47–49: the centurion, the crowds who beat their breasts, acquaintances and the women who saw from a distance). These respective triads, prefixed and affixed,[32] are sympathetic to Jesus (for at least one of the wrongdoers will side with him). In each triad the first party (a single outsider with no previous personal involvement) and the last can be found in Mark, while the middle participant (a lamenting plurality) appears only in Luke. (The Daughters of Jerusalem before the crucifixion and the women from Galilee after the death form also a structural parallelism.)

These triads fit Luke's theological outlook that while some opposed Jesus (the middle triad of mockers taken from Mark), the lives of many others were positively affected by the passion. If for Mark the passion manifests human failure and evil with the overcoming power of God manifested chiefly after Jesus dies, for Luke God's love, forgiveness, and healing are already present throughout the passion. The unprepared and unwilling Simon emerges in Luke in the stance of a disciple; not all the people are hostile to Jesus since a multitude follows him and the Jerusalem women lament for him; one of the two wrongdoers who are led with him to die will be made victorious with him; a Roman centurion will become a spokesman of Jesus' innocence; the crowds will be so touched by his death that they will beat their breasts in penance; and the women from Galilee who have followed him so faithfully will see his death from afar but later see the tomb emptied by his victory.

In the COMMENT I pointed out that the oracle spoken to the Daughters of Jerusalem in 23:28–29, with its prophetic (23:30) and proverbial (23:31) accompaniments, is Luke's way of saying that those responsible for the execution of God's Son will be punished, even in the next generation through the destruction of Jerusalem. It is functionally equivalent to the scenes before Pilate added in Matt ("His blood on us and on our children") and in John ("We have no king but Caesar"). But those self-convicting statements placed respectively on the lips of all the people and of the chief priests are much harsher in their context and import than the reluctant oracle reported from Jesus' lips by Luke. The very fact that it is spoken to women who lament denies that the devastation will be deserved by all who live to see it. If the divine wrath cannot be diverted from Jerusalem because of its prolonged rejection of the prophets and Jesus, Luke shows that not all were hostile and leaves open the possibility that the God who touched the hearts of Simon,

---

[32]In his structural analysis of the Lucan crucifixion narrative, Büchele (*Tod* 66–72) exhibits an exaggerated passion for finding triads, but that should not blind us to his discovery of some genuinely parallel sets of three.

and of one of the wrongdoers, and of the centurion may in turn have been touched by the tears of those who lamented what was being done to Jesus. Modern readers who recognize that issues of responsibility, guilt, and punishment are more complicated than any Gospel portrays may judge that Luke has introduced some helpful nuances.

(Bibliography for this episode may be found in §37, Part 1.)

§40. JESUS CRUCIFIED, PART ONE: THE SETTING

(Mark 15:22–27; Matt 27:33–38; Luke 23:33–34; John 19:17b–24)

Translation

Mark 15:22–27: [22]And they bring him to the Golgotha place, which is interpreted Skull-Place; [23]and they were giving him wine with myrrh, but he did not take it. [24]And they crucify him; and they divide up his clothes, throwing lots for them as to who should take what. [25]Now it was the third hour, and they crucified him. [26]And there was an inscription of the charge against him, inscribed "The King of the Jews." [27]And with him they crucify two bandits, one on the right and one on his left.*

Matt 27:33–38: [33]And having come to a place called Golgotha, which is called Skull-Place, [34]they gave him to drink wine mixed with gall; and having tasted, he did not wish to drink. [35]But having crucified him, they divided up his clothes, throwing lots. [36]And having sat, they were keeping (guard over) him there. [37]And they put up above his head the charge against him, written "This is Jesus, the King of the Jews." [38]Then there are crucified with him two bandits, one on the right, and one on the left.

Luke 23:33–34: [33]And when they came to the place named Skull, there they crucified him and the wrongdoers, the one on the right, the other on the left. [34][But Jesus was saying, "Father, forgive them,

---

*The Koine Greek tradition, the Latin, and the Syriac Peshitta add a v. 28: "And the Scripture was fulfilled that says, 'And with outlaws was he reckoned.'" This is the text from Isa 53:12 that Luke cites in 22:37. MTC 119 comments that Mark very seldom expressly quotes the OT, and that if this verse were originally in Mark, there would have been no reason for Matt or for scribes to omit it. Pace Rodgers ("Mark") minor differences in the Marcan context do not disprove that this verse was copied from Luke, and the reference in Origen, *Contra Celsum* 2.44, can refer to the *fulfillment* of the prediction in Luke.

for they do not know what they are doing."] But dividing his clothes, they threw lots.

[23:38: For there was also an inscription over him: "The King of the Jews, this (man)."]

John 19:17b–24: [17b]He came out to what is called the Place of the Skull, which is called in Hebrew Golgotha, [18]where they crucified him and with him two others, here and there, but Jesus in the middle.

[19]But Pilate also wrote a notice and put it on the cross. Now it was written, "Jesus the Nazorean, the King of the Jews." [20]So many of the Jews read this notice because the place where he was crucified was near the city, and it was written in Hebrew, Latin, and Greek. [21]So the chief priests of the Jews were saying to Pilate, "Do not write 'The King of the Jews,' but that that fellow said, 'I am King of the Jews.'" [22]Pilate answered, "What I have written, I have written."

[23]So the soldiers, when they crucified Jesus, took his clothes and made four parts, a part to each soldier; and (they took) the tunic. Now the tunic was without seam, from the top woven throughout. [24]So they said to one another, "Let us not tear it, but let us gamble about it (to see) whose it is," in order that the Scripture be fulfilled,

> They divided up my clothes among themselves,
> and for my clothing they threw lots.

So then the soldiers did these things.

GPet 4:10–12: [10]And they brought two wrongdoers and crucified the Lord in the middle of them. But he was silent as having no pain. [11]And when they had set the cross upright, they inscribed that "This is the King of Israel." [12]And having put his garments before him, they divided them up and threw as a gamble for them.

COMMENT

Previously, when I treated Jesus before the Jewish authorities and Jesus in the Roman trial, I prefaced each of those major divisions ("Acts") of the PN with a section devoted to background. That procedure did not seem practical here, however. What I call "Jesus Crucified, Part One" consists in Mark/Matt and (to a lesser degree) in Luke of almost a list of discrete items pertinent to crucifixion. The historical, geographical, and archaeological evidence pertinent to each of those items would be more useful to the reader as part of the COMMENT on the verse that mentions it than in an introductory section of background that would necessarily appear many pages before the respective verse. The nature of the material has also caused me to omit an ANALYSIS at the end of this section. In the Synoptics, although some of the items recounted fulfill Scripture or fit into the respective evangelist's overall outline, others are presented without any clear indication of purpose. Indeed no single explanation accounts for the presence of all the items, and different evangelists may have had different reasons for what they included. Once more, then, the investigation of purpose and composition will be more practical if attached to my commentary on the individual items, rather than if it were gathered as an analytic discussion at the end.

In Mark one may detect seven items: (1) name of the place; (2) initial offering of wine; (3) crucifixion; (4) division of clothes; (5) time; (6) inscription of the charge; (7) two bandits. One of those items (#5) is peculiar to Mark. Matt has six of them, in the same order as Mark, and copied from Mark with minor adaptations. Luke has at least four: #1, 3, 7, 4 here at the beginning; and #6 (the inscription) later in 23:38.[1] Overall in this material I find little reason to think that Luke needed a source other than Mark. Yet while Mark/Matt simply list the items without attempting to spell out theological implications or OT echoes, Luke 23:38 weaves one of the items into the narrative (#6); and 23:39–43 expands another (#7) into an important theological episode.

John has a total of five items. At the beginning he lists #1, #3, and #7 simply as details, but then expands #6 and #4 as important episodes with symbolic theological meaning. While it is theoretically possible that John made a selection from Mark's seven, there is enough difference even in those that are parallel to suggest that we are dealing with items fixed early in the tradition and that Mark and John independently reflect that tradition.[2] Let us discuss the seven items in the Marcan order and then in eighth place debate

---

[1]One can debate the presence of #2 (the initial offering of wine) in Luke, since he has only one offering of wine and that is closer to Mark's second offering.

[2]For instance, both Mark 15:29–32 and John 19:19–27 have three individuals/groups who react to Jesus on the cross, but the only shared constituency is the chief priests, who appear as the main component in one reacting group in both Gospels. Mark's three reactions are independent of and subsequent to the introductory list of seven items, and all three are hostile to Jesus. John's first two reactions are related to Mark's introductory items #6 and #4, and the third reaction is supportive of Jesus, not hostile.

the authenticity of the disputed Luke 23:34a where Jesus extends forgiveness.

#1. THE NAME OF THE PLACE (MARK 15:22; MATT 27:33; LUKE 23:33A; JOHN 19:17B)

The scene begins with the arrival of Jesus. Here Mark alone uses a historical present tense for the verb of arrival ("bring"), even as he did in 15:20b–21 for the leading out of Jesus and the compelling of Simon. He will continue to use historical presents in vv. 24 and 27. Thus there is a strong narrative style in the listing of these items. Matt and Luke use *erchesthai* ("to come"); John uses *exerchesthai* ("to come out," which appeared earlier in Matt 27:32). Scholars debate the tone of Mark's *pherein:* Does it always mean "bring" as distinct from "carry"?[3] Does it imply here that Jesus had to be brought (virtually pulled along) because he was too weak; and if so, is that why Matt and Luke avoided it?[4] Or does "bring" simply have the tone of Jesus under compulsion?

Golgotha or Skull-Place. As to the name of the place where Jesus was crucified, both the Semitic (*Golgotha*) and the Greek (*kranion*) forms, each meaning "skull, cranium," seem to have been in the tradition.[5] The Semitic form is omitted by Luke, but that is not unexpected; he omitted "Gethsemane" as well, presumably because such foreign terms were meaningless to his Greek readers. Mark/Matt put the Semitic name first, while John puts the Greek first.[6]

The verb expressing the equivalence in Mark is *methermēneuein* ("to interpret, translate," to be used again in 15:34). Luke substitutes *kalein* ("to call, name," which as a passive participle in this situation is exclusively Lucan). Matt and John both use forms from *legein* ("to say," but rendered here "to call")—Matt's change from Mark is awkward, since now Matt has "called" twice in the same sentence. From this last usage one could get the

---

[3]The verb is less frequent in Matt and Luke, where it does mean "carry." Luke 23:26 has just used it for Simon's carrying the cross. See C. H. Turner, JTS 26 (1924–25), 12, 14.

[4]Did a similar attitude cause scribes to change the Marcan verb to *agein* ("to lead") in Codex Bezae and the Ferrar minuscules?

[5]Despite John's reference to "Hebrew" (as previously in reference to Gabbatha in 19:13), "Golgotha" ("Golgoth" in Codex Vaticanus) is closer to Aramaic *Gulgultā'* than to Hebrew *Gulgōlet.* In the Greek transliteration the second syllable (*gul*) has been dissimilated from the first (BDF 39[6]). For the equivalence with *kranion,* see the LXX rendering of Judg 9:53; II Kings 9:35. The Latin equivalent is *calvaria,* whence the place name "Calvary" popular in English since Wyclif's translation (1382).

[6]Probably the form best known to John's community was the Greek, since he seems to feel it necessary to supply a Greek translation for even common transliterated terms (Messiah, Rabbi). Apparently Mark is following a standard transliterated Aramaic/Greek sequence already illustrated in the *abba, ho patēr* of 14:36.

impression that *kranion* was not simply the translation of "Golgotha" but the actual name used by Greek speakers, an impression furthered by Luke. The grammatical relationship between *topos* ("place") and *kranion* or "Golgotha" varies in each Gospel and is not always clear. In Mark/Matt, for instance, one might judge that "Place" was part of the designation: "Place of a Skull" or "Skull-Place."[7] Luke did not think that "place" was part of the name. John's phrasing in 19:17 is literally "He came out to what is called 'of the Skull' Place which is called in Hebrew Golgotha"; ancient copyists did not agree whether the "which" clause modifies "skull" (which is more likely) or "place."[8]

If one leaves aside those minor points, a major issue involves what the name implies. All the name forms given above are reconcilable with the suggestion that the appearance of the site was similar to a skull because it was a rounded knoll, rising from the surrounding surface.[9] In part because of John's information that a tomb was there (19:41), many have thought that the entrances to cavelike tombs may have supplied the knoll with facelike aspects. We shall discuss in the next paragraph the traditional Jerusalem site of Golgotha. Pilgrims in the 4th cent. spoke of the Calvary that existed there as a *monticulus* or small hill (Jeremias, *Golgotha* 2), and what remains of it today (within a church) stands about 14 ft. high (L.E.C. Evans, "Holy" 112). The utilization of a hill as the place of crucifixion would have served the Roman goal of making the punishment a public warning.

The Site in Jerusalem. Where exactly outside the walls of Jerusalem (p. 912 above) was Jesus crucified? Since John states that Jesus was entombed nearby (a fact confirmed by the need for haste implied in the Synoptic burial narrative), this is the same as the question of the site of Jesus' tomb. The discussion has been focused by queries about the validity of the site chosen by Constantine's architects (drawing on local tradition) for constructing in AD 325–335 a great sacred enclave consisting of the basilica of the Martyrion, a holy garden with a colonnaded rotunda centered on the

[7] See H. Koester, TDNT 8.203. Mark's double use of "place," namely, the Golgotha place (with "the" missing in some mss.) and Skull-Place, has caused some to think that he combined pieces of information. More likely it is simply Marcan tautology.

[8] Also John can be rendered "He came out to a place called Skull," as favored by P[66] and Jeremias (*Golgotha* 1).

[9] The name Skull was given another meaning in later Christian tradition, some of it stemming from Jewish tradition about the Jerusalem Temple area. Origen (*In Matt.* 27:33; #126; GCS 38.265 and 41[1].226) mentions the thesis that Adam was buried here; and a century later Pseudo-Basil (*In Isa.* 5:1; #14; PG 30.348C) mentions the skull of Adam. Jerome (*In Matt.* 4; CC 77.270) knows of the skull-of-Adam tradition but does not accept it. Nevertheless the skull and bones of Adam are depicted at the foot of the crucifix in many paintings and carvings. Still another explanation of the name is that the Skull Hill was a place of public execution where skulls could be found on or near the surface.

tomb (called the Anastasis), and a freestanding Calvary thought to be the hill of Golgotha. What remains from the crusader rebuilding of all this in 1099–1149 is generally called the Church of the Holy Sepulchre. Because (as the name indicates) the primary focus of the ecclesiastical edifice has always been the tomb where Jesus lay, I shall reserve discussion of the history of the site and its churches to the last part of the ANALYSIS of §47 below, the section concerned with the Gospel account of the burial of Jesus by Joseph from Arimathea. Here I am concerned only with what that traditional site (which must be taken seriously as a possible historical remembrance) might tell us about the locale of Golgotha.

A crucial point in the debate is Josephus' placing of the various defensive walls constructed through Jerusalem's history (*War* 5.4.2; #142ff.). The Second North Wall existed in Jesus' time; and the possible genuineness of the site occupied by the Church of the Holy Sepulchre depends on whether it lay outside that wall (and not inside the walls as the church now stands). Excavations since World War II have clarified the situation,[10] for apparently the traditional site stood outside the wall in a section that had served as a quarry since the 8th or 7th cent. BC and had in the 1st cent. BC been partly filled in to serve as a garden and burial place. The site is not far from the Garden Gate in the north wall and fits well the description of John 19:41: "But there was in the place where he was crucified a garden, and in the garden a new tomb in which no one had ever yet been placed." What is now Calvary rose 35–40 feet above the quarry floor, a knoll that should have been easily visible from the walls. Evidence of tombs has been found cut into the rock of the knoll.[11] Thus, extensive excavations have strengthened the case for the traditional site.

The Church of the Holy Sepulchre which is now on that site has emotional drawbacks, e.g., the nasty squabbling among the priests or monks who represent the ancient churches that celebrate rituals there, oppressive grime, darkness, and (through much of the last century) ugly scaffolding because Christians could not agree on repairs. For Protestant evangelicals in particular, the incense and music of exotic liturgies have seemed almost idolatrous. Inevitably there have been attempts to find a more suitable site, the most famous of which is the "Garden Tomb" (associated in the 19th cent. with Thenius, Conder, and the British General Gordon), some 820 ft. N of the existing Turkish walls and the Damascus Gate. A knoll that looks like a

[10]In §37, Part 2, see especially the writings of Bahat, Benoit, Evans, Kretschmar, Lux-Wagner, Riesner, Schein, and Wilkinson ("Tomb").

[11]Bahat, "Does" 32. Plausibly one may reason that the rock of this outcrop had been spoiled by a crack resulting from an earthquake (a split is still visible) and that is why the quarriers left it as unfit for yielding the fine blocks of *melek* limestone that this area supplied.

skull, a landscaped garden, and an ancient tomb have made this choice attractive to visitors repelled by the Sepulchre church. Arguments that the "Garden Tomb" site has no solid tradition from antiquity, that the skull physiognomy does not stem from the 1st cent., that there are many tombs of different periods in this area, and that the Turkish walls are quite far from the walls of Jesus' time have convinced the overwhelming majority of scholars that this candidate for Golgotha is not worthy of serious debate.[12] An equally implausible thesis has been proposed in continued writings by E. L. Martin: The Mount of Olives, near the summit, was the place of execution.[13] His main argument stems from a literalist interpretation of Matt 27:51–54, where one gets the impression that the centurion and those with him have seen the earthquake, the rending of the sanctuary veil, the tombs being opened, and the bodies of the fallen-asleep holy ones being raised. Only from the Mount of Olives could one see the entrance to the sanctuary or "holy place" of the Temple. This assumes that Matt knew which veil was involved and that Martin has read his mind correctly as to which veil, and that all this happened. (Mark is not specific that the centurion saw the rending). There is not the slightest evidence outside Matt that when Jesus died any of these things happened; as I shall contend in §43, we are dealing with apocalyptic symbolism. The attempt to take Heb 13:10–13 literally as a geographical directive to the place where Jesus was "sacrificed" is another failure to recognize symbolism. John's phrasing in 19:20 is particularly obscure (literally: "because near was the place of the city where Jesus was crucified"). Martin wants to interpret that to mean that Jesus was crucified near "the Place [Temple] of the city," for the Mount of Olives was opposite the Temple. This is totally implausible in my judgment: "Place" was used just three verses before in "the Place of the Skull" (Golgotha) and plausibly that is what it means here as well. The most implausible thesis is that of Barbara Thiering:[14] Golgotha was the southern esplanade of the Qumran settlement down by the Dead Sea, over twenty miles from Jerusalem by road (both Pilate and Caiaphas had come there). One will never be able to prove beyond

---

[12]See Vincent, "Garden"; Barkay, "Garden."

[13]He claims in his *A.S.K. Historical Report* that his thesis is revolutionary because the traditional churches, including the Roman Catholic Church, "have accepted as their de facto teaching of dogma (supposedly under the inspiration of the Holy Spirit) that the Church of the Holy Sepulchre built by Constantine and his mother is indeed the crucifixion site." The physical site of the crucifixion in Catholic thought has absolutely nothing to do with dogma, doctrine, or belief. If one looks at the scholars I have listed in n. 10 above, one recognizes that they are not deciding on the basis of religious prejudice. That is a red herring.

[14]*The Qumran Origins of the Christian Church* (Sydney: Australian and New Zealand Studies in Theology and Religion, 1983) 216; repeated in her *Jesus and the Secret of the Dead Sea Scrolls* (San Francisco: Harper, 1992), 113–15. Death took place on Friday in AD 33 after Jesus had married Mary Magdalene for the second time on Wednesday evening.

doubt where Golgotha stood, but no candidate more credible than the traditional site is likely to emerge. Traditions of the 2d and 4th cents. about the place of the burial, which point to the Holy Sepulchre, have more value than such modern guesses that have no serious archaeological support.

#2. THE INITIAL OFFERING OF WINE (MARK 15:23; MATT 27:34)

In Mark/Matt Jesus is offered wine twice. Here, *at the beginning* of the crucifixion process "they," i.e., the Roman soldiers, give him *oinos* (sweet wine) mixed with myrrh or gall, but he does not take/drink it. (Mark uses the imperfect with possibly a conative thrust: were trying to give.) *At the end,* after Jesus' cry of desolation and just before he dies, "someone" among the bystanders fills a sponge with *oxos* (coarse, bitter wine, vinegary in taste), fits it on a reed, and gives it to him to drink (Mark 15:36; Matt 27:48). This is done in a context of mockery, but it is not clear that the action itself is a mockery. We are not told whether Jesus drank it.

In Luke there is only one offering of wine: In the middle of Jesus' time on the cross the soldiers (Luke's first reference to them) mock him, coming up and offering him *oxos*. This resembles the Mark/Matt second offering (no sponge, however). The agents are the soldiers, but that may not be enough to claim an echo of the first offering, since Luke tends to treat the bystanders favorably and may be correcting the Marcan picture of the second offering.

In John there is only one offering of wine: At the end (19:29–30), just before Jesus dies, "they" (the soldiers?) put a sponge soaked in *oxos* on some hyssop and raise it to Jesus' lips; he takes this wine. Clearly this is parallel to the second Mark/Matt offering.

Overall, then, only Mark/Matt have the initial offering of *oinos,* whereas later or toward the end of the crucifixion all four Gospels have the offering of *oxos,* as does *GPet* (see below). Only John specifies that Jesus took that *oxos.* Were there two drinks in the preGospel tradition, and did several evangelists independently simplify the picture? Or in the tradition was there only one drink offered—toward the end, in a context of mockery, and with a Scriptural background? The latter is a simpler solution, but then one must explain why Mark (or the immediate preMarcan tradition) added the initial *oinos.* There is no clear scriptural echo of passion psalms in this initial offering in Mark (Matt adds one, as we shall see). True, Mark has a fondness for doubling scenes and sayings, and the initial offering supplies a type of inclusion (wine at the beginning and the end); but is there a theological motif?

Mark's Use of This Gesture. What Mark describes is not totally lacking in verisimilitude. The idea of a benevolent quaff of wine to numb pain appears already in Prov 31:6–7 where, as an exception to admonishing those in power not to drink, we hear: "Give strong drink to him who is perishing and wine [*oinos*] to those in bitter distress; when they drink, they will forget their misery." Passages in later Jewish writings attest to the offering of scented wine to the condemned as an anesthetic.[15] Mark writes of an admixture of myrrh using the passive participle of *smyrnizein,* a verb related to *smyrna* ("myrrh").[16] Myrrh was used by the Egyptians in embalming; and biblical passages refer to an external use in preparing the body for burial (Mark 14:3; Luke 23:56; John 12:3; 19:39). A wider use as an attractive perfume is attested in Ps 45:9; Prov 7:17; and Song (Canticle) 5:5. Some have thought that it was put in the wine as an anesthetic or narcotic, citing the 1st-cent. AD pharmaceutical of Dioscorides Pedanius. However, in the first book (#77) of *The Greek Herbal of Dioscorides,* ed. R. T. Gunther (Oxford Univ. 1934), 42–43, there is a long list of what myrrh helps (menstruation, colds, dysentery, loss of hair, bad breath, body odor, etc.); but there is only one passing word about a soporiferous effect. Apuleius (*Golden Ass* 8.14) describes a woman drugging a man with strongly soporific wine so that she can harm him in his sleep, but myrrh is not mentioned. Therefore the dulling effect expected from the drink may well have been associated with the wine itself (heavy, sweet wine) rather than with the myrrh. As to the purpose of the admixture of myrrh, strange as it may seem to modern tastes, perfumed wine was prized in antiquity: "The finest wine in early days was that spiced with the scent of myrrh" (Pliny, *Natural History* 14.15; #92). He continues, "I also find that aromatic wine is constantly made from almost the same ingredient as perfumes, from myrrh, as we have said" (14:19; #107).

All this background suggests how Mark's statement about the offer of wine would have been understood. The only surprise in what he describes is that the "they" who offer the wine are Roman soldiers; for in the background references the assistants are often family, friends, or pious helpers. This Gospel picture whereby those who have mocked and scourged Jesus offer a painkilling drink makes intelligible why "he did not take it." In 14:36 in Gethsemane the Marcan Jesus had asked the Father to take the cup of a suffering

[15]TalBab *Sanhedrin* 43a tells of a group of Jerusalem women who, as an act of piety, gave to the condemned a vessel of wine containing a grain of frankincense to numb him. The minor talmudic tractate *Semaḥot* (*'Ebel Rabbati*) 2.9 (44a) reports: "The condemned . . . are given to drink wine containing frankincense so that they should not feel grieved." Tertullian (*De jejunio* 12.3; CC 2.1271) tells how on the morning of his being condemned friends gave a Christian catechumen "medicated" wine as an antidote, but it made him so drunk that he was not able to confess which Lord he served.

[16]Also referred to as *myrra* or *myron* and, when mixed with oil, as *stactē.* It is the resinous gum of the bush known as *balsamodendron myrrha* or, more precisely, as *commiphora myrrha* or *abyssinica.* For details see W. Michaelis, TDNT 7.457–59; G. W. Van Beek, BA 23 (1960), 83–86.

death from him but had come to understand that doing the Father's will
involved drinking that cup. To drink the wine mixed with myrrh given
him by his enemies in order to lessen the pain would be to renege on the
commitment he had made. For the Marcan Jesus the offer of wine is
another manifestation of the *peirasmos* or testing that had begun in Gethsemane.

In my judgment this analysis of Mark's theological intent in which the
refused drink is used to underline Jesus' determination to give himself fully
is more plausible than any of several other suggestions. For example, some
would relate the refusal of wine here to the symbolic statement at the Last
Supper in Mark 14:25: "Amen I say to you that I shall not drink of the fruit
of the vine until that day when I drink it anew in the kingdom of God." Yet
Jesus' refusal to drink the wine mixed with myrrh is scarcely part of that
postponement until later when the kingdom of God has been fully established; for this is not a positive wine that, were Jesus to have drunk it, would
have brought the coming of the kingdom. Davies ["Cup"] has another suggestion: Jesus considers his death as an atonement, and Mishna *Yoma* 8.1
forbids drinking on the Day of Atonement. But there is no evidence that
Mark interprets Jesus' death against the background of the Day of Atonement imagery, as does the Epistle to the Hebrews.

Matt's Use of This Gesture. Some would argue that Mark is alluding to
Ps 69:22, which offers a description of what the enemies of the suffering
just one do to him:

> And they gave for my bread gall [*cholē*],
> and for my thirst they gave me to drink vinegar [*oxos*].

Of the fifteen Greek words in the LXX of the verse, however, only "and"
and the verb "to give" (in a different tense) are found in Mark 15:23. If there
is an echo of the psalm in Mark, it is in the second offering of wine that
involves *oxos* (15:36).

An analysis of the first offering of wine in Matt 27:34 gives a different
result, for that Gospel has replaced Mark's "wine with myrrh" by "wine
mixed with gall [*cholē*]," so that the *cholē* of the first line of the psalm is in
Matt's first offering of wine, and the *oxos* of the second line of the psalm
constitutes Matt's second offering of wine. By parallelism the two lines of
the psalm were saying the same thing in different vocabulary: Gall (*cholē*)
and vinegar or common wine (*oxos*) were unpleasant offerings to the just
one, reflecting hate or contempt. Yet elsewhere Matt (as well as other NT
authors; see John 19:24 below) shows a tendency to break down the parallelism of OT passages into two distinct statements, both of which are shown to

be fulfilled in Jesus.[17] It is Matt, then, not Mark, who makes the first drink recognizably echo Ps 69:22.[18] This represents an abandonment of Mark's emphasis; for while the Marcan readers would discern in the sweet wine perfumed with myrrh the traditional pain-killer, Matt's readers would not think that of the wine mixed with gall. Rather they would recognize that as God had predicted through the psalmist, the just man was being abused by his enemies.[19] I explained above that most likely the reason the Marcan Jesus did not take the anodyne wine offered him was because he had agreed to do the Father's will in drinking the cup. This reason is not applicable to Matt, as the evangelist implicitly acknowledged by inserting a new explanation for Jesus' refusal: "having tasted, he did not wish to drink." He tasted the gall that had been mixed with the wine to mock him and recognized the mockery.[20]

Does the change from myrrh to gall sacrifice all verisimilitude for Matt's narrative? Was gall ever put into wine? Cholē means something bitter (gall, poison, wormwood; see Prov 5:4; Lam 3:15). There is a certain bitterness in the aromatic taste of myrrh as well;[21] and wormwood (*absinthium*) was mixed in ancient wine (Pliny, *Natural History* 14:19; #109), as well as in modern vermouth. Thus the Matthean picture is not absurd, even if readers would recognize the action in the present context as hostile.

While we cannot know with any surety, in summary I suggest that the following scenario best explains the situation in the Gospels pertinent to the wine offered to Jesus on the cross. In the earliest tradition there was *one* offering of common wine (vinegar, *oxos*), probably in mockery of Jesus' thirst on the cross. That is preserved in John's only offering and in Mark/Matt's second offering. It was probably Mark himself who introduced into the crucifixion account an initial offering of spiced wine because that was a practice often followed in such executions. Mark's predilection for doubling is well attested; here the introduction created an inclusive parallelism between the beginning and end of the scene. More important, it enabled Mark

[17]His most famous example is in 21:15, where a parallelism with two names for the same animal in Zech 9:9 (ass, colt) is split into a description of two animals on *both* of which Jesus sits at the same time!

[18]The Koine text of Matt 27:34 goes further in this direction by reading *oxos,* instead of *oinos,* in the first wine offering.

[19]As mentioned previously, I believe that NT argumentation and references to preaching justify our positing that considerable familiarity with Scripture was communicated to Gentile converts. Most Jews who became believers in Jesus are thought by their upbringing already to have had this familiarity.

[20]I find totally implausible the suggestion of Willcock ("When") that Jesus graciously tasted it to show acknowledgment of the kindly purpose for which the wine had been offered. The wine had been offered for a kindly purpose in Mark, not in Matt.

[21]Strained, however, are the efforts of R. C. Fuller ("Drink") and Ketter ("Ist Jesus") to argue that Matt's "something bitter" is really no different from Mark's myrrh.

to signal to the reader Jesus' refusal of what would spare him from suffering and thus to show at the final stage of the drama Jesus' willingness to drink the cup of suffering the Father had given him. Matt, adapting Mark and having recognized the echo of Ps 69:22 in the second drink, introduced another echo ("gall") in the first drink; thus the crucifixion of Jesus fulfilled both lines of what the psalmist had said about the suffering of the just one. As for Luke, his one drink (23:36) is dependent on Mark's account of the second drink (not on an earlier preLucan tradition; see pp. 997–98 below); his omission of Mark's first drink is an example of the usual Lucan simplification, dispensing with Marcan duplication.

There remains a complicating factor. In *GPet* 5:16, toward the end of Jesus' time on the cross and just before (not after, as in Mark/Matt) Jesus' cry of dereliction, "someone of them" (the Jewish people who have crucified him) says, "Give him to drink gall with vinegary wine [*oxos*]." Then having made a mixture, they gave to drink. I shall discuss in APPENDIX I the (relatively few) scholars who give *GPet* priority over the canonical PNs. Following (in an exaggerated manner) Dibelius's idea that the PN arose from reflection on Scripture, they would contend that *GPet*'s strong echo of Ps 69:22 was the original form of the tradition and that Mark decreased the biblical flavor by omitting the reference to gall and introducing a first drink. Matt would have been partially restoring the original tone by bringing back the gall and introducing it into the first drink. To my mind this theory makes Mark act most implausibly. I see rather a tendency to gradually increase the echoes of the psalm. There was already the *oxos* ("common wine, vinegar") in Mark 15:36; Matt added the gall in the first drink; *GPet,* eliminating all non-psalm elements, brought together the gall and the *oxos* into one line. What appears in *GPet* is found elsewhere in 2d-cent. writings, and therefore one cannot be certain whether *GPet* is the font of this combination or echoes it. *Barnabas* 7:3, in describing the crucifixion of the Son of God, reports, "He was given to drink vinegary wine and gall." A few lines later (7:5), in the context of how all this fulfilled the OT preparations spoken by God through the prophets, we find: "Because you are going to give me to drink gall with vinegary wine" (same wording as *GPet*). Irenaeus (*Adv. haer.* 4.33.12) refers to the prediction that he should be given to drink vinegary wine and gall. The echo of the psalm has become almost the only issue.

#3. THE CRUCIFIXION (MARK 15:24A; MATT 27:35A; LUKE 23:33B; JOHN 19:18A)

We now come to the centerpiece of the passion, the crucifixion itself, more often portrayed in art than any other scene in history—with great variation in the shape and position of the crosses, in how Jesus is affixed to the cross, in how he is clothed, in his expressions of anguish, etc. Yet in all comparable literature, has so crucial a moment ever been phrased so briefly and uninformatively?

> Mark: And they crucify him [historical present]
> Matt: But having crucified him
> Luke: There they crucified him
> John: Where they crucified him

Not a word is reported about the form of the cross, about how he was affixed, about the amount of pain. Indeed, in Matt the crucifixion is subordinated to the division of clothes, and in John, to the naming of the site. In Luke and John the crucifixion of Jesus and the crucifixion of the two criminals get the same amount of attention. Thus in what follows we are heavily dependent on evidence from outside the NT.[22]

Crucifixion in General. The English term "cross" prejudices our understanding, for it gives the image of two lines crossing each other. Neither the Greek *stauros* nor the Latin *crux* necessarily has that meaning; they both refer to a stake to which people could be attached in various ways: impaling, hanging, nailing, and tying.[23] Using a stake to impale would normally kill the victim instantly or quickly. Using a stake or pole to crucify would normally effect a slow death since no vital organ would be pierced.

Archaeology supplies evidence that the crucifixion of pirates was known in the port of Athens as early as the 7th cent. BC. Yet Herodotus (*History* 1.126; 3.132,159) seems to associate crucifixion primarily with the Medes and the Persians, and the latter may have been the first to employ it as a punishment on a large scale. With Alexander the Great's spread of Greek power to the East in the late 4th cent., crucifixion became a common Hellenistic practice. The Carthaginian relatives of the Phoenicians practiced cru-

---

[22]In §37, Part 3, see the helpful contributions of Brandenburger, Fitzmyer, Hengel, and H.-W. Kuhn ("Kreuzesstrafe").

[23]*Skolpos* ("picket, stake") and *xylon* ("tree") also appear in references to crucifixion. As for verbs, besides the *stauroun* employed in the Gospels, one encounters *anastauroun, anaskolpizein* ("to fix on a stake"), *kremannynai* ("to hang"), and *proseloun* ("to nail"). Whether deliberately or not, Herodotus uses *anastauroun* (3.125) in reference to corpses, and *anaskolpizein* (1.128; 3.132) in reference to the living. Eventually, however, shades of meaning yielded to stylistic custom: Philo uses *anaskolpizein* and Josephus uses *(ana)stauroun*. See Hengel, *Crucifixion* 24. The Hebrew roots found in crucifixion vocabulary include *tlh* ("hang"), *zqp* ("lift up") and *ṣlb* ("hang, impale").

cifixion, and contact with them in the Punic Wars seems to explain its spread to the Romans. If those who had been killed in other ways were sometimes crucified after death for show in the East, the Roman crucifixion of the living constituted the punishment in itself. Plautus (250–184 BC), who in his plays gives us a Roman world peopled by slaves, soldiers, and rogues, is the first Latin writer to supply vivid, even if brief, references to crucifixion. It was primarily a punishment applied to the lower classes, slaves, and foreigners. Tacitus (*History* 2.72.1–2) speaks of a "slave-type" punishment (*servile modum*); and Cicero (*In Verrem* 2.5.63,66; #163,170) expresses oratorical horror at the thought of daring to crucify a Roman citizen. Actually sometimes that did happen (Hengel, *Crucifixion* 39–40; H.-W. Kuhn, "Kreuzesstrafe" 736–40); but overall, unlike the Carthaginians, the Romans spared the upper classes and nobility from crucifixion. The mind-set may be reflected in reference to Jesus in Philip 2:7–8, which connects taking on the form of a slave with death on a cross.

As for crucifixion by Jews, one of the earliest references to the practice is the execution in the early 1st cent. BC of 800 prisoners by Alexander Jannaeus.[24] As Roman armies began to interfere in Judea, crucifixion of Jews became a matter of policy, e.g., the governor of Syria crucified 2,000 Jews in 4 BC (Josephus, *Ant.* 17.10.10; #295). In the 1st cent. AD Jesus is the first Jew whom we *know* to have been crucified. Otherwise Josephus records no crucifixions of Jews during the first part of the Roman prefecture in Judea (AD 6–40), though there is ample attestation of crucifixion during the second part of that prefecture (AD 44–66).[25]

Despite the number of passing references to crucifixion in secular literature, we learn little by way of detailed information. Comparatively the laconic Gospel accounts emerge as informative (Hengel, *Crucifixion* 25). Partly the situation is explained by the fact that educated Romans would have regarded crucifixion as a barbarous punishment to be talked about as little as possible. (At any period of history those who practice torture are not overly communicative about the details.) "The relative scarcity of references to crucifixion in antiquity and their fortuitousness are less a historical problem than an aesthetic one" (ibid 38). Justinian's *Digest* 48.19.28 looks on

[24]Josephus, *War* 1.4.6; #97; *Ant.* 13.14.2; #380. It is unlikely that Josephus was referring to an impalement that would ipso facto be likely to kill the victim; see §35, n. 4. Consult pp. 533, 541 above for other examples of crucifixions by Jews and for the Qumran interpretation that seems to inculcate this punishment. Halperin ("Crucifixion" 40–42) argues that Jews borrowed crucifixion from the Romans and brought it into Jewish law by involving Deut 21:22–23. He suggests that crucifixion, which became a legitimate form of punishment in Qumran times, was later replaced in rabbinic times by strangulation, a quicker and less agonizing capital punishment.

[25]H.-W. Kuhn, "Kreuzesstrafe" 733. He observes (pp. 686–87) that in the period AD 1–150 incidents of crucifixion are rarely documented elsewhere (Greece, Asia Minor, Syria), except for the crucifixion of Christians in Rome under Nero.

crucifixion as a most aggravated form of the death penalty (*summum supplicium;* see H.-W. Kuhn, "Kreuzesstrafe" 746–51). Cicero (*In Verrem* 2.5.64,66; #165,169) refers to it as a "most cruel and disgusting penalty," and the "extreme and ultimate penalty for a slave." He says (*Pro Rabirio perduellionis* 5.16), "The very name 'cross' should not only be far from the body of a Roman citizen, but also from his thoughts, his eyes, and his ears." Seneca (*Epistle* 101.14) speaks of the "accursed tree." Josephus (*War* 7.6.4; #203) calls crucifixion "the most pitiable of deaths." Besides the NT references to the shame of Jesus' death on the cross (I Cor 1:18,23; Heb 12:2), we have the constant scorn of pagan writers for a religion that so esteems a man executed by the worst of deaths on the infamous cross.[26]

One might think that the reticence of writers about the details of crucifixion could be supplemented by Christian art from the early centuries when crucifixion was still practiced, showing how artists of that period imagined Jesus would have been crucified. The symbolism of a cross (without a corpus) appears in catacomb art, e.g., in the 3d-cent. hypogeum of Lucina, and becomes common by the 4th cent. Yet often the cross sign is only a rough approximation that can tell us nothing about the type of cross Christians thought was used for Jesus. The situation is complicated by the tendency of the older archaeologists to identify anything remotely resembling a cross as Christian.[27] As for depictions of the crucified Jesus, there are only some half-dozen portrayals from the 2d to the 5th cents. (Leclercq, "Croix," with reproductions). One of the oldest, a tiny 2d-cent. carving on a jasper gem, may be a gnostic work; it shows a nude, contorted crucified figure with no onlookers and thus perhaps makes fun of the orthodox Christian belief in the death of Jesus. Another gem, a carnelian of the 2d cent. from Romania, shows a superhuman Christ on the cross almost twice as tall as the surrounding twelve apostles. The 3d-cent. representation found in the Domus Gelotiana of the imperial palace on the Palatine Hill in Rome, a school for pages, is a graffito of a crucified ass; it makes fun of the God worshiped by the Christians and seemingly reuses what may have been a standard form of mockery directed at a royal pretender (Polybius, *History* 8.21; #3; see NDIEC 3 [1979], #34, p. 137). Alas, such reproductions have nothing to teach us about how Jesus was crucified. Granted the sparsity of information, let us nonetheless seek to answer several questions.

On What Type of Cross Was Jesus Crucified? Seneca states (*De conso-*

---

[26]Justin, *Apology* 1.13.4; Origen, *Contra Celsum* 6.10; Augustine, *Civitas Dei* 19.23 (CC 48.690) in reference to Porphyry.

[27]The pre-79 cruciform object at Herculaneum, the celebrated Sator word-square at Pompeii (W. Barnes, NTS 33 [1987], 469–76), the plus signs on Judean ossuaries of the 1st cent., and the Palmyrene cross of AD 134 are all possible examples of this exaggeration.

latione ad Marciam 20.3): "I see crosses there, not just of one kind but fashioned in many different ways: Some have their victims with head down toward the ground; some impale their private parts; others stretch out their arms on the crossbeam." Josephus (*War* 5.11.1; #451) reports that the Roman soldiers under Titus nailed their prisoners in different postures. Occasionally just an upright stake was used, and the condemned's hands were raised vertically and nailed extended above his head. (This is not what happened in Jesus' case,[28] since he carried a cross[beam] to the place of execution.) Where a mass crucifixion took place, sometimes a number of criminals were affixed to something resembling a scaffold or tympanum—a panel of vertical planks. The 5th-cent. depiction of the crucifixion of Jesus on the portal of St. Sabina in Rome shows a type of scaffold. Because of the assumption that the two criminals mentioned on either side of Jesus were all who were crucified on Golgotha, in the present scene three *individual* crosses are usually imagined. While there was an X-shaped cross (*crux decussata,* "crooked"), the fact that Jesus carried a cross(beam) has usually eliminated that from the discussion. If the vertical post already stood at Skull-Place, the crossbeam could have been attached to it in one of two ways. A V-shaped notch was sometimes cut into the very top of the upright post and the crossbeam laid in that, giving the shape of a T (*crux commissa*) in which no part of the cross rose above the crucified one's head.[29] *Barnabas* 9:8 assumes that Jesus was crucified on a tau-shaped cross, and Justin (*Dialogue* 91.2) describes the crossbeam being fitted into the topmost extremity of the upright, an area shaped like a horn. (Justin, however, is interested in the fulfillment of an OT passage dealing with horns that may have guided his description.) Another type of cross was formed if a notch was cut horizontally into the side of the standing pole at some distance from the top, and the crossbeam inserted into that, giving the shape of an elongated plus sign (✝, the *crux immissa*). This would be a cross with four arms; it is assumed by Irenaeus (*Adv. haereses* 2.24.4), who by adding a seat or buttocks-rest to it speaks of five extremities. Tertullian (*Ad nationes* 1.12.7; CC 1.31) compares Jesus' cross to an erect man standing with arms stretched out. This has been the favorite cross of Christian art because Matt 27:37 mentions that "they put up above his head the charge" (see Luke 23:38).

How high from the ground did a cross stand? We find the expression "to go up on the cross" (*anabainein, epibainein, ascendere*). Often the cross was low enough for animals to ravage the feet of the crucified, which may have been only a foot off the ground. Suetonius (*Galba* 9.1) reports that a man

28Pace the Jehovah Witness Bible; see J. F. Mattingly, CBQ 13 (1951), 441–42.
29This is sometimes referred to as a cross with three arms, one vertical descending from the crossbeam, and two horizontal on either side of the point where the vertical bisects the crossbeam.

who claimed to be a Roman citizen was mockingly hung higher than the rest. Three of the evangelists imagine that a reed or hyssop was needed to raise a sponge full of common wine to Jesus' lips. A common *guess* is that Jesus' cross stood some 7 ft. high.

How Was Jesus Affixed to the Cross? Criminals were affixed to the crossbeam by being tied or nailed; then the crossbeam was lifted up by forked poles (*furcillae*) and, with the body attached, inserted into the slot in the upright. Hewitt ("Use" 40) cites evidence that in Egypt tying was more common. Pliny (*Natural History* 28.11.46) includes among magic paraphernalia rope (*spartum*) from a cross; and Livy (*History* 1.26.6) speaks of criminals being tied to a tree and beaten while there. On the other hand, Philo (*De posteritate Caini* 17; #61) alludes to men crucified and nailed to a tree. Lucan (*Civil War* 6.547) has a witch gathering iron that has been driven into the hands (*manus*). A slave in Plautus (*Mostellaria* 2.1; #360) offers a reward if anyone will take his place on the cross, provided the feet be nailed twice and the *arms* (*brachia*) twice. Mishna *Shabbat* 6.10 mentions the nails of a crucified. Seneca (*De vita beata* 19.3) speaks figuratively of people driving their own nails into their crosses.

From these descriptions arise issues pertinent to Jesus. No Gospel account of the crucifixion tells us whether Jesus was tied or nailed. For that we are dependent on descriptions of scenes after Jesus' death. In Luke 24:39 the risen Jesus says, "See my hands and my feet," a statement that suggests they were pierced. More specifically, John 20:25,27 indicates the prints of nails in Jesus' hands. *GPet* 6:21, describing the taking of the corpse from the cross, speaks of drawing "the nails from the hands of the Lord." Ignatius (*Smyrnaeans* 1.2) says that Jesus was "truly nailed." With a clear symbolic interest Ephraem, *Commentary on the Diatessaron* 20.31 (Armenian; SC 121.365) speaks of Jesus' hands as nailed and his feet as tied. To what extent are these passages historical on this point and to what extent do they reflect the passion psalm (22:17): "They have pierced my hands and my feet"? By way of answer to the latter question, none of the above passages that refer to nails only in the hands echoes the LXX wording or imagery of the psalm. Indeed, some scholars, puzzled by that failure to exploit a scriptural passage, have suggested that the evangelists were not using the LXX of the psalm; yet Mark 15:34 clearly quotes the LXX of Ps 22:2. Perhaps Luke 24:39 (the only NT passage to mention the feet) does reflect Ps 22:17; and by the 2d cent. that psalm passage would be cited explicitly.[30]

That Jesus' hands were nailed can be deemed historically plausible, pro-

---

[30]Justin, *Apology* 1.35.5–7; *Dialogue* 97.3–4; Tertullian, *Adversus Iudaeos* 13.10–11 (CC 2.1386).

vided one understands that this is not clinically exact terminology. Nails through the palms would not carry the weight of a body but would tear away. In the classical references above Plautus is more accurate in speaking of "arms," and most assume that the nails went through Jesus' wrists. (Hebrew *yād* covers not only the hand but the forearm.) More of a problem is the historicity of the nailing of the feet. In 1932 Hewitt ("Use" 45) wrote, "There is astonishingly little evidence that the feet of a crucified person were ever pierced by nails." Most of the crucifixion nails discovered by excavations in the border regions of the Roman Empire supply no indications of what limb they had pierced. Yet H.-W. Kuhn ("Gekreuzigte" 303–4) mentions the discovery at the port of Athens (Phaleron) of seventeen skeletons of pirates with iron nails in their hands and feet reflecting an execution in the 7th cent. BC. Far more important for our purposes was the discovery in June 1968 of a tomb at Giv'at ha-Mivtar, just north of the tomb of Simon the Just in Jerusalem. It housed eight ossuaries, containing the bones of almost twenty people. In one ossuary, among the bones of three people (one of them a small child), were those of a man in his late 20s who had been crucified. Both the child and the man were named Yehohanan (YHWHNN), but there was also the designation *BN HGQWL* that has puzzled scholars. Yadin ("Epigraphy") suggested reading *h'qwl*,[31] "the bow-legged," so that the child would have been the son of a man crucified with his legs apart. H.-W. Kuhn ("Gekreuzigte" 312) suggests an echo of the Greek word *agkylos* [Latin *ancyla*], "crooked, bent," describing the bones. The date of crucifixion for the elder Yehohanan was some decades before AD 70. A description of the bones and nails was published by V. Tzaferis, J. Naveh, and N. Haas in IEJ 20 [1970], 18–59; and many depictions of Yehohanan on the cross have been based on their presentation (see the Supplement vol. [1976] of the *Interpreters Dictionary of the Bible*, 200). H.-W. Kuhn ("Gekreuzigte") and Zias and Sekeles ("Crucified") have detected major errors in the 1970 presentation (including the length of the nails). The arms were tied (not nailed) to the crossbeam;[32] the man's legs seem to have straddled the upright beam, so that his feet were nailed to either *side* of it (not to the front); most likely two nails were involved, each piercing first an olive wood plaque, the heel bone, and then the wooden surface of the cross—the olive wood was to prevent the crucified man from pulling his feet free of the nail. The leg bones do not

[31]Naveh ("Ossuary"), who published the inscription, could make no satisfactory sense of *HGQWL*. In the Yadin proposal it is uncertain whether a badly written ' appears as *G* or ' was pronounced and hence written as *G*.

[32]To explain the fact that the wrist bones were undamaged, Haas ("Anthropological" 57–58) had originally theorized that the upper limbs were nailed. For a list of what many consider defects in Haas's publication, see Zias and Charlesworth, "Crucifixion," 279–80.

seem to have been deliberately broken while he was alive on the cross, as originally reported.[33] At least the data from this crucifixion, roughly contemporary with Jesus' crucifixion, should remove skepticism about the plausibility of the suggestion that Jesus' feet were nailed.

Hewitt ("Use" 30–39) surveys how the nails were portrayed in subsequent Christian art. Surprisingly, some very old portrayals of Jesus on the cross, a 5th-cent. ivory box preserved in the British Museum and the wood portal of St. Sabina in Rome (Leclercq, "Croix"), seem to show no nails in the feet. Gradually the nails begin to be portrayed as long—an elongation reflecting theological interest in Jesus' blood. Four nails are more common in the earlier period.[34] Helena, the mother of Constantine, is supposed to have found only three;[35] and that number eventually became standard (Gregory of Nazianzen, Bonaventure)—a nail for each hand, and a third nail piercing Jesus' feet (right foot placed over the left, except in Spanish art).

The nailing of Jesus to the cross would have been painful: "Punished with limbs outstretched . . . they are fastened and nailed to the stake in the most bitter torment, evil food for birds of prey and grim picking for dogs" (free rendition of Pseudo-Manetho [3d cent. AD] *Apotelesmatica* 4.198–200; Hengel, *Crucifixion* 9). No canonical Gospel mentions Jesus' suffering. However, as it reports that they "crucified the Lord," *GPet* 4:10 comments, "But he was silent as having no pain."[36]

Comment is needed on two other minor items pertinent to Jesus affixed on the cross. The body of the crucified could be given physical support in several ways, not as an act of mercy but so that the suffering would last longer. If the condemned could lift himself up to get breath, he would survive longer than if the unsupported body were dead weight hanging from the nailed or tied arms. The report that Jesus died so quickly makes it unlikely that we should think that his body had either of the following supports, but I mention them because they appear in Christian art and writing. A *suppedaneum* or footrest was sometimes attached near the bottom of the upright beam. In the 6th and 7th cents. Christian artists and writers begin to assume

---

[33]Haas ("Anthropological" 57) had reported that the right tibial bone was broken by a single strong blow which might be attributed to the final "coup de grâce." In the light of the newer analysis, the bone-breaking may have occurred in the course of putting the bones in the ossuary.

[34]A counting supported by Cyprian, Ambrose, Gregory of Tours, and *Sibylline Oracle* 8.319–20.

[35]On dubious aspects of this find, see J. W. Drijvers, *Helena Augusta: The Mother of Constantine the Great and the Legend of Her Finding the True Cross* (Leiden: Brill, 1991).

[36]This may well have been one of the passages that led to the orthodox mistrust of this gospel (see APPENDIX I), for it could be read to lend support to the thesis that Jesus was not truly human, or even not real at the time of the crucifixion. More likely, however, the author simply reflects the theme of Jesus' silence (already seen in different settings in the canonical Gospels) combined with the theme of bravery related to the portrayal of Jesus as a martyr. For instance, Polycarp (*Martyrdom* 13.3) prays that God will grant him to remain unmoved in the flames.

that Jesus had one.[37] In the Russian cross this becomes another, shorter crossbeam, traversing the vertical shaft at an angle near the bottom. Midway up the cross there was sometimes a *sedile* ("seat") or *pēgma* ("something stuck on"), i.e., a block of wood to support the buttocks. Seneca (*Epistle* 101.12) writes of taking one's seat on the cross; another expression is to "mount" the cross as if one were riding a horse (*inequitare*). The seat may have been useful as the condemned, tied or nailed to the crossbeam, was being lowered into place; for it could have taken some of the weight during the brief time when the crossbeam was being fitted into the niche prepared for it in the upright.[38]

#4. THE DIVISION OF CLOTHES (MARK 15:24B; MATT 27:35B; LUKE 23:34B; JOHN 19:23–24)

In Mark/Matt the statement that Jesus was crucified is followed immediately by the division of his clothes; indeed, in Matt the crucifixion is grammatically subordinated to the division, almost as if the latter were more important. In Luke and in John the statement that Jesus was crucified is followed by the reference to the crucifixion of two criminals; and the reference to the division of clothes comes slightly later. In John it is prepared for by a second reference to crucifixion (19:23a); in Luke it appears incidentally, simply confirming that Jesus was being treated like a criminal.

All four Gospels indicate that "his clothes" were divided. As mentioned previously, the condemned would normally have been led naked to the place of execution; and so, whether for the sake of Jesus, or of Jerusalem, or of the Jews, an exception has been made. Moreover, the clothes are his own, not the garments of mockery that had been put on him. That exchange was specified in Mark 15:20a; Matt 27:31a, but never specified in John or Luke. (Although Luke had no mocking-clothes put on Jesus by Roman soldiers, when we last heard [23:11] Jesus was wearing the splendid garment with which he was clothed by Herod.)

Before discussing the division described in the Gospels, let us ask whether the division meant that Jesus would have hung naked on the cross. The evan-

---

[37]E. Grube, *Zeitschrift für Kunstgeschichte* 20 (1957), 268–87. One of the oldest portrayals of the crucifixion, the graffito of the crucified ass on the Palatine (2d–3d cents.; p. 947 above) has a *suppedaneum*—an indication that the use was thought to be normal. Yet specimens of 5th-cent. Christian art (the British Museum ivory box, the door panel of Santa Sabina in Rome) lack such a foot support.

[38]Justin (*Dialogue* 91.2) describes it as standing out from Jesus' cross like a rhinoceros horn, but he is interested in the fulfillment of an OT passage dealing with horns (Deut 33:17). As mentioned on p. 948 above, it constituted the fifth extremity of the cross for Irenaeus, while Tertullian (*Ad nationes* 1.24.4; CC 1.31) thought of it as a projecting seat.

gelists are not specific and perhaps would not have known; all that we can discuss are likelihoods. Certainly John, who gives the greatest attention to the scene, is so specific about every item of clothing that one would have the impression that nothing was left. The normal Roman pattern would have been to crucify criminals naked, as attested by Artemidorus Daldianus (*Oneirokritika* 2.53). But did the Romans make a special concession to the Jewish horror of nudity (*Jubilees* 3:30–31; 7:20) and allow a loincloth to be used (*subligaculum*)? That the evangelists think the Romans allowed Jesus to wear his clothes to Golgotha might favor that. Mishna *Sanhedrin* 6.3 records differing rabbinic opinions about whether a male should be stoned naked or with a covering in front. Midrash *Sipre* 320 on Deut 32:21 judges it one of the most shameful things in the world to be (punished) naked in the marketplace. Among the early portrayals of the crucified Jesus (p. 947 above), several of the carved gems have Jesus naked. In the late 2d cent. Melito of Sardis *On the Pasch* 97; SC 123.118) writes of "his body naked and not even deemed worthy of a clothing that it might not be seen. Therefore the heavenly lights turned away and the day darkened in order that he might be hidden who was denuded upon the cross." Church Fathers like John Chrysostom and Ephraem the Syrian tolerate that view. Yet the *Acts of Pilate* 10:1 has Jesus girded with a loincloth after the division of clothes; and both the 5th-cent. ivory box in the British Museum and the cypress door of St. Sabina portray Jesus with a loincloth. I would judge that there is no way to settle the question even if the evidence favors complete despoliation.

The Division and Psalm 22. What the evangelists actually describe in terms of dividing and throwing lots is remarkably similar in the four Gospels.[39] One may ask how much of that language reflects Ps 22:19:

They divided up my clothes [pl. *himation*] among themselves,
and for my clothing [*himatismos*] they threw lots.

The LXX of the psalm verse is quoted exactly (as a fulfillment citation) only in John 19:24; but the seven items enumerated above make a strong appearance in the Gospels' *description* of the dividing:[40]

Mark 15:24b: nos. 1, 2, 4, 6, 7
Matt 27:35b: nos. 1, 2, 6, 7
Luke 23:34b: nos. 1, 2, 6, 7
John 19:23b–24a: no. 2

[39]Mark's final phrases are peculiar to that Gospel ("for them as to who should take what"), using the verb *airein* that was employed three verses before for Simon's "taking" the crossbeam.

[40]There was a sharp debate among Church Fathers as to whether the psalmist had Jesus in mind when he wrote this. Tertullian affirmed it (*Adv Marcion* 4.42.4; CC 1.659), as did the Second Council of Constantinople (4th session; May 12/13, 553) against Theodore of Mopsuestia.

If one compares these statistics, the situation that emerges is curious. Without citing the psalm verse, the Synoptics use half the vocabulary of the psalm in describing the division, with Luke a bit more distant from the psalm than Mark/Matt. As a backup John cites the psalm exactly, but his own description of what the soldiers did has little of the vocabulary of the psalm.

Presumably on the preGospel level (Oswald, "Beziehungen" 56), Christians were including in the PN the customary stripping of the prisoner but doing so in the language of a psalm about the suffering just one. This helped to illustrate God's detailed preparation for the fate of the Son. Mark followed that preGospel pattern; and Matt and Luke copied from Mark, suppressing the historical present tense ("divide") and the awkward ending "as to who should take what." John was familiar with a similar tradition and acknowledged it by a fulfillment citation quoting Ps 22:19 exactly. Yet John made this a major episode in the crucifixion account by narrating a scene that fulfills the psalm in every detail without using the vocabulary of the psalm. In the psalm itself no difference of action is intended between the two lines; for "divided up" and "threw lots" are the same action, with the second phrase simply the way of accomplishing the first. Similarly only one set of apparel is referred to under the names of "clothes" and "clothing." John, however, ignores the parallelism (even as Matt did in reference to the gall and vinegar) and describes two different actions on different items of apparel: the clothes are divided into four parts, whereas the undivided clothing (= tunic) is tossed for.[41]

Some of the Johannine development beyond the psalm represents theological symbolism, as can be seen already from John's schematic arrangement of episodes (p. 908 above). This is Episode 2 in the Johannine crucifixion account. In Episode 1 *Pilate* has given witness to the sovereignty of Jesus by a trilingual proclamation. Now the *soldiers,* whose task to execute criminals aligns them with the forces hostile to Jesus, nevertheless fulfill the Scriptures. (Notice that the division of clothing is framed on both sides by a reference to the soldiers.) The next episode will concern *followers* of Jesus.[42] Where John goes beyond the psalm (and where there may be preJohannine, nonSynoptic tradition) is in having the clothes made into four parts, one to each soldier (19:23b). Squads of four soldiers (Greek: *tetradion;* Latin *quaternion*) seem to have been common.[43] One of the four might well have

---

[41]The Aramaic of a later targum of this psalm has sometimes been invoked as basis for John's exegesis, for it speaks of *lĕbûšā'*, "clothes," in one line and *pĕtāgā'*, "cloak," in the next; but there is no evidence that such a reading existed in the 1st cent.

[42]In n. 2 above I pointed out that like Mark, John has three reactors (Pilate, soldiers, followers) interact with the crucified Jesus, even though the identity of John's reactors differs from that of Mark's.

[43]Acts 12:4 has King Herod Agrippa I deliver Peter to prison in the custody of four squads.

been an officer, and later the Synoptics mention a centurion (Mark 15:39 and par.). Here, then, we have Johannine verisimilitude without any clear theological orientation.[44]

How likely is it that the garments[45] would have gone to the soldiers who were custodians of the condemned? In DJ 48.20.1 the general principle is that the goods of those condemned are confiscated, but 48.20.6 reports a distinction made by Hadrian: The garments that the condemned person is wearing may not be demanded by the torturers. Tacitus (*History* 4.3) describes a slave crucified while still wearing rings. Was this milder 2d-cent. attitude correcting the more rapacious practice of the 1st cent.? As for the method employed to divide the clothes of Jesus, all three Synoptics use *ballein klēron* ("to throw the lot"), an expression appearing in Ps 22:19,[46] where, as in Mark, it is accompanied by the preposition *epi* ("on" = "for"). In reference to the tunic, not the clothes, John 19:24 employs *lagchanein* ("to obtain by chance" = "gamble"),[47] accompanied by the preposition *peri* ("about"). As for what is envisaged, most scholars think that something like dice would have been thrown. De Waal ("Mora"), however, doubts that the soldiers would so conveniently have brought a *pyrgos* ("dice box") to the place of crucifixion. He suggests a *mora* game played by guessing the number of outstretched fingers on the opponent's hidden hands. Seemingly that is how the paraphrase of John by Nonnus of Panopolis (ca. 440) understood *lagchanein:* "putting out the fingers of the hand for it [the tunic]."

The Untorn Tunic. John 19:23–24 attaches considerable importance to a *chitōn,* which evidently he identifies with the *himatismos* ("clothing") of Ps 22:19 and keeps separate from the other four parts of Jesus' "clothes." *Chitōn,* most often rendered as "tunic," would normally be a long garment worn next to the skin.[48] Would the description that John gives of *chitōn arraphos,* "without seam, from the top [to the bottom] woven throughout,"[49] mean that

[44]I find farfetched the attempt to relate the four parts of the clothes to the four women (by the most plausible counting) in 19:25 (see de la Potterie, "Tunique non divisée" 135).

[45]Whether or not the evangelist himself speculated as to what the four items were, scholars have made up for the Johannine lack of specificity. A. Edersheim (*The Life and Times of Jesus the Messiah* [2 vols.; New York: Longmans, Green, 1897] 1.625) suggests: headgear, sandals/shoes, long girdle, and a coarse *talith* or outer mantle. Kennedy ("Soldiers") argues that Jesus would have been led barefoot to Golgotha; and on the basis of John 13:4 that portrays Jesus as wearing something beneath his *chitōn,* he substitutes for the sandals a shirt or inner tunic (the *ḥālûq* mentioned in the Mishna).

[46]In the case of Luke 23:34, however, Codex Alexandrinus and the Lake Family of minuscules have a divergent reading employing the plural *klērous,* and that may be original.

[47]The related *ballein lachmon* appears in *GPet* 4:10 (with *epi*) and Justin, *Dialogue* 97.3 (even if in *Apology* 1.35.8 Justin uses *ballein klēron*). *Lachmos* is a rare word, found chiefly in reflections on this passage.

[48]J. Repond, "Le costume du Christ," *Biblica* 3 (1922), 3–14, discussing John 19:23.

[49]I have tried to follow John's word order. It is not clear what the phrase "from the top" modifies. Most take it with the preceding "without a seam"; but Nestle ("Coat") would take it with the following "woven" (as do the Latin Codex c and Syriac witnesses). He believes John is describing a coat

this was a highly unusual garment or simply a normal garment of special quality? H. Th. Braun[50] discusses weaving technique: A seamless garment was not necessarily a luxury item, for it could be woven by a craftsman who had no exceptional skill. Ca. 400 Isidore of Pelusium (*Epistle* 1.74; PG 78.233B) contended that this style of garment was characteristic of the Galilean poor—was this a guess or did he somehow preserve ancient tradition? According to Aubineau ("Tunique" 105), most of the Church Fathers, judging from the clothes of their own time, deemed John's seamless tunic to have been a very unusual garment, exhibiting either Jesus' majesty or his poverty.

Suggestions have been made that the garment had a sacral character, and the superstitious soldiers feared they would destroy that by tearing it. Some scholars would find a symbolic echo of the Joseph story.[51] Nestle ("Ungenähte") points to the special coat that Joseph had (Gen 37:3) which the LXX understood to be a *chitōn* of many colors. There the Hebrew was probably describing a long tunic, and the Syriac translators apparently understood it as having long sleeves.[52] We have seen above (p. 658) the thesis that in the PN Joseph served as a type or image of Jesus. Gottlieb Klein ("Erläuterung") points to TalBab *Ta'anit* 11b which he interprets to mean that Moses wore a seamless coat (without a border).

Overall two symbolic interpretations have outdistanced the others[53] in the adherents they have won: an allusion to the garment of the high priest, and a symbol of unity. Each must be discussed in detail.

(a) The garment of the high priest. Beginning with Grotius in 1641, scholars have appealed in interpreting John to the description by Josephus of the ankle-length tunic (*chitōn*) of the high priest (*Ant.* 3.7.4; #161): "not composed of two pieces," stitched (*raptos*) at the shoulders and on the side, one

---

without a seam at the top or in the upper part. In a passage to be discussed further on, Josephus (*Ant.* 3.7.4; #161) describes a priestly tunic that "does not consist of two pieces [of cloth] sewn together at the shoulders and at the sides."

[50]*Fleur bleue, Revue des industries du lin* (1951), 21–28, 45–53.

[51]Others look to a pagan background. Saintyves ("Deux" 235–36) points out that the clothing of the gods of vegetation revealed their cosmic nature and that the robes on the statues of the gods had significance (e.g., Macrobius, *Saturnalia* 1.18.22 speaks of garments placed on the statue of Dionysos or Liber to imitate the sun). The gnostic work *Pistis Sophia* 1.9–11 pays great attention to the vesture of light with which Jesus was clothed. It is difficult to know how John's readers, presumably of various backgrounds, would have interpreted John's attention to Jesus' clothes; but the detailed psalm background makes it difficult to believe that the author has suddenly shifted to a totally different background for the tunic.

[52]That seems to be the import of *Midrash Rabba* 84.8 on Gen 37:3 ("reached as far as his wrists"). However, Murmelstein ("Gestalt" 55) cites both the Syriac and the Midrash as evidence for Joseph's wearing a seamless coat. G. Klein ("Erläuterung") denies that the evidence for this is early.

[53]Besides these two, one may mention the seamless tunic as a symbol of Christ himself as one within whom all (including the heavenly and the earthly) were in harmony (Rutherford, "Seamless").

long woven (*hyphasmenos*) cloth. While the pattern of the garment is not far from that in John, the descriptive vocabulary is quite different: Only *chitōn* is the same, and for the high priest that may be an outer garment rather than an inner one, as presumably it was for Jesus. Could John and Josephus be giving us independent Greek renditions of a tradition about the high priest's "woven tunic of fine linen" (Exod 39:27; Exod LXX 36:35)? A factor contributing to interest in it may have been the Roman care to keep control of the high priest's garments, releasing them only for feasts (Josephus, *Ant.* 15.11.4; #403–8; 20.1.1; #6).[54] Those who invoke this background suggest that having had Jesus proclaimed as a king by the title on the cross, John is now symbolizing him as a priest.[55] Some patristic writers compare Jesus to the high priest in Lev 21:10 whose vestment was not rent.[56] In general, however, de la Potterie ("Tunique sans couture" 256–57) is correct that the interpretation of John 19:23 whereby the tunic is the high priestly vestment is a relatively modern insight.[57] (Some who espouse it also hold the following interpretation, for they are not exclusive.)

(b) A symbol of unity. The fact that the tunic without a seam was not torn (*schizein*), an element not in the psalm, has been seen as symbolizing unity among Jesus' followers. De la Potterie ("Tunique non divisée" 131) points to I Kings 11:30–31, where the prophet Ahijah tore his new *himation* into twelve pieces to symbolize the rending of the united kingdom of David and Solomon. John has shown more interest in unity than in priesthood (10:16: "One sheep herd, one shepherd"; 11:52: "To gather together even the dispersed children of God and make them one"; 17:21–22: "That they all may be one"). A parallel symbol could be the net loaded with large fish that was not torn in John 21:11, the only other Johannine use of *schizein*. The related noun *schisma* appears in John 7:43; 9:16; 10:19 for divisions produced among people by Jesus. The idea, then, would be that the Roman soldiers, so prominent at the beginning and end of this episode, did not tear apart what belonged to Jesus. De la Potterie ("Tunique non divisée" 136–37), a strong proponent of this interpretation,[58] thinks that John had in mind the unity of the messianic people of God. In the Western church the unity inter-

---

[54]Noteworthy too is Philo's allegorizing of the high priest, who had a special garment; this is tied in with Philo's identification of the high priest as a symbol of the all-compassing *Logos* (*De ebrietate* 21; #85–86; *De fuga* 20; #108–12; see Bacon, "Exegetical" 423; Conybeare, "New").

[55]For possible references to Jesus as a priest in John, see BGJ 2.765–67, 907–8, 993. Also invoked is Rev 1:13, where one like a Son of Man wears garments possibly symbolic of both priest and king. Hebrews 8–10 has Jesus go to his death in a manner comparable to the high priest's offering sacrifice on the Day of Atonement.

[56]Isidore of Seville (*Quaestiones in Vet. Test. Lev.* 12.4; Pl 83.330); also Severus of Antioch.

[57]Proponents include Barrett, W. Bauer, Calmes, Durand, Haenchen, Hoskyns, Lightfoot, and Loisy.

[58]Other proponents include Bernard, Bultmann, Dauer, Lagrange, and van den Bussche.

pretation is attested early with Cyprian (*De Ecclesiae Cath. Unitate* 7; CC 3.254), who sees in the tunic without a seam, woven from the top, a symbol of the undivided church being unified from heaven above. Slightly later in the East, Alexander of Alexandria criticizes the Arians for having rent the seamless tunic of Jesus.[59]

A decision about exactly what type of symbolism John had in mind may not be possible (that is true too of other Johannine symbolisms), even if there is more evidence for the unity interpretation than for the priesthood symbolism. In either reading one is still forced to deal with the symbolic import of having this undivided tunic *taken away* from Jesus. What is certain is that John has gone beyond the Synoptics in this as well as in the other episodes of the crucifixion.

#5. THE THIRD HOUR (MARK 15:25); THE SOLDIERS KEEPING GUARD (MATT 27:36)

Here we discuss two brief sentences of differing import, found (only) in Mark and Matt, each sequential to the division of clothes: Mark 15:25, "Now it was the third hour, and they crucified him"; and Matt 27:36: "And having sat, they were keeping [guard over: *tērein*] him there." Three issues emerge: Mark's third hour; Mark's second reference to crucifixion; and Matt's soldiers keeping guard.

The Third Hour. Mark has had a long and careful sequence of time indications dividing the day beginning with the Last Supper (see p. 628 above). In particular, this is the first of three time indications in the course of the crucifixion, continued by "the sixth hour" when darkness came over the whole earth in 15:33, and "the ninth hour" when Jesus cried out in 15:34. (On either side of these three, one has *prōi* ["early" = 6 A.M.] for taking Jesus to Pilate in 15:1 and *opsia* ["evening" = 6 P.M.?] for getting Jesus' body in 15:42.) Matt and Luke, who preserve other Marcan patterns of three and other Marcan time indications, omit this reference to the third hour and thus seem to reject the Marcan picture in which Jesus would have been crucified by or shortly after 9 A.M. Already John 19:14 has described Jesus as still standing before Pilate at "the sixth hour," i.e., noon.[60]

In reference to that Johannine passage (p. 846 above) I mentioned and rejected a series of attempts to harmonize Mark and John (also J. V. Miller,

---

[59]Theodoret, *Hist. Eccl.* 1.4.3–5; GCS 19.9. In interpretations focused on unity sometimes the emphasis is christological, e.g., the unity of natures in the one person (Aubineau, "Tunique" 126).

[60]This disagreement is important in the light of John's time agreements with Mark in relation to Peter's denials (cockcrow), the bringing of Jesus to Pilate ("early"), and the burial of Jesus (late on preparation day, just before the Sabbath).

"Time"). Those and others include the following (with each of which I list a basic objection or difficulty):

- arguing that John's sixth hour should be counted from midnight rather than from dawn and so equals 6 A.M.—a horarium already discussed and rejected;[61]
- dismissing John's sixth hour as a theological statement (it is that, but the sixth hour is also the first time indication pertinent to the crucifixion in Matt and Luke);
- making Mark's third hour equivalent to the sixth hour: (a) reading *hote* ("when") for *kai* ("and") with some textual witnesses of Mark 15:25, combined with an ingressive understanding of the aorist ("began to crucify"), so that Mark means that a series of actions related to crucifixion began at 9 A.M.; (b) arguing that Mark's third hour covers from 9 A.M. to noon (a thesis refuted by the Marcan pattern of third, sixth, and ninth hours, which requires a distinction between the third and sixth; moreover, Mark spells out a duration when he wishes one, e.g., from the sixth to the ninth hour in 15:33);[62]
- arguing that Mark's third hour describes the moment when Pilate decided to crucify Jesus, while John's sixth hour describes the moment of the execution of that decision[63] (actually Pilate's presence and action were concluded by Mark ten verses before he mentioned the third hour);
- arguing that Mark's "third" hour is a mistaken reading for the "sixth"[64] (one would then have two Marcan references to the sixth hour);
- arguing that in many passages "hour" is eschatological, i.e., the hour of Jesus' final struggle as in Mark 14:35,41 (once more, however, the sequence of the third, sixth, and ninth hours indicates specific time indications within that struggle).

My overall conclusion is that Mark's 9 A.M. and John's noon cannot be reconciled in any of the ways cited. Both indications may be theological; one may be chronological and the other theological or liturgical; but both cannot be chronologically exact.

The only time indication appearing in all four accounts of the crucifixion

[61]§35, n. 45. J. P. Louw (*Scriptura* 29 [1989], 13–18) argues strongly that one cannot harmonize by claiming that Mark 15:25 represents a Roman way of reckoning hours while John 19:14 represents a Greek one. "All the data from ancient Greek and Latin texts substantiate a single unified system of counting the hours of the day from sunrise to sunset" (NTA 34 [1990] #88).

[62]A desperate proposal by Cowling, "Mark's" recognizes this: While Mark's third hour was a three-hour time watch (9 to noon), the sixth and ninth hours mentioned by Mark were actual hours (noon and 3 P.M.). Blinzler (*Trial* 266) questions whether any of these "hours" can be made the equivalent of a three-hour watch period.

[63]See Theophylact, *Enarratio in Ev. Joannis* (on John 19:14; P 124.269A) and Euthymios Zigabenus, *Commentarium in Marcum* (on Mark 15:25; PG 129.845A).

[64]This is the reverse of the thesis that John's "sixth" hour was a copyist's mistake for "third." I mentioned both proposals in §35, n. 46.

is "the sixth hour" (noon). Possibly that stood in the preGospel tradition but was used differently: in the Synoptics for darkness coming over the whole land; in John for the sentencing of Jesus to be crucified. Moving beyond that to history, we should recognize that Mark's 9 A.M. time for crucifixion has much less likelihood than that Jesus hung on the cross in the early afternoon. Mark himself may give an indication that Jesus was not crucified so early; for with evening drawing on (between 4 and 6 P.M.?), Pilate wonders that Jesus has died so soon (Mark 15:44).

If "the third hour" was not part of the early tradition, Mark (or the immediate preMarcan tradition) would have added it to fill out the pattern of the third, sixth, and ninth hours. Was that purely for structural purposes or was there a theological motif? Gnilka (*Markus* 2.317) would detect here the chronological determinism of apocalyptic thought in which there are periods fixed by God (seasons and times, years, months, and weeks), even if there is no close parallel to Mark's counting of daytime hours. Without following that thesis completely, one can recognize that the exact Marcan time frame in this fateful day shows how carefully God took care of the events surrounding the death of the Son.

A second possibility is that the time frame responds to liturgical patterns in Mark's church. The most famous of several attempts to explain the whole of Mark as a liturgical arrangement is P. Carrington's *The Primitive Christian Calendar* (Cambridge Univ., 1952); he held that Mark consisted of readings arranged according to a church calendar. Less farfetched is that in Mark's church background there were fixed hours of prayer,[65] perhaps especially for an annual commemoration of the death of the Lord. Christian prayer hours are noted in Acts 3:1 (ninth hour); 10:9 (sixth hour); and 10:30 (ninth hour). The site of Golgotha may have been remembered because of the Jewish tendency to honor (perhaps with annual feasts) places associated with the deaths of martyrs. The liturgical suggestion is attractive but is little more than a guess.[66]

Mark's Second Reference to Crucifixion. In Mark 15:24 we find "and they crucify him"; in 15:25, "Now it was the third hour, and they crucified him"; in 15:27, "And with him they crucify two bandits." Matt has the first and third references to crucifixion but not the second. Why the Marcan re-

---

[65]Karavidopoulos ("Heure") and others may be correct in proposing that this was the practice of the Church of Rome, but it could have been a wider Jewish-Christian practice. Daniel (6:11) had the custom of praying three times a day; and TalBab *Berakot* 26b attributes such timed praying to the patriarchs.

[66]Although Gnilka ("Verhandlungen" 9) recognizes that there was liturgical influence on Mark, he thinks that the Marcan time references were added for historicizing purposes.

petitiveness? Theses that Mark has combined an extraneous tradition by incorporating the second reference or that the second reference, which alone uses an aorist, should be translated "began to crucify" are not necessary. Most likely we have another instance of free-flowing Marcan narrative style. There will be two references to Jesus' crying out in Mark 15:34,37. (Notice too the double reference to crucifixion in John 19:18,23.)

Nevertheless, there remains a problem. Matt and Luke copied from Mark neither element of 15:25: not "the third hour" nor the second crucifixion reference. Some would explain the silence in Matt and Luke by textual criticism. Blinzler (*Trial* 268–69) proposes that the form of Mark read by Matt and Luke (independently) lacked 15:25, which was the addition of a later editor. One could then attribute to that editor and that later period the liturgical interest discussed above. Or one could explain the addition as the result of an editorial misinterpretation. For example, one encounters in Christian writing the motif that Jesus spent six hours on the cross, presumably counted from the sixth hour until evening when Joseph from Arimathea came. Did the hypothetical Marcan editor mistakenly count the six hours back from the time of Jesus' death about the ninth hour (3 P.M.) and thus emerge with crucifixion at the third hour? As attractively simple as the proposal of interpolation is, the positing of a different form of Mark available to Matt and Luke is a rather desperate solution.[67]

The absence of both elements of Mark 15:25 in Matt and Luke is best explained as deliberate omission. If the absence of the Marcan verse were manifested by Luke alone, that would be a minor problem, for Luke has already excised the first offering of wine. But Matt has retained all the other Marcan preliminary incidents. Why did he suddenly excise both elements in 15:25? One may plausibly explain the omission of the second reference to crucifixion on the grounds that Matt and Luke often dispense with Marcan repetition, e.g., the repetition of prayer in Mark 14:35–36 where independently they eliminated the first Marcan description. But one needs another explanation for the omission of "the third hour" (when Mark's references to the sixth and ninth hours are preserved). Independently did Matt and Luke

---

[67]Similarly I have little confidence in the thesis of J. P. Brown (JBL 78 [1959], 223) that originally in Mark, in the place where 15:25 now stands, there was a different wording pertinent to *watching Jesus on the cross,* and that verse gave substance to Matt 27:36 (perhaps through Matthean rewriting). To establish the existence of such a Marcan verse, besides Matt 27:36 with its *tērein,* one can point to Luke 23:35, which in the same sequential position as Mark 15:25 and Matt 27:36 reads: "And the people were standing looking on [*theōrein*]." Also one could argue for the originality of an alternative reading of Mark 15:25 (supported by Codex Bezae and the OL) that substitutes for "and they crucified him" the reading "and they were guarding [*phylassein*] him." But the vocabulary of these three witnesses to the hypothetical lost Marcan verse is too diverse, and the Bezae reading of Mark may result from an attempt to harmonize with Matt.

decide that Mark's placing of the crucifixion at such an early hour ran against a well-established tradition associating the sixth hour with Jesus' crucifixion? They may have found Mark's introduction of a complete time frame too radical an innovation; or, if the Marcan frame was liturgical in origin, they may not have repeated it because they had no such liturgical prayer pattern in their own churches.

The Soldiers Keeping Guard (Matt 27:36). Precisely where Mark 15:25 should have come (after the clothes division, before the inscription), Matt records a different verse not found in Mark: "And having sat, they were keeping [guard over: *tērein*] him there [*ekei*]." There is verisimilitude here, for Petronius (*Satyricon* 111) describes a soldier assigned to watch over crucified robbers (see Matt 27:38) lest their bodies be taken down (also Phaedrus, *Fables of Aesop*, Perotti's Appendix 15.9). What is described by Matt fits into the plan of his PN: These soldiers will be recalled as Jesus dies (27:54) so that they can join the centurion in testifying to the Son of God. In other details this verse is harmonious with Matthean styles and motifs. As for the sitting and guarding position of the soldiers, only Matt explains Peter's presence in the courtyard of the high priest thus: "He sat with the attendants to see [*idein*] the end" (26:58; see 26:69). Only Matt uses the verb *tērein* in the PN (here; 27:54; in 28:4 for the custody of the tomb). Thus, with SPNM 279–80 one can explain this verse as a Matthean creation. These soldiers will raise the value of the Roman testimony to Jesus, for the recognition of his divine sonship will be based not only on what happened at his death but on what happened throughout the crucifixion, as well known by those assigned to keep guard.

#6. The Inscription and the Charge (Mark 15:26; Matt 27:37; Luke 23:38; John 19:19–22)

The four Gospels agree that the crime with which Jesus was charged existed in a written form at the place of crucifixion. Mark and Luke call it an *epigraphē* ("inscription"), with Mark adding *epigegrammenē* ("inscribed") in a typical periphrastic construction. Matt and John both use the passive participle *gegrammenos* ("written"—they also agree on including "Jesus" in the wording); John uses *titlos* ("notice"), a Greek translation of the technical Latin term *titulus* (perhaps through the vulgar Latin *titlus*). John's more precise terminology is in harmony with his tendency to make this a formal episode. *Titlos* for John seems to include the board and the message written on it, but the term could refer just to the message.[68] There is

---

[68]See F. R. Montgomery Hitchcock, JTS 31 (1930), 272–73.

another sense of *titlos* as a royal "title," and that may not be completely absent from John.

Three Gospels mention the existence of the inscription/title in their introductory material pertinent to the crucifixion. Luke mentions it only later as the basis of the soldiers' mockery of Jesus (by analogy with Mark's making the *substance* of the inscription the object of Jewish mockery in 15:32). What the evangelists portray here is not an official notification related to Roman records but a technique of informing the general public: If crucifixion was meant to deter crime, it would be useful to have the specificity of the crime publicized. A plaque (*tabula;* Greek *pinax*) was prepared indicating the charge against the prisoner, i.e., the crime or *causa poenae* of which he had been convicted. Mark/Matt speak of *aitia,* the term used in John (18:38; 19:4,6) in Pilate's statements that he found no *case* against him. Blinzler (*Trial* 254) imagines the writing would have been in red or black lettering on the white gypsum surface of a board. From our chief references to a *titulus* outside the NT,[69] it appears that such an inscription was frequent but not necessary, that there was considerable latitude in the wording (which could contain a note of sarcasm), and that it could be displayed in several ways. Eusebius exemplifies one wording: "This is Attalus the Christian." Sometimes the *titulus* was carried before the condemned as he went to be crucified or was marched around the amphitheater; other times it was hung around his neck. In TalBab *Sanhedrin* 43a (p. 376 above) a herald is supposed to have gone out to give cry to Jesus' crime.

The Gospel Reports. Mark does not describe the position of the inscription; John describes it as "put on the cross"; Luke has it "over [*epi*] him"; Matt specifies that it was "put up [*epitithenai*] above [*epanō*] his head." Harmonizing the evidence, most artists have imagined a *crux immissa* (✝) with the inscription on the section of the upright that rose above Jesus. That may well have been what all or most of the evangelists intended, since all think that those who were passing or were nearby could read it. The fact that in the (quite limited) secular evidence we have no instance of the title being placed in such a position has led some scholars to dismiss the Gospel localization as fiction. Surely, however, were the evangelists freely creating, they could have placed the title in another position and have had it readable. Verisimilitude suggests that writers living in the 1st cent. AD would not describe a totally implausible scenario without theological reason.

The inscription/title contains the only words pertinent to Jesus claimed to have been written during his lifetime. We observe, however (with amuse-

---

[69]Suetonius, *Caligula* 32.2; *Domitian* 10.1; Tertullian, *Apology* 2.20 (CC 1.91); Cassius Dio, *History* 54.3.7; Eusebius, EH 5.1.44.

ment if we think of literalistic approaches to the Gospels), that all four evangelists report them differently (as does *GPet* 4:11):

> Mark: The King of the Jews
> Matt: This is Jesus, the King of the Jews
> Luke: The King of the Jews this (man)
> John: Jesus the Nazorean, the King of the Jews[70]
> *GPet:* This is the King of Israel

Mark does not report who did the inscribing, but the surrounding actions are
those of Roman soldiers. Matt attributes the written charge to a "they" who
have to be the guarding soldiers. Luke places the inscription in a setting
where he mentions (Roman) soldiers for the first time. In none of the Synoptics is there a suggestion that the inscription itself was made for the purpose
of mockery, although once inscribed the wording was used in mocking Jesus.
One gets the impression from the inscription and the use made of it that to
the last moment Jesus was the victim of false accusation.

The Episode in John. John not only develops the inscription into a major
episode but changes its import. Pilate writes the title. That indication is not
directly contradictory to the Synoptic picture because most readers would
understand that Pilate had it written and put up by the soldiers. Nevertheless
the immediacy of the attribution to Pilate and the ensuing impression that
he and the chief priests are at Golgotha arguing with one another enable
John to turn the scene at the cross into a personal encounter, prolonging the
struggle in the trial. Once more Pilate and "the Jews" debate over Jesus. In
the apparent conclusion of the trial the chief priests forced Pilate to condemn
Jesus who he knew was not guilty; now with irony Pilate turns the tables on
his Jewish protagonists by proclaiming to be true the charge they had
made.[71] The implication of Pilate's deliberate reuse of the Jewish charge is
spelled out in the *Acts of Pilate* 10:1: "After the sentence Pilate ordered the
charge against him to be written as a title in Greek, Latin, and Hebrew, just
as the Jews had said that, 'He is the King of the Jews.'" In the Johannine
dramatization the Roman governor has regained his imperiousness after having been cowed by threats at the end of the trial. Without effort the laconic
answer (given in Greek) to the chief priests of the Jews can be rendered into

---

[70]In John 19:21 the title is repeated as "The King of the Jews," a form that agrees with Mark and
must have been the basic wording in the tradition.

[71]John plays on the complexities of the charge. In the Roman trial Pilate's question, "Are you the
King of the Jews?" (18:33) was not of his own making but came from the Jewish nation and chief
priests who gave Jesus over to him (18:34–35). Jesus never answered "I am a king" but "You say
that I am a king" (18:37) to underline that his kingdom was not of this world as had been implied.
Yet now at the cross the chief priests claim: "That fellow said, 'I am King of the Jews.'" And it is
in response to their affirmation stating that Jesus himself made the claim that Pilate affirms Jesus'
kingship (presumably in the sense that Jesus envisioned the kingdom).

a Latin epigram worthy of an authoritarian prefect: *Quod scripsi, scripsi.* The chief priests had accepted Caesar as king; now they must be satisfied with a rebuff by Caesar's representative.

John's formulation of the wording of the title is the most solemn and most memorable, as attested by the traditional artistry of the cross with an INRI from the supposed Latin *Iesus Nazarenus Rex Iudaeorum.* The solemnity is increased by the indication that the title was trilingual.[72] Inevitably there have been attempts to argue that John's form of the title, including the trilingual pattern, is historical. A peculiar variant is the thesis of Regard ("Titre"), who maintains that Matt preserves in literal translation the Hebrew form of the inscription, Luke preserves the Greek form, and John, the Latin form! Equally romantic is the thesis of Lee ("Inscription") that the full title, "This is Jesus of Nazareth, the King of the Jews," was written in Semitic (Aramaic) consonants; but the longer style of Greek and Latin writing (which included vowels) meant that only abbreviated forms appeared on the inscription in those languages, whence the briefer Gospel variants. He invokes the eyewitness of Simon the Cyrenian for the wording—something the Gospels decline to do. There have been attempted reconstructions of the Hebrew[73] and even discussions of whether the relic of the title (Johannine form) venerated at the Church of Santa Croce in Gerusalemme in Rome might not be authentic.[74]

Leaving all this aside, we can be reasonably sure that soldiers would not have taken care to transcribe a criminal charge in three languages. Multilingual inscriptions were in vogue in antiquity but in solemn settings, e.g., imperial proclamations. Gordian III's tomb, erected by Roman soldiers, was inscribed in Greek, Latin, Persian, Hebrew, and Egyptian. (Jerusalemites would have been familiar with the edict against entering forbidden sections of the Temple inscribed in Greek and Latin [Josephus, *War* 6.2.4; #125]; and it is not impossible that by irony that edict contributed to John's thought.) If the Synoptics informatively reported the existence of an inscription because its wording would become the occasion for the mockery of Jesus, John has moved in another direction which in part mocks "the Jews." Only in John's trial scene was the significance of the title "The King of the Jews" explored:

---

[72]The Koine textual tradition of Luke 23:38 reads "inscribed over him in Greek, Latin, and Hebrew letters." Fitzmyer (*Luke* 2.1505) vocalizes the opinion of the vast majority of scholars: "Almost certainly a gloss taken over from John 19:20."

[73]Most of the medieval paintings show a Hebrew text, sometimes vocalized on the basis of John's Greek (see Wilcox, "Text"). S. Ben-Chorin, *Bruder Jesus* (Munich: Deutscher Taschenbuch, 1977), 180, has a peculiar suggestion: *Yeshu Hanozri Wumelek Hayehudim,* the first four letters of which constitute a play on the tetragrammaton *YHWH.* Blinzler (*Trial* 254) turns to Aramaic (which is most often, if not always, what John's "Hebrew" means): *Yēšūaʿ Nazorayāʾ malkāʾ diyehūdayē* (= my modification of Blinzler's Germanic transcription).

[74]*The Month* 155 (1930), 428.

It is a false title if it refers to a kingdom of this world, but Jesus is a king in the sense that he has come from above into this world to bear witness to the truth (John 18:36–37). Here the Johannine Pilate, who has no power over Jesus except what has been given him from above (19:11), is brought to make a formal proclamation of the truth. When Jesus challenged him in the trial, "Everyone who is of the truth hears my voice," Pilate evaded by asking what is truth (18:38a). But no one escapes so easily from judgment in the presence of Jesus, and now Pilate is brought to profess publicly what he would not confess privately.

In this proclamation IĒSOUS NAZŌRAIOS has all the formality of "Tiberius Caesar," and the trilingualism increases the imperial or regal atmosphere. For the Christian readers "Jesus the Nazorean" colors "The King of the Jews" to give a fuller picture. The latter, if rightly understood, has truth; but Jesus himself gave an "I am" to his identification as the former in 18:5,7–8. Thus in the title that culminates the Roman governor's judgment on Jesus there is an echo of a designation of Jesus spoken when Roman soldiers first came on the stage of the PN to arrest him. The three languages have symbolic force. Hebrew is the sacred language of the Scriptures of Israel; Latin is the language of the Roman conqueror (indeed the word John uses is *Rōmaisti*); Greek is the language in which the message about Jesus is being proclaimed and written. Ancient scribes saw possibilities in the symbolism: Some Koine textual witnesses changed the order to Hebrew, Greek, and Latin, giving the place of dignity at the end to the imperial language; but John's primacy is not determined by what is powerful here below. We may compare Pilate's present role to that of Caiaphas in John 11:49–52; 18:14. High priest that year and therefore someone who could prophesy, Caiaphas was brought by God unknowingly to speak the truth about Jesus: "It is better that one man die for the people." Having encountered the truth (Jesus), Pilate is brought to make an imperial proclamation prophetically true in its wording.[75] In John 19:16 "the Jews" had said, "We have no king but Caesar"; but ironically the Roman has proclaimed a king other (and greater) than Caesar. Even more clearly than the Synoptics, John uses Pilate to vocalize a theological evaluation.

John 19:20 tells us that this dramatic title was read by many of the Jews because "the place where [Jesus] was crucified was near the city."[76] The

[75]Pseudo-Cyprian (*De montibus Sion et Sinai* 9; PL 4.915C) says that Pilate made manifest a prophetical saying.

[76]Literally "near was the place of the city where Jesus was crucified." Martin ("Place" 3) uses the tangled Greek word order to argue for the Mount of Olives as the crucifixion site, near the place (i.e., Temple; see 11:48) of the city. There is nothing in the context, however, to encourage reading "place" here as the Temple; more logically it is the Place of the Skull of 19:17b. The grammar does not necessarily support Martin's reading since *eggys* ("near") can govern the genitival phrase "of the

Synoptic crucifixion accounts have three mockeries of Jesus by those who dispute his claims; John's closest parallel in terms of content is the present scene where "the chief priests of the Jews" challenge Pilate's proclamation of "The King of the Jews." In the triumphal Johannine portrayal of the crucifixion Pilate is adamant in favor of Jesus. The verbs in "What I have written, I have written" are both perfect in tense, the first equivalent to an aorist, the second connoting a lasting effect (BDF 342[4]). Compare the response of the Seleucid king Demetrius in I Macc 13:38: "The things we have guaranteed to you have been guaranteed." On Pilate's lips both Roman authority and Roman respect for a written statement find expression.

In John this is Jesus' final encounter with his Jewish adversaries, and the "chief priests of the Jews" still refuse him any acknowledgment. That is given by the representative of the Gentiles. Jesus had said (12:32) that when he was lifted up from the earth, he would begin to draw all to himself; and that has now begun. John's portrayal of the crucified Jesus is harmonious with the famous Christian interpolation in Ps 96:10: "The Lord reigns *from the wood* [of the cross]."[77]

GPet. The inscription on the cross is used in *GPet* 4:11 in a way that differs from both the Synoptic and Johannine presentations. Since the Jewish people, not the Roman soldiers, crucify Jesus, they inscribe, "This is the King of Israel." Previously they had mocked Jesus, "Judge justly, King of Israel," but there is no suggestion that the inscription itself is a mockery. "The King of Israel" is not a political title as is "the King of the Jews." For the Christian who wrote *GPet* Jesus is truly the King of Israel; and so the Jews have proclaimed the truth in that inscription, even if they mock Jesus' claim to it.

Is there a historical kernel in the canonical title or inscription? As Bammel ("Titulus" 355–56) points out, many critical scholars dismiss the inscription as a Christian invention: Bousset because it shows disparagement of the Jews; Haenchen because it contains a Jewish-Christian confession of Jesus.[78] Such objections pertain more to the Johannine developments of the title than to the simple existence of the inscription "The King of the Jews" in relation to the crucifixion of Jesus.[79] The use of the title here is related to its use in

---

city." Schnackenburg (*John* 3.271) points to the separation of words that belong together as a mark of Johannine style and as proof that the scene was composed in Johannine circles.

[77]This reading is not found in the MT or LXX but is implied in *Barnabas* 8:5 and known to Justin (*Dialogue* 73.1), Tertullian (*Adv. Marcion* 19.1; CC 1.533), and the Latin tradition.

[78]To the contrary, the Jewish scholar Winter ("Marginal" 250–51) argues that the Gospel wording of the title is historical, since had Christians created the wording, they would have been more precise about Jesus' theological identity. He points to the Christian phrasing that was the subject of the previous note: "The *Lord* reigns from the wood [of the cross]."

[79]Mark's form of the wording is surely the most original among the Synoptics, for Matt and Luke simply expand on it. The same form is found in the discussion between the chief priests and Pilate in John 19:21.

the Roman trial. Was the trial usage enshrined in the inscription; or did the memory of a crucifixion inscription shape the account of the trial; or were both historical; or were both formulations of Christian faith? That the title "the King of the Jews" is completely a Christian invention is implausible, since it never appears as a Christian confession.[80] Jesus' recorded reaction to it, "You say (so)," indicates that this is not a phrasing he would choose. There is, on the other hand, nothing implausible about it as a charge that a Roman governor, deciding a case according to extraordinary proceedings typical of provincial administration in a minor area like Judea, could relate to the general policy of the *Lex Iulia de maiestate* in the ordinary jurisprudence of Rome (pp. 717–19 above). That a claim to kingship would bring a violent Roman reaction can be seen from the mass crucifixions performed by Varus, the Roman governor of Syria, against self-proclaimed kings and their followers after the death of Herod the Great (Josephus, *Ant.* 17.10.8,10; #285,295). H.-W. Kuhn ("Kreuzesstrafe" 735) thinks the inscription is a historicizing of the characteristic evaluation of Jesus by the Romans. But how did the characteristic evaluation get started? Did Christians not preserve any memory about the basic details of the most important event in their faith? Objections to historicity have often been based on the (dubious) claim that Christians would have had no access to what was said in the Sanhedrin and the Roman trials, but here we are dealing with a public sign. I see no convincing objection to its historicity as the expression of the charge on which the Romans executed Jesus.

#7. Two Bandits or Wrongdoers (Mark 15:27; Matt 27:38; Luke 23:33c; John 19:18b)

Mark has one more historical present in 15:27, "And with him they crucify two bandits," forming an inclusion with 15:24, "And they crucify him." This is not a sign that what is in between is inserted (pace Matera, *Kingship* 27); it is a sign that Mark is concluding his list of preliminary items. In what follows Mark will start again his sequential narrative. Matt's "Then there are crucified with him two bandits" (27:38) is less obviously an inclusion with "having crucified him" of 27:35; but Matt's listing of the preliminary items has already been sequential, as suggested by "Then." While Mark/Matt thus place the reference to the two co-crucified at the end of listed items pertaining to the crucifixion, Luke and John agree in putting it at the beginning in the same sentence that announces the crucifixion of Jesus at the place of

---

[80]The use of the designation by the magi in Matt 2:2 does not contradict this, for that occurs before they are enlightened by information from the Scriptures. The magi, like Pilate, have recognized a certain truth about Jesus, but in 2:2 are scarcely depicted as Christians.

the Skull; and thus make the presence of the co-crucified somewhat more incidental or, at least, less climactic in the list. It is noteworthy that all four Gospels mention that two others were crucified with Jesus and agree on their relative position on either side of Jesus.[81] Yet the Gospels are not very informative about details pertinent to the crucifixion of the co-crucified. This terseness has given free rein to patristic commentators and artists to portray the crucifixion of the two criminals as different from the crucifixion of Jesus and thus highlight the uniqueness of the Lord. For instance, often the criminals are depicted as affixed to a different style of cross, as tied rather than nailed, or as without inscriptions of their crime.[82] They were even given names, e.g., for the good (right side) and the bad (left side): Joathas and Maggatras (Capnatas, Gamatras) in OL mss. of Luke 23:32 (and derivatives); Zoatham and Camma in an OL ms. of Matt 27:38; Dysmas and Gestas in *Acts of Pilate* 9:4.[83] All of this goes beyond the Gospels, which mention them without explanation, but also without embarrassment over the fact that Jesus is being treated as one among several criminals.[84] What is noticeable is that the criminal code of the Mishna was not in effect; *Sanhedrin* 6.4 would not have two people judged in the same day.

Why were the co-crucified included in the Gospel accounts? The simplest answer is that their presence illustrates the indignity to which the innocent Jesus was subjected. He had protested in Mark 14:48 and par. that he was being arrested as if he were a bandit (*lēstēs*); now in the language of Mark/Matt he is crucified amid bandits. Luke has taken great pains to show that Jesus is *dikaios* ("innocent, just"); yet he is crucified among *kakourgoi* ("wrongdoers, malefactors"—a term that Luke may have chosen to avoid the political implications of *lēstēs* for his readers in the 80s and 90s after the violence in Judea in the 50s and 60s).

There are other motifs.[85] Just as Mark/Matt mention the inscription among the preliminary items and then return later to the wording of the inscription as a source of mockery, so also these two bandits will appear later

---

[81]In the Synoptics, right and left; in John, "here and there," with Jesus in the middle.

[82]Chrysostom, *Homily on John* 84 (85); PG 59.461.

[83]One also finds Titus and Dumachus (whom Jesus met as a child!) in the *Arabic Gospel of the Infancy* 23; see Metzger, "Names" 89–95. The most curious nomination is supplied by B. Thiering (n. 14 above): Judas Iscariot and Simon Magus!

[84]Matera (*Kingship* 62) would see an echo of the request of James and John to sit at Jesus' right and left in his glory, a request (Mark 10:35–37) that follows immediately upon Jesus' third prediction of his passion. Yet the imagery of an honored seat or throne is so different from what we have here that mention of right and left is not sufficient to establish a parallel, and indeed the vocabulary for "left" is not the same.

[85]Besides those mentioned above, Paton, "Kreuzigung," would see here a continuation of the Sacaean-feast mockery that was proposed by some as background for the Roman mockery of Jesus (p. 876 above). However, Dio Chrysostom (*De Regno* 4.66–70), the major source of information for that feast, mentions only one man being mocked, stripped, scourged, and hung.

in Mark 15:32b and Matt 27:44 as deriding Jesus. In Luke the motif of future usage is even stronger. That Gospel already mentioned the two wrongdoers on the road to crucifixion (Luke 23:32), so that the present reference (23:33) is a reiteration of their presence—all this because they will play a role in a major episode in 23:39–43 where one will mock but the other will confess Jesus and be rewarded by him. In John their future utility in the crucifixion account (even if different from the utility in the Synoptics) is probably also a motif. We shall hear nothing of their mockery, but after Jesus is dead their bones will be broken while his will not (19:31–36). That difference will highlight a scriptural passage pertinent to Jesus. The future of the wrong-doers (Lucan terminology) in *GPet* 4:13–14 involves elements similar to both Luke and John, as we shall see.

What is the relationship between the Gospel references to the two co-crucified and Isa 53:12: "With outlaws [*anomoi*] was he reckoned"? Clearly the evangelists looked on Jesus being crucified between criminals as an in-dignity suffered by God's Son, but did this particular Isaian passage generate the Gospel report? Not all the items pertinent to the crucifixion were gener-ated by reflection on OT texts, e.g., Mark's first offering of wine, if we may judge from vocabulary (p. 942 above). Here too there is no vocabulary simi-larity between the Isa passage and the Gospel description of the co-crucified. (The same may be said of a proposed similarity to Ps 22:17: "A company of evildoers [*ponērouomenoi*] has encircled me.") Luke is the only Gospel that cites Isa 53:12 (in 22:37 at the Last Supper), but there is no vocabulary indication that Luke saw that passage fulfilled in the crucifixion of Jesus between two wrongdoers.[86] One of those wrongdoers will emerge in a highly favorable light and not as an *anomos*. The only other Lucan use of *anomoi* (Acts 2:23) suggests that the outlaws were those who crucified Jesus, not those who were crucified with him. The application of Isa 53:12 to the pres-ent scene is first clear in the textual variant that constitutes Mark 15:28 (see footnote on p. 933 above). Presumably that is a 2d-cent. interpretation, from a time when there was a tendency to find hitherto unnoticed OT connections for Gospel passages.

Of what crime were the co-crucified accused? John is the least informative with his reference to "two others," an unfortunate silence that offers no in-centive for associating these two with Barabbas, whom John called a *lēstēs*. For Mark/Matt they are "two bandits" (pl. of *lēstēs*); yet those Gospels never

---

[86]The initial reference to the wrongdoers in Luke 23:32 shows signs of Luke's writing in vocabu-lary and syntax, and that is true also of the present verse (23:33) where the wrongdoers are crucified. Untergassmair (*Kreuzweg* 42) points to the initial *kai* + *hote* + a finite verb ("And when they came") as occurring seven times in Luke-Acts. The *men . . . de* ("one . . . other") construction in the latter part of the verse is also Lucan (Fitzmyer, *Luke* 1.108), even if *hon men . . . hon de* occurs only here.

cify Jesus and divide his clothes, in v. 34a Jesus prays unexpectedly and graciously for these agents. Who are the "they" who "do not know what they are doing"? I have argued (pp. 856–59 above) that although Luke has not yet mentioned Roman soldiers, he assumed a general awareness on the part of readers that the Romans crucified Jesus. And so I agree with Harnack, Flusser, and others that this act of forgiveness covered the Romans who physically affixed Jesus to the cross but did not understand that they were doing this outrage to God's Son. Yet Luke never presents the Romans as solely responsible for the crucifixion; they did the physical action, but "the chief priests and the rulers and the people" (the Jewish agents of 23:13 who are the last-mentioned antecedent for any "they" in the crucifixion) cried out to crucify Jesus (23:21). On the route to the place of crucifixion Jesus spoke to the Daughters of Jerusalem, "If in the green wood *they do such things*"; and that had to refer to Jewish antagonists symbolized by Jerusalem. In Acts 3:17; 13:27 those who acted in ignorance when they executed Jesus are explicitly identified as the Jewish populace and their rulers. Therefore, in Luke 23:34a the "they" for whom Jesus is praying includes both the Romans and the Jews in proportion to their respective roles in Jesus' death.

More needs to be said about the Lucan Jesus' praying for the Jewish agents who have been so consistently hostile to him. How can he say that "they do not know what they are doing"? The chief priests and their cohorts have heard Jesus preach and have quite deliberately rejected his proclamation. They are part of a Jerusalem that Jesus has denounced for killing the prophets (13:34). Yet it was to obdurate Jerusalemites Jesus attributed ignorance, "Would that even today you knew the things that make for peace; but now they are hidden from your eyes" (19:42). Seemingly in the Lucan understanding, no matter how much the evil was plotted, the perpetrators can always be said not to have known (i.e., appreciated God's goodness or plan) or else they would not have acted as they did. In opposing Jesus' followers to the point of stoning them, a Paul who was allied with the chief priests said: "I myself was convinced that it was necessary *to do* many *things* against the name of Jesus the Nazorean" (Acts 26:9). Yet surely Luke would judge that Paul did not know what he was doing. Perhaps with Daube ("For they" 60) one might sum up Luke's attitude thus: If there were those who did not know because they had not been told, there were also those who did not know because, although they had been told, they did not grasp. It is noteworthy, however, that even though the latter group do not know what they are doing, they need forgiveness.

As for punishment, Luke 12:48 makes a distinction, "The person who has not known and has done things to deserve a beating shall receive a light beating." Presumably that refers to the more elementary lack of knowledge, for the words of Jesus to the Daughters of Jerusalem shows that punishment can become inevitable for more reprehensible evildoers. If Luke 23:34a is authentically Lucan, then, one has to distinguish between a forgiveness that is possible and a punishment that is inevitable. But was not an appeal for forgiveness combined with a sense of inevitable punishment a message of the OT prophets in the last days before the fall of the kingdoms of Israel and of Judah?

How does a prayer for forgiveness because they do not know what they are doing match the ethical attitudes of the world contemporary with the NT? As Daube ("For they" 61–62, 65) points out, some cite the Socratic principle: No one ever does wrong but from ignorance of himself, of his place in the world, or of ultimate good. Then they move too quickly to assume the Greek origin of the prayer attributed to Jesus. True, the Jewish attitude toward ignorance in sinning is complex. There are passages that reflect benevolence if the ignorance is a lack of information so that the actions really become inadvertent or indeliberate. Num 15:25–26, in describing the atonement made by priests for the people of Israel, offers the assurance that forgiveness for sins of inadvertence shall be granted even to the resident aliens among them, "since the fault of inadvertence affects all people."[89] Yet deliberate actions, those done with a high hand, are judged severely, and the lack of full understanding was not widely accepted as an excuse. In 1QS 10:16–21, even though a Qumran psalmist says, "I will pay no man the reward of evil" and thus seems to eschew vengeance, he goes on to show that he is eagerly awaiting divine judgment on those who depart from the way. More benevolently in the MT of Isa 53:12 the Servant makes intercession for the sins of all without distinction of how the sins were committed (see TalBab *Soṭa* 14a). In Jonah 4:11, despite all the horrors inflicted on others by the brutal Assyrians, it is asked rhetorically whether God should not have pity on the population of Nineveh, "people who do not know their right hand from their left." *Test. Benjamin* 4:2 states: "The good person ... shows mercy to all, even though they be sinners."[90] An important distinction is made by Philo (*In Flaccum* 2; #7): "For a person who goes astray because of ignorance of a better way, allowance may be made; but the person who with knowledge does what is wrong has no defense but is already convicted in his conscience." Would Luke 23:34a be putting the Jewish authorities in the first category? Or more likely would the prayer be in disagreement with Philo's attitude toward the second category? If Judaism was not at one on

---

[89]Heb 5:2 praises the high priest for treating gently those who do not know and are deceived.
[90]We must be cautious: There is Christian influence on the *Testaments of the Twelve Patriarchs*.

this issue, neither was later Christianity; and, as we shall see below, that may be one of the reasons why this prayer is not found in all copies of the NT.

The Authenticity of the Verse. It is omitted in important textual witnesses, some of them very early.[91] Yet other major Greek codices and early versions have it. This is an instance where the weight of textual witnesses on one side almost offsets that on the other side. What emerges is that already in the 2d cent. some copies of Luke had the prayer, while others did not. From that situation the following possibilities for the origin of the prayer in 23:34a emerge:

- It was spoken by Jesus (in the crucifixion context or elsewhere) and preserved only by Luke. Some later copyists, finding it unacceptable, removed it.
- It was spoken by Jesus but was not preserved by Luke. It circulated as an independent saying and only in the 2d cent. was inserted in the present context by a copyist who thought that it fit well the sentiments of this Gospel. Other copyists did not know of it. (A similar history is supposed for the story of the woman caught in adultery, which eventually was inserted at the beginning of John 8.) This position is held by MTC 180.
- It was not spoken by Jesus but was formulated by Luke (or in the immediate preLucan tradition) as an appropriate vocalization of what Jesus must have thought: He actually forgave silently. Some later copyists, finding it unacceptable, removed it.
- It was not spoken by Jesus but was formulated in postGospel Christian thought as appropriate to Jesus and inserted by a copyist in Luke's PN as a fitting context.

To discern whether the evidence favors Lucan composition, which is our interest here, we shall discuss sequence, style, alternative origins, and why copyists might have omitted it.

(a) *Sequence.* Despite Schweizer's appeal to overall Lucan structure in favor of the prayer (p. 972 above), this prayer attributed to Jesus is intrusive, breaking up two sentences (vv. 33 and 34b) where the subject is "they," i.e., the crucifiers. Yet as Harnack ("Probleme" 257) points out, that intrusion could be Luke's own work because he is inserting a nonMarcan saying amid

---

[91]P[75], Codices Vaticanus, Bezae, the corrector of Sinaiticus, Koridethi, and the Syr[sin] and Coptic versions. Nestle ("Father") thinks that the placing of this saying of Jesus as next-to-last in the order of the Seven Last Words of Jesus in Tatian's *Diatessaron,* as discussed at the beginning of this subsection, suggests that it was a later insertion, and that Tatian's original attitude would have been influenced by the lack of the passage in the OS. The author of the *Apostolic Constitutions* used Tatian; and after recounting the "My God" word from Mark/Matt at the ninth hour, he reports, "After a short while he cried out with a loud voice, 'Father, forgive them, for they do not know what they are doing,' and adding, 'Into your hands I commend my spirit,' he breathed out and was buried before sunset in a new tomb" (5.14.17).

material borrowed from Mark. Indeed, it is quite effective to find in the midst of hostile actions by the crucifiers a prayer by Jesus for their forgiveness. In that sequence the prayer is met by further hostility (stripping him of his clothes). Even if this verse is not from Luke, the present sequence made sense to someone, i.e., to the later copyist who inserted it.

(b) *Style*. As the verse now stands, the name Jesus is necessary to indicate the change of agent. The imperfect "was saying" (*elegen*) is not unusual in Luke to introduce a question or demand. Jesus prays with great frequency in Luke (Fitzmyer, *Luke* 1.244–45); and among the Synoptics a prayer addressed to God in the Greek vocative "Father," without any modifier or Semitic translation, is a Lucan peculiarity (10:21; 11:2; 22:42; 23:46). In the Lucan PN, if we count the present instance, Jesus prays "Father" three times.[92] Thus the format of the prayer is very Lucan. This is also true of the rest of the vocabulary in the prayer (Untergassmair, *Kreuzweg* 46). The pattern "forgive . . . for" (*aphes . . . gar*) is exactly the same as in the Lucan form of the Lord's Prayer (11:4).[93] As for "what they are doing," we find in 6:11 the scribes and Pharisees discussing "what they will do to Jesus" (see also 19:48). The Lucan Jesus paints a picture of a God who is generous in forgiving, even before repentance is expressed (15:20; 19:10). In 6:27–29 Jesus teaches his disciples. "Love your enemies; do good to those who hate you; bless those who curse you; pray for those who maltreat you." In 12:10 he says, "Everyone who speaks a word against the Son of Man will be forgiven." Logically, then, what is *done* against the Son of Man can also be forgiven. If one wonders why Jesus asks the Father to forgive instead of extending forgiveness himself (as in 5:20; 7:48), he may be motivated by a desire that his prayer be imitated by Christians who suffer unjustly, e.g., Stephen in Acts 7:60. Thus if one wishes to posit that a 2d-cent. copyist inserted a prayer into Luke, that copyist took great care to imitate Lucan style and thought and was so successful that the end product was perfectly Lucan.

(c) *Suggested alternative origins*. If the prayer were not an original part of the Lucan Gospel, where would it have come from? One suggestion is that it was formulated from the general NT attributions of ignorance to Jesus' enemies, e.g., I Cor 2:7–8: None of the rulers of this world understood the secret wisdom of God, "for if they had, they would not have crucified the Lord of Glory." Yet the ignorance motif is clearer in Luke-Acts than in any other NT writing. If one is tempted to posit that a copyist read passages

---

[92]On the Mount of Olives that the cup might be taken away; here for the forgiveness of his persecutors; and before he dies, entrusting his spirit into the Father's hands.

[93]Elsewhere in Luke "forgive" has the object "sins"; yet the "them" being forgiven here are "the sinful men" of 24:7 into whose hands the Son of Man has been delivered to be crucified.

like Acts 3:17 and 13:27 and then formulated this prayer, one has even better reason to posit that the prayer was a formulation by Luke himself.

Others have proposed that Christians developed this prayer of Jesus in reflection on the MT of Isa 53:12: "He bore the sins of many and made intercession for the transgressors." This reflection would have had to be on the Hebrew, for the LXX of the second clause reads: "He was given over because of their sins." If Luke 23:34a was written by Luke, since he normally worked from the LXX, one would have to posit that the reflection on the MT was done by Jesus himself or by preLucan Christians. If the verse was not written by Luke but added by a copyist, could it have been developed by postLucan Jewish Christians who still read Hebrew? Flusser ("Sie wissen" 404–7) thinks so, offering the continued Christian mission to the Jews as a context in which the prayer for their forgiveness could have been persuasive. He points to the *Gospel of the Nazarenes* as a possible locus—a gospel known in the 2d–4th cents. to Hegesippus, Eusebius, and Jerome, all of whom also exhibited knowledge of the prayer. In that gospel (#35; HSNTA 1.153; rev. ed. 1.164) we read that the prayer of Jesus for forgiveness led to the conversion of 8,000 Jews, as recorded in Acts (2:41 + 4:4). In the same vein Hegesippus (reflective of 2d-cent. Jewish Christianity) describes how in Jerusalem in the early 60s James, the brother of the Lord, knelt and prayed as he was being stoned by the scribes and Pharisees: "Lord, God, Father, forgive them for they do not know what they are doing" (cited in Eusebius, EH 2.23.16). The Nag Hammadi *Second Apocalypse of James* places related motifs on the lips of James: "Judges, you have been judged; and you did not spare, but you were spared" (V.57,21–24); "He will not judge you for those things that you did, but will have mercy on you" (V.59,6–8). Was the prayer first attributed to James, the great hero of the Jewish Christians (the "bishop of bishops" of the Ps-Clementines [*Epistle of Clement,* Preface]) and then later shifted to Jesus? Or did the influence go the other way: A saying of Jesus favorable to the Jews was preserved in Jewish-Christian circles and made part of the martyrdom of James, the brother of Jesus? We note that nothing in the Hegesippus account denies that Jesus had uttered such a prayer.

A middle component important for relating the James of Hegesippus and Jesus in relation to the prayer is Stephen. In Acts 7:60 he too knelt and prayed, "Lord, do not hold this sin against them." Just as in Acts 7:56 Stephen saw the heavens opened and the Son of Man standing at the right of God, the James of Hegesippus affirms that the Son of Man is sitting at the right of the Power and will come on the clouds of heaven (EH 2.23.13). Thus there is a connecting line from the death of Jesus, through the death of Stephen, to the 2d-cent. picture of the death of James. The association of a prayer for forgiveness with the Hellenist spokesman Stephen, who was antiTemple, weakens the thesis that it was preserved only in Jewish-Christian circles. A common factor among the three figures is a martyr's death. True, a prayer for forgiveness of persecutors is not characteristic in the Jewish martyr pattern set by the victims of Maccabean times: They warned that God would ultimately punish their persecutors, depriving them of the resurrection (II Macc 7:14,19,31,35–36; *IV Macc* 9:30; 10:11; 11:3). Yet forgiveness, such as that expressed in Luke 23:34a, became a mark of suffering Christians. Ignatius (*Eph.* 10:2–3) urges: "Offer prayers in response to their blasphemies . . . be gentle in response to their cruelty and do not be eager to imitate them in return. . . . Let us eagerly be imitators of the Lord." Justin Martyr (*Apology* 1.14) affirms, "We pray for our enemies and endeavor to persuade those who hate us unjustly." In the late 2d cent. the Lyons martyrs are said to have prayed "even as did Stephen, the perfect martyr, 'Lord, do not hold this sin against them'" (EH 5.2.5).

In relating the prayer to martyrdom, once more one must inquire about the direction in which the motif traveled. For instance, was the prayer originally associated with the protomartyr Stephen, and then read by copyists back into the story of Jesus' death to increase the martyrological element there? There are serious difficulties with that thesis. Surkau (*Martyrien* 90) points out that Luke's PN is more martyrological than Mark's or Matt's, so that it would make sense to posit that the prayer was already on the lips of the Lucan Jesus rather than retrojected from Stephen's martyrdom. Moreover, a study of Luke's use of Mark's PN shows that he has colored the account of Stephen's death by transferring to it motifs that Mark associated with Jesus' death (blasphemy, false witness, hostility to the sanctuary/holy place, the role of the high priest). Thus one would tend to think that the influence went from Jesus' prayer to Stephen's prayer. In Luke-Acts there is attributed both to Jesus and to Stephen another prayer in which the respective speaker commits his spirit into heavenly care (Jesus to the Father in Luke 23:46; Stephen to the Lord Jesus in Acts 7:59). One cannot dismiss, then, the possibility that Luke-Acts had a prayer uttered both by Jesus and by Stephen that God would be lenient to the executors. This prayer would subsequently have been attributed by Jewish Christians to James, the brother of the Lord, their martyr hero, and become a pattern for the attitude of other Christian martyrs as well.

The discussion thus far has shown that there is nothing to disprove the Lucan authorship of 23:34a and no convincing alternative explanation of its origin. Were there not textual witnesses that lacked it, there would be no serious doubt among scholars about its appertaining to the Lucan PN. Yet if one wishes to argue that Luke wrote this prayer, there remains one major objection.

(d) *Why would copyists have omitted this beautiful passage from mss. that contained it?* The lack of the prayer in Mark/Matt might have made copyists uneasy, but that alone would scarcely have caused them to take the drastic step of excision. Did they find the prayer contradictory to the threatening words spoken by Jesus to the Daughters of Jerusalem in 23:29–31, indicating that punishment was inevitable? Was such a prayer deemed contradictory because the Father had not granted forgiveness to the Jews but had caused Jerusalem to be destroyed in 70? The latter issue was echoed by the Church Fathers, e.g., Jerome (*Epistle* 120.8.2; PL 22.993) explains that the prayer won some years of reprieve for the Jews before the destruction and during that time thousands came to believe.

While the above issues may have entered the picture, the primary suggestion for a motif why copyists might have omitted the prayer is that they found it too favorable to the Jews. In relation to that, two factors are important. The first is the Christian conviction that Jews continued to be hostile persecutors long after the death of Jesus. In I Thess 2:14–16 we hear that Jews drove out Christians and prevented the proclamation of the Gospel. According to Acts (13:45,50; 14:2,19; 17:5,13; 18:12) Jews constantly stirred up trouble for Christian preachers. John 16:2 claims that Christians were expelled from the synagogue and put to death.[94] Josephus (*Ant.* 20.9.1, #200) reports that the high priest Ananus II had James, the brother of Jesus, stoned in the early 60s. In the 2d cent. and later, Christians thought that they were captured for martyrdom because Jews denounced them to the Romans. The *Martyrdom of Polycarp* speaks of the customary wrathful zeal of the Jews against the saint (12:2; 13:1). Justin, who had been in Palestine, addresses his Jewish adversaries: "You hate and murder us also . . . as often as you get authority." (*Dialogue* 133.6). The forgiving prayer of Jesus in 23:34a might have troubled copyists who shared this picture of the Jews as relentless persecutors.

A second factor that could have influenced copyists' judgment is the morality of the prayer, as already discussed at the beginning of our treatment of 23:34a. Since the Jewish authorities acted so deliberately against Jesus, surely they knew what they were doing and how then could they be forgiven without genuine repentance? Ongoing persecution of Christians was a sign that such repentance was not forthcoming, and so 2d-cent. copyists would have been making their judgments in a context of the strong antiJewish feeling exhibited in the *Didache, GPet,* Aristides' *Apology, Doctrine of Addai,* and the Syriac *Didascalia Apostolorum.* Later John Chrysostom would

---

[94]No information is given as to whether the putting to death was direct or indirect (i.e., by informing the Romans that these people were no longer entitled to the tolerance extended to Jews).

write: "After you killed Christ . . . there is no hope left for you, no rectifica-
tion, no forgiveness, no excuse" (*Adv. Judaeos Oratio* 6.2; PG 48.907). Since
agreement with church thought and practice influenced the process of receiving writings as canonical Scripture, copyists who shared this theology
might well have decided against a prayer asking God to forgive Jesus' Jewish
persecutors.[95] The Syriac *Didascalia* 2.16.1 (Connolly ed., p. 52) echoes
Luke 23:34a but shows hesitation: "Our Savior was pleading with his Father
for sinners, 'My Father, they know not what they do, nor what they speak;
but *if it be possible,* do you forgive them.'" Epp ("Ignorance") points out
that although Codex Bezae (which originally omitted 23:34a) contains the
Acts texts about the ignorance of the Jewish participants in the death of
Jesus, it seems to make that ignorance more blameworthy.

Overall, after surveying the pros and cons, I would deem it easier to posit
that the passage was written by Luke and excised for theological reasons by
a later copyist than that it was added to Luke by such a copyist who took the
trouble to cast it in Lucan style and thought. Except perhaps in Jewish-
Christian circles, there would have been few 2d-cent. copyists anxious to
have Jesus pray for forgiveness for the Jews.[96] Harnack ("Probleme" 261),
who argued most strongly for the genuineness of Luke 22:43–44, is less
certain (even if favorable) about 23:34a; he insists, however, that it should
not be stricken from copies of the Gospel text.

It is ironical that perhaps the most beautiful sentence in the PN should be
textually dubious. The sentiment behind it is the essence of responding to
hostility in what came to be thought of as a Christian manner. This word of
Jesus would surely have been a prime factor leading to Dante's judgment on
Luke as "the scribe of the gentleness of Christ." For some, if Jesus did not
utter these words, they have no Christian religious importance. For others,
if Luke did not write them, they are merely apocryphal sentiment. For still
others, while an affirmative answer on either or both of those points would
be appreciated, the long use of these words by Christians means they have
acquired normative authority.[97] If they were added by a scribe, that scribe's
insight would have become an authentic interpretation of the Lucan Christ.
Alas, too often not the absence of this prayer from the text, but the failure to
incorporate it into one's heart has been the real problem. Flusser ("Sie wissen" 393) begins his treatment of this verse on the plaintive note that the

[95]Harnack, Harris, and others count this a very important factor. See BGJ 1.335 for the similar
issue of scribal hesitation about including a story where Jesus forgave an adulteress.

[96]Yet there is no way to be certain: A copyist might have inserted this as a prayer for the Romans
and never have dreamed that his words could be read as forgiveness for the Jews.

[97]That reflects a tenet in which continuous church usage serves as the criterion of what is canonical Scripture.

crusaders quoted to the Jews a word (apocryphal) of the Lord, "There will yet come the day when my sons will come and revenge my blood." Yet in their Latin NT the crusaders could find presented as a genuine word of the Lord Luke 23:34a—a word that should have given them a very different outlook.

(*Bibliography for items in this episode may be found in §37, Parts 3 and 4.*)

§41. JESUS CRUCIFIED, PART TWO: ACTIVITIES AT THE CROSS

(Mark 15:29–32; Matt 27:39–44; Luke 23:35–43;
John 19:25–27)

Translation

Mark 15:29–32: 29And those passing by were blaspheming him, wagging their heads and saying, "Aha, O one destroying the sanctuary and building it in three days, 30save yourself by having come down from the cross."

31Similarly also the chief priests, mocking him to one another with the scribes, were saying, "Others he saved; himself he cannot save. 32Let the Messiah, the King of Israel, come down now from the cross in order that we may see and believe."

Even those who had been crucified together with him were reviling him.

Matt 27:39–44: 39But those passing by were blaspheming him, wagging their heads 40and saying, "O one destroying the sanctuary and in three days building it, save yourself, if you are Son of God, and come down from the cross."

41Similarly also the chief priests, mocking him with the scribes and elders, were saying, 42"Others he saved; himself he cannot save. He is the King of Israel—let him come down from the cross, and we shall believe. 43He has trusted in God. Let him be delivered if He wants him, for he said, 'I am Son of God.'"

44In the same way even the bandits who were crucified together with him were reviling him.

Luke 23:35–43: 35And the people were standing there observing.

But there were also rulers sneering, saying, "Others he saved; let him save himself, if this is the Messiah of God, the chosen one."

³⁶Moreover, also the soldiers mocked, coming forward, bringing forward to him vinegary wine, ³⁷and saying, "If you are the King of the Jews, save yourself." ³⁸For there was also an inscription over him: "The King of the Jews, this (man)."

³⁹Moreover one of the hanged wrongdoers was blaspheming him, "Are you not the Messiah? Save yourself and us."

⁴⁰But in answer the other, rebuking him, said, "Do you not even fear God? Because you are under the same condemnation; ⁴¹and indeed we justly, for we are receiving what is worthy of what we did, but he did nothing disorderly." ⁴²And he was saying, "Jesus, remember me whenever you come into your kingdom." ⁴³And he said to him, "Amen, I say to you, this day with me you shall be in paradise."

John 19:25–27: ²⁵But there were standing near the cross of Jesus his mother, and his mother's sister, Mary of Clopas, and Mary Magdalene. ²⁶So Jesus, having seen his mother and the disciple whom he loved standing nearby, says to his mother, "Woman, look: your son." ²⁷Then he says to the disciple, "Look: your mother." And from that hour the disciple took her to his own.

GPet 4:13: But a certain one of those wrongdoers reviled them [the Jews], saying, "We have been made suffer thus because of the wrong that we have done; but this one, having become Savior of men [human beings], what injustice has he done to you?"

COMMENT

In the first part of the crucifixion scene (Part One), the evangelists set the stage, naming place and time and situating Jesus on the cross amid two bandits or wrongdoers. In Part Two they begin the action of the drama by showing us how those who were present at the Place of the Skull reacted to the crucified Jesus. The reactions they describe run the gamut from negative to positive according to the individual evangelist's theological outlook on the passion. In *Mark/Matt* the reaction is entirely negative: Three groups are listed and all mock Jesus. This is another example of the patterns of three that we have seen throughout the PN:[1] Jesus makes predictions about the fate of three among those who follow him (about Judas, the disciples, and Peter); in Gethsemane Jesus prays three times and comes back to find his followers sleeping three times; Peter denies Jesus three times; in Mark the period on the cross is divided into the third, sixth, and ninth hours. The negative reaction whereby not a single person close to the cross is favorable to Jesus fits the overall pessimism that has dominated the Marcan PN since Jesus left the Last Supper and began to proclaim a warning of scandal (Mark 14:27). For the most part, Matt has preserved the dour outlook of the Marcan PN; and in this scene at the cross Matt hews very close to Mark, making only minor changes and adding an OT echo (27:43) that only intensifies the hostility.

In *Luke* the reaction to Jesus on the cross is mixed, negative and positive. Luke preserves the Marcan pattern of three mockeries of Jesus; but he surrounds those three by an ameliorating framework, describing at the beginning "the people" who are neutral bystanders, and at the end one of the cocrucified who is sympathetic to Jesus. The latter gives Luke a chance to have the mockery terminate with an act of salvation by Jesus, another instance of Luke's treating the suffering of Jesus as salvific.

For *John* this is the third crucifixion episode. In the first, as the crucifixion began, "the chief priests of the Jews" were silenced by Pilate;[2] in the second, by treating Jesus as a criminal to be despoiled of his clothes, the soldiers unknowingly fulfilled the Scriptures. Now we find a mixture of friends, disciples, and relatives standing near the cross and constituting a believing community from whom Jesus establishes his true family. Here there is no mockery of Jesus on the cross; he has triumphed over his enemies.

I shall divide my treatment into three subsections. The first will comment on the threefold mockery of Jesus common to the Synoptics, even if Luke modifies the Marcan schema. The second will discuss the addendum to the schema in Luke 23:40–43 where one of the hanged wrongdoers takes Jesus' side against the other wrongdoer who mocked him by blaspheming—in

[1]Important here, at least for Matt and Luke, is another pattern of three: the three temptations of Jesus by Satan at the beginning of the ministry matching the three mockeries of Jesus at the end of his life. At the cross, two of the mockeries in Matt (27:40,43) and two in Luke (23:35,37) are phrased as "if" clauses, even as are the three temptations in Matt 4:1–11 and Luke 4:1–13. Indeed, Matt's mockery, "If you are Son of God" (compare Luke's "If you are the King of the Jews") is verbatim the same as the "If you are Son of God" in two of the temptations. The tone of the two triads is the same.

[2]In the artistic Johannine chiastic balance (p. 908 above), just as after the introduction "the chief priests of the Jews" face Pilate in Episode 1 to make a request concerning Jesus that Pilate frustrates, so before the conclusion "the Jews" shall reappear in Episode 5 to make of Pilate another request concerning (the now dead) Jesus that he will again frustrate. But they do not confront Jesus as he hangs on the cross.

other words, the positive side of the Lucan picture. The third will comment on John's very positive scene at the foot of the cross.

THE THREEFOLD MOCKERY OF JESUS (MARK 15:29–32; MATT 27:39–44; LUKE 23:35–39)

While this is a common Synoptic portrayal, there are small Matthean variations from Mark and larger Lucan ones. I shall use a table to make an overall comparison. The 1, 2, and 3 at the left represent the three mockeries in the order in which they occur in each Gospel; the a, b, and c represent respectively the mockers, the substance of the mockery, and the challenge to Jesus to save himself. Under Matt only *differences* from Mark are noted.[3]

		Mark	Matt	Luke
				the people observe
1	a.	passersby blaspheme		rulers sneer
	b.	destroying sanctuary	+Son of God	Messiah of God; chosen one
	c.	save yourself; come down		saved others; save self
2	a.	ch. priests, scribes mock	+elders	soldiers mock
	b.	Messiah, King of Israel	King of Israel	King of the Jews
	c.	saved others, not himself come down so we believe	Son of God be delivered	save yourself
3	a.	two co-crucified deride	bandits	one co-hanged wrongdoer blasphemes
	b.			Messiah
				other co-hanged sympathizes; will go to paradise

[3]A minor difference that I found too complicated to include is that Matt binds the mockeries more closely together than does Mark. He repeats Mark's "Similarly" to introduce the second mockery, but adds "In the same way" to introduce the third mockery. The same effect is achieved by having the "Son of God" title in both the first and second mockeries.

Before I comment on individual mockeries, an overall glance should make clear that Luke's expansion is for the most part dependent on Mark—the only serious possible exception is the substance of the dialogue between Jesus and the sympathetic wrongdoer. Luke has created a *preface* to the threefold mockery by adapting Mark's passersby into the people and giving them a neutral role. He has created a *sequel* to the threefold mockery by splitting up Mark's two co-crucified and making one of them sympathetic. Since he does not have passersby, Luke has made up the lacuna in the triadic structure by substituting soldiers. Indeed, Luke has made the middle mockery a compendium of Marcan scenes he had previously not drawn on: mockery by Roman soldiers immediately after the Roman trial (Mark 15:16–20a), the offering of wine (15:23 + 36), and the inscription of the charge "The King of the Jews" (15:26). With that overall observation, let us turn to the components one by one.

Mark/Matt's First Mockery (Mark 15:29–30; Matt 27:39–40). No study of this initial mocking as Jesus hangs on the cross can afford to overlook its dramatic character. Both Gospels have illustrated amply the fierce hostility of the Jewish authorities determined on Jesus' death. Indeed, in the instance of a crowd that had come to request Pilate to release a prisoner at the feast, the determined authorities succeeded in stirring up that crowd to ask for the release of Barabbas and the crucifixion of Jesus. But here we encounter simple Jewish passersby[4] who are not indicated to have encountered Jesus previously and who have not been preprogrammed by the authorities; yet their first reaction is to blaspheme the crucified on the basis of what they have heard about him.[5] "Blaspheme" is a significant word for Mark, supplying interesting inclusions with previous usages.[6] At the beginning (Mark 2:6–7 = Matt 9:3) Jesus was accused of blaspheming because he forgave sins, a power appropriate to God alone. At the end in his trial by the Sanhedrin (Mark 14:61–64 = Matt 26:63–66) Jesus was convicted of blasphemy because he said he was the Messiah, the Son of the Blessed, the Son of Man who would be seen at the right of the Power. Early in Mark (3:22,28–30 =

[4]Mark/Matt do not identify the passersby as Jewish; but in a Jerusalem locale the failure to give them another identity would scarcely allow readers any other conclusion.

[5]We have already commented on Matt 27:25 that has "all the people" take responsibility for the death of Jesus ("His blood on us and on our children"). Mark is not so systematic, but would the overall impact of this narrative lead to any other conclusion about the reprehensible involvement of the people?

[6]I pointed out above (p. 523) what becomes obvious here: *Blasphēmein* has in the attested usage of this period no implication of pronouncing the sacred name YHWH. It involves an insult and is most often reflective of arrogance by the blasphemer or the blasphemed. Here it is not significantly different from the *empaizein* ("to mock") and *oneidizein* ("to revile") that Mark/Matt use in the second and third mockeries, except perhaps in intensifying the irreverence.

Matt 12:24,31–32) scribes from Jerusalem were associated with the commission of an everlasting sin by blaspheming against the Holy Spirit who was at work in Jesus' exorcisms—they thought of him as possessed by an unclean spirit. Now at the end as Jesus hangs on the cross, passersby blaspheme against Jesus, challenging his power to destroy the sanctuary and build it in three days.[7] Thus the picture of hostile misunderstanding is consistent in Mark from beginning to end.

Before giving voice to their blasphemy, the passersby communicate by their body language as they wag their heads in derision. As we shall see below (p. 989) they thus imitate an action that the OT associates with the behavior of the wicked toward the suffering just. They begin their voiced contempt with a vivid expletive, "Aha" (a Marcan dramatic touch that the more sober Matt omits).[8]

The avowed subject matter that gives rise to the first Mark/Matt mockery is the charge that Jesus would or could destroy the Temple sanctuary and rebuild it in three days—a charge made in a vocative participial form almost as if the "one-destroying-the-sanctuary" had become a proverbial identifying description of Jesus. This wording obviously echoes the testimony given against Jesus at the trial by the Jewish Sanhedrin[9] (false and inconsistent testimony for Mark 14:57–59; legally sufficient testimony for Matt 26:60–61). The way the charge is placed on the lips of passersby suggests that it was well known and that whatever Mark may have meant originally by calling the testimony that invoked it false, he did not mean that Jesus never said it. How this claim of Jesus got to be so well known, the reader is probably not expected to ask. The reaction of the passersby to it in the present form indicates that its offensiveness is not integrally related to the phrases "made by hand" and "not made by hand," those interpretative precisions that were present in Mark 14:58 but absent here (and absent in both Matthean reports of the saying).

If we recall that there were two themes in the Mark/Matt Jewish Sanhedrin trial, we can see that there is a deliberate effort to recall the whole trial here.

---

[7]This blasphemy is more reprehensible because in Mark 7:22 Jesus pointed out that it is a vice which stems from the hearts of people.

[8]Greek *oua* is used in Epictetus to express wonder. Yet, finding scornful wonder unsatisfactory, Bishop ("*oua*") suggests relating the Marcan expression to Arabic *'uāʿ*, a warning to "look out" by the rider of a donkey or a camel—the passersby are warning Jesus to look out for himself. Without meaning to be harsh, I deem this pedantic fantasy. Expletives have emotional intelligibility without one's tracing their etymology; a dictionary will not be very informative about the "Aha" I used to translate *oua*.

[9]The use here of "in [*en*] three days" in place of "within [*dia*] three days" of Mark 14:58 (Matt 26:61) is a meaningless variant. The Matthean word order here with "in three days" before "building" (a reversal of the order in Mark's mockery) is the same order as in the trial saying.

Trial Themes	Marcan Mockeries	Matthean Mockeries
1. Sanctuary destruction	1. same	1. same + Son of God
2. Messiah, Son of Blessed or God	2. Messiah King of Israel	2. King of Israel Son of God

Mark, who has already used "blaspheme" to recall the judgment at the trial, recalls the first trial theme in the first mockery and the second trial theme in the second mockery. Matt recalls both trial themes in the first mockery[10] and then repeats "Son of God" in the second mockery. Various reasons for Matt's emphasis on the "Son of God" motif suggest themselves. First, probably by the time Matt was writing, the physical Jerusalem sanctuary had been destroyed, and hostile Jewish incredulity was now primarily concentrated on christology, so that the issue of whether Jesus was the Son of God had come to the fore in church-synagogue debates. Second, Matt recounts the temptations of Jesus at the beginning of the Gospel, and in those "if you are Son of God" is a major motif (see n. 1 above).[11] I have noted that this mockery scene in Mark uses the theme of blaspheming as an inclusion with beginning passages in his Gospel; Matt uses "if you are Son of God" as his inclusive phrase. A third reason for Matt's emphasis on Jesus as the Son of God may involve an echo from the OT Book of Wisdom in its description of the mocking of the just by the wicked—an echo involved with the themes of being saved and delivered that are best discussed at the end of the second Mark/Matt mockery below (pp. 994–95), where Matt makes an insertion that facilitates such a discussion.

Already here, however, an echo of the OT theme of the mockery of the just is clear. On p. 953 above, in studying the division of Jesus' clothes, we saw a recall of the wording of Ps 22:19. Below we shall see that the only words spoken on the cross by the dying Jesus in Mark/Matt will quote Ps

---

[10]Mark's first mockery juxtaposes "destroying the sanctuary" and "save yourself" without specifying grammatically that *if* Jesus can do the one, he should be able to do the other. Matt's addition of "if you are Son of God" clarifies that. Moreover, it reminds us that in Matt's Sanhedrin trial the charge of destroying the sanctuary was not false (as it was for Mark) but led directly to the high priest's question as to whether Jesus was the Son of God.

[11]In the mockeries at the cross Matt catches both major satanic misunderstandings of the nature of the Son of God: At the beginning of the Gospel the temptations of the devil culminated in the offer of a power befitting the world's standard for God's Son (Matt 4:8–9); in the middle of the Gospel Peter was called Satan because he thought suffering irreconcilable with Jesus' being the Son of the living God (16:16,22–23). Donaldson ("Mockers") advocates strongly that in the mockeries Matt with his emphasis on the Son of God has gone beyond the picture of the suffering just man in Mark.

22:2. And so it is not surprising that we have another reverberation of Ps 22 here:[12]

> Ps 22:8a: All those observing [*theōrein*] me sneered [*ekmyktērizein*] at me;
> 8b: they spoke with the lips; they wagged [*kinein*] the head.

In their first mockery of Jesus on the cross Mark/Matt echo Ps 22:8b in the phrase about the wagging of the heads;[13] and as we shall now see, Luke draws upon 22:8a as he reshapes the Marcan passage.

The "People" Who Watch (Luke 23:35a). As I explained at the beginning of this section, Luke supplies a framework for the three mockeries by adding reactions both before and after. If the "passersby" who begin the Marcan scene are a hostile group (of Jews) who blaspheme, Luke begins with a more benevolent (Jewish) "people."[14] By carefully painting this group into the crucifixion scene and its aftermath, Luke is preparing for the quick acceptance of Jesus by large numbers of Jerusalemites in Acts 2:41,47; 4:4; 6:1. In composing the framework Luke combines Mark's picture[15] with Ps 22:8a and writes: "And the people were standing there observing."

In itself the appearance of people at an execution could be negative, representing curiosity-seekers come to enjoy the spectacle, as in *III Macc* 5:24 where a multitude comes out early to see Jews put to death. But the sequence of Luke's references to the people in the crucifixion account indicates a more positive attitude here. Surely "the people" near the cross in 23:35 is the same "large multitude of *the people*" that followed Jesus to the crucifixion site in

---

[12]The bracketed Greek words represent LXX vocabulary of the psalm passage that is used in the Gospel account of the mockery. Yet the Gospel use of Scripture here is so allusive that we cannot always be certain whether the evangelist is reading the LXX or the MT. (McCaffrey, "Psalm" 86, also invokes the possibility of targumic readings.) Beyond allusions to Ps 22 and Wis 2 cited in my text, Prof. E. Boring has called to my attention Jer 48:27 (LXX 31:27) addressed as a reproof to Moab: "Is Israel a laughing stock to you? Was she caught *among thieves* that you wag your head whenever you speak of her?"

[13]This can scarcely be doubted because of frequent uses of Ps 22 in the PN; but "wagging the head" is found in other passages of affliction and they may have been in mind too, e.g., Lam 2:15: "*All who pass along* the way clap their hands at you; they hiss and *wag their heads* at the daughter of Jerusalem." Both the italicized phrases are found in Mark 15:29. Bailey ("Fall" 105) stresses this background in Lam, and certainly there would be irony in having the Jerusalemites mock Jesus in the same way that their enemies once mocked Jerusalem.

[14]An exception to the generally favorable Lucan presentation of "the people" (APPENDIX V, A) is 23:13 that joins "the people" to the chief priests and the rulers—a group that together brought Jesus to Pilate to be punished (23:14). Implicitly they would have been part of a "they" that is hostile to Jesus throughout the Pilate trial (23:18,21,23) and to whose will Pilate gives over Jesus (23:25). Attempts to make Luke totally consistent in treating this (Jewish) people fail to recognize that Luke 2:34 described Jesus as a contradictory sign "set for the fall and rise of many in Israel."

[15]Besides changing the Marcan passersby to the standing people, Luke omits Mark's ill-natured "wagging their heads" and moves Mark's "were blaspheming" from the first mockery to the third, attaching it to the hostile wrongdoer (23:39). Since Luke omitted the theme of the destruction of the sanctuary from the interrogation of Jesus before the Sanhedrin, he omits it from the mockery as well.

23:27. While Luke did not indicate their attitude or reason for following, the fact that that multitude accompanied "women who were beating themselves and lamenting" for Jesus would not give the impression that they had a negative attitude toward Jesus.

Here the people are portrayed as "standing [*histanai*] there observing [*theōrein*]." Once again neither verb in that Lucan description would reveal the attitude of "the people" toward the crucified Jesus. In Greek that reflects Semitic background the verb *histanai* often conveys no more than presence, virtually equivalent to "to be" in a place. At times, however, Luke uses it to paint a living tableau, as in 23:10 where he says that before Herod "the chief priests and the scribes had been *standing* there insistently accusing him [Jesus]." Now, in contrast to Mark's transient first group, the passersby, Luke's people "standing there" are an enduring presence throughout the crucifixion,[16] for as Jesus dies we read in 23:48: "All the crowds who were gathered together for the observation of this, having observed these happenings, returned striking their breasts." There we see the results of the observation (*theōrein*) that began as Jesus was mocked. Whether or not the people were already sympathetic in contrast to the three groups of mockers, their observation led to repentance. Thus for Luke—and this will once more be emphasized in relation to the two malefactors—observing Jesus on the cross could harden the hostility of some and soften the hearts of others.

Luke's First Mockery; Mark/Matt's Second Mockery (Luke 23:35b; Mark 15:31–32a; Matt 27:41–42). Having left out Mark's first group of mockers (the blaspheming passersby), Luke had to rearrange to get his threefold mockery. He followed the Marcan order in the sense that Mark's second group of mockers, i.e., the chief priests and scribes mocking Jesus about being the Messiah, become Luke's first group of mockers: the rulers sneering at Jesus about being the Messiah. Let us begin by looking in detail at the Lucan passage.

The opening words are literally: "There were sneering, however [*de*], also [*kai*] the rulers." Probably under the influence of the awkward *kai,* some ancient scribes[17] and a few modern commentators[18] have understood that the people's watching in 23:35a was malevolent and thus complemented the sneering of the rulers. In the majority interpretation (defended above) in which the watching is not meant to be hostile, there are several ways to

---

[16]Matt 27:36 in a different way also includes at the cross an enduring watching presence: the soldiers who sat keeping guard over him there.

[17]Codex Bezae, which has antiJewish tendencies, omits Luke's "there were also rulers," so that the people are standing there, watching, and sneering at him. The Lake and Ferrar families of minuscules have the rulers sneering at him "with them" (= the people).

[18]Plummer (*Luke* 532) counts the people's watching as the first of "four kinds of ill-treatment." Structurally, *in one episode* we should be suspicious of four, rather than three, mockeries!

explain the *kai*. One could resort to explaining it as part of Luke's borrowing from Mark (15:31: "*also* the chief priests") without paying sufficient attention to the awkwardness thus accidentally created. More simply the force of the *kai* may be adverbial, not having the implication that the rulers were sneering too as others had, but that not only were the people standing there watching but also the rulers were sneering and saying. In a way the *kai* would be calling attention to the parallel structure of the two parts of v. 35, each having a subject accompanied by a finite verb with the force of an imperfect tense,[19] and an explicative participle continuing the action of the verb.

In Mark/Matt the verbs of insult in the three mockeries are *blasphēmein*, *empaizein*, and *oneidizein* in that order. Luke uses *ekmyktērizein*, *empaizein*, and *blasphēmein*—is the last the culmination? His preference for *ekmyktērizein* ("to sneer") over Mark's *oneidizein* ("to revile") may have been dictated by the appearance of *ekmyktērizein* in Ps 22:8a. (Notice that one is thus presupposing that Luke saw that Mark was using Ps 22:8b, but has preferred to use 22:8a—a subtle editing!) Nevertheless, the verb was already in the Lucan vocabulary since he is the only author in the NT who employs it (16:14). It is marvelously expressive; for it is related to *myktos*, "nose," and so has some of the connotation of English "to look down one's nose at" or "to turn up one's nose at." *Archontes*, "rulers," is peculiar to Luke in the PN (23:13 and here) and in Luke-Acts sometimes corresponds to the components of the Sanhedrin (APPENDIX V, B6). Thus it is equivalent to Mark's second group of mockers: "the chief priests . . . with the scribes," to which Matt adds the "elders" to fill out the components of the Sanhedrin. Yet Luke's preference for the umbrella term "rulers" supplies a nice contrast to "the people." For Luke the Jewish reaction to Jesus is divided in the passion (as in subsequent history): The people are not hostile as a whole, but the rulers are. That is quite different from Matt's view where "all the people" (27:25) side with the authorities.

Mark has the chief priests "mocking him to one another" and speaking about Jesus in the third person. Gnilka (*Markus* 2.320) thinks they are at a distance from the cross, but that would destroy the setting where the first and third mockers are immediately present to Jesus. It is appropriate that members of the Sanhedrin, under various designations, appear as the main protagonists in the first Luke mockery and the second Mark/Matt mockery since the scene is meant to remind the readers of the challenge to Jesus in the Sanhedrin trial or interrogation. Mark has set the pattern: Charges against Jesus by the Jewish authorities as they interrogated him are resumed

---

[19]The pluperfect of *histanai* in 23:35a has that import, even as the perfect has a present import (BDF 97[1]).

to mock him as he hangs on the cross but will ultimately be the subject of God's vindication of Jesus after he dies. We have already discussed in relation to the Mark/Matt first mockery the charge that Jesus claimed he would destroy and build the sanctuary. Let us now turn to the titles about which Jesus was queried in the Jewish proceedings, namely, "the Messiah," "the Son of the Blessed/God." In the mockery at the cross the following titles appear:

> Mark 15:32:   Messiah, King of Israel
> Matt 27:42–43: King of Israel, Son of God
> Luke 23:35–37: Messiah of God, chosen one, (3d mockery) King of the Jews

Why does MARK mention only "Messiah," and not "Son of the Blessed/God," especially when in the vindication of Jesus after he dies the Roman centurion will confess him as the Son of God?[20] The latter feature, taken by itself, is intelligible: A Gentile would not use "Messiah" in confessing Jesus. Could that be a key to the answer? Does Mark portray the Sanhedrin authorities mocking what is of concern to them, i.e., "the Messiah," and the Roman centurion confessing the same reality but under the title of "Son of God"?

Does a similar approach explain in part what Mark adds to "Messiah," even though it was not mentioned at the Sanhedrin trial, i.e., the title "King of Israel"?[21] On this title Matt follows Mark although he keeps it quite separate from "Son of God," while Luke shifts to "the King of the Jews." The Lucan title clearly echoes the charge against Jesus in the Roman trial, as evidenced by the fact that Luke has attributed it to (Roman) soldiers. Has Luke thus given us the key to Mark's mind, namely, that having echoed the Jewish trial of Jesus with the sanctuary and Messiah motifs, Mark wants to echo the Roman trial as well? But why then would Mark not have written "the King of the Jews" instead of what he did write, "King of Israel"? Does he (followed by Matt) intend that Pilate and Romans use the political title "the King of Jews" (15:2,9,12,18,26)[22] but that Jews use the more theological "King of Israel"? Our evidence for that surmise would be by external comparison: In *GPet* 4:11 the inscription on the cross set up *by Jews* is "This is the King of Israel."[23] While it is attractive to think that Mark wants to echo

---

[20]In discussing these titles I shall be asking questions rather than firmly offering solutions. The logic of the evangelists is obscure here, and perhaps the choice of titles was not as deliberate as most solutions suppose.

[21]Of the seven Marcan uses of *Christos* ("Messiah") four are followed by a title in apposition: Son of God/Blessed (1:1; 14:61), son of David (12:35), King of Israel (here). Luke 23:2 has Jesus charged before Pilate with claiming to be "Messiah king."

[22]For the use of this title by the Hasmonean and Herodian secular kings, see p. 731 above.

[23]Also according to John 12:12–13 Jesus was praised by the Jewish crowd as he entered Jerusalem: "Blessed be the one who comes in the Lord's name and the King of Israel."

the Roman trial, the suggestion that he does so by giving us the known Jewish equivalent of "the King of the Jews" implies great subtlety.

MATT's preference for "Son of God" has already been discussed (p. 988 above) since he has used it twice, introducing it into the first mockery as well as substituting it for Mark's "Messiah" in the second mockery. It remains puzzling to this commentator why Matt did not leave "Messiah" alongside "Son of God." Nothing in Matt's account would favor the thesis that "the King of Israel" translates the charge in the Roman trial since, unlike Mark's mockery where that title comes after the sanctuary and Messiah charges, in Matt it appears between the two references to "Son of God."

Although LUKE's "the King of the Jews" (the third mockery) offers less of a problem as a title, the additions to Mark's "Messiah" are puzzling; for Luke speaks of "the Messiah of God, the chosen one." It is noteworthy that Luke 9:20 placed the confession of "the Messiah of God"[24] on Peter's lips when the parallel in Mark 8:29 had simply "the Messiah" (and Matt 16:16 had "the Messiah, the Son of the living God"). If at the cross the Jewish rulers are sneeringly throwing back at Jesus a claim that his followers made for him, Luke has taken care to hint to the reader that the title is primarily theological. As for the other Lucan addendum, "the chosen one" (*ho eklektos*),[25] in the account of the Transfiguration Luke (9:35) had God call Jesus "my Son, my chosen one [*eklelegmenos*]," where the parallel in Mark 9:7 had "my Son, my beloved [*agapētos*]." Matt 17:5 followed Mark but added "in whom I am well pleased," a full form used by the three Synoptics in describing the heavenly voice at Jesus' baptism. In both the Transfiguration and the baptism designations readers are meant to recognize a combination of royal christology (Ps 2:7: "You are my son") and Suffering Servant christology (Isa 42:1: "Behold my servant . . . my chosen one in whom my soul delights"). Since that combination represents postresurrectional Christian reflection on Jesus' career, the Jewish rulers in Luke are sneering at the most profound evaluation of Jesus by his followers.

---

[24]See also "His Messiah" in Acts 3:18, and "the Messiah of the Lord" in Luke 2:26—the latter (or "Messiah Lord") is attested as a Jewish designation in *Ps. Solomon* 17:36(32)—see BBM 676.

[25]Perhaps because "the chosen [elect] one" was not a familiar title to them, copyists adapted the phrase, e.g., some Koine mss. smooth Luke 23:35 to "the Messiah, the chosen one of God," while P[75] has "the Messiah, the chosen Son of God." (Is the latter an attempt to incorporate the two titles that Luke has used in the Jewish interrogation of Jesus: Messiah and the Son of God [22:67,70a]?) "The chosen one of God" as a title for Jesus has impressive textual support in John 1:34. Was "the chosen or elect one" a title in preChristian Judaism? The title appears a dozen times in *I Enoch* between 45:3 and 61:10, i.e., in the "Parables" section that has not been found among the many Qumran copies of *I Enoch* and that shows signs of Christian interpolation; yet see pp. 509–10 above. The title does appear in 4Q Mess Ar in reference to a newborn child who will have a great future, but without enough context to identify that figure as the Messiah—so J. A. Fitzmyer, FESBNT 127–60 vs. J. Starcky.

The Challenge to Save Himself or Be Delivered (esp. Matt 27:43). In relation to Mark/Matt's second mockery and Luke's first mockery we have discussed the personages (Sanhedrin authorities) and the titles that gave rise to the mockery. But there is a challenge that runs through the first two mockeries in Mark/Matt and all three in Luke, namely, a challenge, worded in various ways, that Jesus should save himself,[26] come down from the cross, or be delivered by God. Matt 27:43 adds to what has been borrowed from Mark a whole verse dealing with this challenge. Let me list the various phrasings, followed by the Gospels in which they occur and an indication (1, 2, or 3) as to which of the three mockeries contains them in that particular Gospel.[27]

i.   Save yourself: Mark 1, Matt 1, Luke 2–3
ii. Others he saved; himself he cannot save: Mark 2, Matt 2
       Others he saved; let him save himself: Luke 1
iii. Come down from the cross: Mark 1–2, Matt 1–2
iv. He has trusted in God. Let him be delivered if He wants him (Matt addendum to 2)

Several items are immediately notable. First, I have been treating Luke's first mockery as equivalent in certain features to the Mark/Matt second mockery; under *ii* it is apparent that the equivalence extends to the challenge as well. Yet Luke does not appreciate the Marcan wording "himself he cannot save." For Mark that is an artistic hardening of attitude by the second mockers (the Sanhedrin authorities) over the first (mere passersby)—the authorities in Mark are certain of Jesus' impotence. But the Jesus of the Lucan PN, while not as omnipotent as the Johannine Jesus, is portrayed as more in control of his destiny than the Marcan Jesus; and Luke would find "cannot save" too strong. Second, Luke, who three times employs the Marcan theme of Jesus' saving himself, avoids the Marcan challenge that Jesus should come down from the cross. Did Luke regard "Save yourself by having come down from the cross" as tautology?

I have shown above (p. 989) how Ps 22:8 gave shape to the first Mark/Matt mockery and to Luke's description of "the people" that prefaces the mockeries. The next verse of the psalm has influenced the challenge to Jesus:

---

[26]Pesch (*Markus* 2.488) thinks that the inability to save himself may have been a standard test betraying the false messiah, but the evidence he advances (*Apocalypse of Elijah* and Hippolytus) is over a century later and found in a Christian context.

[27]Note that under *i,* the third Lucan mockery has adapted the challenge (borrowed from Mark) to the context in which it is addressed to Jesus by a wrongdoer "hanged" with him: "Save yourself and us." The challenge in the second Lucan mockery is also in the second person ("Save yourself"); and Codex Bezae would conform the challenge in the first mockery (23:35b) as well, changing it from the third person to the second: "You saved others, save yourself."

Ps 22:9a: He hoped in the Lord; let Him deliver him;
      9b: Let Him save him because He wants him.

The reference in 9b to God *saving* the just has been adapted in challenges *i* and *ii* to Jesus (who claims to be God's Son or the Messiah). Challenge *iv,* a form reported only in Matt 27:43, makes clear use of 22:9a as well.[28] Since the sarcastic reason why challenge *iv* is presented to Jesus is that "he said, 'I am Son of God,'" Matt probably has in mind too another scriptural mockery of the just sufferer by the ungodly:

Wis 2:17a: Let us see if his words are true,
     17b: and let us test [*peirazein*] what will be his outcome.
     18a: For if the just one is God's son,
     18b: He will help him and deliver him from the hand of those standing against him.[29]

Clearly the OT atmosphere of the challenge hurled at Jesus is strong.

There are also motifs, however, derived from the Gospel accounts of Jesus' ministry. The "he saved others" of challenge *ii* globally describes a range of actions, for "save" is frequent in narratives of Jesus' forgiving sins and healing.[30] Perhaps especially significant is the Gospel use of "save" for Jesus' delivering people from death (Mark 5:23; Luke 8:50)—the Jesus who has saved others from death should be able to save himself from death.[31] But the challengers show no cognizance that Jesus' admonition to his disciples had exactly the opposite import: "Whoever wishes to save his life will lose it" (Mark 8:35 and par.). Similarly the challenge "come down from the cross" is exactly the opposite of the demand that Jesus posed to his disciples to take up the cross and follow him.[32] In Mark the challenge to come down from the cross is placed "in order that we may see and believe." But the Marcan readers have already heard Jesus speaking of such outsiders in Isaian language (Mark 4:12 from Isa 6:9): "They may indeed see but not perceive."

---

[28]SPNM 287–88 debates in detail which linguistic form of the psalm text motivated Matt and concludes: "Although influence from both the Hebrew and the LXX may be present, there is no necessary relationship with either version." The issue is complicated both by Matt's freedom in adapting and by his having other passages in mind. Aytoun, "Himself," would trace "Himself he cannot save" in challenge *ii* to the last line of Ps 22:30(29), a very obscure line which reads literally, "His soul he does not make alive," and which Aytoun interprets to mean that the sufferer did not save himself.

[29]The context in Wis 2:19–24 goes on with the resolution of the ungodly to torture and condemn the just to a shameful death, "for according to his own words, God will take care of him."

[30]E.g., Matt 1:21; Mark 3:4 and par.; Luke 7:50; 8:48; 17:19; 18:42.

[31]The suggestion that Jesus cannot save himself is particularly ironic in Matt, where the readers have already heard Jesus say, "Do you think that I am not able to call upon my Father, and He will at once supply me with more than twelve legions of angels?" (Matt 26:53).

[32]Mark 8:34; Matt 10:38; 16:24; Luke 9:23; 14:27.

Matt 27:42 concentrates only on the belief element: "Come down from the cross, and we shall believe."[33] The irony is that if he came down, he would ipso facto become unbelievable.

I have already pointed in n. 1 to the verbal parallels between these three mockeries of Jesus at the end of Matt and the three temptations of Jesus at the beginning. "If you are Son of God . . . come down from the cross" is very close to "If you are Son of God, throw yourself down [from the pinnacle of the Temple]" (Matt 27:40; 4:6). Matt's readers are meant in each to recognize that if Jesus does what the challenger wants him to do, he will cease to be the very thing that the claim concerns: He will not be God's Son. Rather, only when he remains on the cross to die will Jesus be truly believed in as God's Son (Matt 27:54; Mark 15:39).

Luke's Second Mockery (Luke 23:36–38). In place of Mark's first set of mockers, "the passersby," Luke substituted "the people" and gave them a neutral role framing the mockeries. Logically this meant that if Luke was to keep the pattern of three, he had to introduce a substitute group of mockers (see the table on p. 985 above). Consequently after the sneering rulers who make up the first Lucan mockery, we now find "Moreover, also the soldiers mocked."[34] The appearance of these soldiers at last specifies the vague "they" who have been in charge of the execution of Jesus since Pilate gave him over.[35] Although Luke does not identify them, surely he means us to think of *Roman* soldiers (pace Walaskay, "Trial" 92). In the third Lucan passion prediction (18:32) Jesus said he would be handed over *to the Gentiles* and mocked. Eleven other uses of *stratiōtēs* ("soldier") in Luke-Acts refer to soldiers that Roman officers, like centurions and tribunes, had under them.[36] The title they use here to mock Jesus is "the King of the Jews," a title that never originates with Jews in the Gospels and which echoes Pilate's charge (23:3) in the Roman trial. Thus, while the Marcan first and second

[33]The same challenge would be vocalized by the disbelieving Celsus 150 years later: "Why does he not at any rate now show forth something divine and deliver himself from this shame?" (Origen, *Contra Celsum* 2.35).

[34]The opening of all three Lucan mockeries of Jesus on the cross (23:35b,36,39) is marked by a postpositive *de*, translated: "But . . . Moreover . . . Moreover . . ." Despite the custom of describing these three insults as "mockeries," the verb *empaizein*, which is most properly translated "to mock," appears only in the second action. Previously all three Gospels used it in the third passion prediction (Mark 10:33–34; Matt 20:19; Luke 18:32). Luke used *empaizein* in both the previous PN scenes in which Jesus was derided (before the Jewish trial [22:63], and in the presence of Herod [23:11]), while Mark 15:20 and Matt 27:29,31 used it only for the mockery after the Pilate trial.

[35]Luke 23:26: "they led him away"; 23:33: "there they crucified him"; 23:34: "they threw lots."

[36]The only exceptions in the total Lucan practice are in Acts 12:4,6,18 with the soldiers of King Herod Agrippa I. Yet since that king had taken over the governing role previously held by Roman prefects, one may say that *stratiōtēs* is always used by Luke for soldiers of the civil governing authority. The term should not be confused with the *stratēgos* used by Luke-Acts for the "captains of the Temple," who are priestly figures accompanied by Jewish militia, charged with Temple order (APPENDIX V, B4), or with *strateuma* that Luke 23:11 uses for Herod's troops.

mockeries progress from passersby to chief priests and the scribes, the Lucan first and second mockeries progress from Jewish rulers to Roman soldiers. The Jewish rulers sneer at Jesus under the religious title "the Messiah of God"; the Roman soldiers mock him under the political title "the King of the Jews." The fact that both challenge him to save himself from the cross shows that Jews and Romans alike misunderstand Jesus' identity.

Several features in the Lucan account require attention. The *first* is a parallelism between this Lucan scene at the cross where Jesus is mocked by Roman soldiers and the Mark/Matt scene in the praetorium after the Pilate trial where Jesus is mocked by a Roman cohort (§36 above). Here in Luke and there in Mark the verb *empaizein* ("to mock") is used, and the mockery is centered on the title "King of the Jews." The scribes of Codez Bezae and the OS noticed this relationship; for in their text of the Lucan scene at the cross, just as in Mark's postPilate mockery, the soldiers say, " 'Hail [*chaire*], O King of the Jews,' . . . after having put on him also a thorny crown." Mark may be said to have four settings in which mockery takes place: Jewish trial, Roman trial, on the cross, and as Jesus dies (15:36–37).[37] The first and the third are by Jews, the second by Romans, and the fourth simply by "someone." Luke's sense of orderliness has caused him to reduce the mockeries to two: one before the Jewish trial by the Jewish captors who were holding Jesus, and the other on the cross by Roman soldiers.

The *second* feature deserving attention is the action of the soldiers "coming forward, bringing forward to him vinegary wine [*oxos*]." That the soldiers have to come forward (*proserchesthai*[38]) implicitly recognizes that Luke has kept the Roman military in the background until now. *Prospherein* is the second Lucan verb in a row compounded with *pros*, whence my repetitious translation "bring forward." The verb is often used for a religious, respectful presentation of gifts (as in Matt 2:11), so that the action described here is not in itself mocking. Only when we hear the words of the soldiers does it become clear that their offering of cheap wine[39] is a burlesque gift to the king.

On p. 940 above I described the Mark/Matt accounts of two offerings of wine to Jesus on the cross. *At the beginning* in Mark 15:23 (= Matt 27:34)

[37]The relation between Luke's account and the last Marcan crucifixion episode which involves the offering of wine will be discussed shortly.

[38]This verb, occurring 10 times in Luke, 10 in Acts (compared with 5 in Mark, 1 in John), still does not have Matthean frequency (52 times) or import (p. 253 above).

[39]It is difficult to ascertain the impression conveyed by the offering of *oxos*, the coarse, diluted, vinegary, dry red wine (related to *oxys*, "sharp") which was the *posca* or ordinary drink of the Roman soldiers, e.g., of those stationed at Hermopolis in Egypt, as attested by papyri finds. For Matt and probably also for Mark the use of the word *oxos* in the PN is an echo of Ps 69:22 (see p. 1059 below); but does Luke intend his readers to make such a connection, and would they have done so?

they (Roman soldiers) offer *oinos* or sweet wine, mixed with myrrh (gall), presumably with the benevolent purpose of lessening Jesus' pain; but he does not take it. *At the end* in Mark 15:36 (= Matt 27:48) a bystander fills a sponge with *oxos* or bitter wine, fits it on a reed, and (in a context of mockery) gives it to Jesus to drink; but we are not told whether or not he drank it.[40] Not unexpectedly Luke simplifies by recounting only one offering of wine, basing his narrative mostly on Mark's second wine offering—the first was ineffectual, after all, since Jesus refused it. Indeed, the only possible echo of Mark's first offering would be Luke's specification of what Mark only implies: The soldiers were the agents. Luke also makes specific the mockery hinted at by the context in which Mark places the second offering.[41] By bringing mockery and *oxos* here, Luke thus eliminates several items of Marcan repetition.

A *third* feature is the information "For there was also an inscription over him: 'The King of the Jews, this (man).'" Luke uses this to explain why the soldiers were moved to say to Jesus, "If you are the King of the Jews"—they could read the title before their eyes on the cross. As we saw on p. 963 above, Mark 15:26 (= Matt 27:37) mentions the inscription at the beginning of the crucifixion account simply as a pertinent item, without supplying theological or narrative explication. John 19:19–22, on the other hand, develops the title as the centerpiece of the first narrative episode in the crucifixion account, working with the dramatic import of the languages employed and the angry protest of the chief priests of the Jews that caused Pilate to insist on its affirmation of Jesus' kingship of the Jews. Luke's treatment stands midway between these two approaches, for Luke uses Mark's details with an instinct for their narrative import not unlike John's.[42] Since in Luke the inscription feeds the soldiers' mockery, it is not simply a notice of the accused's crime; it is a public derision of his pretensions. That is caught in the *houtos* ("this") that Luke adds to the Marcan wording of the inscription: "The King of the Jews—this character!"

Thus in my judgment the mockery by the soldiers, peculiar to Luke, is totally a formation by that evangelist from Marcan raw material, exhibiting

---

[40]In John 19:29–30 "they" (the soldiers?) put a sponge soaked in *oxos* on some hyssop and raise it to Jesus' lips; he takes that wine. There is no mockery involved. Nothing suggests that Luke knew the Johannine tradition or drew on John's account.

[41]The challenge in the Marcan mockeries to come down from the cross may have reminded Luke of the taunt that accompanied Mark's final offering of wine, about wanting to see if Elijah would come to take him down.

[42]Indeed, ancient scribes wrongly translated that functional similarity to John into a verbal relationship. As reported in §40, n. 72, in Luke 23:38 instead of "an inscription over him," the Koine textual tradition substituted "inscribed over him in Greek, Latin, and Hebrew letters"—surely a gloss taken over from John. Without that gloss Luke's text betrays no dependence on John.

his customary flair for rearranged organization, simplification through avoidance of repetition, and preference for smoother narrative flow.

The Third Mockery (Mark 15:32b; Matt 27:44; Luke 23:39). Mark/Matt ended the setting of the crucifixion (§40) by speaking of two bandits who were crucified alongside Jesus; Mark/Matt close the second part of the crucifixion scene by coming back to these co-crucified. In all three Synoptics this is the shortest mockery of Jesus on the cross. (For Mark that is not surprising since the three prayer scenes in his Gethsemane account also grow progressively shorter.) Mark introduces a new verb, *oneidizein* ("to revile, reproach") in the imperfect, and the continuous force of that tense plus the force of the initial *kai* gives a pungency to the brevity: Even the co-crucified kept on reviling Jesus. Since Mark supplies no wording for this reproach, Matt assumes that it was done "in the same way" as the preceding mockeries.[43] When Mark (15:27) introduced these figures, he spoke of them as "two bandits" (pl. of *lēstēs;* also Matt 27:38); but he does not reproduce that terminology here: They are simply co-crucified. Evidently Mark is not interested in the crime of which these figures are guilty, but only in their miserable fate on the cross. He is not interested in the content of what they said but only in the fact that they reviled Jesus. The force of the third mockery, then, is the cumulation of hostility: Not only the haphazard passersby and the determined Sanhedrin enemies of Jesus, but even the wretches that share his fate speak ill of him. On the cross Jesus has no friends; he is a solitary righteous man closely surrounded on all sides by enemies. Once again Ps 22 may be in the background, for in v. 7 the righteous speaks thus: "I am one reviled [*oneidos*] by human beings and considered as nothing by people [*laos*]." Words of the same stem as *oneidizein* are standard in OT accounts describing the mockery undergone by the just (Ps 69:10; 89:51–52; Wis 5:3).

The Lucan version of the third mockery has meaningful differences from Mark.[44] When Luke introduced the criminals who would be crucified with Jesus in 23:32,33, he called them wrongdoers (pl. of *kakourgos*), and he repeats that designation here.[45] Unlike Mark, he wants to emphasize not only their wretched fate but the fact that they have done something reprehensible. One of them will be saved, and the readers must see that Jesus' bountiful

---

[43]The Greek *to d' auto,* although separated from the verb, is translated by some almost as if it were in an objective relationship: "reviling him in the same way."

[44]A minor difference is that Luke does not speak of those who were "crucified together" with Jesus but of the "hanged," i.e., the verb *kremannynai* that will be used of Jesus' death in Acts 5:30 and 10:39 ("hang him on a tree"). This verb, which is more biblical, echoes the description in Deut 21:22,23 of the punishment of a capital offense, but we cannot be sure that the Deut allusion is intended here.

[45]Luke is the only Gospel that never uses *lēstēs* ("bandit") for those whose arrest accompanies Jesus' passion—either for Barabbas (John 18:40) or for the co-crucified (Mark 15:27 and Matt 27:38,44).

graciousness is not simply sympathy for suffering but true mercy toward sinners. Indeed, Luke has the first wrongdoer live up to his designation. The Jewish rulers in the first mockery sneered disbelievingly: "If this is the Messiah." The Roman soldiers in the second mockery mocked Jesus: "Save yourself." Now the evildoer who hangs at Jesus' side repeats both in his blasphemy: "Are you not[46] the Messiah? Save yourself and us." For all the injustice involved, the Jewish rulers and the Roman soldiers had on their side the legal formalities of interrogation and trial, but the wrongdoer (as his fellow will remind him) is on the other side of the law. His blaspheming Jesus is even more gratuitous than that of the passersby of whom Mark 15:29 used that verb. It is a Jesus who has been vilified without cause who will now show mercy.

THE SALVATION OF THE OTHER WRONGDOER (LUKE 23:40–43)

Thus far in the present scene, which describes activities at the cross, Luke has been reworking Marcan material, even when he was creating the introductory verse (23:35) about the people watching. That neutral group, placed before the three hostile mockeries, alerted Luke's readers that the picture at the cross was not totally negative. To match that introductory verse Luke now terminates the scene with an episode centered on a figure who is more than neutral, namely, "the other" wrongdoer[47] who serves as a witness to Jesus' innocence. More important, this episode gives Jesus an opportunity to speak from the cross the last words of his life directed to people. During the mockeries he did not answer those who demanded signs; now he speaks to a wrongdoer who acknowledges being a criminal. The others derided

---

[46]Twenty of 53 NT uses of *ouchi* occur in Luke-Acts (Mark 0; Matt 9; John 5); it expects a positive answer: In this wrongdoer's view Jesus claims to be the Messiah. This theme echoes Mark's second mockery (15:32), where Jesus is addressed sarcastically as "the Messiah, the King of Israel." Codex Bezae omits "Are you not the Messiah?" The Koine tradition of Luke ("If you are the Messiah"), on the other hand, conforms the third Lucan mockery to the second, which reads: "If you are the King of the Jews." Agnes Lewis ("New") points to the OS[sin] reading "Are you not the Savior," a reading harmonized with "Save yourself and us." G. G. Martin ("New") points to *GPet* 4:13 that speaks of Jesus as "the Savior of men [human beings]." Do *GPet* and OS[sin] reflect a common tradition, or has the former influenced the latter? How to date them in respect to each other is uncertain; both are 2d cent.

[47]Luke never supplies another designation. The popular "good thief" is imperfect on two scores: first, the use of *lēstēs* ("bandit") for the co-crucified, while found in Mark/Matt, is avoided by Luke; second, Luke does not use "good" to describe this wrongdoer but "bad" (*kakos*). In an attempt to be more precise, some would favor "penitent" for "good"; yet, as I shall mention, while the wrongdoer acknowledges his guilt, he is never explicit about sorrow. Inevitably there have been attempts to be more precise, supplying different sets of names for the two criminals (p. 969 above). The saved wrongdoer has been identified as "the one on the right" (Mark 15:27) of Jesus, and the blaspheming wrongdoer as the "one on his [Jesus'] left."

Jesus as an implausible king; now Jesus answers that this day he himself will be in paradise. The wicked wrongdoer picked up the challenge "Save yourself" (by coming down from the cross) and added to it "and (save) us"; Jesus will save one of the "us" but by remaining on the cross and entrusting himself to his Father.

Where did Luke get this episode? There is no evidence that Mark (or Matt or John) knew of it.[48] Did Luke draw it from an independent tradition? Some (Fitzmyer, Jeremias, Taylor) answer affirmatively, pointing to nonLucan features, e.g., paradise. Yet, as the footnotes will show, there are Lucan features as well; and so it is not impossible to think of the scene as a Lucan theological creation.[49] Or one may argue for an intermediary view: Luke has drawn an element from independent tradition and developed it into the present episode. As for that element, there are two chief proposals: (a) The thesis that the account in *GPet* 4:13 represents preLucan tradition. In that tradition only one of the wrongdoers played an active role; and he reviled *the Jews,* voicing some of the themes but not much of the wording found in Luke. It is proposed that Luke combined this independent tradition with Mark's two co-crucified revilers. However, one then has to suppose that there were two very different early traditions concerning the co-crucified, the one in Mark and the one in *GPet,* each seemingly unknown to the preserver of the other until both fell into Luke's hands. Also one must think that by chance the early tradition posited for *GPet* fits in extremely well with the theology of that apocryphal gospel, which makes the Jews the only adversary in the passion. Is it not far more likely that *GPet* has drawn remotely on Luke and turned the Lucan episode in an antiJewish direction? That suggestion would fit in with the general approach I have advocated toward *GPet,* namely, that it draws on the canonical Gospels (not necessarily from their written texts but often from memories preserved through their having been heard and recounted orally). (b) The thesis that Luke has taken from the tradition an "Amen" saying of the forgiving Jesus who promised a sinner a place with him in paradise.[50] Luke would then have adapted this saying to the context

---

[48]From patristic times on there have been attempts to harmonize Luke's picture with that of Mark/ Matt where both the co-crucified revile, e.g., the proposal that both started out hostile but one changed his mind, or the contention that Mark's picture of both *reviling* is not contradictory to Luke's picture in which only one *blasphemes.* Of those two harmonizations the former is not true to what is stated in the respective Gospel narratives, while the latter ignores the equivalence of reviling and blaspheming (in parallelism in II Kings 19:22).

[49]As I shall point out, the Genesis story of Joseph imprisoned amid the (good) chief butler who was restored to his post and the chief baker who would be hanged on a tree might have inspired Luke to describe two different fates for the wrongdoers. In the infancy narrative the Genesis story of Abraham and Sarah inspired Luke's description of Zechariah and Elizabeth.

[50]This is more plausible than the suggestion of Robbins ("Crucifixion" 41) that the saying originally referred to "a converted Gentile sharing the destiny of a martyr, a recurrent feature in martyr

of the cross by applying it to one of the wrongdoers of whom he read in Mark. We know that Luke had access to a collection of the sayings of Jesus; and the proposed adaptation is not without parallel in Lucan procedure, for most posit that in 22:29–30 Luke took a saying which promised thrones in the kingdom to the Twelve and adapted it to the context of the Last Supper.

What is certain is that whether pure creation or tradition in whole or in part, the episode of the benevolent wrongdoer has been adapted by Luke to his theological purpose in at least three ways: (a) He has used it to supply the other side of a positive framework for the negative mockeries. (b) He has presented "the other wrongdoer" as another impartial witness to Jesus' innocence in a chain stretching from Pilate and Herod before Jesus' death to the centurion after the death. (c) He has given another instance of healing forgiveness exercised during the passion in a chain that includes the servant of the high priest (whose ear Jesus healed) and those who nailed Jesus to the cross (forgiven as not knowing what they did). The first words that the Lucan Jesus spoke to the people were in the synagogue at Nazareth, as he proclaimed release to the captives and liberty to those who were oppressed (4:18); it is only fitting that his last words addressed to another human being should fulfill that promise by offering paradise to a wrongdoer hanged on a cross. If Luke got this episode from a source (which I doubt), one recognizes why he favored that source: It had the same theology he had. Well does Fitzmyer ("Today" 210ff.) appeal to this episode to refute the thesis that Luke has no soteriological theology of the cross.

The Other Wrongdoer Speaks to His Blaspheming Companion (Luke 23:40–41). While in Mark/Matt no answer is given to the reviling by the co-crucified, in Luke the sarcasm and repeated blasphemy by the one wrongdoer receives a direct response[51] from his companion. Luke likes to contrast two figures, e.g., Mary and Martha (10:38–42), the rich man and Lazarus (16:19–31), the Pharisee and the publican (18:9–14), JBap and Jesus (7:33–34)—see also the parable of the two sons in Matt 21:28–32. Here there is also a resonance of the story in Gen 40 about the chief baker and the chief butler (cupbearer) imprisoned with Joseph in Egypt.[52] The chief butler was given a place at Pharaoh's court, while the chief baker was hanged on a tree. Joseph, after interpreting positively the butler's dream of the future, added, "Remember me . . . when it will be well with you and act [do] mercifully

---

stories of later Judaism." The salvation of a persecutor is a later feature in Jewish and Christian martyr stories, and there is nothing here to suggest a Gentile background.

[51]Among the Gospels the pattern "in answer . . . said" is Lucan, reflecting LXX usage.

[52]See p. 658 above for other similarities between Joseph and Jesus in the PN, e.g., Joseph was sold to enemies by Judah/Judas, one of the twelve (sons of Jacob), for twenty or thirty pieces of silver.

toward me."[53] If in the Genesis story the butler eventually takes Joseph up with him to a prestigious place in the court, in the Lucan story Jesus takes the wrongdoer up with him to paradise.

We have seen that the three mockeries of Jesus resemble Satan's three temptations of Jesus. Jesus rebuked (*epitiman*) Satan for his effrontery (Luke 4:35,39,41), and so it is not surprising to find the same verb (more commonly used in Luke than in the other Gospels) employed here as the second wrongdoer rebukes the first. The rebuke gains emphasis from *oude,* "not even," a particle used five times in Luke to begin a sentence, as it does here. Interpreters disagree about the word modified by it in Luke's question: Does "not even" modify "you" (Marshall), or "God," or "fear" (Plummer, Fitzmyer)? The last is the most likely since *oude* immediately precedes the verb "fear"; but the general import is clear, no matter what word it modifies. In 12:4–5 the Lucan Jesus warned that the only one who should be feared is God, who has the power after someone's death to cast that person to hell; and that type of fear,[54] based on divine justice, is involved here. Certainly the wrongdoer speaks of something more than simple pious fear, for the warning that fear is imperative is called forth by blasphemy that has been spoken against the Son of God.

The clause "Because you are under the same *krima*" is elliptic and somewhat obscure. García Pérez ("Relato" 263) feels impelled to resort to Aramaic, but his highly speculative approach produces a translation ("Do you not fear God *when* you stand condemned?") that is not much better than the one that can be derived from the Greek. The awkwardness of the Greek is alleviated if one recognizes that "Because" is tantamount to "After all." What comparison is involved in "the same"—the same as Jesus? García Pérez (287ff.) would reject that implication, arguing that the phrase is no more than a reminder that the blaspheming wrongdoer is being punished for what he did. Yet in what follows, the idea seems to be that all three are condemned to die on the cross: two deservedly, one unjustly. Part of the problem of understanding precisely what Luke means centers on *krima.* Generally in the NT it refers to the judicial action (judgment or sentencing), but it can refer to the negative result of the action (execution). I use "condemnation"

---

[53]Beyond the similarities in the biblical narrative, it is noteworthy that contemporary with Luke's writing, Josephus in *Ant.* 2.5.1; #62 speaks of Joseph's fellow prisoners as condemned (*katakrinein*) for crimes, and *Ant.* 2.5.2; #69 has Joseph undergoing the fate of a wrongdoer (*kakourgos*) despite his virtues, while Luke 23:40 has the two wrongdoers and the same condemnation (*krima*). In later Jewish tradition the request in the Joseph story to be remembered was taken to refer to a future world, even as for Luke the remembrance involves paradise. See Nestle, "Ungenähte" 169; Gottlieb Klein, "Erläuterung"; and Derrett, "Two" 201–9.

[54]*Phobeisthai* ("to be afraid") is used more frequently by Luke (23 times) than by any other Gospel (Mark 12, Matt 18, John 5).

to refer to the whole complex. Luke would have us think that the two wrong-doers were tried even as Jesus was, were judged (23:24 uses *epikrinein* for Pilate's judgment that the demand to crucify Jesus should be met), and were led off to be crucified (23:26,32). Thus all three had the same judicial experience.

In v. 41 the eloquent wrongdoer admits that he and his companion are being *condemned justly*—an implicit contrast with the statement that will be made after Jesus' death in Luke 23:47: "Certainly *this man was just.*" In typical Lucan language the wrongdoer confesses, "We are receiving what is worthy of what we did"[55]—an implicit contrast with Pilate's affirmation about Jesus in Luke 23:15: "There is nothing worthy of death that has been done by him." (Similarly in Acts 25:11 Paul denies that he has done anything worthy of death.) While the wrongdoer was certainly able to know that crucifixion fitted his crime and that of his companion, how can he be so certain of the rest of his assertion (again phrased in Lucan language[56]): "But he did nothing disorderly." How does he know what Jesus did? Certainly in this genre we should not resort to a naturalistic explanation, e.g., the wrongdoer had previously known Jesus[57] or he had heard that Pilate had declared Jesus innocent. Rather this wrongdoer in Luke has somewhat the same function that Pilate's wife had in Matthew 27:19: Though a Gentile who had never seen Jesus before, she could affirm that he was a "just man." She knew that through (divine revelation in) a dream; however, for Lucan characters, such as this wrongdoer or the centurion after Jesus' death, the first time they see Jesus his innocence is transparent. Only those whose eyes are blinded by ignorance do not recognize that (Acts 3:17).

Is the recognition of his own guilt and of Jesus' innocence equivalent to repentance (*metanoia*) on the part of the wrongdoer? If so, the implicit forgiveness extended to him by Jesus would be comparable to that extended in Luke 15:20 by the father to the prodigal son who did not have enough time to express fully his confession: "I have sinned against heaven and before you" (15:21). Or has this wrongdoer not yet reached *metanoia*? That

---

[55]"Receive" is *apolambanein,* which is used 4 or 5 times by Luke, 1 by Mark, and 0 by Matt and John. *Axios* plus the genitive ("worthy of") is used 11 times in Luke-Acts, 2 in Matt, and 6 in the rest of the NT. "What we did" begins with a genitive, not an accusative; the attraction of the relative pronoun to the case of the antecedent is a Lucan grammatical feature (Fitzmyer, *Luke* 1.108, under 6). *Prassein* ("to do") is a verb used 19 times in Luke-Acts, 2 in John, 0 in Matt and Mark.

[56]"But" is *de* paired with the preceding *men* ("indeed")—a classical usage affected by Luke (Fitzmyer, *Luke* 1.108). "Did" is *prassein,* used again. Among the Gospels *atopos* (literally, "out of place") occurs only in Luke. Indeed, here in its place Codex Bezae reads the more usual *ponēros* ("evil"), offering a contrast with Peter's judgment on the "men of Israel" in Acts 3:17: Jesus did nothing evil; but they did evil, even if in ignorance.

[57]Some apocryphal gospels expand the narrative of the baby Jesus in Egypt, having his family encounter favorably this "robber" at that time. See n. 70 below.

incomplete stage would require greater forgiveness—the kind implied by Paul in Rom 5:8: "God demonstrated His love for us in that while we were still sinners, Christ died for us." The Lucan Jesus healed the ear of the high priest's servant who was hostile to him. His very presence healed the enmity that had existed between Herod and Pilate. He spontaneously pleaded with his Father for forgiveness for those who crucified him. In none of those three cases did he look for *metanoia*. Obviously, then, interpreters cannot demand that *metanoia* must have existed in the heart of this crucified wrongdoer who recognized that Jesus had not done anything disorderly, deserving condemnation.

The Other Wrongdoer Speaks to Jesus (23:42). Having rebuked his companion, the "other" (wrongdoer) now directs a persistent ("was saying") plea to Jesus. His manner of address, "Jesus," is stunning in its intimacy, for nowhere else in any Gospel does anyone directly address Jesus simply by his name without a specifying or reverential qualification.[58] Such familiarity has struck some interpreters as illogical on the part of a convicted evildoer who encounters Jesus for the first time, but one may doubt that such an issue even occurred to Luke. In the PN the address "Jesus" is a moving artistic touch, for the personal name conveys the sincerity of the request. Beyond that, this usage reflects irony. The first person with the confidence to be so familiar is a convicted criminal who is also the last person on earth to speak to Jesus before Jesus dies. The familiarity is not irreverent, for the wrongdoer assumes that Jesus has the kingly power to dispense at will royal benefits.

The requested benefit is phrased in terms of remembrance[59] whenever Jesus comes (aorist subj: has or will come) into/in his kingdom. "Into/in" reflects a famous textual problem. P[75], Codex Vaticanus, and the Latin tradition support *eis*, "into," while the Koine tradition, including Codices Sinaiticus and Alexandrinus, support *en*, "in." In the Greek of this period the demarcation line between the two prepositions is not precise, but here most interpreters see a difference of theological import.

---

[58]These are the vocative addresses to Jesus in the Gospels: "Jesus Nazarene" (Mark 1:24; Luke 4:34); "Jesus Son of God" (Mark 5:7; Luke 8:28); "Jesus Son of David" (Mark 10:47; Luke 18:38); "Master Jesus" (Luke 17:13). Those patterns help to explain the Koine textual variant in Luke 23:42: "And he was saying, 'Jesus, *Lord,* remember me . . . ,'" and the Codex Bezae variant: "Having turned to *the Lord,* he said to him. . . ."

[59]The verb *mimnēskesthai* ("to remember") occurs six times in Luke, compared to six times in all the other Gospels together. (Also the *hotan* ["whenever"] that follows it occurs more frequently in Luke than in any other Gospel.) Requests for remembrance are attested in early Jewish funerary inscriptions (IEJ 5 [1955], 234). Indeed the quest to be remembered graciously in a more favorable situation is attested also in other religious tradition. Diodorus Siculus (1st cent. BC), *Bibliotheca* 34/35.2.5–9, tells us of a Syrian who engaged in the magic arts and prophesied that the goddess had told him he would become king. At a dinner where some mocked him, the request was made by

(a) *Eis*, "into," (favored by Fitzmyer, Metzger, RSV, NAB, *New Jerusalem Bible*) would mean that the wrongdoer thought that Jesus was on his way to his kingdom and wanted to be remembered as soon as Jesus got there. (The use of *eis* following *erchesthai*, "to come," occurs some twenty-five times in Luke-Acts and is a set expression for arriving at a place.) How would the wrongdoer know with conviction that Jesus was truly a king? Once more it must be remembered that we are dealing with a popular narrative that does not spell out the logic. The soldiers have mocked Jesus as "the King of the Jews." Following that, the wrongdoer recognizes an injustice done to Jesus and concludes that in fact he will rule over a kingdom.[60] How will this come about? Luke does not explain the wrongdoer's understanding: Does he expect God to step in and stop Jesus from dying? Or will God make Jesus victorious immediately after death in a kingdom on this earth or in a kingdom in heaven? Sometimes scholars try to determine the answer by asking what a Jewish criminal (not likely to have been a learned theologian) would have understood about Jesus' destiny in AD 30/33. That is an unsatisfactory approach: In AD 80–95, when Luke was writing, Christian readers of the *eis* phrase would have understood the wrongdoer to mean "into your heavenly kingdom" because they knew Jesus had just assigned places (thrones) in the kingdom (22:29–30) and that he went to heaven (Acts 1:9–11; 7:56). One may object that they also would have known that Jesus did not ascend into heaven until Easter Sunday evening (Luke 24:51) or till forty days after Easter Sunday (Acts 1:3,9–11). However, the very fact that Luke could describe the ascension into heaven at two different dates leaves open the possibility that he saw no problem reproducing another early Christian belief that Jesus ascended (in an invisible, otherworldly way) into heaven from the cross as he died.[61] That

---

others who gave him a gift: "Whenever you become king, remember this good deed." He did become king and rewarded them.

[60]There is debate whether *basileia* here means "kingdom" or "kingly power, rule," sometimes with the assumption that the *en* reading (understood as a reference to the parousia) is facilitated if the words refer to Jesus (coming back) with kingly power. In fact, however, both prepositions can be meaningful with either connotation of *basileia*, even if "kingdom" reads more easily with *eis* and "kingly power" with *en*. Some would claim that the semitism *bemalkût* ("in the rule of" = "as king": Dan 6:29) underlay the Greek *en basileia* (G. Dalman, *The Words of Jesus* [Edinburgh: Clark, 1902], 133–34). The contention that later scribes who no longer understood the Semitic background changed it to *eis basileian* is dubious because those scribes would be introducing a theology of ascent into heaven from the cross which was not prominent in later times.

[61]Applying a psalm to Jesus, Peter in Acts 2:27 says that God would not let the Holy One see corruption. The idea of several goings of Jesus to the Father is found also in John: elevation through the cross in 12:32–33, and ascension on Easter in 20:17. The Gospel narratives describe everything after the death of Jesus as a sequence affecting Jesus' followers who remained within history; nevertheless the evangelists seem to have understood that from God's stance everything from the death on the cross to the outpouring of the Spirit (from Good Friday evening to Pentecost) was unified and timeless. In dying Jesus had passed beyond time. On all this see G. Bertram, "Die Himmelfahrt Jesu vom Kreuz aus und der Glaube an seine Auferstehung," in *Festgabe für Adolf Deissmann* (Tübingen: Mohr, 1927), 187–217, esp. 215–16.

belief is found in Heb 10–11, in John's language of being "lifted up" on the cross in return to the Father (3:14–15; 8:28; 12:32,34; 13:1; 16:28), and even in Luke 24:26 where the risen Jesus speaks of having entered (past tense) into his glory after suffering. Would entering (*eiserchesthai*) into his glory be the same as coming (*erchesthai*) into his kingdom?[62] In Dan 7:13–14 "one like a Son of Man" comes to the Ancient of Days and is given *honor* and *kingdom,* and that is related to 7:22, where the saints come to possess the kingdom. The *eis* reading of Luke 23:42 is quite consonant with such an interpretation.

(b) *En,* "in" (favored by Lagrange, Lake, Plummer, G. Schneider), offers a wider range of possibilities than the *eis* reading. García Pérez, who prefers it, points out instances where it means "into";[63] and he observes that '*th* (Hebrew) or '*t'* (Aramaic), while they normally mean "come," can be polyvalent, slipping over toward "go." Since I am dubious that Luke was translating from Semitic, I judge it better to work with the Greek meaning: "Remember me whenever you come in [or with] your kingdom [or kingly rule]." That "remember" fits such a context is apparent from Ps 106:4: "Remember me, Lord, in the course of favoring your people. Visit me [LXX: us] with your salvation."

Most often those who accept the *en* reading understand Luke to be referring to the parousia, and that seems to be implied by the subvariant of the *en* reading in Codex Bezae: "in the day of your coming." Once again, one should not evaluate this interpretation on the basis of whether a Jewish criminal in AD 30/33 would be expecting the second coming of the Messiah (the title used in blasphemy by the first wrongdoer), for seemingly the *second* coming was a peculiarly Christian concept.[64] The real issue is that in 80–95 Christian readers of Luke certainly expected the parousia. Indeed, defenders of the *eis* reading argue that the more familiar concept of the parousia caused scribes to change from the original *eis* (with its now less familiar concept of ascent into heaven from the cross) to *en.*[65] That the coming of the kingdom was appropriate language for the endtime is apparent in the Lord's Prayer (Luke 11:2): "May your kingdom come." To the objection that the crucified wrongdoer speaks of Jesus' kingdom, not of God's, one may point to Luke

---

[62]P[75] actually substitutes "kingdom" for "glory" in 24:26.

[63]"Relato" 272–84: he cites instances from the LXX and Luke 1:17c; 4:1; 9:46.

[64]If one leaves out the "second" element, Ps 72:12–14 describes the role of the future, yearned-for king: "He shall rescue the poor . . . from fraud and violence he shall redeem them." The day of the Lord's coming was not always a day of expected wrath (as it is in Rev 6:17).

[65]This argumentation is on the level of reader comprehension in the 80s. But if one thinks of 23:43 as a saying on the lips of the historical Jesus, he may have thought he would return in parousia immediately after his death. Luke 22:16 seems to anticipate fulfillment in the kingdom of God very shortly after the Last Supper.

22:29 where the Father has assigned Jesus a kingdom (also 1:33), and to Matt 16:28 which refers to the parousia as "the Son of Man coming in his kingdom."

Not all those who advocate the *en* reading refer it to a distant future coming of Jesus in the parousia to establish his kingdom on earth. Some think of Jesus coming after this wrongdoer's death to take him to heaven, somewhat along the lines of John 14:3: "And when I go and prepare a place for you, I will come again and will take you to myself, that where I am you may be also." This interpretation comes close to the picture in the *eis* reading, for both understand the ultimate destiny to be heaven. The main remaining difference would be whether after dying Jesus takes the man with him directly to heaven from the cross in order to enter into the kingdom, or after dying Jesus goes to heaven and then returns with kingly power to take the man back with him to heaven.

Overall I judge that Jesus' response in 23:43, which we shall now discuss, rules out the parousia by its emphatic "today." It allows the second form of the *en* interpretation just discussed, as well as the *eis* interpretation. The idea of Jesus ascending into (*eis*) the kingdom from the cross seems to me the most plausible. In the fearful judgment of God about which he has warned the blaspheming wrongdoer, the "other" wrongdoer expects Jesus to be vindicated and to gain his kingdom; he is asking to be remembered at that moment.

Jesus' Response to the Other Wrongdoer (Luke 23:43). The mark of disciples is that they are spontaneously willing to respond to Jesus' invitation to follow him (Luke 5:11,27–28; 9:23,57–61; 18:22,28). By asking to be remembered by Jesus this wrongdoer has anticipated the invitation and already expressed his desire to follow Jesus. Jesus responds with an "Amen" saying. In discussing the origin of this scene, I mentioned the possibility that instead of being entirely a Lucan creation, or entirely a borrowing from preLucan tradition, the scene may have been created on the basis of a traditional saying, namely, this Amen-pronouncement of future blessing with its peculiar use of "paradise." At the beginning of the PN, Mark/Matt had their final "Amen" saying when Jesus predicted Peter's three denials. (Comparable is the "Amen, Amen" saying in John 13:38.) Luke had no "Amen" saying there, so that his sole usage of this style in the PN, which is also his final use of it,[66] consists of the last words spoken to a human being by Jesus in

---

[66]Luke avoids Semitic words (omitting *Abba, Hosanna, Rabbi*), and so it is surprising that he includes *Amēn* 6 times (a word that some 8 times is left untranslated in the LXX). Yet this frequency in Luke is lowest among the Gospels (13 times in Mark, 31 in Matt, 25 in John [in the doubled format "*Amēn Amēn*"]). See the overall analysis in O'Neill, "Six" 1–6. Two of Luke's 6 usages have reference to the kingdom; this is the only one addressed to an individual.

his preresurrectional life. On p. 137 above, I mentioned briefly various theories about the meaning of an "Amen" saying, and pointed out that the one aspect that cannot be debated is the atmosphere of solemnity projected by the "Amen." These last words of the Lucan Jesus exhibit divine graciousness beyond any anticipation, including that of the crucified wrongdoer who petitioned Jesus. In Luke 11:9, Jesus promised "Ask and it will be given you"; here it is given more abundantly. The fact that Luke prefixes an "Amen" to the fulfillment tells us much about the Lucan conception of the merciful Jesus.

Although "this day" in Greek follows immediately after "say," it does not refer to the time of saying but to the time of being with Jesus in paradise; "this day" responds to the "whenever" in the wrongdoer's request.[67] On the one hand "this day" has an eschatological tone, so that E. E. Ellis[68] is correct in saying that of itself the phrase does not necessarily mean the day of crucifixion but could refer to a period of salvation inaugurated by the death of Jesus. Yet the context, in which the response goes beyond the request, favors the literal meaning of "this very day" (which, in any case, is eschatological), not some indefinite future in God's plan. Luke signals that by the immediately following references (23:44) to the sixth hour (noon) and the ninth hour (3 P.M.), i.e., hours of that same day which is now hastening to a close. In 2:11; 4:21; and 19:9 Luke has used "this day"[69] of a chronological day that is also an eschatological moment of salvation.

The wrongdoer asked to be remembered by Jesus; more is granted in terms of being *with* Jesus; for the response given by Jesus includes not only deliverance but intimacy. Acknowledging the disciplelike spontaneity manifested by the wrongdoer, Jesus is giving him the role of a disciple. In 22:28–30 the Lucan Jesus said to the Twelve, "Now you are the ones who have remained *with* me in my trials," and as a reward he gave them to eat and drink at his table in the kingdom. On that analogy Jesus' promise that the wrongdoer would be *with* him involves more than being in his company in paradise; it involves sharing his victory (Plummer, *Luke* 535).[70] The Lucan usage of the phrase "with me" may not reach the mysticism of the Pauline

---

[67]So Blathwayt, "Penitent." Scribes made closer the connection of the "this day" to what precedes. In the OS[sin] the malevolent wrongdoer says in Luke 23:39: "Are you not the Savior? Save yourself alive *today*, and also us." In Codex Bezae the benevolent wrongdoer asks Jesus to be remembered "in the *day* of your coming," and Jesus begins his response by saying, "Have courage."

[68]NTS 12 (1956–57), 37. See "the day of the Lord" in OT prophecies (Isa 2:11; Jer 30:3; etc.). Heb 13:8 describes Jesus Christ as "the same yesterday, *today*, and forever."

[69]*Sēmeron* occurs in Luke-Acts a total of 20 times, compared to 8 in Matt and 1 in Mark.

[70]The *Arabic Gospel of the Infancy* has the infant Jesus in Egypt encounter the two future wrongdoers who would be crucified with him; Jesus says to his mother that Titus (the benevolent wrongdoer) "will *go before me* into paradise" (23:2).

usage; but in Luke, as in Paul (I Thess 4:17; Philip 1:23; II Cor 4:17), to be with Christ describes a fate after death.

"Paradise," the designated destiny in the "Amen" saying, has been a much-discussed term. Does it represent heaven, i.e., the highest heaven in which Jesus is eternally at God's right hand, or some inferior or temporary celestial state? In Hebrew *pardēs* is a Persian loan word (*pairi,* "about"; *daêza,* "wall": a walled enclosure or park), and three times in the OT it clearly describes a garden (Neh 2:8; Eccles 2:5; Cant 4:13). The Greek *paradeisos* in the LXX reproduces both Hebrew *pardēs* and *gan/gannâ* ("garden," as in the Garden of Eden).[71]

Those who argue that "paradise" in Luke 23:43 is not the highest heaven of God's full presence and thus the ultimate destiny include Calvin, Maldonatus, Jeremias, Leloir, O'Neill, etc. They offer several arguments: (a) Many uses of "paradise" imply a lesser form of closeness to God, e.g., the paradise of Gen 2:15; 3:8 where God walked with Adam and Eve; the paradise of II Cor 12:3–4 where it is equal to the third of seven heavens (12:2), a place to which Paul was swept up in mystical vision. Paradise is also the third heaven in *II Enoch* 8, the place where the just wait for final judgment; see also *Life of Adam and Eve* (*Apocalypse of Moses*) 37:5. (b) There can be no full salvation or redemption until Jesus has been raised from the dead.[72] Thus the wrongdoer would not have been taken definitively into the presence of God already on Good Friday. As a parallel one might point to the Matthean account of the events that took place when Jesus died (27:52–53): The tombs were opened, and many bodies of the holy ones who had fallen asleep were raised; they came out of their tombs; and *after* his resurrection they entered into the holy city—a type of salvation in two steps, with the second step following the resurrection of Jesus on Easter Sunday. (c) The wrongdoer cannot go to the highest heaven, for he has not expressed repentance clearly. (De la Calle, "Hoy" 299, draws a parallel between paradise and purgatory.) See, however, pp. 1004–5 above where I list examples of Luke's theology of divine forgiveness even before repentance is expressed. A Jesus who was known as a friend of sinners (7:34), who received sinners and ate with them (15:2), may not have been squeamish about taking a sinner into the highest heaven once that sinner had asked to follow him.

"Paradise" understood as the highest heaven or final bliss in God's pres-

---

[71]See Weisengoff, "Paradise" 163–66; also J. Jeremias, TDNT 5.766–68. In the first centuries of Judaism after the exile references to paradise become reasonably frequent, as attested by apocrypha; but there is less use in the early rabbinic literature—a frequency proportion that suggests we are dealing with the terminology of popular expectation.

[72]Bertram ("Himmelfahrt" 202) reports that according to Chrysostom the Manichaeans used "This day with me you shall be in paradise" (as well as "Father, into your hands I place my spirit") to prove that resurrection from the dead was not really necessary.

ence has an even larger number of proponents (Ambrose,[73] Cornelius a Lapide, Fitzmyer [seemingly], J. Knabenbauer, MacRae, etc.) and is supported by impressive arguments:[74] (a) In early Judaism paradise and Eden took on the significance of ultimate happiness. In Isa 51:3 the future glory of Zion is compared to Eden, the garden of the Lord. Grelot ("Aujourd'hui" 198–200) points to Aramaic fragments of *I Enoch* for the "paradise of righteousness," i.e., the place where the saintly go. In *Ps. Sol.* 14:3 the Lord's holy ones live forever in the garden of the Lord.[75] In *II Enoch* 65:10 paradise is an eternal residence. See also *Test. Dan.* 5:12; *Test. Levi* 18:10–16. Jewish tombstones mention the Garden of Eden, surely meaning a full heavenly existence (Nestle, "Luke xxiii"). (b) Such a meaning responds better to the wrongdoer's request to be remembered in Jesus' kingdom. He is scarcely hoping for an inferior heavenly status. II Tim 4:18 shows the heavenly kingdom to be the final state. (c) It seems inconceivable that after his death Jesus went only to a lower heaven. (d) "Be with me" (*met' emou*) must be close in meaning to the expressions of ultimate bliss "with the Lord" in I Thess 4:17 (*syn Kyriō*) and II Cor 5:8 (*pros ton Kyrion*). (e) The parable of Lazarus and the rich man (Luke 16:19–31) shows two places in the other world: Hades, which is a situation of torment, and the bosom of Abraham; and the division between them is permanent. There is no real reason to think of the bosom of Abraham as provisional and to make a distinction between it and heaven. See also the parable of the rich barn builder in 12:16–20. (f) There is nothing alien in the thought of a complete (rather than partial) act of graciousness by God to the dying. TalBab, '*Aboda Zara* 18a, reflects a (later) Jewish outlook in a similar situation. The Roman executioner of a saintly rabbi asked would he have life in the world to come if he did something that would make the rabbi's death less tortured. The rabbi responded affirmatively; and when he died a voice from heaven affirmed that both rabbi and executioner have life in the world to come. Thus one may gain eternal life in a single hour. (g) "The paradise of God" in Rev 2:7 is parallel to these other descriptions: no "second death" (2:11); power over the nations (2:26); having one's name in the book of life (3:5); and, in particular, sitting with Christ on his throne (3:21). Rev 22:2 uses paradise imagery for the state of perfect and lasting bliss with God. By bringing this wrongdoer with him into

[73]A famous interpretation is given by Ambrose, *Expositio Evang. secundum Lucam* 10.121 (CC 14.379): "Life is to be with Christ; for where Christ is, there is the kingdom."

[74]Besides the arguments I shall list, some would add another argument supporting the idea that Jesus took the wrongdoer from the cross directly into supreme bliss, namely, that this is consonant with Luke's de-emphasis on the parousia. In interpreting Lucan thought I find this postulated de-emphasis exaggerated, and there is nothing in this scene to support it.

[75]Fitzmyer, *Luke* 2.1507, adventurously prints "in Paradise" as if it were a quote from *Ps. Sol.* 14:3.

paradise, Jesus is undoing the results of Adam's sin which barred access to the tree of life (Gen 3:24).[76]

Thus the second understanding of paradise in Luke 23:43, namely, as being with Christ in the full presence of God, has very high probability. What then would be the lesson from Jesus' action? To answer that, some have resorted to symbolism, e.g., this wrongdoer was a Gentile or represented the Gentiles, and so the story points to the conversion of the Gentiles on the world's last day. Others have sought historical antecedents, finding in this wrongdoer a Zealot who was attracted by Jesus' claim to kingship (Hope, "King's Garden"). Some Church Fathers contrasted this brave wrongdoer with the apostles who had fled. However, that comparison represents a mélange of the Gospels, for they do not flee in Luke. The only contrast clearly intended by Luke is with the first wrongdoer, who remains hostile toward Jesus' claim to kingship. Still other scholars think that Luke is teaching his readers how to receive suffering patiently and make it an occasion of winning Jesus' favor. The most frequently held view is the most obvious: This story teaches the unmotivated graciousness of God exercised by and in Jesus. The action implicit in 23:43 is consonant with the activity of the Lucan Jesus, who during his public ministry forgave sins (5:20; 7:48) and brought salvation (19:9). The fact that Jesus can speak with such authority about the hanged wrongdoer's fate shows that he has God's power of judgment, which he wields graciously.[77]

Nevertheless, some would almost look down on this Lucan presentation, for they contrast it with Pauline soteriology whereby the death of Jesus is the factor that brings about forgiveness. The observation is made that in Luke Jesus is not dying for the sinner but joining the sinner to him in salvation. Variations of this view are held by Conzelmann, Talbert, and Untergassmair, to name a few. The forgiveness extended here, however, is certainly in view of the death of Jesus, since only after death will Jesus take the wrongdoer with him to paradise. One should also insist that for Paul not simply the brute fact of death by crucifixion but the forgiving intention of Jesus was important. Rom 5:6–8 speaks of the love of Christ for us as part of his salvific death. Thus a loving forgiveness extended by the crucified Jesus to a wrongdoer is really not so far from Paul's notion that Christ died for us while we were still sinners. The Jesus who speaks here continues the general pattern of mercy shown previously in the Lucan PN when Jesus healed the servant's ear in the arrest scene, when Jesus expressed concern about the

---

[76]Garrett ("Meaning" 16) points out that in the Lucan portrait of Jesus' death there is both Adam imagery and Moses imagery (Luke 9:30–31: "his exodus").

[77]Neyrey (*Passion* 139–40) portrays this verse as a judicial pronouncement by one whom Acts 10:42 describes as "ordained by God to be judge of the living and the dead."

future fate of the Daughters of Jerusalem on the way to the place of execution, and when Jesus prayed for forgiveness for those who crucified him. Frequently called the episode of "the good thief,"[78] this is rather another aspect of the good Jesus.

FRIENDS AND DISCIPLES NEAR THE CROSS (JOHN 19:25–27)

In the Synoptic Gospels we saw a pattern of three mockeries of Jesus by those at the cross. In Mark/Matt there were only hostile agents (passersby, chief priests with scribes/elders, and crucified criminals), while Luke framed the three hostile agents (rulers, soldiers, and one crucified wrongdoer) with the people as neutral observers and the other wrongdoer as sympathetic. John too has a pattern of three groups of agents at the cross—a pattern evidently fixed early in the narrative tradition of the crucifixion—even if a separate Johannine episode is built around each. In 19:19–22 the chief priests of the Jews hostilely complained about the title "the King of the Jews" (a topic that appears in the second Lucan mockery). In 19:23–24 the soldiers treated Jesus as a criminal, dividing his clothes. Now in a move that goes beyond Luke, a third Johannine group of participants consists of friends and disciples of Jesus. If one analyzes the action, Jesus was made triumphant over the first group, for Pilate resisted their request; unwittingly, by their actions the second group fulfilled the Scripture pertinent to Jesus; Jesus reconstitutes the principal members of the third group, the mother and the beloved disciple, as a family in discipleship. Thus in a certain way Jesus is the supreme agent throughout the three episodes, fulfilling the plan given to him by the Father.

Those Standing Near the Cross (John 19:25). The opening sentence in this episode provides a double contrast. A *men . . . de* construction offers at least a moderate contrast between the women standing (pluperf. of *histanai* used in an imperf. sense) near (*para*) the cross and the soldiers who "did these things" (19:24). The other contrast is implicit: These women are "standing near the cross" before Jesus dies, while a partially comparable group of women is mentioned in Mark 15:40 after the death of Jesus as "observing from a distance." (In that situation Luke 23:49 will make the contrast sharper by having those women among those "*standing* from a distance."[79]) To what extent is this latter contrast real and intentional? Are the

---

[78]Consonant with the "good thief" designation is the touching and attractive observation that in the end he also stole heaven. Unfortunately, there is nothing in any Gospel's description of the two co-crucified that would suggest that they were thieves. The *lēstēs* ("bandit") designation in Mark/Matt does not refer to a thief.

[79]In the present scene Luke 23:35 has reported that "the people were standing there observing," so that functionally John 19:25 almost combines two Lucan verses.

same women involved? Were they near the cross or far off or both?[80] Is there one underlying tradition that has developed in different ways in the Synoptic and Johannine Gospels? To study this in more detail we must recognize that John has two components in his group near the cross: first, women who are there but do not become involved in the dialogue; second, Jesus' mother and the beloved disciple to whom Jesus addresses himself. The first component is described in v. 25, with the overlapping figure of Jesus' mother, who is introduced there; and the second component is described in vv. 26–27. Let us compare the first component to the Synoptic lists of those who look on far off.

How does one punctuate "his mother and his mother's sister Mary of Clopas[81] and Mary Magdalene"? Is John 19:25 referring to two, three, or four women? If *two women* are involved, there would be a twofold apposition: his mother = Mary of Clopas; his mother's sister = Mary Magdalene. This interpretation has serious unlikelihoods: for instance, that the mother of Jesus, Mary wife of Joseph, would be referred to as Mary of Clopas. Another unlikelihood is that Mary of Magdala would be the sister of Mary of Nazareth, so that their parents named both daughters Miriam. No other Gospel reference to Mary Magdalene suggests that she was a close relative of Jesus (his aunt). If *three women* are involved,[82] there would be one apposition, namely, his mother's sister = Mary of Clopas—the personal name would be parenthetical to the designation "sister." This solution still leaves the problem of the two sisters being named Miriam. Most likely, then, we are to think of *four women,* as understood by Tatian and the Syriac Peshitta, which insert

[80]The standard harmonization is that having stood near the cross before Jesus' death (John), they moved to a distance after the death in order to observe (Synoptics).

[81]The designation "of Clopas" offers four possibilities, as Bishop, "Mary Clopas," points out: (1) Sister of Clopas: this is the least likely hypothesis since there is little evidence of a woman identified through her brother; (2) Mother of Clopas: in Arabic sometimes a woman is identified through her son's name; (3) Wife of Clopas (Moffatt; [later] Phillips; RSV; NEB; NAB): a designation less likely after a woman has become a mother; (4) Daughter of Clopas (Jerome; early Arabic versions; Goodspeed and [early] Phillips translations; Bacon ["Exegetical" 423]): particularly an unmarried woman might be identified through her father. Bishop thinks the choice is between 3 and 4, and argues for 4, in favor of which his later article "Mary (of) Clopas" cites the Diatessaron. Imaginatively Bishop proposes that later she became the mother of James and Joses and went with her father Clopas (= short form of Cleopater) toward Emmaus in Luke 24:18. In fact, however, the name Clopas is not found elsewhere in the NT; and it is not the same as the name Cleopas in Luke 24:18. It is never associated in the NT with Mary, the mother of Jesus, despite patristic attempts to make him her relative (by blood or marriage).

[82]*Gospel of Philip* #28; II 59,6–11: "There were three women who always walked with the Lord: Mary his mother, and her[?] sister, and Magdalene (the one who was called his companion). His sister and his mother and his companion were each a Mary." See Klauck, "Dreifache." It is tempting to speculate that Mary (wife of) Clopas was a sister of Jesus (see Mark 6:3); and therefore all the women near the cross, except Magdalene, were relatives of Jesus. Like most temptations, it is better resisted.

an "and" between the second and third designations.[83] The reason why the personal name of Jesus' mother is not given may be that like the disciple whom Jesus loved (also never named), she has a predominantly symbolic role. But why, then, is the sister of Jesus' mother not named? Was she so well known that naming was unnecessary, or was her name not preserved in the tradition? We have no way of knowing.

Having decided on the number four, we may now compare John's list of women near the cross with two Synoptic PN lists, one of women who are mentioned after Jesus' death as standing or observing from a distance and the other of women in the burial scene who observed Jesus being placed in the tomb by Joseph from Arimathea. In constructing Table 8 to facilitate this comparison, I shall also include (in italics) a third list consisting of the women who in all four Gospels came to the empty tomb on Easter. With varying intensity there is an implication that the women who were at Golgotha for Jesus' death and also observed his burial in the tomb before the Sabbath came to that same tomb after the Sabbath. Consequently the Easter lists are helpful in settling ambiguity as to whom the evangelists were referring in their previous descriptions. While Table 8 of the three scenes (I: death; II: burial; III: Easter) may seem complicated, since it must include so many lists of the grouped followers of Jesus, a discussion is facilitated if readers pay attention to the capital letters at the extreme left as a way of comparing respective figures: Horizontal line A has the figure that occurs most frequently when all the scenes are considered; B has the figure second in frequency; etc. As one reads down vertically, the numeral next to a name indicates the order in which that person appears in the scene indicated at the top of the column. Thus in the first vertical column (Scene I under discussion here), the order of the list of names in John's text is: (1) Jesus' mother, (2) his mother's sister, (3) Mary of Clopas, (4) Mary Magdalene, (5) the disciple whom Jesus loved. John has no women at the burial (II).

There is a remarkable consistency of certain names in the various Gospel accounts of Scenes I, II, and III. Horizontal *line A* shows that Mary Magdalene is the most frequently named, appearing in nine of the eleven vertical lists and thus not named only in the two Lucan scenes that refer to Galilean women without using personal names.

Another woman named Mary (across *line B* in the table) appears with high consistency, even if the designation given her varies. Twice in Matt she is simply called "the other Mary." When she is further identified in the

---

[83]There is no need, however, to claim that John wants to contrast the four women with the four soldiers of the preceding episode since in neither instance does John apply the term "four" directly to the individuals.

TABLE 8. THE WOMEN AND OTHERS: ON *FRIDAY* (I) BEFORE OR AFTER JESUS' DEATH; (II) AT THE BURIAL; AND ON *EASTER* (III) AT THE EMPTY TOMB

	I John 19:25 be-fore death	III *John 20:1,2* *Easter*	I Mark 15:40–41 after death	II Mark 15:47 burial	III *Mark 16:1* *Easter*	I Matt 27:55–56 after death	II Matt 27:61 burial	III *Matt 28:1* *Easter*	I Luke 23:49 after death	II Luke 23:55 burial	III *Luke 24:10* *Easter*
A	4. Mary Magdalene	*1. Mary Magdalene*	1. Mary Magdalene	1. Mary Magdalene	*1. Mary Magdalene*	2. Mary Magdalene	1. Mary Magdalene	*1. Mary Magdalene*			*1. Mary Mag-dalene*
B	3. Mary of Clopas		2. Mary mother of James the younger and of Joses	2. Mary of Joses	*2. Mary of James*	3. Mary mother of James and of Joseph	2. the other Mary	*2. the other Mary*			*3. Mary of James*
C	2. his mother's sister		3. Salome		*3. Salome*	4. mother of the sons of Zebedee					*2. Joanna*
D		2. "We"	4. many other women who had come up with him to Jeru-salem			1. many women who had fol-lowed Je-sus from Galilee			2. the women who were following with him from Gali-lee (see 8:1–3)	1. the women who had come with him out of Galilee	*4. the other women*
E	1. his mother 5. disciple whom Jesus loved								1. all those (masc.) known to him		

Synoptics, it is through her sons James and Joses/Joseph.[84] The possibility that this Mary is the same person known to John as Mary of Clopas (her husband or father) is good.

Occasionally still another woman is remembered by name (*line C* in Table 8), but here the identifications vary widely. For Mark in Scenes I and III Salome is the third woman. (In an echo of Tatian's Diatessaron preserved in Middle Persian, found among the Turfan fragments in the Gobi desert, Salome is the second woman alongside Mary in Scene III; and the third woman is Arsenia—see W. L. Petersen in TTK 187–92, esp. 189.) Is Matt's "mother of the sons of Zebedee" (elsewhere only in Matt 20:20) a knowledgeable identification of the woman called Salome in Mark? Even if one were to suggest that, there is no reason to equate either of these with the Joanna known only to Luke, whom elsewhere (8:3) he describes as the wife of Chuza, Herod's steward. The peril in attempting to identify Salome, the mother of the sons of Zebedee, or Joanna with the woman whom John calls "his mother's sister" (i.e., the sister of Mary of Nazareth) is obvious; yet upon that dubious identification depends the thesis that would make the sons of Zebedee cousins of Jesus. There are varying names for candidates in the lists of the Twelve; so also various women who were attached to Jesus were remembered; and for reasons that we cannot determine, different ones were preserved in traditions of different Gospels.

Line D in the table shows that the evangelists were aware that a group of women was involved in the various events we are discussing, and that generalization should make us cautious when we try to equate individuals in the lists.

Line E in the table has entries so peculiar to one Gospel that seemingly they have no parallel elsewhere in the lists but have considerable theological import to the respective evangelists. We are chiefly interested here in "his mother" and "the disciple whom Jesus loved," who are the protagonists in John 19:26–27. Luke's "all those [masc.] known to him" will be discussed

---

[84]The variant whereby "Joses" is used in Mark and "Joseph" in Matt also occurs in the names of "the brothers" of Jesus in Mark 6:3 and Matt 13:55. Since James is also the name of a "brother" of Jesus, many would identify the sons of the woman at the cross with "the brothers" of Jesus. That identification, when accepted, has produced the most diverse explanations: (a) Mary the mother of James and Joses/Joseph is not the same as Mary the mother of Jesus. Consequently these men are not blood brothers of Jesus but more distant relatives, perhaps cousins because this other Mary was the wife of Joseph's brother Clopas. On Clopas, see Hegesippus (ca. AD 150) in Eusebius EH 3.11 and 3.32.1–6. (b) The two Marys are the same person; but because Mary the mother of Jesus was not a believer (Mark 3:21,31–35; 6:4), Mark prefers to designate her by her other children (Jesus' brothers) rather than as Mary the mother of Jesus. (See the treatment in Crossan, "Mark" 105–10.) This is a dubious interpretation of Mark's overall view of Mary; moreover, it has to suppose the three other evangelists went in the opposite direction because they gave Mary a favored role in Christian memory. It is incredible that if Luke understood the Mary to whom he refers in 24:10 as "Mary of James" to be the mother of Jesus, he would have designated her thus.

fully in its proper sequence in §44 after the death of Jesus. Let me note here only that the "all" has been taken literally by some scholars to include the Twelve (without Judas?), in harmony with the praise given them in Luke 22:28 as having remained with Jesus in his trials. Nevertheless, that inclusive adjective can suggest the presence (at a distance from the cross) of male disciples beyond the Twelve (cf. 10:1). We saw another hint of that in Mark's account (14:51–52) of a would-be disciple who, after the Twelve had fled (14:50), remained, only to flee away naked himself. Might John's picture of "the disciple whom Jesus loved" fit into that tradition, with the understanding that *an overall, vague recollection of the involvement in the PN of male disciples beyond the Twelve was used by the individual evangelists to exemplify their theologies of the passion*? Mark would have used it to fortify his thesis of human weakness and failure during the passion; Luke, to strengthen an optimistic portrayal of (at least partial) fidelity by those who had followed Jesus; John, to embody symbolically an ideal discipleship that never wavered. Even by this standard of remote parallels in the tradition, there is no hint in the Synoptics that would support the Johannine picture of Jesus' mother as present at the cross.[85] Luke, who will later mention her presence in Jerusalem before Pentecost (Acts 1:14), would have been likely to name her among the Galilean women if he knew that she was present at the crucifixion. As we shall see, she serves John as a symbol of discipleship; and we have to be content to deal with the following verses on a theological level, without being able to resolve further the questions of the preGospel antiquity of the picture of the mother and the disciple at the cross or its historicity.

But before I turn to the verses dealing with those two figures, how would I use Table 8 to evaluate the other part of the picture John gives in v. 25, where he names the three women present with Jesus' mother but assigns to them no active part in what follows? Of the three scenes in which women are named in the PN (in relation to the crucifixion, observing the burial, coming to the empty tomb on Easter), the one most agreed upon by the evangelists involves Mary Magdalene (explicitly or implicitly with companions) coming to the tomb on Easter and finding it empty. Women are absent from John's burial scene, and there is disagreement between John and the Synoptics about the time and place of their presence at the crucifixion: John 19:25 mentions Jesus' mother's sister, Mary of Clopas, and Mary Magdalene (along with Jesus' mother and the disciple whom he loved) as standing *near the cross before Jesus died,* while Mark 15:40 mentions Mary Magdalene, Mary mother of James the younger and of Joses, and Salome as observing

---

[85]In n. 84 I judged unfavorably the thesis that "his mother" is to be identified with the Synoptic "Mary mother of James and Joses/Joseph."

from a distance after Jesus died. Now, in this crucifixion context John is primarily interested in the other figures, the mother of Jesus and the disciple whom he loved, whom John must place near the cross before the death since Jesus speaks to them. Apparently, in order to group in the death scene those previously involved with Jesus, John has taken a form of the Mary Magdalene/another Mary/another woman tradition and attached it to his own special scene; and in so doing he betrays the fact that the three-women tradition was well established in relation to the crucifixion. (Certainly John's way of listing the women is not a back-formation from his mention of Mary Magdalene at the empty tomb; as for the origin of the Synoptic list of the women after the crucifixion, see p. 1195 below.) I say "a form" of the women tradition because the lists in Mark and John are surely related (two of the three women may well be the same) and yet John has the names in a different order, designates the second Mary differently, and identifies a different third woman. That makes it unlikely that John has copied from Mark; plausibly both evangelists drew on a more ancient preGospel tradition. The fact that in John the three women are only mentioned and not addressed suggests that the localization of them near the cross is secondary and that the Marcan presentation of them after the death observing from a distance is closer to the ancient tradition. John's relocation, besides having the convenience of consolidation, shows that the Son of Man lifted up on the cross has begun drawing all to himself (John 12:32–34). By placing the three women in the company of Jesus' mother and the disciple whom Jesus loved (whom Jesus is about to reconstitute as a family of disciples), John is more positive toward them than any Synoptic Gospel, even though hitherto he has never mentioned them in the following of Jesus, nor indicated that they were among "his own" at the Last Supper (13:1), or present during the passion.

The Mother of Jesus and the Beloved Disciple (John 19:26–27). Although "his mother" is mentioned in 19:25 with the other women as standing near the cross, she does not become a protagonist until 19:26, where she is joined to the beloved disciple. A verb compounded of *para* and *histanai* is used of these two in v. 26, even as *histanai* ("to stand") and *para* ("near") were used of the four women in v. 25—one has the impression that two traditions are being sewn together. We last heard of this other disciple in 18:15–16 where, not having gone away with the rest, he followed Jesus to the court of the high priest and got Peter in. Now, after Peter has denied Jesus, this disciple is the only faithful male to follow Jesus to the cross. His presence here is peculiar to John and indeed most critical scholars would attribute it to the evangelist, not to preGospel Johannine tradition. Yet the Gospel itself, in its second reference to him at the crucifixion (19:35), makes him the eyewitness and presumably the tradition bearer who guarantees the

scene. In discussing v. 25 I offered some Synoptic parallels that give plausibility to the thesis that the disciple may already have been mentioned incho-
atively in the preJohannine crucifixion story, even if it was the evangelist
who has elaborated and systematized the disciple's theological import as the
preeminently beloved disciple. While the language and characterization of
this episode involving the mother and the disciple are totally Johannine, we
shall see below that functionally it has a Synoptic counterpart.

Jesus begins to speak upon *seeing* his mother and the disciple. (In the
Synoptics the women see [different verb] Jesus afar off; here he sees the two
figures near.) The mother is the first mentioned in the pair, and Jesus speaks
first to her; that priority suggests that she is the primary concern of the episode. The disciple is more important in the total Gospel picture, and Jesus'
interest in his role is predictable; but the role of Jesus' mother cannot be
anticipated from what has hitherto been narrated and must be clarified. We
last heard of her at Cana (2:1–12), where her initial concern was to fill the
needs of the wedding party by an implicit demand for Jesus to act. He disso-
ciated himself from her concerns, placing first the hour assigned to him by
the Father. Only her response, "Do whatever he tells you," and Jesus' granting her request at the end were favorable to her having a positive future
relation to Jesus. The fact that Jesus' brothers mentioned in her company in
2:12 are severely judged in 7:3–7 as never having believed in him would
leave the reader ambiguous about the role of Jesus' mother even if she is
never so judged. That ambiguity is resolved here, for the mother stands with
the other women (indeed, first among them) who are clearly attached to Jesus even to his death; and she is about to be put in close relationship to the
ideal disciple.

The relatedness of this episode to that at Cana is clear: These are the only
two Johannine passages in which the mother of Jesus appears; that same
designation is used for her in both instances (with no personal name); in
each she is addressed as "Woman," an address perfectly proper for a man to
a woman, but never found for a son to his mother;[86] and while Cana occurred
before the hour had come (2:4), this episode occurs after the hour has come
(13:1). Jesus' words to his mother in 2:4 were that he and she had no common concern; his words to her here have the opposite import. They call attention to and *reveal* a role that puts her in intimate relationship to the ideal
disciple; for "Look: your son" is another instance of John's revelatory use

---

[86]See BGJ 1.99. That this address may not have seemed properly reverent to scribes of a later
period who had a more developed mariological sense may explain a tendency to omit "Woman"
from John 19:26 (some Coptic mss. and one OL).

of "Look"[87] detected by de Goedt ("Schème"; see BGJ 1.58). Similarly "Look: your mother" is a revelation to the beloved disciple. The atmosphere is testamentary as the dying Jesus makes disposition of the two unnamed figures who are known only through their relation to him (*his* mother, the disciple whom *he* loves). The importance of what is done is highlighted in v. 28, where we read, "After this, Jesus having known that already all was finished . . ." Thus what Jesus does in relationship to his mother and the disciple is his last-willed act, and is an act of empowerment that both reveals and makes come about a new relationship. We are reminded of Ps 2:7: "You are my son; today I have begotten you," which also involves a revelatory empowerment.

What is the new relationship that did not exist before? What is the importance of instructing Jesus' mother to be the mother of the beloved disciple, and instructing him to be her son? One line of interpretation stretching from Augustine to Aquinas to Lagrange has found in this episode a manifestation of filial piety: The dying son is worried about his mother's future, and he is leaving her to his closest friend to be taken care of. She is to be treated by the disciple as he would treat his own mother.[88] I find little in Johannine thought to recommend this interpretation. Johannine disciples are not of this world (17:14), and what will happen to them in terms of material welfare until they die is an issue that the Johannine Jesus regards as extraneous (21:22). To interpret the relationship between the Johannine Jesus and his mother in terms of filial care is both to reduce Johannine thought to the level of the flesh and to ignore the distancing from the concerns of natural family that took place at Cana in 2:4.[89]

Many more interpreters of John have moved to a theological level in order to understand the scene. Most of the time that has meant probing the symbolism of the two figures addressed by Jesus. Already at an early period in Christian exegesis, she who is called "Woman" here was compared to Eve, the woman of Gen 2–4. Even as the old Eve was the mother of all the living (Gen 3:20), so does this new Eve become the mother of the disciples of

[87]*Ide* ("look," used in John 19:4,14) is found in the best textual witnesses, but there is respectable support for *idou* ("behold"). Barrett (*John* 552) and others find similarity to an adoption formula; see Tobit 7:12 (Sinaiticus): "Henceforth you are her brother and she is your sister." Yet there is no precise parallel where the mother is addressed first; and it is Paul, not John, in whose theology adoptive sonship has a role.

[88]Schürmann ("Jesu" I5) argues that the task is *not* mutual: Mother, care for your son; Son, care for your mother. Rather it means: Mother, see the son who will care for you; Son, see the mother you will care for.

[89]I am not saying, of course, that historically Jesus was not a loving son to his mother. If she was in Jerusalem for Passover, her son would have been concerned about her. But the never named "his mother" of John has been lifted to the level of theological significance; and the issues are those of spirit, not of flesh.

Jesus, i.e., those endowed with eternal life. The beloved disciple was looked on as a son given to Mary to replace Jesus who was crucified, even as the old Eve said, "God has given me a son to replace Abel whom Cain killed" (Gen 4:25; see also 4:1: "With the help of the Lord, I have begotten a man").[90] That symbolism has been fortified by an appeal to Rev 12 (often with the assumption that this book is related to John) where the woman who struggles with the dragon (12:9: = the ancient serpent of Gen 3) is the mother of the Messiah (12:5); but after he is taken up to God and to his throne, she has other offspring (12:17: "Those who keep the commandments of God") who stand with her in the war waged against her by Satan.

Working with Rev 12:2, where the woman in her birth pangs is pregnant with the Messiah, others have appealed to the image of Mary in the Lucan infancy narrative and identified the Johannine mother of Jesus with Lady Zion who brings forth a new people with joy.[91] If the beloved disciple represents the Christian,[92] Mary is taken to be a figure of the church (Ambrose, Ephraem) who is a mother to Christians, giving them life in baptism. In the 9th–11th cents. the interpretation moved from the symbolic Mary to Mary as a person exercising spiritual motherhood from heaven.[93] In advocating such symbolic interpretations some scholars make no distinction between what may have been intended in a 1st-cent. milieu by the evangelist and the usage made of the passage to meet the needs of the subsequent church. The symbolic interpretation has continued into modern exegesis. R. H. Strachan (*The Fourth Gospel* [3d ed.; London: SCM, 1941], 319) thinks the mother represents the heritage of Israel now being entrusted to the Christians (beloved disciple). Bultmann (*John* 673) identifies the mother with Jewish Christians and the disciple with Gentile Christians, and has the former finding a home with the latter.[94] This interpretation overlooks John's complete lack of interest in the distinction between Jew and Gentile, a lack of interest signaled not only by silence on the subject, but by the principle that human parents beget only flesh, while the Spirit comes from divine begetting (John

---

[90]For a full exposition, see Feuillet, "Adieux" 474–77.

[91]Isa 49:20–22; 54:1; 66:7–11; Feuillet, "Adieux" 477–80; "Heure" 361–80. For a discussion as to whether this is valid imagery for the Lucan infancy narrative, see BBM 319–28.

[92]Origen, *In Jo.* 1.4(6); GCS 10.9: "Every man who becomes perfect no longer lives his own life, but Christ lives in him. And because Christ lives in him, it was said to Mary concerning him, 'Here is your son, Christ.'"

[93]On all this, see BGJ 2.924–25 and the literature cited there, esp. Koehler, Langkammer. The latter ("Christ's" 103–6) argues (against C. A. Kneller) that the idea of Mary's spiritual motherhood was not found in Ambrose but belonged to scholasticism and the Middle Ages. What is found in Ambrose is the portrayal of John 19:26–27 as the private and public "last will" of Jesus—a private legacy to the beloved disciple (John, son of Zebedee) and a public legacy to all Christians.

[94]Meyer ("Sinn") recognizes correctly that the beloved disciple becomes the brother of Jesus in this scene; but he argues that the unmentioned natural brothers of Jesus represent Jewish Christianity which was being replaced. He thinks that the symbolic sense of the woman figure is irrelevant!

3:3–6). Perhaps the most serious exegetical difficulty about these symbolic approaches has been pointed out by Schürmann ("Jesu" 20): The scene does not primarily concern the two figures in themselves but the new relationship that exists between them. Before I offer a theological interpretation of that relationship, let me comment on the last part of 19:27.

"From that hour the disciple took her to his own" has been the subject of much discussion, a good example of which can be seen in the opposing positions taken in lively controversy by Neirynck ("*Eis*") and de la Potterie ("Parole" and "Et à partir"), two ranking Roman Catholic scholars. Neirynck, famous for his attempts to establish Johannine dependency on Mark, argues strongly on the basis of Greek usage that "took to" (*lambanein eis*) is a verb of motion as in 6:21 and that *ta idia* ("his own") means "to his own home," just as in 16:32. De la Potterie argues that before the 16th cent. no one took these words in a material sense,[95] and that the phrase must mean that the disciple accepted her into a type of spiritual intimacy.[96] In "Et à partir" 120 he speaks of "interior and spiritual space." Wis 8:18 shows a similar expression for taking Wisdom to oneself. "From that hour" means a beginning (inceptive aorist: he began to take); and there is an eschatological dimension, for the woman represents the eschatological people. De la Potterie ("Et à partir" 125) ends his interpretation by criticizing the historical critical method which cannot penetrate the sense of the text.

I would take a stance between the two positions. Neirynck shows through grammatical and vocabulary parallels what the text could mean if one ignores Johannine theology. But I think it absolutely incredible that such a dramatic revelatory scene involving Jesus' mother in a new relationship with the beloved disciple concludes simply with his taking her to his house. I would reject not only the extravagant aspects of this interpretation, e.g., that they left at that moment and were not present for the death (despite 19:35 which has the disciple at hand after the death of Jesus), or that we may conclude from this that the disciple was a Judean who had a house nearby. The

[95]Certainly there were early interpretations that the beloved disciple took Mary to his house. Indeed, this was taken so literally that at Panaya Kapulu in modern Turkey (some five miles from ancient Ephesus) a house is shown where Mary is supposed to have resided with John (= the beloved disciple) when he moved to Ephesus. De la Potterie, however, would trace that to 19:26–27a, the mother-son relationship, not to the phrase "to his own." A factor that makes the debate with Neirynck a bit more acerbic than it need be is de la Potterie's habit of referring to what he has "shown" (*montrer*) in previous writings, e.g., "Et à partir" 84,98–99,101, when he means what he has argued for. An argument does not a demonstration make!

[96]See also "Parole" 31, where de la Potterie speaks of the spiritual space in which the beloved disciple lives as his comprehension of Jesus. I find difficult to translate his favored rendering of "the disciple took her to his own," namely: "Le Disciple l'accueillit dans son intimité." De la Potterie combines this interpretation with the representative value of Mary as the New Zion and figure of the church ("Parole" 38–39)—see n. 98 below.

interpretation is flawed more deeply because it assumes that the evangelist was interested in where these two figures went to live. That is a question of this earth, of the realm below; and it has no place in Johannine thought (3:31). Those who are interested in Jesus' earthly origins are portrayed as disbelieving Jews in 6:42; those interested in the earthly habitat of the mother of Jesus would not be considered much better. The idea of providing a house for Jesus' mother does not lead well into 19:28 ("After this, Jesus having known that already all was finished . . ."), as if providing lodgings were the ultimate purpose of Jesus' life.

On the other hand some of the historical criticism that de la Potterie rails against permits us to distinguish between later mariological mysticism that flavors his interpretation and the type of theological issue that a 1st-cent. evangelist might be interested in. One does not need to invoke "interior and spiritual space" to understand "his own." What is peculiar to the beloved disciple, what is "his own," is neither his house nor his spiritual space but the fact that he is the disciple par excellence. "His own" is the special discipleship that Jesus loves.[97] The fact that the mother of Jesus is now the disciple's mother and that he has taken her to his own is a symbolic way of describing how one related to Jesus by the flesh (his mother who is part of his natural family) becomes related to him by the Spirit (a member of the ideal discipleship). Those who harmonize the Gospels may object that Luke 1:38 shows Mary to be already a disciple at the annunciation, since she says, "Behold I am the slave of the Lord; let it be to me according to your word." But there is no reason to think that John's readers knew of this Lucan scene— a caution made apparent through historical criticism.

I remarked above that I agree with Schürmann that the significance of this episode lies in the new relationship between the mother of Jesus and the beloved disciple, not in symbolism attached to Mary through the history of interpretation.[98] My contention that this new relationship involves the issue

---

[97]In 16:32 Jesus predicted that the other disciples would be scattered each *to his own*—theirs was not the special discipleship that would enable them to stay with Jesus. The "his own" of the beloved disciple is just the opposite.

[98]New Eve, the church, the mother of every Christian who must become a beloved disciple, the mother of the church or of the eschatological people, or the ever-virgin who had no children of her own (besides Jesus) to whom she could be entrusted—valid though some of those may be for later theological issues. In my judgment A. Kerrigan, "Jn. 19.25–27 in the Light of Johannine Theology and the Old Testament," *Antonianum* 35 (1960), 369–416, by arguing that Jesus conferred a universal maternity directly on Mary, confuses Johannine theology and that of the later church. More possible (but still very uncertain) is the thesis of Zerwick ("Hour") that the "messianic" context in John, created by the Scripture citations in the surrounding episodes, makes it likely that John thought of Eve and her posterity and saw Mary as the mother of the church (pp. 1192–94). However, John's Gospel, while not neglecting other sheep not of this fold, was concerned primarily with the community of the beloved disciple. When the Gospel was taken into the canon, the scope of the motherhood

of how Jesus' natural family was related to a family created by discipleship (in Johannine language, through birth from above) gains support from the fact that this precise issue was one that the Synoptic evangelists struggled with. In the Synoptic tradition Mary appears actively only once during the public ministry, when she and the brothers of Jesus come seeking Jesus (Mark 3:31–35; Matt 12:46–50; Luke 8:19–21). In Mark followed by Matt, their request to see Jesus is not treated favorably,[99] for Jesus has a different agendum that concerns his Father's will. Pointing to his disciples, he identifies them as his family: "Whoever does the will of God is brother and sister and mother to me" (3:35). Mark leaves the reader with the impression that the natural family is separated from the family of discipleship. (We saw that Cana represented for John a rejection by Jesus of his mother's concerns for the needs of the wedding party in favor of an agendum set by the "hour" [determined by the Father].) Luke's reinterpretation (8:19–21) of the basic Marcan scene gives a very different picture of the natural family. By omitting all contrast between the natural family and the family through discipleship, Luke makes the mother and brothers model disciples, hearing the word and keeping it, thus exemplifying the seed planted in good ground, as explained in the immediately preceding parable (8:15). John's second scene involving the mother of Jesus, this scene near the cross, accomplishes in relation to the first scene at Cana what Luke's reinterpretation accomplishes in relation to the Marcan scene—it brings the natural family (Jesus' mother) into the relationship of discipleship by making her the mother of the beloved disciple who takes her into his own realm of discipleship. The woman whose intervention at Cana on behalf of earthly needs was rejected because the hour had not yet come is now given a role in the realm engendered from above after the hour has come.[100] There remains a touch of similarity to Mark in that the natural "brothers" do not become disciples (John 7:3–7) but are replaced by the beloved disciple who, by becoming the son of Jesus' mother, becomes Jesus' brother.

---

was broadened. M.-E. Boismard, RB 61 (1954), 295–96, is quite cautious on relating messianic activity and Gen 3:15 to this scene, and on insisting that Catholics should not seek all Mary's maternal privileges in the literal meaning of this text. On the other end of the spectrum, Preisker ("Joh") seems almost polemic in arguing against Marian mother-goddess cult here; for him Mary becomes simply a member of the community on earth. Yet to have been made mother of the beloved disciple constitutes a unique status!

[99]Only Mark (3:21) associates this seeking at Capernaum with the fact that "his own" (= family at Nazareth) think that he is beside himself and set out to seize him.

[100]Even if that role is not as advanced as the roles assigned to the mother of Jesus in later mariology (see n. 98 above), to be constituted the mother of the beloved disciple by Jesus' dying wish is a privileged role in discipleship. Failure to recognize the importance of this causes H. M. Buck ("Fourth" 175–76) to misunderstand the scene completely: Jesus is no longer his mother's son; he is

Luke modified the gloom of Mark's picture of the hostile reactions to Jesus on the cross by using one wrongdoer who was rewarded with a place in paradise (heaven). John's positive example looks not to heaven but to the earthly continuation of beloved discipleship. For John there is no discontinuity between the ministry of Jesus and the postresurrectional period in regard to this unique discipleship. The beloved disciple did not come into existence after the resurrection but was already there during the crucifixion itself. As we shall see below (p. 1082), the gift of the Spirit, associated with what we may call the foundation of the church, takes place for this discipleship already at the cross (19:30).[101] By relating his mother (natural family) to the beloved disciple, Jesus has enlarged the discipleship in a significant way as a sign that it will grow and contain many from diverse backgrounds. This interpretation of the episode in 19:25–27 makes intelligible the fact that in the next verse (19:28) Jesus is said to know that all things are now finished.

ANALYSIS

The amount of material that had to be the subject of comment in this part of the crucifixion scene, which I have entitled "Activities at the Cross," tempted me strongly to make a separate section of John 19:25–27. Nevertheless, I became more and more convinced that the Johannine passage had to be treated alongside the Synoptic mockery episode if we were to appreciate structural and functional relationships and to trace the development of Christian reflection on the crucifixion. Most of the important points about structure and theology have already been discussed in the COMMENT so that the analytic treatment will be quite brief. Some additional observations need to be made about historicity and theology.

A. **Historicity**

Crucifixion was designed to be a public event producing a chastening effect on observers, and so we can be certain that there were people around

wholly the son of the Father. "In giving her a new son, John would exclude the Mother from participating in the work of Christ."

[101]If this unique discipleship and the community it produced constitute the "church" for John (although the Gospel does not use that term), the ecclesiastical aspect of this episode in 19:25–27 may be related to the unity interpretation of the previous episode (19:23–24) where the tunic was not torn (p. 957 above). Chevallier ("Fondation" 343) complains that his fellow Protestants neglect the ecclesiastical symbolism of Mary even though Calvin did not. He sees in 19:25–27 the formation of a church with two different types of sheep—a new family with Mary representing the historical Israel and the beloved disciple representing a new type of discipleship (p. 348).

the cross of Jesus. In the cast of characters involved in the Gospel accounts, the most certain to have been present historically are the soldiers. In the crucifixion before the death of Jesus, soldiers in Mark constitute the "they" who do all the activities described between 15:16 and 15:27; but they are given no part in the Marcan mockery of Jesus on the cross. Matt follows Mark but explicates the obvious by telling us that the soldiers keep guard on Jesus (27:36). John 19:23–24 is an expanded account of the soldiers dividing Jesus' clothes (normal treatment of a criminal). Only Luke 23:36–38 gives the soldiers a part in the mockery of Jesus on the cross. While it is not unlikely that soldiers might join in reviling a pretentious crucified criminal, without doubt this is Luke's form of the mockery of Jesus by the Roman soldiers which is recounted during and after the Pilate trial in the other Gospels. The historicity of this Lucan mockery must be related to the historicity of that other mockery (pp. 874, 877 above).

Certainly, too, there would have been passersby (Mark/Matt) and onlooking people (Luke), i.e., John's "many of the Jews," since the place of crucifixion was chosen for accessibility and was probably alongside a road that led to and from a city gate (John 19:20: "near the city"). It is not implausible that some of those present would observe in a neutral manner (Luke) and some would gratuitously express contempt (Mark/Matt). Nevertheless, the language in which the latter reaction is described is so redolent of OT passages describing the mockery of the just[102] that it is impossible to decide whether a specific memory from Golgotha was at the root of the Mark/Matt scene.

The presence of some of the Sanhedrin members who had promoted Jesus' death is not at all implausible: One could speculate that they would have wanted to see the denouement of what they had set in motion.[103] The jump from verisimilitude to historical fact is warranted if one accepts the historicity of the role of Joseph from Arimathea (§46 below). While not all members of the Sanhedrin would have been scrupulously religious, is it plausible that the chief priests and many of the scribes and elders would have been at the scene of the death of a crucified criminal on Passover? JEWJ 74–79 has attempted to show that the activities surrounding the crucifixion described by the Synoptics were possible on the feast day. Be that as it may, I shall follow my standard practice of insisting that after the Last Supper the Synop-

---

[102]In addition to the passages cited in the COMMENT, it is worth noting that the verb *empaizein* ("to mock") appears in the burgeoning martyr tradition (I Macc 9:26; II Macc 7:7,10) which, as Surkau and others have shown, contributed to the Christian image of Jesus' death.

[103]Yet there was the danger that they would be present at the place of execution when Jesus or one of his companions died, and contact with a corpse would render them ritually impure for celebrating the feast.

tics never mention Passover or show consciousness that they are describing the feast day itself. Therefore the only historical problem that springs *from the text of the Gospels* is whether the chief priests would have been active in the crucifixion scene on the eve of Passover (John 19:31). In John 19:21 the activity of the priests is described; and yet one would have expected them to have been in the Temple, slaying lambs for the Passover meal that would take place on the evening of the day of crucifixion. If prima facie such priestly involvement on Golgotha seems implausible, we should admit uncertainty as to the rules governing the activity of Sadducee priests on Passover eve. But perhaps we are asking inappropriate questions, given the intention of the evangelists. That fact that Mark 15:31 joins the scribes to the chief priests and Matt 27:41 feels free to add the elders should warn us that the Gospels are freely describing the continued activity of the Sanhedrin without precise memories; and the dramatic and theological function of having Jesus mocked by those whom Luke globally calls "the rulers" really makes impossible a precise historical judgment.

If we turn to the historicity of the mockery of Jesus by the co-crucified, we also run into problems. There is no convincing reason to reject the assertion of the four evangelists that there were others crucified with Jesus, and it is not impossible that crude criminals would have expressed contempt for Jesus' religious pretensions. Yet Mark/Matt assign no direct words to this reviling of Jesus, and Luke 23:39 has one of the hanged wrongdoers use virtually the same words that appeared in the first and second mockeries. Surely then there was no precise memory about this reviling of Jesus, and the dominant interest was to show the just maltreated by the unjust. Luke's peculiar episode where the other wrongdoer is sympathetic to Jesus and speaks to him defies historical judgment. There is no way to show that this could not have happened, but one must explain why no other canonical evangelist is aware of it. On pp. 1001–2 above I suggested that the traditional element in the Lucan scene may be the "Amen" saying (23:43) whereby Jesus promises paradise to a sinner. Luke may have adapted that saying (which could have been spoken on another occasion) to the setting of the crucifixion and have made one of the Marcan co-crucified the subject of the forgiveness.

The most difficult element to verify historically among the activities at the cross is the presence of the friends of Jesus, including his mother and the disciple whom he loved, as described in John 19:25–27. The fact that this picture fits John's theology of a believing community (church) already in existence before Jesus dies does not automatically establish that John invented the scene. We shall see in §44 below that the presence of friends or companions of Jesus *at a distance,* as recounted in the Synoptic Gospels, corresponds to a scriptural motif (Ps 38:12[11]; 88:9[8]); and so it is very difficult to decide on the basis of theology that one picture is more historical than the other, or that either is necessarily historical. Nothing in the other Gospels would support the presence of Jesus' mother at Golgotha, but there is some evidence that disciples who were not members of the Twelve[104] were involved in the PN. As for Roman custom, some appeal to later rabbinic evidence that often the crucified was surrounded by relatives and friends (and enemies) during the long hours of agony.[105] Yet in the reign of terror that followed the fall of Sejanus in AD 31, "The relatives [of those condemned to death] were forbidden to go into mourning" (Suetonius, *Tiberius* 61.2; see also Tacitus, *Annals* 6.19). Under various emperors of this period relatives were not allowed to approach the corpse of their crucified one (§46 below). Thus we cannot be sure that Roman soldiers would have permitted the contact with Jesus described in John 19:25–27.[106]

B. **Some Added Theological Notes**

I have already commented (p. 984 above) that in the reactions of people at the cross a pattern of three (flowing from older tradition) can be found in all our Gospels, even if in John the pattern emerges as three distinct episodes (19:19–22; 19:23–24; 19:25–27).[107] Clearly the fact that in *Mark* (*followed by Matt*) the three reactions to Jesus on the cross are all hostile mockeries fits in with Mark's theology of the PN where Jesus is entirely deserted by friends and maltreated by enemies. There is a dramatic progression in the mockers from haphazard passersby through Sanhedrin members to even fellow condemned criminals. The content of the mockeries has several theological dimensions. On the one hand the mockeries pick up the themes of the Sanhedrin trial of Jesus (destroying the sanctuary, claiming to be Messiah [+ Son of God in Matt]) when Jesus was ridiculed as a false prophet; they are thus transitional to what will happen when Jesus dies on the cross and fulfills his prophecy, as the veil of the Temple sanctuary is rent and he is

[104]Within the Fourth Gospel itself there is little reason to think that the disciple whom Jesus loved was a member of the Twelve.

[105]Stauffer (*Jesus* 111, 179[1]) cites TalJer *Giṭṭin* 48C; Tosepta *Giṭṭin* 7.1. The key passage in both works seems to be Tosepta *Giṭṭin* 5.1 about a man who was crucified and while still breathing gave a writ of divorce to his wife. If I understand the logic, the assumption is that wife or family would have been at the cross to witness this.

[106]In the COMMENT I pointed to the likelihood that a very early tradition involved Mary in a scene that contrasted natural family and the family constituted by discipleship. The Synoptics, however, have that scene during the public ministry, and so John may have adapted it and brought it into a new setting at the cross.

[107]Since there is little evidence that John drew his three episodes from Mark's three mockeries, a good case can be made that the pattern of three existed in preGospel narration of the crucifixion. We saw in §27 that a pattern of three denials by Peter existed as far back as we can trace the story. Of course, traceable antiquity in narration should not be confused with historicity.

confessed as the Son of God. On the other hand the mockeries clarify the strongly religious nature of the real conflict between Jesus and his Jewish opponents. If Pilate interrogated Jesus concerning the charge of being "the King of the Jews" and afterward the Roman soldiers mocked him under that title, that issue has disappeared in Mark/Matt as far as the Jewish mockers of Jesus on the cross are concerned.[108]

Luke's picture is more complicated. His framing the three hostile mockeries with a neutral preface (the observing people) and a benevolent conclusion (the sympathetic wrongdoer) fits entirely with Luke's dislike of a totally negative picture. In general (but see n. 14 above) in the PN he distinguishes between some Jewish rulers who are strongly opposed to Jesus and the Jewish people who are not. As I have stressed (p. 1012 above), the salvation of the one wrongdoer by Jesus is typical of Luke's view that God's mercy is already active in the PN. Nevertheless, in rearranging the three hostile mockeries within that framework, Luke's sequence of Jewish rulers, Roman soldiers, and one wrongdoer does not preserve the theological thrust of Mark's progression. No longer is the concentration solely on the Jewish religious issues stemming from the Sanhedrin investigation, for now there is intermingled the charge of "the King of the Jews" stemming from the Roman trial and leveled by Roman soldiers. Because the most consistent theme in the three hostile mockeries is the challenge to *save,* these mockeries have become a preamble to what is the most important feature in this Lucan scene: the acceptance of that challenge by Jesus, who saves the sympathetic wrongdoer at the end of the episode.

John's arrangement of activities at the cross in the three episodes results in a theologically dramatic pattern. The sovereign Jesus reigning from the cross is victorious or accomplishes God's purpose in all three (p. 1013 above). Among those who are involved in the episodes there is a progression from the hostility of the chief priests who regard Jesus as a fraudulent king, through the insensitivity of the soldiers who treat Jesus as a criminal, to the fidelity of family and friends who are constituted in a new status by an act of Jesus' love. This last episode is the culmination of Jesus' ministry, which ends on a positive note of success. If his own people did not accept him, there are a new "his own" who do accept him and are thus empowered to become God's children in a new relationship to God's Son (John 1:11–13).

(*Bibliography for this episode may be found in §37, Parts 5 and 6.*)

---

[108]"The King of Israel" in Mark 15:32 has a messianic tone without the political coloring of "the King of the Jews."

§42. JESUS CRUCIFIED, PART THREE: LAST EVENTS, DEATH

(Mark 15:33–37; Matt 27:45–50; Luke 23:44–46;
John 19:28–30)

Translation

Mark 15:33–37: ³³And the sixth hour having come, darkness came over the whole earth until the ninth hour. ³⁴And at the ninth hour Jesus screamed with a loud cry, "*Elōi, Elōi, lama sabachthani?*" which is interpreted, "My God, my God, for what reason have you forsaken me?" ³⁵And some of the bystanders, having heard, were saying, "Look, he is crying to Elijah." ³⁶But someone, running, having filled a sponge with vinegary wine, having put it on a reed, was giving him to drink, saying, "Leave (be). Let us see if Elijah comes to take him down." ³⁷But Jesus, having let go a loud cry, expired.

Matt 27:45–50: ⁴⁵But from the sixth hour darkness came over all the earth until the ninth hour. ⁴⁶But about the ninth hour Jesus screamed out with a loud cry, saying, "*Ēli, Ēli, lema sabachthani?*"—that is, "My God, my God, to what purpose have you forsaken me?" ⁴⁷But some of those standing there, having heard, were saying that "This fellow is crying to Elijah." ⁴⁸And immediately one of them, running and taking a sponge full of vinegary wine and having put it on a reed, was giving him to drink. ⁴⁹But the rest said, "Leave (be). Let us see if Elijah comes saving him." ⁵⁰But Jesus, again having shouted with a loud cry, let go the spirit.

[Luke 23:36: Moreover, also the soldiers mocked, coming forward, bringing forward to him vinegary wine.]

23:44–46: ⁴⁴And it was already about the sixth hour, and darkness came over the whole earth until the ninth hour, ⁴⁵the sun having been eclipsed. The veil of the sanctuary was rent in the middle.

46And having cried out with a loud cry, Jesus said, "Father, into your hands I place my spirit." But having said this, he expired.

John 19:28–30: 28After this, Jesus having known that already all was finished, in order that the Scripture be completed, says, "I thirst." 29A jar was there laden with vinegary wine. So, putting on hyssop a sponge laden with the vinegary wine, they brought it forward to his mouth. 30So when he took the vinegary wine, Jesus said, "It is finished"; and having bowed his head, he gave over the spirit.

GPet 5:15–19: 15But it was midday, and darkness held fast all Judea; and they were distressed and anxious lest the sun had set, since he was still living. [For] it is written for them: "Let not the sun set on one put to death." 16And someone of them said, "Give him to drink gall with vinegary wine." And having made a mixture, they gave to drink. 17And they fulfilled all things and completed the(ir) sins on their own head. 18But many went around with lamps, thinking that it was night, and they fell. 19And the Lord screamed out, saying, "My power, O power, you have forsaken me." And having said this, he was taken up.

COMMENT

In §38 I gave an overall picture of the arrangement of the final Act of the Gospel PNs, consisting of Jesus' crucifixion/death. There remain, however, difficulties in determining the demarcation of individual sections, and in the present section it is not easy to decide how best to do justice to the flow of the Mark/Matt narrative. In Mark we have seen the importance of a horarium that calls attention to almost every three-hour period. Although it would be tempting to divide Mark's account on the basis of such time designations, no subdivisions proportionate in length or content would emerge here, since the opening verse of this section (15:33) has within itself two three-hour notations (sixth and ninth hours).

A more plausible basis for subdividing the present Marcan section is to draw on the mention before Jesus' death of a darkness over all the earth (15:33) and the mention after Jesus' death of a rending of the Temple sanctuary veil (15:38). This gives us two God-given, eschatological signs forming an inclusion on either side of Jesus' death agony.[1] Yet from another viewpoint, the rent sanctuary veil is an integral part of the postcrucifixion sequence that constitutes the next scenes (§§43–44 below); for the centurion who reacts to it is parallel to the women who look on from afar—both exemplify responses to the changed situation produced by Jesus' death and God's intervention. Thus, it is not clear whether the present section should be Mark 15:33–38 (with vv. 33 and 38 as an inclusion), or 15:33–37 (with v. 38 beginning the next section: 15:38–41).

Recognizing that neither method of subdividing Mark is perfect, in this commentary that compares PNs I have chosen the latter because Matt's organization of material favors it. To the rending of the sanctuary veil which Matt has taken from Mark 15:38, he has added a series of cosmological signs (27:51–53: earthquake, opened tombs, rising of the dead) that cannot easily be joined to the last events preceding the death on the cross.

Both Luke and John have arrangements of the predeath material that are easier to diagnose. In Luke 23:44 the initial *kai* ("And"), accompanied by the first time indication given in this evangelist's crucifixion account, signals a new subdivision, as does the shift to indirect description from the direct speech that preceded. In 23:44–45, *before* Jesus dies, Luke has joined the darkness over the whole earth with the rending of the sanctuary veil—two signs that Mark had inclusively placed on either side of the death. Through this rearrangement the two ominous divine interventions constitute one vignette to which Jesus reacts by an act of confidence in God's loving care (23:46).[2] Thus Luke is able to make the total scenario after Jesus' death positive, with the trio of the centurion, the crowds, and the onlooking Galilean women all favorable to Jesus (23:47–49), even as there was a trio of Simon, the multitude, and the Jerusalem women favorable to Jesus before he was crucified (23:26–31). In John's complicated chiastic pattern (p. 908 above), 19:28–30 constitutes Episode 4, easily distinguishable from the two subsequent postdeath episodes in 19:31–42 (to be discussed in §§44, 46–47 below).

This commentary will treat the incidents in this section in the order listed below; here the apocryphal *GPet* has an unusual amount of material parallel to Mark/Matt:

---

[1]As we shall see in the ANALYSIS, several scholars would interpret such an inclusion as a Marcan framework placed by the evangelist around preMarcan material. /

[2]Matera ("Death" 475) thinks that by moving the rending of the sanctuary veil to before Jesus' death Luke is trying to avoid the impression that this death marks the end of the Temple and its cult. Luke's effort fits in with his plan to narrate scenes in Acts where the apostles and Paul go to the Temple. I would agree that Luke lessens the immediacy of the end of the Temple cult; but God's rending the veil just before the death of Jesus is a sign that the end is inevitable in harmony with

- Darkness at the sixth hour (Synoptics; *GPet*)
- Jesus' death cry, Elijah, and the offering of vinegary wine in Mark/Matt (*GPet*)
- Jesus' death cry in Luke
- Jesus' last words and the offering of vinegary wine in John
- Death of Jesus (all)

The second of the above incidents will require the longest treatment because there is a complicated misunderstanding about the coming of Elijah that occurs only in Mark/Matt.

DARKNESS AT THE SIXTH HOUR (MARK 15:33; MATT 27:45; LUKE 23:44–45A; *GPet* 5:15,18)

As one reads the startling description of darkness covering the whole earth from noon to 3 P.M. (sixth to ninth hours), several possible interpretations spring to mind. This could be a factual account involving either a natural phenomenon (eclipse, storm, etc.) or a totally unparalleled miracle.[3] Or it could be a purely figurative description, reflecting either OT eschatological language, or Hellenistic imagery associated with the death of famous men, or both. While all these possibilities will have to be discussed, such discussion will be subordinate to our primary concern, namely, the use to which each evangelist puts the darkness motif.

Darkness in Mark/Matt. There is no way to know whether the individual evangelists, Mark and Matt, thought that there was physical darkness at midday on Golgotha—more than likely they did, for they attach to it an "hour" specification similar to those they attach to events they posit as real—but the dominant focus in the two Gospels is symbolic and theological.

Mark: The intervening three hours since the soldiers crucified Jesus at 9 A.M. (15:25) have been filled with the mocking of Jesus on the cross by the passersby, by the chief priests, and by the co-crucified. No human beings have shown mercy to God's Son, and now at noon in the realm of nature the whole earth goes into darkness. Although some interpreters make the point that Mark has the darkness end before Jesus dies, Mark does not state that; what he emphasizes is that the darkness extended till the very moment (hour) when Jesus died, namely, the ninth hour when Jesus gave his scream of aban-

---

words spoken to the "Daughters of Jerusalem" about the destruction of Jerusalem in the next generation (23:28–31).

[3]In summarizing the history of interpreting the darkness, Grández ("Tinieblas" 183) calls attention to the influence of the Pseudo-Areopagite (ca. AD 500), who pointed to the analogy of the great miraculous interventions of God in the OT, especially in the exodus.

donment and expired (15:34,37; 3 P.M.). Thus, even on the most obvious level of symbolism, the darkness adds to Mark's dour description of the crucifixion which is the culmination of the PN.

However, there is a deeper level of reference. The preceding mockeries of Jesus echoed OT descriptions of the suffering just one, especially Ps 22:8. The dying scream of Jesus introduced by the darkness will quote the opening line of the same psalm (22:2). The reaction to that cry by someone who runs to give Jesus vinegary wine fulfills Ps 69:22. Thus the context presses readers to think of an OT background for this unusual darkness employed dramatically by God. Chaotic darkness preceded God's creation of light in Gen 1:2–3. One of the exodus plagues was darkness "over all the land" for three days, called down by Moses as a punishment for the Egyptians (Exod 10:21–23).[4] The (first) Passover context of that plague makes it a likely parallel for the darkness at the Passover of Jesus' death.[5] As for darkness symbolizing divine wrath, in a bitter reproach to Jerusalem God proclaims, "Her sun sets at midday; she is shamed and disgraced" (Jer 15:9). In Wis 5:6 those who have been mocking the just one, doubting that he is a "son of God," are brought to exclaim, "We have strayed from the way of truth, and the light of justice did not shine for us, and the sun did not rise upon us." In Jer 33:19–21 (lacking in the LXX), if day and night no longer follow the normal sequence, that would be a sign that God is breaking the covenant. Perhaps the best OT parallel may be found in the darkness that marks "the day of the Lord," conceived of as a day of judgment and punishment: "a day of wrath . . . a day of darkness and gloom" (Zeph 1:15). Joel 2:2 warns: "It is near, a day of darkness and of gloom" (see also 2:10); and Joel 3:4 (RSV 2:31) predicts, "The sun will be turned to darkness . . . at the coming of the great and terrible day of the Lord." Amos 8:9–10 seems particularly pertinent, even if the vocabulary differs from Mark's: "And on that day, says the Lord God, the sun shall set at midday, and the light shall be darkened on earth in the daytime. . . . I will make them mourn as for an only son and bring their day to a bitter end." Against this background one can interpret Mark to mean that while the mockers demanded of Jesus on the cross a sign (i.e., that he come down from the cross), God is giving them a sign as part of a judgment on the world, namely, a warning of punishment that was now beginning. Although

[4]Some stress that the Egyptian darkness was for *three* days and the Golgotha darkness for *three* hours; Mark, however, does not mention "three hours" but the sixth and the ninth hours. Grayston ("Darkness") carries the evil symbolism of the darkness further to include death (Ps 88:11–13 and Job 38:19: part of the horrors of the underworld).

[5]Matching Luke's mention (23:45a) of the *sun* having been eclipsed (or failed) is the Passover parallel suggested by Irenaeus (*Adv. haereses* 4.10.1) involving the sacrifice of the paschal lamb before the setting of the sun (Deut 16:5–6).

throughout Mark's PN God has not been visibly active, now that Jesus is drinking the dregs of the cup that his Father has given him, divine intervention begins to be seen.

Since the noun *gē* means both "earth" and "land," it is debatable whether Mark describes darkness over the whole earth or only over the land (of Judea, as *GPet 5:15* understood it).[6] Some favor the latter as less troublesome to explain since darkness over the whole earth for three hours at the time of Jesus' death should have been noted in ancient historical or astronomical records, and it was not. However, such a historical objection should not influence our interpretation of a scene that primarily has theological import. While the target of the OT oracles of judgment on the day of the Lord was usually Israel or Judea, the prophets scarcely confined the apocalyptic signs to one small corner of the earth. In the Marcan context soon there will be brought on the scene a Roman centurion who will deliver a resounding vindication of Jesus (15:39); surely, then, Mark sees this as a climactic day for all peoples and the whole earth.

Matt: In 27:45 he follows Mark closely, albeit presenting a smoother Greek.[7] However, features in the Matthean context serve to strengthen the Marcan symbolic and eschatological message. In Matt alone (27:25) "all the [Jewish] people" accepted responsibility before Pilate for sentencing Jesus to death by crucifixion; it is not unexpected, then, that God sends the darkness as a warning of imminent judgment. Matt (27:51–53) will follow the death of Jesus with eschatological signs (earthquake, opening of tombs, raising the dead) even more dramatic than Mark's rending of the sanctuary veil. Surely, then, the darkness is more of the same. Does Matt's strong emphasis on "all the [Jewish] people" mean that his "all the *gē*," which is a change from Mark's "the whole *gē*," refers to the land of Judea rather than all the earth? Probably not—even though the explanation for Matt's changing Mark here cannot be purely one of stylistic preference since elsewhere Matt uses "whole" (*holos*) for geographic expanse. "Over all the *gē*" is very common LXX usage and heightens the OT background for the darkness. In particular,

---

[6]Among those who favor "land" are Erasmus, Luther, Billerbeck, Ewald, Klostermann, Knabenbauer, Olhausen, and Plummer. Among those who favor "earth" are Gnilka, Grayston, and Lohse, with Loisy claiming that in the Gospels the expression "over the whole *gē*" or "over all the *gē*" never has a meaning restricted to "land" (Grández, "Tinieblas" 204—I would not have that certainty about Luke 4:25). Unconvincing is the argument that in relation to Moses Exod 10:22–23 has the plague "over all the land of Egypt," and so here the divine punishment by analogy should come over all the land of Judea. Should not the divinely sent plague be greater in relation to Jesus, God's Son, and thus "over the whole earth"?

[7]Since earlier Matt had no third-hour notice comparable to Mark's, his change of Mark's "the sixth hour having come" to "from the sixth hour" is just a chronological adjustment. He uses the *apo . . . heōs* ("from . . . until") pattern ten times to describe a period of time (SPNM 292).

it appears in Exod 10:22, one of the passages cited above to throw light on Mark's meaning.

Darkness in *GPet*. Although *GPet* 5:15 describes the same event as Mark 15:33 and Matt 27:45, it does so in almost totally different vocabulary (except for the basic word "darkness"). If we suppose that *GPet* drew on the canonical Gospels (at least through a memory of having heard a Gospel orally), some of the changes may be intentional, rather than haphazard. *GPet*'s interpretation of *gē* as Judea is in line with the fierce antiJudaism of this apocryphal Gospel that thus far has had the Jewish king Herod command Jesus' death (1:2), and the *Jewish people* drag along the "son of God" now that they have power over him (3:6), and mock, spit upon, strike, and scourge the Lord (3:9), only finally to crucify him, dividing his clothes (4:10,12). They forbid the breaking of the bones of the co-crucified wrongdoer who showed sympathy to the Lord, so that he might die tormented (4:14).

Another motif has influenced the vocabulary of *GPet*'s description: "But it was *midday,* and . . . the *sun had set*." The italicized words echo the description of the day of the Lord in (the LXX of) Amos 8:9 which, as we have already suggested, may have given rise to the symbolism in Mark.[8] Characteristically *GPet* makes scriptural motifs found in the canonical Gospels more explicit. Further emphasis on the Scriptures is seen in *GPet*'s direct citation of what is written: "Let not the sun set on one put to death." Although *GPet* has previously used the same citation verbatim and, indeed, specified that it was "in the Law" (2:5), the citation has no exact counterpart in the Pentateuch or anywhere in the OT. The closest one comes is Deut 24:15 (LXX 24:17), which insists that the day's wages are to be paid before the sun sets. That refrain about sunset[9] has been combined with the idea (but not the vocabulary) of Deut 21:22–23 whereby a hanged corpse must not remain on the tree overnight. This general scriptural injunction may have been behind the canonical Gospel accounts since they all describe a burial before the Sabbath, which began at sunset, but only *GPet* has cited the Scriptures on this point. Was that because *GPet*'s readers were Gentiles who would not understand the Jewish mentality on this point if it had been left implicit? More likely (and perhaps in addition) it represents an antiJewish implication of hypocrisy: Those who crucified Jesus were extremely careful

---

[8]This passage shows me the impossibility of considering *GPet* the original PN on which Mark and Matt were dependent. Why would either or both of those have discarded the scriptural phrasing "midday" used by *GPet* in favor of "the sixth hour," not attributable to any of the OT passages that are background for the darkness?

[9]See it in Eph 4:26: "Let not the sun set on your anger."

about such minutiae as the exact hour of sunset, but they did not hesitate to mock the Son of God (3:9).[10] Still one more echo of sacred literature may be detected if the author of *GPet* knew *II Enoch* 67:1–3.[11] There darkness covers the earth when Enoch speaks and is taken up to heaven.[12] Such a parallel would enhance the apocalyptic coloring of the phenomena that occurred while Jesus was on the cross.

Beyond the scriptural, the treatment of darkness in *GPet* illustrates the popular storytelling facet of this apocryphon. We are told in 5:18 that many went around with lamps because they thought night had come, and even still they fell. This depiction emphasizes vividly that the darkness was intense and, as a sign from God, it had the power to paralyze the enemies of Jesus. To all appearances these Jewish opponents had mastery over him, but God has now begun to visit their sins on their heads (5:17). In Deut 28:29 God curses the people if they are disobedient: "Even at midday you will grope like a blind man in the dark, unable to find your way."

Darkness in Luke. As in Mark the darkness is timed as coming about the sixth hour until the ninth hour; but between the darkness and the death cry of Jesus there is interposed the rending of the sanctuary veil, which is associated with the eclipsing of the sun. Besides this dissolution of the Marcan connection between the darkness and the death, Luke 23:44–45 brings to a head other problems about the darkness; for it has joined before Jesus' death two signs taken from Mark 15:33 (darkness before Jesus' death) and 15:38 (rending of the sanctuary veil after Jesus' death). This rearrangement is undoubtedly a reflection of Luke's penchant for a (logically) more orderly account (Luke 1:3) and shows an understanding that the two signs are of similar origin, reflecting God's wrath. Luke wanted to concentrate the negative elements before the moment when Jesus would entrust his spirit into his Father's hands (23:46). Everything in Luke that will follow that act of trust will be positive, acknowledging God's benevolence.

If the Lucan reordering is reasonably intelligible, the Lucan wording is a greater problem. Luke 23:44 is borrowed from Mark 15:33 (as almost all acknowledge) since twelve of its sixteen words are found in Mark.[13] Yet there is some interesting tinkering: Mark is the one who usually overuses

---

[10]In interpreting the canonical Gospels, one must make some allowance for a realization by the evangelists that those who did harm to Jesus did not know his true divine identity. In *GPet*, however, the Jewish perpetrators know they have done evil (7:25; 8:28; 11:48).

[11]Preserved in Slavonic and never attested before the 14th cent. AD, this pseudepigraphon is very difficult to date, but many would attribute it to about the 2d cent. AD, when *GPet* was also being written.

[12]The passage continues: When the people saw this, they glorified God and went to their homes—cf. Luke 23:48. For the influence of *II Enoch*, see Clarke, "St. Luke."

[13]Several of the words are not normal Lucan style, e.g., from Mark Luke takes "over the whole earth," whereas elsewhere (4:25; 21:35) he prefers "all the earth."

"and"; but here in 44b Luke has added a second "and," creating coordination. More important is Luke's addition of "already" (*ēdē*), from which one might surmise that Jesus had been on the cross before noon (sixth hour) and thus find an implicit harmonization with Mark's horarium. Yet we should also note the addition of "about" (*hōsei*) which, with a time expression, is a common Lucan usage (9:28; 22:59; Acts 10:3). Feldkämper (*Betende* 273) observes that thus Luke shows an appreciation that one cannot assign an exact hour to an eschatological sign like midday darkness.

A major issue is the clarification that Luke supplies in 23:45a, which seems to be independent of Mark.[14] Evidently ancient scribes were also puzzled by this clarification, for mss. attest basically two different readings:

- *tou hēliou eklipontos:* aorist (or occasionally pres.: *ekleipontos*) genitive absolute: P[75], Codices Vaticanus, Sinaiticus, Ephraem rescriptus, some Sahidic witnesses.

    Translation (a): the sun having been eclipsed

    Translation (b): the sun having failed

- *kai eskotisthē ho hēlios:* coordinated main clause: Codices Alexandrinus, Bezae, Koridethi; Marcion; Latin and Syriac witnesses; Koine tradition.

    Translation (c): and the sun was darkened/obscured

Because, as we shall see, there is a major astronomical problem about positing an eclipse of the sun at the time of Jesus' death, the second reading is much easier (even as is Translation [b] of the first reading) and for that reason may have been favored by scribes eager to improve the acceptability of the passage. The first Greek reading has more impressive textual support and should be given preference under the rule of choosing as original the more difficult reading.[15]

There remains the problem of how the first reading is to be translated. Translation (b) is possible, for "to fail, die out, give out" is a normal translation of *ekleipein*,[16] and many modern Lucan scholars from Lagrange to Marshall and Fitzmyer have preferred it. Although a banal explanation of the darkness, it avoids the awkwardness of attributing a mistake to Luke, for an eclipse of the sun cannot take place during the period of the full moon that

[14]It is very difficult to derive Luke's Greek (either reading given above) from Mark despite the attempt of Buckler ("Eli" 378) to relate it to the *Elōi* (variant texts: *Ēli*) and *egkatelipes* of Mark 15:34.

[15]Because of the influence of Origen (see below) older commentators favored the second reading; but with the advent of Tischendorf in the last century and a sharper sense of textual criticism the first reading has come into general favor. Grández ("Tinieblas") offers a history of opinions on this point.

[16]An interesting example is in the LXX of Sir 22:9(11), which describes a dead person as one who has lost (*ekleipein*) the light or whose light has failed.

begins Passover.[17] Also the maximum length of an attested full solar eclipse seems to be seven minutes and forty seconds (Driver, "Two" 333), considerably less than the three hours posited by the Synoptic Gospels. Any suggestion that God suspended natural possibilities and caused an extraordinarily long eclipse over the whole earth at a time when none could happen runs against the silence of ancient authors contemporary with the supposed event, like Seneca and Pliny, who normally would have noted such an extraordinary wonder. If there was no eclipse of the sun at the death of Jesus,[18] what other known phenomenon could have caused the darkness or the obscuring of sunlight? Many explanations have been offered: sunspots, solar storms, the *ḥamsīn* or sirocco winds bringing a dust storm,[19] a thunderstorm, the aftermath of a volcanic eruption in Arabia or Syria, etc. The Lucan passage, however, gives no hint of winds or storms (contrast Acts 2:2). Moreover, some of these suggestions emanate from people who have lived in Palestine and know the local weather phenomena,[20] but Luke does not betray that type of knowledge.

On the other hand, there is a Lucan pattern that favors Translation (a), "The sun having been eclipsed," even if that translation means that Luke's description is not scientifically accurate.[21] In his infancy narrative Luke reported that "an edict went out from Caesar Augustus that a census should be taken of the whole world" (2:1). So far as known evidence indicates, there never was such a universal census under Augustus, despite the ingenious

[17]Already this problem was seen by Origen (*Commentariorum Series* 134; *In Matt.* 27:45 [GCS 38.271–74]), who favored the reading that the sun was darkened. Elsewhere Origen hinted that the idea of an eclipse was introduced by antiChristians to discredit the Gospels. (We remember he thought the same of the reading in Matt 27:16–17 that gave "Jesus" as the personal name of Barabbas.) See B. M. Metzger, "Explicit References in the Works of Origen to Variant Readings in the New Testament Manuscripts," in *Biblical and Patristic Studies,* eds. J. N. Birdsall and R. W. Thomson (Memory of R. P. Casey; New York: Herder, 1963), 78–95, esp. 87. Julius Africanus, who was born in Jerusalem and knew Origen, wrote his *Chronikon* about AD 221; in 5.50 (Rowth ed. 2.297) he reported that Thallos (a historian of the early 1st cent. AD?) called this darkness an eclipse of the sun, but such a designation was without foundation.

[18]In times past J. J. Scaliger (1598) and A. Calmet (1725) and others have thought of a moon eclipse, sometimes combined with a sun eclipse! Appealing to Acts 2:20, "The sun shall be turned to darkness, and the moon to blood," Humphreys and Waddington ("Dating") suggest that Luke combined a sandstorm with a partial moon eclipse that took place on April 3, AD 33.

[19]This is mentioned or favored by distinguished scholars, e.g., Lagrange, Benoit, Fitzmyer. Driver ("Two") argues that since the Temple was open on the eastern side (Mishna, *Middot* 2.4), the wind that brought the dust could have torn the sanctuary veil!

[20]Certainly that is true of Lagrange's proposal of a sirocco; and already, writing ca. 396, Jerome, who lived there, mentions an unusual darkness that took place around Pentecost (*Contra Ioannem Hierosolymitanum* 42 [PL 23.393C]).

[21]The fact that Origen argued against the eclipse interpretation shows that it had support in his time; and there were famous church writers (Chrysostom, Cyril of Alexandria) who accepted it, even if they posited a special act of God in producing it. G. B. Caird, Danker, and Sawyer argue for the eclipse translation, and it is found in the NAB, *Jerusalem Bible,* and NEB.

attempts of interpreters to defend Lucan accuracy (see BBM 394–95, 547–56). There were many edicts of Augustus and many regional censuses; and Luke, by confusion or artistic license, was drawing on them to create a background for Jesus' birth at Bethlehem. Similarly Luke 2:2 describes this as "the first census under Quirinius as governor of Syria" and tells us that it brought Jesus' parents from Galilee to Bethlehem. There was a census (but of Judea, not of Galilee) under Quirinius as governor of Syria; yet it was carried out more than ten years after the most plausible date for Jesus' birth, which seems to have taken place during the reign of Herod the Great. Luke has taken a known event (that was associated with Herod's son) and by confusion associated it with the time of Jesus' birth.[22] In light of these procedures in the infancy narrative, it is not implausible that having read about darkness at noon in Mark, Luke associated it with a well-known eclipse of the general period in which Jesus died and made the latter the cause of the former.[23] The verisimilitude of such an association, including the exaggerated length of the darkness, is apparent when one reads some of the often exaggerated literary descriptions of a solar eclipse. For instance, Plutarch (*Pelopidas* 31.2) describes an eclipse of the sun in 364 BC thus: "Darkness took hold of the city in the daytime." Sawyer ("Why" 128) reports the depiction of a solar eclipse at Antioch in 1176 that lasted for three minutes and twenty seconds: "The sun was totally obscured; night fell and the stars appeared . . . the darkness lasted for two hours; afterwards the light returned."

Was there a *noted* eclipse in this region within a year or two of Jesus' death (AD 30 or 33) of which Luke could have heard or read? A solar eclipse, lasting 1½ minutes, took place in parts of Greece, Asia Minor, and Syria on Nov. 24, AD 29.[24] There are possible pertinent references to it in ancient authors, but the date they assign varies. Concerning an eclipse that happened in the reign of Tiberius (AD 14–37), Origen (*Contra Celsum* 2.33) reports

---

[22]In this instance I would opt for confusion over artistic license because Luke shows confusion about this census in Acts 5:36–37. There he attributes to the famous Gamaliel a speech (apparently given in the late 30s) that mentions the uprising of Theudas (which took place a decade later!) and *after* that uprising mentions the census associated with the uprising of Judas the Galilean (= the census under Quirinius in AD 6). Indeed, the association of Gamaliel with this speech may be another instance of Luke's bringing known events and people into the story in appropriate but not absolutely accurate places and roles.

[23]Probably Luke did not know that there could not have been an eclipse at Passover. Killermann ("Finsternis") points out that Albert the Great, who had scientific abilities, may not have known that Passover occurred at the full moon. Yet Thucydides (*History* 2.28) speaks of an eclipse of the sun at the *new* moon as seemingly the only time when such an occurrence could take place.

[24]Reflecting the view that Luke was an Antiochene, Sawyer ("Why" 127) suggests that Luke had experienced this eclipse as a youth. That hypothesis, however, complicates the issue of Lucan accuracy, for he should have remembered that it took place in the autumn, not in the spring when Jesus was crucified.

that Phlegon made a record of it along with an earthquake "in the 13th or 14th book, I think, of his Chronicles [*Olympiades*]."[25] (Phlegon, a Greek from SW Asia Minor, was a historian who lived in the reign of Hadrian, AD 117–135.) Eusebius in his *Chronicle* for the 18th–19th year of the reign of Tiberius (GCS [2d ed.] 47.174–75)[26] reports that Phlegon says that in the 4th year of the 202d Olympiad there was a great eclipse of the sun, outdoing all that preceded. It became like a night at midday. The specified year would have run from July 1, AD 32 to June 30, AD 33.[27] Eusebius goes on to connect this with an earthquake in Bithynia that caused buildings to fall in Nicaea and with signs in the Jerusalem Temple reported by Josephus; clearly he is constructing a scenario to match the Gospel reports. Some have appealed to Chinese astronomical records to support the darkness (see Grández, "Tinieblas" 198).

If Luke has confusedly or by art connected a vague memory of such a solar eclipse (that factually occurred several months or years before Jesus' death) with the Marcan tradition of a darkness on the day of Jesus' death, we should not think he was offering a purely naturalistic explanation for the latter. Luke would have assumed that this eclipse was controlled by God, who employed it to signal the death of the Son. No less than Mark, Luke would have seen this darkness resulting from the eclipse as one of the eschatological signs of the last times mentioned in the OT.[28] In the Lucan infancy narrative Jesus was hailed as "a rising light [*anatolē*] from on high, appearing to those who sat in darkness and the shadow of death" (1:78–79). Indeed, among the evangelists only Luke has previously mentioned darkness in the PN; for as Jesus was being arrested, he exclaimed that this was the "hour" of his enemies "and the power of darkness" (22:53). The symbolism of the return of darkness as Jesus died should have been apparent to Luke's readers.

There may have been another dimension to Luke's communication, however, that goes beyond the OT background and beyond the eschatological motifs apparent in Mark/Matt. The connection between a noted eclipse and the darkness at noon before the death of Jesus may have served to underline the impact of that death upon the Roman Empire (which, like "the ends of the earth" in Acts 1:8, is what Luke would have meant by "the whole

[25]Yet in commenting on Matt (n. 17 above) Origen is careful to point out that Phlegon did not say that the eclipse took place at the full moon.

[26]Tiberius reigned from 14 to 37; was Eusebius thinking of AD 31–32? Holzmeister ("Finsternis") raises the issue of a possible confusion between a moon eclipse on April 3, AD 33, and the sun eclipse on Nov. 24, AD 29.

[27]Some like Maier ("Sejanus") use this evidence to argue for the death of Jesus in April 33, but such reasoning does not remove the impossibility of a solar eclipse at Passover.

[28]Luke's mind-set is apparent in Acts 2:17–21, when on Pentecost Peter cites from Joel 3:1–5 (RSV 2:28–32) signs (including darkening of the sun) showing that what happened to Jesus marks "the last days."

earth" in 23:44). Luke showed interest in the universal effect of Jesus' birth in 2:1 by connecting it with the edict "from Caesar Augustus that a census should be taken of the whole world," and he may be showing a parallel interest at Jesus' death. We can see that by considering how Luke's readers in the Hellenistic world with little background in OT "day of the Lord" imagery might have understood the darkness, eclipse, and rending of the sanctuary veil described in 23:44–45. There is abundant Greco-Roman evidence that extraordinary signs were commonly thought to accompany the death of great or semidivine men.[29] If we confine ourselves to authors who wrote within 100 years before or after Jesus' death, we find that Plutarch (*Romulus* 27.6) reports that at the demise or departure of Romulus "the light of the sun was eclipsed." Similarly Ovid (*Fasti* 2.493) uses the expression "the sun fled," and Cicero (*De re publica* 6.22): "the sun . . . appeared to be extinguished." When Julius Caesar was put to death, Plutarch (*Caesar* 69.4) speaks of an obscuring of the sun; and Josephus (*Ant.* 14.12.3; #309) describes it as an occasion on which "the sun turned away."[30] Indeed, Pliny (*Natural History* 2.30; #97) mentions this death to exemplify a wide expectation: "portentous and long eclipses of the sun, such as when Caesar the dictator was murdered."

Because Mark/Matt report the rending of the sanctuary veil after the death of Jesus, we shall leave until §43 below a discussion of that phenomenon even though Luke mentions it in 23:45b. I have rendered that verse as a separate sentence, to avoid having to translate *de*. If that particle is conjunctive, the darkening/eclipse and rending of the veil are yoked as negative signs in heaven and on earth. If it is adversative, setting up a contrast with the negative darkness,[31] then the rending (perhaps understood as opening a path through the veil into the sanctuary of the Father's house) is connected with Jesus' loud cry as he places his spirit into his Father's hands.

JESUS' DEATH CRY; ELIJAH; OFFERING OF VINEGARY WINE (MARK 15:34–36; MATT 27:46–49; *GPet* 5:19,16)

Jesus' final words on the cross (his only words in Mark/Matt) appear in three different forms in Mark/Matt, Luke, and John respectively; and we

[29]Grández ("Tinieblas" 199–200) lists some thirty passages from twenty-five Hellenistic authors pertinent to this, from which I shall make a selection. From a later period there are also some rabbinic parallels (St-B 1.1040–42).

[30]Similarly Ovid (*Metamorphoses* 15.785) describes "the sad face of the sun," and Virgil (*Georgics* 1.467) reports that the sun "veiled its shining head."

[31]More frequently the particle is mildly adversative; other times it is truly conjunctive, having the force of "also" after a preceding *kai* ("and"). There is also a third possibility, namely, that it is simply transitional, meaning "now" or "then." That connotation would seem to me to favor joining

shall have to devote a subsection to each of the three. The discussion of the Mark/Matt form will be done under three subheadings: meaning of the death cry,[32] its wording, and the misunderstanding about Elijah combined with the offering of vinegary wine.

Meaning of Jesus' Death Cry. At 3 P.M., after three hours of darkness over the whole earth, the crucified Jesus speaks for the first and only time. (Although it is often said that Mark has Jesus die at this hour, the "ninth hour" is affixed to Jesus' scream with a loud cry, not to his death, even if we may assume that he expired shortly thereafter—especially if the "loud cry" of v. 37 is simply a resumption of the "loud cry" of v. 34.) "Speaks" is not precise, for Mark uses the verb *boan* and Matt uses *anaboan;* moreover, they both refer to what emerges from his mouth as *phonē megalē* ("a loud cry," which will be repeated two or three verses later as Jesus dies). The range of *boan* and *anaboan* includes solemn proclamation, the acclamation or shout of a crowd, and a desperate cry for help.[33] In Luke 9:38; 18:38 *boan* is used to describe a man crying out loudly or insistently to Jesus, and in 18:7 for voices crying out to God for help. In Mark/Matt Jesus speaks in Semitic the words of Ps 22:2a, "My God, my God, for what reason have you forsaken me?" The second part of that verse (22:2b) in Hebrew refers to God being far from "the words of my cry." Clearly, then, the scream and loud cry lend desperate urgency to Jesus' petition. Moreover, to those familiar with crucifixion, such a cry would not have seemed unusual. Blinzler (*Trial* 261) describes as part of what made crucifixions particularly gruesome "the screams of rage and pain, the wild curses and the outbreaks of nameless despair of the unhappy victims." Yet it was not in rage but in prayer that Jesus screamed his loud cry, even as the martyrs in Rev 6:10 shouted with a loud cry their prayer for God to intervene. Indeed, prayers made with a loud cry are relatively frequent in the biblical story.[34]

In the Gospels, however, there is still another dimension. The scream, crying out, and loud cry of Mark 15:34; Matt 27:46; Luke 23:46; and *GPet* 5:19, as well as the loud cry, shouting, and letting go of the breath/spirit

---

the rending to the darkness; but Sylva ("Temple" 243) uses it otherwise, translating thus: "Then, the curtain of the Temple tore down the middle, and Jesus, crying with a loud voice, said. . . ."

[32]Although I recognize the resultant awkwardness, I have tried to be consistent in translating *phōnein, phōnē* as "cry"; *krazein* as "shout"; *kraugazein* as "clamor, yell"; and *boan* or *anaboan* as "scream." See also pp. 824, 826, 843 above.

[33]See usage in all four Gospels for JBap's proclamation in the desert; also Acts 17:6; 25:24.

[34]Luke 17:15; 19:37–38; I Kings 8:55; Ezek 11:13; Neh 9:4; etc. Midrash *Sifre* on Deut 3:23 (*Pisqa* 26) says that prayer has ten names, and the first one it lists is "cry." Whether Mark would have expected his readers to know that the ninth hour when Jesus uttered his prayer was the Jewish ritual time for the afternoon prayer (see Pesch, *Markus* 2.494) depends in part on whether Mark's arrangement of time reflects a church prayer ritual in commemoration of the day of the Lord's death.

of Mark 15:37; Matt 27:50,[35] constitute an apocalyptic sign similar to the eschatological elements of darkness, rent sanctuary veil, earthquake, and risen dead that accompany the death of Jesus in the various Gospels. In John 5:28 the *cry* of the Son of Man causes all those who are in the tombs to hear; and in 11:43 the *clamor* and *loud cry* of Jesus help to call forth Lazarus from the tomb. In I Thess 4:16 the *cry* of the archangel accompanies the coming of the Lord to raise the dead, while in *IV Ezra* 13:12–13 the Man from the Sea *calls* the multitude to him. In judgment the Lord *speaks, roars,* and *cries out,* at times producing earthquakes, in Amos 1:2; Joel 4:16 (3:16); Jer 25:30; and Ps 46:7, even as in Rev 10:3 the angel *shouts* with a loud voice as he reveals the seven thunders.[36]

A particular eschatological aspect is the final battle with evil.[37] In language echoing Isa 11:4, according to II Thess 2:8 the Lord Jesus slays the Lawless One (*anomos*) with the breath/spirit (*pneuma*) of his mouth. Acts 8:7 employs *boan* and *phonē megalē* to describe the shriek of unclean spirits as in defeat they come out of the possessed.[38] (Note that on the cross four verses after Matt 27:46 Jesus will let go the *spirit.*) Does the violent description of Jesus' outcry suggest that in his death struggle with evil he feels himself on the brink of defeat so that he must ask why God is not helping him? In any good drama the last words of the main character are especially significant. It is important for us, then, to ask how literally we should take, "My God, my God, for what reason have you forsaken me?" (Ps 22:2).

There is much to encourage us to take it very literally on the level of the evangelists' portrayal of Jesus. (The question of historicity, i.e., whether Ps 22:2 represents how Jesus actually felt at the moment of death, will be

---

[35]It may well be that with these phenomena Mark (followed by Matt) intends an inclusion with his use of some of the same terms at the beginning of the Gospel: e.g., Mark 1:2 cites Malachi, the basis of the Elijah expectation; 1:3 uses *phonē* and *boan* of JBap in the desert; 1:10–11 has the *pneuma* descend on Jesus as a *phonē* speaks from heaven.

[36]In some dozen passages in Rev a "loud cry" accompanies revelation to the seer.

[37]A. Fridrichsen, J. M. Robinson, and Schreiber are among the many who see the Marcan passion as a climax of the conflict with the demonic. While at times this theme may be exaggerated, I would defend it against Best (*Temptation*), who insists that the victory of Jesus over Satan in the temptation was total and that accordingly Mark has no struggle with or victory over the demonic in the passion. As I have argued (pp. 157–62 above), the Synoptic reference in Gethsemane to *peirasmos* (14:38) continues a struggle with Satan or the devil begun with the *peirazein* of 1:13.

[38]Hitherto only the demons have known that Jesus is the Son of God. Danker ("Demonic") would explain that when in Mark 15:37 Jesus expels the demon (lets go the spirit) with a great cry, the centurion who has seen the expulsion of the demon can now confess Jesus as the Son of God (pp. 67–68). On p. 48 he cites with approval the view of Best that the cry of dereliction reflects the fact that Jesus himself has become the object of the wrath of God. Even though I see an aspect of the struggle with the demonic in the crucifixion, I judge that these views go beyond Mark's detectable intention. Jesus is never shown as having a demonic element within; no demonic spirit comes forth or is expelled from Jesus in Mark 15:37; and Jesus is not the object of the wrath of God.

treated in the ANALYSIS.[39]) In the tragic drama of the Mark/Matt PN Jesus has been abandoned by his disciples and mocked by all who have come to the cross. Darkness has covered the earth; there is nothing that shows God acting on Jesus' side. How appropriate that Jesus feel forsaken! His "Why?" is that of someone who has plumbed the depths of the abyss, and feels enveloped by the power of darkness. Jesus is not questioning the existence of God or the power of God to do something about what is happening; he is questioning the silence of the one whom he calls "My God."[40] If we pay attention to the overall structure of the Mark/Matt PN, that form of addressing the deity is itself significant, for nowhere previously has Jesus ever prayed to God as "God." Mark/Matt began the PN with a prayer in which the deity was addressed by Jesus as "Father," the common form of address used by Jesus and one that captured his familial confidence that God would not make the Son go through the "hour" or drink the cup (Mark 14:35–36; Matt 26:39). Yet that filial prayer, reiterated three times, was not visibly or audibly answered; and now having endured the seemingly endless agony of the "hour" and having drunk the dregs of the cup, Jesus screams out a final prayer that is an inclusion with the first prayer. Feeling forsaken as if he were not being heard, he no longer presumes to speak intimately to the All-Powerful as "Father" but employs the address common to all human beings, "My God."[41] (The fact that Jesus is using psalm language—a fact to which Mark does *not* call our attention—does not make less noticeable the unusualness of such terminology on Jesus' lips.) Mark calls our attention to this contrast between the two prayers and makes it more poignant by reporting the address in each prayer in Jesus' own tongue: "*Abba*" and "*Elōi*," thus giving the impression of words coming genuinely from Jesus' heart, as distinct from the rest of his words that have been preserved in a foreign lan-

[39]Braumann ("Wozu" 158) distinguishes four stages of interpretation: 1. What would Jesus have meant by the psalm if he spoke it? 2. What did it mean on a preMarcan level? 3. What did Mark mean by it? 4. What did Mark's readers understand?

[40]Lacan ("Mon Dieu," espec. 37, 53) has intriguing reflections on this point. While human suffering makes us think God is absent, that may be because we have shaped God in our image and likeness. The cross teaches us that the self-revelation of the true God, for whom humility is power, takes place in human weakness. The silence confirms that there is a God. Vigorous poetic theological affirmations about the Word collapsing into a scream for the lost God have marked the christology of H. U. von Balthasar, for whom the citation of Ps 22:2 is a major factor; see Zilonka, *Mark* 207–21.

[41]Eissfeldt ("Mein Gott") detects six different shades of meaning for this expression in the OT, ranging from a reference to a house idol to a way of describing the covenant God of Israel (Deut 4:5). In the psalms in particular it expresses closeness, involving God in the ups and downs of the life of the petitioner (pp. 10–15). Often, as here on Jesus' lips, it implies a warm interiorized association. Gerhardsson ("Jésus" 222) warns what the prayer of Jesus in Mark/Matt is not, namely: a radical cry in a universe that seems empty of God, or a pious outpouring by one who does not realize what he is saying, or a saying uttered simply in order to fulfill the Scriptures. Rather, the one who speaks feels no consolation but has not lost his sense of the will of God expressed in the scriptural word.

guage (Greek). As he faces the agony of death,[42] the Marcan Jesus is portrayed as resorting to his mother tongue.

There is an external indication that also favors taking literally the pessimistic pathos of Jesus' last words. In discussing the opening *"Abba"* prayer of the Marcan PN, I called attention to a parallel description in the Epistle to the Hebrews (4:14–16; 5:7–10) of Jesus' prayer to the One who had the power to save him from death. While many aspects of the Hebrews passage had echoes in the Mark/Matt Gethsemane prayer, there are other aspects that have resemblances to the prayer on the cross (p. 232 above). It is on the cross that Jesus has learned even more fully "obedience from the things he suffered." It is here that he has made "strong clamor," and it is here that he will be "heard from [anxious] fear" and made perfect. These parallels in Hebrews encourage us to take literally the psalm passage in which Mark/Matt vocalize Jesus' desperation.[43]

While I find this interpretation of Mark convincing, in fairness it should be noted that from the early Church Fathers[44] to contemporary scholars and preachers many have resisted the surface import that would have Jesus expressing the sentiment of being forsaken by God. Very often in this opposition the assumption is made that the psalm was historically cited by Jesus, and no distinction is made between what Mark/Matt implied and what Jesus himself felt. Zilonka (*Mark* 8–94) shows how the literal "forsaken" interpretation was rejected by Roman Catholic scholars as a whole during the church rejection of historical criticism in the antiModernist period ca. 1910.

Some deny the obvious meaning of the words, e.g., Sagne ("Cry") employs the Book of Job to explain: "The cry of Jesus on the cross is not a reproach against God, but the explosion of suffering in love"! Another form of rejecting the idea that Jesus was forsaken recognizes that citing Ps 22:2 implies desperation, but has Jesus expressing this not in his own name but in the name of sinners or of the Jews.[45] Others shift the meaning from des-

---

[42]Braumann ("Wozu" 161–62) insists that Jesus' feeling forsaken refers not simply to suffering but to death. Léon-Dufour ("Dernier" 669) comments that Jesus did not enter death with all the answers derived from the beatific vision but with a "Why?"

[43]Read ("Cry") would find further support for the stark tone of Mark in the formulas of II Cor 5:21: "made him to be sin for us" and Philip 2:8: "he humbled himself becoming obedient to death, even death on a cross."

[44]Hasenzahl (*Gottverlassenheit*) combines his curiously disparate approach to the Mark/Matt "last word" of Jesus with reflections on the christological understanding of the Greek psalter, a combination that warns us how difficult it is to move back from the later Christian reflection to what Mark intended.

[45]So, for example, C. M. Macleroy (ExpTim 53 [1941–42], 326): In love Jesus has identified with us and our sins; he experienced the separation from God that our sins bring into our lives. Isa 53:6 enters this view: "The Lord laid upon him the iniquity of us all." Kenneally ("Eli" 132) attributes variations of the view to Origen, Athanasius, Augustine, and Cyril of Alexandria. A complicat-

peration to loving surrender by harmonizing Mark/Matt with Luke or John, so that, for example, Luke's "Father, into your hands I place my spirit" becomes the correct interpretation of "My God, my God, for what reason have you forsaken me?" Or they may soften the import of the Aramaic or Greek verbs used by Mark/Matt. (In fact, those verbs have various shades of meaning, and we shall see that this enterprise was shared by ancient copyists.) Buckler ("Eli" 384) points out that the Semitic verbs (*šbq* and *'zb*) mean not only "leave, forsake" but also "leave a bequest, hand over to" (*'zb* in Pss 10:14; 49:11), and by complicated exegesis has Jesus refusing a royal role in relation to God's people. It has even been suggested that the Semitic transliteration given by Mark/Matt constitutes a wrong reading of what Jesus actually said.[46]

On theological grounds others challenge more directly a literal interpretation of Mark/Matt. The charge is made that to take literally the wording about God forsaking or abandoning Jesus would be to deny Jesus' divinity.[47] Certainly Mark did not imply such a denial, for immediately after Jesus' prayer in 15:34 we find the climactic confession of Jesus as God's Son (15:39). Still another objection finds despair being attributed to Jesus in a literal interpretation of the prayer. Despair, understood as the loss of hope in God or of salvation, is considered a major sin, and the NT affirms that Jesus committed no sin.[48] This is a rather pointless objection, however, for nothing in the Marcan passage suggests a sense of the loss of salvation or forgiveness

---

ing factor for Church Fathers and later Roman Catholic scholars was the rendering of the second part of Ps 22:2 in the LXX and Vulgate: "Far from my salvation are the words [i.e., recounting] of my sins" (reading *š'gh* [*šĕ'āgâ*], "cry," as *šg'h* [*šĕgî'â*], "sin"). That sentiment could not be attributed literally to the sinless Jesus! On the other hand, Wilkinson ("Seven" 75–76) cites with approval Schmiedel's view relating this passage to Jesus' bearing the sin of the world: The horror of that sin has obscured the closeness of his communion with the Father. P. Rogers ("Desolation" 57), who lists various views of times past, attributes to Luther the thesis that Jesus on the cross was at the same time supremely good and supremely sinful.

[46]Sidersky ("Passage") shows how the transliteration *sabachthani* ("forsaken me"), seemingly from Aramaic *šbq*, could represent a form of (Hebrew-Aramaic) *škh*: "Why have you forgotten me?"—a question that appears in Ps 42:10. In a later article ("Parole") he points to another possibility: The original was a form of (Hebrew) *zbh*: "Why have you sacrificed me?" Cohn-Sherbok ("Jesus' Cry") thinks of the original as a rhetorical question involving Aramaic *šbh*: "Why have you praised me?" and sees this as a victory cry ushering in the messianic kingdom—that leads people to ask where is Elijah. Such suggestions, of course, invalidate the evangelist's own interpretation of what the Semitic wording means.

[47]Baker ("Cry") finds acceptable Jesus' being "forsaken" (a withdrawal of the light and joy of God's presence) but not absolutely "abandoned" (breaking of the unity between Father and Son); yet such precision of thought is not transparently conveyed by the respective English verbs. Kenneally ("Eli" 130–31) finds erroneous all suggestions that the hypostatic union was broken, that God withdrew actual grace, and that Jesus lost the beatific vision. These fears are couched in the language of later theology and cover ideas that were scarcely in the mind of Mark or his readers. A more realistic issue is that nonChristian apologists of the early centuries might well have found a contradiction between Jesus being divine and yet uttering such a despondent prayer of weakness.

[48]II Cor 5:21; Heb 4:15; I Pet 2:22; John 8:46; I John 3:5.

(or even the need thereof). Jesus is praying, and so he cannot have lost hope; calling God "My God" implies trust. Because he saw how Jesus died, the Marcan centurion confesses that Jesus was God's Son; Mark could not have meant that Jesus' despair prompted such a recognition. Thus, despair in the strict sense is not envisaged.[49] Rather the issue is whether the struggle with evil will lead to victory; and Jesus is portrayed as profoundly discouraged at the end of his long battle because God, to whose will Jesus committed himself at the beginning of the passion (Mark 14:36; Matt 26:39,42), has not intervened in the struggle and seemingly has left Jesus unsupported. (That this is not true will become apparent the second that Jesus dies, for then God will rend the sanctuary veil and bring a pagan to acknowledge publicly Jesus' divine sonship.) Jesus cries out, hoping that God will break through the alienation he has felt.

Other factors enter into scholars' rejection of the literal import of Jesus' prayer. That import seems to contradict the untroubled communion with God expressed elsewhere by Jesus. The Johannine Jesus says, "I am never alone because the Father is with me . . . I have conquered the world" (16:32–33). The Lucan crucified Jesus has just expressed the conviction that this day he would be in paradise. But those statements are in other Gospels that have christologies different from that of Mark/Matt.[50] For Luke and John, God is patently with Jesus in the passion so that Jesus can give voice respectively to surety and victory on the cross before he dies. For Mark/Matt, despite a long-range confidence that God will make the Son of Man victorious, Jesus reaches a low point at death; and God exercises overwhelming power only after Jesus dies. In fact, the comparative argument can be used to favor a literal interpretation of the Mark/Matt prayer as truly agonized, e.g., the tone of despondency is probably what caused Luke not to copy this psalm prayer from Mark and to substitute another much more positive psalm prayer: "Father, into your hands I place my spirit." Similarly John whose Jesus says, "The Father and I are one," would find alien a tradition in which he screams, "My God, my God, why have you forsaken me?"

Perhaps the most frequently offered argument for softening the dour import of the Mark/Matt death cry is based on the general context of Ps 22.

---

[49]Reimarus used this verse to argue that Jesus died a frustrated, defeated revolutionary. There have been novelistic attempts to make despair the last temptation of Jesus; but that also appears in L. Boff, *Way of the Cross* (Maryknoll: Orbis, 1980), 95–97: "Jesus' absolute hope is understandable only in the light of his absolute despair."

[50]Of course, many of those who raise the objection of a lack of harmony with other words of Jesus suppose that all "Seven Last Words on the cross" were historical and that therefore the fact that they appear in different Gospels is irrelevant—the words have to agree because they all came from the same Jesus. Lofthouse ("Cry") lists this and other noncritical arguments against attributing to Mark 15:34 the sense of Jesus' feeling forsaken.

Jesus cites the opening verse of a psalm that continues for thirty more verses. By the end the psalmist will take a positive view: Rejoicing, he will proclaim that he has survived the danger and that after all God did not spurn him or "turn His face away" (Ps 22:25).[51] Accordingly some would invoke a hermeneutic principle that a NT citation of a specific OT passage supposes that the readers will be familiar with the context of that passage and so understand implied references to that context. At times that principle has validity, but it is not universally true. Applied here, it would mean that Mark expected his readers to recognize that a psalm was being cited, to know the whole psalm, and to detect from a reference to the agonized opening verse the triumphant fate of the one who prays—in short, to take almost the opposite meaning of what Jesus is portrayed as saying! Elsewhere in citing psalms,[52] Mark/Matt have shown the ability to quote a verse with exact appropriateness to the point under consideration, and there is insufficient reason to think they have not followed the same procedure here. If one wishes to draw on the context of the whole psalm without positing such an extraordinary *contresens* usage of Ps 22:2, one can supplement the literal sense of that quoted verse by two observations. First, the positive ending of the psalm helps to show that in attributing to Jesus such a sentiment of abandonment Mark did not think that Jesus was guilty of despair or had lost hope. Mark knew that the passion culminated in victory even if it plumbed the depths of lonely suffering; for that reason it was appropriate for him to portray Jesus at his lowest moment in the passion uttering the most tragic verse[53] of a psalm that ends on a triumphant note. Second, the speaker in the psalm is one who has been committed to God since birth (22:10–11) and has constantly relied on God (22:9). That makes particularly poignant the present predicament where

---

[51]Burchard ("Markus") and Trudinger ("Eli") argue strongly for the positive import of the whole psalm in interpreting Jesus' citation. Trudinger (253–56) appeals even to the title where, he says, *lmnṣḥ* does not mean "To a musical conductor" but "To the One who brings about victory," i.e., by making the suffering just one victorious. On the other hand, Léon-Dufour ("Dernier" 672) lists arguments against this type of interpretation: The situation of one near death on a cross does not imply a long prayer consisting of a whole psalm, and there is no emphasis that a psalm is being cited.

[52]Possible citations of or allusions to Psalm 22 in the Marcan PN are found in Mark 15:24,29,30,31. See APPENDIX VII for more detail on the citation of psalms.

[53]The import of the verse is sharpened when we consider the survey of Caza ("Relief" 181) showing that the psalter as a whole stresses that God does *not* abandon those who seek help (Pss 9:11; 16:10; 37:25,28; 94:14). She describes this as the only instance where God abandons the righteous just. Outside the psalter, however, we hear in II Chron 32:31 that in the face of the Babylonian ambassadors, "God forsook him [King Hezekiah] to test him, that He might know all that was in his heart." Moreover, the Matthean Jesus has shown an awareness that the wrong confidence in divine help can be a deception. In the temptations at the beginning of the Gospel, the devil cited Ps 91:11–12 to the effect that if Jesus was Son of God, God would command the angels to support him and not let him dash his foot against a stone. There Jesus replied that the Lord God should not be put to the test.

for the first time God has not responded and seemingly has forsaken the suppliant. Obviously that general situation is most appropriate to Jesus on the cross.[54]

Overall, then, I find no persuasive argument against attributing to the Jesus of Mark/Matt the literal sentiment of feeling forsaken expressed in the psalm quote. The interpretation of this prayer at the end of the PN should follow the same course as the interpretation of the opening prayer of the PN in Mark 14:35–36 and Matt 26:39. There many would reject the literal meaning that Jesus really wanted the hour to pass from him and was not eager to drink the cup of suffering. They could not attribute to Jesus such anguish in the face of death. If one accepts literally that anguish at the opening moment when Jesus could still call God "*Abba*, Father," one should accept equally literally this screamed protest against abandonment wrenched from an utterly forlorn Jesus who now is so isolated and estranged that he no longer uses "Father" language but speaks as the humblest servant.

Wording of Jesus' Death Cry. In Mark/Matt there are two wordings of Ps 22:2. The first is a transliteration of the Semitic in Greek characters; the second is a translation of the import of that verse into Greek. The Semitic transliteration must be compared to Hebrew (MT) and Aramaic forms of the psalm verse; the Greek translation must be compared to the LXX translation of the psalm verse. The following Semitic renditions of Ps 22:2 are pertinent to our study:

Hebrew (MT):	*'Ēlî, 'Ēlî, lāmâ 'ăzabtānî*
Aramaic:	*'Ĕlāhî, 'Ĕlāhî, lĕmā' šĕbaqtanî*[55]
Mark:	*Elōi, Elōi, lama sabachthani*
Matt:	*Ēli, Ēli, lema sabachthani*[56]
Codex Bezae:	*Ēlei, Ēlei, lama zaphthani*[57]

[54]In my judgment none of this justifies interpreting Mark 15:34 in terms of Jesus enduring the wrath of God. In his survey of interpretations, P. Rogers ("Desolation" 57) attributes to Anselm of Canterbury in his *Cur Deus Homo?* the thesis that Jesus was abandoned to satisfy the angry justice of God. Modern advocates often uphold it in continuity with the understanding that "the cup" of 14:36 is "the cup of wrath." But the issue in Jesus' prayer on the cross is God's failure to act, without any suggestion as to why. Nothing in the Gospel would suggest God's wrath against Jesus as the explanation.

[55]This is a reconstruction, graciously checked for me by J. A. Fitzmyer; 1st-cent. Aramaic would permit *'Ēlî* or *'Ĕlāhî*. The later (ca. 450) Targum on the Psalms (Lagarde ed.) reads: *'Ēlî, 'Ēlî, miṭṭûl mâ šĕbaqtanî*, employing an interrogative (*mṭwl mh*) not attested in 1st-cent. Aramaic. See the transliteration in Codex Washingtonensis of Matt: *Ēli, Ēli ma sabachthanei*.

[56]Variant ms. readings harmonize the form of God's name in Mark/Matt so that both read *Elōi* or *Ēli*. Similarly there are attempts to harmonize the *lama* and *lema* difference, and witnesses in the Koine tradition read *lima* in Mark. The exotic *sabachthani* is written *sabaktanei* in Codex Vaticanus of Matt, *sabapthanei* in Vaticanus of Mark, and *sabachtanei* in Sinaiticus of Matt, *sibakthanei* in Alexandrinus of Mark.

[57]Thus in both Mark and Matt; *Ēlei* is an unimportant orthographic variant of *Ēli*.

The minor differences between Mark and Matt have been the subject of much discussion, both as to the language that each is transcribing (Aramaic or Hebrew) and as to originality.[58] Clearly *sabachthani* in Mark/Matt resembles the verb in the Aramaic rather than in the Hebrew of the psalm; consequently most scholars agree that the psalm is being cited in Aramaic. Yet apparently both Gospels are using mixed forms: The *Elōi* of Mark is close to Aramaic, while the *Ēli* of Matt echoes Hebrew; the *lama* of Mark echoes Hebrew, while the *lema* of Matt resembles Aramaic. Although it is not impossible that the tradition recorded a mixed Hebrew-Aramaic quote,[59] that is not a necessary conclusion. First, there were dialects both of Hebrew and Aramaic where forms differed from what might be called the more classical standards of the two languages, e.g., Galilean Aramaic, a form of which Jesus would probably have spoken. Specifically, Rehm ("Eli") would maintain that the *Ēli* of Matt is not Hebrew but spoken Aramaic, while Mark's *Elōi* represents traditional Aramaic. Even without that distinction both *'Ēl* and *'Ēlāh* are attested for "God" in Aramaic documents.[60] Second, transliteration of Semitic vowels and consonants was not an exact procedure. (The standardized transcription of the MT used above does not render exactly Hebrew pronunciation in Jesus' time.) Rehm would argue that the *shewa* (short "e" vowel) in the Aramaic *lĕma'* could be transcribed either as *e* or *a*, so that Mark's *lama* is not really an echo of Hebrew. Some scholars have even maintained that the Mark/Matt *sabachthani* does not transcribe Aramaic *šĕbaqtanî*.[61] On purely linguistic grounds, however, it is perfectly possible to contend that the Marcan transliteration represents Aramaic or an Aramaic dialect, not mixed Hebrew-Aramaic. This would be in harmony with Mark's tendency elsewhere to present transliterated Aramaic, not Hebrew.[62] While Matt's transliteration could also represent Aramaic, it is not unlikely that that more bookish evangelist has conformed at least the name

[58]While in harmony with the theory of Marcan priority, there are many defenders of Mark's form as more original, a surprising number of scholars support Matthean originality: Allen, Dalman, Hauck, Huby, Jeremias, Klostermann, Rehm, Taylor, Zahn, etc.

[59]This is a view shared with nuances by many scholars (Gundry, Lagrange, Stendahl, Strecker, etc.), a few of whom would maintain that Jesus spoke such a mixture. Among those who contend that in the tradition Ps 22:2 was originally cited in Aramaic are Cadoux and McNeile; those for original citation in Hebrew include Dalman, Gnilka, Kilpatrick, Taylor, and Wellhausen.

[60]E.g., Targum Onqelos.; see n. 55 above for the Targum on the Psalms.

[61]Normally *ch* should transliterate Semitic *ḥ* not *q* (usually rendered by *k*). Yet in the transliteration one must allow the influence of *th* on the consonant before it, so that a *k* rendering of Semitic *q* has been shifted to a *ch* (Rehm, "Eli" 275). See n. 46 above.

[62]See *talitha koum* (5:41); *ephphatha* (7:34); *hōsanna* (11:9,10); *abba* (14:36); *Golgotha* (15:22). *Korban* (7:11) has most often been thought to reflect (mishnaic) Hebrew, but *qrbn* (*qorbān*) is now attested in an Aramaic ossuary inscription discovered near Jerusalem in the 1950s (FESBNT 93–100).

of God to the form used in prayer in the sacred Hebrew language.[63] It is generally agreed that in the Lord's Prayer Matt (6:9) has changed the more ancient "Father" address (Luke 11:2; representing the *'Abbā'* of Aramaic) to "Our Father (who are) in heaven," a form conformable to traditional synagogue usage. The same type of influence may have been at work here. The transliteration of Mark in Codex Bezae is interesting, for here we have a further step by a scribe who has totally conformed the passage to Hebrew.[64]

The solution just proposed for the variants in the Mark/Matt and Bezae transliterations has been rejected by others on the assumption that these are the ipsissima verba of Jesus and that he would have recited the psalm in Hebrew. Beyond the unprovable assumption of historicity (see ANALYSIS), such an approach presupposes other uncertainties, e.g., that Jesus could read[65] and that he knew the Scriptures in Hebrew. From the discovery of the Qumran (11Q) Targum of Job we have clear evidence that Aramaic translations of some biblical books were in existence several centuries before Jesus' time. If he used these words, there is no convincing reason that he could not have spoken them in Aramaic; and no matter what language he used, there is good reason to think that an early Aramaic-speaking Christian community might have preserved them in Aramaic. The contention that the Hebraized form in Codex Bezae represented the scribe's access to a preMarcan tradition is not plausible.

Let us turn now from the transliteration of the Semitic of Jesus' words in Mark/Matt to the translation[66] of those words into Greek. The following list compares the Gospel text with the rendition of Ps 22:2 in the LXX:

[63]We shall have to come back to Matt's reason for changing the Marcan reading when we discuss the misinterpretation of Jesus' words to mean that he was Elijah (p. 1061 below).

[64]Here I agree with Rehm ("Eli" 275), although other scholars challenge the derivation of Bezae's *zaphthani* from Hebrew *'ăzabtānî*. (Admittedly the transliteration is odd; first the initial *ayin* was lost, and then the normal *b* transliteration became *ph* under the influence of the following *th*.) Nestle ("Mark xv") and Gnilka ("Mein Gott") would derive *zaphthani* not from the root *'zb* (forsake) but from the root *z'p* (rage against). They argue that Bezae translates the transliterated *zapthani* by a form of *oneidizein* ("Why have you reviled me?"), and that *oneidizein* is not used in the LXX to render *'zb*. Yet neither does it render *z'p;* and in the Greek translations of Symmachus and Lucian it does render *'zb*.

[65]For this Luke 4:16–21 is the sole evidence. Fitzmyer (*Luke* 1.526–27) reports the debate among scholars whether that is a free Lucan creation based on Mark 6:1–6a or represents independent tradition. He regards 4:17–21 as "better ascribed to Luke's own pen" because it betrays a distinctive Lucan concern. Nevertheless, Meier (*Marginal* 1.268–78) is probably to be followed in contending that Jesus was taught how to read and to expound the Hebrew Scriptures.

[66]Mark uses *methermēneuein* ("to interpret") as he did in reference to Golgotha in 15:22. Matt (27:33) avoided it there, even as he changed it here. SPNM 296 suggests he found it too cumbersome; yet Matt used it in 1:23.

LXX: *ho theos, ho theos mou, prosches moi hina ti egkatelipes me*
Mark: *ho theos mou, ho theos mou, eis ti egkatelipes me*[67]
Matt: *thee mou, thee mou, hinati me egkatelipes*
Codex Bezae: *ho theos mou, ho theos mou, eis ti ōneidisas me*[68]
GPet: *hē dynamis mou, hē dynamis, kateleipsas me*

From the fact that a translation is given one may judge that the audience was no longer expected to understand the Semitic wording (and indeed *GPet* no longer reports it). In discussing the initial PN prayer in Mark (p. 175 above), we saw that the presence of both transliterated Aramaic and a Greek translation (14:36: *Abba ho Patēr*) may have represented a history of the prayer being recited in Aramaic first, then (in a mixed community) in both languages, finally in Greek alone. It is tempting to posit a similar history for the final Marcan prayer of Jesus; but obviously the circumstances in which Christians would pray this prayer as Jesus prayed it would have to be restricted, e.g., in times of martyrdom or extreme suffering. As for the wording, the LXX ("God, My God, attend to me, to what purpose have you forsaken me?") represents a literal translation of the MT Hebrew except for the omission of the first possessive pronoun and the insertion of a clause petitioning attention (*prosches moi*).[69] Even though Mark/Matt used the wording of the LXX, they stayed closer to the Hebrew in avoiding the LXX peculiarities. (Scholars like Black, Gundry, and Stendahl [SPNM 297] regard Matt's *hinati* ["to what purpose"] as a stylistic improvement on Mark's *eis ti* ["to/for what reason"]; yet in 26:8 Matt followed Mark 14:4 in using *eis ti*. More likely Matt is conforming to the LXX Greek.[70]) Some have speculated that they knew a shorter form of the LXX psalm verse different from the 4th-cent.-AD one known to us; others have thought that Mark/Matt adapted the LXX to the Hebrew wording[71] or to the Semitic tradition of Jesus' words. Either solution makes it unlikely that the earliest Gospel tradition of Jesus' words had only Greek (as in *GPet*) and that the Semitic transliteration was added later to give verisimilitude.

---

[67]Codex Vaticanus omits the second *ho theos mou.*

[68]This is the reading in Mark only.

[69]Some would attribute these LXX changes to a misinterpretation of one of the *'Ēlî* words in the Hebrew as a preposition *'ĕlî,* "to me."

[70]Braumann ("Wozu" 159–61) and Burchard ("Markus" 8) insist that Mark's *eis ti* means "to what end," not "why." It is more difficult to explain Matt's substitution of the rare Attic vocative *thee* for Mark's (and the LXX) use of the nominative *ho theos* as a vocative (BDF 147). Yet the same type of substitution occurred in Jesus' initial PN prayer to the Father in Matt 26:39 over against Mark 14:36.

[71]Presumably that is what Aquila did, for his Greek rendition did not have the *prosches moi.*

Codex Bezae. As in the Semitic transliteration so also here for Mark this codex has a remarkable rendition in *ōneidisas:* "Why have you reviled me?" This Western reading is echoed in the *exprobasti* of an Old Latin witness, the *maledixisti* of Codex Bobiensis (Burkitt, "On St. Mark"), and the *in opprobrium dedisti* of Porphyrius. Harnack ("Probleme" 261–64) offers argumentation for accepting the Bezae Greek verb as original, with the result that the standard Mark *egkatelipes* ("forsaken") would be later harmonizing with the LXX. Would the Bezae scribe have dared to change Mark's *egkatelipes* if he found it, given the support of Matt and the LXX for that reading? More often it has been argued that the Bezae scribe did change Mark because he found the notion of God's forsaking Jesus theologically offensive. That solution, however, is not without problems: Why then did he not change Matt as well? Is God's reviling Jesus any less offensive than God's forsaking him? There is probably no totally satisfactory diagnosis of the oddness of Bezae, but some factors are interesting. Even though Harnack thinks *ōneidisas* cannot have been a translation of Bezae's Semitic transliteration *zaphthani,* the verb *ōneidizein* is used by Symmachus and Lucian to translate *'zb* (n. 64 above); and so the scribe may not have thought his *ōneidizein* very adventurous over against the *egkataleipein* rendering. It may have been for him a matter of more familiar Greek—and perhaps more usual theological Greek, for words related to *ōneidizein* describe the sufferings of Christ in Rom 15:3 and Heb 13:13 (see also Heb 10:33; 11:26). The Romans passage cites Ps 69:10, and so the idea that Jesus was reviled may have been fixed in Christian memory. Mark used this verb in describing the third mockery of Jesus on the cross: "Even those who had been crucified together with him were reviling him" (15:32b; Matt 27:44). Is God now being suspected of offering still another mockery in the series, or is there a chance that the Bezae scribe understood Jesus to be asking, "My God, My God, why have you (allowed their having) mocked me?" In that case there would be less a problem of why Bezae allowed Matt to read: "Why have you forsaken me?" Both questions would have the import of asking why God has allowed such things to be done to Jesus.

There is a minor but fascinating corollary to this Western reading pointed out by Skehan ("St. Patrick"). The apostle to Ireland is recorded to have had ca. AD 400 a peculiar way of praying in Latin: "When I would cry 'Heliam (Heliam)' with my strength, behold the splendor of that sun would come down upon me." Patrick, in invoking the sun, is using a transliterated form of Greek *Hēlios* (perhaps in part drawing on a picture of Elijah [Latin *Elias*] having gone up there with his chariot [II Kings 2:11]), but at the same time is echoing the prayer of Jesus. Codex Bobiensis of N. Africa may give us a key to where he got his wording:[72] in Mark 15:34–36 it has Jesus praying "Heli, Helianm" (= Greek *Ēli, Ēli: "My God"*), and the bystanders referring to "Helion . . . Helias" (= Greek *Ēlian . . . Ēlias:* "Elijah"). Was there a moment in the Western Latin interpretation of Jesus' prayer that he was thought to have addressed a reproach to the sun for having forsaken him or reviled him? That would make perfect sense immediately following the verse about darkness having covered the whole earth!

Rendition in GPet 5:19. Without any accompanying transliteration of Semitic, *GPet* reports Jesus' last words as, "My power, O power, you have forsaken me." Clearly this is closer to Mark/Matt than to Luke or to John. Three possibilities (with variations) are immediately apparent: (1) *GPet* represents an original tradition that was secondarily modified by Mark/Matt; (2) *GPet* is secondary and represents a modification of Mark/Matt; (3) Both *GPet* and Mark/Matt are derivative from an original tradition. At an earlier period in *GPet* research this issue would probably have been resolved on the basis of a theological analysis of the document as a docetic work in which Jesus was simply a human shell inhabited by a divine power. Basis for this view was found in 4:10, where "the Lord" had no pain when he was crucified. Most often, then, the present passage was interpreted as if it reflected the theology ascribed to Cerinthus (Irenaeus, *Adv. Haer.* 1.26.1) whereby the divine being (Christ) who descended upon Jesus at the baptism withdrew from him before he died. Such an analysis made it hard for most scholars to ascribe originality or priority to the wording of the death cry in *GPet*. Today, however, this docetic interpretation of *GPet* has largely been abandoned.[73] The description that Jesus had no pain is seen as a martyrological touch showing the bravery of the one about to die, and it is recognized that the Cerinthian interpretation of the death cry is most unlikely since Jesus clearly remains divine after the "power" has left him (see 6:21; 10:40). Accordingly the decision about the three possibilities listed above has to be made on other grounds.

As we consider the possibilities individually, we must keep in mind the overall relationship that we have already seen between *GPet* and the canonical Gospels. That past experience makes too simple an acceptance of possibility (1) quite unlikely, for hitherto we have found nothing to make us think that Mark or Matt depended on *GPet*. True, a specific passage, itself a citation of Scripture, might provide an exception. Nevertheless, even on that limited basis it is hard to see how Mark/Matt could have drawn their form of Jesus' last cry from that in *GPet*. One would have to think that at a later

---

[72]This represents the African Old Latin tradition, and British bishops who attended a church council in N. Africa could have spread knowledge of this type of translation.

[73]Brown, "Gospel of Peter" 325, 340; see APPENDIX I.

period of Gospel development they or one of them[74] introduced an Aramaic wording that they had not found in their source. Moreover, they would have edited the wording to favor a lower christology, for they would have introduced the notion of God forsaking Jesus—a notion more offensive theologically than that of Jesus' power deserting him.

Possibility (2) has seemed likely in other instances, at least in the sense that the author of *GPet* may have heard a reading of Matt or of Mark and have written from memory of that oral communication rather than from a written copy. Here as a likely sign of the influence of Mark/Matt on *GPet,* we notice that these words of Jesus come after a reference to darkness holding fast all Judea (5:15a), i.e., largely the same sequence as in Mark/Matt, even if *GPet* contains a much more dramatized description (5:15b–18) than that found in Mark/Matt and the offering of vinegary wine comes before Jesus' words rather than after them. *GPet* 5:19 reports that the Lord "screamed out, saying," employing the same Greek as in Matt 27:46 (but without "a loud cry"). In the citation of Jesus' words *GPet* stays close to Mark/Matt and/or to the LXX in the choice of the verb *kataleipein,* which does not differ in meaning from their *egkataleipein.* The two points that would need to be explained if one were positing *GPet* dependence on Mark/Matt are the *GPet* shifts from a question to a statement[75] and from "My God, my God" to "My power, O power." Since the question in Mark/Matt already implies that a forsaking has taken place, the shift to "you have forsaken me" in *GPet* is not very significant, except to the extent that it shows a looser attitude toward exact citation of Scripture (Ps 22:2 is a question in both the MT and LXX). The deliberate change from "God" to "power" is the real issue. The christology of *GPet* is extremely high (e.g., never referring to "Jesus" but always to "the Lord"; thinking of the risen Jesus as a figure whose head was higher than the heavens [10:40]); and so the author might have found offensive the notion that God forsook Jesus. That very explanation, however, runs against a frequent explanation of why *GPet* hit upon "power" as a substitute for "God," namely, that it was a title for God, as in Mark 14:62 and Matt 26:64 where Jesus speaks of the Son of Man sitting at the right of "the Power" (Luke 22:69: "of the power of God").[76] If one is going to see the use of "power" as a deliberate alteration of Mark/Matt and of the LXX in order to make Jesus being forsaken seem less offensive, one must interpret the term literally.

[74]Matt is closer to *GPet* than is Mark—thus one might have to posit that in this instance Matt borrowed from *GPet* and Mark borrowed from Matt!

[75]Actually one could read the verbal form in *GPet* as a question, but there is no grammatical reason to do so as there is in Mark/Matt.

[76]It should be noted that "my Power" as a reference to God is more awkward than "the Power."

Possibility (3) for the words of Jesus (combined with [2] for the context) may offer fewer hurdles in the sense that one could dispense with positing intentional excision of "God" on the basis of a theological stance. If Ps 22:2 was associated with the death cry of Jesus and various interpretations of that psalm verse flourished side by side, the *GPet* author may have chosen the one known to him in his oral tradition without deliberate rejection of the one in the LXX followed by Mark/Matt. There is evidence for another rendering of Ps 22 that could have been known to the author of *GPet*. The Hebrew word for God *'Ēl* was derived from the verbal root *'wl* (*'yl*), which also gave rise to a number of words involving strength. The construct noun *'ēl* appears in the expression "the strength of hand(s)" in Prov 3:27; Neh 5:5; Micah 2:1. Thus the *'ēlî* of Ps 22:2 could have been read to mean something like "My strong one" or "My strength." In the 2d cent. AD, contemporary with *GPet*, as part of a Jewish attempt to produce a Greek translation more faithful to the Hebrew, Aquila rendered Ps 22:2 as "My strong one [*ischyre*], my strong one," a translation which Eusebius thought could be more eloquently rendered, "My strength" (*Demonstratio evangelica* 10.8.30; GCS 23.476). If the author of *GPet* had heard Matt read orally and remembered that the dying Jesus cited the psalm, might he not have recorded that with a rendition of the psalm known to him—a rendition that was less offensive theologically and made perfect sense? He could have meant that Jesus felt his physical strength had left him, a feeling that did not have to be expressed in a rhetorical question as in Mark/Matt. Or did the author of *GPet* go further and, since the word *dynamis* was used for Jesus' miraculous power (Mark 5:30), imply that Jesus now could not deliver himself because he had lost the power to produce miracles—a power always delimited by purpose since Jesus never used it for his own convenience? Or could the author have intended to go even further, in the direction of Philip 2:7 and Jesus' emptying himself, not of his divinity,[77] but in terms of experiencing human powerlessness like that of a slave? Not long after *GPet* was written Tatian was speculating that the godhead must have been hidden from the one slain on the cross, for if it had been revealed the one to be slain would not have feared and the slayers would not have been able to slay.[78] In all this *GPet* would be a witness of how the tradition of Jesus' death cry was being reinterpreted and understood in popular circles in the 2d cent.

Elijah and the Offering of Vinegary Wine. Just before Jesus' death

---

[77]In mid-2d cent. Justin may have been polemicizing against a wrong understanding of the loss of *dynamis* when he wrote that Jesus already had the power when he was born (*Dialogue* 88.2) and that some hidden power of God belonged to him in his crucifixion (49.8).

[78]Reported by T. Baarda, "A Syriac Fragment of Mar Ephraem's Commentary on the Diatessaron," NTS 8 (1961–62), 287–300, esp. 290.

Mark 15:35–36 and Matt 27:47–49 combine these two elements in a very awkward sequence. The Elijah element is found only in Mark/Matt while the *oxos* or vinegary wine[79] is a universally common element in the PN, being mentioned in all the canonical Gospels and *GPet.* A few general remarks about this situation may be useful before we try to unravel the difficult Mark/Matt account.

A major factor in the offering of vinegary wine to Jesus on the cross is an echo of Ps 69:22 describing how the just one is mocked by his enemies:

> And they gave for my bread gall,
> and for my thirst they gave me to drink vinegar.

This psalm is certainly in mind in Matt and *GPet,* for both mention gall,[80] the other psalm component besides the vinegary wine. Plausibly too the psalm is in mind in John 19:28–30: There Jesus' "I thirst" is explicitly set in the context of the completion of Scripture; and when he has drunk the wine, he says, "It is finished." While Mark is much less specific, the whole context of 15:36 echoes Scripture passages, including Ps 22:2. Only Luke's description of the offering of vinegary wine gives the reader no hint of the psalm being fulfilled: In 23:36 amid the three mockeries of Jesus on the cross the vinegary wine is offered to him by (Roman) soldiers. (The difficulty of relating Mark and Luke to Ps 69:22 suggests that the scene was not invented through reflection on that psalm.) In moving the action from immediately before Jesus' death, where it stood in Mark, Luke has given up some of its patent symbolism.

Another aspect of the offering of vinegary wine that is common to most of the narratives is mockery. That is not surprising since in Ps 69:22 gall and vinegar function as deliberate raillery. Even Luke, who has obscured the psalm background, maintains the element of mockery. Curiously, while John 19:28–30 manifests a strong scriptural component, it is alone in portraying no clear mockery. That may be because John is the one who has best woven the offering of wine into the storyline and accordingly has sacrificed one of the original aspects of the gesture.

From these observations the following scenario may be constructed. In an early stage of the crucifixion tradition a reference to an offering of vinegary wine was preserved or introduced because it showed how, just before he

---

[79]*Oxos* was a cheap, bitter red wine or vinegar distinct from the previously offered *oinos,* which had been mixed with myrrh or gall and was mentioned respectively (and only) in Mark 15:23 and Matt 27:34. See p. 940 above. It is difficult to decide whether to translate *oxos* as "vinegar" or as "wine." The choice depends on whether the primary element is mockery or drink. In Ps 69:22 I have used "vinegar" because mockery is the main theme; I have decided not to prejudice the Gospel situation and have used "vinegary wine" throughout.

[80]Matt 27:34 (mixed with *oinos*); *GPet* 5:16; see p. 944 above for the differences.

died, Jesus was mocked even as was the suffering just one in Ps 69:22. That this item could have had a separate history from the other death phenomena may be seen from the Qumran Hymns, where the liars who persecute the just assuage their enemies' thirst with vinegary wine (1QH 4:10–11). Awkwardly, the preMarcan tradition (or less likely, Mark) combined this wine offering with an eschatological reference to Elijah—so awkwardly that it is very difficult to analyze the storyline. I say "less likely, Mark" because the awkwardness of the combination[81] suggests that Mark did not create either component, for then he could have adapted one to the other to make a smoother storyline. The awkwardness is more easily explicable if Mark were joining two already formed traditions.[82] Indeed, Mark may not have fully understood their interrelation. While Matt followed Mark in this, modifying some of the awkwardness, Luke eliminated the Elijah component and moved the offering of vinegary wine to an earlier point in the narrative, i.e., into the tradition of the three mockeries of Jesus on the cross (§41 above). The author of *GPet* kept the Mark/Matt death context for the offering of vinegary wine, but he eliminated the Mark/Matt awkwardness by eliminating or forgetting the Elijah component. Independently of Mark (presumably), John drew on the vinegary wine tradition combined with last words, but made the combination more intelligible by supplying a scriptural reference to Jesus' thirst, so that Jesus' final words could refer to the completion of Scripture. He either did not know or rejected the Elijah tradition. Let us now begin to test that scenario by studying the Mark/Matt sequence.

If immediately after Jesus cried out the words of Ps 22:2, Mark had incorporated into his account of the death of Jesus this affirmation, "Someone, running, having filled a sponge with vinegary wine, having put it on a reed, was giving him to drink" (i.e., what now stands in Mark 15:36a), there would be little problem. One would have concluded that this was a discrete reference to Ps 69:22, giving biblical background for the mockery of the just one by his enemies. Problems are caused by what Mark 15:35 actually reports immediately after Jesus cried out the words of Ps 22:2, namely, "And some of the bystanders, having heard, were saying, 'Look, he is crying to Elijah.'" This misunderstanding is reiterated in 15:36b, "Let us see if Elijah comes to take him down." The first problem is why from Jesus' "*Elōi, Elōi, lama*

---

[81]It is not clear how the cry to Elijah (15:35) stems from hearing Jesus cite Ps 22:2 (15:34), or why (mistakenly) hearing a cry to Elijah should cause someone to offer vinegary wine to Jesus (15:36a), or whether and why that offering is involved with pausing to see whether Elijah comes to take Jesus down.

[82]I do not find persuasive Matera's thesis (*Kingship* 29–32) that there were three separate traditions (citation of Ps, offering of wine, Elijah). In Mark/Matt, *GPet*, and John (thus, in four out of five of our witnesses) a death psalm-citation (with variant wording) is related to the offering of vinegary wine; and that conjunction may well represent the oldest traceable tradition.

sabachthani" the bystanders conclude that he was calling on Elijah. The second problem is how their misinterpretation is related to someone running and getting vinegary wine to offer.

FIRST, the names *Elōi* and *Ēli* and *Ēlias* (Elijah). This problem is a superb test of the hermeneutical approach one takes to Mark's account. Scholars who know Semitic ask themselves about the verisimilitude (or even the historicity) of a moment when Semitic speakers heard Aramaic *'Ĕlāhî* (transcribed by Mark *Elōi*) and mistook it for the prophet's name *'Ēlîyāhû,* sometimes abbreviated *'Ēlîyâ.* (Less often asked is how these Semitic speakers heard *lĕmā' šĕbaqtanî* [which Mark transcribes *lama sabachthani* and translates "Why have you forsaken me?"] and understood it to be an appeal for Elijah to come and take Jesus down.) There have been ingenious and sometimes desperate attempts to find a dialectal pronunciation of God's name or of Elijah's name that could more plausibly explain how the Jewish bystanders confused one with the other.[83]

Matt, who probably knew both Aramaic and Hebrew, may already have seen the problem; for the *Ēli* that he uses in transcribing God's name, besides introducing into Jesus' Aramaic words a more traditional Hebrew designation for God (pp. 1052–53 above), provides a form of address that bystanders could more plausibly have misunderstood as the prophet's name *'Ēlîyâ.*[84] Some scholars argue on this score for the originality of Matt's Semitic (Hebrew) transliteration of God's name over Mark's form (15:34), but this solution faces serious objections.[85]

The approach to understanding Mark described above is problematic in my judgment and may be responding to a false problem. In part it supposes that Mark, besides preserving a few Aramaic words, is describing in Greek a scene that would make sense if readers understood the underlying Semitic language. In all probability, however, Mark was writing for readers who did

---

[83]Rehm ("Eli" 276–77) argues on the analogy of other shortened personal names that the already shortened *'Ēlîyâ* could have been further abbreviated to *'Ēlî.* See Kutscher's view in the following note.

[84]Guillaume ("Mt. xxvii") carries this further when he argues that the first person possessive suffix on "my God," although written *iy* (transcribed *î*), was actually pronounced *iya* like the ancient Semitic suffix written that way. This view has been challenged by E. Kutscher, *The Language and Linguistic Background of the Isaiah Scroll* (1Q Isaᵃ) (Studies on the Texts of the Desert of Judah 6; Leiden: Brill, 1964), 181–82. Kutscher's own explanation of the Matthean text is that Elijah's name was pronounced *'Ēlî,* as in Jewish inscriptions in Rome.

[85]E.g., how then does one explain Mark's wording? It becomes necessary to posit that someone (Mark or a later copyist) changed *Ēli,* the Hebrew transliteration that was more original (whether he found it in Matt or in a preMarcan tradition), and made more sense as a basis for the Elijah misunderstanding, to the Aramaic transliteration one now finds in Mark, namely *Elōi.* Why? Was it on the principle that Mark always uses Aramaic transliterations? I find such an approach implausible: Someone (Mark or a copyist) who knew that much Semitic would have been perceptive enough to realize that he was producing a mess in regard to the Elijah misunderstanding.

not know Semitic. After all, he regularly translated Aramaic words for them and in 7:3–4 felt compelled to explain some elementary Jewish customs. If one remains on the level of the Greek, readers would have had little problem understanding Mark's scene (so also L. Schenke and Brower). Having heard in exotic Aramaic Jesus' words "*Elōi . . .* ," and having been told that this was misunderstood by hostile Jewish bystanders as an appeal to *Ēlias* (Greek transcription for "Elijah"), they would have assumed that the Semitic under-lying the Greek form of the prophet's name was close to the transliterated Aramaic *Elōi* that Jesus used. That is what hearers of Mark's Gospel who know no Aramaic have been doing ever since.

Whether Mark himself knew that the Semitic form of the prophet's name was not like Jesus' Aramaic for "My God" we do not know, for it is not clear that Mark could read or understand either Aramaic or Hebrew.[86] Therefore Mark may not have realized that to any reader who knew Semitic his *Elōi* transliteration could not be confused with *Elias,* the name of the prophet Elijah. Matt, who seemingly did know the Semitic languages, probably saw the problem and that is why he changed the name of the divinity to (translit-erated) Hebrew *Ēli,* which could more easily have been confused.

If the call for the coming of Elijah did not originate on the Semitic level of the tradition from a genuine misunderstanding of the name of God, how did that element arise and what function did it have as a separate component in the death narrative? An important factor is that the expectation of the coming of Elijah fits into the Marcan series of apocalyptic events sur-rounding Jesus' death, namely, the loud cry, darkness over the whole earth, rending of the veil of the Temple sanctuary. (The list is longer in Matt: earth-quake[s], opening of tombs, rising of the saintly dead.) Elijah was very prominent in popular expectations of the endtimes, as miracle worker in time of mortal need, as forerunner of the God's coming, as anointer of the Mes-siah.[87] (Probably all these were related to the last prediction in the prophetic books: "Behold I will send you Elijah the prophet before the day of the Lord comes, the great and terrible day" [Mal 3:23, or 4:5 in the RSV].) One may

[86]The fact that Mark preserved a few Aramaic words does not answer this question. One of his six Aramaic transliterations (n. 62 above) is a place name; two are healing formulas that would have been memorized by Greek-speaking Christians in Aramaic (since they were probably thought to have healing power as exotic words); two others are prayer formulas. To give an example of how one can parrot formulas from another language that one does not speak or read, when the Latin Mass was being celebrated, ordinary English-speaking Roman Catholics could use and understand *Dominus vobiscum* without knowing Latin. Similarly, many of today's Jews would know some basic Hebrew prayer formulas without having the ability to speak or read Hebrew.

[87]See Cohn-Sherbok, "Jesus' Cry"; Gnilka, "Mein Gott." A *baraita* or older tradition in TalBab *Baba Qamma* 60b says, "When dogs howl, the angel of death has come to the city; if the dogs frolic, Elijah the prophet has come to the city." TalBab *Aboda Zara* 17b and 18b connect Elijah and deliverance from the Romans.

object, however, that the coming of Elijah cannot be associated with the other apocalyptic signs surrounding Jesus' death because the others are described as happening while the Elijah expectation is a misunderstanding. Yet we remember that the Elijah expectation has been presented as a misunderstanding before, precisely in relation to the suffering of the Son of Man and the resurrection of the dead (Mark 9:9–13; Matt 17:9–13): "Why do the scribes say that Elijah must come first?" To which Jesus replied, "I tell you that Elijah has come." (Matt adds that they did not know him—so also the Son of Man will suffer at their hands.) On the cross, when the Son of Man is finally suffering his fate, Mark/Matt show a series of signs foretold by the prophets for the last times, but the only response of the bystanders is to repeat the misunderstanding about Elijah (whereas, as Brower, "Elijah," insists, the readers know that Elijah has come as JBap). Although they have seen the darkness and heard the loud cry of Jesus, they interpret him as crying out to Elijah.[88] They turn the expected coming of Elijah into mockery of Jesus: "Let us see if Elijah comes to take him down" (Mark 15:36b), even as a few hours before they had derided Jesus, "Come down now from the cross" (15:32; see 15:31). Matt increases the hostility of the mockery by having some of those standing there employ the contemptuous *houtos* in reference to Jesus: "This fellow is crying to Elijah" (27:47). The wording they use to cast doubt on Jesus is: "Let us see if Elijah comes saving him" (27:49), echoing an earlier mockery directed to Jesus, "Save yourself, if you are Son of God" (27:40; also 27:42: "Himself he cannot save"). Ironically, while Elijah will not intervene on Jesus' side, soon God will, and in a very visible way that all shall see.

SECOND, the offering of vinegary wine. We have already discussed the offering of vinegary wine (*oxos*) as an echo of Ps 69:22; but now we must be concerned with the storyline in Mark 15:36; Matt 27:48–49; and *GPet* 5:16–17. All the accounts suppose that there was vinegary wine at hand (John 19:29 will make that explicit: "A jar was there laden with vinegary wine"). That is not implausible since *oxos* is Greek for the *posca* or red peasant wine drunk by Roman soldiers (MM 452–53). In itself the offering of *oxos* to Jesus need not have been hostile, for vinegary wine is implicitly a desirable drink in Num 6:3 and Ruth 2:14. Plutarch, in his life of Cato Maior (1.7) says, "Water was what he drank on campaigns, but occasionally in a raging thirst he would request vinegary wine."[89] Nevertheless, the context in Mark makes it likely that the wine offering was not a friendly gesture.

---

[88] The noun *phonē* is used to describe Jesus' cry in Mark 15:34; the verb *phonein* is used in 15:35: "He is *crying* to Elijah." Although some have understood the latter to mean "He is calling for Elijah," that would normally require *prosphonein*.

[89] For other references, see Colin, "Soldato" 105.

If Mark is echoing the use of *oxos* in Ps 69:22, he is recalling how the just one was given bitter food by his enemies. The accompanying sarcastic skepticism about waiting to see if Elijah would come to take Jesus down (Mark 15:36b) suggests mockery. But the scene is very complicated. Who is the "someone" who runs to get the vinegary wine? The fact that this wine is a soldier's drink, and that Luke explicitly has soldiers offer the wine, has caused many commentators to suppose that Mark means a Roman soldier,[90] only to point how unlikely it would be for a Roman soldier to know about Elijah. This identification may be a false track, for the inner logic of the Marcan narrative suggests that the "someone" is one of the bystanders mentioned in the previous verse. The objection that the Roman soldiers who normally guarded the crucified and kept away sympathizers would not have allowed such a gesture supposes what is not clear, namely, that the gesture was sympathetic. Still it becomes complicated when this same "someone" speaks and says, *"Aphete.* Let us see if Elijah comes to take him down."[91] What is the connection between the "someone's" action of offering wine and what he says? *The speaker seems to be offering a reason for giving Jesus a drink.* The force of *aphete* would normally be "Let him be" or "Leave him alone"; but whom would the "someone" be stopping since he is the only one who is acting? Are we to suppose some unmentioned hostile movement on the part of the other bystanders which the "someone" is forestalling by offering *oxos*? In that case the offering is meant to revive Jesus lest he die too soon, before they had a chance to see whether Elijah will come. (Vinegary wine could certainly revive; for, as Colin, "Soldato" 128, points out, the acrid odor of the vinegar under the condemned's nose would have that effect.) Or is the "someone," who is embarrassed at being seen doing something good for Jesus, trying to pretend that he is on the side of the skeptical bystanders? That, however, may be to construct too complicated a scenario. *Aphete* is sometimes simply a rough intensive, serving virtually as an auxiliary verb to an imperative, as in Mark 10:14: "Let the children come to me." The meaning here would then be, *"Do* let us see . . . ,"[92] and perhaps one would not be expected to press the issue of how the wine drink would ac-

---

[90]Veale ("Merciful") bases this supposition on combining Mark and John. Metzger ("Names" 95) reports that in Codex Egberti (10th cent.) the one who offered the wine is given the name Stephaton.

[91]Lee ("Two" 36) would have the bystanders speak by (implausibly) supposing that Mark was composed in Semitic and that the final *waw* of the plural form *'mrw* was lost by haplography, being mistaken for the initial *nun* of the jussive underlying "Leave." Such erudite improvements on Mark go back to antiquity, for the Syriac versions of 15:36 read a plural for "saying," instead of the very well attested singular.

[92]MGNTG 1.175. Taylor (*Mark* 595) opts for this, and Moffatt's translation is close: "Come on, let us see."

complish the speaker's goal. I have left the translation of Mark 15:36b literal to show the problem.

Here again Matt, who changed Mark's *Elōi* to *Ēli,* presumably because he recognized that it would not easily be confused with the name of the prophet Elijah, tries to straighten out the storyline he found in Mark. In 27:48 he makes it clear that the one who runs to get the wine is one of those standing there who thought Jesus was crying for Elijah (and thus consciously or unconsciously prevents the Roman-soldier interpretation). The runner is no longer the speaker; rather "the rest said." *The speakers are offering a reason not to give Jesus a drink.* Accordingly now the *aphete* can be translated literally, "Let (him [= Jesus] be)." The other (Jewish) observers think that the volunteer wine-offerer is distractingly interfering or even doing something hostile to Jesus (echoing the hostile atmosphere of Ps 69:22 that Matt's mention of gall in 27:34 shows the evangelist had in mind) and perhaps trying to hasten Jesus' death.[93] They want Jesus left alone to linger long enough for them to see if his prayer to Elijah is answered.

GPet 5:16 is closer to Matt in presenting a smooth storyline. One of the Jews responsible for crucifying Jesus (no Roman soldiers have been mentioned) proposes to maltreat Jesus by giving him to drink gall with vinegary wine. There is no ambiguity about the malevolent goal of the *oxos* since gall is the first-mentioned element. This mixture, clearly evocative of Ps 69:22, the Jews themselves mix. Accordingly *GPet* 5:17 passes a condemnatory judgment on them: "And they fulfilled all things [i.e., the Scriptures about maltreating the just] and completed the(ir) sins on their own head." This is another instance of the antiJewish sentiment that is much more prominent in *GPet* than in the canonical Gospels.

Before we leave the discussion in Mark/Matt, we should notice *an additional line at the end of Matt 27:49* found in some important textual witnesses (Codices Vaticanus and Sinaiticus, the Irish-British family of Latin mss., Harclean Syriac, and Chrysostom): "But another, having taken a lance, stabbed at his side, and there came out water and blood." Pennells ("Spear") argues for the genuineness of this text. It would lead into 27:50, where Jesus shouts out with a loud cry and expires. Pennells thinks that embarrassment at the picture of Jesus shouting when he was stabbed and dying of a spear wound led to suppression of the passage or its transfer to after Jesus' death, as in John 19:34. Most textual critics, however, have judged that it was an erudite Alexandrian addition to Matt copied from John 19:34 (with which it shares ten words out of thirteen): "One of the soldiers stabbed his side with

---

[93]Taylor (*Mark* 596) calls attention to Goguel's evidence for a belief that the death of a crucified person was hastened by drinking.

a lance, and immediately there came out blood and water." Presumably the Johannine passage was copied into the margin of a ms. of Matt and then subsequently introduced into the text, even though it is not totally clear why a copyist introducing a Johannine vignette into Matt would have moved this episode from after the death of Jesus, where John had it, to before the death.[94] However, the situation may have been more complex. In the early 14th cent. (Council of Vienne, Pope Clement V) because of the importance of the water and blood as symbols for baptism and eucharist, there was a dispute as to whether they came from Christ before or after his death. The Spiritual Franciscans supported the Matthean pre-death order, with Ubertino da Casale citing a Latin ms. that was seemingly at Paris and independent of the Irish-British family. Burkitt finds evidence for the Matthean reading in an epistle of Jerome to Pope Damasus. An 11th-cent. minuscule (72) Gospel in the British Museum (Harley 5647) has a scholion claiming that Tatian supported it—that would bring the Matthean addendum back to the 2d cent. before the likelihood of Alexandrian improvement. There has been a learned dispute concerning whether Tatian introduced the lance blow of John 19:34 into his consecutive harmony before the death of Jesus (even though that positioning would contradict John's explicit indication that Jesus was dead and is not supported by one of our chief guides to Tatian's harmony, i.e., Ephraem's commentary) and so was responsible for the idea that gave rise to the Matthean addendum. On all this see the articles in §37, Part 8, by Burkitt ("Ubertino"), Pennells, Vogels, and van Kasteren; the last-mentioned thinks that the Matthean addendum predated Tatian. While there is little chance that the addendum was originally part of Matt, its very existence in mss. of Matt is a testimony to how early Christians harmonized the Gospel accounts of the passion.

JESUS' DEATH CRY IN LUKE 23:46

From the complications surrounding the death scream in Mark/Matt, we turn to the simpler Lucan account. The vinegary wine offering has been moved earlier (Luke 23:36); Elijah is not mentioned;[95] and only the death cry itself is recounted: "Father, into your hands I place my spirit."

---

[94]Another minor difference is that John mentions "blood and water" while the Matthean addendum has "water and blood." Was that change effected in Matt under the influence of I John 5:6, "Jesus Christ came . . . by water and blood"?

[95]Büchele (*Tod* 52–53) argues that Luke eliminated the call for Elijah because in Luke's mind Jesus himself had the Elijah role (so also Bornkamm, Conzelmann, Schreiber). That is not so clear; after all, a Lucan reference to the coming of Elijah here would have been an inclusion with the role of JBap as Elijah at the Gospel's beginning (1:17). The thesis that Luke suppressed the Elijah episode because it did not fit his portrayal of Jesus as a martyr (W. Robinson, Schneider) would seem to

Although the Lucan cry differs totally in wording from the Marcan cry, there is good reason to think that Luke is editing the Marcan account. Before the death of Jesus Luke groups the darkness over the whole earth and the rending of the sanctuary veil (see p. 1038 above). These two negative apocalyptic signs, taken over by Luke from Mark, symbolize God's judgment on those who have mocked Jesus in 23:35b–39. Jesus' last words (23:46) are connected to these signs by an "and"—in response to them he cries out to his Father his words of trust and dies without apprehension. Just as at the beginning of the PN Luke omitted the passage where the Marcan Jesus began to be greatly distraught and troubled, expressing himself in the adapted language of Ps 42:6 ("My soul is very sorrowful unto death"), so at the end of the PN Luke excises the Marcan Jesus' desperate cry of abandonment from Ps 22:2. Luke's motive in this excision is primarily theological; he is also being consistent with his standard editorial policies by not reporting Mark's Aramaic wording from Ps 22:2 and by having only one loud cry, contrasted with Mark's two (even as he had only one cockcrow contrasted with Mark's two).[96]

As for wording, the softening of Mark's portrayal begins already with Luke's preference for the verb "to cry out" (*phōnein*) over Mark's "to scream" (*boan*). The latter is too violent an action to be attributed to the Lucan Jesus.[97] Luke follows Mark's lead in having the dying Jesus pray in the language of the psalter but chooses Ps 31:6 over 22:2. The Lucan wording is identical with the LXX of the psalm ("Into your hands I shall place my spirit") except that the form of the verb (*paratithenai*) has been changed from the future to the present and "Father" has been made part of the citation.[98] The psalmist in Ps 31 is praying for deliverance from his enemies and their snares—praying with assurance, for the cited verse continues: "You have redeemed me, O Lord." Deliverance from hostile enemies is also the theme in Ps 22 cited by the Marcan Jesus; but Mark has attributed to Jesus

---

depend on reading the episode positively as if the participants wanted Elijah to help Jesus. If they made the reference to Elijah in mockery, the episode would fit very well into a martyr presentation. More simply Luke may have omitted the reference because he could not see how Mark could derive a call to Elijah from Jesus' citation of the psalm.

[96]Even one "loud cry" (*phōnē megalē*) is adventurous for Luke. Jesus, who has prayed often, has never prayed before with such vehemence, for hitherto a "loud cry" has been the mark of exclamations by demons, a leper, the multitude of the disciples, and the enemies of Jesus. Yet words from the *phōn*- root are not strange to the Lucan PN (22:60,61; 23:20,21,23), and greater emphasis is appropriate for Jesus' last word.

[97]The cognate combination "to cry out with a loud cry" occurs also in Acts 16:28 in reference to Paul.

[98]The verb *paratithenai* means "to place toward, place beside, commit." Abramowski and Goodman ("Luke xxiii") describe discussions among Syriac-speakers (Nestorians, Ephraem) on how to translate it, preferring for dogmatic reasons "to commend" rather than "to lay down." As for "Father," the inclusion of a direct address may have been catalyzed by "O Lord" in the second line of the psalm verse.

the most desperate verse of that psalm, while Luke has attributed to him a trusting verse. We have heard in Luke of the scribes and chief priests seeking to lay "hands" on Jesus (20:19; see 22:53), and Jesus predicted that the Son of Man would be "given over" (*paradidonai*) into the "hands" of sinful men (9:44; see 24:7); but the denouement of the PN comes when Jesus proclaims that it is into the "hands" of the Father himself that he "places over" (*parati-thenai*) his spirit, i.e., all that he is and has. "Spirit" is not simply a partial component of the human being (as in "soul" and body); it is the living self or life power that goes beyond death. In Jesus' case, however, "spirit" goes beyond the usual anthropological definitions, for he was conceived by the Spirit that came upon Mary (Luke 1:35), and at his baptism the Holy Spirit descended upon him in a bodily form (3:22), so that he was full of the Holy Spirit (4:1) and moved about Palestine in the power of the Spirit (4:14). When Jesus "places over" his spirit to the Father, he is bringing round to its place of origin his life and mission.[99]

If Luke has dramatically shifted the theological tone of the death scene by preferring Ps 31:6 for Jesus' last words over Mark's Ps 22:2, another significant shift is visible when we compare the Marcan Jesus' address "My God" to the Lucan Jesus' "Father" (also Luke 10:21; 11:2), an address by which the psalm citation has been personalized. In part Luke's choice here of "Father" is by way of inclusion with the first words of Jesus in Luke 2:49: "Did you not know that I must be in my *Father's* house." By comparison with Mark's PN, however, there is another inclusion. The movement in the Marcan Jesus' prayer from the opening scene in Gethsemane, where he used "Father" (14:36), to the dying scene, where he uses "My God" (15:34), is one of increased alienation. But the Lucan Jesus has been utterly consistent throughout the PN, praying to "Father" at the beginning on the Mount of Olives (22:42) and to "Father" at the end at the crucifixion place named Skull. Indeed, within the Lucan crucifixion account there is still another in-clusion: At the very moment he was being crucified, Jesus prayed "Father" (23:34) even as he does at the moment he dies on that cross—two prayers peculiar to the Lucan Jesus.

Luke is taking great care in describing the death of Jesus so that this pic-ture will be impressed on the minds of his readers who would be followers of Jesus: As they come to die, their sentiments must imitate the sentiments of their master when he faced death. In Acts 7:59–60 Stephen, the first Christian martyr, will be described as shouting (*krazein*) with "a loud cry," having said, "Lord Jesus, receive my spirit." The effectiveness of Luke's les-son is seen a half-century or more later in Justin, *Dialogue* 105: "Hence God

---

[99]Feldkämper (*Betende* 277–79) is very helpful on these points.

also teaches us by His Son that we should struggle [*agōnizesthai;* see *agōnia* in Luke 22:44] in all ways to become righteous and at our departure [*exodos;* Luke 9:31] to ask that our souls may not fall under any such [evil] power. For when Christ was giving out [*apodidonai*] his spirit on the cross, he said, 'Father, into your hands I place my spirit.' This also have I learned from the memoirs."

Some would see another symbolism here, drawing upon the later-attested Jewish custom of reciting Ps 31:6 at evening prayer.[100] Assuming that this custom was already in vogue, Hendrickx (*Passion* 123) writes imaginatively: "Jesus who died at the ninth hour (three o'clock in the afternoon) recited this prayer at the moment the trumpets were sounded for the evening prayer, the end of which was precisely 'Into your hands I commit my spirit.' Joining the people in their evening prayer, Jesus expressed his confidence and certainty that his death was only a 'going to sleep,' and therefore the beginning of life with the Father." I doubt that: The date when the psalm began to be used as evening prayer is uncertain; the Lucan portrait of Jesus crying out with a loud cry scarcely suggests evening prayer; and even in Luke there are apocalyptic signs that militate against thinking of Jesus' death as only a "going to sleep." After all, the Lucan Jesus proclaimed this whole period as the hour of his enemies and "the power of darkness" (22:53). Jesus' death prayer confidently proclaims that the power of darkness has not been able to separate him from his Father. When he is seen again after his death, he clearly speaks from the realm of his Father: "I send the promise of my Father upon you" (24:49; Acts 1:4; see Acts 1:7). And when he shall come back as the Son of Man at the end, he will come "in the glory of the Father" (Luke 9:26).

JESUS' LAST WORDS AND THE WINE OFFERING IN JOHN 19:28–30A

John's account (Episode 4 in the structural outline on p. 908 above) is longer than Luke's but shorter than Mark/Matt's. Although there are obscurities in it because of the double reference to being finished, it has a straightforward storyline when compared to the obscurities of Mark/Matt. By way of simplification John lacks the Synoptic crucifixion time-indicators (sixth, ninth hours) and apocalyptic elements (darkness, loud cry, rending of sanctuary veil, earthquake); on the positive side John integrates closely the offering of vinegary wine into the echo of a psalm. The theological outlook, as we shall see, is typically Johannine.

Before we comment on the individual verses in detail, a glance at the

---

[100]For references see St-B 2.269. TalBab *Berakot* 5a reports the dictum of Abaye that at bedtime even a scholar should recite one verse of supplication, e.g., "Into your hand I place my spirit; you have redeemed me, O Lord, God of truth."

overall arrangement of the episode would be useful. This episode begins in 19:28a with the assurance that "already all was finished [*tetelestai, from telein*]." Then (19:28b) after a statement of thirst made by Jesus "in order that the Scripture be completed [*teleiōthē, from teleioun*]," there is in 19:29 an offering of vinegary wine. In 19:30a when Jesus takes it, he affirms, "It is finished [*tetelestai*]." It might seem illogical to have three separate indicators involving finishing, completing, and finishing; but what happens here is interrelated, and John wants to be massively insistent on how Jesus dies only after he has terminated what he came to do.

"After this, Jesus having known that already all was finished" (19:28a). The episode opens with a stereotyped Johannine phrase "After this," that indicates logical and sometimes chronological sequence (BGJ 1.112). The clause "Jesus having known" is a bit awkward;[101] and one is tempted to translate it as "having realized" or "having become aware," so that a particular incident or action might be identified as leading Jesus to this perception. Yet it is dubious that John would have wanted to present Jesus as learning anything, for whatever the Johannine Jesus does or says flows from what he saw with the Father before his incarnation and, indeed, before the world began (5:19; 8:28; 17:5). John is letting the reader know what Jesus already knew.

Indeed, the atemporality of Jesus' knowledge (that serves as a key to understanding the thrust of what he knows, i.e., "that already all was finished") is illustrated by two other passages in John with which the present passage forms an inclusion. The lifting up of Jesus on the cross is the keynote of the second part of John, which many call "The Book of Glory" (BGJ 1.cxxxviii; 2.541–42). That Book begins in 13:1: "Before the feast of Passover, Jesus, having known that the hour had come for him to pass from this world to the Father. . . ." Both 13:1 and 19:28a have a temporal reference that leads up to the "Jesus having known"; what is known in each case has a finality; yet some six chapters of activity separate them. Part of the solution is that the opening of the Last Supper and the death of Jesus on the cross are all part of the same "hour." Intermediate between them is 18:4, a transitional verse from the supper to the passion-crucifixion: "So Jesus, having known all the things to come upon him. . . ." The "So" is implicitly a temporal reference since it is consequent to Jesus' having come out from the supper to the garden across the Kidron and to Judas' having brought out assembled forces against him. Once more Jesus has known this and all that will follow—a

---

[101]There is varied word order in the better textual witnesses that support *eidōs*, "having known," over against *idōn*, "having seen," of the Koine tradition. In what follows "already" is missing in some witnesses and appears in varying sequence in others. Evidently the early copyists saw some of the difficulties explained above.

portrait perfectly in harmony with the leitmotif of the Johannine passion that Jesus is in control: "I lay down my life . . . I lay it down of my own accord" (10:17–18). In all three instances the participle "having known" comes at a crucial moment in the progress of the action where the reader might need assurance that Jesus was in control. The participle is phrased in terms of what has happened but leads into something significant that is about to happen.

If there is temporal development, in John that comes not in Jesus' knowledge but in whatever has occurred or is occurring to enable the report "already all was finished." The "all" (*panta*) is neuter plural and (at least, in part[102]) has to refer to all that God gave Jesus to do: "The Father loves the Son and has given all [*panta*] into his hand" (3:35; also 5:17,20; 6:37,39). Taken together, the opening phrases of 19:28a, "After this . . . already all was finished," must include a reference to the preceding episode where Jesus constituted his mother and the disciple whom he loved into a new family relationship (pp. 1025–26 above) and made them a "his own" who were empowered to become God's children—thus fulfilling the Prologue's stated purpose for the Word's becoming flesh (1:12).[103]

Yet previous instances of the expression "Jesus having known" have led into what follows. And so we must allow the likelihood that "all was finished" (19:28a) goes beyond Jesus' action in the preceding episode and includes the completion of Scripture about to be narrated in 19:28b–29. That likelihood is increased by the second use of "finished" in 19:30a, forming an inclusion that covers what occurs between. True, the verb "to finish" (*telein*) occurs only here (19:28a,30a) in John, and so there is no Johannine precedent for its including Scripture fulfillment. Yet *telein* is used elsewhere in the NT for the death of Jesus as fulfilling the prophets (Luke 18:31; 22:37; Acts 13:29), and certainly in John the crucifixion of Jesus echoes themes in Scripture. John 3:14 affirmed that just as Moses lifted up the serpent in the desert, so must the Son of Man be lifted up. This "lifting up," an image twice more applied to the Son of Man in John (8:28; 12:32–34, with the latter specifically referring to the kind of death Jesus would die), is the language used for the fate of the Suffering Servant in Isa 52:13. One may also make a case that the Johannine language for Jesus' laying down his life (*psychē*) in 10:11,15,17–18 stems from Isa 53:10 with its reference to the Servant's

---

[102]The "in part" allows for the scholarly dispute whether the object in the finishing is on the christological plane (Becker) or on the biblical plane, or on both planes. See the careful discussion in Bergmeier, "TETELESTAI."

[103]In Exod 40:33, at the conclusion of the building of the tabernacle, we read: "Moses finished [*syntelein*] all the works"; thus there is biblical precedent for God's chosen instrument "finishing" the work God gave him to do.

giving his life (*psychē*) as an offering for sin.[104] In summary, there is no major obstacle to giving "all was finished" a double content, referring back to the previous episode when Jesus, lifted up, began drawing to himself disciples as he had promised (12:32) and referring forward to the completion of Scripture that is about to take place.

"In order that the Scripture be completed, (he) says, 'I thirst' " (19:28b). The interpretation just offered brings this purpose clause into close relationship with the first half of the verse as part of what was finished.[105] The verb "to complete" is *teleioun,* applied to Scripture only here in John, who normally employs *plēroun,* ("to fulfill") for Scripture, as in 12:38; 13:18; 15:25; 17:12; 19:24. Accordingly Bergmeier ("*TETELESTAI*" 284) and others ask if *teleioun* did not come to John from a preGospel source. But I would judge that the use of the verb here is deliberately Johannine. First, *teleioun* is from the same stem as *telein* and so lexicographically helps to show that Scripture completion is part of Jesus' finishing all things. Second, *teleioun* has been used previously in John for Jesus' completing the work that the Father gave him to do (4:34; 5:36; 17:4) and so makes clear that Jesus' finishing all things also includes his christological task. Third, *teleioun* is more appropriate than *plēroun* for this particular reference to Scripture because this is the final fulfillment, the *telos,* the end.[106]

In this interpretation the *hina* ("in order that") clause, as to be expected in Greek grammar, is governed by the preceding verb form(s) ("having known . . . was finished"). There remains the issue of the relationship of that clause to what follows. Important grammars (BDF §478; MGNTG 3.344) cite this as an example of where the final clause precedes the main clause so that the fulfillment of Scripture is related to Jesus' saying "I thirst." This additional relationship where *hina* points forward as well as backward is favored by the realization that the subject "Jesus" and the main verb "says" encompass between them all the clauses we have been discussing. The main objection to having the *hina* clause point forward is that what Jesus says is not an explicit citation from Scripture. Is it an implicit citation? Since the immediate response to it is the offering of vinegary wine, many think of Ps 69:22, "For *my thirst* they gave me to drink vinegar." That would mean that despite the phrasing "in order that the Scripture be completed, (Jesus) says,

---

[104]Mark 10:45 would have the Son of Man give his life (*psychē*) as a ransom for many, and so this employment of Isaian language is probably preGospel in its origins.

[105]Yet because I think the purpose clause also points to what follows, I would not agree with a translation that relates "finished" with "in order that" so closely as does O. M. Norlie, *Simplified New Testament* (Grand Rapids: Zondervan, 1961): "Jesus, knowing that everything had been done [*tetelestai*] to fulfill the Scriptures, said . . ."

[106]*Telos* occurs in 13:1, which we have already noted as an inclusive parallel to 19:28a (p. 1070 above): "He now showed his love for them to the very *end.*"

'I thirst,'" the scriptural element is not in Jesus' words but in the response they provoke. We shall see below, however, doubts that John presents this offering as mockery. Accordingly while a reference to Ps 69 may have existed on a preGospel level for the wine offering and may still be discreetly present in the *reaction* to Jesus' "I thirst," we need to discuss further whether there is not also (or, indeed, primarily) a scriptural element in the thirst itself expressed by Jesus.[107]

What Scripture passage could John have had in mind in the "I thirst"? Worth consideration is the possibility that John was familiar with the tradition that the dying Jesus prayed in the language of Ps 22:2, "My God, my God, for what reason have you forsaken me?" a tradition that Mark took over into his Gospel. At the beginning of the PN John seems to have known the prayer tradition also taken over by Mark wherein Jesus asked his Father "that, if it is possible, the hour might pass from him" (Mark 14:35). The attribution of that sentiment to Jesus was irreconcilable with Johannine christology; and so elsewhere in the Fourth Gospel we find a scene that constitutes a commentary on it by having Jesus refuse to pray such a prayer and substitute another: "And what should I say? Father, save me from this hour? But for this (purpose) have I come to this hour. Father, glorify your name" (12:27–28). Similarly here the theme of Ps 22:2 which has Jesus forsaken by God would be irreconcilable with Johannine christology. (We find virtually a corrective commentary on it elsewhere in the Fourth Gospel: "I am never alone because the Father is with me" [16:32].) Has John substituted for it by appealing to another verse in Ps 22, namely "Dried up like baked clay is my strength [or throat]; my tongue cleaves to my jaws; You have brought me down to the dust of death" (22:16)? While thirst is not mentioned in the verse, clearly the sufferer suffers from it to the point of death.

Why would John not have quoted Ps 22:16 literally if that was what he had in mind? A possible answer is that the reluctant psalmist is accusing God of having brought him to this situation, while John sees Jesus as the master of his fate. Jesus' stating "I thirst" just before he dies may mean that he is deliberately fulfilling the situation envisaged in the psalm, an impression harmonious with his affirmation in 10:17–18 that he lays down his own life and no one takes it from him. It would also make Jesus responsible for the reaction in terms of the offering of vinegary wine and any Scripture fulfillment in that action (perhaps Ps 69:22 and, in addition, the Passover

---

[107]Jesus on the cross could indeed have been thirsty, but surely John is not disinterestedly describing a factual thirst. In seeking symbolism some would find a connection to the words that Jesus spoke at an earlier noontime to the Samaritan woman, "Give me to drink" (4:6–7). In my judgment the relationship is too obscure to be helpful.

lamb motif—see below). This proposal of Ps 22:16 as the referential point of John 19:28b is speculative but is in harmony with Johannine patterns and thought. Other candidates have been suggested;[108] but a primary reference to Ps 22, followed by a possible secondary reference to Ps 69, would mean that John has adapted to his christology the psalms we know other Christians and evangelists were thinking of. To the scriptural background one should add another note of Johannine christology. At the beginning of the PN, instead of having Jesus pray that the Father might take the cup of suffering from him (as in Mark 14:36), John portrayed Jesus as rebuking Peter for drawing his sword to resist the arresting party: "The cup the Father has given me—am I not to drink it?" (John 18:11). "I thirst" in 19:28b shows that same determination to drink the cup.

Offering of Vinegary Wine on Hyssop (19:29). The Johannine vignette of this action differs from the Synoptic accounts[109] in some significant ways. In Mark/Matt (with varying clarity) a Jewish bystander fills the sponge with vinegary wine and offers it to Jesus on a reed in a mockery somehow connected with Jesus' calling upon Elijah. We are not told how he got the wine, which was often associated with Roman soldiers, or had handy a suitable reed. In Luke (earlier and not as part of the death scene) Roman soldiers came forward and offered the wine in mockery of the King of the Jews.[110] Soldiers would have had both the wine and a lance to put the sponge filled with it up to Jesus' lips; but Luke is silent about all that. John takes the trouble to explain that a jar was there laden with vinegary wine. The "they" who fill a sponge with that wine are not specified. The last dramatis personae mentioned were Jesus' mother and the beloved disciple, but 19:27 seems to put a terminus to the mother's involvement in the scene. Consequently almost all commentators have assumed that readers are to think of the Roman soldiers who were active in 19:23–24 and who would have had access to both the wine and Jesus. Obviously only one of the soldiers would have brought the wine to Jesus' lips, so that the "they" include those who sug-

---

[108]Bornhäuser (*Death* 153), Hoskyns (*John* 531), Beutler ("Psalm" 54–56), and Witkamp ("Jesus") suggest Ps 42:3, "My soul [i.e., I] thirsts for God, the living God." Another candidate is Ps 63:2: "O God (you are) my God whom I seek; for you my flesh pines and *my soul thirsts*." One cannot exclude these possibilities, especially since John may have had a collective sense of completing Scripture. Bampfylde ("John") argues that the Scripture is Zech 14:8 (in conjunction with Ezek 47), which underlay John 7:38: "As the Scripture says, 'From within him shall flow rivers of living water'" (see BGJ 1.320–23). There is great likelihood that some form of this last proposal is applicable to John 19:34 (although what precise Scripture underlies John 7:38 is disputable) but much less likelihood that it is appropriate here.

[109]The parallel is clearly between John and the second Mark/Matt offering consisting of *oxos*. For my estimate of Freed's strange view that John is offering an interpretation of Mark's first offering, see BGJ 2.928.

[110]Interestingly, although Luke and John differ in many ways in describing their one offering of wine (*oxos*), they both use the verb *prospherein* ("to bring forward") to describe the action.

gested the idea and helped. These military men would have been capable of mockery, for in the midst of the trial before Pilate Roman soldiers mocked Jesus (19:2–3). In the more recent scene (19:23–24), however, they were simply carrying out the customary treatment of the criminal without any special brutality. Nothing in 19:29 suggests mockery; rather the soldiers seem to be responding spontaneously to Jesus' request for a drink. (See p. 1063 above for *oxos,* "vinegary wine," as a thirst-quenching drink.) In 19:23–24 John reported that the soldiers divided Jesus' clothes in the manner in which they did "in order that the Scripture be fulfilled"—an indication that even though they may not have known it, they came under the direction of Jesus who was orchestrating the passion as part of laying down his own life. Their response to his statement of thirst comes under the same orchestration, as we shall see.

The truly puzzling item in the Johannine picture is the indication that the sponge laden with wine is put on hyssop. Mark/Matt mention a reed, presumably a long, strong stalk; Luke and *GPet* mention no instrument for reaching Jesus' mouth.[111] What does John mean by "hyssop"? On a wider scale it is not easy to be certain what the Bible means by "hyssop."[112] Hyssop is a plant of the labiate family, related to mint and thyme; but "true" hyssop known to Europeans (*Hyssopus officinalis L.*) does not grow in Palestine. Biblical descriptions of hyssop (Heb. *'ēzōb;* Gr. *hyssōpos*) may not always refer to the same plant, e.g., it can be portrayed as a small bushy plant that can grow out of cracks in the walls, a plant that I Kings 4:33 implies is the humblest of shrubs. As for the hyssop associated with Passover and sprinkling, most think of *Origanum Maru L.* or Syrian marjoram,[113] a shrub that reaches about a yard in height, with a relatively large stem and branches with leaves and flowers that are highly absorptive and thus suitable for sprinkling (Lev 14:4–7; Num 19:18). Nothing in the biblical accounts suggests that this hyssop could bear the weight of a soaked sponge. In varying ways scholars seek to avoid this difficulty and to justify the accuracy of the Johannine account.[114]

---

[111]Part of the difference among those writings may stem from a different image of how high the cross was. The *crux humilis* was about seven feet high. Is John thinking of the higher *crux sublimis?*

[112]Already the rabbis disputed what was meant by hyssop in the Mishna; in TalBab *Šabbat* 109b the two candidates proposed are artemisia and marjoram, with the latter favored.

[113]A number of writers (Galbiati, "Issopo" 393) distinguish two species, with the marjoram (*Origanum majorana*) as a smaller, garden variety of the plant.

[114]Some argue that the marjoram stem gets woody after a while; Nestle ("Zum Ysop") argues that a tall stalk of hyssop stood near the cross and points to a Transjordanian village with the name "House of Hyssop" (Josephus, *War* 6.3.4; #201). Still, most doubt that it would be sufficiently stiff. Milligan ("St. John's" 29) raises the possibility that both in OT references and here a bunch of hyssop was tied to a rod; yet there would scarcely have been such a prepared instrument at the place of crucifixion, and the spontaneity of the action does not allow for the preparation of one. Others suggest that in this instance "hyssop" refers to *Sorgum vulgare L.,* which can grow to six feet in

Influenced by Matt 27:34 ("wine [*oinos*] mixed with gall") a few scribes and church writers (Eusebius, Hilary, Nonnus, and Chrysostom) read John 19:29 to mean that the hyssop was mixed with the wine.[115] Another ancient attempt at avoiding the difficulty has attracted much more attention: An 11th-cent. cursive ms. (476) reads *hyssos* ("javelin") for *hyssōpos*. (This can be related to the *pertica*, "pole, rod, long staff," found in some OL mss.) Without knowing this Greek ms., J. Camerarius (d. 1574) suggested this emendation; and a javelin reading has been accepted by Tischendorf, Blass, Lagrange, Bernard, and (with equivalents) by some translations (Moffatt, Goodspeed, NEB). But there are many objections: Galbiati ("Issopo" 395) contends that *hyssos* would render the Latin *pilum,* a weapon of the Roman legionaries, not of the cohort troops at Pilate's disposal. When John does speak of a spearlike weapon (19:34), he uses *logchē,* not *hyssos.* Although "javelin" makes better sense than "hyssop," MTC 253 points out correctly that *hyssos* resulted from a copyist's dropping out a syllable because of the letters that begin the next word.[116]

A much better solution is to accept the fact that John means the biblical hyssop despite the physical implausibility caused by the fragility of that plant. In treating the offerings of wine to Jesus on the cross in Mark/Matt, we saw that in the first wine offering Matt highlighted the scriptural component (possibly implicit in Mark) by changing the "wine with myrrh" of Mark 15:23 to "wine mixed with gall" (Matt 27:34), despite the implausibility of that, in order to have it match the first line of Ps 69:22 that has the suffering just one given gall by his enemies. Despite the implausibility of the hyssop as a support for the sponge, John may be effecting his own change in the offering of wine for the same purpose of echoing Scripture.[117] The most famous reference to hyssop is in Exod 12:22, which specifies that hyssop should be used to sprinkle the blood of the paschal lamb on the doorposts of the Israelite homes. This is evoked by Heb 9:18–20 to describe how the death of Jesus ratified a new covenant, reminding those addressed that Moses used hyssop to sprinkle the blood of animals in order to seal the earlier

---

length, and argue that this is the reed of Mark/Matt. This is but one of some seventeen other plants that have been proposed (see Wilkinson, "Seven" 77).

[115]Nestle, "Zum Ysop" 265, points out that hyssop served as a medicine and food component. Pliny (*Natural History* 14.19; #109) describes a drink made by throwing three ounces of Cilician hyssop into a gallon and a half of wine. Galbiati ("Issopo" 397–400) argues that the original Greek of John had both hyssop and reed (*kalamos*), with the hyssop used to bind the sponge to the reed. Then the hyssop was misunderstood as a flavoring.

[116]By haplography *hyssōpōperithentes* became *hyssōperithentes.* I find improbable the suggestion of G. Schwarz ("*Hyssōpō*") that a rare and only later-attested Aram. '*ēz* ('*izzā*') "rod" (= Mark/Matt "reed") was misread in John as '*ēzôb* "hyssop."

[117]The scribal reading mentioned above in which the vinegary wine is *mixed* with hyssop is an implicit recognition of this.

covenant. Did John introduce hyssop into the offering of wine to show Jesus fulfilling the scriptural role of the paschal lamb? Other passages that suggest a lamb role for Jesus in the Johannine PN are 19:14, where Jesus is judged at noon, the very hour when the slaughter of lambs for Passover began in the Temple area (p. 847 above); and 19:33,36, where the fact that Jesus' bones are not broken fulfills the Scripture pertinent to not breaking the bones of the paschal lamb (Exod 12:10; p. 1185 below).[118] Plausibly the reference to hyssop in John 19:29 is meant to alert readers to an inclusion with the Gospel's opening description of Jesus by JBap: "Behold, the lamb of God who takes away the sin of the world" (1:29). If so, then Jesus' having brought about that offering of wine by his "I thirst" would have both finished the work that the Father had given him to do and completed the Scriptures.

"So when he took the vinegary wine, Jesus said, 'It is finished' " (19:30a). The suggestion just made that John had a positive understanding of the offering of vinegary wine on hyssop explains not only that Jesus provoked this offering by saying, "I thirst," but also that he took the proffered wine when it was brought forward to his mouth—something mentioned only in John. In 18:11 Jesus said that he wanted to drink the cup the Father had given him; when Jesus drinks the offered wine, he has finished this commitment made at the beginning of the PN. When Jesus drinks the wine from the sponge put on *hyssop,* symbolically he is playing the scriptural role of the paschal lamb predicted at the beginning of his career, and so has finished the commitment made when the Word became flesh.

In 19:28a we heard of "Jesus, having known that already all was finished"; now in 19:30a Jesus phrases that directly, "It is finished."[119] These two *tetelestai* passages surround Jesus' saying "I thirst." A parallel pattern exists with the loud cry in Mark 15:34 and 15:37 surrounding Jesus' saying "My God, my God, for what reason have you forsaken me?" From another point of view, although in Mark/Matt and in Luke, Jesus' last words are a psalm citation, in John the psalm echo, "I thirst," is the-next-to-the-last saying of Jesus, while "It is finished" constitutes the very last words. Since "I thirst" comes under the rubric of "all being finished," we might think of it and "It is finished" as functionally constituting one saying.

Taken thus, the Johannine last words of Jesus from the cross are an interesting contrast to those reported by Mark/Matt and by Luke. In *Mark/Matt*

---

[118]Milligan ("St. John's" 25–26) would add another Passover feature: He tries to claim that it was vinegar, not wine, that was offered to Jesus, and that vinegar was used in the Passover ritual. In the Johannine storyline could readers be expected to think that the soldiers would have vinegar during their guarding the crucified? The connection of vinegar with Passover is highly dubious.

[119]I find dubious the attempt of Robbins ("Crucifixion" 39) to find a biblical background for this use of *telein* in the twofold *syntelein* of Job 19:25–27; the thrust of the two passages is quite different.

the citation of Ps 22:2 expresses Jesus' strong sense of having been forsaken by God, who has not visibly assisted him during the PN. Ps 22 ends on a note of victory, but Mark does not let that show through until after Jesus' death—death on a cross is the low point before a triumph to come. Although some think Matt changes the climax to victory,[120] I find nothing in the text to justify that. Matt's theology of Jesus' death is not significantly different from Mark's. In *Luke* the citation of Ps 31:6 expresses Jesus' unshakable trust in God who is always a loving Father to him. Throughout the PN, even when abused, Jesus has acted consistently with his behavior during his lifetime by healing, forgiving, and reaching out to the suffering. The first words Luke recorded from the lips of Jesus (2:49) expressed astonishment that his parents would not know that he would be "in my Father's house," and throughout the ministry Jesus prayed with great frequency. It is fitting that the last words recorded are a prayer indicating that he will be taken into the Father's hands.

In *John* Jesus, who has come from God, has completed the commission that the Father has given him, so that his death becomes a deliberate decision that all is now finished, taken by one who is in control. His own "I thirst," echoing Ps 22:16, has caused the offering of vinegary wine on hyssop, fulfilling not only Ps 69:22 but also the exodus motif of sprinkling the lamb's blood. Jesus said that the testimony given on his behalf by the Father (5:37) was harmonious with the Scriptures that also testified on his behalf (5:39). Accordingly his "It is finished" refers both to the work the Father has given him to do and to the fulfillment of Scripture. As "Lamb of God" he has taken away the world's sin, thus fulfilling and completing the role of the paschal lamb in OT theology.

THE DEATH OF JESUS IN ALL THE GOSPELS

The Gospel death notices are extremely laconic:

Mark 15:37: But Jesus, having let go [*aphienai*] a loud cry, expired [*ekpnein*].

Matt 27:50: But Jesus, again having shouted [*krazein*] with a loud cry, let go [*aphienai*] the spirit.

Luke 23:46b: But having said this, he expired.

John 19:30b: And having bowed his head, he gave over the spirit.

GPet 5:19b: And having said this, he was taken up [*analambanein*].

---

[120]Senior (*Passion . . . Matthew* 141) writes of the Matthean Jesus: "And with the shout a final act of integrity: the sacred life-breath of the Son of God is handed back in trust to the God who had given it." For me that is Lucan, not Matthean, death theology.

Each death notice consists of two parts: first, an introductory participial clause, in four of the five witnesses involving speaking; second, a main verb describing the death.

The Introductory Clause. Mark/Matt have the emission of a loud cry, the second time in each that this phrase has been used. I have already pointed out that John's "finished," also used two times (the second by Jesus himself), is functionally parallel to the Mark/Matt duplication. Luke and (probably independently) *GPet* settle for a neutral reference back to Jesus' previous words.

The Marcan "loud cry" without words before death has been the subject of much speculation. Source critics have wondered whether this was not the most ancient reminiscence, so that all the last words (psalm citations) attributed to Jesus were subsequent additions. Doctors have discussed whether it is compatible with asphyxia as the physiological cause of Jesus' death. (For both these points see ANALYSIS below.) There are serious difficulties, however, in appealing to the Marcan expression to decide such issues. We saw above (pp. 1044–45) that a "loud cry" is one of the eschatological features surrounding the death of Jesus, and thus is not simply a factual reminiscence.[121] The twofold reference to a "loud cry" in 15:34,37, which are also the two verses in which the name Jesus appears, reflects Mark's predilection for doubling that we have already encountered (cf. the two references to "they crucify" in 15:24,27). Indeed, it is legitimate to ask if by his aorist participle "having let go a loud cry" Mark envisages a separate cry from the one he vocalized in 15:34 (with "My God, My God, for what reason have you forsaken me?"). Or after an interruption (the wine offering and Elijah misunderstanding) is Mark not simply resuming thus: "But Jesus, having let out *that* loud cry [in 15:34], expired"? We saw in 15:1 a Marcan aorist participle "having made their consultation" that was probably simply resumptive of the juridical deliberations in 14:53–64 after the interruption provided by Peter's denials in 14:66–72. If there was for Mark no second loud cry but only a reference back to the first, we can dispense with the theorizing about the preMarcan character of the wordless cry uttered by Jesus before he died.

Matt (27:50) adds a *palin* ("again") to what he takes over from Mark,[122] and so clearly he understood that there was a second cry. I find dubious the interpretation of this by Senior in SPNM 304–5. Despite the wording pertinent to being forsaken in Ps 22:2, he stresses the note of confidence in the psalm. When Jesus cries out again before he dies, he is expressing his "con-

---

[121]Of course, a death rattle may have come from Jesus' lips before he died, but Mark's "loud cry" is no simple report of that.

[122]An unusual procedure; *palin* occurs seventeen times in Matt, twenty-eight in Mark.

fident and triumphant faith." Matt's introduction of *krazein* ("to shout") echoes such sentiments as Ps 22:6, "To You they shouted out, and they were
saved," and 22:25, "But when he shouted out to Him, He heard him." Not
only do I disagree with such a positive interpretation of the fundamental
import of the Matthean Jesus' use of Ps 22:2; but I would argue that if
krazein comes to Matt from the psalm, one should derive it from the verse
immediately after 22:2: "I shout by day, and you do not answer" (22:3).
Bieder (*Vorstellung* 52) is closer to truth, in my judgment, when he interprets this Matthean cry as similar to the Marcan cry, emerging not from
victory but from the abyss of feeling forsaken.

Although Luke is following Mark, he changes "having let go a loud cry"
to "having said this." Since Luke has already used the expression "loud cry,"
his failure to reproduce it a second time does not stem from dislike for it. If,
like Matt, Luke interpreted Mark (probably wrongly) to mean a second loud
cry, he may once more characteristically be avoiding Marcan doubling. Or
Luke may have recognized that Mark was simply referring to the first cry
resumptively after an interruption and thought the resumption was confusing
and unnecessary. Since Luke had no wine or Elijah interruption, he could
refer back to that cry more simply: "having said this."

We have already discussed John's resumptive saying "It is finished." In a
certain sense it is the equivalent of the introductory saying clauses in the
Synoptics that we have just been discussing. But John too has a participial
clause: "having bowed his head." In itself it might be simply a picture of
exhaustion, but that would be irreconcilable with John's insistence on a Jesus
who is master of his own fate. After all, this is a Jesus who needed no help
from Simon the Cyrenian but carried the cross by himself to Golgotha
(19:17). Some Johannine commentators (Braun, Loisy) have contended that
bowing the head is the action of a man who is going to sleep, and certainly
sleep is a possible image for death in John (11:11–14). Yet sleep does not fit
the dynamic image of Jesus in the Johannine PN. This is the only Gospel
that shows standing near the cross of Jesus a group of his followers to whom
he has spoken (19:25–27). The participial "bowing his head" modifies the
main action of giving over the spirit. Might it not indicate the direction of
the giving, namely, down to those who stood near the cross?

Description of the Death. None of the evangelists uses the ordinary verbs
for dying: *apothnēskein* or *teleutan*.[123] Mark and Luke have the simplest
description, employing *ekpnein* ("to breathe out"). In the light of his theory

---

[123]In itself this is not enough to show that all the evangelists wanted to emphasize the voluntary
aspect of Jesus' death. Taylor (*Mark* 596) finds a voluntary element in Matt and John but not in Mark.

(that I judge overdone) of demon expulsion at Jesus' death, Danker ("Demonic" 67–68) takes the *ekpnein* to mean that Jesus "expelled the *pneuma* [demonic spirit]" and associates the loud cry with the demon coming out. Luke, who repeats Mark's wording here, surely did not understand that. The Lucan Jesus, who was conceived in Mary by coming of the Holy Spirit (1:35), could never have been inhabited by a demon; it was Judas into whom Satan entered (22:3). Less imaginatively, Taylor (*Mark* 596) finds in *ekpnein* the suggestion of a sudden, violent death, presumably because he interprets it to mean a strong exhalation following a loud cry. Again I doubt that Luke, who uses this verb, is attributing a violent death to Jesus. More simply, since *ekpnein* is a euphemism for "die" in Sophocles, Plutarch, and Josephus (BAGD 244), even as is my literal English rendition "expire," both Mark and Luke may have used the verb as a neutral description.

Matt's wording prima facie may seem to emphasize that Jesus voluntarily "let go the spirit." Probably Matt took over *aphienai* ("to let go") from Mark's "let go a loud cry" (15:37), where the verb reflects an action more tortured than voluntary. Matt may have drawn *pneuma* ("spirit") from an analysis of Mark's *ekpnein*. Actually *aphienai* (with *psychē, "soul, life"*) is used neutrally for dying in the LXX (Gen 35:18; I Esdras 4:21), even as is the exodus or going forth of the spirit (Sir 38:23; Wis 16:14). Thus all Matt may be saying is that Jesus let out the life force or last breath, a resigned act that consisted in offering no further resistance, even if it did not exactly convey a voluntary death.

GPet, although it has been hewing closely to a Matthean form of these last events before Jesus' death, departs significantly from the canonical Gospels in the verb used to describe the death: "He was taken up" (*analambanein,* a verb associated with the ascension in Acts 1:2,11,22; I Tim 3:16; Mark 16:19). There is here no denial of the resurrection (for that will be described graphically in 9:35–10:42), and no docetism as if the real Jesus who was only spiritual went away, leaving an appearance of a body (for in 6:21–24 Jesus' body still has the power to make the earth shake). There are two possible understandings. The first is that this being "taken up" reflects early Christian theology that Jesus' entry into heaven was directly from the cross, even though those who held this view could also describe Jesus as rising from the dead and subsequently ascending into heaven—a theology that testifies to the subtle understanding that after his death Jesus had passed out of time. As we have seen, Luke in 23:43 can imply that Jesus went to paradise on the day of his death, but still subsequently describe a resurrection and two ascensions (24:51; Acts 1:11)! Precisely because this theology stems from the earlier Christian period[124] and in later centuries a chronological sequence was taken much more literally, I doubt that *GPet* is being so subtle with its *analambanein* in 5:19b. A second explanation is that by the 2d cent. the verb "taken up" could be merely a euphemism for dying, even as today one might tenderly report the death of elderly people to their grandchildren by saying that they have been taken to heaven. Vaganay (*Évangile* 257) gives examples from Irenaeus, Origen, and the OS[sin] of "take up, receive" as equivalent to "die." If one opts for this second explanation, *GPet,* like Matt, will have simply found a more graceful way to report that Jesus died.

John's "he gave over [*paradidonai*] the spirit" is often interpreted in the light of Luke's "Father, into your hands I place [over: *paratithenai*] my spirit." Certainly in the abstract that interpretation is possible. Jesus is going to his Father; and there is a certain fittingness in having the long chain of those giving Jesus over (p. 211 above) come to an end with Jesus giving himself over. Yet this is the Johannine Jesus who is already one with the Father—he may go to the Father, but can he give his spirit to the Father? Remembering what we said about "bowed his head," would we not have a better sequence if, while going to the Father, Jesus gives his spirit to those who are standing near the cross? In 7:37–39 Jesus promised that when he was glorified, those who believed in him were to receive the Spirit. What more fitting than that those believers who did not go away when Jesus was arrested (18:8), but assembled near the cross, should be the first to receive it? This would mean that although the other evangelists described Jesus as breathing forth or giving out his spirit or life force, John rethought the tradition by equating "spirit" with the Holy Spirit. Such serious Johannine interpreters as Bernard, Bultmann, and Lagrange reject this. A major objection is that elsewhere in NT thought only the *risen* Christ gives the Holy Spirit. However, while not raised from the dead, the Jesus of John is lifted up on the cross and already passing from this world to the Father (13:1; 17:11). He is already enjoying much the same status that in the other Gospels comes when he is raised from the dead. Another objection is that the giving of the Holy Spirit is explicitly placed on Easter Sunday evening in John 20:22. Yet one must recognize John's way of combining commonly known Christian presentations with those peculiar to his own community's memory. In the Easter Sunday scene of 20:19–23 he preserves the tradition shared by other Gospels that the risen Jesus appeared to the Twelve (see 20:24), the forebears of the larger church. In that larger church tradition nothing is reported about special followers of Jesus who were not members of the Twelve but

---

[124]Another witness is Hebrews. In 9:11ff. Jesus seems to pass from the cross directly into the heavenly Holy Place with his own blood; yet 13:20 refers to the resurrection.

stood near the cross—some of them (especially the beloved disciple) were the forebears of the Johannine community. It is very much Johannine style that while not rejecting the Twelve (especially Peter), priority is given to the disciple whom Jesus loved. Plausibly then, John means that when Jesus bowed his head down toward those who stood near the cross, i.e., believers who were remembered as the antecedents of the Johannine community, he gave over to them the Holy Spirit. They would have been the first to have been made children of God by the victorious Jesus, when he was lifted up on the cross but before he was risen from the dead.

ANALYSIS

Four issues will be discussed here: A. composition of this section in Mark; B. the tradition and/or historicity of Jesus' last words; C. the physiological cause of Jesus' death; and D. imaginative rewriting of the Gospel accounts so that the crucifixion is nullified or denied.

A. **Theories of How Mark 15:33–37 Was Composed**

As pointed out in the COMMENT, there are many Marcan features in this section. This results in the usual range of theories of composition, depending on whether one assumes that a Marcan feature implies Marcan creation. Boismard (*Synopse* 2.426) thinks that the earliest text was much shorter: At the ninth hour, Jesus, having let go a loud cry, expired (15:34a,37). As elsewhere Pesch (*Markus* 2.491) attributes the whole of 15:33–39 to the preMarcan PN and divides it (as always) into three subsections (33, 34–36, 37–39). For Bultmann (BHST 273–74) the whole section is secondary and "strongly disfigured by legend," with the possible exception of v. 37. Taylor (*Mark* 651) regards 34–37 as part of the primary (A) narrative, with v. 33 as B material. Many scholars regard 34 and 37 (Jesus speaking or acting with a loud cry) as a doublet, only one of which is original, or perhaps as a Marcan frame encompassing earlier material in 35–36. Matera (*Kingship* 57) sees 35–36, bracketed by vv. 34 and 37, as the third mockery reported in Mark, following those done by the Roman soldiers in the praetorium (15:16–20a) and by the three groups who came to Golgotha (27–32). (I would have to comment that the mockery in 15:36 is of much lesser intensity that the two preceding mockeries and not fully parallel.) Within 15:35–36 Matera finds a further bracketing by the reference to Elijah in both verses.

(Again I comment that the first reference to Elijah is at the end of v. 35, and therefore we are scarcely dealing with a beginning/conclusion. Moreover, the Elijah references are not repetitious as are the "loud cry" references, but are in a progressive description. They are wrongly described as bracketing.) Although I find Matera's framework forced, I find him more plausible when he suggests that Mark found the use of Ps 22 already in vogue,[125] and worked that use into a coherent narrative. Lührmann (*Markus* 263) seems to regard much of the material in the passage as old, even if it was Mark who established the relationship between Elijah and the rest.

Here as previously I doubt that we have adequate methodology to discern with precision preMarcan sources rewritten by Mark from Mark's own creation. Already in the COMMENT I suggested a more plausible scenario involving all the Gospels, and for convenience' sake I shall now summarize that.

Two separate traditions, namely, (a) the last cry of Jesus, combined with the offering of vinegary wine; (b) mockery about Elijah, were put together by Mark or in preMarcan tradition to give us the scene that now exists in *Mark/Matt*—a joining that has produced a somewhat confused storyline in which the Elijah motif is awkwardly related both to Jesus' cry and to the wine. The Mark/Matt scene is filled with scriptural reminiscences: The words of Jesus' cry are a citation of Ps 22:2 where the just one addressed his plaint to God; "vinegary wine" is the same word (*oxos*) that Ps 69:22 used for the vinegar drink offered in mockery to the just one by his enemies; the coming of Elijah is an eschatological expectation expanding the last of the prophets' words in Mal 3:23 (RSV 4:5). The author of *GPet* knew the tradition of Jesus citing Ps 22:2 but presents a different rendering of the divine name. Since the *GPet* translation does not seem to be a theological correction of Matt or of Mark (for the meaning is not substantially different), it may represent another form of the early tradition on which Mark also drew.

The account in *Luke* seems to be an attempt to improve Mark's account by eliminating the Elijah element, by moving the mocking offering of vinegary wine to the set of three mockeries of Jesus on the cross narrated earlier (§41), and by making the wording of Jesus' cry harmonious with Lucan theology of the passion. Accordingly the Lucan Jesus does not use the language of being forsaken by God from the LXX of Ps 22:2 but the language of entrusting oneself into God's hands from the LXX of Ps 31:6. *John* shows

---

[125]Yet on p. 60 he speaks of the early use of the psalm in passion "apologetic." More plausible is that the early use reflected an attempt by Christians to reconcile their own beliefs with the expectations they had learned from Scripture—not at first apologetic against others but for self-understanding.

no knowledge of the Elijah motif but may have known the tradition of Ps 22:2 plus the vinegary wine (in a preMarcan form?)—his reporting that Jesus said, "I am never alone because the Father is always with me" (16:32) appears to be a dissenting comment on the theme that Jesus could feel forsaken by God. John echoes Pss 22:16; 69:22 and Exod 12:22 in Jesus' expression of thirst and the reaction to his plaint by offering vinegary wine. (Of all the Gospel accounts this is the smoothest storyline.) Accordingly Jesus' last words, "It is finished," besides embodying his fully controlled laying down of his life, signal the complete fulfillment of Scripture. This highly polished episode betrays Johannine composition.

B. The Last Words of Jesus: Oldest Tradition and/or Historicity

There are three different Gospel reports of Jesus' last words (Mark/Matt, Luke, John); of these at most only one can represent the oldest discernible tradition. Jesus' citation of Ps 22:2 seems to have been known by all the evangelists (even if two did not reproduce it), and the transliterated Aramaic form in Mark can be defended as earlier than the form in Matt. Often, then, Mark's "*Elōi, Elōi, lama sabachthani?*" is affirmed to be the oldest knowable Christian tradition of Jesus' last cry and even to have been spoken by Jesus. Neither affirmation can be assumed, so the issue must be discussed. While I shall work with the scenario of Gospel development summarized in the two preceding paragraphs, many of the points to be made below will have validity even if that scenario is rejected.

A citation of Ps 22:2 may be the oldest tradition reported in the Gospels; but was that citation supplied by Christian reflection on the crucifixion or did it come from Jesus himself? It is not inconceivable that historically a Jesus tortured by his sufferings gave voice to his desperation by using a psalm prayer describing the despondent condition of a suffering just one. Since the prayer cited by Jesus was the opening line of the psalm (22:2), Christians would have followed Jesus' lead by mining the psalm for passages to interpret the other events of the crucifixion (see APPENDIX VII, B2).

Let us look at the arguments for and against historicity.[126] The fact that the prayer was remembered in Aramaic is often thought to favor derivation from Jesus, even as *Abba* is most frequently treated as an ipsissimum verbum of Jesus. Yet an Aramaic-speaking Christian community did compose prayers in Aramaic, e.g., *Maranatha* (I Cor 16:22). Some reject that observa-

---

[126]Zilonka (*Mark* 46–47) lists six arguments supporting the historicity of the citation of Ps 22:2 in Mark 15:34 as Jesus' actual words, arguments proposed by Roman Catholic scholars of the early 1900s; later (169) he points out that by the 1970s none of the six had survived the impact of modern historical criticism.

tion, claiming that there is no evidence that the NT attributed to Jesus such prayers created by Christians. Yet on that score Acts 2:27 warrants study. Although it appears in a sermon by Peter, the citation of Ps 16:10 is phrased in first-person language that implies Jesus as the speaker: "You will not forsake [*egkataleipein* as in Ps 22:2] my soul to Hades, nor will you give your holy one to see corruption." The pessimism of "My God, my God, for what reason have you forsaken me?" has been offered as another argument for historicity: No Christian would dare to put such a despairing cry on the Savior's lips! That cry, however, is not an expression of despair in the strict sense (pp. 1048–49 above), and early Christians would scarcely think it blasphemous or unworthy to portray Jesus as praying a psalm. The argument that the sentiments of Ps 22:2 make sense as Jesus faces death supports the possibility that Jesus cited the psalm; only rarely, however, do the evangelists portray the inner feelings of Jesus.[127]

If the original tradition about Jesus' last words did not have Ps 22:2, what would have caused Mark or a preMarcan Christian to choose that passage to be inserted? If Mark were the inserter, one could offer as a reason the conformity of this psalm citation with Mark's pessimistic view of the passion, for 22:2 constitutes a perceptive commentary on the fact that God did not intervene to save his faithful one from dying. If a preMarcan Christian were the inserter, since from the very first it was a principle that Jesus died "in accordance with the Scriptures" (I Cor 15:3), one could suggest that the whole of Ps 22 was one of the first Scriptures to become entwined with features in the passion; then the use of 22:2 would have been simply one more step.[128] An argument against attributing to Jesus himself the citation of Ps 22:2 is the fact that other evangelists (Luke and John) felt free to change Jesus' last words (which should have had special solemnity) to other psalm citations or allusions. Such substitution would have come easier if it were recognized that the citation of Ps 22:2 arose from Christian reflection on the passion, compared to which a citation from another psalm would have equal right to be considered appropriate. When the arguments pro and con are weighed, no one can say that the case for "*Elōi, Elōi, lama sabachthani?*" as the ipsissima verba of Jesus is established.

If it is possible that the citation of Ps 22:2 came from Christian reflection

---

[127]Floris ("Abandon" 284) argues that Ps 22 reflects not the crisis of Jesus as he faced death but the crisis of his disciples as they sought to understand how in God's plan he could have died such a death.

[128]Attention has been called to Midrash *Tehillim* on Ps 22:2 (section 6). It states that on the three days of the fast decreed in Esther 4:16 (a fast that Midrash Rabbah on the Esther passage associates with Passover), one should say on the first day, "My God," and on the second day "My God," and on the third day, "Why have you forsaken me?" But this is too late a witness to allow us to call on that custom to explain why an early Christian would have placed Ps 22:2 on Jesus' lips.

on the death of Jesus, what other possibilities for Jesus' last words are there, by way of preMarcan tradition and/or historicity? Logically there would seem to be three: 1. Jesus remained silent; 2. Jesus uttered a loud wordless cry; 3. Jesus uttered some basic words. Let us consider those one by one.

1. SILENCE. In Mark/Matt from the time Jesus was crucified until now, Jesus has said nothing. Clearly, then, it would not be inconceivable that he died without saying anything. (Indeed, by not speaking Jesus could have seen himself as fulfilling the description of the Suffering Servant in Isa 53:7 who opened not his mouth as he was led to the slaughter.) In that case all three Gospel accounts of Jesus' last words would represent Christians' use of the psalms as they reflected on what Jesus' attitude must have been. While not illogical, this proposal has no direct support in the Gospel texts, for Jesus speaks aloud in all of them.

2. WORDLESS CRY. That Jesus screamed out a loud cry is attested in varying ways by the three Synoptics and *GPet.* In all those witnesses words are then supplied for the cry; but in Mark 15:37 and Matt 27:50 there is a second (resumptive?) reference to "a loud cry," this time without words. Is a wordless cry the earliest memory so that the psalm words reported in the Gospels represent later Christian supplementation? Among those who have advocated a form of this are Bacon, Bertram, Boman, Bultmann, Hauck, Loisy, Pallis, Strathmann, Wansbrough, and J. Weiss. Unlike 1 above, here a subsequent supplying of words would have been in harmony with and not against the direction of what is thought to have been original. One could find support for the proposal in Heb 5:7 that has Jesus utter "a strong clamor . . . to the One having the power to save him from death," but reports no words in that clamor. I would reject the contention that a dying crucified man would not have had the strength to utter words even if he might give forth a death rattle or gasp—an argument sometimes used to support this proposal.[129] Occasionally one sees another contention that the attribution of a death scream or cry to Jesus is less theological than having him recite a psalm passage and therefore might be more historical. That overlooks the fact reported in the COMMENT that "a loud cry" has an apocalyptic tone, and so could be one of the signs of the last times (like darkness, rending the sanctuary veil, earthquake, opened tombs) through which Christians expounded the significance of the death of Jesus (Schützeichel, "Todesschrei").

3. BASIC WORD(s). Working from the words of Jesus reported in the Gospels, scholars have hypothesized a more basic saying or cry. The thesis of Sahlin ("Verständnis") has attracted considerable attention, e.g., Boman,

---

[129]Yet the fact that crucified men could and did speak before they died (p. 1044 above) does nothing to support extravagant suggestions in the other direction, e.g., that Jesus recited the whole of Ps 22 from the cross! (Holst, "Cry" 287).

Léon-Dufour. He proposed that Jesus said in Hebrew, "*Ēlî 'attā*'" ("You are my God"), found four times in the psalter (22:11; 63:2; 118:28; 140:7; also Isa 44:17).[130] The bystanders thought he was speaking Aramaic, "*Ēlîyā' tā*'" ("Elijah, come"). Words used to reproduce and translate the spoken Hebrew were confused in subsequent Greek renditions, leading to the citation of Ps 22:2.[131] A memory of the original might be seen in the fact that Mark/ Matt chose a verse from a psalm in which "*Ēlî 'attā*'" appeared.[132] Sahlin goes on to theorize that Jesus himself was thinking of Ps 118:28, "You are my God, and I will give thanks to you," i.e., the conclusion of the Hallel psalms begun at the Last Supper (Mark 14:26).[133] Without the complexities involved in Sahlin's ideas, some would have Jesus crying aloud simply "*Ēlî*," ("My God") in Hebrew, so that both the expansion to Ps 22:2 and the Elijah misunderstanding came from that (see Boman, "Letzte" 112). The movement from "*Ēlî 'attā*'" to Ps 22:2 may have been facilitated by an established relationship of theme; for Midrash *Mekilta* on Exod 15:2 (*Shirata* 3), a midrash written relatively early in the Christian era, says that *'Ēlî*, "My God," signifies the rule of compassion or mercy and cites Ps 22:2, "My God, to what purpose have you forsaken me?" The advantage of either form of this proposal is that it traces back to Jesus or the earliest tradition a basic wording that has some similarity to the oldest Gospel tradition. Also the proposal agrees with all the Gospels in having Jesus speak words before he dies. If one is not going to accept that Jesus himself cited Ps 22:2 before he died (a possibility not to be discounted), this proposal seems the best alternative. More than that one cannot claim.

C. The Physiological Cause of the Death of Jesus

Crucifixion pierces no vital organ, and so inevitably one must wonder what physical or organic factor caused Jesus to die. The extremely brief Gospel descriptions of the death of Jesus are of little help in answering this question. Mark and Luke say noncommittally that he expired; Matt probably

[130]That such a prayer would not be inappropriate when facing death is maintained by Léon-Dufour ("Dernier" 678), who calls attention to the invocation of the name of God in the Shema, the most frequently recited Jewish prayerful confession ("Hear O Israel, the Lord our God ['*Ĕlōhênû*], the Lord is one"), and to the later tradition that Aqiba said "The Lord is one" as he died.

[131]An early Marcan (or preMarcan) transliteration into Greek read *Ēli atha,* translated into Greek as *theos mou ei sy* ("You are my God")—this is reflected in the presence of only one *theos mou* in Codex Vaticanus. The *ei sy* became *eis ti,* and the enigmatic "My God, for what reason" was interpreted as part of Ps 22:2 and completed in the wording of that psalm.

[132]Some would argue that John did so as well since they connect "I thirst" with Ps 63:2: "O God, my God . . . for you my soul thirsts."

[133]See p. 123 above for doubts about the Passover supper use of Hallel psalms in the early 1st cent. when Jesus died and/or whether Mark would have expected his readers to know about such a custom.

means no more. John emphasizes Jesus' control over his own death as he gives over the spirit; *GPet* highlights God's intervention, for the passive ("Jesus was taken up") is a circumlocution for divine activity—both of these are clearly theological portrayals. At the beginning of §18 I pointed out that those skilled in the law (advocates, professors of law, etc.) have produced many studies of the trial of Jesus with the assumption that from their profession they could shed light on the legalities of the proceedings. Often they wrote without any awareness that the NT records could not be treated as if they were exact court records. It is not surprising that many of those skilled in medicine (doctors, professors of anatomy, etc.) have written to explain the cause of Jesus' death, using the Gospel accounts as if the details preserved therein were exact observations that made a diagnosis possible. For instance, they have noted that Jesus could utter one or more loud cries (Mark/Matt, Luke, *GPet*), that he was thirsty (John), that he died surprisingly soon (Mark 15:44–45; John 19:33), and that after death blood and water flowed from a lance wound in his side. Often the medical writers have expressed their conclusions without recognizing that any or all these features might embody theological symbolism rather than historical description.[134]

Frequently ancient Christian writers did not bother speculating about a physical cause because they regarded the death as miraculous and totally under the control of Jesus, who did not have to die. Tertullian (*Apology* 21.19; CC 1.126) explains that Jesus "with a word expressing his own will dismissed his spirit, forestalling the work of the executioners." As late as the 20th cent., most often physiological explanations have been combined with christological and spiritual factors.

A survey of medical explanations by Wilkinson ("Incident" 154) reports that the first discussion of the death of Jesus as a physiological issue was that of F. Gruner in 1805. In 1847 J. C. Stroud, M.D., in *The Physical Cause of the Death of Christ* (rev. ed., 1871), proposed what became a classic thesis, i.e., the violent rupture of Jesus' heart, giving preachers the opportunity to stress that literally the Lord died of a broken heart brought on by his vision of human ingratitude, sin, etc. Without detracting from a death by Jesus' consent, Stroud theorized that after a hemorrhage had taken place

---

[134]In his article "Autopsy," which bears the subtitle "Biblical Illiteracy Among Medical Doctors," D. E. Smith is devastatingly critical of Edwards et al. (a Methodist pastor and two Mayo Clinic professionals) for the lack of criticism manifested in their 1986 article "On the Physical Death of Jesus." He asks (p. 14) how a scientific publication, the *Journal of the American Medical Association,* could publish a piece that the vast majority of biblical scholars would immediately evaluate as "not scientific" and "pseudo-intellectual." Smith is harsh, but he has exposed a real problem; see nn. 138, 139, and 141 below. Nevertheless, Smith's own guidelines (pp. 4–5) as to what is historical (the decisions of the Jesus Seminar, and P. Winter's judgment that what is described in the Gospels about the Jewish legal proceedings does not correspond to "normal Jewish procedure") need greater professionalism on the biblical side.

through the heart wall into the pericardial sac, there was a clotting of blood, separating it from serum. The lance thrust opened the pericardial sac, releasing the two substances which appeared as blood and water. Stroud's thesis was endorsed by Dr. W. Hanna, *The Last Days of Our Lord's Passion* (1868), and was still being defended by A. R. Simpson ("Broken") in 1911. However, gradually new medical experience showed that cardiac ruptures do not occur spontaneously or under the pressure of mental agony but are the result of a previously diseased condition of the heart muscle. Moreover, the coagulation of blood in the pericardium would have required more time after death than the Gospel account allots. The articles of Merrins and Sharpe represent medical refutations of the Stroud broken-heart thesis, even though in their own way they preserve the element of the supernatural and the volitional.[135]

The next thesis that became a classic identified the cause of death as suffocation. Its most famous proponent was the French surgeon P. Barbet.[136] His 1950 study of the crucifixion drew on his own research in the 1930s and on earlier research in the 1920s by Dr. LeBec; but he also drew heavily on the Shroud of Turin as an accurate representation of the corpse of the crucified Christ. Experimentation had been done on Austrian-German soldiers of World War I who were hung alive by two hands from a post. If one were to translate the gruesome results to crucifixion, the following scenario would be plausible. Attached to the cross by wrists and ankles, the victim would shift his weight from arms to legs.[137] If there were no rest for the buttocks and no support for the feet, the dead weight of the body would soon cause the crucified to slump down exhausted. The intercostal muscles that facilitate inhaling would become too weakened to function, so that the lungs, unable to empty, would fill with carbon dioxide. Death would result from asphyxia. Barbet (*Doctor* 119–20) maintained that after death a horizontal lance thrust from the right pierced Jesus above the fifth rib and perforated the fifth intercostal space, piercing the right auricle of the heart (which always has blood) and the pericardium (the serum of which appeared like water). Aspects of the asphyxiation theory were thought to be confirmed by Nazi experimenta-

---

[135]The responses of Young to Sharpe and of Southerland to both Sharpe and Young show the intensity of the debate in the early 1930s. One finds a medical discussion rejected on the grounds that the physician did not do sufficient justice to the Johannine statement that Jesus gave over his own spirit.

[136]Much earlier S. Haughton, who was both a minister and a doctor, in *The Speaker's Commentary on the New Testament,* ed. F. C. Cook (London: Murray, 1881), 4.349–50, argued that Jesus died both from asphyxiation and from the rupture of the heart (Stroud).

[137]In this theory the breaking of the legs would hasten death, because then they could not be used to lift the weight of the body.

tion at Dachau, and the approach was reiterated in the 1960s by another French physician, J. Bréhant. A variation of the same approach was advocated by Dr. W. D. Edwards of the Mayo clinic in 1986: The major pathophysiologic effect of crucifixion was an interference with respiration and thus asphyxia.[138] Gilly (*Passion* 120–21) attributed the death of Jesus to progressive asphyxiation when, under the effect of all the preceding suffering, the respiratory muscles were tetanized.[139]

Yet many other proposals have been made.[140] As for the lance thrust, Primrose ("Surgeon") argued that frontal scourging damaged the abdomen so that when the stomach was pierced both blood and water emerged. Lossen ("Blut") argued that the lance hit not only Jesus' arteries in between the ribs in the third intercostal area (producing blood), but also his lung (from which came serum watery in appearance). In a series of articles (especially "Wound" [1957]) Sava, a Brooklyn physician, maintained that Barbet's experiments were invalidated because he worked with corpses that were dead over twenty-four hours. Pericardial fluid would have to pass through the lung to get to the surface of the chest, and a fresh corpse would not have exhibited the gaping tunnel imagined by Barbet for that passage. Moreover, the pericardium would hold only six or seven cubic centimeters of fluid. In Sava's own theory ("Wounds" [1954]) the scourging caused a hemorrhage in the pleural cavity between the ribs and the lungs, producing fluid that ultimately separated into light serous and dark red parts.

As for the cause of death, Edwards combined asphyxia and hypovolemic shock;[141] and indeed insufficiency of blood to the various parts of the body enters into various composite theories, e.g., Marcozzi ("Osservazioni") proposed suffocation related to circulatory failure. Sometimes it has been suggested that the shock caused acute dilation of the stomach so that it contained dark watery fluid. Both psychological and physical reasons would have produced this shock, e.g., the spiritual agony in Gethsemane, exposure

[138]Edwards (1461) does not exclude dehydration and congestive heart failure as possible contributing factors, and on 1463 he says, "It remains unsettled whether Jesus died of cardiac rupture or of cardiorespiratory failure." The water flow from the lance wound probably represented serous pleural and pericardial fluid (1463). Thus, in some ways, despite its main thrust toward asphyxia, the article combines many of the solutions of the past century, including some that most had thought happily discarded.

[139]A. M. Dubarle, EspVie 96 (#5, Jan. 30, 1986), 60–62, in a biting review, hopes that in his medical practice Gilly does not make the numerous mistakes that he manifests in all other areas in this book.

[140]Summaries of these can be found in Wilkinson, "Physical," and Blinzler, *Prozess* 381–84.

[141]His article ("On the Physical"), written in combination with others, gives with great assurance but remarkable lack of critical sense a combination of details from the biblical accounts, from the Shroud of Turin, and from handbooks dealing with crucifixion practices. One would need to issue cautions at almost every turn.

for three to six hours on the cross, and the loss of blood in the scourging.[142] On the assumption that the Gospel accounts give detailed history, some have tried to refute this suggestion by pointing to Jesus' vigor before he died and his loud cry. Yet E. Sons (*Benedictine Monthly* 33 [1957], 101–6) has responded that a type of shock seen in World War II, resulting from extreme physical punishment, left full consciousness unto death. A clot resulting from the damage to blood vessels during the scourging has been proposed.

In my judgment the major defect of most of the studies I have reported on thus far is that they were written by doctors who did not stick to their trade and let a literalist understanding of the Gospel accounts influence their judgments on the physical cause of the death of Jesus. There is no evidence that the evangelists personally knew anything about that matter, and discussion of it could better be carried on simply by employing the best of medical knowledge to determine how any crucified person is likely to have died (and not citing a single biblical detail in confirmation). The recent study by Zugibe ("Two"), a medical examiner and pathologist, comes close to that goal. He has challenged the asphyxia theory of LeBec, Barbet, and others by contending that the experiments on which they drew consisted of men hung with their hands almost directly over their heads. He has conducted experiments with volunteers whose arms in simulated crucifixion were spread out at an angle of 60° or 70° to the trunk of the body, and no asphyxia resulted. He contends that shock brought on by dehydration and loss of blood is the only plausible medical explanation for the death of the crucified Jesus. Obviously no certitude has been reached by the various medical commentators; and while experiments in actual crucifixion may be the only way to come to higher probability, we trust that this barbarism is now safely confined to the past.

D. Imaginative Rewriting That Nullifies the Crucifixion

Despite shortcomings, the medical studies described above take seriously the unanimous Gospel witness that Jesus died on the cross. Hesitantly, but with the hope it may be of assistance, I have decided to present a brief survey of theories that rewrite the Gospel presentation into a radically different scenario. It is an embarrassing insight into human nature that the more fantastic the scenario, the more sensational is the promotion it receives and the more intense the faddish interest it attracts. People who would never bother reading a responsible analysis of the traditions about how Jesus was crucified,

---

[142]Wilkinson ("Physical" 104–5) explains this well. Ball and Leese ("Physical" 8) maintain: "Mental agony, associated with oligaemic shock produced by injury, could have been a lethal combination producing the sudden death of Christ by cardiac syncope."

died, was buried, and rose from the dead are fascinated by the report of some "new insight" to the effect he was not crucified or did not die, especially if his subsequent career involved running off with Mary Magdalene to India. Whether sparked by a rationalism that seeks to debunk the miraculous or by the allure of the novel, often such modern imaginings reproduce ancient explanations that dismissed the death of Jesus on the cross, explaining it away through confusion or a plot.

1. CONFUSION. By the 2d cent. a number of suggestions were being circulated that someone other than Jesus was crucified on Golgotha. According to Irenaeus (*Adv. haer.* 1.24.4) the gnostic Basilides maintained that Jesus did not suffer. "Rather a certain Simon of Cyrene was compelled to bear his cross for him . . . and through ignorance and error it was he who was crucified." If this view was in circulation in the 1st cent., it may have been one of the reasons why John ignored the Simon tradition and insisted that Jesus carried the cross by himself (pp. 916–17 above).

Thomas, whose name John three times explains as "Twin" (11:16; 20:24; 21:2), was confusingly identified in Syriac-speaking Christianity, especially of the Edessa region, with Jude (Judas), one of the four "brothers" of Jesus mentioned in Mark 6:3 and Matt 13:55. Thus was created the figure of Jude Thomas, the twin brother of Jesus, a portrait popular in gnostic circles.[143] The idea that Jesus had a look-alike may have been one of the factors that led to the thesis that someone who looked like Jesus was crucified instead of him. A gnostic form of that is the contention that the bodily appearance of Jesus was crucified, but the real Jesus (who was purely spiritual) was not.[144] Cerinthus made the distinction in terms of the earthly Jesus and the heavenly Christ, for Irenaeus (*Adv. haer.* 1.26.1) reports Cerinthus' view that Christ descended on Jesus at the baptism and "in the end Christ withdrew again from Jesus—Jesus suffered and rose again, while Christ remained impassible inasmuch as he was a spiritual being." In the Nag Hammadi *Apocalypse of Peter* (VII.81.7–25) we read that Peter saw two figures involved in the crucifixion: Executioners were pounding on the hands and feet of one; the other was up on a tree laughing at what was going on. "The Savior said to me, 'The one whom you saw on the tree, happy and laughing, is the living Jesus; but the one into whose hands and feet they drive the nail is his fleshly part. It is the substitute being put to shame, the one who came to being in

---

[143]It is attested in such writings as *The Book of Thomas the Contender* (II.138.2,4); *The Gospel of Thomas* (II.32.11); *Acts of Thomas* 1.

[144]Tatian's view was ambiguously close to a gnostic outlook. Baarda (n. 78 above), reporting on the then recently available Syriac version of Ephraem's commentary on Tatian's *Diatessaron*, finds therein the thesis that the godhead was separated from the slain one and hidden from him by a force/power (see *GPet* 5:19). A. d'Alès, RechSR 21 (1931), 200–1, reports that some 4th- and 5th-cent. writers thought that the divinity left Jesus' body accompanying his soul.

his likeness.'" *The Second Treatise of the Great Seth* (VII.51.20–52.3) affirms: "I visited a bodily dwelling. I cast out first the one who was in it, and I went in . . . He was an earthly man; but I, I am from above the heavens." The confusion this caused among the unenlightened during the passion is graphically described: "It was another, their father, who drank the gall and the vinegar; it was not I . . . It was another, Simon, who bore the cross on his shoulder" (VII.56.6–11).

The Koran (4.156–57) criticizes the Jews for "saying, 'We killed the Messiah, Jesus the son of Mary, the messenger of Allah,' when they did not kill or crucify him;[145] but he/it was counterfeited [or: a double was substituted] before their eyes. . . . [146] And certainly they did not kill him." Islamic apologists have pointed out that Mohammed would have had no trouble accepting the crucifixion of Jesus; therefore the fact that he did not accept it shows he got revelation on the subject from God. But we do not know how much orthodox Christianity Mohammed knew; the Arabian Christianity he was acquainted with probably came from Syria and was heterodox. It may have brought with it the gnostic substitution views described above. (Tröger, "Jesus" 217, maintains that certainly the Islamic commentators on the Koran were familiar with gnostic texts.) The suggestion of a counterfeit leads us to another aspect of the approaches that deny to Jesus death by crucifixion.

2. PLOT. The idea of the crucifixion as a deception was in circulation in antiquity. In 1966 attention was called to a defense of Islam written ca. 1000 by 'Abd al-Jabbār.[147] The part directed against Christianity drew knowledge of the latter not only from the canonical Gospels but also from translated Syriac writing(s) of the 5th cent.; these seem to represent the compositions of an early Jewish-Christian sect that did not regard Jesus as divine (2d-cent. Nazarenes?). According to the underlying account Judas agreed to point out Jesus the Nazarene to the Jews; and so amid a great crowd assembled for the Passover "Judas Iscariot took the hand of a man and kissed his hand," running away after that. The Jews seized the man who had been pointed out and

---

[145]Whether the emphasis is on the "not" or the "him" is uncertain. If the latter, a substitution interpretation is facilitated. Tröger ("Jesus" 215) reports that all Islamic interpretations revolve around a substitution. The more common interpretation posits that someone else was crucified: a disciple, a well-known Sergius, or someone (e.g., Judas) who was changed to look like Jesus. Some modern Shiite theologians maintain that although Jesus' body died his spirit had been taken to heaven. Tröger (218) maintains that Mohammed himself "in no way wanted to deny Jesus' crucifixion and death as historical fact." He probably wanted to say that in reality the true prophet lives because he cannot be killed.

[146]The very obscure sentence I have omitted seems to say that the Jews themselves are uncertain about it.

[147]S. Pines, *The Jewish Christians of the Early Centuries of Christianity According to a New Source* (Proceedings of the Israel Academy of Sciences and Humanities 2.13; Jerusalem: Central Press, 1966), esp. 54, 56. S. M. Stern, "Quotations from Apocryphal Gospels in 'Abd al-Jabbār," JTS NS 18 (1967), 34–57, esp. 44–45.

brought him before Pilate, but the man sobbed and wept and denied that he had ever claimed to be the Messiah. Al-Jabbār, interpreting it to mean that Judas deliberately pointed out the wrong man, uses this to prove that Mohammed was right. Was deception by Judas what the 5th-cent. writing meant, or is it being read into the document in light of the Koran? If deception was the meaning, did it go back to the earliest stages of the Jewish-Christian group, or was their understanding of the crucifixion contaminated between the 2d and 5th cents.? In any case, by 1000 Judas had entered into plot theories as the one responsible for a scenario quite different from the standard account of Jesus' death on the cross.[148]

Sometimes Jesus himself was seen as the deceiver. Above we recorded Irenaeus' report of Basilides' thesis that Simon of Cyrene was crucified instead of Jesus. Simon could be mistaken for Jesus because "Jesus for his part assumed the form of Simon and stood by laughing."

A special form of the plot thesis is that one or the other drinks of wine offered to Jesus—among the Gospels only John 19:30 has Jesus take the wine—was a narcotic that numbed him so that he appeared dead but could be revived after his executioners departed. Heppner ("Vermorderte") reports on a variant proposed by G. B. Wiener (1848), and resuscitated in the 1920s, that Jesus was given morion wine, also called death wine. *Mōrios* was a plant used in making philters, a type of sleep-producing nightshade, sometimes identified with the mandragora plant. Pliny (*Natural History,* 21.105; #180) speaks of it as a poison that kills more quickly than opium and when mixed with wine produces senselessness. Heppner (664–65) tells of an apocryphal work that describes Judas' sister giving it to Jesus because she saw how much trouble he had caused. Thiering (*Qumran* 217–19) maintains that the high priest Jonathan kindly offered Jesus wine mixed with poison (*cholē,* "gall") so that he would not suffer further. After tasting it, he lost consciousness and appeared to die. Simon Magus (a doctor) who had been crucified with Jesus and whose legs had been broken was put in the cave tomb with him (along with Judas). She assures us: "Within the tomb, Simon Magus worked quickly, despite his broken legs. He squeezed the juice from the aloes and poured it with myrrh down the throat of Jesus. The poison that was not yet absorbed was expelled, and by 3 A.M. it was known that he would survive."

In 1965 H. J. Schonfield created a sensation with his book *The Passover Plot,* proposing a vast conspiracy. Jesus set the stage for his entry into Jerusalem and intentionally forced Judas to betray him. He chose the day of his death as Passover eve so that his body would be taken down from the cross

---

[148]Variants of the Judas-plot theory can be found in APPENDIX IV; in many of them he did not want Jesus to die and assumed that Jesus would be delivered, only to be seized with remorse when Jesus was actually killed.

quickly. The drink given Jesus was doctored to produce unconsciousness, thus permitting him to be revived when Joseph from Arimathea claimed his body. His plan backfired because of the spear wound, so that actually Jesus died soon afterward, but not from crucifixion. Undoubtedly many of those who hastened to buy the book thought they were getting the latest scholarship. The survey above shows that there is not likely to be much new under the sun in such exercises of the imagination. These theories demonstrate that in relation to the passion of Jesus, despite the popular maxim, fiction is stranger than fact—and often, intentionally or not, more profitable.

(*Bibliography for this episode may be found in §37, Parts 7, 8, and 9.*)

§43. JESUS CRUCIFIED, PART FOUR: HAPPENINGS AFTER JESUS' DEATH
a. EXTERNAL EFFECTS

(Mark 15:38; Matt 27:51–53; [Luke 23:45b])

Translation

Mark 15:38: And the veil of the sanctuary was rent into two from top to bottom.

Matt 27:51–53: [51]And behold, the veil of the sanctuary was rent from top to bottom into two. And the earth was shaken, and the rocks were rent, [52]and the tombs were opened, and many bodies of the fallen-asleep holy ones were raised. [53]And having come out from the tombs after his raising they entered into the holy city; and they were made visible to many.

[Luke 23:45b: ([44]And it was already about the sixth hour, and darkness came over the whole earth until the ninth hour, [45a]the sun having been eclipsed.) [45b]The veil of the sanctuary was rent in the middle. ([46]And having cried out with a loud cry, Jesus said, "Father, into your hands I place my spirit.")]

GPet 5:20–6:22: [5:20]And at the same hour [midday] the veil of the Jerusalem sanctuary was torn into two. [6:21]And then they drew out the nails from the hands of the Lord and placed him on the earth; and all the earth was shaken, and a great fear came about. [22]Then the sun shone, and it was found to be the ninth hour.

10:41–42: (Those present at Sunday dawn were hearing a voice from the heavens addressed to the gigantic figure of the Lord who has been led forth from the sepulcher): [41]"Have you made proclamation to the fallen-asleep?" [42]And an obeisance was heard from the cross, "Yes."

COMMENT

Between Jesus' death (§42 above) and the burial by Joseph of Arimathea (§§46–47 below), there are two sets of happenings or reactions to the death. (a) External, often physical, effects of an extraordinary nature (Mark 15:38; Matt 27:51–53; *GPet* 5:20–6:22). These physical effects are to be discussed in the present section (§43), namely: rending of the sanctuary veil, shaking of the earth, rending of the rocks, opening of the tombs, raising of the bodies of the fallen-asleep holy ones, their entrance into the holy city and being made visible to many. None of them are recounted after Jesus' death by John [1] or by Luke, although the latter has the rending of the sanctuary veil before Jesus dies (Luke 23:45b). (b) Reactions by people who were present (Mark 15:39–41; Matt 27:54–56; Luke 23:47–49; John 19:31–37; *GPet* 7:25–8:29[2]). The reactors include the centurion, those who kept watch over Jesus, the assembled crowds, the women, the hostile "Jews," and the soldiers who come to take the bodies away. Although their responses are often closely related to the physical happenings (e.g., the centurion reacts to the rending of the sanctuary veil), treatment of them will be reserved to the next section (§44).

In (a) we find an obvious pattern for subdivision. The rending of the veil of the sanctuary, found in Mark, Matt, Luke, and *GPet,* will be treated first. Some six special phenomena reported only by Matt among the canonical Gospels (one or two of them are echoed in *GPet*) will constitute the second subdivision. Commentators from the NT period onward have shown great ingenuity in interpreting these events, and considerable discussion will be required in my COMMENT to keep the luxuriant overgrowth of such interpretations (interesting though they may be) distinct from what each evangelist wished to convey by the happenings he described and what plausibly would have been understood by his 1st-cent. hearers/readers.

THE VEIL OF THE SANCTUARY WAS RENT (MARK 15:38; MATT 27:51; LUKE 23:45B; *GPet* 5:20)

An interpretation of what the Gospels narrate here is, in my judgment, relatively simple. Complications stem from the introduction of an interpreta-

---

[1] The closest John comes to something external and physical is the flow of blood and water from Jesus' pierced side (19:34).

[2] In fact, *GPet* has mixed the two sets of reactions. Amid external effects in 5:20–6:22 (veil torn, earth shaken, sun returning), we find "a great fear came about"; but most of the personal reactions (by the Jews; by Peter and his companions) come afterward. For an analysis of what *GPet* has done, see p. 1136 below.

tion of the veil found in Hebrews, and from attempts to discern which veil of the historical Temple is meant and what significance that would add. The existence of a different tradition involving the fracture of the Temple lintel has also entered the discussion. These issues will be treated one by one.

The Role of This Phenomenon in the Gospel Narratives. The language used to describe the rending of the veil (*katapetasma*) is remarkably stable:

Mark: And the veil of the sanctuary was rent into two from top to bottom.
Matt: And behold, the veil of the sanctuary was rent from top to bottom into two.
Luke: The veil of the sanctuary was rent in the middle.
GPet: The veil of the Jerusalem sanctuary was torn into two.

Twelve of the thirteen Greek words in Mark/Matt are identical; the one difference is at the beginning. Mark's simple *kai* ("and") will be used by Matt to introduce six additional phenomena that he will add in 27:51b–53; but this first phenomenon, the only one he draws from Mark, he chooses to highlight by the *kai idou* ("And behold"), which he uses elsewhere some dozen times[3] but which is never employed by Mark. Luke, besides moving the rending of the veil to before the crucifixion, has simplified Mark's duplication ("from top to bottom" and "into two") into one expression: "the middle,"[4] meaning "in or down the middle." Granting *GPet*'s proclivity for different vocabulary, it is notable to find only one significant change, *diarēgnynai* ("to tear [apart]") for *schizein* ("to rend"). Here *GPet* may have been influenced by the use of *diarēgnynai* in Mark/Matt for the high priest's tearing his clothes at Jesus' blasphemy during the Sanhedrin trial.[5] *GPet* was seemingly addressed to an audience with little knowledge of Palestine, and so it may have been useful to specify "the *Jerusalem* sanctuary." Faced with such similar wording, let us now turn to interpreting each Gospel.

Mark. Twice before, both times in the PN, Mark has spoken of *naos*, "the sanctuary."[6] Before the chief priests and the whole Sanhedrin, there was given against Jesus false testimony, namely, that he had been heard saying, "I will destroy this sanctuary made by hand, and within three days another not made by hand I will build" (14:58). As Jesus hung on the cross, those

---

[3]The frequency of the pattern would cause me to query the attempt of Witherup ("Death" 577) to make this expression in v. 51a part of the time sequence of chap. 27 (v. 46: ninth hour; 48: immediately; 57: evening).

[4]Luke uses *mesos* more than do Mark/Matt together. Whether this change also has theological significance will be discussed below.

[5]Unfortunately we do not have this trial preserved in the extant copy of *GPet* (which begins with the Herod/Pilate trial); it might have followed Matt's usage (26:65 [Mark 14:63]).

[6]Although what Jesus says about or does in "the Temple" (*to hieron*) is not unrelated to his attitude toward "the sanctuary," the immediate evocation is more likely to have been of passages using the same vocabulary.

who passed by were blaspheming him, "Aha, O one destroying the sanctuary and building it in three days . . ." (15:29). Part of the import of the present narrative, which constitutes a third reference to the sanctuary, must be that Jesus is vindicated: Rending the veil of the sanctuary has in one way or another destroyed that holy place. (Another almost identical sequence of three passages deals with the issue of Jesus' claim to be the Messiah, the Son of God—14:61; 15:32; 15:39: at the Sanhedrin, on the cross, after death—and there too the last one vindicates Jesus.) Nevertheless, Mark does not explain exactly how rending its veil destroys the sanctuary, and so we must analyze the image, as to both the rending and the sanctuary veil.

(1) The rending. Clearly the passive "was rent" makes God the agent.[7] At the beginning of Jesus' ministry the heavens were "rent" so that the voice of God could speak from them and declare of Jesus, "You are my beloved Son" (1:10–11); now God from heaven intervenes again, rending the veil of the sanctuary so that the centurion in the next verse will be brought to confess, "Truly this man was God's Son."[8] In 15:34 Jesus with a loud cry screamed out his sense of being forsaken by God, only to be mocked by those standing there. By the violent rending (*schizein*) God responds vigorously, not only to vindicate Jesus whom God has *not* forsaken, but also to express anger at the chief priests and Sanhedrin who decreed such a death for God's Son. Several early Christian witnesses confirm this interpretation of the rending as an angry act. In *Test. Levi* 10:3, when God can no longer endure Jerusalem because of the wickedness of the priests, the veil of the Temple is rent so that their shame can no longer be covered.[9] In *GPet* the signs that surround the death of Jesus, including the veil of the sanctuary being torn in two (5:20), show that he is just (8:28) and lead the Jews, the elders, and the priests to say, "Woe to our sins. The judgment has approached and the end of Jerusalem" (7:25). Indeed, that same gospel, by using the verb "tear" (as noted above), suggests a connection between the high priest's *tearing* of his clothes before the Sanhedrin as he demanded Jesus' death (Mark 14:63) and God's *rending* of the veil at Jesus' death, with the latter as an angry response

---

[7]Later traditions will attribute the rending to the Temple itself or to the angels, but in either case the ultimate agency is God's.

[8]Motyer ("Rending") uses this parallelism in an exaggerated way, attempting to find in the present scene a Marcan Pentecost: Because there was a descent of the Spirit (1:10: *pneuma*) when the heavens were rent at the beginning of Mark, this also happens at the end in the rending of the veil, as is hinted at when Jesus expires (15:37: *ekpnein*).

[9]In a series of articles M. de Jonge has explored early Christian exegesis of the rending of the veil, using the *Testaments of the Patriarchs* as a prime example. Whether one thinks of this as a Jewish work glossed by Christians or as a Christian composition, there was a Christian at work in the passages I shall be citing here.

to the former.[10] After all, at that very moment in the Sanhedrin trial Jesus warned the high priest that he and his fellow judges would see the Son of Man coming (14:62)—a coming in judgment that has commenced at the cross.

If wrath is the dominant symbolism of the rending in Mark 15:38, is there also an element of sorrow at what has happened to Jesus and/or to what is happening to the sanctuary and Jerusalem? Codex Bezae and the OL add to Mark's "rent . . . into two" the word "parts." Was the scribe who initiated the addition thinking of II Kings 2:12 where Elisha, inconsolable at the departure of Elijah, tears his cloak into two pieces (different Greek word)? The connection could have been suggested by the references to Elijah in Mark 15:35–36 when Jesus died. Daube ("Veil" 24) uses this to argue for the theme of sorrow and points also to TalBab *Mo'ed Qatan* 25b, which lists the mournful occasions where one rends one's clothes, not to be sewn up again: One of them is the destruction of the Temple and of Jerusalem, i.e., first for the Temple and then an enlarged rending for Jerusalem.[11] Referring to the rending of the sanctuary veil as the work of an angel (see p. 1120 below), Melito's homily *On the Pasch* 98 says that while the people did not rip their clothes at the death of Jesus, an angel ripped his. The evidence is not conclusive, but one should not discount the added motif of sorrow.

(2) The sanctuary veil. The general function of such a veil would be to shut the holy place off from the profane, and rending the veil would mean destroying the special character or holiness that made the place a sanctuary. Against the background of the sanctuary as a divine dwelling place—an idea shared by pagans and Jews alike—rending the veil could mean that the deity or the deity's presence had left. According to Ezek 10 the glory of God left the Temple in anger at the idolatries practiced there, just before God employed the Babylonians as instruments in destroying the Temple. In *II Baruch,* a Jewish apocryphon describing the destruction of Jerusalem by the Romans (whom it portrays as the Babylonians), an angel takes away the veil and other furniture of the Holy of Holies (6:7) before the voice is heard inviting, "Enter enemies and come adversaries, for he who guarded the house has left it" (8:2). A Christian form of this picture can be found in Tertullian (*Adv. Iudaeos* 13.15; CC 2.1388), who reports that a holy spirit

---

[10]This connection made in antiquity by *GPet* is more plausible than the attempt of Bailey ("Fall" 104) to make parallel the "unveiling" of Jesus (Mark 15:24: "They divide up his clothes") and the "unveiling" of the sanctuary—a proposed parallel that involves no vocabulary and little symbolic similarity.

[11]As part of the connection between the rending of the sanctuary veil and the rending of clothes, Daube points to Aramaic/Hebrew *pargōd,* meaning both "curtain" and "tunic."

(i.e., angel) used to dwell in the Temple before the advent of Christ who is the temple; also *Didascalia Apostololorum* 6.5.7 (Funk ed. 312): "He deserted the Temple [leaving it] desolate, rending the veil and taking away from it the holy spirit." The Marcan love for duplication has a strong literary effect here: The veil is rent "from top to bottom" and "into two" and so will not be reparable. Thus, for Mark the rending of the sanctuary veil means that with the death of Jesus the sanctuary as such went out of existence; the building that continued to stand there was not a holy place. Yet in addition to indicating symbolically what had already happened, the rending of the sanctuary veil retained value as a sign of what was yet to come and as an ominous warning of a judgment that would not be turned back. (Those who were reading Mark when or after the Romans physically destroyed the sanctuary of the Jerusalem Temple must have seen in this the fulfillment of what was signified earlier by the rending of the veil. After all, the Marcan Jesus had told them to be on the lookout for signs in the sacred precincts [13:14]: "When you see the desolating abomination standing where it ought not . . . then let those in Judea flee to the mountains.") As a negative sign after the death, the rending stands parallel to the darkness before Jesus' death. The day of the Lord with its burden of judgment was being heralded.

Matt. Here, on the one hand, the ominous, apocalyptic character of what has already been effected through the death of Jesus is intensified. Matt's readers have heard Jesus chastise Jerusalem for killing the prophets, predicting, "Behold your house is forsaken and deserted" (23:37–38). How much more divine wrath for killing the Son (21:33–41)! To illustrate this, the rending of the sanctuary veil is accompanied by the shaking of the earth and the rending of the rocks which, as we shall see in the next subsection, are familiar apocalyptic portents of the last times portrayed in the OT and early Jewish writings. On the other hand, the opening of the tombs, the raising of the many bodies of the fallen-asleep saints, and their being made visible to many in Jerusalem, while also part of the expected apocalyptic context, are positive signs. Matt is showing that the divine judgment has begun with both the negative and the positive.

Luke. Although the rending of the sanctuary veil in this Gospel, narrated in 23:45b, occurs immediately before the death of Jesus (see §42), I noted that I would reserve treatment of the phenomenon until here. The postponement was not because I intend to interpret Luke through Mark, but because Luke's moving of the rent veil to a position between the darkness over the whole earth and Jesus' final words has produced an ambiguity that can be appreciated better now that we have discussed the symbolism of this portent in Mark/Matt. If Luke found the Marcan localization to be unsatisfactory, perhaps in some way he interprets the rent veil differently. After the Lucan relocation, two lines of interpreting the rent veil become possible: (a) It retains some of its negative force and is joined to the darkness that precedes it as a double sign of divine displeasure; (b) It has acquired positive force and is joined to Jesus' last words as a contrasting positive reaction to the darkness. I pointed out on p. 1043 above that deliberately I had not translated the particle *de* in 23:45b because on purely grammatical grounds it is not possible to make a decision whether the *de* has a conjunctive sense, yielding an introductory "And (also)," which favors the (a) interpretation, or an adversative sense, yielding a "But," which favors the (b) interpretation. (In my translation I tried to reflect the existence of *de* without prejudicing the exegesis by setting v. 45b off as an independent sentence.[12]) Let us now evaluate each interpretation.

(a) Yoking the rending of the veil with the darkness. Luke 23:47–49 (to be treated in §44 below) will present after the death of Jesus three types of people who respond compassionately and thus affirm the salvific import of the death. I regard that grouping as a Lucan construction to match the three favorable responses to Jesus before he was crucified, a grouping also peculiar to Luke (23:26–32). In such an optimistic context after Jesus' death, Luke could not allow the ominous rending of the veil that he found in Mark to remain, and so he has moved it to where there was already an ominous context, placing it before the death to form a unit with the darkness that covered the whole earth from about the sixth until the ninth hour while Jesus suffered on the cross (23:44–45). Combined with the darkness/eclipse, the rent sanctuary veil offers a pattern of dire portents in the heavens and on the earth. That arrangement suited Lucan theology in another way.[13] At the Lucan Sanhedrin trial there was no prediction that Jesus would destroy the sanctuary, and so at the cross there was no need to portray a fulfillment of that prediction after Jesus' death. In Luke's outlook the Temple did not lose its sacred value through anything that happened in Jesus' lifetime, for the story of that life began and ended with a scene in the Temple complex (1:9 [*naos*]; 24:53 [*hieron*]). Indeed, in the early days of Christian life at Jerusalem believers in Jesus went daily to the Temple to pray (Acts 2:46; 3:1). Only with Stephen do we hear that the Most High does not dwell in the house built by Solomon's hands (7:48–49), and Stephen is the one who is condemned before the authorities for speaking against the holy place, say-

---

[12]Sylva ("Temple" 242) treats the independent sentence in NEB as meaning that the rending of the veil "may stand alone, not closely connected with what precedes or what follows it." That is not my understanding of the phenomenon; it must be related to one or the other.

[13]For what follows see the helpful observations of F. Weinert, CBQ 44 (1982), 69–70.

ing, "This Jesus the Nazorean will destroy this place."[14] By changing the Marcan picture where the rending of the veil was God's violent response to the death of Jesus, Luke has avoided desacralizing the Jewish sanctuary at the time of the death. The rending of the sanctuary veil before Jesus' death is a forewarning that the continuing rejection of Jesus will bring the destruction of the holy place, especially when rejection comes to the point of killing those (like Stephen) who proclaim him.[15] For Mark the rending of the veil after the death of Jesus both effected a present destruction of the holiness of the sanctuary and served as a sign of a future, less symbolic destruction. For Luke the rending of the veil, now placed before the death of Jesus, remains on the level of an ominous sign pointing to the future (which he narrates in Acts).

(b) Yoking the rending of the veil with Jesus' last words. This approach has been expounded by Pelletier and impressively by Sylva. While part of the supporting argumentation involves the role of the veil in Hebrews (which I shall discuss below), let me present the case here on purely Lucan grounds. If one gives an adversative thrust to the *de* of v. 45b ("But the veil of the sanctuary was rent in the middle"), one can interpret this phenomenon as a reaction to the darkness over the whole earth: The veil has been rent so that Jesus can go from the surrounding darkness through to his Father to place his spirit into his Father's hands, as he himself says immediately after the veil is torn. Several factors favor this interpretation. The veil is no longer rent "into two from top to bottom" as in Mark—a more violent image—but rent "in the middle," as if one would pass through. At the beginning of this Gospel (1:35) the coming of the Holy Spirit on Mary brought the conception of the Son of God; at the beginning of the ministry (3:21–22) the heaven was "opened" and the Holy Spirit descended on Jesus as a voice from heaven declared, "You are my beloved Son." Now this Son in his last words cries out to his Father, returning this spirit to God's hands. But why through the rent sanctuary veil? We remember that shortly after his birth Jesus was presented to the Lord in the Jerusalem Temple (2:22–27). At age twelve he was found by his parents in the Temple; and when chastised, he replied that he

---

[14]This is characterized as false witness in Acts 6:13–14. That is not because the saying is not true, but because the agency is misunderstood: Jesus himself takes no action to destroy the holy place, but the attitude of the rulers, and especially of the priests, toward him and his followers is the occasion of a divine judgment that strips the holy place of its holiness. Stephen, who is martyred, marks a turning point in the Christian attitude toward the Temple. Even though later in Acts Paul will go to the Temple (21:26), he has already stated (17:24) that the Lord of heaven and earth does not dwell in man-made sanctuaries (*naos*).

[15]Green ("Death" 556) finds a slightly different emphasis: "The time of the temple is not over. . . . But it is no longer the center around which life is oriented. Rather than serving as the gathering point for all the peoples under Yahweh, it has now become the point-of-departure for the mission to all peoples."

must be in his Father's house. Luke, then, has portrayed the Temple, "a house of prayer" (19:46), as the place of divine presence, and so Jesus may be shown as now passing (himself or his spirit) through the rent veil to the heavenly sanctuary which contained that presence. We know from Hebrews that some early Christians did think in this fashion (see below). An added argument is brought from the death of Stephen in Acts 7:55–59: He sees the heavens opened and the Son of Man standing at God's right; and as he dies he says, "Lord Jesus, receive my spirit." He was offering his spirit through the opened heavens to Jesus, who was now in heaven where he had gone earlier (1:11), even as Jesus offered his spirit through the rent veil to his Father in the sanctuary. Luke changed Jesus' last words from the Marcan cry of abandonment to a prayerful affirmation of trust; why could he not have changed the Marcan rent veil from a negative sign of destruction of the sanctuary to a positive sign of access to God?

This interpretation is possible, but I do not think it correct[16] because it pays insufficient attention to the exact wording that Luke has used, i.e., namely, "rent" (*schizein*) and "sanctuary" (*naos*). Both as Jesus' ministry begins and as Stephen dies, when Luke is describing the aperture of the heavens as a passageway for the spirit (to descend upon Jesus or to go up from Stephen), he uses a verb for opening. In fact, at the baptism (3:21) he changes Mark's expression (1:10) "the heavens rent [*schizein*]" to the less violent "open." Luke's only other Gospel use of *schizein* besides this sanctuary-veil passage shows how he understands its force; in 5:36 he introduced this verb into the parable of rending a piece from a new garment (Mark 2:21 had *airein*). The only two uses in Acts (14:4; 23:7) show a crowd rent in two, divided for and against Jesus. Thus never does Luke use *schizein* for an opening through which one passes, and his preserving here this verb which he found in Mark (contrary to his practice in 3:21) suggests that he has retained its negative force. Also one should be careful in generalizing from Luke's statements about the Temple (*hieron*) to his use here of the sanctuary (*naos*), copied from Mark.[17] His only other Gospel usage of "sanctuary" (in 1:9,21,22 for the place where Zechariah performs his priestly duties) suggests an awareness of the distinction between the two. There is no evidence that Luke thought of Jesus in priestly terms, and therefore it would be quite unusual to have the Lucan Jesus passing (himself or his spirit) through the sanctuary where only priests go. Luke had a positive

---

[16]On grounds other than the ones I propose, Green ("Death" 550–52) also disagrees with Sylva and emphasizes that since the very negative darkness comes before the rending of the veil, it must interpret that rending.

[17]I cannot help noticing the title of Sylva's article: "The *Temple* Curtain and Jesus' Death in the Gospel of Luke" (my italics).

attitude toward the Temple (as also posited in the [a] interpretation above); but he has preserved a sign of the destruction of the sanctuary, i.e., the place where priests and especially the high priest ministered to God's presence, for he knows that the priests and especially the high priest will continue their hostility to Jesus, persecuting Peter, John, Stephen, Paul, and other Christians (Acts 4:6; 5:17; 7:1; 9:1–2,21; 22:30; 23:14; 24:1; 25:2).

In summary, then, without dismissing altogether this second interpretation (b) of Luke, I definitely favor the first interpretation (a) where the rending of the sanctuary veil (like the darkness) is a negative indicator of God's wrath, even if for Luke that wrath is not immediately destructive as it is in Mark. Because there is an element of ignorance among those who put Jesus to death (Luke 23:34; Acts 3:17), a period of grace is granted before it will become Christian truth that God does not dwell in houses made by hands, and that Jesus of Nazareth has destroyed this holy place (Acts 7:48–49; 6:13–14).

Having commented upon the three Synoptic accounts of the rending of the sanctuary veil, I would now normally turn to expound the other phenomena narrated by Matt (27:51b–53) alone. I cannot pass so easily, however, from my interpretation of the rent sanctuary veil as a negative portent, which seems clear in Mark/Matt (and more probable in Luke), without commenting on various complementary issues that cause some scholars to give it another interpretation. Since I have already discussed diverse interpretations in Luke (a discussion necessitated by Luke's change of the Marcan locus), I am primarily concerned in what follows with a diverse interpretation of the rent veil in Mark.

The Veil in Hebrews. This epistle never employs the words *naos* ("sanctuary"), *hieron* ("Temple"), or *schizein* ("to rend"); but using the imagery of the preTemple Tent or Tabernacle, it paints a remarkable portrait of Jesus as the high priest of the New Covenant functioning as did the OT high priest on the Day of Atonement (Yom Kippur). In that description there occur the only other NT references (three) to the *katapetasma* ("veil") of which the three Synoptic death scenes speak. In Heb 6:19–20 Jesus, a high priest forever according to the order of Melchizedek, is described as a forerunner who has entered "the inner place of the veil" (an inner sanctum cut off from the outer by a veil). In 9:2–3 the description of the Israelite Tabernacle includes the outer (section of the) Tent called the Holy Place, and "behind the second veil there is the [section of the] Tent called the Holy of Holies."[18] In 10:19–20 the readers are assured: "We have confidence of entrance into the Holies

---

[18]The description assumes, but does not describe, a first veil at the entrance to the Holy Place.

in the blood of Jesus, an entrance which he inaugurated for us as a new and living way through the veil, i.e., his flesh."[19]

For our purposes it is not necessary to go into all the disputes about how to interpret this imagery. The following scenario is plausible. Once a year the Jewish high priest went through the *katapetasma* or veil that separated the Holy Place from the inner Holy of Holies; in the latter he incensed the gold cover (*kappōret*) of the Ark of the Covenant[20] and sprinkled it with the blood of a bull and goat previously sacrificed (Lev 16:11–19). Similarly, according to Hebrews, Christ the high priest passed through the *katapetasma,* which is his flesh, to the Holy of Holies which is the highest heavens, taking his own blood, in order to consummate there the sacrifice begun on the cross. By so doing he opened the way for believers to enter the heavenly sanctum. Is Eph 2:13 ("You who were once far off have become near by *the blood* of Christ") an independent form of the same idea?

In reflecting on the Mark/Matt account of Jesus' prayers in Gethsemane and on the cross, we found a parallel in Heb 4:14–16; 5:7–10 when Jesus, a high priest tested as we are, "brought prayers and supplications with a strong clamor and tears to the One having the power to save him from death." That parallelism was best explained by positing a very early tradition of Jesus' praying to God before he died, a tradition that was developed through the use of psalms into a narrative in Mark and *independently* into a hymn in Hebrews. In the present instance, then, it is not unlikely that there was an early theological insight that the death of Jesus redefined God's presence among the chosen people, a presence hitherto found in the veiled sanctuary (Holy of Holies) of Israelite liturgical ordinance. In the line of development that led to Mark's presentation, this insight was combined with Jesus' threats against the Jerusalem sanctuary, prophesying destruction unless his proclamation of God's kingdom was heeded. The rejection of that proclamation by crucifying the proclaimer effected the destruction of the sanctuary, symbolized by the irreparable rending of the veil that marked its distinctness as the place of God's presence. This symbolic destruction, serious as it was, foreshadowed the final physical destruction of the Temple by the Romans. In the independent line of development that led to Hebrews, this insight was combined with the theology of Christ as the high priest of the New Covenant. Once more (implicitly) the Jerusalem sanctuary had lost all signifi-

---

[19]From the analogy of the Israelite high priest we have to assume that like the veil, the flesh was something Jesus had to pass through (the incarnation of God's Son?) to get to heaven.

[20]This existed in the pre-exilic sanctuaries but not in the Temple of Jesus' time. That, along with the fact that the building of the Temple was not commanded by God as was the erection of the Tabernacle, may explain why Heb drew its imagery from the latter.

cance but not by destruction; now God's presence in the heavenly sanctum is depicted as opened to all who follow Jesus through the veil.

Such an understanding of the relationship of the *katapetasma* passages in Hebrews and in Mark 15:38 presents no major problem for the interpretation of Mark already given above. These NT works would be offering independent developments of an early tradition[21] in which the emergent final imagery is quite different: in Mark, a destructive rending of the veil causing the sanctuary to lose its holiness; and in Hebrews, a positive opening of the veil to God's presence in a heavenly Holy of Holies. Problems arise, however, when the positive outlook of Hebrews is introduced into the explication of Mark 15:38, so that the Marcan passage emerges with (a) only a positive interpretation, e.g., the veil was rent so that Jesus could lead others into the sanctuary, or (b) both a negative and a positive interpretation.[22] How is one to evaluate these suggestions?

I judge (a) impossible. Admittedly, it would be pleasing to have an entirely positive Marcan picture emerge from the death of Jesus (like the Lucan picture in 23:47–49) and thus to remove the antiJewish implications of a destructive divine judgment on the Jerusalem sanctuary. But interpretation (a) illegitimately neglects the relationship between the use of *naos* in Mark 15:38 with the two preceding Marcan *naos* passages, both of them in the PN and both of them referring to the destruction of the *naos* by Jesus. It also does not do justice to an element of violence implied by rending (*schizein*). Completely to overlook these factors on the basis of imagery in Hebrews that never mentions *naos* or *schizein* is unjustifiable.

Prima facie, interpretation (b) is more deserving of attention, for it re-

[21]While independently two authors could have hit on the change of the site of God's presence, their hitting upon the key symbol of the *katapetasma* in relation to the death of Jesus without the influence of a common tradition is less likely. Also, as will become evident from my citation of Jewish literature, descriptions of divine punishment of Jerusalem traditionally involved the Holy of Holies and its furnishings; and early Christian tradition evidently turned to this same symbolism. Besides the (inner) veil passages there is Rom 3:25 with its reference to the *hilastērion* (*kappōret*).

[22]Commentators often do not distinguish between (a) and (b); they also disagree (as will be explained) on whether the outer veil was rent to allow access to the Holy Place or the inner veil was rent to allow access to the Holy of Holies. Yet among those who in one way or another assign a positive interpretation to the rending of the veil in one or the other Synoptic Gospel are Bartsch, Benoit, Caird, Ellis, Gnilka, Linnemann, Motyer, Pelletier, Sabbe, Schneider, Taylor, Vögtle, and Yates. Lindeskog ("Veil" 134) argues, as I do, for a common tradition behind the Synoptics and Heb but thinks the import of that early tradition was positive. Not all positive interpretations are the same as that offered by Heb. For instance, *Test. Benjamin* 9:4 has the curtain (*haplōma*) of the sanctuary rent, with the result that the spirit of God is poured out upon all the Gentiles like fire. Ephraem (*Comm. on the Diatessaron* 21.4–6; SC 121.376–78) lists a number of activities of this Spirit, e.g., using the rent veil to clothe honorably the naked body of Jesus on the cross. Jerome (Epistle 120, *Ad Hedybiam* 8; CSEL 55.490) and other Church Fathers would have heavenly mysteries revealed when the veil was rent and in this connection sometimes quote I Cor 13:12 and II Cor 3:16–18. A gnostic interpretation along this line is found in *Gospel of Philip* II,3; 85.5–21.

spects the negative thrust demanded by the Marcan sequence.[23] Yet one must prove that Mark 15:38 is patient of the positive explication found in Hebrews. Two basic arguments are offered by those who respond affirmatively. First, they note that in the first reference to *naos* in Mark 14:58 there is both negative and positive: not only the destruction of the *naos* made by hand, but the building of another *naos* not made by hand. (Generally they ignore the fact that the second reference to *naos* in 15:29 has only the negative part, an emphasis which suggests that as the narrative continues Mark's primary concern will be to show the destruction of the *naos*.) The deduction, however, that therefore there should be both a negative and positive fulfillment in the rending of the veil in 15:38 (Vögtle, "Markinische" 374–75) is weak, for the positive element (if it need be present) may lie in the centurion's confession of Jesus as Son of God in 15:39 and have nothing to do with the veil. That confession in 15:39 is the center of the second argument offered by proponents of interpretation (b). We shall see in §44 below that the centurion who recognizes Jesus' true identity may represent the Gentiles ready to acknowledge what the Jews denied. But some would press this further and argue that Jesus, having gone through the rent veil into the heavenly sanctuary, is beginning to lead others through that veil.[24] In evaluating this, one must be disturbed by the complete lack of entering language in Mark 15:38–39 and of even an implied reference to heaven. (Mark's imagery is not at all like that of Luke's scene where Jesus promises that one wrongdoer will be with him this day in paradise [23:40–43].) If we return to Mark 14:58, the positive image of Jesus' *building* another sanctuary not made by hand would not make us think of a heavenly sanctuary, for surely that has existed timelessly. Mark is more likely depicting replacement by a sanctuary consisting of believers, as in other NT passages that imagine a Temple of living stones (p. 440 above). In that interpretation Mark 15:39 would be showing the first new believer after the death of Jesus and thus the commencement of the building of another sanctuary. Such an exegesis of 15:39 does nothing to support a positive reading of the rent sanctuary veil in 15:38. Overall, then, I see no solid reason for bringing over from Hebrews a positive interpretation of Mark 15:38[25] whereby the veil has been rent to allow Jesus to enter the heavenly sanctum, leading others behind him.

The Veils in the Temple of Jesus' Time. Interpretations other than the

---

[23]Theoretically one could debate whether the rending of the veil can be negative and positive at the same time, but symbols are notoriously resistant to the law of noncontradiction.

[24]Appeal is made to Acts 7:55–56, where Stephen looks up to heaven: "Behold, I perceive the heavens opened and the Son of Man standing at the right of God."

[25]Those who settle for or favor a negative interpretation (with varying nuance and in reference to one or the other Gospel) include Danker, Dormeyer, Grundmann, Juel, Lohmeyer, Lührmann, Marshall, Maurer, Schenke, Schmid, Schreiber, and Zahn.

one I advocate for Mark 15:38 have been advanced on the basis of the special significance that the veil had in the Herodian Temple. This argument is based on the suppositions that the evangelists knew this significance and that we are able to recover it; consequently a number of erudite articles have been devoted to a historical investigation of the issue. Before I finish this discussion, I shall raise a hermeneutical challenge to the whole approach; but for the moment let me lay out the available facts. Fitzmyer (*Luke* 2.1518) would count thirteen curtains or veils in the Temple, but the issue may be even more complicated. Many statements about the veils are based on Pentateuchal descriptions of the arrangement of the Tabernacle. Since the Tabernacle or Tent of the desert wanderings was not rigidly built but movable, curtains rather than permanent dividers played an important role. But the Pentateuchal descriptions of the Tabernacle are overlaid with memories of a more permanent building at Shiloh constructed when the Israelites gained control of the highlands of Judea and Samaria. As for the Temple, we have some detailed descriptions of Solomon's Temple, less detail about Zerubbabel's Temple, and for the Herodian Temple which existed in Jesus' time some passages in Josephus and Philo (as well as much later memories in the Mishna and Talmud, often colored by idealism).[26] The descriptions of an earlier Temple are often colored by the writer's experience of the Temple now standing and are further complicated by the desire to show that the Temple, which was essentially a human (royal) enterprise, followed in its structures the directives God had given through Moses for the Tabernacle. Clearly doors were used as dividers in the Temple; but we cannot always decide whether the mention of curtains and veils is an anachronism, or cloth dividers were kept in many Temple doorways and apertures, even if now otiose, for the sake of tradition. For instance I Kings 6:31–34 speaks of doors, while II Chron 3:14 speaks of a veil leading into the Holy of Holies. Josephus (*Ant.* 8.3.3; #71–75) describes doors with veils or woven hangings; and *Aristeas* 7.86 depicts the outer veil (*katapetasma*) as shaped to match the doors, which evidently were left opened, for winds moved and bulged out the veil. Overall we must be cautious when we read scholars' descriptions of the sanctuary veils that existed at Jesus' time and check whether they are based on contemporary descriptions of the Herodian Temple or are a mélange of earlier descriptions of uncertain applicability.

For the present discussion two or three veils are important. Within the innermost court of the Herodian Temple area stood the sacred Temple itself, divided into two rooms. The portal led into the Holy Place (*Hêkāl*); and at

---

[26]Let me leave aside the complication that the Herodian Temple was not finished in Jesus' time, and so even use of the Josephan descriptions of the finished Temple may be anachronistic. On the complications of the various descriptions of the veils, see Légasse, "Voiles."

the end of that room was the entrance into a further and smaller chamber, the Holy of Holies (*Děbîr;* see sketch in NJBC 76.42 of the Solomonic Temple, which set the pattern). The two veils that concern us are those that hung at the entrance from the outside court to the Holy Place (the outer veil) and the entrance from the Holy Place into the Holy of Holies (the inner veil).[27] A third veil comes into the discussion because in the Tabernacle there was a veil (that I shall call the precinct veil) at the entry to the whole sacred precinct or compound; and biblical descriptions are not always clear as to which entrance (to the compound or to the structure) is involved and correspondingly whether the precinct veil or the outer veil is meant. (Légasse, "Voiles" 568–71, denies that there was a precinct veil in the Solomonic or Zerubbabel Temples.) Which of these veils might have been meant in the Synoptic accounts that speak of the rending of the *katapetasma?* OT vocabulary for the outer and inner veils is not rigorously consistent: *Katapetasma* is used for both outer and inner veils[28] but more often for the inner veil, while *kalymma* is used for the outer veil (and the precinct veil) but, so far as I can discover, not for the inner veil.[29]

Vocabulary, then, slightly favors interpreting the Synoptic reference to the *katapetasma* as having the inner veil in mind (if specificity was intended). The fact that *katapetasma* in Hebrews clearly refers to the inner veil covering the entrance to the Holy of Holies also points in that direction.[30] Yet many contend that the Synoptics were referring to the outer veil that marked the entrance from the court outside into the Holy Place.[31] The outer veil, not the inner, would have been visible from a distance. Consequently those who understand Mark 15:39 (that the centurion saw that thus Jesus expired) to

[27]Mishna *Yoma* 5.1 describes a double curtain with a space between, but Légasse ("Voiles" 580–81) judges this a fictive description.

[28]But to my knowledge it is not used for the precinct veil, unless Num 3:26 refers to that.

[29]In these listings I do not attempt to be exhaustive: (1) Descriptions of the precinct veil are found in Exod 27:16; 35:17; 38:18; 39:40; 40:8,33; Num 4:26, using *mesek* in Hebrew and *kalymma* ("curtain") in LXX Greek, although Philo (*De vita Mosis* 2.19; #93) speaks of a *hyphasma* or woven piece. (2) Descriptions of the outer veil are found in Exod 26:36–37; 35:15; 39:38; 40:5,28; Num 3:25,31; 4:25, using *mesek* in Hebrew and *kalymma, katakalymma, kalymma katapetasmatos,* and *epispastron* ("draw curtain") in LXX Greek. Philo calls it a *kalymma* in *De vita Mosis* 2.21; #101, but *katapetasma* (once modifying it as "the first" veil) in *De specialibus legibus* 1.171,231,274. Seemingly the outer veil is meant in Lev 21:23 and Num 18:7, which use *pārōket* in Hebrew and *katapetasma* in Greek. (3) Descriptions of the inner veil are found in Exod 26:31–33; 30:6; 35:12; 39:34; 40:21; Num 4:5, using *pārōket* in Hebrew and *katapetasma* in LXX Greek (and Philo). It is noteworthy that while the Hebrew description of the outer and inner veils in Exod 36:35–37 distinguishes them as *mesek* and *pārōket,* the LXX (37:3–5) uses *katapetasma* for both.

[30]Church Fathers and subsequent scholars who think that Mark/Matt are referring to the inner veil include Chrysostom, Theodoret, Cyril of Alexandria, and Aquinas; and Billerbeck, Hauck, Lindeskog, Plummer, Schneider, Senior, Swete, Taylor, and Turner.

[31]These include Origen and Jerome; and Bartsch, Benoit, Driver, Ernst, Fitzmyer, Huby, Lagrange, Lohmeyer, McNeile, Pelletier, and Vincent. Yates ("Velum" 232) thinks that Matt and Luke meant the outer veil but finds Mark unclear.

mean that he also literally saw the rending of the veil (Matt 27:54: saw "these happenings")[32] would argue that the outer veil must have been involved. What difference does it make? That depends on whether the outer veil had a special significance. Pelletier ("Grand") depicts the outer veil as a huge linen draw-curtain in an entrance porch that was ninety feet high (whence the significance of "from top to bottom"). According to Josephus (*War* 5.5.4; #213–14) it had four different colors symbolizing the elements of the universe (fire, earth, air, water) and portrayed the panorama of the heavens.[33] (However, Philo [*De Vita Mosis* 2.17–18; #84–88], who also speaks of the symbolism of the four elements, describes curtains all the way around the Tabernacle, and so one could get the impression that the symbolism was not confined to the outer veil.) Lindeskog ("Veil" 136) manages to draw some of the same symbolism from what lay behind the inner veil, now no longer the Ark of the Covenant but a special stone designated as foundational—a stone that was involved in the creation of the world, the gate to hell and heaven (Mishna *Yoma* 5.2; TalBab *Yoma* 54b). From all this it has been argued that the rending of the sanctuary veil had cosmic significance as interpreted by the extra phenomena in Matt 27:51b–53 (earth shaken, rocks rent, tombs opened),[34] or had salvific import for all since it involved a rending of the heavens offering access to the presence of God. Ulansey ("Heavenly") employs the idea of heavenly symbolism for the veil to enhance the inclusion between the rending of the veil and rending of the heavens at the beginning of Mark (p. 1100 above).

Despite the enormous amount of research dedicated to the outer/inner veil issue and to the esoteric symbolism of the respective veils, along with Dormeyer and Lamarche, I reject the value of the whole enterprise in relation to the Gospel description. One can attribute at most possibility to the scholarly decisions as to which veil the evangelists might have had in mind (if all three

[32]See p. 939 above for the theory of E. L. Martin. In the same vein D. Brown ("Veil") points out that if the inner veil were rent, the only ones who would have known of it were the priests, who alone were allowed into the Holy Place; and according to the Synoptic accounts at this moment they were at Golgotha. In any case would they have been likely to advertise such an event if it took place at the time of Jesus' death? Occasionally those who push the historical issue to the extreme contend that the priests who did reveal the rending of the inner veil were those who became followers of Jesus (Acts 6:7)!

[33]In support of the heavenly symbolism Pelletier ("Veil" 171) also points to Sir 50:5–7, where Simon the high priest comes from within the *katapetasma* and is compared to a star, the sun, the moon, and a rainbow. In "Voile" he calls attention to the *parapetasma*, a similar huge, colored wool veil hanging in the portal of the temple of Olympia in Greece, reported by Pausanias (*Descriptio Graecae* 5.12.4) to have been donated by the Syrian king Antiochus (IV?). According to I Macc 1:22 and Josephus (*Ant.* 12,5.4; #250) Antiochus IV took away the veil of the Jerusalem Temple ca. 169 BC.

[34]Clearly Jesus' death was thought to be of cosmic significance, and I would interpret the special Matthean phenomena as symbolizing that. It is another question whether the rending of the veil had this significance.

had the same veil in mind). How much confidence can we have that the general description "the veil of the sanctuary," used by the three evangelists, conveyed any precision about outer/inner? More radically, what assurance do we have that the evangelists knew about the number of veils, or details about them and their symbolism? None of them had ever been inside the Holy Place. Had any of them ever been to Jerusalem and seen the outer veil from a distance?[35] How widely were esoteric interpretations of the veils known? Still more radically, is there any likelihood that the readers of the Gospel would have known about all this? Mark (7:3–5) had to explain to his readers elementary Jewish purity customs. Can we seriously think he expected them to interpret the rending of the veil against an unsupplied background of the curtain arrangements in the Herodian edifice and of the way they were colored? From the beginning of this commentary I have argued that detectable comprehensibility to a 1st-cent. audience is an important (even if not sufficient) guide to interpretation. It is one thing to posit that the Christians (Jewish and Gentile) in that audience would have known the basic themes of the Jewish Scriptures pertinent to Jesus; it is another to posit that they would have understood details of cosmic symbolism that are not contained in the biblical descriptions of the Temple. On that principle I would contend that we should not introduce into the exegesis of Mark 15:38 and par. esoteric information about the historical veils in the Jerusalem Temple.

Phenomena Marking Temple Destruction (Especially in Josephus and Jerome). Under this somewhat awkward title I shall deal with material that does cast light on how the report of the rending of the sanctuary veil would fit into people's understanding in the 1st cent. and how it was interpreted by early Christians.[36]

It was widely understood in antiquity that God or the gods frequently gave extraordinary signs at the death of noble or important figures. The blood of a Maccabean martyr quenched the fire set by his torturers to burn him (*IV Macc* 9:20), and there was an eclipse of the moon on the night when Herod the Great put to death Matthias who had stirred up youth to purify the Temple by removing an eagle Herod had placed there (Josephus, *Ant.* 17.6.4; #167). Sometimes in the instance of Jewish martyrs who died piously a voice was heard from heaven proclaiming their blessed destiny in the world to come (TalBab *Berakot* 61b; '*Aboda Zara* 18a). As for the Greco-Roman mind-set, in relation to the darkness covering the earth at noon before Jesus

[35]Luke in 1:5–10,21–22 and Acts 3:2,11 shows knowledge of priestly customs and of details of Temple layout; but was that personal knowledge or simply part of the tradition he received? He adds nothing locative to Mark's picture of the veil.

[36]Most helpful in what follows are the studies by de Jonge, McCasland, Montefiore, Nestle, and Zahn listed in §37, Part 10. See also Lange in Part 11.

died, I cited (p. 1043) eclipses thought to have marked the death of Romulus and of Julius Caesar. Beyond that Virgil (*Georgics* 1.472–90) adds terrestrial and celestial wonders at the death of Caesar: Etna pouring forth molten rock; clashes of arms in the German skies; the Alps quaking; an awesome voice speaking in the forests; pale specters in the dark night; the temple ivories weeping and the bronzes sweating; frequent lightnings in a cloudless sky; and comets. Cassius Dio (*History* 60.35.1) reports portents at the death of Claudius, including a comet seen for a long time, a shower of blood, a thunderbolt striking the soldiers' standards, the opening by itself of the temple of Jupiter Victor.

Similar signs are associated by Cassius Dio with the fall of Alexandria to Octavian in 30 BC (51.17.4–5), so that besides the death of men, the "death" of prestigious places and institutions was marked by the gods. Important for our consideration is one of the most famous instances of this.

Josephus (*War* 6.5.3; #288–309) tells of some eight wonders that occurred between AD 60–70 and served as ominous, God-given portents of the coming desolation of the Jerusalem Temple by the Romans, even though many of the Jews foolishly took them as positive signs. In the HEAVENS there were a sword-shaped star; a *comet*[37] that continued for a year; at 3 A.M. a light as bright as day shining around the altar and the sanctuary; chariots and *armies seen throughout the country in the clouds* before sunset (told with special emphasis that this is not a fable). In the TEMPLE area there were many signs: a cow giving birth to a lamb; the massive brass eastern *gate of the inner court opening* by itself at midnight, even though scarcely movable by twenty men; *at Pentecost* the priests in the inner court hearing a *collective voice, "We are departing from here"* (i.e., the sanctuary[38]); years of woes against Jerusalem and sanctuary uttered by Jesus bar Ananias, whom the Jerusalem authorities seized, beat, and handed over to the Romans to be put to death, only to have him released by the governor as mad. Tacitus, who would have been in Rome during the last years of Josephus' life there, wrote (*Hist.* 5.13) in reference to Titus' destruction of the Jerusalem Temple that there were ill-omened signs that the Jews foolishly looked on as favorable. They included armies fighting in the heavens; fire lighting up the Temple; doors of the Holy Place abruptly opening; a superhuman voice declaring that the gods were leaving it and at the same time a great movement of those departing.[39]

---

[37]I am italicizing motifs that will come into the subsequent discussion.

[38]In many references in the following pages the presence of an angel or angels (spirit or spirits) in the Holy of Holies is assumed. Sometimes these may be the angels who adore the divine presence (as in Isa 6:2–3) or who guard the sanctuary; other times, like the angel of the Lord, they may represent an anthropomorphic description of God.

[39]Although Montefiore ("Josephus" 152) judges Tacitus to be an independent witness, McCasland's view ("Portents" 330–31) that Tacitus drew on Josephus is probably correct.

From the preceding paragraphs it should be clear that the 1st-century readers of the Gospels, whether Jewish or Gentile, would have had no great problem with the rending of the sanctuary veil (or the additional phenomena in Matt 27:51b–53) that the Gospels associated with the death of Jesus in AD 30/33. In the post-70 era, Christians would soon have become aware of the portents that Jews associated with the destruction of the Jerusalem Temple by the Romans.[40] Because of the common motif of the destruction of the Jerusalem sanctum, they easily mingled the two traditions of ominous divine signs. Let us discuss some traces of that mingling and of how it functioned interpretatively.

Below (p. 1120) I shall cite a poetic piece from Melito of Sardis (ca. AD 170) that describes what happened at Jesus' death: The earth was trembling, the heavens feared, the angel rent his clothes, the Lord thundered from the heaven, and the Most High gave a cry. Although what Melito lists is related to the added phenomena in Matt 27:51b–53, the imagery has some similarities to Josephus' portents before the destruction of the Temple. Similarly and contemporaneously, *The Ascents of James* (Pseudo-Clementines 1.41.3.) reports that the whole world suffered with Jesus: The sun was darkened; the stars were disturbed; the sea was roiled up; the mountains were moved; the graves were opened; and the veil of the Temple was rent as if lamenting the destruction hanging over the place. Tertullian (*Adv. Marcion* 4.42.5; CC 1.660) connects the rending of the Temple veil to the breaking out of an angel leaving the daughter of Zion.[41] Eusebius (EH 3.8.1–9) cites the whole passage from Josephus about the portents of the destruction of the Temple;

[40]In addition to the Josephus list, we have other traditions. *II Bar* 6–8 relates that before the destruction of the Temple by the Babylonians (= Romans) angels came and took out the furniture of the Holy of Holies, including the veil, ephod, *kappōret*, altar, and priestly vestments. Only then did a voice come from the midst of the Temple allowing entrance to the adversaries because the guardian had left the house. TalJer *Yoma* 6.43c says that among the portents, *forty years before the destruction of the Temple* (see pp. 365–66 above) its doors opened of their own accord. Rabbi Johanan ben Zakkai rebuked the Temple for thus troubling itself, since Zech 11:1 had already prophesied: "Open your doors, O Lebanon, that the fire may devour your cedars." (We remember that the Solomonic Temple was built of cedar of Lebanon.) TalBab *Yoma* 39b reports that at that time sacred lots came out unluckily, the crimson strip over the Temple entrance remained red rather than turning white on the Day of Atonement, and one of the seven-branched candlestick lamps went out. TalBab *Giṭṭin* 56b narrates that Titus entered the Holy of Holies, rent the veil with his sword, and blood spurted out. Despite the final Christian layer, the *Lives of the Prophets* is thought by many to contain old Jewish traditions. There (Torrey ed., 44) Habakkuk says: "The veil of the inner sanctuary will be torn to pieces, and the capitals of the two pillars will be taken away." For "capitals," see n. 45 below.

[41]*Transitus Mariae* (difficult to date) 10 (JANT 195) has the women who ministered in the Temple flee into the Holy of Holies during the crucifixion darkness. There they see an angel come down with a sword to rend the veil in two and hear a loud voice uttering a woe against Jerusalem for killing the prophets. When they see the angel of the altar fly up into the altar canopy with the angel of the sword, they know "that God has left His people." See also *Gospel (Questions) of Bartholomew* 24–27 (HSNTA 1.491; rev. ed. 1.542–43).

elsewhere (*Demonstratio Evangelica* 8.2.121–24; GCS 23.389–90) he says that the Pentecost portent reported by Josephus took place after the death of the Savior and then calls attention to a scene that occurred during the governorship of Pilate, leaving a confusing indicator of the time span of the narrated events. In his *Chronicle* (p. 1042 above) Eusebius links to the general period of Jesus' death the eclipse reported by Phlegon (related to Luke 23:45a), an earthquake in Bithynia (related to Matt 27:51b), and Josephus' Pentecost portents (related to the veil)! The obscuring of the time difference between what happened to Jesus in AD 30/33 and what happened near the destruction of the Temple in AD 70 (a forty-year generational span) will become characteristic of other Christian writers. Among the different authors and their traditions the melding may have happened because of: (a) Jewish references to certain occurrences forty years before the destruction; and/or (b) a theology that saw the death of Jesus as the cause for the (later) destruction of the Temple; and/or (c) a recognition that the rending of the sanctuary veil was an anticipatory sign of the destruction of the whole, as foretold by Jesus.

Jerome has a very important role in the development of the veil tradition, not only because of his use of the Josephus material but because of his access to early apocryphal Christian witnesses. Of import are a half-dozen references covering a range of almost thirty years (between 380 and 409) that are not always consistent and may reflect a growing tradition in Jerome's own mind.[42] I shall treat them in chronological order to the extent that dating can be ascertained. In Epistle 18a (*Ad Damasum Papam* 9; CSEL 54.86) Jerome comments on Isaiah's vision (6:4) of the Lord's throne in the Temple where the Seraphim are singing praise to God's holiness: "And the lintel [over the door frame] was shaken at the voice with which they shouted, and the house was filled with smoke." Jerome quotes a Greek Father (Gregory Nazianzen?) who sees this fulfilled in the (Roman) destruction of the Temple and burning of Jerusalem. Yet others hold that the Temple lintel was heaved over when the veil of the Temple was rent, and the whole house of Israel was confused by a cloud of error. It was to this same period that Josephus was referring when he wrote about the priests hearing the voices of the heavenly hosts from the inmost part of the Temple, "Let us cross out from these abodes." In Epistle 46 (*Paulae et Eustochii ad Marcellam* 4; CSEL 54.333) Jerome associates the rending of the Temple veil with Jerusalem being surrounded by an army and the departure of the angelic guardianship. He again cites Josephus but now in such a way that Josephus seems to say that the voices of the heavenly hosts broke forth "at that time when the Lord was crucified."

---

[42]See Zahn, "Zerrissene" 733, 740, 751, 753.

In his *Commentarium in Matt.* 4 (on 27:51; SC 259.298) Jerome makes reference to a gospel he has often mentioned (i.e., the gospel written in Hebrew characters, although it was actually in Aramaic, used by the Nazoreans of the Berea or Aleppo region).[43] In that gospel he says, "We read that the Temple lintel of infinite size was shattered and fractured." Then he repeats the Josephus reference about the outcry of the angelic hosts. In Epistle 120 (*Ad Hedybiam* 8; CSEL 55.489–90) Jerome again cites Josephus, as well as referring to the gospel written in Hebrew letters where: "We read not that the veil of the Temple was rent, but that the Temple lintel of great size was heaved over." In his *Commentarium in Isaiam* 3 (CC 73.87), once more in reference to 6:4, he speaks of the lintel of the Temple being heaved over and all the hinges broken, fulfilling the threat of the Lord in Matt 23:38 that the house would be left deserted.[44] Later in the same writing (18; CC 73A.775), commenting on the uproar from the city and Temple (Isa 66:6), which is part of the sound of the Lord repaying enemies, Jerome sees an undoubted reference to the period when Jerusalem was surrounded by Roman armies. Once more he cites the Josephus passage about the outcry of the angelic hosts who presided over the Temple.

I have gone into this in some detail because it casts interesting light on the factors that entered Christian interpretation. Clearly the Jewish tradition about the portentous phenomena surrounding the destruction of the Temple (in this case phrased by Josephus) has colored the understanding of the phenomena accompanying the death of Jesus. Both sets of actions express God's wrath, and those of AD 30/33 foreshadow the greater destruction in 70; indeed, the line between the two is blurred. The rending of the sanctuary veil which functioned on a symbolic level ultimately becomes the physical shaking or upheaving of the Temple lintel, as occurred in the destruction of the building by the Romans. A catalyst in connecting the Christian presentations of 30/33 and 70 is OT prophecy referring to events in the Temple whenever the wording, no matter what it meant originally (Isa 6:4 was positive!), was applicable to either set of phenomena. If one follows the chronological flow of Jerome's passages, he first mentions the breaking of the Temple lintel in interpreting Isa 6:4 and then later mentions that he found this (instead of the rending of the veil) in an apocryphal gospel. Surely, then, Jerome saw a relationship between the reading in that gospel and the exegesis of Isaiah.

[43]See M. J. Lagrange, RB 31 (1922), 161–81, 321–44. Confusingly, sometimes Jerome treats this *Gospel of the Nazoreans* as if it were the Semitic original behind Greek Matt. (It is not the same as the *Gospel of the Hebrews* known to the Alexandrian Fathers, which is independent of Greek Matt.) He claims to have translated it into Greek (and Latin?); but we are not sure always whether he is citing it directly, or from quotes in others, or from memory.

[44]He specifies that forty-two years after the passion the Temple was destroyed.

The phenomena surrounding Jesus' death in Mark 15:33,38 echo OT passages (particularly those giving the signs of the day of the Lord). So also do other phenomena which developed in popular circles and of which we have knowledge from the Fathers and apocryphal writings; but there a different set of OT passages comes into play.[45] These remarks serve as a helpful introduction to the first attested set of other phenomena occurring after the death of Jesus that were used to supplement Mark's rending of the sanctuary veil, namely, those listed in Matt.

SPECIAL PHENOMENA IN MATT 27:51–53 (AND *GPet*)

Previous PN scenes also have had material peculiar to Matt, namely, the death of Judas and the thirty pieces of silver, the dream of Pilate's wife, Pilate's washing his hands, and "his blood on us and on our children"— material that I have suggested came from vivid popular tales of the passion. Here, alone among the canonical Gospels, Matt has an additional list of astounding phenomena that greeted the death of Jesus.[46] While, like the rending of the sanctuary veil, these phenomena reflect apocalyptic eschatology, they are even more imaginative. *GPet,* which echoed special Matthean material in the washing of the hands, echoes at least one of these phenomena (the shaking of the earth).[47]

In order to study the Matthean passage carefully, it is helpful to set up the verses in a line-by-line structure:

51a: And behold, the veil of the sanctuary was rent from top to bottom into
       two.

---

[45]For the lintel in place of the veil, two articles by Nestle ("Sonnenfinsternis" and "Matt 27,51") are fascinating. In the context of describing the day of the Lord when the end comes to God's people Israel, the Hebrew of Amos 8:3 speaks of the "songs" (*šîrôt*) of the holy place being turned to howls. The LXX refers to the "ceiling panels" (*phatnōmata*) of the sanctuary, while Jerome's Vulgate has "door hinges." (Aquila has the door pivots [*strophigges*], seemingly reading *sîr* for *šîr.*) In classical Greek the word the LXX uses for "wail" (*ololyzein*) often refers to the cry of goddesses and to things sacred. The MT of Amos 9:1 has the Lord standing by the altar, saying, "Strike the pillar capitals and the thresholds will shake." The LXX (seemingly reading the consonants *kprt* for *kptr* of the MT) has the lid of the Ark of the Covenant struck and the porch pylons shaken, while Jerome's Vulgate has the door hinges struck and the lintels shaken. If one puts together the LXX and the Vulgate of these passages, one has references to ceiling panels, strange cries in the sanctuary area, and shaken lintels—partially the makings of Jerome's combination of the fractured lintel and the Josephus phenomena. Some of the combinations antedated Jerome. Describing the martyrdom *at the altar* of the priest Zechariah, father of JBap, *Protevangelium of James* 24:3 says, *"The panels of the ceiling of the sanctuary wailed,* and they [i.e., the priests or (variant) the panels] *rent* their clothes *from top to bottom."* This combines Amos 9:1, 8:3, and Mark 15:38 or Matt 27:51a.

[46]Both among the Church Fathers and modern scholars (see §37, Part 11) these phenomena have been the subject of an extraordinary amount of discussion. Good surveys of views are found in Aguirre Monasterio and Maisch.

[47]This fact strengthens my view that in part *GPet* is a folk-gospel.

b: *And the earth was shaken,*
c: *and the rocks were rent;*
52a: *and the tombs were opened,*
b: *and many bodies of the fallen-asleep holy ones were raised.*
53a: And having come out from the tombs
b: after his raising
c: they entered into the holy city;
d: and they were made visible to many.

I have italicized four lines (51bc,52ab) so that readers can see both their similarity to each other (four coordinated simple sentences or main clauses, beginning with *kai,* in which the verb is an aorist passive) and their differences from the more complicated 51a (which Matt took over from Mark) and from 53.[48] It is almost as if the basic aorist passive pattern of 51a, indicating divine action, has been taken over to construct a small poetic quatrain consisting of two couplets (51b and c are interrelated, as are 52a and b) with the earthquake of 51bc leading into the results described in 52ab. V. 53 has the appearance of a drawn-out reflection on the events of 52ab.[49] Poetic refrains are often a part of the popular presentation of an event, and are attested in NT references to the aftermath of the death of Jesus.[50] A close poetic parallel is found in *On the Pasch* of Melito of Sardis, composed ca. AD 170. In the context of describing the Lord's death and the darkness that accompanied it, Melito (98; SC 123.118) writes four couplets in which, while the first lines decry the insensitivity of the Jews, the second lines describe the corresponding terrestrial or celestial phenomena thus:

[48]While v. 51a also has an aorist passive, the basic action is modified by a long descriptive phrase. V. 53 begins with a participial construction plus a phrase, and the first principal verb is active, not passive. The thesis formerly held by Schenk (*Passionsbericht*) that a seven-line Jewish apocalyptic hymn describing the resurrection of the dead lay behind vv. 51b–53d is unsatisfactory on many scores. To get seven lines beginning with *kai* ("and") he had to delete v. 53b and to add a *kai* at the beginning of 53c. Also he had to change the participle in 53a to a finite verb, and to ignore the shift from the passive to the active. The attribution of such a hymn to Jewish sources neglects the temporal force of the aorist: These apocalyptic actions have happened (in Jesus, as Christians believe) and are not simply anticipated in the future. The same objection faces the attempt to make the hymns of the Lucan infancy narrative Jewish rather than (Jewish) Christian compositions; see BBM 350. See the rejection of Schenk's thesis by Senior, "Death of Jesus" 318–19; Aguirre Monasterio, *Exégesis* 69–71. Senior, "Matthew's Special Material" 278, reports that Schenk has abandoned this theory.

[49]I have deliberately not punctuated 53abc to illustrate the problem of whether 53b should be read with 53a or 53c.

[50]I Pet 3:18–19, consisting of five or six poetic lines, has an eschatological tone: The one who died in the flesh and was made alive in the spirit goes and preaches to the spirits in prison. Eph 4:8, consisting of three lines, portrays Christ ascending on high, leading a host of captives. Perhaps the NT analogue closest in form to Matt 27:51b–52b is I Tim 3:16, composed of six lines (short main clauses) in a pattern of three couplets: Christ is the unnamed subject and all the verbs are in the aorist passive. Frequently this poem is interpreted as ranging from the incarnation to the ascension, but the whole could refer to the death of Jesus and its aftermath. See (p. 1115 above) the *Pseudo-*

The earth was trembling . . .
The heavens feared[51] . . .
The angel rent his clothes[52] . . .
The Lord thundered from heaven,
and the Most High gave a cry.

Notice that the contextual reference to darkness is followed by allusions to an earthquake and a loud cry.

With these general remarks about format, let me now turn to a closer consideration of the phenomena themselves. (Although I favor the view that the quatrain in vv. 51b–52b is preMatthean and that v. 53 is a Matthean development beyond the quatrain, I shall leave that issue until we have discussed the contents.)

The Four Terrestrial Phenomena in 27:51bc,52ab as Reactions to Jesus' Death. Previously we have heard of the darkness over all the earth at noon and the rending of the sanctuary veil. If we add these two to the four phenomena recounted in vv. 51b–52b, there are in Matt a total of six apocalyptic signs associated with the death of Jesus.[53] (Two more will be associated with the raising of Jesus in v. 53, yielding eight in all.) A few years later Ignatius (*Trall.* 9:1) would write that Jesus "was truly crucified and died, with those in heaven and on the earth and under the earth looking on."[54] It may not be too romantic, then, to see in Matt 27:51b–52b a progression from signs in the heavens (darkness) to signs on the earth (rent sanctuary veil, earth shaken, rocks rent) to signs under the earth (opening of the tombs and raising of the dead). Those who surrounded the cross mockingly demanded a sign from heaven in the coming of Elijah (27:49); God, who refused that sign, has now amply responded in a majestic way appropriate to the divine power.

The issue of the historical reality of such signs is surely beyond our calculation, but even on the surface level of the Gospel narrative by their very nature they are of varying visibility. Only a few people could have seen the rending of the sanctuary veil or the actual raising of the bodies of the dead holy ones. Despite Matt's generalizing "many," only some Jerusalemites

---

Clementine Recognitions 1.41.3, which has a stylized pattern; it is not clear whether this is derivative from Matt or from an independent variant tradition of signs accompanying the death of Jesus.

[51]Probably a reference to the darkness that covered all the earth.

[52]This refers to the rending of the sanctuary veil. Tertullian (*Adv. Marcion* 4.42.5; CC 1.660): "The veil of the Temple was rent by the breaking forth of an angel leaving the Daughter of Zion." See Bonner, "Two" 183–85.

[53]*Did* 16:6 speaks of three signs of the last days: "First, a sign of an opening in heaven; then, a sign of the voice of the trumpet; and third, the resurrection [*anastasis*] of the dead."

[54]Ignatius (*Eph.* 19), with its references to the virginal conception, a star, and forms of magic (cf. magi), shows knowledge of the type of popular material that Matt 2 incorporated into the birth narrative; he may also have known popular material incorporated into Matt's PN.

could have seen these holy ones when they were made visible in the holy city. The three-hour darkness over all the earth at noon, however, and the shaking of the earth (and probably the concomitant rending of the rocks) should have been visible to all in the area, at least. Perhaps Matt acknowledges that, for, when in 27:54 he reports that "the centurion and those with him keeping (guard over) Jesus" had seen all "these happenings" and were greatly afraid, he singles out the shaking (of the earth) as an example. That specification helpfully acknowledges that the earthquake is the principal factor in 27:51b–53, governing the other three phenomena. (It is the only one of the four preserved clearly in *GPet*.) The quake causes the rending of the rocks (Matt repeats the *schizein* used for the rending of the sanctuary veil) and the opening of the tombs. In themselves these first three of the four phenomena could have been natural occurrences since Palestine is prone to earthquakes; yet, as with the darkness over all the earth (described by Luke as the result of an eclipse), the timing shows that a divine passive is being employed in the verbs and that God is active in all this. That is placed beyond doubt by the fourth phenomenon, the raising of the saintly dead.[55] The four need to be discussed one by one to see their eschatological import.

Earth Shaken (27:51b).[56] In Matt alone a star greeted the birth of "the King of the Jews" (2:2,9); and so it is not surprising by way of inclusion that at the death, besides darkness coming over all the earth (27:45), the earth itself would shake. On pp. 1041–42 above we saw that both Origen and Eusebius, in describing the eclipse recounted by Phlegon, made reference to a severe earthquake. Probably Matt's reference to a shaking of the earth, combined with Isa 6:4, explains a shift in imagery in later Christian tradition from the rending of the sanctuary veil at Jesus' death to a fracturing and overturn of the Temple lintel (p. 1117 above). There are numerous OT examples of shaking the earth as a sign of divine judgment or of the last times, e.g., Judg 5:4; Isa 5:25; 24:18; Ezek 38:19. In the context of God's blazing wrath being manifested toward the people of God who are so evil, Jer 4:23–24 reports: "I looked at the earth and it was waste and void; at the heavens and their light was gone; I looked at the mountains and they quaked, and all

---

[55]We must reject, then, any attempts to treat the four phenomena differently: If by modern standards the first are less supernatural and easier to accept than the last, both the structure and the import of the Matthean scene place them all on the same level of divine intervention.

[56]Although in general Riebl (*Auferstehung*) favors a preMatthean Semitic antecedent for the description of the phenomena, on pp. 49–50 she acknowledges that the vocabulary of "And the earth was shaken [*seiein*]" is quite Matthean. A related noun, *seismos* ("shaking"), is used for Matt's second earthquake associated with the opening of Jesus' tomb in 28:2, while the verb *seiein* is kept for the shaking or trembling of the guards (28:4) in response. Previously the verb was used for the stirring of Jerusalem when Jesus entered (21:10). Witherup ("Death" 580), in my judgment, presses too far when he sees "shaking" to be loaded with christological significance, even if it does represent reaction to events concerning Jesus.

the hills were moved." The combination of darkness and earthquake as part of judgment is found too in the description of the day of the Lord in Joel 2:10: "Before them the earth shall tremble and the heavens shake; the sun and moon shall be darkened, and the stars shall withdraw their light."[57] *Test. Levi* 3:9 extends the reaction to the lower regions: "And the heavens and the earth and the abysses are moved before the face of His great majesty." In *I Enoch* 1:3–8, as part of the great shaking of the earth that greets God's coming forth from heaven to judge the world, even the heavenly Watchers tremble—an interesting detail to compare to Matt's second earthquake (28:2–4) when an angel of the Lord opens the tomb of Jesus and the guards are shaken with fear. When the Lord comes in response to the cry of the just one on the day of his distress, we read in Ps 77:19: "The earth trembled and quivered" (also II Sam 22:7–8). In Matt 24:7–8 (Mark 13:8) earthquakes mark the beginning of the travails of the last times. Thus, Matt's readers, if they were familiar with any of this background, should have had little difficulty recognizing in the shaking of the earth that accompanied the rending of the sanctuary veil an apocalyptic sign of God's judgment evoked by the cruel death to which the Son of God was made subject. As for readers with primarily a Greco-Roman background, Virgil reported that the Alps quaked at the murder of Caesar (p. 1114 above). Indeed, when Lucian wants to burlesque the death of a famous man, he combines an earthquake with a talking vulture flying off to heaven as signs that greeted his departure (*De morte Peregrini* 39).

Rocks Rent (27:51c).[58] This might be considered an example of poetic parallelism, using other words to say the same thing as "the earth was shaken." Nevertheless, often the power of God in smashing the solid rocks is a special item in describing judgment. The phrase "the rending of the rocks" occurs in the LXX of Isa 2:19 in the description of where those who flee the day of the Lord will hide their idols. In I Kings 19:11–12 as part of what might be expected in a theophany, we hear of a strong wind splitting the mountains and crushing the rocks, and after that an earthquake. Zech 14:4 describes the final judgment, with God coming to stand on the Mount of Olives and "rending" it into two halves; Nahum 1:5–6 reports that when the wrath of God is let loose, the mountains are shaken and the rocks are

---

[57]Also Joel 4:15–16 [RSV 3:15–16]; Isa 13:9–13; Hag 2:6,21; Rev 6:12; *Assumption* [*Testament*] *of Moses* 10:4–5.

[58]Although *petra* ("rock") is more frequent in Matt (five times) than in the other Gospels, the verb *schizein* is used elsewhere in Matt only for the rending of the sanctuary veil two lines earlier, where he borrowed it from Mark. The latter uses it not only here but at the baptism for the rending of the heavens (1:10).

smashed asunder. In *Test. Levi* 4:1, a poetic passage with a format not unlike
that of Matt 27:51b–52b, as God effects judgment on human beings, "the
rocks are rent, and the sun darkened."

Tombs Opened (27:52a).[59] For Matt, God's action of opening the bowels
of the earth after the death of Jesus is an inclusion with God's opening the
heavens in the beginning of the ministry at the baptism of Jesus (3:16).[60] The
connection of the tomb openings with the preceding rending of the rocks is
splendidly visible in the Dura Europos synagogue wall-paintings that portray
the raising of the dead as part of the enlivening of the dry bones in Ezek
37—a 3d-cent. AD tableau[61] that is very helpful in understanding how Matt
and/or his readers might imagine the scene he is narrating.[62] There in the
splitting of a mountain covered by trees (almost surely the Mount of Olives
rent by an earthquake[63]), rocks are rent, thus opening up tombs burrowed
into the sides of the mountain and exposing bodies of the dead and their
parts. A figure is depicted who may be the Davidic Messiah (see Ezek
37:24–25) bringing about this raising of the dead. Earlier and contemporary
with the writing of Matt there is testimony to the importance that Ezek 37
had for the just who died for their convictions about God. At Masada, where
Jewish Zealots made their last stand against the Roman armies in AD 73, in
the floor of the synagogue were found fragments of a scroll on which was
written Ezekiel's account of his vision of the raising of the dead bones. Consequently, even apart from the Dura Europos picturization, Ezek 37:12–13
may be the key passage behind Matt's description both in this line and in
what follows, for it offers the only *opening* of tombs (as distinct from the
simple raising of the dead) described in the OT:[64] The people of God are

[59]When I discuss the burial of Jesus, I shall give statistics on the various words for tomb and
sepulcher; here *mnēmeion* is employed, a term that Matt will use three times for the tomb of Jesus.

[60]By contrast Mark 1:10 and 15:38 make the inclusion between the *rending* of the heavens and
of the sanctuary veil.

[61]The Dura synagogue was built ca. AD 200. The paintings, including the Ezekiel painting on the
north wall, stem from the period following the enlargement in AD 244.

[62]H. Riesenfeld, *The Resurrection in Ezekiel xxxvii and the Dura-Europos Paintings* (Uppsala:
Lundequistska Bokhandeln, 1948); R. Wischnitzer-Bernstein, "The Conception of the Resurrection
in the Ezekiel Panel of the Dura Synagogue," JBL 60 (1941), 43–55, esp. 49; U. Schubert, "Jüdische"
3–4; A. Grabar, "Le thème religieux des fresques de la synagogue de Doura (245–256 après J.C.),"
RHR 123 (1941), 143–92. Aguirre Monasterio (*Exégesis* 84–97) relates to the Dura frescoes various
targumic and Jewish liturgical reflections on Ezek 37. None of this material is a totally reliable guide
to 1st-cent.-AD folkloric understanding of the raising of the dead, but it may well be closer to that
understanding than is modern exegesis of OT texts pertaining to the subject.

[63]See Zech 14:4, where God comes to exercise judgment on the Mount of Olives. Matt's insistence in the next verse (27:53) that they entered the holy city (of Jerusalem) may have been influenced by Zechariah's locale for the judgment.

[64]Note that Ezek 37:7 mentions an earthquake (see Grassi, "Ezekiel"). Yet I am very skeptical of
a connection between Ezek 37:6, "I will give my spirit (in)to you, and you shall live," and Matt
27:50, Jesus "let go the spirit." The imagery of the two passages is different. The fallen-asleep holy

assured that they will come to know the Lord because: "I will open your tombs [*mnēma*], and I will bring you up out of your tombs, and I will lead you into the land of Israel." Previously each description of an individual phenomenon in Matt's list of four in 27:51b–52b, while partially repeating in poetic parallelism what preceded (the shaking of the earth rent the rocks and thus opened the tombs), also provided a new vista. That is true here as well, for the sign has now moved from the heavens (darkness) and the earth (rent sanctuary veil, shaken earth, rent rocks) to under the earth. Which tombs were opened? The answer to that is involved with the identity of the "holy ones" in the fourth phenomenon.

Many Fallen-Asleep Holy Ones Raised (27:52b).[65] "Asleep" is a frequent NT euphemism for the dead (I Thess 4:13; I Cor 15:20; John 11:11; II Pet 3:4). In the context of judgment *I Enoch* 91:10 envisions that "the just shall arise from their sleep" (also *IV Ezra* 7:32); and *II (Syriac) Baruch* 21:24 regards Abraham, Isaac, and Jacob as asleep in the earth. (Some Church Fathers, like Augustine and Chrysostom, imagined that Matt meant that these bodies were awakened from their death-sleep by Jesus' scream and loud cry as he died [27:46,50].) Elsewhere in the NT the "holy ones" or "saints" are believers in Jesus (I Cor 14:23; Rom 1:7; Acts 9:13; Heb 13:24), even as sometimes in the OT they are the people of Israel (Isa 4:3; Dan 7:21; 8:25). In this passage they must be Jews who died after a saintly life.[66] *I Enoch* 61:12 places in parallelism "all the holy ones who are in heaven" and "all the elect ones who dwell in the garden of life." *Test. Levi* 18:10–11 foresees that the anointed high priest of the last days "will open the gates of paradise . . . and will give to the holy ones to eat from the tree of life." Noting that Matt speaks of the "bodies" of the holy ones rather than simply of the "holy ones," some have tried to distinguish between this resurrection and that of the whole person, as if this were an in-between resurrection before the final resurrection. However, no such distinction is being made by the use of "body," since the resurrection of dead bodies from the tombs is simply

---

ones are raised in the earth-shaking moment of Jesus' death; I cannot see that Matt means that they received Jesus' released spirit. Aguirre Monasterio (*Exégesis* 184) contends that Matt uses a highly unusual expression for dying; but then, one may ask, if Matt intended a parallel to Ezek 37:6, why did he not choose a verb that would have facilitated that?

[65]*Egeirein* ("to raise") is used thirty-six times in Matt, thirteen of which refer to the resurrection of the dead.

[66]They are those whom Matt elsewhere (13:17; 23:29) associates with prophets of old under the title "the just [*dikaioi*]"—a vocabulary switch that may indicate the nonMatthean origin of this piece. (Syr[sin] and Ephraem read "just" in place of "holy ones" in the present passage.) Although a few Church Fathers would include Gentiles, the context in Matt indicates clearly that he is thinking of Jews—why would Gentiles go into "the holy city"? Wis 5:5 writes thus of the destiny of the pious Jewish deceased: "See how he is accounted among the sons of God [angels], how his lot is among the holy ones [also angels, or virtuous human dead?]."

set imagery.[67] Hitherto the apocalyptic signs have been negative (darkness, rent sanctuary veil, earthquake), but this sign shows the positive side of the divine judgment centered on the death of God's Son: The good are rewarded as well as the evil punished.

Jews who believed in bodily resurrection would have expected that all the holy ones (just) should have been raised and received the kingdom (Dan 7:22; Luke 14:14), or even that all human beings should have been raised and been assigned different fates by God (Dan 12:2; John 5:28–29). A selective raising as here is very peculiar and has led to speculation:[68] What tombs were opened and which holy ones were raised? The Matthean context (27:53–54) in which the opening of the tombs is part of the phenomena visible to the centurion and other guards on Golgotha and in which those raised become visible in the holy city indicates that Matt is thinking of tombs of holy ones in the Jerusalem area close to where Jesus died.[69] Although some commentators have proposed that Matt is describing the deliverance of the great known figures of OT history whose reward has been delayed until the redemption brought by Jesus,[70] relatively few of them were supposed to be buried in the Jerusalem area. Because of the speculation connecting "Skull-Place" with Adam's skull (§40, n. 9), that patriarch has been proposed (Epiphanius). And because Peter in Acts 2:29 mentions the tomb of David being "with us to this day" in Jerusalem, that saintly king has been another candidate (Augustine). Appeal has been made to Matt 23:37 with its charge that Jerusalem killed the prophets, suggesting the possibility of their having been buried there. Other commentators have thought of holy ones closer to Jesus' time or involved with him, even if there is only legend about their burial place. In antiquity JBap was nominated as one of the raised bodies, although that was queried by later commentators (Cornelius a Lapide) on the grounds that several churches (Rome, Amiens) claimed to have relics of his preserved head. The *Gospel of Nicodemus* (*Acts of Pilate*) 17:1

[67]See Isa 26:19 for the dead rising and those in the tombs being raised. Tatian's *Diatessaron* recognized the equivalence of this terminology by reading "the dead" in place of "many bodies of the fallen-asleep holy ones"; see W. L. Petersen, NTS 29 (1983), 494–507.

[68]Matt uses "many" frequently, and of itself the usage is not necessarily partitive (see 9:10; 13:17; 24:11). "Many bodies of the fallen-asleep holy ones" contains an epexegetical genitive (the "many bodies" are "the fallen-asleep holy ones"), but the context makes it clear that not all the just of every time and place have been raised.

[69]Other tombs are found adjacent to Calvary and to Jesus' tomb in the Church of the Holy Sepulcher in Jerusalem, and the presence of a burial area nearby is assumed in the Gospel accounts of Jesus' interment.

[70]Heb 11:39–40, after going through the exploits of many great OT figures, says, "And all these, though proved by faith, did not receive the promise . . . so that apart from us they should not be made perfect." Ignatius (*Magn.* 9:2) writes of the OT prophets: "When the one arrived for whom they were rightly waiting, he raised them from the dead." See more specifically *Martyrdom (Ascension) of Isaiah* 9:17–18 (p. 1131 below).

says that Jesus raised Simeon, the aged man who took the baby Jesus into his arms (Luke 2:25–28), as well as Simeon's two sons who had died recently. Indeed their tombs could still be seen opened, and these risen worthies were alive and dwelling in Arimathea!

All such speculation is unnecessary, for this popular, poetic description is deliberately vague—its forte is atmosphere, not details. Note that the features of fear, lack of recognition, doubt, and demanded proof that accompany the resurrection and appearances of Jesus are *not* found in Matt 27:52–53. The identity of the risen Jesus as the same one whose crucifixion and death had been witnessed was important for NT writers; but here the awesome power of God's action, not the identity of the raised, is the issue. The coming of the kingdom of God in the ministry of Jesus was understood not as the final manifestation of the kingdom (i.e., the culmination when the Son of Man would gather before him all the nations, assigning those who are to inherit the kingdom prepared for them from the foundation of the world, as in 25:31–34) but as an inbreaking inaugurating and anticipating it. Similarly, this raising of "many bodies" as Jesus dies is not the universal final resurrection but an inbreaking of God's power signifying that the last times have begun and the judgment has been inaugurated (see D. Hill, "Matthew" 80–82). At the Sanhedrin trial Jesus warned the high priest and the authorities judging him, "From now on you will see the Son of Man sitting at the right of the Power and coming on the clouds of heaven" (26:64). The darkness, the rent sanctuary veil, the shaken earth, the rent rocks, the opened tombs, and the raised bodies of the holy ones are the apocalyptic trappings that illustrate the partial fulfillment of the divine judgment implied in that prophetic warning, as the All-Powerful One responds to the death of the Son of Man who is the Son of God.

When one appreciates the symbolic, poetic, and popular apocalyptic character of the four lines of 27:51b–52b with the phenomena they describe, they offer no major problem. They are clearly attached to the death of Jesus on Friday afternoon,[71] whence the ominous judgmental tone that precedes the raising of the holy ones. But the situation has been complicated by Christian theological attempts to understand chronologically the various aspects of

---

[71]We shall see that v. 53 changes the focus to Easter. Hutton ("Resurrection"), drawing on *GPet* 10:41 where "the fallen asleep" are mentioned after the resurrection of Jesus, would see all these phenomena as stemming from a transposed resurrection account. Besides the extremely dubious thesis that *GPet* is more original than Matt, the elements of wrathful judgment in v. 51bc belong with the darkness over all the earth at noon and the rent veil of the sanctuary rather than with the resurrection, if we can judge from the canonical accounts. Against Hutton's advocacy of the priority of the *GPet* account, see Aguirre Monasterio, *Exégesis* 115–51; and Maisch, "Österliche" 102–3— also Senior, "Death of Jesus" 314–18, who points out that even the resurrection appearance of angels in Matt 28:2–4 functions differently from the angelic appearance in *GPet* 10:39.

Jesus' death and going to his Father. One attempt, reflected elsewhere in the NT and early church writings, fills in the interstice between death on Friday and discovery of the empty tomb early Sunday by having Jesus descend into hell; and we shall discuss that in the next paragraph. Another attempt makes all victory flow from the resurrection of Jesus, and we shall discuss that in relation to the next verse (Matt 27:53).

THE DESCENT INTO HELL. Where was Jesus from the time he died and was buried until he appeared at Easter? One early Christian answer, already discussed above (§41) in relation to Luke's "This day with me you shall be in paradise" (23:43), was that he went to God or was in heaven. That, I would argue, was the original background understanding of the poetic Matthean verses we have been discussing—Friday was the time of victory and the cross itself the site of judgment, so that *functionally* the raising of the fallen-asleep holy ones at Jesus' death had the same import as the Lucan Jesus' taking the wrongdoer who had been crucified with him into paradise on the same day on which they both died. Another view, however, was that Jesus did not enter into heaven until after the resurrection localized on Easter; and sometimes in that scenario the in-between time was taken up with a descent into the netherworld.[72] There he was thought to have crushed the evil spirits locked up in the depths of the earth since primeval sins (*I Enoch* 10:12) and/or to have freed from confinement the dead holy ones (or, at least, the repentant) who were waiting (in prison or a type of limbo called hell) for redemption or access to heaven.[73] This speculation must have begun early, for it seems to be presupposed in a series of (admittedly obscure) NT passages,[74] even if often there is a lack of specificity as to when the descent occurred. I Pet 3:18–19 speaks of Christ having been put to death in the flesh but made alive in the spirit, in which "having gone, he made proclamation [*kēryssein*] to those spirits in prison." I Pet 4:6, after a reference to him who is ready to judge the living and the dead, says, "For this is why the gospel was preached

---

[72]The creedal phrase "He descended into hell" appears in the East (formula of Sirmium) and West (Old Roman Creed used at Aquileia) by the 4th cent., even though there is no unanimity as to what it means, in part because of debates over Origen's position that the souls of the wicked could be converted after death. On all this see W. J. Dalton, *Christ's Proclamation to the Spirits* (AnBib; Rome: PBI, 1965; 2d ed. 1989).

[73]Early Jewish imagery of what followed death was not uniform and indeed often had changed drastically from biblical (pre-exilic) times when *Sheol* was no more than a tomb, a place of darkness and gloom (Job 10:21) where the bodies of all the dead were inert, without hope (Job 17:13,15). See N. J. Tromp, *Primitive Conceptions of Death and the Nether World in the Old Testament* (Rome: PBI, 1969). Closer to the views described in the text above would be *IV Ezra* 4:35–42, where the souls of the just ask how long they have to remain in their chambers; and an archangel explains: In Hades the chambers are like the womb, for, when the premeasured number of the ages and times is completed, these places will give back those committed to them from the beginning.

[74]Many of these are poetic, consisting of several lines (perhaps from a larger poem), even as I have posited that Matt 27:51b–52 is poetic.

even to the dead, in order that, though judged in the flesh according to human beings, they might live according to God in the spirit." Eph 4:8–10 indicates that there was a descent into the lower parts of the earth before Christ ascended on high leading a host of captives (see also Rom 10:6–7; Philip 2:9).

None of the above about the descent into hell seems to have anything to do with the picture in Matt 27:52 with its opened tombs and the raising of the fallen-asleep holy ones at the time of Jesus' death, but we have evidence that the two images were intertwined by the early 2d cent., if not earlier.[75] Besides references to the darkness holding fast all Judea and the ripping of the sanctuary veil, *GPet* 6:21 reports that "all the earth was shaken," betraying knowledge of one of the peculiarly Matthean phenomena. Then in *GPet* 10:41–42, as the Lord is led forth from the sepulcher, a voice from heaven speaks, "Have you made proclamation [*kēryssein*] to the fallen-asleep?"; and from the cross there is an obedient response, "Yes." Obviously this proclamation (language of I Pet 3:19) to those asleep (language similar to Matt's) had to have happened between the time Jesus died and the time he rose. The combination of Matt's language with that of the descent is even more obvious in Justin (*Dialogue* 72:4) as he claims the fulfillment of a spurious citation of Jeremiah:[76] "The Lord God of Israel remembered His dead, the fallen-asleep in the earth of the grave; and He went down unto them to preach to them the good news [*euaggelizein*] of His salvation."[77] Justin (*Apology* 1.35 and 48) makes reference to documents (acts) of the trial of Jesus before Pilate; and that same type of legendary material is known to us in later form in the *Acts of Pilate* (*Gospel of Nicodemus*). There (17ff.) the raised Simeon and his sons, whose opened tombs can still be seen (clearly an echo of Matt's phenomena), are brought from Arimathea where they now live to give a sworn, written statement to the Jewish authorities about the miracles that Jesus did in Hades, by defeating Hades and Satan and leading forth to paradise all the famous figures of the OT and JBap. When we discussed the popular Judas traditions that Matt 27:3–10 had taken over and shaped into a narrative about the price of innocent blood, we pointed to other developments of this death-of-Judas material in Acts and Papias. It is not surprising to find the same situation here in diverse popular traditions about the apocalyptic signs that accompanied the death of Jesus. Even if later writers connected these traditions, in Matt's account which shows imaginatively

---

[75]This approach is still supported by some, e.g., Bousset, R. C. Fuller; Gschwind, Neile, Pesch, and Schniewind.

[76]The Jeremiah passage with a similar interpretation is also found in Irenaeus, *Adv. haer.* 4.22.1.

[77]Later Eusebius (EH 1.13.20) cites an apocryphal letter of Abgar of Edessa: "He was crucified, descended into Hades . . . raised up the dead; and though he descended alone, he ascended with a great multitude to the Father." The Greek *Apocalypse of Ezra* 7:1–2 reports: "I was set down in a grave, and I raised up my elect ones, and I summoned up Adam from Hades."

how Jesus' resurrection broke the power of death, there is nothing to suggest that the author himself knew about the descent into hell/Hades (see Fascher, *Auferweckung* 38; Aguirre Monasterio, *Exégesis* 153–71).

Coming out of the Tombs, Entry into the Holy City, and Appearances (27:53). I have already pointed out that the style of writing changes noticeably when we pass from the short coordinated lines of the quatrain (27:51b–52b), phrased in the aorist passive, to the complex participial, active phrasing (much closer to Matt's normal style) in 27:53. The moment that is the focus of theological interest also changes. Is not Jesus "the first fruits of the fallen-asleep" (I Cor 15:20), "the first-born from the dead" (Col 1:18)? Does not the oldest preserved Christian writing on the subject (I Thess 4:14) give the proper order: "Jesus died and rose; so through Jesus God will lead out with him those asleep"? How, then, can the many bodies of the fallen-asleep holy ones have been raised (Matt 27:52b) before Jesus himself was raised? We encountered this difficulty in discussing Luke 23:42–43, which implied that Jesus would come into his kingdom this very Friday of his death and take along to paradise the wrongdoer hanged with him. Dismayed by such a view that appeared to neglect the resurrection and Easter, scribes seemingly changed the Lucan "into your kingdom" to "in your kingdom," shifting the reference to the parousia; and commentators explained that paradise was not really the highest heaven, to which Jesus and his companion would go only after the resurrection. Similar maneuvering has been at work in Matt 27:53, centered on the phrase in 53b about the resurrection, on the earthly or heavenly reference of "the holy city" in 53c, and on the types of bodies that were made visible in 53d.

"After his raising" (27:53b).[78] Normally in relation to Jesus' resurrection the verb *egeirein* has been translated transitively by "raise," and *anistanai* intransitively by "rise,"[79] with the noun *anastasis* (forty-two times in the NT) rendered as "rising, resurrection." But here we have the sole NT occurrence of *egersis,* "raising." Are we to take it intransitively, so that the "of him [Jesus]" which follows it is possessive, equivalent to "after Jesus' rising"?[80] Or are we to give it a (more expected) transitive force, so that the "of him" is objective, i.e., "after the raising of Jesus"? Since these two possibilities

[78]This is the most difficult phrase in Matt 27:51–53, but we should reject attempts to remove or neutralize it, whether ancient (Codex 243; Palestinian Syriac) or modern (Klostermann). While one might judge that this phrase is an editorial addition to v. 53, that addition would have been made by the time the Gospel first appeared; and so it must be treated as a part of Matt. See n. 106 below.

[79]I do not wish to enter here into the complicated issue of the agent of the resurrection, God or Jesus; see NJBC 81.133. The raise/rise distinction given above is too simple, especially for *egeirein* since the meaning of the verb shifts according to the outlook of the individual NT authors, and the passive can mean both "be raised" and "rise."

[80]A good parallel is the LXX of Ps 139:2, "You know my *egersis*" i.e., my rising up; similarly Zeph 3:8: "the day of my *anastasis.*"

have the same connotation (setting 27:53 in whole or part in an Easter context), decision between them is unimportant. More crucial is a third interpretation that treats *egersis* as transitive with an implied object: "after his raising [them, i.e., the bodies of the fallen-asleep holy ones]."[81] This is the rendering that offers the fewest interpretive problems, for it does not change the time focus from the death of Jesus on Friday involved in the preceding verses. Yet the very ease of this interpretation makes us suspicious that we are dealing with an erudite improvement. Moreover, grammatically this involves a double objective genitive, namely, "the raising of him [of them]." It is more prudent, then, to deal with either of the first two interpretations that have 53b refer to the resurrection of Jesus and, thus, to an Easter context.

If we translate 53b to mean "after his [Jesus'] resurrection," how do we punctuate the first main clause in 53abc? A number of scholars attribute all the action of v. 53 to the Easter period after Jesus' resurrection (Blinzler, R. C. Fuller, Sickenberger, Wenham), with the grammatical effect of treating 53b as a parenthetical aside modifying the whole. While this would yield an attractively simple picture, it does not do justice to the fact that "after his raising" does not appear first in the sentence, where it could modify all that followed. Moreover, were the whole action of v. 53 postresurrectional, it should more logically have been recounted in the next chapter of Matt that begins on Easter.[82] With more respect for grammar we might put a comma after 53b so that it is joined to 53a: "After having come out from the tombs after Jesus' resurrection [by or after Sunday[83]], they. . . ." This would mean that even though they were raised on Friday, the holy ones waited inside their tombs until Sunday when Jesus had risen from the dead—an extraordinary courtesy! A less illogical view can be derived by putting a comma after 53a and thus joining 53b to 53c (so A. Schlatter, T. Zahn): "And having come out from their tombs [on Friday], after Jesus' resurrection [Sunday] they entered into the holy city; and they. . . ." That would remove from the Friday of Jesus' death (when the other phenomena in 27:51b–52b occurred) only one composite scene, consisting of two phenomena: the entrance into the holy city and the appearances of 53cd. While I favor this last rendering of v. 53, the important issue is that this verse has moved to Easter from the Friday of 51–52 at least the aftermath of the emerging from the tombs,

---

[81]Some minuscule Greek mss. and the Ethiopic version have made this explicit by reading "the raising of them" instead of "the raising of him."

[82]A number of scholars (Hutton, Resch, Seidenstecker, Trilling, Zeller) argue that this verse or the whole of 27:51b–53 belongs with the account in chap. 28 and has mistakenly been placed here.

[83]I am being cautious because the Gospel resurrection accounts do not say that Jesus rose from the dead on Sunday (even if that is implied elsewhere in some of the "third day" formulas). They indicate that he had been raised by Sunday since on that day the tomb was found empty.

namely, the appearances, and thus has produced a setting that gives priority to Jesus' resurrection. The *meta* ("after") of 27:53b has a causative tone: Jesus' resurrection made possible the entry of the raised holy ones into the holy city and their appearances there.[84]

"The holy city" (27:53c). The difficult temporal issue just discussed has to imply that the risen dead passed days in some locale; and so it becomes important to determine what Matt envisions by reporting that the bodies of the fallen-asleep holy ones, once raised, entered "the holy city." (In part, a response to this will be affected by whether the risen dead were mortal or immortal, an issue to be discussed in relation to the next clause [53d] in Matt.) The use of that designation for Jerusalem in passages such as Isa 48:2; 52:1; Rev 11:2, as well as earlier in Matt (4:5–6), rules out all other terrestrial candidates.[85] Nevertheless, not a few interpreters balk at the thought of many known risen dead being seen in Jerusalem—that large-scale a phenomenon should have left some traces in Jewish and/or secular history! Consequently, they appeal to the use of "holy city" for a new, heavenly Jerusalem in Rev 21:2,10; 22:19 ("the city that is to come" of Heb 13:14), and interpret Matt 27:53c to mean that the risen dead entered heaven after Jesus' resurrection.[86] Certainly that would agree with portrayals where the risen Jesus leads a host into heaven (e.g., Eph 4:8). The *Martyrdom (Ascension) of Isaiah* 9:7–18 describes how the righteous from the time of Adam onward had to wait until the incarnation of Christ before they could receive their crowns; he plundered the angel of death by rising from the dead, and when he ascended to the seventh heaven, they ascended with him. *Test. Dan* 5:12 would have "the holy ones" refreshing themselves in Eden and the just rejoicing in the New Jerusalem. Yet there is a fatal flaw in this heavenly "holy city" interpretation of Matt 27:53c: "They were made visible to many" in 53d can scarcely apply to heaven! Nor does it refer to earthly appearances after an unmentioned going to heaven (see Winklhofer, "*Corpora*" 41–43), for Matt betrays no interest in the in-between. Surely appearances in the earthly Jerusalem are intended.

[84]SPNM 317. Notice the thought of Ignatius (*Magn.* 9:1), writing not long after Matt: "the Lord's Day on which also our life sprang up through him and his death." The purpose of the risen holy ones is not to testify against Jerusalem, for there is nothing negative in this scene of appearances, and Matt would scarcely use "holy city" for Jerusalem in a scene of condemnation by the "holy ones." The select seers of the holy city share the sanctity of those seen. In the verb *emphanizein* there is an element of revealing, making clear: The raised holy ones are a testimony to Jesus' victory over death.

[85]Why does Matt use the designation "the holy [*hagios*] city" rather than speaking directly of Jerusalem? Is he playing on an established designation that contains the same word he has just used for "holy ones" (*hagioi*) in 52b?

[86]See Gschwind, *Niederfahrt* 192. Eusebius (*Demonstratio evangelica* 4.12.4; GCS 23.169), using Matthean terminology, reports that after the resurrection many bodies of the fallen-asleep holy ones rose (*anistanai*) and were brought along with him into the holy and *truly heavenly* city (also 10.8.64; GCS 23.483).

"They were made visible to many" (27:53d). Taken by itself the poetic reference to the raising of the fallen-asleep saints in Matt 27:52ab would undoubtedly be interpreted as a resurrection to eternal life.[87] What is added in 53d about appearances in Jerusalem does not necessarily challenge that interpretation. After all, Jerusalem appearances were attributed to the risen Jesus, who certainly enjoyed eternal life.[88] The idea that the bodies of the fallen-asleep saints were made visible (passive of *emphanizein* indicating that God was the agent[89]) to many in the holy city but implicitly not to all corresponds to what Peter states in Jerusalem in Acts 10:40–41: "God raised Jesus on the third day and gave him to become visible [*emphanēs*] not to all the people but to us." However, there are major differences. NT writers remember the identity of those to whom the risen Jesus was made visible and place a terminus on those appearances, even describing Jesus' departure, ascending to heaven (I Cor 15:5–8; Luke 24:51; Acts 1:3,9; Mark 16:19). There is no other NT memory of Matt's raised holy ones; those in the holy city to whom they appeared are never identified, and we are never told when or if they went to heaven. Consequently in early Christian thought an alternative understanding of the risen holy ones was advanced: They were not raised to eternal life, but (like those raised by Jesus during his ministry) they were only resuscitated to ordinary life. A miracle was performed but not the miracle of a resurrection like that of Jesus. They were "made visible" in their ordinary bodies, and they would die again.[90] This conception lies behind the already mentioned claim in the *Gospel of Nicodemus* that those raised included Simeon and his two sons, who had died recently (and thus presumably had not corrupted—note that those resuscitated by Jesus during the ministry had just died). The ordinary character of their renewed existence is confirmed by the report that they were living at Arimathea. Eusebius (EH 4.3.2) quotes from the apologist Quadratus, who lived during Hadrian's reign (117–138), concerning those who had risen from the dead: "After Jesus' departure they existed for a considerable time, and certain of them have

[87]That eternal life is involved is maintained by many Church Fathers, e.g., the Alexandrians (Clement, Origen, Cyril), Epiphanius, Eusebius, Gregory of Nyssa, and Anselm.

[88]These appearances of Jesus are narrated by Luke and John; Matt has an appearance by the tomb to Mary Magdalene and the other Mary (28:1,9–10) but no appearance of Jesus in the city. It has been suggested that the appearance of these many risen dead in the holy city makes up in Matt for that lack.

[89]As Witherup ("Death" 581) points out, this verb (*emphanizein*) in the passive can have an active meaning ("appear"); but in the instance of the raised dead only God can make them appear. Nevertheless, Witherup's observation illustrates that this is not the same kind of passive found previously in the four verbs of the quatrain (27:51b–52b).

[90]Held by Chrysostom, this view had its strongest following in the West: Tertullian, Ambrose, Augustine, Aquinas (*Summa Theologiae* IIIa, q. 53, a. 3), and Suarez; and it still has defenders: Cullmann, Fascher, Lagrange, Vosté, and Witherup. A third and lesser-known interpretation posits that apparent bodies were involved, neither mortal nor immortal (Luke of Bruges, AD 1606).

reached even our own days." While this folklore partially resonates with the popular character of the vivid phenomena associated with the death of Jesus,[91] it is quite foreign to the apocalyptic thrust of those phenomena. If we remember that the criterion of interpretation must be what Matt intended by his narrative (not what we think happened), the concatenation of signs in the heavens, on the earth, and under the earth scarcely allows us to think that the culmination was a resuscitation to ordinary life. Those who were resuscitated by Jesus during his ministry did not have to appear or to be made visible to some; that description makes sense only of those who are raised to another sphere, even as Jesus was raised and appeared.

Overall, then, the following seems the best interpretation of 27:53: To vv. 51b–52b, a poetic piece describing four eschatological phenomena associated with Jesus' death, Matt had added two other interrelated eschatological phenomena associated with Jesus' resurrection, namely, emerging from the tombs to enter Jerusalem and being made visible to many. Thus, those who were raised to eternal life at the death of Jesus made their appearances after his resurrection. These holy ones entered Jerusalem, the holy city near which God will judge all at the end of time; and their appearances both attested that Jesus had conquered death and promised that eventually all the holy ones would be raised. Matt does not report what happened to them after the Jerusalem appearances any more than he reports what happened to Jesus after his last appearance (28:16–20). Presumably it was self-evident that both he and they, having been delivered from death, dwell with God henceforth.[92] The issue of why Matt expanded the tradition I shall leave to the ANALYSIS below.

ANALYSIS

All the phenomena that we have discussed in this section represent a theological interpretation of the import of the death of Jesus, an interpretation in the language and imagery of apocalyptic. I have pointed out in the COMMENT

[91]Previously I have cited parallels in Greco-Roman descriptions of the death of famous people or institutions to show that the Gospel phenomena would be intelligible to readers from that background, no matter what theological value they might assign to such portents. Cassius Dio (*History* 51.17.5) reports that at the fall of Alexandria to the Romans, "the disembodied spirits [*eidōlon*] of the dead were made visible."

[92]Epiphanius (*Panarion* 75.7.6–7; GCS 37.339) speaks of the raised holy ones going together with Jesus into the holy city, i.e., both into the earthly Jerusalem to appear and into the heavenly Jerusalem to be with God. Bieder (*Vorstellung* 54) reports the thesis of Diodorus of Tarsus that they were taken up like Elijah.

that to make a matter of major concern their literal historicity is to fail to understand their nature as symbols and the literary genre in which they are presented.[93] A comparable example would be for readers ca. AD 4000 to debate the literal historicity of George Orwell's book *1984:* Orwell was a most perceptive interpreter of the destructive forces set loose during his lifetime, but his was a discriminative vision, not a history of what actually happened in a specific year. (Or, if one wishes an example from NT times, one can scarcely posit the literal historicity of the apocalyptic signs that Peter sees fulfilled at Pentecost in Acts 2:19–20, e.g., the moon having turned to blood.[94]) Granted that for Christian faith the self-giving of God's Son changed human relationships to God and thus transformed the cosmos, apocalyptic imagery was in many ways a more effective medium for communicating such truths that lie beyond ordinary experience than would have been discursive disquisition. Apocalypticists, with all their vivid images, still write within the limiting sphere of human approximation; they betray an awareness that they have not exhausted the wealth of the otherworldly— an awareness that a more precise and prosaic exposition sometimes obscures.

A. The Evangelists' Theologies in Recounting the Rending of the Sanctuary Veil

Although the three Synoptics narrate this, there can be little doubt (even if we judge simply from vocabulary) that one basic report was copied into the two other Gospels; and on the analogy of what we have seen elsewhere, there is nothing to cause us to doubt that the basic report was Mark's. Mark has used and even phrased this phenomenon to correspond to his arrangement of the Gospel story and his own theological purpose. On the macroscale of the whole Gospel the rending of the heavens in 1:10–11 marked the beginning of God's gracious intervention as the Spirit descended on Jesus and the heavenly voice declared, "You are my beloved Son"; and the rending of the sanctuary veil at the end of the Gospel marks God's wrath at the Jerusalem authorities who, having mocked that identification, crucified this same

---

[93]The issue of the literal historicity of the opening of the tombs, the raising of the bodies of fallen-asleep saints, and their appearances to many in the holy city (Matt 27:52–53) is not the same as the issue of whether Jesus' body corrupted in the tomb and whether he was seen by many. See p. 1132 above for the very different atmosphere in the accounts of these two events.

[94]To some, not to affirm the historicity of the rending of the sanctuary veil, or of the earthquake, or of the appearances of the risen dead, all narrated in relation to Jesus' death, is to deny a divine guidance or inspiration of the Gospel accounts. Strangely, that judgment detracts from the unique power of God which it seeks to protect: If human beings could give a rich exposition of the significance of Jesus' death in a language and genre other than history, on what grounds would one deny God's freedom to supply guidance to such expression?

Son. The very next verse will show that God will now turn to outsiders to recognize what the leaders of Jesus' people could not: "Truly this man was God's Son." On the microscale of the PN, the mockery during the Sanhedrin trial and on the cross (14:58; 15:29) of Jesus' claim that he would destroy this "sanctuary" has now been answered, showing that Jesus spoke the truth: The veil that marked off the sanctuary as holy space has been rent from top to bottom into two—there is no longer truly a sanctuary in the Jerusalem Temple, for God is no longer present there.[95] While Mark attached this wrathful judgment to the moment of Jesus' death, both he and his readers, if they lived as the Roman legions under Titus burned the Jerusalem Temple, would have seen the rending of the sanctuary veil as a portent of this more physical destruction to come.

Marcan use and even rephrasing, however, does not establish Marcan creation. In the COMMENT, by comparing Mark's symbolism of the rent veil to the symbolism of Jesus' passing through the veil in Hebrews (p. 1107 above), I found good reason to suggest that at a preMarcan stage Christians perceived that the death of Jesus redefined God's presence among the people chosen to be God's own. Even as early Jewish literature portrayed corrective divine judgment by focusing on the devastation of the Jerusalem sanctum (the holiness of which God stopped protecting), so Christian reflection on judgment centered on the symbolism of the veil in that sanctum, demarcating God's holy presence. (I contended that one need not decide whether originally the outer or inner veil was meant: There is nothing in the Gospel narratives to specify that, and the readers of the Gospels may not even have known of such a differentiation, even if the readers of Hebrews were directed to the inner veil.) The preMarcan tradition probably already saw the rending of the veil as hostile, and Mark intensified that by having the rent veil "of the sanctuary" confirm the preceding PN references to Jesus' destroying the sanctuary. The author of Hebrews saw positive possibilities in the veil: Jesus passed through the veil carrying his own blood to offer an eternal sacrifice in the heavenly sanctum, and as a forerunner led others to follow him. In either interpretation (Mark's or Hebrews') the earthly sanctuary, the one built by hand, no longer had meaning.

Luke and Matt both combined the rending of the sanctuary veil that they took over from Mark with other apocalyptic signs. Without adding new signs *Luke* did this by relocating the rending to before the death of Jesus and join-

---

[95]The word "sanctuary" is Mark's primary tool in connecting the texts involving Jesus' claim at the Sanhedrin trial and its fulfillment at his death. See p. 1099 above for the possibility that there is a secondary connection between the high priest's *tearing* his garment at the blasphemy in Jesus' claim before the Sanhedrin to be the Son of the Blessed and God's *rending* the veil of the sanctuary, an area accessible to priests alone, in order to show that it is God's Son who has been blasphemed.

ing it to the darkness. God spread darkness at noon over the whole earth (Luke 23:44–45a) in anger at the approaching death on the cross of a Jesus whom years ago in the Temple precincts Simeon had hailed as "a light to be a revelation to the Gentiles and to be a glory for your people Israel" (2:32). Similarly in anger[96] God rent the veil of that sanctuary where years ago the priest Zechariah had heard the angel Gabriel proclaim the beginning of the turning of many sons of Israel to the Lord their God (1:8–23, esp. 1:16). Through the Lucan relocation the immediate destructiveness of the rending which Mark emphasized in his prophecy-fulfillment pattern has yielded to its other role (secondary in Mark) as a sign of future destruction. For Luke there is a grace period for repentance (Acts 3:17–21), but ultimately and inevitably the days are coming when the Jerusalemites will say to the mountains, "Fall on us" (Luke 23:30). Drawing on popular tradition, *Matt* has related God's rending of the sanctuary veil to other God-given apocalyptic signs that intensify the judgment provoked by the crucified death of God's Son.

But before we analyze the additional Matthean signs, we should consider *GPet,* which exemplifies further developments reflecting popular imagination. As in the common Synoptic portrayal, *GPet* 5:15 placed the darkness that "held fast all Judea" at midday before the Lord "was taken up" (5:19), but not without dramatizing the effect of the darkness: "Many went around with lamps, thinking that it was night, and they fell" (5:18). After recounting the Lord's departure, but "at the same [midday] hour,"[97] *GPet* 5:20 reports the tearing of the veil of the Jerusalem sanctuary; and only in 6:22 are we told, "Then the sun shone, and it was found to be the ninth hour." In other words, the Synoptic ambiguity about when the darkness ended (pp. 1034, 1039 above) has been exploited to have the three-hour absence of the sun envelop the death scene and its immediate aftermath.[98] Within that framework comes the shaking of the earth, but not as part of a poetic quatrain expressing an apocalyptic judgment by God, as in Matt. The earth shakes when the body of the Lord is placed upon it, an effect that produces "great fear" (6:21b).[99]

---

[96]In the COMMENT I explained why I did not accept the yoking of the rent veil with Jesus' final, trusting prayer, so that it becomes a positive sign of the opened heavens.

[97]Note the implication that Jesus died at midday. The sixth or noon hour is the one time notice found in the four canonical accounts of the crucifixion, even if what happens at noon varies: sentencing by Pilate (John); darkness, after a crucifixion at 9 A.M. (Mark); darkness without an implication that crucifixion had taken place long before (Matt, Luke).

[98]Thus *GPet*'s combining the torn veil with the darkness differs from the Lucan combination just discussed. The fact that *GPet* 6:22 reports "the sun shone" after the death notice that Jesus "was taken up" (5:19) makes it clear that the twice-mentioned law about the sun not setting on one who has died (2:5; 5:15) has not been violated.

[99]In my approach to *GPet* I posit that occasionally the preMatthean popular tradition that was drawn on by Matt has continued its development, and it is from that later stage of development that *GPet* has drawn. Yet *GPet* has also drawn on a memory of the contents of Matt. In the present

Just before he was taken up the Lord had screamed, "My power, O power, you have forsaken me" (5:19); but this exercise of theological insight adapts the earthquake to show that the dead body retains divine power,[100] a body that 10:40 will describe as so gigantic that the head stretched beyond the heavens. *GPet* is giving us an early attestation of the developing fascination with the death phenomena that we saw (pp. 1115–18 above) in full flower in the patristic period.

B. Matthew's Theology in Recounting the Special Phenomena

Matt inherited from Mark two eschatological phenomena (darkness over all the earth at noon and the rent veil of the sanctuary) as signs of divine judgment in reaction to the death of the Messiah, God's Son. To them he added another six phenomena, also signs eschatological or even apocalyptic in nature. Four of them are found in 27:51b–52b in a poetic quatrain of paratactic main clauses subdivisible into two couplets, one threatening (earth shaken, rocks rent), the other encouraging (tombs opened, bodies of the holy ones raised). The COMMENT showed the extent to which the four signs echoed Scripture. Like the phenomena borrowed from Mark, the phenomena in the quatrain offered a dramatic way in which ordinary people familiar with OT thought could understand that the death of Jesus on the cross had introduced the day of the Lord with all its aspects, negative (divine wrath, judgment) and positive (conquest of death, resurrection to eternal life).[101] The quatrain represented a form of Christian thought (often early) that could attach God's response to one of the moments used to describe Jesus' passing beyond time, without spelling out the response chronologically by allotting different results to the individual steps in a sequence of crucifixion, resurrection, ascension, and gift of the Spirit. Early attempts to identify the shaking of the earth with an otherwise known earthquake of the late 20s and to identify which dead were raised, even if they have their own theological thrusts, represent a failure to preserve the symbolic character of the set scriptural language of apocalyptic.

---

instance, faced with at least those two possible derivations, I think *GPet* can best be explained as dependent on Matt. In the instance of the related tradition that between death and resurrection the Lord had made proclamation to those asleep (10:41), however, I think *GPet* was drawing on further developments in the popular tradition, for I find no proof that Matt knew of "the descent into hell" (pp. 1127–28 above).

[100]While this might be devalued as a magical view, it could also be a simply expressed appreciation of the incarnation and its enduring results.

[101]The import of the phenomena is eschatological rather than christological, for God is the agent rather than Jesus. However, the fact that God does this because of Jesus' death has implications for Jesus' identity, and that is recognized by the confession of him as God's Son given by the centurion and the guards with him in Matt 27:54. As for soteriology, here Jesus' death does not raise the dead; God raises them on the occasion of that death.

The style of the quatrain in 27:51b–52b is not typically Matthean; and the vivid, imaginative character of the phenomena suggests a preMatthean poetic piece circulating in popular circles.[102] (In n. 50 above I pointed to other poems or short hymns treating the death-resurrection-ascension event.) I have contended that the veil of the sanctum was a symbol associated with Jesus' death on a preMarcan level, for it appears in another way in Hebrews. Perhaps already the aorist passive phrasing "the veil was rent," preserved in the three canonical Gospels and only slightly adapted in *GPet,* was also preMarcan.[103] Imitation of the pattern could have given rise to a quatrain in the same aorist passive style, piling on one another other apocalyptic portents interpreting Jesus' death. That quatrain could have come to Matt from the same circles that supplied some material in the infancy narrative (especially the story of the magi, the star, and the wicked king in chap. 2) and the account of Judas' death haunted by the fear of innocent blood.[104] Such material is almost totally composed from interwoven echoes of Scripture and to a degree unattested elsewhere in Matt gives free rein to symbols. The fact that Jerusalem is involved in all these scenes suggests that here, however much modified by Matt, we may be hearing elaborations of the Jesus story that originated among Jerusalem Christians. The objection that despite semitizing features, the detectable preMatthean quatrain existed in Greek (not in Semitic) does not disprove Jerusalem origins. The Lucan infancy hymns, which may also have been of Jerusalem Christian genesis, are known only in semitized Greek, despite (unconvincing) attempts to reconstruct Semitic originals (BBM 350–55).

[102]Those who posit a preMatthean unit (behind either the quatrain or the whole of 27:51b–53) include Aguirre Monasterio, Bartsch, Bieder, Fischer, Haenchen, Hauck, Hirsch, Plummer, and Riebl. On the issue of preMatthean vocabulary and style, see Aguirre Monasterio, *Exégesis* 29–56.

[103]Mark, then, by adding "sanctuary," would have brought this phrase into a sequence whereby it fulfilled two preceding passages predicting the destruction of the sanctuary.

[104]Consonant with his usual aversion to positing any clearly defined preMatthean tradition (other than Mark or Q), Senior ("Death of Jesus" 320; "Matthew's Special Material" 282–85) argues for Matthean composition of the quatrain. He claims that the main argument for the preMatthean position is the parataxis of the four lines, and offers an example of parataxis shaped by Matt in the four lines of Matt 7:25. The weakness of that argument can be shown if we translate the latter verse literally: "And fell the rain, and came the rivers, and blew the winds, and it struck against that house." First, this quadruple structure is less regular than that of 27:51b–52b, as we see in the shift of the subject pattern in the last clause. Second, the word order is different, and it is precisely the word order in vv. 51b–52b (with the verb last) that suggests to Riebl (*Auferstehung* 58–60) a (written) Semitic antecedent. Third, despite the four-line pattern, the description of what happens in 7:25 is factual (i.e., the phenomena are those of ordinary experience), while the contents of 27:51b–52b are highly imaginative and echo Scripture, even as does the other popular material peculiar to Matt mentioned above. The contention that every once in a while Matt on his own suddenly erupted into creating such material is far less credible than the contention that he incorporated popular material that had developed around Jesus' birth and death. Fourth, if Matt both created the quatrain in vv. 51b–52b and mentioned more phenomena in v. 53, why did he change the style so sharply from one of those passages to the other?

To the four phenomena in the quatrain Matt 27:53 added two more (entry of the raised holy ones into the holy city, being made visible to many) in a verse noticeably different in construction from 51b–52b and closer to Matt's own style. Some would contend that we have here another piece of preMatthean tradition, but more likely Matt supplemented the quatrain with his own commentary.[105] Why? One can suggest two likely motives.

Matt's first motive involved extending the eschatological symbolism to Easter and connecting it to Jesus' own resurrection. Matt would have been acting under the influence of a strain of Christian thought that characterized Jesus as the firstborn or first fruits of the dead (p. 1129 above)—an aspect seemingly neglected by localizing the raising of the fallen-asleep holy ones on Friday before Jesus' resurrection. Without changing that presentation, Matt has done more justice to the priority of Jesus by having the holy ones who had been raised on Friday enter the holy city and be made visible only "after his raising."[106] The freedom of early Christians to attach eschatological symbolism to any one of the events in the sequence death–resurrection–ascension–gift of the spirit (which from God's viewpoint are only different aspects of one timeless moment) is illustrated further in Acts 2:16–20. That passage sees fulfilled at Pentecost what was prophesied by Joel: before the coming of the day of the Lord, wonders in heaven above and signs on earth below (blood, fire, a cloud of smoke, sun turned to darkness, moon turned to blood). The Acts passage is the Lucan equivalent of Matt 27:51b–53 in emphasizing apocalyptic signs. Besides exhibiting a flexibility about the salvific event to which the signs could be attached, it casts light on the interpretation of Matt in two other ways. First, it cautions against too facilely historicizing the symbolism. As I noted at the beginning of the ANALYSIS, there have been few attempts to claim that on Pentecost the moon actually turned to blood, while there have been many attempts to treat the Matthean eschatological signs as historical. Moreover, the Acts passage is explicitly a citation of Scripture, and that observation leads us further in our quest to determine why Matt felt impelled to supplement the quatrain in vv. 51b–52b that he received from popular tradition.

[105]Arising from vocabulary there are two objections to attributing v. 53 to Matt. Elsewhere he does not use *emphanizein* ("to make visible"); but the adjective *emphanēs* is used in Acts 10:40 in relation to the risen Jesus, and so we may be dealing with established resurrection-appearance language. Elsewhere Matt does not use *egersis* ("raising"), but he probably wants to continue from *egeirein* in v. 52b: The holy ones were raised previously, and now Matt focuses on Jesus' own raising. Positively for Matthean composition, only Matt among the Gospels has used "holy city" for Jerusalem, namely, when the devil took Jesus there to tempt him and challenge whether he was really God's Son (4:5–6; cf. 5:35). The present instance of entering "the holy city" will be followed by a confession of Jesus as God's Son.

[106]Because I regard this phrase as a key to Matt's theological outlook, I reject the suggestion (see Riebl, *Auferstehung* 54–56) that it represents postMatthean editing.

Matt's second motive in adding v. 53 was the fulfillment of Scripture. Above I pointed out how much Ezek 37 with its creative description of the enlivening of the dry bones influenced Jewish imagination in picturing the resurrection of the dead. The first part of Ezek 37:12–13, "I will open your tombs," probably shaped the third line of the quatrain of Matt 27:51b–52b, "And the tombs were opened." But the Ezek passage continues: "And I will bring you up out of your tombs, and I will lead you into the land of Israel. Then you shall know that I am the Lord." Even as elsewhere Matt enhances the scriptural background and flavoring of material taken from Mark, so here scripturally he goes beyond the quatrain by offering in 27:53 the fulfillment of the rest of the Ezek passage: "And having come out from the tombs, . . . they entered into the holy city [of Jerusalem]." Another biblical passage may have shaped Matt's addition, especially the last clause "and they were made visible to many," i.e., Isa 26:19 (LXX): "Those in the tombs shall be raised, and those in the land [or on the earth] shall rejoice." Thus in what he has added to Mark (both the quatrain taken over from popular tradition and his own commentary on it), Matt has developed the theological insight. In apocalyptic language and imagery borrowed from Scripture he teaches that the death of Jesus and his resurrection ("raising") marked the beginning of the last times[107] and of God's judgment, shaking the earth as an accompaniment to the threatening darkness that spread over it, and raising the holy ones to a new life. These holy ones are Jews; in the next part of the scene to which we shall now turn Matt will present Gentiles (the centurion and the guards who were with him) and their confession of faith. From Jesus' birth (which involved Joseph and the magi) to his death, Matt is interested in showing that Jesus brought salvation to both Jew and Gentile alike.[108] Thus, in Ezekiel's language, through God's Son they come to "know that I am the Lord."

(*Bibliography for this episode may be found in §37, Parts 10 and 11.*)

[107]In a certain way the last times began for Matt with the birth of the Messiah; but there were different aspects of the last times, and here we come to the eschatological moment of punishment and reward.

[108]Perhaps it is worthwhile to stress once more, however, that the positive, salvific aspects of this picture are centered in the raising of the dead and the confession by the centurion, not in the rending of the sanctuary veil.

(Mark 15:39–41; Matt 27:54–56; Luke 23:47–49;
John 19:31–37)

Translation

Mark 15:39–41: 39But the centurion who had been standing there opposite him, having seen that he thus expired, said, "Truly this man was God's Son." 40But there were also women observing from a distance, and among them Mary Magdalene, and Mary mother of James the younger and of Joses, and Salome 41(who, when he was in Galilee, used to follow him and serve him), and many others who had come up with him to Jerusalem.

Matt 27:54–56: 54But the centurion and those who with him were keeping (guard over) Jesus, having seen the (earth)shaking and these happenings, feared exceedingly, saying, "Truly this was God's Son." 55But there were there many women observing from a distance, such ones as had followed Jesus from Galilee, serving him, 56among whom was Mary Magdalene, and Mary mother of James and of Joseph, and the mother of the sons of Zebedee.

Luke 23:47–49: 47But the centurion, having seen this happening, was glorifying God, saying, "Certainly this man was just." 48And all the crowds who were gathered together for the observation of this, having observed these happenings, returned striking their breasts. 49But all those known to him were standing from a distance, and the women who were following with him from Galilee, seeing these things.

John 19:31–37: 31Then the Jews, since it was preparation day, in order that the bodies might not remain on the cross on the Sabbath, for that Sabbath was a great day, asked Pilate that their legs be broken and they be taken away. 32So the soldiers came and broke the legs of the one and of the other who had been crucified with him; [33]but having come to Jesus, when they saw him already dead, they did not break his legs. [34]However, one of the soldiers stabbed his side with a lance, and immediately there came out blood and water. [35]And the one who has seen has borne witness, and true is his witness; and that one knows that he speaks what is true in order that you too may believe. [36]For these things happened in order that the Scripture might be fulfilled: "Its (his) bone shall not be fractured." [37]And again another Scripture says, "They shall see whom they have pierced."

GPet 4:14 (after 4:13 where one of the crucified wrongdoers reviled the Jews for making the Savior suffer unjustly): And having become irritated at him, they ordered that there be no leg-breaking, so that he might die tormented.

6:21: And then they drew out the nails from the hands of the Lord and placed him on the earth; and all the earth was shaken, and a great fear came about.

7:25–8:29: [7:25]Then the Jews and the elders and the priests, having come to know how much wrong they had done to themselves, began to beat themselves and say, "Woe to our sins. The judgment has approached and the end of Jerusalem." [26]But I with the companions was sorrowful; and having been wounded in spirit, we were in hiding, for we were sought after by them as wrongdoers and as wishing to set fire to the sanctuary. [27]In addition to all these things we were fasting; and we were sitting mourning and weeping night and day until the Sabbath. [8:28]But the scribes and Pharisees and elders, having gathered together with one another, having heard that all the people were murmuring and beating their breasts, saying that, "If at his death these very great signs happened, behold how just he was," [29]feared (especially the elders) and . . .

COMMENT

I shall subdivide my remarks here under four headings: Mark/Matt, Luke, John, and *GPet*. While the Synoptics have in common two reactions, namely, of the centurion (Matt includes fear) and of the Galilean women, Luke has a different form of the first plus an extra reaction (of the repentant crowds) intercalated between them, thus warranting special treatment. John has a different presentation in which "the Jews" react by wanting the bodies taken away—a request that shifts attention to the dead body of Jesus which becomes the source of blood and water, as witnessed by the beloved disciple. *GPet* has four reactions in a scattered pattern and of a mixed nature: fear as in Matt, repentant Jews as in Luke, mourning disciples, and threatened Jewish authorities.

REACTIONS OF THOSE PRESENT ACCORDING TO MARK/MATT

After the eschatological divine actions that have preceded, an initial *de* ("But") shifts the scene to human reactions. There is no hostility in either of the two that are recounted (centurion, women), but scholars disagree strongly about the tone of each.

Reaction of the Centurion (Mark 15:39; Matt 27:54). This figure spontaneously praises Jesus as God's Son. Previously Mark 15:16–24 and Matt 27:27–35 told us of Roman soldiers who mocked Jesus in the praetorium and led him away to Golgotha; there they gave him wine, crucified him, and divided up his clothes. (Matt 27:36 added that they then sat and kept guard over him.) Neither Gospel has mentioned the presence of an officer of centurion rank.[1] Yet now we learn from Mark that he had been standing there right in front of Jesus in a position to observe what had been going on,[2] and presumably in charge of the execution. (The latter point will be confirmed in 15:44 when Pilate summons the centurion to ask if Jesus is dead.) Only *his* reaction is described, as if the other soldiers were no longer present: Evidently for Mark it is more effective to have a single spokesman evaluate Jesus. Matt fills in the scene by adding to the evaluators of Jesus the soldiers who had been sitting, "keeping (guard over) him." Since 27:36 prepared for this addition, Matt's narrative flow is an improvement over Mark's unexpected introduction of a figure who all along had been "standing there opposite him." More important, Matt has thus established the legal propriety of "Truly this was God's Son"; it is now a confession not by one man but by a

---

[1]Only Mark in the NT, with his penchant for Latinisms, uses (3 times) the loan word *kentyriōn* from the Latin *centurio*, related to *centum* ("a hundred"), a word found also in Greek literature (e.g., Polybius, *History* 6.24.5). Matt and Luke prefer the more properly Greek *hekatontarchēs* (variant *hekatontarchos*, related to *hekaton* "a hundred"), which appears 20 times in the NT (4 in Matt, 16 in Luke-Acts).

[2]In II Kings 2:15 and Sir 37:9 the phrase *ex enantias* ("opposite, in face of") is used with *idein* ("to see").

plurality of witnesses (who match the plurality of Sanhedrin-trial witnesses arraigned against Jesus' exalted dignity).

What the centurion saw. Mark 15:39 reports that the centurion's reaction followed his "having seen that he [Jesus] thus expired." What does that mean? Two verses before (15:37) Mark wrote, "But Jesus, having let go a loud cry, expired." Accordingly one could equate the "thus" of v. 39 with letting go a loud cry in v. 37. Codices Bezae, Freerianus, and Alexandrinus, although differing in Greek wording, all present the centurion as having seen him *crying out* and expiring. In order to explain how "seeing" a cry would lead to the centurion's very high christological evaluation, some commentators imaginatively guess at the unmentioned content of the cry. Stock ("Bekenntnis" 292) points to OT passages where a cry accompanied divine action (see p. 1045 above) and raises the possibility that Jesus' cry without words could have been revelatory. But in the storyline is it plausible that the Roman centurion (or Mark's readers) would have recognized that? Danker ("Demonic" 69) contends that an evil spirit came out of Jesus with a loud cry as he died, and it was the sight of this that impressed the centurion. In §42, n. 38, I explained why I did not find convincing Danker's interpretation of Jesus' expiring with a loud cry; yet even if one were to accept his theory, such a defeat of the forces of evil might cause the centurion to exclaim that Jesus was good or innocent, but why would it lead him to give to Jesus the highest christological evaluation in the Gospel? During Jesus' ministry, through his God-given power, demons came out from the possessed with a loud cry (Mark 1:26; cf. 3:11; 5:13); if now through this power the same thing happened to Jesus, why would the centurion be so easily moved to confess Jesus' unique filial relationship to God? Others would push the area covered by the *"thus* expired" of 15:39 back further to include 15:34–36, i.e., Jesus' articulated cry, "My God, my God, for what reason have you forsaken me?", and the continued mockery by the bystanders until Jesus expired ("Let us see if Elijah comes to take him down.") Such an extension is helpful because "My God" is invoked there, and the centurion's confession involves Jesus' relationship to God.[3] Nevertheless, that extension does not really explain the exalted content of the centurion's confession, for nothing in those verses shows that in fact God had not abandoned Jesus, and certainly God did not intervene to save him from death.

Far more plausible is that "having seen that he thus expired" in 15:39 was meant to include not only the expiration in 15:37 (and what immediately

---

[3]In discussing the relationship of the vocalized loud cry in 15:34 and the unvocalized loud cry in 15:37, I found it more likely that Mark did not think of two cries but in 15:37 was simply resuming his storyline (after an interruption in 15:35–36) by recalling the loud cry he had mentioned in 15:34.

preceded it in 15:34–36),[4] but especially 15:38 and what followed the expiration: the rending of the sanctuary veil. The objection that this event can scarcely be considered part of "thus *expired*" does not give sufficient force to the "thus" that Mark has placed in an emphatic position. In the centurion's sight Jesus who had cried out "My God" just before he expired was truly God's Son because God had responded dramatically and thus had shown that Jesus had not been abandoned—a divine response that at the same time ironically granted the request of those who had mockingly invited a heavenly intervention. But could the centurion have *seen* this? Some object that the inner sanctuary veil leading to the Holy of Holies could have been seen only by Temple priests, and the outer veil only from the east (the Mount of Olives) and not from the skull-shaped hill of Golgotha to the north. I reject the very applicability of such an objection. If it is meant on the level of history, it confusedly misreads an apocalyptic sign as a factual occurrence (§43, ANAL-YSIS). If it is meant on the level of story flow, it supposes that Mark and his readers knew the architectural and geographical layout of the Temple in relation to Golgotha, a supposition that I challenged above (p. 1113) in discussing the veils. There is no reason to think that the ancient Marcan audience (any more than most people today) would have had a problem with the centurion's seeing the rending of the veil. And it would have made sense to them that this tremendous sign led him to understand that Jesus was not only innocent but indeed so closely related to God that the deity had begun to destroy the sanctuary of the people who had dared to mock him.

The first known interpreter of Mark read the scene to include what happened *after* Jesus' death, for in Matt 27:54 the centurion and those keeping guard have seen "the (earth)shaking and these happenings"[5]—in other words most of the apocalyptic signs wrought by God to interpret Jesus' death: the earth shaken, rocks rent, tombs opened, bodies of the fallen-asleep saints raised.[6] Matt emphasizes the earthquake partly because it is related causally to some of the other signs, and partly because it would have been

---

[4] I would favor pushing the "thus expired" back to 15:33 and the darkness that came over the whole earth from the sixth hour. That is surely something that the centurion would have seen. In all this and throughout this section I am thinking on the level of the story flow, not on the level of historicity.

[5] Codices Vaticanus and Bezae read the present participle *ta ginomena,* while the Koine tradition reads the aorist participle *ta genomena,* "these things that had happened."

[6] The signs I have listed reflect the likelihood that "the shaking and these happenings" are to be taken sequentially, i.e., the "happenings" are what Matt listed after the earthquake. There is no adequate reason in interpreting Matt to include how Jesus died (pace Vanni, "Passione" 88). I am uncertain about the rending of the veil since that is the same type of eschatological sign as the others. As I explained in §43 above, plausibly Matt 27:53 means that while the dead came out of the tombs on Friday, they came into Jerusalem and appeared on Sunday or later after Jesus' resurrection. In describing what the centurion saw on Friday, Matt jumps back over that verse (which he had appended) to Friday's events.

the most clearly visible. This shift of emphasis from the rent veil (the implied focus of Mark's attention) raises the possibility that Matt was aware of the topographical problems about seeing the veil. Whether or not that is so, however, Matt's signs should not be historicized any more than Mark's; and the centurion's sight of "these happenings" should not be challenged on the grounds of geographical implausibilities—how many tombs could have been seen from Golgotha? Understandably Matt reports that the sight of the shaking earth and the other happenings caused exceeding fear,[7] as well as an exclamation (taken over almost verbatim from Mark) giving voice to the awe: "Truly this was God's Son."

What is meant by "God's Son"? I have translated literally the expression *huios theou* in Mark and *theou huios* in Matt to make intelligible the problem that interpreters have had with it. It is anarthrous, i.e., does not have the definite article before either noun, unlike the comparable arthrous designation (i.e., with the definite article) in the high priest's question at the Sanhedrin trial: "Are you . . . *the* Son of *the* Blessed/God?" (*ho huios tou eulogētou* in Mark; *ho huios tou theou* in Matt). A large number of scholars contend that this predicate in the centurion's confession of Jesus means something less than "the Son of God."[8] Let me list their three important arguments and explain why I disagree.

(1) Some argue that Mark, who thus far has never had a human being confess Jesus as "the Son of God," would not allow that here. One may reason in the other direction, however: Mark does have the demon-possessed recognize that Jesus is "(the) Son of (the Most High) God" (3:11; 5:7; cf. 1:24);[9] would he have had the centurion confess less in response to God's impressive action at the time of Jesus' death? That such a confession has not been uttered before is no obstacle, for the full understanding of Jesus' identity was not possible before the Son of Man had suffered (see 9:30–32). Also Mark is supplying an inclusion framing the Gospel: At the beginning God said, "You are my beloved Son" (arthrous: 1:11); at the end a human being finally recognizes that truth.[10] Within the PN the confession is surely meant

---

[7]*Sphodra* ("exceedingly") occurs 7 times in Matt, 1 in Mark, and 1 in Luke. Shaking of the earth and fear among the guards will reappear as a Matthean motif in 28:2–4 when the angel of the Lord rolls back the stone from Jesus' tomb.

[8]RSV (1st ed.), NEB, Phillips, and Moffatt render it as "a son of God." In §37, Part 12, for the less-than-full christological predicate, see Harner, Johnson; also C. Mann, ExpTim 20 (1908–9), 563–64. For the full-valued "the Son of God," see P. H. Bligh, Bratcher, Glasson, Goodwin, Guy, Michaels, Stock.

[9]Since Mark 1:11 had God reveal Jesus to be the Son, most agree that this confession by demoniacs is not to be considered false. Rather demons know supernaturally what humans can know correctly only when they have understood the role of the cross as a component in Jesus' identity (his suffering humanity)—a component that is also part of the identity of those who would be his disciples.

[10]There may be another inclusion if "Son of God" in 1:1 (missing in some mss.) is genuine.

to pick up the issue raised at the Sanhedrin trial where Jesus answered "I am" when asked whether he was the Son of the Blessed. Why would Mark now have less than that confessed by the centurion? As for Matt, this first argument is not applicable, for he has had Jesus confessed by the disciples as "God's Son" (anarthrous: 14:33) after the walking on the water, and by Simon Bar-Jona as "the Son of the living God" (arthrous: 16:16) at Caesarea Philippi. The confession by the centurion and the guards is a continuation of the confession of believers.

(2) Grammatically some would argue that the anarthrous predicate has to have less force than the arthrous and is indefinite, equaling "a son of God," a rank shared by other human beings. That claim about indefinite import, however, is far from certain. I have just pointed out that in chaps. 14 and 16 Matt used the anarthrous and arthrous titles interchangeably;[11] he does so again in 26:63 (arthrous) and 27:40,43 (anarthrous). In Luke 1:32,35, in revealing to Mary what Jesus will be called, the angel Gabriel uses "Son of the Most High" and "Son of God" without the article; and no one can doubt that he intends the highest christology. As for the use of the title with the copula verb, there are instances where the designation "Son of God" in an exclusive sense is anarthrous when in whole or in part it precedes the verb, as it does in the centurion's confession, e.g., Matt 4:3,6 (= Luke 4:3,9); Matt 27:40; John 10:36. Indeed, after a famous study by E. C. Colwell more precision has entered the evaluation of the anarthrous predicate. Colwell's rule, viz., definite predicate nouns which precede the verb usually lack the article,[12] caused him (p. 21) to find in Mark 15:39 a confession of "the Son of God." Harner ("Qualitative" 75) has sought to refine the grammatical picture by arguing that anarthrous predicate nouns that precede the copula verb may function primarily to express the *nature or character of the subject.* The Marcan centurion, then, does not mean that Jesus was *a* son of God, for in that case the designation would have followed the verb. But neither does the centurion mean that Jesus was the exclusive Son of God in the full christological sense, for then the predicate would have been arthrous. Rather he means that Jesus was the kind of Son of God who is marked by (and therefore can be known through) suffering and death. While Harner's grammatical distinctions are probably too refined, he correctly implies that "Truly . . . God's Son" would include a Marcan rejection of any false notion of divine

[11]One could make a case that there is a progression from the disciples' anarthrous confession to Simon Peter's more solemn arthrous confession; but surely Matt was not having the disciples confess, "You are a son of God" (like other human beings), after Jesus walked on the water and calmed the storm.

[12]"A Definite Rule for the Use of the Article in the Greek New Testament," JBL 52 (1933), 12–21. E. S. Johnson ("Is Mark" 4), in his examination of 112 instances of definite predicate nouns preceding the verb, found that 15 had the article and 97 did not.

sonship (especially one that would exclude suffering) in circulation among Christians. But Harner's evaluation should have extended "the kind of Son of God" qualification to the whole PN context. In the logic of the Marcan storyline the centurion must be referring back to "the Son of the Blessed" question at the Sanhedrin trial, for that is the only other time that divine sonship has been a topic in the Marcan PN.[13] Jesus is in fact the kind of Son of God that the Jewish leaders asked about, the affirmation of which they regarded as blasphemous. That is the import of "Truly," the first word in the centurion's confession: In the issue that led to Jesus' death truth was on Jesus' side.[14]

(3) Often it is argued that a pagan Roman[15] soldier would not have had the religious background to confess Jesus as the unique Son of the true God. He could have recognized that Jesus was a good or holy man and a child of God in that sense, or at most a divine hero, worthy to be worshiped.[16] Once more this is the wrong kind of historicizing. We are not to ask what a soldier meant at Golgotha in the year 30/33; that is impossible to discover. (If the scene is historical and he spoke this sentence, did he speak Latin, where there is no definite article [*filius Dei*], or Greek? If the latter, would he have known the niceties of Greek grammar [Colwell's rule]? See Guy, "Son.") We are to ask what this scene meant to the Marcan readers in the late 60s or 70s. For them the centurion would have had representative value both as a Gentile and as a Roman official with responsibility who would not have reacted out

[13]In the mockery at the cross that the centurion might have heard, the chief priests and the scribes challenged Jesus' being "the Messiah, the king of Israel," without mentioning the Son of God. Once again Matt's storyline is an improvement, for in 27:40,43 he had both passersby and the chief priests mock Jesus' claim to be the Son of God.

[14]Stock ("Bekenntnis" 104) points out that *alēthēs* had this force of solving a dispute in its only previous Marcan use (14:70b) where the bystanders affirm to Peter, "Truly you are one of them, for indeed you are a Galilean."

[15]Troops under the control of the prefect of Judea were often not ethnically Roman or Italian (§31, n. 64), and centurion rank did not require Roman citizenship. Yet this centurion comes with his soldiers from the praetorium of the Roman prefect (Mark 15:16,20) and will be summoned by Pilate to report on Jesus' death (15:44). Therefore, he must be thought of by the readers as a Roman representative of Pilate. That was understood early: *GPet* 8:31 gives to the centurion who with soldiers was sent by Pilate to guard Jesus' tomb the name Petronius, which was the name of a Roman legate of Syria ca. AD 40. *Acts of Pilate* 16:7 gives the centurion the name Longinus, a name borne by Romans of the Cassia gens (C. Schneider, "Hauptmann" 5). Metzger ("Names" 95) reports that a picture in the 10th-cent. Codex Egberti calls the man Stephaton who put the vinegary wine on the sponge to offer to Jesus.

[16]As for declaring Jesus good, Matt 27:19 has Pilate's wife recognize that Jesus is a just man, and Matt 27:23–24; Luke 23:14; and John 19:6 all have Pilate declare Jesus innocent. Some appeal to Luke's form of the centurion's confession (23:47: "Certainly this man was just") as proof that Mark meant this; but below I shall argue that Luke is changing, not translating, Mark. As for declaring Jesus a divine hero, P. H. Bligh ("Note") points out that a pagan would be familiar with the designation *sebastos* ("worthy to be worshiped") attached to Augustus, or even the *huios sebastos* attached to Tiberius.

of sheer pity or credulity.[17] As Jesus hung on the cross, the chief priests with scribes were saying, "Let the Messiah, the King of Israel, come down from the cross in order that we may *see* and *believe*" (Mark 15:32). Now a Gentile has seen what God has done and has believed. The Q tradition knows of a centurion who on the spot showed such faith that Jesus promised to many from East and West places at table with Abraham, Isaac, and Jacob, while the children of the kingdom would be thrown into outer darkness (Matt 8:5–13; Luke 7:1–10). This centurion at the cross is Mark's equivalent. At the end of the risen Jesus' appearances in the other Gospels, there is a directive to proclaim Jesus' gospel beyond the confines of Judaism to the Gentile world (Matt 28:19–20; Luke 24:47; [Acts 1:8]; John 20:21 [by implication]; Marcan Appendix 16:15). For Mark, who does not recount appearances of the risen Jesus, this centurion serves as a symbol for the incipient fulfillment of Jesus' promise in 13:10 that the gospel would be preached to all the nations. Is there also an OT echo? Granted the use of Ps 22 in the PN (APPENDIX VII), especially in Jesus' last words a few verses before (15:34), was Mark thinking of Ps 22:28: "All the ends of the earth shall remember and turn to the Lord, and all the families of the nations shall bow down before Him"? That the confession is made by a Roman soldier is also important. In narrating the activity of the soldiers in the crucifixion, 15:26 reported an inscription bearing the charge against Jesus, "The King of the Jews," echoing the charge in the trial before Pilate (15:2). Now the chief among the soldiers tacitly ignores that false political issue and returns affirmatively to the charge in the Sanhedrin trial, "the Son of God [the Blessed]."[18]

As for verisimilitude,[19] Mark's readers need not have found strange this

[17]Manus ("Centurion's" 269): "In a world where the army was used to expand the empire and acquire hegemony over weak nations, the rank and status of a centurion was a respectable one." Johnson ("Is Mark") offers helpful sociological background, e.g., a Hellenistic audience would have looked upon a centurion as one whose capability had enabled him to advance to a respected officer's position. (Note the admirable integrity and sympathetic stance of the tribune in Acts 23:16ff. and of the centurion in 27:43.) But then Johnson goes on to misapply historical information in order to deny that the centurion confessed Jesus' unique sonship. Johnson is undoubtedly right that many Roman soldiers serving in Judea would have had contempt for crucified criminals, have been anti-Jewish, and have despised Jewish beliefs as superstition. But Johnson does not ask whether Mark's audience would have adverted to that. Would they not have regarded it as all the more convincing that one who had no reason to be favorable to Jesus had recognized the truth about him? Later the centurion Longinus was looked on as a Christian saint (honored on March 15) whose relics were preserved in Mantua.

[18]The preceding context demands that this confession be interpreted over against the Jewish denial. I think Bligh ("Note" 53) historicizes wrongly when he sees it made over against the Roman soldier's allegiance to the emperor: "This man, not Caesar, is the Son of God." I see nothing to suggest that the Marcan audience would think of this contrast.

[19]Petronius, *Satyricon* 111, mentions a soldier who stayed watching the cross lest someone take away the body for burial.

affirmation of faith by a Roman centurion involved in Jesus' crucifixion. Acts 10 recounts how another centurion, Cornelius, came spontaneously to faith in Jesus,[20] and 16:25–34 tells of Paul's jail guard at the Roman colony of Philippi who was instantly converted by Paul's not seeking to escape. In Jewish martyr stories divine intervention on the martyr's behalf and/or the way in which the martyr was willing to suffer for the truth sometimes converted their captors or persecutors,[21] and that became a feature of Christian martyr stories as well. Certainly the acceptance of Jesus' heavenly origins by a Roman centurion after a divine sign has no lesser degree of verisimilitude than the acknowledgment in Luke 23:42 of Jesus' heavenly kingdom by a crucified wrongdoer without any divine sign. Neither figure had the religious background of the Jewish authorities; both could see the truth.

By way of summary, then, there is no convincing objection to the thesis that the predicate in the confession of the Marcan centurion meant "the Son of God" in the full sense of the term. I chose to deal with the various objections because some have been convinced by them. I would rather have answered the basic question in the same manner I dealt with the issue of what the high priest meant when he asked Jesus, "Are you . . . the Son of the Blessed/God?" There is no likelihood that Mark's audience would make a distinction between what their creedal statement (Jesus is the Son of God) meant ca. 70 and what the high priest and the centurion meant when they used "Son of God" in a story situated in 30/33. The audience would have heard one of the two figures scoffing at what they believed, and the other affirming it.

Turning briefly to Matt, I find no reason to think that "God's Son" in Matt's form of the centurion's confession means something different from Mark's use of the term. The participle "saying" that introduces the Matthean confession is dependent on "feared exceedingly." In other words, religious awe engendered by the eschatological signs is the context in which Jesus is hailed as God's Son. The "Truly" that is the first word of the confession was used previously in the acknowledgment of Jesus' divine sonship by the disciples in Matt 14:33. We saw that Ezek 37 greatly influenced Matt's reference to the rocks being rent, the tombs being opened, and the bodies being raised. Now that these phenomena have occurred, the centurion and the guards who saw them recognize who Jesus is, fulfilling Ezek 37:13 (LXX): "Then you shall know that I am the Lord, when I have opened your sepulchers to lead forth my people from the sepulchers." The contrast between a

---

[20]True, Acts 10:1–2 reports that he was already a devout God-fearer, but the real import of the story is the unexpectedness of faith coming to this Gentile centurion (see 11:18; 15:7).

[21]Dan 3:28; 6:24; *III Macc* 6:20–29; see Pobee, "Cry." After the martyr Eleazar had undergone a horrible death, the author of *IV Macc* 7:6–15 recognizes the extraordinary import of this noble figure by a series of laudatory titles.

Roman confession and Jewish rejection is even stronger in Matt than it was in Mark. Jewish rejection of what the Roman affirmed is heightened by the fact that Matt's Sanhedrin trial had the high priest using this very title "the Son of God" (26:63: *ho huios tou theou*); and as Jesus hung on the cross (Jewish) passersby, chief priests, scribes, and elders all mocked his claim to be "Son of God" (27:40,43: *huios tou theou; theou huios;* see Vanni, "Passione" 89). Gentile acceptance is heightened by the fact that after Jesus' death Matt has plural confessors of "God's Son" (centurion, those keeping guard), thus forming an inclusion with the period after Jesus' birth when the Gentile magi came and worshiped "the King of the Jews," while the Jewish king Herod and "all the chief priests and scribes of the people" were hostile.[22]

"Truly THIS MAN WAS *God's Son."* The predicate has been the most discussed aspect of the Mark/Matt centurion's confession, and in treating it above we saw the importance of "Truly." Yet we would not do justice to Mark's theology if we neglected the grammatical subject and the verb of the dramatic declaration. All the other Gospel confessions of Jesus are in the present tense; and so the use of the imperfect tense, "was," in this final confession is both unique and significant. Mark/Matt do not mean that Jesus' divine sonship is something confined to the past, but the verb shows that the confession is an evaluation of the past.[23] Jesus was God's Son throughout a ministry which began when God affirmed that truth (Mark 1:11), even if no human being has hitherto recognized it. The grammatical subject in Mark, "this man," is a rarely found description of Jesus. Mark used it previously only in 14:71 when Peter stated, "I don't know this man"—a denial by the chief disciple shared the wording of a confession by a new disciple! (The preceding verse in the denial [14:70] was Mark's last use of "Truly," which reappears here.) That "this" is placed first in the confession has partially a locative force, calling attention to the one in front of whose crucified body the centurion stands. (Note how the bandits crucified on either side of Jesus [15:27] are ignored.) To a greater degree, however, the "this" is designatory: this one who died in this way. Combined with "was" the demonstrative serves Mark's theology that the revelation of God's Son took place on the cross. As for the nominal subject "man [*anthrōpos*],"[24] Mark has frequently contrasted "man [= human being]" and "God" (7:8; 8:33; 10:9,27; 11:30; 12:14) as opposed alternatives. In those passages human values are so different from God's as to distort religious truth. Jesus acted and spoke with power/authority (*exousia:* 1:22,27; 11:28), but the scribes accused him of

---

[22]Matt 2:4,20; the latter contains a plural: "those who sought the child's life," showing that all the parties of 2:4 were involved.

[23]For many of the observations made here, see Stock, "Bekenntnis" 296–97.

[24]Davis ("Mark's") is particularly helpful on this point.

blaspheming by claiming to do things that God alone could do (2:7: note that they too see human and divine origin as opposed alternatives). The reader is being told that the reason Jesus was not blasphemous is that in him the contrariety between the human and the divine does not exist. He is the Son of Man whose values are those of God and not of human beings: the Son of Man who came to serve, not to be served (10:45), and who has acknowledged that his role is to suffer on the cross (8:31; 9:31; 10:33). Before the Sanhedrin Jesus answered affirmatively the high priest's question about his being the Son of the Blessed (God) in terms of seeing the Son of Man (14:61–62); now the Roman centurion has seen "this man" and identified him as the Son of God.[25] Manus ("Centurion's" 264) phrases well the totality of the picture in Mark 15:39: "Mark makes the Roman centurion a faithful *representative* of Gentile Christianity which saw the significance of Jesus as the son of God revealed par excellence in the drama of the cross." He is the first of that believing community which in the language of 14:58 constitutes another sanctuary not made by hand, replacing the Jerusalem sanctuary made by hand, the veil of which has just been rent into two from top to bottom.

Matt 27:54 has a slightly different thrust since it omits "man" from the grammatical subject, which is now simply "this" and is moved to the end in the Greek word order: "Truly God's Son was this."[26] Yet the reference to the crucified Jesus is maintained. As he hung on the cross others might utter a mockery tantamount to "This was God's Son?" as a derisive question expressing incredulity (see 27:40,43); Matt's centurion responds with his prefixed "Truly."

Reaction of the Women (Mark 15:40–41; Matt 27:55–56). The second response to Jesus' death is described at twice the length of the first; yet nothing is uttered by those described, so that their presence has to speak for itself—a factor producing disagreement among interpreters and opening the possibility that the presence may mean different things in different Gospels.[27]

The identification of the women. According to Mark, among the "women

[25]The grammatical order in the confession of Mark 15:39 is appropriate ("this man" as subject; "God's Son" as predicate); for throughout the Gospels "Son of Man," as Jesus' self-designation, is normally a subject, while "the Son of God," said of him by others, is usually a predicate. The confession of the centurion has been hailed as "the" climax of Mark's Gospel. The critique of that position by Stockklausner and Hole ("Mark 15:39") is a bit overdone in my judgment. Yet they are right in insisting that the resurrection is also important to Mark, so that 15:39 is better characterized as *a* climax.

[26]In the third of Peter's denials, where Mark 14:71 had "I don't know this man," Matt 26:74 took the alternative of eliminating "this": "I don't know the man." Is Matt's twice avoiding Mark's "this man" in the PN accidental; or is the designation, which could be understood as "this fellow," an undignified reference to Jesus in Matt's eyes?

[27]In his effort to detect a new structure in the ending of Matt, Heil ("Narrative" 420) attempts to join the reaction of the women (27:55–56) to the burial and resurrection account so that Matt 27:55–28:20 forms a unit. I judge this wrong for three reasons: (a) as I shall argue (pp. 1300–1),

observing from a distance" were: (i) Mary Magdalene, i.e., Mary from Magdala on the NW shore of the Sea of Galilee; (ii) "Mary, of James the younger and of Joses, the mother"; (iii) Salome—these "used to follow and serve him" when he was in Galilee[28]—and (iv) many others who had come up with him to Jerusalem. Mark has never before mentioned that women had followed Jesus throughout his public ministry; and so in naming three of them he has to supply some background information. Unfortunately, what he supplies is phrased confusingly, mentioning a plural group both at the beginning and the end of 15:40–41. One gets the impression that none of the women who were observing from a distance were native to Jerusalem. Of three it is said specifically that when he was in Galilee they used to follow and serve him.[29] Other women who are not said to have done that (although Mark may have meant that they did) had come up with (*synanabainein*) Jesus to Jerusalem, i.e., presumably from Galilee in the coming up (*anabainein*) described in 10:32–33, where Jesus warned his companions that he would suffer. We are left to wonder whether Mark meant that the three named women had also come up with him in the same journey.[30]

Matt simplifies the picture by having one mention of a plural group, combining the features of the twofold Marcan reference:[31] (i) the *"many* women observing from a distance" are those who "had followed Jesus *from* Galilee, serving him"—here all are Galileans; all have served him; all have followed him to Jerusalem. Among them are: (ii) Mary Magdalene; (iii) "Mary, of James and of Joseph, the mother"; (iv) the mother of the sons of Zebedee.

In order to compare the names of the individually identified women, please consult Table 8 (p. 1016 above), presented in relation to John's scenario of women standing near the cross. That table lists the women mentioned in three interrelated scenes: on Friday in the vicinity of the cross, and again at the burial; on Easter at the empty tomb. In line D of the table I point

---

Heil's discovery of three unequal parts (each with three subsections) represents overstructuralization foreign to Matt; (b) this analysis runs against the clear storyline which associates 27:55–56 primarily with what has preceded in the crucifixion, rather than with the burial and resurrection to follow; and (c) the analysis ignores the inclusive parallel between Matt 27:57–28:20 (note the beginning with 27:57) and 1:18–2:23 to be pointed out below (Table 9; p. 1302).

[28]These verbs in the imperfect have pluperfect force. Any attempt (see Schottroff, "Maria") to make the verbs inchoative with the idea that Mark means that these women are still following and serving Jesus in this crucifixion scene does not do justice to Mark's specification that this took place in Galilee. Only in 16:1 will Mark inform us that the women still wish to render service to the dead Jesus.

[29]*Diakonein* ("to serve, minister to") here probably means to take care of material needs, particularly food and drink (see Mark 1:13,31).

[30]Turner ("Marcan" 26.240) thinks that they did not but came later, just at Passover time, hoping to meet Jesus in Jerusalem. Pesch (*Markus* 2.508) recognizes that the literal grammar of Mark favors distinctions in the degrees of the women's adherence; Schottroff ("Maria" 13) rejects that.

[31]This is a clear instance of the implausibility of the thesis that Mark drew on Matt and Luke: Both of them give a simple description, so that Mark would have had to introduce confusion.

to a tradition (phrased differently by the various Gospels) of a larger group of Galilean women associated with Jesus who were present in Jerusalem, presumably having come for the Passover feast. Of the women identified by name,[32] line A shows Mary Magdalene to be the most frequently recalled; and here Mark/Matt name her first. Line B shows the high frequency of another woman named Mary, most often identified through her sons James and Joses/Joseph.[33] On this line, however, Mark confusingly offers three different designations for Mary: at a distance from the cross: "Mary, of James the younger and of Joses, the mother"; at the burial: "Mary of Joses"; and at the empty tomb: "Mary of James." Many theories have been advanced to explain how such diversity arose;[34] but fortunately a decision on that point is not of importance for our discussion here.

Line C of the table shows that there is too much variation among the Gospels about the other named women to allow comparative identifications. Mark alone mentions a Salome (here and 16:1—in Palestine at this period "Salome" was a common name). She appears also in the second fragment of

---

[32]Hengel ("Maria" 248) points out a tendency in the three scenes to list three women by name, similar to the tendency to list three of the Twelve: Peter, James, and John. Such listing probably reflects the relative importance within the larger group of those three, and the first named in each list may be respectively the first to have been granted an appearance of the risen Jesus (I Cor 15:5 for Cephas/Peter).

[33]I explained the likelihood that she is the woman whom John calls Mary of Clopas (her husband or father). As for the variants "Joses" in Mark and "Joseph" in Matt, and the similar variation in the names of the brothers of Jesus, see §41, n. 84.

[34]To illustrate scholarly ingenuity, let me list some of the proposals, with some queries: (a) The longer first designation of this Mary was original, and the second and third were shortened from the first. This is probably the most widely held view. But why then was the order of sons in the first (James before Joses) not followed? (b) The second and third designations of Mary were original, and the first was a composite from them (R. Mahoney, Matera, Schenke). This is related to the thesis that the women's presence at the tomb was more original than their stance (far-off or near) at the cross. On what basis, then, did the composer of the first designation of Mary, working from the second and third, change the order of names and add "the younger" to James' name? (c) Only the third reference to Mary was original, for the first and second lists of the women's names are easily omitted. Why then does the wording of the first and second references to Mary differ from the third? (d) Codex Vaticanus has two definite articles: "The Mary of James the younger and the mother of Joses." Pesch and Schottroff read this as a designation of two women, so that the second and third references are respectively to one and the other of them. Matt, however, read Mark to mean one woman: "the other Mary" (27:61; 28:1). (e) One woman is meant but her designation should be understood as "Mary *the wife* of James the younger and mother of Joses" (Finegan, Lohmeyer). Such a double designation of one person, however, is quite unusual. (f) Crossan ("Mark") contends that the preMarcan level spoke of "Mary of James" in the first and third references. Mark added "Joses" in the first and created the second ("Mary of Joses") because James and Joses were listed together among Jesus' brothers (6:3). (Later in PMK 146, however, Crossan contends that the third reference to the women in 16:1 was created on the basis of the first in 15:40.) (g) This Mary was Mary the mother of Jesus (as in John 19:25–27); but Mark, who denigrated the importance of family relationship to Jesus (3:31–35), preferred to designate her by her other sons (6:3). One has no other example of such a way of referring to Mary the mother of Jesus, and seemingly neither Matt or Luke detected her under this sobriquet. Although this survey of views that I find wanting is sobering, I have dared to make a suggestion of my own in §47, p. 1277.

SGM (3.15–16) at the moment when Jesus comes to Jericho (Mark 10:46a): "Present there were the sister of the young man whom Jesus loved, and his mother, and Salome; and Jesus did not receive them." Bauckham ("Salome" 257ff.) points out that she is subsequently remembered, particularly in gnostic works, as one of the (four) named women disciples of Jesus (e.g., *First Apocalypse of James* V.40.25–26). Is she to be kept distinct from the Salome of the *Protevangelium of James* 19:3, who may have been a child of Joseph by a previous marriage (see 9:2) and thus a "sister" of Jesus (same legal father)?[35] Or (whether historically or by subsequent imagining) did a sister of Jesus become one of the Galilean women who followed him?

On Line C Matt mentions the mother of the sons of Zebedee, a woman named in the NT by Matt alone. Is she Matt's identification of Mark's Salome? Or at a distance from the cross (he names no third woman in the burial and empty tomb scenes) is Matt substituting for Salome (a figure never mentioned by him) another, more significant woman? Previously Matt has twice changed what he received from Mark in a way that could give the designation "the mother of the sons of Zebedee" evocative significance here. In the issue of obtaining first places in Jesus' kingdom, as a substitute for the sons themselves (Mark 10:35), Matt 20:20 had the request made by "the mother of the sons of Zebedee." By changing the "Peter, and James, and John" of Mark 14:33, Matt 26:37 had Jesus take along with him in Gethsemane "Peter and the two sons of Zebedee." After those references redolent of failure, does Matt reintroduce at a distance from the cross "the mother of the sons of Zebedee" as a promise of a future role both for her and her sons in the following of Jesus?

In the ANALYSIS I shall discuss the issue of the presence of the women in the three scenes (the cross, the burial, the empty tomb) to determine which may have been the more original localization. Here we shall concentrate on the role the women play in the extant Mark/Matt narrative of the aftermath of Jesus' death. Two issues have been the subject of scholarly debate: their discipleship and the import of their "observing."

Were the women who observed from a distance disciples? On the level of terminology, Matt uses *mathētēs* for Jesus' adherents some sixty-five times (about two-thirds of the time independently of Mark or Q). While he envisions the extension of discipleship to all nations (Matt 28:19) and wants his readers to become disciples along the model of those whom he describes, it is never clear that he uses the term during Jesus' ministry to refer to any others than the Twelve, who were all men. (See 10:1: "His twelve disciples.")

---

[35]Mark 6:3 refers to the sisters of Jesus. Epiphanius (*Panarion* 78.8.1; 78.9.6; GCS 37.458,460) names in that category Mary and Salome, who were daughters of Joseph. See §41, n. 82.

Mark's first mention of Jesus' having disciples (2:15) has the explanatory clause "for there were many who were following him." One could get the impression in 3:14 that it was out of this larger group of disciples that he appointed the Twelve. Having called to himself the crowd with his disciples (8:34) Jesus stressed the importance of the cross in following him; and in 9:35 he talked to the Twelve about the need to be a servant of all. Would the indication in 15:41, then, that the three named women "used to follow him and serve him" in Galilee mean that in Mark's estimation they could be called "disciples," even though their presence with Jesus has never before been mentioned? Schottroff ("Maria") says yes; Gerhardsson ("Mark" 219–20), after describing very positively all that the women did, states: "But they are not painted as proper disciples, even less as future apostles."[36] We need to recognize that we may be asking something that Mark never asked of himself, and that two questions may be in order to cover that situation. Would Mark consider these women disciples, were he asked? (I suspect so.) Did Mark think of them when in describing the ministry he wrote the word "disciples"? (Perhaps not.)

No matter how one answers such questions (if they are answerable from the available evidence) and beyond the terminological level, the discipleship issue affects the interpretation of the present scene in a particular way. As part of her thesis that these women were disciples, Schottroff would argue that they were at the Last Supper, went to Gethsemane, were part of the "all" who fled, and now bravely have come back. I can see nothing in Mark to support that contention. Mark 14:17 says that Jesus came to the supper with the Twelve and gives no indication in that scene that he had anyone else in view.[37] In 14:26 those who were at the supper were the ones who went out to the Mount of Olives; and in 14:50, fulfilling the prophecy made to them in 14:27, they were the "all" who fled. In chap. 14 Mark is interested pedagogically in showing the failure of the Twelve, not of women he has never mentioned to his readers. The "all" who fled from Gethsemane are never present again in the Marcan PN or indeed again in the Gospel. In 14:28 Jesus said that after his resurrection he would go before them into Galilee;

---

[36]Also E. Schweizer, EvT NS 42 (1982), 294–300 in disagreement with Schottroff.

[37]That there must have been others at the supper (cooks, waiters) is irrelevant in diagnosing the import of the Gospel narrative, for only mentioned characters function on that level. The presence of women (disciples) at the supper has sometimes entered current debates about the ordination of women to the priesthood. Lest someone suspect that by denying Mark's intention to include at the supper the women observers whom he would first mention at the crucifixion, I am in a covert way commenting on the ordination issue, let me observe that I have stated many times that the issue of whether women should be eucharistic celebrants cannot be decided either positively or (as is done more frequently) negatively on the basis of those whom the evangelists describe as present at the Last Supper. The evangelists' description of the supper corresponds to issues they were dealing with; it is with great peril applied to later church problems that never entered their minds.

and it is to them as an absent audience that on Easter the women are instructed by the (angelic) young man: "Go tell his disciples and Peter, 'He is going before you to Galilee'" (16:7). Clearly the women who are to carry the message are not part of those disciples; that is why they have to be introduced to the readers in 15:40–41.

How were the evangelist's readers meant to evaluate the women's observing from a distance? Some wrong evaluations have been proposed. Sentimentally, some would imagine that their presence must have comforted Jesus. That is thoroughly implausible: They are not introduced until after his death; they are set at a distance, giving the readers little encouragement to think he would have seen them; Jesus' cry in 15:34 portrays a man who has not been consoled. Another suggestion is that they were being held up as examples of bravery because they dared to come to Golgotha. Schottroff ("Maria") stresses that those who sympathized with leaders of revolutionary movements were liable to punishment. This is also implausible. Mark's readers are scarcely meant to recall without prompting this unmentioned background, given the fact that Jesus has never been presented as a leader of a revolutionary movement and no attempt by either Jewish police or Roman soldiers to arrest any of his followers has been reported. Observing "from a distance" is scarcely an opening description designed to make readers think of bravery. Indeed, the last person to whom that phrase was applied was Peter in Mark 14:54, who was following the arrested Jesus "from a distance"[38]—as the three denials indicate, he did not want to be identified as a follower of Jesus. From an understandable desire to uncover some of the unrecorded aspects of women's roles in Christian beginnings, others propose that these women observers are to be contrasted with the male disciples of Jesus. Cowardly males fled; noble women remained. If one wishes to make that comparison, "observing from a distance," even if not a description designed to make one think spontaneously of noble behavior, is better than "they all fled" (14:50). However, what evidence is there that Mark's narrative would encourage readers to contrast male disciples whose fleeing was mentioned some sixty verses before with these women who are not said to have *remained* (precisely because we have been told nothing of their previous presence)?

The clear contrast that Mark gives his readers in adjacent verses, as distinct from those imposed on his text, is between the centurion who has been standing there opposite Jesus and the women who were observing from a distance. From having seen how Jesus expired, the centurion, who presum-

---

[38]This is the only other Marcan PN use of *apo makrothen* and the only other use in the whole Gospel for Matt.

ably never knew Jesus before, is brought to confess him as God's Son. From what they have observed from a distance, these women who followed and served Jesus are silent and give no evaluation of him. If we remember that Mark does not spare the inadequacies of those associated with Jesus (family, disciples), it would be consistent for Mark to present the role of these women followers as inadequate. Indeed, his description of them may echo Ps 38 where a suffering figure describes how his enemies lay snares for his life and he gets no help from those close to him: "Those who were close to me stood *from a distance*" (38:12).

To test the thesis that Mark has not portrayed the role of these women observers so positively as many have assumed, let us look ahead to the two other Marcan scenes in which they will reappear (three scenes within fifteen verses). In 15:42–47 Joseph from Arimathea, one who was looking for the kingdom of God and had the courage to get Jesus' body from Pilate, will lay it in a tomb. These women will observe where he was placed without any helping intervention by word or deed. The only intervention on Jesus' behalf that Mark will attribute to them will come in 16:1 when after the Sabbath the three will buy spices in order to go and anoint Jesus.[39] Alas, the initiative will result in failure. When in 16:5–8 the young (angelic) man informs the three that Jesus has risen and that they are to go and tell his disciples and Peter that he is going before them to Galilee, they do not have the courage to obey. They say nothing to anyone, for they are afraid. When the centurion saw how Jesus expired, he immediately confessed aloud Jesus' divine identity. The three women are not moved to proclaim Jesus even when they are directed to do so by heavenly intervention![40] Mark's portrayal of the male disciples of Jesus illustrated that despite close following of Jesus during the ministry, they failed because they did not have the strength to remain with him during the bearing of the cross. Seemingly Mark has now used the female followers of Jesus to illustrate that observing the crucified sympathetically but from a distance was insufficient to guarantee the fidelity demanded of disciples; indeed, not even the news of the resurrection in itself accomplished that. Neither group has exemplified taking up the cross to follow Jesus, and that is absolutely necessary.[41] Both groups would have been meant

[39] I presume this act would strike Mark's readers favorably unless they were meant to regard it as foolishly superfluous after 14:3–8 where already a woman had poured pure nard ointment over Jesus' head, anointing his body beforehand for burial.

[40] For the thesis that the women fail at the empty tomb, see A. T. Lincoln, JBL 108 (1989), 283–300.

[41] Despite a series of scholarly attempts to portray the women in Mark as models of fidelity, the Gospel treats men and women with relative impartiality: Occasionally men and women are effective in their reaction to Jesus (9:38–39; 14:9), but the customary followers of Jesus, male and female,

to instruct Mark's readers. Those readers who had been persecuted and failed by fleeing or denying Jesus could identify with and, at the same time, gain hope from the male disciples who, after all, were promised that they would see Jesus in Galilee and who (as all knew) afterward became believing proclaimers of the Gospel, eventually showing themselves willing to bear the cross. Those who had escaped persecution and who might pride themselves that they had not failed are possibly being warned that noninvolvement and the reluctance to confess the risen Jesus publicly were reprehensible. But they too would not have been left without hope: The fact that the names of these women were remembered in the tradition suggests that eventually the risen Jesus gave them the strength to proclaim him—as the writer of the Marcan Appendix affirms (Mark 16:9–10).

In general throughout the ministry Matt has treated Jesus' relatives and disciples much less pessimistically than Mark treated them.[42] Is a more favorable treatment given by Matt to these Galilean women followers as well? Nothing in the present scene or in the burial scene (27:61) would indicate substantial difference from Mark; and in 28:1, instead of having the women intervene after the Sabbath by buying spices in order to go and anoint Jesus (Mark 16:1), Matt attributes to them the less indicative motive of desiring to see the sepulcher.[43] At the tomb itself, however, Matt's presentation of the women (28:8–10) is dramatically the opposite of Mark's. The women still have fear, but they obey the angel and run with great joy to give Jesus' disciples the angel's message. When Jesus himself appears to them, they take hold of his feet and *worship him* (the same wording used to describe the magi's reaction in 2:11). The Matthean readers, then, having got an impression that these women onlookers at the crucifixion and burial did not immediately react as well as did the centurion or Joseph of Arimathea, would discover that in the end they showed the fidelity of true followers of Jesus. In Matt, as in Mark, the women would be parallel to the male disciples (the Twelve), not contrasted to them; but now the parallelism is much more positive. Though the disciples had fled from Gethsemane, once the angel's mes-

---

fail at crucial moments. See E. S. Malbon, *Semeia* 28 (1983), 29–48; also C. C. Black, *Disciples* 278, n. 37.

[42]As regards the *family,* Matt did not include the pejorative Mark 3:20–21, although he copied what went before (Matt 10:2–4 = Mark 3:16–19) and after (Matt 12:24–29 = Mark 3:22–27). Also Matt 13:57 omitted the negative phrase about Jesus' relatives in Mark 6:4. As regards *disciples,* for example, Matt 14:33 had the disciples confess Jesus' divine sonship whereas Mark 6:52 had their hearts hardened. Matt 8:25; 9:32 avoided the rudeness toward Jesus on the part of the disciples reported in Mark 4:38; 5:30–31.

[43]In part the change from Mark is dictated by the presence of hostile guards at the sepulcher so that the women would not have been allowed near the body. Yet also Matt may have recognized the superfluousness of the Marcan intervention since Jesus had already been prepared for burial (26:12).

sage (repeated by the risen Jesus) was relayed to them, they obeyed and went to Galilee. When Jesus appeared to them despite the continued doubt of some, they worshiped him and were made apostles (28:16–20).

REACTIONS OF THOSE PRESENT ACCORDING TO LUKE

Luke 23:47–49 differs from Mark/Matt in having three reactions after Jesus' death on the cross instead of two, and this arrangement is clearly a Lucan artistic construction. Before Jesus was placed on the cross, as he was being led out to the place named Skull, Luke 23:26–31 also described three reactions. Thus Luke has set the crucifixion in a triptych, with three respondents grouped benevolently on either side of the cross. (Within the crucifixion scene itself [23:35–43] he preserved the pattern of three negative mockings that he found in Mark, even if before and after he framed them with the neutral "people" and the well-disposed wrongdoer.) On the way to crucifixion the reactors were: (i) Simon the Cyrenian who brought the cross behind Jesus, i.e., probably in Luke's estimation an individual who became a disciple by taking up or bearing the cross (as if it were his own) and following after Jesus (9:23; 14:27); (ii) a large multitude of the people who followed Jesus to the site of execution, evidently sympathetic but not revealing their mind by word or deed; (iii) women, addressed as "Daughters of Jerusalem," who were beating themselves and lamenting for him. In the present scene the reactors are also an individual and the people and women: (i) the centurion who, on the basis of what he has seen happen, glorifies God and affirms that Jesus was just; (ii) all the crowds who, after observing, returned to their homes striking their breasts; (iii) all those known to him standing at a distance and the women followers from Galilee, seeing these things, evidently with sympathy but not revealing their mind by word or deed. The first and third of these reactions have been adapted from Mark; the second is a Lucan contribution corresponding to that Gospel's more favorable attitude toward the Jewish people. Let us consider the three reactions one by one.

Reaction of the Centurion (23:47). Having seen *this happening,* he was *glorifying God* and affirming that Jesus was *just.* The italicized expressions represent differences from Mark's account of the centurion. Such differences have caused Creed, Fitzmyer, Taylor, and others to maintain that here Luke drew from a source other than Mark,[44] a source often deemed more original

---

[44]Hanson ("Does" 77–78) holds that the Lucan form is an adaptation of Mark but argues against Kilpatrick that the Proto-Luke hypothesis (i.e., there was a combination of Q and a Lucan special source into which Luke brought Marcan material) is not refuted by this scene. Manus ("Centurion's" 268) agrees with B. S. Easton that Luke's *dikaios* is primary and suggests it may represent "an original understanding of Jesus' personality probably current in the primitive Q community especially in the Palestinian-Syrian region."

because the Lucan confession seems more appropriate on the lips of a Roman Gentile than Mark's "God's Son." In my judgment none of that is necessary: Luke, with adaptations to fit his theological outlook, has drawn totally on Mark and not on another source. A basic argument for Lucan dependence on Mark may be drawn from two sets of words, viz., the introductory description of the centurion and his confession. The introductory words "But the centurion, having seen" are the same in Mark and Luke with the exception that Luke has substituted for the Latinized *kentyriōn* (related to *centum*, "hundred"), used by Mark alone, the proper Greek for "centurion": *hekatontarchēs* (related to *hekaton*, "hundred"), which with its variant *hekatontarchos* is used sixteen times in Luke-Acts and never in Mark.[45] As for the centurion's confession, Luke's word order is very close to Mark's even if the key word of the predicate is different:

| Mark 15:39: | *alēthōs* | *houtos ho anthrōpos* | *huios theou ēn* |
| Luke 23:47: | *ontōs* | *ho anthrōpos houtos* | *dikaios ēn* |

Both evangelists place the adverb in an emphatic position at the beginning;[46] and both use the imperfect tense of the verb, so unusual in a confession. If such similarities point to Luke's use of Mark, how do we account for the differences italicized in the initial sentence above?

Three Differences from Mark. The FIRST DIFFERENCE lies in what the centurion has seen: namely, in Mark, "that he [Jesus] thus expired"; and in Luke, "this happening."[47] For Mark "thus expiring" included Jesus screaming a cry of abandonment, a mocking response by the bystanders (vinegary wine, jibe about Elijah), again the loud cry, Jesus expiring, and the veil of the sanctuary being rent by God. Luke has presented a different sequence: The eschatological warnings of the darkness and the rent veil were joined (23:44–45) before Jesus' death; and by contrast Jesus cried aloud a prayer of trust, expiring on the note of "Father, into your hands I place my spirit" (23:46). The violent apocalyptic content of Mark's "thus" does not immediately precede Luke's description of the centurion's "having seen this happen-

---

[45]Mark, as we saw, offered little preparation for the appearance of the centurion standing there opposite Jesus, although he did have a whole Roman cohort called together to mock Jesus in Pilate's praetorium (15:16). Luke has offered even less preparation, for only during the mockery of Jesus on the cross (23:36) were readers alerted that Roman soldiers were involved.

[46]Mark's *alēthōs* is virtually synonymous with Luke's *ontōs* ("really, certainly"); but the latter, implying what flows from one's very being, is appropriate in the confession that Jesus is just, for throughout the Gospel (10:29; 16:15; 18:9; 20:20) Luke has challenged those whose justice or righteousness is superficial or self-deceptive.

[47]*To genomenon*, the aorist participle neuter singular from *ginesthai* ("to happen, come about"), meaning "what happened." The plural form *ta genomena* ("these happenings") will be used in the next verse. Matt 27:54 had the centurion and the guards see *ta ginomena*, the present participle neuter plural (n. 5 above).

ing," nor does anything like Matt's list of extraordinary happenings.[48] The Lucan centurion saw Jesus' composure facing death, a Jesus whose trusting relationship with God could not be interrupted, even by death.[49]

The SECOND DIFFERENCE is that the Lucan centurion, "having seen" the happening, responded by "glorifying God." After Jesus' death Luke thus achieves an inclusion with the beginning of the Gospel where after Jesus' birth the shepherds returned (to their fields) "glorifying God for all they had . . . seen" (2:20). Indeed, during the Lucan account of the ministry, "glorifying God" has been a standard reaction to seeing Jesus manifest divine power.[50] Surely Luke's readers would not stop to ask themselves, as do some modern commentators, whether it is plausible that a Gentile soldier would so easily praise the God of Israel. They would perceive that from the beginning to the end of Jesus' life those who had eyes to see consistently lauded God. Moreover, they would deem it appropriate that the final glorification came from a Gentile, thus anticipating the reception of the Gospel by the ends of the earth to be narrated in the Book of Acts (where in 13:48 Gentiles will glorify the word of God). The motif of "glorifying God," then, is clearly Luke's addition to what he received about the centurion from Mark, and there is no need to posit a special source.

The THIRD DIFFERENCE is what is predicated in the centurion's confession, i.e., in Luke that this man (Jesus) was "just,"[51] as contrasted with Mark's "God's Son." Why without authorization from a source would Luke have changed from Mark's christological formula to a "lower" estimate of Jesus? Some scholars deny that a change is involved, arguing that *dikaios* represents Luke's understanding of Mark's anarthrous *huios theou*. Indeed, they use Luke as an argument for translating Mark to mean "a son/child of God" (p. 1148 above). In antiquity Augustine (*De consensu evangelistarum* 3.20; CSEL 43.346) wrote: "Perhaps the centurion had not understood Jesus as the only-begotten equal to the Father but had spoken of him as the son of God because he believed him to be just, even as many just people are said to be sons of God." In modern times, Plummer (*Luke* 539) interprets the Marcan and Lucan confessions to mean the same: Jesus "was a good man and quite right in calling God His Father." This type of interpretation confuses what

---

[48]In that list Matt showed how Jesus' death effected the raising of the fallen-asleep holy ones; the belief in a similar afterlife effect is seen in Luke's "This day with me you shall be in paradise" (23:43). Are we to think that the Lucan centurion heard that?

[49]Some would extend "this happening" that the centurion saw back to include Jesus' prayer of forgiveness for his executioners (23:34).

[50]Luke 5:25–26; 7:16; 13:13; 17:15 (by a Samaritan); 18:43. *Doxazein* ("to glorify") with *theos* ("God") as an object occurs 1 time in Mark, 2 in Matt, 1 in John, 11 in Luke-Acts.

[51]Although *dikaios* could be a nominal predicate ("the just one") lacking the article because it was placed before the copulative verb (n. 12 above), there is little reason not to accept the customary adjectival rendering.

may have gone on historically in the centurion's mind[52] with what Luke would have him say and mean on the narrative level. I contended that the Marcan centurion confessed Jesus as the Son of God in the full sense, and I see little likelihood that Luke misunderstood Mark. (In recording what happened before the Sanhedrin, Luke 22:70 spoke of "the Son of God," correctly interpreting Mark's "the Son of the Blessed"; are we to think that Luke has not recognized Mark's resumption of that theme here?) To maintain that Luke is dependent on Mark in the present scene, one must deal with Luke's deliberately changing Mark and preferring a designation of Jesus that was more appropriate for his own purposes.

The Meaning of the Lucan Centurion's Confession. Scholars have debated the connotation of *dikaios* used as a predicate here. Often it is rendered "innocent":[53] This man was not guilty of the charge on which he was executed. Obviously in the context of crucifixion this is something that an unprejudiced observer might conclude without any special religious insight. Though the authoritative Liddell and Scott *Greek-English Lexicon* (9th ed.) does not give "innocent" as a translation for *dikaios,* BAGD (196.3) does, even if only in reference to this verse.[54] Certainly it is not an indefensible rendering; and although I prefer "just," the semantic range of "just" includes innocence. I stress this because some of the campaigners against the "innocent" translation (Hanson, Karris) write almost as if "innocent" and "just" were totally different ideas.[55] The rival translation of *dikaios* as "just, righteous, upright" has equal if not greater support among scholars and translations.[56] In favor of it Beck ("Imitatio" 42) contends that no other Luke-Acts usage of *dikaios* is reducible simply to "innocent," i.e., not guilty.[57] The ad-

---

[52]Goodwin ("Theou" 129) represents an older scholarship that thought the centurion might have said both things.

[53]Danker, Fitzmyer, Kilpatrick, Klostermann, Marshall; and the NT translations of Fenton, Goodspeed, Moffatt, Weymouth, RSV, NRSV, NAB, NAB (rev.), and NEB.

[54]In the LXX occasionally *dikaios* renders *nāqî,* "clean, without guilt," especially in set phrases like "innocent blood"; Gen 20:5; Prov 6:17; Joel 4:19; etc. In the NT "innocent" is a possible understanding of *dikaios* applied to Jesus in the context of his death in Matt 27:19; I Pet 3:18.

[55]For instance, Karris ("Luke 23:47" 68–70), who is worried that detecting elements of martyrdom in Luke's presentation of Jesus' death favors the "innocent" translation, unnecessarily dismisses the martyrological background. Were martyrs so identified as criminals that "just" might not apply to them as well as "innocent"? Brawley (*Luke-Acts* 141, n. 24) challenges Karris's contention (65) "that *diakios* does not mean innocent, but means righteous," asking whether one can substantiate such a sharp differentiation from the Greek.

[56]Beck, Dechent, Hanson, Karris, Lagrange, C. Schneider; and the NT translations of Wyclif, Coverdale, Rheims, KJV, *New Jerusalem Bible.* With the same import but paraphrastic are "perfect" (Tyndale) and "great and good" (*Jerusalem Bible*). Because "righteous" might evoke Pauline ideas of "righteousness," I prefer "just," which also reminds readers of "justice," a fundamental quality of the king in the OT. The centurion is commenting on "The King of the Jews."

[57]Epp ("Ignorance" 61–62) points out, however, that in the Codex Bezae of Acts 16:39 there is an addition excusing the Roman officials who did not know that Paul and Silas were *dikaioi,* i.e., innocent.

jective has a wide range of positive meaning for Luke, being used to describe the saintly (Elizabeth and Zechariah in 1:6, and Simeon in 2:25), even the saintly dead (14:14–15). By attempting to answer several questions let us explore its meaning for Luke in the centurion's confession.

Why might Luke have preferred not to preserve Mark's full christological confession of "God's Son"? Translating *dikaios* as "innocent," some commentators have contended that Luke found this affirmation more appropriate for a pagan bystander. (The argument is less appropriate if it means "just," for that designation, as we shall see, had OT background.) Others would attribute to Luke an apologetic motive: a Roman confirmation that Jesus was innocent and not politically subversive. C. Schneider ("Hauptmann") maintains that Luke feared a syncretistic reading of the "God's Son" confession: What a pagan spokesman would mean by spontaneously confessing Jesus under that title might be thought by Luke's readers to be acceptable, whereas Luke would insist on a recognition of Jesus' unique divine sonship, and so in his Gospel would restrict proclaiming the title to committed Christians. In my judgment, such motives, if present at all, had little influence on Luke's preference for *dikaios*. (See Beck, "Imitatio" 41, who rejects them.)

The key to the change from Mark's "God's Son" lies in the import *dikaios* had in the Lucan storyline and for Luke's theology. In Mark that very high evaluation of Jesus was prompted by God's startling intervention after Jesus' death (rending the sanctuary veil). But what precedes the confession in Luke is Jesus' trusting prayer to his Father, something less likely to lead to a full acknowledgment of Jesus' divinity.[58] Moreover, in terms of having a Gentile confess Jesus, Luke could be more flexible than Mark/Matt because of the range offered by his planned Book of Acts. If the first two evangelists wanted to have in the finale of their story a Gentile come to full faith in Jesus (anticipating the destiny of the Christian mission), the present scene before the burial was their last opportunity. (Resurrection appearances, which theoretically might offer another opportunity, were fixed in the tradition [e.g., I Cor 15:5–8]; and none of the preserved tradition hints at an appearance to a Gentile.) Luke, however, had a whole second book, much of which would be devoted to the spread of faith among the Gentiles; and that would historically be a more appropriate context to describe a conversion leading to a

---

[58]On the other hand, some would argue that since the Lucan Jesus has just addressed God as "Father," it would have been appropriate for the Lucan centurion to recognize him as "God's Son." That might be valid reasoning if Luke understood the expression to mean "*a* son of God." But in the storyline a pagan soldier would not easily understand from a prayer to God as Father that Jesus was *the* unique Son of God.

confession of Jesus in the church language of "Son of God."[59] In fact Acts does devote almost a whole chapter (10, especially 10:34–48) to how a Roman centurion became a believer. Such flexibility allowed Luke here to adapt the centurion's confession, which he took over from Mark, to another theological message.

Why, conformable to his own thought patterns, did Luke choose *dikaios* to phrase his message? There are several plausible reasons; and I shall devote a paragraph to each, for they are not mutually exclusive. *First,* the Lucan Jesus had prayed, "Father, into your hands I place my spirit," echoing Ps 31:6. In that same psalm (v. 19) we read, "Let the lying lips be struck dumb which speak insolently against the just one [*dikaios*] in pride and contempt."[60] The prayer of the Lucan Jesus also echoes Wis 3:1: "The souls of the just are in the *hand* of God"; and the context there, beginning in 2:12, is the plot of wicked adversaries to destroy a *dikaios* who professes to have knowledge of God calling himself a child (*pais*) of God, saying that God is his father (2:13,16). The adversaries say, "If the just one [*dikaios*] is the son of God [*huios theou*], He will help him" (2:18). On p. 995 above we saw that Matt 27:43 drew on this passage, and so it was probably widely known to early Christians. The combined ideas that the just entrusted himself to God's hand (as Jesus did in prayer at his death) and that the just one was God's son may explain why Luke could regard *dikaios* as an interchangeable alternative for Mark's *huios theou* in the centurion's reaction to Jesus' death prayer. Earlier in Luke direct divine revelation has been associated with identifying Jesus as the Son of God (1:35; 3:22; 9:35). There is no indication of such a divine intervention in the Lucan picture of the centurion, and so the *dikaios* alternative may have seemed more logical.

A *second* contributing factor would have been the use of *dikaios* as a christological title in the early church, drawing upon OT practice. In the idealizing of the expected Davidic king, he is described as *dikaios* in Jer 23:5; Zech 9:9; *Ps Sol.* 17:32,[61] as is the Suffering Servant in Isa 53:11. In a context where Jesus has been condemned as the King of the Jews and made to suffer an ignominious death, Luke may have deemed both those scriptural echoes of *dikaios* appropriate. By using "just" of Jesus the centurion was preparing Luke's readers for the references to Jesus as "the just one" in Acts

[59]So Büchele, *Tod* 54; Walaskay, "Trial" 93.

[60]The righteous *dikaios,* especially as persecuted without warrant by accusers (notice the combination of "just" and "innocent"), is a frequent figure in the psalter: Pss 5:13; 7:10; 11:3,5; 34:16,18,20,22; 37:12,16,17,21,25,29,32,etc.

[61]Justice is often listed as a fundamental element in divine and human kingship, e.g., Pss 72:1–2; 97:1–2; Isa 9:6.

3:14 and 7:52, a title given him in relation to his having been put to death. Other uses in Acts 22:14; James 5:6; I Pet 3:18; and I John 2:1 show that the solemn statement of the centurion, "Certainly this man was just," would have had some of the tone of confessing Jesus as "the just one."[62]

A *third* and perhaps principal factor behind Luke's choice of *dikaios* was his desire to make the centurion's confession fit into a chain of reactions that run through Luke's presentation of the Roman proceedings against Jesus. That Jesus was not guilty of the charges leveled against him has been a Lucan concern throughout.[63] Pilate was shown repeatedly affirming it (23:4,14,22), even citing Herod as support (23:15); and in two of those references (23:4,14) Pilate spoke of "this man" as the centurion does. Patently the centurion's confession adds to the testimony. In judging Jesus he does not have the authority of Pilate; yet his testimony to Jesus is convincing against the background of implied conversion. The only PN information about Roman soldiers hitherto given by Luke (23:36–38) is that they mocked Jesus, coming forward (as if in obeisance?), bringing him vinegary wine, and saying, "If you are the King of the Jews, save yourself." When now suddenly the chief among them confesses Jesus really to be "just," a term traditionally used for the Davidic king, one has to think that he has been persuaded, despite his strong inclination to the contrary. A major element in the persuasion has been the sight of Jesus accepting death with a prayer that illustrated his claim to be close to God. Thus moved, the centurion has gone beyond Pilate's "Not guilty" to affirm that Jesus was what he claimed to be. This unexpected conversion to the truth about Jesus places the centurion in another chain of reactions to Jesus, deeper than those of Pilate and of Herod. As described by Luke 23:20, Simon the Cyrenian would have known nothing of Jesus previously and should have been inclined unfavorably toward Jesus after the crucifiers had taken hold of him to impose Jesus' cross. Yet Simon is (symbolically) portrayed as being converted instantly, bringing the cross behind Jesus in the position of a follower. Similarly, the co-crucified wrong-doers (23:39–43) would not have been sympathetic toward this royal pretender, and indeed one of them blasphemed Jesus: "Are you not the Messiah? Save yourself and us." Yet the other, despite his criminal past, was converted to acknowledge not only that Jesus had done nothing disorderly but also that he had a kingdom and was close enough to God to be able to grant a share in that kingdom. When we preface these two figures to the centurion, we find that before, during, and after the crucifixion agony of Jesus an unlikely

[62]On the adjectival and nominal predication of *dikaios,* see n. 51 above.

[63]Does that reflect apologetics (responding to actual or feared Roman accusations that the "founder" of this Christian group was a convicted royal usurper) or simply Christian conviction not without implications for missionary endeavor?

figure (an imposed-upon stranger, a convicted wrongdoer, and a previously mocking soldier) had instantly come to recognize the truth about the one being crucified. None of them confesses Jesus' identity in such a familiar fixed formula of christology as "the Son of God" but rather in the implied christology of personal attachment. Such a sequence of "conversions" served both as a challenge and an encouragement to Luke's readers. Beyond this inner PN chain of reactions, the centurion is part of still another sequence. The first one to see Jesus in Jerusalem was Simeon who praised God and said, "My eyes have seen this salvation that you have made ready in the sight of all the peoples: a light to be a revelation to the Gentiles" (2:28–32). The first one to see Jesus in Jerusalem after his death is this centurion who glorifies God and by confessing Jesus becomes an example of the salvation brought to the Gentiles.

Reaction of the Crowds (23:48). Only Luke records this; but it is so typical of his arrangement, wording, and theology that no special source need be posited. Structurally this reaction is closely parallel to that of the centurion:[64]

centurion	having seen	happening	was glorifying	saying
crowds	having observed	happenings	returned	striking breasts

Implicitly the centurion and the crowds are in the same "observation" place near the cross, reserved by Luke for those who have not previously been committed to Jesus, as distinct from the place at a distance where Jesus' acquaintances and women followers stand in the next verse. These "crowds" represent the "people" whom Luke has mentioned before and during the crucifixion, as may be seen when we look at the key words in three passages:[65]

23:27:   There was following him [Jesus] a large multitude of the *people*
23:35:   And the *people* were standing there OBSERVING
23:48:   All the crowds who were gathered together for the OBSERVATION

(In the first and the third passage there is a subsequent reference to women, Jerusalem and Galilean respectively.) Earlier, in the Roman trial (23:13–18) the people, like the chief priests and the rulers, were hostile to Jesus, asking for his death (also the hostile "crowd" in 22:47). In the three crucifixion passages, however, they develop from sympathetic following and observing to repentance. Like the centurion, what moves them to change is having observed "happenings." Some would regard the plural here as a meaningless

---

[64]Feldkämper, *Betende* 280. The parallelism is increased by a gloss (to be discussed below) that has the crowds speak words.

[65]Untergassmair, *Kreuzweg* 92.

variant of the "happening" seen by the centurion,[66] covering only Jesus' prayerful death. Yet Luke may mean to add to that "happening" the centurion's own confession, so that the crowds would have been moved by observing not only the death but his reaction to it. (In 5:25–26 there is a tandem arrangement: The healed paralytic going home glorifying God is part of what causes all to be amazed and glorify God.) The crowds striking their breasts after the crucified death of Jesus are parallel to the Jerusalem women who before the crucifixion beat themselves[67] and lamented for Jesus (23:27–28). In that earlier moment there was an element of mourning for one about to die, but here the crowds are expressing repentance.[68] Their mourning is not simply for the passing of a human life but for the unjust execution of one who was visibly close to God.

The repentance of the crowds is not a conversion on the level of that of the centurion, for they neither glorify God nor confess Jesus. Acts 2:38 shows that for Luke repentance is not sufficient unless it is followed by confessing the name of Jesus. That the crowds "return" (presumably to where they came from[69]) leaves their future obscure. Jesus' words, spoken before crucifixion to the Daughters of Jerusalem who accompanied the large multitude of the people, presented divine punishment as inevitable for them and their children (Luke 23:27–31); yet punishment does not preclude forgiveness, for afterward Jesus prayed the Father to forgive even his crucifiers (23:34). In many ways this scene echoes the peculiarly Lucan parable of the Pharisee and the publican (18:9–14). During the Pilate trial both the authorities (chief priests, rulers) and the people shouted for condemnation. The authorities have shown no sign of grief after Jesus' death, for, like the Pharisee of the parable, they trust in themselves that they are just. The crowds of the people have seen the centurion proclaim that certainly Jesus was just; and like the publican they beat their breasts, implicitly signifying, "Be merciful to us sinners."

Copyists were not content to leave implicit what the crowds would say. A 2d-cent. addition is found in the OS[sin.cur] and OL (St. Germain, ms. g). In variant forms words like these appear on the lips of the crowds: "Woe to us!

---

[66]One suggestion is that a plural subject prompted the switch to a plural object. Luke uses the singular "happening" in 8:34–35; 24:12; and the plural "happenings" in 9:7.

[67]In 23:48 Luke uses the transitive verb *typtein* ("to strike"), used previously in the Roman mockery of Jesus (Mark 15:19; Matt 27:30) as the soldiers were striking the head of Jesus. In 23:27 Luke used the reflexive of *koptein* ("to beat"), the same verb that is used after the death of Jesus in *GPet* 7:25 (reflexively) and 8:28 (transitively). Just after Zech 12:10 (the passage about looking upon the one whom they have pierced cited by John 19:37), Zech 12:12 uses *koptein* to describe the lamenting of the Davidic families in Jerusalem.

[68]Need for repentance is a strong Lucan theme: 10:13; 11:32; 13:3,5; 15:7,10; 16:30; 17:3–4.

[69]For the absolute use of *hypostrephein,* without a destination, see Luke 2:20,43; 8:37,40; Acts 8:28.

What has happened to us because of our sins? (The judgment and) The end of Jerusalem has approached." A similar saying is found in Ephraem's *Commentary on the Diatessaron* (20:28; SC 121.362) and *GPet* 7:25.[70] The added words complete the parallelism between the centurion and the crowds, for now they both speak: the Gentile soldier in a confession of faith; the Jewish crowds in self-judgment.[71]

Reaction of Those Standing at a Distance (23:49). With adaptations Luke has taken over from Mark that there were Galilean women observing from a distance—nine of eighteen words in this verse are found in Mark 15:40–41. Luke has those women (and all those known to Jesus) "standing from a distance," an expression composed of "stand," a verb that Mark 15:39 used in a compound form for the centurion, and the phrase "from a distance" that Mark 15:40 used of the women observers.[72] Since Luke has already utilized "observe" (*theōrein*) for the crowds whose presence he introduced between the centurion and the women, here he exemplifies stylistic alternation by returning to "see" (*horan*), the verb he used for the centurion.[73] Luke does not give the names of the women either here or at the burial (23:55–56) but only in reference to the empty tomb (24:10: perhaps an indirect confirmation that the empty tomb locale was original for all or some of them [p. 1018 above]). For the readers' comprehension, however, the absence of names in the present Lucan episode is not significant since in this Gospel (alone) "the women who were following with him from Galilee" were introduced in the course of the Galilean ministry.[74] In 8:1–3 we were told how, as Jesus went through city and village proclaiming and announcing the good

[70]See MTC 182 for precise wordings. Harris ("Origin" 9) calls attention to a Syriac version of I Macc (found in a 5th-cent.-AD account of martyrdom) where Mattathias says, "Woe to us! What has befallen us? To look upon the misery of our people and the ruins of the holy city!" (See I Macc 2:7.) He proposes that this gave rise to the OS gloss, which in turn influenced the *Diatessaron, GPet,* and the OL. Harnack (*Bruchstücke* 57), however, contends that this and other Gospel glosses were drawn from *GPet.*

[71]In a contrary direction a 9th-cent. witness tells us that the *Gospel of the Nazoreans* (24, HSNTA 1.150; rev. ed. 1.162) reported: "At this word of the Lord [Luke 23:34?] many thousands of the Jews standing around the cross believed."

[72]Luke employs *makrothen* ("at a distance") twice alone and twice with *apo* ("from"). Whereas Mark/Matt used *apo makrothen* for Peter's following Jesus to the courtyard of the high priest, Luke 22:54 omitted *apo.* "Standing from a distance" is atrocious English but preserves the distinction.

[73]The participle *horōsai* in 23:49 is feminine by attraction but surely is meant to apply as well to "all those known to him." Fitzmyer (*Luke* 2.1521) would distinguish between a more intent "looking on" here and the "gazing" of the idle crowds as at a spectacle in the previous verse; but Untergassmair (*Kreuzweg* 105) is to be followed in not seeing any real difference between the two verbs. The crowds are scarcely pictured as idle, and the transformation toward repentance that they undergo from *observing* (noun and verb) is significant. For the two verbs, see BGJ 1.502–3.

[74]Perhaps to emphasize the connection between the women here and those previously introduced, the Koine tradition has the participle in the aorist ("had followed") instead of the present tense. Luke's *synakolouthein* almost combines the two verbs in Mark 15:41: *akolouthein* and *synanabainein* ("to come up with"), and thus simplifies Mark even as did Matt.

news of the kingdom of God, the Twelve were *with* him; "and some women who had been cured from evil spirits and infirmities: Mary called Magdalene from whom seven demons had gone out; Joanna wife of Herod's *epitropos* ["steward"? "companion"?], and Susanna, and many others who were serving [*diakonein*] them out of their own means." When finally at the empty tomb, in his third PN reference to these women, Luke will identify those of whom he has spoken at the cross and burial, he will interweave Mary Magdalene and Mary of James from the list in Mark (16:1; see Table 8 on p. 1016) with his own tradition of the names of the Galilean women and thus emerge with this list: "Mary Magdalene, and Joanna, and Mary of James, and the rest (of the women) with them" (Luke 24:10).

In introducing the women in 8:3 Luke used *diakonein,* the same verb Mark (15:41) uses here, but added his own tonality. Mark's usage would have the women taking care of material needs like food and drink (n. 29 above), but Luke specified this as having been done "out of their own means." They were not just distributing but providing. In this Luke anticipated the action of women of the early church, such as Lydia whose hospitality to Paul he will describe in Acts 16:14–15 (see also Luke 10:7; 24:29). This, plus the fact that Luke has told us these women were cured by Jesus, would cause Luke's readers to think of them as committed disciples[75] when they read of them standing from a distance in the crucifixion scene, even though no more than Mark does Luke have them previously active in the PN or reactive here by either word or deed. The fact that women are described as "standing" there, not having "returned" or gone away as did the crowds of the previous verse, prepares readers for participation still to come. Indeed in the next two scenes in which the women reappear Luke will go beyond Mark's portrayal (where they remain inactive during the burial and disobedient at the empty tomb). At the burial the Lucan women will not only see where Jesus is buried but will immediately go and prepare spices and ointments, so that as soon as the prescribed Sabbath rest is over they can set out for the tomb with the spices (23:56; 24:1). In the ensuing scene, upon leaving the empty tomb, they will relay the angels' message concerning the living Lord to the Eleven and all the rest (24:9). True, unlike Matt, Luke will narrate no appearance of Jesus to the women at the tomb; but his wording in Acts 13:31 leaves open the possibility that there was a subsequent appear-

---

[75]Rosalie Ryan ("Women" 56–57) points out that some women scholars (E. Tetlow, E. Schüssler Fiorenza) accuse Luke of a patriarchal attitude toward women which would restrict them to household or "at home" tasks. Ryan argues convincingly that 8:1–3 describes these women and the Twelve similarly, as being "with" Jesus (almost a technical element in discipleship) and proclaiming the good news of the kingdom.

ance to them: "He appeared to those who came up with him from Galilee."[76] Thus the whole Lucan picture of the women from Galilee in the PN is positive: Unlike the Daughters of Jerusalem (the parallel group before the crucifixion) who with their children cannot be spared God's wrathful judgment on the city, these women will be gathered together in Jerusalem with the Eleven and the mother and brothers of Jesus, devoting themselves to prayer and thus preparing for the coming of the Spirit at Pentecost (Acts 1:13–14).

Male acquaintances. The major Lucan change from Mark 15:40–41 in terms of those who are at a distance from the cross observing/seeing is that Luke prefaces to the Galilean women another group: "all those known [*gnōstoi*, masc.] to him [Jesus]."[77] The "all" is Lucan hyperbole as in the preceding verse: "all the crowds." In itself, the masculine would normally be read as generic, i.e., "those known" would consist of men but could also include women. Nevertheless, since it is followed by an explicit reference to women, most interpreters concentrate on who were these *men* "known" to Jesus (e.g., Ketter, "Ehrenrettung").

Some wonder if Luke had any specific group of individuals in mind. Psalm passages dealing with the suffering just one could have prompted the usage, e.g., Ps 38:12: "My friends and my neighbors approached opposite me and stood there, and *those who were close to me stood from a distance*"; Ps 88:9: "You have *distanced from me those known to me;* they have made me an abomination to themselves." Above I cited negative psalm passages of this type as background for Mark's account that does not present a favorable picture of the participation by the women from Galilee. I am dubious about their applicability here, granted Luke's positive portrayal of the reactions after the death of Jesus. Of course, he could have taken over the background and changed the meaning. Even more likely, the psalm usage of *gnōstoi* could have stayed in his mind and colored what he wrote. In either case a psalm echo in the last verse of the Lucan account of the crucifixion would be a reminder that Jesus died in accordance with the Scriptures (I Cor 15:3).

If Luke did have a specific group in mind, what men did he envision (on the level of storyline, with the level of history left to the ANALYSIS below)? *Gnōstos/oi* occurs a dozen times in Luke/Acts, but almost always in a set expression about something being known; consequently the term itself has no consistent reference. Many think that Luke might mean or include the

---

[76]Acts uses *synanabainein*, the word Mark 15:41 used for the women. For them Luke uses *synakolouthein* (23:49: "to follow with") and *synerchesthai* (23:55: "to go/come with").

[77]The best texts read *autō* ("to him"); the Koine tradition reads *autou* ("his"). A frequent translation covers both possibilities: "all his acquaintances."

Eleven (Twelve minus Judas). Unlike the other Gospels Luke has not told the readers that the Eleven (apostles, disciples) fled or were let go at the time of Jesus' arrest (even if he never mentions their presence in the PN after that and shows Peter as the only one to attempt to follow Jesus to the high priest's courtyard). If here the *gnōstoi* are associated with the women from Galilee, the Twelve were associated with them in 8:1–3. In 24:9, coming from the empty tomb, the women will report to "the Eleven and all the rest"; and before Pentecost in Acts 1:13–14 the women will again be associated with the Eleven. But would Luke, who so often mentions the Twelve or Eleven by title, refer to them in this crucial scene in such a vague way, the only time he does so in Luke-Acts?[78] Perhaps one could answer that Luke was aware of the common tradition that the Eleven were not present at Skull Place, and so did not dare mention them by name. His referring to them only after the death of Jesus and placing them at a distance could have been part of the same delicate sensitivity. Yet what would such an obscure, indirect reference accomplish, since most readers would easily miss the application to the Twelve?

Another proposal is that *gnōstoi* include the relatives of Jesus, male and female, and that this is partially parallel to John's inclusion (19:25–27) of the mother of Jesus at the cross. Acts 1:14 will associate in one phrase "the women and Mary the mother of Jesus and his brothers," even as the present verse associates the *gnōstoi* and the women. Contributing to this interpretation is the only other truly parallel use of *gnōstoi* (to refer to a group of people) in Luke, namely, at the beginning of the Gospel in 2:43–44. There, when Jesus was lost, left behind in the Temple, his parents looked for him "among relatives and *gnōstoi.*" The passage, while not identifying the two groups, does associate them. Yet that argument may backfire, for II Kings 10:11 and Neh 5:10 also associate *gnōstoi* with relatives without identifying the two groups, so that one may ask if *gnōstoi* would be used for close relatives. Moreover, Luke gives no reference to the "brothers" of Jesus in the PN[79] or in the resurrection appearances on Easter Sunday, a reference that would tell his readers that these people, who did not follow Jesus about during his ministry, had come to Jerusalem for the Passover at which he died. (Acts 1:14 is set at another festal time close to fifty days later.)

A third suggestion, and the one that seems to me the most plausible, is that Luke uses this vague description to designate other disciples and/or

---

[78]Some, pointing out that Luke uses *mathētēs* ("disciple") less than the other Gospels, suggest that *gnōstoi* substitutes for that here. But nowhere else is this the case.

[79]The word *adelphoi* does occur at the Last Supper, in 22:32 when Simon Peter is told to strengthen his brothers; but the context in 22:28–32 makes it clear that this is a reference to other members of the Twelve.

friends of Jesus (beyond the Twelve). We remember that among the Gospels Luke alone is specific that beyond the Twelve there are seventy(-two) others whom Jesus sent out on an evangelizing mission during the Galilean ministry (10:1,17). It is not implausible that such Galileans are being associated here with the Galilean women. When the Galilean women come from the empty tomb, they will report the angels' message "to the Eleven and *all the rest*," indicating the presence at Jerusalem in these days of a wider group of Jesus' followers than the women and the Twelve. Luke 24:13, immediately after that report, will speak of two of these going to Emmaus and later the same day reporting back to the Eleven in Jerusalem (24:33). Later Acts 1:13–15, having listed the Twelve, the women, and Jesus' mother and brothers, will refer to a group of 120. Vague terms are used by Luke to describe the larger group ("others," "all the rest"), and plausibly the present passage is another instance ("all those known to him"). If this interpretation is correct, Luke would indirectly agree with John 19:26–27 that places at the cross the unnamed disciple whom Jesus loved (and perhaps even with Mark 14:51–52 that describes a certain young man following Jesus from Gethsemane).

In any case, one should not let scholarly speculation about these men onlookers overshadow Luke's primary interest in v. 49, i.e., the women who are part of his parallelism with the other women before the crucifixion.

REACTIONS OF THOSE PRESENT ACCORDING TO JOHN

We begin here Episode 5 in the chiastic structure of John's crucifixion and burial account (p. 908 above). Given John's sensitivity to narrative continuity, it is not surprising that here he does not simply list two or three reactions but weaves them into a consecutive story. Characteristic of Johannine christological concern is the fact that the "reaction" that comes from Jesus (blood and water) overshadows the reactions of others to his death. John's account is unique in mixing with those reactions a request to have the bodies be taken away—a request that the other Gospels (and John again) will describe in the burial scene (§46) in relation to Joseph from Arimathea. I shall keep a detailed discussion of how the bodies of the crucified would be buried until that scene (which treats the burial of Jesus) and treat here only a few burial details essential to making John's account intelligible.

The Request Made to Pilate (19:31). In this verse John has elements similar to the opening of the burial scene in Mark 15:42–45. Both passages have the clause "since it was preparation day [*paraskeuē*],"[80] in connection

---

[80]Part of this clause is found also in Luke 23:54. Some would use the fact that Mark and John share three identical Greek words (but not in the same order) to affirm Johannine dependence on

with the oncoming Sabbath. Earlier John 19:14 spoke of this Friday as "preparation day for Passover" (echoing a set Hebrew formula *'ereb pesaḥ*); there he was interested in the sixth hour (noon) on the preparation day, seemingly because it was the time for the beginning of the slaughter of the paschal lambs. Now after Jesus' death John is interested in this Friday as the day before the Sabbath. (I remind the readers that while *paraskeuē* means "preparation," the underlying Hebrew *'ereb* means "evening, vigil.") The seemingly more important fact that the next day was Passover is echoed only in the statement "that Sabbath was a great day."[81] Has Passover lost its meaning to remain only "a feast of the Jews" now that the Lamb of God is slain? In any case the two Johannine references to "preparation day" in 19:14 and here form a type of inclusion around the crucifixion, the first occurring as Jesus was sentenced to death, the other just after that death.

It is interesting that (implicitly) Mark and (explicitly) John and *GPet* relate the urgency about getting Jesus buried to the fact that the next day was the Sabbath. In fact the law behind the desire of the Jews "that the bodies might not remain on the cross on the Sabbath" (John—a law phrased in *GPet* 2:5 as "The sun is not to set on one put to death") is Deut 21:22–23, which insists that on *any day* (not just on the Sabbath) the bodies of hanged criminals should not remain overnight on the tree.[82] Nevertheless, Mark, John, and *GPet* probably reflect practical fact, namely, that on special days there was greater pressure for observance. In terms of Roman behavior Philo (*In Flaccum* 10.83) indicates an expectation that at festivals the authorities would allow bodies to be taken down, and in terms of Jewish sensibilities profanation of special holy days would be a greater concern. There may well have been extra pressure to get Jesus off the cross before a Sabbath in Passover week.

As we shall see in the first episode pertaining to the burial (§46), the Gospels are unanimous in having Joseph from Arimathea request the body

---

Mark. A set time expression that could have been widely used in the tradition is not a decisive indication.

[81]That this is the significance of "great Sabbath" is a surmise, for no such designation occurs in early Jewish literature (I. Abrahams, *Studies in Pharisaism and the Gospels* [New York: Ktav reprint, 1968], 2.68). John 7:37 used "the great day" to designate a special day (the last) during the feast of Tabernacles. Some (Bultmann, Leroy) would find here evidence that John had previously misrepresented the chronology by indicating that Friday (daytime) was the day before the one on which the Passover meal would be eaten (Friday evening/Saturday), for now John has joined the Synoptic dating in which Friday evening/Saturday would be the day after the Passover meal had been eaten (Thursday evening) and "great" because the offering of sheaves would take place on that day (Lev 23:6–14; see APPENDIX II). This judgment that the Johannine writer was guilty of contradictory statements within a few lines is suspect, especially when the issue involved (dating of feasts) is one on which John has previously shown care.

[82]For the applicability of this law to the crucified, see pp. 532–33, 541 above.

of Jesus from Pilate, and ultimately be given it to bury. Although differing in details, Mark, John, and *GPet* agree that the way in which the request and granting came about involved complications. *GPet* 2:3–5, as part of its (unhistorical) portrait of Herod as judicially supreme in Jerusalem, has Joseph request Pilate and Pilate in turn request Herod for the body. In Mark 15:44–45, after Joseph has made his request, Pilate is amazed that Jesus could have already died and calls for the centurion to verify the death—clearly the centurion who, we were told in 15:39, had been "standing there opposite" Jesus and who had "seen that he thus expired." In John, before Joseph comes on the scene, "the Jews" ask Pilate to have the legs broken and the bodies taken away. (Crurifragium could have the effect of a coup de grace [Harrison, "Cicero" 454].) In the course of doing that, the soldiers see that Jesus is dead. Thus Mark and John are in agreement that Jesus' death was verified by Roman military personnel before his burial, but in Mark that is at Pilate's specific request. Apologetics may have influenced the Marcan picture (§46); John's goal is primarily theological, as we shall now see.

Neither in John 19:21 nor 19:31 are "the Jews" said to come/go to Pilate; and although in the Synoptics (also *GPet* 2:3) Joseph comes/goes to Pilate, that is not said of him in John 19:38. Accordingly some contend that John mistakenly imagines that Pilate was personally present at Calvary. In the Roman trial scene, however, John meticulously situated Pilate inside and outside the praetorium because it suited his dramatization of Pilate's role; and so, rather than positing historical error, we may assume that here John finds it more dramatic to keep the characters close to center stage where the cross of Jesus stands. We may see a parallel in the Johannine treatment of the women followers of Jesus, not at a distance as in the Synoptics but "near the cross" (19:25).

Although in asking Pilate to act, "the Jews" aim to fulfill the Law, they also betray hostility,[83] like the hostility suggested in the parallel Episode 1 (Table 7, p. 908 above) when at the beginning of the crucifixion *their* chief priests demanded that Pilate change the title on Jesus' cross (19:21). Now they ask first that the legs be broken and only then that the bodies be taken away.[84] One might contend that "the Jews" were asking simply that the crucifixion punishment be terminated; yet leg-breaking was not so integral a part

---

[83]Legality and hostility were also combined in John 19:7: "We have a law, and according to that law he ought to die."

[84]Careless Johannine grammar in 19:31 has them ask literally "that their legs be broken and taken away." One need not aggravate the hostility of "the Jews" by assuming that they knew Jesus was already dead. In crurifragium (perhaps a name coined by Plautus, *Poenulus* 4.2; #886) sometimes other bones were broken as well as the leg bones.

of the crucifixion that it had to be included.[85] When John 19:38a describes favorably Joseph's asking to "take away" Jesus' body (same verb: *airein*), nothing is said about breaking legs. If *GPet* 4:14 can be looked on as an early interpretation of the leg-breaking tradition found in John, there the action is definitely in an atmosphere of hostility by the Jews, even if the *GPet* logic of what they want is different.[86] All this makes it possible that "the Jews" in John, as part of their request that the bodies of the crucified be removed, ask that one final act of suffering be imposed.[87] The fact that in John the project of "the Jews" to have the legs broken does not succeed in the case of Jesus will be presented as a triumph of God's planning foretold in the Scriptures (19:36).

The Soldiers' Action (19:32–34a). John does not tell us explicitly that Pilate granted the petition of "the Jews"; but that is implied both in the "So" at the beginning of v. 32 and in the fact that the soldiers set about doing what was requested. Why do the soldiers first deal with the two co-crucified on either side of Jesus, leaving him who was in the middle (19:18) till the last? The answer is not that they saw that Jesus was already dead, for that observation does not come until v. 33 after they have broken the legs of the co-crucified. Rather the arrangement is dictated by the dramatic goal of having Jesus dealt with last. In the storyline the observation of death causes the soldiers to reject the petition of "the Jews" by not breaking the legs of Jesus. According to the structure of the Johannine crucifixion and burial account (p. 908 above), this Episode 5 before the Conclusion is parallel to Episodes 1 and 2 after the Introduction. In Episode 1, as I have already noted, the chief priests of "the Jews" petitioned Pilate about changing the wording of the title on the cross, even as here "the Jews" petitioned him about the leg-breaking and removal. In both instances the Roman reaction frustrates the malevolent purpose. In Episode 2 the soldiers decided not to tear the tunic of Jesus, thus fulfilling the Scriptures (Ps 22:19); here they decide not to break the bones of Jesus, thus fulfilling the Scripture (perhaps Ps 34:21— see discussion of 19:36).

---

[85]Despite early reports to the contrary, Zias and Sekeles ("Crucified") state in reference to the crucified Yehohanan ben *hgqwl* (p. 950 above), who was roughly contemporary with Jesus: "The evidence does not support the contention that the victim was administered a coup de grace that broke the lower limb bones." Harrison ("Cicero") shows from Cicero's usage that crurifragium had the connotation of being a brutal punishment deserved by low types (e.g., pirates).

[86]They do not want the legs broken (legs of Jesus or legs of the wrongdoer who sided with Jesus?), so that the torment will last longer. *GPet* uses *skelokopein* while John uses *katagnynai ta skelē*. In *GPet* the leg-breaking incident occurs before the death of Jesus and is tied in with a parallel to Luke's account of one of the co-crucified who was sympathetic to Jesus.

[87]DNTRJ 325–29 points out that in Jewish thought disfigurement was an obstacle to resurrection, but I doubt that John is attributing to "the Jews" an attempt to prevent Jesus' resurrection. We cannot even be sure of the attitude of 1st-cent. Jews on this point. Certainly among the Pharisees there was an increasing sensitivity about keeping bodies whole and not allowing them to be mutilated, but did

With his report that the soldiers saw Jesus "already dead" (19:33), John affirms what Mark 15:44 will state more directly when it has Pilate amazed that Jesus "had already died."[88] This strong attestation of the death of Jesus in John was not for apologetics (to prove that Jesus rose *from the dead*) but for christology: Even from his dead body life-giving elements will come forth (symbolized by blood and water). A special action by "one of the soldiers" leads to that development, even as in the functional parallel in Mark 15:39; Matt 27:54 the centurion is the agent for the christological confession, "Truly this (man) was God's Son." It is not surprising that harmonizers have identified the two, using the lance (*logchē*) of the Johannine soldier to give the name Longinus to the Matthean centurion.[89] Harmonization with this Johannine scene is represented also by the gloss in Matt 27:49 (p. 1065 above) where before Jesus died, while some of those standing by were saying that Jesus was crying to Elijah, one of them put a sponge full of vinegary wine on a reed, giving Jesus to drink: "But another, having taken *a lance, stabbed at his side,* and *there came out water and blood.*" (The italicized words are shared by the Matthean gloss and John.[90]) Piercing the crucified evidently provided assurance of their death: "As for those who die on the cross, the executioner does not forbid the burying of those who have been pierced [*percussos*]" (Quintilian, *Declamationes maiores* 6.9). The action by the soldier in John 19:34 has the illogic of ordinary life: Like the other soldiers he has seen that Jesus is dead, yet to make sure he probes the body for a telltale reaction by stabbing Jesus' side. Probably that is what is meant rather than the delivery of a coup de grace aimed to pierce the heart (pace Lagrange, *Jean* 499), even though the verb *nyssein* ("to prick, thrust in") can cover both prodding (as to awaken a sleeping man) and plunging deeply.[91]

---

they think that broken limbs prevented resurrection? After all, there was breakage as bones were gathered up and placed in ossuaries.

[88]The early tradition of a quick death for Jesus (whereas often the crucified survived for days) has fed medical speculation about the state of Jesus' health and the actual medical cause of his death (since crucifixion pierced no vital organ); see pp. 1088–92 above.

[89]The earlier (A) recension of the *Acts of Pilate* 16:7 has the name while the later recension (B) 11:1 has: "But Longinus the centurion [*hekatontarchos* as in Matt, not *kentyriōn* as in Mark], standing there, said, 'Truly this was God's Son' [as in Matt]."

[90]Michaels ("Centurion's") would see a progressive sequence involving the *Acts of Pilate* passages in the preceding note and the gloss.

[91]*Nyssein* is used in Codex Bezae of Acts 12:7 for pricking Peter's side to awaken him, and in Sir 22:19 for pricking the eye and causing tears; but by Josephus (*War* 3.7.35; #335) for stabbing a Roman soldier and killing him. Notice that the lightweight lance (*lancea, logchē*) is used, not the heavy spear (*pilum, hyssos*). I disagree with Wilkinson ("Incident"150) that the desire of Thomas to put his hand in Jesus' side (20:25,27) shows that a wide, deep wound was envisioned by John. Thomas, who has not seen Jesus, is made to speak exaggerated language to illustrate his desire for crass physical proof. The Vulgate and Peshitta used the verb "opened," probably reflecting a misreading (*ēnoixen* for *enyxen*), facilitating an interpretation whereby the sacraments and even the church came forth from Jesus' side (see BGJ 2.949–52). Augustine states (*In Jo.* 120.2; CC 36.661): "He did not say 'struck' or 'wounded,' or something else, but 'opened.'"

John uses *pleura* ("side") in the singular, though more normally in Greek it is plural. That has led some to suggest that John is recalling Gen 2:21–22, where God takes a *pleura* from Adam and forms it into a woman.[92] The Ethiopic version and the *Acts of Pilate* (B recension, 11:2) specify the right side, and both art and medicine (seeking the cause of Jesus' death) have utilized that indication. If taken historically it works against the coup-de-grace theory, for a blow at the heart would be aimed at the left side; but Barbet (*Doctor* 120) argues that Roman soldiers were trained to strike at the heart through the right side because the opponent's left would be protected by a shield. More plausibly in the light of ancient mentality, there may have been scriptural background for this imaginative detail, e.g., Ezek 47:1: "And water came down from the right side." Symbolic interpretations of the side and the wound serve as a good introduction to a discussion of the flow of blood and water produced by the lance—one of the best remembered, even if not easily understood, dramatic symbols in John.

"Immediately there came out blood and water" (19:34b).[93] Following the death of Jesus Mark/Matt had eschatological signs that led to the confession by the Roman centurion. John has this sign brought about by a Roman soldier. Leaving historical and compositional issues to the ANALYSIS, I shall concentrate here on what the text as it now stands was meant to convey. There will be no attempt, therefore, to distinguish what the episode meant in the source and what it meant for the evangelist, as does Schnackenburg (*John* 3.289: not symbolic in the source); or, a fortiori, on what it meant for the final redactor if he was the one who added the "blood and water" of 19:34 or the witness of 19:35. Nor shall I discuss the incredibly rich developments in subsequent reflections by Church Fathers and theologians on the pierced side (or even, pierced heart[94]) as a symbolic source of salvation, divine love, and the sacraments.[95]

---

[92]A. Loisy, A. Feuillet; see BGJ 2.949 for the motif of the New Eve.

[93]The position of "immediately" varies in the textual witnesses; and a few, versional and patristic, plus the gloss to Matt 27:49, read "water and blood." That is probably a harmonization with I John 5:6,8; but M.-E. Boismard (RB 60 [1953], 348–50) argues that it may be original, with scribes having conformed it (in all but one Greek ms.!) to the more normal expression "blood and water." B. Kraft, BZ 13 (1915), 354–55, writing on the order "water and blood" in a Coptic fragment of Irenaeus published by P. de Lagarde in 1886, shows that this was not Irenaeus' own reading in the 2d cent. but stems from the later copyist influenced by a Coptic version he had before him. A. Barberis, *Sindon* 10 (#11; 1967), 31–33, influenced by Chrysostom's insistence that water came out first, then blood, argues that there were two flows: blood and water from the lance blow, and then more blood during the removal from the cross and burial, as can be proved from the Shroud of Turin—thus both textual readings could be affirmed by the sequence blood-water-blood!

[94]Lavergne ("Coup" 7) uses "heart" in the title of his article; and this statement appears in the summary: "In this word 'heart' in place of the more usual 'chest' is contained the real meaning of this work [i.e., article]."

[95]The literature is considerable but one may sample profitably: J. Heer, "The Soteriological Significance of the Johannine Image of the Pierced Savior," in *Faith in Christ and the Worship of Christ,*

A considerable amount of modern literature devoted to the blood and water has been medical in character: If one supposes that John is describing an actual happening, what physiological cause could have caused a corpse to emit blood and a fluid that looks like water? The ANALYSIS of §42 devoted subsection C to "The Physiological Cause of the Death of Jesus" and digested the pertinent discussions. Clearly none of that discussion dedicated to discovering the natural cause of the blood-and-water phenomenon is germane to John's purpose in recording it, for he presents the flow of blood and water from the dead Jesus as something so wonderful that he must assure readers that behind it lies the guaranteed testimony of an eyewitness. Even though that testimony pertains primarily to the theological import of the blood and water, it would scarcely have been invoked if what is described was normal or easily explicable. Against Richter ("Blut") who thinks that the flow of blood and water indicated simply a truly human death, Minear ("Diversity" 164) correctly points out that the language of seeing and bearing witness in 19:35 has consistently been used in John (1:34; 3:11,32–33) for heavenly witness. While one may quibble about the applicability of "miracle" if that term is too narrowly defined as beyond the powers of nature, a long tradition[96] that evaluated this flow as miraculous is closer to John's intention than is the modern postmortem medical analysis.[97]

Recognizing that John's intent in speaking of blood and water is theological, scholars have been divided on the precise message intended. Was John using Hellenistic symbolism to portray Jesus as divine? There was an old Homeric legend that the gods had in their veins a type of blood mixed with water, e.g., Aphrodite bled lymph blood diluted with water.[98] Origen (*Contra Celsum* 2.36) reports the mocking question whether Jesus had in his veins the divine liquid that was the blood of the gods. One can never be sure what was understood by those among John's readers who had a pagan Hellenistic

---

ed. L. Scheffczyk (San Francisco: Ignatius, 1986), 33–46; A. A. Maguire, *Blood and Water. The Wounded Side of Christ in Early Christian Literature* (Studies in Sacred Theology 108; Washington: Catholic Univ., 1958), which goes to the 4th cent.; and S. P. Brock, "'One of the Soldiers Pierced . . .' The Mysteries Hidden in the Side of Christ," *Christian Orient* 9 (1988), 49–59, which covers the theologians of the Syriac church.

[96]Represented by Origen, Aquinas, Cajetan, Cornelius a Lapide, and Lagrange, to name a few.

[97]Ancient medical lore has also been brought into the discussion. Greek thought from Heraclitus to Galen stressed that proper proportions of blood and water in the human body guaranteed health. *IV Macc* 9:20 describes a martyr's death in terms of his blood smeared on a wheel, and fluid from his body quenching the burning coals. Midrash *Leviticus Rabbah* 15.2 on Lev 13.2ff. says, "A human being is evenly balanced, half water and the other half blood."

[98]P. Haupt, *American Journal of Philology* 45 (1924), 53–55; E. Schweizer, EvT NS 12 (1952–53), 350–51. Alexander the Great, hit by an arrow and in great pain, quoted from Homer (*Iliad* 5.340): "What flows here, my friends, is blood and not 'Serum [*ichōr*] such as flows from the veins of the blessed gods'" (Plutarch, *Alexander* 28.3).

background; but since nowhere else does John depend on such blatantly pagan imagery to explain Jesus, I see little reason to suppose that it was a major factor here.

Was John using the blood and water with an anti-gnostic intent? We know that in the 2d cent. there were docetic gnostics who denied that Jesus really died on the cross (§42, ANALYSIS D), and in the *Acts of John* 101 Jesus is represented as denying that blood really came from his body. Irenaeus ca. 180 used 19:34b against docetists (*Adv. haer.* 3.22.2; 4.33.2). In the 1st cent., however, when John wrote, did such docetic gnosticism exist among those who claimed to believe in Jesus?[99] True, the flow of blood and water (if the latter [*hydōr*] was understood as equivalent to *ichōr,* fluid from the wound) might convey the idea that Jesus was truly dead. Yet Hultkvist (*What*) has used this emission to argue that Jesus was not dead but only in a coma resulting from severe hemorrhage. In any case was not Jesus' death already established by the soldier who both saw that he was dead and probed his body? The next verse with its "that you too may believe" suggests that depth of faith, not correction of error, was the main goal.

Was John thinking here of Jesus as the paschal lamb or, more generally, of him as a sacrificial victim, and trying to show that he fulfilled the requirement that the blood of the victim should flow at the moment of death so that it could be sprinkled?[100] But then why the flow of water? The Scripture citation in 19:36 will show that John may well have in mind the paschal lamb imagery, but that is connected to the unbroken bones, not to the flow of blood.

Some have suggested that primarily John is calling attention to OT background (see Lefèvre, "Seitenwunde," for a rich variety). Above (p. 1178) I pointed to the thesis that Gen 2:21–22 (Eve from the side of Adam) was behind the whole scene.[101] Others think of the Suffering Servant *pouring* out his soul (life) to death in Isa 53:12 (if that is what the hiphil of ʿ*rh* means). Another proposed set of passages involves the exodus imagery of Moses

[99]Richter and others think of gnosticism as a major adversary in the Gospel. In BGJ and BEJ I contended that there was a much clearer concern about incipient gnosticism at the later date when the Johannine Epistles were written and that is visible in the reference to water and blood in I John 5:6.

[100]Mishna, *Pesaḥim* 5.3,5. So Miguens ("Salió" 13–16) and Ford ("Mingled"). Miguens (17–20) points to the similarity between the soldier's stabbing Jesus' side with a lance and the insistence of Jewish law that the priest should slit the heart of the victim and make the blood come forth (Mishna, *Tamid* 4.2) Wilkinson ("Incident" 150) rejects Ford's thesis that the blood should flow in order that it could be sprinkled—on the level of history that would not interest the soldier; on the level of narrative that would not interest the author.

[101]Brock ("One") shows that this imagery was popular in the Syriac-speaking church along with the symbolism that the piercing with the sword opened up the garden of the tree of life that was fenced in with a sword after Adam's sin (Gen 3:24). See also R. Murray, *Orientalia Christiana Periodica* 39 (1973), 224–34, 491.

causing water to flow from the rock and the Ezek 47 image of water flowing from Jerusalem—a connection facilitated when John 19:34 is read in the light of 7:38, where living water *flows* from within Jesus. This last proposal has added significance as background for the most embraced explanation, namely, that here John is continuing and developing a symbolism he used earlier.

In John 7:37–38 Jesus cited a Scripture passage seemingly in reference to himself: "From within *him* shall flow rivers of living water."[102] There the evangelist interrupted to explain that Jesus was referring to the Spirit which those who believed in him were to receive, for as yet there was no Spirit since Jesus had not been glorified. In Jesus' death we now have the hour of his glorification as he has been lifted up on the cross in return to the Father (12:23–24,28–32; 13:1; 17:1,10–11). That death is signified by the blood, and the promised Spirit flowing from within him is signified by the water.[103] This interpretation is not contradictory to the idea that Jesus gave over his Spirit to those at the cross in 19:30, but is another aspect of a multifaceted Spirit-giving through the death, resurrection, and ascension of Jesus. (Note that in each case the Spirit comes from Jesus and thus is the Spirit of Jesus.) At the cross his mother and the disciple whom he loved represented the forebears of the Johannine community—a community of the specially beloved who had already come into existence before he died and were the first to receive the Spirit. Now that he has been lifted up in death he is drawing *all* to himself (12:32), and all those who believe in him shall receive the Spirit (7:39). The same OT passages that were background for the flow of living water from within him in John 7:38 (Num 20:11; Ps 78:15–16; Ezek 47:1; see BGJ 1.321–23) would have been influential in John 19:34b. And granted the importance of Zech 9–14 in the PN, one might single out Zech 13:1: "On that day a fountain shall be opened for the House of David and for the inhabitants of Jerusalem, for the removal of sin and impurity"; and

---

[102]Others take the "him" to refer to the believer (BGJ 1.320–21). The Scripture is often identified as Num 20:11 where Moses strikes the rock and the waters flow forth. In Midrash *Exodus Rabbah* 3.13 on Exod 4:9 Moses is said to have struck the rock twice because he first brought forth blood and then water, but we do not know that this exegesis was in circulation in the 1st cent.

[103]So also Vellanickal, "Blood." In a combination of oversimplification and oversubtlety, de la Potterie ("Symbolisme" 208, 214–15) objects to making the death (blood) historical and the water (Spirit) symbolic; he prefers to distinguish between the blood as "sign" of death and as "symbol" of life. John, however, never makes a linguistic distinction between sign and symbol. I would interpret the blood to be symbolic of the death *as John understands that historical event,* i.e., theologically: a glorified and life-giving death on the uplifting cross. Well does Origen (*Contra Celsum* 2.69) observe that this is a different type of dead man who "showed even as a corpse signs of life in the water and the blood." The potentiality of water to symbolize the Spirit was recognized early (see Irenaeus, *Adv. haer.* 4.14.2).

Zech 12:10: "I will pour out on the House of David and on the inhabitants of Jerusalem a spirit of pity and compassion" (see below under 19:37 for further use of this passage).[104]

I began this discussion of the flow of blood and water by pointing to the functional equivalence of John 19:34 and Mark 15:39 in that each features a Roman soldier in an episode that interprets Jesus' death. We may add that each Gospel passage hints at the wide salvific effect of that death, Mark by having a *Gentile* confess Jesus, and John by fulfilling Jesus' promise to draw all to himself through the pouring out of the Spirit to all believers. Yet Mark's centurion commented on the death christologically, while John's soldier remains silent. The functional equivalent of Mark's interpreting centurion is John's testifying eyewitness in the next verse, to which we now turn.[105]

The True Witness of the One Who Has Seen (19:35). A parenthetical comment[106] highlights the importance of what has preceded. Just as Mark's centurion, having "seen that he thus expired" (a "thus" that includes the eschatological intervention of God in rending the sanctuary veil), interpreted that sight christologically and salvifically, so now John has "one who has seen" a prophetic sign that followed the death of Jesus and bears true witness "in order that you too may believe." What was seen by this Johannine seer was primarily the stabbing of Jesus' side and the outflow of blood and water (19:34), but the seeing would have placed that action in the whole context of 19:31–33. Who was the seer? John's extremely indirect style here makes the answer to that uncertain; in part it hinges on whether he refers to two different people in 19:35a and 35b respectively.

As for 19:35a, "And the one who has seen has borne witness, and true is his witness," there have been two males singled out at the cross to whom this might apply. The closest antecedent is the soldier (Minear, "Diversity" 163–64); but it seems odd within a Johannine framework that such a solemn affirmation would be attributed to him without some indication that he came

---

[104]For the relation of I John 5:6–8 to this interpretation of "blood and water" in 19:34b, as well as to the role of the witness in 19:35, see BEJ 577–80. Beyond the interpretation of "blood and water" as the Spirit flowing from the glorified death of Jesus, there is also the possibility of a *secondary* sacramental symbolism, whether both elements symbolize baptism, or the blood symbolizes the eucharist and the water, baptism. Both sacramental interpretations were in vogue by the late 2d and early 3d cents. (BGJ 2.951); and the idea that the sacraments flowed from the death of Jesus would not be impossible for John himself. Yet this symbolism is difficult to prove.

[105]The equivalence would be strengthened by the thesis to be mentioned (although it is held by very few) that John's "the one who has seen has borne witness" was the soldier who pierced Jesus' side.

[106]A few Latin witnesses omit the verse and Nonnus implies a somewhat different reading; Blass ("Über") argues on text-critical grounds that it is so dubious that nothing can be made to depend on it—a view that is repeated in BDF 291[6], where Blass was a major contributor. In fact, however, this view has practically no following among commentators.

to believe. The importance of the testimony better fits the disciple whom Jesus loved, mentioned a few verses earlier (19:26–27) as standing nearby the cross. That he is meant is confirmed by 21:24, which speaks of the beloved disciple (who has been referred to in 21:20–23): "This is the disciple who bears witness about these things and who has written these things, and we know his witness is true."[107]

More difficult to identify is the figure mentioned in 19:35b: "and that one [*ekeinos*] knows that he speaks what is true in order that you too may believe." (The purpose clause probably modifies the whole sentence, including the bearing witness of 35a, rather than simply "speaks.") The use of *ekeinos* suggests to many a new subject who knows that the eyewitness ("he" = the beloved disciple) speaks what is true. Let me summarize briefly some of the identifications of *ekeinos* as a new subject (for detail see BGJ 2.936–37). Some think that *ekeinos* is God or Jesus (mentioned in 19:33),[108] both of whom John occasionally tags as *ekeinos* (but only when the context is clear), or even the Paraclete (the Spirit symbolized by the water) who is the witness par excellence (15:26).[109] The real objection to each of these is that the highly oblique context does not prepare us for the respective agent.[110] The Johannine writer has also been proposed as the *ekeinos:* The writer knows that the eyewitness (the beloved disciple) speaks the truth. Something similar is found in 21:24: "We know that his [the beloved disciple's] witness is true." However, a self-reference as *ekeinos* is more awkward than the use of "we";

[107]There is considerable debate about whether the writer is indicating that the witness borne (*martyrein, martyria*) by the beloved disciple in 19:35a involves the witness embodied in the written Gospel or simply that of the basic tradition behind the Gospel. In favor of an indication that the disciple wrote the Gospel is invoked the "who has written these things" clause of 21:24; yet that might mean no more than "has caused these things to be written," as in 19:19 where "Pilate also wrote a notice and put it on the cross." Lavergne ("Coup" 11) reports that he researched the ninety-nine uses of *martyr-* words in Plato, and that Plato seems to employ *martyria* (eight times) only in the instance of written testimony. Chase ("Two") argues that in 19:35 there is nothing to indicate that the disciple wrote, for a written account would not add to his trustworthiness. Rather this is an almost viva voce comment of the one presiding over reading the Gospel aloud to a body of disciples, just as a comment is made by "we" in 21:24 or, indeed, by "I" in 21:25.

[108]Nestle ("John xix") lists in favor of this view Abbott, Sanday, Strachan, and Zahn, and reports that it goes back to Erasmus. Lavergne ("Coup" 9–10) thinks that *ekeinos* (seemingly = God, until Jesus is risen) lends divine affirmation to the veracity of the human witness of 19:35a. There is a chain of witnesses in John 5:31–38 culminating in the Father.

[109]Kempthorne ("As God") argues that God is the witness, not God looking down from heaven but in the person of the Spirit; and he cites in support I John 5:6, which speaks of Jesus having come by water and blood and then states: "And the Spirit is the one who bears witness for the Spirit is the truth." Yet cannot one go further? As John indicates, the Spirit bears witness through others (15:26–27); and so if one argues that the beloved disciple is the *ekeinos* of 19:35b, the reason that he can bear witness is because he is the embodiment of the Paraclete-Spirit.

[110]Among them the "Jesus" identification has the most following, since Jesus is mentioned by name in this scene. But it would be odd to have Jesus who has died certify the truth of witness to what happened after his death.

accordingly many attribute 19:35 to a redactor who as a third party states that the evangelist (*ekeinos*) knows that the eyewitness speaks the truth.[111]

Others, ancient and modern (Nonnus of Panopolis, Bacon, Bultmann, Schnackenburg, etc.) challenge the idea that *ekeinos* changes the subject. One can point to an anaphorical use of the pronoun as "he" (BDF 291[6]; MGNTG 3.46); and in this pattern the reference would be to the beloved disciple himself, the chosen instrument of the Paraclete-Spirit. This last identification makes the best sense within the framework of Johannine theology: The beloved disciple who in 19:35a has seen and borne witness is the one who speaks in 19:35b "in order that you too may believe."[112] Undoubtedly what is to be believed is the christological and salvific import of the death of Jesus, even as the evangelist writes this Gospel "that you may believe that Jesus is the Messiah, the Son of God, and that, believing, you may have life in his name" (20:31). At the beginning of John's narrative of Jesus' earthly career, JBap was the one who *saw* and *bore witness* that Jesus is the Son of God (1:34); by way of inclusion at the end of that career the beloved disciple has seen and borne witness to the same truth.[113] The beloved disciple is more perceptive than any other follower of Jesus, and in a certain way here he anticipates resurrection faith. True, he himself will not come to believe in the risen Jesus until he sees the garments in the empty tomb (20:8); but his perception that the Jesus who has died on the cross is life-giving will help people to believe, even as the sight of the risen Jesus in other NT works brings people to faith. (This is a point made by Harder, "Bleibenden," when he compares I Cor 15:6 and John 19:35.)

Fulfillment of Scripture (19:36–37). Some verses earlier we heard of Scripture being "fulfilled" (19:24: *plēroun*) or "completed" (19:28: *teleioun*) in regard to the events preceding Jesus' death. Now by inclusion we hear of Scripture being fulfilled in regard to the events following Jesus' death.[114] The introduction in v. 36 relates the Scripture to "these things" that have happened. Logically the plural refers to at least two items: that Jesus' legs were not broken (19:33), and that his side was stabbed by a lance (19:34a), for the citation in v. 36 refers to the former, and the citation in v. 37 to the

---

[111]They think of the redactor responsible for chap. 21 of John, especially 21:24. For the contrary thesis that this redactor was copying from 19:35 which was a reflection of the evangelist, see ANALYSIS B below.

[112]The present subjunctive is textually preferable to the aorist here. An even more acute problem of deciding between the two tenses occurs in the parallel clause of 20:31 (BGJ 2.1056).

[113]On the basis of this insight leavened by the thesis that the beloved disciple was John, son of Zebedee, it became a convention to paint the crucifixion as a triptych with the two witnessing Johns in the side panels.

[114]Otherwise in the events of the Johannine PN it has been Jesus' own words that were "fulfilled" (18:9,32). In Matt Scripture is fulfilled in relation to the arrest of Jesus without resistance (26:54,56), and in relation to Judas (27:9–10).

latter. (Commonly it is claimed that there is no citation referring to the flow of blood and water [19:34b] which is covered by v. 35, but we shall return to that point later.)

The FIRST CITATION (19:36) is "Its [or his: *autou*] bone shall not be fractured [*syntribēsetai*]." The ambiguity of the *autou* has been preserved in my translation, for much discussion has centered on whether the primary referent is the paschal lamb ("its") or the persecuted psalmist ("his"). This passage constitutes an example of how we should not easily or univocally assume that OT passages creatively gave rise to Gospel events. John's description in 19:33 used *skelos* ("leg") and *katagnynai* ("to break"; *GPet* 4:14 used *skelokopein*), while the citation in 19:36 uses *osteon* (*ostoun:* "bone") and *syntribein* ("to fracture, shatter"). More than likely the application of Scripture by the evangelist came after the basic description of the Johannine episode was set (ANALYSIS B below). There are several Scripture passages employing *osteon* and *syntribein* that have been proposed as candidates for the one John had in mind, and we need to discuss those.

(a) A Pentateuchal passage phrasing the law governing the paschal lamb:[115]
- Exod 12:10 (LXX); 12:46: You [pl.] shall not fracture [*syntripsete*] a bone from it [*ap' autou*].
- Num 9:12: They shall not fracture [*syntripsousin*] a bone from it.

In support of this being the primary reference one may recall John's description of Jesus as the Lamb of God (1:29,36), a time setting a few hours before the Passover meal, and possible implicit references to the paschal lamb in 19:14 (noon: the hour when the slaughtering of paschal lambs in the Temple began) and 19:29 (hyssop: used to sprinkle the lamb's blood).[116] The imagery of Jesus dying as the paschal lamb or as a sacrifice whose blood cleanses from sin had wide circulation among early Christians (I John 1:7; I Cor 5:7; I Pet 1:19; Rev 5:8–9). Against the thesis that John was referring to a paschal-lamb passage is the fact that the passive singular of the verb used by John 19:36 is not found in the examples above, which have plural active forms of the verb. Some would posit a deliberate change by the evangelist, e.g., to make the OT texts sound more like a prophecy. Others would posit

[115]Antipathy toward having a fractured bone presumably stems from the desire that what is offered to God should be perfect. From a comparative religion survey Henninger ("Neuere") points out that bones were not broken because bone and marrow had to be kept intact for reanimation, but admits that there is no evidence of that thesis in Israel's view of the lamb.

[116]Some would add 19:31 ("in order that the bodies might not remain on the cross") in the light of Exod 12:10 that when the next day comes, nothing must remain of the lamb killed in the evening. Also see APPENDIX VI on parallels (esp. #12) between the death of Jesus and the sacrifice of Isaac.

that he used a Greek translation other than that found in the LXX.[117] Of the various Scripture passages cited or alluded to plainly in the Johannine PN, this would be the only one from the Pentateuch.

> (b) The description of the suffering just one in Ps 34:21:
> > The Lord watches over all their bones,
> > and not one of them [*ex autōn*] will be fractured [*syntribēsetai*].

The Johannine passive verb is found here but not the Johannine subject ("his bone"). Other formal Scripture citations in the Johannine PN have been from the psalms.[118] Even though Ps 34 is never cited in the NT in relation to Jesus' passion,[119] the motif of this psalm (God answers the call of the afflicted and delivers the just: 34:7,20) would fit the Johannine scene well: God's providence prevented the soldiers from breaking Jesus' legs contrary to the request of his enemies. A number of scholars (Dodd, Haenchen, Seynaeve, Torrey, B. Weiss) favor this as the passage intended by John. With Hemel-soet, Rehm, and others I think the evidence favors the paschal-lamb image as the primary reference; but I see no reason why John may not have intended to echo the psalm as well.[120] After a detailed study of the language, Menken concludes: "The best explanation for the peculiar form of the quotation in Jn 19,36 seems to be that here elements from Ps 34(33),21 have been combined with elements from the Pentateuchal texts."[121] Moreover, both lamb and persecuted psalmist fit into Johannine theology.

The SECOND CITATION (19:37) is "They shall see [*opsontai eis*] whom they have pierced [*ekkentein*]" (Zech 12:10).[122] As with 19:36 there is a dissimi-

---

[117]Appeal has been made to the Codex Vaticanus LXX form of Exod 12:10, which reads *syntrip-setai*, a future middle singular with a passive sense: "A bone from it shall not be fractured." Yet the "from it" (*ap' autou*) is not the same as John's *autou*, and the verb is still not the same as John's future passive singular (*syntribēsetai*). In fact, Menken ("Old" 2104) may be correct in arguing that the Vaticanus *syntripsetai* is nothing more than another way of writing the more widely attested LXX plural form of the verb in Exod 12:10, *syntripsete*, since *ai* and *e* were pronounced the same at this time.

[118]John 19:24 cited Ps 22:19; John 19:28–29 seemingly cited Ps 22:16 and 69:22.

[119]It is cited in I Pet 2:3; 3:10–12 (see also *I Clement* 22:1–7; *Barnabas* 9:2).

[120]Bultmann, Schnackenburg, and others think that the Johannine source cited the psalm, but the evangelist saw a reference to the paschal lamb. Since I do not think one can reconstruct such a source, I would rather see the possibility that one of these biblical texts may have been in Johannine use earlier than the other.

[121]"Old" 2106. Indeed, on pp. 2114–16 he makes an interesting case that already in *Jubilees* 49:13 (the Ethiopic rather than the Latin) we find echoes of the Pentateuchal passages pertinent to the lamb combined with Ps 34:21: "There is no fracturing of bone from the middle of it [the paschal lamb], not a single one, because not a single bone will be fractured from the children of Israel."

[122]This is introduced by "And again [*palin*] another [*heteros*] Scripture says." Lavergne ("Coup" 13–14), drawing on an older sense of *palin* as "back, backwards," argues that this should be translated: "And in an inverse sense another Scripture says." The first Scripture passage forbade that damage should be done to Jesus, while the second speaks of his being pierced. There is a contrast from the contents even without Lavergne's translation. This is John's only use of *heteros*, "another";

larity of vocabulary between the description in the episode (19:34a: *nyssein*, "to stab at") and the citation in 19:37, and in the episode no plural group is said to see Jesus after the lance blow. The citation, once more then, did not give rise to the episode but has been added to bring out the theological depth of an existing account. Although clearly Zech 12:10 is being cited, the wording given by John in the citation does not agree verbatim (see italics) with either the MT, "They shall *look on me* whom they have pierced"[123] or the standard (Vaticanus) LXX: "They shall *look upon* [*epiblepsontai*] *me* because they have *danced insultingly.* "[124] Most often in reference to the parousia and sometimes in combination with Dan 7:13, the Greek form of the Zech 12:10 passage cited in John with its *opsontai* and *ekkentein* is found in Rev 1:7, and echoed in *Barnabas* 7:9 and Justin *Apology* 1.52.12 (cf. *Dialogue* 64.7). Since most of these are scarcely dependent on John, we cannot think that John simply changed the standard LXX reading by adapting it to the MT. Rather he and the other witnesses were citing another early Greek form of Zech 12:10.[125] John has cited only one line of a long verse in Zech. The words in 12:10 that precede the cited line speak of God's pouring out a spirit of compassion on the House of David and the inhabitants of Jerusalem. The words in 12:10 that follow the cited line report that they wail over him as a beloved and firstborn son. How would those other words in the verse be meaningful to John? I reported at the beginning of this subsection dealing with the Scripture citations that conventionally this second Johannine citation (v. 37) is thought to refer to the stabbing of Jesus' side with a lance (v. 34a), but not to the flow of blood and water (v. 34b) or to the witness of the one who has seen (v. 35). But why then were the Scripture citations not placed after vv. 33–34a, rather than after vv. 34b–35, to which they had no

---

its equivalent appears as a formula with variations in early rabbinic literature for stringing together applicable citations, e.g., Midrash *Mekilta* (*Beshallaḥ* 2.84) on Exod 14:4. An *eis* ("into") follows "see," perhaps with the innuendo of penetrating to the meaning of the stab wound. De la Potterie ("Volgeranno" 113), as part of his tendency to take Johannine prepositions (over)literally, renders "into the interiority of."

[123]In the context the "me" in the Hebrew is Yahweh, a reading so difficult that most regard the text as corrupt. Some forty-five Hebrew mss. (collated by Kennicott and de Rossi) have "him," but that may represent copyists' attempt at improvement. The verb *opsontai* (from *horan*) used by John is not employed in Septuagintal Greek to render the hiphil of *nbṭ* used by the MT.

[124]The LXX probably misread Hebrew *dqr* ("pierce") as *rqd* ("skip about"). The root derivation of English "insult" traced through the Latin involves dancing or leaping derisively about someone.

[125]The 5th–6th-cent. Vienna codex (L) preserves a Greek reading closer to John and to the MT: "They shall look upon me whom they have pierced." The late P. W. Skehan, a distinguished specialist in the LXX, wrote me in personal correspondence: "I have no doubt whatsoever that the Vienna codex reading is both pre-Hexaplar [before Origen] and proto-Lucianic [see NJBC 68:69: a 2d- or 1st-cent.-BC Palestinian revision of the LXX, bringing it closer to the Hebrew], and that it underlies John." One would still have to posit that the *epiblepsontai* ("look upon") of this reading was changed to the *opsontai* ("see") of the Christian readings, and for that reason Menken ("Textual" 504) prefers to posit that underlying John is a Greek translation from the Hebrew which was independent of the LXX.

reference? Why would "these things," which introduces the citations in v. 36, not refer to what happened in the immediately preceding verses, especially to the startling flow of blood and water from the side of Jesus? Moreover, the citation in v. 37 speaks of "*see* whom they have pierced" and the only "seeing" that takes place after the stabbing of Jesus' side occurs in v. 35 in reference to the beloved disciple who has borne witness to the flow of blood and water. It is much more logical, then, to think that the citation in v. 36 (bone not fractured) refers to vv. 32–33, and the citation in v. 37 (see whom they have pierced) refers to vv. 34–35.

In that scenario the whole of Zech 12:10 was part of the Johannine outlook (so also Hemelsoet, Venetz). The opening words of 12:10 that have God pouring out a spirit of compassion in connection with the House of David would be related to the water (= Spirit) coming out of the side of Jesus (v. 34b). The seeing of the one pierced in 12:10 by a plural subject ("they") would be fulfilled by the one soldier of v. 34a who, having seen that Jesus was already dead, stabbed Jesus' side and thus caused the outflow, and by the beloved disciple who saw all this.[126] The wailing over the one pierced as "a beloved and firstborn son" mentioned at the end of 12:10 could be related to v. 35b where *ekeinos* "speaks what is true in order that you too may believe." Believe what? John 20:31 fills in the object: "that you may believe that Jesus is the Messiah, the Son of God." Rev 1:7 associates Zech 12:10 with the coming on the clouds of heaven, a motif often associated with the Son of Man coming in judgment. In John's realized eschatology, however, the judgment is already taking place, for the pierced one who hangs on the cross is the Son of Man who has been lifted up (3:14; 8:28; 12:32–34). Moreover, as 3:18–21 makes clear, there is always a twofold aspect, positive and negative, in the judgment constituted by seeing and encountering Jesus; and that will divide those who encounter the pierced one as well. Those who accept the witness of the beloved disciple see and believe, and thus receive the Spirit that flows forth from the glorified Jesus, the Son of God. But for "the Jews" who caused the piercing by their demand to have Jesus' legs broken, the pierced one is in Johannine thought a sign of punishing judgment.[127]

---

[126]Menken ("Textual" 504) argues that despite the wording of Zech 12:10 where the "they" who look seem to be the same as the "they" who have pierced, there is evidence in Jewish interpretation for not identifying the two groups. In John the Roman soldier in fulfilling the request of the Jews and the order of Pilate does the piercing, while both he and the beloved disciple do the seeing.

[127]See BGJ 9.954–55; de la Potterie, "Volgeranno" 116. Menken ("Textual" 511) recognizes that there is a difference in the seeing of the pierced Jesus by believers and unbelievers, but strangely (p. 505, nn. 43, 44) he makes a point that John does not say that either "the Jews" or the Roman soldiers looked on the pierced Jesus. I think that is a meaningless distinction because, as a matter of fact,

REACTIONS OF THOSE PRESENT ACCORDING TO GPET

In this commentary on the canonical PNs, my interest in *GPet* is in seeing how lines of development visible in (or even before) the NT Gospels continued in the 2d cent. The breaking of the legs recounted in John 19:31–33 appears in *GPet* 4:14 in other vocabulary *before* the death of Jesus and is combined with the Lucan picture of one of the crucified wrongdoers being sympathetic to Jesus. In the combined story Jewish malevolence is intensified over the implicit malevolence in the request of John 19:31. There is nothing in *GPet* about the Johannine lance wound in Jesus' side[128] or the flow of blood and water.

In Mark/Matt the reactions of people come after the external phenomena that manifest God's reaction to the death of the Son (sanctuary veil rent, earth shaken), so that the people are responding to the phenomena as well as to the death. *GPet* mixes the phenomena and the reactions. In 6:21 the shaking of the earth which takes place when Jesus' body is placed on it understandably produces fear among the Jews. (Notice that now the power that produces the shaking is no longer simply divine intervention as implied by the passive in Matt 27:51, but resides in Jesus' dead body, even as John has the dead body the source of a life-giving flow.) Among the canonical Gospels fear is a reaction to Jesus' death only in Matt 27:54, where too it follows a reference to the earth shaking. In Matt it is the Roman soldiers who "feared exceedingly"; in *GPet,* since the crucifixion is done by Jews, they are the subject of "a great fear."

A phenomenon mentioned by the Synoptics *before* the death of Jesus was darkness over the whole earth. Even more dramatically *GPet* 5:15–18 describes that event also before the death; but only *GPet* specifies that the end of the darkness came after the death of Jesus (6:22, following 5:19): "Then the sun shone, and it was found to be the ninth hour." This caused the Jews to rejoice and to give to Joseph Jesus' body for burial (6:23). Thus in *GPet* the extraordinary phenomena have produced both fear and joy.

More reactions of people are found in *GPet* 7:25–8:29. In considering them, one must remember they come after the *burial* of Jesus, not only after his death as in the canonical Gospels. In sequence *GPet* describes four groups: (a) "the Jews and the elders and the priests" in 7:25; (b) Peter and his companions in 7:26–27; (c) "the scribes and Pharisees and elders" in 8:28a, continued by 8:29–30; (d) "all the people" in 8:28b. Since both (a)

John does not say that the witness (beloved disciple) looked on the pierced Jesus either. The judgment touches those who are the dramatis personae in the whole scene.

[128]In *GPet* 6:21 (which shares with John 20:25 a reference to nails) only hand wounds are indicated.

and (d) beat themselves or their breasts, are they related? How is one to reconcile that the elders among the Jews and the priests in (a) show repentance, while the elders among the scribes and Pharisees in (c) do not? Part of the confusion stems from the fact that in these verses *GPet* has run together reactions to the death of Jesus (as in the Synoptics) and a story of how the Jewish authorities got soldiers from Pilate to watch the burial place of Jesus (as in Matt 27:62ff.). Nevertheless, *GPet* 7:25–8:29 offers an interesting insight into the author's attitude toward the Jews, whom (having left the Romans completely out of the execution) he has described as responsible for the crucifixion and death of Jesus. One gets the impression that overall *GPet* envisions two Jewish groups, one unrepentant and the other repentant. In portraying *unrepentant* "scribes and Pharisees and elders" (8:28a) who will approach Pilate about the sepulcher of Jesus (8:29ff.), *GPet* is close in spirit to John, who has malevolent "Jews" ask that the legs be broken, and even closer in theme to Matt, who in 27:62ff. has "the chief priests and Pharisees," who ultimately will pay people to lie, approach Pilate about the sepulcher of Jesus—in both cases the intent is to prevent the resurrection. The *GPet* "scribes and Pharisees and elders" fear because they have heard the people's reaction to Jesus (8:28–29); this echoes the beginning of the passion in Mark 14:1–2; Matt 26:3–5; and Luke 22:1–2 where the chief priests and scribes or elders seek to seize and kill Jesus in stealth lest there be a disturbance among the people, for, as Luke explains, "they feared the people." As for *repentant* Jews, one gets the impression that *GPet* differentiates between "the Jews and the elders and the priests" who beat themselves in 7:25 and "all the people" who beat their breasts in 8:28b. The former do so because by their sins they have made inevitable God's wrathful judgment and the end of Jerusalem, and thus they have done wrong to themselves. The latter do so, after they have murmured against the authorities, because the great signs have shown them how just Jesus was. In having this differentiation *GPet* is close to the twofold Lucan picture of reactions to Jesus before the crucifixion and after his death, as can be seen in the italicized words in what follows. According to Luke 23:27–32, as Jesus was led off to be crucified with two *wrongdoers,*[129] there was a large multitude of *the people* and the Daughters of Jerusalem who were *beating themselves* and lamenting, but Jesus warned them of apocalyptic destruction to come. After Jesus' death in Luke 23:48 "all the crowds" struck *their breasts.*[130] In its pictures of the unrepentant Jewish leaders and people and of various types of repentant ones, *GPet* has contin-

---

[129]Note that in *GPet* 7:25 the Jews have *done wrong* to themselves.

[130]See pp. 1168–69 above for textual variants in Luke 23:48 that are very close to what is found in *GPet*. Vaganay (*Évangile* 269–70) discusses the relationship between these variants and *GPet* and opts for a common source, while Harnack argues that the variants are dependent on *GPet*.

ued portrayals found in the canonical Gospels but darkened the hostile background.

An intriguing novelty among the reactions in *GPet* (7:26–27) is that of Peter and his companions (*hetairoi,* seemingly the Twelve on the basis of 14:59) in the aftermath of the death and burial and before the resurrection.[131] The canonical Gospels, having left the Twelve and Peter in Gethsemane or the court of the high priest, pick up their story only on Easter after the discovery of the empty tomb. In mentioning them *GPet* preserves the canonical Gospel convention of not having them present at the crucifixion; indeed it explains their absence by reporting that they had gone into hiding because the Jews were seeking them as wrongdoers. No canonical Gospel reports an attempt to arrest Jesus' followers along with him, and the closest one comes to *GPet* on this point is in John 20:19 where the disciples have the doors of the place shut "for fear of the Jews." The particular charge against the disciples in *GPet* is that they wished to set fire to the Temple sanctuary. Closest to that is Acts 6:12–14, where Stephen is brought before the Sanhedrin accused of saying that Jesus of Nazareth would destroy this (holy) place. That *GPet* has Peter and his companions sorrowful, wounded in spirit, mourning, and weeping is an understandable dramatic touch. What is more significant is that it has them fasting "night and day until the Sabbath." All three Synoptics (Mark 2:20 par.) have Jesus say of his disciples that when the bridegroom was taken away from them they would fast, and by the time of *GPet* some custom of fasting in relation to the time of Jesus' death was in place.[132] The "night and day" phrase seems to indicate a Jewish pattern of the day beginning in the evening. "Until the Sabbath" is confusing because *GPet* 2:5 has Jesus crucified on the day before the Sabbath. Such a curiosity helps to reinforce a picture of the author of *GPet* as skilled in popular drama but weak on details about 1st-cent. Jewish life.

Analysis

As usual there are two basic issues to be discussed: historicity and composition, with the latter applicable mostly to John.

---

[131]That Peter relates this reaction as "I" and includes his companions as "we" is unheard of in the canonical Gospels. Vaganay (*Évangile* 271) cites this as a clear mark that *GPet* belongs to the pseudepigraphical apocryphal-gospel genre. Note too in *GPet* the dramatic emotions in this reaction: "wounded in spirit" (cf. II Macc 3:16); "mourning and weeping" (Marcan Appendix 16:10).

[132]Tertullian, *De ieiunio* 2.2; CC 2.1258; *Apostolic Constitutions* 5.18 (Funk ed., p. 289); Syriac *Didascalia Apostolorum* 21.13 (Connolly ed., pp. 180, 183). *Gospel of the Hebrews* 7 (HSNTA

A. **The Historicity of the Reactors and of Their Reactions**

After the death of Jesus the canonical Gospels describe three groups who are present and react by actions, words, or observation: (1) Roman soldier(s) and/or centurion (all); (2) Jewish crowds and/or authorities (Luke, John, *GPet*); (3) Followers of Jesus (all, *GPet*). In evaluating the historicity of these reactors and their reactions we shall be bedeviled by a major problem. With rare exception there is little implausibility in what is described, so that one may speak of general verisimilitude. Nevertheless what is described fits in closely with the interests of the evangelists; otherwise they would not have included it. Conformity with the theology and dramatic organization of a Gospel does not establish creation by the evangelist but makes historicity extremely difficult to prove.

1. Roman Soldiers. That these would have been present is certain; and if verification of Jesus' death was desired (Mark, John), they would have carried it out. The issue of historicity becomes more complicated when one focuses on the role of a particular soldier (John) or officer (Synoptic centurion). Since in word or deed (as distinct from functional theological import) John's soldier has no surface similarity to Mark's centurion, there is insufficient reason to think that John drew on Mark. Reasonably one could maintain that old tradition spoke of a soldier in the aftermath of Jesus' death, and that Mark and John represent different developments of that. For example, it would have been commonly known that among the group of four commissioned to carry out the execution one soldier would have been in charge, and independently in different places storytelling could have dramatized the role of that soldier in relation to Jesus' death. By way of contrast with the hostile Jews, a natural tendency would have been to present the Roman as impartial or favorable.

There is no way to establish the historicity of what the centurion actually says in the Synoptics, for it is scarcely accidental that what he affirms fits well the theological purposes of the individual evangelists. Mark had a heavenly voice identify Jesus as God's Son at the beginning of the Gospel (1:11); it is fitting, then, that at the end, after Jesus' death, a human being (Gentile) acknowledge that: "Truly this man was God's Son" (15:39). Matt, who had Gentile magi acknowledge Jesus at the beginning of the Gospel, has by inclusion Gentiles (the centurion and those with him) acknowledge Jesus at the end of the Gospel, an acknowledgment as "Son of God," a title that he has used in the PN more frequently than any other evangelist (26:63; 27:40,43). In the COMMENT I sought to show that Luke's form of the centuri-

---

1.165; rev. ed. 1.178) has James, the brother of the Lord, fasting from bread after the Last Supper until Jesus would appear to him.

on's confession, "Certainly this man was just" (23:47), was an adaptation of Mark's form of the confession and thus neither independent nor original. It suited Luke's theological purposes to have outsiders recognize that Jesus was a just man, indeed, *the* just one, both before and after Jesus' death on the cross.

The historicity of John's account is complicated by 19:35 that stresses the presence and veracity of an eyewitness, seemingly the beloved disciple. Many scholars doubt the historicity of this figure, but I would contend that plausibly there was behind the Johannine community and its tradition a disciple of Jesus, not a major figure by outside standards (e.g., not one of the Twelve) but one whose subsequent role in Johannine life showed that he was specially loved by Jesus. Even if there was an eyewitness, is everything that John ascribes to the soldier historical, since the focus of the beloved disciple's witness would have been on theological import? There is no implausibility in the soldier's not breaking Jesus' legs but rather stabbing his side with a lance to make sure he was dead. Nevertheless, the difficulty of confirming John's information is exemplified by the fact that no other Christian work written within a hundred years of Jesus' death mentions the wound in the side.[133] Even more complicated is the historicity of the flow of blood and water effected by the lance blow. Barrett, Dodd, and others judge simple creation unlikely; and one could argue for the historicity of this peculiar physical phenomenon[134] which originally (on a preGospel level) did no more than confirm Jesus' death. Of course, as I have insisted in the COMMENT, the evangelist does not present the outflow in that way; for him it is a heaven-given revelatory sign of great theological import, fulfilling a prophecy of Jesus.

2. Jewish Crowds and/or Authorities. The presence of onlooking spectators at a crucifixion could be expected. Stories of unjust persecution and martyrdom tend to posit such a group, e.g., *III Macc* 5:24 (which is scarcely historical) describes crowds assembled for the spectacle of Jews being put to death. The likelihood of the attendance of priests and other authorities (posited by *GPet* and probably by John [cf. 19:31 with 19:20–21]) is complicated by unanswerable questions related to the feast. Did not the priests have Temple duties if this was the day before the Passover meal would be eaten in the evening, i.e., slaying the lambs? Would they not have become ritually

---

[133]Luke 24:39 mentions hands and feet; *GPet* 6:21 mentions the hands.

[134]The medical situation was discussed in §42, ANALYSIS C. From one point of view dead bodies do not bleed because the heart ceases to pump blood through the arteries. Yet in the period shortly after death, especially where gravity favors a flow (e.g., a body kept erect), blood can drain from an opening made in veins or auricles of the heart, for in undamaged vessels it would not have coagulated. What is described as water mixed in with the blood could have been some type of accumulated bodily fluid. Few doctors are willing to say that what John describes is impossible.

impure by being close to crucified dead men? As for the historicity of the reactions attributed to them, it is not unlikely that some of his fellow Jews would have been hostile to Jesus in death as they were in life. Yet the role attributed to "the Jews" in John 19:31 is stereotypically hostile, and their request to Pilate at the end of the crucifixion scene is an inclusive parallel to their request to him at the beginning (19:21). Luke 23:48 describes the repentance of the Jewish crowds, and historically it is not unlikely that some among the local onlookers would have thought that Jesus was treated unfairly by the Romans or by the Jewish authorities or by both. Nevertheless, the Lucan portrayal of the crowds (as a component in a pattern of three reactions) after Jesus' death fits in perfectly with his generally more sympathetic portrayal of the Jerusalem populace during the PN, and constitutes an artistic inclusion with the mention of the sympathetic multitude of the people (as a component in a pattern of three reactions) before Jesus' death.

3. Followers of Jesus. John alone (19:25) places these near the cross of Jesus before his death, and in §41 (ANALYSIS A) I warned that it would be unusual for the Romans to permit family and sympathizers such proximity. As for their presence at a distance after the death (Synoptics), at certain periods of heightened Roman fears of conspiracy or of recurrent revolts it would have been unwise to signal sympathy with the convicted.[135] But as I pointed out in §31 (A and B), there is no record of organized revolts in Judea during the prefecture of Pilate; he was not a ferociously cruel governor (pace Philo); nor is there real evidence that there were plans to arrest Jesus' followers as if he were the leader of a dangerous movement. Consequently a priori there is nothing implausible in the Synoptic picture of women followers (Galileans, perhaps not even known in Jerusalem) observing from a distance, not expressing in any way their attitude toward the crucifixion.[136] (In the COMMENT I expressed disagreement with the thesis that their presence was held up by the evangelists as an act of bravery.)

What complicates the issue of historicity is the interconnected presence of these women in the three scenes of the crucifixion, the burial, and the empty tomb (Table 8, p. 1016). The strongest Gospel attestation is that on Easter morn Mary Magdalene (and some other women) found the tomb of

---

[135]Tacitus (*Annals* 6.19) and Suetonius (*Tiberius* 61) point to hypersensitivity under Tiberius after the downfall of Sejanus in AD 31. See also Philo, *In Flaccum* 9; #72; Josephus, *War* 2.13.3; #253 for later periods.

[136]Luke has males known to Jesus also standing at a distance; John has the beloved disciple as an eyewitness. Again this is not implausible (so Gerhardsson, "Mark" 222); and neither evangelist mentions the presence of members of the Twelve, whose flight and absence has every chance of being historical.

Jesus empty. Despite significant academic dissent both Gospel evidence and scholarly opinion favor the historicity of the emptiness of the tomb and indeed of Magdalene as the first witness to the fact that Jesus' body was no longer there.[137] It has long been noted that were fictional invention involved (for apologetic purposes to support the reality of the resurrection), the discovery of the tomb by males, not females, would have been a more likely result, granted limitations on the validity of women's testimony.[138] Ironically, however, the historicity of the Galilean women at the tomb on Easter morn has been used to cast doubt on their presence at Golgotha on Friday, either after the death on the cross or at the burial. Did the evangelists or their forebears simply guess that if the women found the tomb on Easter, they must have seen where Jesus was buried on Friday, and that if the women were there for the burial of the body, they must have observed the death? (The early tendency to relate death, burial, and resurrection is attested in I Cor 15:3–4.) Yet "guess" may be pejoratively tendentious, for the interrelationship posited in that question exhibits respectable logic. To find Jesus' tomb Christians had to know where he was buried, and the women who found the tomb are never recorded as having to ask others where it was.

In any case I judge the interrelationship more complicated. As I argued above (§41), John in 19:25–27 seems to have combined his own scene involving the mother of Jesus and the beloved disciple with another tradition of three Galilean women at the crucifixion, thus indirectly attesting the antiquity of the latter. His form and ordering of the women's names (Jesus' mother's sister, Mary of Clopas, and Mary Magdalene) does not appear to be borrowed from Mark's enumeration (Mary Magdalene, Mary mother of James the younger and of Joses, and Salome). A plausible explanation is that there was a preGospel tradition about Galilean women who observed the crucifixion from afar (John has moved them close to the cross because of the combination he makes with his scene of the mother and the beloved disciple to whom Jesus speaks). In line with the storytelling pattern of three, a reference to three was fixed, of whom two were named: Mary Magdalene

---

[137]Magdalene's finding the tomb empty (all Gospels; *GPet*) is a different issue from that of her being the first to see the risen Jesus (Matt, John, Mark 16:9). The intermingling of the two may be responsible for a certain ambiguity about whether there were other women with her when she found the tomb. Probably the earliest memory had her alone see the risen Lord (John; Mark 16:9); but she and other women went to the empty tomb, so that by simplification Matt 28:9–10 has Jesus appear to them. In all this investigation of the most ancient tradition I am referring simply to finding the tomb empty, not to the narrative of angelic appearances at the tomb where a revelation is given that Jesus has been raised and thus explains why the tomb is empty. See NJBC 81:124.

[138]Josephus, *Ant.* 4.8.15; # 219; Mishna *Roš Haššana* 1.8; TalBab *Šebuʿot* 30a. See Gerhardsson, "Mark" 218.

and another Mary.[139] Inevitably, in varying degree the presence of three women in the crucifixion tradition influenced the account of the story of the finding of the empty tomb by Mary Magdalene and others, so that the others in the Easter-morn scene began to be identified harmoniously with the women at the crucifixion—once again not an illogical assumption. In §47 below I shall explain why I think the specification of the women at the burial (absent from John) is a back-formation from the filled-out tradition of the women finding the tomb empty.

B. The Composition of the Synoptic and the Johannine Accounts

In terms of the composition of the SYNOPTIC scene, I need only summarize what has already been stated in various places in the COMMENT. In my judgment Matt and Luke are clearly derivative from Mark. *Matt* has added persuasiveness to the Roman confession of Jesus as God's Son by having it come from the other guards as well as from the centurion. *Luke* has expanded Mark's two reactions to three in order to match the three parties who react to Jesus on the way to the place of execution (23:26–31). In each set of three there is an individual (Simon, centurion), a multitude or crowd, and a group of women (Jerusalemites, Galileans). *Mark's* own arrangement is not without artistry: A Gentile centurion stands close by, opposite Jesus, while the Galilean women followers observe from a distance. The positive reaction in 15:39 is placed on the lips of a Gentile, whose confession of Jesus as God's Son reverses the denial of it by the Jewish high priest at the trial (14:61) and supplies human acknowledgment near the end of the Gospel of what the heavenly voice proclaimed at the baptism as the Gospel began (1:11). The role of the women in 15:40–41 is passive and transitional to the burial in the next scene (§46).[140]

JOHN's account needs more discussion because in the COMMENT I refrained from entering into most issues of composition. Haenchen (*John* 2.202) contends that here John employs a tradition different from Mark's; yet I pointed to many functional parallels. In my judgment that is too short a scene to allow a judgment as to whether Mark and John represent two totally separate formations or two independent developments of the same small preGospel nucleus (Michaels). What I regard as extremely unlikely is that here John knew only Mark and drew upon it creatively.

[139]As the women were taken into the individual Gospels the name of the third was variously specified: Salome (Mark), mother of the sons of Zebedee (Matt), Joanna (see Luke 24:10), and Jesus' mother's sister (John), leaving us uncertain whether these are four different candidates.

[140]So Matera (*Kingship* 50–51), who speaks of these verses as a Marcan creation. I think it more judicious to speak of a Marcan formation of an older tradition about the women, as I explained above under historicity.

As for the issues of source, contribution of the evangelist, and redaction there is, as usual, no scholarly agreement. Let me exemplify the problems by offering Bultmann's thesis with my own *parenthetical* observations based on discussion in the COMMENT. Bultmann holds that John 19:31–34a,36–37 came to the evangelist shaped by the community, and compared to the Synoptics this is a relatively late formation centered on the fulfillment of Scripture. (Because of sharp vocabulary differences between the Scripture citations in vv. 36–37 and the episodes in vv. 32–34a, I argued that the former did not give rise to the latter and were appended to the episodes after they were already formed.) Bultmann proposed that 19:34b (flow of blood and water) and 19:35 (eyewitness is true) were added to the evangelist's completed Gospel by the Ecclesiastical Redactor[141] as a reference to sacraments, one of the peculiar concerns of the Redactor's theology. (I contended that the possible sacramental significance of the blood and water is secondary; the main meaning is related to 7:38–39, i.e., the flowing of the living water of the Spirit from a Jesus glorified in death, and so is perfectly harmonious with symbolism found in the body of the Gospel.) Bultmann would apply the Scripture citations in 19:36–37 to vv. 32–34a but not to the later-inserted 34b–35. (I argued that the Scripture citation in 19:36 clearly refers to vv. 32–33, and the citation in 19:37 from Zech 12:10 really makes sense only if it refers to the whole of vv. 34–35. Overall, then, I would side with Venetz, "Zeuge," and others who judge 19:34b–35 to be the work of the evangelist rather than of the redactor.)

Granted that the detection of stages in the formation of John 19:31–37 is far from certain, our evidence points to 19:31–34 as narrative tradition that came to the evangelist.[142] In the course of incorporating it into the Gospel he rewrote it and added the parenthetical comment in 19:35, as well as the Scripture citations in 19:36–37, in order to bring out additional theological perspectives. I prefer to speak of preJohannine tradition rather than to reconstruct a source with exactitude. Both the preGospel stage(s) of the Johannine tradition and the Gospel were shaped in the Johannine community and reflect a continuity, with new insights being based on earlier ones. Therefore, I am skeptical when a difference of meaning is said to exist between the putative source and the Gospel. If, as in the case of the Scripture citation of 19:36, two different symbolic images may have

---

[141]If we speak simply of a redactor (leaving aside the mind-set that Bultmann would attribute to the Ecclesiastical Redactor), this is an old theory. Haensler ("Zu Jo"), like Belser before him, maintained that this was added to the Gospel by Aristion, mentioned in Papias' list of the presbyters (EH 3.39.4,7).

[142]In discussing historicity I pointed to the possibility that this preGospel tradition would have contained the breaking of the legs, a lance probe, and the flow of blood and water as a sign of death.

been combined, we do more justice to the state of our knowledge to justify both interpretations on the Gospel level. It is for this reason that in the COMMENT I have made none of my interpretation depend on what the preGospel level meant.

(Bibliography for this episode may be found in §37, Parts 12 and 13.)

CONTENTS OF ACT IV, SCENE TWO

§45. SECTIONAL BIBLIOGRAPHY
for Scene Two of Act IV:
The Burial of Jesus (§§46–48)

Part 1 treats the burial in general [§§46–47], while Part 2 concentrates on the special Matthean scene of the guards at the sepulcher [§48]. For writings on the site of the burial and the Church of the Holy Sepulchre, see above in SECTIONAL BIBLIOGRAPHY §37, Part 2.

Part 1: Overall Bibliography on the Burial of Jesus (§§46–47)

Bakhuizen van der Brink, J. N., "Eine Paradosis zu der Leidensgeschichte," ZNW 26 (1927), 213–19.

Barrick, W. B., "The Rich Man from Arimathea (Matthew 27:57–60) and 1QIsaᵃ," JBL 96 (1977), 235–39.

Bartina, S., "*Othonia* ex papyrorum testimoniis linteamina," *Studia Papyrologica* 4 (1965), 27–38.

Bender, A. P., "Beliefs, Rites and Customs of the Jews, connected with Death, Burial and Mourning," JQR 6 (1894), 317–47, 664–71; 7 (1895), 101–18, 259–69.

Blinzler, J., "Die Grablegung Jesu in historischer Sicht," in *Resurrexit,* ed. É. Dhanis (Vatican: Editrice Vaticana, 1974), 56–107.

———, "*Othonia* und andere Stoffbezeichnungen im 'Wäschekatalog' des Aegypters Theophanes und im Neuen Testament," *Philologus* 99 (1955), 158–66 (in ref. to John 20:5).

———, *Prozess* 385–415 (lacking in his *Trial*).

———, "Zur Auslegung der Evangelienberichte über Jesu Begräbnis," MTZ 3 (1952), 403–14 (reaction to the German form of Bulst, "Novae").

Bornhäuser, K., "Die Kreuzesabnahme und das Begräbnis Jesu," NKZ 42 (1931), 137–68.

Braun, F.-M., "La sépulture de Jésus," RB 45 (1936), 34–52, 184–200, 346–63. Collected in book form in 1937.

Broer, I., *Die Urgemeinde und das Grab Jesu* (SANT 31; Munich: Kösel, 1972).

Brown, R. E., "The Burial of Jesus (Mark 15:42–47)," CBQ 50 (1988), 233–45.

Büchler, A., "L'enterrement des criminels d'après le Talmud et le Midrasch," REJ 46 (1903), 74–88.

Bulst, W., "Novae in sepulturam Jesu inquisitiones," VD 31 (1953), 257–74, 352–59 (on the Shroud of Turin). German form in MTZ 3 (1952), 244–55.

Burkitt, F. C., "Note on Lk. xxiii 51 in the Dura Fragment," JTS 36 (1935), 258–59.

Calleri Damonte, G., "Aloe officinalis o aquilaria agallocha?" *Sindon* 22 (#29; 1980), 48–56.

Charbel, A., "A Sepultura de Jesus como Resulta dos Evangelhos," *Revista de Cultura Biblica* (Sao Paolo) 2 (1978), 351–62.

Cousin, H., "Sépulture criminelle et sépulture prophétique," RB 81 (1974), 375–93.

Craig, W. L., *Assessing the New Testament Evidence for the Historicity of the Resurrection of Jesus* (Lewiston, NY: Mellen, 1989), 163–96.

Curtis, K.P.G., "Three Points of Contact between Matthew and John in the Burial and Resurrection Narratives," JTS NS 23 (1972), 440–44.

Daube, D., "The Anointing at Bethany and Jesus' Burial," ATR 32 (1950), 186–99. Reprinted in DNTRJ 310–24.

de Jonge, M., "Nicodemus and Jesus: Some Observations on Misunderstanding and Understanding in the Fourth Gospel," BJRL 53 (1970–71), 337–59. Cited as reprinted in his *Jesus Stranger from Heaven and Son of God* (SBLSBS 11; Missoula: Scholars Press, 1977), 29–47.

de Kruijf, T. C., "'More than half a hundredweight' of Spices (John 19,39 NEB). Abundance and Symbolism in the Gospel of John," *Bijdragen* 43 (1982), 234–39.

Dhanis, É., "L'ensevelissement de Jésus et la visite au tombeau dans l'évangile de saint Marc (xv,40–xvi,8)," *Gregorianum* 39 (1958), 367–410. Reprinted in *Christus Victor Mortis,* ed. É. Dhanis (Rome: Gregorian, 1958), 167–210.

Ducatillon, J., "Le linceul de Jésus d'après saint Jean," RThom 91 (1991), 421–24.

Figueras, P., "Jewish Ossuaries and Second Burial: Their Significance for Early Christianity," *Immanuel* 19 (1984–85), 41–57.

Gaechter, P., "Zum Begräbnis Jesu," ZKT 75 (1953), 220–25.

García García, L., "'Lienzos', no 'vendas', en la sepultura de Jesús," *Burgense* 32 (1991), 557–67.

Ghiberti, G., *La Sepoltura di Gesù. I Vangeli e la Sindone* (Rome: P. Marietti, 1982).

Giblin, C. H., "Structural and Thematic Correlations in the Matthean Burial-Resurrection Narrative (Matt. xxvii.57–xxviii.20)," NTS 21 (1974–75), 406–20.

Hachlili, R., and A. Killebrew, "Jewish Funerary Customs during the Second Temple Period, in the Light of the Excavations at the Jericho Necropolis," PEQ 115 (1983), 115–26.

Heil, J. P., "The Narrative Structure of Matthew 27:55–28:20," JBL 110 (1991), 419–38.

Hemelsoet, B., "L'ensevelissement selon Saint Jean," in *Studies in John* (J. N. Sevenster Festschrift; NovTSup 24; Leiden: Brill, 1970), 47–65 (on John 19:31–42).

Hepper, F. N., "The Identity and Origin of Classical Bitter Aloes (Aloe)," PEQ 120 (1988), 146–48.

Holtzmann, O., "Das Begräbnis Jesu," ZNW 30 (1931), 311–13.

Jackson, C., "Joseph of Arimathea," *Journal of Religion* 16 (1936), 332–40.

Jeremias, J., *Heiligengräber in Jesu Umwelt* (Göttingen: Vandenhoeck & Ruprecht, 1958).

Joüon, P., "Matthieu xxvii,59: *sindōn kathara,* 'un drap d'un blanc pur,'" RechSR 24 (1934), 93–95.

Kennard, J. S., Jr., "The Burial of Jesus," JBL 74 (1955), 227–38.

Klein, S., *Tod und Begräbnis in Palästina zur Zeit des Tannaiten* (Berlin: H. Itzkowski, 1908).

Krauss, S., "La double inhumation chez les Juifs," REL 97 (1934), 1–34.

Lai, P., "Production du sens par la foi . . . Analyse structurale de Matthieu 27,57–28,20," RechSR 61 (1973), 65–96.

Lieberman, S., "Some Aspects of Afterlife in Early Rabbinic Literature," in *H. A. Wolfson Jubilee Volume* (2 vols.; Jerusalem: Central Press, 1965), 2.495–532. Reprinted in his *Texts and Studies* (New York: Ktav, 1974), 235–73.

Liebowitz, H., "Jewish Burial Practices in the Roman Period," *The Mankind Quarterly* 22 (1981–82), 107–17.

Mahoney, R., *Two Disciples at the Tomb* (Bern: Lang, 1974), 121–40 on John 19:31–42.

Masson, C., "L'ensevelissement de Jésus (Marc xv,42–47)," RTP NS 31 (1943), 193–203. Reprinted in his *Vers les sources de l'eau vive* (Lausanne: Payot, 1961), 102–13.

Mercurio, R., "A Baptismal Motif in the Gospel Narratives of the Burial," CBQ 21 (1959), 39–54.

Meyers, E. M., "Secondary Burials in Palestine," BA 33 (1970), 2–29.

Murphy-O'Connor, J., "Recension: *Die Urgemeinde* . . . par I. Broer," RB 81 (1974), 266–69 (on Joseph of Arimathea).

O'Rahilly, A., "The Burial of Christ," IER 58 (1941), 302–16, 493–503; 59 (1942), 150–71.

———, "Jewish Burial," IER 58 (1941), 123–35.

Pesch, R., "Der Schluss der vormarkischen Passionsgeschichte und des Markusevangeliums: Mk 15,42–16,8," in *L'Évangile selon Marc, Tradition et rédaction,* ed. M. Sabbe (BETL 34; Gembloux: Duculot, 1974), 365–409.

Prete, B., "'E lo legarano con bende' (Giov. 19,40)," BeO 10 (1968), 189–96.

Price, R. M., "Jesus' Burial in a Garden: The Strange Growth of the Tradition," *Religious Traditions* 12 (1989), 17–30.

Puech, É., "Les nécropoles juives palestiniennes au tournant de notre ère," in *Dieu l'a resuscité d'entre les morts* (Les quatres fleuves 15–16; Paris: Beauchesne, 1982), 35–55.

Scholz, G., "'Joseph von Arimathäa' und 'Barabbas,'" LB 57 (1985), 81–94.

Schreiber, J., "Die Bestattung Jesu. Redaktionsgeschichtliche Beobachtungen zu Mk 15, 42–47," ZNW 72 (1981), 141–77.

Senior, D., "Matthew's Account of the Burial of Jesus (Mt 27,57–61)," FGN 2.1433–48.

Shea, G. W., "On the Burial of Jesus in Mark 15:42–47," *Faith & Reason* 17 (1991), 87–108.

Sylva, D. D., "Nicodemus and his Spices (John 19,39)," NTS 34 (1988), 148–51.

Turiot, C., "Sémiotique et lisibilité du texte évangélique," RechSR 73 (1985), 161–75 (on Matt 27:57–28:15).

Vaccari, A., "'*edēsan auto othoniois*' (Ioh. 19,40)," in *Miscellanea Biblica B. Ubach,* ed. R. M. Díaz (Montserrat, 1953), 375–86.

Vander Heeren, A., "In narrationem evangelicam de sepultura Christi," ColB 19 (1914), 435–39.

von Dobschütz, E., "Joseph von Arimathia," *Zeitschrift für Kirchengeschichte* 23 (1902), 1–17.

Part 2: The Guard at the Sepulcher in Matt 27:62–66 (§48)

(See also the bibliography of APPENDIX I on *GPet*)

Craig, W. L., "The Guard at the Tomb," NTS 30 (1984), 273–81.

de Zulueta, F., "Violation of Sepulture in Palestine at the Beginning of the Christian Era," JRS 22 (1932), 184–97.

Kratz, R., *Auferweckung als Befreiung. Eine Studie zur Passions- und der Auferstehungstheologie des Matthäus (besonders Mt 27,62–28,15)* (SBS 65; Stuttgart: KBW, 1973).

Lee, G. M., "The Guard at the Tomb," *Theology* 72 (1969), 169–75.

Metzger, B. M., "The Nazareth Inscription Once Again," *New Testament Studies* (Leiden: Brill, 1980), 75–92. Orig. pub. in *Jesus und Paulus,* ed. E. E. Ellis and E. Grässer (W. G. Kümmel Festschrift; Göttingen: Vandenhoeck & Ruprecht, 1975), 221–38.

Pesch, R., "Eine alttestamentliche Ausführungsformel in Matthäus-Evangelium," BZ NS 11 (1967), 79–95, esp. 91–95 on Matt 28:11–15.

Schmitt, J., "Nazareth (Inscription dite de)," DBSup 6 (1958), 334–63.

Smyth, K., "The Guard on the Tomb," HeyJ 2 (1961), 157–59.

Walker, N., "'After three days' [Matt 27:63]," NovT 4 (1960), 261–62.

Walter, N., "Eine vormatthäische Schilderung der Auferstehung Jesu," NTS 19 (1972–73), 415–29 (on Matt 28:2–4).

§46. THE BURIAL OF JESUS, PART ONE: JOSEPH'S REQUEST FOR THE BODY

(Mark 15:42–45; Matt 27:57–58; Luke 23:50–52; John 19:38a)

Translation

Mark 15:42–45: ⁴²And, it being already evening, since it was preparation day, that is, the day before Sabbath, ⁴³Joseph from Arimathea having come (a respected council member who was also himself awaiting the kingdom of God), having taken courage, came in before Pilate and requested the body of Jesus. ⁴⁴But Pilate was amazed that he had already died; and having called over the centurion, he questioned him if he was dead for some time. ⁴⁵And having come to know from the centurion, he granted the corpse to Joseph.

Matt 27:57–58: ⁵⁷But it being evening, there came a rich man from Arimathea whose name was Joseph, who had also himself been a disciple of Jesus. ⁵⁸This man, having come before Pilate, requested the body of Jesus. Then Pilate ordered (it) to be given up.

Luke 23:50–52: ⁵⁰And behold a man, Joseph by name, being a member of the council, a good and just man—⁵¹he was not in agreement with their decision and course of action—from Arimathea, a city of the Jews, who was awaiting the kingdom of God. ⁵²This man, having come before Pilate, requested the body of Jesus.

John 19:38a: ³⁸ᵃBut after these things Joseph from Arimathea, being a disciple of Jesus but hidden because of fear of the Jews, asked Pilate that he might take away the body of Jesus, and Pilate permitted (it).

GPet 2:3–5: ³But Joseph, the friend of Pilate and of the Lord, had been standing there; and knowing that they were about to crucify him, he came before Pilate and requested the body of the Lord for burial. ⁴And Pilate, having sent to Herod, requested his body. ⁵And Herod said, "Brother Pilate, even if no one had requested him, we would have buried him, since indeed Sabbath is dawning. For in the Law it has been written, 'The sun is not to set on one put to death.'"

5cAnd he gave him [Jesus] over to the people before the first day of their feast of the Unleavened Bread.

6:23: And the Jews rejoiced and gave his body to Joseph that he might bury it, since he was one who had seen how many good things he did.

COMMENT

The treatment of Jesus' burial will be divided into three sections. The first section (§46) centers on the request for the body made by Joseph to Pilate. Discussion of this request will necessitate a treatment of Roman and Jewish attitudes toward burial of the crucified, and an understanding of the motives of Joseph from Arimathea. The second section (§47) will treat the placing of Jesus' body in the tomb, with some who knew Jesus observing the burial (the women) and others taking part in it (Nicodemus). Here there will be reflection on Jewish burial customs that might distinguish an honorable burial from a dishonorable one. The third section (§48), which constitutes an epilogue and runs over into the resurrection account, will be devoted to Matt's story of the guard placed at the sepulcher.

In all this the clear and unanimous Gospel presentation is that Jesus was given a distinguishable burial in a place that could be remembered. His was not the type of common burial in which corpses could be confused;[1] nor was he buried and then reburied, so that the women went to the wrong tomb on Easter and that is why they found it empty.[2] These last two suggestions,

[1]We must be careful to recognize limitations in our knowledge of burial practices in Jesus' lifetime. Even before recent sensitivity about the limited applicability of the Mishna to Jesus' time, and therefore about mishnaic rules for burying the bodies of the condemned, Büchler ("Enterrement" 74–75) recognized that the references to burial in Josephus indicated a different situation in the 1st cent. from that envisaged by later information.

[2]Following in the footsteps of G. Baldensperger, *Le tombeau vide* (Études d'histoire et de philosophie religieuses; Univ. de Strasbourg, 30; Paris: F. Alcan, 1935), Kennard ("Burial" 233) would make Joseph's own tomb separate from the tomb in which the women saw Jesus placed, and make Joseph the one who reburied Jesus, unbeknown to the women. Answering such flights of the imagination belongs to the "empty tomb" sections of books on the resurrection. See P. De Haes, *La résurrection de Jésus dans l'apologétique des cinquante dernières années* (Analecta Gregoriana 59; Rome: Gregorian Univ., 1953), esp. 215–33; Craig, *Assessing* 163–96. A different type of twofold burial is advocated by Bulst ("Novae") in order to make the Gospel evidence fit the image of the Shroud of Turin; his theory is vigorously criticized by Blinzler ("Zur Auslegung").

typical of rationalist attempts to disprove the reality of the resurrection, find no support in the Gospel text or in primitive Christian tradition.[3] Passages like Rom 6:4 and Col 2:12 treat the burial of Jesus as an accepted basis for theological conclusions, and the prePauline tradition (stemming from the 30s?) in I Cor 15:3–5 fixes the burial of Jesus in an established chain: Christ died, he was buried, he was raised, and he appeared. How does this Christian memory of a distinguishable burial fit into what we know of Roman and Jewish attitudes toward the bodies of those executed by crucifixion? (Mark gives no hint that there was anything extraordinary in the fact that Jesus was buried, and so presumably information about ordinary attitudes on this issue would be pertinent.) Let us look at that issue before we treat the individual Gospel accounts of the request made to Pilate by Joseph from Arimathea.

ROMAN ATTITUDES TOWARD THE BODIES OF THE CRUCIFIED

In investigating Roman customs or laws dealing with the burial of crucified criminals, we find some guidance in DJ 48.24,[4] which gives the clement views of Ulpian and of Julius Paulus from the period ca. AD 200. The bodies of those who suffer capital punishment are not to be refused to their relatives (Ulpian) nor to any who seek them for burial (Paulus). Ulpian traces this attitude back to Augustus in Book 10 of *Vita Sua*, but he recognizes that the generous granting of bodies may have to be refused if the condemnation has been for treason (*maiestas*). The exception was verified a few years before Ulpian in the treatment of the martyrs of Lyons reported in Eusebius (EH 5.1.61–62): The bodies of the crucified Christians were displayed for six days and then burned so that the ashes might be scattered in the Rhone. Christian fellow-disciples complained, "We could not bury the bodies in the earth . . . neither did money or prayers move them, for in every possible way they kept guard as if the prevention of burial would give them great gain."

If we move back from the 2d cent., what was the Roman attitude at the time of Jesus toward the bodies of crucified criminals? Despite what Ulpian tells us about Augustus, he was not always so clement. Suetonius (*Augustus* 13.1–2) reports, with the obvious disapproval of 2d-cent. hindsight, that Augustus refused to allow decent burial for the bodies of those who fought for

---

[3]The first Christian passage known to me that could give any support to any of these hypotheses is the peculiar inscription of Archbishop Hypatius of Ephesus from the year 536. In reference to the self-abasement of Jesus, it observes that not only did he humble himself on a cross, but after his death, "as the tradition of the evangelist runs, he was thrown out [*aporiptein*] naked and without burial; then in the property of Joseph was he buried, laid in that man's tomb." Bakhuizen van der Brink ("Paradosis" 217) suggests that the root of this "tradition" may be in the parable of Mark 12:8 about the son of the owner of the vineyard: "Taking, they killed him and threw him out [*ekballein*]."

[4]Also T. Mommsen, *Römisches*, 987–90.

Brutus: "That matter must be settled with the carrion-birds." Since Augustus would have looked on Brutus as a traitor, the parallel to the question of what would happen to those convicted of treason (*maiestas*) is significant. In the reign of terror that followed the fall of Sejanus (AD 31), Tacitus reports the actions of Tiberius: "People sentenced to death forfeited their property and were forbidden burial" (*Annals* 6.29). Beyond such imperial vengeance, severity is assumed to be normal by Petronius (*Satyricon* 111–12), as in Nero's time he writes the story of a soldier at Ephesus who neglected his duty of preventing the bodies of dead criminals from being removed from the cross. While he was absent in the night making love to a widow, parents came stealthily, took the body down, and buried it, causing the soldier to fear the severest punishment. Evidently it was almost proverbial that those who hung on the cross fed the crows with their bodies (Horace, *Epistle* 1.16.48).

Discerning Roman legal practice for a province like Judea is difficult. The law cited above (DJ) was *juxta ordinem,* i.e., customary law in Rome for dealing with Roman citizens. Decisions in the provinces dealing with non-citizens were most often *extra ordinem,* so that such a matter as the disposition of crucified bodies would have been left to the local magistrate. Before Jesus' time, in Sicily, much closer to Rome, Cicero (*In Verrem* 2.5.45; #119) reports that a corrupt governor made parents pay for permission to bury their children. Philo (*In Flaccum* 10.83–84) tells us that in Egypt, on the eve of a Roman holiday, customarily "people who have been crucified have been taken down and their bodies delivered to their kinfolk, because it was thought well to give them burial and allow them ordinary rites." But the prefect Flaccus (within a decade of Jesus' death) "gave no orders to take down those who had died on the cross," even on the eve of a feast. Indeed, he crucified others, after maltreating them with the lash. Looking at the total picture, what can we say of the likely attitude of Pilate dealing with Jesus, who was crucified on the charge of being "the King of the Jews" in the time of Tiberius? I have contended in §31B that Pilate was not overly brutal, and as a Roman governor he would not have been likely to punish needlessly a criminal's family. But in charges of treason Roman governors were anxious that the convicted criminal not be regarded as a hero to be imitated. Whether the case of Jesus should be considered an example of *maiestas* (§31D) is debatable; but if it was, little indeed would be the likelihood that the prefect of Judea would have given the body of this crucified would-be-king to his followers for burial.[5] True, even according to Mark (who does not have Pilate affirm Jesus' innocence as do the other evangelists) Pilate suspects that the

---

[5]If a governor wanted to be merciful, he would more likely have given the body to the family of the crucified. It is interesting that no Gospel even raises this possibility, although, of course, only John has family members present for the crucifixion (19:25–27: the mother of Jesus and her sister).

accusation against Jesus is from motives other than those professed (15:10). Nevertheless, in the logic of the story, having committed himself to a public action, Pilate would have had to be apprehensive about possible idolizing of Jesus by his followers and about the severity of the emperor in matters relating to *maiestas*.

JEWISH ATTITUDES TOWARD THE BODIES OF THE CRUCIFIED

As we have seen (pp. 532–33 above), there is solid evidence that in Jesus' era crucifixion came under the Jewish laws and customs governing hanging, and in particular under Deut 21:22–23: "If there shall be against someone a crime judged worthy of death, and he be put to death and you hang him on a tree, his body shall not remain all night on the tree; but you shall bury him the same day, for cursed of God is the one hanged." The conflict between Roman and Jewish attitudes is phrased thus by S. Lieberman: "The Roman practice of depriving executed criminals of the rite of burial and exposing the corpses on the cross for many days . . . horrified the Jews."[6] In the First Jewish Revolt the Idumeans cast out corpses without burial. Commenting with disgust on this, Josephus states, "The Jews are so careful about funeral rites that even those who are crucified because they were found guilty are taken down and buried before sunset."[7]

The crucial issue in Judaism, however, would have been the type of burial. The hanged person was accursed, especially since most often in Jewish legal practice this punishment would have been meted out to those already executed in another way, e.g., stoning.[8] In the OT we see a tendency to refuse to the wicked *honorable* burial in an ancestral plot (I Kings 13:21–22). Even a king like Jehoiakim, despite his rank, having been condemned by the Lord for wickedness, had these words spoken of him by Jeremiah (22:19): "The burial of an ass shall be given him, dragged and cast forth beyond the gates of Jerusalem." Jer 26:23 refers to a prophet condemned (unjustly) and slain by the king being thrown "into the burial place of the common people" (see also II Kings 23:6). *I Enoch* 98:13 excludes from prepared graves the wicked who rejoice in the death of the righteous, and Josephus (*Ant.* 5.1.14; #44) has Achar at nightfall given "the ignominious burial proper to the con-

---

[6]"Some" 2.517. Evidently when the authorities refused to grant the body for burial, sometimes Jews took it into their own hands and stole the body; the later rabbinic *Semaḥot ('Ebel Rabbati)* 2.11 forbids that.

[7]*War* 4.5.2; #317. Such practice applied even to suicides and the bodies of enemies (*War* 3.8.5; #377) and to all those who were condemned by Jewish laws to be put to death (*Ant.* 4.8.24; #264–65).

[8]See the debate in Mishna *Sanhedrin* 6.4: "All that were stoned were then hanged, according to Rabbi Eliezer; but the Sages say, 'No one is hanged except the blasphemer and the idolater.'"

demned" (see also 4.8.24; #264). The account of the death of Judas in Matt 27:5–8 shows that the Jews of Jesus' time[9] would think of a common burial place for the despised, not a family tomb. By the time of the Mishna (*Sanhedrin* 6.5), there is a reference to two places of burial which "were maintained in readiness by the court, one for those who were beheaded or strangled, and the other for those who were stoned or burned." Tosepta *Sanhedrin* 9.8 states, "Even if the criminal were king of kings, he may not be buried in the grave of his fathers, but only in that prepared by the court." (Some have thought that the wording of that passage was polemically phrased against Christians.) Once the flesh of the deceased criminal had decomposed, the bones could be gathered and buried in the ancestral burial place (Mishna *Sanhedrin* 6.6). (Obviously, the common burial place provided by the court is not thought of as an indistinguishable common grave or charnel house where corpses could be confused, for the bones had to be recoverable.) Some aspects of the mishnaic practice were surely ideal or reflect a post-NT situation (see n. 1 above); but the bones of the crucified Yehohanan ben *ḥgqwl*, found in a 1st-cent. burial place at Giv'at ha-Mivtar in 1968 (p. 950 above), were in an ossuary[10] adjacent to the ossuary of Simon the builder of the Temple, so that the honorable second burial of the crucified was not so late a practice as once thought.

How would this attitude that criminals should receive (at first) shameful burial be applicable to those crucified by Gentiles? In the Bible and the Mishna there is an assumption that the condemned person was punishable by death under Jewish law, which is God's law. In a political situation where the death penalty was imposed by Gentiles, however, the opposite could be true: An innocent or noble Jew might be crucified for something that did not come under the law of God, or indeed for keeping the divine law. We find this issue raised in TalBab *Sanhedrin* 47a–47b when Abaye complains, "Would you compare those who are slain by a [Gentile] government to those who are executed by the Beth Din? The former, since their death is not in accordance with [Jewish] law, obtain forgiveness; but the latter, whose death is justly merited, are not [thereby] forgiven." Such a distinction had to be made much earlier, or there could have been no tradition of an honorable burial for the Maccabean martyrs.[11] Thus we cannot discount the possibility of an honorable first burial of one crucified by the Romans.

What would have been the Jewish attitude toward the crucified Jesus? A desire to get his body off the cross before sunset is implicit in the appeal of Joseph to Pilate in the Synoptics and explicit in John 19:31; *GPet* 2:5; 5:15.

---

[9]Whether fact or legend, Matt's story clearly took shape among Palestinian Jewish Christians.

[10]For ossilegium, see Meyers, "Secondary"; Figueras, "Jewish."

[11]M. Hadas, *The Third and Fourth Books of the Maccabees* (New York: Harper, 1953), 104–13.

Yet would the tendency have been to give Jesus an honorable or dishonorable burial? According to Mark/Matt the Sanhedrin found him worthy of death on the charge of blasphemy, and Josephus (*Ant.* 4.8.6; #202) would have the blasphemer stoned, hung, "and buried ignominiously and in obscurity." *Mart. of Polycarp* 17:2 has Jews instigating opposition lest the body of Polycarp be given to his adherents for honorable burial. On the other hand, Jesus was executed by the Romans not for blasphemy but on the charge of being the King of the Jews. Could this have been regarded as a death not in accordance with Jewish law and so not necessarily subjecting the crucified to dishonorable burial?

With that background we are now ready to seek to understand the Gospel narratives of Joseph's request to Pilate.

THE REQUEST FOR BURIAL ACCORDING TO MARK 15:42–45

For the whole burial scene Mark is the key account among the Synoptics since there is no solid reason to think that Matt or Luke knew anything beyond what Mark supplied them. In this first section also John is very close to the Marcan picture; and if John is independent of Mark, that similarity would cause us to think that here Mark has not departed greatly from common preGospel tradition. A careful and detailed discussion of Mark, then, may save time in discussing the other Gospels.

Time Indication (15:42). Mark gives two time indications plus an explanation of the second. The first is "it being already evening [*opsia*]."[12] What precise hour of the day is meant? According to the last time specification given (15:34,37) Jesus had screamed out at the ninth hour (3 P.M.) and then expired. Jewish law would have the crucified taken down and buried before sunset, which would mark the beginning of another day. By narrative flow, then, the setting is somewhere between 3 P.M. and sunset. In itself *opsia* does not convey precise information about relationship to the opening of the next day.[13] Mark's "already" and the following "since" are the only hints that Joseph was conscious of temporal pressure and must have hastened. The actions now about to be described (going before Pilate who would call in the

---

[12]*Ginesthai* in the genitive absolute as a way of indicating time that had already "become" is a formulation Mark uses nine times.

[13]An example of its imprecision is found in Matt 14:15,23b where "it being evening" both precedes and follows the multiplication of the loaves as if the action had taken no time. In passages like Matt 14:15 and 20:8 "evening" seems to be late afternoon, whereas in 16:2 the sun seems to have already set. As for Marcan usage, previous instances of *opsia* were accompanied by precisions fixing the time. In 1:32 *opsia* was refined by "when the sun had set"; in 14:17, when *opsia* had come, Jesus and the Twelve came and sat for the Passover supper, a meal that could not be eaten until the next day had begun.

centurion, buying a linen cloth, taking the body down, tying it up, and putting it in a burial place) would have taken not much less than two hours. Consequently, by logic rather than by simple translation, interpreters assume that Mark has in mind late afternoon, no earlier than ca. 4:30 P.M. What should be emphasized is that *opsia* fits into a series of time references that Mark has been giving us in relation to the death of Jesus (15:1,25,33,34: early, 3d, 6th, 9th hours), so that sequence more than precision is intended.[14] Indeed, if we had chosen to begin the discussion of the PN with the Last Supper, the "evening" reference in 14:17 that began the supper account could form an inclusion with the "evening" here to mark the beginning and the end.

The second Marcan time indication, "since it was preparation day [*paraskeuē*]," besides showing that it was still Friday and that the next day had not begun, makes more intelligible why Mark went to the trouble of telling us that it was *already* evening. While discussing *paraskeuē* in John 19:14 (§35), I indicated that it rendered Hebrew *'ereb* ("vigil, day before") but added the tone of making ready for an important next day. To explain this concept to his (Gentile) readers Mark adds a rendering that is more than a literal translation: "that is, the day before Sabbath." The initial *ho estin* ("that is") has been used by Mark eight times before; and in 3:17; 5:41; 7:11,34, 15:22,34 it signaled the rendering of Aramaic words into Greek for intelligibility. Evidently, then, Mark did not deem Greek *paraskeuē* sufficiently enlightening in itself for his readers; he translated it in relation to the Sabbath, for even Gentiles would know that Jewish people regarded the Sabbath as holy and did not work on that day.[15] (Indeed, if *paraskeuē* was preMarcan [p. 1238 below], Mark may have clarified it by explanatory phrases both before ["it being already evening"] and after.) On p. 1174 above, in treating the almost identical "since it was preparation day" in John 19:31, I judged it unlikely that either evangelist thought that the necessity of getting the crucified off the tree (cross) occurred only on the eve of a Sabbath (or of a feast day). Rather their mutual stress on the oncoming Sabbath reflects both the intensified sense of Jewish outrage that a sacred day would be profaned[16] and the greater chance that at such a time to avoid trouble the Romans might consent

---

[14]The "already" (*ēdē*) of 15:42, placed before *opsia*, is in relation to the previous time indication of the 9th hour, even if indirectly it suggests urgency.

[15]Interestingly, when Josephus uses *paraskeuē* (*Ant.* 16.6.2; #163), he also explains it as being before the Sabbath.

[16]In later rabbinic times the necessity for respecting the Sabbath in terms of burial is illustrated by the legend that at the death of Rabbi Judah ha-Nasi on the eve of the Sabbath all the inhabitants of Israel assembled to mourn, and by divine providence the day was miraculously extended until each Israelite was able to reach home and kindle the Sabbath light (*Midrash Rabbah* on Ecclesiastes 7:12; #1).

to have the bodies taken down. It is worth noting that *GPet* 2:5 agrees that it was the day both before the oncoming (dawning) Sabbath and "before the first day of their feast of the Unleavened Bread" (i.e., similar to John 19:14, which explains it as the day before Passover), although it is the Sabbath time indication that is cited in this *GPet* verse in relation to burial before sunset.

The Marcan Description of Joseph from Arimathea (15:43). The fact that all the Gospels mention Joseph here for the first time, that Arimathea (a non-Galilean site[17]) was his birthplace or identifying residence, and that he is pictured as having "come" on the scene after the death of Jesus makes it clear that none of the evangelists thinks of this man as a Galilean follower of Jesus or as someone who had hitherto been involved in the PN. In both these features he differs from the Twelve[18] and from the women (and those known to him in Luke) who observed the death of Jesus from afar. Perhaps because of this Mark supplies more than the usual information about him, but unfortunately in an extremely convoluted sentence.[19]

"A respected council member" (*euschēmōn bouleutēs*) is the first item of information. Mark's Gentile readers could understand this: In their own region they would have had a city or town council (*boulē*), and in inscriptions honoring public administrators *euschēmōn* occurs frequently.[20] That Joseph was an outstanding member of the city council that ran Jerusalem would have been the impression given. Using *synedrion* ("Sanhedrin") Mark has twice in the PN (14:55; 15:1) referred to the authoritative body at Jerusalem that found Jesus guilty, a body which consisted of "all the chief priests, and

---

[17]Matt and *GPet* (by intuitive interpretation of the tradition and probably not on the basis of private historical information) tell us that the tomb near Golgotha where Jesus was buried was Joseph's own tomb. However, since many Jews wanted to be buried in the Jerusalem area near the Temple, the Jerusalem location of Joseph's tomb does not necessarily tell us that Joseph lived in the Jerusalem area. Luke calls Arimathea "a city of the Jews" (23:51), meaning that it was in Judea. By many it has been identified with Ramathaim-zophim of I Sam 1:1. In his *Onomasticon* Eusebius suggested Remphthis or Rentis, 9 miles NE of Lydda. (I Macc 11:34 associates Lydda and Rathamin [Ramathaim] as districts.) Yet W. F. Albright, *Annual of the American Schools of Oriental Research* 4 (1922–23), 112–23, rejects the Rentis identification and proposes Ramallah. Another suggestion is Beit Rimeh, 5 miles E of Rentis and about 12 miles NW of Bethel. None of these sites is in Galilee.

[18]*GPet* 6:23 and 7:26 heighten the difference: Joseph is present for the burial while the Twelve are in hiding.

[19]Gnilka (*Markus* 2.331) points out awkward grammar, e.g., the duplicated verbs "having come [*erchesthai*] . . . came in before [*eiserchesthai pros*]." Although Mark means that Joseph stemmed from Arimathea, he could be read to mean that he came from Arimathea to go in before Pilate.

[20]Used only here in Mark, *euschēmōn* means "prominent, honorable, outstanding." In Acts 13:50 Jews incite "prominent" citizens against Paul and Barnabas; in Acts 17:12 "prominent" Greek women as well as men become believers in Jesus. In I Cor 7:35; 12:24, and in the only LXX instance (Prov 11:25) the meaning is "fitting, honorable." The attempt of Schreiber ("Bestattung" 143, n. 4) to connect the description of Joseph as *euschēmōn* with the rich people who put large sums in the treasury (Mark 12:41–44) and with the godless rich of Isa 22:16 who have hewn tombs for themselves and "habitations in the rock" is implausible. There is no connection in vocabulary, and in Mark he is not said to be rich or the owner of the tomb. The Marcan description is clearly positive.

the elders, and the scribes" (14:53). As I showed above (§18, B2), in the course of history that body was referred to in Greek with a certain inter-changeableness both as *boulē* and *synedrion;* and Josephus (*War* 2.17.1; #405) uses *bouleutēs* for council members associated with the ruling authorities in Jerusalem. Most probably, then, Mark wanted his readers to know that Joseph was a distinguished member of the Sanhedrin,[21] even though previously Mark has portrayed *all* the Sanhedrists as having sought testimony against Jesus in order to put him to death (14:55: "the whole Sanhedrin"), as having judged him guilty, punishable by death (14:64), and as having given him over to Pilate (15:1: "the whole Sanhedrin"). "All" and "whole" may well be Marcan hyperbole, but their use creates a mindset among readers about the Sanhedrin opposition to Jesus. Thus there is nothing in Mark's first item of information about Joseph to make readers think of him as a follower or supporter of Jesus.

"Who was also himself awaiting [*prosdechesthai:*[22] looking for] the kingdom of God" is Mark's second item of information about Joseph. The "himself" may connote an element of the unexpected, granted the previous information. The "also" indicates that he is being compared to others who were awaiting the kingdom. Before Jesus' death Mark described those who mocked him as king (and thus were not awaiting the kingdom) and after Jesus' death those who were in various ways sympathetic to him. In the immediately preceding 15:39–41 the latter consisted of the centurion who, though previously not a follower of Jesus, was moved to confess him, and the women who followed him in Galilee. Joseph was "also" one of this type, but Mark does not make clear whether the similarity is to the women (al-

---

[21]Patently this is the way Luke (23:50–51) understood Mark. Those who object to this conclusion ask why, having employed *synedrion* twice, Mark shifts to *bouleutēs* to describe a member thereof. Beyond the greater intelligibility of *boulē* to Greek readers mentioned above, it is noteworthy that no NT author ever uses a denominative from *synedrion* to describe a Sanhedrin member, e.g., *synedros* or *synedriakos*. Could Mark in practice have thought of *bouleutēs* as the standard term for such a figure? The suggestion of Winter ("Marginal" 244) that Joseph was not a member of the Great Sanhedrin but of the Beth Din or lower court whose duty it was to see that those executed received decent burial is doubly defective: Not only does Mark's Greek offer no reason to think of a separate body, but there is no solid evidence that such a diversity of bodies existed in the Jerusalem of Jesus' time (see §18, B2). Even more incautious is Shea's conclusion ("Burial" 89–90) that Joseph was a member of the high priest's consistory or cabinet that consisted of priests and laymen—a conclusion that ignores our lack of precise knowledge about the makeup of a Sanhedrin in Jesus' lifetime (§18, C1).

[22]Never found in Matt or John, but seven times in Luke-Acts. This is a periphrastic construction that lends force to the verb. Schreiber ("Bestattung" 143–45) interprets *prosdechesthai* in the light of Mark 4:12, "seeing but not perceiving," so that Joseph becomes a pious legalist who ignores Exod 23:1,7 about killing the innocent but is concerned about the body! How anyone can read this description as negative defies imagination. Given the eminent value according to "the kingdom of God" in Mark, readers would surely interpret "awaiting the kingdom of God" positively. If Mark was describing a plotting legalist, as Schreiber contends, then independently Matt and Luke have completely misunderstood Mark by seeing Joseph as a positive figure.

ready followers) or to the centurion (not a follower at this moment but open to becoming one). This is Mark's only use of *prosdechesthai,* and so we have to look at other synonymous expressions related to the kingdom to see what the readers of Mark or of Matt would have understood by "awaiting the kingdom of God."

Surely the disciples of Jesus, specifically the Twelve, would have been covered by that phrase, since to them was given "the mystery of the kingdom of God" (4:10–11). Therefore many interpreters from early times to the 20th cent. have understood Mark as affirming that Joseph was a disciple.[23] If that was what Mark meant, why did he take such an indirect and obscure way of saying so?[24] He showed no such indirection in reporting the burial of JBap (6:29): "His *disciples* . . . came and took his corpse and put it in a tomb." Actually, "awaiting the kingdom of God" could describe a common Jewish anticipation covering many others beyond the disciples of Jesus. In 1QS[b] 5:21 there is a blessing for the Prince of the Congregation: ". . . that he may establish the kingdom of His [God's] people forever." The Qaddish, an early Jewish prayer, asks, "May He establish His kingdom in your days." In Mark itself (12:34) there was a scribe who asked Jesus about the commandments and admired Jesus' knowledge of the Law but who did not specifically follow him—the scribe was said to be "not far from the kingdom of God." Thus for Mark those who awaited the kingdom covered both disciples and pious observers of the Law who were outside the discipleship. Was the latter category closed to Joseph because he was one of the Sanhedrin that was "seeking testimony against Jesus in order to put him to death" (14:55)? It is noteworthy that Mark does not say, as does Matt 26:59, "seeking *false* testimony against Jesus. . . ." For Mark, clearly the chief priests and the scribes acted with deceit (14:1); and the chief priests were envious and malicious (15:10,31). But there were other members of the Sanhedrin who had to be led by the high priest to say that Jesus had culpably blasphemed (14:63–64) and so should be punished by death. If the Marcan Joseph was among those

---

[23]Matt 27:57 describes Joseph as a disciple of Jesus (as does John 19:38a). But is Matt interpreting Mark's meaning or changing it? Luke did not see such an implication in Mark.

[24]One answer proposes deliberate obscurity on Mark's part because he found it hard to present a Sanhedrin member who was at the same time a disciple of Jesus. This is not a satisfactory solution, granted that Mark could have avoided such a difficulty by not writing that "the whole Sanhedrin" condemned Jesus. Shea ("Burial" 91), following Blinzler ("Grablegung" 69), would argue that Mark did not call Joseph a disciple because he confined that term to those who accompanied Jesus on his journeys. This is too narrow an appreciation of what discipleship meant for Mark. E. Best, *Following Jesus: Discipleship in the Gospel of Mark* (JSNTSup 4; Sheffield Univ. 1981), 39, makes clear that following Jesus, which is the characteristic of a disciple in Mark, involves the imitation of Christ; it is primarily a spiritual following rather than a geographical one. "The disciples are on a journey, or pilgrimage, on which they travel after Jesus seeking a dedication like his . . ." (p. 246). If Mark thought that Joseph (who was awaiting the kingdom of God) believed in Jesus, there is nothing in that description that would have stopped Mark from describing him as a disciple.

Sanhedrin members, he might be described as a pious Jew who awaited the kingdom of God in the sense that he sought only to obey the commandments, much as the scribe of 12:28.[25]

From all that Mark has reported so far, then, there is a possibility and even likelihood that Mark is not describing Joseph as a disciple of Jesus. We have to ask now whether that interpretation is refuted by the next two clauses in 15:43, namely, that it took courage for him to come in before Pilate, and that he requested the body of Jesus. The logic of my response will be easier to grasp if I treat the two clauses in reverse order.

The end of Mark 15:43 tells us that Joseph "came in before Pilate and requested the body of Jesus."[26] One can understand a disciple of Jesus requesting his body for burial; but why would a pious, law-observant member of the Sanhedrin who was not a disciple of Jesus want to bury the body of a crucified blasphemer? It would have been a matter of obeying God's will, for the deuteronomic law required that even a criminal's body not be left on the cross after sunset, a situation all the more binding because the next day was the Sabbath. Sometimes an objection is raised that if Joseph's request were granted, contact with the corpse would have rendered him impure, a status that a pious Jew would have wanted to avoid. As we shall see below, probably he would not have done the burying alone and would have had servants helping him; but let us not resort to that explanation, since servants are not mentioned in the narrative. Those who wrote the deuteronomic law did so knowing that anyone who handled a corpse would become impure;[27] clearly burial was seen as a necessary good that overshadowed the accompanying impurity. I showed above when treating Jewish attitudes how seriously the burial of corpses was taken in Jesus' time. A later example from the Mishna (*Nazir* 7.1) debates whether the high priest himself, upon encountering a stray corpse, would have to bury it even at the cost of becoming contaminated. Thus Joseph's concern about burying Jesus was perfectly consistent with Jewish piety.[28] A particular objection has been raised as to

[25]One of those who consented to the execution of Stephen was Saul of Tarsus (Acts 8:1), clearly a person who awaited the kingdom of God—not a disciple of Jesus, but open to becoming one when enlightened. The thesis that Joseph was a pious Sanhedrist who only in developing Christian tradition was thought to have been a disciple at the time of the burial was impressively presented by Masson, "Ensevelissement"; I developed it further in my article "Burial."

[26]All three Synoptics use the verb *aitein* ("to request") here, the same verb that Mark used earlier in 15:8 when the crowd came up to Pilate and "began to request (that he do) as he used to do for them," i.e., release at the feast a prisoner whom they requested.

[27]On this issue of impurity see the detailed discussion in Mishna *Oholot*.

[28]Why did Joseph not request the bodies of the criminals crucified on either side of Jesus? We have to assume that the story in the Synoptics has been narrowed down in its focus to Jesus, ignoring the two others who were no longer theologically or dramatically important. Craig, *Assessing* 176, raises the possibility that if Joseph were both a delegate of the Sanhedrin and a secret disciple, he obtained all three bodies but disposed of the criminals' bodies in a common grave.

whether such piety would allow Joseph to bury a crucified criminal on Passover Day. As we have seen, however, Mark mentions Passover only in reference to Jesus' meal on Thursday night and then seems to ignore the Passover-daytime setting in describing all the subsequent activity of the Sanhedrin and the crucifixion. In fidelity to what Mark emphasizes, there is no reason to bring the Passover into our quest for intelligibility in the burial scene, any more than we needed to bring that dating into the trial scene.

Why, if Joseph was not a disciple of Jesus, did it take courage on his part to approach Pilate?[29] The Marcan Pilate, who had perceived that Jesus had been given over to him by the Sanhedrin out of envious zeal (5:10: *phthonos*), conceivably might have been suspicious if a Sanhedrist bothered him again. Or was Joseph afraid that in asking for Jesus' body, he might be mistaken as a sympathizer in the cause of "the King of the Jews" and thus be tainted by *maiestas,* in Roman eyes a crime taken very seriously? Cicero (*Phillipic* 1.9; #23) admitted that while originally he had disapproved of the *Lex Iulia de maiestate* (p. 717 above), that law should be scrupulously observed for the sake of peace. Suetonius (*Tiberius* 58) tells us: "A praetor asked Tiberius whether in his opinion courts should be convened to try cases of treason [*maiestas*]. Tiberius replied that the law must be enforced, and indeed he did enforce it most savagely." Tacitus (*Annals* 6.8) mentions Tiberius' inane suspicions about everyone who had been friendly with Sejanus, who was guilty of treason. If in such a context it took courage for Joseph to come in before Pilate to request the body of a criminal crucified as a would-be king, what would save him was that he was a respected member of the Sanhedrin that had given this criminal over for prosecution. Incidentally, in the light of Roman attitudes explained at the beginning of this section, the Marcan account is far more plausible than are the Matthean and Lucan accounts. A prefect would not have been likely to give the body to a disciple of Jesus (Matt) or to a member of the Sanhedrin who had argued for finding Jesus not guilty (Luke).[30]

---

[29]The *tolmēsas* of Mark 15:43 apparently remained difficult even if one thought of him as a disciple or at least as favorable to Jesus, for it was omitted both by Matt (for whom Joseph was a disciple) and by Luke (for whom Joseph did not agree with the Sanhedrin decision against Jesus). In an article that indulges in constant harmonization and assumes that every detail is historical, Shea ("Burial" 95) would explain that the courage of Joseph (a disciple of Jesus) in coming "in before" Pilate was exhibited in ignoring the ritual impurity that John 18:29 (he means 18:28b) says would be incurred if "the Jews" entered the praetorium. Since Mark never mentions such impurity, how would Mark's readers even think of that possibility? As for John, he does not say that Joseph *came in* before Pilate.

[30]Scholz ("Joseph" 82–84), drawing on the Marcan use of *paradidonai* ("to give over"), sees Pilate's giving Jesus to Joseph as a positive action, for a worthy burial—even though no Gospel uses the verb *paradidonai* for this action! See the discussion on p. 1226 below. The argument that Pilate might simply have chosen to be gracious to Joseph the disciple of Jesus fits neither what Mark tells us about Pilate's cynical behavior at the trial (15:10,15), nor Josephus' account of Pilate, nor Roman

Why, if Joseph was not a disciple of Jesus, did he give Jesus an honorable burial? This objection, in my judgment, is based on a false premise. It assumes that the *sindōn* or "linen cloth" that Mark 15:46 describes as being bought and used by Joseph to tie up and bury Jesus was fine or expensive material (thus Shea, "Burial" 96–97). That is far from verifiable, granted the wide range of the uses of *sindōn* for garments of different shapes, size, and uses. Indeed, to make it clear that the disciple Joseph treated Jesus' body properly Matt (27:59) has to add that the "linen cloth" was "clean white." I shall argue in §47 below that Mark describes the sparest type of burial, marked by haste and lacking in amenities.

The contention that Mark was presenting Joseph as a pious Sanhedrist but not as a disciple of Jesus makes sense of a detail that is the Achilles' heel of the disciple interpretation. No canonical Gospel shows cooperation between Joseph and the women followers of Jesus who are portrayed as present at the burial, observing where Jesus was put (Mark 15:47 and par.).[31] Lack of cooperation in burial between two groups of Jesus' disciples is not readily intelligible, especially when haste was needed. Why did the women not help Joseph if he was a fellow disciple, instead of planning to come back after the Sabbath when he would not be there?[32] Lack of cooperation between the women followers of Jesus and a Sanhedrist responsible for the death of Jesus whose only wish was to get the criminal's corpse buried is quite intelligible. He would not have allowed them near precisely because they were followers of Jesus. *GPet* 12:50 dramatizes what Mark implies by specifying that (on the day of death) *the Jews* had prevented Mary Magdalene from rendering at the tomb the customary burial services to the beloved.

This interpretation of Mark also makes sense of some other notices about the burial of Jesus that may represent ancient tradition. (With effort all the

---

crucifixion customs. If one wants to posit that Joseph was Jesus' disciple, the Marcan Pilate's behavior makes sense only if Pilate did not know this hidden fact; but then one has removed much of the daring that caused positing discipleship in the first place.

[31]This discussion seeks to make sense of the present narrative where Joseph and the Galilean women appear in the same scene. If one argues that the women were absent from the preMarcan burial narrative (p. 1277 below), the thesis that Joseph was a disciple would present a problem about why they stayed away. I have contended that there was a preGospel tradition that three Galilean women (one of them was Mary Magdalene) observed from afar the death of Jesus on the cross. There is a very strong tradition that Mary Magdalene went to the tomb on Easter morning. If the Joseph who took down the body of Jesus from the cross was a disciple, why did she not come to the burial and help him when haste was important?

[32]Shea ("Burial" 105) would explain the lack of cooperation on the grounds that Jewish women were not supposed to talk with men in public, especially with strangers (Joseph is a stranger because he was a Judean disciple of Jesus and they were Galilean ones!), and sexes were segregated at funerals. Where in the Gospels (except in John 4 where Jesus speaks to a Samaritan woman) is there any problem about women talking to men? As for funeral customs, John (20:14–15) has no difficulty about Magdalene at the tomb addressing a man whom she thinks is a gardener.

following are capable of being explained in another way, but their wording favors a burial of Jesus by Jews condemnatory of Jesus rather than by his disciples.) A sermon in Acts 13:27–29 reports: "Those who lived in Jerusalem and their rulers . . . requested Pilate to have him killed; and when they had fulfilled all that was written of him, *they* took him down from the tree and placed him in a tomb."[33] John 19:31 tells us that *the Jews* asked Pilate that the legs of the crucified be broken and they be taken away. A variant reading at the end of John 19:38 continues the story: "So *they* came and took away his body."[34] Similarly in *GPet* 6:21 we read, "And then they [the Jews] drew out the nails from the hands of the Lord and placed him on the earth."[35] Justin (*Dialogue* 97.1) phrases the burial thus: "For the Lord too remained on the tree almost until evening [*hespera*], and towards evening *they* buried him"—in a chapter where the context suggests that the "they" may be the Jewish opponents of Jesus rather than his disciples. The plural may be simply a generalization of the memory of Joseph who was one of "the Jews," i.e., not a disciple of Jesus at this time but a pious Sanhedrist responsible for sentencing Jesus and acting in fidelity to the deuteronomic law of burying before sunset those hanged (crucified) on a tree. Let us move on now to how this Sanhedrist had his request answered.

Pilate's Reaction to Joseph's Request (15:44–45). A common contention[36] is that in all or in part these verses were added to Mark by a redactor for apologetic purposes, i.e., to prove by the double witness of Pilate and the centurion that Jesus was truly dead, so that his resurrection was not simply a resuscitation from a coma. The main argument for such a suggestion is Synoptic: The amazement of Pilate and the verification of death by the centurion are not reported by either Matt or Luke, and so many would conclude that this account must have been absent from the form of Mark known to them. Some (Gnilka, Schenk) would maintain that even if 15:44–45a were

---

[33]R. H. Fuller, *The Formation of the Resurrection Narratives* (New York: Macmillan, 1971), 54–55, recognizes the antiquity of the tradition but interprets the burial hostilely as the "last act of the crime." That is not really clear in Acts and may have been totally absent from the underlying tradition.

[34]Boismard (*Jean* 444) would have the Jews the subject in this earliest form of the Johannine tradition. Murphy-O'Connor ("Recension") rejects the Jews as subject, for they would have wanted to avoid ritual impurity. (He fails to take into account the serious responsibility of pious Jews to bury such a body even at the price of impurity.) For him the "they" are the anonymous disciples of John's Gospel (even though no such plural anonymous group is mentioned in the context), so that Joseph's role in the burial (19:38) is a later interpolation. If the "they" is original, Boismard's identification is far more plausible.

[35]In the continuing story (6:23) they "give his body to Joseph that he might bury it"—thus seemingly a melding of two traditions. *Acts of Pilate* 12 reports that the Jews became so hostile when they heard that Joseph had asked for Jesus' body that they imprisoned Joseph; this is a further development of the later Gospel portrayal of Joseph as a disciple of Jesus or sympathetic to him.

[36]Klostermann, Lohmeyer, Loisy, etc.; see BHST 274.

redactional, 15:45b ("He granted the corpse to Joseph") had to be in the original Mark both because the request of Joseph to Pilate for the body of Jesus needed an answer and because Matt reports an answer. If I may begin with this proposed exception, I see little to recommend it. The request of Joseph needs only an implicit answer, which is all that it receives in Luke. While Matt has an answer by Pilate (27:58b: "Then Pilate ordered [it] to be given up"), his wording differs totally from that of Mark 15:45b, so that Matt's dependence on the latter is dubious.

Let us take Mark 15:44–45 as a unit, then. Besides the absence of this unit in Matt and Luke, what arguments support or challenge the thesis that it was added to Mark by a later redactor?[37] First, to what extent are the style and vocabulary characteristic of Mark? The introduction of the previously mentioned Roman prefect in v. 44, "But Pilate" (*ho de Pilatos*), is exactly the same as the introduction of the previously mentioned Magdalene in v. 47, "But Mary" (*hē de Maria*). When the Marcan Pilate first encountered Jesus, he was amazed (15:5: *thaumazein*) that Jesus refused to answer him; here in Pilate's last encounter with the issue of Jesus, he is amazed again.[38] In the popular Greek of this era the verb often governs a "that" (*hoti*) clause, but here the more classical "if, whether" (*ei*) is employed in an indirect question (BDF 454[1]; ZAGNT 1.164). The wording of the two Marcan indirect questions about Jesus' death in vv. 44 and 45 has caught commentators' attention: "amazed that he had already died [*ei ēdē tethnēken*]" and "questioned if he was dead for some time [*ei palai apethanen*]." The first with *ēdē* offers no difficulty as Marcan style, but nowhere else does Mark use *palai*.[39] Yet in the redactor thesis, the redactor would have written both questions and presumably would have varied the wording of the second to avoid repetition. The same explanation would be applicable if Mark wrote these verses. In describing how Pilate summons the centurion, v. 44 uses *proskaleisthai* ("to call over/in," used more by Mark [9 times] than by Matt or Luke), *kentyriōn* (only Mark, 3 times), and *eperōtan* (25 times in Mark, as much as Matt and Luke together); the last verb was used of Pilate previously in Mark 15:2,4, and of the high priest in 14:60,61. In v. 45 "having come to know" represents the only place in the NT where *apo* ("from") is used with *ginōskein*. In Greek "He granted the corpse [*edōrēsato to ptōma*] to Joseph" has auditory parallelism to "Joseph . . . requested the body [*ētēsato to sōma*]." This is the

---

[37]I.e., someone who subsequently added the verses to a completed Gospel—the Gospel that had already been used by Matt and Luke—early enough for the verses to appear in all known copies. Personally I doubt that there is sufficient evidence in the rest of Mark for positing such a figure.

[38]Gnilka (*Markus* 2.333) would have this verb point to the numinous. Yet beyond the overall Marcan belief that Jesus is wonderful, I see nothing in the storyline of the two uses by Pilate to suggest religious awe. Why would a quick death make Jesus more divinely mysterious?

[39]It is textually dubious in 6:47, supported by Codex Bezae and P[45].

only time Mark uses *dōreisthai,* but this verb "to grant" is very appropriate for an act of clemency (see II Peter 1:3–4). The more precise word for a dead body, *ptōma,* used by Mark to express the results of Pilate's investigation (Jesus is now a corpse[40]), was employed by Mark previously (6:29) to describe the burial of JBap's corpse. The parallel between the fate of the precursor and that of Jesus will be continued in 15:46 (which is undoubtedly Marcan), for of both burials the expression "placed him/it in a burial place/ tomb" is used. A final stylistic argument pertinent to the identity of the composer of vv. 44–45 is that the participle that begins the next verse (15:46) "And having bought" logically modifies Joseph, but the last subject in 15:45 was Pilate. If 15:44–45 were added by a redactor so that originally v. 46 continued v. 43, the subject there was Joseph. I find this scarcely a convincing argument, for the last *word* in v. 45 was "Joseph," and so the opening of v. 46 is simply picking up that as a subject. Such a construction *ad sensum* is not unusual. Moreover, 15:46 does not perfectly continue the storyline of v. 43 because in such a sequence one is not told that Pilate granted Joseph's request. Overall, then, Blinzler is correct ("Grablegung" 59) in arguing that one cannot settle the redactional question by appealing to style or vocabulary. There are several touches that might be judged unMarcan, but they are outnumbered by distinctively Marcan words and patterns. Overall it seems more logical to posit that Mark wrote the passage than to introduce a redactor who imitated Mark so closely.

Another argument that has entered the discussion of the authorship of Mark 15:44–45 involves plausibility. I shall discuss the issue, but frankly I do not understand what the plausibility of the contents or the lack thereof tells us about who wrote this passage. At most one might argue that if the action described in these verses were seen to be thoroughly implausible, on that score Matt and Luke might independently have decided to eliminate it even though they found it in Mark. (In fact, few have argued in that way, for the action is not thoroughly implausible.) The first question is whether Pilate would have been likely to check on the death of a criminal. We know little of the practice of Roman governors pertaining to such an issue,[41] but John 19:32–34 shows that another evangelist did not think it implausible to have a Roman soldier test to see if Jesus was dead. Mark's plausibility has to be determined in terms of the practical issue: Was the length of time that Jesus

---

[40]Daube ("Anointing" 195) argues that *ptōma* (which some judge crude) was particularly suitable for a mutilated dead body, a disgrace in the eyes of the rabbis (Mishna *Sanhedrin* 9.3). Craig (*Assessing* 177) sees here the possibility of a Latinism reflecting the official language of the governor's order: *donavit cadaver.*

[41]Mishna *Yebamot* 16.3 shows how cautious the rabbis were: Even if a person was publicly crucified, evidence establishing death may be offered only after an interval for the soul to have gone out of the body.

had hung on the cross so short that his death might have amazed an authority? Mark 15:25 had Jesus crucified at the third hour, so that Jesus was on the cross some six hours before he died (15:34,37). Seneca (*Epistle* 101.10–13) takes for granted that the crucified could last a long time, and Origen reports that it was not rare for the crucified to survive the whole night and the next day.[42] Surely, then, Jesus did die sooner than most (and according to John 19:32–33 sooner than his crucified companions). That factor could have amazed the governor, making him suspicious that a deceit was being practiced. On the other side of the coin, is it plausible that Jesus died so soon? In fact, crucified men lasted different lengths of time, depending on their own state of health,[43] on the severity of the precrucifixion torture inflicted on them (e.g., flagellation), and on the way in which they were crucified (nails, supports). Josephus (*Life* 75; #420–21) tells of seeing three of his friends hanging on crosses; he went and told Titus, who gave orders that they should be taken down; two of them died while under the treatment of physicians, while the third survived. (Note how the chief Roman official responds to a request about the crucified.) Overall, then, it was not impossible that Jesus died relatively quickly, and there is nothing egregiously unlikely about Pilate's reaction to Jesus' reported death in 15:44–45.

In the light of this discussion there is only one major objection to maintaining that Mark wrote 15:44–45: How could Matt and Luke independently have been led to omit the passage? That such independent omission did occasionally occur we saw in treating Matt 14:51–52, another two-verse passage, describing the naked flight of the young man who wanted to follow Jesus. Apparently each evangelist found the scene too scandalous a portrait of a disciple to retain. Here, as mentioned, it is most often contended that the reaction of Pilate in 15:44–45 was included for apologetic purposes to show that Jesus was truly dead.[44] Did the later evangelists think that the apologetics had backfired by even raising the question of the truth of Jesus' death and by showing that a Roman governor doubted it? That independently such a reaction could have caused each evangelist to omit this passage from Mark is not a perfect solution; but in my judgment it is more likely than the theory that a shadowy redactor (otherwise not well established) added the verses to Mark early enough for them to appear in all known copies but after Matt and Luke had drawn upon the Gospel.

---

[42]So Barbet (*Doctor* 68, without supplying the reference). Barbet similarly points to an Arabic text which affirms that in 1247 at Damascus a crucified man lasted till the second day.

[43]C. F. Nesbitt (*Journal of Religion* 22 [1942], 302–13), pointing to the prevalence of malaria in the Jordan valley and around Tiberias, speculates that Jesus was not well or strong!

[44]Alternative proposals involve antidocetism (Klostermann) or purely decorative narrative embellishment (Blinzler). The former purpose could apply, I would think, only if the verses are redactional and late.

THE REQUEST FOR BURIAL ACCORDING TO MATT 27:57–58

This account is less than half the length of Mark's and, in my judgment, totally dependent on it. Accordingly we have to pay attention not only to what Matt includes and adapts, but also to what he omits.

Time Indication (27:57a). In observing how Matt reduces a whole Marcan sentence to a phrase, we remember that Mark 15:42 in an awkward juxtaposition had two time indications plus an explanation of the second: "And, it being already evening, since it was preparation day, that is, the day before Sabbath." As might be expected, Matt eliminates the awkwardness as he skillfully reuses the three Marcan elements to cover the three days from the burial on Friday evening to the empty tomb on Sunday morning. (To illustrate the reuse, while giving Matt's wording, I shall italicize what he took over from Mark.) The first Marcan time indication is reused by Matt here to introduce Joseph and the request for the body on Friday: "But *it being evening.*"[45] The second Marcan time notice Matt will use in 27:62 to introduce the special material he will report about the Pharisees and the guard at the tomb on Saturday: "on the next day, *that is,* after *preparation day.*" The final Marcan element, the explanatory phrase about Sabbath,[46] Matt will use in 28:1 to introduce his story of the empty tomb on Sunday: "But late [*opse*] *on Sabbath*, at the dawning [= beginning] of the first day of the week." (On how time was calculated for days of the week, see p. 1353 below.)

The Matthean Description of Joseph from Arimathea (27:57b). We spent pages discussing what Mark 15:43 meant by "a respected council member who was also himself awaiting the kingdom of God." The most plausible interpretation was that although like other members of the Sanhedrin Joseph rejected Jesus, he was a pious man wishing to fulfill the Law, whence his desire to get the body of Jesus buried before sunset. In rejecting the thesis that Mark was presenting Joseph as a disciple of Jesus, I asked why he would have phrased that information so ambiguously in terms of "awaiting the kingdom of God." But I might also have asked the reverse question: If Mark did not mean that Joseph was a disciple, why did he describe him as "awaiting the kingdom of God," since that language could be applied to disciples of Jesus? The answer to that question and to Matt's description of Joseph lies in the great likelihood that after the resurrection Joseph did become a Christian and that is why his name was remembered in all the Gospel accounts. Knowing that but also thinking that Joseph was

[45]While not preserving all the Marcan PN time indications, Matt has kept the inclusion whereby "evening" marks the beginning of the Last Supper (26:20) and the ending of the crucifixion by burial.

[46]Mark 16:1, beginning the empty tomb story, has another reference to the Sabbath: "And when the Sabbath was over." Matt avoids the duplication.

not a disciple before the burial, Mark deliberately described him in language appropriate both for a law-observant Jew and for a (future) disciple of Jesus. Matt, judging that subtleties are pedagogically perilous because readers in fact do not understand, eliminates Joseph's preEaster, Sanhedrin history[47] and anticipates his postEaster career as a Christian: "There came a rich man *from Arimathea* whose name was *Joseph, who had also himself* been a disciple[48] of Jesus." (Again elements from Mark are italicized.) The consecutive narrative in Matt is important: The women who had followed Jesus from Galilee were observing the crucified from a distance (27:55–56); now comes a rich man who also himself had been a disciple of Jesus—two types of adherence. Moreover, over against the most famous male *disciples* of Jesus (the Twelve) who had fled, Matt presents one male *disciple* who has remained with Jesus to the death. In the Matthean portrayal earlier information has been lost, but Joseph as a Christian model has been clarified.

In his omissions of Marcan material, Matt has exercised not only "council member" but also "respected," the special status that in Mark's story helped to make intelligible why Pilate granted the request. In its stead Matt offers "a rich man." That Joseph had wealth is related to his having his own new tomb (27:60),[49] an ownership that by the time Matt wrote had become a Christian tradition about the place where Jesus had been buried (e.g., *GPet* 6:24: "called the Garden of Joseph"). How did Joseph's being rich affect his

---

[47]Did Matt think that impossible? More likely he thought it not fitting to repeat.

[48]Literally a verb: "had been discipled to Jesus." Anticipating the postresurrectional situation is a major characteristic of Matt's Gospel both in its christology and its treatment of Jesus' followers, e.g., in adding Son-of-God confessions (Matt 14:33; 16:16, compared to Mark 6:52; 8:29). That this is misunderstood by ultraconservatives is visible in the editorial introduction to Shea's posthumous "Burial": The thesis that in calling Joseph a disciple Matt is anticipating the man's postEaster career is treated as challenging the veracity of Matt. Such anticipated postresurrectional insights *are* the truth for Matt.

[49]A scriptural background for Matt's tomb of a rich man has been found by some in the description of the Suffering Servant. The MT of Isa 53:9 reads: "And he gave [i.e., placed] with the wicked his grave, *and with the rich man in his deaths*." Many suspect corruption in the last clause and have suggested Hebrew emendations that would yield a better synonymous parallelism: "and with the doers of evil his tomb." Clearly the emendations would do nothing to support Matthean use of this verse, which is dependent on "rich man"; moreover, for Matt Jesus was buried in the new tomb of Joseph, a disciple of Jesus, and thus neither with nor by the wicked. The later targum ("And he shall deliver the wicked into Gehenna, and those that are rich in possessions that they have obtained by violence unto the death of destruction"), while retaining "rich," is no closer to Matt in meaning. Neither is the LXX ("I will give the wicked in place of [*anti*] his burial and the rich [pl.] in place of his death"), which presumably refers to God's retributive putting to death the Servant's wicked opponents in place of him. Barrick ("Rich") appeals to the 1QIs[a] reading, which he understands to mean "And they made his grave with wicked (men), but his body (lay) with a rich (man)." That interpretation requires interpreting the scrolls *bwmtw* not as his "burial monument," but as "his back," i.e., "body." It correctly recognizes that only by antithetic parallelism can the verse come into play in Matt, but still does not explain how Matt would have seen the first part of the verse fulfilled. As we have seen, in instances of biblical citation Matt likes every detail fulfilled. One can doubt, then, that Matt had this Isaian passage in mind.

role as a model Christian disciple? When Matt read the Marcan "awaiting the kingdom of God," did he think of the words of Jesus he had recorded earlier in 19:23–24: "A rich man will enter the kingdom of heaven with difficulty . . . it is easier for a camel to come through the eye of a needle than for a rich man to enter the kingdom of God"? If so, Matt may have decided in this scene after Jesus' death to portray one rich man who met the challenge of "Come, follow me," unlike the young man whose many possessions turned him away (19:21–22). Matt never reports the curse Luke 6:24 attributes to Jesus, "Woe to you rich, because you have received your consolation." [50] Matt has no warning not to invite rich neighbors to the banquet (Luke 14:12), no parable of a rich man who foolishly builds larger barns (Luke 12:16–21), no parable of a rich man contrasted with Lazarus (Luke 16:1–13). Unlike Simon Peter, James, and John in Luke 5:11 who leave "everything" to follow Jesus, those worthies in Matt 4:20,22 leave specific things (nets, boat, father). Senior (*Passion . . . Matthew* 151) points out that Matt refers to a much wider range of coins than Mark and has such terms as "gold," "silver," and "talent" some 28 times, compared to 1 time in Mark and 4 in Luke. One may suspect, then, that among Matt's community there were rich people, and Joseph could serve for them as a model disciple.

Joseph and Pilate (27:58). We have already discussed the problem of Matt's omitting the contents of Mark 15:44–45. [51] What Matt gives us here, therefore, is a shortened form of Mark 15:43b (and, some would say, a rewriting of Mark 15:45b). In the clause "having come before [*proserchesthai*] *Pilate*," Matt preserves from Mark the use of a second verb "to come" to describe Joseph, but has simplified Mark's redundant *eiserchesthai pros* ("to come in before"). In *"requested the body of Jesus"* Matt preserves also the Marcan *aitein* which he used previously in 27:20 when the crowds requested Barabbas from Pilate in place of Jesus, whom they wanted destroyed. Now, by contrast, the request is addressed to Pilate by a disciple wanting to save the body of Jesus from destruction.

In 27:58b, "Then Pilate ordered (it) to be given up," Matt has the same idea as Mark 15:45b ("he granted the corpse to Joseph") but expressed in entirely different vocabulary. [52] The Matthean Pilate has acquiesced without expressing any hesitation or questioning Joseph, even though Joseph is a

---

[50] The pertinent Matthean beatitude (5:3) is "Blessed are the poor *in spirit*, for theirs is the kingdom of heaven"—a beatitude that can include the rich—unlike the Lucan beatitude (6:20): "Blessed are you poor."

[51] I argued that more probably the version of Mark used by Matt had those verses, but Matt omitted them because it did not help the Christian presentation of the resurrection to have it known that the Roman governor queried whether Jesus was actually dead.

[52] If the form of Mark that Matt used had vv. 44–45, then Matt has decided to paraphrase the last clause in those verses.

disciple of Jesus. Two factors should be considered in recognizing that such acquiescence is not implausible granted the Matthean storyline. First, there is a difference between Mark's portrayal of Pilate and Matt's. During the trial of Jesus the Marcan Pilate was a cynical judge who did not greatly exert himself on Jesus' behalf: Even though he recognized the prejudice of Jesus' enemies, he gave Jesus over and released Barabbas to satisfy the crowd (Mark 15:10,15). I argued above that this Pilate would not have taken the risk of releasing the body of "the King of the Jews" to a known disciple of that king. But during the trial the Matthean Pilate was told by his wife that Jesus was a just man, and he acted out a public washing of hands to remain innocent of Jesus' blood (27:19,24). Such a well-disposed Pilate might have continued to show his conviction that Jesus had been unjustly treated by ordering that his body be given to a disciple precisely because he recognized that Jesus had no political following. Second, the Matthean Joseph, unlike the Marcan, was a rich (and presumably influential) man whom a governor might not wish to offend by refusing his request. Pilate's affirmative response implies the agency of Roman soldiers, for they would be the ones who would turn over the body. *Apodidonai* ("to give up/back") is a Matthean verb (18 times, compared to 1 in Mark, 8 in Luke); and besides the sense of surrendering the body, it may have the connotation of giving it back to Jesus' supporters, since Joseph is a disciple.[53] (Did Matt mean us to think that Pilate knew this about Joseph?) Throughout the PN we have seen Jesus "given over" (*paradidonai*) from one hostile actor to another in a chain leading to the cross.[54] Now finally he is not given over again but given back to one who loves him.

THE REQUEST FOR BURIAL ACCORDING TO LUKE 23:50–52

Some scholars posit a special source for Luke in this section of the burial narrative (Grundmann, Schneider, B. Weiss); but I see no convincing reason to think that Luke had any written source beyond Mark here (so Büchele, Taylor) even if, as usual in the PN, Luke exercised greater freedom toward Mark than Matt did in what he took over. Luke begins his burial account with an initial "And" (*kai*), just as he began his accounts of the Roman trial (23:1) and of the crucifixion (23:26). Before we treat what Luke records in the burial, we should note his opening omission of the two time indications

---

[53]The verb appears in Philo (*In Flaccum* 83) in a passage about bodies being taken down from crosses and delivered to relatives to be given burial rites.

[54]*Paradidonai* in reference to Judas before the PN (26:2,15,16,21,23,24,25); then 26:45,46,48; 27:2,3,4,18,26.

and explanatory phrase that began Mark's account (15:42). The omission of Mark's *opsia* ("evening") is not surprising since Luke-Acts never uses *opsia* (5 times in Mark, 7 in Matt, 2 in John). As for Mark's "it was preparation day, that is, the day before Sabbath," Luke will reuse those phrases in the second part of the burial scene (§47 below); for *after* the actual burial, Luke (23:54) states: "And it was preparation day, and Sabbath was dawning." Placed there, it shows implicitly Joseph's success in keeping the law of burying crucified bodies before sunset, as well as the law of the Sabbath rest.[55] At the beginning of the Gospel Luke portrayed a number of pious Jews who were carefully law-abiding and still open to participate in the Jesus event (Zechariah, Elizabeth, Simeon, Anna: 1:5–6; 2:25,36–37). By way of inclusion at the end of the Gospel he presents Joseph as the same kind of Jew.

The Lucan Description of Joseph from Arimathea. The use of an initial *kai idou* ("And behold") in 23:50 is standard Lucan style.[56] Although Luke depends on Mark here, he rearranges the material, supplementing it by inferences, and so gives a longer presentation of Joseph than that found in any other Gospel. "A man, Joseph by name [*onomati*]" involves a Greek name-identification formula used 27 times in Luke-Acts (Mark 1, Matt 1, John 0); indeed the Gospel opened in 1:5 with "a priest, Zechariah by name." In the phrase "being [*hyparchōn*] a member of the council" Luke inserts his own style (*hyparchein* occurs 40 times in Luke-Acts, 3 in Matt, 0 in Mark, John), while preserving Mark's *bouleutēs,* which he clearly understands to mean a member of the Sanhedrin responsible for Jesus' death (v. 51). But Luke postpones Mark's "awaiting the kingdom of God" until after he has affirmed in plain language the character of this Sanhedrist as "a good and just [*dikaios*[57]] man," a description that replaces Mark's "respected" and gives more attention to Joseph's moral character than to his dignity in the Sanhedrin. This description fits the Lucan Joseph into a pattern of pious Jews described at the beginning of the Gospel: Zechariah, mentioned above, and his wife Elizabeth were "just before God" (1:6); Simeon was not only "a just man" but also "awaiting the consolation of Israel" (even as the Lucan

---

[55]Luke 23:56ab shows us explicitly that the latter law (which Gentile readers would know about) was important, for after the burial the women returned to where they were staying to prepare spices and myrrh, "And then on the Sabbath they rested according to the commandment."

[56]It occurs in Luke twenty-six times; see Fitzmyer, *Luke* 1.121. Feldkämper (*Betende*) would begin with 23:49 and thus by way of inclusion have the Galilean women at the beginning and the end (23:55–56) of the burial scene. Yet v. 49 has the women standing from a distance seeing the things that took place *as Jesus died.* The better diagnosis is that the Lucan structure has the two scenes, one of death and the other of burial, each ending with the Galilean women observing or looking.

[57]Of the many possible renderings of *dikaios* ("righteous, upright, saintly"), "just" seems appropriate here, set over against the injustice of the Sanhedrin.

Joseph is both "just" and "awaiting the kingdom of God").[58] Thus, unlike Matt who makes Joseph a disciple, Luke preserves Mark's subtlety of describing a pious, law-observant Jew—a person who at the time of burial was not a disciple of Jesus but had the moral qualifications to become one once he would recognize that the awaited had come. Mark never explained how someone "awaiting the kingdom of God" could have been part of a Sanhedrin that found Jesus guilty of blasphemy and worthy of death; but Luke resolves the problem: Joseph "was not in agreement [*sygkatatithesthai*] with their decision [*boulē*] and course of action."[59] In his analysis Luke is echoing important scriptural language, for the OT uses of *sygkatatithesthai* in Exod warned Israel: "You shall not be in agreement with the wicked as an unjust [*adikos*] witness" (23:1) and "You shall not be in agreement with them [the pagan inhabitants of the land] and their gods" (23:32).[60] Luke 22:66,70 had all the members of the Sanhedrin interrogate Jesus, and 23:1 had "the whole multitude of them" lead Jesus to Pilate. Yet here is one Sanhedrist who did not violate the warning commands of God to Israel by agreeing against Jesus with unjust judges in the Sanhedrin or with the Romans.[61]

In v. 51b Luke returns to copying from Mark basic information about Joseph. To Mark's notice that Joseph was from Arimathea, Luke adds for the sake of his Gentile readers "a city of the Jews," meaning that this was in Judea, even as he had spoken of "Capernaum, a city of Galilee" (4:31). Does Luke also desire readers to note that although Jesus had been condemned and mocked as "the King of the Jews" (23:3,37), there was a good and just man from "a city of the Jews" who buried him? I shall mention in §47 that Luke develops the role of the women observers more than do Mark/Matt: Joseph from a Judean city and the women out of Galilee form a pair in the Lucan burial narrative. Only at the end of the description of Joseph does

[58]In 1:27 Luke has the virgin Mary espoused "to a man whose name was Joseph." In this architectonic arrangement where at the end of the story Luke has Joseph from Arimathea resemble pious Jews at the beginning of the story, is he also meant to remind us of his namesake, or is the similarity of name accidental?

[59]The play that the *bouleutēs* did not agree with the *boulē* (Luke-Acts 9 times; 0 in Mark, Matt, John) is surely intended. This is an inference by Luke in an attempt to make sense of the Marcan information and scarcely something about which he had private information. Were the latter true we would have expected Luke to prepare us for such an exception in his account of the Sanhedrin proceedings. In fact, as I point out in the text above, Luke describes the actions of the Sanhedrin against Jesus with the same universality found in Mark 14:53,55,64; 15:1 ("all, whole").

[60]The only other OT use is in the Susanna story of Dan 13:20 where the lascivious elders want her to "consent" to them.

[61]There is no need to harmonize historically the Lucan "all" or "whole" with this exception by positing that Joseph was not present in the Sanhedrin when the vote was taken. That suggestion runs against Luke's literary intent; clearly he wants to portray Joseph as a man of courage in dissenting.

Luke add from Mark "who was awaiting the kingdom of God" (even as Luke 2:25 kept "awaiting the consolation of Israel" till the end of the description of Simeon). In fact Luke has been interpreting that clause all throughout the description, but now at last readers can fully understand it in the way Luke wants it understood.[62]

Joseph and Pilate (23:52). "This man, having come before Pilate, requested the body of Jesus" represents an example of Luke and Matt (27:58) in exact verbal agreement for nine Greek words. This, plus another instance of agreement in the next section (§47), brings some scholars, e.g., F.-M. Braun ("Sépulture") to posit that Matt and Luke have a source independent of Mark. Others, like Büchele, posit the influence of oral tradition on the two evangelists. In general I am more favorable to the latter solution, but appeal to it is probably unnecessary in the present instance. The last five Greek words (= "requested the body of Jesus") are verbatim from Mark; in fact, the mutual agreement of Matt and Luke *against* Mark consists only of two words. The first, *Houtos* ("This one/man"), which is scarcely significant, arises from the need to supply a subject after having broken down the complicated Mark 15:43 into more manageable segments, a simplifying process that is normal for both Matt and Luke. The second agreement is the use of the participle *proselthōn* (*proserchesthai*) with the dative rather than Mark's finite *eisēlthen* (*eiserchesthai*) with *pros*. Employing a participle is part of the grammatical recasting for purposes of simplification. Reducing Mark's tautological accumulation of prepositions (*eis-* as part of the verb, plus *pros*) to *pros-* as part of the verb is an obvious improvement that could have occurred to each evangelist independently, especially since both use the verb *proserchesthai* far more frequently than Mark does (Matt 52 times; Luke-Acts 20; Mark 5).

Like Matt, but presumably independently, Luke omits the material in Mark 15:44–45 about Pilate's amazement that Jesus was dead and his questioning of the centurion to know the truth. Indeed, even more radically than Matt, Luke has nothing corresponding even in idea to Mark 15:45b: "He granted the corpse to Joseph." (The fact that Joseph has made his request for the body to Pilate, however, confirms my contention above [p. 857] that Luke meant his readers to think that the Romans did the physical execution.) Only from the opening of the next verse in Luke (23:53: "And having taken down"; see §47), do readers learn that the Lucan Pilate acceded to Joseph's request.

---

[62]Burkitt ("Note") points out that a small 3d-cent. uncial fragment of the *Diatessaron* found at Dura Europos contains the Greek of Luke 23:51, and it clearly is not a translation from the OS of that verse. This helps to show that Tatian drew for his harmony on Greek texts of the Gospels not unlike those known to us.

ASKING[63] FOR BURIAL ACCORDING TO JOHN 19:38A

In the previous Johannine scene, in order that the bodies might not remain on the cross on the Sabbath, "the Jews . . . asked [*erōtan*] Pilate that their legs be broken and they be taken away [*airein*]" (19:31). John indicated implicitly that Pilate ceded the first part of this petition, for the soldiers came and began breaking the legs of those crucified with Jesus (19:32). Yet we were told nothing about the enactment of the second part of the petition: "that they be taken away." That seems to be picked up now in 19:38a: Joseph "asked [*erōtan*] Pilate that he might take away [*airein*] the body of Jesus."[64] Readers will recognize rivalry between the two petitions for taking away the body, since John explains that Joseph was a hidden disciple of Jesus who feared "the Jews." If Pilate knew that, then by acceding to Joseph's petition he was at the same time denying the second part of the petition of "the Jews" in 19:31, for certainly they did not want Jesus to get an honorable burial. Such independence of action would be consonant with Pilate's previous disdain for the initiatives of "the Jews" against Jesus (18:31; 19:15,21–22). Or are we to think that Pilate did not know Joseph's hidden sympathies and regarded his petition simply as a reminder that what "the Jews" had asked had two parts? In that case in ceding to Joseph, Pilate thought he was ceding to "the Jews."

There is no way to be certain how John intended us to understand Pilate's attitude; however, the obscurity may indicate that at a preGospel stage in Johannine tradition Joseph was not (yet) a disciple of Jesus but the spokesman for "the Jews" who presented the petition of 19:31 "that their legs be broken and they be taken away" and that both parts of the petition were granted to him. Later, as Joseph came to be distinguished from the hostile Jews (because he became a believer and thereby a disciple), a second petition reusing the language of the first (*erētan* and *aitein* in both) was fashioned for Joseph.[65] This hypothesis would mean that the material in 19:31–37

---

[63]The Synoptics all used *aitein* ("to request"); twice (19:31,38) John uses *erōtan* ("to question, ask, petition").

[64]Notice that neither "the Jews" nor Joseph is said to come to Pilate, an action posited in all three Synoptics and *GPet*. On whether John thought that Pilate was present at the place of crucifixion, see p. 1175 above. The "after these things" of 19:38a is a vague Johannine connective and clearly editorial.

[65]On p. 1219 above I mentioned a variant reading in John 19:38b (Codex Sinaiticus, Tatian, OL, some Sahidic) with a plural subject: "So *they* came and took away his body." This reading, supported by Boismard and Bultmann as original, might echo this earlier stage of Johannine tradition where Joseph worked together with the other Jews who presented the petition in 19:31. Or it may simply be a scribal improvement to prepare the way for the appearance of Nicodemus in 19:39–40; of him together with Joseph it will be said, "So they took the body of Jesus."

(which has no Synoptic parallels) and at least some of what is in 19:38–42 (which has Synoptic parallels except for the role of Nicodemus) constituted a consecutive story; it militates against any simple hypothesis that in 19:31–42 John has joined two disparate bodies of material.

The Johannine Description of Joseph from Arimathea. Be all that as it may, in its current form John 19:38a, like the later Synoptics, represents a stage of the tradition about Joseph where his subsequent career as a Christian has been read back into his status before Jesus' burial. We have seen that faced with Mark's difficult portrayal of a pious Sanhedrist who by implication must have voted against Jesus, Matt simplified by omitting the Sanhedrist and making Joseph a disciple before the burial, while Luke left him a Sanhedrist but one who was not in agreement with the decision of the others. John's portrayal has some of both those approaches. First, as in Matt, Joseph is a disciple of Jesus.[66] Second, and closer to Luke, he was a hidden disciple for fear of "the Jews." It is fascinating that in the next part of the Johannine scene (§47) Joseph will be associated in the burial with Nicodemus, a teacher of the Jews (3:1; = Sanhedrist) who is sympathetic to Jesus and dissents from the judgment of his fellow Jewish authorities (7:50–52). If we put John's Joseph and Nicodemus together, they represent the different views of Joseph in Matt and Luke! Indeed, the statement that hitherto the Johannine Joseph was governed by "fear of the Jews" creates a certain resemblance to what is reported about Joseph by Mark alone (15:43), namely, that it took courage for him to go to Pilate.

Joseph and Pilate. We have already discussed how Joseph's asking Pilate that he might take away the body of Jesus duplicated the request of "the Jews" in 19:31. In wording different from either Mark's "granted the corpse" or Matt's "ordered (it) to be given up," John reports the acquiescence: "Pilate permitted [*epitrepein*[67]]." In this Gospel that has given Pilate a greater role than any other, his final action is in favor of a hidden disciple of Jesus. The fact that we cannot tell whether Pilate knew or did not know this is not unbefitting a Pilate whom John has dramatized as the man caught in between and never wanting to decide—the man who asked "What is truth?" (18:38) in response when he who is the truth (14:6) stood before him, issuing the challenging invitation, "Everyone who is of the truth hears my voice"

[66]Curtis ("Three" 442–43) would have John dependent on Matt here, even though the vocabulary is significantly different. (John uses the noun while Matt 27:57 uses the verb *mathēteuein*, Matthean in three of its four NT occurrences.) The attitude toward Joseph in all the Gospels implies that he became a Christian, and easily that could have led two writers independently to speak of him in the language of discipleship.

[67]This is John's only use of the verb (Mark 2 times; Matt 2; Luke-Acts 9).

(18:37). We do not know even at the end whether, however faintly, Pilate had heard.

THE REQUEST FOR BURIAL ACCORDING TO GPET, AND THE GROWTH OF THE JOSEPH LEGENDS

We have seen in the canonical Gospels a line of development that moved Joseph from being a pious Sanhedrist observing the law of burying the crucified toward a more sanctified status as a model disciple of Jesus. *GPet* gives us a 2d-cent. glimpse of other and further developments. Here we are told even before the trial that Joseph was a friend of the Lord (2:3), indeed perhaps one who traveled with him, for he had seen the many good things Jesus had done (6:23). In the preserved portion of *GPet* there is no indication that he was a Sanhedrist, although he is described as "standing there" during the proceedings against Jesus under Herod and knows that they are about to crucify him.[68] Indeed, since he is not identified as "from Arimathea" and is a friend of Pilate, readers of the extant *GPet* fragment would not even know that he was a Jew, unless they recognized "Joseph" as a characteristically Jewish name.

In "he came before Pilate and requested the body of the Lord for burial" (2:3) *GPet* hews close to Matt 27:58. Note that now there is no need for courage (Mark 15:43) because Joseph is a friend of Pilate. *GPet* differs sharply from the canonical Gospels in dating Joseph's visit to the Roman before Jesus is crucified and in depicting Pilate as unable to grant the request. In a scene illustrative of the author's ignorance of the political realities of 1st-cent. Judea, Pilate must in turn request from Herod the body of Jesus—Herod is the supreme judge and ruler. Whereas in Luke 23:12 Herod and Pilate had been at enmity toward each other before putting Jesus on trial, the *GPet* Herod addresses "Brother Pilate" (2:5);[69] and speaking as an observant Jew (!), he gives the Roman a short instruction on the niceties of Jewish law pertinent to burial before the Sabbath.[70] That instruction tells us that *GPet* situates the trial and death of Jesus on Friday, and only subsequently in 2:5c do we learn that this is (also) the day "before the first day of

---

[68]Caution is required in judging this information in 2:3, for the way Joseph is mentioned suggests that he appeared earlier in the lost part of the narrative.

[69]The two never converse in the canonical Gospels. The "Brother" formula could be protocol among sovereigns (Josephus, *Ant.* 13.2.2; #45); but was also used in the greetings of ordinary letters.

[70]As in Mark 15:42, Luke 23:54, and John 19:31, the urgency about burial is because the next day is the Sabbath. I have already commented that *GPet* 7:27 shows forgetfulness or confusion when, after the death of Jesus, it has Peter and the other members of the Twelve (see 14:59) "mourning and weeping night and day *until the Sabbath*."

their feast of the Unleavened Bread" (in partial agreement with John [19:14] for whom this is the "preparation day for Passover"). Further instruction cites in paraphrase the specific law that underlies the urgency to get Jesus buried, a law that has been tacitly supposed in the canonical Gospels: "The sun is not to set on one put to death" (see Deut 21:22–23).

In response to the request transmitted through Pilate, Herod never directly says that the body will be granted to Joseph; but that happens even if in a roundabout way. In 6:21 the Jews who executed Jesus draw the nails from the hands of the Lord and place him on the earth. When all the earth shakes, a great fear comes about among them. Only after the long darkness that holds fast all Judea (5:15) ends, when the sun shines (6:22), do the Jews rejoice and give the body to Joseph that he might bury it. At an earlier stage of the tradition (as I would reconstruct it) the Jews (of whom Joseph was one) got the body of Jesus; but now they give it to Joseph (who seems not to be one of them) "since he was one who had seen how many good things he [the Lord] did" (6:23). It is not clear what the "since" (*epeidē*) means: Did the Jews give the body to Joseph since he was a person who would be sympathetic to Jesus because of what he saw—an interpretation that would make the Jews thoughtful—or in a *constructio ad sensum,* does the "since" clause supply the reason why Joseph had requested the body?

GPet represents only the beginning of a florid Joseph legend. In the *Acts of Pilate (Gospel of Nicodemus)* 12 the Jews arrest and imprison Joseph because of his burying the body of Jesus. In 15–16 Joseph defends himself before the chief priests, telling how Jesus appeared to him during that imprisonment. Then in 17 Joseph narrates that Jesus descended into hell and raised the dead; Joseph leads the chief priests to Arimathea to see the raised Simeon and his sons. But the most astonishing development of the legend comes from the medieval period in the ecclesiastical histories of Glastonbury in England and of its monasteries.[71] Having been a companion of Philip the Apostle in Gaul, Joseph crossed to England where he was allotted an island (Glastonbury, also Avalon of Arthurian fame) in the swamps. Some 31 years after the death of Jesus and 15 years after the assumption of Mary, he built a church of wattle in honor of Mary. By 1400 it was claimed that Joseph brought the Holy Grail to England or indeed a vessel containing the blood of Jesus. This gave Britain status as having a church founded in apostolic times, matching the claims of Spain to have been evangelized by James the brother of John (7th-cent. tradition eventually localized at Compostela) and of France to have been visited by Mary (Magdalene), Lazarus, and Mar-

---

[71]On all this see J. Armitage Robinson, *Two Glastonbury Legends* (Cambridge Univ., 1926); R. F. Treharne, *The Glastonbury Legends* (London: Cresset, 1967).

tha (11th cent., especially in the Marseilles region). Joseph passed into Arthurian legends, becoming part of Galahad's vision of the Holy Grail in T. Malory's *Morte d'Arthur* (15th cent.). A final touch of the Joseph legend has him as Jesus' merchant uncle who took the boy Jesus with him on a journey that brought them to Britain.[72] W. Blake enshrined speculation about that visit of Jesus in the magnificent poem "Jerusalem" (which in turn became a stirring hymn):

> And did those feet in ancient time
> Walk upon England's mountains green?
> And was the holy Lamb of God
> On England's pleasant pastures seen?
> And did the Countenance Divine
> Shine forth upon our clouded hills?
> And was Jerusalem builded here
> Among these dark Satanic Mills?

Who could have foreseen such a career (in literature but, alas, not in fact) for one who began simply as a "respected council member who was also himself awaiting the kingdom of God"?

ANALYSIS

With §46 we have begun three sections dealing with the burial of Jesus. The third section (§48) deals with what happened on the Sabbath day after the burial in terms of the women resting and of the Pharisees arranging a guard on the tomb. Consequently only the first two sections (46 and 47) treat the burial itself. My arrangement of those as Part One and Part Two is purely for the convenience of presenting my COMMENTS in units of manageable size. From the viewpoint of the evangelists those two parts belong together and form a relatively brief, unified account of Jesus' burial. To determine how this account developed, it will be useful to study both the internal structure and the external relation to the crucifixion and resurrection accounts.

---

[72]E. Jung and M.-L. von Franz, *The Grail Legend* (Boston: Sigo, 1986), 344.

A. **Internal Structure of the Burial Accounts**

Despite their relative brevity and the unified story they tell, the accounts seem to be of composite origin. What Joseph from Arimathea does is a major factor in all of them, but on a secondary level there is the presence and action of another figure or figures. In Mark/Matt the secondary presence consists of the two Marys who are described in one verse and have the minimal functions of observing (Mark) or of sitting opposite the sepulcher (Matt). In Luke the description of the women is longer: They followed (Joseph as he took Jesus down and placed him in the tomb); and after seeing, they returned (to where they were staying) and got spices and myrrh ready. The attention that Luke pays to these women gives them almost parity with Joseph in the burial story. In John the women are absent, but the other figure is Nicodemus. Although he and Joseph work together in preparing the body and placing Jesus in the tomb, Nicodemus initiates the burial process by bringing the myrrh and aloes and thus becomes the dominant figure. In *GPet* the elements of the burial story are scattered: before the crucifixion, the request for the body of Jesus (2:3–5); after Jesus' death, the darkness, the earthquake, and moving the body to the sepulcher (6:21–24); and after the Pharisees have asked Pilate for a guard to watch the sepulcher, the rolling of the stone against the door of the tomb (8:32). Here, in addition to Joseph, Jews or Jewish authorities play an important role both in granting the request and in sealing the tomb.

The balance between Joseph and the other figure(s) in the burial accounts often betrays the theological interest of the evangelists. The burial by Joseph in itself really does no more than conclude the crucifixion, but the presence of other or secondary figure(s) allows other functions. The women who are present in the Synoptics point to Easter and their discovery of the empty tomb. Indeed, in Luke this orientation becomes the dominant interest in a burial which concludes with the women getting ready spices and myrrh that they plan to use on Easter. As we shall see in §47, the presence of Nicodemus helps John to portray the burial as a triumph, a presentation appropriate in a Gospel that has shown the crucifixion to be a victorious exaltation. The magnified role of the Jews in the burial in *GPet* (Herod grants the request for the body; the Pharisees, elders, and scribes take part in rolling the stone against the door of the tomb) is not surprising, granted the fact that in this gospel *they* have tried, condemned, and crucified Jesus. Previously we have seen the strong antiJewish prejudice of *GPet,* and here their continued activity helps to display that the malevolence of the Jewish authorities toward the Son of God did not stop with his death.

These observations about the internal structure of the burial accounts are complemented when we study the external relation of those accounts to the narratives that immediately precede and follow.

B. External Relation to the Crucifixion and Resurrection Accounts[73]

Some scholars maintain that the appearances of the risen Jesus were once proclaimed separately from the PN, which ended with the crucifixion or the burial of Jesus. Theoretically that is possible, but there is little extant evidence to support the thesis. If we leave aside 2d-cent. and later gnostic works (sometimes called "gospels") that present themselves as revelations of the risen Jesus without a foregoing narrative of Jesus' earthly ministry, the canonical Gospels and *GPet* join appearance material to the crucifixion and burial. The predictions of Jesus about the fate of the Son of Man (APPENDIX VIII, A2), which in their basic outline may be independent of the canonical PNs, join resurrection to death. The early prePauline tradition in I Cor 15:3–5 strings together that Christ died, was buried, was raised, and appeared. The passive of *thaptein* used there also appears in a speech in Acts 2:29 comparing David with Christ; and Acts 13:29 affirms: "Having taken him down from the tree, they placed him into the tomb."

While that evidence militates against separating crucifixion, burial, and resurrection as if they were totally distinct traditions, it does not really solve the issue of the antiquity and relationship of burial and resurrection *narratives*.[74] We can recognize that early Christians maintained that Jesus was buried after he died on the cross, but the NT evidence from outside the Gospels and Acts does not report where Jesus was buried, what was done in the burial, and by whom. To illustrate the problem we recall that while most scholars acknowledge the antiquity of the reports of the appearances of the risen Jesus, many think that the narratives of the women at the empty tomb are of relatively late origin in the 1st cent. (And we can distinguish further between earlier knowledge of the fact that Mary Magdalene found the tomb

[73]I am primarily interested here in what this relationship tells us about the composition of the burial account. In the last paragraph of this B subsection, however, I shall give attention to how the burial account functions between the crucifixion and the resurrection in the respective Gospels.

[74]Dhanis ("Ensevelissement" 375) discusses the view of scholars who think that the preMarcan PN contained a burial narrative reflected in whole or in part by Mark 15:42–47 (e.g., Cerfaux, Michaelis, Taylor [probably], Vaganay). Some of those (e.g., Taylor) would not think it contained an empty tomb narrative. Matera (*Kingship* 50–51) joins Broer and Schenke in arguing that the narrative of the burial in Mark 15:42–47 and that of the empty tomb in 16:1–8 were originally separate. I shall speak of a preGospel account of the burial and a preGospel tradition of Magdalene's finding that the tomb was empty, but I reiterate my conviction that we cannot delineate exactly a whole preMarcan PN (§2, C2). Nor am I certain that on the preGospel level there was a developed *narrative* about the empty tomb.

empty and a later developed narrative about how angels revealed the meaning of the empty tomb.) Is the *narrative* of the burial in the tomb and the presence of the women there to be dated to the same formative period as the empty-tomb narratives, as a type of back-formation from them? For instance, did the report that the women knew on Easter where the tomb was and how it was sealed lead to the surmise that they must have observed the burial? Yet the theory of back-formation does not explain the substance of the burial narrative centered on Joseph from Arimathea. In the light of our discussion above about the internal structure of the burial accounts, one might answer that objection by theorizing that a basic Joseph-burial narrative belonged to the crucifixion story and only the mention of the women in Mark (followed by Matt and Luke) was back-formed from the empty-tomb story. If John was independent of Mark, the presence of a short reference to Joseph taking away the body in John 19:38 and the absence of women from the burial would lend support to that theory.[75] I spoke of a "basic burial narrative" because further development within the course of Gospel writing is clear from the differences between Mark's early presentation of Joseph as a pious Sanhedrist and the later evangelists' portrayal of Joseph as already a disciple of Jesus or as a Sanhedrist who did not agree with the decision of the others against Jesus.

Below I shall work with this theory to see what we can detect as the most ancient material in the Joseph-burial story. But before I do that, let me comment briefly on how the individual evangelists fit the burial scene into their PN structure. What has been suggested about the composition of the burial account gives us the key to Mark's use: The burial is a connective between the death of Jesus and the narrative of the tomb left empty by the resurrection of Jesus, with Joseph pointing back to what has happened and the women pointing forward to what will happen. Luke follows Mark closely here; and indeed by increasing the role of women, Luke equalizes the thrust. There is also a Lucan structural touch in the enhanced parallelism between 23:47–49 and 50–56a: Each ends with the women from Galilee who have observed what has happened. (By varying the names of the women, Mark and Matt do not facilitate the parallelism.) Matt and John make unique structural use of the burial narrative in relation to the crucifixion and resurrection. Matt's burial scene (27:57–61) is not simply a continuation of the crucifixion story. Rather, along with the peculiarly Matthean episode of the guard at the tomb (27:62–66), it is joined with the three resurrection episodes (28:1–10, 11–15,

---

[75]I shall leave to the ANALYSIS in §47 a discussion of the origin of the role of Nicodemus, found only in John. Many features in *GPet,* e.g., having Pilate ask Herod for the body, and having Pharisees, elders, and scribes work on the Sabbath by rolling a large stone to the entrance of a tomb, are the polemic creations of popular storytelling.

16–20) to constitute a five-episode ending of the Gospel to match the five beginning episodes in the infancy narrative (1:18–25; 2:1–12, 13–15, 16–18, 19–23). That analysis of structure (which I favor) and rival approaches to Matthean structure will be discussed in detail in subsection A of the ANALYSIS of §48 (especially Table 9) when we consider the guard at the tomb and the continuance of that guard motif in the resurrection narrative. If structurally Matt's burial scene strongly points forward, John's burial scene (19:38–42) points backward. It is Episode 6 in the chiastically structured Johannine crucifixion account (Table 7, p. 908), closely yoked with Episode 5 (19:31–37) as the final two episodes partially matching the opening two (19:19–22, 23–24). In the COMMENT of §47 readers will see the importance of that structural pattern in establishing the role of Nicodemus in the burial as a positive act of praise. Here, however, let us concentrate on ascertaining the preGospel material underlying the burial accounts as they now stand.

C. PreGospel Burial Tradition

We shall discuss three elements: the time indication; the description of Joseph from Arimathea; and the burial that he gave to Jesus.

1. TIME INDICATION. A reference to the day on which the burial took place as *paraskeuē*, "preparation day," is found in all the canonical accounts;[76] and it contains the implication that the burial had to be over before the Sabbath began.[77] That this time indication was preMarcan is suggested by several factors. First, it renders Hebrew *'ereb* ("vigil, day before"), and so could reflect a Semitic-speaking stage in Gospel formation. Second, Mark offers two specifications of *paraskeuē*: "it being already evening" and "that is, the day before Sabbath." He has scarcely created a term that he would have had to explain in this manner; rather he uses it because it is traditional. Third, John (whom we have elsewhere found independent of Mark) uses the term three times, once in reference to the moment of Pilate's sentencing of Jesus (19:14) and twice in reference to the burial (19:31,42). If John had invented the term, logically we would have expected him to give it the same meaning throughout. Rather he uses its ambiguity in order to make it the preparation for Passover in 19:14, but agrees with Mark (Matt and Luke) in making it the preparation for Sabbath in the two burial narrative references. A plausible

---

[76]In Matt (27:62) the phrase "after the preparation day" introduces the episode (§48) about the guard at the sepulcher.

[77]Logically the day for which preparation was being made had to be significant. In the Synoptics, unlike John, that day (which would begin in the evening) could not be the one on which the paschal meal would be eaten.

explanation is that the preSabbath meaning here was too traditional to change.

2. DESCRIPTION OF JOSEPH FROM ARIMATHEA. In all the burial accounts there is a felt need to identify this figure, and that implies that Joseph had not previously played a known role in the Jesus story.[78] In the COMMENT on Mark 15:43 I suggested that "a respected council member who was also himself awaiting the kingdom of God"[79] meant that Joseph was a religiously pious Sanhedrist who, despite the condemnation of Jesus by the Sanhedrin, felt an obligation under the Law to bury this crucified criminal before sunset. That Mark created such an identification is most unlikely since it runs counter to his hostile generalizations casting blame on all the members of the Sanhedrin for the injustice of sentencing Jesus to death (14:55,64; 15:1). As for John, in treating the relationship between 19:31 and 19:38a, I suggested that at an earlier stage of Johannine thought Joseph was associated with "the Jews" who asked that the bodies be taken away—and thus with the group that had demanded Jesus' death (19:7).[80] Only because of his post-resurrectional discipleship did his request for the body of Jesus come to be seen as a rival request to that of "the Jews."[81] This suggestion would mean that in very different language the preGospel traditions behind Mark and behind John were in harmony in their view of Joseph, a view that fitted the final outlook of neither evangelist.

3. RAPID AND MINIMUM BURIAL BY JOSEPH.[82] By the little they narrate about Joseph's actions, the evangelists (even those who make him a disciple of Jesus) give an impression of an expeditious burial without frills.[83] Joseph requests the body of Jesus from Pilate; the request is granted; Joseph takes

[78]Even the later Gospels, which report that Joseph had been a disciple or a well-disposed Sanhedrin member, point to no previous scene in which his presence had been mentioned. For *GPet* see n. 68 above.

[79]Braun ("Sépulture" 37) argues that this was the original information about Joseph and that everything else the Gospels report represents Christian touching-up of the portrait.

[80]This is not the usual solution, for many scholars see the request by the Jews in 19:31ff. and the request by Joseph as two rival traditions incorporated into John. For instance, Boismard (*Jean* 444–45) diagnoses each tradition with its subsequent additions down to the half-verse. In another complicated construction, Loisy (*Jean* 496) suggests that the tradition which began in 19:31 was continued by 19:40a,41–42 so that the "they" who buried Jesus were "the Jews." To this were added the separate themes of the burial by Joseph (19:38) from the Synoptics and of the burial by Nicodemus.

[81]By hindsight it could be seen that although the intention of the Jewish request was hostile, once the request was granted, Joseph's carrying out the burial actually worked for good. That nuance could be caught by presenting the request twice, once with hostility and once with better intent.

[82]In dividing the burial narrative into two parts to get units of convenient length for comment, I have placed the actual burial in the second part (§47). Here I give only a bare outline, leaving detail till there.

[83]John has a more elaborate burial according to Jewish custom, but that is at the initiative of Nicodemus. John's beginning account of Joseph's own actions (19:38ab) does not differ in substance from Mark's account.

the body, wraps it with cloth(s), and places it in a tomb (nearby). No mention is made of washing the body or anointing it immediately before burial.[84] Only as the basic account is modified in the later Gospels under the impact of the increasing ennoblement of Joseph is it stated that the cloth was clean white, that the body was washed (*GPet*), that there were spices (John: but even then, no anointing), and that the tomb was new and even Joseph's own. While the need for haste was certainly a motive for the frugality of the burial in the basic account, such a burial also matches the account's portrait of Joseph: one who was motivated by God's rule (kingdom) expressed in the law that the crucified should be taken down and buried before sunset, but one who at this stage had no reason to honor the condemned criminal.

I have been outlining a detectable preGospel account of the burial of Jesus by Joseph. (Whether the presence of other dramatis personae constitutes ancient tradition, along with details about the tomb, will be discussed in the ANALYSIS of §47.) How much of that is history? That Jesus was buried is historically certain. That Jewish sensitivity would have wanted this done before the oncoming Sabbath (which may also have been a feast day) is also certain, and our records give us no reason to think that this sensitivity was not honored. That the burial was done by Joseph from Arimathea is very probable, since a Christian fictional creation from nothing of a Jewish Sanhedrist who does what is right is almost inexplicable, granted the hostility in early Christian writings toward the Jewish authorities responsible for the death of Jesus. Moreover, the fixed designation of such a character as "from Arimathea," a town very difficult to identify and reminiscent of no scriptural symbolism, makes a thesis of invention even more implausible.[85] The very fact that the later Gospels had to ennoble Joseph and to increase

---

[84]Attempts have been made to harmonize the claim that Joseph was a disciple with the frugal burial that he gave Jesus, e.g., that he did extend many of the amenities but the evangelists did not think it necessary to mention them (Blinzler—but why then did the later evangelists mention a few amenities, but not the most expected?); that out of respect for the significance of blood, they did not wash the bloodied corpse (Bulst and Shroud of Turin enthusiasts); that Joseph tried to buy spices but the stores were out of stock (Gaechter, Shea). The desperate character of some of these proposals is obvious; more objectionably they would interpret the Gospels by what is *not* narrated by the evangelists because basically (even if unconsciously) those who propose them disagree with what is narrated.

[85]R. Mahoney (*Two* 112) does not think that the Gospel reports are so persuasive in establishing the historicity of Joseph and his role in the burial. The known absence of Jesus' disciples at the burial, he claims, could have been reason for inventing a prominent Jew of unimpeachable credentials. But why invent a Sanhedrist, given the Christian tendency to universalize Sanhedrin guilt visible in Mark 14:53 ("all"); 14:55 ("whole"); 14:64 ("all")? Another possibility he suggests is that an empty tomb outside Jerusalem—I presume he means the one associated with Jesus' burial—was connected with this otherwise unknown figure. Yet the fact that the tomb was Joseph's appears only in the late layers of Gospel development; the very early tradition does not identify the tomb. If Mark and John bear witness to a preGospel tradition about Joseph, so old that already by Gospel-writing time his identity is being modified, that tradition has to go back to the first decade or two of Christianity, which is a bit early for etiological creation.

the reverence of the burial given to Jesus shows that Christian instincts would not have freely shaped what I have posited for the basic account. While high probability is not certitude, there is nothing in the basic preGospel account of Jesus' burial by Joseph that could not plausibly be deemed historical.[86]

(Bibliography for this episode may be found in §45, Part 1.)

---

[86]Bultmann (BHST 274) characterizes Mark 15:42–47: "This is an historical account which creates no impression of being a legend apart from the women who appear again as witnesses in v. 47, and vv. 44–45 which Matthew and Luke in all probability did not have in their Mark." Taylor (*Mark* 599) judges that quotation an understatement but agrees about the women. In the next section I too shall conclude that the presence of the women here is probably a back-formation from their presence in the empty-tomb tradition.

§47. THE BURIAL OF JESUS, PART TWO: PLACING THE BODY IN THE TOMB

(Mark 15:46–47; Matt 27:59–61; Luke 23:53–56a;
John 19:38b–42)

Translation

Mark 15:46–47 [46]And having bought a linen cloth, having taken him down, with the linen cloth he tied up and put him away in a burial place that was hewn out of rock; and he rolled over a stone against the door of the tomb. [47]But Mary Magdalene and Mary of Joses were observing where he was placed.

Matt 27:59–61: [59]And having taken the body, Joseph wrapped it up in a clean white linen cloth [60]and placed him in his new tomb which he had hewn in the rock; and having rolled a large stone to the door of the tomb, he went away. [61]But Mary Magdalene was there and the other Mary, sitting off opposite the sepulcher.

Luke 23:53–56a: [53]And having taken (it) down, he wrapped it up with a linen cloth and placed him in a rock-hewn burial place where no one was yet laid. [54]And it was preparation day, and Sabbath was dawning. [55]But the women who had come with him out of Galilee, having followed after, looked at the tomb and how his body was placed. [56a]But having returned, they got spices and myrrh ready.

John 19:38b–42: [38b]So he came and took away his body. [39]But there came also Nicodemus, the one who had first come to him at night, bringing a mixture of myrrh and aloes, about a hundred pounds. [40]So they took the body of Jesus; and they bound it with cloths together with spices, as is the custom among the Jews for burying. [41]But there was in the place where he was crucified a garden, and in the garden a new tomb in which no one had ever yet been placed.

⁴²So there, on account of the preparation day of the Jews, because the tomb was near, they placed Jesus.

GPet 6:24: And having taken the Lord, he washed and tied him with a linen cloth and brought him into his own sepulcher, called the Garden of Joseph.

8:32: And having rolled a large stone, all who were there, together with the centurion and the soldiers, placed (it) against the door of the burial place.

COMMENT

In treating the type of burial given to Jesus by Joseph, we find that while the Synoptics differ among each other in details, the difference of Mark from John is quite sharp. The issue has an added importance as a test for the hypothesis advanced in the preceding section (§46) that in an early form of the tradition (represented by Mark and perhaps by the preJohannine layer) Joseph was not a disciple of Jesus before the burial but a pious Sanhedrist whose interest was to fulfill the law of having the crucified bodies buried before sunset. As explained there (p. 1209), from the prophets through to the Mishna there was an insistence that one found guilty according to Israelite law or by Jewish courts should not receive an honorable burial. An honorable burial would not be given to Jesus by a Sanhedrist who had voted for him to be condemned to death on the grounds of blasphemy. In discussing the issue, however, we are partially hampered by uncertainty as to what constituted honorable burial in the time of Jesus. The Mishna (*Šabbat* 23.5) mentions burial customs such as washing and anointing the corpse, laying it out and binding up the chin, and closing the eyes. Details of honorable burial can be detected from Jewish narrative literature: trimming the hair, clothing the corpse with care, covering the head with a veil, perhaps tying the hands and feet in view of carrying the corpse. But how many of these practices were customary in Jesus' time? There is little certitude, especially since a change in burial style is reported to have been introduced between then and the Mishna.[1] As for customs mentioned in the NT, in an honorable burial

---

[1]Rabban Gamaliel II (ca. AD 110) is supposed to have opted for simpler burial customs (TalBab *Mo'ed Qaṭan* 27b)

Tabitha (Acts 9:37) is washed and laid out at her home, while in a dishonorable burial no washing is mentioned for Ananias and Sapphira (Acts 5:6,10). No canonical Gospel mentions the washing of Jesus' body (though *GPet* 6:24 does), and that would probably have been the most basic service that could be rendered to one who had died on a cross and would be covered with blood. (Mishna *Oholot* 2.2 specifies that blood on a corpse is unclean.) Anointing and spices surely were features of an honorable burial. Those are not mentioned in the Synoptic accounts of Jesus' burial; but John 19:40 reports, "So they took the body of Jesus; and they bound it with cloths together with spices, as is the custom among the Jews for burying." Acts 8:2 reports that the devout men who buried Stephen made great lamentation over him, but no lamentation over Jesus by Joseph or even by Galilean women followers is mentioned.[2] Thus Mark's account is singularly lacking in elements that would suggest an honorable burial for Jesus, while John's account clearly envisions a customary and, therefore, honorable burial. With that in mind let us study the individual accounts in detail.

BURYING JESUS ACCORDING TO MARK 15:46–47

The first of these two verses describes the physical burial of Jesus; the second lists the women observers.

Buying a Linen Cloth, Taking the Body Down, Tying it Up with the Cloth, and Burying it (15:46a). Once Pilate had granted the corpse (*ptōma*) to Joseph, he[3] is pictured as buying a *sindōn,* a word that can indicate the kind of cloth and/or what was made of it. Primarily *sindōn* indicates linen material of good quality,[4] and secondarily something like a tunic, drape, veil,

---

[2]I find weak the explanation for this difference on the basis that Jesus was condemned by the Sanhedrin and Stephen was not. Stephen was brought before the Sanhedrin and false witness was borne against him, and he was interrogated by the high priest (6:12–14; 7:1), so that the Sanhedrin members may well be the "they" who were enraged at him, cast him out of the city, and stoned him (7:54–58).

[3]The subject in v. 45 was Pilate, but "Joseph" was the last word in the verse and so becomes the subject of the participle with which Mark begins v. 46.

[4]So Blinzler, "*Othonia*" 160; Gaechter, "Zum Begräbnis" 220; Joüon, "Matthieu xxvii" 59. It is not justified, however, to claim that *sindōn* was of such quality that readers would have to recognize the burial as honorable. (*Byssos* is the really fine linen.) To specify that the *sindōn* he took over from Mark would befit a burial rendered to Jesus by a disciple, Matt (27:59) adds "clean white" (*katharos*). The argument of Shea ("Burial" 98) that if Joseph were not a disciple of Jesus and were just burying a criminal, he would have wrapped the body in ragged, torn, dirty winding sheets makes little sense on two scores. First, this is a hasty, impromptu gesture by Joseph. Are we to suppose that he would go home (to Arimathea?) or go into the city to friends' homes asking them for some dirty cloths? Rather he went and purchased what was readily available, and stores surely did not sell torn cloths for interring criminals. Second, a cloth of at least durable quality would have been needed to take down and carry a bloodstained body without tearing through, for this is how we are left to imagine that Jesus' corpse was transported. Luke 7:12,14 envisions a body being carried on a bier

or sheet of that material. From such general usage it is not easy to be precise about the size and shape of the *sindōn* envisaged here, and all that may be meant is that Joseph bought a piece of linen. Although all three Synoptics use the term in the burial, the only other NT instance of the word is in Mark 14:51–52 where a *sindōn* was wrapped around the young man in such a way that it was left in the hands of those who seized him when he fled away naked. On that analogy many imagine the *sindōn* of Jesus' burial to have been like a sheet or large towel in shape. Blinzler ("Grablegung" 80), however, insists that *sindōn* could refer to several pieces of cloth, corresponding to the consistent plural of *takrîk* in the Mishna for burial garments[5] and to the usage in the Greek *Life of Adam and Eve* 40 (late 1st cent.?) where God instructs Michael to go into paradise and "bring me three cloths of linen and silk . . . and spread them out over Adam. . . . And they brought other linens and prepared Abel also." Nevertheless, nothing in the Synoptic account would make one think of more than one cloth;[6] and certainly talmudic literature attests to the use in burial of a *sādîn*[7] or single linen cloth, e.g., Rabbi Judah ha-Nasi was buried in one (TalJer *Kil'ayim* 9.3 [32b]).

Some have puzzled whether Joseph had sufficient time to go and buy such a cloth, since we were told in 15:42 that it was "already evening."[8] Probably it is useless to ask "Was there enough time?" questions of a narrative that designedly gives an overall impression of haste, interspersed with time indications that are not precise. Nevertheless, attempts to answer are not without interest. Blinzler ("Grablegung" 61) contends that Joseph would not have touched the dead body himself and thus become impure (see Num 19:11); rather he would have had others to accomplish the task. Therefore one should take the verbs that describe his action causatively: "having had a linen cloth bought"—a cooperation that would have sped up the process. Similarly, although Mark seems to have Joseph himself "take down"[9] Jesus,

---

in an honorable burial. Büchler ("Enterrement" 78–79, 83) reports that in mishnaic times a bier or couch would be used for a nearby burial, and a coffin for a distant burial; to use something crude like a bier of cords would be the type of treatment accorded to a criminal's corpse.

[5]For example, *Kil'ayim* 9.4; *Šabbat* 23.4; *Sanhedrin* 6.5.

[6]If readers knew that there should have been plural burial garments, the mention of only one might convey the minimal character of the burial. But I see no reason to suspect that Mark's readers had such knowledge. The *Gospel of the Hebrews* (frag. 7; HSNTA 1.165; rev. ed. 1.178), which seems to be independent of the Synoptic Gospels, speaks of one *sindōn*.

[7]*Sindōn* occurs only four times in the whole Greek OT, and this is the word it translates. To get a plural sense the plural of each is used in those instances.

[8]An added problem exists for those who think that Mark has Jesus die on the day which began with the Passover meal. Could one purchase cloth on such a feast day? JEWJ 77 argues, as usual, that it was possible, on the basis of Mishna *Šabbat* 23.4.

[9]The verb *kathairein* used by Mark is the technical expression for removing someone from the cross (Josephus, *War* 4.5.2; #317; Philo *In Flaccum* 83).

Joseph would have had him taken down by others. Sometimes confirmation for this is found in the words spoken at the empty tomb in Mark 16:6: "See the place where *they* placed him."

The only burial preliminary reported by Mark is that Joseph "tied up"[10] Jesus' body in the linen material, i.e., the absolute minimum one could do for the dead. This frugality puzzles many who think that the Marcan Joseph was a disciple of Jesus. (Midrash *Sipre* on Deut §221 indicates that it can be better to leave the body exposed all night than to bury it without proper preparation, although whether such permissiveness would apply in Jerusalem, the holy city, is debatable.) Some would posit that the Gospel account is abbreviated and that surely the readers would know that Joseph must have washed the blood off. No such imaginings (see §46, n. 84) are necessary if Joseph was not a disciple and felt no obligation to care for the crucified criminal beyond burying him. At Bethany Mark 14:8 had Jesus' body anointed by a woman beforehand for burial, and this was proleptic precisely because Mark had no tradition of an anointing (or of other kind acts) done for Jesus' body after his death.[11] The anointing at Bethany before the passion was the only item appropriate to an honorable burial that the Marcan Jesus is said to have received; and Mark's audience would have been expected to remember it since "Wherever the gospel is proclaimed in the whole world, what she has done will be told in memory of her."

To describe the burial of a corpse the verb *katatithenai* ("to lay down, put away"), found in the Koine text of Mark, is rare in the NT, occurring in the Gospels only here. Nestle-Aland (26 ed.) prefers to read *tithenai* with Codices Sinaiticus and Vaticanus, the verb used by Matt and Luke (and John 19:42). However, it is hard to imagine a scribe changing an original *tithenai* to an unusual *katatithenai* and breaking the comparative Gospel harmony, while a change of an original Marcan *katatithenai* to *tithenai* in order to harmonize with Matt and Luke is quite understandable scribal procedure. A variety of synonymous Greek words[12] is used in the Gospels to designate the

---

[10]*Eneilein* means to confine a thing or person inside something, e.g., a prisoner in fetters, or a child in swaddling; Ghiberti (*Sepoltura* 49) would interpret it to mean that the body was tightly wrapped. Presumably, then, the linen material not only covered Jesus but was wrapped around him.

[11]So Daube, "Anointing." He suggests that a story that originally had a woman anointing Jesus' feet (Luke 7:38—or perhaps weeping on them?) was placed just before the PN in Mark/Matt; and, because Jesus' body was not anointed before burial, that woman's action gradually came to be understood as an anticipatory anointing of Jesus' *body* (Mark 14:8; Matt 26:12) in preparation for death and burial. At the end of the trajectory Matt eliminates the postburial anointing intended by the women (Mark 16:1; Luke 23:56a), thereby making the woman's action the only anointing of Jesus.

[12]One should dismiss as hypercriticism attempts (e.g., E. Hirsch) to use them to detect different Marcan sources; for in Mark 5:2,3,5, even as here, *mnēma* and *mnēmeion* are interchangeable. Similarly implausible is the attempt of Bornhäuser (*Death* 185) to distinguish *taphos* as the trough (in which Jesus was laid) inside the burial vault (*mnēmeion*).

place where Jesus was buried; and it may be helpful to identify the different translations that I have used to distinguish the respective Greek words and to offer some statistics of usage:[13]

mnēma ("burial place"): Mark 2; Luke 2; *GPet* 6.
mnēmeion ("tomb"): Mark 5; Matt 3; Luke-Acts 7; John 9; *GPet* 3.
taphos ("sepulcher"): Matt 4; *GPet* 7 (*entaphiazein*, "to put in a sepulcher": Matt 1, John 1; *thaptein*, "to bury": I Cor 15:4; Acts 2:29).

Mark reports that the burial place was hewn out of the rock, a practice attested in Isa 22:16 and frequent in NT times, with quarries often serving as apt sites for such tunneling. As noted on p. 937 above, Golgotha was probably a knoll that rose up from a quarry floor, a rock protuberance not useful for being quarried itself but convenient for cutting out tombs.

Rolling a Stone against the Door of the Tomb (15:46b). The description found here raises the issue of whether Mark (and/or the other evangelists) envisaged a tomb tunneled into the rock vertically or horizontally, since both types of Jewish tombs have been found, with vertical shafts more common for private burial. Two indications are pertinent. The first is that Joseph "rolled over a stone against the door [*thyra*] of the tomb." The "stone" is mentioned in all the Gospels (not here but after Easter in Luke 24:2; John 20:1). Matt and *GPet* specify that the stone was large, while Mark 16:4 explains that it was "very large." The three Synoptics use a form or forms of the verb "to roll" (*proskyliein, apokyliein, anakyliein; GPet* uses simple *kyliein*). Mark/Matt have Joseph roll the stone; Luke and John do not identify the agent; *GPet* 8:32 has the stone rolled and placed against the door of the tomb by all those who were there along with the centurion and the soldiers. While one might cover over with a stone the hole that serves as the mouth of a vertical shaft, the language of rolling a stone against the door ill befits that type of tomb.[14] The second indication is that the "other disciple" in John 20:5 bent down to look into the tomb but did not enter. Both these indica-

---

[13]The statistics cover usage in both passion and Easter accounts *in relation to Jesus' body*, not general NT use. The first two nouns listed are related and have the root meaning of "memorial." The better reading at the beginning of Mark 15:46b is *mnēma*, with Sinaiticus and Vaticanus; but Nestle-Aland (26th ed.) has accepted *mnēmeion* from the Koine, which in my judgment has been conformed to the *mnēmeion* at the end of the verse.

[14]John 20:1 uses the verb *airein* to describe the removed stone, but one need not translate that "taken off," as if John envisaged a vertical shaft tomb with the stone on top. The verb there means "taken away" as it does in the next verse in reference to Jesus' body. The normal purpose for such a stone was to prevent animals from gaining entry, especially those that would eat the bodies. In the Marcan picture, however, where Joseph was a Sanhedrist (and not discernibly a disciple of Jesus), closing the tomb may have had the purpose of keeping out the women followers of Jesus who were observing where Jesus was placed. Echoes of that may be heard in the insistence that the stone was (very) large, that the women on Easter were worried about who would roll away the stone for them (Mark 16:3), and that guards sealed the stone (Matt 27:66; *GPet* 8:33).

tions fit well a tomb tunneled into the side of a rock face and entered by a small windowlike door at ground level, at most a yard high, so that adults would have to bend down to look or crawl in. (Today the "Tombs of the Kings," a half-mile north of the old-city wall in Jerusalem, in a quarry, offer an excellent example of this type of burial place.[15]) This door might be closed by a boulder rolled up against it; or for more elaborate tombs there was a wheel-shaped stone slab that could be rolled in a track across the entrance, with the practical effect of a sliding door. Apparently Matt 28:2 supposes[16] a boulder, since the angel who rolls away the stone sits on it—a wheel-shaped stone would most likely have been rolled back into a rock recess or flat along the outside of the tomb and thus not available for sitting.

What was the tomb of Jesus like inside? Often tombs that were entered by a horizontal shaft opened into several cavelike rooms, high enough for adults to stand,[17] and connected by tunneled passageways. (Such a tomb might begin with one burial room and be expanded to others as need arose; in picturing Jesus' tomb the claim that it was a new tomb should be remembered in this connection.) In such tombs there were several ways of accommodating burial, sometimes appearing in combination, even if it is not always clear that repositories of different styles were in use at the same era. Popular, particularly in the Jerusalem area, since Hellenistic times were *kōkîm,* i.e., loculi (i.e. large, deep pigeon holes) about 1½ or 2 feet in width and height, burrowed horizontally into the rock wall of the cave to a depth of 5 to 7 feet, each able to receive a corpse, head first. Another plan involved a stone bench on which bodies (or more often ossuaries) could be placed, cut out around three sides of the rooms. Still another plan involved an arcosolium or semicircular niche about a yard up from the floor, formed by cutting away the side walls of the cave to a depth approaching two feet. The niche with its half-moon shape had at the bottom a flat shelf on which a corpse could be laid, or sometimes a trough into which the body could be placed.[18] No Gospel

---

[15]The Tombs of the Sanhedrin in this same region are also in a quarry. For excellent illustrations and explanations of tombs, see FANT 181–219.

[16]We should remember that there is no proof that any of the canonical evangelists, who were not themselves eyewitnesses and were writing from thirty to seventy years after the event, had seen the tomb of Jesus. Under the influence of tombs that he had actually seen, each may be describing what he supposed the tomb of Jesus to have been (so Ghiberti, *Sepoltura* 63).

[17]The height was often achieved by digging out pits in the floor. Particularly helpful in understanding such tombs is Puech, "Nécropoles." For a range of tomb types uncovered in recent archaeology, as well as for mishnaic specifications, see Liebowitz, "Jewish" 108–11.

[18]Already from the 1st cent. AD the burial chambers of the wealthy might have large stone sarcophagi, either cut in the rock (a development from the carved-out arcosolium) or, more rarely, freestanding. This form of burial became more popular in the 2d cent. AD. Besides wooden biers and coffins used to transport bodies, archaeology shows that primary burial within a tomb was often in wood (a requisite in Mishna, *Mo'ed Qaṭan* 1.6) until the time of decomposition was over and

account tells us what type of burial accommodation was envisaged; but the story of the women at the empty tomb in Mark 16:5 may suppose an anteroom with a bench since it describes a young man sitting inside on the right. Jewish graves within sixty feet of the traditional tomb of Jesus (the Holy Sepulchre) were of the *kōkîm* type, while in the nearby area a family tomb of Jesus' era consisted of a chamber with arcosolia shelf graves on either side. John 20:12 may suppose that Jesus' body was placed on a bench or on the shelf of an arcosolium, for there are two angels, one seated at the head and the other at the foot of the place where Jesus had lain. Reconstructions of Jesus' tomb based on a knowledge of the venerated site in the Church of the Holy Sepulchre point to an arcosolium.[19] Even though much has been learned recently about the architectural history of that site (as I shall recount below in subsection C of the ANALYSIS), further detailed knowledge of Jesus' tomb cannot be expected from that source.

Mark tells us nothing about who owned the burial place or why Joseph was free to use it. Two proposed answers to those questions reflect back on the issue discussed in §46, namely, whether Mark describes a Joseph who was not yet a follower of Jesus. The *first* of the two seeks to make sense of Mark's silence about elements that would make the burial of Jesus honorable—a silence that implies that Jesus was buried as one who had been crucified after being found guilty by a Sanhedrin. Outside the walls of Jerusalem,[20] adjacent to the place of crucifixion there may well have been burial places for convicted criminals, i.e., hollows quarried in the rock wall of the hill used for execution. On days when the Romans let the bodies be taken down from the cross, burial places close by would have been a necessity if the bodies were to be put away before sunset. A distinguished member of the Sanhedrin, Joseph may have had access to tombs that served for those whom the Sanhedrin judged against. Into one of these tombs nearby the cross,[21] then, the Marcan Joseph, acting quite consistently as a pious law-observant Jew, could have placed the corpse of Jesus. Objections to this proposal are based on information in the other Gospels (e.g., Matt's claim that

reburial was possible. Soft-limestone ossuaries or bone boxes were for reburial, and many of these have been recovered from the period just before AD 70. This was partly for practical reasons (gathering the bones allowed reuse of tombs), but more importantly for religious reasons (belief in resurrection and afterlife); see Figueras, "Jewish." Sometimes the bones from more than one corpse were placed in the same ossuary.

[19]O'Rahilly, "Burial" 152; Puech, "Nécropoles" 54; Bahat, "Does" 32.

[20]By Tannaitic times (ca. 2d cent. AD) it became customary to have the cemetery for criminals at a distance (Klein, *Tod* 64–99). In NT times, burial of them simply outside the city seems to have been sufficient (Mark 12:8; Acts 14:19).

[21]The "nearby" is by implication in the Synoptic Gospels since none mentions carrying Jesus' body to the place of burial, an action that could not have traversed any distance granted the hour and oncoming Sabbath. (Carrying a body on the Sabbath would have violated the Law; see John 5:10;

the tomb was Joseph's own) and on archaeological evidence. In the Church of the Holy Sepulchre in Jerusalem there are some remains of what has been traditionally identified as the tomb of Jesus. If the tomb is genuine, it seems to imply a more elaborate burial place than would have been provided for the interment of criminals.[22]

The *second* answer draws on Matt 27:60 that has Joseph use his own tomb. This answer has the attraction of offering a simple explanation of why the burial place was available to Joseph for such an impromptu burial. There are many objections to it as well as some supporting evidence. By way of objections, the information is supplied in the NT only by Matt,[23] and it could be part of Matt's expansion of the role of Joseph. If, going beyond Mark, he made Joseph a disciple of Jesus, did Matt identify the burial place as Joseph's own tomb precisely because that would explain why it was available for use in burying Jesus? Yet elsewhere Matt has access to popular tradition about Jerusalem (Matt 27:6–8: the "Field of Blood" bought with Judas' silver as a burial ground for strangers); and perhaps here as well he had access to old tradition about the tomb. Joseph's use of his own tomb can be reconciled with the thesis that he was not yet a disciple of Jesus by supposing that in his anxiety to have Jesus buried before sunset, he was willing to have his own tomb serve as a temporary receptacle for the body of the crucified until the Sabbath was over.[24] (There is nothing, however, in the Marcan account to suggest that this was a temporary burial.) How likely is it that an influential Sanhedrist would have had his private tomb so close to a place of execution? Blinzler ("Grablegung" 85) tries to avoid the problem by contending that we are not certain that Golgotha was a regular place for public execution. Or are we to think that choosing a place of burial with the greatest proximity to the holy city[25] was more important to the pious than the undesirability of adjacent Golgotha? (Externally impressive tombs from the 1st cent. are still

---

Mishna, *Šabbat* 10.5.) John 19:41–42 makes explicit the proximity of the tomb to the site of the crucifixion.

[22]If Mark 16:5 implies that the tomb had an antechamber, that too would suggest an elaborate structure. However, Mark's use of *mnēma* and *mnēmeion* (with the root meaning of "memorial"; n. 13 above) for the burial place or tomb of Jesus is scarcely probative. As BAGD 524 indicates, these words can be generic terms for "grave" or "tomb." In Acts 13:29 the burial of Jesus in a *mnēmeion* is a hostile action seemingly by Jesus' Jewish enemies. Moreover, if one opts for the "memorial" connotation, that may reflect Christian veneration of the spot.

[23]No other canonical Gospel states that this was Joseph's own tomb. That is affirmed by *GPet* 6:24 but almost surely in dependence on Matt.

[24]This possibility would be enhanced if the information that this was a new tomb never used before (Matt 27:60; Luke 23:53; John 19:41) is historical, for then Joseph would not be contaminating deceased family members by placing among them the corpse of a criminal.

[25]Mishna *Baba Batra* 2.9 insists that graves must be kept at fifty cubits (about seventy-five feet) from a town.

standing in the Kidron valley parallel to the southern end of the walls of Jerusalem, a choice spot even if it is close to the undesirable Gehenna.)

While the first answer has the methodological advantage of not depending on outside information, the choice of one over the other represents little more than a guess, since there could be other possibilities for which we have no evidence, e.g., Joseph's use of a friend's tomb. Probably Mark never expected his readers to ask about the availability of the tomb.

The Two Marys (15:47). Having ended the story of Joseph with his closing the tomb, Mark turns our attention to two other figures in the burial story. Readers should consult Table 8 (p. 1016) that compares these Galilean women (and the way they are identified) in three interrelated Marcan scenes: observing from a distance as Jesus died (15:40–41: three named women); here (two named women); and going to the tomb on Easter to anoint Jesus' body (16:1: three named women). The first two of the three women described in the initial scene ("Mary Magdalene, and Mary mother of James the younger and of Joses") are mentioned here at the burial,[26] but the second in an abbreviated form: "Mary of Joses."[27] These two (plus Salome) will be in the Easter scene as well: They observed Jesus die; here they are observing his burial in this tomb; they will find the same tomb empty. Notice that Mark does not have them involved in the burial,[28] or lamenting as women of the time were wont to do, or even expressing sympathy; he is interested only in their observing. The imperfect tense "were observing" means that the women were there for a time, and thus probably throughout the brief burial process. It should not be weakened to a conative imperfect (B. Weiss), "were trying/wishing to observe," especially if that gives the implication that they did not in fact observe. (Why, then, would Mark have mentioned them? He is portraying a chain of witnesses connecting the locale of the burial and that of the resurrection.) The clause with the perfect tense of *tithenai,* "where he was/had been placed," gives prominence to the "where" precisely because these women will come to the same place at Easter. Yet one should not press that to mean that the women observed only the place and not the actual putting away (15:46: *katatithenai*) of the body. (Why, then, would Mark have

[26]Some scholars think that Mark has two women in order to fulfill the Law's requirement (Deut 19:15: "Only on the evidence of two or three witnesses shall a charge be sustained"), but that does not explain why he did not retain the three women. Moreover, there were limitations on women as legal witnesses (p. 1195 above).

[27]See §44, n. 34, for theories to explain the long and short forms of this Mary's designation. There are many variant readings of the son's name(s) here, but "Mary of Joses" is the best attested (Codex Vaticanus and some Koine witnesses).

[28]In my interpretation where the Marcan Joseph is not a friendly disciple of Jesus, the women disciples would not have been permitted to participate. Nevertheless, the basic impression in the extant narrative is one of noninvolvement.

used the imperfect "were observing"?) Notice that Luke 23:55, which shows knowledge of Mark 15:47, refers to the women's seeing not only where but also how the body was placed.

BURYING JESUS ACCORDING TO MATT 27:59–61

In relation to Mark this account has been affected by Matt's portrayal of Joseph as a disciple of Jesus before the burial, so that clearly he is burying his master, not a convicted criminal. Pilate has ordered that the body be given back to Joseph, presumably by Roman soldiers (27:58). Consequently Joseph needs simply to take (*lambanein*) the body from them, not take it down from the cross as in Mark 15:46 (*kathairein*). The Marcan Joseph's hasty improvisation of buying linen material at the last moment is omitted; presumably the rich Matthean Joseph was prepared for an affirmative answer from Pilate and had the material at hand. Matt's indirect employment of Mark's information that the linen was just now bought is found in his speci-fication that the *sindōn* was *katharos*. Normally this would mean "clean"; and I have kept that meaning in the translation, understanding it as a sign of a reverential attitude in the burial. The additional element of "white" stems from the careful discussion by Joüon ("Matthieu xxvii"), who contends that the adjective refers to the heavily bleached character of the linen and its pure whiteness.[29]

Again more reverentially, Matt describes what was done to the body of Jesus (not to "him" as in Mark). The use of *entylissein* ("to wrap up") by Matt is one of the famous agreements with Luke (23:53) over against Mark's *eneilein*. The verb *entylissein* is also found in John 20:7, and so by the last part of the 1st cent. probably had become part of the standard language perti-nent to Jesus' burial. Independently Matt and Luke may have turned to it in preference to Mark's matter-of-fact "tie up." Matt and Luke (and John 19:42) also agree in using the normal *tithenai* instead of Mark's rare *katatithenai;* did they find a pejorative tone in that verb, one of the connotations of which is to rid oneself of a burden?

The chief innovation in Matt about the place of burial is that the tomb is Joseph's own and new. The first item, fitting the picture of a disciple being generous in the burial of his master, may reflect deduction by Matt: If Joseph was free to use the tomb and was rich, surely it was his own tomb.[30] Or was

[29]See Rev 15:6; 19:8,14; the related verb *katharizein* is used in Ps 51:9 in parallelism with wash-ing and producing a state whiter than snow.

[30]For the imaginative use of this as a different tomb from that in which the women saw Jesus placed, see §46, n. 2; for proposed background in Isa 53:9, see §46, n. 49.

this a factual memory? (Above, in discussing what kind of a tomb Mark envisioned, we saw the strong and the weak points of that claim.) Or after becoming a Christian did this wealthy Jew purchase the tomb in which he had buried Jesus? The answer to the origin of Joseph's ownership may lie in still another direction. *GPet* 6:24 shows the development of a place name "the Garden of Joseph." On that analogy by Matt's time had the tomb associated with Joseph's activity in burying Jesus been pointed out as "Joseph's tomb" and had that been simplified to the tomb that Joseph owned?[31]

As for the newness of the tomb, John 19:41 is in agreement with Matt: "There was . . . in the garden a new tomb in which no one had ever yet been placed." Once more Curtis ("Three" 443) would use this as proof of John's dependence on Matt. I would judge it rather as a sign that both evangelists are influenced by a developing Joseph tradition,[32] for the same idea is conveyed by Luke 23:53 and John 19:41 in the language of a place or tomb in which no one had ever yet been laid/placed. The account of the burial and tomb in all the Gospels is influenced by the subsequent account of the discovery of the empty tomb and the proclamation that Jesus had risen. Just as in the later Gospels the empty-tomb account shows the influence of apologetics countering adversaries' arguments against the resurrection, so also the burial account. Jesus' body could not have become confused with another body in the tomb and then lost, for this was a new tomb.[33]

Matt's description of the closing of the tomb is not significantly different from Mark's. Matt uses Mark's *lithos* for the "stone" that closes the tomb and that will be rolled back by the angel in connection with the great earthquake on Sunday morning (28:2), not the *petra* he used in describing the earthquake and the rending of the "rocks" that led to the raising of the holy ones when Jesus died (27:51–52)—material that came from the popular non-Marcan source available to Matt. To Mark's account Matt adds here the detail that the stone was large (information that Mark holds back until he describes

---

[31]For the likelihood that the tomb of Jesus would have been remembered and venerated, see C in the ANALYSIS below.

[32]Similarly, independently both seem to have been influenced by a tradition about a postresurrectional appearance of Jesus to Mary Magdalene.

[33]Shea ("Burial" 102) misses the apologetic factor and tries to use the newness historically as a proof that Jesus was buried in an expensive tomb. There is little in the Gospel accounts to support Bultmann's suggestion (*John* 680) that the newness shows that the tomb has not yet been profaned and so is suitable for the holiness of Jesus' body. As pointed out in n. 24 above, some would relate the newness to Jewish concern that remains of venerated family ancestors would have been contaminated if the body of a crucified criminal were introduced into an already used tomb. Both Gospels (Matt, John) that call the tomb "new," however, present Joseph as Jesus' disciple; and in that situation the body of Joseph's venerated master would scarcely have brought dishonor to a family tomb already in use.

the open tomb in 16:4).[34] Understandably the tomb of a rich man would be of a scale to require a large stone for closure. Matt also adds that Joseph "went away" after he closed the tomb, so that the women who are next mentioned implicitly remain there alone.[35] Just as for Mark, so also for Matt, readers should review Table 8 in §41 in order to see the connection among the three scenes in which the Galilean women appear: at the death of Jesus observing from a distance (27:55–56 with three named women); here at the burial (two named); and going to see the sepulcher on Easter (28:1: same two named). Following Mark's example, Matt names at the burial only the first two of the women he named in the initial scene (27:56: "Mary Magdalene, and Mary mother of James and of Joseph") and abbreviates the designation of the second woman to "the other Mary." What is different is that Matt does not say, as Mark did, that the women were observing where Jesus was placed. Is that because Matt has a Jewish sense of how very limited would be the legal value of their witness? Or would readers assume that since the women "were" (imperfect) there, sitting just opposite the sepulcher, naturally they observed the burial? In any case, the women seem to have gone away by the next day when (in a scene peculiarly Matthean) a guard of soldiers secures the sepulcher and seals the stone at its door (27:65). It is worth noting that in reference to the women Matt 27:61 introduces the word *taphos* ("sepulcher") instead of the *mnēmeion* ("tomb") that he used in reference to Joseph; this new term will run through the account of the guard (27:64,66) into the Easter-morning visit of the women (28:1).

BURYING JESUS ACCORDING TO LUKE 23:53–56A

Luke's account in this scene is almost evenly divided between the burial by Joseph and what the women were doing, for Luke gives the latter more attention than do Mark/Matt.

Burial by Joseph (23:53–54). Unlike Matt, Luke has not made Joseph a disciple of Jesus before the burial; yet the Lucan Joseph did not agree with

---

[34]R. H. Fuller (*Formation* 54) would attribute the rolling away of this stone to the earliest form of the resurrection tradition. Yet that does not justify other scholars' attempts to use the size of the stone as historical information that constitutes another proof that the tomb of Jesus was luxurious. It is bad methodology to ignore the purpose for which the evangelists narrate details and to use those details to create a historical picture that the evangelists may never have envisaged. The reason for mentioning the size of the stone is to increase the miraculous element in the stone's being rolled back when the women visit the tomb on Sunday.

[35]That the function of "went away" is to shift the readers' attention to the women is far more plausible than the thesis of Schreiber ("Bestattung" 160) that Matt is contrasting Joseph's departure to observe the Sabbath with the continuing action of the Jewish authorities who spend time on the Sabbath getting a guard placed on Jesus' tomb (27:62–66). Actually Matt does not mention "Sabbath" with either action.

the decision in the Sanhedrin against Jesus. Joseph's motive in burying Jesus, therefore, beyond piety (Mark's view) would have had to involve respect and pity. Like Matt, Luke omits the first Marcan clause "having bought a linen cloth," presumably for a similar reason: Knowing that an injustice was being done, Joseph had already begun to make some reparation by preparing for the burial. Unlike Matt (who has those under Pilate's orders get the body of Joseph) but like Mark, Luke has Joseph take the body down. As explained in relation to Matt, Luke also prefers what had become the more standard verb *entylissein* ("to wrap") over Mark's *eneilein* ("to tie up") for describing how Jesus' body was enveloped in a *sindōn*. Again with Matt he prefers the more usual *tithenai* to Mark's *katatithenai* ("to put away, lay down") for *placing* Jesus' body in the grave. Yet, with Mark, Luke uses *mnēma* ("burial place") vs. Matt's *mnēmeion* ("tomb"), modifying it, however, with the elegant rare adjective "rock-hewn." Luke, unlike Matt, does not call the burial place "new," but achieves the same effect through a clause: "where no one was yet laid," resembling John 19:41: "in which no one had ever yet been placed."[36] Some would trace this clause that terminates 23:53 to the special Lucan source (see Fitzmyer, *Luke* 2.1523); but I see the unusual number of peculiar minor agreements (Matt and John, Luke and John, Matt and Luke, all over against Mark) in this section as a sign that the apologetic use of the burial narrative had catalyzed the development of a commonly used description and that this influenced the evangelists as they wrote about the burial. (In the case of Matt and Luke this caused them to substitute independently for what Mark had.) Beyond apologetics, Luke may have favored this particular expression, "where no one was yet laid," as an echo of the clause he had used to describe the entry of Jesus as king into Jerusalem on a colt "on which no person has ever sat" (19:30,38). I shall suggest below that there was a regal character to the burial in John; and Senior (*Passion . . . Luke* 151–52) may not be wrong in finding a similar aspect in Luke, as "the King of the Jews" is placed in a tomb.

Luke omits Mark's information that Joseph closed the tomb by rolling over a stone against its door and will not mention the stone until the Easter-morning scene (24:2) when the women will come and find it rolled away. Rather Luke places here, after the burial, one part of the time indication[37] that Mark 15:42b ("since it was preparation day, that is, the day before Sab-

---

[36]Luke's "laid" is from *keisthai* (Luke 6 times; Mark 0; Matt 3; John 7); John's "placed" is *tithenai*.

[37]John 19:42 also has a time indication ("on account of the preparation day of the Jews") at the end of the burial account. But John has it just before he says that they placed Jesus in the tomb, whereas Luke has his reference to preparation day just *after* the placing of Jesus in the burial place. Moreover, quite differently from Luke, John had a previous time indication in 19:31 (preparation day before the Sabbath) before the taking down from the cross. In that detail John was closer to Mark.

bath") placed before the burial. In Mark that indication, combined with "it being already evening," explained the urgency for getting Jesus' body off the cross and into the tomb. Luke's placing of the time indication ("it was preparation day, and Sabbath was dawning") has a twofold effect. First, it assures the readers that the Law was followed, for Jesus' burial was completed before the Sabbath. Also it helps to explain why the women whom Luke is about to mention could not stay at the tomb but went away to get spices and myrrh ready: They had to obey the Sabbath rest that was about to begin (23:56b). Luke employs *epiphōskein* in the imperfect: "the Sabbath *was dawning*," a verb that involves *phōs* ("light") and reflects a mindset where days begin in the morning as the sunlight begins to shine. This verb seems odd in the context of the Jewish calendar where the day begins after sunset and so with the onset of darkness. Despite efforts to explain the usage in terms of other lights that shine at night,[38] surely it merely reflects unthinking customary idiom, which is not always precise. (Matt 28:1 employs the same verb for the "dawning" of the first day of the week: not early Sunday morning but late Saturday night, which is the beginning of Sunday in the Jewish calendar.)

What the Women Saw and Did (23:55–56a). As with the other Synoptic Gospels, readers should once more consult Table 8 in §41 to see the interrelationship of the three scenes in which the Galilean women appear: first, standing from a distance and seeing those things that happened at the death of Jesus (23:49: no individual named[39]), here (none named), and going to the tomb with spices on Easter morning (24:1, with three named in 24:10). In the present scene by speaking of "the women who had come up with him out of Galilee," Luke is repeating almost verbatim the designation he used in the first scene,[40] reminding us that these women made with Jesus the great journey from Galilee to Jerusalem that began in 9:51. While Mark/Matt simply identify the women as Galileans, Luke's repetition goes beyond that by assuring the continuity of these death, burial, and resurrection scenes with Jesus' ministry in Galilee (so Talbert, *Reading* 225) and thus the consistency of his whole career. Interestingly, those males known to Jesus, whom Luke (Luke 23:49) alone mentioned at the death scene as "standing from [*apo*] a

---

[38]Fitzmyer (*Luke* 2.1529) lists these: the dawning light of the first star, or of the planet Venus, or of the Sabbath candle.

[39]I explained in discussing 23:49 that it was not necessary for Luke to name "the women who were following with him from Galilee" because (alone among the Gospels) during the Galilean ministry Luke had introduced such women as Mary Magdalene and Joanna, whom in the present context he will name only in 24:10 at the end of their activities.

[40]Despite the fact that Luke 23:55 repeats the description of the women from 23:49, Taylor (*Passion* 96, 102–3), who recognizes a dependence on Mark in 23:49, would assign 23:55 as well as 56a to the special Lucan source.

distance," now have completely disappeared from the narrative. The connection of the women to the two scenes, however, is heightened: They are not only at both but have "followed after" (23:55), i.e., presumably after Joseph as he took down the body and placed it in the burial place (23:53).[41] In v. 55 Luke is also more specific than Mark about what the women saw:[42] not only the site of the tomb, but also how the body of Jesus was placed therein. The latter means that they saw that it was wrapped up with a linen cloth (23:53) but not anointed; that is why they did not stay at the tomb but "returned" to make preparations for anointing.[43]

Whither did they return? Presumably to where they were staying in Jerusalem, a spot where they had spices and myrrh that they could get ready, since unlike Mark 16:1 Luke does not report that they had to buy those commodities. (Indeed, with Sabbath dawning, there would not have been time to make a purchase.) Useless are the ingenious attempts to harmonize Luke, where the women had the spices before the Sabbath began, with Mark, where the women did not buy the spices until after the Sabbath was over.[44] Luke, having read Mark, deliberately changed the sequence as part of his writing a more "orderly account" (1:3). Presumably Luke wanted readers to think that in their loving foresight these women had already acquired what would be necessary. In first introducing them in 8:2–3 Luke described them as providing for or "serving" (*diakonein*) Jesus in his public ministry "out of their own means." They have served him in death no less than in life.

What the women got ready is described in verse 56a by the plural form of the Greek words *arōma* and *myron* ("spices and myrrh"). The plural of *arōma* appears in the Johannine burial account (19:40), as does *smyrnon* (19:39), another word for myrrh. I shall leave until my discussion of John's burial account a detailed discussion of these fragrant materials because a problem exists whether John means pulverized spices or oil scented with

[41]Literally *katakolouthein* means "to follow down," but Luke scarcely means down the slopes of Skull-Place; in Acts 16:17 it is used for following after Paul.

[42]Luke uses *theasthai* ("looked at"), not the *theōrein* ("were observing") of Mark 15:47.

[43]The participial construction that begins 23:56a binds it close to 23:55, so that grammar confirms the logical connection between what they saw and what they did. The verb "to return," *hypostrephein*, is very Lucan, occurring thirty-two times in Luke-Acts but never in the other Gospels.

[44]E.g., the thesis that what they had on Friday (Luke) was not enough, so they had to buy more on Sunday (Mark)—Luke 24:1 is specific that the spices that the women took to the burial place on Sunday morning were those that they had prepared (on Friday), and so not some newly purchased ones. Nor is it permissible to argue that the "*de* [56a: 'But'] . . . *men* [56b: 'then']" construction is not to be taken as temporally sequential, so that Luke can be read in an inverted manner: They kept the Sabbath (56b) and then prepared spices (56a). The reason for this supposed inversion is that Luke wanted to finish narrating the burial before he turned to the empty-tomb sequence (Vander Heeren, "In narrationem"). However, Luke connects the preparation of the spices with the returning from the burial place; such an inversion would have to assume that they stayed at the tomb the whole Sabbath and "returned" to where they were staying only on Sunday!

them. Since Luke's *myron* virtually always implies liquid, there is little reason to doubt that he means scented oil and/or ointment which will be applied (by pouring?) on the corpse. Luke has read Mark 16:1 that the purpose of the women's going to the tomb on Easter morning was to bring spices (*arōma*) to anoint (*aleiphein*) Jesus; and although he is not that specific in 24:1, Luke surely wants readers to understand the same goal.

Some scholars, doubting that the women could get the spices and myrrh ready (23:56a) before sunset, have wondered whether Luke was confused about Jewish time reckoning and thought that Friday evening belonged to preparation day rather than to the Sabbath. (This thesis would give the women till midnight to finish getting the spices ready before the Sabbath began.) But Luke 22:13–14 suggests an understanding that the hour of the evening meal marked the next day (the day after the Passover lamb had been sacrificed: 22:7). The very mention of the "dawning" Sabbath in 23:54 requires an atmosphere of haste not of leisure; and so whether or not modern scholars think there was enough time before the Sabbath for getting spices ready, Luke wanted his readers to think so. From the opposite direction comes another objection to Luke's account of the spices. Why did the women have to get the job done before the Sabbath in the light of Mishna *Šabbat* 23.5 which says that on the Sabbath "They may prepare all the requirements for a corpse, anoint it, and wash it, provided only that they do not move any one of the limbs"? Besides the possibility that there was a more stringent Sabbath demand in NT times, that mishnaic rule would not be applicable to the body of Jesus, for it supposes a situation in which it has not been possible to get the corpse interred before the Sabbath so that it is still in the possession of the buriers. A more applicable mishnaic rule would be *Šabbat* 8.1 that forbids taking out on the Sabbath "sufficient oil to anoint the smallest member."

BURYING JESUS ACCORDING TO JOHN 19:38B–42

I mentioned at the very beginning of this section that John's account was very different from Mark's, for in John Jesus receives an honorable burial. Already (because he had modified Mark's picture so that Joseph became Jesus' disciple) Matt had moved toward a less stark description of the burial: The linen was "clean white" and the tomb "new." No Synoptic, however, suggests the use of spices on Jesus' corpse between death and burial as does John, where about a hundred pounds are brought. At the same time John respects the tradition about Joseph, for *alone* he does no more in 19:38b than he does in Mark. Following Pilate's permission in 19:38a, the Johannine

Joseph "came [*erchesthai* as in Mark 15:43a] and took away [*airein* while Mark 15:46 has *kathairein*] his body."

What makes the difference in John's account, beginning in v. 39, is the presence of Nicodemus. He is the one who came "bringing a mixture of myrrh and aloes, about a hundred pounds." Indeed, his very presence makes Joseph's action more positive, if the *lambanein* of the combined action ("they took the body") in 19:40 has a more favorable tone than the *airein* of Joseph's solitary action ("he took away the body") in 19:38b.[45] John does not specify how Joseph and Nicodemus cooperated other than in the very act of burial. Did Nicodemus buy the large amount of spices on short notice, the moment he heard that Jesus had died, or did he already have them,[46] foreseeing that Jesus would not be spared by the Romans? Lagrange (*Jean* 503) supposes that Joseph and Nicodemus had agreed on a division of labor: Joseph went to Pilate, while Nicodemus went to the spice store. Gaechter ("Zum Begräbnis" 221–23), with his usual harmonizing, proposes that both went to the store: Joseph bought the linen cloth (Mark 15:46), and Nicodemus bought the spices. All this speculation runs against John's intention: There is a spontaneity and unexpectedness in "But there came also Nicodemus." The effects of the death of Jesus are finding independent expression in the reactions of various people: in a Joseph who had hitherto been only a hidden disciple because of fear of the Jews, and now in a Nicodemus "who had first come to him [Jesus] at night." The fact that like Joseph in all the Gospels, Nicodemus is said to have "come" (to the site of execution after Jesus' death) means that he was not present during the passion. Like the Marcan Joseph, Nicodemus was a Sanhedrist, "a teacher of Israel" (3:10); yet, although he was interested in the kingdom (3:1–5), he had only enough courage to come to Jesus at night, as John reminds his readers. Like the Lucan Joseph, Nicodemus disagreed with his fellow Sanhedrists over their judgment against Jesus; yet he did so not by professing Jesus' innocence but by raising a technicality of the Law (7:50–52). Implicitly he was rich like the Matthean Joseph, for he had the means to bring a large amount of spices. And finally like John's own Joseph, he does a public action for Jesus that demonstrates more courage than hitherto exhibited.

---

[45] So Hemelsoet ("Ensevelissement" 54–55), who points to 1:12 where all who "receive" (*lambanein*) Jesus become children of God.

[46] A few textual witnesses, including Codex Sinaiticus, read "having" a mixture of myrrh and aloes, instead of "bringing." Does the fact that there is already a mixture (*migma*) suggest preparation? The variant *heligma,* found in Codices Sinaiticus* and Vaticanus (and thought original by Barrett), means "roll" or "package"; it throws little light on this issue, since it probably represents a scribe's effort to understand how the spices were carried. Another, minor variant is *smigma,* a form of *smēgma,* ("ointment"), a scribal guess about the nature of the spices. Bernard (*John* 2.653) would explain *heligma* as a corruption of *smigma.*

Our discussion, however, must go into more detail, for many questions are raised by John's account. How are we to understand the symbolism of the hundred pounds? What is meant by "myrrh and aloes"—small pieces of incense or a liquid, and if the latter, was there an anointing? What does John intend by the "cloths" which bind the body of Jesus together with the spices? How does John mean us to judge Nicodemus' gesture? Let us treat these questions one by one.

"About a hundred pounds" (19:39b). The Roman *litra* or pound was about twelve ounces, and so the amount would be about seventy-five of our pounds.[47] This is still an extraordinary amount. If powdered or fragmented spices are meant, such a weight would fill a considerable space in the tomb and smother the corpse under a mound. Puzzlement about where such a quantity could have been got on short notice and how it was brought has caused scholars to seek to explain the amount away. For instance, A. N. Jannaris (ExpTim 14 [1902–3], 460) proposes reading *hekaston* for *hekaton,* yielding "myrrh and aloes, about a pound *each.*" De Kruijf ("More" 236–38) takes *litra* as a measure not of weight but of volume; and, on the analogy of John 12:3 where *litra myrou* involves liquid in an alabaster vessel, he argues that it represents six to ten fluid ounces (roughly ⅓ to ½ pint). The result would be four gallons, more or less, of perfumed oil.[48] De Kruijf holds that this interpretation would remove some of the unrealistic extravagance of the quantity. A major difficulty is that here John does not use *myron,* a word that implies oil, but, as we shall see below, terms that more likely imply powder. Others (e.g., Lagrange, *Jean* 503) accept the meaning "pound" but wonder if there has not been a scribal error about the number (an error that has left no evidence in the textual copies!). Rather it is better to recognize that large numbers are employed in various Johannine scenes as symbolically suggestive of messianic abundance, e.g., in 2:6 the six water jars each containing two or three measures (all totaled, 120 to 180 gallons), and in 21:11 the 153 fish. What specifically would be symbolized here? De Kruijf ("More" 239) thinks of reverent faith. Others point to large amounts of spices at royal burials. Five hundred servants were required to carry the spices (pl. of *arōma*) at the burial of Herod the Great (Josephus, *War* 1.33.9; #673; *Ant.* 17.8.3; #199). Later rabbinic sources (TalBab 'Aboda Zara 11a; *Semahot* ['*Ebel Rabbati*] 8.6 [47a]) speak of seventy or eighty minas being burned at the death (ca. AD 50?) of Rabban Gamaliel the Elder, who "was worth more than a hundred useless kings." The biblical background is Jer 34:5 where the Lord promised the soon-to-be exiled King Zedekiah that "as spices were

---

[47]Josephus (*Ant.* 14.7.1; #106) gives a lower weight for the pound that would make the amount about fifty of our pounds.

[48]Working with mishnaic measures, O'Rahilly ("Burial" 310) calculates about three gallons.

burned for your fathers, the former kings before you, so shall spices be burned for you." The idea that Jesus was accorded a burial fit for a king would correspond well to the solemn proclamation that on the cross he was truly "the King of the Jews" (John 19:19–20) and to the contention that he was buried in a garden (19:41; see below). When Mary, the sister of Martha, used one pound of myrrh (*myron*) to anoint Jesus' feet, Judas Iscariot, "one of the disciples" of Jesus, complained about the waste of money (John 12:3–5); ironically now Nicodemus, who is just emerging as a disciple of Jesus, has used a hundred pounds of myrrh (*smyrna*) on Jesus' body.

"A mixture of myrrh [*smyrna*] and aloes [*aloē*] ... together with spices [pl. of *arōma*], as is the custom among the Jews for burying" (19:39b–40).[49] Jews did not eviscerate the cadaver, as did the Egyptians in mummification. So far as we can tell for this period (p. 1243 above), a customary honorable burial would have involved washing the body, anointing with oil, and/or placing spices within the wrappings of the body,[50] and clothing it. Does John imply that Jesus' body was anointed by Joseph and Nicodemus? He does not use a verb for anointing (*aleiphein*) as he did in 12:3 where he described the action of Mary of Bethany that was somehow associated with Jesus' death and burial (12:7), an action that Mark/Matt thought was the only preburial anointing of Jesus (Mark 14:8 [*myrizein*]; Matt 26:12).[51] In part the answer to whether John implies an anointing here depends on the meaning of *arōma,* always employed in the plural in the accounts of Jesus' burial. Does it mean "spices," i.e., dry powders and small pieces; or does it mean "oil made fragrant by spices"?[52] In Mark 16:1 *arōma* is clearly brought for anointing and so involves oil. (That is probably true also of *arōma* in Luke 23:56a; 24:1.) In burying, however, dry spices could also be sprinkled around the corpse and where it was laid to offset the odor of decomposition. That may be what is meant in the description of the burial of King Asa (II Chron 16:14): "They laid him on a bed and filled (it) with spices and kinds of myrrh." (See also Prov 7:17 where different fragrant particles, not oil, are sprinkled on a couch.) The description in John 19:40 of binding the body of Jesus "with cloths together with spices" does not seem to envision a liquid poured over the cloths. But we cannot settle the

---

[49]While among the canonical PNs only Matt uses *taphos* ("sepulcher"), John's verb for "burying" is *entaphiazein* ("to put in a sepulcher"; also Matt 26:12), which extends to preparing for burial.

[50]So Liebowitz, "Jewish" 108. Anointing would not necessarily consist of rubbing the oil on the corpse, for it could be dripped from a vessel over the body from head to foot. The purpose of the spices was in part to offset the stench of corruption and perhaps even to retard the decomposition.

[51]Mark 16:1 has the women after the Sabbath buy spices (plural of *arōma*) to go and anoint (*aleiphein*) Jesus.

[52]See O'Rahilly, "Jewish" 128–32. A formula for an anointing oil made by blending spices with olive oil is given by Exod 30:23–25.

issue till we look at the relationship between the plural of *arōma* and the "myrrh and aloes" mentioned in the previous verse. (Myrrh and aloes may have been a frequent combination; it occurs in Song of Songs 4:14.) Is this *arōma* a third substance alongside them, or is it a summarizing name for them? If the latter, are they dry particles or oil? Unfortunately the answers to these questions, which I shall now attempt, involve considerable complexity.

SMYRNA. There are two terms in the Greek Bible for "myrrh," *myron* and *smyrna;* and both of them are used in the accounts of the burial of Jesus, the former by Luke, and the latter by John.[53] By *myron* the LXX often renders Hebrew *šemen* ("oil"), and *myrizein* appears in Josephus (*Ant.* 19.9.1; #358) for being scented with ointment.[54] Ointment or vegetable oil mixed with a fragrant substance was used for cult, cosmetic, and burial purposes. A clear biblical example of *myron* employed for the pulverized spice is not found. It is the noun used for myrrh in the Bethany scene (Mark 14:3–8; Matt 26:6–12; John 11:2; 12:3–5; also Luke 7:37–38), where perfumed oil is envisioned. It is used in the Lucan burial scene in 23:56 in combination with *arōma* and contributes to our thinking that Luke meant liquid.

By *smyrna* (the word John uses here) the LXX renders Hebrew *mōr* (related to the root *mrr,* "bitter").[55] This myrrh is a dry powder made by pulverizing the gummy resin that exudes from the low, stubby *commiphora abyssinica,* a bush of the balsam family that grows in S. Arabia and N. Somaliland. Besides having medicinal properties, because it emits a strong scent it was used for incense (teamed with frankincense in Matt 2:11), cosmetics, and perfume (see the verb *smyrnizein* for scented wine in Mark 15:23; see p. 941 above). The use in burial was to offset unpleasant odors. It could be heaped up as powder (Song 4:6; "mountains of myrrh" and "hills of incense") or be dripped down in liquid form (Song 5:5).

ALOĒ. Modern botanists do not always agree about the classification and/ or the place of origin of the candidates most often suggested for the biblical references to "aloes," so that some of the information offered by biblical dictionaries and encyclopedias is disputed.[56] Attempts to discern what John meant have gone in two different directions. The first candidate, sometimes

[53]Helpful here are the articles in TDNT by W. Michaelis, *"myron, myrizō"* (4.800–1), and *"smyrna, smyrnizō"* (7.457–59). Also G. W. Van Beek, "Frankincense and Myrrh," BA 23 (1960), 70–95.

[54]*Šemen* is also rendered by *elaion* ("olive oil, oily ointment"). *Myrizein* (poetic *smyrizein*) is related to the Indo-European root *smur* (Eng. "smear"); *aleiphein* is a synonym.

[55]The Greek form may have been assimilated to *Smyrnē,* the city name of "Smyrna." It is not etymologically related to myron.

[56]See Hepper, "Identity." There are some 360 different species of the genus aloes; some were cultivated in antiquity and transported by merchants, and thus were transplanted to new areas.

called lign-aloes (from Latin *lignum,* "wood"), is the highly aromatic powdered wood from the inner core of the *aquilaria agallocha,* the eaglewood
tree native to SE Asia and similar to sandalwood; it was imported into Bible
lands and used in incense and perfume. OT references (Ps 45:9; Prov 7:17;
Song 4:14)[57] associate "aloes" with fragrant substances like cassia, cinna-
mon, and nard, even as John associates it with myrrh. Accordingly many opt
for this as John's reference even though in literature outside the Bible and
still in most references today this is not what is meant by "aloes." The second
candidate is genuine or medicinal aloes, namely, the dried liquid from a genus of succulent plants in the lily family called *aloë officinalis* or *aloë vera
L.,* of which there are many species. *Aloë succotrina* appears frequently as
the possible species, for the name reflects origin in the Red Sea island of
Socotra off the coast of Yemen, a site on the trade routes to Palestine.[58] The
dried juice of this plant, sometimes referred to as bitter aloes, supplied an
acrid, unpleasant-smelling medicine[59] that could also be used for embalming. Yet, of course, Jesus was not embalmed. Objecting that the plant
is rare on Socotra and has never been widely cultivated, Hepper proposes a
different species, *aloe vera (L.) Burm f.,* a widely cultivated, genuine aloes
plant that grows in SW Arabia. From it two products are derived: a mucilagi-
nous gel and a bitter yellow exudate, both of which can be reduced to a
solid and pulverized, one for medicinal purposes as a skin curative, the other
offering the possibility for use in burial.

No certainty is possible, but the coupling with *smyrna* makes it likely that
John is thinking of two fragrant substances.[60] Moreover, since most biblical
allusions to fragrant aloes seem to envision a pulverized substance, the combination increases the likelihood that John's "myrrh and aloes" in 19:39 is
not a reference to oil or ointment but to dry spices.[61] Accordingly I have
translated the *arōma* (pl.) of 19:40 as "spices"—not a third substance but a

---

[57]The tree that produces fragrant aloes does not grow in Palestine, and so Num 24:6 offers a
problem since (unless there is a textual error as frequently posited) the tree in that passage seems to
be growing in the Jordan valley. Calleri Damonte ("Aloe" 51–52) shows how widely known this
wood-aloes was in antiquity.

[58]Oman and Socotra are mentioned in antiquity as traditional sources of aloes. Nevertheless,
Hepper ("Identity") maintains that the plant in question is misnamed, for what is correctly called
aloe succotrina Lam. is S. African in origin. The correct name, he states, is *aloe perryi Baker.*

[59]Pliny (*Natural History* 27.5; #14–20) discourses on the medical uses of aloes as an astringent,
laxative, and cure for headaches, hemorrhages, and hemorrhoids.

[60]Vardan, a 12th-cent. Armenian writer, quotes Papias: "Aloes is a kind of incense" (F. X. Funk,
Patres Apostolici [2 vols.; Tübingen: Laupp, 1901], 1.375).

[61]Pliny (*Natural History* 13.3; #19) gives the Greek *diapasma* as the technical name for a dry
mixture of aromatics, and *magma* as the name for thick unguent. See Calleri Damonte ("Aloe"
49,55): Jewish burials in Rome show the use of aromatic substances. He thinks that the aromatic
powder was put on the bottom and along the sides of the place destined to receive the body, and that
after the wrapped body had been lowered into this place, more powdered spices were sprinkled over
it from above.

generic reference to the previously mentioned fragrant, pulverized "myrrh" and "aloes" that would be sprinkled in with and/or over the burial wrapping around Jesus. Thus, while John differs from the Synoptics in giving a more elaborate burial to Jesus, none of the Gospels posits that Jesus was anointed with oil between death and burial.[62] This conclusion is of no use, however, in harmonizing the accounts. Granted that Jesus was not anointed on Friday, if a hundred pounds of spices (myrrh and aloes) were buried with him, there would be no point to the women purchasing or preparing further spices for use on Easter, as they do in Mark and Luke.[63]

"Bound [*dein*] it with cloths [pl. of *othonion*]" (19:40). Once again it is difficult to determine exactly what John wishes to convey. *Dein* was used in John 11:44 for tightly wrapped hands and feet, a binding that must have involved strips going around the limbs several times and holding them fast. Is such a close multiple binding meant here as well?[64] The Marcan *eneilein* ("tied up") and the Matthean/Lucan *entylissein* ("wrapped up") allowed the imagery of one piece of linen cloth (*sindōn*) covering the body of Jesus, and therefore perhaps a less tightly constrained corpse. We saw that there was nothing in the Synoptic description to suggest a plurality of burial clothes. What does John intend with his plural form *othonia?* (Even beyond this, John writes of another and separate garment in the empty-tomb story of 20:7, a *soudarion* which had been on Jesus' head.[65]) Although some (e.g., Bulst) have thought of bandage-width strips of cloth or bandages similar to mummy wrappings, we do not know that the Jews of this period wrapped strips around dead bodies in the way envisaged. When John wished to describe linen strips binding the hands and feet of a corpse (11:44), he used the plural of *keiria*, not of *othonion*. Moreover, the meaning "strips" is not

[62]Thus, not in the manner in which he had been anointed before Passover (Mark 14:3; Matt 26:7; John 12:3). In part because of the baptismal motif in the first appearance of Nicodemus (John 3:5), Mercurio ("Baptismal" 50–54) would detect a baptismal element in the spices for anointing in the Johannine burial account. This imaginative thesis loses all likelihood if no anointing was intended.

[63]Above I rejected the thesis that the women in Mark observed only the place where Jesus was laid, not the burial proceedings—a thesis used in Lagrange and others to harmonize Mark and John, on the grounds that the Marcan women would not have seen Nicodemus' spices. Harmonization with Luke 23:55 is even more incredible, for there they looked at "how his body was placed."

[64]Ghiberti (*Sepoltura* 50–52) points out that in the papyri *dein* has the sense of impeding motion. One may respond to Feuillet and Lavergne that attributing to it a symbolic sense (a bound prisoner who will be liberated by resurrection—also Prete, "E lo legarano" 192) does not mean that it has no literal sense.

[65]In the empty tomb it is rolled up by itself. This is a loanword in Greek from the Latin *sudarium*, related etymologically to *sudor* ("sweat"), which served for drying. Presumably it was a type of napkin or kerchief. Lazarus had his face covered or surrounded by one (11:44); and some think the function was to keep the corpse's jaw from falling down, as described in Mishna *Šabbat* 23.5. Luke 19:20 has a servant wrap up a sum of money in a *soudarion;* Acts 19:12 has such a cloth touched to Paul's skin and applied to the sick.

traditional.[66] The plural of *othonion* may designate category or size (BDF 141) rather than the number of pieces, e.g., a 4th-cent.-AD papyrus (Rylands Catalogue vol. 4, #627, pp. 117–22) points to *othonion* as a general category and *sindonion* (a garment made of *sindōn* material) as a species. Vaccari ("*edēsan*") accepts this relationship between the generic *othonia* and the specific *sindōn* as applicable to the Gospels; but Blinzler ("Othonia") thinks that *sindōn* is the generic material out of which *othonia* or pieces are made. In the Codex Vaticanus Greek of Judges 14:12–13 the plural of *sindōn* and the plural of *othonion* are interchangeable designations for the same thirty garments; and García García ("Lienzos") thinks that John's *othonia* refers to Mark's *sindōn*. (In a variant Ducatillon, "Linceul," thinks *othonia* includes not only the *sindōn* but also the *soudarion* or headpiece that will be mentioned in the tomb after the resurrection and the *keiriai* or binding strips that are implied.) These interpretations, which vary both as to content and plausibility, at least warn that we should not too facilely portray as contradictory the Marcan (and general Synoptic) term and the Johannine term for the burial garment of Jesus.[67] On the level of the impressions they would make on readers, however, the Synoptics seem to picture a single burial cloth while John speaks of several cloth wrappings. Whether John's picture of plurality would enhance the impression of an honorific burial cannot be decided. In order to envision and depict how Jesus was buried, rather than drawing on historical tradition, the individual authors may simply have used the burial clothing with which they themselves were familiar.

How to Evaluate the Gesture by Nicodemus? His past history is important. First, he had come to Jesus *at night.* Despite the attraction he felt for Jesus as a teacher from God (3:2), he was not willing to reveal publicly (by day) his interest. On the level of Johannine symbolism he still belonged to the realm of darkness when he came to the light of the world (8:12; 9:5). Later he protested about the illegality of the procedure of his fellow (Sanhedrin) authorities against Jesus (7:50–51). This was a step forward since he

[66]Only since the 1870s have "linen strips" and "bandages" made their appearance in vernacular Bibles as translations of *othonia,* in place of the traditional "linen cloths." In part, this new translation depends on taking *othonion* as a diminutive in meaning as well as form from *othonē* ("linen cloth, sheet"; Acts 10:11; 11:5). But the vague connotation of diminutive forms at this period (BDF 111³) could mean that there is no difference between *othonē* and *othonion,* other than that the former designates the material, and the latter an article made of it. For details, see Bartina, "*Othonia*"; Blinzler, "*Othonia*"; and Vaccari, "*edēsan.*"

[67]I see no reason to think that John knew of the Marcan *sindōn* and changed it to *othonia,* for there is no clear theological import in the latter. The difference may reflect different traditions behind Mark and John. Whether Luke 24:12 (about which there is a textual problem) was written by Luke or added by a later scribe, its composer sensed no contradiction in having Peter see only *othonia* in the tomb where Luke 23:53 placed Jesus wrapped in a *sindōn;* and certainly Luke 24:12 came from a source other than Mark from which Luke 23:53 drew *sindōn.*

was no longer secretive, but still he did not alert Jesus' opponents that he respected Jesus as a teacher. These actions during the ministry would not place Nicodemus significantly higher than those among the authorities whom John 12:42–43 criticized: They believed in Jesus; but from fear of the Pharisees and lest they be ejected from the synagogue, they did not confess him publicly. "They loved the glory [= praise] of men more than the glory of God." For John such pusillanimous faith was tantamount to lack of faith; for as Jesus says in 5:44, "How can people like you believe, when you accept glory [= praise] from one another but do not seek that glory which is from the One God."

The disputed issue is whether Nicodemus' behavior at the burial is another negative example of failure, of insufficient faith, and of lack of understanding, or represents a positive change to an expression of more adequate faith. This dispute is of major import, for on it depends the whole thrust of the burial in John. The positive position is the majority opinion,[68] and I share it; but to clarify the issue a discussion of the negative position advocated by Sylva and by de Jonge is necessary. Sylva ("Nicodemus") contends that bringing spices in such an amount signals a failure to understand that Jesus lives beyond death, as do the verb *dein* ("to bind," used also for Lazarus in 11:44) and the employ of burial garments that the risen Jesus would have to discard (20:6–7). De Jonge ("Nicodemus" 34) describes both Joseph and Nicodemus as "having come to a dead end," for they regard the burial as definitive and are not able to look beyond the tomb. John means us to contrast these men who lack understanding and faith with the beloved disciple whose witness (19:35) will further the belief of Christians at a period beyond the grave.

In debate with these theses I contend that such a negative view of Nicodemus' actions represents a confusion about types of faith. Inevitably in John when the beloved disciple appears alongside another figure in the same scene, the beloved disciple exhibits a more perceptive faith; but that does not mean that the other figure does not believe, as shown by the many times the beloved disciple and Simon Peter are yoked together in implicit contrast. We saw that the witness borne by the beloved disciple as the blood and water came out from the side of Jesus (19:34–35) constituted a certain analogy to the witness of the apostles to the risen Christ (Acts 10:40–42), even though clearly the faith of the disciple was not yet full belief in the risen Jesus (which came after 20:8). The faith of Nicodemus is not on that level, for he does not bear witness and we do not know what Nicodemus anticipated for the future in terms of resurrection—we remember that in John Jesus has not

---

[68]Besides the standard commentaries, see for the general development of Nicodemus: K. Stasiak, "The Man Who Came by Night," TBT 20 (1982), 84–89; J. N. Suggit, "Nicodemus—the True Jew," *Neotestamentica* 14 (1981), 90–110. As for the negative view, besides himself and de Jonge, Sylva lists as supporters only P. W. Meyer and G. Nicholson. One may add W. A. Meeks (JBL 91 [1972], 54–55).

clearly predicted a resurrection as he had in the Synoptic narratives. In the Nicodemus scene John is not concerned with preparing for the resurrection (he has no women witnesses here) but with culminating the triumph of the crucifixion. There is nothing negative about the act of burying Jesus, for once he died, he had to be buried. John's conviction that Jesus is "the resurrection and the life" (11:25) did not make burial unnecessary; rather it made burial insignificant. The issue is whether John intended the way in which Nicodemus buried Jesus to be understood as something positive that glorified Jesus or as something negative that misrepresented him. The fact that some of the vocabulary used for burying Lazarus is reused here has no negative connotation, since John (19:40) indicates that he is describing what was customary.[69]

Previously in John's Gospel believers who adhered to Jesus and were identified as his disciples have been contrasted with those who believed but were afraid to have it known that they were disciples. At this "hour" of the death and burial of Jesus the beloved disciple in 19:31–37 is the example par excellence of the first group of believers. Hitherto Joseph and Nicodemus in 19:38–42 have belonged to the second group; but now they are presented as transformed through Jesus' victory on the cross, so that they move out of the latter group to constitute a new category, no longer contrasted to the first group but complementary to them. We are left with the expectation that the public action of Joseph and Nicodemus will lead them to bear witness to Jesus after the resurrection. If the previous fault of Joseph mentioned by John is that although a disciple, he hid because of the fear of "the Jews," in the present narrative that is true no longer. His petition to "take away the body of Jesus" (19:38a) is presented as a rival to the petition of "the Jews" to do exactly the same thing (19:31), and he wins out over them. Surely he has shown himself as no longer cowed by fear of "the Jews." If the previous fault of Nicodemus mentioned by John is that he had come to Jesus at night and thus, by implication, privately, now he has come before sunset and thus publicly. If till now he was one of those authorities who put the glory of men before the glory of God, he has changed his priority. The amount of spices that he brings would do honor to a king and, as Bacon ("Exegetical" 424) says, testifies to the sincerity of this belated reverence. There is not a word in the account to suggest that either of these men thought the burial to be the definitive end of Jesus. Indeed, although John knows of a stone before

---

[69]The fact this was a custom "among the Jews" does not suggest malice but simply indicates that Nicodemus did what was expected. From the viewpoint of language, more significant may be that instead of simply taking away (*airein*) the body of Jesus, as the Jews requested (19:31) and as Joseph did (19:38b—see §46, n. 65), once Nicodemus comes, he and Joseph "take" or "accept" (*lambanein*) the body of Jesus.

the entrance to the tomb (20:1), he does not have Joseph and Nicodemus close or seal the tomb. Moreover, it is a violation of the whole flow of the Johannine crucifixion-burial narrative to suggest that the final episode is no more than "a dead end." John transformed the crucifixion into the triumph of Jesus; so also he has transformed the burial into a triumph. One who reigned as a king on the cross receives a burial worthy of his status.

It is important to recall the structure of this narrative sketched on p. 908. The first two episodes showed how the enemies of Jesus contributed unwittingly to his victory on the cross. In 19:19–22 the demand made to Pilate by Jewish chief priests caused Pilate to proclaim solemnly that Jesus truly was "the King of the Jews"; and in 19:23–24 the Roman soldiers fulfilled what was written of Jesus in the Scriptures. The last two episodes show how different types of believers glorify Jesus by drawing out the implications of his death. In 19:31–37 the beloved disciple, to whom the Spirit was given over as Jesus died (19:30), bears witness to the fact that a demand made to Pilate by the Jews caused Roman soldiers to bring about the fulfillment of Jesus' promise of living water (as well as the fulfillment of the Scriptures in regard to other details about Jesus' death). This is meant to make others believe. In 19:38–42 Joseph and Nicodemus have gained the courage to glorify Jesus publicly by a regal gift of spices and by the place in which they bury him. This is the fulfillment of Jesus' own words: "When I am lifted up from the earth, *I shall draw all to myself*" (12:31–34). Joseph and Nicodemus are the first two drawn from among those who had hitherto not publicly adhered to Jesus as believers must. This is meant as encouragement to still others within the synagogue to follow the same route.

"A garden, and in the garden a new tomb in which no one had ever yet been placed. So there, on account of the preparation day of the Jews, because the tomb was near, they placed Jesus" (19:41–42).[70] While John shares developments of the burial tradition found in Matt (27:60: "new tomb") and in Luke (23:53: "where no one was yet laid"), he also has developments not attested elsewhere. That the burial was near the place where Jesus was crucified probably represents a deduction comparable to what was implied by the other Gospels (n. 21 above).[71] What is more significant and peculiar to John among the canonical Gospels is that the tomb was in a

[70]This time John does not indicate whether the preparation day is for the Passover (19:14) or for the Sabbath (19:31). Tatian and some Syr mss. opted for the latter by adding: "because Saturday had begun."

[71]I find farfetched the attempt (e.g., A. Loisy) to see here an echo of the paschal-lamb motif from Exod 12:46, which specifies that the lamb must be eaten on the spot and none of the flesh carried away. Even more farfetched is the attempt (Price, "Jesus" 17) to relate "tomb in which no one had ever yet been placed" to I Sam 6:7, where the Ark of the Covenant is borne by cattle "on which there has never come a yoke."

garden (*kēpos*),[72] a tradition that appears, perhaps independently, in *GPet* 6:24 as "the Garden of Joseph."[73] For *GPet* the name is explicable because the sepulcher was Joseph's own. John, however, betrays ignorance of that ownership—the reason he offers for the burial of Jesus in this particular tomb is because it was near the place where he was crucified. If the site later came to be known popularly as "the Garden of Joseph," the Johannine basis would lie in the tradition that Joseph used a tomb in that garden to bury Jesus. Let us discuss first the possibility or verisimilitude of such a garden burial, and then its significance in Johannine thought.

Possibility/verisimilitude. Jewish burials were made outside the city, and that means outside the city gates. Very likely Jesus was crucified and buried north of Jerusalem. A major junction in the north wall of the city (where the eastern section of it swung farther north to include the Antonia area) was called Gennath (Josephus, *War* 5.4.2; #146), a name connected with the Garden Gate (Hebrew *gan*, Aramaic *gannā'* = "garden"), one of the four gates in the north wall. Indeed, the route from the likely site of Pilate's praetorium (the Herodian palace; §31, C2) to the most likely site of Golgotha would have brought Jesus eastward along the city-side of the north wall, to exit the city through the Garden Gate. An intelligible reason for such a designation of the gate was that there were gardens in this northern area. Certainly there were important burials to the north of the walls, e.g., those of the royal high priests John Hyrcanus and Alexander Jannaeus (*War* 5.6.2 and 5.7.3; ##259, 304). Krauss ("Double" 8) indicates that it was not uncommon for Jews to put to rest their dead in fields or gardens (particularly when they planned later to collect the bones for "reburial" in an ossuary); and TalBab *Yebamot* 86b mentions a garden and graveyard in close proximity.[74] Ca. AD 350 Cyril

[72]In John 18:1 this term was applied to a locale on the Mount of Olives and may mean an orchard. The garden motif is picked up again in John 20:15 with Mary Magdalene's surmise that Jesus is the "gardener" (*kēpouros*) who might have carried Jesus' body off from the tomb. In the *Secret Gospel of Mark* 2:26 the tomb of the unnamed woman's brother was in a garden; that has a good chance of reflecting a combination of John's accounts of the burials of Lazarus and of Jesus (p. 296 above).

[73]As Price ("Jesus") shows, the tradition of the garden had a rich subsequent history. Tertullian, *De Spectaculis* 30 (CC 1.253), reports a Jewish polemic contention that the gardener of this plot took Jesus' body away from the tomb lest crowds of visitors damage his lettuces or cabbages. *The Book of the Resurrection of Christ by Bartholomew the Apostle* 1.6–7 (Coptic, 5th to 7th cents.; JANT 183) tells us that the gardener's name was Philogenes, whose son Jesus had healed. He offered a tomb close to his vegetable garden to the Jews who were looking for a place to bury Jesus, all the while planning to take the body away and bury it honorably. But when he came back at midnight he found the tomb surrounded by angels and saw the Father raise Jesus. The Muslim antiChristian apologist 'Abd al-Jabbār, writing ca. 1000 (p. 1094 above), reports that Jesus was crucified in a field of melons and vegetables—a theme he may have picked up from Jewish attacks on the worship of the crucified Jesus as idolatrous, phrased in the language of Jer 10:3–5 (a wooden idol set up like a scarecrow in a cucumber field; Price, "Jesus" 24). In the *Toledoth Yeshu* polemics, Judas buried Jesus in a garden under a brook (ibid 27).

[74]Garden burial seems to have been a Greek custom as well; so M. Smith, *Clement* 105.

of Jerusalem (*Catechesis* 14.5; PG 33.829B) reported that the remains of a garden that had previously existed were still visible adjacent to the Martyrion basilica that Constantine had recently built to honor the traditional site of Jesus' tomb (subsection C in the ANALYSIS below). Thus there is nothing implausible in John's scenario that there was a garden in the area north of Jerusalem where Jesus was crucified, and that he was buried in a tomb in that garden.

Significance. Does John intend an inclusion by having his PN begin in 18:1 with Jesus going out across the Kidron with those who were his disciples to where there was a garden (*kēpos*), and by ending his PN in a garden where Jesus is buried by two men who are just becoming public disciples? That is certainly a possibility. Some scholars have also tried to find a parallel between the garden across the Kidron and the paradise (*paradeisos*) of Genesis 2:8 where God placed the first human being and where sin was first committed. Because of the vocabulary dissimilarity I did not find that proposal convincing; nor do I accept such a parallel here, despite the attempt to reinforce it through the Adam parallelism that Paul detected in Christ's death (Rom 5:12–21) and/or through the thesis that Golgotha was named after Adam's skull (§40, n. 9).

Above I pointed out that huge amounts of spices were used in regal burials. Is the fact that the kings of Judah were buried in garden tombs (II Kings 21:18,26) part of the same picture? From the LXX of Neh 3:16 we learn that the sepulcher of King David was in a garden, and Acts 2:29 shows that David's tomb was popularly familiar in NT times. Was the garden burial of Jesus remembered because it was seen as symbolically appropriate for the Son of David? Was the tradition recalled by John in particular because of his emphasis that Jesus of Nazareth on the cross was triumphantly proclaimed as "the King of the Jews"? The evidence for this thesis is not sufficient to establish proof, but such a symbolism would be a most appropriate conclusion to John's PN.

ANALYSIS

As I have stressed, my division of the treatment of the burial of Jesus into two parts (§§46 and 47) is only for convenience in commenting, since in fact the Gospel accounts are relatively brief and unified. In the ANALYSIS of §46 I have already discussed the composition of the accounts and reconstructed a preGospel tradition of the burial by Joseph that could have been shared by

Mark (which influenced Matt and Luke) and John. Building on that general discussion, I shall concentrate here on the preparation and interment of the body (the last part of the Joseph burial) and on the activity of other dramatis personae (the addendum to the Joseph burial). The ANALYSIS will close with a summary of what is known about the history of the Church of the Holy Sepulchre and the site on which it stands—a summary that represents what Christian tradition in Jerusalem can tell us about the burial place.

A. **Preparation and Interment of the Body**

The Marcan description of the finale of the burial by Joseph is laconic: Joseph took down the body, tied it up in a linen cloth, and put it away in a burial place hewn out of rock. (Harmoniously with their ennoblement of Joseph, Matt and Luke embellish the description of the cloth and/or the tomb.) After the burial, Mark tells us that Joseph rolled over (*proskyliein*) a stone against the door of the tomb. (Matt adds that he went away.) John's account is complicated by the intervention of Nicodemus, who cooperated with Joseph and thus changed the style of the burial to one done according to Jewish customs. Nevertheless, if one confines oneself to what John attributes to Joseph alone in 19:38b and one skips over the role of Nicodemus and his spices in the joint action of 19:40–42, the finale of the story of the burial activities in John runs like this: Joseph came and took away the body; he (they) bound it with cloths; he (they) placed it in a nearby garden tomb, *a new one in which no one had ever been placed.* The italicized clause at the end of my summary of the finale represents an embellishment of the tomb almost identical with the embellishments that Matt and Luke add over Mark, and so may be looked on as a later stage in Johannine composition. The nonitalicized portion of the summary shows how close John is to Mark. On the basis of the agreements between Mark and John, therefore, I suggested on pp. 1239–40 above a preGospel tradition of the Joseph-burial finale that had Joseph taking (down) the body, wrapping it with cloth(s), and placing it in a tomb (implicitly nearby). Mark and John have incorporated this tradition in quite different vocabulary.[75] This difference not only helps to establish

---

[75]Mark: *kathairein* ("to take away"), *eneilein* ("to tie up"), *sindōn* ("linen cloth"), *katatithenai* ("to put away"). John: *lambanein* ("to take"), *dein* ("to bind"), *othonion* (pl.: "cloths"), *tithenai* ("to place"). It is mind-boggling to theorize that John copied from Mark the brief core of the action but changed almost every key word. Why? One has to posit either John's independence of Mark (with both drawing on the same preGospel tradition) or a remote dependence based on having heard or read Mark in the past. The latter suggestion falters on the fact that the more vivid Marcan details that people tend to remember are not preserved in John, e.g., that the tomb was hewn out of the rock or that the stone was rolled over against the door of the tomb. Luke and Matt, which are dependent

that John did not copy from Mark but also suggests that the common tradition was shaped in the Semitic-speaking stage of preGospel formation, so that there were already different formulations in the Greek stage of the pre-Marcan and preJohannine tradition. This perception of early origin, although not in itself proving historicity, contributed to my judgment at the end of the ANALYSIS of §46 that "there is nothing in the basic preGospel account of Jesus' burial by Joseph that could not plausibly be deemed historical."

But now on the basis of some differences between Mark and John in their descriptions of the finale of the burial, let me raise questions about other details that might have been in the preGospel Joseph-burial account.

DID THE PREGOSPEL ACCOUNT HAVE JOSEPH TAKE JESUS DOWN FROM THE CROSS? The Gospels agree that Joseph needed Pilate's permission but disagree as to whether Pilate's soldiers took the body down and give it to Joseph (Matt implicitly, perhaps John; the Jews in *GPet* take the body down and give it to Joseph) or took it down himself (Mark, Luke). It would help to settle the issue if we knew what the Romans usually did once they had made the concession of allowing discrete burial. Did they show their mastery of the situation by not letting anyone touch the body till they actually gave it over, or did they spare themselves the extra labor and contemptuously make the petitioner do the physical work of detaching the corpse from the cross? I see no way to decide, although the first seems a bit more probable especially when there were to be different disposals of the bodies of the crucified so that the Romans themselves would have had to take down at least some from the cross.

WHAT DETAILS ABOUT THE TOMB WERE INCLUDED IN THE PREGOSPEL BURIAL ACCOUNT? Mark (followed by Matt and Luke in slightly different vocabulary) specifies that the tomb was hewn out of rock. John does not; instead he states that the tomb was in a garden near the site of the crucifixion. In my judgment these details about the tomb are not on the same level as the indications that it was new (Matt, John), that no one had ever been laid/placed in it before (Luke, John), and that it was Joseph's own (Matt, *GPet*). The latter indications stem either from apologetic interests associated with the empty tomb or from the ennoblement of Joseph, and so are more likely to represent a later formative stage. (Lateness does not rule out all possibilities of factuality.) I mentioned in the COMMENT that rock-hewn tombs were common in the area north of Jerusalem which is the most plausible site for Golgotha, and that there was a Garden Gate that led out to that area, presum-

---

on Mark (not by past memory, however, but by direct use of written Mark), preserve the first of those features, and Matt preserves the second.

ably so called because there were gardens or orchards there.[76] If Christians retained a memory of the tomb of Jesus (and that is plausible), these details, as well as the hint that this was a horizontal-shaft tomb with the door blocked by a rock, could be factual. That would not mean necessarily that they were part of the early preGospel tradition of the Joseph burial; they could have still been added at a later stage (whether preMarcan or Marcan, preJohannine or Johannine) as it was fleshed out. Or they could reflect verisimilitude, e.g., rock-hewn tombs closed by rolling stones were frequent in the garden area north of Jerusalem and so presumably Jesus was laid in a tomb like that. Similar comments might be made about the indication (explicit in John, implicit in the others) that the tomb was near where Jesus was crucified. A Joseph who was not a disciple would not have taken the trouble nor have had the time before the Sabbath to carry the crucified criminal's body far away; consequently the tomb was (factually or plausibly) near Golgotha. Once more I see no way to settle this issue. Because I do think that Christians remembered the tomb in which Jesus was buried, I tend to favor factuality over verisimilitude in explaining the origin of these details. Yet the fact that Mark and John do not share any of them makes it less likely that they were to be found in the detectable early preGospel tradition that underlay both Gospels.

DID THE PREGOSPEL ACCOUNT HAVE JOSEPH CLOSE THE TOMB WITH A STONE? Mark, followed by Matt (who makes the stone large), has Joseph himself roll over the stone against the door of the tomb. Neither Luke nor John specifies who was responsible for the stone being there. *GPet* has those interested in the guarding of the tomb, i.e., Roman soldiers and Jewish authorities, roll a large stone to the door of the tomb. At the time on Easter morning that the women get to the tomb, all five works agree that the stone was or is moved.[77] There is reason to judge, then, that in the preGospel tradition of Mary Magdalene's discovery of the empty tomb, reference was made to the tomb being already opened because the stone that had closed it had

---

[76]True, John may well give a theological significance to the garden setting of the burial (p. 1270 above), and so one might argue that this detail is not unmotivated and should be put together with the others that were brought into the burial picture for apologetic or theological reasons. The theological import, however, in this instance is not so clear that it can easily be judged to have given rise to the mention of a garden; more likely the theological possibilities arose from the fact that a garden was mentioned in recounting the burial.

[77]Mark: *apokyliein, anakyliein;* Matt and Luke: *apokyliein;* John *airein;* GPet *kyliein.* I am dubious to what extent the removed burial stone is echoed in 1 Pet 2:4, which invites people to come "to him, a living stone, rejected by human beings but before God chosen and precious." Mercurio ("Baptismal" 48–49) points to this as one of the baptismal motifs in the Gospel descriptions of the burial, along with the water that flows from Jesus' side, the linen cloth, and the garden (of paradise!).

been rolled/moved back.[78] It would not have been either a great or an illogical leap to assume that the person who buried Jesus put the stone at the door of the tomb, and therefore it may well be that Joseph's closing of the tomb was read into the burial story as a back-formation from the empty-tomb tradition. Such a back-formation would not necessarily mean that such action by Joseph was not historically factual—what is logically surmised to have happened more often than not actually did happen—any more than acceptance of the factuality of Joseph's actions would necessarily mean that the tomb closing was included in the preGospel tradition about the burial. John's independent tradition does not mention the stone in the burial account but only in the empty-tomb story; that fact suggests that there was no tomb closing in the preGospel Joseph-burial story and supports a back-formation theory. Nevertheless, one must allow the possibility that John omitted the closing of the tomb for theological reasons, since the stronger the identification of Joseph as a disciple before the burial, the less likely a tendency to have him close the tomb with finality, as if he were not open to the resurrection. That is why the closing of the tomb becomes an action by Jesus' opponents in *GPet*, as is the *sealing* of the tomb in Matt 27:66.

WERE SPICES MENTIONED IN THE PREGOSPEL ACCOUNT OF THE BURIAL? The issue of the spices is more complicated. In connection with Nicodemus, John mentions myrrh (*smyrna*), aloes, and spices as part of the burial in which Joseph cooperates. Luke mentions spices and myrrh (*myron*) being prepared by the women after the burial on Friday evening before the Sabbath began. Mark (16:1) has the women buy spices on Easter morn after the Sabbath is over before they go to the tomb. The fact that none of the three Gospels that refer to "spices" (pl. of *arōma*)[79] associates them with Joseph's personal action makes it dubious that there was a mention of spices in the preGospel tradition of a burial by Joseph. Was the use of spices part of the preGospel empty-tomb tradition and read back into the burial? Or were there other burial traditions beyond the burial by Joseph that we have been discussing? That question leads us into a discussion of the second topic in

---

[78]Speculation as to how it was opened belongs to a later stage in the development of the story with the introduction of the angel(s) to interpret the meaning of the empty tomb, so that the story could become an effective means of proclaiming the risen Lord. As for the agent of the removal, Mark, Luke, and perhaps John imply that the angel(s) who appear in/at the tomb did this; Matt describes an angel who descended from heaven rolling back the stone; *GPet* has the stone roll of itself.

[79]They may not interpret the spices in the same way. I argued in the COMMENT that John is thinking of pulverized, dry myrrh and aloes, while Mark (clearly) and Luke (probably—*myron* is usually oil) think of a liquid oil or salve for anointing.

this ANALYSIS: the fact that all the Gospels have other actors besides Joseph in their burial accounts.

B. **Presence and Activity of Dramatis Personae Other than Joseph**

The Synoptic Gospels have in common the presence of Galilean women at the tomb; and using Luke 24:10 to clarify 23:55, we can see that implicitly they agree that two of those women were Mary Magdalene and Mary mother of James and Joses/Joseph. Nicodemus is active only in John. In *GPet* 6:21,23 the Jews "drew out the nails from the hands of the Lord and placed him on the earth . . . and gave his body to Joseph that he might bury it"; and in 8:32 Roman soldiers and scribes, Pharisees, and elders "having rolled a large stone . . . placed (it) against the door of the burial place." (The *GPet* story goes on to have the latter agents seal the burial place and keep watch over it.) If, as I speculated, Joseph from Arimathea was originally a Sanhedrist who was not on Jesus' side, it is not surprising that Christian tradition about the burial would want to complement him with figures more favorable to Jesus, like the women or Nicodemus.[80] On the other hand, once Joseph was imagined to have been a pre-burial Christian and it was believed that the risen Jesus broke the bonds of the tomb, some of the negative character of the burial process (attempting to get rid of Jesus) would quickly be attributed to his enemies. Were other preGospel traditions that gave a role to these additional dramatis personae in the burial of Jesus brought into the Gospels by way of combining them with the Joseph story? Or was the presence of such dramatis personae a product of deduction from the empty-tomb resurrection narratives, and/or of theological creation, and/or, in the case of enemies, of apologetics? Whether or not they appeared in the preGospel traditions, was their presence historical? These are questions with which we must now wrestle as we treat separately the origins of the role of the Galilean women and of Nicodemus in the burial accounts. That of the Jews in closing the tomb will be kept until the next section (§48) where wc treat Matt's account of the request of the chief priests and the Pharisees to guard the tomb, along with its parallel in *GPet*.

1. THE GALILEAN WOMEN. Readers should refresh their memory of the discussion centered around Table 8 on p. 1016. It was pointed out that of the three appearances of these women in the PN (at a distance from the cross, observing the burial, coming to the empty tomb on Easter), the one most agreed upon by the evangelists involved Mary Magdalene (explicitly or im-

---

[80]Another reaction, as we saw, was to transform Joseph into someone more favorable to Jesus.

plicitly with companions) coming to the tomb on Easter and finding it empty. That, plus another early tradition that Mary Magdalene was accorded the first Jerusalem appearance of the risen Lord, was the primary factor in preserving the memory of the Galilean women.[81] What does the disagreement among the evangelists, especially between Mark and John, about the appearance of these women in the earlier PN scenes mean? On pp. 1019, 1195 above I discussed their presence at the crucifixion and argued that John 19:25 and Mark 15:40 pointed to the likelihood of a preGospel tradition that three women were present at (a distance from) the cross: Mary Magdalene, another Mary (variously identified), and a third woman.

It is more difficult to argue for an early common tradition involving their presence at the burial. Negative signs are that they are absent from John, that in Mark (the basic Synoptic account) they have no active participation in the burial, and that they observe the burial in the tomb so that they can come back to the tomb on Easter and make up for what was lacking in the burial. The thesis of back-formation, then, is very attractive: namely, that from the role of Mary Magdalene and companions in the empty-tomb tradition and from the early tradition of the presence of three Galilean women at the crucifixion it was logically assumed that they were at the burial. They were included in the Marcan story of the burial (followed by Matt and Luke) in order to make the burial story more clearly a connective between the crucifixion and the resurrection. Primarily Joseph's action was the culmination of the passion and crucifixion account; and the women's observation prepared for the resurrection from the tomb. (John's burial account, which does not mention the women, clearly brings the crucifixion to a close; it serves as Episode 6 of the crucifixion narrative in a chiastic pattern [p. 908], but does little to prepare for Mary Magdalene's visit to an empty tomb.) In the larger Marcan picture, however, the women by their presence at the crucifixion, the burial, and the empty tomb interrelate all three scenes.

In §44, n. 34, I surveyed ingenious attempts to use variations in the names of the women (especially of the other Mary) to determine the scene in which they were more original. Not surprisingly that technique has been used here as well, e.g., Gnilka (*Markus* 2.331) would maintain that while the Marcan list of names in the empty-tomb story (16:1) is secondary and drawn from the list at the crucifixion (15:40), the list of names here at the burial is older tradition, for only two are mentioned. Blinzler ("Grablegung" 61) considers the list both here and at the empty tomb to be original. While regarding this

---

[81]The subsequent career of Mary Magdalene became the subject of florid legendary development, not unlike the legends that grew up around Joseph from Arimathea. However, the fact that she is primarily a figure of the resurrection accounts would render a report on those legends out of place in a book on the PN.

approach based on names as, at best, complementary to other argumentation, I suggested that the two older traditions of the names had three women at the crucifixion (Mary Magdalene, another Mary, a third woman[82]), and Mary Magdalene (and vaguely other women) at the empty tomb. Eventually the names of the women at the empty tomb were harmonized with the names given to the women at the cross, but in an abbreviated form since they had already been mentioned.[83] Thus, if we look once more at Table 8, Mark's "Mary Magdalene, and Mary mother of James the younger and of Joses, and Salome" in 15:40 became "Mary Magdalene, the Mary of James, and Salome" in 16:1.[84] According to the thesis that the reference to the women at the burial is a back-formation from their presence at the empty tomb, the shortening has continued: only "Mary Magdalene and Mary of Joses," with a decision to name here the other son from 15:40 who was omitted from the reuse in 16:1.[85] Matt has gone further in his simplification, using at the burial (27:61) the same shortened form (Mary Magdalene and the other Mary) that he will use at the tomb (28:1). These suggestions about the procedure of the evangelists in this complex matter remain highly speculative, however.

2. NICODEMUS. This additional character in the burial is found only in John, where he has appeared in two previous scenes (3:1ff.; 7:50–52). To explain his presence here (when he is totally absent from the Synoptic burial account) an astounding number of suggestions have been made by scholars. Most simply some have thought that there was a historical Nicodemus who did just what John described but who was forgotten in the tradition of the larger church. (More than the other evangelists, John shows a knowledge of Jerusalem and of Jesus' followers there.) We have seen the likelihood that as the tradition grew, Joseph was transformed from a pious law-observant Sanhedrist who before the burial was not a follower of Jesus into a disciple or one sympathetic to Jesus. Was the original picture more complex, with several Jewish Sanhedrin members anxious to have Jesus buried before sunset, including a Joseph who was not a disciple and a Nicodemus who was

[82]I doubt that the third woman was identified in the preGospel tradition because every Gospel names her differently; see §44, n. 139.

[83]That harmonization did not happen in John which, by naming only Mary Magdalene (who speaks as "we") at the tomb, preserves the older situation.

[84]If we compare the respective Matthean texts, we find that "Mary Magdalene, and Mary mother of James and of Joseph, and the mother of the sons of Zebedee" in 27:56 became "Mary Magdalene and the other Mary" in 28:1. Luke, with his own sense of order, having named the Galilean women in the course of the ministry in 8:1–3, simply refers to them in general at the crucifixion and burial, naming them once more (in a shortened form) only as the empty-tomb story ends (24:10).

[85]This last step would have been on the literary level; the earlier steps could have been wholly or partly in the oral shaping of the Gospel traditions. The explanation I have offered answers many of the objections that I raised against other theories about the names in §44, n. 34.

sympathetic to Jesus throughout the public ministry; and were the two amalgamated into Joseph in simplified preaching that has left its effect on the Synoptic accounts? The main difficulty with such historical suggestions is that in Mark the burial by Joseph is hasty and minimal; in John the presence of Nicodemus and his spices makes the burial customary and honorific—if one argues that the Synoptic tradition forgot Nicodemus, it also forgot the very nature of the burial. Another thesis is that although Nicodemus was original in the Johannine scenes of Jesus' ministry, he was added here for symbolic purposes. For example, with the reminder that earlier Nicodemus had come at night (19:39 echoing 3:1–2), did John want readers to recollect the initial dialogue between Jesus and Nicodemus about "water and spirit" (3:5) as they reflected on the meaning of the water that came out of Jesus' side in 19:34? Still another thesis is that Nicodemus was entirely an imaginative Johannine creation. It is pointed out that he was much like Joseph: Both were Sanhedrin members; both were attracted to Jesus; both kept hidden their sympathy for him. Was Joseph too established a figure in the tradition to allow dramatization, so that John fashioned a doppelgänger who might function elsewhere besides the burial?[86] Or alongside Joseph, who during Jesus' lifetime was a hidden disciple for fear of the Jews, did John want to set a figure like Nicodemus personifying the synagogue leaders who were familiar at a later period to the Johannine Christians, showing publicly their sympathy for Jesus only after a moment of great trial (and thus finally breaking the concealment pattern of 12:42)?

None of these theses can claim great probability. In fact, the two episodes involved in the burial, John 19:31–37 and 19:38–42, are among the most difficult in the Gospel for discerning the history of Johannine composition. Yet some observations can be made with surety (even if they do not enable a decision): The role of Nicodemus was absent from the preGospel Joseph-burial account; when added it changed the style of the burial from minimal to customary; the role of Nicodemus is very Johannine in the triumphal orientation it gives to the burial as the culmination of the enthroning crucifixion. Both in this episode, then, as in the preceding one with the eyewitness of 19:35 (i.e., the beloved disciple of 19:26–27), we have present a crucial, very Johannine character not known to the Synoptics who establishes the theological symbolism of the scene.

Like many other commentators on John (Barrett, Dodd, Schnackenburg,

---

[86]An objection to the supposed inability to dramatize the Joseph image is constituted by what happens to Joseph in *GPet,* where he becomes a friend of Pilate (2:3) "who had seen how many good things he [Jesus] did" (6:23). There Joseph becomes like "many of the Jews" in the ministry of the Johannine Jesus—"having seen what Jesus did, they believed in him" (John 11:45, as contrasted with those in 12:37).

etc.) I recognize that one should not jump to the conclusion that exclusively Johannine characters are not historical because their role suits the theology of the Gospel. After all, John makes similar dramatic theological use of characters whose existence is confirmed by the other Gospels, e.g., Simon Peter. As for the peculiarly Johannine characters, I would argue that John did not simply invent the disciple whom he describes as loved by Jesus; I take him to have been a relatively insignificant disciple when compared with those named in the common tradition, e.g., the Twelve, but one who achieved major importance within the confines of Johannine tradition, where his ongoing closeness to Jesus was perceived as the model for community behavior. I see no reason for denying Nicodemus a possible historicity; but that judgment does not guarantee that he had a role in the burial, any more than the historicity of the beloved disciple guarantees that factually he appeared in every scene in which he is described. A decision on that point must be aided by other factors, e.g., not only whether the Johannine character is absent from the Synoptic parallel (which in itself is not too decisive[87]), but whether the presence of the Johannine figure is in conflict with the Synoptic presentation. The present situation is close to that.

C. The Church of the Holy Sepulchre in Jerusalem

Let me close this analysis of what may be ancient in the burial narrative with the light cast on the tomb of Jesus by what we know of the traditional site at which both Golgotha and the tomb were venerated in Jerusalem and of the series of churches built there.[88] Certainly the site possesses verisimilitude, for we have already seen that it is appropriately located for what the Gospels tell us about the place of Jesus' execution and burial. It was north of the Second North Wall of Jesus' time, near the Garden Gate; excavations have shown that there was a quarry at the site which had begun to be filled in so that it served as a garden for cereals and trees (figs, carobs, olives) and for burials, mostly of the *kōkîm* type (see COMMENT above). But beyond verisimilitude, which could apply to several sites, why has this candidate, the Church of the Holy Sepulchre, emerged first in its claim that within its walls are both Golgotha and the tomb? (Seemingly in the first millennium neither site was *inside* the basilica church erected at this spot: The site of

[87]It is not truly significant that Luke 24:12 (if authentic) mentions only Peter running to the tomb while John 20:2–4 has the beloved disciple alongside Simon Peter (even though this combination is purely Johannine and quite symbolic). As Luke 24:24 shows, it was in the Lucan tradition that "some of those with us [thus more than one] went away to the tomb."

[88]In the SECTIONAL BIBLIOGRAPHY of §37, under Part 2 (Geography), see especially the articles of Bahat, Kretschmar, Ross, and Wilkinson ("Church"), which reflect the foundational studies of Coüasnon and Corbo. I am indebted to Bahat and Wilkinson for much that I digest in this section.

the crucifixion was in a courtyard and that of the tomb in a rotunda separated from the church by a garden.) The very name the church now bears suggests that the primary claim is centered on the tomb, and I shall concentrate on that here.

We may begin with reflections on the likelihood that Christians would remember correctly which was the tomb of Jesus, even though in this early period there is little evidence that they preserved precisely a memory of the sites of other phenomena associated with him. In the Gospels there are clear signs of theological interest in the tomb. Acknowledging the existence of an old tradition that on Easter morn Mary Magdalene found empty the tomb in which Jesus had been buried, many scholars would posit an ongoing development into full-scale narratives with the presence of an angel or angels who served to interpret the significance of the empty tomb as an indicator of the resurrection. However, interest in the symbolism of the tomb would not necessarily be accompanied by a knowledge of the exact site. The information that Mark gives, namely, that it was hewn out of rock, would scarcely help to make the site identifiable; only John's report that the tomb was in a garden near Golgotha and Matt's indication (by surmise?) that it was Joseph's own tomb might serve that purpose. Nevertheless, we have to turn to evidence outside the Gospels to establish the likelihood of a remembered spot.

There was in this period an increasing Jewish veneration of the tombs of the martyrs and prophets.[89] The putative tombs of the Maccabees were venerated, since they were considered martyrs for the worship of the true God (p. 1210 above). Indeed, by the 4th cent., Christians in Antioch had taken over these tombs from the Jews as places of prayer and pilgrimage.[90] *The Lives of the Prophets,* a work with a complicated history but which may have roots in 1st-cent.-AD Judaism, is careful in most of its accounts to tell us where the prophet was buried. Of particular interest is 1:9, which tells us that the tomb of Isaiah in Jerusalem was "near the tomb of the kings, west of the tomb of the priests in the southern part of the city" (= the Kidron valley). As for the tomb of Haggai (14:2), "When he died he was buried near the tomb of the priests, in great honor, even as they were." Zechariah, who was the martyred son of a priest, was taken by the priests and buried with his father (23:1). The Kidron valley and the area north of Jerusalem are dotted with monumental tombs from this period, commemorating (accurately and inaccurately) the memory of prophets, holy men, sages, priests, and roy-

---

[89]See Jeremias, *Heiligengräber,* esp. 145.
[90]Chrysostom, *De Maccabeis* 1.1 (PG 50.617); Homily 11, *De Eleazaro* 1.1 (PG 63.523–24).

alty. I have already mentioned the "Tombs of the Kings" (in reality, the tomb complex of Queen Helen of Adiabene, who died about twenty-five years after Jesus) that offer an excellent parallel in many features for studying the kind of place in which Jesus was probably buried (cut in a quarry; containing both *kōkîm* and arcosolium burials; closed by a rolling stone). A particular reason for remembering the tomb of Jesus would lie in Christian faith that the tomb had been evacuated by his resurrection from the dead. If one may appeal to later mishnaic attitudes, *Berakot* 9.1 offers encouragement for thinking that the Jewish followers of Jesus would not forget the site of that tremendous happening: "When a place is shown where wonders happened in Israel, say, 'Blessed is the One who wrought wonders for our ancestors in this place.'" Unfortunately *GPet* shows no reliable knowledge of 1st-cent. Palestine; otherwise one might appeal to 6:24, which gives a place name, "the Garden of Joseph," as proof that Christians could point out the tomb site.

Some historical factors could have affected the remembrance of the spot. A close relative of Jesus, James "the brother of the Lord," was a major figure in the Jerusalem Christian community (Gal 2:9) from just after Jesus' resurrection (I Cor 15:7: "He appeared to James") until AD 62 when he was put to death by the high priest Ananus II (Josephus, *Ant.* 20.9.1; #200). In that period he might well have had a family interest in the tomb, an interest that could have been a living tradition among the relatives of Jesus who are supposed to have been prominent in Palestinian Christianity into the 2d cent. (Eusebius, EH 3.19–20). Burial in the quarry garden that marked the traditional site stopped within fifteen years of Jesus' death, for it was incorporated into Jerusalem when Herod Agrippa I (AD 41–44) pushed the city walls farther north. Even more difficult would have been retention of a memory of the site during the major change that occurred after the Second Jewish Revolt with Hadrian's rebuilding of Jerusalem as the Roman city of Aelia Capitolina. Jews were not allowed in this new city, but the Christian community was able to continue because the bishopric now passed into the hands of Gentile Christians (EH 4.6.3–4). In 135 in the general area of the tomb site an immense platform was built—a rectangular filled-in area on which the Romans constructed a temple to Aphrodite (although some scholars, drawing on Jerome, speak of a temple to Jupiter). The choice to erect a pagan temple right over the tomb of Jesus may have been accidental and not a deliberate affront to what after all was only a minor sect.[91] Yet it may also

[91]L. D. Sporty (BA 54 [1991], 28–35) thinks rather of an affront to Judaism. If one looked from the Mount of Olives along an east-west line from what was the Golden Gate of the Temple compound through the site of the Holy of Holies to where the Aphrodite temple was built, the pagan

have served to landmark the now-buried site for the next two hundred years (Kretschmar, "Kreuz" 424). As for Golgotha, according to Jerome, it protruded above the platform and constituted a base for a statue of Aphrodite. In the latter part of the 2d cent. the site of the buried tomb could be shown to Melito of Sardis when he came to Jerusalem, and he described it as in the midst of the broad streets of the Roman city (pp. 912–13 above).

In 325, according to Eusebius and Cyril of Jerusalem, who were contemporary with the event, local tradition about the site of the crucifixion and burial guided the builders commissioned by the Emperor Constantine who wished to uncover the holy places and honor them with a church (see L.E.C. Evans, "Holy" 123). When they demolished the Hadrianic structures and dug out the fill, they found the cave tomb, a discovery described by Eusebius in his *De vita Constantini* (3.30–32; GCS 7.91–93—see S. Heid, *Römische Quartalschrift* 87 [1992], 1–28). Cyril of Jerusalem, who preached in the Constantinian basilica ca. 350, also speaks of the tomb as having been a grotto or cave.[92] Besides building a long basilica running east-west called the Martyrion (completed in 336), the Constantinian architects worked on the burial cave and Golgotha, thus creating a sacred complex with three major sites. As for the holy cave, the interior tomb chamber with the burial niche was left intact; but the builders cut away much of the outer antechamber of the cave as well as the exterior rock face until only a blocklike structure was left standing on a level surface. They then adorned the exterior with an edicule having small marble columns and a gold roof, thus turning it into a shrine. Eventually this became the center of a colonnaded rotunda, entitled the Anastasis (Resurrection),[93] set in a garden courtyard west of the Martyrion basilica. Golgotha or the Calvary knoll was in the southern corner of the courtyard, touching on the west end of the basilica.

The Persian invaders of 614 stripped some of the precious adornments off the edicule but were not interested in the underlying rock tomb, which fortunately was not damaged by the fire that accompanied the depredation. Nor does another major fire in the 10th cent. seem to have damaged the tomb itself. Catastrophe came in 1009 when the Fatimid Caliph of Cairo, Ḥākim,

---

temple would have stood at a dominantly higher point on the western end of the line towering over the Jewish religious ruins—a visible sign of Rome's triumph over Judaism. The choice of the Constantinian architects to build their church on the site of the Aphrodite temple which they destroyed and thus on the same east-west line would have shown the triumph of Christianity over both the Roman and Jewish religions.

[92]*Catechesis* 14.9 (PG 33:833B); in 14.22 (PG 33.853A) he claims that the stone that closed the tomb was still there.

[93]Bahat ("Does" 40) makes the interesting suggestion that the rotunda imitated the shape of the Temple to Aphrodite that had stood above the site in the forum of Hadrian's Aelia Capitolina; and indeed it is likely that some of the columns from that temple were used. He points to rotunda-shaped Aphrodite temples elsewhere, including Rome.

as part of his attempt to abolish Christianity, destroyed the whole complex and had the tomb virtually levelled, leaving traces of the original rock walls only on the north and south (fortunately enough to enable subsequent investigators to detect the plan of the edicule). In a rebuilding forty years later a replica of the tomb was erected and the Anastasis rotunda partially restored, but the Constantinian basilica was not rebuilt.

When the crusaders arrived in 1099, they began to build a church to house both the Anastasis and Calvary; and this was completed in 1149. Having the general form that is still standing, it exhibited the pointed arches and other features that were beginning to appear in the European churches of the era. Golgotha was squared off and a marble casing placed over it (although the original rock of the knoll is still visible in the back); so that it now stood within the church like a high boxed chapel not far from the edicule that covered the rebuilt tomb. Once more the area of the holy sepulcher became a burial spot, this time for the crusader kings of the Latin Kingdom of Jerusalem. The crusaders were driven out in 1187. Over the centuries earthquakes and fires marred their great church and weakened it; and attempts to shore it up left an ugly tangle of supporting girders and wooden beams. It was only with the reconstruction begun in 1959 that the long history of structures underneath became apparent. And beneath nearly 1,700 years of architectural endeavors, not visible to the pilgrim's eye, which sees a marble covering, there are still the very meager remnants from the walls of a cave that has the best claim to have been the burial place hewn out of rock into which a pious Sanhedrist placed the corpse of the crucified Jesus.

(Bibliography for this episode may be found in §45, Part 1.)

§48. THE BURIAL OF JESUS, PART THREE: ON THE SABBATH; THE GUARD AT THE SEPULCHER

(Matt 27:62–66; Luke 23:56b)

Translation

Luke 23:56b: 56bAnd then on the Sabbath they rested according to the commandment.

Matt 27:62–66: 62But on the next day, which is after the preparation day, there gathered together the chief priests and the Pharisees before Pilate, 63saying, "Lord, we remembered that that deceiver said when he was still living, 'After three days I am (to be) raised.' 64So order the sepulcher to be made secure until the third day, lest, having come, the disciples steal him and say to the people, 'He was raised from the dead,' and the last deception will be worse than the first." 65Pilate said to them, "You (may) have a custodial guard. Go, make secure as you know how." 66Having gone, they made the sepulcher secure with the custodial guard, having sealed the stone.

[28:2–4 (after the Sabbath, at the sepulcher): 2And behold there was a great earthquake; for an angel of the Lord, having come down out of heaven and having come forward, rolled away the stone and was sitting upon it. 3Now his appearance was as lightning, and his garb white as snow. 4But from fear of him those keeping guard quaked and became as dead men.]

[28:11–15 (after the women have been met by the risen Jesus and told to go to his brothers, the disciples): 11But while they were going, behold some of the custodial guard, having entered the city, announced to the chief priests all the things that had happened. 12And having gathered with the elders and having taken a decision, they gave many silver pieces to the soldiers, 13saying, "Say that,

'His disciples, having come at night, stole him while we were sleeping.' [14]And if this be heard by the governor, we shall persuade (him) and make you free from worry." [15]Now having taken the silver pieces, they did as they were instructed. And this word has been spread about among the Jews until this day.]

GPet 8:28–9:34: [8:28]But the scribes and Pharisees and elders, having gathered together with one another, having heard that all the people were murmuring and beating their breasts, saying that, "If at his death these very great signs happened, behold how just he was," [29]feared (especially the elders) and came before Pilate, begging him and saying, [30]"Give over soldiers to us in order that we may safeguard his burial place for three days, lest, having come, his disciples steal him, and the people accept that he is risen from the dead, and they do us wrong." [31]But Pilate gave over to them Petronius the centurion with soldiers to safeguard the sepulcher. And with these the elders and scribes came to the burial place. [32]And having rolled a large stone, all who were there, together with the centurion and the soldiers, placed (it) against the door of the burial place. [33]And they marked (it) with seven wax seals; and having pitched a tent there, they safeguarded (it). [9:34]But early when the Sabbath was dawning, a crowd came from Jerusalem and the surrounding area in order that they might see the sealed tomb.

[9:35–11:49: [9:35]But in the night in which the Lord's Day dawned, when the soldiers were safeguarding (it) two by two in every watch, there was a loud voice in heaven; [36]and they saw that the heavens were opened and that two males who had much radiance had come down from there and come near the sepulcher. [37]But that stone which had been thrust against the door, having rolled by itself, went a distance off to the side; and the sepulcher opened, and both the young men entered. [10:38]And so those soldiers, having seen, awakened the centurion and the elders (for they too were present, safeguarding). [39]And while they were relating what they had seen, again they see three males who have come out from the sepulcher, with the two supporting the other one, and a cross following them, [40]and the head of the two reaching unto heaven, but that of the one being led out by hand by them going beyond the heavens. [41]And they were hearing a voice from the heavens saying, "Have you made proclamation to the fallen-asleep?" [42]And an obeisance was heard from the cross, "Yes." [11:43]And so those people were seeking a common perspective to go off and make these things clear to Pilate; [44]and while they were still considering it through, there appear again the opened heavens and a certain man having come down and entered into the burial place. [45]Having seen these things, those around the centurion hastened at night before Pilate (having left the sepulcher which they were safeguarding) and described all the things that they indeed had seen, agonizing greatly and saying, "Truly he was God's Son." [46]In answer Pilate said, "*I* am clean of the blood of the Son of God, but it was to you that this seemed (the thing to do)." [47]Then all, having come forward, were begging and exhorting him to command the centurion and the soliders to say to no one what they had seen. [48]"For," they said, "it is better for us to owe the debt of the greatest sin in the sight of God than to fall into the hands of the Jewish people and be stoned." [49]And so Pilate ordered the centurion and the soldiers to say nothing.]

COMMENT

In this last section of my commentary on the PN I have placed together a half-line from Luke and a scene from Matt. Although these two items have nothing in common by way of content, they have a similar function. No activity was narrated by Mark between the burial of Jersus in the presence of Mary Magdalene and Mary of Joses, when it was already evening on the day before Sabbath (15:42), and the coming of Mary Magdalene and Mary of James and Salome to the burial place when the Sabbath had elapsed (16:1–2). Both the evangelists who drew on Mark fill in by mentioning what took place on the Sabbath that intervened between the two Marcan references.[1]

---

[1]No theologian has been more interested in the import of what happened on this Holy Saturday than Hans Urs von Balthasar; yet his reflections (guided by the mystical experiences of Adrienne von Speyr) have not been centered on what the canonical evangelists assign to this day. For von Balthasar (*Mysterium Paschale* [Edinburgh: Clark, 1990; German orig. 1969]) the crucified one, condemned as a sinner and utterly abandoned by God, descended among the dead on Saturday in order to show solidarity with those who had abandoned God in sin—a divine "yes" breaking down

Luke's effort is brief and uncomplicated. He has interpreted Mark's silence about the women on the Sabbath to mean that they rested on that day. By specifying this and relating it to observance of "the commandment,"[2] i.e., "Remember to keep holy the Sabbath day . . . on it you shall not do any work" (Exod 20:8–10), Luke portrays the women as carefully law-observant. Thus at the end of the Gospel the Lucan picture of the burial and resurrection of Jesus in Jerusalem features pious, law-observant characters of the same type as depicted at the beginning during Jesus' infancy and boyhood visits to Jerusalem (2:22–24,25,37,41–42). By inclusion Luke vocalizes his theology that Jesus' whole career from beginning to end was marked by respect for the Law and that he attracted followers of this mindset among the Jews.

Matt also fills in the Sabbath in an inclusive way that makes the end of the Gospel match the beginning; for in the ANALYSIS, subsection A, below, I shall show that he has arranged five episodes from 27:57 to 28:20 so as to parallel the structure of his infancy narrative. The story of the guard at the sepulcher, which begins on the Sabbath, is an essential element in the five-episode arrangement. The whole of the COMMENT will be devoted to interpreting this guard story in Matt, and readers may find it useful to know ahead of time some of the conclusions I shall reach in the ANALYSIS pertinent to the basic contours. A consecutive story about the guard at the sepulcher came to Matt from the same collection of popular tradition that he tapped for previous additions he made to Mark's PN, such as the suicide of Judas and the blood money (27:3–10); the dream of Pilate's wife (27:19); Pilate's washing his hands of Jesus' blood while the people accepted responsibility for it (27:24–25); the extraordinary phenomena on earth and in heaven when Jesus died (27:51b–53). I shall contend that the author of *GPet* drew not only on Matt but on an independent form of the guard-at-the-sepulcher story, and in *GPet* 8:28–11:49 the basic story is still found consecutively (even if details in the story are modified by later developments). Matt, however, divided up the guard story to constitute the second episode (27:62–66 before the resurrection) and the fourth episode (28:11–15 after the resurrection) in the burial-resurrection narrative,[3] just as the Herod story was divided up to con-

---

the gates of hell by embracing the "no" of obdurate dead sinners and providing hope for the salvation of all. A magnificent concept, but paradoxically different from Matt's interest in showing that sin continued on the Sabbath. It is *GPet*, not Matt, which states that between the sealing of the tomb at the dawning of the Sabbath (9:33–34) and the emergence of the Lord from the tomb on the dawning of the Lord's day (9:35; 10:39–40) proclamation had been made by the crucified one to the fallen-asleep (10:41). Matt 27:52 placed the raising of the fallen-asleep holy ones on Friday afternoon before the burial of Jesus.

[2]The Lucan phrase "according to the commandment" is omitted by Codex Bezae, perhaps to avoid giving the impression that believers in Jesus were bound by the Sabbath ordinance.

[3]A small segment is interwoven in the third episode (28:2–4 as part of 28:1–10); a similar phenomenon occurs in the infancy narrative where Herod is mentioned in the third episode.

stitute the second and fourth episodes in the infancy narrative. The guard-at-the-sepulcher story, when told as a unit in popular circles, did not have to be related to the other empty-tomb story (the women come to the tomb) that we find in Mark; but both Matt and *GPet* have interrelated the two stories, Matt by interweaving them, *GPet* by telling them one after the other (see 12:50–13:57 for the women story). Like the listing of the extraordinary pheomena in Matt 27:51b–53, the guard story had as its primary focus a miraculous divine confirmation of Jesus' victory, so that development of the apologetic element (that the body was not stolen) came later logically and (probably) temporally. Questions about historicity and/or about the most ancient elements in the guard story will also be left until the ANALYSIS.

Let us turn now to detailed commentary on the *earlier part* of the Matthean guard story, i.e., the part that belongs to the burial narrative, which I shall divide into two subsections: first, the petition made to Pilate; and second, the granting and execution of the petition. A third subsection will simply survey the *latter part* of the guard story as it is continued in the Matthean resurrection narrative. The much longer narrative in *GPet* will not be the subject of detailed commentary but will be brought in to supplement remarks on Matt.[4]

THE PETITION MADE TO PILATE (MATT 27:62–64)

Time Indication. Since the petition concerns guarding the sepulcher lest it be tampered with, logically it had to be presented before the tomb's being (found) open on Sunday morning after the Sabbath.[5] *GPet* takes the choice of having it presented before the Sabbath dawned (see 9:34). If the author was calculating time by Jewish standards, he would mean that the petition was made late Friday afternoon; if not, he might mean it was made in the early hours of Saturday before dawn. However, nothing can be concluded about this point granted the confusing indications about the Sabbath in *GPet*.[6] Matt takes the choice of having the petition presented on the Sabbath itself. The time variation between *GPet* and Matt suggests that there may

---

[4]This choice is dictated by the nature of the volume as a commentary on the *canonical* Gospels. Sometimes I have not hesitated to add a subsection on a short segment in *GPet*, but the twenty-two verses of the guard story constitute over one-third of what is preserved of *GPet*.

[5]In the canonical burial-of-Jesus narratives Matt alone uses *taphos* ("sepulcher"), and two of his four uses are in the guard story, with the fourth in 28:1 that joins the story to the account of the women coming on Easter. In the Easter account *mnēmeion* ("tomb") is the most frequently used canonical word (Mark 4, Matt 1, Luke 5, John 7)—Mark and Luke have *mnēma* once each.

[6]For example, in 7:27 after Jesus' death and burial, the author tells us that the disciples "were sitting mourning and weeping *night and day until* the Sabbath," even though he already had "Sabbath dawning" when Jesus was sentenced to death (2:5)!

have been no precise time indication in the guard story, an absence that allowed each writer to fit it in where he thought best in the interstice between Friday and Sunday. Indeed, the time indication in Matt 27:62 ("after the preparation day"—a very indirect way of referring to the Sabbath) betrays Matt's editing hand. In discussing the elements of time indication for the burial story in Mark 15:42 (already evening, preparation day, the day before Sabbath), I pointed out that in the corresponding passage (27:57) Matt used only one of the Marcan indications (evening) and that he reserved the others till later, namely, "preparation day" until the present scene (27:62) and "Sabbath" until the next scene at the empty tomb (28:1, where he economizes on the mentions of "Sabbath" in Mark 15:42 and 16:1).

Those Involved. Matt 27:62 reports that "there gathered together the chief priests and the Pharisees."[7] *Synagein* ("to gather together") echoes other Matthean PN passages (26:3,57; 27:17,27) where those who were or would be adversaries of Jesus gathered together. (*GPet*'s account of the guard story uses the same verb [8:28]—an indication that if that author drew on an independent form of the guard story, he also had heard Matt and was influenced by familiar Matthean expressions.) If we combine "the chief priests" here with their reappearance in 28:11–12, where they are associated with "the elders," we recognize that we are dealing with the traditional adversaries of Jesus in the Matthean PN, where the designation "chief priests" appears fifteen other times and "elders" seven other times. Gnilka (*Matthäus* 2.487) is correct in seeing here the components of the Sanhedrin. The startling exception is the reference to "the Pharisees," who appear only here in the Matthean PN.[8] In other words, this story about the guard at the sepulcher violates the traditional (and even historical) remembrance that the Pharisees were not active in the death of Jesus. That the Pharisees appear only here in *GPet* (8:28: independently or drawing on Matt?) suggests that we cannot trace a form of the guard story that does not have them. Kratz (*Auferweckung* 57–59) sees no particular significance in the appearance of the Pharisees here, but to others it suggests that the story of the guard at the sepulcher was vocalized at a period when the Pharisees had become the chief opponents of Christians (after 70?), whether or not the story had earlier antecedents.[9]

Some have wondered whether a gathering of the chief priests and the

---

[7]The corresponding passage in *GPet* 8:28 has "the scribes and Pharisees and elders . . . gathered together" against Jesus. Later Matt 28:12 will introduce "the elders" into his story, even as *GPet* 8:29 will reiterate that "the elders" were present.

[8]Elsewhere in the canonical PNs only in John 18:3. In Matt "the chief priests and the Pharisees" were last teamed in 21:45–46 when they sought to arrest Jesus because his parables threatened them.

[9]Yet we must note that the Pharisees, after being mentioned at the beginning both in Matt and *GPet,* are never referred to again; the chief priests and the elders in Matt and the elders and scribes in *GPet* remain hostile figures throughout the story.

Pharisees before Pilate would have been a violation of the Sabbath. Certainly Matt calls no attention to such a violation, for his circumlocution "on the next day, which is after the preparation day" avoids mention of the Sabbath.[10] Truly implausible behavior is found in what *GPet* has happen in the period of time about "when the Sabbath was dawning" (9:34). After the elders and scribes had joined in sealing the tomb, they pitched a tent there and along with soldiers safeguarded the tomb all through the Sabbath into the night when the Lord's Day (Sunday) dawned (*GPet* 8:33–10:38). On the Sabbath they were joined by a crowd from Jerusalem who came out to see the sealed tomb (9:34). The picture of so many observant Jews spending the Sabbath at a tomb is another factor (along with chronological confusion about the Jewish calendar) that makes us doubt that *GPet* was written by a knowledge-able Jewish Christian.

Recollection of Jesus and What He Said. Matt 27:63 has the Jewish authorities address the prefect as "Lord," a politeness never attested in previous encounters in the PN. They speak to him of Jesus as "the deceiver" (*planos*) and of what is likely to be claimed by his disciples about his resurrection as a "deception" (27:64: *planē*). Neither of these words is used elsewhere by Matt, and the corresponding verb "to deceive" (*planan*) is never used in any Synoptic PN. Among the Gospels the verb is applied to Jesus only in John 7:12,47. On p. 544 above I pointed out that Jewish polemic identifying Jesus as the deceiving prophet of Deut 13:2–6; 18:20, attested in the Talmud and other Jewish literature, seemingly does not belong to the pre-70 strata of the NT. Thus we have another indicator that the formulation of the guard story may be relatively late.[11]

In Matt 27:63 the adversaries quote to Pilate Jesus' words: "After three days I am (to be) raised." Nowhere in Matt (or in any other Gospel) has Jesus actually said those words. In the three passion predictions of 16:21; 17:22–23; and 20:18–19 (see APPENDIX VIII) he spoke of the *Son of Man* being raised *on the third day*. The expression "three days" did occur in the sign-of-Jonah passage (12:40: "the Son of Man will be in the heart of the earth three days and three nights"), a sign addressed to the scribes and Pharisees (12:38),[12] and in the destruction-of-the-sanctuary claim attributed to

---

[10]That this day was part of the festal period of the Unleavened Bread which began with the Passover meal on Thursday night/Friday, while a logical deduction from Matt's earlier chronological indications, is even further from the Matthean picture here.

[11]Of note is the absence of all reference to Jesus' claims in the *GPet* form of the guard story. Perhaps in the psychology of the *GPet* storyline, since the people have been saying how just Jesus was (8:28), we are to imagine that his adversaries thought it wise not to attack him directly.

[12]Giblin ("Structural" 414–19) argues at length for the Jonah passage as the antecedent for the saying of Jesus that the chief priests and the Pharisees report to Pilate. It has the Son of Man "in the heart of the earth," and that is where the Jewish authorities want to keep Jesus in response to his

Jesus at the Jewish trial and on the cross (26:61; 27:40: "within three days I will build [it]"). Yet even there we do not find "after three days," which might imply resurrection on Monday, the fourth day.[13] But perhaps we should not press stringently the issue of exact wording;[14] for the time indication is from the viewpoint of the total narrative rather than from a historical moment on the Sabbath when the Jewish authorities were speaking. In the burial-resurrection sequence Matt 27:57,62; and 28:1 indicate distinct days, with the last being "the dawning of the first day of the week"—after those three indicated days Jesus will have been raised. Indeed, Matt 28:6, "For he has been raised just as he said," will go out of its way to point out the truth of a prediction that the Jewish authorities in 27:63 characterized as coming from a deceiver! What is really surprising in our present scene before Pilate is that the chief priests and the Pharisees know not only the substance of Jesus' saying but understand it correctly as referring to his resurrection. Although in the storyline Jesus' disciples have heard many more predictions of Jesus' being raised up than have the chief priests and the Pharisees, none of the Gospels attributes that much insight to them before the resurrection, or sometimes even after they have encountered the risen Jesus![15] Clearly the story has been formulated in a context where Christians have been proclaiming the resurrection and their opponents understand what they are claiming.

A Petition Phrased because of Fear about Jesus' Disciples. Matt 27:64 begins by having the Jewish authorities ask Pilate to issue an order that would last until the third day. The verb *keleuein* ("to order") was used by Matt a few verses before (27:58) in place of Mark's *dōreisthai* (15:45: "to grant") to cover Pilate's giving up Jesus' body to Joseph. Having issued an order that favored Jesus' disciple, Pilate is now asked for an order hostile to the disciples. The time limitation in the request, while determined by Jesus' prediction, has the psychological effect of facilitating an affirmative answer: A Roman governor would not commit forces for an indeterminate time. When it comes to what Pilate was asked for and why, Matt 27:64 and *GPet* 8:30 agree broadly. The substance but not the wording of the petition is the

---

bold warning to them at the trial (26:64): "You will see the Son of Man sitting at the right of the Power and coming on the clouds of heaven."

[13]Walker ("After") points out that the Jewish authorities are quoting this on Saturday and on that day they ask that the sepulcher be made secure "until the third day," which would mean Monday. He suggests that some of the traditional expressions referring to three days are calculated from Thursday.

[14]Elsewhere in the Gospels even when Jesus cites his own words, the quotation is not necessarily verbatim (see John 18:9).

[15]This is where literalist attempts at historicity stumble. Lee ("Guard" 63) argues that the words of Jesus, including a statement about the destruction of the Temple sanctuary within three days, were betrayed to the chief priests by Judas. That assumes that Judas reached an understanding of this or of the other sayings as a reference to the resurrection!

same: Pilate was asked for help (*GPet* specifically "soldiers") in securing or safeguarding (Matt: *asphalein; GPet: phylassein*) the sepulcher/burial place (Matt: *taphos; GPet: mnēma*). The wording of the reasoning behind the request is virtually identical: "Lest, having come, the/his disciples steal him."[16] There is once again variation of vocabulary but not of substance in the apprehension that having stolen the body, the disciples would use this to mislead "the people" (*ho laos* in both) to believe in Jesus' resurrection (passive of *egeirein* in Matt; active of *anistanai* in *GPet*). Matt ends the petition with a gnomic statement: "The last deception will be worse than the first" (phrased in the language used previously in 12:45: "And the last state of that man becomes worse than the first"). This sarcastically implies that Jesus' whole career was false, but ironically leaves the logical problem of why the Jewish authorities have taken so seriously a claim made by such a deceiver. *GPet* ends the petition on a different note. Consonant with its picture of "all the people" murmuring at Jesus' death and professing that he was just (8:28), *GPet* has the authorities afraid that the people might "do wrong" (*poein kaka*) to them. Here the language is ironic, for *GPet* 4:10 (and Luke) showed Jesus crucified among the *kakourgoi* or "wrongdoers."

While I shall reserve issues of historicity till the ANALYSIS, verisimilitude is worth discussing here. How plausible would this story appear in reporting a fear that Jesus' body might be stolen? And if we may anticipate, how plausible is it that Pilate would move to block such a depredation? Tomb violation was not unusual in antiquity, usually in search of treasure; but the present instance would involve the transfer of a corpse. That was done occasionally for honest reasons (to move the recently deceased to a better tomb) or dishonest reasons (for sorcery or magic), and the suggested motivation of the disciples (deception) in the charge before Pilate falls into the latter category. That Pilate's help could plausibly be enlisted to prevent a tomb violation designed to create a superstitious devotion is seen from an inscription that has had a fascinating history, an inscription that some have thought was provoked by what happened to the tomb in which Jesus was buried.

---

[16]*GPet* has "his disciples," and so does the Koine textual tradition of Matt (probably by contamination from Matt 28:13 where the lie has "his disciples" stealing the body); it is absent from Codices Vaticanus and Sinaiticus. (The Koine tradition of Matt also adds "at night," but again in imitation of 28:13). While I think that the author of *GPet* was familiar with Matthean phrasing, too much should not be deduced about literary dependence from this clause, which is about the longest verbatim literary agreement between *GPet* and a canonical Gospel. That the disciples came and stole Jesus away (a description repeated in Matt 28:13; see John 20:2,15) became an established charge in polemic discussions, as Matt 28:15 testifies (also Justin, *Dialogue* 108.2); and the fixed phrasing of that charge could have been known to the author of *GPet* without direct dependence on Matt. Yet most of the vocabulary is quite at home in Matt, and the "having come" plus a verb of motion is very Matthean (twenty-seven times).

In the 19th cent. among some antiquities acquired at Nazareth (but not necessarily originating there) was a marble slab about 2' by 1.25' containing 22 lines of Greek inscription. It was sent to the Paris Bibliotheque Nationale in 1878 and published by F. Cumont in *Revue d'Histoire* 163 (1930), 241–66. It bears the title *Diatagma Kaisaros*. This is not a standard designation of an imperial pronouncement, and scholars have been intrigued by what kind of a pronouncement this was and the Caesar who made it.[17] That it is a translation from Latin is generally suggested, but there is no agreement that it can be classified as one of the rigorously defined juridical statements known from later imperial times: *edictum, rescriptum, decretum, mandatum.* We may have an extract from an edict that was made only for a section of the empire,[18] and there is no way to determine whether it was a response to a question proposed to Rome. As for the "Caesar," as Metzger ("Nazareth" 86–87) notes, the range of suggestions has run from Augustus, who became emperor in 30 BC, to Septimius Severus, who died in AD 211. Nevertheless, the imprecision of the title *Diatagma Kaisaros* suggests a period before imperial style became fixed, and paleography favors the period 50 BC to AD 50. Consequently the early emperors Augustus, Tiberius, and Claudius have been advanced most often.[19] Augustus frequently designated himself as "Caesar"; and were it not for a desire to see here an application to Jesus (which would require an emperor later than Augustus), his candidature might have convincing support.

The thrust of the inscription[20] is that sepulchers and graves should remain unmolested in perpetuity. Those who have infringed on the inviolate character of burial should be tried and punished. Such criminals include anyone who has cast out bodies that have been buried in a tomb and/or who "with malicious deception has transferred them to other places." The governing principle is: "It shall be especially obligatory to honor those who have been buried. Let no one remove them for any reason." One can understand why the fact that the inscription was first known at Nazareth and that it warns against moving bodies has led some to think this was the emperor's answer to Pilate's report that the discovery of Jesus' empty tomb caused a squabble between Jesus' followers and Jews who did not believe in Jesus and that they

---

[17]The inscription has been the subject of an enormous bibliography. At the time Schmitt wrote in 1958 ("Nazareth" 6.361–63) there were already some seventy entries, and the count had risen to ninety by the time of Metzger's 1975 article ("Nazareth" 91–92).

[18]De Zulueta ("Violation" 193–94) points out that *violatio sepulchri*, even though punished by fines, was not treated as a criminal issue throughout the empire until 2d cent. AD.

[19]If the inscription was copied during the reigns of Augustus or Tiberius, it was not originally set up in Nazareth, for Galilee was not under direct Roman rule in that period.

[20]See transcription and translation in de Zulueta ("Violation" 185) and Metzger ("Nazareth" 76–77).

were arguing as to why Jesus' tomb was empty. That ca. AD 49 (?) Claudius "expelled Jews from Rome beause of their constant disturbances impelled by Chrestus" (Suetonius, *Claudius* 25.4) has often been interpreted as an attempt by that emperor to settle a fight in the synagogues of Rome between Jews who believed that Jesus was the Christus and those who did not. The "Nazareth Inscription" has been seen as another such imperial involvement, perhaps by Claudius again. This suggestion is farfetched, reflecting imagination more than evidence. There is no serious evidence that Pilate made any such report, or that Rome would have been interested in the problem, or that such a debate occurred right after Jesus' resurrection. Yet the inscription does fill in the background of the guard-at-the-tomb story. On the one hand, it shows that tomb violation was very serious, and that a Roman governor might have committed soldiers when there was reason to anticipate the theft of the body of one whose death had public notoriety. On the other hand, common knowledge that those who stole a body would be seriously punished by the Romans might make readers realize the ridiculousness of the Jewish claim that disciples who fled when Jesus was arrested had now gained the courage to steal Jesus' body.

PILATE GRANTS THE PETITION (MATT 27:65–66)

In *GPet* 8:30 the Jewish authorities had asked Pilate: "Give over soldiers to us in order that we may safeguard his burial place." That vocabulary is reused to describe the prefect's reaction: "Pilate gave over [*paradidonai*] to them Petronius the centurion with soldiers to safeguard the sepulcher" (8:31). The verb *paradidonai* so often used in the PN for the giving over of Jesus, is now used differently, and perhaps ironically. Since *GPet* had Jews crucify Jesus, this is the first mention of Roman soldiers. Not surprisingly there appears here the Roman centurion (*kentyriōn* as in Mark 15:39, not *hekatontarchēs* as in Matt 27:54) who was featured in the Synoptic crucifixion stories. He is only a transferred memory, however; for despite his bearing the personal name Petronius[21] and being mentioned five times in the guard story (*GPet* 8:31,32; 9:38; 11:45,47), the centurion neither does nor says anything by himself.

Matt 27:65 has Pilate respond in direct discourse, *"Echete koustōdian.*

[21]See §44, n. 15. This is a known Roman name, e.g., a Petronius was governor of Syria in AD 39–42; but some have looked on it as a play upon the name of the author of *GPet*, namely, the *Petros* of 14:60, even as a daughter named Petronilla was attributed to the first of the Twelve. Metzger ("Names" 95) reports that the 13th-cent. Syriac *Book of the Bee* offers names for all the soldiers sent to watch the tomb: They "were five [in number], and these are their names, Issachar, Gad, Matthias, Barnabas, and Simon; but others say they were fifteen, three centurions and their Roman and Jewish soldiers."

Go, make secure as you know how." I left the first two words in Greek because of their disputed meaning. Most often they have been understood to mean: "You have a custodial guard of your own"—in other words, Pilate refuses to help and tells the chief priests and the Pharisees that they have troops of their own whom they can use to make the sepulcher secure. Numerous arguments of varied weight militate against such an interpretation wherein those who guarded the tomb would be Jewish troops mustered by Jewish authorities: (1) *GPet* 8:31 has clearly understood Pilate to give Roman soldiers to safeguard the burial place. (2) If the Jewish authorities had military of their own to secure the sepulcher, why did they need Pilate's help in the first place? (3) Matt uses the term *koustōdia* to refer to the military who guarded the sepulcher: a Latin loanword in Greek that in early Christian literature appears only in this story (27:65; 28:11). Such a Latinism fits well the picture of a Roman prefect assigning Roman troops.[22] (4) Matt 28:12 will call those who guarded the sepulcher "soldiers," using the plural of *stratiōtēs,* while 28:14 will refer to Pilate as the *hēgemōn* ("governor"). Previously (27:27) Matt used these two Greek terms to refer to "the soldiers of the governor," and surely here he is thinking of the same Roman soldiers. In 22 of 26 NT uses of *stratiōtēs,* it refers to Roman soldiers; in another 3 (Acts 12:4,6,18), to soldiers under the command of King Herod Agrippa I—never does it refer to soldiers controlled by the Jerusalem Jewish authorities. (5) If those involved were Jewish soldiers under the control of Jewish authorities, why would they be responsible to the Roman governor for falling asleep and failing to keep watch, as 28:14 implies?[23]

Much more likely Matt means that Pilate gave the Jewish authorities Roman soldiers to help make the sepulcher secure.[24] The key word *echete,* then, has to be translated not as "You have a custodial guard" but as "You (may) have a custodial guard," or "You are granted a custodial guard," or "Take a

[22]Lee ("Guard" 173) romantically contends that Caiaphas heard *custodia* from Pilate's own lips when he spoke to the high priest in Latin! In talmudic Aramaic *qûṣṭôdyā'* appears as a loanword from Latin; that may weaken the argument used here, if it is an echo of earlier Aramaic usage.

[23]Craig ("Guard" 274) contends that a Jewish guard is intended because Matt 28:11 has them report to the chief priests—if Roman troops were involved, as in *GPet,* they would have reported to Pilate. On two grounds I find that argument quite unconvincing. First, the Roman troops granted by the Matthean Pilate were put under the directives of the chief priests and the Pharisees in 27:65 ("You [may] have a custodial guard. Go, make secure as *you* know how"), so naturally the troops report to the chief priests about what happened. The chief priests reassure them that if they cooperate with the lie about sleeping, they will not be made scapegoats by having the chief priests tell Pilate that the soldiers he gave them were unreliable. Second, in *GPet,* where clearly Roman troops are involved, they *first* consult with Jewish elders whom they have awakened (10:38; 11:43) about how to report to Pilate before *together* they go to give a report to Pilate (11:45)—a sensitivity about responsibility to the Jewish authorities.

[24]There is an interesting interpretative addition to 27:65 in the 9th-cent. minuscule Codex 1424: "And he gave over to them armed men in order that they should sit opposite the cave and keep guard over it day and night."

custodial guard." The verb *echein* is being used in the set sense of an affirmative response to a request: "You have it."[25] Thus in Matt, as in *GPet,* Pilate gives Roman soldiers to the Jewish authorities to enable the Jewish authorities to make the sepulcher secure in the way they best know how. Symbolically this is important; for when the resurrection frustrates this security, readers are to recognize that God has frustrated both Roman and Jewish power.

Matt and *GPet* agree that the sepulcher or burial place was made secure by putting seals on the stone that was used to close the door. In Matt (27:60), before the Sabbath began, Joseph of Arimathea had rolled a large stone to the door of the tomb; and it was that stone that "they" sealed.[26] It is not clear whether the authorities were part of the "they" and thus working on the Sabbath, or the Roman troops were agents who did the sealing under their direction. Before the Sabbath has dawned, *GPet* 8:31–33 has the elders and scribes come to the burial place; and, together with the centurion and (Roman) soldiers and all who were there, they roll a large stone against the door of the burial place and seal it. In both Matt and *GPet* the implication is that wax was put on the stone in such a way that opening the tomb would break the wax, and in that wax the imprint of a seal was made. A special element in *GPet* is that there were seven seals. The number seven is commonly symbolic in the Bible, but it is difficult to be certain whether here the seven is just part of the folkloric imagination or has special symbolism.[27] One might appeal to Rev 5:1–5, which has a scroll sealed with seven seals that can be opened by no one in heaven or on earth save by the lion of the tribe of Judah, the root of David who has triumphed—that could reinforce the obvious meaning of *GPet* that everything was done to make opening the tomb difficult (but the power of God would break through all these human precautions).

CONCLUSION OF THE GUARD STORY IN THE RESURRECTION NARRATIVE (MATT 28:2–4, 11–15)

GPet preserves the guard story as a unit, so that the resurrection section of this story (9:35–11:49) follows immediately after the tomb sealing; and

---

[25]See BAGD p. 33, I,7b; also Smyth, "Guard" 157–58. Both cite Papyrus Oxyrhynchus (vol. 1, papyrus 33, col. 3, line 4) where the magistrate Appianus asks for a special favor, and the emperor (Marcus Aurelius?) responds *eche,* i.e., "Take it" or "You have it." One may also point to the *Acts of the Scillitan Martyrs* 13 where the proconsul Saturninus makes a grant to Speratus, *"Moram . . . habete":* "You have a delay" (MACM 88).

[26]The Greek of Matt 27:66 is awkwardly abbreviated; scribes of the Western textual tradition have tried to improve "with the custodial guard" (*meta tēs koustōdias*) by changing it to "with the guards" (*meta tōn phylakōn*).

[27]Several suggestions have been made. Because chief priests are involved, some would cite Zech 3:9; 4:10 where a special stone is set before Joshua the high priest with seven facets, representing

the whole story precedes the standard account of the women coming to the tomb on Easter morning (12:50–14:60). Matt chooses to weave the two together in an alternating pattern (see ANALYSIS). Neither solution can disguise that the guard-at-the-tomb and the women-coming-to-the-tomb were two different accounts. To detect what belongs to the guard-at-the-tomb story in Matt we need to look at what he has added to Mark's account of the women coming to the tomb. Mark has Mary Magdalene and the other women come very early on the first day of the week and find the large stone rolled back, the tomb opened, and a young man (angel) seated inside. Matt has the women come late Saturday night ("when the first day of the week was dawning," i.e., beginning); as they get to the sepulcher, there is a great earthquake; an angel of the Lord comes down and rolls back the stone—an angel whose appearance is like lightning.[28] These extraordinary occurrences cause those keeping guard (*tērein* as in Matt 27:36) to quake and become as dead men. There is wry irony here: The quaking of the earth that accompanied the angel's coming causes the guards to quake; those whose presence is to certify that Jesus stays dead become as dead themselves. As to time, the corresponding scene in *GPet* 9:35–37 also takes place in the night that ends the Sabbath and begins the "Lord's Day."[29] A loud voice sounds in the heavens, which open (comparable to Matt's earthquake); and two males (angels have male attributes in Jewish thought) come down from there and approach the sepulcher. The stone rolls by itself to the side, and both enter the sepulcher. The guarding soldiers awaken the centurion and the elders to relate what they have seen. Then *GPet* has a sequence that is without parallel in Matt. The two angelic men, whose heads reach from earth to heaven, bring out from the sepulcher Christ who is even taller; and they are followed by a talking cross who can assure the heavens that proclamation has been made to the fallen-asleep (see Matt 27:52).[30]

The next major segment of the story in Matt (28:11–15) has some of the custodial guard enter Jerusalem to announce (*apaggellein*) to the chief priests all the things that happened (*ta genomena*). Again this is wry irony:

---

the eyes of the Lord that range over the whole earth. Because the tomb is in the earth, reference is also made to *4 Baruch* 3:10 where God has sealed the earth with seven seals in seven periods of time.

[28]In the story of the women coming to the tomb Mark 16:5 has the young man dressed in a white robe; Luke 24:4 has the two men (angels: see Luke 24:23) in dazzling apparel. This corresponds to the second part of the Matthean description (28:3b) of the angelic garb as white as snow. The "lightning" part of the description in 28:3a belongs to the guard-at-the-tomb story.

[29]By the time that *GPet* was written, the first day of the week (Matt) had become the Lord's Day.

[30]I have stated that it is not my purpose to write a commentary on *GPet;* yet since the talking cross may strike modern readers as ridiculous, I should call attention to other early dramatizations of the cross as the sign of the Son of Man (Matt 24:30) or as a cosmic sign and tree of life, e.g., *Epistola Apostolorum* 16; *Apocalypse of Peter* 1; anonymous homily *On the Pasch* 51.9–10 (SC 27:177–79); see Mara, *Évangile* 188–89; Schmidt, *Kanonische* 71.

Apaggellein was used in 28:8,10 for announcing the good news of the resurrection, and the centurion's seeing "these happenings" (*ta ginomena*) produced a confession of faith in God's Son (27:54). The chief priests gather together (*synagein*) with the elders and take a decision (*symboulion lambanein*) to give silver (pl. *argyrion*) to the soldiers to lie. Here Matt is using language that creates inclusions with earlier actions in the PN. In 26:3 the chief priests and the elders gathered together (*synagein*), and the result of the meeting was that they paid silver (pl. *argyrion*) to Judas to give Jesus over. In 27:1 the chief priests and the elders took a decision (*symboulion lambanein*) against Jesus that they should put him to death, a decision that caused Judas to bring the silver back (27:3), only to be treated callously by the authorities. Thus for Matt the Jewish authorities have remained consistent in their identity and manner of proceeding.

The lie that the soldiers are to tell is phrased in the set terms that the Jewish authorities used when they first approached Pilate about making the tomb secure (27:64): Jesus' disciples came and stole him—at night while the soldiers were sleeping. And if Pilate hears about this fictional dereliction of duty, the authorities are prepared to avert his wrath (presumably by another lie). Matt's readers would not be surprised by this resort to falsehood if they remembered 26:59: "The chief priests and the whole Sanhedrin were seeking false testimony against Jesus so that they might put him to death." In the polemical picture being painted, lies were used to put Jesus to death, and lies will be used to kill his memory. The soldiers take the silver, even as did Judas in 26:15, and do as they are instructed,[31] so that the false "word has been spread about among the Jews until this day" (28:15)—a type of antigospel. In the Synoptic Gospels this is one of the few instances of "the Jews" used in this manner, to designate an alien and hostile group (cf. Mark 7:3), reflecting an era when the followers of Jesus (even if of Jewish birth) no longer considered themselves to be Jews.

Again the account in *GPet* (11:43–49) is more elaborate. In response to the miraculous opening of the tomb by the angels and their bringing Jesus out from the tomb, accompanied by the talking cross, those who have observed (who include the soldiers and the elders) are trying to get a common perspective or way of looking at the phenoemna (*syskeptesthai*) so that they can go off and make these things clear (*emphanizein*) to Pilate. But then they

---

[31]Pesch ("Alttestamentliche" 95) calls attention to a set Matthean pattern of carrying out commands; see Matt 1:24–25; 21:6–7; 28:15; and 28:19–20. Matt will reuse the verb *didaskein* from 28:15 in Jesus' command to his eleven disciples: "Going therefore, make disciples of all nations . . . *teaching* them to observe all I have commanded you" (28:19–20). The Jewish authorities teach the soldiers to lie; Jesus has his disciples teach people to keep the commandments. In Matt's mind there is no doubt about who really observe the Law.

see the opened heavens and another heavenly being[32] come down and enter the burial place. This second phenomenon settles their decision: Even though it is night, they go to Pilate and tell him what they have seen, including their understanding that this shows that Jesus was God's Son. (Notice that while Matt had the centurion and those who were with him keeping [guard over] Jesus confess this, *GPet* has the confession made by both the guards and the Jewish authorities.[33]) Pilate's reaction, "*I* am clean of the blood of the Son of God, but it was to you that this seemed (the thing to do)," accepts their professed understanding of Jesus, but points out that they were the ones primarily responsible for death ("blood") of him whose standing they now grudgingly acknowledge. That very fact, however, leads the Jewish authorities to emphasize their anguished fear of being stoned if the Jewish people hear the truth. (Notice that the *GPet* has these authorities admit implicitly that the blasphemy which deserved stoning was not by Jesus but by them.) And so Pilate, despite his recognition that Jesus was the Son of God, commands the centurion and the soldiers to remain silent. If for Matt a lie has been spread among the Jews, for *GPet* the failure of both the Romans and the Jewish leaders to tell the truth has misled the people.

ANALYSIS

Since Luke's contribution to this episode is only a half-verse that helps the transition to the empty-tomb or resurrection narrative, we may concentrate here on Matt (and corresponding passages in *GPet*). In §46 (ANALYSIS A) I discussed the structure of the Gospel burial narratives but alerted readers that the complicated issue of Matthean structure would be reserved until here, since the guard-at-the-sepulcher story is an important segment of Matt's burial narrative. After treating Matthean burial structure and composition, I shall conclude with the question of the historicity of the guard story.

A. Structure of Matt's Burial Narrative and Origins of the Guard-at-the-Sepulcher Story

SOME THEORIES ABOUT STRUCTURE. As we have seen, the Marcan and Lucan burial narratives consisted of two segments: one dealing with Joseph

---

[32]In 11:44 an *anthrōpos*, whereas 9:36; 10:39 used *anēr*. This heavenly being will be referred to in the next section as a *neaniskos* or "young man" (13:55).

[33]The form of the centurion's confession in Luke 23:47, "Certainly this man was just," has its parallel in the people's reaction in *GPet* 8:28: "Behold how just he was."

from Arimathea concluding the story of the crucifixion, and the other dealing with the Galilean women serving as a transition to the empty-tomb and
resurrection story.[34] Matt 27:57–61 has the same two segments and follows
Mark closely. Accordingly an author like Senior who rarely recognizes any
source for Matt other than Mark will think of what follows about the guard
at the tomb (27:62–66) as simply a Matthean creative appendage to the
burial. Thus in "Matthew's Account" 2.1446–48, he proposes a structure
consisting of a bipartite burial account (27:57–61 and 27:62–66) and a bipartite empty-tomb account (28:1–10 and 28:11–15). The principal difficulty
with this is that it splits off by itself the resurrection appearance of Jesus in
Galilee (28:16–20), even though that has been foreshadowed in the first segment of the empty-tomb account (28:7).

A much more elaborate proposal has been made by Heil, first in "Narrative," an article dedicated to Matt 27:55–28:20, and then in a book (*Death*)
treating the whole of Matt 26–28, with reflections on the Matthean Gospel
structure in general. Using his own form of narrative criticism, he detects an
extremely complicated literary structure based on "a pattern of alternation
or 'interchange' in which each scene frames and is in turn framed by contrasting scenes" ("Narrative" 419–20). He divides the burial/resurrection
into three parts of unequal length: (1) 27:55–61; (2) 27:62–28:4; (3) 28:5–
20, with each of those subdivided into three subsections (thus nine segments
in all). An example of the framing in the first part is that there is a subsection
on the women from Galilee in 27:55–56 and another in 27:61 serving as a
framework for the action of Joseph the disciple in 27:57–60. Yet, as already
pointed out in §44, n. 27, to create this framework Heil has to ignore the
narrative flow, since the women in 27:55–56 are related to the crucifixion,
specifically said to be observing the death of Jesus and its aftermath, not to
the burial. On a larger scale I find Heil's divisions very artificial; and while
they detect some Matthean patterns, they often sacrifice other and larger
issues. In an unpublished critique of Heil given at the 1991 Catholic Biblical
Association Meeting at Los Angeles, J. R. Donahue pointed out that Heil's
division does not respect the genres of different elements in the burial/resur-
rection narratives. In an incisive critique Senior ("Matthew's Account," especially 2.1439–40) speaks of the "nearly mechanistic nature" of Heil's literary
pattern; and since Heil's book would extend such a pattern through the whole
of Matt, many may well share Senior's doubt that the evangelist was capable
of formulating such an elaborate plan. Senior suspects Heil is unconsciously
fitting "the text to the Procrustean bed of the alleged pattern." That suspicion,

---

[34]John does not have the women segment, and his whole burial narrative (including Nicodemus)
concludes the crucifixion story illustrating the triumph of Jesus. It is part of the chiastic crucifixion
structure outlined on p. 908 above.

applied to Heil's nine segments in Matt 27:55–28:20, is increased for me by his subsequent discovery of nine segments in Mark 14:53–16:8 (*Biblica* 73 [1992], 331–58).

What I propose below moves in another, simpler direction. I disagreed with Senior's splitting off the resurrection appearance in 28:16–20 from the burial and empty-tomb structure. I disagreed with Heil's including in his plan the crucifixion episode 26:55–56. My diagnosis of structure will cover burial, empty tomb, and resurrection without additions or exclusions, thus 27:57–28:20. (These are also the confines of the Matthean unit accepted by the independent structural studies of Giblin, Lai, and Turiot.) It will attempt to do justice to the way Matt has woven together material taken from Mark and material from other sources (guard-at-the-tomb story and resurrection appearance—which he did not create). Let me use the origin of the guard-at-the-tomb story as an entrée into the Matthean structural plan.

ORIGINALLY A CONSECUTIVE STORY. Two easily observable facts indicate that at one time there was a consecutive story about the guards, not interwoven with the story of the women at the tomb (as it now is in Matt). First, a consecutive story exists in *GPet;* and it is very difficult to assume that the author of *GPet* selected out elements from Matt's interwoven account, made a consecutive story out of it (8:28–11:49), and then prefaced it to the residual story of the women at the tomb (12:50–13:57).[35] Second, extracting from Matt anything pertaining to the tomb that is not in Mark gives us the guard story, so that the interweaving of the two stories in Matt does not produce a closely integrated sequence that has the marks of being original.

This last point leads into an analysis of the Matthean structure that, in my judgment, shows that without doubt Matt himself interwove two accounts. I sided in BBM 51 with those who recognized that after an introductory genealogy, Matt's infancy narrative has a five-episode structure, each with a formula citation of Scripture. They are set in an alternating pattern with those who are favorable to Jesus, namely Joseph and the mother, highlighted in the first, third, and fifth episodes, while the enemies of Jesus, especially Herod, are highlighted in the second and fourth episodes. If we use A to designate the favorable episodes and B to designate the hostile episodes, we may schematize the pattern as in Part One of Table 9. Part Two illustrates a

---

[35]The author of *GPet* may well have known Matt's account of the guard (a judgment based on his use of Matthean vocabulary), but a plausible scenario is that he also knew a consecutive form of the story and gave preference to that. In order to join it to the women-at-the-tomb story, the author of *GPet* had to make one adaptation: the awkward second angelic descent from heaven in 11:44. The two angelic males of the first descent (9:36) belonged to the guard story, but they left the tomb supporting Jesus. As we know from all the canonical Gospels, the women story that the *GPet* author was about to tell required angelic presence at the empty tomb when the women arrived (see *GPet* 13:55); and so he had to have another angelic man come down.

TABLE 9. COMPARING THE MATTHEAN BIRTH AND BURIAL/RESURRECTION ACCOUNTS

Part One: The Birth Account

A[1]	1:18–25	(Isa 7:14)	First angelic dream revelation to JOSEPH about the child to be born of Mary as the Messiah
B[1]	2:1–12	(Micah 5:1)	The magi come to **Herod**, the chief priests, and the scribes, who supply information but actually plot hostilely against Jesus; the magi find child and mother at Bethlehem and worship; they go back another way
A[2]	2:13–15	(Hosea 11:1)	Second angelic dream-revelation to JOSEPH to take the child and his mother to Egypt
B[2]	2:16–18	(Jer 31:15)	**Herod** kills the male children of Bethlehem in an unsuccessful attempt to kill Jesus
A[3]	2:19–23	(Isa 4:3?)	Third angelic dream-revelation to JOSEPH that those who sought the child's life are dead; he is to take the child and his mother from Egypt to Nazareth

Part Two: The Burial/Resurrection Account

A[1]	27:57–61	Burial by Joseph, a DISCIPLE, with the WOMEN FOLLOWERS observing
B[1]	27:62–66	**Chief priests** and Pharisees get **custodial guard** from Pilate to secure the sepulcher against Jesus' claim to be raised
A[2]	28:1–10	WOMEN FOLLOWERS go to sepulcher; earthquake; angel comes from heaven and rolls back stone; guards quake and become as dead; angel reveals to women who are to tell DISCIPLES; the women see Jesus
B[2]	28:11–15	**Custodial guard** announce all these things to **chief priests**, who with the elders bribe them with silver to lie that the disciples stole the body
A[3]	28:16–20	On a mountain in Galilee Jesus appears to the eleven DISCIPLES and commissions them to go to all nations

similar alternating pattern in the Matthean burial/resurrection narrative.[36] There the disciples/women motif runs through the A episodes, and the chief priest/Pilate/guards motif runs through the B episodes.

Clearly in both instances a hostile story and a friendly one have been interwoven in a positive-negative-positive-negative-positive pattern. In each instance there is an episode where the two stories come together: toward the end of B[1] in the infancy narrative, and at the beginning of A[2] in the sepulcher/resurrection narrative.[37] True, in the latter there is no guidance so sure as the five formula citations in the infancy narrative;[38] but it is worth noting that each of its five episodes has a verb of motion at the beginning, and the first three have time indications.[39] This structural inclusion between the beginning and end of the whole Gospel is, in my judgment, evidence that the present interwoven arrangement of the Matthean guard-at-the-sepulcher story does not represent the original flow of that story (which was once consecutive). The interweaving rearrangement in Matt's sepulcher/resurrection narrative also means that Matt has departed from Mark, who used the burial primarily as a connective between the crucifixion and the resurrection accounts.[40] While there are continuing echoes from the crucifixion, the burial in Matt is primarily the opening part of a structure that points to the resurrection episodes. Finally, the five-part structure alerts us that the negative element of Jewish rejection of the resurrection (dominant in the B episodes, the first of which happens to be the one we are commenting on) is not primary. Greater emphasis is given to A episodes and what God has done; the negative is present as a foil to exhibit that God can overcome. Despite their murderous intent against the newborn King of the Jews, Herod, the chief priests,

[36]This structural parallel between the two narratives, which I advocated in BBM 105, was suggested earlier by J. C. Fenton, "Inclusio and Chiasmus in Matthew," StEv I, 174–79. From another viewpoint, Giblin ("Structural") has argued correctly that the Matthean resurrection narrative does not begin with 28:1 but with 27:57. He points to an inclusion between *mathēteuein* ("been a disciple") in 27:57 at the beginning and that verb ("make disciples") in 28:19 at the end.

[37]The complex nature of this middle episode gets special treatment from Giblin, "Structural" 409–11.

[38]The sepulcher/resurrection narrative is more interested in the fulfillment of Jesus' own word that he would be raised after three days than in the fulfillment of the prophets. Of course, that word in the form in which the Jewish authorities remember it was probably uttered in comment on the OT prophet Jonah who was three days and three nights in the belly of the whale.

[39]27:57: *erchesthai;* 27:62: *synagein;* 28:1: *erchesthai;* 28:11: *poreuesthai* and *erchesthai;* 28:16: *poreuesthai*—all five initial verses have a postpositive *de* ("But"). As for time: 27:57: "it being evening"; 27:62: "on the next day, which is after the preparation day"; 28:1: "late on Sabbath at the dawning [i.e., beginning] of the first day of the week."

[40]Also, if the Marcan burial scene had an apologetic element designed to show that Jesus was truly dead (Pilate's investigation) and that was omitted by Matt, the Matthean guard story, which is an addendum to the burial scene, has a compensating apologetic thrust in showing that Jesus truly came forth from the sepulcher.

and the scribes (2:20: "those who sought the child's life") were thwarted; and the child was brought back safely from the exile in Egypt. Despite their attempt to keep the King of the Jews in his sepulcher, Pilate, the chief priests, and the elders are thwarted; and the Lord is brought back safely from the netherworld.

A STORY FROM THE SAME BODY OF POPULAR MATERIAL FROM WHICH MATT DREW OTHER PN ADDENDA. Throughout the Matthean PN I have contended that Matt occasionally supplemented the Marcan material available to him by stories that bore the stamp of popular, imaginative reflection on the events surrounding the death of Jesus[41]—stories marked by vivid imagery (blood, dreams), by extraordinary heavenly phenomena (earthquake, dead rising), and, alas, by extreme hostility toward Jews. There are elements of Matthean style in these stories,[42] and so the evangelist has rewritten and reshaped them; but there are enough elements peculiar to them to make me think that Matt did not create them.

Among such stories I mentioned *the episode of Judas hanging himself* (27:3–10) with its thirty pieces of silver, the insensitivity of the chief priests and the elders who are scrupulous about blood money but care nothing for the guilt involved in giving over an innocent man to death, and the allusion to the "Field of Blood" to this day; *the incident of Pilate's wife's dream* about a just man (27:19); *the description of Pilate washing his hands* of the blood of an innocent man, while all the people say, "His blood on us and on our children" (27:24–25); and after the death of Jesus *the poetic quatrain* that has the rocks rent, the tombs opened, and the many bodies of the fallen-asleep holy ones raised (27:51b–53). I find clear signs that the guard-at-the-sepulcher story belongs to the same vein of vivid popular material. There is a strong antiJewish feeling as the chief priests, the Pharisees, and the elders are shown as unprincipled scoundrels; a dramatization of Pilate; an earthquake; an offering of silver to purchase contemptible behavior;[43] a tradition

[41]I remind readers that I use the term "popular" to cover a transmission of Jesus material other than by the preaching, kerygmatic transmission that marked much of the Synoptic material or by the marshaling of synagogue-trial evidence that shaped the Johannine material. I intend nothing pejorative historically, theologically, or intellectually in the designation. Indeed, in the popular stories detectable in Matt perceptive theological issues are being raised, and the quality of the language is often quite striking. Notice, for example, the quasi-technical use of *echete koustōdian* ("You [may] have a custodial guard") in this Matthean guard story (Smyth, "Guard" 157).

[42]Pesch ("Alttestamentliche") is insistent on this point (unfortunately, however, not distinguishing adequately between Matthean reformulation and Matthean creation).

[43]The episode of Judas and the silver followed Matt 27:1 when "all the chief priests and the elders of the people took a decision [*symboulion lambanein*] against Jesus that they should put him to death." In Matt's guard-at-the-sepulcher story (28:11–12) the chief priests gather with the elders and, "having taken a decision," give silver to the soldiers.

that has endured until this day. The parallels to the Matthean supplementary material increase if we look to the form of the guard story in *GPet*.[44] There Pilate says, "*I* am clean of the blood of the Son of God, but it was to you that this seemed (the thing to do)" (11:46), even as in Matt 27:24 he said, "I am innocent of the blood of this man. You must see to it." Proclamation to "the fallen-asleep" after the death of Jesus is a theme in *GPet* 10:41–42, comparable to the raising of "the fallen-asleep" in Matt 27:52.[45] The five-episode structural parallel between the Matthean sepulcher/resurrection narrative and the Matthean infancy narrative also supports the thesis that popular material was the source for the guard story, since the infancy narrative has the same kind of popular material. It contained revelation through dreams and angels, and indeed in the magi episode a heavenly communication to Gentiles of what hostile Jewish authorities could not see (even as there was revelation to Pilate's wife). The star that came to rest over the place where the child Jesus could be found belongs in the same context as the dead rising from the tombs and coming into the holy city to be seen by many on the occasion of Jesus' resurrection.[46]

In stressing that Matt took over and broke up a popular story so that he might combine it with material he had from Mark about the burial and resurrection, I do not suggest that he simply copied the story as he heard or read it. In the COMMENT we saw that the existing account has Matthean vocabulary and constructions. The evangelist did not use a paste-and-scissors method of composition; he rethought and rephrased material that he took over to give a unity of purpose and style. In studying the infancy narrative I found the same phenomenon in the Matthean retelling of the magi story (see BBM 192).

A STORY THAT IS PRESERVED IN MATT IN A LESS DEVELOPED FORM THAN IN GPET. I have argued that Matt broke up a consecutive guard-at-the-sepulcher story to interweave it with the women-at-the-tomb story, while

---

[44]Of course, Matt was not the only author influenced by popular imaginative reflection on Christian happenings. Kratz (*Auferweckung* 33–35) points out that several NT stories have the motif of frustrated guards who cannot prevent the holy one they are watching from getting out, e.g., Acts 5:19,23 (a story involving deliverance from prison by an angel of the Lord); Acts 12:4–11 (also involving an angel of the Lord, a gate that opens of itself, and a wicked king); Acts 16:23–34 (an earthquake, with prison doors that open of themselves, and chains that come loose).

[45]See APPENDIX I, n. 18. One could add also that the extraordinary phenomena in the *GPet* form of the story (the stone rolling of itself; the gigantic size of the angels and the even more gigantic size of the risen Lord; the talking cross) match the affinity for the spectacular in the special Matthean material.

[46]Comparison of Matt's infancy narrative to Luke's, e.g., comparing the magi to the shepherds, or the flight to Egypt to the peaceful return through Jerusalem to Nazareth, illustrates that whether or not the Lucan narrative is historical, the Matthean is more folkloric.

GPet preserved the original consecutive form of the guard story.[47] That does not mean, however, that the *GPet* story is more original. It is quite possible that by the 2d cent. when *GPet* was written (and thus after the time when Matt had drawn on his source), the guard-at-the-sepulcher story had continued to develop in extraGospel narration and become a longer and more elaborate composition. While I disagree firmly with Crossan's contention that much of the *GPet* passion account antedated the canonical passion accounts and was one of their main sources (see APPENDIX I below), I agree with him that the relationship is not to be treated simply in terms of literary dependence of *GPet* on the canonical Gospels. In this particular instance, in my judgment, what is found in *GPet* is best explained in terms of the author's knowing the canonical Gospels (perhaps by distant memory of having heard them), especially Matt, as well as an independent form of the guard-at-the-sepulcher story, and of his own activity in combining these two sources of material.[48] Let us look at the various elements in this explanation.

By detailed comparisons it will be argued in APPENDIX I that the *GPet* author has heard or read Matt and knew traditions of Lucan and Johannine origin. Here let me simply give some instances of possible echoes of Matt in the long *GPet* account of the guard at the tomb (8:29–11:49).[49] *GPet*'s "Truly he was God's Son" is closer to Matt's "Truly this was God's Son" than to Mark's "This man was God's Son." Matt speaks of the elders 7 times in the PN, as compared with Mark's 3, Luke's 1 (John 0); *GPet* has 3 references to them in the guard-at-the-sepulcher story. Probably too in the *GPet* account there have been interwoven elements borrowed from *Matt's form* of the popular material listed above. (This is much harder to show, however, for this material too could have traveled independently after Matt drew on it.[50]) For instance, Matt 27:52 mentions the fate of "the fallen-asleep" in a

[47]This has been proposed by B. A. Johnson and Walter and accepted by many others. Proponents are divided on whether the pre-*GPet* form stopped with 11:49 (so that, as I think, the *GPet* author joined it to the separate women-at-the-tomb story) or continued to 13:57. The *GPet* form of the women story has many similarities to the canonical forms and could represent simply an imaginative retelling of memories from them.

[48]In a study of intertextuality in the *Protevangelium of James,* W. S. Vorster (TTK 262–75) argues that the author of that 2d-cent. apocryphon creatively combined canonical material with other tradition.

[49]There are also echoes of peculiarly Lucan material (the people beating their breasts; two angelic men [*anēr*]). If one extended the search to the subsequent women-at-the-tomb story in *GPet* 12:50–13:57, one would find there more echoes of Luke (at the dawn [*orthrou*]), as well as of John ("afraid because of the Jews"; bending down to see inside the sepulcher).

[50]Both Matt and *GPet* mention the Pharisees at the beginning of the story and only there (and also nowhere else in the PN); both Matt (28:1–2) and *GPet* (9:35–36) have angelic descent from heaven in connection with the opening of the sepulcher at the "dawning" of Sunday (*epiphōskein:* Matt's only use). I would suspect that these are elements that Matt found in the original guard-at-the-sepulcher story and that therefore the author of *GPet* could have also found them there without depending on Matt.

poetic quatrain that has a good chance of being more original than the *GPet* dramatization of it in 10:41. The fact that Herod and the Jews conducted both the trial and crucifixion in *GPet* meant that Matt's scene of Pilate's washing his hands and declaring himself innocent of Jesus' blood could not stand within the trial; apparently *GPet* broke up the incident, putting the washing of the hands earlier (see 1:1) and the declaration of being clean of Jesus' blood after the opening of the sepulcher. (When I say "broke up," I do not conceive of this as a literary reshuffling of a Matthean story that the *GPet* author had in a ms. before him; I think rather of his having heard Matt read in the past and from that hearing having images in his mind which he unconsciously reshuffled under the impact of other stories of the passion he heard, such as that of the guard at the sepulcher.)

Yet there are many elements in the long *GPet* story that are not found in Matt. The author himself could have added them to a story he took from Matt, since this is a popular, folkloric Gospel and the author probably had an affinity for the dramatic and extraordinary. Nevertheless, that solution does not explain important facts. The role of Pilate in the *GPet* sepulcher story is dramatically different from the role he played in 2:4–5: There he had to request from Herod the body of the Lord for burial; here he has complete authority over the sepulcher. Moreover, when one compares the Matthean account of the guard at the sepulcher that is some ten verses in length with the twenty-two-verse account in *GPet* (over one-third the length of the total *GPet* PN!), one notices that no other part of the *GPet* passion or resurrection account has been expanded so extensively by comparison with a corresponding canonical scene. Therefore, on the presumption that the author of *GPet* acted with some consistency, we have the right to suspect that here he had a source besides Matt, namely, a more developed account of the guard at the sepulcher. (That point is also supported by the consecutiveness of the story in *GPet*.) The supplying of the centurion's name, the seven seals, the stone rolling off by itself, the account of the resurrection with the gigantic figures, the talking cross, the confession of Jesus as God's Son by the Jewish authorities, and their fear of their own people—all those elements could plausibly have been in the more developed form of the story known to the author of *GPet* and absent from the form known to Matt. (True, Matt need not have reported the whole story; but why would he have omitted many of those items?)

The likelihood that the author of *GPet* had available two forms of the guard-at-the-sepulcher story, Matt's and another, is increased by evidence for still another form of part of the material. Codex Bob(b)iensis of Mark 16:3/4 has a Latin addition: "Suddenly at the third hour of the day darkness came about through the whole earth, and there came down from heaven angels; and rising in the shining brightness of the living God, they went up [ascended] with him; and immediately light came about."[51] This story is set just before the women come up to the empty tomb. Clearly it is parallel to *GPet* 9:36; 10:39–40, which is set in the same context; but it is much simpler. D. W. Palmer (JTS NS 27 [1976], 113–22) has proposed that originally this Bob(b)iensis story was attached to the hour of Jesus' death when the darkness came over the whole earth, and that angels came down to take Jesus from the cross. (Remember that *GPet* 6:22 mentions that after Jesus' body was taken from the cross, the sun shone, ending the darkness.) If that were the case, the independent story underlying *GPet* may have been composite, already combining the phenomena that took place at the cross (see pp. 1118–19 above) with those pertaining to guards at the sepulcher, a combination not found in the form of the sepulcher story known to Matt.

Besides elements drawn from Matt and from an independent form of the guard story, other elements in *GPet* may reflect the author's own editing of what he received: e.g., the expression "the Lord's Day" and the confusing time frame centered around the Sabbath.[52] And certain elements may have been a combination. For example, on the one hand the use of "the Jews" at the end of the guard story by Matt in 28:15 is untypical and may have been original in the form of that story known to him. The appearance of *Ioudaios* at the end of the *GPet* account in 11:48 might mean that it was also original in the form of the story known to the *GPet* author so that he did not need to borrow it from Matt. On the other hand *GPet* uses that term a total of six times, and so it was part of the author's own style as well. Some students of *GPet* would contend that my suggested interplay of dependence on Matt (and other Gospels) orally remembered, of dependence on a separate, more developed form of the guard story transmitted in popular circles, and of personal additions constitutes too complicated a scenario for explaining what appears in *GPet*. To the contrary, in the instance of such an imaginative tale, I would find that scenario plausible in an ancient world where repetition of stories orally and reminiscences from having heard them were more common than reading stories oneself. It is a scenario surely more believable than imagining that the author of *GPet* worked at a desk with copies of the vari-

[51]This 4th/5th-cent. codex copies from an archetype of the 2d or 3d cent. The grammar of the Latin is obscure and probably has been corrupted in copying. Still other witnesses to independent forms of this material might be suggested, e.g., it is not clear that this *Ascent of James* (mid-2d cent.?) section of the *Pseudo-Clementine Recognitions* (Latin 1.42:4) is dependent on Matt: "For some of those who were guarding the place with diligence called him a magician when they could not stop him from rising; others pretended that he was stolen."

[52]The fact that Matt has the whole first part dealing with the request to Pilate take place on the Sabbath while *GPet* has it happen before the Sabbath had dawned indicates that the original story had no precise time indication. Elsewhere the author of *GPet* shows an ignorance of Jewish chronology (n. 6 above), and here his having the Jewish elders and crowd watching the tomb on the Sabbath is quite implausible.

ous canonical Gospels propped up in front, carefully making changes, in order to craft a tale of a talking cross.

THE BASIC THRUST OF THE GUARD STORY. Three goals enter the discussion: polemics, apologetics, and apocalyptic eschatology. The ending of the Matthean account has a polemic bent: It refutes a story circulating among the Jews, namely, that Jesus' disciples stole his body and then fraudulently proclaimed the resurrection.[53] But that is surely not the primary thrust of the basic story. If one left out the theme of paying the soldiers to spread a lie (a theme absent from the *GPet* form of the guard story), the placing of a guard at the tomb and the failure of that precaution to prevent the tomb from being opened by divine intervention would still have meaning. The polemic element may represent the latest or final stage of the use of the guard story, developed at the period when Jewish polemic had begun to describe Jesus as a "deceiver" (27:63: *planos*) and when in the Matthean area there was an ongoing struggle between Christian missionaries and Jewish teachers of Pharisaic persuasion (27:62: Pharisees) to persuade the people (27:64: "say to the people").[54] Laying aside the polemics, we still find a strong apologetic tone: This story proves that Jesus fulfilled the word he spoke, "After three days I am (to be) raised"; there can be no doubt, then, about the truth of the Good News that would be proclaimed by the disciples to all nations until the end of the age (Matt 28:19–20). Yet again Jesus' prophecy is absent from the *GPet* form of the guard story,[55] and apologetics does not explain all the elements. Accordingly many have been led to think that the oldest and most basic element in the story that underlies both Matt and *GPet* may be an eschatological message phrased in apocalyptic imagery. The message is that God makes the divine Son triumph over his enemies, even when they consist of the seemingly all-powerful ruler and the supreme religious authorities—

---

[53]Some would contend that as an apologetic proof, the Matthean story is weak since the guard was not placed until the Sabbath, and thus the body could have been stolen between burial late Friday afternoon and the sealing on Saturday. They point out that this "hole" in the story has been plugged in *GPet*, where the burial place is closed with a stone, sealed, and guarded before the Sabbath began. I am not convinced by either observation. The Matthean story is brief and popular; we are left to assume that the Jewish authorities would have taken the elementary caution to have the sepulcher checked to see that the body was still there before they sealed it on Saturday. That would have been part of their securing it as they "know how" (27:65). If the authorities were smart enough to remember and understand a statement of Jesus about resurrection made long ago, they were scarcely so naive as to guard an empty tomb. As for *GPet* with its very confused time sequence, I doubt that better apologetics caused the author to move the sealing story up to Friday afternoon. That dating is related to another motive for sealing the tomb, namely, a reaction to what the people were saying in response to Jesus' death that had just taken place (8:28–29). Since *GPet* will portray the body of Jesus coming forth from the tomb, the author scarcely needed an earlier sealing of the burial place to prove that the body was still there.

[54]Gnilka (*Matthäus* 2.488) denies the missionary background, but offers no reasoning.

[55]In the *GPet* storyline the wish to safeguard the burial place "for three days" (8:30) need imply only that after such a period the imposter would surely be dead.

the same message found in the story of Herod's attempt to kill the child, as narrated at the beginning of the Gospel. The startling things that happen (in Matt, the earthquake and an angel coming down and rolling away the stone; in *GPet* much more) are a dramatization of the great power of God compared to puny human obstacles.[56] At the beginning of the Gospel Matt included a story depicting how the child who is Emmanuel ("God with us") would meet dangerous opposition in his predestined task of saving his people from their sins (1:21) and would need divine intervention. At the end of the Gospel he depicts at the tomb a foretaste of the eschatological struggle, warning readers that the risen Jesus who says, "I am with you all days until the end of the age" (28:20), will still face dangerous opposition that God's power, now manifestly given to him (28:18), will have to overcome.

B. **Historicity of the Matthean Story of the Guard at the Sepulcher**

A few prolegomena to this discussion are necessary. The main focus will be the Matthean account, not the *GPet* account that I regard as a later, more developed form. In principle some would reject any possibility that the Matthean account might be historical because it contains the supernatural, viz., an angel descending from heaven to roll back the stone. I do not deem it methodologically sound to let such an a priori rejection of the supernatural determine historicity, and indeed that principle would rule out the discussion of any resurrection narrative. In my judgment the possibility or plausibility of this story must be discussed on the same basis as that of any other Gospel story. Other a priori principles have been invoked to deny historicity. For example, the observation that this is a late and popular story (found only in Matt, not in Mark), or that it has an apologetic bent, would cause many to dismiss it out of hand as a fabrication. I argued above that apologetics is not the primary thrust; and even if it were, why are apologetics and historicity incompatible? After all, an argument based on something that really happened may have been advanced against the Jewish opponents of Christianity. As for the late appearance of the story in the Gospel tradition, there are other possible reasons besides fictional creation that could supply an explanation (e.g., that the presence of a guard was unimportant until enemies ad-

---

[56]Recognizing that this was the original thrust of the guard story, Kratz (*Auferweckung* 74) sees in a second stage of narration a definite increase in an apologetic motif that was only there lightly at the beginning, and then in a third stage a development of the epiphanic character of the story (especially visible in the opening of the tomb and the angelic intervention). As for *GPet* as a whole, one may have to recognize that in material expanded from canonical Gospel memories there is less of the astounding than in material that has an independent source. Accordingly one has mixed emphases in the final form of the *GPet* PN (see D. F. Wright's article "Apologetic and Apocalyptic," the title of which catches the diversity).

vanced the lie that the body had been stolen).[57] Similarly, circulation in popular circles rather than in public preaching does not always point to nonhistoricity.

Having refused to treat this issue on such a priori grounds, I am not always impressed by the force of the a posteriori arguments against historicity. For example, the lie that the soldiers are bribed to spread ("His disciples, having come at night, stole him while we were sleeping") is sometimes dismissed as absurd. It is claimed that to sleep on duty was a capital offense in the Roman army; and so the soldiers would have known that they were contributing to their own demise, despite the promise that the chief priests would persuade the governor and thus could deliver them from worry. On the level of storyline, however, as I pointed out, the chief priests are corrupt; and readers are meant to assume that they would lie to Pilate and probably bribe him not to punish the soldiers. On the level of background facts, it is not clear that sleeping on duty was always punished by death. Tacitus (*Histories* 5.22) tells of careless sentries whose sleeping on watch almost allowed the enemy to catch their general; but they seem to have used the general's scandalous behavior (he was away from duty, sleeping with a woman) to shield their own fault. In other words, bargains could be struck; and it is not implausible that Pilate might not have been so strict about the behavior of troops temporarily placed at the service of the Jewish authorities if those authorities chose not to push for punishment.

Yet there is a major argument against historicity that is impressive indeed. Not only do the other Gospels not mention the guard at the sepulcher, but the presence of the guard there would make what they narrate about the tomb almost unintelligible. The three other canonical Gospels have women come to the tomb on Easter, and the only obstacle to their entrance that is mentioned is the stone. Certainly the evangelists would have had to explain how the women hoped to get into the tomb if there were a guard placed there precisely to prevent entry.[58] In the other Gospels the stone is already removed or rolled back when the women get there. How can we reconcile that with Matt's account where, while the women are at the sepulcher, an angel comes down out of heaven and rolls back the stone? There are other internal

---

[57]Lee ("Guard" 171) suggests that a servant of the high priest (the one to whom the risen Jesus gave his linen burial cloth according to the *Gospel of the Hebrews* 7 [HSNTA 1.165; rev. ed. 1.178]) later became a Christian and that only then did the story become known. Besides the dubious expedient of combining such diverse information, this argument does not take into account that while the lie might have been secret, the posting of the guard would have been publicly known. Moreover, it may imply (wrongly) that the guard consisted of Jewish Temple police among whom would have been the servant of the high priest.

[58]Lee ("Guard" 171) suggests that the guards had fled from the tomb before the women got there, but that is not what Matt reports.

implausibilities in Matt's account (e.g., that the Jewish authorities knew the words of Jesus about his resurrection and understood them, when his own disciples did not; that the guards could lie successfully about the astounding heavenly intervention); but they touch on the minor details of the story. The lack of harmony with the other Gospels touches on the heart of the story, i.e., the very existence of a guard. Can one save historicity by going back to a preGospel situation and contending that the Jewish Sanhedrin member who buried Jesus, Joseph from Arimathea, may have taken some precaution to protect the sepulcher, and that this developed into the story that Matt now tells? That is a very hypothetical suggestion, however; for neither Matt nor *GPet* connects the guard with Joseph, and even some minor precaution should have left a trace in the other Gospels as an obstacle to the women on Easter. Absolute negative statements (e.g., the account has no historical basis) most often go beyond the kind of evidence available to biblical scholars. More accurate is the observation that as with other Matthean material (e.g., Herod's slaughtering the children at Bethlehem and the flight to Egypt—a story with functional parallels to the present story) there is neither internal nor external evidence to cause us to affirm historicity.[59]

That, of course, does not mean the story is without value.[60] I have suggested that the polemic and apologetic functions were probably secondary, and that the more fundamental thrust was an apocalyptic eschatological dramatization of the power of God to make the cause of the Son successful against all human opposition, no matter how powerful. John has a partially similar dramatization in 18:6, where in the garden across the Kidron a cohort of Roman soldiers under a tribune and Jewish attendants fall to the ground before Jesus when he says, "I am." Truth conveyed by drama can at times be more effectively impressed on people's minds than truth conveyed by history.

The treatment of the guard-at-the-tomb story closes my consecutive com-

[59]The same may be said of the raising of the holy ones and their appearance to many in Jerusalem (Matt 27:52–53). It is remarkable that Blinzler (*Prozess* 415), who tends to be extremely conservative about historicity, acknowledges difficulty in claiming it in relation to the guard story. Let me point out that if some popular material that Matt has used to supplement the PN and make it more vivid should be judged to be unhistorical, we have no way of knowing whether the evangelist was aware of that. He included a body of material, but was he in a position to evaluate the historical value of each episode?

[60]W. L. Craig has written very perceptively on the resurrection of Jesus and has deflated some of the presuppositions that underlie facilely repeated arguments against its reality. In his attempt (unsuccessful in my judgment) to defend the historicity of the guard story, it is disappointing that he seems to see worthless legend as the alternative to a historical account ("Guard" 274). The Bible is a collection of literatures of many different genres, and we devalue it if we emphasize history in a way that would demean other types of biblical literature. Jonah is an OT book of extraordinary value even if no man bearing that name was ever swallowed by a large fish or put a foot in Nineveh. Gnilka (*Matthäus* 2.488–89), who thinks that Matt brought this story (which he had found) into the Easter narrative in order to refute Pharisee attacks on the resurrection, judges it a dubious way to defend the Gospel. But was defense its chief purpose?

mentary on the PN of the Gospels. Matt's interweaving of that story with his recital of the resurrection reminds us that the PN is not the end of the Gospel account of Jesus—none of the canonical Gospels ends without a further account that gives assurance (in various ways) that he has been raised from the dead. The last line in Matt's guard story reflects a tragic situation of polemic and counter-polemic that accompanied the Christian proclamation of the risen Lord: "And this [false] word has been spread about among the Jews until this day" (28:15). This acrid reproach, however, is not the finale of Matt's Gospel. That comes five verses later when the risen Jesus says, "Behold, I am with you all days until the end of the age" (28:20). Matt's real concern is to have this last and true word spread about among Christians until this day.

(Bibliography for this episode may be found in §45, Part 2.)

APPENDIXES

APPENDIX I: *THE GOSPEL OF PETER* —
A NONCANONICAL PASSION NARRATIVE

Some 250 miles S of Cairo and 60 miles N along the Nile from Nag Ham-madi[1] is Akhmîm (ancient Egyptian Chemmis and Hellenistic Panopolis), the site in antiquity of a Pachomian monastery, and from the 5th cent. of a necropolis. In 1886–87 a French archaeological expedition found in one of the monks' graves a small codex (6" × 4½"). On its 33 two-sided parchment leaves 4 fragmentary Greek texts[2] were copied by different hands between the 4th and 9th cents. After an opening recto page with a Coptic cross and an alpha-ōmega lettering, pages 2 through 10, stemming from the 7th–9th cents.,[3] are devoted to a work that begins in mid-sentence with an account of the trial of Jesus and ends in mid-sentence at the sea where (presumably) the risen Jesus will appear to Simon Peter, Andrew, and Levi. Apparently this incomplete segment was all that the copyist had of the work. Since in it Simon Peter speaks in the first person (14:60; cf. 7:26), scholars guessed that it was part of the *Gospel of Peter* mentioned by several early church writers, an apocryphon that was known to have been in circulation in the Antioch area before AD 200.[4] In the 1970s two small fragments of Papyrus

---

[1]This is the site where in Dec. 1945 Egyptian peasants found within a jar a collection of thirteen Coptic codices (books) that had been buried about AD 400—these codices contained fifty-two discrete tractates, probably from one of the 4th-cent. monasteries associated with St. Pachomius (292–348), which stood within a five-mile radius of the find (Chenoboskion, where Pachomius began his life as a hermit, and Pabau, which was the headquarters monastery). These tractates constitute the NHL.

[2]Besides *GPet,* which comes first, the other three in order are the *Apocalypse of Peter; I Enoch* (1:1–32:6); and, on a (34th) page pasted to the back cover, the *Acts [Martyrdom] of St. Julian.* For the page allotments, see Crossan, *Cross* 4–5. The original publication was in *Mémoires publiés par les membres de la Mission archéologique française au Caire* Vol. 9, ed. U. Bouriant (Paris: Leroux). Fascicle 1 (1892), 91–147, describes the fragments, with 137–42 offering a Greek transcription and a French translation of *GPet;* Fascicle 3 (1893), 217–35, provides a study and critically annotated transcription of *GPet* by A. Lods, and Plates II–VI reproduce a facsimile of the Greek.

[3]The pages have 17–19 lines each (14 on the 10th page with 3 lines left blank at the end). J. Armitage Robinson divided the text into 14 chaps.; Harnack, into 60 vv. It is now normal to use *both* systems of reference simultaneously, e.g., v. 14, which ends chap. 4 (= 4:14), is followed by v. 15 opening chap. 5 (= 5:15).

[4]So far as we know, this was the only gospel attributed to Peter in antiquity. There is no preserved quotation of any words from it, however, that we might check against the Akhmîm text. Some have doubted whether the Petrine gospel mentioned by Origen in reference to infancy-narrative material (p. 1337 below) was the same work of which we find the passion narrative in *GPet.* An affirmative answer is suggested by Latin fragments preserved from Origen's *Commentary on Matthew* which show similarities to *GPet*'s mindset about the passion, e.g., 125 says that Jesus did not suffer any-

Oxyrhynchus 2949 (with some 16 discernible words from about 20 partial lines) were shown to agree partially with 2:3–5 of the Akhmîm copy,[5] proving that the latter had transcribed a work that was known in 2d-cent. Egypt and helping to confirm the identification. Throughout this commentary, then, I have used the designation *GPet* to refer to the Greek text of Akhmîm with the assumption that it substantially reproduces a section of this ancient *Gospel of Peter.*

The contents of this APPENDIX will be as follows:

A. Literal Translation of GPet (with the right margin indexing the pages where I have commented on the passages being translated)
B. Sequence and Contents of *GPet*
   1. Sequence Table (comparing *GPet* to the canonical Gospels)
   2. Comparing the Contents of *GPet* and Those of the Canonical Gospels
   3. Overall Proposal about Composition Based on Sequence and Contents
C. Aspects of the Theology of *GPet*
   1. The Ancient Debate about the Docetism of *GPet*
   2. Discernible Theological Features in *GPet*
D. When and Where was *GPet* Composed?
Bibliography[6]

A. *Literal Translation of* GPet[7]

[1:1]But of the Jews none washed his hands, neither Herod nor one of his   834
judges. And since they did not desire to wash, Pilate stood up. [1:2]And then
Herod the king orders the Lord to be taken [sent?] away, having said to
them, "What I ordered you to do to him, do."

[2:3]But Joseph, the friend of Pilate and of the Lord, had been standing   1232
there; and knowing they were about to crucify him, he came before Pilate
and requested the body of the Lord for burial. [2:4]And Pilate, having sent
to Herod, requested his body. [2:5]And Herod said, "Brother Pilate, even if
no one had requested him, we would have buried him, since indeed Sab-   1350
bath is dawning. For in the Law it has been written, 'The sun is not to set   1174, 1213
on one put to death.'"   1233

[2:5c]And he gave him over to the people before the first day of their feast   1213, 1360
of the Unleavened Bread. [3:6]But having taken the Lord, running, they were   1233

---

thing (GCS 38.262, line 26; cf. *GPet* 4:10); 140 has Jesus "received" after death (*receptus;* GCS 38.290, line 22; cf. *GPet* 5:19: *anelēphthē*).

[5]See Coles and Lührmann in the SECTIONAL BIBLIOGRAPHY.

[6]The works in the SECTIONAL BIBLIOGRAPHY that I have found the most helpful are those of Swete, Vaganay, Beyschlag, and Mara.

[7]This translation is based on the Greek text supplied by Maria Mara, with one significant change, i.e., preferring *par[alē]mphthēnai,* not *par[apē]mphthēnai* in 1:2. Neirynck prints this Greek text at the end of "Apocryphal" (171–75).

pushing him and saying, "Let us drag along the Son of God now that we   912
have power over him." 3:7And they clothed him with purple and sat him   864–65
on a chair of judgment, saying, "Judge justly, King of Israel." 3:8And a   1392
certain one of them, having brought a thorny crown, put it on the head of   866–71
the Lord. 3:9And others who were standing there were spitting in his face,
and others slapped his cheeks. Others were jabbing him with a reed; and
some scourged him saying, "With such honor let us honor the Son of   869
God."

4:10And they brought two wrongdoers and crucified the Lord in the mid-   971
dle of them. But he was silent as having no pain. 4:11And when they had   1338
set the cross upright, they inscribed that "This is the King of Israel."   964, 992
4:12And having put his garments before him, they divided them up and
threw as a gamble for them. 4:13But a certain one of those wrongdoers   1000–1
reviled them, saying, "We have been made suffer thus because of the
wrong that we have done; but this one, having become Savior of men,
what injustice has he done to you?" 4:14And having become irritated at   1333
him, they ordered that there be no leg-breaking, so that he might die tor-   1176
mented.

5:15But it was midday, and darkness held fast all Judea; and they were   1037–38
distressed and anxious lest the sun had set, since he was still living. [For] 1136–37
it is written for them: "Let not the sun set on one put to death." 5:16And
someone of them said, "Give him to drink gall with vinegary wine." And   940–44
having made a mixture, they gave to drink. 5:17And they fulfilled all things   1065
and completed the(ir) sins on their own head. 5:18But many went around   1340
with lamps, thinking that it was night, and they fell. 5:19And the Lord
screamed out, saying, "My power, O power, you have forsaken me." And   1054–58
having said this, he was taken up.   1081

5:20And at the same hour the veil of the Jerusalem sanctuary was torn   1098–1101
into two. 6:21And then they drew out the nails from the hands of the Lord   949
and placed him on the earth; and all the earth was shaken, and a great fear   1219
came about. 6:22Then the sun shone, and it was found to be the ninth hour.
6:23And the Jews rejoiced and gave his body to Joseph that he might bury   1232–33
it, since he was one who had seen how many good things he did. 6:24And   1278
having taken the Lord, he washed and tied him with a linen cloth and
brought him into his own sepulcher, called the Garden of Joseph.   1224, 1253

7:25Then the Jews and the elders and the priests, having come to know
how much wrong they had done to themselves, began to beat themselves   1168–69
and say, "Woe to our sins. The judgment has approached and the end of   1189–91
Jerusalem." 7:26But I with the companions was sorrowful; and having
been wounded in spirit, we were in hiding, for we were sought after by   290, 1213
them as wrongdoers and as wishing to set fire to the sanctuary. 7:27In addi-   1345
tion to all these things we were fasting; and we were sitting mourning and   1327
weeping night and day until the Sabbath.

8:28But the scribes and Pharisees and elders, having gathered together   1287–89
with one another, having heard that all the people were murmuring and
beating their breasts, saying that, "If at his death these very great signs
happened, behold how just he was," 8:29feared (especially the elders) and   1299
came before Pilate, begging him and saying, 8:30"Give over soldiers to us   1291–92
in order that we may safeguard his burial place for three days, lest, having   1333
come, his disciples steal him, and the people accept that he is risen from   1292
the dead, and they do us wrong." 8:31But Pilate gave over to them Petronius   1294

the centurion with soldiers to safeguard the sepulcher. And with these the
elders and scribes came to the burial place. 8:32And having rolled a large
stone, all who were there, together with the centurion and the soldiers,   1247
placed (it) against the door of the burial place. 8:33And they marked (it)   1273
with seven wax seals; and having pitched a tent there, they safeguarded   1296
(it). 9:34But early when the Sabbath was dawning, a crowd came from   1290
Jerusalem and the surrounding area in order that they might see the
sealed tomb.

   9:35But in the night in which the Lord's Day dawned, when the soldiers   1297
were safeguarding (it) two by two in every watch, there was a loud voice
in heaven; 9:36and they saw that the heavens were opened and that two   1333
males who had much radiance had come down from there and come near   1299
the sepulcher. 9:37But that stone which had been thrust against the door,
having rolled by itself, went a distance off to the side; and the sepulcher   1274
opened, and both the young men entered. 10:38And so those soldiers, having seen, awakened the centurion and the elders (for they too were present,   1295
safeguarding). 10:39And while they were relating what they had seen,
again they see three males who have come out from the sepulcher, with
the two supporting the other one, and a cross following them, 10:40and the   1297
head of the two reaching unto heaven, but that of the one being led out by   1335
hand by them going beyond the heavens. 10:41And they were hearing a   1339
voice from the heavens saying, "Have you made proclamation to the
fallen-asleep?" 10:42And an obeisance was heard from the cross, "Yes."   1287, 1307
11:43And so those people were seeking a common perspective to go off   1295
and make these things clear to Pilate; 11:44and while they were still consid-   1298
ering it through, there appear again the opened heavens and a certain man   1299
having come down and entered into the burial place. 11:45Having seen   1301
these things, those around the centurion hastened at night before Pilate   1295
(having left the sepulcher which they were safeguarding) and described
all the things that they indeed had seen, agonizing greatly and saying,
"Truly he was God's Son." 11:46In answer Pilate said, "*I* am clean of the   1299
blood of the Son of God, but it was to you that this seemed (the thing to   1305, 1307
do)." 11:47Then all, having come forward, were begging and exhorting him
to command the centurion and the soldiers to say to no one what they had
seen. 11:48"For," they said, "it is better for us to owe the debt of the greatest
sin in the sight of God than to fall into the hands of the Jewish people and
be stoned." 11:49And so Pilate ordered the centurion and the soldiers to   1299
say nothing.

   12:50Now at the dawn of the Lord's Day Mary Magdalene, a female
disciple of the Lord (who, afraid because of the Jews since they were   1345
inflamed with anger, had not done at the tomb of the Lord what women   1218
were accustomed to do for the dead beloved by them), 12:51having taken   1345
with her women friends, came to the tomb where he had been placed.
12:52And they were afraid lest the Jews should see them and were saying,
"If indeed on that day on which he was crucified we could not weep and
beat ourselves, yet now at his tomb we may do these things. 12:53But who
will roll away for us even the stone placed against the door of the tomb in   1327
order that, having entered, we may sit beside him and do the expected
things? 12:54For the stone was large, and we are afraid lest anyone see us.   1247
And if we are unable, let us throw against the door what we bring in memory of him; let us weep and beat ourselves until we come to our homes."

13:55And having gone off, they found the sepulcher opened. And having come forward, they bent down there and saw there a certain young man   1299
seated in the middle of the sepulcher, comely and clothed with a splendid robe, who said to them, 13:56"Why have you come? Whom do you seek? Not that one who was crucified? He is risen and gone away. But if you do not believe, bend down and see the place where he lay, because he is not here. For he is risen and gone away to there whence he was sent."
13:57Then the women fled frightened.   1327

14:58Now it was the final day of the Unleavened Bread; and many went out, returning to their homes since the feast was over. 14:59But we twelve disciples of the Lord were weeping and sorrowful; and each one, sorrowful because of what had come to pass, departed to his home. 14:60But I,
Simon Peter, and my brother Andrew, having taken our nets, went off to   1331
the sea. And there was with us Levi of Alphaeus whom the Lord . . .

B. *Sequence and Contents of* GPet

To study the relationship of *GPet* to the canonical Gospels, it is important to understand both its contents and the sequence in which they are presented. Below I shall offer: (1) a table to help with the sequence; (2) some lists comparing *GPet* to each of the canonical Gospels; and (3) an overall proposal about the composition of *GPet* based on 1 and 2. In all that pertains to such a comparison of sequence or wording one factor must be kept firmly in mind. The Akhmîm codex gives us a copy made some six hundred years after the original of *GPet* was written; and we can be sure that copyists made changes in that long course of transcription[8]—probably all the more freely because this work, circulated privately, was widely deemed as heterodox, and was not read publicly, as were the canonical Gospels where greater supervision was exercised and changes would have been noticed. When the vocabulary or even the sequence of *GPet* agrees with that of the canonical Gospels, there is always the danger that some copyist has substituted the more familiar canonical wording or patterning for what originally stood in *GPet*.

1. SEQUENCE TABLE

Table 10 (pp. 1323–1325) follows the sequence of *GPet;* in the first column whatever is double underlined is found in *GPet* only. Although I see little to recommend the compositional theory of D. Crossan, we shall have to discuss it below in this subsection under B3. Therefore, I have thought that it might be useful to readers if I were to put dotted lines around episodes

---

[8]I mentioned above that the 2d-cent. Papyrus Oxyrhynchus 2949 form of this gospel, which has only sixteen words, has discernible differences from the comparable *GPet* passage.

in the first column that Crossan regards as secondary editing or redaction in *GPet;*[9] in his theory all the rest would have existed before the canonical evangelists wrote and would have been known by them. There is no column for Mark because the basic Marcan sequence is the same as Matt's, and *GPet* has no scene peculiar to Mark.

GPet follows the classical flow from trial through crucifixion to burial and tomb, presumably with postresurrectional appearances to follow. The *GPet* sequence of individual episodes, however, is not the same as that of any canonical Gospel, as one can see in sections I, IV, and V of the chart. Yet in some short sequences *GPet* is closer to Mark/Matt than to the other Gospels. For example in II, although *GPet* places the way of the cross before the mocking and scourging (the opposite of the Mark/Matt order), it is clearly closer to those two Gospels than to Luke which omits the mockery here (and the scourging altogether), or to John which has shifted the mocking and scourging into the middle of the Roman trial. Again in the latter part of III the *GPet* sequence of darkness, vinegary-wine drink, Jesus' scream "My power," and the torn sanctuary veil approaches that of Mark/Matt which have the same four items but with the scream and the wine drink reversed.

When one looks at the overall sequence in the twenty-three items I listed in Table 10, it would take great imagination to picture the author of *GPet* studying Matt carefully, deliberately shifting episodes around, and copying

[9]For Crossan, there are two types of additions: (1) *insertions,* or scenes made from canonical Gospel material and introduced into the Cross Gospel, even though they virtually contradicted what was already there; (2) *redaction* passages created to prepare for and facilitate the insertions and thus to smooth over the apparent contradictions. Because he has different analyses in (a) *Four* 134 and later in (b) *Cross* 21, I offer both here in parallel columns:

(a) REDACTION for →	INSERTION	(b) REDACTION for →	INSERTION
2:3–5ab →	6:23–24	2:3–5ab →	6:23–24
7:26–27 →	14:58–60	7:26–27; 14:58–59 →	14:60
9:37; 11:43–44 →	12:50–13:57	11:43–44 →	12:50–13:57

In Table 10 in the text below I have been able to indicate with dotted boxing all these additions except 11:43–44 (and the 9:37 of [a], which apparently Crossan no longer considers an addition). Note that in Crossan's theory the placing of the redactional preparation has little to do with where the insertion will appear (indeed the second and third horizontal rows presume a very peculiar mind if one analyzes the sequence of verses). Moreover, the classification of the insertions as canonical is rather loose attribution. *GPet* 14:60 has a remote resemblance to John 21:1–2 and to a name in Mark 2:14, but are we to think that the *GPet* final author really gathered such unrelated material from a ms. of Mark and a ms. of John to create 14:60? (Koester, KACG 220, despite a general liking for Crossan's approach, objects to his treatment of 14:60.) Also Crossan's attribution of 2:3 to the latest stage of *GPet* composition gets no help from the fact that this passage appears in the oldest known copy, Papyrus Oxyrhynchus 2949.

TABLE 10. SEQUENCE IN THE GOSPEL OF PETER AND THE CANONICAL GOSPELS

GPet	Matt	Luke	John
I. 1:1–2:5: Trial before Herod (with Pilate present)	**27:11–26 Only Pilate**	**23:2–25 Pilate & Herod**	**18:28–19:16a only Pilate**
1:1 Herod <u>refused</u> to wash hands	27:24 (Pilate)		
1:2 <u>Herod ordered Lord taken away</u>			
2:3–5b Request for Lord's body: Joseph→Pilate →Herod	27:57–58 Joseph→Pilate	23:50–52 Joseph→Pilate	19:38a Joseph→Pilate
2:5c Herod gave Lord over <u>to the people</u>	27:26 Pilate to soldiers	23:25 Pilate to their will	19:16a Pilate to them
II: 3:6–9: Way of cross; mocking; scourging	**27:27–32**	**23:26–32**	**19:2–3, 16b–17a**
3:6 They (Jews) <u>pushed and dragged</u> Son of God	27:31b Roman soldiers led	23:26 They led	19:16b They took along
3:7–9 Purple clothing, judgment chair, mocked King of Israel, thorny crown, spat, slapped, struck with reed, mocked Son of God	27:27–31a all items except slap; King of Jews as title (see 27:19 [judgment seat]; also 27:39–43 on cross)	(see 23:35–37 on cross)	19:2–3 crown of thorns, purple robe, King of Jews, slaps
III. 4:10–6:22: Crucifixion	**27:33–56**	**23:33–49**	**19:17b–37**
4:10 Crucified amid wrongdoers; <u>silent, no pain</u>	27:38 amid bandits	23:33 amid wrongdoers	19:18 amid others
4:11 Title on cross: King of <u>Israel</u>	27:37 Jesus, King of Jews	23:38 King of Jews	19:19 Jesus the Nazorean, King of Jews
4:12 Divided garments	27:35	23:34b	19:23–24
4:13 Penitent wrongdoer		23:40–43	

TABLE 10. Continued

GPet	Matt	Luke	John
4:14 <u>No</u> leg-breaking			19:31–33
5:15 Midday darkness; <u>anxiety lest sun set</u>	27:45 (6th–9th hours)	23:44–45a (6th–9th hours)	
5:16–18 Drink: gall with vinegary wine; they fulfilled all things; <u>sin on their head; thought it was night</u>	27:34, 48 Two drinks: (sweet) wine with gall and vinegary wine	23:36 Drink: vinegary wine	19:28–30 Drink: vinegary wine; *he* finished all things
5:19 Lord screamed, "My power"; he was taken up	27:46 "My God"		
5:20 Veil of sanctuary torn	27:51a	23:45b	
6:21 <u>Drew out nails; placed him on earth</u>; earth shaken; fear	27:51b, 54		
6:22 <u>Sun shone</u>; 9th hour	27:46 (9th hr.)	23:44 (9th hr)	
IV. 6:23–11:49: Burial	**27:57–66**	**23:50–56**	**19:38–42**
6:23–24 <u>Jews</u> gave body to Joseph; he <u>washed</u> him; linen cloth; "his own" sepulcher; garden	27:58b–60 (no garden); his tomb	23:53–54 (no "his own"; no garden)	19:38b–42 (no linen cloth; no "his own")
7:25 Sorrow of Jews; beat themselves		23:48 crowds striking breasts	
7:26–27 <u>Peter and companions: sorrow, fasting</u>			
8:28–11:48 Guards at tomb; angelic opening; <u>came out with gigantic Lord and talking cross</u>; guards silenced	27:62–66; 28:2–4, 11–15		

TABLE 10. Continued

GPet	Matt	Luke	John
V. Women at empty tomb; Appearances of the Lord			
12:50–13:57: Women at empty tomb	28:1, 5–10	24:1–11, 22–23	20:1–2, 11–18
14:58–60: After feast 12 go home; Peter et al. at the sea			21:1–23 Peter et al. at the sea see risen Lord

in episodes from Luke and John to produce the present sequence. In the canonical Gospel PNs, we have an example of Matt working conservatively and Luke working more freely with the Marcan outline and of each adding material; but neither produced an end product so radically diverse from Mark as *GPet* is from Matt. Some scholars think the author of the Long Ending of Mark knew Matt and Luke; be that as it may, he produced a sequence of resurrection appearances that is more detectably close to the sequence in Luke than is the sequence of *GPet* to any of the four Gospels. The opposite hypothesis that the four canonical evangelists drew on all or part of *GPet* is even more incredible in respect to sequence. Are we to believe that four different writers used *GPet* as a main source, and none preserved the *GPet* sequence for more than two or three of twenty-three episodes I listed in the table?[10] The difficulty of hypotheses of careful literary dependence in either direction will become more apparent in what follows.

2. COMPARING THE CONTENTS OF *GPet* AND THOSE OF THE CANONICAL GOSPELS

I shall now give some lists to accomplish this purpose.[11] Some general cautions: Most of the time I shall refer to "Jesus," but readers should remember that *GPet* never uses the personal name; its most frequent alternative is "the Lord." Except where specific Greek words are given, what is being

---

[10]I see no greater likelihood in Crossan's thesis that the canonical evangelists drew only on part of *GPet*. All the items from 2:5c through 6:22 would have been in the part that he thinks they used, and the *GPet* diversity of sequence from the canonical Gospels is quite sharp in much of that area.

[11]Swete (*Euaggelion* xvi–xx) offers lists which I have checked against my own; obviously there will be differing judgments about what is important enough to include.

compared are items or episodes, not wording. *GPet,* even when describing an incident also found in a canonical Gospel, uses remarkably different vocabulary. It is very rare that it agrees with any of the Gospels in more than two or three consecutive words.

(a) Items shared by *GPet* and more than one of the canonical Gospels (an asterisk indicates that the respective item is absent from John and is therefore a Synoptic feature):[12]

- Use of generalized term "the Jews" (Matt, John)
- Pilate's role in Jesus' death is not so important as that of the Jewish authorities
- Joseph has dealings with Pilate over the burial of Jesus' body
- Joseph was a friend/disciple of Jesus or did not vote against him
- Getting the body off the cross is related to the approaching Sabbath
- Jesus mocked as king with purple/scarlet clothing, crown of thorns, scourging, spitting, striking
- Judgment chair/seat with relation to Jesus or to Pilate (Matt, John)
- Crucifixion of Jesus between two criminals
- Inscription on the cross that Jesus was King of the Jews/Israel
- Gambling to divide his clothes/garments
- Mention of the 6th hour and *darkness over the earth/Judea
- Offered a drink of vinegary wine
- *Jesus' final words as "My power/my God" (Mark/Matt)[13]
- *Veil of the sanctuary rent/torn
- Joseph buries Jesus in a tomb *in a linen cloth
- A (*large) stone covers the tomb entrance; eventually rolled/taken away
- On Sunday Mary Magdalene (and others) come to tomb
- There they are addressed by explicitly or implicitly angelic figure(s) who explain the absence of Jesus' body

(b) Items shared by several canonical Gospels but absent from *GPet* (an asterisk indicates that the respective item is also absent from John and is therefore a Synoptic feature):

- Pilate's major role in the trial of Jesus and his finding Jesus not guilty
- Barabbas and the cries of the crowd to crucify Jesus
- Carrying of the cross by Jesus and/or *Simon of Cyrene
- *Several mockeries of Jesus hanging on the cross

---

[12]I shall begin with the canonical Roman trial of Jesus and its parallel in *GPet*'s Herodian trial, but with the reminder that we do not have the whole of the latter. I shall give relatively little attention to comparing postresurrectional appearances at the end of the list, for *GPet* breaks off there and we do not know what would have been recounted.

[13]Of the Seven "Words" of Jesus on the cross, *GPet* has nothing resembling the three in Luke or the (diverse) three in John; its one "word" is only partially similar to the Mark/Matt one "word."

- *Confession of Jesus (Son of God, just) by the centurion immediately after death[14]
- Women at the cross or onlooking from a distance; *women at burial
- Jesus appearing to Mary Magdalene at tomb (Matt, John)
- Jesus appearing to disciples/Twelve in Jerusalem (Luke, John)

While these items are not so numerous as those in (a), several of them (Barabbas, mockeries on the cross, some of the appearance narratives) are major components in the canonical passion and resurrection accounts.

(c) Items peculiar to *GPet* and Mark. In the extent of narrative covered by *GPet,* Mark has three outstanding items absent from the other canonical Gospels, i.e., a crucifixion reference to the 3d hour; Pilate's asking if Jesus had already died (15:44–45); and after the angelic message at the tomb, to translate literally, the women "said nothing to no one." All three are lacking in *GPet.* In the PN proper the most noticeable peculiarity shared by Mark and *GPet* is the use of *kentyriōn* for "centurion."[15] Only in the story of the women at the tomb on "the Lord's Day" does *GPet* come close to vocabulary peculiarities in Mark. In *GPet* 12:53 the women ask the rhetorical question, "Who will roll away for us even the stone placed against the door of the tomb?"; in Mark 16:3 they ask, "Who will roll away for us the stone from the door of the tomb?" Both works have the sentence, "For the stone was large," even if the word order is different and Mark alone has the adverb *sphodra* ("very"). Both works describe the (heavenly) being inside the sepulcher/tomb as a *neaniskos* ("young man"). Both works combine the verbs *phobeisthai* and *pheugein* to describe the *frightened flight* of the women from the tomb (*GPet* 13:57; Mark 16:8) but again in different order. Only in *GPet* 14:60 and Mark 2:14 do we hear of Levi of Alphaeus. These few similarities (several of which also contain differences) are insufficient to show that *GPet* was a primary written source for the Marcan evangelist (Crossan's thesis) or, in the other direction, that the author of *GPet* had Mark before him as he wrote.

I need to add more on this last point because of the work of Neirynck, who has a strong penchant to relate to Mark almost all the canonical material pertinent to the women at the tomb—a thesis with which I disagree. In "Apocryphal" 144–48 he discusses in detail the relation of the women-at-

---

[14]These confessions of Jesus' identity come later and in other circumstances in *GPet* (8:28; 11:45).

[15]*GPet* 7:27 has the combined verbs *penthein* and *klaiein* ("to mourn and weep") to describe the reaction of Peter and his companions to the death of the Lord. In the material we are considering here, only in the Long Ending of Mark (16:10) does that combination appear, and again it is to describe the reaction of those who had been with Jesus.

the-tomb story in *GPet* 12:50–13:57 to Mark 16:1–8.[16] There are three major difficulties in positing dependence on Mark: (1) Even Neirynck ("Apocryphal" 144) has to state that this is the most "Markan" section in *GPet,* an admission which does not sufficiently alert readers to how little distinctively Marcan is found in the rest of *GPet.* As Gardner-Smith has pungently observed (see "Gospel" 264–70), if the author of *GPet* had read Mark, he had certainly forgotten the details. Unless the evidence for dependence on Mark in the tomb story is truly compelling,[17] I would think it logical to avoid inconsistency by rejecting Mark as a source for *GPet.* (2) In judging the *GPet* and Mark agreement in the tomb story, we note a good deal of difference in internal sequence and word order. These differences should not be overlooked in studying the comparison Neirynck makes between the two: He has had to make changes in the Marcan verse sequence to draw attention to the parallels. (3) If one lays aside differences of order and sequence and compares only vocabulary, there are about 200 Greek words in the *GPet* passage concerning the women at the tomb and about 140 in the Marcan. If one is generous and ignores differences of case endings and tenses, my count is that *GPet* and the Nestle text of Mark share about 30 words. If one sets aside other places in the story where Matt or Luke is closer to *GPet* in vocabulary than is Mark, *of these 30 words* Matt has about 14 and Luke about 17; and since those numbers are not always overlapping, the statistic means that the author of *GPet* could have got two-thirds of the vocabulary he shares with Mark from either Matt or Luke. As for the relatively few words that *GPet* shares only with Mark (among the canonical Gospels), we must keep in mind the possibility of noncanonical origin. For example, the *neaniskos* of the tomb story is found only in *GPet* and Mark; but *SGM* also portrays a *neaniskos* in a tomb, and so the image of the young man did circulate in apocryphal tradition. In my judgment, then, the tomb-story similarities leave too slim a basis for positing *GPet* dependence on Mark.

(d) Items peculiar to *GPet* and Matt. Here the list, presented in *GPet* se-

---

[16]There is no question that in shaping 12:50–13:57 the author of *GPet* was influenced by canonical Gospel material (even Crossan admits that); there are in this story echoes of Luke and of John, and of passages where Mark and Matt agree, combined with many features that are peculiar to *GPet* (that Magdalene was a female disciple, that the Jews inflamed with anger had previously stopped the women from what they were accustomed to do, that they wanted to weep and beat themselves, that the young man inside was comely). But is there evidence that the author of *GPet* used Mark?

[17]What I have listed in the preceding paragraph above is really all that is parallel in that story. Neirynck would increase the basis for dependence by sheer hypothesis: The "he is risen and gone away to there whence he was sent" in *GPet* 13:56 is a replacement of Mark's "Go tell his disciples and Peter that he is going before you into Galilee; there you will see him as he told you" (16:7). That assumes what needs to be proved, namely, that the author knew Mark. In any case, much of Mark 16:7 is in Matt 28:7. The absence of this directive to go to Galilee in a *GPet* sequence where, in fact, the disciples will go to the sea to fish (14:60) is for me a strong indication that the author did not have even written Matt before him.

quence, is quite long and dramatically different from the relationship between *GPet* and Mark (notice that only toward the end does Matt's sequence of these peculiarities begin to differ from *GPet*'s):

- the washing of hands in relation to Jesus' innocence (*GPet* 1:1; Matt 27:24)
- Gall as part of the wine drink given to Jesus (*GPet* 5:16; Matt 27:34)
- *Anaboan* (*GPet* 5:19; Matt 27:46: "to scream out") for Jesus' last words
- A shaking of the earth in relation to Jesus' death (*GPet* 6:21; Matt 27:51)
- The sepulcher/tomb in which Jesus is buried is Joseph's own (*GPet* 6:24; Matt 27:60)
- "Gathering together" of Jewish authorities including Pharisees (*GPet* 8:28; Matt 27:62)
- Request by Jewish authorities to Pilate to protect the grave "lest, having come, his/the disciples steal him"; Pilate's granting soldiers (*GPet* 8:30–31; Matt 27:64–65)
- The use of *taphos* ("sepulcher"), particularly in that story
- The sealing of the stone that closed the door of the tomb (*GPet* 8:33; Matt 27:66)
- The appearance from heaven of "males" or an angel involved with the rolling away of the stone from the door of the tomb
- Dealing with the "fallen-asleep" after Jesus' death (*GPet* 10:41; Matt 27:52)[18]
- The fright of the guard; consultation with the Jewish authorities; agreement that the guards would keep silence or lie
- Pilate's statement that he was clean/innocent of Jesus' blood (*GPet* 11:46; Matt 27:24)

On the other side of the picture there are many items peculiar to Matt not found in *GPet:* the dream of Pilate's wife, "His blood on us and on our children," rocks split, tombs opened, many of the fallen-asleep holy ones raised and made visible to Jerusalemites, Jesus' appearance to women at the tomb. When these are added to those listed under (b) where Matt is most frequently a component of the "several canonical Gospels," and to overall differences of vocabulary, we recognize how difficult it is to imagine a relationship in which one author had a written ms. of the other before him and copied from it.

---

[18]Denker (*Theologiegeschichtliche* 93–95) contends that Matt's raising of the fallen-asleep differs from *GPet*'s proclamation to the fallen-asleep because the latter does not change the fate of the dead. How does one know that? Harnack (*Bruchstücke* 69) correctly observes that the proclamation was not one of judgment: These are the asleep who by that very designation are able to be wakened. *Odes of Solomon* 42:3–20 describes the opening of the doors of Sheol by the Son of God and the salvific going forth of those who were in darkness (see Crossan, *Cross* 365–68).

(e) Items peculiar to *GPet* and Luke:

- Herod had a role in the trial of Jesus[19]
- Friendly relations between Herod and Pilate (*GPet* 2:5; Luke 23:12)
- Jesus given over to Jews after trial; Roman soldiers mentioned only later
- Co-crucified are "wrongdoers"; one is favorable to Jesus
- Jesus' death related to approaching end of Jerusalem (*GPet* 7:25; Luke 23:28–31)
- Jewish people lament, beating themselves/breasts (*GPet* 7:25; 8:28; Luke 23:27,48)
- Jesus recognized as "just" (*dikaios: GPet* 8:28; Luke 23:47)
- "Dawning" of the Sabbath (*GPet* 9:34; Luke 23:54)
- Many/crowds returned to homes (*hypostrephein: GPet* 14:58; Luke 23:48)

The list is not so long as the Matthean list, and in these few shared items there are major differences in *GPet:* Herod's trial role is greater than Pilate's; Herod is already on friendly terms with Pilate; the favorable wrongdoer speaks from the cross to the Jews, not to his companion. Moreover, there are notable items peculiar to Luke missing from *GPet:* Jesus' address to the Daughters of Jerusalem; all three of the Lucan Jesus' "words" (sayings) on the cross; eclipse; the women getting the spices and myrrh ready; resting on the Sabbath; the rhetorical question by the angelic men at the tomb and the reminders of what Jesus said in Galilee; all the postresurrectional appearances of the Lucan Jesus. When these differences are added to the failure of *GPet* to follow unique patterns in the Lucan sequence, it is clear that in content and sequence *GPet*'s relationship to Luke is more distant than *GPet*'s relationship to Matt.

(f) Items peculiar to *GPet* and John:

- It is the day before the 1st day of Unleavened Bread/Passover
- Their feast; a feast of the Jews
- The issue of not breaking Jesus' bones (somewhat unclear in *GPet* 4:14)
- The Jews carry lamps/lanterns (*GPet* 5:18; John 18:3)
- Nails in the hands (*GPet* 6:21; John 20:25; only implicit in Luke 24:39)
- Sepulcher/tomb in garden
- Jews speak to Pilate of Jesus as Son of God (*GPet* 11:45; John 19:7)
- Women or disciples are afraid of the Jews after Jesus' death

---

[19]I follow here the surface likelihood that the Herod the king of the *GPet* PN (1:1–2:5c) is the Herod who features in only Lucan passion references (23:6–12,15; Acts 4:25–28), Herod Antipas the tetrarch of Galilee. I would allow, however, that he might be the Herod the Great of the Matthean magi story who tried to put the child Jesus to death, for I suspect that the author of *GPet* and/or his audience might not distinguish between the wicked Herods of Christian memory. See Brown, "Gospel of Peter" 337.

- Women or disciples bend down to look in sepulcher/tomb
- Simon Peter and others at the sea (site of an appearance)

Several times above I gave the Johannine chapter and verse because the placing of the parallel item was so different; and indeed these are truly *items,* for there is no consecutive story shared by the two works (unless there will be one in the appearance to Simon Peter where *GPet* breaks off at the end[20]). The Pilate trial in John 18:28–19:16a, with its inside-outside the praetorium pattern, is a carefully constructed whole, and none of that appears in *GPet*'s account of the trial. Similarly there is a discernible chiastic arrangement of the episodes in John's crucifixion-burial account that is totally absent from *GPet.* If *GPet* shares with John such items as the title on the cross, the division of garments, and the vinegary wine, it contains nothing of the Johannine dramatization of those items into discrete episodes; and it offers no echo of the other episodes: the mother and the beloved disciple at the foot of the cross; the lance stabbing of Jesus' side from which came out blood and water; Nicodemus and the hundred pounds of myrrh and aloes. It is virtually inconceivable that the author of *GPet* had John before him and copied so little distinctively Johannine; and it is scarcely less conceivable that the author of John had *GPet* as his main source in constructing his PN.

(g) Items peculiar to *GPet,* not found in any canonical Gospel:

- Herod as the principal judge whom Pilate must ask for the body
- Specific Law passage cited about sun not setting on one put to death
- Jews, not Romans, carried out all the crucifixion acts from thorny crown and scourging to deposition from cross
- When crucified, the Lord was silent as having no pain
- The darkness at midday caused many to need lamps, thinking it was night, and to fall
- Peter and companions in hiding, sought as wrongdoers who would set fire to the Temple
- Petronius the centurion who safeguarded the sepulcher; seven wax seals
- The stone rolling by itself; the extravagant height of the heavenly men; depiction of the Lord's resurrection; his having preached to the fallen-asleep; the talking cross
- Admission of sin by Jewish authorities; their fear of being stoned by Jewish people
- Women who came to tomb feared lest the Jews should see them

---

[20]The opening of the broken-off story sounds promising, but note that the named other disciples in *GPet* 14:60 (Andrew, Levi of Alphaeus) are different from the others in John 21:2 (Thomas, Nathanael, the sons of Zebedee, two other disciples).

- On final day of the Unleavened Bread they returned to their homes
- Presence of Andrew and Levi of Alphaeus at the sea

Having presented this series of lists illustrating various ways to reflect upon the relationship of *GPet* to the canonical Gospels, I now turn to evaluating the evidence to see which proposal might do most justice to the evidence.

3. OVERALL PROPOSAL ABOUT COMPOSITION BASED ON SEQUENCE AND CONTENTS

In the more than a century since *GPet* has been available, scholars have been divided on whether the author drew on the canonical Gospels (any or all),[21] or composed on the basis of independent tradition.[22] Combinations of dependence and independence have also been proposed, and to them one must now add the thesis of Crossan that all four canonical evangelists drew on an early form of *GPet* (which he calls the "Cross Gospel"; see 10:42),[23] and that afterward additions were made to produce the present form of *GPet*—additions that increased conformity between *GPet* and the canonical Gospels (see n. 9 above). In "Gospel of Peter" I wrote a detailed refutation of Crossan's thesis,[24] and throughout the commentary on individual scenes I showed why I did not think *GPet* presents a more original form of the PN than do the canonical Gospels. Rather than repeat the detailed discussions here, let me mention three major objections. *First,* if all four canonical evangelists used the Cross Gospel as a major source, why is it that no one of them followed *GPet*'s vocabulary and word order for more than two or three

[21]This has been the majority view, e.g., Beyschlag, Burkitt, Dodd, Finegan, Harris, M. R. James, Lührmann, Mara, Maurer, Meier, Moffatt, J. Armitage Robinson, Swete, Turner, Vaganay, Wright, Zahn. Although a few (e.g., Mara) have thought that the author may have heard the canonical Gospels, most have assumed that he was working with written copies. If only some Gospels were specified as a source, most often they were Matt and Mark.

[22]Thus, to a greater or lesser degree (some allow knowledge of Mark), Cameron, Crossan, Denker, A. J. Dewey, Gardner-Smith, Harnack, Hilgenfeld, Koester, Moulton, Völter, von Soden, and Walter. Varying proposals have been made about the underlying independent tradition: e.g., separate stories shaped by OT reminiscences, or even a continuous preGospel PN on which the canonical evangelists also drew. Independence has been advocated with different suggestions about when *GPet* was composed, e.g., anterior to some or all the canonical Gospels, or about the same time.

[23]The Cross Gospel consisted of the three units in *GPet:* 1:1–2 + 2:5c–6:22; 7:25 + 8:28–9:34; 9:35–10:42 + 11:45–49 (Crossan, *Cross* 16). As for the dependence of canonical Gospels on it, he schematizes this theory (18): Mark's main source was the Cross Gospel; Matt used the Cross Gospel and Mark, and so did Luke; John used the Cross Gospel, Matt, Mark, and Luke. A. J. Dewey ("Time"), who rejects Crossan's theory, proposes three different stages of *GPet* composition, with the last completed after the fall of Jerusalem in 70, but does not spell out a relationship of the canonical Gospels to this early PN.

[24]See also the negative reactions of Neirynck ("Apocryphal"); Green ("Gospel"); and D. F. Wright ("Four"). The latter (p. 60) raises the interesting objection that the Cross Gospel and the insertions and redactions seem to share the same vocabulary and style.

words? (The glaring exception is a segment of seven words, "Lest having come, his/the disciples steal him," shared by *GPet* 8:30 and Matt 27:64.[25]) Matt and Luke, according to Crossan, worked with Mark as well—why then did they work so differently in preserving a much greater residue of Marcan vocabulary and word order? *Second,* if the canonical evangelists copied items from *GPet,* why did they leave out the items listed in (g) above that include some of the most eyecatching elements in *GPet,*[26] especially when those items were in lines contiguous to what the evangelists copied? If Mark copied the centurion (*kentyriōn*) from *GPet,* why did he not copy the centurion's name, Petronius? Why would Matt copy from *GPet* the fact that the sepulcher was sealed and omit that there were seven seals? *Third,* how is it that if Matt, Luke, and John all drew nonMarcan material from *GPet,* they never agree against Mark in what they added? Look at lists (d), (e), and (f) above for the diverse items in which each Gospel agrees with *GPet.*[27] When Matt and Luke drew nonMarcan material from Q, they produced an enormous amount of agreement—only rarely do we have to recognize Q material in one Gospel that is not in the other. How could they have dealt so differently with *GPet?* Are we to think that Luke and John read *GPet* 4:13–14, and that Luke excerpted and developed the element of one penitent wrongdoer while John excerpted and developed the element of no leg-breaking, without either giving the slightest indication of being aware of the other element in this two-verse passage?—a silence even more incomprehensible in Crossan's theory where John knew Luke as well as *GPet!*

Obviously in the instance of the second and third objections against Crossan's theory, it is much easier to theorize that the author of *GPet* knew the canonical Gospels, made the material he borrowed more vivid by imaginative additions, and picked up from each Gospel various items not found in the other. However, a literary dependence of *GPet* on all or three of the canonical Gospels really does not explain the first objection about vocabulary, nor the lack of agreement in sequence, nor lists (b) and (g). If he had the four Gospels before him, why would the author of *GPet* have omitted Barabbas, Simon of Cyrene, the women at the crucifixion and at the burial, and Jesus' appearances at the tomb or in Jerusalem, especially when several

[25]For the minor variant of Matt's "the" vs. *GPet*'s "his," see §48, n. 16.

[26]Less than one-third of them belong to material that Crossan excludes from the original form of *GPet,* and so two-thirds of them would have been known to the canonical evangelists when they used *GPet.*

[27]Crossan (*Cross* 19) thinks he has found one exception where two Gospels agree with *GPet* against Mark: Luke 24:4 and John 20:12 have two individuals at the empty tomb in agreement with *GPet* 9:36 vs. one in Mark 16:5. But since he posits that John knew Luke, how does he know that John did not copy this point from Luke rather than from *GPet?* (By p. 361 he seems to recognize this possibility.) Since the Lucan two males and the Johannine two angels are not in the same setting or position as the *GPet* two males, I regard this one exception as entirely dubious.

Gospels had such items? And where did he get so many items not found in any Gospel? And how can we explain the massive "switching" of details in *GPet* compared to similar details in the canonical Gospels? For example, John 19:38 describes Joseph from Arimathea as a disciple of Jesus, while in *GPet* 12:50 Mary Magdalene is the one who is a disciple of the Lord. Luke 23:6–12 has Pilate send Jesus to Herod so that Herod and Pilate became friends; in *GPet* 2:3–4 where Pilate sends to Herod, it is Joseph from Arimathea who is a friend of Pilate. While Matt 27:19 and John 19:13 have Pilate sitting on the *bēma* to judge Jesus, *GPet* 3:7 mockingly has Jesus seated on the *kathedra* invited to judge righteously. In John 19:33 we are told that the Romans did not break the bones of Jesus because he was already dead; *GPet* 4:14 has the Jews command that the bones of the crucified (Jesus) not be broken, presumably so that he will live and suffer longer. Other such "switchings" can be named (see Brown, "Gospel of Peter" 335). One might explain some as redactional preferences by the *GPet* author who was deliberately changing the written Gospels before him, but not such a multiplicity.

A final objection to the thesis that the *GPet* author composed by using the written canonical Gospels is that we have an example of a 2d-cent. scholar working on written copies of the four Gospels and combining them to make a consecutive PN, namely, Tatian's *Diatessaron*. The end product is clearly recognizable in vocabulary and sequence as a harmonization, and shows none of the aberrant variation visible in *GPet*.[28]

After working with the table and lists above (and the massive vocabulary difference), I am convinced that one explanation makes better sense of the relationship between *GPet* and the canonical Gospels than any other.[29] I doubt that the author of *GPet* had any written Gospel before him, although he was familiar with Matt because he had read it carefully in the past and/ or had heard it read several times in community worship on the Lord's Day,

[28]Already Swete (*Euaggelion* xxii–xxv), who placed *GPet* after the canonical Gospels, recognized the problem of difference from Tatian; and at least for him it meant that one could not explain *GPet* in terms of the author having used the *Diatessaron*. He raised the possibility of dependence on a preTatian harmony of the passion history of a looser type. Rather than positing such an intermediary whose existence we cannot prove, it seems more economical to argue that, unlike Tatian's literal harmonization of written Gospels, *GPet* is itself a free harmonization of canonical Gospel memories and traditions.

[29]I do not claim more than that. Personally I cannot reconstruct the exact history of the composition of a long commentary volume I myself wrote twenty-five years ago: What did I know before I began and where did I obtain it? As I wrote, how many new ideas did I get from reading other authors (as distinct from their confirming and sharpening views I already had)? How many times did I profit from papers I heard? I can recognize when I have quoted others directly, but I cannot trace their indirect influence on phrases that I used and the way I organized material. How can I possibly hope to detect the exact composition of a section of the *Gospel of Peter* copied some 600 years after the original was written, especially when that original, composed about 1,850 years ago, is now lost?

so that it gave the dominant shaping to his thought. Most likely he had heard people speak who were familiar with the Gospels of Luke and John—perhaps traveling preachers who rephrased salient stories—so that he knew some of their contents but had little idea of their structure. The spoken background of *GPet* is echoed in the fact that about one-third of its verses are in direct discourse. Under (c) I reported that I see no compelling reason to think that the author of *GPet* was directly influenced by Mark. (We must remember that before AD 150 very few churches would have had copies of several canonical Gospels to read in public, and a written copy of any Gospel would have been accessible to very few individuals. Indeed, the category of "better known" or "more famous" might be more appropriate than "canonical" at this period.) Intermingled in the *GPet* author's mind were also popular tales about incidents in the passion, the very type of popular material that Matt had tapped in composing his Gospel at an earlier period. All this went into his composition of *GPet,* a gospel that was not meant to be read in liturgy but to help people picture imaginatively the career of Jesus.[30] Tatian's *Diatessaron* shows that there was a tendency in the 2d cent. to create one consecutive story (albeit on a scholarly, literary level), and the *Protevangelium of James* gives an imaginative recasting of the infancy story from echoes of Matt and Luke combined with imaginative popular developments.[31] Therefore, the work I am proposing would not have been an oddity in the early days of Christianity.

Beyond the early days, however, I would argue that it is not an oddity at any time; and I would like to offer a contemporary comparison with the hope that it may make more intelligible to readers my theory of composition. (While I have tried to describe what follows in such a way that all can recognize its possibility, allow me to state my assurance that the people I am describing existed in large numbers in pre–Vatican-II Roman Catholicism.) Let me suppose that we selected in our own century some Christians who had read or studied Matt in Sunday school or church education classes years ago but in the interim had not been reading their NT. Yet they had heard the canonical passion narratives read in church liturgies. Also they had seen a passion play or dramatization in the cinema, on TV, or on the stage, or heard

---

[30]Below under C1 I shall narrate the story of Bishop Serapion and the trouble that was caused at Rhossus when some people began reading in public the *Gospel according to Peter.*

[31]In terms of literary classification I would regard the *Protevangelium* as a cousin of *GPet* in the same species of apocryphal gospels. The compositional instincts are much the same, but the author of *Prot. Jas.* had access to written copies of Luke and Matt. On the one hand, it is more elaborately expanded over the canonical Gospels than is *GPet;* on the other hand, when it cites them, it does so with greater preservation of exact vocabulary. Dramatically both works describe eschatological events that the canonical Gospels were content to leave wrapped in silence: the actual birth of Jesus in *Prot. Jas.* 19 and the actual resurrection in *GPet* 10:39–41. Theologically these vivid descriptions left both works open to heretical interpretations: encratism and docetism respectively.

one on the radio; and they had attended a church service where preachers were using imagination to fill in PN lacunae and were combining various Gospel passages, e.g., a Good Friday three-hours or Seven-Last-Words service. If we asked this select group of Christians to recount the passion, I am certain that they would have an idea of the general outline, but not necessarily be able to preserve the proper sequence of any particular Gospel. Certainly the complicated Johannine chiastic structures would not be retained by them. They would remember some catch phrases (e.g., pieces of silver, cockcrow, "He is risen") but otherwise largely rephrase the story in their own words, perhaps elevated above the level of ordinary conversation because of the solemnity of the occasion—words often of a faintly traditional biblical echo but not exactly the same as in the written Gospels. The more traditional among these selected narrators might never refer to the main character as "Jesus" but as "Christ" or "our Lord." They would remember one or two of his sayings ("words") on the cross, probably the ones they liked best, but surely not all of them. They would recall the more vivid Gospel episodes (Judas' hanging himself; Pilate washing his hands; the good thief [even if he is never called that by Luke]; John and Mary at the foot of the cross [even if the Gospel of John never mentions those names]) without much ability to report in which Gospel those episodes appeared. They would realize that the tomb had been opened by divine intervention but might dramatize the rolled-away stone in different manners. They might remember characters like Pilate, Herod, and the high priest but not really be precise about how they were intertwined in the trial and crucifixion or where they were at a given moment. There would be a tendency to portray more hostilely the enemies of Jesus (particularly the Jewish opponents, given the remarkable endurance of antisemitism) and attribute to them evil motives. And amid the remembrances of the passion from the Gospels there would be an admixture of details and episodes not in the Gospels, e.g., Judas' motives might be supplied; perhaps Peter's repentance; some of the background of the good thief and his name (Didymus); an elaboration of the centurion's role and perhaps the name Longinus. In other words, we would get from our test group of Christians modern parallels to *GPet,* which, as I have contended throughout the commentary, was not produced at a desk by someone with written sources propped up before him but by someone with a memory of what he had read and heard (canonical and noncanonical) to which he contributed imagination and a sense of drama.

Thus far, I have discussed the issue only from the viewpoint of sequence and content. Let me add some observations about the theological outlook of *GPet* before I discuss when and where such a gospel might have been composed.

C. *Aspects of the Theology of* GPet

We have in *GPet* only a section of the original *Gospel of Peter,* and so we must be very careful about judging the theology and outlook of the original author, especially when his silence about something would enter the judgment, e.g., his failure to mention Barabbas or Simon of Cyrene. The "author of *GPet*" really means the person responsible for the Akhmîm fragment. Origen (*In Matt.* 10.17 on 13:55; GCS 40.21) reported that according to the *Gospel of Peter* Joseph, husband of Mary, had children by an earlier marriage.[32] To know fully the thought of such an apocryphon that covered the whole career of Jesus, one would need more than what is preserved in the section of the passion-resurrection account we have in *GPet.*

1. THE ANCIENT DEBATE ABOUT THE DOCETISM OF *GPet*

We may begin with the only extended discussion of the work in antiquity. Eusebius (EH 6.12.2–6) tells us that Serapion, who was bishop of Antioch ca. 190,[33] wrote a book, *Concerning What Is Known as the Gospel according to Peter* (*Peri tou legomenou kata Petron euaggelion*), refuting the gospel's false statements that had led into heterodoxy certain members of the church at Rhossus (a Mediterranean coast town some 30 miles NW from Antioch across the mountains). After this brief analysis Eusebius cites a passage from Serapion's book.[34] In principle the bishop rejected books that falsely bore the name of an apostle; but he came to Rhossus assuming the orthodoxy of the congregation, and so without careful examination he gave permission for the continued reading of the gospel attributed to Peter even though there had been a dispute over the work (about Petrine authorship?). Subsequently Serapion was alerted to the danger of heresy in relation to the work, and so now he was warning the Rhossus community to expect him to return soon. (The heresy had something to do with an otherwise unknown Marcianos, presumably a local character, who was not consistent in his thought.) Serapion, having learned from docetist students of this gospel, had gone through it. He found that most of it was in accordance with the true teaching of the Savior, but some things (which he was going to list) were added.

---

[32]That outlook is clearly found in the *Protevangelium of James,* which Origen cited alongside *GPet* as a source. Evidently these 2d-cent. apocrypha shared material. Harnack (*Bruchstücke* 90) would attribute to *GPet* noncanonical stories and sayings of Jesus' ministry found in Christian writings that seem to have had a knowledge of the *GPet* PN (Justin, *Didascalia,* etc.; see D below). That is too uncertain a criterion.

[33]EH 5.22 dates him to the tenth year of the reign of Commodus (180–192).

[34]Some of Eusebius' own mind goes into the analysis; presumably the citation represents exactly Serapion's mind almost 150 years earlier.

An impression was gained that Serapion had classified the gospel attributed to Peter as docetic; and so when *GPet* was discovered, most interpreters were prone to read as docetic several ambiguous passages therein (so J. A. Robinson, Zahn, J. R. Harris, Turner, Moulton, Swete, etc.). The tide has now turned and most recent writers do not find docetism in *GPet* (so Schmidt, Mara, Denker, McCant, Crossan, Head).[35] We may point out that Serapion (although not overly clear) never said that the gospel he encountered was docetic; rather he said that docetists used it and pointed out passages in it that could be read docetically—with the benefit of their guidance Serapion could detect additions, but he still judged that most of the apocryphon was quite orthodox. The passages cited as docetic in *GPet* are capable of a nondocetic interpretation. To summarize what I wrote in the commentary, *GPet* 5:19, "My power, O power, you have forsaken me," is not plausibly an indication that the divinity left the body of Jesus before death[36] because the body of the dead Jesus still has miraculous power to cause an earthquake (6:21), and the one who comes forth from the tomb is supernatural and has preached to the fallen-asleep between his death and resurrection (10:40–42). *GPet*'s statement in 4:10 that the Lord on the cross "was silent as having no pain" need not be an affirmation of docetic impassibility, for a similar description of a Christian martyr implies bravery and divine assistance (*Martyrdom of Polycarp* 8:3).[37]

2. Discernible Theological Features in *GPet*

If one lays aside the ancient docetic issue, what are some of the noticeable theological features of *GPet?*

(a) It manifests a very high christology. The personal name Jesus is never used, nor even "Christ." "Lord" is the most consistent designation (14 times); also "Son of God" (4 times). Those who scourge Jesus refer to him as the Son of God (3:9); a co-crucified wrongdoer recognizes that he is the "Savior of men" (4:13); all the Jewish people recognize how just he was

---

[35]Although I side with these scholars, I cannot simply affirm that the 2d-cent. gospel read by Serapion was not docetic in its theology. I would need to see the whole work, of which *GPet* gives us only a section. If the gospel attributed to Peter had an infancy narrative, as Origen affirms, the outlook there would have been crucial in determining docetic tendencies. If the Petrine evangelist was not consistent, he may have exhibited docetism in that area even if not in the crucifixion account.

[36]Wright ("Apologetic" 405–6) agrees with this judgment but offers a complicated explanation of 5:19a: The saying that the power has left (not forsaken) the Lord should be understood as equivalent to 5:19b, "And having said this, he was taken up." If I have understood Wright, the divine power is the identifying factor of the Lord which is taken up to God. I do not think that does justice to "left *me*."

[37]Wright ("Apologetic" 402–3) contends that while the *GPet* expression does not imply docetic impassibility, it does imply divine impassibility, i.e., not that the Lord was not human but that the Lord was truly divine.

(8:28); Roman soldiers and Jewish elders who were trying to safeguard the tomb have to acknowledge that Jesus is the Son of God (10:38; 11:45), as does Pilate (11:46). The divine power is so inherent in Jesus that when his dead body touches the earth it quakes (6:21); and his raised body stretches from earth to above the heavens, outdistancing the angels (10:40).

(b) There is a strong antiJewish animus, especially against the religious authorities. Only John among the canonical PNs can match *GPet* in the frequency (six times) of its alienated use of "the Jews" as another, often hostile group. Although there are instances of Jewish repentance (7:25; 8:28), Herod and the Jews will not wash their hands (of the blood of Jesus: 1:1); they are the ones who condemn him, mock and spit at him, slapping his cheeks (2:5c–3:9). They complete their sins on their own head (5:17). Scribes, Pharisees, and elders watch his tomb even on the Sabbath in an attempt to prevent the resurrection (8:28,32–33; 10:38). Although they have seen the risen Jesus and know that he is the Son of God, they persuade Pilate to keep it quiet, acknowledging that what they are doing is "the greatest sin in the sight of God" (10:38–11:49).

(c) There is knowledge of the Scriptures, mostly implicit.[38] The one explicit biblical citation is in 2:5, echoed in 5:15: "In the Law it has been written, 'The sun is not to set on one put to death.'" Actually that passage is not found in the Pentateuch (or any biblical book), but is a paraphrase of Deut 21:22–23, combined with some of the phraseology of Deut 24:15 (LXX 24:17). *GPet* 5:16 ("Give him to drink gall with vinegary wine") echoes Ps 69:22 ("And they gave for my bread gall, and for my thirst they gave me to drink vinegary wine"). This time the citation is not explicit and again it is not exact. As I pointed out above (p. 944), the combination of the *cholē* and *oxos* is so established in Christian writing of the early 2d cent. that there is no way to be sure that *GPet* has used the LXX of this verse. The description of the darkness in *GPet* 5:15, different from that in the Synoptic Gospels, echoes in key phrases ("It was midday . . . lest the sun had set") the LXX of Amos 8:9. On the other hand, *GPet*'s words concerning the clothing of Jesus in 4:12 ("Having put his garments before him, they divided them up and threw as a gamble for them") is not close to the LXX wording of Ps

---

[38]Swete, *Euaggelion* xxvii, offers a list of OT passages used in *GPet* and other early Christian writings. The great interest in *GPet*'s use of the OT stems from Dibelius, "Alttestamentlichen," who, even though he judged *GPet* dependent on the Synoptics, found its use of Scripture more original than that of John and indeed illustrative of a process that gave rise to gospels. (See my hesitations about this on p. 944 above.) Following in the steps of Dibelius, Denker (*Theologiegeschichtliche* 77) points to a major use of Isaiah and the Psalms; but many of his judgments in this study are based on very debatable allusions. In part, the high evaluation of the allusive or implicit employment of Scripture stems from the thesis that this was earlier than the appeal to the fulfillment of named passages. Often, however, the preference for different styles of OT citation may have been a matter of ambiance rather than of antiquity: the popular ambiance vs. the scholarly and apologetic.

22:19 ("They divided up my clothes among themselves, and for my clothing they threw lots"), with only the verbs *diamerizein* and *ballein* the same. The Lord's scream in 5:19, "My power, O power, you have forsaken me," is even further from the LXX of Ps 22:2 than are Mark/Matt, and the author of *GPet* does not give us a Semitic transcription as do those Gospels. Is he making his own translation from Hebrew? Or is he echoing another Greek rendition that was in circulation at this time (p. 1054 above)? If I see no way to be certain that the author of *GPet* used the LXX Scriptures, as did the canonical evangelists, neither do I know that he read Hebrew, even though an occasional Hebrew play behind his Greek has been proposed.[39] Indeed, the author's use of Scripture does not tell us how much he *read* the OT, as distinct from having heard it talked about or references made to it in Greek as part of his religious background. Are we reading in his work the echo of certain OT texts or allusions already intimately associated with the passion events he was narrating rather than the fruits of his actually consulting a collection of biblical books?[40]

(d) There seems to be confusion about Jewish feasts. The author knows of "the first day of *their* feast of the Unleavened Bread" (2:5c), by which he means the feast of the (Jewish) people, a feast that as a Christian he would seemingly not consider his. This first day would logically be the oncoming Sabbath of 2:5, the day after Jesus' death. Yet when Jesus does die he reports (7:27) that the disciples of the Lord were fasting and sitting mourning and weeping "night and day until the Sabbath." Apparently he is not sensitive to Sabbath observance; for he reports that on Saturday morning a crowd (obviously of Jews) came from Jerusalem and environs to see the sealed tomb of Jesus, and that the whole night between Friday evening and Saturday dawn was spent by scribes, Pharisees, and elders in a tent safeguarding the tomb, staying there until the angels descended on the Lord's Day (see 8:33–10:38). The sequence from 12:50–13:57 to 14:58 would give readers the impression that the Lord's Day (Sunday) was the final day of the Unleavened Bread, even as Saturday had been the first day—thus apparently a two-day feast, not the seven-day feast known in the Bible (Lev 23:6, etc.). This could be just careless writing, but the more obvious impression is that the author knew little about Jewish practice.

---

[39]The *cholē* ("gall") of Ps 69:22 renders Hebrew *rō'š*, a word with several meanings, the most frequent of which is "head." Was *GPet* 5:16–17 playing on the two meanings of the underlying Hebrew: "'Give him to drink *gall*' . . . completed the(ir) sins on their own *head*"?

[40]Deut 21:22–23, employed as background by *GPet,* seems to have been used by Aristo(n) of Pella (ca. 140) in antiJewish apologetic in his "Dialogue between Jason and Papiscus," as cited by Book 2 of Jerome's *Commentary on Galatians* (on 3:14; PL 26.361–62). Cambe ("Récits") argues that *GPet* may be like many other works of the 2d cent. in using *Testimonia* or collections of passages detected as applicable to Jesus, in this case to his passion, death, and resurrection.

(e) There are hints of already established Christian cultic patterns. Sunday is known as "the Lord's Day" (9:35; 12:50). A fasting on the Sabbath, that in the story is related to the time between Jesus' death and his resurrection, may well reflect practice in the author's time.

D. *When and Where Was* GPet *Composed?*

The story of Bishop Serapion and the existence of the Oxyrhynchus fragments show that before 200 a form of *GPet* was known both in Syria and in Egypt. Indeed, Serapion indicates that the work had been in circulation for a while, for he sought guidance about the docetism of the work "from the successors of those who first used it." Parallels in *GPet* with traditions about the passion exhibited by the *Epistle to Barnabas*,[41] by Justin,[42] and by the *Ascension of Isaiah*[43] confirm that composition later than 150 is unlikely.

If we turn from that as one terminus (the date before which) to the other terminus (the date after which), a virtual certainty is that it could not have been composed in Palestine in the 1st cent. In a writing that involves a historical setting, whether that writing is 90 percent fact or 90 percent fiction, one expects at least minimum plausibility about circumstances with which everyone would be familiar. Those who today try to write more Sherlock Holmes stories are writing fiction, even as was A. Conan Doyle; but living much later and outside England, they might easily make errors about London of the late 1800s that he would never have made. Yet none of them would make the massive error of depicting the England of that period as a republic ruled by a president, for everyone likely to write or read such a story would know that England was a monarchy. It is scarcely conceivable that a Palestinian of the 1st cent. AD could have imagined that Herod was the supreme ruler in Jerusalem and that the Roman governor Pilate was subject to him. The Roman prefectures of AD 6–40, 45–66, and the Jewish Revolt would have made the matter of governance unforgettable at least before

---

[41]*GPet* 5:16: "Give him to drink gall with vinegary wine"; *Barn* 7:5: "to give me gall with vinegary wine."

[42]*GPet* 3:7 and *Apol.* 1.35 have Jesus seated on the judgment seat. *GPet* 4:12 and *Dial.* 97 use the awkward expression *lachmon ballein* ("throw a gamble") in reference to Jesus' garments. *GPet* 10:41 has proclamation made to the fallen-asleep between Jesus' death and resurrection; *Dial.* 72.4 has God remembering the fallen-asleep in the earth of the tomb: "He went down to them to evangelize them about their salvation." It is debated whether Justin drew on *GPet* and whether this was the "Memoirs [*Apomnēmoneumata*] of Peter" that he mentions (*Dial.* 106.3); recently Pilhofer, "Justin," has argued affirmatively for both.

[43]*The Martyrdom and Ascension of Isaiah* is a composite work. In 3:15–17 two angels open the grave of Jesus on the third day and bring him out on their shoulders, a scene comparable to *GPet* 10:39–40. This passage belongs to the "Testament of Hezekiah" section of the Isaian apocryphon, which is sometimes dated to ca. 100 or slightly afterward (see M. A. Knibb, OTP 2.149).

100. I suspect even Jews outside Palestine would have been aware of the governance of Judea in that century, so that if one wishes to posit that *GPet* was written in the 1st cent., odds would have to favor its having been written outside Palestine[44] by a nonJew with a good knowledge of the Jewish Scriptures and of Jesus.[45] There are solid reasons, however, for placing such an author in the 2d cent. rather than the 1st. The first of these would be the likelihood explained above that the author used echoes from the canonical Gospels of Matt, Luke, and John (all of which were composed by 100), a usage implying that *GPet* was probably composed after 100.[46]

Moreover, the span between 100 and 150 would fit the theological features we have just discerned. Admittedly, comparative development is always a very uncertain gauge for dating works since older and newer theologies are often contemporary in different corners of Christianity. Yet there are several works of the early 2d cent. that share theological views of *GPet* that go beyond anything found in most of the NT, which was written in the 1st cent. I pointed out that *GPet* shares with the *Protevangelium of James* (very widely dated to ca. 150) a tendency to dramatize visibly the divinity of Jesus (*Prot. Jas.* in describing the birth, *GPet* in describing the resurrection from the tomb), a dramatization absent from the canonical descriptions of those moments in Jesus' life. The preference for "the Lord" in place of "Jesus" as a way of referring to the Nazorean has a canonical Gospel adumbration in Luke but is thoroughgoing in *GPet;* it is visible also in *Didache* (8:2; 9:5; 11:2; 12:1; etc.). The designation of Sunday as "the Lord's Day" (*GPet* 9:35; 12:50), which appears in one of the latest NT books (Rev 1:10), was becoming widespread in the early 2d cent. (*Did.* 14:1; Ignatius, *Magn.* 9:1).[47] The period of fasting attached to the day of Jesus' death (*GPet* 7.27) has a paral-

---

[44]Mara (*Évangile* 31) is quite correct when she writes, "L'auteur est complètement dépaysé." Readers are told that this takes place in Judea (5:15), but *GPet* has none of the local place names that appear in the canonical PNs. The one local reference that he has (5:20), one not found in the Synoptic Gospels, "the veil of the *Jerusalem* sanctuary," is information for readers who otherwise might not know which sanctuary was involved. *GPet* is silent about the going of the twelve disciples *to Galilee* after the resurrection: They go home, and Simon Peter and Andrew are suddenly at the sea. Has the author any precise idea of where Galilee and the sea are or of distances from Jerusalem?

[45]To my mind this shows the utter implausibility of Crossan's thesis that *GPet* embodies the oldest Christian PN, for then later canonical evangelists who had a much better knowledge of Palestinian milieu and history than that exhibited in *GPet* would still have respected *GPet* enough to make it their main source! Of course, if one accepts the view Crossan offers in *Cross* 405, "It seems to me most likely that those closest to Jesus knew almost nothing whatsoever about the details of that event [the passion]," one has removed most external controls for judging dating.

[46]The Greek of *GPet* marked by occasional classical features (atticisms, optative) has at times been used to date it. F. Weissengruber (in Fuchs, *Petrusevangelium* 117–20) claims that this combination of narrative style and revived classicism is particularly at home in the first half of the 2d cent.; but many would doubt that such precision over against 1st-cent. Greek is possible.

[47]There is some dispute as to whether these passages refer only to Easter Sunday or to Sunday in general (W. Stott, NTS 12 [1965–66], 70–75).

lel in the mindset of *Did.* 8:1, which inculcates fasting on Wednesday and Friday.[48] The *Epistle of Barnabas* and Melito of Sardis manifest an antiJudaism comparable to the animus in the pages of *GPet*. (Perler, "Évangile," asserts strongly the literary dependence of Melito on *GPet*.) Beyschlag, then, is justified in detecting in *GPet* the atmosphere of the first half of the 2d cent.[49]

As for the place of composition, although Mara (*Évangile* 217–18) has suggested Asia Minor, and the Oxyrhynchus fragments raise the possibility of Egypt (pointed to earlier by D. Völter), Syria is most often proposed. A.F.J. Klijn[50] states that before 150 there was in Syria a text of the Gospels and Acts that showed agreement with the *Diatessaron, Epistula Apostolorum,* and *GPet*. The Serapion story shows that *GPet* was known at Rhossus and Antioch, and at least in certain circles had been known for a long time. Origen mentions *GPet* after he visited Antioch. *Didascalia Apostolorum* was written by a bishop in Syria ca. 200–225; the Syriac form (especially chap. 21 = Latin 5) shows a knowledge of *GPet* (directly or through a florilegium of gospel passages?). Parallels with the *Didache* (most likely composed in Syria) and the high christology of Ignatius of Antioch may also be cited. Parallels in style and content between *GPet* and the *Protevangelium of James* have been mentioned; and H. R. Smid thinks the latter "was possibly written in Syria."[51] The *GPet* author was influenced strongly by Matt, a Gospel most likely composed in the environs of Antioch.[52] A knowledge of Lucan and Johannine PN elements would also be consonant with this area.[53] Whether or not the author of Luke was a native of Antioch (so Fitzmyer, *Luke* 1.47), Acts certainly shows knowledge of the Christian community at Antioch. I favor the ancient tradition that associates the final composition of John with Ephesus rather than the opinion of some modern scholars (based almost entirely on parallels of ideas) that fastens on Antioch. Nevertheless, theological vocabulary attested only in John among the Gospels appears in the writings

[48]Seemingly by the 120s at Rome under Sixtus (I) and/or Telesphorus fasting on the days before Easter had begun to be introduced. See *Decretales Pseudo-Isidorianae,* ed. P. Hinschius (1883; reprinted Aalen: Scientia, 1963), 109–10.

[49]*Verborgene* 46; this has been the most common dating by past investigators, and is continued by Denker (between the two Jewish wars), Johnson, and Mara. See also Head, "Christology."

[50]*A Survey of the Researches into the Western Text of the Gospels and Acts: Part II, 1949–69* (NovTSup 21; Leiden: Brill, 1969), 25.

[51]*Protevangelium Jacobi* (Assen: Van Gorcum, 1965), 22.

[52]J. P. Meier, in the work he did with R. E. Brown (*Antioch and Rome* [New York: Paulist, 1983], 45–84), thinks of Matt as a representative of the outlook of the Antiochene church of 70–100, and Ignatius and *Didache* as representative of the church there after 100.

[53]I prefer this cautious phrasing. Our limited knowledge forces us to look for an *area* where these Gospels could have been known; however, we should allow for the contrary possibility that composition took place in a "backwater" area by an author whose travels had brought him into contact with diverse Christian presentations of Jesus.

of Ignatius, so that most likely someone in the Antioch area in the early 2d cent. could have known some of the peculiar features of the Johannine PN. Finally, the attribution of this gospel to Peter may be indicative. It is very clear that Peter functioned prominently in the church of Antioch, for there in the 40s occurred the clash between Peter and Paul described in Gal 2:11–14. As Meier points out (*Antioch* 24), despite Paul's rhetoric, it was he who left Antioch, rarely ever returning; Barnabas went over to Peter; and the Gospel of the Antioch area, Matt (16:18), points to Peter as the foundation rock of Christ's church. Thus a writer in that area, dramatizing the passion of Jesus, might very well have fastened on Peter as spokesman.[54]

Beyond the general locale, what type of Christian background does *GPet* reflect? Theoretically it is possible that the author came from one background, e.g., Jewish Christian, and directed his words to another, Gentile Christian; but with so little available evidence we must lay aside such a complication and look at *GPet* as if the author and his addressees were of the same ambiance. Because of the influence of Scripture on *GPet,* some (e.g., Denker, *Theologiegeschichtliche* 78) have proposed a Jewish-Christian setting. Yet from the earliest days works employing Scripture were addressed to Gentile audiences (Galatians), and by the 2d cent. the use of the Scriptures was a lingua franca among Christians. *Barnabas* is filled with scriptural citations and allusions; yet the author of a major commentary on it suggests that it was written for Gentile Christians in the Syro-Palestine area probably by a Gentile.[55] As I pointed out under C above, the author of *GPet* seems confused about Jewish customs and clearly regards the Unleavened Bread as a feast of the Jews, an alienated group of which he does not seem to be a member.[56] If the Sabbath is mentioned in relation to the Jews (but without much knowledge of what they could not do on that day), Sunday has become the Lord's Day. It is almost as if the author and his audience are spiritually

[54]The pseudonymous character of *GPet* was often misunderstood or misrepresented in earlier scholarship. In their desire to defend the worth of the canonical Gospels against this new discovery, some looked down on the author as a forger, e.g., Vaganay's objectionable custom of referring to the author as "le faussaire," in a commentary that otherwise made an important contribution. In the 2d cent. there was a growth of traditions identifying the apostles Matthew and John as authors of Gospels that almost certainly they did not write; those attributions were eventually prefixed to the respective Gospels. The author of *GPet* has gone further in incorporating his attribution within the text of the gospel he was writing, even as did the author of the *Protevangelium of James* (25:1). The desire for apostolic patronage and dramatic plausibility are likely motives we may attribute to the *GPet* author; there is absolutely nothing to show that he wanted to deceive. It is worth adding that contemptuous attitudes toward the *GPet* author have not been confined to scholars who thought him a secondary user of the canonical Gospels; Gardner-Smith ("Date" 407) considered him "credulous, muddle-headed, incompetent."

[55]P. Prigent, *Épître de Barnabé* (SC 172), 22–24, 28–29.

[56]Again caution is necessary, however; I think that the fourth evangelist was born a Jew, but would not consider himself a Jew because synagogues of his acquaintance had expelled believers in Jesus, and thus had virtually or actually said to them that they were no longer Jews (John 9:28,34).

related to those described by Ignatius of Antioch (*Magn.* 9:1) as "no longer observing the Sabbath but living according to the Lord's Day." Perhaps we are at that moment in Christian development when it no longer mattered much whether one's ancestry was Jewish or Gentile; believers in Jesus of both backgrounds considered themselves Christians, while "Jews" were a particular group of nonChristians. Was there ongoing conflict with those Jews? The presence of polemics against Jews in *GPet* and of implicit apologetics does not necessarily prove that. An inherited hatred for another religious group can be passed on for generations even when there is no longer contact with that group. Yet we must admit that some references to the Jews in *GPet* may have a note of self-protection as if they were an ongoing enemy: Peter and his companions hid after Jesus' death, for they were being hunted as wrongdoers who would set fire to the (Temple) sanctuary (7:26); Mary Magdalene was not able to do anything for Jesus' body on the day of burial because the Jews were inflamed with anger (12:50). The issue is complicated by other passages that show Jews acting as penitents (7:25; 8:28). Consequently judgments about the relationship to the Jews in the ambiance of *GPet* remain highly speculative.

Moving to a different aspect, I would see the ethos of *GPet* as later but not far removed from the ethos that Matt had tapped in the 80s–90s for what I have called the popular material (§48, n. 41) that he used to supplement Mark's PN: the stories of Judas' suicide and the silver pieces contaminated by innocent blood, of the dream of Pilate's wife, of Pilate's washing his hands of the blood of this man while all the people took responsibility, of the phenomena that accompanied Jesus' death (shaking of the earth, opening of tombs, emergence of the fallen-asleep holy ones), and of the guard at the sepulcher frightened by a descending angel and earthshaking—as well as the infancy story of the magi and the star and the wicked Herod slaughtering the Bethlehem male children. In the commentary above, as I dealt with the episodes peculiar to Matt's PN, I pointed out *GPet*'s parallels to many of them; and in particular I argued that the author of *GPet* had not only heard the heavily edited Matthean form of the guard-at-the-sepulcher story but also had access to a later, more developed form of the story which still preserved the continuity of the original. I would argue, then, that *GPet* is a gospel reflecting popular Christianity, i.e., the Christianity of the ordinary people not in the major center of Antioch, where public reading and preaching would have exercised greater control, but in the smaller towns of Syria, not unlike Rhossos where Serapion became acquainted with it.[57] *GPet* was

---

[57]Harnack (*Bruchstücke* 37) imagined *GPet* to belong to a party outside the church in the sense that it did not feel itself bound by the traditions and ordinance of the larger church. That is not what I mean: Christians of all periods who have thought themselves loyal to the large church have had

not heterodox, but it incorporated many imaginative elements that went beyond the canonical Gospels and the writings of bishops like Ignatius. Through most centuries, including our own, the ordinary Christian view of Jesus has differed considerably from what was proclaimed from pulpits as based on Scripture. Elements of popular piety and imagination have tended to fill the portrait with a coloring that one could not justify intellectually from the written Gospels, but which in its own way was an extraordinary enrichment.[58] Even today the image of the birth of Jesus held by most Christians is far closer to what is portrayed by innumerable Christmas cribs or crèches that ultimately owe their inspiration to Francis of Assisi, than to what is portrayed in either Matt or Luke. So also the image of the passion and death of Jesus held by most Christians from the first century on would go beyond what is found in any canonical Gospel or in all of them put together.

A fundamental objection to *GPet* since its discovery over a century ago has been that it is not historical, an objection often made by those who assume wrongly that everything pertaining to the passion in the canonical Gospels is historical. The canonical PNs are the product of a development that has involved considerable dramatization, so that exact history is not a category applicable to them.[59] Nevertheless, I have no doubt that Mark's PN has a greater historical component than has *GPet's* PN,[60] in part because it represented something like a common preaching that was associated with apostolic tradition—a line of descent that exercised a control over basic facts, despite rearrangements and simplification. That is why it received official church recognition (canonical status) and was seen to be part of God's provision for the Christian people (recognized as inspired). Gospel stories such as those of *GPet*,[61] composed in more popular circles, were not under

---

theological views that were not the same as those of the official teachers (even though they were not always aware that this was the case), not because they were disobedient but because of folk piety and imagination. Those at Rhossos who were beginning to read from *GPet* publicly were still within the large church, or the bishop of Antioch would not have been asked for his view of the matter.

[58]The popular played a special role not only because *GPet* stood outside the canon-forming preaching process but also because of its apocalyptic coloring. See J. H. Charlesworth, "Folk Traditions in Jewish Apocalyptic Literature," in *Mysteries and Revelations,* eds. J. J. Collins and J. H. Charlesworth (*Journal for the Study of Pseudepigrapha,* Supp. 9; Sheffield: Academic, 1991), 91–113.

[59]May I point out that this is not necessarily a liberal view, e.g., it was espoused in reference to the Gospel accounts of Jesus' whole ministry both by the Roman Pontifical Biblical Commission and by the Second Vatican Council (NJBC 72:35,15).

[60]Mara (*Évangile* 30) says that the author of *GPet* does not appear to have been restrained by the truth of the facts he recounts, but he was held by the truth of their interpretation. However, that might imply that the *GPet* author could distinguish whether what he recounted was historically true.

[61]In my remarks I have in mind narrative apocryphal gospels such as *GPet, Protevangelium,* and *Infancy Gospel of Thomas.* One might envision differently noncanonical collections of sayings attributed to Jesus that often had a much more cerebrally planned focus. Although popularly there

the same controlling influences, and imagination was allowed freer rein. Nevertheless, at times they could function quite happily in enabling ordinary Christians to imagine the passion. Two major difficulties might cause malfunction. If flights of imagination went to the point of becoming heterodox (and the 2d cent. was precisely a time when the lines between heterodoxy and orthodoxy were being sharply drawn), church authorities would tend to ban the stories that lent support to such aberrant ideas. In Serapion's time some were using *GPet* for docetist propaganda, perhaps along the lines that a dying Jesus who, as it were, felt no pain, was not really human or did not really die.[62] But it was a second difficulty that initially brought *GPet* into dispute. If I am right in contending that *GPet* came into existence as a popular production, not conceived in the womb of church preaching, it was never designed to become official proclamation, any more than is a passion play. But now Christians at Rhossus were beginning to read *GPet* publicly and thus to give it a status alongside the canonical Gospels, something that Serapion had never encountered in the major center of Antioch. (Even though some there knew of *GPet,* he the bishop did not.) The very nature of the canon—the collection of books that the church has committed itself to live by as a norm—will always call such innovation into question.

What is a balanced reaction to *GPet* today? I have criticized a condemnatory attitude prevalent among some earlier commentators on *GPet* who considered the author a heretic, or someone hostile to the larger church with its developing canon of only four Gospels, or a forger attempting to gain credence for an unhistorical approach to Jesus. On the other hand, I have explained that I see no solid reason to hail it as the oldest PN, nor am I sympathetic to a simplistic tendency to regard extracanonical works as the key to true Christianity as contrasted with a narrow-minded censorship represented by the canonical NT. Nevertheless, while appreciating Serapion's dilemma and the sense of pastoral responsibility that led him ultimately to react against *GPet* and thus for all practical purposes to end its career, I think we may at the same time be grateful to the mourner who buried with a monk of the late patristic period a strange little book of spiritual readings dealing

---

is a tendency to speak of the tractates found in the Nag Hammadi collection as gnostic "gospels," very few of them claim to be gospels or are at all similar to the canonical Gospels.

[62]I would hope that today Christians would recognize another heterodox tendency in *GPet:* its intensified antiJewish depictions. There is antiJudaism in the NT as a result of polemics between Jews who believed in Jesus and those who did not, but it is more restrained than that of *GPet* and *Barnabas.* This is an instance of what I think of as a larger truth: Frequently among ordinary Christians there was (and is) more hostility toward Jews than detectable among official spokesmen—a situation that may have been true, vice versa, in Judaism as well, if we may judge from comparing the more official Mishna and Talmuds with the popular *Toledoth Yeshu.* Several times I have cited passion plays as examples of the tendency to enrich the story of Jesus' death with *popular* imagination, and often a strong antiJudaism appears in those plays.

with the afterlife and thus belatedly supplied us with a fascinating insight into how dramatically some ordinary Christians of the early 2d cent. were portraying the death of the Messiah. Beneath the drama, in its own way *GPet* proclaimed that Jesus was the divine Lord, victor over all that his enemies could do to him by crucifixion.

Bibliography for Appendix I:
The Gospel of Peter

This is only a working bibliography; fuller bibliographies composed in different years may be found in Vaganay, Mara, Fuchs, and Crossan (*Cross*); Greek vocabulary concordances may be found in Fuchs and Vaganay.

Beyschlag, K., *Die verborgene Überlieferung von Christus* (Siebenstern Taschenbuch 136; Munich, 1969), 27–64.

Brown, R. E., "The *Gospel of Peter* and Canonical Gospel Priority," NTS 33 (1987), 321–43.

Cambe, M., "Les récits de la Passion en relation avec différents textes du IIe siècle," FV 81 (4; 1982), 12–24.

Coles, R. A., "[Papyrus] 2949. Fragments of an Apocryphal Gospel (?)," in *The Oxyrhynchus Papyri Vol. 41,* eds. G. M. Browne et al. (London: British Academy, 1972), 15–16.

Crossan, J. D., *Four Other Gospels* (Minneapolis: Winston, 1985), esp. 124–81 on *GPet.*

————, *The Cross That Spoke. The Origins of the Passion Narrative* (San Francisco: Harper & Row, 1988).

————, "Thoughts on Two Extracanonical Gospels," *Semeia* 49 (1990), 155–68. On *GPet* and *Secret Mark.*

Denker, J., *Die theologiegeschichtliche Stellung des Petrusevangeliums* (Europäische Hochschulschriften, Series 23, 36; Bern/Frankfurt: Lang, 1975).

Dewey, A. J., "'Time to Murder and Create': Visions and Revisions in the *Gospel of Peter,*" *Semeia* 49 (1990), 101–27.

Dibelius, M.,"Die alttestamentlichen Motiven in der Leidensgeschichte des Petrus- und Johannesevangeliums," Beihefte zur ZAW 33 (1918), 125–50. Also in DBG 1.221–47.

Fuchs, A., *Das Petrusevangelium* (Studien zum Neuen Testament und seiner Umwelt B.2; Linz, 1978). Contains a concordance.

Gardner-Smith, P., "The Date of The Gospel of Peter," JTS 27 (1926), 401–7.

————,"The Gospel of Peter," JTS 27 (1926), 255–71.

Green, J. B., "The Gospel of Peter: Source for a Pre-Canonical Passion Narrative?" ZNW 78 (1987), 293–301.

Harnack, A. (von), *Bruchstücke des Evangeliums und der Apokalypse des Petrus* (2d ed.; Leipzig: Hinrichs, 1893).

Head, P. M., "On the Christology of the Gospel of Peter," VC 46 (1992), 209–24.

Johnson, B. A., "Empty Tomb Tradition and the Gospel of Peter" (Th.D. Dissertation; Harvard Divinity School, 1966).

———,"The Gospel of Peter: Between Apocalypse and Romance," in *Studia Patristica* 16.2 (7th Oxford Congress, 1975; TU 129; Berlin: Akademie, 1985), 170–74.

Koester, H., "Apocryphal and Canonical Gospels," HTR 73 (1980), 105–30, esp. 126–30 on *GPet.*

Lambiasi, F., "I criteri d'autenticità storica dei vangeli applicati ad un apocrifo: il Vangelo di Pietro," BeO 18 (1976), 151–60.

Lührmann, D., "POx 2949: EvPt 3–5 in einer Handschritt des 2./3. Jahrhunderts," ZNW 72 (1981), 216–26.

McCant, J. W., "The Gospel of Peter: Docetism Reconsidered," NTS 30 (1984), 258–73.

Mara, M. G., *Évangile de Pierre* (SC 201; Paris: Cerf, 1973).

Neirynck, F., "The Apocryphal Gospels and the Gospel of Mark," in *The New Testament in Early Christianity,* ed. J.-M. Sevrin (BETL 86; Leuven Univ., 1989), 123–75, esp. 140–57, 171–75 on *GPet.* Reprinted in NEv 2.715–72.

Perler, O., "L'Évangile de Pierre et Méliton de Sardes," RB 71 (1964), 584–90.

Pilhofer, P., "Justin und das Petrusevangelium," ZNW 81 (1990), 60–78.

Rodríguez Ruiz, M., "El evangelio de Pedro. Un desafío a los evangelios canónicos?" EstBib 46 (1988), 497–525.

Schaeffer, S. E., *The "Gospel of Peter," the Canonical Gospels, and Oral Tradition* (Union Theological Seminary [NYC] Ph.D. Dissertation, 1990; UMI Dissertation Service, 1991).

Schmidt, K. L., *Kanonische und Apokryphe Evangelien und Apostelgeschichten* (Basel: Majer, 1944), esp. 37–78 on *GPet.*

Stanton, V. H., "The 'Gospel of Peter' and the Recognition in the Church of the Canonical Gospels," JTS 2 (1901), 1–25.

Swete, H. B., *Euaggelion kata Petron: The Akhmîm Fragment of the Apocryphal Gospel of St Peter* (London: Macmillan, 1893).

Turner, C. H., "The Gospel of Peter," JTS 14 (1913), 161–95.

Vaganay, L., *L'Évangile de Pierre* (EBib; 2d ed.; Paris: Gabalda, 1930).

von Soden, H., "Das Petrusevangelium und die kanonischen Evangelien," ZTK 3 (1893), 52–92.

Wright, D. F., "Apologetic and Apocalyptic: the Miraculous in the *Gospel of Peter,*" in *The Miracles of Jesus,* eds. D. Wenham and C. Blomberg (Gospel Perspectives 6; Sheffield: JSOT, 1986), 401–18.

———,"*Four Other Gospels* [by J. D. Crossan]: Review Article," *Themelios* 12 (2, Jan. 1987), 56–60, esp. 58–60.

Zahn, T., "Das Evangelium des Petrus," NKZ 4 (1893), 143–218. Reprinted as a book.

APPENDIX II: DATING THE CRUCIFIXION (DAY, MONTHLY DATE, YEAR)

Discussion of this issue makes sense only if we assume that the evangelists are reliable for the minimal chronological references that they all (plus *GPet*) supply, namely, that Jesus died in Jerusalem on a day before the Sabbath at Passover time during the prefecture of Pontius Pilate. We shall use those temporal indications individually as the keys to determining the following information about the crucifixion:

A. The Day of the Week
B. The Date in the Month
    1. Clarification of Five Preliminary Issues
    2. Gospel Evidence for Dating the Crucifixion in Relation to Passover
    3. Attempts to Deal with the Discrepancies
    4. A Brief Survey of the Opinion Adopted in This Commentary
C. The Year
Bibliography

Although by its very nature, discussion of chronology is technical, it often gives insight into how scholars think the evangelists worked.

A. *The Day of the Week*

Mark 15:42 identifies the day on which Jesus dies as "the day before Sabbath" (*prosabbaton*). Matt, while not mentioning the Sabbath in relation to the crucifixion, clearly indicates that the day after Jesus' death (27:62) is the Sabbath; for as it comes to an end, the first day of the week begins (28:1). Just after Jesus is buried, Luke 23:54 states that Sabbath is about to dawn. John 19:31 records precautions being taken lest the bodies remain on the cross for the oncoming Sabbath. *GPet* 2:5 indicates that Jesus would die and be buried before Sabbath dawned. It is not surprising, then, that the vast majority of scholars have accepted that the crucified Jesus died on Friday, and indeed sometime in the afternoon.[1]

---

[1]Pertinent specific hour indications include these: The Synoptics have Jesus on the verge of dying by the ninth hour (3 P.M.: Mark 15:34; Matt 27:46; Luke 23:44); *GPet* 5:15–20 places Jesus' death in the context of midday; John 19:14 has Jesus before Pilate's praetorium at the sixth hour (noon).

A few dissenters have opted for Thursday or even Wednesday,[2] chiefly on the basis of Matt 12:40: "The Son of Man will be in the heart of the earth three days and three nights" (echoed in 27:63). A backward calculation from Saturday night through Friday night could lead to the conclusion that Jesus had to be in the tomb Thursday night to fulfill the prophecy (or even Wednesday night in the light of Matt 28:1, which has the women coming to the tomb just after Sabbath is over and Sunday is beginning, and thus before Saturday nighttime). But that prophetic word is based explicitly on Jonah having been in the belly of the fish three days and three nights (Jonah 2:1) and is secondary to prophecies of the Son of Man being raised on the third day (Mark 9:31; 10:34; etc.) which make resurrection by Sunday reconcilable with death and burial on Friday. All the discussion that follows, therefore, is based on the daytime of Friday as the time of the crucifixion.

B. *The Date in the Month*

No monthly date is specified by the Gospels. Yet in the context of the final few days of Jesus' life all make a reference to Passover, and the Synoptics refer to the feast of the Unleavened Bread. It might be well, then, at the outset to recall the history of these two feasts.

In the ancient biblical texts describing Passover (Exod 12:1–20; Lev 23:5–8; Num 28:16–25), its date depended on the sighting of the new moon that began Nisan,[3] for the celebration of the feast came at the full moon of that month. At the twilight that ended the 14th of Nisan and began the 15th, the lamb (or goat) was slaughtered and its blood sprinkled on the doorposts of the house. During that nighttime belonging to the 15th (the night of the full moon), the lamb was roasted and eaten with unleavened bread and bitter herbs. This 15th of Nisan also began the week-long feast of the Unleavened Bread. Already six hundred years before Jesus these feasts had been joined

---

[2]Hoehner ("Day" 241–49) lists B. F. Westcott, J. K. Aldrich, R. Rush for Thursday, and W. G. Scroggie for Wednesday. Davison ("Crucifixion") argues for Wednesday on the grounds that the Sabbath mentioned by all the Gospels as following the daytime of the crucifixion was an "annual Sabbath" rather than a weekly Sabbath. "Annual Sabbath" is used by him to designate those days within festal periods on which there was rest from work and a sacred assembly. He finds "two annual Sabbaths" connected with Passover or Unleavened Bread, namely, the first day and the last of the seven-day period (Lev 23:7–8). The first Passover "annual Sabbath" in the year in which Jesus died was Wednesday night/Thursday, and it was in the Wednesday daytime immediately preceding that "Sabbath" that Jesus was tried and was crucified—a Wednesday daytime that was the 14th of Nisan. Unfortunately he offers little proof for this.

[3]Also called Abib (Exod 13:4), Nisan was the first month of the year, although in another calendrical reckoning the New Year came in the seventh month (Tishri).

as a combined festal period that brought people to the Temple in Jerusalem;[4] and eventually the slaughtering of the lambs was considered a task of the priests, thus taking on the characteristics of a sacrifice.

The chronological relationship between the death of Jesus and the date of those two feasts is complicated by the fact that at face value there is a contradiction between the Synoptics and John. The meal that Jesus ate on Thursday evening before he was arrested, according to the Synoptics, was the paschal (Passover) meal, whereas in John 18:28, on Friday morning when Jesus was being tried before Pilate, the Jewish authorities and people refused to "enter into the praetorium lest they be defiled and in order that they might eat the Passover (meal)"—a feast that according to John 19:14 was to begin the next day (i.e., Friday evening). Thus, the paschal meal for the Synoptics was on Thursday evening and Jesus died in the daytime after it; for John it was on Friday evening and Jesus died in the daytime before it. Before entering in detail into the complexities of this seeming contradiction, let us review preliminary issues on which we need to be clear.

1. CLARIFICATION OF FIVE PRELIMINARY ISSUES

(a) There is a dispute about how hours were counted in the PN, namely, the third, sixth, and ninth hours in relation to the sentencing and crucifixion. Were the evangelists who mention one or all of those counting from 6 A.M. (thus 9 A.M., noon, 3 P.M.), or were they counting from midnight (thus 3, 6, and 9 A.M.)? Most scholars accept the 6 A.M. starting point. However, in order to harmonize contrary Gospel data, a few (like Walker, "Dating" 294) appeal to two systems, e.g., John 19:14 is thought to count from midnight in having Jesus before Pilate at the sixth hour (= 6 A.M.); and Mark 15:25, to count from dawn in having Jesus crucified at the third hour (= 9 A.M.). In the commentary we have seen that such harmonizations are implausible and unnecessary, so that calculation from 6 A.M. should be accepted throughout, even if that leaves the accounts in conflict. It is not demonstrable that any

---

[4]Passover was the more ancient of the two, originating in the pastoral culture when Israel was seminomadic, moving about with its flocks to find grazing. Unleavened Bread, marking the beginning of the barley harvest, was adopted later during the agricultural phase after the entrance into Canaan. Originally Passover was not a feast (in the OT only Exod 34:25 calls it one) when people had to go as pilgrims to the central shrine, for the lamb was killed and eaten at home; only when joined to Unleavened Bread did it become one of the three pilgrimage feasts. For the joining of the themes of the two, see Deut 16:2–3 which, after speaking of the animal chosen for Passover sacrifice, says, "For seven days you shall eat with it unleavened bread." By the 1st cent. AD, as we shall see, the names were becoming interchangeable. By the next century "Passover" had become the name for the whole feast, so that "the feast of the Unleavened Bread" never appears in Tannaitic literature (Zeitlin, "Time" 46), e.g., Midrash *Mekilta* (Pisḥa 7) on Exod 12:14 speaks of "The seven days of the Passover feast"; and Mishna *Pesaḥim* 9:5 says that after Egypt, "The Passover of all subsequent generations had to be observed throughout seven days."

evangelist had a personal, chronologically accurate knowledge of what happened. Most likely they found a time indication like "the sixth hour" (mentioned by all) in the tradition and attached it to different moments in the passion according to their respective dramatic and theological interests. Fortunately this issue of counting hours is not of great import for our present discussion.

(b) There is also a dispute concerning the beginning of the day: When an evangelist spoke of the day before the Sabbath, was he thinking of a day that began at sunset Thursday (and so included Thursday evening/Friday daytime), or at midnight (which in our modern calculation ends Thursday and begins Friday), or even at sunrise on Friday?[5] Once more in attempts to harmonize, some would argue for different systems (a Jewish one, a Roman one, or a local Greek one) employed by different evangelists. In the commentary I have rejected this harmonizing route for escaping difficulties. The issue before us involves a Jewish feast, and there can be little doubt that in the liturgical calendar the day began in the evening. Moreover, the account of the burial of Jesus on Friday afternoon with its tone of haste makes little sense unless all the evangelists were calculating that a day was about to begin soon. When it is important, to help readers of the following discussion to keep in mind the difficult concept of a day that began in the evening, instead of writing of Wednesday, Thursday, and Friday in reference to the pertinent crucifixion actions, I shall write of "Wednesday nighttime/Thursday daytime" to cover a day that ran from approximately 6 P.M. Wednesday to 6 P.M. Thursday; similarly of "Thursday nighttime/Friday daytime," and of "Friday nighttime/Saturday daytime"—using for these the abbreviations Wn/Thd, Thn/Fd, Fn/Sd.

(c) Frequently one finds the statement that although John has Jesus die on the day before Passover, the Synoptics have Jesus die on Passover itself. The last part of that statement is not precise: No Synoptic Gospel ever mentions Passover or Unleavened Bread in its account of the hours of the arrest, trials, crucifixion, death, and burial of Jesus. In describing the time period in which Jesus dies, the Synoptic Passover references are to the preparations for the Last Supper or to eating the Supper.[6] The last Gospel references among the

---

[5]For information see Zeitlin, "Beginning," with the caution that his use of the Mishna to determine the pre-70 (AD) period may need qualification. Parenthetically let me note that even though the Jewish calendric day began in the evening, popular parlance could be affected by a way of thinking in which a day is seen to start with sunrise—something that is still true today when the calendric day begins at midnight. This has left its mark in the use of "dawning" for the evening-beginning of a Sunday in Matt 28:1 and *GPet* 9:35: Neither writer is thinking of Sunday around 5 A.M.; both are thinking of Saturday just after sunset. Notice that Matt has omitted Mark's (16:2) "very early" and "when the sun had risen"; and in *GPet* 11:45, after the events happen, it is still night.

[6]The advance notice in Mark 14:1–2, namely, that "The Passover and the Unleavened Bread was (to be) after two days" and the authorities did not want to seize and kill Jesus on the feast (a passage

Synoptics to "Passover" are in Mark 14:16; Matt 26:19; and Luke 22:15, and the last references to the "Unleavened Bread" are in Mark 14:12; Matt 26:17; and Luke 22:7—all these *before* the section that we have been considering as the PN, which begins after the Last Supper. (We shall see later the importance of being precise on this point.) The expression "feast" does occur in the confines of the PN (Mark 15:6; Matt 27:15, and the spurious Luke 23:17) pertinent to the custom of releasing one prisoner "at a/the feast." Yet even if that refers to "*the* feast" of Passover (as I think), it is not definitive as to which day is meant before or during the eight-day festal period of Passover/Unleavened Bread.

(d) Hebrew *pesaḥ* and Greek *pascha* are ambivalent terms, referring not only to a feast day but also to the slaughter of a lamb or goat and the subsequent meal. For the sake of clarity (*only in what follows in this subsection B of the present* APPENDIX), where useful I shall use "Passover" for the festal day and "pasch/paschal" for the sacrificial slaughtering and the meal. In five Marcan uses of *pascha* in the time period of Jesus' last days, the usage varies: 14:1 tells us that the Passover feast was "after two days"; 14:12 mentions first the time when they sacrificed the pasch(al animal), and then a preparation to eat the pasch(al meal); 14:14 expresses Jesus' desire "to eat the pasch with my disciples"; 14:16 says, "They prepared the pasch/Passover" (presumably the paschal meal but also with a sense of celebrating the Passover feast).

(e) Recognition of that ambivalence leads us to a true ambiguity that may be said to have its roots in the instruction of Exod 12:6 that the lamb or goat be kept until the 14th day of the month (Nisan, in later nomenclature) and then slaughtered "between the two evenings." In the early period of Israelite history when the slaughtering was done by the head of a family, presumably that meant the animal was killed between twilight (just as the sun set) and darkness. Therefore the slaughtering was at the end of one day (the 14th) and the meal at the beginning of the next (the 15th). Later, when the practice developed of having the priests sacrificially slaughter the lambs in the Jerusalem Temple confines, more time was required to slay thousands of these animals brought forward by the families who intended to observe the feast. Consequently the slaughtering started on the early afternoon of the 14th (when the sun had *begun* to set), and sometimes almost six hours might separate the slaughtering on the 14th of Nisan and the meal which took place in the evening beginning the 15th. Thus the question of which day was considered Passover becomes relevant for our discussion of the time of Jesus.

---

to be discussed below), might seem a possible exception. In fact, however, that passage would not encourage us to place the arrest and death of Jesus on the feast itself.

(In modern Judaism, where there is no longer a sanctuary sacrifice of an animal, and the meal features the unleavened bread, Passover is the 15th of Nisan, the first day of the Unleavened Bread festival, a day that begins in the evening with that meal.) References in the OT, the NT, Josephus, and Philo are not always precise on this point partly because of the historical development just described, and partly because *pesah* and *pascha* refer to the feast, the slaughtering, and the meal, as explained in (d). On the one hand, Lev 23:5–6 states with precision: "The Passover of the Lord falls on the 14th day of the first month, at the evening twilight. The 15th day of this month is the Lord's feast of the Unleavened Bread." Num 28:16–17 is also clear: "On the 14th day of the first month falls the Passover of the Lord; and the 15th day of this month is the pilgrimage feast." Similarly Josephus (*Ant.* 3.10.5; #248–49) affirms: On the 14th of Nisan "we offer the sacrifice called *pascha*. . . . On the 15th day the Passover is followed up by the feast of the Unleavened Bread." Again Philo (*On the Special Laws* 2.27–28; #145,149,150,155) speaks of the Passover as occurring on the 14th of the month, and the feast of the Unleavened Bread as beginning on the 15th. On the other hand, Josephus can fail to make distinctions: "When the feast of the Unleavened Bread came around, they sacrificed the pascha" (*Ant.* 9.13.3; #271);[7] and "When the day of the Unleavened Bread came around, on the 14th of the month" (*War* 5.3.1; #99). Presumably it is in this imprecise category that Mark 14:12 (copied by Luke 22:7) belongs: "On the first day of the Unleavened Bread when they sacrificed the paschal lamb," since technically they sacrificed the lamb on the 14th, and the first day of the Unleavened Bread (when they *ate* the lamb) was the 15th.[8] Evidently by the 1st cent. AD the two feasts had so fallen together that frequently in ordinary speech distinctions were not made. In any case this discussion cautions against the statement that although John has Jesus die on the day before Passover, the Synoptics have Jesus die on Passover itself (a statement against which I argued for another reason in [c] above). If technically according to the religious calendar the 14th of Nisan when the lambs were slaughtered was Passover, and the paschal meal was eaten at the beginning of the 15th which was the first day of the Unleavened Bread, then according to John Jesus died on Passover, and according to the Synoptics he died on the day after Passover, namely, on the first day of the Unleavened Bread! At least in this subsection where we are seeking precision, however, to avoid any confusion caused by the issue of which day was considered Passover, I shall speak in a way that I hope is unobjectionable. John has Jesus die in the afternoon of the day

[7]Also *Ant.* 18.2.2; #29: "The feast of the Unleavened Bread which we call Passover."
[8]Similarly by that distinction Matt 26:17 would be imprecise since it has the disciples asking on the first day of the Unleavened Bread where Jesus wants the paschal meal to be prepared.

when the lambs were being slaughtered in the Temple area and before the paschal meal (and thus on the 14th of Nisan), and the Synoptics have Jesus die in the daytime following an evening paschal meal eaten with his disciples (and thus on the 15th of Nisan).

2. GOSPEL EVIDENCE FOR DATING THE CRUCIFIXION IN RELATION TO PASSOVER

In the Synoptics and in John there are advance notices to the coming Passover that would serve as the setting for Jesus' passion, and then proximate references associating with Passover individual episodes from the Last Supper to the sentencing of Jesus. They will be treated in this order: (a) Synoptic advance notices; (b) Synoptic proximate references; (c) Johannine advance notices; (d) Johannine proximate references.

(a) *Synoptic Advance Notices.* Many would commence the Marcan PN with 14:1–2: "But the Passover and the Unleavened Bread was (to be) after two days; and the chief priests and the scribes were seeking how, after having seized him by deception, they might kill him. For they were saying, 'Not on the feast,[9] lest there be a disturbance of the people'" (see Matt 26:1–5; Luke 22:1–2). The time indicator in the first line is often given importance not only because Mark is thought to be the oldest of the Gospels, but because some would judge this to be the beginning of the preMarcan PN which is older still. Nevertheless, there are major difficulties about it. There are four more references to *pascha* in the Marcan passion sequence (14:12,14,16), and all those refer to the paschal sacrifice/meal. Do those four and this one reference to the Passover feast come from the same source? If not, which is more original?

There are two obstacles to connecting them. First, the notice in 14:1–2 is the first layer of a typical Marcan "sandwich" arrangement of three episodes that may be schematized thus:

A. An incipient or desired action that will require time to be completed.	→	B. A separate episode filling in the time and complementing the theme of A.	→	A'. Resumption of the action of A.

---

[9]There is a debate whether "the feast" means Passover, Unleavened Bread, or both. As we have seen the classic usage applied "feast" to Unleavened Bread; but in the 1st cent. AD the usage was changing, so that "feast" was being used more frequently (and soon exclusively) for Passover rather than for Unleavened Bread. When Mark picks up the theme in 14:12–16 he mentions Unleavened Bread once more and Passover four times more; it is doubtful that he saw a calendric distinction between them, but Passover dominates his mind.

In Mark 14:1–11 the passage plotting the death of Jesus that we have been discussing (14:1–2) serves as *A;* it is followed by the *B* scene of the woman pouring ointment over Jesus' head at Bethany (14:3–9), which anticipates anointing his body for burial (14:8); then 14:10–11 has the role of *A'* picking up the action of A as Judas comes to the chief priests and offers to give Jesus over to them. If one were to take the sequence of the three episodes literally, one would ask how much time of the after-two-days-till-Passover was taken up by them. If one recognizes that the sequence is purely literary, the anointing by the woman becomes an undatable episode[10] set as filler (whence the name "sandwich" construction) between two parts of a single episode of a plot against Jesus by the Jewish authorities assisted by Judas, which carried the indicator that Passover was "after two days." (Although Matt 26:1–14 follows the tripartite Marcan sequence, Luke 22:1–6 omits the anointing-by-the-woman episode [see 7:36–50] and makes a single piece of the plot and betrayal by Judas.)

Second, if the "after two days-before-Passover-and-Unleavened-Bread" was attached to the plot, did it specify the date when the priests and scribes were seeking how to seize and kill Jesus or the date when Judas came to them? And what precise date is being calculated by a relationship to "the Passover and the Unleavened Bread"? Is Mark thinking of two days until the 14th of Nisan or until the 15th? (We shall see below Mark's imprecise way of referring to these feasts.) Calculating back an interstice of two days from those two dates apparently would fix the date given in 14:1 as the 12th or 13th of Nisan. Yet Holtzmann, Swete, Turner, and others argue that "after two days" is not so easily calculated. Just as "after three days" in Mark 8:31; 9:31 is fulfilled in resurrection on the third day, they think that "after two days" may have meant Passover on the second day—a reasoning that might fix the date in 14:1 as the 13th. (That resurrection analog, however, has its own problems.)

(b) *Synoptic References to the Passover Supper.* Mark 14:12 goes on from what was just discussed to report: "And on the first day of the Unleavened Bread, when they were sacrificing the pasch(al lamb), his disciples said to him, 'Where do you wish that, having gone away, we shall prepare in order that you may eat the pasch(al lamb/meal)?'" Then two disciples go into Jerusalem city and find a guest room for Jesus to eat the pasch(al lamb/meal) with his disciples (14:16). "And when evening had come, Jesus comes with the Twelve; and reclining with them and eating, he said . . ." (14:17–18). Above under B,1e we saw that frequently there was imprecision about dating Passover when it was run together with the feast of the Unleavened Bread.

---

[10]John 12:1–8 has Mary anoint Jesus' feet at Bethany "six days before Passover."

Lev 23:6 would locate "the first day of the Unleavened Bread" on the 15th of Nisan; indeed, in the OT the 14th of Nisan is never called "the first day of the Unleavened Bread."[11] Yet the rest of Mark's description corresponds to what we know of the 14th of Nisan, e.g., the slaughtering of the lambs and making preparations for the paschal meal. Eating the pasch would come at a moment after that day(time) was over and the 15th had begun. (The Matthean and Lucan accounts point in the same direction; and in none of the Synoptics is Passover mentioned again after this, as noted in B,1c above.) Thus the meal described (the Last Supper) that Jesus ate with the Twelve should have been the paschal meal (and is specifically so in Luke 22:15). By the logic of calendric sequence—but not by Synoptic Gospel affirmation— what follows in the rest of the night (going to Gethsemane, arrest, Jewish trial) and in the next daytime (Roman trial, crucifixion, death, burial) should have taken place on that same one day: the 15th of Nisan, a Thn/Fd. (Most commentators would add "on Passover," but we have seen above that at this period technically Passover may have been the 14th, the day of the sacrific- ing of the lamb rather than the day of eating it. Less disputably the 15th was technically the first day of the Unleavened Bread.)

Many scholars accept this 15th of Nisan as the most plausible dating for the crucifixion, including Baur, W. Bauer, Dalman, Edersheim, Jeremias, J. B. Lightfoot, Schlatter, and Zahn. Often, at least implicitly, part of their logic is that Mark preserves the oldest tradition. The main reason for doubting this chronology is the amount of activity that the Synoptics de- scribe as taking place on what should have been a solemn festal day: a crowd coming out to Gethsemane to arrest Jesus; a session of the Sanhedrin to sentence Jesus to death; both Sanhedrin authorities and crowds going to see the Roman governor; Simon of Cyrene coming in from the fields (Mark 15:21); many passersby at the crucifixion site (15:29); buying a linen cloth (15:46). JEWJ 74–79 argues that one can find indications in Jewish tradition allowing every one of these actions on a feast; but beyond debates about his individual points,[12] the conglomeration of so much activity on a feast day has seemed highly implausible. Moreover, all this action against Jesus on the festal day seems to run against the expressed wish of the chief priests

---

[11]For disputed rabbinic passages see JEWJ 17, n. 2. In Mark 14:12 some would try to understand Greek *prōtē* ("first") as *pro:* "the day *before* the Unleavened Bread"; or posit a misunderstood Ara- maic original which should have been translated: "before the first of the Unleavened Bread" (see *GPet* 2:5c). Most likely we are dealing with careless Marcan writing, where what he really means in 14:12 is defined by the second phrase, so that he might be paraphrased: "And on the beginning day of Unleavened Bread/Passover, when they were sacrificing the lamb."

[12]Many of the Jewish texts cited come from long after the time of Jesus and so are dubiously applicable. In particular, some have queried Jeremias's defense of a Sanhedrin session on a feast, for which he appeals to the immediate need to rid the people of a false prophet (JEWJ 78–79).

and the scribes that arresting Jesus and killing him should not take place on the feast lest there may be a disturbance among the people (Mark 14:1–2).

(c) *Johannine Advance Notices.* Having reported a Sanhedrin meeting that resulted in a plan to kill Jesus (11:45–53) and in Jesus' escaping off to Ephraim (11:54), John indicates that "the Passover of the Jews was near, and many went up to Jerusalem from the country before the Passover in order that they might purify themselves" (11:55). Although the situation is similar to that of the Synoptic advance notices discussed in (a) above, the "was near" of John is vaguer than the "after two days" of Mark 14:1. This nearness of Passover causes many people to come up to Jerusalem for the feast in order that they might purify themselves, but John gives no indication as to how long that would take—presumably no less than seven days.[13] We are next told (John 12:1) that six days before Passover Jesus came to Bethany where Mary anointed his feet, an ointment kept for his entombment.[14] Note that John makes sequential the same episodes that Mark 14:1–11 has intermingled. There Mark placed the anointing in a framework with a notice that Passover was after two days; how seriously then are we to take John's dating of the anointing scene to six days before Passover? All we know is that John (unlike his practice in 1:29,35,43; 2:1) does not spell out a sequence of days before he comes to Passover eve; for there is only one intervening day specifically mentioned, namely, the next day of 12:12ff. on which a crowd greets Jesus with palm fronds as he comes into Jerusalem.

(d) *Johannine References to the Immediately Oncoming Passover.* John has one proximate Passover reference in the context of Jesus eating with his disciples, namely, in 13:1 "before the feast of Passover" appears at the beginning of a general introduction to the second part of the Gospel which commences with an evening meal on the night before Jesus dies. In disagreement with the more specific Synoptic chronological references to the meal, John's phrasing does not suggest that Jesus is eating the paschal meal with his disciples. Rather after part of the meal is over Judas leaves and thus causes some to think that Jesus has told him to go out and buy what is needed for the feast (13:29). Since the only feast John mentions is Passover (not Unleavened Bread), and the meal is the major factor in Passover, surely this is an indication that the paschal meal still lies in the future. John departs even more from the Synoptics by continuing his chronological references

---

[13]For the custom of being purified before celebrating a feast, see Num 9:10–11; II Chron 30:16–18; Josephus, *War* 1.11.6; #229; Acts 21:24–27. Num 19:11–12 requires a seven-day period to purify the uncleanness contracted from contact with a corpse, with water cleansing on the third and seventh days. In relation to Unleavened Bread this would probably take place on the 10th and 14th of Nisan.

[14]Might this be compared to a cleansing on the first day of the seven-day period mentioned in the preceding note?

into the following daytime and applying them beyond Jesus' circle to "the Jews" in general. On the next morning, before Pilate's praetorium as he is about to begin the trial of Jesus, the Jews (leaders and people: see 18:35,38) are portrayed (18:28) as avoiding impurity so that they may eat the pasch(al lamb/meal). And when the trial is coming to an end,[15] as Pilate leads Jesus outside and sits on the judgment seat, we are told that it is preparation day for Passover (19:14).[16] There is little doubt, then, that John presents the whole fateful night and following daytime (which we saw to be Thn/Fd) as the 14th of Nisan, the day before the paschal meal would be eaten.[17]

Scholars who favor John's chronology over that of the Synoptics probably constitute a majority, e.g., Blinzler, Brooke, Burkitt, Cadoux, Dibelius, Hoskyns, T. W. Manson, C. G. Montefiore, G. Ogg, Peake, Rawlinson, Sanday, Strachan, Streeter, and Taylor—this despite the tendency of their adversaries to cite the general principle that one cannot expect a historical account from John. In my judgment that principle is just as invalid as the older thesis that the Fourth Gospel was written by the most intimate of eyewitnesses (John, son of Zebedee) and therefore is the most historical of all the Gospels. None of the four canonical Gospels is pure history; all preserve older traditions transformed by theological reflection and gathered for missionary or pastoral purposes. When they disagree, no overall principle settles the issue of the more plausible. The Johannine chronology is supported by *GPet* 2:5c, where Jesus is given over for execution "before the first day of their feast of the Unleavened Bread," and by TalBab *Sanhedrin* 43a: "On the eve of Passover Yeshu was hanged." (However, both those references may be influenced indirectly by John.[18]) Probably the most persuasive argument for those who accept John's dating of the crucifixion is that then the many activities described on Thn/Fd do not occur on a feast day. However, it may be false to suppose that the 14th of Nisan, the day when the lambs were being sacrificed

[15]In the midst of the trial John 18:39 speaks of a Jewish custom of releasing a prisoner at Passover, but from that reference one cannot tell whether Passover is about to begin or has already begun.

[16]C. C. Torrey (JBL 50 [1931], 227–41) attempted to avoid the import of this by arguing that *paraskeuē* ("preparation day") was simply equivalent to Hebrew/Aramaic *'ereb*/*'ărûbā'* ("eve"), specifically the eve of the Sabbath, or Friday. Therefore John did not mean the preparation day for Passover but a Friday in Passover week. S. Zeitlin (JBL 51 [1932], 263–71) shows that this is not justifiable on the basis of Semitic evidence, and I have argued on p. 846 above that the Greek connotation of "preparation" should not be dismissed even in a set expression.

[17]Although by the more ancient calendric calculation, the 14th of Nisan when the lambs were sacrificed may have been considered Passover (B,1e above), for John the 15th, when the meal was eaten, was the Passover.

[18]In early-2d-cent. Christianity we know of the "Quartodecimans" who argued that Easter should always be celebrated the 14th of Nisan, no matter what day of the week it fell on. G. Ziener, "Johannesevangelium und urchristliche Passafeier," BZ 2 (1958), 263–74, would see the Fourth Gospel originating in a primitive Jewish-Christian Passover celebration of the Quartodeciman type—thus the Johannine dating may have had no more than liturgical value. However, most would see the relationship in the opposite direction: John's dating contributed to the Quartodeciman practice.

in the Temple area, was not a festal day. Even if it was looked on purely as the "preparation day for Passover" (John 19:14), according to later Jewish law, as explained in the commentary, some of the activities would be forbidden on the eve of a feast day as well, e.g., a Jewish trial for a capital offense. We are not certain, however, how much of this highly protective attitude toward legalities was in effect in the 1st cent.[19]

3. ATTEMPTS TO DEAL WITH THE DISCREPANCIES

We have seen that all the Gospels place Jesus' death on the day before the Sabbath, thus a Thn/Fd. We have also seen that because of their indications pointing to the supper that Jesus ate with his disciples as a paschal meal, logically the Synoptic evangelists imply that this Thn/Fd was the 15th of Nisan. Johannine passages referring to events both on Thursday night and in the daytime on Friday indicate that the Thn/Fd was the 14th of Nisan, the eve (preparation day) of the 15th when the paschal meal would be eaten. Attempts to deal with this discrepancy between the Synoptics and John run the gamut from contending that both chronologies are true, through favoring one over the other, to the view that neither is true. The easiest solution is to accept one of the two presentations as more plausible—a judgment that does not necessarily solve the issue of historicity, even though many commentators combine the search to find what an evangelist intended with a discussion of what happened.[20] However, often on the dubious assumption that the Gospels must be historical, there is a desire to harmonize the two pictures. Let us sample some of the more prominent proposals.

(a) The Synoptics and John are both correct, and one can harmonize them **by rearranging the sequence.** Often this solution is based on the ancient thesis that the author of John knew the Synoptics and wrote to supplement them, assuming that his passages would be intercalated with theirs (but, alas, forgetting to supply any key for doing so). The Arabic form of Tatian's *Diatessaron* places John 13:1–20 (a meal dated before Passover) before the Synoptic account of the Last Supper (the paschal meal). That still leaves the reference in John 18:28 where the Jews have not yet eaten Passover. To be plausible, then, the rearrangement has to be combined with other proposals: e.g., the Jewish authorities postponed the celebration of their paschal meal

---

[19]We know that by this time there was a certain respect for eves. Judith 8:6 has no fasting on the eve of the Sabbath and the eve of the new moon, but does not mention the eve of the great feasts. Later Mishna *Pesaḥim* 4.5 reports that in Judea they used to carry on their occupations on the eve of Passover until noon, but in Galilee they used to do no work at all.

[20]Still a further issue is whether any of the evangelists had personal knowledge of the precise day on which Jesus died. One can doubt that without descending into the nihilism of assuming that no writer knew or cared about anything that happened in Jesus' passion.

until they had disposed of Jesus, their archenemy (as old as Chrysostom).[21] Overall, I find that this solution presupposes an interest in harmonized sequence totally foreign to the evangelists, and in some of its combinations posits implausible Jewish behavior.

(b) The Synoptics and John are both correct because **there were two Passover celebrations one day apart.**[22] Some would support this possibility on the basis of an acknowledged provision in the Law that those who were unable to celebrate on the 14th of Nisan could celebrate on the 14th of the next month (Num 9:10–11). Actually, however, that "escape clause" may militate against the likelihood of another escape through legally tolerated adjacent days for Passover in Nisan itself. (Num 9:13 can be harsh on those who do not eat at the appointed time precisely because an alternative has been made available.) Those who take the approach of two Passovers often point out that Passover (the full moon) was calculated from the *sight* of the new moon at the beginning of Nisan, a sighting that may have varied in different regions. (In fact, ancient Jews had an exact knowledge of astronomy that may have helped the naked eye.) Another contention, quite justified in itself, is that the various OT accounts describing how to celebrate feasts were not always consistent since they embody different practices changing over centuries, and that there was dissension among Jews about how to interpret them. Certainly there was a dispute about some chronological details pertinent to Passover/Unleavened Bread and about when to celebrate the feast of Weeks.[23] In judging the variants of this approach one should recog-

---

[21]Another proposal is that of Heawood ("Time" 42–44) who argues that John's having the Jews avoid contamination "in order that they might eat the Passover" is confused and really means: in order that they might complete the purifications of the feast of the Unleavened Bread—cleansings that followed the Passover meal on the 15th. Zeitlin ("Time" 46–47) is perfectly correct in rejecting this introduction into John of "Unleavened Bread," a nomenclature that he never employs and that was going out of use as the name of the feast at the time John wrote (n. 4 above).

[22]A few have offered as an analogy the fact that Jews in the Diaspora celebrated the feast of Weeks over a two-day period (to be sure that they had the right day) while those in Jerusalem celebrated a single day. The analogy limps, for Jesus' celebration of Passover took place in Jerusalem, and he was not a Diaspora Jew. The reference in TalBab *Megilla* 31a to two Passover days to make allowance for the Diaspora in Babylon belongs to a redactional level, probably about five centuries after Jesus.

[23]Mishna *Pesahim* 4.5 preserves a memory of a dispute between the schools of Shammai and Hillel about whether work before Passover had to stop on the night that began the 14th of Nisan or only at sunrise. As for the feast of Weeks, after the first day of the feast of the Unleavened Bread came the day for waving the sheaf of the firstfruits of the barley harvest. Lev 23:11 says: "On the day after the Sabbath the priest shall do this"; and Lev 23:15–16 calculates the feast of Weeks (Pentecost) as the fiftieth day of a period beginning after that Sabbath. There was dispute over whether the indicated "Sabbath" is to be taken as equivalent to the holy day of rest constituted by the 15th of Nisan itself. That would put the waving of the firstfruits on the 16th, no matter what weekday that was (a view associated with the Pharisees; held by Josephus [*Ant.* 3.10.5; #250] and Philo [*De specialibus legibus* 2.30; #176], and implicit in the LXX of Lev 23:11), or as the first Saturday to occur from the 15th on, so that the ceremony of firstfruits was always on a Sunday (a view associated with the Sadducees: see Tosepta *Roš Haššana* 1.15). Interestingly H. Montefiore

nize that the Synoptics attach time references to Jesus' private meal with his disciples, while John describes a public chronology. Nevertheless, celebrating a true paschal meal in Jerusalem had to depend on when the priests killed lambs in the Temple and thus made them available for the meal—a public factor that militated against private calendric decisions. Variants of the two-Passover approach include the following:

(1) Perhaps Galileans celebrated Passover one day earlier than was customary in Jerusalem (every year? this year?).[24] Jesus and his followers from Galilee would then have celebrated Passover as described in the Synoptics, while the public Jerusalem calendar would be reflected in John. Mishna *Pesaḥim* 4.5 shows that by the 2d cent. AD there was a difference between Galilee and Judea as to when work must stop on the eve of Passover, but that there was a difference in the 1st cent. about which day to celebrate Passover remains an unsubstantiated guess.

(2) Perhaps the Pharisees followed one calculation (and Jesus was closer to them), while the Sadducees (priests) followed another that governed public life (the one indicated by John). For instance, it is theorized that when the day for eating the pasch fell on the Sabbath (as in the Johannine calculation), limitations about work on the eve of the Sabbath prevented the priests from getting the required number of lambs slaughtered; and so they had to begin the sacrifice a day earlier, on Thursday afternoon. Similarly Chenderlin ("Distributed" 392) argues that the Jerusalem authorities may have had to make a provision for two sacrificing days in Nisan because they could not kill enough lambs on one day to meet the needs of hundreds of thousands of pilgrims that came. (Yet beginning slaughtering at noon on the 14th was already a concession to cover such practicalities.) Facing this priestly procedure, the theory continues, and bound by the law that nothing of the slaughtered lamb could remain till the next morning, the Pharisees and their sympathizers had to eat the lamb on the night of the first day even though that was not the regular time (in the year of Jesus' death it was the night of Thn/Fd, the 14th), while the less legalistic Sadducees could wait till the second, regular night which began the 15th (Fn/Sd). Against such theorizing is the fact that the Sadducees did observe the written law, and we have no reason

---

("When"), on the basis of I Cor 15:20 which has Christ the firstfruits raised from the dead, argues that waving of the sheaf on the 16th of Nisan took place this year on the Sunday when the tomb was found empty; thus Fn/Sd was the 15th, and Thn/Fd the 14th as in Johannine chronology. However, according to the other calculation the waving always took place on a Sunday, no matter the date in Nisan.

[24]Dockx ("Le 14 Nisan" 26–29), after discussing a number of the harmonizing variants I shall present, judges this to be the only really defensible proposal. He speculates that Galileans did not accept as binding the decisions of a calendar committee that met in Jerusalem on the 29th of every month. Mishna *Roš Haššana* 1 is the source for those who picture how the new moon that marked a new month was calculated at Jerusalem; see Shepherd, "Are Both" 127.

to think they could ignore Exod 12:10. Moreover, it is peculiar to place the whole burden of solving the Gospel discrepancies on the availability of a slain lamb, when no Gospel ever mentions that a lamb was part of the meal. Certainly Mark shows no awareness of a calendric dispute between Sadducees and Pharisees, for his first notice about the oncoming Passover (14:1) has the chief priests cooperating with scribes (a group that elsewhere he associates with the Pharisees: 2:16; 7:1,5) in a plot against Jesus that presupposes the same understanding of the feast.

(3) Because chronological calculations varied throughout the Diaspora where Jews were scattered more than 1,000 miles from Jerusalem, perhaps there was a policy of a consecutive two-day Passover, in order to be sure that the correct day was covered. More specifically Shepherd ("Are Both") proposes that Diaspora Jews used fixed astronomical calculations according to which Thn/Fd was the 15th of Nisan, while Palestinians depended on a sighting of the new moon and Fn/Sd was the 15th for them. In such explanations Jesus, knowing that he would be dead by the second of the two days, opted this year for the first (even though he was not a Diaspora Jew). He celebrated the paschal meal on the 14th of Nisan whereas many other Jews of his time had the meal on the 15th (Fn/Sd). Such theories seem to imagine the priests cooperating with a calendric calculation they did not accept by slaughtering lambs on the day before each of these Passovers! *The problem with all these solutions is that we do not have any evidence for the celebration in Jerusalem of two adjacent days as Passover.* The solutions have been invented to reconcile Gospel discrepancies and cannot call on established Jewish practice for support.

(c) The Synoptics and John are both correct because **the Synoptics were not describing a paschal meal.**[25] Rather they were describing a nonpaschal meal eaten by Jesus with his disciples on the 14th of Nisan, even as John was. Some scholars have thought that on the night before he died Jesus ate a specially blessed meal[26] or a meal of the type eaten by religious confedera-

---

[25]Less frequently the argument proceeds in the opposite direction, namely, that both in the Synoptics and *in John* Jesus ate the Passover meal with his followers; and when in the following daytime John 18:28 reports that the Jews did not want to be defiled by entering the praetorium so that "they might eat [*phagein*] the pasch(al lamb/meal)," that means the subsequent meals of the seven-day festal period. Chenderlin ("Distributed" 369–70) argues for this, pointing out that the verb for the Passover/pasch proper was *thyein* ("to sacrifice") or *poiein* ("to do"). Given, however, that the OT shows specific concern about purity preparatory for eating the paschal meal itself (e.g., Num 9:6–13 with 9:11 using *phagein*), this is a forced interpretation. Moreover it deals poorly with John 19:14, which calls the day when Jesus was judged the "preparation (day) for Passover"—clearly such language involves preparation for a very special day, not for any day in a week-long festal season. Finally the thesis does not do justice to John 13:29, which is a strong indication that the meal Jesus is eating is not the meal of the (Passover) feast, for which things may still need to be bought.

[26]Often reference is made to Qiddush (Kiddush) or purification meals, i.e., food eaten on the eves of Sabbath and festivals ritually to sanctify those days (see Walker, "Dating" 294). Taylor (*Jesus*

tions (Haburoth).[27] However, beyond the fact that we know very little about the practice of these proposed meals in the 1st cent. AD (so that it becomes a case of explaining *obscurum per obscurius*), such suggestions do not do justice to the Synoptic data about preparing *for the pasch* or to Luke 22:15: "I have desired to eat this pasch(al meal) with you." Accordingly, a more common suggestion is that on the evening that ended the 13th of Nisan and began the 14th, according to both the Synoptics and John, Jesus ate a prepaschal meal,[28] one that he designed himself in order to anticipate the regular paschal meal to be eaten the next night (which he knew that he could not eat because he would be dead). The evidence that JEWJ 41–62 has gathered to prove that the Last Supper was a paschal meal[29] is often cited in the prepasch theory: It was a paschal meal in everything but the lamb (which could not be obtained because it would not be slaughtered till the next afternoon); and that was why Jesus could speak about eating this pasch with his followers. Yet the Synoptic story flow does not favor such a private anticipation of the paschal meal: (Two) disciples are commissioned to go into the city and find a house where Jesus may eat the pasch with his disciples (Mark 14:12–16 and par.). Such preparation involves public contact and scarcely allows that when they come that night, they will be eating a type of private pasch a day earlier than everybody else. To my mind this theory is one more example of an ad hoc creation for purposes of harmonization. If one did not have John, those now inclined to find a prepaschal meal in the Synoptic accounts of the Last Supper would never have thought of that thesis and would be arguing for a paschal meal.

Moreover, whether one thinks of a paschal or a prepaschal meal, the Passover parallels in JEWJ are weak support. Many of them are drawn from mishnaic descriptions of Passover that are dubiously applicable to Jesus' time, as has been pointed out by Bokser ("Was") who has specialized in

115–16) reports that G. H. Box opted for the Sabbath Qiddush, while W. E. Oesterley and G.H.C. Macgregor preferred the Passover Qiddush. Taylor (also Geldenhuys, "Day" 651) rejects these proposals on the grounds that such a meal was eaten in the evening on which the Sabbath or the Passover began, thus regularly on Friday for the Sabbath and also on a Friday this particular year if one follows John's chronology for Passover. There is no evidence that either could be anticipated one day and eaten on a Thursday evening as in the Synoptics. For rabbinic debates about various times for reciting the Qiddush, see TalBab *Pesahim* 105a ff.

[27]JJTJ 246–59 discusses the Pharisee *ḥăbûrâ*, trying to reconstruct the history of such communities in Jerusalem in the 1st cent. AD; but almost all the evidence is rabbinic, and it is very difficult to know how much later organization has been retrojected into the picture.

[28]See Blank, "Johannespassion" 151–52; Bornhäuser, *Death* 63–64. Occasionally I have the impression that proponents of the prepaschal meal are thinking of a meal that was an accepted custom for the evening that ended the 13th of Nisan and began the 14th. I do not know of concrete evidence for the existence at this time of such a set prepaschal meal.

[29]Eaten in the confines of Jerusalem; at night; with an appropriate number (at least ten); reclining; with those present washed and thus ritually pure; wine; the suggestion of giving something to the poor; interpretative words over the bread and wine.

trying to reconstruct the early festal meal. Personally I find quite persuasive his thesis[30] that the Passover seder as we know it from Jewish sources did not develop until after AD 70 when the lamb could no longer be killed sacrificially and the loss of this chief element from the meal caused greater symbolic emphasis to be given to other elements by way of compensation. On the other hand, we must be careful in applying Bokser's arguments to a discussion of the Gospel Last Supper accounts. They prove that it is not possible to show that historically Jesus ate a paschal meal with his disciples, as Jeremias and many others sought to do. They do not tell us whether the evangelists who knew the Jewish situation after 70 were coloring their description of Jesus' last meal with imagery from the "lamb-less" paschal meals that began to be celebrated then. How soon after 70 did seder-like features of the Passover develop in Judaism? How soon did echoes of them come into Christian descriptions of the Last Supper? Was there already an inchoate development of seder symbolism in the "lamb-less" Passovers celebrated away from Jerusalem in the Diaspora that would have facilitated both processes? Readers should keep those issues in mind when they consider in the next major subsection (3) the view that I have adopted in this commentary. Before turning to that, however, one other attempt to harmonize the Gospels should be mentioned.

(d) The Synoptics and John are both correct to the extent that they preserve memories of the chronology of **the Qumran calendar** that Jesus followed in his last days. Although many have theorized that simultaneously there was adherence to different religious calendars by Jews in Palestine in the 1st cent. AD, our first concrete proof of that came with the discovery of the Dead Sea Scrolls at Qumran in 1947. Clearly those who produced the Scrolls (identified by most as Essenes) adhered to the *solar* calendar supposed in the *Book of Jubilees,* an ancient calendar that had been replaced in the Jerusalem Temple (probably in the 2d cent. BC) by what we customarily think of as the standard Jewish lunar calendar. The Qumran calendar, based on a rough solar year of 364 days with intercalated additions, was ingeniously permanent so that feasts fell on the same weekday every year. For example, on the presumption that days are reckoned as beginning in the evening, the 15th of Nisan (the date of the paschal meal) would always begin Tuesday night and continue through Wednesday daytime. With Jaubert and Ruckstuhl as advocates and many others (Delorme, Skehan, Schwank, E. Vogt) expressing interest or support, a harmonizing arrangement of Gospel details was proposed to show how Jesus might have followed the Qumran (Essene) solar calendar. In this theory the solar calendar is reflected in the

---

[30]B. M. Bokser, *The Origins of the Seder* (Berkeley: Univ. of California, 1984).

TABLE 11. COMPARISON OF THE (QUMRAN) SOLAR CALENDAR AND THE LUNAR CALENDAR
FOR DATING EVENTS IN THE PASSION NARRATIVE

Day	Gospel Happening	*Nisan* Date
Tues. day →	preparation for paschal meal (Mark 14:12–16)	solar 14 lunar 11

Tues. eve →
 	
night →
(Tu./Wed.)
 	
Wed. day →
	Last Supper paschal meal (Mark 14:17–18; Luke
	   22:15) eaten before (lunar) 15th Nisan (John 13:1)
	Gethsemane; arrest of Jesus
	Inquiry before Annas (Mark 14:53a; John 18:13)
	Peter's denials; mockery by servants (Luke 22:54–65)
	Sent to Caiaphas (John 18:24); 1st Sanhedrin session
	   (Luke 22:66–71)
	Mockery of Jesus by authorities (Mark 14:65)
		solar 15
		(paschal meal)
		
		lunar 12

night → (Wed./Th.) Th. morn. → Th. P.M. →	(*Jesus in custody of high priest*) 2d Sanhedrin session (Mark 15:1a) Jesus taken to Pilate (Mark 15:1b; Luke 23:1) Opening of Pilate trial (Luke 23:2–5) Jesus taken to Herod (Luke 23:6–12) Return to Pilate and trial resumed (Luke 23:15ff.); adjournment	solar 16 lunar 13

night →
(Th./Fri.)
Fri. morn →
	(*Jesus in Pilate's custody*)
	Pilate's wife's dream (Matt 27:19)
	Pilate trial resumed; Barabbas
	Pilate sentences Jesus (Mark 15:15)
	   noon before Passover (John 19:14)
	   (Jewish priests slay lambs in Temple precincts)
	Crucifixion, death, burial by Joseph
		solar 17
		
		lunar 14

Fri. eve. → Sat. morn. →	Jesus in the tomb Jews eat their paschal meal (John 18:28b) Priests and Pharisees ask Pilate to guard sepulcher (Matt 27:62–64)	solar 18 lunar 15 (paschal meal)

time references of the Synoptics, while Johannine indications were governed by the corresponding dates on the official lunar calendar followed by the Jerusalem authorities. I schematize the results in Table 11 above.[31]

I shall now list arguments advanced in defense of this adventurous reconstruction and at the same time give a response to them marked off by dashes: (i) It allows more time for events that seem impossibly crowded in the Gospels—but thus undoes the motive of haste and stealth that the Synoptics

---

[31]The Gospel references I give there suppose some intuitive understanding by the readers: Even if an event occurs in several or all Gospels, e.g., Peter's denials, I give the reference most appropriate to the sequence, e.g., only Luke has those denials followed immediately by a mockery of Jesus. If you are truly puzzled why I have given one reference rather than another, please consult the treatment of the episode in the commentary.

assign to the Jewish authorities. (ii) It meets the mishnaic demands requiring trials over more than one day for a capital offense with an interstice before sentencing—yet (pp. 357–63 above) there is no real evidence that these later Jewish laws were in effect at this time. (iii) It enables the anointing of Jesus by the woman at Bethany to be both "six days before Passover" (John 12:1) and only two or three days before Passover (Mark 14:1,3)—but only at the price of ignoring how Mark has put together 14:1–16, as explained above. (iv) There is Christian tradition that supports a memory of the Last Supper on Tuesday evening, especially in *Didascalia Apostolorum* 21 (5.13; Connolly ed. p.181)—but is this a historical reminiscence of Jesus' following an Essene calendar, or a desire to fulfill the prophecy that Jesus was three days and three nights in the heart of the earth (Matt 12:40), as explained under A above?

This summary of supporting arguments does not do justice to the amount of learned ingenuity that has gone into the defense of the Essene-calendar hypothesis. Nevertheless, I firmly join those who in articles or in book reviews have rejected it (Benoit, Blinzler, Gaechter, Jeremias, Ogg, Schubert, Trilling, etc.). The harmonizing of events displayed in the table puts genuine preGospel traditions together with literary editing by the evangelists that should be left out of a historical reconstruction. In the commentary I contended that Luke's arrangement (which is very important in this theory) flows from his desire to put in more logical order (Luke 1:3: *kathexēs*) what he found in Mark and is totally secondary. The idea of two trials in Mark rests on a misreading of Mark 15:1. One should not attempt to fit into a chronology clearly imaginative stories that Matt has borrowed from popular tradition, e.g., the dream of Pilate's wife. Moreover, what evidence is there that Jesus at any other time in his life followed anything other than the official calendar? Calendric adherence was a matter of deep religious identity; no accusation against Jesus by his enemies accuses him of Essene sympathies or of calendric irregularities. What would prompt Jesus and his disciples to depart so seriously from the official calendar in this instance? Where did they get the lamb for Passover, days before the official time for slaughtering?[32] In short this solution has less plausible basis than most other harmonizations and only creates new difficulties.

[32]Ruckstuhl ("Zur Chronologie" 50–51) calls upon Josephus (*Ant.* 18.1.5; #19), an unclear passage: Seemingly the Essenes sent offerings to the Temple, but observed different rules of purification, and so were barred from the precincts of the Temple frequented by others. What is uncertain is whether Josephus means that therefore they went elsewhere (in Jerusalem?) to offer sacrifices under their own rules or that they ceased altogether to offer sacrifices at Jerusalem. Granted the hostility of the Jerusalem priests toward the Qumran sectarians attested in the Dead Sea Scrolls, it seems very dubious that Qumran Essene priests were permitted publicly to sacrifice paschal lambs in Jerusalem, so that a nonEssene like Jesus could get one if he decided to follow the solar calendar. See Blinzler, *Prozess* 118–20; HJPAJC 2.570,582,588.

As I close this subsection, my judgment is that the various attempts to reconcile the chronological discrepancies between the Synoptics and John are implausible, unnecessary, and misleading.[33] The two Gospel traditions have given us irreconcilable chronological notices. Logically, then, neither or only one set of notices can be historical. In what follows I shall go beyond that judgment to suggest why the evangelists produced diverse chronologies, a suggestion that will cast light on the oldest historical tradition.

4. A BRIEF SURVEY OF THE OPINION ADOPTED IN THIS COMMENTARY

The word "brief" appears in the title for two reasons: First, in refuting the many harmonizing solutions above I have laid out for the readers the basic facts that must be dealt with; second, the long commentary on the PNs that is the substance of this book fills in what is only outlined here.

Before the Gospels were written, Paul reported as a received tradition (presumably dating back to the 30s when he became a follower of Jesus) that on the night in which Jesus was given over he took bread and said, "This is my body," and after supper, "This cup is the new covenant in my blood" (I Cor 11:23–25). In other words, he knew an early tradition of a final supper before Jesus' death (with eucharistic words in a form closest to what Luke reports). In the same letter Paul challenges his readers/hearers to clear out the old yeast inasmuch as they are unleavened, "for Christ, our pasch(al lamb), has been sacrificed" (5:7). He states that Christ has been raised from the dead, "the firstfruits of those who have fallen asleep" (15:20). It seems clear that the death and resurrection of Jesus were associated in Paul's mind with the symbolism of the opening days of the feast of Passover/Unleavened Bread. Since a pilgrimage feast is the most plausible explanation of why Jesus and his Galilean disciples were together in Jerusalem, I would regard as historical that Jesus' final supper and crucifixion took place just before or at Passover—a fact that Christians very quickly capitalized on theologically by relating his death to the sacrifice of the paschal lamb. Paul is not the only nonGospel witness to this. Later on, but not in obvious dependence on the Gospels, I Pet 1:19 speaks of "the precious blood of Christ as of a lamb without blemish or spot," echoing Exod 12:5. Although (perhaps under the influence of apocalyptic conventions) Rev 5:6–14 uses a Greek word for

---

[33]Unfortunately many who have justifiable religious interests in the Gospels feel impelled to harmonize them. Yet if one believes that the Gospels are the inspired word of God, why does one seek to improve what they offer by harmonizing their diversities so that one can present to others a unified picture that they do *not* give? If one believes that the Christian church was guided in recognizing that the Gospels are canonical or normative, why does one seek to produce a harmony in their stead? In the 2d cent. Tatian did that, but eventually the whole church refused to substitute his harmony for the four diverse Gospels.

lamb (*arnion*) that is not employed by the LXX for the paschal lamb, such an identification may lie behind Rev's picture of Christ (in a liturgical context of incense, prayers, and hymns) standing as a slain lamb whose blood purchased people from every tribe for God. Many times in the commentary on the passion we have seen that an old insight has found its way *into narrative* differently in Mark and in John. That is true here of the preGospel theological identification of Jesus as the paschal lamb.

In Mark 14 Jesus' Last Supper with his disciples is presented as a paschal meal. This is clear from Mark 14:12–16, the preparation for the meal; and so I think that Luke (22:15) correctly interprets Mark when he has Jesus begin the supper by saying that he has desired to eat this pasch with his disciples. Whether the theological identification has been carried through to the extent that Synoptic readers would recognize Passover features in details of how the meal is eaten and the cup is drunk I do not know.[34] Clearly, however, in this paschal supper the words spoken in reference to the bread and wine give to Jesus' body and blood ("poured out for many") the central place that normally would have been accorded to the lamb sacrificed in the Temple, a lamb that is never mentioned at the Last Supper. In other words we have here a theologoumenon, i.e., the presentation of the Last Supper as a paschal meal is a dramatization of the preGospel proclamation of Jesus as the paschal lamb. Granted that Mark has written this up in narrative form,[35] was Mark responsible for the basic theologoumenon? Or before Mark's writing had Christians already begun to picture the "Lord's Supper" (I Cor 11:20) eaten "on the night in which he was given over" (11:23) as a paschal meal? The day that began in the evening with the paschal meal would have been the 15th of Nisan and the first day of the week-long feast of the Unleavened Bread.[36] We have noted that Mark has no echo of that feast-day dating in any detail of Jesus' passion subsequent to the supper;[37] indeed, without

[34]Nor, as a matter of fact, does anyone else know because of two serious gaps in our information: How quickly were the adaptations of the post-70 period when the lambs were no longer sacrificed (adaptations spelled out in the Mishna written about 200) introduced into the Jewish ritual of the paschal meal, and to what extent were the intended Christian readers of the years 60–90 (when the Synoptic Gospels were written) familiar with the contemporary Jewish Passover celebration? Throughout the commentary I have contended that the explanation given by Mark in 7:3–4 suggests that his readers knew little about Judaism. Luke has a good book-knowledge (LXX) of Judaism, but there are few indications of what his readers knew. There is a good chance that the Jewish-Christian section of Matt's community knew contemporary Judaism well, even if polemically.

[35]Therefore the presence of Marcan style in 14:12–16 does not solve the issue of whether the basic insight is Marcan or preMarcan.

[36]By the calculation of many it would have been Passover. As explained in B,1e above, however, there is inconsistency in 1st-cent. references as to whether the 14th or the 15th was Passover, and for that reason I am avoiding the term.

[37]As I have pointed out, during the Pilate trial Mark 15:6 and Matt 27:15 speak of the custom of releasing one prisoner "at a/the feast." Yet that reference need mean no more than during the eight-

manifesting any consciousness that he needs to offer an explanation, he narrates activities that are extremely difficult to reconcile with this being the feast day. Moreover, he has not modified the conflict with such a feast-day dating for the arrest and crucifixion implicit in the 14:2 reference to the plot of the chief priests and scribes *not* to seize and kill Jesus "on the feast." If Mark had created the paschal dating for the meal, one would have expected him to have thought through the implications and have brought about greater consistency in the narrative. It seems more likely that Mark has taken over an understanding of the supper as a paschal meal and not attempted to change the basic narrative of the passion in the light of it—and this (perhaps consciously) because he thought of the paschal characterization of the meal as liturgical theology and not as history.[38] In my judgment, then, although Christians began early to think of the Last Supper as a paschal meal, that picture does not give us historical information that Jesus died on the 15th of Nisan; and indeed I suspect Mark recognized that. Therefore, despite all the ink poured out on the subject, in chronological discussions we should treat with extreme caution (and perhaps give up) the so-called Synoptic dating of the crucifixion on the 15th of Nisan (a dating which, in fact, those Gospels never apply to anything more than the Last Supper[39]).

In John 1:29 (1:36) the theological insight of Jesus as the paschal lamb finds direct expression when John the Baptist hails him as "the Lamb of God who takes away the sin of the world."[40] The Gospel never spells out how Jesus the lamb takes away the world's sin; but I John (which often recalls old Johannine traditions) in related passages (1:7; 2:2) says: "The blood of Jesus, His Son, cleanses us from all sin" and "He himself is an atonement for our sins, and not only for our sins but also for the whole world." This indication that by his death the Lamb of God is effective against the world's sin finds reinforcement in the frequent incidence of paschal-lamb imagery

---

day festal period of Passover/Unleavened Bread, and certainly does not highlight the day of the trial as the feast day par excellence.

[38]Blank ("Johannespassion" 151–54) appeals to the theory of Schille that Mark reflects the cultic setting of the annual Christian Passover that was the occasion for reciting the PN. Grappe ("Essai" 106–8) sums up efforts to use what is known about the Quartodecimans (n. 18 above) to reconstruct the early Jewish-Christian Passover practice.

[39]The only reference in the Marcan passion context that is not attached to the meal is in 14:1: "But the Passover and the Unleavened Bread was (to be) after two days." As I explained, the "sandwich" nature of the material that follows in 14:1–11 means that without the Passover references preparatory to the coming meal in 14:12–14, we would not be able to tell precisely from Mark the date of the day on which Jesus died (14th or 15th of Nisan). The same may be said of Matt and Luke, which here are very dependent on Mark.

[40]BGJ 1.58–63 points out that "Lamb of God" may be a polyvalent symbol, intended to recall not only the paschal lamb (its most plausible reference) but also the motif of the Suffering Servant going to his death like a sheep led to slaughter (Isa 53:7) and even the apocalyptic lamb. Vocabulary issues are discussed there.

in the Johannine PN. The soldiers do not break the bones of Jesus (John 19:33), thus fulfilling the scriptural description of the paschal lamb, "Its bone shall not be fractured" (19:36: Exod 12:10,46; Num 9:12; p. 1185 above). Hyssop is used to raise the sponge of vinegary wine to Jesus' lips, even as hyssop was used to sprinkle the blood of the paschal lamb on the doorposts of the Israelite homes (Exod 12:22). Probably also, in using "the sixth hour" (the one "hour" calculation common to all four accounts of the death of Jesus) for that moment on the "preparation day for Passover" when Pilate sentenced Jesus to death, John 19:14 is alluding to Jesus as the paschal lamb; for that was when the priests began to slay the lambs on the 14th of Nisan preparatory for the paschal meal on the 15th.[41] In other words, like Mark, John has woven the preGospel insight of Jesus as the paschal lamb into his narrative. Unlike Mark, he has not done this in reference to the Last Supper, for in the Johannine account there is nothing overt that points to it as a paschal meal, and no reference to the eucharistic body and blood of Jesus which might take the place of the missing lamb.[42]

How does this analysis affect our evaluation of John's chronology? We used John's seven passion references to Passover (three in advance and four proximate, as discussed under B2,cd above) to determine that John portrays the Thn/Fd of Jesus' Last Supper, trial, and death as the 14th of Nisan, the eve of Passover. Only one of those (19:14, discussed last in the preceding paragraph), the one that speaks specifically of the "preparation day for Passover," is related to Jesus being portrayed as the paschal lamb, and that is by subtle allusion. Thus the odds do not favor John's having created the chronology to fit that theological insight.

Such an observation, however, is not enough to establish historicity: The chronology of the 14th of Nisan, even if it did not stem from Johannine theological dramatization, could still be the product of imagination and a wrong guess. Yet it is virtually impossible to find a plausible alternative date. We have seen the dubiousness of the 15th of Nisan, and there is no remembrance whatsoever to suggest that the crucifixion might have come later than that. Indeed, as indicated in n. 23 above, the firstfruits ceremony which does come later in the festal period (the 16th or Sunday) was associated with

---

[41]See the discussion on p. 847 above. I pointed out that in portraying Jesus at the feast of Tabernacles, even as here in reference to Passover, John seems to have expected his readers to perceive allusions to the symbolism of the feast that had developed beyond what is spelled out in the OT.

[42]Jeremias, of course, would find implicit Passover references; but see n. 34 above, and the larger issue of the dubious applicability of the mishnaic Passover seder to the 1st cent. Whether, at an earlier period in the development of Johannine Gospel tradition, there was a Passover motif in the Last Supper is related in part to whether one accepts the thesis that the passage about eating the flesh and drinking the blood of Jesus in John 6:51–58 once stood in the chap. 13 context of the supper (see BGJ 1.287–91).

Jesus' resurrection, so that he must have died earlier than that. Nor is there good reason for thinking Jesus died earlier than the 14th. Not only is there no Gospel recollection to that effect, but also no earlier day such as the 13th or 12th was part of the Passover feast or associated with the death of the paschal lamb. If Jesus were put to death on one of those days, why would the earliest preserved recollection about the Last Supper on the night in which Jesus was given over to death (I Cor) have coexisted with a reference to him as our paschal lamb who has been sacrificed? I suppose that one could theorize that if Jesus died in the general ambiance of Passover, Christians might have begun to think of him as the paschal lamb; but the explicit reference to the night in which he was given over is part of a tradition that Paul received and thus takes us back to Christian thought of the very early days.[43] Thus there are solid reasons for judging as historical that Jesus died on Thn/Fd, the 14th of Nisan, the day on which paschal lambs were sacrificed, and the eve of the 15th of Nisan[44] on which the paschal meal would be eaten.

C. THE YEAR

Except for the romantic few who think that Jesus did not die on the cross but woke up in the tomb and ran off to India with Mary Magdalene, most scholars accept the uniform testimony of the Gospels that Jesus died during the Judean prefecture of Pontius Pilate, which is usually dated between AD 26 and 36.[45] How do we narrow down that span? The infancy narratives of Matt and Luke (not models of objective history) indicate that Jesus was born before Herod the Great died—a disputed death date, even if the vast majority accept 4 BC.[46] We do not know how long before that death, but many would appeal to the witness of Matt 2:16 that Herod sought to kill children "two years of age and under" and so opt for Jesus' birth date as about 6 BC. During John's account of the public ministry of Jesus (8:57), "the Jews" say to him, "You are not yet fifty years old"—if one overlooks the hyperbolic tone of that statement and counts from the Matthean and Lucan birth indications, it suggests that Jesus was active publicly before AD 44. Luke 3:23 says

---

[43]I realize, of course, that the pasch(al lamb) reference in I Cor 5:7 is not necessarily as old as the material in I Cor 11:23–25; but they are related, and there is no hint of novelty in Paul's presentation of the paschal-lamb imagery (which is certainly not a development of the mission to the Gentiles), so that we cannot separate them by a long span of time.

[44]Or, as John 19:14 calls it, the "preparation day for Passover."

[45]The evangelists (except Mark) mention the high priesthood of Caiaphas; but that is of no assistance in dating the crucifixion, since Caiaphas was high priest before and after Pilate's prefecture, from 18 to 36/37. Eccentric dating for Jesus' death is supplied by R. Eisler (AD 21) and J. Steward (AD 24).

[46]See BBM 166–67, 607–8, 666–68; also R. E. Brown, *CBQ* 48 (1986), 482–83.

that when Jesus began his ministry he was about 30 years old (thus ca. AD 24?). Luke 3:1–2 has John the Baptist receive the word of God in the 15th year of the reign of Tiberius Caesar; but that dating is not without difficulties. Fitzmyer (*Luke* 1.455) lists five problematic factors in calculating that date, but many would opt for Aug./Sept. AD 28–29. At times Lucan chronological calculation is not accurate (e.g., for the census under Quirinius; see BBM 547–56). Also we do not know how long was the interval between the Baptist's receiving the word and the beginning of Jesus' ministry: several years or a few months? The fact that after twenty verses Luke turns to Jesus has led many calculators to opt for the lower range and start Jesus' ministry in late 28; but this is not totally harmonious with Luke's idea that Jesus was about 30. In John 2:20, when Jesus has cleansed the Temple and predicted the destruction of the sanctuary, the Jewish opponents object that the Temple sanctuary has taken 46 years to build. Josephus (*Ant.* 15.11.1; #380; and *War* 1.21.1; #401) gives two different dates for the start of the rebuilding, namely 23/22 BC and 20/19 BC, to which a 46-year addition would yield AD 24/25 and 27/28 respectively.[47] Even though there are problems about John's placing this Temple-cleansing scene early in the ministry when the Synoptics place it in the very last days of Jesus' life, many scholars accept the latter date as historical and use it to confirm Luke's chronology pointing to the year AD 28 as the commencement of Jesus' public activity.

If Jesus began his ministry about then (and it is a big "if"), how long did that ministry last before he was crucified? The Synoptic Gospels offer no way of calculating the length of the ministry, and from the brevity of the Marcan account one might assume that it lasted a relatively short time. A Passover is mentioned in John 2:13; another in 6:4; and a third in relation to Jesus' death (11:55 etc.). Given John's highly theological concentration on Passover motifs, are those references to an annual feast historical? If the answer is yes, are those three Passovers (which John *mentions* for his own purposes) the only Passovers of the public ministry? If the answer is yes, how long was Jesus active before the first-mentioned Passover? The answer to that might determine whether we are to think of a two-year or a three-year ministry. If we add two or three years to 28/29, depending on which month in those years Jesus began to be active, we emerge with a range between 30 and 33 for the death of Jesus. The uncertainties that I have indicated about every stage of the reasoning make such calculations very unreliable, to say the least;[48] yet they have had their impact. Blinzler (*Prozess* 101–2) has listed

---

[47]Hoehner ("Year" 339) would reckon from the beginning of the rebuilding of the *sanctuary* proper in 18/17 BC and emerges with AD 30—a date that favors crucifixion in 33.

[48]Some would supplement calculations from the Gospels with affirmations by church writers like Tertullian and Clement of Alexandria that Jesus died in the 15th or 16th year of Tiberius. Those

the options of about 100 scholars for the year of Jesus' death: None whom he lists has opted for AD 34 (actually Zeitlin has) or 35, while between one and three respectively have opted for the years 26, 27, 28, 31, 32, and 36.[49] Thirteen opted for AD 29, fifty-three for 30, and twenty-four for 33[50]—thus close to the range just mentioned.

Astronomy has played an important role in narrowing down the possible years for Jesus' crucifixion. If Jesus died on the 14th of Nisan, in which years during Pilate's prefecture did that fall on Thn/Fd? That question is not so easy to answer, even though the mathematical accuracy of ancient astronomy was very respectable. Sighting the new moon was essential for determining Nisan, and one has to calculate when such a sighting would have been possible *in Palestine.* Even then, bad atmospheric conditions could have interfered with the sighting and delayed what should have been the beginning of the month. The Jewish calendar was a lunar calendar, and to keep it in approximate synchronism with the solar year leap months had to be added. JEWJ 37 warns that we have no historical records about the adding of leap months in AD 27–30. And a translation into our months must use the Julian calendar, not the much later Gregorian. It is not surprising, then, that astronomers have emerged with different results; indeed, JEWJ 39–41 gives an extraordinary account of opinions switching back and forth in the period from the 1920s to the 1940s. Having no personal competence, let me report here points of partial agreement between the careful studies of Jeremias (JEWJ 38) and the Oxford scholars Humphreys and Waddington,[51] namely, that the 14th of Nisan:

---

not only are likely to be derivative directly or indirectly from the Gospels, but also are problematic in themselves, especially with respect to how the beginning of Tiberius' reign was being reckoned.

[49]The date of the conversion of Paul, often calculated about AD 36 (on the basis of Gal 1:18–2:1), limits the choice of the upper end of the scale. Obviously Jesus had to have died sometime before that. However, Kokkinos ("Crucifixion") is not intimidated from arguing for Jesus' death in 36, based on the year 33 for the marriage of Herod Antipas to Herodias (which took place before the death of JBap), on 33/34 as the sabbatical year echoed in Luke 4:17–20 as part of Jesus' sermon, and on the birth of Jesus in 12 BC, making him close to fifty years old in AD 36 (John 8:57).

[50]It is useless to list all the names. Among the more famous or knowledgeable authorities who have opted for AD 30 are Benoit, Belser, Brandon, Conzelmann, Dibelius, Flusser, Haenchen, Holtzmann, Jeremias, Leitzmann, Metzger, Olmstead, Schürer, Wikenhauser, and Zahn. Among those who opted for AD 33 are Bacon, Besnier, Hoehner, Husband, Gaechter, Maier, Ogg, Reicke, Renan, and Turner.

[51]"Dating" 744; "Astronomy" 169; the italicized dates are the ones they would regard as most probable astronomically. The study of these two scholars claims to be of particular value because every effort was made to take into account the variables. However, not unlike the medical doctors who studied the death of Jesus (§42, ANALYSIS C), these learned scientists tend to take literally the various Gospel statements without raising the kinds of questions I have posed in the text above. Moreover, they give a great deal of attention to apocalyptic descriptions of the moon appearing like blood when Jesus died (Acts 2:19–20; apocryphal *Report of Pilate [Anaphora],* found in JANT 154), an appearance that Humphreys and Waddington relate to a lunar eclipse on April 3, AD 33— one of the two probable dates for the death of Jesus.

in AD 27 fell on Wn/Thd or with some possibility on *Thn/Fd*
in AD 30   "   " *Thn/Fd* or   " less   "   on Wn/Thd
in AD 33   "   " *Thn/Fd*

If we exclude 27 not only as weak astronomically but also as too early for Jesus' death in the light of almost all the Gospel indications about his life and ministry listed above, that leaves two possibilities for the 14th of Nisan as a Thn/Fd, namely (translated into the Julian calendar), *April 7, 30* or *April 3, 33*.[52] In general there has been a tendency to reject 33 as implying too old a Jesus and too long a ministry, since he would have been almost 40 when he died and have had a public ministry of some 4 years. If he died in 30, he would have been about 36 and have had a ministry of somewhat less than two years. Neither date fulfills every detail in the Gospel evidence about Jesus' birth and ministry; but since many of those details are theologically intended and approximate, I see no problem about either. In some ways the political situation in 33 (after the fall of Sejanus in Rome in Oct. 31) would explain better Pilate's vulnerability to the pressures of the populace,[53] but that is too uncertain an argument to create a preference. I see no possibility of coming to a decision choosing one of the two years.[54]

Bibliography for Appendix II:
Dating the Crucifixion

Writings on this topic are very numerous; and since dating is a tangential issue for my commentary, in this bibliography I have made no attempt at completeness.

Beckwith, R. T., "Cautionary Notes on the Use of Calendars and Astronomy to Determine the Chronology of the Passion," CKC 183–205.

Black, M., "The Arrest and Trial of Jesus and the Date of the Last Supper," in *New Testament Essays,* ed. A.J.B. Higgins (T. W. Manson Memorial; Manchester Univ., 1959), 19–33.

Blinzler, J., "Qumran-Kalendar und Passionschronologie," ZNW 49 (1958), 238–51.

Bokser, B. M., "Was the Last Supper a Passover Seder?" *Bible Review* 3 (2; 1987), 24–33.

[52]For a contrary voice, see Olmstead ("Chronology" 4, 6) who argues that in 33 the 14th of Nisan was not on a Thn/Fd: "The year of crucifixion can be only 30 AD. . . . Friday, April 7, 30 AD is established as firmly as any date in ancient history."

[53]See §31, B1; this thesis is defended by Maier ("Sejanus") and Hoehner ("Year"). Maier cites the earthquake and eclipse reported by Phlegon, and Eusebius' dating the death of Jesus in the 19th year of Tiberius, both of which can be calculated as evidence for AD 33 (p. 1042 above).

[54]It is interesting that in CKC the very assured astronomical reckoning of Humphreys and Waddington ("Astronomy") is followed immediately by the very skeptical article of Beckwith ("Cautionary") that calls into doubt almost every means used to calculate the year of Jesus' death.

Chenderlin, F., "Distributed Observance of the Passover—A Hypothesis," *Biblica* 56 (1975), 369–93; 57 (1976), 1–24.

Davison, A., "The Crucifixion, Burial, and Resurrection of Jesus," *Palestine Exploration Fund* 38 (1906), 124–29.

Dockx, S., "Le 14 Nisan de l'an 30," *Chronologies néotestamentaires et Vie de l'Église primitive* (Paris-Gembloux: Duculot, 1976), 21–29.

Doyle, A. D., "Pilate's Career and the Date of the Crucifixion," JTS 42 (1941), 190–93.

France, R. T., "La chronologie de la semaine sainte," *Hokhma* 9 (1978), 8–16.

Geldenhuys, N., "The Day and Date of the Crucifixion," *Commentary on the Gospel of Luke* (NICOT; Grand Rapids: Eerdmans, 1954), 649–70.

Grappe, C., "Essai sur l'arrière-plan pascal des récits de la dernière nuit de Jésus," RHPR 65 (1985), 105–25.

Heawood, P. J., "The Time of the Last Supper," JQR 42 (1951–52), 37–44.

Hinz, W., "Chronologie des Lebens Jesu," ZDMG 139 (1989), 301–8.

———, "Jesu Sterbedatum," ZDMG 142 (1992), 53–56.

Hoehner, H. W., "The Day of Christ's Crucifixion," BSac 131 (1974), 241–64.

———, "The Year of Christ's Crucifixion," BSac 131 (1974), 332–48.

Humphreys, C. J., and W. G. Waddington, "Astronomy and the Date of the Crucifixion," CKC 165–81.

———, "Dating the Crucifixion," *Nature* 36 (1983), 743–46.

———, "The Jewish Calendar, a Lunar Eclipse and the Date of Christ's Crucifixion," *Tyndale Bulletin* 43 (1992), 331–51.

Jaubert, A., *The Date of the Last Supper* (Staten Island, NY: Alba, 1965). French orig. 1957.

———, "Jésus et le calendrier de Qumrân," NTS 7 (1960–61), 1–30.

Kokkinos, N., "Crucifixion in A.D. 36: The Keystone for Dating the Birth of Jesus," CKC 133–63.

Maier, P. L., "Sejanus, Pilate, and the Date of the Crucifixion," CH 37 (1968), 3–13.

Montefiore, H. W., "When Did Jesus Die?" ExpTim 72 (1960–61), 53–54.

Mulder, H., "John xviii 28 and the Date of the Crucifixion," in *Miscellanea Neotestamentica II,* eds. T. Baarda et al. (NovTSup 48; Leiden: Brill, 1978), 87–105.

Olmstead, A. T., "The Chronology of Jesus' Life," ATR 24 (1942), 1–26.

Ruckstuhl, E., *Chronology of the Last Supper* (New York: Desclée, 1965).

———, "Zur Chronologie der Leidensgeschichte Jesu," *Studien zum Neuen Testament und seiner Umwelt* 10 (1985), 27–61; 11 (1986), 97–129. Reprinted in his *Jesus im Horizont der Evangelien* (Stuttgart: KBW, 1988), 101–84.

Saldarini, A. J., *Jesus and Passover* (New York: Paulist, 1984).

Shepherd, M. H., "Are Both the Synoptics and John Correct about the Date of Jesus' Death?" JBL 80 (1961), 123–32.

Smith, B. D., "The Chronology of the Last Supper," *Westminster Theological Journal* 53 (1991), 29–45.

Stemberger, G., "Pesachhaggada und Abendmahlsberichte des Neuen Testaments," *Kairos* 29 (1987), 147–58.

Story, C.I.K., "The Bearing of Old Testament Terminology on the Johannine Chronology of the Final Passover of Jesus," NovT 31 (1989), 316–24.

Walker, N., "The Dating of the Last Supper," JQR 47 (1956–57), 293–95.

———, "Yet Another Look at the Passion Chronology," NovT 6 (1963), 286–89.

Zeitlin, S., "The Beginning of the Jewish Day during the Second Commonwealth," JQR 36 (1945–46), 403–14.

———, "The Date of the Crucifixion According to the Fourth Gospel," JBL 51 (1932), 263–71.

———, "The Time of the Passover Meal," JQR 42 (1951–52), 45–50.

APPENDIX III: PERTINENT PASSAGES DIFFICULT TO TRANSLATE

Throughout the commentary I have struggled with the normal difficulties of translation and grammar. A few passages or phrases are so difficult, however, that they require extended discussion. To have done that in the respective COMMENTS would have meant lengthy digressions, distracting from the chain of thought. Accordingly I have moved these severe translation difficulties to this APPENDIX. They include:

A. Mark 14:41 (*apechei*)
B. Heb 5:7–8 (*apo tēs eulabeias*)
C. Matt 26:50 (*eph ho parei*)
D. John 19:13 (*ekathisen epi bēmatos*)

A. *Translation of Mark 14:41:* (apechei: p. 208)

The words of Jesus to his sleepy disciples in Mark 14:41 contain a number of short phrases that are difficult to translate because of problems of grammar and idiom. I translated several of these (which are also found in Matt 26:45) as questions: "Do you go on sleeping, then, and taking your rest?" Here I concentrate on the single word that follows in Mark (which Matt omits, probably because he could not understand it): *apechei*. Couchoud ("Notes" 129) says that it "has resisted a battalion of commentators."[1] Indeed, beginning with J.M.S. Baljon (1898) a number of scholars have forthrightly judged *apechei* an "absurd reading" (K. W. Müller, "*Apechei*" 93). The verb *apechein* consists of the preposition "from" and the verb "to have." In papyri dealing with commerce it is used to describe receiving in full an amount that had been owed and giving a receipt (LFAE 110–12): It is thus that one "has from" the payee. Such a meaning is echoed in the refrain of Matt 6:2,5,16: "They [the hypocrites] have *received* their reward [*misthos*]."

---

[1]See in the SECTIONAL BIBLIOGRAPHY (§4, Part 2) articles by Anonymous (= Bornemann), Bernard ("St. Mark xiv"), Boobyer, de Zwaan, Hudson, Müller, Smisson, and Zeydner; also Feldmeier, *Krisis* 209–15.

The verb can also mean "to be distant from, to abstain from, to keep away from."

Translations offered for *apechei* in Mark 14:41 can be divided into those that understand the verb to have a subject which the translator supplies and those that take the verb impersonally. A modifying factor in the theories is how *apechei* relates to what precedes and, more especially, to what follows (v. 41c: "The hour has come; behold the Son of Man is given over into the hands of the sinners"). I shall now list some suggested interpretations without seeking to be exhaustive. The translations illustrating the various proposals are my own (not necessarily those offered by the scholars holding the interpretation), simplified for the sake of comparison.

(1) *Supplied personal subject.* Most supply "Judas" for the unmentioned subject.[2] "Judas is receiving [or has received] the money" (de Zwaan, Smisson). Judas was promised money in Mark 14:11, and his arrival is announced in 14:42 (the next verse here). A variant of this is Boobyer's suggestion: "Judas is taking possession of me." Another variant is that of Anonymous (Bornemann): "Judas is far away." Euthymius Zigabenus (*In Matt.* 26:45; PG 129.685D) offers other subjects: "The devil has got power over me" or "What concerns me [i.e., the Scriptures] has been fulfilled" (cf. Luke 22:37). Dormeyer (*Passion* 132) proposes: "The Father [addressed in 14:36] has received my prayer"—yet we remember that the prayer was for the hour to pass, not to arrive as it does in 14:41c. "God is far away" is proposed by Feldmeier (*Krisis* 212–15). A fundamental question may be asked about all such suggestions that supply subjects: Would the ordinary Marcan reader spontaneously have recognized the proposed subject?

(2) *The reading in Codex Bezae.* Instead of *apechei* followed by *ēlthen hē hōra,* Bezae offers this reading: *apechei to telos kai hē hōra.*[3] While *telos* means "end" and *hōra* means "hour," the meaning of *apechei* with this addition remains unclear. The Latin of Bezae reads *sufficit finis et hora*—see Jerome's rendering of *apechei* as "It is enough" or "It suffices" under (3) below. OL renderings include *consummatus est finis* and *adest finis,* "The end is completed" or "is at hand." BAA 225 assumes Bezae means "Far-off is the end and the hour," which is the exact opposite of what is affirmed about "the hour" in v. 41c in the best Greek mss. Zeydner (*"Apechei"* 440) thinks *telos* can be rendered as an object: "One has received the end." A

---

[2]Anonymous ("Erklärung" 105) observes that Jesus is reluctant to mention Judas' name because of his betrayal.

[3]Variations are found in Codices Washingtonensis and Koridethi, family 13 of minuscules, OL, and OS^sin; see the listing in de Zwaan, "Text" 460. *Hē hōra* comes from the next clause in the best-attested Greek of Mark 14:41: "The hour has come."

translation combining Greek readings (Bezae and Vaticanus) could give: "Is the end far away? Why, the hour has come!" (Hudson "Irony"). Taylor (*Mark* 556), who favors the Bezae reading as a key to the original, offers, "The end is pressing; (and) the hour has come"; but it is hard to justify "is pressing" for *apechei,* without resorting to alternatives mentioned in (5) and (6) below. Others (MTC 114–15) would wisely query whether Bezae represents any more than an ancient guess at what *apechei* meant (influenced by *telos echei* in Luke 22:37), rather than an entrée to the original text of Mark.

(3) *Impersonal renderings.* Let me list some proposals. "Is it far away?" a question answered immediately by "(No), the hour has come." (One gets the same meaning by anticipating *hōra* as subject: "Is the hour far away? It has come.") "It is all over; the hour has come" is offered by Lagrange and Gnilka. Others propose "It is settled" or "It is paid" in reference to Judas' treachery (cf. Boobyer, "*Apechei*" 45). Bauer (BAGD 85), working back from the attested *ouden apechei,* "Nothing hinders," mentions the thesis that *apechei* means "It hinders," i.e., the sleep of the disciples is a hindrance.

Most important is Jerome's Vg rendering: "It is enough."[4] Such a rendering makes good sense, especially after an interrogative or exclamatory interpretation of the preceding verbs: "Are you sleeping and resting? Enough of that." Yet was Jerome giving a translation of *apechei* that he knew was justified by Greek? Or, heavily influenced by the OL, did he find this word puzzling and use *finis* (see [2] above) to craft a meaning that made good sense? Or did he find or substitute another Greek verb that he translated (see [5] below)? The brute fact is that there is practically no evidence in all Greek literature (independent of comments on Mark 14:41) that *apechei* means "It is enough."[5] The lexicon of Hesychius is said to offer *aporchē* or *exarchei* (which mean "enough") as meanings of *apechei;* but this listing is not given in the critical edition of K. Latte, *Hesychii Alexandrini Lexicon* (2 vols.; Copenhagen: Munksgaard, 1953), 1. lines 6103–16. In any case, Hesychius (6th cent.?) was a Christian and might have been influenced by the Vulgate or a ms. tradition of Mark similar to Bezae. We are left, then, with two postNT examples for the proposed "It is enough" meaning of *apechei,*[6] and

[4]This rendering may be found in Augustine and in most later translations: Luther, RSV, NAB, German *Einheitsübersetzung*, etc.

[5]Papyrus Strassbourg 4.19 (6th cent. AD) is sometimes cited, but *apechei* is an erroneous reading there, according to K. W. Müller ("*Apechei*" 85). The reading in the British Museum papyrus 1343.38 (8th cent.) is also dubious.

[6]So F. Field, *Notes on the Translation of the New Testament* (Cambridge Univ., 1899), 39; Müller, "*Apechei*" 84–85.

both of them have problems.[7] The first is in one of the *Anacreonta* (16[15 or 28].33); these are odes of the postclassical period in the style of Anacreon, and this particular ode may stem from the 2d cent. AD. In the context of a man rhapsodizing to a painter who is doing a picture of the man's girl friend, we find *apechei* near the end as the man thinks he is almost seeing the girl in the flesh. While it could mean "It is enough," alternatively it could express the idea that the painter has earned his pay and should stop. The second is in Cyril of Alexandria's commentary on Haggai (2:9; PG 71.1048B), where *apechei* appears in the context of a statement that God has no need for silver and gold. Rather than "It is enough," it could mean that God already has possession of these things. Thus, in both these instances the translation "It is enough" may reflect a preconception (influenced by knowledge of Mark 14:41) that *apechei* can mean that. Such sparsity of evidence calls this translation into doubt and, indeed, raises questions about efforts to translate *apechei* impersonally.[8]

(4) *Textual corruption.* Couchoud ("Notes" 130–31) proposes that the text of Mark 14:41 was originally longer, containing phrases now found in 14:42, e.g., "Behold the one who gives me over has come near." His eye caught by similar words, a scribe wrongly transposed the lines. When the mistake was noticed, the correct reading was put at the bottom of the already copied page, with a note in the margin next to 14:41: *apechei to telos,* "The end (of this line) is farther on." This note got into the text and was mistaken for a statement of Jesus, a mistake compounded when another copyist dropped *to telos* because, thus read, the statement now contradicted "The hour has come." Other brilliant proposals could be listed, but there is no way to establish that such a mistake did indeed occur.

(5) *Mistranslation from Semitic* (on the assumption that the Greek Gospel is a literal translation of an Aramaic or Hebrew original or source). C. C. Torrey,[9] presupposing that *apechei* means "It is enough," suggested that the Greek writer interpreted wrongly Aramaic *kaddu* ("already"), under the influence of the Syriac meaning of that word ("enough"). Black (BAA 225–26), however, argues that in both Aramaic and Syriac *kaddu* means "already" and no such mistake would have been made. Rather, assuming that the Bezae rendering (2 above) is a reliable guide to Mark's Greek and that *apechei* in Bezae means "far off," Black suggests that the Greek writer misread *dhq*

---

[7]I shall leave aside here shrewd emendations proposed by Couchoud ("Notes" 129); he observes that in the first passage *apechō* and in the second *apeche* would be a more sensible reading than *apechei.*

[8]De Zwaan ("Text" 467–68) gives a chart of over fifty papyri uses of *apechein;* they are overwhelmingly in the active mood with the meaning "to have received." Most are in the first person singular; none of those in the third person singular (*apechei*) is impersonal.

[9]*Our Translated Gospels* (New York: Harper, 1936), 56–58.

("to press, urge") as *rhq* ("to be far away"). The Aramaic original of Mark meant: "The end and the hour are pressing." Zeydner (*"Apechei"* 441–42) points to the pa'el of *šlm*, which means both "to finish" and "to pay a debt"; presumably it was misunderstood in the latter sense although it was meant in the former: "It is finished" (see John 19:30). The basic difficulty mentioned at the end of (4) above is aggravated here: Not only are we uncertain of the existence of an underlying Aramaic, but we are uncertain about the Aramaic usage of Jesus' time.

(6) *Substituting other Greek verbs* (on the assumption that *apechei* must stem from scribal misreading because it makes such poor sense). (a) *Epechei* from *epechein*, "to hold fast, stop"; so that the reference was to the end of Jesus' struggling in prayer to have the hour pass. This reading would be facilitated were there an indication of indirect discourse: He said to them (that) he was finished. (b) *Epestē* from *ephistanai*, "to be at hand." A. Pallis[10] thinks that *epestē* was first wrongly read as *apestē*, then as *apechei*. The original would have been a statement "It is at hand," matching "The hour has come" and the arrival of Judas (14:43). (c) *Enestē* from *enistanai*, "to be at hand." This suggestion and the preceding are influenced by the OL *adest finis*.[11] (d) *Arkei* from *arkein*, "to be enough," thought to be the basis for Jerome's *sufficit*. (e) *Etelesthē* from *telein*, "to be concluded," supported by the OL *consummatus est finis*. (f) *Apechei*, not from *apechein*, but as a grammatically justifiable imperfect of *apochein*, "to pour out" (K. W. Müller, *"Apechei"* 95–99). In 14:35 Jesus prayed for the hour to pass; in 14:36 he prayed for the cup (of divine wrath) to be taken away; now he acknowledges in reverse order that he must undergo both: "(God) has poured out (his wrath in the cup); the hour has come."

Such a list of possibilities, no one of them truly convincing, is discouraging until one realizes that the import of most of them is the same. *Apechei* says something that coincides with "the hour has come; behold the Son of Man is given over into the hands of the sinners." That is true for readings such as "Judas has received the money"; "The end is pressing/has been completed"; "It is settled"; "It is enough"; "God has poured out." In my translation I have chosen a well-attested meaning of *apechein*: "The money is paid," which fits in with the promise to pay Judas in 14:11. I have no assurance that this is right, but it does fit in with the immediacy of what follows. The great *peirasmos* has begun for Jesus; the hour has come; he is given over to sinners.

---

[10]*A Few Notes on the Gospels according to St. Mark and St. Matthew* (Liverpool: Booksellers, 1903), 22–24.

[11]De Zwaan ("Text" 464) would argue that even the *epechei* reading in (a) renders *adest*.

B. *Translation of Heb 5:7–8 (p. 227)*

We are told in Heb 5 that Jesus prayed "⁷ . . . to the One having the power
to save him from death, and having been heard from fear, ⁸despite his being
Son, he learned obedience from the things that he suffered." The phrase that
ends v. 7, "from fear" (*apo tēs eulabeias*) is difficult to translate in a way
that does justice to word usage and grammar and still fits into the flow of
thought. *Apo* ("from") is normally used in the meaning range of something
coming away from something else. In this passage many want to translate it
as "on account of, because of" (BDF 210¹), or even "after" (Andriessen).
Eulabeia, related to *lambanein,* has a root meaning of "acceptance," which
in reference to God comes to mean "fear of God, piety, reverence." BAGD
321 insists that in the NT it probably means only "awe"; but Bultmann
(TDNT 2.751–53) points out that in classical literature *eulabeia* slipped over
into "anxiety, anxious fear," which meaning he would assign to the usage in
Heb 12:28.¹² Nevertheless, the fact that *apo* meaning "because of" and *eulabeia* meaning "(anxious) fear" are quite debatable should be kept in mind
when judging the following suggested translations:

- "having been heard because of his (reverential) fear": This requires that one
  understand Jesus' being saved from death as something other than his not
  dying; what follows in v. 8 becomes a modifying comment: Even though he
  was heard, he still had to learn obedience. The Vulgate, Greek Fathers, Luther,
  and most modern translations take this interpretation.
- "having been heard (and delivered) from (anxious) fear": This rendering, held
  by Dibelius, Héring, Manson, etc. (yet firmly rejected by BDF 211), presupposes an ellipsis, but has the advantage of making the following verse a complementary illustration of the human struggle.
- "to save him from [*ek*] death and—having been heard—from (anxious) fear":
  (thus Brandenburger, "Texte" 216): This has the same thrust as the preceding
  interpretation, but has "save" govern *ek* and *apo* clauses almost in apposition.
- "having been heard. Apart from his (reverential) fear and despite his being
  Son, he learned obedience": Two factors that might have spared his having to
  learn from suffering are in apposition; yet then one might have expected: "despite his exhibiting (reverential) fear and his being son. . . ." See Matt 6:7 for
  the absolute use of "heard."
- "death. Having been heard, from [*apo*] anxious fear—despite his being Son—
  from [*apo*] the things that he suffered, he learned": This involves an apposition
  between the two *apo* phrases that in Greek are awkwardly separated.
- "(not) having been heard": Many have accepted Harnack's brilliant but textu-

¹²"Fear of death" in Heb 2:15, clearly meaning anxiety, is an important parallel, even if it uses
phobos.

ally unattested addition of a negative to explain why Jesus had to learn from suffering: His prayer to be saved from death was not heard. This makes Hebrews agree with the Mark/Matt Gethsemane scene.

In my judgment, except for the last suggestion, which is an emendation (always a desperate resort), the basic thrust of the whole is not crucially changed whether "from fear" emphasizes the anxiety of the sufferings of Jesus or, understood as reverence, colors his status as Son.[13]

C. *Translation of Matt 26:50* (eph ho parei: *p. 256)*

Already in §13, n. 22, I listed the many authors who had written articles on this verse, and many of those articles concentrated on this phrase. (The others are on the meaning of *hetairos* that precedes it.) *Parei* from *pareinai* ("to be present"; less likely from *parienai,* "to come here") means "You are here" or "Are you here?" *Ho* is a neuter relative pronoun ("which") and, preceded by the preposition *epi,* would give the basic meaning "unto which, for which." I shall list below some attempts to resolve the ambiguity of a clause that reads literally: "Friend, for which you are here." Occasionally I shall use italics in *my* translations (not necessarily those of the authors cited) to clarify a grammatical point.

(1) The pronoun taken as a relative for which the translator must supply an implied nominal antecedent. From the context of Judas' identifying Jesus by a kiss so that he can be given over to the arresting party we get some of the proposed antecedents: "Friend, (that is a betrayal kiss) for which you are here" or "Friend, for that (betrayal) you are here." The Matthean Jesus already knows what Judas is doing, and so such a statement would be more likely to indicate his knowledge (indicative) than his surprise (exclamatory). As in all suggestions (including those to be mentioned below) where words must be supplied, an obvious difficulty is Matt's failure to give the antecedent he intended. Acts 10:21 illustrates how easily and clearly this could have been done: "What is the reason [*tis hē aitia*] because of which you are here?"

(2) The pronoun taken as a relative in which a demonstrative is hidden (BAGD, p. 585, I 9), meaning "that which" or "what." Under this rubric many would posit an aposiopesis, i.e., a phrase emotionally broken off, either because Judas was kissing him and interfering with his speaking, or because Jesus, overcome, could not continue, "Friend, that for which you are here. . . ." The supposed emotion could be related to the (dubious) thesis

---

[13]For more detail, besides the authors noted at the beginning of §11B, see P. Andriessen and A. Lenglet, *Biblica* 51 (1970), 207–20, esp. 208–12; P. Andriessen, NRT 96 (1974), 282–92.

that "Rabbi" and the kiss were unusual and therefore hypocritical signs of respect and friendship. Perhaps classifiable here would be the *eph ho* value proposed by Lee: "for that purpose, for such an errand"; thus, "Friend, for *that* you are here!"

(3) The same pronominal value as in (2) but with a helping verb supplied by the translator. Klostermann proposes, "Friend, (are you misusing a kiss) for that for which you are here?" The demonstrative relative as the object of a supplied verb often becomes an indirect question, as in a possibility mentioned by Zorell: "Friend, (I know) for what you are here." This type of proposal sometimes becomes elaborate (e.g., Belser): "Friend, (do you think that I do not know) for what you are here?" An ancient example is supplied by a Christian who was put to death under Marcus Aurelius (MACM 28–29): *Egō de eph' ho pareimi* ("Let me do that for which I am here" or, less likely, "I have that for which I am here"). A complicated interpretation of this sort is proposed by Wellhausen in his commentary on Matt: "*Friend,* do you kiss me with the goal *for which* it is evident that *you are here?*" The objection that Matt should have supplied a verb if he meant something like this gathers force when we see how easily Josephus (*War* 2.21.6; #615) did it: "He carried out [*diepratteto*] that for which he was there."

Most often the supplied verb is an imperative, "Friend, (do) that for which you are here." This has the advantage of brevity and brings Matt in harmony with Jesus' words to Judas in John 13:27, "Do [*poiēson*] quickly that which you do."[14] An imperative fits in which the other imperatives in the Matthean context: "Get up; let us go; behold, there has come near the one who gives me over" (26:46). Benoit and the NAB accept the imperative "do" interpretation, and Eltester is close to it with his hortative, "Friend, that for which you are here (let it be done)." One may wonder why Matt, who eight verses before wrote clearly, "Let your will be done [*genēthētō*]," did not use a *genēthētō* here; but Eltester would answer that this is a greeting, and greetings are often elliptic. Somewhat desperate is Blass's suggestion of a textual corruption where the original did not have *hetaire* ("Friend") but either *aire* or *hetaire aire:* "Take that for which you are here."

(4) The relative taken as an interrogative pronoun in a direct question: "Friend, for what are you here?"—a translation favored by the majority of the Church Fathers. An interrogative use of the relative pronoun *hos* is well attested in indirect questions, e.g., John 13:7, "You do not know now what I am doing." But grammarians are not agreed that such a usage is found in

---

[14]We should not be overly impressed that a scribe of the 9th-cent. Irish Latin Codex Armagh moved in this direction: "Amice, *fac* ad quod venisti"—he was probably influenced by the *fac* in John.

a direct question.[15] Reading Matt as a direct question offers a parallel to Luke's *question* addressed by Jesus to Judas (22:48); and we remember that Sir 37:2, which was offered on p. 257 above as plausible background for Matt's use of *hetairos,* is a question. Rehkopf argues strongly for the interrogative, following Deissmann who dismisses the grammarians as overly influenced by classical Greek (and some of the scribes as overly influenced by neo-atticism). For him the question that appears in the OL and Vulg is proof that ancient translators understood Hellenistic Greek to allow such a construction.[16] However, one is never sure when the ancient scribes stopped translating and became creative in dealing with difficult phrases. Moreover, Eltester ("Freund" 73) asks whether one is sure that the Latin reading "Amice ad quod venisti" is a question and not simply a Latin preservation of the ambiguity of the Greek; the Clementine Vulg, after all, seems to have found it necessary to clarify: "Amice, ad *quid* venisti." (Yet the OS[sin] and Origen did read a question.)

Deissmann's favorite argument ("Friend" 493; LFAE 125–31) stems from an inscription consisting of two phrases separated by a space on a drinking vessel: *eph ho parei . . . euphrainou,* which he translates, "For what are you here? Drink!" Since the beaker is rounded, however, one could just as easily read the *euphrainou* before the *eph ho parei:* "Drink! That's what you are here for." Owen, Klostermann, Spiegelberg, J. P. Wilson, and BDF 300 opt for the latter rendering and thus remove the proposed example of a direct interrogative use of the relative. Wilson ("Matthew") compares it to the exclamatory usage in Menander, *Epitrepontes* 363 (Loeb p. 424): "O Heracles, what has been done [to me]."

(5) A set colloquial phrase. Precisely because of the toast on the drinking goblet, BDF 300[2] proposes that there may have been a set phrase *eph ho parei,* "That's what you are here for." We could then understand, "Friend, (as the saying goes), that's what you are here for" to be Jesus' ironic way of letting Judas know that his plan has been seen through. A *Gegengruss* (Eltester), or countergreeting, *hetaire, eph ho parei,* could be offered by Jesus to match Judas' *chaire, rabbi.* More complicated is the proposal of F. W. Danker[17] that *eph ho* is a copyist's error for *eph hō*[18] and that the latter was a set commercial idiom for the contractual basis on which obligations are

---

[15]"Hardly" says BDF 300[2] of Matt 26:50; dubious are Lee ("Matthew xxvi"), Owen, and Zorell; "An unambiguous example of it is yet to be found" says BAGD, p. 584, I 9; an open question says ZAGNT 1.89.

[16]Deissmann, "Friend" 492. The Vulg, read as a question, influenced many translations: Wycliffe, Luther, Tyndale, KJV, RSV.

[17]BAGD 583, 2d col., based on NTS 14 (1967–68), 424–39.

[18]This, with an iota subscript, is a variant in some mss. and in the *Textus Receptus.*

met and something is done. Thus, "That's the deal," or interpreted interrogatively here, "Friend, what deal did you make?"

Despite the obscurities of grammar, the various interpretations cover a narrow range of meaning. No matter what the phrase may have meant in preMatthean tradition (if it existed there), it cannot now serve as a question seeking information—Jesus already knows. Nor is it likely to be a statement of indignation. Either it expresses Jesus' sadness and pain at betrayal (and that may be the thrust of the question in Luke), or it shows with irony or sarcasm that Jesus knows. I think the Matthean context (especially 26:25) favors the latter. I find attractive the suggestion at the beginning of (5) above (for which we have concrete evidence) that this was a set phrase, usually in a context of convivial joy, but now used in the opposite situation. People could encourage others to a drink of companionship, "Friend, rejoice. That's what you are here for." To the irony that Judas comes with a kiss and says, "Hail, Rabbi," Jesus responds with equal irony, "Friend, that's what you are here for."

D. *Translation of John 19:13* (ekathisen epi bēmatos: *p. 844 above*)

These words[19] come near the end of the Roman trial of Jesus when Pilate has failed in several attempts to have Jesus released and when "the Jews" begin to blackmail him with the threat: "If you release this fellow, you are not a friend of Caesar" (19:12). "Now Pilate, having heard these words, led Jesus outside and . . . in/into a/the place called Lithostrotos." Should the Greek words given above in the subsection title which fit into the lacuna be translated *intransitively,* e.g., "and sat down on the judgment seat," or *transitively,* e.g., "and sat him [Jesus] on the judgment seat" (or "on a platform" that served as a place of judgment)? In the COMMENT of §35 I opted for the intransitive translation but kept detailed discussion until here.

The Greek *bēma,* representing the Latin *tribunal,* has two basic meanings pertinent to the present context. It can refer to the *sella curulis* or "judgment seat" on which a Roman judge sat to conduct a trial for a serious crime. Josephus (*War* 2.14.8; #301) mentions the *bēma* that Florus placed in front of the palace where he stayed in Jerusalem; presumably it was on an elevation with steps leading up to it. But through the custom of using the name of the part for the whole, *bēma* can also refer to the platform, usually semi-

---

[19]See the articles in the SECTIONAL BIBLIOGRAPHY (§30, Part 3) by Balagué, Corssen, de la Potterie, Derwacter, Kurfess, O'Rourke, Robert, Roberts, Trebolle Barrera, and Zabala; also Excursus XVII in Blinzler, *Prozess* 346–56; and the various commentaries on John.

circular and made of stone or wood, in the center of which was the judgment seat. What Matt 27:19 means by *bēma* is clear: The message from Pilate's wife comes to him while he is seated on the judgment chair, and one gets the impression that the whole trial was conducted from that chair.[20] A trial was conducted in one of two positions: a *sessio de plano* (off the bench, literally, "on level ground") for lesser crimes or more informal proceedings, and a *sessio pro tribunali* (seated on the judgment chair) for serious crimes; but the judge did not move from one position to the other in the midst of a trial. *If the intransitive meaning is followed* in John 19:13, does Pilate take his seat on the *bēma* only at the end of the trial? Was everything up to this point informal so that the trial begins in 19:13? Of course, John is not acting as a court reporter describing the technicalities; he is writing as a dramatist with the complicated scenario of Pilate moving back and forth, inside and outside the praetorium. He may have included a juridical term to convey the impression that the most solemn and serious moment of the trial had come. In my judgment, to have Pilate simply sit on the platform rather than on the judgment chair does not harmonize with the very careful localization (Lithostrotos, Gabbatha) and timing (at noon before the Passover meal) that John gives to this moment. *If one follows the transitive translation,* wherein Pilate has Jesus sit on the *bēma,* one has a greater possibility for rendering it as "platform."

Among modern scholars the transitive translation with Jesus on the *bēma* began to make inroads with an 1872 dissertation by J. Groenigen at Utrecht and has many followers.[21] Other commentators (with whom I agree)[22] have examined the arguments for the transitive reading and found them wanting. Thus they translate 19:13 intransitively with Pilate on the *bēma* (or primarily intransitively since a few allow a double meaning[23]—yet Johannine double meanings do not normally allow contradictory views). Clearly one is not going to settle this question by counting authorities, so let us turn to the main arguments.

[20]See also the trial of Paul before Festus in Acts 25:6, 17; and Josephus, *War* 2.9.3–4; #172, 175.

[21]E.g., Beutler, Boismard, Bonsirven, F.-M. Braun, Charbonneau, Corssen, de la Potterie, Fenton, Gardner-Smith, Guichou, Haenchen, Harnack, Kurfess, Lightfoot, Loisy, G.H.C. Macgregor, MacRae, Mader, Meeks, O'Rourke, Roberts, and Schwank.

[22]E.g., Balagué, Barrett, W. Bauer, Benoit, Bernard, Blinzler, Bultmann, Bruce, Derwacter, Holtzmann, Hoskyns, Knabenbauer, Lagrange, Lightfoot, A. Richardson, Robert, Zabala, and Zahn.

[23]Some think that John was deliberately ambiguous by way of theological irony, e.g., J. Ashton, *Understanding the Fourth Gospel* (Oxford: Clarendon, 1991), 228, following R. H. Lightfoot. Trebolle Barrera ("Posible") points out that Hebrew *yšb* is intransitive in the *qal* and transitive in the *hiphil,* and that in some coronation scenes (I Kings 8:20; II Kings 4:20) Greek translators were divided as to whether it should be rendered intransitively or transitively. He thinks John was influenced by the possibilities of the Hebrew.

(1) The verb form *ekathisen* can be either transitive (set [something/some-body] on) or intransitive (sat on).[24] In the sentence flow, however, if it were transitive, one would have expected a pronominal object that is lacking here: "He led Jesus outside and set *him* on the *bēma*." De la Potterie has tried to construct an argument that in NT Greek where the second verb has the same object as the first, the object need not be repeated. Blinzler (*Prozess* 347) contends, however, that the examples given by de la Potterie are all ones where no pronoun is needed after the second verb because there is no ambiguity, i.e., the second verb cannot be intransitive. For instance, in Eph 1:20: "(God) having raised Christ from the dead and seated (him) at his right hand," even though no pronominal object is expressed in Greek, the verb must be transitive (seated, not sat) because God cannot sit at His own right hand. Interestingly, some scribes in the Koine tradition still felt it wise to add a pronominal object after the verb of seating in Eph 1:20, perhaps to facilitate public reading. (No scribe ever adds a pronoun in John 19:13, and that may mean that scribes never thought of reading the verb transitively; no Greek Father read it transitively, nor did any one of the main ancient versions.) On the other hand, when a transitive meaning is meant and there could be ambiguity, the object is regularly expressed, e.g., II Kings 11:19; II Chron 23:20; the LXX of Dan 4:37b(34). Balagué ("Y lo" 66), then, would give the opposite rule from de la Potterie: Unless the context is totally clear, when *kathizein* does not have an object expressed, it is always intransitive. It is noteworthy that Josephus uses the same expression as John (*kathizein epi bēmatos*) of Pilate (*War* 2.9.3; #172) and of Vespasian (3.10.10; #532), and in both cases it is intransitive.

(2) The meaning of *bēma*. As I mentioned above, some would see as a major argument against the intransitive meaning the fact that in the middle of a trial a Roman judge would not suddenly take his seat on the judgment chair. I argued, however, that John is writing for dramatic effect and so with this picture of Pilate sitting down, John is saying no more than the most solemn moment had come. In the opposite direction, some who take the scene as history cannot imagine Pilate profaning the sacred symbol of Roman justice, the *sella curulis,* by seating a criminal on it for buffoonery, as supposed in the transitive meaning. Yet supporters of the transitive meaning can also answer that we are not dealing with history but with drama in which, for the sake of irony, John might have chosen to have Jesus the judge seated on a judgment chair. One can question, however, whether Johannine irony would employ the intrinsically implausible to make its point. Feeling

---

[24]Derwacter ("Modern" 27) reports that 47 out of the 50 NT uses of *kathizein* are intransitive, and that all 4 other NT uses with *bēma* are intransitive.

the force of that argument, some supporters of the transitive meaning (de la Potterie, "Jésus" 226–31) argue that the *bēma* on which Jesus was placed was not the judgment chair but the judicial platform or the area in front of the Roman judge. That thesis supposedly receives support from the lack of a definite article before *bēma* in John 19:13. Yet the article is also lacking in the two instances cited above from Josephus where *bēma* does mean judgment chair. There is always the possibility that *kathizein epi bēmatos* (no article) has been influenced by the Latin *sedere pro tribunali* (a language that lacks a definite article). Also by analogy, in the LXX "to sit on the throne" (*kathizein epi* [*tou*] *thronou*) can be used with or without the definite article. If one can draw no argument from the lack of an article in John 19:13, Zabala ("Enigma" 21) is quite correct in arguing against the transitive interpretation that *kathizein epi bēmatos* does not mean "to install as judge."

(3) An argument for the transitive interpretation is drawn by de la Potterie from the phrase that follows *ekathisen epi bēmatos,* namely, *eis topon.* As part of a thesis that he has argued for many years, namely, that in John prepositions are used with precision, de la Potterie presses *eis* to mean "into the place called Lithostrotos" and holds that the whole phrase modifies the first verb "led," not the second verb "sat." The basic idea, then, would be that Pilate led Jesus out into the place called Lithostrotos and sat him on the judicial platform. There are several difficulties with this view. John's precise use of prepositions is dubious (see BGJ 1.5); *eis* ("into") and *en* ("in") are often semantically indistinguishable in the Greek of this period (BDF 205; 207[1]). *Kathizein eis* after a verb of motion like "led" can have the sense of sitting down or resting in a place, as in I Sam 5:11, or be equivalent to "sitting there," as in II Sam 15:29. See also II Thess 2:4 where *eis . . . kathizein* is used for "sit in the Temple of God." In John 19:13 what goes with "led Jesus" is "outside"; the "in [*eis*] a place called Lithostrotos" goes with Pilate sitting on a judgment seat. Robert ("Pilate" 281) argues for *eis* being used pregnantly with *kathizein,* meaning "to go and sit down." O'Rourke ("Two") points out that in a series of verbs, when a phrase follows the second verb, it is usually to be construed with the second verb. Even Meeks, who favors the transitive use of *kathizein,* considers this argument based on a literal sense for *eis* very weak.

(4) The picture of Pilate seating Jesus on the *bēma* is defended as a continuation of the mockery of Jesus in 19:5: The "Look, your king" in 19:14 echoes "Behold the man" in 19:5. One needs to be precise, however. After the mockery of Jesus as king was carried out by soldiers in 19:2–3, the *Ecce homo* of 19:5 may have been more directly intended to show how foolish the charge against him was. As for "Look, your king" in 19:14, the intention was not to mock Jesus but to make "the Jews" take responsibility for execut-

ing their own king. Since the *bēma* is not a throne, mockery of a Jesus seated
on the *bēma* should have been phrased not simply as "Look, your king,"
but "Look, your judge." That observation leads us to discuss an important
argument for the transitive interpretation that some would draw from two
early passages, one in *GPet,* the other in Justin, where Jesus is portrayed as
seated and is mocked as a judge.

GPet 3:7 has as its subject the Jewish people: "And they clothed him with
purple and sat him on a chair of judgment, saying, 'Judge justly, King of
Israel.'" Does this text really support the transitive reading of John 19:13 if
we suppose that the *GPet* author knew or had heard that passage? Notice the
changes and their implications: *GPet* has the Jewish people, not Pilate, as
subject; the clear reference to a chair (*kathedra kriseōs*) means that *bēma*
was not understood as a platform; a context of mockery that is not clear in
John has been effected by adding elements from the mockery of Jesus by
the Roman soldiers found in John 19:2–3; although Jesus is called king, he
is mockingly told to *judge* justly (*dikaiōs;* see Matt 27:19); and, most important, in order to make *kathizein* transitive, a pronominal object (*auton*) is
placed after it—the grammatical element that is notably absent in John.
Thus, this is more a rewriting than an exegesis of John 19:13, fitting the
motif into a new dramatic context, quite different from that in John. As often
in *GPet* what motivates the rewriting is a desire to bring out similarities to
the OT. Here the passage in mind is Isa 58:2, where God complains that the
Israelites act as if they were a righteous nation (which they are not): "They
ask of me just [*dikaios*] judgment." There is no echo of that text in John.

Little needs to be added about the other passage, i.e., Justin, *Apology*
1.35.6. Having cited Isa 58:2, Justin refers to Jesus being crucified by the
Jews who spoke against him and denied he was the Messiah: "And as the
prophet had said, having dragged him along [*diasyrein*], they sat (him) on a/
the *bēma* and said, 'Judge us.'" Justin is close to *GPet* 3:6 that has the Jewish
people say, "Let us drag along [*syrein*] the Son of God now that we have
power over him." Most of the observations made above about *GPet* apply
here. There is no pronominal object following *kathizein;* but this exemplifies
the rule that the object may be omitted when there is no ambiguity: The Jews
as a plurality cannot sit on the *bēma.*

In my judgment, from these two passages a serious argument for the *intransitive* reading of John may be derived. Without the type of changes in
setting and detail they exhibit, one cannot read the phrase about the *bēma*
transitively. In *GPet* and Justin only two parties are involved (the Jews and
Jesus), and in *GPet* after the Jewish people seat Jesus on the chair, they speak
to him. In John 19:13 three parties are involved, Pilate, the Jews, and Jesus.
After Pilate has led Jesus out and the action involving the *bēma* has taken

place, Pilate speaks to the Jews, not to Jesus. If the action were transitive and Pilate had seated Jesus on the *bēma,* the same dynamism seen in *GPet* and Justin should have taken place: Pilate would have spoken to Jesus, not to the Jews, and have challenged him to act as judge. In the commentary I argued that the solemn setting of place and time in John 19:13–14 encourages one to read this as a culminating moment in the trial where Pilate sits on the *sella curulis* to render judgment and a capital sentence. The weakness of the arguments for the transitive interpretation means that there is no cause to change that picture.

APPENDIX IV:
OVERALL VIEW OF JUDAS ISCARIOT

Outline:

A. The Career of Judas
   1. The Existence of Judas
   2. Attempts to Enlarge the Role of Judas
   3. Did Judas Participate in the Eucharist?
   4. What Did Judas Betray?
   5. What Was Judas' Motive for Giving Over Jesus?
   6. How Did Judas Die? (Acts and Matt; Papias)
B. The Name Iscariot
   1. Ways of Writing the Name
   2. Various Explanations
Bibliography

The NT tells us relatively little about Judas; but, as we saw in our commentary on the PN (especially §29), what it reports is highly dramatic. Working with the few details that are given and applying insight and imagination, writers from the beginning to the present have fleshed out the picture. Among major writers on Judas in recent years one may name Haugg, Halas, Gärtner, Vogler, and Klauck. It seems worthwhile, therefore, to devote an appendix to Judas, drawing together material pertinent to this major PN figure and thus going beyond what was germane to the line-by-line commentary.

A. *The Career of Judas*

This Judas is mentioned 22 times in the NT: Mark 3, Matt 5, Luke-Acts 6, John 8. If that listing of NT works is correct chronologically, interest in Judas was progressive. Mark names him among the chosen Twelve in 3:19, but not again after that until Judas begins the process of giving Jesus over in 14:10–11. The later Gospels enhance the picture by reporting details that might be relevant to why he gave Jesus over. Let us now analyze that material and scholarly surmises based on it.

1. THE EXISTENCE OF JUDAS

The name of one of the twelve sons of Jacob-Israel, *Yĕhûdâ* is rendered as *Ioudas* in the LXX. Patriarchal names were popular in NT times, and several figures in the NT bear the name Judas.[1] Thus in itself the name of this man is not suspect. Yet "Judas" is etymologically related to "Jew" (*Yĕhûdî, Ioudaios*);[2] and thus the one who gave Jesus over could be regarded by those hostile to him as the quintessential Jew. Augustine holds that as Peter represents the church, Judas represents the Jews (*Enarratio in Ps 108*. 18,20; CC 40.1593,1596; *Sermon 152*. 10; PL 38.824). As Lapide (*Wer* 11–42, esp. 11–16) documents, this was exploited as antiJewish polemic in dramatic literature and art, e.g., depicting Judas with grossly exaggerated "Semitic" features and generalizing his love for money. In another direction, the fact that the consonants of his name (*Yhwdh*) give in Hebrew the numerical value of thirty may have contributed to Matt's count of thirty pieces of silver. The figurative possibilities of the name have led a number of scholars to the thesis that Judas never existed but was originally a symbolic figure (J. M. Robertson, W. B. Smith, G. Volkmar—see Schläger, "Ungeschichtlichkeit"; Campbell, *Did* 42). Arguments advanced include these: the paucity of NT data concerning him; the contention that Judas' role was primarily parabolic as an admonition to the faithful of the possibility that they might betray Jesus (Plath, "Warum" 181–82); the staged nature of the scenes in which he appears (e.g., Matt 26:21–25 where one after the other the disciples ask "Is it I, Lord?", with Judas coming last); Judas' appearance in a scene in a later Gospel from which he was absent in an earlier Gospel (compare the Bethany anointing in Mark 14:4; Matt 26:8; John 12:4–5); the differing stories about his death; silence about him in Paul, in most of the Apostolic Fathers, in Aristides, and Justin. G. Volkmar suggested that the image of Judas was created from the early Christian experience of being handed over to Roman authorities by the Jews; and Wrede ("Judas" 132) discusses whether this might not be possible. Strauss in the 1864 ed. of his *Leben Jesu* had moved close to a mythical explanation of Judas, and many others (e.g., Wrede, Heitmüller) think large parts of the Judas story are fictional. Enslin ("How") considers the stories of Peter's denials and Judas' betrayal to have been Marcan creations from II Sam 15–17. J. B. Bauer ("Judas") argues that early Christians thought that Judas went away (Acts 1:25: "to

---

[1] Sometimes this is disguised as "Jude" to avoid confusion with Iscariot. One of the "brothers" of Jesus bears the name Judas (Mark 6:3—presumably the author designated in Jude 1:1), as does a disciple whom John 14:22 declares not to have been the Iscariot—presumably the latter is the "Judas of James" in the lists of the Twelve in Luke 6:16; Acts 1:13.

[2] The tribe of Judah was the major component in the Southern Kingdom, an area that became the province of Judea under the Romans.

his own place"), and various stories of his death filled in their ignorance of his fate. John 17:12 is cited as an example that in Christian estimation Jesus had lost him.

Much of the argument for total or almost total nonhistoricity flows from interpreting silence. Is the fabrication of Judas a plausible way to represent what could easily have been stated? The theme of Judas = the Jew is never suggested in the NT. The figure of Judas scarcely helped the Christian image; indeed an opponent like Celsus could point to him as an erroneous choice by the supposedly divine Jesus (Origen, *Contra Celsum* 2.11). The differing Synoptic lists of the Twelve all mention him, and that is surely preGospel tradition. Judas is firmly embedded in both the Synoptic and Johannine PNs. If he were a fictional creation, that would have had to take place within the first decade of Christian tradition! As for the gradually expanding career in the later Gospels, that may well represent imagination filling in the blanks; but it constitutes no argument against the basic historicity of the character.

Another nuance in this discussion concerns Judas' role. For instance, Grayston (*Dying* 395–99) admits that Judas was not invented by Mark and was a member of the Twelve, but by innuendo raises the possibility/likelihood that he played no active role in giving over Jesus to the Jewish authorities. Grayston maintains that the earliest Christian tradition claimed that God had given Jesus over (*paradidonai*) or, in conflict with the Jews, that the Temple hierarchy had given Jesus over. Only in response to internal Christian dangers was Judas given a role in the PN as giving Jesus over to death. I read the evidence about *paradidonai* differently. The range of subjects who are said to have given over Jesus was discussed on pp. 211–13 above. It is perfectly possible that varying circumstances in the preaching caused one subject or the other to be emphasized; but there is no convincing evidence that the language was not polyvalent from the beginning, and that a subject like Judas was created at a later level. Dorn ("Judas") offers an admirably careful discussion of the issue; he points out that although Judas surely existed as one of the Twelve in Jesus' lifetime, there is little likelihood that in the tradition he was included among the Twelve who bore witness to the risen Jesus. Some deed that challenged his discipleship had taken place between the ministry and the resurrection. If Judas were only the first to flee, would that sufficiently account for the unanimous Gospel tradition that he gave Jesus over, for an old tradition that the circle of the Twelve had to be filled out as if Judas' position was definitively vacant, and for the association of Judas' damnable fate with the "Field of Blood"? Thus in my judgment, attention to all the evidence supports the thesis that one of the Twelve named Judas gave Jesus over to the authorities who arranged his death. In the tradition little more than that may have been known about Judas, except that he died a sudden, violent death and that his name was associated in the Jerusalem area with "the Field/Acreage of Blood."

2. ATTEMPTS TO ENLARGE THE ROLE OF JUDAS

If some scholars have minimized Judas to the point of dispensing with him, others have gone in the opposite direction, giving him greater importance than the NT warrants. For instance, the facts that he is called son of Simon (John 6:71), that he is present at the Bethany anointing, as are Martha, Mary, and Lazarus (John 12:2–4), and that Mark 14:3 localizes the Bethany anointing at the house of Simon the leper have led J. A. Sanders (NTS 1 [1954–55], 29–41) to theorize that Judas was the older brother of Martha, Mary, and Lazarus in the Bethany family of Simon the leper—indeed "a masculine Martha gone wrong" (p. 41)! There have been several attempts to identify Judas as the disciple whom Jesus loved in John's Gospel, and Hueter (*Matthew*) thinks Judas may have written that Gospel. A. Wright ("Was Judas") argues that the cardinal number *heis,* used of Judas in the phrase "one of the Twelve,"[3] was colloquial for the ordinal (BDF 247¹), so that Judas was "first of the Twelve." Arguments proposed for supporting Judas' priority include: his position at the Last Supper (John 13:26, close enough to be reached by Jesus); his control of the common purse (John 12:6); and the possibility proposed by Wright that he was a priest, enabling him to enter the Temple as far as the sanctuary into which he threw the silver pieces (Matt 27:5). But why would the Christian community, which did not suppress the memory of Judas' having given Jesus over, suppress the memory of his being first among the Twelve? In fact there is little to support the primacy of Judas. All lists of the Twelve put Simon Peter first; Matt 10:2 uses the ordinal *prōtos* of him, and he plays a far greater role in the Gospels than Judas. Indeed, even John (brother of James) is named more frequently than is Judas (30 times [plus 4 as son of Zebedee] compared to 22). As for holding the purse (if that is factual), nothing in the values proclaimed by Jesus would make

---

[3]Burn ("St. Mark") reports that Wright had distinguished support from F. Field, but that J. F. Isaacson counterargued that in Hellenistic Greek, as opposed to Attic, *ho eis* can mean "one of the" because there are clear instances where the definite article can be indefinite. A. T. Robertson (*Expositor* 8th Ser., 13 [1917], 278–86) rejects the thesis of Wright but correctly observes that *ho heis tōn dōdeka* is the best reading in a passage like Mark 14:10. He accepts H. B. Swete's attempt to do justice to the article, giving the meaning: that one, the only one of the Twelve to go to the chief priests to give Jesus over. J. R. Harris (*Expositor* 8th Ser., 14 [1917], 1–16) does not accept Wright's thesis either—in some early traditions Judas is third or sixth among the Twelve—but has problems with Robertson's view of *ho heis.* Wright (*Expositor* 8th Ser., 14 [1917], 397–400) answers, particularly concentrating on Harris's fanciful attempt to relate Judas Iscariot to Issachar in terms of where either figure is placed among the twelve (tribes or apostles).

that role primary. Finally, following Wright's thesis, if *heis* applied to Judas in John 6:71 means "first of the Twelve," what does it mean when applied to Thomas (John 20:24)?

3. DID JUDAS PARTICIPATE IN THE EUCHARIST?

Besides the scholarly attempts to minimize and maximize the career of Judas, attention has been given to differing presentations in the few scenes in which Judas appears, e.g., the Last Supper. Bornhäuser (*Death* 65–66) would contend that Jesus' indirect way of indicating to the disciples where he would eat the supper (Mark 14:13–15 and par.) reflected his desire to conceal the locale from Judas. Yet Judas was at the supper. Was Judas still there when Jesus distributed his body and blood to his disciples, and did he accept that gift even though he had decided to give Jesus over? (For a survey of the intensive discussion of this, see Halas, *Judas* 104–36.) Those who affirm Judas' participation often point to I Cor 11:27–32, where Paul speaks in strong condemnation of whoever eats the bread or drinks the cup of the Lord unworthily: "That person eats and drinks judgment on himself by not discerning the body. That is why . . . some have died." They would detect in Paul's general admonition a remembrance of Judas who ate unworthily and soon died. No Gospel account specifically describes Judas receiving the bread/body or wine/blood. John does not describe the eucharist at the supper, and so nothing can be made of the morsel given to Judas in John 13:26. Jesus' dipping (food) into the dish with Judas in Mark 14:20; Matt 26:23 is described as quite distinct from the eucharist. In Mark 14:18–21; Matt 26:21–25 Jesus' warning predicting betrayal by Judas (overtly in Matt) *precedes* the words over the bread and wine (Mark 14:22–25; Matt 26:26–29). Neither evangelist describes the departure of Judas from the meal (mentioned only by John 13:30), even though Judas is not among the disciples who go with Jesus to Gethsemane (but arrives later: Mark 14:43; Matt 26:47). One has no way, then, of telling whether in the mind of these two evangelists Judas left after the warning (and before the eucharist) or after the eucharist. Luke's account causes the problem: There Jesus' warning predicting betrayal (by Judas: 22:21–23) *follows* the words over the bread and wine (22:17–20). Surely one would guess that Judas was there for both. Yet Luke never mentions Judas by name during the supper; and his lack of concern with any possible impropriety implied in the sequence just described is apparent from the statement the Lucan Jesus makes to his disciples after the woe on the betrayer in 22:22: "You are the ones who have remained with me in my trials . . . you will sit on thrones judging the twelve tribes of Israel"

(22:28,30). If one is likely to think that Judas received the eucharist and then heard Jesus curse him, did he leave after the curse and before the promise?

There have been the usual attempts to solve the problem by rearranging texts. Hein ("Judas") posits two meals: Judas was at an earlier meal when he decided to give Jesus over, but he was not at the Last Supper and hence did not receive the eucharist. Hein finds evidence for two meals in Ephraem's *Commentary on the Diatessaron* 19.3–4 (SC 121.332–33) and the *Apostolic Constitutions* (5.14.1–6; Funk ed., p. 271), which permit a distinction between the night of the washing of the feet and the night of the eucharist—a distinction that grew up in liturgy, perhaps? Preisker ("Verrat" 152–53) argues that Mark 14:10–11 (Judas going to the chief priests to agree to give Jesus over) is out of chronological order (so also E. Hirsch, Klostermann, Wellhausen), for it originally came at the end of the Last Supper as in John 13:30. The (hypothetical) original Lucan order was 22:25,28–30,21–23,3–6; and thus Judas gave Jesus over after the eucharist. Such rearrangements suppose that scribes, scandalized by finding Judas receiving the eucharist with an already fixed plan to betray Jesus, tried to soften the account. I would judge most of this as unproductive guessing about an issue that may have been very foreign to the evangelists' concern.

4. WHAT DID JUDAS BETRAY?

In my commentary (pp. 211–13 above), I insisted that the verb *paradidonai,* applied to Judas, means "to give over," not "to betray."[4] Judas gave Jesus over by two actions according to the Synoptics: He went before or with the arresting party to show them where and when to seize Jesus (in a remote place on the Mount of Olives late at night); and once there he identified who Jesus was, distinguishing him from others who were there (the disciples). Some scholars have found either or both of these functions illogical and have argued that Judas betrayed Jesus in another way. Let us first consider the contention of illogicality. Would not Jesus' whereabouts and identity have been well known to the authorities or, at least, could they not have had police follow and arrest Jesus without Judas' help? To that objection one can respond by the following: There were masses of people in Jerusalem for the feast, making supervision difficult; Jesus normally did not stay in Jerusalem but outside the walls (Mark 11:11; among friends in John 12:1–2); in the Synoptic accounts this is the first time Jesus has come to Jerusalem and he has not been there long; even in John, where he has been in Jerusalem fre-

---

[4]The classical verb for betraying is *prodidonai.* The only time a word from that stem is applied to Judas in the NT is Luke 6:16 (*prodotēs*). Did the overwhelming preference for *paradidonai* stem from usage in Isa 53:12 [LXX]: "He was given over for our sins."

quently and could have been well known, Jesus has several times eluded arrest and hidden himself (John 7:30,45–46; 8:59; 10:39–40; 11:54). Thus it is not illogical on the level of verisimilitude that the Jewish authorities could use help from Judas as to where and when they might take Jesus without a riot.

As we turn to the theories of those who favor the idea of betrayal, the underlying presumption is that Judas gave the Jewish authorities secret knowledge about Jesus that enabled them to build a case against him. Let me list some sayings or deeds of Jesus that Judas is supposed to have betrayed: that Jesus claimed he would destroy the sanctuary (Goguel); that Jesus claimed to be God's Son (Grundmann) or the Messiah, thus breaking the messianic secret (Bacon, Bornhäuser, A. Schweitzer, Seitz); that Jesus hoped to inaugurate the kingdom of God with or immediately after the Last Supper (Bacon, Preisker; see Mark 14:25; Luke 22:28–30 [Ps 122:5]); that Jesus had let himself be anointed (Bacon; see Mark 14:3,8 [I Sam 16:13]); that Jesus celebrated the Passover at an illegal time or in an illegal way (M. Black); that Jesus had approved the use of the sword (Stein-Schneider; see Luke 22:36–38; Isa 53:12). All these suggestions are speculation, based mostly on motifs that appear directly or indirectly in the Jewish proceedings against Jesus. The fatal objection to all of them, in my judgment, is that were this true, Judas should have appeared as a witness against Jesus to make the charge plausible.

Derrett ("Iscariot," with the announcement that he is approaching the NT with a fresh mind and the correct approach) discusses Judas in light of the *měsîrâ*. The Hebrew and Aramaic root *msr* means "to deliver up"; and as the Jews lived under foreign rule, words from that root were used to describe the giving over of Jews to the *Gentile* rulers. At the end of the 2d cent. AD Mishna *Terumot* 8.12 insists that such behavior is inexcusable under any circumstances. Earlier and more applicable to the NT is the hostility of the Qumran *Temple Scroll* (11Q Miqdaš 64:7–8): "If someone delivers his people to a foreign nation . . . you shall hang him on a tree, and he shall die."[5] How is any of this applicable to Judas? Did he realize, when he gave Jesus over to the Jewish authorities, that he was indirectly giving him over to Pilate? On the level of verisimilitude one would expect that he would know the normal procedure of the Sanhedrin in capital cases. On the other hand, according to Matt 27:3, having seen that the Jewish authorities were

---

[5]In general, however, the root *msr* at Qumran rarely applies to giving a person over, as it does in CD 19:10. It is not clear whether CD 9:1 refers to this same issue: "Everyone who vows another human being to destruction by the laws of the Gentiles shall himself be put to death." Contrast P. Winter, RQ 6 (1967–69), 131–36, and I. Rabinowitz, RQ 6 (1967–69), 433–35.

going to give Jesus over to the Romans, Judas changed his mind with re-morse—almost as if he did not know that this would be the outcome.

It is better to accept the Gospel evidence that the iniquity of Judas was to give over his teacher and friend to the *Jewish* authorities by showing them how they could arrest Jesus without public disturbance. They already knew enough about Jesus to be seriously hostile toward him. The Gospels agree that Judas had turned against Jesus by the time of the Last Supper. When did he begin to incline in that direction? That is uncertain; for, although John 6:70–71 has Jesus refer to Judas as "a devil" in mid-ministry, it is not clear that such a designation means that Judas was already planning to give Jesus over (Zehrer, "Judasproblem" 259).

5. WHAT WAS JUDAS' MOTIVE FOR GIVING OVER JESUS?

Mark gives no indication of why Judas did what he did. The later Gospels mention two factors that might constitute motivation. *First,* in Matt 26:14–15 Judas asks the chief priests, "What will you give me if I give him over to you?" In John 12:4–6, where Judas complains that the ointment used by Mary on Jesus should have been sold for money for the poor, the evangelist gives a clear indication of insincerity: Judas "was a thief; he held the money box and could help himself to what was put in." These two episodes were connected in the medieval *Golden Legend* of Jacob of Voragine: The thirty pieces of silver specified in Matt as the price given by the chief priests were deemed to be Judas' self-reward as a tithe on the 300 denarii that the oint-ment should have been sold for (Mark 14:5; John 12:5). However, we cannot be certain the portrayal of Judas as avaricious is not a later denigration of his character on the principle that one who did such an evil act must have embodied all evil.[6] In itself there is nothing implausible in the idea that Judas was in charge of the money box, despite the argument that Jesus would more likely have given that job to a former tax collector such as Levi/Matthew.

Lüthi ("Problem") thinks that the charge that Judas was a thief hinted at the diabolic, and that leads us to the *second* motivation offered in the Gos-pels. Luke 22:3 introduces the scene in which Judas goes to the authorities by reporting, "Then Satan entered into Judas called Iscariot." Before the Last Supper John 13:2 informs the reader, "The devil had already put into the heart of Judas, son of Simon, the Iscariot, to give Jesus over"; 13:27 stresses

---

[6]Bartnik ("Judas") points to the theologizing of Judas as the archetypal sinner. Klauck (*Judas* 74) wonders whether Judas as thief is not a retrojection of early Christian dislike of possessions (Acts 2:44–45; 4:32–35). In that case, however, one might have expected Luke-Acts to emphasize Judas' avarice. "The wages of his wickedness" in Acts 1:18 is too general to indicate avarice.

that "after the morsel of food, Satan entered into Judas." Thus Luke and John present Judas as the instrument of Satan, the main agent in giving Jesus over (see Billings, "Judas"). For John, Judas gave the Prince of this world entrée into Jesus' inner circle. Further indication of the diabolic is the designation of Judas as "the son of perdition" (John 17:12, a term used by II Thess 2:3 for the antiGod figure) and as a devil (John 6:70). In addition, the idea that Jesus knew Judas "from the beginning" may be related to the judgment that the devil was a murderer "from the beginning" (John 6:64; 8:44). Of course, this is a theological judgment made in retrospect; it does not help to diagnose Judas' personal outlook.

A familiar theme is that what Judas did served the fulfillment of Scripture, as indicated in Mark 14:18–21 and par.; 14:43–45,49 and par.; John 13:18; Matt 27:9. Yet this is even more clearly a theological explanation.

Scholars (as well as novelists and dramatists—see Hughes, "Framing") have not hesitated to make up for the reticence of the NT in proposing motives for Judas' behavior. Zehrer ("Judasproblem" 262) points out that a number of factors have been cited as likely to have scandalized Judas and caused him to reject Jesus: the claim of Jesus to be the Messiah; the more blasphemous claim to be God's Son; Jesus' illegal celebration of the Passover meal at an anticipated date; and his sayings about the Temple. (Zehrer himself rejects these). Using the NT material, Origen, facing Celsus' objection that in choosing Judas the supposedly divine Jesus had made a mistake, argued that Judas had started out as a good disciple; avarice and lack of faith opened the way for the devil (*Commentary on John* 32.14 on 13:18; GCS 10 [Origen 4].448; see S. Laeuchli, CH 22 [1953], 253–68). In the other direction, some (e.g., E. Stauffer) have thought that Judas might have been working with the Sanhedrin for a long time, even if the Gospels portray him as making his decision about the time of the Last Supper.[7] A favorite suggestion is that Judas had grown impatient with Jesus' failure to inaugurate the kingdom, an impatience born from zeal (those who think Judas was an ardent nationalist) or from ambition (those who note the sequence in Luke 22:21–24 where the woe against the betrayer is followed by a dispute as to which of the disciples is the greatest). Yet in regard to that suggestion, Judas plays no role in the several NT passages dealing with kingship for Jesus or ambition among the disciples (e.g., John 6:15; Acts 1:6; Mark 9:33–34; 10:37). Some who think that Judas still believed in Jesus propose that Judas

---

[7]The tendency to see Judas as evil early on accelerated. In the *Arabic Gospel of the Infancy* 35, Judas is possessed by the devil as a child and strikes the boy Jesus. In the influential 13th-cent. *Golden Legend* of the Dominican Jacob of Voragine (Feast of St. Matthew, Feb. 24) there is a prophetic warning to Judas' parents on the night of his conception that this child will be evil; and he is that all through his life, especially when he becomes a friend of Pilate.

gave him over with the expectation that Jesus would now be forced to show his power, overcome the authorities, and inaugurate God's rule (Cox, "Judas" 420–21). As support they invoke Matt 27:3–5, where Judas seems stunned when the authorities are handing Jesus over to Pilate. A particular version of this is advocated by Stein-Schneider ("Recherche" 415–20): Judas, a faithful disciple, hoped to stop a revolt that Jesus' actions had caused, and with money sought to get the chief priests to let him go. Even more idiosyncratic is the thesis of G. Schwarz (*Jesus* 12–31) that Judas was only obeying the orders of Jesus (John 13:27) to give him over to Caiaphas who was known to Judas (the unnamed disciple of John 18:15b). The morsel of bread given to Judas by Jesus at the supper was a gesture of thanks, and Judas' kiss was a gesture of farewell as in Ruth 1:14. (Schwarz's mixture of texts from various Gospels, none of them given the meaning the evangelists intended, is surrounded by his retroversion of segments of the PNs into the original Aramaic!) Others opine that Judas had now lost faith in Jesus and felt it his religious duty to stop this false teacher.[8] Luke 22:6 uses the verb *exomologein* in describing Judas' dealings with the chief priests. Often translated that Judas "consented," the verb can have the connotation of "acknowledge, confess," and so has been understood by some in terms of the priests forcing Judas to confess his complicity in the following of Jesus before they accepted his service.

A group of gnostics developed the strange idea of gratitude toward Judas since he forced the powers of this world to act against Jesus and thus made salvation possible (Ps-Tertullian, *Adv. Omnes Haer.* 2.5; CC 2.1404). Occasionally that idea is invoked more subtly in modern discussions (Lapide, "Verräter" 79), chiefly to remove any thought of attributing blame for the crucifixion. Most Christians went in the opposite direction of portraying Judas as an odious figure. Judas has gone through history a marked man because he was guilty of the innocent blood of Jesus. Besides making him a hated symbol of the Jews,[9] Christians used him to exemplify the evil of those who gave Christians over to Roman persecutors.[10] In the 2d cent. the *Martyrdom of Polycarp* 6.2 judges that those who gave that saint over to the arresting party "should undergo the same punishment as Judas." Although

---

[8]Ps-Tertullian (*Adv. Omnes Haer.* 2.6; CC 2.1404) describes gnostics who thought Judas was trying to unmask Jesus as an evil person. The medieval Jewish legends of the *Toledoth Yeshu* have Rabbi Jehuda ish Bartola (Judas Iscariot) helping the Jewish people to overcome the magic defenses of the wicked Jesus. Judas took Jesus' body from the tomb; and when the lying claim of resurrection was made, Judas refuted it by showing the body.

[9]Notice the combination in a curse from patristic times invoked on anyone who would disturb a grave: Let him have the curse of Judas and of those who say, "Away with him . . . crucify him" (NDIEC 1 [1976] #61, pp. 100–1).

[10]The *Shepherd of Hermas* (*Sim.* 9.19.1–3) states that there is no repentance possible for "those who give over the servants of God." *Hermas* is easier on those who are devoid of faith.

there is no official church teaching that any specific person has gone to hell, that citation agrees with the suggestion in Acts 1:25 ("Judas turned aside to go to his own place") that Judas was condemned.[11] Similarly Irenaeus (*Adv. haer.* 5.33.3–4), after citing an early 2d-cent. fragment from Papias wherein Jesus spoke about the abundance of the last times, says that Judas expressed disbelief and the Lord hinted that he would not be among those to see that abundance.

6. How Did Judas Die? (Acts and Matt; Papias)

In §29, as part of the treatment of Matt 27:3–10, I gave a translation of the reference to Judas' death in Acts 1:16–20,25. From the early 2d cent. Papias supplies still a third account that I shall discuss below. In §29 I compared the Matt and Acts accounts chiefly from the viewpoint of trying to determine an earlier form of the tradition; here we shall be concerned with historicity.

(a) *The Acts Account in Relation to Matt 27:3–10.* As can be imagined, faced with two such different reports of Judas' death as those recounted by Matt and Acts (and perhaps even an independent third account with still further differences), debunkers have had marvelous grist for their mills, as already visible in D. F. Strauss's *Leben Jesu* (1835). Highly respectable conservative scholars (e.g., Benoit) have also been led to recognize that the descriptions of the death of Judas have been filled in from OT examples of the deaths of wicked men. Inevitably, too, there have been learned conservative attempts to defend the historicity of both the Matt and Acts accounts by harmonization or reinterpretation.

In antiquity, already among the copyists of the NT text and among Church Fathers there were attempts, explicit or implicit, to solve the two chief differences between Matt and Acts, i.e., the manner of death (hanging in Matt; falling prone and bursting open in Acts), and the purchase of the field/acreage (by the chief priests after Judas' death in Matt; by Judas himself in Acts). As to the first difference, the idea that Judas did not die when he hanged himself (e.g., the rope broke) and that Acts describes the death that took place later is already implicit in the OL of Acts 1:18: "He bound himself

[11]This would be harmonious with the judgment in Mishna *Sanhedrin* 10.2 that Ahithophel (who turned against David and hanged himself) has no place in the world to come. In the opposite direction Origen's distrust of eternal punishment may be illustrated in his view that Judas' suicide reflected a naked soul confessing and beseeching mercy (*In Matt.* 117 on 27:3; GCS 38.245). Halas (*Judas* 46) points to the *Acts of Andrew and Paul* where, after having given back the money, Judas met Jesus and was sent into the desert for penance; there he met and worshiped the demon (JANT 472).

by the neck; and having been cast down on his face, he broke open in the middle." Similarly the Vulgate reads: "And having been hanged, he snapped in the middle." Such harmonization is still proposed by modern scholars, but often with more nuance. There is harmonization in the theory of Derrett ("Miscellanea") who draws on a reference from many centuries later in *Seder Rabba de Bereshith* 30 to someone in hell having his belly burst and (the bowels) drop out before his face. Derrett pictures a Judas hanging head downward and bursting!

The second difference (the purchase of the land) also continues to be the object of ingenious explanation. Haugg (*Judas* 180) would understand Acts to allow an interpretation in which Judas gave the money and others used it to buy the field. Sigwalt ("Eine andere"), Silva ("Cómo murió"), and Sickenberger ("Judas") in varying degrees fasten on the fact that while Matt 27:7 uses *agorazein* to say that "they bought," Acts 1:18 uses *ktasthai* for what Judas did; and to the latter they attribute a more indirect sense of acquired or having been in the market for. Sickenberger goes further to suggest that if one allows for itacism, the Acts form *ektēsato*, instead of being derived from *ktasthai*, could come from *ktizein* ("to create, make; found"), so that Judas would be described as the founder who made the purchase possible (with reference to this sense of the verb in post-1000 Byzantine inscriptions). In my judgment such harmonization distorts the obvious meaning of the Acts text, written in complete ignorance of the Matt story.

More interesting is the effort (sometimes independent of harmonization) to interpret the four extremely difficult Greek words in Acts 1:18: *prēnēs genomenos elakēsen mesos,* which I translated "laid prostrate, he burst open in the middle." Literally the first words are "become prostrate"; and some would propose "fell prostrate," in part to harmonize with Matt's account of hanging. Among other scholars who want to emend, A. D. Knox ("Death") would read *mesos genomenos elakēsen prēnēs,* "And arriving in the midst of it [the acreage he had bought], he fell headlong." J. W. Cohoon (JBL 65 [1946], 404), arguing that all four Greek words are mistranslations of putative Hebrew originals, emerges with "becoming insane, he hanged himself from a tree" and thus achieves perfect consonance with Matt. On immediately following pages of JBL (405–6) E. J. Goodspeed witheringly refutes this suggestion as the product of uncontrolled imagination and bad grammar.

Most of the serious debate has centered on *prēnēs,* "prostrate, headlong, prone [Latin *pronus*]." In a famous article on *prēnēs* Chase pointed to similar-sounding verbs: *pimprasthai,* "to burn"; *prēthein,* "to swell"; and although *prēnēs* is not attested with a meaning related to those verbs, he argued that it would be a natural formation for "swollen"[12] and that *ginesthai* (*genomenos*) was common with medical terms. Chase's suggestion of translating *prēnēs genomenos* as "having swollen up" gives a much easier reading; it has found its way into BAGD and the Liddell-Scott Greek dictionary as a possibility and been accepted by scholars of the rank of Harnack, Harris, and Nestle. These points have been offered in support: (a) Judas is described as swollen (*prēstheis*) in both citations of the Papias story (see below).[13] (b) In Codex C of the *Gospel of Nicodemus* (*Acts of Pilate* B; JANT 116), after the report that when the cock that Judas' wife was cooking began to crow, Judas "straightaway made a halter of rope and hanged himself," there is a marginal addition that has *elakisen epristhē ebremesen*—the idea is that he burst open after having swollen; and Chase would see *ebremesen* as a confusion from *erragē mesos* "and bestrewed or poured forth from the middle." (c) The punishment of the faithless wife involved a curse that would cause her to have her belly swell up (Num 5:21–22,27).[14] (d) Swelling up is a death that God inflicts on various unworthy people.[15] In evaluation it should be noted that argument (b) is very speculative and (d) is weak, for while many evil figures are smitten in the intestines with intense pains and worms,[16] relatively few are said to swell up. In rejecting Chase's translation, H. J. Cadbury (JBL 45 [1926], 192–93) argues that in no case in Greek medical or nonmedical literature does *prēnēs* mean swollen (also A. D. Knox, Lake).

In my judgment neither translation of Acts 1:18 ("and laid prostrate, he burst open in the middle" or "having swollen up, he burst open in the middle") suggests even remotely that Luke was aware that Judas had hanged himself, as reported in Matt. Many of those who struggle to harmonize these accounts do so on a principle foreign to the Bible itself, i.e., what is narrated must be historical; and so, if there are two differing accounts, they must be able to be harmonized. These two accounts cannot be harmonized; consequently both cannot be historical, and in fact neither may be.

In the ANALYSIS of §29 we saw the extent to which the OT (explicitly cited or implicitly supposed) contributed to Matt's story of Judas' hanging himself, the thirty pieces of silver, and innocent blood. In particular, the im-

---

[12]Desautels ("Mort" 236) claims that the meaning of *prēnēs* depends on whether it is derived from a *pro-* root (fall *forward*) or a *pra-* root (become swollen).

[13]*Prēstheis* is reflected in the Georgian and Armenian versions of Acts.

[14]Also Josephus *Ant.* 3.11.6; #271); see Eb. Nestle, "Fate." More distantly Ps 109:18 would have cursing penetrate the wicked's entrails like water.

[15]In the Ahiqar legend, according to the Syriac version (8:41) "Nadan swelled up like a bag and died." The Arabic version (8:38) and the Armenian have him swell up and burst open. See also the description of the death of the wicked Emperor Galerius by Eusebius (EH 8.16.5). *Acts of Thomas* 33 has the great evil serpent who had tested Eve swell, burst, and die so that poison poured out.

[16]See the list in n. 28 below.

age of Ahithophel (II Sam 15–17), the trusted advisor who tried to give David over to Absalom and who failed and hanged himself, implicitly influenced the Matthean description of Judas' death.[17] In Acts too, Scripture (explicitly cited or implicitly supposed) has shaped the story. In Acts 1:20 two psalm citations (69:26; 109:8) are related to Judas' vacated office (*episkopē*) or place among the Twelve and to the choice of another to take his place. Implicit references have also been detected.[18] Wilcox and Manns think there is a reflection of the tradition preserved in the Targum Neofiti of Gen 44:18 where Judah (= Judas) warns: If Simeon and Levi killed people to avenge the rape of Dinah (see 34:25), a woman who was not numbered among the tribes of the brothers and who had no share in the Promised Land, "how much more for the sake of Benjamin, our brother who is of the *number* of the tribes and who has a *share* [*ḥōleq*] and inheritance in the division of the land." This is seen as related to the description of Judas in Acts 1:17: "He was numbered among us and allotted a share of the ministry."[19] The reference to the killing of a brother is thought to have become intertwined with the story of Cain in Gen 4 where he kills his brother Abel in a field (LXX *pedion,* "plain") and there is emphasis on the blood.[20] The validity of this suggested background depends greatly on the antiquity of the composition of Targum Neofiti that scholars like J. A. Fitzmyer would date to a period considerably after the NT. Also Dupont ("Douzième") has severely challenged Wilcox's approach to Acts 1:15–26.[21]

As for the manner of Judas' death in Acts 1:18, Benoit ("Death" 194) would invoke Wis 4:19 where God punishes the evil: "He shall rend them, [leaving them] speechless and prostrate [*prēneis*]."[22] But he also recognizes the influence of the death of the antiGod figure Antiochus IV Epiphanes in

---

[17]The explicit formula citation from Zech/Jer in Matt 27:9–10 is related to the fate of the money paid for innocent blood and the purchase of the field, but not to how Judas died.

[18]One of these is Ps 16:5–6 (share of inheritance).

[19]Part of the theory is that *ḥōleq* was related to the *ḥăqēl* of *ḥăqēl dĕmāʾ* (Hakeldamach in Acts 1:19).

[20]Some think these texts served as background for the Matt story as well. When God asks Cain about Abel, Cain shows no remorse: "Am I my brother's keeper?" Functionally this resembles the reaction of the chief priests and elders in Matt 27:4: "What is that to us?" Manns ("Midrash" 198) thinks that both Matt's and Acts' accounts of Judas' death were passed on orally in Aramaic, whence the resemblance to the Aramaic of Targum Neofiti.

[21]On 142–44 Dupont shows that most of the vocabulary in the crucial Acts 1:17 is thoroughly Lucan, and that the idea of being allotted a share is thoroughly biblical, so that one need not appeal to Targum Neofiti. E. Richard (CBQ 42 [1980], 330–41) also rejects Wilcox's approach.

[22]Wis 2:13,18 describes the just one mocked as son of God, a parallel to the mockery of Jesus on the cross (Matt 27:43). Betz ("Dichotomized") in a complicated argument invokes Qumran language about the community member who continues his evil ways (1QS 2:16–17): "He will be cut off from the midst of all the sons of light. . . . His allotted portion will be in the midst of the accursed forever." The connection between Acts' *elakēsen mesos* and being "cut off from the midst" is tenuous, however.

II Macc 9:5–10; he too fell, and subsequently his body corrupted. Thus if Matt's Judas dies a death resembling that of the evil traitor Ahithophel, Luke's Judas dies in a manner resembling the demise of another evil figure.[23] Before drawing any conclusions about historicity from this, let us look briefly at a third ancient account of Judas' death.

(b) *The Account Given by Papias.* In the 4th book of the *Logiōn kyriakōn exēgēseis*, written considerably before 150, Papias described the death of Judas; and although the book is no longer extant, the pertinent passage was quoted by Apollinaris of Laodicea (4th cent.). That citation has, in turn, been preserved in catenae or collections of patristic passages on the Scriptures. Lake ("Death" 23) gives the Greek text of two versions of Apollinaris' citation of Papias taken from Cramer's catena published in Oxford in 1844,[24] one from the catena on Matt 27, the other from the catena on Acts 1. It is the Acts catena that is most often translated. There Apollinaris, having stated that Judas did not die by hanging but was taken down and died the death described in Acts 1:18, assures the reader that Papias tells the story more clearly:[25]

Judas lived his career in this world as an enormous example of impiety. He was so swollen in the flesh that where a wagon could pass easily he could not pass. Indeed not even his oversized head alone could do so. His eyelids were so puffed, they say, that he could no longer see the light at all; nor could his eyes be detected even by an optician's instrument, so far had they sunk below the outer surface. His private organ was gross and loathsome to behold in a degree beyond shame. Carried through it from every part of his body, there poured forth together pus and worms, to his shame even as he relieved himself. After so many tortures and punishments, his life, they say, came to a close in his own acreage [*chōrion*]; and this acreage because of the smell has been until now a desert and uninhabited. Indeed, even until this day none can pass by that place without holding the nose with one's hands—so massive was the flow from his flesh and so widespread over the earth.

The catena on Matt 27 has two parts. The second part (less directly attributed to Papias) is almost the same as the catena on Acts just quoted. The first part, attributed directly to Papias, is much briefer.

[23]II Macc was composed in Greek. Acts' accounts of the deaths of Judas and of Herod Agrippa I (12:23: "eaten by worms") would have been understood not only by Greek-speaking Jews but by those who knew Greco-Roman accounts of wicked deaths. See n. 28 below.

[24]See also J. Kürzinger, *Papias von Hierapolis* (Regensburg: Pustet, 1983), 104–5.

[25]While Apollinaris knows of the hanging, nothing in what he quotes suggests that Papias knew.

> Judas lived his career in this world as an enormous example of impiety.
> He was so swollen in the flesh that he could not pass where a wagon could
> easily pass. Having been crushed by a wagon, his entrails poured out.

Harris ("Did Judas") argues for the originality of the longer form, pointing
out that Bar Salibi, independently of Apollinaris, ascribes to Papias details
mentioned in it. Lake ("Death" 25) prefers the short version and thinks that
the longer version arose from piling up horrors from the gruesome deaths of
notoriously evil men.

Is the Papias account (in either form) independent of the account in Matt
and Acts? Certainly there is no sign of dependence on Matt.[26] Parallels with
Luke are somewhat more possible: Judas is *prēstheis* ("swollen") in Papias
and *prēnēs* ("prostrate") in Acts.[27] Yet in Papias Judas is never said to burst
open as he does in Acts. If both write of *chōrion* ("acreage"), the acquisition
of it by Judas is absent from Papias. In Acts 1:25 "his own" modifies "place"
(*topos*), not *chōrion* as in Papias. A closer parallel involves Ps 69:26, cited
explicitly in Acts 1:20 ("Let his habitation become a desert, and let there be
no dweller in it"). It is echoed implicitly in Papias' account near the end of
the long form where Judas' acreage has been until now a desert and uninhabited. Another passage from Ps 69 (69:24) is sometimes thought to have influenced the Papias account: "Let their eyes be darkened so that they cannot
see, and may their loins tremble continually." The second psalm passage
cited in Acts 1:20 is 109:8; and some would find the influence of 109:18 on
Papias: "May cursing soak into his body like water, and like oil into his
bones." I mentioned part of Wis 4:19 in relation to the Acts account ("He
shall rend them, [leaving them] speechless and *prostrate*"); other lines of
that verse have been thought similar to Papias' report in picturing a dishon-
ored corpse and unceasing mockery. These relationships are very tenuous in
my judgment. It is probably best to remain content with saying that the Papias account has been influenced by accounts of the death of evil men in
biblical and perhaps even nonbiblical stories.[28] I would judge (along with

[26]Notice the vocabulary difference between Papias (long form) "until this day" (*mechri* [*tēs*]
sēmeron) and Matt 27:8: "to this day" (*heōs tēs sēmeron*).

[27]The resemblance would be much closer if Chase is right that *prēnēs* can mean "swollen."
Klauck (*Judas* 121) thinks Papias is secondary to Acts.

[28]See Benoit, "Death" 194. The long form of Papias is closer to the full account of the death of
Antiochus Epiphanes in II Macc 9:5–10 (worms, vile stench) than is Acts 1:18. The death of Nadan
in the Arabic form of the Ahiqar legend (8:38) has a much expanded description of the effect of
swelling on the body. Herod Agrippa is struck down and eaten by worms in Acts 12:23. Josephus
(*Ant.* 17.6.5; #168–69) includes in the death of Herod the Great ulceration of the bowels, rotting of
the private organ producing worms, and malodorous breath. Besides going mad, the brutal governor
of Cyrene, Catullus, has his ulcerated bowels fall out (Josephus, *War* 7.11.4; #451–53). According
to Herodotus (*Hist.* 4.205) the cruel Cyrenaean Queen Pheretime has maggots or worms come out
of her body. The same fate befalls Cassander who acts against the family of Alexander (Pausanius,

Hilgenfeld, Lake, Nellessen, Overbeck, Schweizer, van Unnik and others) that the Papias account, even the long form, is probably independent of Acts as well as of Matt.

3. *Summary.* By the 2d. cent. there were three or four different deaths ascribed to Judas: suicide by hanging (Matt); bursting open in the middle (Luke); swelling up and being crushed by a wagon so that his entrails poured forth (Papias, short form); and suffering from a loathsome disease that affected all his organs (Papias, long form). Is any one of them historical? The long form of Papias is clearly legendary. The Lucan account is obscurely brief and may describe what is not possible. Herber ("Mort" 47–49) reports medical studies in France as to whether one can burst open without an external cut.[29] Many countries have the legend of swelling and bursting because evil or the evil spirit is inside. We remember that in Luke 22:3 Satan had entered into Judas; the death in Acts 1:18 may reflect that. As for the short form of Papias, an accident is certainly possible; but the immense swelling is melodramatic. Of course, the debate about which Papias passage is the more ancient affects the value of the passages for history. Matt's suicide by hanging is certainly possible, but the almost exact parallel with Ahithophel affects an evaluative judgment.

Disappointing as it may be, historical probability cannot be assigned to any of the different deaths. I suggested in §29 that early Christians had the tradition that Judas died suddenly, shortly after the death of Jesus. If one can derive probability from the evidence, that note should be applied to the idea that these Christians did not know in detail how Judas had died. The suddenness of the death of Judas persuaded Christians that such a death was a punishment from God, and that persuasion catalyzed narratives evocative of other scriptural deaths that were deemed punishments by God.[30] The common antecedent of the four accounts, then, is not one form of death but the sudden violence of the death that needed interpretation by the Scriptures.

B. *The Name Iscariot*

The Judas who gave Jesus over is often distinguished from others in the NT named Judas or Jude by the designation "Iscariot." What does that designa-

---

Graeca Descriptio 9.7.3–4). The hostile Emperor Galerius is punished with an abscess in his private organ, ulcerated bowels, a multitude of worms, and an intolerable stench (Eusebius, EH 8.16.3–5).

[29]Not really relevant to the Judas issue is Mishna *Sanhedrin* 9.5 where a recalcitrant criminal is force-fed with barley till his belly bursts. TalBab *Shabbat* 151b cites as an example that three days *after death* the belly bursts and the insides come out.

[30]As pointed out in n. 28 there were also Greco-Roman models. The death of the *theomachoi*, the contenders against the gods, was a classical motif. One may compare the words of Jesus about Judas, "It would have been better for that man if he had not been born" (Mark 14:21; Matt 26:24)

tion mean? Does it tell us anything about Judas' background, career, attitudes, or death? Morin ("Deux") gives an interesting history of the many attempts to explain the name, beginning already with Origen (ca. 254: *In Matt.* 78 on 26:14; GCS 38.187) who was reporting what he had heard. Before listing the many proposals, some no more than guesses, let me first note the various ways in which the appellation appears in NT mss.

1. WAYS OF WRITING THE NAME

The designation "Iscariot" for Judas appears 10 times in the NT (Mark 2; Matt 2; Luke 2; John 4),[31] never, however, in the confines of the PN (calculated from Gethsemane to the grave). There are several different ways of writing the name; all of the forms in the list below appear preceded by *Ioudas:*[32]

- *Iskariōth:* Mark 3:19; 14:10; Luke 6:16
- *(ho) Iskariōtēs:* Matt 10:4; 26:14; John 12:4
- *ho kaloumenos Iskariōtēs:* Luke 22:3
- *Simōnos Iskariōtou:* John 6:71; 13:26[33]
- *Simōnos Iskariōtēs:* John 13:2
- *Skariōth:* Codex Bezae and Lat of Mark 3:19
- *Skariotes:* Codex Bezae and Lat of Matt 10:4; 26:14
- *apo Karyōtou:* Codex Bezae of John 12:4
- *Simōnos apo Karyōtou:* Codex Bezae of John 13:2,26; Sinaiticus (original hand), Koridethi, and Family 13 (minuscules) of John 6:71
- *Simōnos Skariōth:* Codex Bezae and OL of John 6:71

From such variations three questions emerge: (a) *Which is more original,* Iskariōth *or* Iskariōtēs? Since *Iskariōth* is closer to Hebrew name style and *Iskariōtēs* closer to Greek style (Klauck, *Judas* 40), the latter may well have resulted from conforming to the Greek gentilic adjectival ending, e.g., *Simōn ho Kananitēs* (in some mss. of Mark 3:18 and Matt 10:4 adjacent to Judas' name), or to a Greek nominal ending for a role or profession, e.g., *stratiōtēs,* "soldier." Yet Arbeitman ("Suffix") points out that Greek words ending in *-tēs,* when taken over into Hebrew/Aramaic, appear with both the endings

---

to Sophocles' statement (reported by Stobaeus, *Florilegium* 121.9): "Not to have existed is better than to suffer great sorrow."

[31]Dibelius ("Judas") thinks this is sufficiently frequent to suggest that the name probably contains a damning judgment.

[32]Not all the minor variants are listed. Helpful with these variants are Halas, *Judas* 8–10; Haugg, *Judas* 72–78; and Torrey, "Name" 51.

[33]Only John gives the name of Judas' father. Mss. differ in these passages on the case ending of *Iskariōt-;* I have offered the best-attested reading.

-*ṭys* and -*ōṭ,* corresponding to the two forms *Iskariōtēs, Iskariōth.*[34] (b) *How important are the variant readings in Codex Bezae* (apo Karyōtou, Skariōth *types)?* Are they reflections of the underlying Semitic designation of Judas, or are they scribal attempts to interpret the Greek *Iskariōth?* The fact that the *apo Karyōtou* readings occur only in John suggests the latter. An interchange between Eb. Nestle and F. H. Chase (ExpTim 9 [1897–98], 140, 189, 240, 285–86) raises the possibility that this interpretation arose with an early translation of John into Syriac (see the Harclean Syriac), and moved from there through a Codex Sinaiticus corrector into Bezae and the Latin evidence—all part of an ancient guess that *Iskariōth* contained a geographic designation. Similarly the *Skariōth/Skariōtēs* readings may be scribal interpretations, but they militate against the geographical understanding of *Iskariōth* as a man from ____, since *'îš* ("man") would not have been dispensed with so easily. (c) *Does the Johannine reading (4th in the list)* Ioudas Simōnos Iskariōtou *indicate that Simon, Judas' father, was called Iscariot?* Dorn ("Judas" 48) answers affirmatively, judging that Iscariot was a family name, derived from the place whence its bearers came (see below). If so, the name tells us nothing about Judas' career. While the two genitives in Greek might favor "Judas, son of Simon Iscariot," Ingholt ("Surname" 154) argues that in the Semitic original an adjective describing the first member of such a series can be put after the second name and possibly attracted to the case of the second name, thus "Judas, son of Simon, the Iscariot." Although that argument in itself is not totally persuasive, such a reading, which is found only in two passages of John, is not an adequate base for dismissing the other evidence that it was Judas who was remembered as the Iscariot.

From these three questions the safest conclusion is that the variations in ms. reporting of the designation are of no great help in discerning its original meaning. While Judas' father's name was probably Simon, the son was known as Iscariot. Forms with *apo* are early scholarly guesses that *Kariōth* designated Judas' place of origin. There is no significant difference between *Iskariōth* and *Iskariōtēs.* At most the forms *Skariōth* and *Skariōtēs* may reflect on the limited value to be given to the first syllable in putative originals (see below).

As we turn to proposed derivations of "Iscariot," the fact that the designation is used throughout accounts of Jesus' ministry may be important. Theories that make the meaning of the name depend on the final moments of the Gospel story (e.g., his giving Jesus over, the way Judas died) have to suppose

---

[34]He contends that the final *â* of a form like *saqqarâ* becomes *ô,* whence the -*ōt(h)* ending in Greek.

that the name was retrojected into earlier descriptions of Judas in the Gospels, including the choice of him as one of the Twelve. Theories that explain the designation "Iscariot" in terms of Judas' origin (family or locale), trade, appearance, outlook, or political allegiance do not have that difficulty—Judas would have had the sobriquet when he was called as a disciple by Jesus.

2. VARIOUS EXPLANATIONS

(a) *Minor Explanations.* For the sake of brevity I list here ancient and modern explanations that had or have limited following and, in my judgment, little likelihood.[35] I associate with them names of scholars who have either mentioned or defended them. Origen mentioned a theory that related "Iscariot" to Judas' being hanged or strangled; much later J. B. Lightfoot also moved in this direction: *'askĕra'* from the root *skr/sgr,* "to stop up." Jerome suggested *zeker Ya,* "memorial of the Lord," which, to be faithful to Origen, could mean remembrance of the way Judas was punished by the Lord in death. The thirty silver pieces have pointed some to the root *śkr* ("hire, pay"). Lightfoot suggested *scortea,* a leather apron worn by couriers over their clothing, with the assumption that Judas' purse which held the common funds (information only in John 12:6) was sewn into it or perhaps was in a box covered with leather. He called attention to a loanword from *scortea* attested in much later talmudic Aramaic *'isqôrĕtîyā'.* Derrett ("Iscariot" 9–10) would derive "Iscariot" from *'isqā' rē'ût,* "one who makes a business [money] out of friendship," a derivation involved with giving Jesus over for silver. The Aramaic noun *'ēseq, 'isqā',* meaning "business," is not attested in any Aramaic before AD 100 (courtesy of J. A. Fitzmyer from his dictionary material). The word offered by Derrett for friendship, *rē'ût,* is Hebrew and not Aramaic. Derrett does not explain how an Aramaic noun (from a later period) in the emphatic state would be in a construct chain with a Hebrew noun. As part of his debatable retroversion of NT Greek into original Aramaic, G. Schwarz (*Jesus* 231) argues that the second part of the Greek for "Iscariot" represents this chain of Semitic development: *qrywt = qryt' = qrt',* and that the *qrt'* in the (postChristian) targums can refer to Jerusalem, so that Judas can be the man from Jerusalem.

A number of suggestions derive "Iscariot" from a proper name: from Issachar (*Yiśśākār;* Jerome); from Jericho (*Yĕriḥô*); from Sychar in Samaria (John 4:5 [see BGJ 1.169]; Schulthess); from Kartah in Zebulun (*Qartâ;* Josh 21:34; H. Ewald). A few of these would need to depend on NT writings

---

[35]Some of the ancient proposals are not defensible from the standpoint of scientific rules governing transcription from Hebrew to Greek.

of "Iscariot" lacking the initial syllable *Is-;* they would also have to reflect an adjectival ending being appended to a proper name.

(b) *Man of Kerioth.* The most popular explanation of "Iscariot" appeals to a putative Hebrew form *'îš Qĕrîyôt,* suggesting that Judas came from a town called Kerioth. The Codex Bezae form *apo Karyōtou* shows that the idea was ancient. Serious objections have been offered: (i) Why was *'îš* transliterated and not translated as "man" or even a relative pronoun, e.g., "Philip the one who was from Bethsaida" in John 12:21? (ii) Was there a town of Kerioth in Judea or Galilee? Most point to Josh 15:25 for a Kerioth in the southern part of Judah (remember Judas = Judah) between En-Gedi and Beersheba; indeed some analyses of Judas and his motives have been based on his being the only Judean among the Twelve. The Hebrew of that verse has *Qĕrîyôt Ḥeṣrôn*—Jerome and the Aramaic targum take these as two towns; but the LXX *hoi poleis Aserōn* understands the first noun as the plural of *qiryâ,* meaning "the cities [or villages] of Hezron." Many modern commentators think the latter is correct; and if so, Kerioth in Judea disappears. A Moabite city named *Qĕrîyôt* is mentioned in the Hebrew of Amos 2:2 (LXX *poleis* again) and of Jer 48:24,41 (LXX 31:24,41: Keriōth). Not many, however, would suggest that Judas came from the Transjordan. In either case, moreover, there is no evidence that cities mentioned from 1,200 to 600 years before were still extant in Judas' time. (iii) The assumption that *'îš* plus a city named X would mean "man of X" is dubious. The normal way to express that in Hebrew would be with a gentilic adjective, e.g., *'îš Qĕrîyôtî,* or "a certain man from" (*'îš ḥad min Qĕrîyôt*). Sometimes defenders of the *'îš Qĕrîyôt* approach point for justification to *'îš Ṭôb* in II Sam 10:6,8, but the expression there means "men of Tob." Another proposed example is problematic chronologically since it is from later Mishnaic Hebrew; Jose b. Joʿezer of Sereda is *'îš Ṣĕrēdâ* (see *Soṭa* 9.9; *'Eduyyot* 8.4; *'Abot* 1.4). Overall the objections make the "man of Kerioth" understanding of Iscariot very dubious.

(c) *Sicarius.* The Greek term *sikarios* appears in Acts 21:38; it is related to Greek *sikarion,* Latin *sica,* "dagger"; Josephus uses it to describe fanatical revolutionaries who used daggers. Celada, Lapide, Schulthess, and Wellhausen are among the many who derive "Iscariot" from a form of this term. Cullmann ("Douzième" 139) thinks that Judas Iscariot (in the Synoptic lists of the Twelve), Judas the *Kananitēs* (a Sahidic variant in John 14:22), and Judas the *Zēlōtēs* (contaminated by Simon the *Zēlōtēs:* Luke 6:15; Acts 1:13) are all the same person. For Cullmann *Sicarius* would be transliterated as *Iskariōth* and translated as *Zēlōtēs,* while transliterated Aramaic from the root *qnʾ,* "to be zealous," would have yielded *Kananitēs.* Many who accept such a derivation appeal to the *Skariōth* and the *Skariōtēs* forms of Judas' name (Codex Bezae and the Latin of Mark 3:19; Matt 10:4; 26:14) for the dispensability of the first syllable of *Iskariōtēs* and for a form closer to *sikarios*. This derivation is harmonious with the guess that a political under-standing of the kingdom made Judas, a revolutionary, impatient with Jesus and brought him to the act of giving over Jesus. Etymologically there are objections: Are we to suppose a metathesis in the first two syllables of the *sikarios* form (*sika-* to *iska-*)? But why, since *sika* could easily have been pronounced? Ingholt ("Surname" 156) would go back to an Aramaic form *'isqaryā'ā'* (or *'iskaryā'ā'* if the Syriac is a guide). From the viewpoint of intelligibility, nothing in the described career of Judas in the NT would en-courage one to think of him as a political revolutionary who would deserve this title. More seriously, the evidence in Josephus (pp. 688–92 above) places the first existence of the *sicarii* and the Zealots in Palestine two or three decades after Judas' death.

(d) *The One Who Gives Him Over.* The root *sgr/skr* in the intensive verbal forms (pi'el, hiph'il) means "to give up or over, surrender to" (= LXX *para-didonai*). Some have pointed to Isa 19:4, "I will give over [*sikkartî*] the Egyptians," suggesting that a form of this verb describing Judas as the one who gave Jesus over was the origin of the name Iscariot. Morin ("Deux" 353) adds the evidence of *sgr/skr* in this sense in the Aramaic Sefire inscrip-tions and in the Qumran *Genesis Apocryphon,* arguing that it is a standard verb for delivering criminals to authorities. In his theory "Iscariot" might be related to an Aramaic pa'el verbal form with an object like "him" (*yĕsaggar/ yĕsakkar yātêh* [which he renders *yŏtêh*]) or to an aph'el form (*yaskar yātêh*). Several objections arise: the *sgr* form is more common than the *skr* form; and while *g* in Semitic can be rendered by a *k* in Greek, a rendering by *g* would be more normal. Moreover, one would have to assume that no NT author recognized that *Iskariōth* rendered the idea of giving Jesus over. Morin struggles manfully to prove that Mark 3:19 (*Ioudan Iskariōth hos kai paredōken auton*) could denote: "Judas Iscariot, that means, 'The one who handed him over.'" But Mark has written a "that means" clause just two verses before: *Boanērges ho estin huioi brontēs* ("Boanerges, that means Sons of Thunder")—that is the normal way to write it and, in my judgment, indicates that 3:19 should be translated according to the face value of the Greek, not as "that means" but as "Judas Iscariot *and it was he* who gave him over." If within thirty years "Iscariot" was not recognized as meaning "gave over," the chances are that it did not originally mean that.

(e) *The Deceiver.* Already in 1861 E. W. Hengstenberg proposed as back-ground *'îš šĕqārîm,* "man of lies," from the root *šqr* ("deceive"). "Lie" would be *šeqer* or *šiqrā';* "liar" would be *šaqqār.* Torrey ("Name" 59–61) advo-cates *šaqray,* "liar," as a basis for "Iscariot," once the word is made definite (*šĕqaryā'* or *'išqaryā'*). Ingholt ("Surname" 157), while not favoring this derivation, thinks it etymologically possible (see also Gärtner, *Iscariot* 7). Yet the Syriac Peshitta did not recognize this root in its transcription of *Iskari-ōth*. In addition to the problem of a derivation that would have been true not of Judas' whole career but only of the end, one may wonder about a sobriquet that had little resemblance to what Judas did—no NT account has Judas lie about Jesus.

(f) *The Ruddy-Colored One.* The root *sqr* is associated with having a brown color or ruddy complexion.[36] Ingholt ("Surname" 158–62) favors this derivation and points to Aramaic forms like *saqray, sĕqārā',* and *'isqārā'.* Palmyrene tesserae have personal names followed by *'sqr'* or *'šqr';* and Arabic has *el Ašqar* meaning "the one with a ruddy complexion." Depictions of Judas in the 9th cent. show him with red hair. In Acts 13:1 one hears of "Symeon called Niger," and so a color appellation is not impossible. Ehrman ("Judas") adds the evidence of TalBab *Giṭṭin* 56a that the head of the *sicarii* or the Judean revolutionary party in AD 70 was Abba Saqqara, nephew of Yohanan ben Zakkai. Arbeitman ("Suffix") backs this derivation suggesting that *saqqārâ* yielded the *Iskar-* in Iscariot. Despite the support for this theory, one must realize that knowing the color of Judas' hair or complexion is not a significant gain.

Almost one hundred years ago G. Dalman (*Words* 52) stated, "It is a very plausible conjecture that 'Iskariōth' was already unintelligible to the evangelist." I doubt that we have moved much beyond that judgment; and if one or two new derivations of "Iscariot" have been advanced since then, even were they true, they would not tell us much about Judas.

Bibliography for Appendix IV:
Judas Iscariot

Bibliography pertinent to the death of Judas in Matt 27:3–10 (sometimes involving comparison with Acts 1:15–26) is found in §25, Part 3.

Arbeitman, Y., "The Suffix of Iscariot," JBL 99 (1980), 122–24.

Bacon, B. W., "What Did Judas Betray?" HibJ 19 (1920–21), 476–93.

Bartnik, C. S., "Judas l'Iscariote, histoire et théologie," *Collectanea Theologica* 58 (1988), 57–69.

Betz, O., "The Dichotomized Servant and the End of Judas Iscariot (Light on the dark passages: Matthew 24,51 and parallels; Acts 1:18)," RevQ 5 (1964–66), 43–58.

Billings, J. S., "Judas Iscariot in the Fourth Gospel," ExpTim 51 (1939–40), 156–57.

---

[36]From the root *sqr* Iscariot has been related to the idea of "the dyer."

Brownson, J., "Neutralizing the Intimate Enemy: The Portrayal of Judas in the Fourth Gospel," SBLSP 1992, 49–60.

Buchheit, G., *Judas Iscarioth: Legende, Geschichte, Deutung* (Gütersloh: Rufer, 1954).

Burn, J. H., "St. Mark xiv.10," ExpTim 28 (1916–17), 378–79 (response to A. Wright on Judas, first of the Twelve).

Chase, F. H., "The Name of Judas Iscariot in the Fourth Gospel," ExpTim 9 (1897–98), 285–86.

———, "On *prēnēs genomenos* in Acts i 18," JTS 13 (1911–12), 278–85, 415.

Cox, W. A., "Judas Iscariot," *The Interpreter* 3 (1906–7), 414–22; 4 (1907–8), 218–19.

Cullmann, O., "Le douzième apôtre," RHPR 42 (1962), 133–40. German in *Oscar Cullmann: Vorträge und Aufsätze 1925–62,* ed. K. Fröhlich (Tübingen: Möhr, 1966), 214–22.

Derrett, J.D.M., "The Iscariot, *Mᵉsira,* and the Redemption," JSNT 8 (1980), 2–23. Reprinted in DSNT 3.161–83.

———, "Miscellanea: a Pauline Pun and Judas' Punishment," ZNW 72 (1981), 131–33. Reprinted in DSNT 4.187–89.

Dorn, K., "Judas Iskariot, einer der Zwölf," in Wagner, *Judas Iskariot,* 39–89.

Dupont, J., "La Destinée de Judas prophétisée par David, Actes 1:16–20," CBQ 23 (1961), 41–51. Reprinted in his *Études sur les Actes des Apôtres* (LD 45; Paris: Cerf, 1967), 309–20.

———, "Le Douzième Apôtre (Actes 1:15–26)," in *The New Testament Age,* ed. W. C. Weinrich (Honor of B. Reicke; 2 vols.; Macon, GA: Mercer, 1984), 1.139–45. Reply to Wilcox, "Judas-Tradition."

Ehrman, A., "Judas Iscariot and Abba Saqqara," JBL 97 (1978), 572–73.

Enslin, M. S., "How the Story Grew: Judas in Fact and Fiction," in *Festschrift to Honor F. Wilbur Gingrich,* eds. E. H. Barth and R. E. Cocroft (Leiden: Brill, 1972), 123–41.

Gärtner, B., *Iscariot* (Facet, Biblical Ser. 29; Philadelphia: Fortress, 1971; German orig. 1957).

Goldschmidt, H. L., and M. Limbeck, *Heilvoller Verrat? Judas im Neuen Testament* (Stuttgart: KBW, 1976).

Halas, R. B., *Judas Iscariot* (CUA Studies in Sacred Theology 96; Washington, D.C.: Catholic Univ., 1946).

Harris, J. R., "St. Luke's Version of the Death of Judas," AJT 18 (1914), 127–31.

Haugg, D., *Judas Iskarioth in den neutestamentlichen Berichten* (Freiburg: Herder, 1930).

Hein, K., "Judas Iscariot: Key to the Last Supper Narratives?" NTS 17 (1970–71), 227–32.

Herber, J., "La mort de Judas," RHR 129 (1945), 47–56 (on Acts 1:18).

Hueter, J. E., *Matthew, Mark, Luke, John . . . Now Judas and His Redemption (In Search of the Real Judas)* (Brookline Village, MA: Branden, 1983).

Hughes, K. T., "Framing Judas," *Semeia* 54 (1991), 223–38.

Ingholt, H., "The Surname of Judas Iscariot," in *Studia orientalia Ioanni Pedersen Septuagenario* (Copenhagen: Munksgaard, 1953), 152–62.

Klauck, H.-J., *Judas—ein Jünger des Herrn* (QD 111; Freiburg: Herder, 1987).

Knox, A. D., "The Death of Judas," JTS 25 (1923–24), 289–90 (on Acts 1:18).

Lapide, P. E., "Verräter oder verraten? Judas in evangelischer und jüdischer Sicht," *Lutherische Monatshefte* 16 (1977), 75–79.

Lüthi, K., *Judas Iskarioth in der Geschichte der Auslegung von der Reformation bis zur Gegenwart* (Zurich: Zwingli, 1955).

———, "Das Problem des Judas Iskariot—neu untersucht," EvT NS 16 (1956), 98–114.

Manns, F., "Un midrash chrétien: le récit de la mort de Judas," RevSR 54 (1980), 197–203.

Menoud, P. H., "Les additions au groupe des douze apôtres, d'après le livre des Actes," RHPR 37 (1957), 71–80.

Morin, J.-A., "Les deux derniers des Douze: Simon le Zélote et Judas Iskariôth," RB 80 (1973), 332–58, esp. 349–58 on Judas.

Nellessen, E., "Tradition und Schrift in der Perikope von der Erwählung des Matthias (Apg 1,15–26)," BZ 19 (1975), 205–18, esp. 207–11 on Judas.

Nestle, Eb., "Another Peculiarity of Codex Bezae," ExpTim 9 (1897–98), 140.

———, "The Fate of the Traitor," ExpTim 23 (1911–12), 331–32, on Acts 1:18. German in ZNW 19 (1919–20), 179–80, with minor updating.

Pfättisch, J. M., "Der Besitzer des Blutackers," BZ 7 (1909), 303–11.

Plath, M., "Warum hat die urchristliche Gemeinde auf die Überlieferung der Judaserzählungen Wert gelegt?" ZNW 17 (1916), 178–88.

Preisker, H., "Der Verrat des Judas und das Abendmahl." ZNW 41 (1942), 151–55.

Roquefort, D., "Judas: une figure de la perversion," ETR 58 (1983), 501–13.

Schick, C., "Aceldama," PEFQS (1892), 283–89.

Schläger, G., "Die Ungeschichtlichkeit des Verräters Judas," ZNW 15 (1914), 50–59.

Schwarz, G., *Jesus und Judas. Aramaistische Untersuchungen zur Jesus-Judas Überlieferung der Evangelien und der Apostelgeschichte* (BWANT 123; Stuttgart: Kohlhammer, 1988).

Sickenberger, J., "Judas als Stifter des Blutackers; Apg. 1,18f.," BZ 18 (1929), 69–71.

Sigwalt, C., "Eine andere Erläuterung von dem 'Besitzer des Blutackers,'" BZ 9 (1911), 399. Reaction to Pfättisch.

Silva, R., "¿Cómo murió Judas, el traidor?" CB 24 (212; 1967), 35–40.

Stein-Schneider, H., "À la recherche du Judas historique," ETR 60 (1985), 403–24.

Torrey, C. C., "The Name 'Iscariot,'" HTR 36 (1943), 51–62.

Vogler, W., *Judas Iskarioth* (Theologische Arbeiten 42; 2d ed.; Berlin: Evangelische Verlag, 1985).

Wagner, H. (ed.), *Judas Iskariot* (Frankfurt: Knecht, 1985).

Wilcox, M., "The Judas-Tradition in Acts 1:15–26," NTS 19 (1972–73), 438–52.

Wrede, W., "Judas Ischarioth in der urchristlichen Ueberlieferung," *Vorträge und Studien* (Tübingen: Mohr, 1907), 127–46.

Wright, A., "Was Judas Iscariot 'The First of the Twelve'?" *The Interpreter* 13 ([Apr 1917] 1916–17), 18[2]–25[2].

Zehrer, F., "Zum Judasproblem," TPQ 121 (1973), 259–64.

APPENDIX V: JEWISH GROUPS AND AUTHORITIES MENTIONED IN THE PASSION NARRATIVES

Outline:

A. Jewish Groups Mentioned in the Passion Narratives
   1. Terms for Such Groups and Their Respective Gospel Usage
   2. Individual Gospel Portrayals
B. Jewish Authorities Described as Hostile to Jesus
   1. High Priest, Chief Priests
   2. Scribes
   3. Elders
   4. Captains of the Temple
   5. Pharisees
   6. Rulers

According to Mark 14:43 there was accompanying Judas and aligned against Jesus "a crowd . . . from the chief priests and the scribes and the elders." Acts 13:27–28 charges that "those who live in Jerusalem and their rulers" asked Pilate to have Jesus killed. While the canonical Gospels allot to Pilate and the Roman soldiers a direct role in the death of Jesus, these two texts and others also attribute a hostile role to a collective Jewish group (crowd, people, nation, Jews, Jerusalemites, sons of Israel) and to specific Jewish authorities (chief priests, scribes, elders, captains of the Temple, Pharisees, rulers). This APPENDIX is intended to give an overall view of the role attributed by the Gospels to the collective group and to the individual authorities.[1]

---

[1]My primary concentration is on what each writer tells us about the hostile groups and figures. Far more complicated is the extent to which these reports are historical. If Mark used written sources, did those sources agree on hostile characters? Did Mark himself have knowledge of these different characters, or was he simply reshuffling what he received from source or tradition? Matt and Luke add to and change Mark's cast of characters. Is that on the basis of independent knowledge or simply a literary reshuffling? What factors contemporary to the evangelists (as distinct from historical factors from Jesus' time) caused them to name, magnify, and/or omit certain hostile characters? Although I do not seek to answer those questions here, in the body of the commentary, where possible, I dealt with them as I treated individual passages.

A. *Jewish Groups Mentioned in the Passion Narratives*

In historical fact, of the four to seven million Jews contemporary with Jesus in the Roman empire, only an infinitesimal percentage would have heard of him during his lifetime. Even of the Jews living in Judea and Galilee in AD 30/33, only a minute percentage would have stood before Pilate's praetorium to demand Jesus' crucifixion or have mocked him on the cross. Factually, then, many NT statements are exaggerated generalizations. For instance, Matt 27:25 has "*all* the people" say, "His blood on us and on our children," while Acts 2:36 urges, "Let *all* the house of Israel know with surety that God has made both Lord and Messiah this same Jesus whom *you* crucified." (In §18F I discussed the issue of antiJudaism in such passages and the malevolence toward Jews they produced in subsequent centuries.) The situation has not been helped by popular preaching that has confusingly fused groups that the Gospels keep separate, e.g., by suggesting that the same Jewish crowd that welcomed Jesus as he entered Jerusalem turned against him on Good Friday. Accordingly it will be a useful exercise to seek precision about the groups of Jews described by the evangelists and the roles attributed to them. Let us begin by listing the terms used by the various Gospels and then study the tone of the usage in each Gospel.

1. TERMS FOR JEWISH GROUPS AND THEIR RESPECTIVE GOSPEL USAGE

There have been important studies of specific collective terms used in the PN (e.g., Crowe and Kodell on *laos,* "people"); but only when we take into account the range of terms used by the various writers do we get the whole picture. I list below terms used to describe Jewish groups active during Jesus' passion, i.e., from the time he left the supper until he was placed in the grave. Although our chief concern is the testimony of the canonical Gospels, I shall add Acts[2] and *GPet.*

- Crowd (*ochlos*):[3] Mark, Matt, Luke, *GPet*
- Nation (*ethnos*): Luke,[4] John

---

[2] Although I am primarily interested in the references to the passion of Jesus in Acts, the parallelism that Acts makes between the hostility to Paul and the hostility to Jesus is worth noting. Via ("According" 137) points out, "Those who oppose Jesus are basically the same as those who oppose Paul." In the latter capacity are the following: "crowd(s)" (7 times); "Gentiles" (*ethnoi* 3); "Jews" (passim); "chief priest(s)" (5); "elders" (3); "rulers" (2); "soldiers" (1); the Sanhedrin (7). In Palestine Paul was tried by two Roman procurators and a Herodian king.

[3] James (*Trial* 1.246–47) distinguishes two meanings of *ochlos:* the populace in general (not necessarily gathered together), and a crowd or concourse of people. He tries to argue that in the sense of populace, the *ochlos* was friendly to Jesus, e.g., Matt 27:15, as compared with Mark 15:8. This is too subtle: Matt means the same as Mark, but has moved the reference to the crowd earlier to create a smoother reading. The crowd is the representative of the populace; that is why Matt 27:25 can refer to the crowd of 27:24 as "all the people."

[4] In Acts 4:25,27 *ethnos* is used in the plural for Gentiles hostile to Jesus.

- People (*laos*): Matt, Luke, Acts,[5] *GPet*
- The Jews: Matt, John, Acts, *GPet*
- Men of Israel, sons of Israel, nation of Israel: Matt, Acts
- Inhabitants of Jerusalem, Daughters of Jerusalem, crowd from Jerusalem: Luke, Acts, *GPet*

2. INDIVIDUAL GOSPEL PORTRAYALS

The above list is helpful in showing that a Jewish group or groups collectively played a major role or roles in the Gospel narratives of the passion. However, a particular term is capable of quite different use, describing in one Gospel a group favorable to Jesus and in another Gospel a group hostile to him, or within the same Gospel describing a group favorable during the ministry in Galilee but hostile during the passion in Jerusalem. Therefore we must study each Gospel individually in its portrayals of a collectivity hostile to Jesus during the passion.

Mark. Before the PN the crowds (*ochlos*) that encounter Jesus are not hostile to him. Even when Jesus comes to Jerusalem the crowd (or every crowd) is astonished by his teaching, hears him gladly, so that the crowd causes fear among the authorities who are seeking to destroy Jesus (11:18,32; 12:12,37). Yet in the PN besides describing the hostile *ochlos* that comes with Judas to arrest Jesus, Mark uses that term three times more in the PN (15:8,11,15) to describe a crowd that becomes increasingly hostile to Jesus as he stands before Pilate. On a surface level of plausibility one may query whether the crowd that comes to arrest Jesus and the crowd that cries out for his crucifixion consist of the same people; but on the narrative level "the crowd" has become one of the actors in the drama, and at the end in Mark it is not friendly to Jesus. To describe a collectivity hostile to Jesus Mark does not use in the PN "the people,"[6] "the nation," or "the Jews."

Matt. In its overall usage of "crowd" Matt is close to Mark. Before the PN crowds are not antagonistic to Jesus. Indeed, as Jesus enters Jerusalem, Matt (21:8–9; no Marcan parallel) shows him greeted enthusiastically by crowds as the Son of David; and, as in Mark, the authorities who want to act against Jesus are hampered by a crowd favorable to him (21:26,46). Yet once the PN begins there appears in the arrest scene a crowd(s) hostile to Jesus, and in the trial before Pilate there are three references to a Jewish crowd(s)

---

[5]Besides attributing to the people a role in the death of Jesus, Acts (6:12) shows the people in Jerusalem hostile to Stephen.

[6]There is one Marcan reference to "the people" after Jesus' arrival in Jerusalem, and that group is favorable to Jesus (14:2).

that opts for Jesus' crucifixion.[7] By the use of other terms the Matthean PN, more strongly than the Marcan, portrays a collective Jewish antagonism toward Jesus; for Matt describes as hostile "all the people"[8] (27:25), "the Jews" (28:15), and "the sons of Israel" (27:9).

Luke. Before the Last Supper the chief priests and (Temple) captains agree to pay Judas money to give Jesus over "without a crowd being present" (Luke 22:6), a passage implying that the crowd might favor Jesus (also 19:3). Of the three appearances of *ochlos* in the Lucan PN, the crowd in the arrest scene with Judas (22:47) is hostile; the crowd addressed by Pilate in 23:4 is not characterized; and in 23:48 "all the crowds who were gathered together" mourn for what was done to Jesus. The "Daughters of Jerusalem" in 23:27 are women who lament for Jesus. But the most important index of Lucan thought about a Jewish collectivity's relation to Jesus is the use of *laos,* "people." Of 141 NT instances, 84 or sixty percent are in Luke/Acts (36 in Luke; 48 in Acts). At the beginning of Luke (1:17) the first angelic annunciation (of the birth of JBap) envisions the making ready for the Lord of a prepared people, and indeed what happens in the Gospel can be described thus: "The Lord God of Israel has visited and redeemed His people" (1:68; see also 2:32). In what precedes the passion, after Jesus has cleansed the Temple precincts and taught there (19:47–48), the effort of the authorities to destroy him was frustrated "because all the people hung on hearing him speak" (also 20:6,19,45; 21:38; 22:2). Grammatically "the people" who appear before Pilate in 23:13 are among the "they" who cry out against Jesus in 23:18; but in 23:35 the people are said to have stood by watching the crucifixion while others mocked Jesus. Thus in the Lucan Gospel taken by itself, one finds little emphasis on a collective group hostile to Jesus.

The evidence of Acts, however, is to the contrary. In Acts 2:22–23 the "men [*andres*] of Israel" are spoken to as those who took part in the crucifixion and killing of Jesus. The people or the men of Israel addressed in Acts 3:12 are said (3:13–15) to have given over Jesus, to have denied him before Pilate, to have asked for a murderer rather than the Holy One, and thus to have killed the author of life. In 4:27 "the peoples of Israel" are described as having gathered together with the Gentiles against Jesus. In Acts 10:39

---

[7] I use "crowd(s)" because of a peculiar Matthean phenomenon. In 26:47 "a numerous crowd [sg.]" arrives to arrest Jesus, but in 26:55 he addresses himself to "the crowds [pl.]." Before Pilate "crowd" is singular in 27:15, plural in 27:20, and singular in 27:24. This variant is simply a way of generalizing; there is no specific difference of meaning or indication of different sources.

[8] The Matthean use of "the people" (*laos*) is more complicated than the Marcan. Although Matt describes at Jerusalem a "people" favorable to Jesus (26:5, parallel to Mark 14:2; see n. 6 above), the frequent designation "the elders of the people" may have the effect of aligning the people with those hostile authorities. At the end of the PN, however, the chief priests and the Pharisees fear that the disciples' preaching of the resurrection might win over "the people" (27:62–64).

"the Jews" are said to have put Jesus to death by hanging him on a tree. Jerusalemites and their rulers are blamed for Jesus' death in 13:27–28. The reader of the whole work Luke-Acts, then, would probably come away with a strong sense that there was a Jewish collectivity very hostile to Jesus.[9]

John. Neither "crowd" nor "people" is used to describe those working against Jesus in the PN. But John 18:35 uses "nation" for those who with the chief priests gave Jesus over to Pilate. The phrase "the Jews" is used at least nine times in the PN to describe those hostile to Jesus and who want his death. The latter usage makes the Johannine picture of collective agency very strong.[10]

GPet. Here the involvement of a Jewish collective group in the crucifixion of Jesus goes beyond the usage of "crowd" (9:34), "people" (hostile to Jesus in 2:5; potentially favorable in 8:28,30; 11:48), and "the Jews" (hostile to Jesus in 1:1; 6:23; 7:25; 12:50,52; favorable in 11:48). There is in *GPet* no hostile Roman involvement in the crucifixion, so that the responsibility is totally Jewish: the Jewish king Herod (1:2; 2:5), the Jewish authorities ("the scribes and Pharisees and elders" in 8:28 [8:31]), and the Jews or Jewish people.

The evidence is unanimous, then, that a collective Jewish group, least tendentiously identified as a crowd, cooperated with the Jewish authorities in the arrest and/or approved the crucifixion of Jesus. That unanimity does not establish without doubt that such hostility by a group of Jewish people toward Jesus is historical, but it does show how hypothetical and without serious evidence is the contention of Maccoby ("Jesus" 55–56) that historically the Jewish crowd was for Jesus and that Christian writers distorted this fact. Rather, it is surprising that granted the Christian tendency to generalize Jewish responsibility, the Gospels have given overall a mixed picture where among the Jewish people present some were for and some were against Jesus—a picture that has considerable plausibility. Moreover, where a crowd or the people are shown against Jesus, most of the time such hostility is not portrayed as spontaneous but as resulting from persuasion by the religious authorities.

[9]Sometimes treatments of the role of the people in the Lucan PN do not take sufficiently into account the statements in Acts and thus exaggerate the positive side of the overall Lucan view. Compare writings by Brawley (*Luke-Acts,* esp. 133ff.), Cassidy ("Trial" 70,173–74), Rau ("Volk"), Rice ("Role"), and Tyson (*Death* 26–47). See pp. 389–90 above on Luke.

[10]Unfortunately the discussion of "the Jews" in John has been sidetracked by Bultmann's dehistoricizing identification of "the Jews" and "the world." Bultmann's approach to John largely ignores the struggles with the synagogue that shaped the Fourth Gospel. (Granskou, "Anti-Judaism," is a particularly unhelpful treatment of "the Jews" in this Bultmann heritage.) By using "the Jews" to refer to those hostile to Jesus, John identifies the synagogue authorities and their followers of the last third of the century (as encountered in the history of the Johannine community) as the heirs of the authorities and populace who were hostile to Jesus in Judea and Galilee during his lifetime.

B. *Jewish Authorities Described as Hostile to Jesus*

In their accounts of the arrest the Gospels mention as opposed to Jesus and as agents of the arrest the chief priests, the scribes, the elders, the captains of the Temple, and the Pharisees. A survey of these and of the frequency with which one encounters them in the different versions of the PN is important for evaluating what we are being told about the primary moving force against Jesus. Nevertheless, this survey must be interpreted with nuance. Because Mark mentions the scribes more than the elders, one might get the impression that the scribes played a greater role than did the elders in having Jesus condemned—and the opposite impression from Matt where the statistics are the reverse. Nevertheless, despite the statistical information that I shall supply, caution is suggested when we realize that the original hearers/readers of the various Gospels would scarcely have been conscious of such statistics and were much more likely to form overall impressions. The fact that the Pharisees are absent from Mark's PN need not mean that Mark's hearers/readers would have thought (or even that Mark would have wished to convey) that the Pharisees had no responsibility for that death. The twelve references to Pharisees in the Marcan account of the public ministry, presenting them as unsympathetic and hostile to Jesus, would probably have carried over and influenced the judgment of the hearers/readers about which Jewish authorities wanted Jesus' death.[11] Therefore, some observations based on careful distinctions may not really be pertinent to what the Gospel meant to those who first received it. Here the conclusion of Kingsbury[12] is very appropriate: "Within the story-world of Mark, the religious authorities—the scribes, Pharisees, Herodians, chief priests, elders, and Sadducees—formed a united front opposed to Jesus and therefore constitute, literary-critically, a single, or collective, character. If Jesus is the protagonist, they are the antagonists." I would ask my readers to keep that very much in mind below, as I introduce precisions.

In what follows the number of "times," given in parentheses after the respective Greek designation of the authorities, does not refer to the total occurrence of those authorities in the Gospels but in the chapters pertaining to the lethal plotting of the authorities against Jesus that directly precedes the Last Supper, the PN itself, and the guard-at-the-tomb story, namely, Mark 14, 15; Matt 26, 27, 28; Luke 22, 23; John 11, 12, 18, 19.[13]

[11]Van Tilborg (*Jewish* 6) argues that Matt did not wish to create any distinction between various groups like the Pharisees and the Sadducees.

[12]"Religious," 63. Kingsbury is very clear (even as I hope I have been in this APPENDIX) that he is not dealing with history but with the impression created by the Gospel storyline.

[13]Notice that this coverage goes beyond what I have been considering as the confines of the PN since it includes presupper plotting.

1. HIGH PRIEST, CHIEF PRIESTS

Archiereus, archiereis (sg. "high priest"; pl. "chief priests": Mark 17 times, Matt 19, Luke 9, John 19—including 4 in John 11:47–53,57). In all the Gospels the chief priests are the most active opponents of Jesus during the PN. None of the Gospels mentions here those who were simple priests.[14] Therefore we must assume that it is not the priestly activity of these opponents that makes them hostile to Jesus, but their role as *chief* priests. There was only one high priest at a time in Judaism, with the incumbent theoretically determined by hereditary descent from Aaron through Zadok. According to Num 35:25 high priesthood was for a lifetime: "until the death of a high priest who has been anointed with sacred oil" (also *IV Macc* 4:1). But now the situation had been complicated for about two hundred years as foreign rulers deposed high priests frequently and replaced them by others who were not necessarily of the same family.[15] Jews seem to have reacted to such changes according to their theological persuasion, with some giving honor to the de jure candidate even after deposition, and others accepting the de facto occupant.[16] TalBab *Yoma* 8b looks back bitterly (and with exaggeration) on this period: "Because money was being paid for the purpose of obtaining the position of high priest, they were changing every twelve months." During the years AD 18–37 (a tenure of exceptional length) and hence at the time of Jesus' death, the high priest was Caiaphas, mentioned in the PN by Matt and John, although John also refers to Annas, the father-in-law of Caiaphas, as high priest. Both these figures have been discussed in detail in the COMMENT of §19. Otherwise in the PN the Gospels have the plural "chief priests," a usage familiar to us from Josephus (*War* 2.12.6; #243; *Life* 38; #193). The Dead Sea Scrolls speak of "head priests" under a chief head priest (1QM 2:1). Among the "chief priests" would have been deposed high priests, along with some members of the priestly families from which the high priest was chosen, and probably some who had been entrusted with

---

[14]That is noteworthy since in John 1:19 priests are hostile to JBap, and in Acts 4:1–3 priests are involved in the arrest of Peter and John.

[15]McLaren (*Power* 202–3) contends that the Romans adopted the practice initiated by Herod, changing the incumbent high priest when it was considered appropriate or expedient. The increased turnover of office-bearers resulted in ex–high priests who were a phenomenon of the 1st cent. AD. "Chief priests" is language of that century.

[16]E. P. Sanders (*Judaism* 322–23) makes some excellent observations about the complexity of attitudes toward the high priest. The secular authority expected him not to let things get out of control and would change incumbents till a satisfactory one was found; yet the high priest had his own interests (and those of his people) and could agitate against the authority to whom he owed his office. The pious wanted the high priest to be on their side; they preferred that he be pious, but he had authority by virtue of his office, even when he championed an unpopular cause and despite a dubious political pedigree and dealings.

special sacerdotal duties.[17] In short, the term designates a Jerusalem priestly aristocracy with positions of privileged power over the Temple and its treasury.

In the Synoptic picture Jesus would have had no encounter with the chief priests in his public ministry until he came to Jerusalem for the first time (Mark 11:1; Matt 21:1; Luke 19:28), so that up to that moment they figure only in the passion predictions (Mark 8:31; 10:33; and par.; see APPENDIX VIII, A2). Jesus irritated them, and they began seeking to destroy him the very day he arrived in Jerusalem (Matt 21:15) or the next day (Mark 11:18) or soon afterward (Luke 19:47). John's picture is more complicated since he has Jesus come to Jerusalem several times, and on some of those occasions the chief priests are described as plotting against him (7:32,45; 11:47–57; 12:10). We are not told all their motives but his public presence and statements in the Temple are mentioned as provoking opposition. Besides the issue of whether Jesus is the Messiah, what the chief priests say about Jesus and Pilate fits well with the apprehensions of a powerful, monied priestly aristocracy, e.g., "We have found this fellow misleading our nation, forbidding the giving of taxes to Caesar" (Luke 23:2); "If we permit him (to go on) thus, all will believe in him, and the Romans will come and take from us both the place [i.e., the Temple] and our nation" (John 11:48). While the chief priests participate in virtually every phase of the PN, we should not forget that they are not shown as acting alone, as Via ("According" 126–33) has pointed out. They worked in and through the Sanhedrin, whence the importance of considering other authorities such as the scribes and elders.

2. SCRIBES

Grammateis (Mark 5, Matt 2, Luke 3, John 0).[18] Since scribes are never mentioned in John, we are dealing with a Synoptic description. We must divide it into a preJerusalem ministry and a Jerusalem ministry. Unlike the chief priests, scribes play a role in Jesus' life before he comes to Jerusalem (Mark 10 times, Matt 10, Luke 6), and in almost half these instances they

---

[17]See HJPAJC 2.232–36; Sanders, *Judaism* 327–29. In my description I have combined two different theories (priestly families or special duties) of who "the chief priests" were; I see no reason for having to choose between them.

[18]Acts uses this plural of *grammateus* three times for hostile Jewish authorities in Jerusalem. J. Jeremias (TDNT 1.741) points out that in treating 1st-cent. situations neither Philo nor Josephus uses *grammateis* in the way in which the Gospels and Acts use it for those learned in the Law (with the exception of the reference to "sacred scribes" in *War* 6.5.3; #291).

are joined to the Pharisees.[19] Indeed, in Mark 2:16 we hear of "the scribes of the Pharisees" (also Acts 23:9), and in Luke 5:30 of "the Pharisees and their scribes." They are portrayed as teachers (Mark 1:22; 9:11) concerned with religious issues; and so they question, usually in an unfriendly manner, the behavior of Jesus or of his disciples (Mark 2:6–7,16; 7:1,5; 9:14). Scribes "from Jerusalem" (3:22) are portrayed as fiercely hostile to Jesus during his ministry in Galilee. Already in the passion predictions (8:31; 10:33) the Marcan Jesus begins to mention the scribes (in Jerusalem) who will have a part in the death of the Son of Man.[20]

In the three Synoptics, almost from the moment of Jesus' arrival in Jerusalem, scribes are associated with the chief priests as opponents of Jesus (Mark 11:18,27; Matt 21:15; Luke 22:2). More than the other evangelists, Matt (chap. 23) makes a connection between these Jerusalem scribes and those encountered in the earlier ministry by having Jesus in Jerusalem utter eight "woes" castigating the scribes *and the Pharisees* (see Luke 20:46). In Mark 14:1 and Luke 22:2 scribes are associated with the chief priests in the plot that will gain Judas' help, and the initial statistics given above show that they continue to be active throughout the PN, especially in Mark. Since in the Synoptic view Sanhedrin meetings consist of chief priests, scribes, and elders, the references to Jerusalem scribes who want Jesus dead presumably envision scribes who were part of the Sanhedrin, whether or not that is specified.

To summarize, then, we find two types of scribes in the Synoptics.[21] There

---

[19]This situation is greatly complicated by the fact that after 70 rabbis who followed Pharisee attitudes toward the oral law were central in the Judaism known to the evangelists, and so in the Gospel descriptions of Jesus' ministry (which had taken place decades earlier) there was a tendency to give Pharisees a similar prominence—sometimes for polemic reasons, sometimes by simple anachronism. Therefore, the precise historical relationship between the scribes and Pharisees in Jesus' time is hard to discern. There is no accord on the outlook of the individual evangelists or how they reached it. Here are some sample theories. A.F.J. Klijn (NovT 3 [1959], 259–67) contends that while scribes are often a separate group in Mark, Matt tends to substitute Pharisees; and Luke omits references to scribes or combines them with Pharisees. Cook (*Mark's*) contends that Mark found in three different sources references to hostile leaders and understood little of them. He shuffled them about in his own account (see n. 1 above); but in fact scribes and Pharisees were identical, so that the scribes described in the PN were Pharisees. Working on a different level of Gospel interpretation, D. Lührmann (ZNW 78 [1987], 169–85) thinks Mark assumed that his readers were informed about the scribes and the Pharisees. Shown mostly in Galilee, the Pharisees argued with Jesus about applications of the oral law; scribes, more prominent in Jerusalem, contested the authority of Jesus in promulgating the kingdom. The latter was the issue that most concerned the Marcan community.

[20]J. C. Weber (JBR 34 [1966], 214–22) thinks that there was no historical continuity between the opponents of Jesus in Galilee and those in Jerusalem.

[21]Scribes are mentioned less in the PN of Matt than in the PNs of Mark and Luke. This may be because the Matthean church had Christian scribes and therefore a positive attitude toward that designation (see Matt 13:52; R. D. Crossan, "Matthew" 176). Cook (*Mark's* 141) maintains that all Luke's references to scribes were taken over from Mark or added under the influence of Mark.

are scribes of Pharisee leaning whom Jesus encounters chiefly in Galilee and whom he puzzles, annoys, and even angers because of his attitude toward what they regard as religious practice fixed by the Law. There are also scribes in Jerusalem who are part of the Sanhedrin; and together with the chief priests they want Jesus dead.[22] (Issues of behavior contrary to the Law that are so prominent in the ministry are not the charges against Jesus in the Jewish proceedings.) Yet I must ask whether Mark's readers would have been expected to notice this distinction. Or were they to think that the scribes who want Jesus dead in the PN were the same as the scribes with Pharisee affiliation encountered earlier? I suspect the latter. In Matt this is even more likely because of the woes delivered in Jerusalem against the scribes and the Pharisees.

3. ELDERS

Presbyteroi (Mark 3 times, Matt 9, Luke 1, John 0).[23] We may leave aside from our discussion *presbyteros* used in several senses; elder in age (Luke 15:25); synagogue authorities who are part of the local scene (Luke 7:3); Christian church authorities patterned on the synagogue authorities (Acts 14:23); and the ancients who are the sources of tradition (Mark 7:3,5). Pertinent to our inquiry, however, is that among those who want Jesus dead in the PN are "elders" or frequently in Matt "elders of the people." (Is this designation precisely to keep them distinct from other elders described above? These elders never appear during the Galilean public ministry of Jesus, and at Jerusalem are mentioned only in the company of the chief priest(s). Indeed in five of the thirteen PN occurrences of "elders" the scribes are also mentioned, so once more we are dealing with the components of the Sanhedrin as conceived by the Synoptics.

The Gospels never explain who the elders were or their particular role in Jerusalem, but the history of *zĕqēnîm* ("elders") in the OT casts light on them. Elders served as town leaders (Judg 8:14), not only in matters of com-

---

[22]D. R. Schwartz, *Studies* 89–101, contends that scribes are representatives of priestly law and competitors of the Pharisees. Could that be true at least of the scribes in Jerusalem? But then the Pharisees would have no voice in the Sanhedrin described by the Synoptics.

[23]Before the PN Luke has three references to *presbyteroi* as Jewish authorities, and Acts has seven more. Yet Gaston ("Anti-Judaism" 141) maintains that Luke's knowledge of "elders" comes only from Mark and was conventionally expanded from there in Acts. Josephus does not use *presbyteroi* for members of the Jerusalem Sanhedrin (G. Bornkamm, TDNT 6.654). One needs to look for synonyms describing those who function as NT "elders," e.g., *hoi prōtoi,* "the first men"; *hoi en telei,* "those in the leading position"; *gnōrismoi,* "notables"; *hoi dynatōtatoi,* "the most powerful/influential"; *hoi episēmoi,* "the eminent/distinguished"; *hoi prouchontes,* "the respected/esteemed." Also *gerousia* for *presbyterion,* "council of elders." (See McLaren, *Power* 204–6 for the Josephus references.) Yet some of these could be the same as *archontes,* "rulers," to be discussed in subsection 6 below.

munity policy but also in administering justice (Ruth 4:2,9,11). There were also "elders of Israel" (II Sam 3:17; 5:3), perhaps representatives drawn from various tribes or regions. At the end of the monarchy we find elders as a powerful group in Jerusalem, e.g., in the meeting that would decide the fate of Jeremiah, when the princes and the people were speaking to the priests and the prophets, "certain of the elders of the land" rose and commented (Jer 26:16–17). A letter of Jeremiah (29:1) to the exiles taken captive by Nebuchadnezzar was addressed, "To those who are left of the elders of the exiles, to the priests and the prophets, and to all the people." Jer 19:1 speaks of "the elders of the people" (a terminology that reappears in Matt 21:23; 26:3,47; see n. 8 above). After the exile the pedigree of those who came back was very important, and the registries of the heads of houses were preserved (Ezra 8:1–14). Then we find in Judea an aristocracy of elders who can be considered as rulers in certain matters, e.g., property is forfeited by order of the officials and the elders in Ezra 10:8. We have seen in §18,B1 that there appear in the documents of this postexilic period references (e.g., I Macc 12:6, II Macc 1:10) to a Gerousia or Senate (respectively reflecting the Greek and Latin words for "old" and hence a body of elders). The high priest's leadership of a Gerousia (eventually known as a Sanhedrin) was facilitated because the nobles who functioned as elders in deliberations were mostly of the Sadducee outlook. Josephus (*Ant.* 18.1.4; #17) tells us that the Sadducees were not numerous, but included in their ranks people of the best standing. In AD 66 Josephus (*War* 2.17.3; #411) shows the men of influence or power [*dynatoi*] deliberating with the chief priests and the most notable Pharisees about the course of action to take with Rome. These would be similar to "the elders" who appear in the Synoptic PN, following the initiative of the priests against Jesus. The elders were a nonpriestly aristocracy, a nobility by heredity and wealth, who were consulted on important matters affecting the people. Perhaps Joseph from Arimathea was one of them. It is difficult to discern why Matt mentions them more frequently than the other Gospels in the PN, and sometimes in place of Mark's scribes.[24]

Before we pass on to another group of authorities, it may be worth noting that the triad of chief priests, elders, and scribes (that is the order of precedence) is mentioned five times in Mark (8:31; 11:27; 14:43,53; 15:1); twice in Matt (16:21; 27:41); and twice in Luke (9:22; 20:1); never in John. Only Mark 11:27 is not in direct relation to the passion of Jesus.

[24]Doeve ("Gefangennahme" 465–66) thinks Matt is giving historically correct information that only Sadducees (chief priests and elders) were involved in Jesus' death, whence the down-playing of the scribes. But why then does Matt (27:62) make the only Synoptic PN reference to the Pharisees, and why does he assemble (chap. 23) Jesus' woes on the scribes and Pharisees in a Jerusalem setting just before Jesus' death?

4. CAPTAINS OF THE TEMPLE

Stratēgoi (Mark 0, Matt 0, Luke 2, John 0). In the plot of the authorities to seize Jesus by stealth and kill him, Mark 14:1 has the chief priests and scribes conspiring; Matt 26:3 has the chief priests and elders of the people conspiring; and in both Mark 14:10 and Matt 26:14 it is with the chief priests that Judas deals. But Luke 22:4 has Judas conferring with the chief priests and *stratēgoi*. This term reflects the Greek for leading an army (related to English "strategy") and is usually rendered as "captains." In the arrest of Jesus, while Mark 14:43 has a crowd come with Judas "from the chief priests and the scribes and the elders" (= Sanhedrin members), and Matt 26:47 has the crowd "from the chief priests and elders of the people," Luke 22:52 has present on the scene "the chief priests and captains of the Temple and elders." This gives the impression that these captains have a military or policing function in relation to the Temple and have Sanhedrin status. They appear three more times in Acts as Jerusalem authorities. In 4:1–3 "the priests, and the captain [sg.] of the Temple, and the Sadducees" come upon Peter speaking in Solomon's Portico and arrest him and John. In Acts 5:21–24 the high priest and those with him call together "the Sanhedrin and all the Senate [*Gerousia*] of the sons of Israel," but the attendants cannot produce Peter since he is gone from the jail. "When the captain of the Temple and the chief priests hear these words," they are perplexed. Then (5:26) "the captain with the attendants" goes out and brings Peter and John before the high priest. While these references in Acts confirm the Gospel picture, they give preference to a single figure, the captain, who seems able to command the attendants.

In Josephus (*War* 6.5.3; #294) when the massive bronze gate of the Temple has swung open by itself, the watchmen run and report the matter to the *stratēgos*. In *Ant.* 20.6.2; #131 the governor of Syria puts the high priest Ananias and the *stratēgos* Ananus in chains and sends them to Rome (ca. AD 50). *Ant.* 20.9.3; #208 speaks of "the scribe of the captain Eleazar; he was the son of Ananias the high priest." This picture has been further filled in from the Mishna, where next to the high priest in rank there is a *sagan* (a Hebrew term appearing in the OT in the pl. for "prefects" and rendered in the LXX by *stratēgoi* or *archontes*). He seems to be the priest who is in supreme charge of order in and around the Temple, serving at times as a deputy for the high priest (indeed perhaps the high priest's son and heir to the office—see JJTJ 160–63; HJPAJC 2.277–79). We can feel more at ease using this mishnaic evidence since the much earlier War Scroll of Qumran, contemporary with Jesus' time, speaks of the high priest and his deputy (*mišneh*) at the head of twelve chief priests (1QM 2:1–2).

Luke's fluctuation between a plural and a singular is confusing: Were there subordinate captains under the captain, or has the term become generalized to imitate "chief priests" and "scribes"? Yet his overall picture is plausible. Next to the high priest there was another priest who was a prominent member of the Sanhedrin with special policing authority in Temple affairs, whence the designation "the captain of the Temple," and a special role in arrests and trials. Since the captain seems to have been one of the chief priests, there would be no need to enlarge the Synoptic understanding of the three groups that make up the Sanhedrin: the chief priests, the scribes, and the elders. Did Luke have a special tradition about the role of such a Temple captain (or captains) in the arrest of Jesus; or has such a figure, mentioned in the story of the arrest and trial of Peter, been taken back from Acts and by analogy applied to the arrest of Jesus?

5. PHARISEES

Pharisaioi (Mark 0, Matt 1, Luke 0, John 1).[25] Despite the frequent references to Pharisees in the public ministry of Jesus in all the Gospels, most often in a posture unfriendly or sharply hostile to Jesus, and despite the blistering criticism of them in Matt 23, they are noticeably absent from the three Synoptic passion predictions, from the plotting with Judas, and indeed from almost the whole PN! Before the PN Matt mentions them after Jesus has entered Jerusalem as plotting with the chief priests to arrest him (21:45–46), but the parallel verses in Mark and Luke omit "the Pharisees." That suggests we are dealing with Matthew's own generalization, not with ancient tradition. In the three Synoptic PNs the only mention of the Pharisees is in the story unique to Matt about the guard at the tomb (27:62), a story that also contains the only Synoptic PN reference to "the Jews" (28:15). I have suggested in §48 that this was a popular story reflecting the antiJewish attitude and vocabulary of many ordinary Christians in Matt's time. In the Johannine account of the ministry, while Jesus is in Jerusalem, the Pharisees join the high priest in an attempt to arrest Jesus (John 7:32–49), in calling together the Sanhedrin to discuss him (11:47), and in orders about his arrest (11:57).

---

[25]A normal counterpart to the Pharisees would be the Sadducees, but the *Saddoukaioi* (alluded to in the NT 14 times [Matt 7; Mark 1; Luke 1; Acts 5]) are never named in the PN, even though according to all three Synoptics (Mark 12:18; Matt 22:23,34; Luke 20:27) Jesus encountered them when he came to Jerusalem. K. Müller ("Jesus . . . Sadduzäer" 9–12) insists that Jesus would have been offensive to Sadducee theology on issues other than the well-known ones of the angels and bodily resurrection, e.g., in his independent attitudes toward cleanliness (Mark 7:1–8), Qorban (7:9–13), and oaths (Matt 23:16–22). Earlier in this APPENDIX I indicated that among other characters mentioned in the PN as hostile to Jesus surely all or most of "the chief priests" and probably "the elders" were Sadducee in outlook, but the affiliation of the Jerusalem "scribes" is uncertain. Sanders (*Judaism* 318) offers evidence for his contention: "Not all aristocrats were Sadducees, but it may be that all Sadducees were aristocrats."

In these scenes through stress on the Pharisees John may be making tradition about the priestly opposition to Jesus more contemporary in the 80s and 90s, after the loss of priestly power through destruction of the Temple, when the Pharisees had emerged as the main Jewish opponents of the Johannine community. But even after such references, remarkably there is only one mention of the Pharisees in the whole Johannine PN (18:3): Judas takes attendants of the chief priests and (of the) Pharisees when he sets out to arrest Jesus.

A conclusion drawn from all the evidence is that there was no firm Christian memory that the Pharisees as such played a role in the crucifixion of Jesus.[26] Some of the scribes (and perhaps even some of the priests) who were called together against him as part of the Sanhedrin may have been Pharisee, rather than Sadducee, in the way they interpreted the Law; but their part in consigning Jesus to die was not associated in Christian recall with their being Pharisees. Not surprisingly, then, the basic issues of Law observance portrayed as matters of dispute during the ministry between Jesus and the Pharisees do not appear in the Jewish legal procedure against Jesus.

Nevertheless, the ordinary readers of the Gospels would be expected by the evangelists to make a connection between the opposition to Jesus by the Pharisees and scribes during his ministry and the determination to put Jesus to death by the chief priests, scribes, and elders when he came to Jerusalem—Jewish authorities are opposed to Jesus throughout. Historically that might mean that reports of Pharisee opposition to Jesus assisted the Sanhedrin authorities in their own agenda: They knew that if they handed Jesus over to the Romans with their own judgment that he should die, they would not face protest instigated by the Pharisees. If a Pharisee like Saul (Paul) persecuted the followers of Jesus (Gal 1:13), he would have needed assistance and authorization. Acts 9:1–2; 22:5; 26:12 mention the high priest, chief priests, and elders as participants in the same persecution. If that cooperation is historical, it warns us not to overcompartmentalize the Jewish opposition to Jesus.

6. Rulers

Archontes (Mark 0, Matt 0, Luke 2, John 0).[27] This designation for Jerusalem Jewish authorities hostile to Jesus occurs in the PN only in Luke

---

[26]As I indicated in n. 19 above, it is very difficult to reconstruct historically the role of the Pharisees in Jesus' lifetime; and in §18, C2, I agreed with those who contended that the Pharisees were not a dominant force politically or liturgically in Jerusalem. Sanders (*Judaism* 398) estimates that numerically there were three times as many priests and levites as there were Pharisees.

[27]With considerably greater frequency *archontes,* often translated as "magistrates," appears in Josephus as a designation for officials in Jerusalem. McLaren (*Power* 207) would argue that these were administrators but not involved in reaching decisions.

23:13,35; but, as we shall see, there are other Johannine and Lucan references that cast light on what is meant. Part of the difficulty is that *archontes* can cover a wide range of princely rulers, local officials, and men of importance.[28] But we shall confine ourselves to *archontes* in Jerusalem who deal with Jesus, as they appear in John and in Luke-Acts.[29]

John's *archontes* seem to function with powers and concerns that elsewhere in the Gospels are given to Sanhedrin members. In John 3:1 Nicodemus, a man of the Pharisees and an *archōn* of the Jews, comes sympathetically to Jesus at night. In 7:26, when Jesus speaks publicly, the people ask, "Can it be that the *archontes* know that this is the Messiah?" But hearing such talk in the crowd, the chief priests and the Pharisees send attendants to seize Jesus (7:32). When the attendants come back empty-handed and half-believing in him, the Pharisees answer them scornfully, "Have any of the *archontes* of the Pharisees believed in him?" (7:48), only to have Nicodemus point out the unfairness of this judgment (7:50). In 12:42, having reported Jesus' judgment upon blindness and disbelief, John comments, "Yet many of the *archontes* believed in him; but for fear of the Pharisees they did not confess it, lest they be put out of the synagogue." The evidence is a bit confusing as to what extent the *archontes* are coterminous with chief priests and Pharisees; also some *archontes* are for Jesus and some against him. Difficulties stem from the fact that John is writing in general terminology at a later time for an audience that presumably is not particularly interested in the subdivisions of Jewish authorities, and from the fact that he is intermingling with the opposition to Jesus the tactics of later synagogue opposition to the Johannine Christians.

Turning to the Lucan writings, we find that Acts 4:26–27 aligns against Jesus the kings and the *archontes* in Jerusalem, and seems to identify the former as Herod and the latter as Pilate. But this very literal attempt to apply a psalm passage to the passion produces a description that is not really characteristic of the Lucan view of *archontes*. In Acts 13:27–29 Paul states that "those who live in Jerusalem and their *archontes*" condemned Jesus (*krinein*) and asked Pilate to have him killed; they eventually took him down from

[28]In the Gospels and Acts, for instance, we have Beelzebul *archōn* of demons and the satanic "*archōn* of this world"; *archontes* of the Gentiles who exercise authority (Matt 20:25); *archontes* in the Gentile cities (Acts 14:5; 16:19); Moses is an *archōn* (Acts 7:35); Jairus is the *archōn* of the local synagogue (Luke 8:41); there is an *archōn* or higher magistrate to whom disagreeing parties go and then are given over by him to the judge (Luke 12:58); and there are references to a local *archōn* without much specifying context (Matt 9:18,23; Luke 14:1; 18:18).

[29]Tcherikover ("Was" 73–74) argues persuasively that the *archontes* of Jerusalem cannot be equated with the archons of the Greek city-states; but then he argues that one description of them covers the evidence in Josephus and the NT, namely, that they were members of the priestly families. I doubt that the usage in John and in Luke allows such precision.

a tree and laid him in a tomb.[30] Since that description coincides with what the Sanhedrin members did in Luke's PN, *archontes* is presumably an umbrella term for chief priests, captains of the Temple, elders, and scribes (Luke 22:52,66). In Luke 23:35 the *archontes* scoff at Jesus on the cross, and the parallel passages in Mark/Matt attribute such mockery to the chief priests and the scribes. Acts 23:5 treats the high priest as an *archōn* of the people. Acts 4:5–8 mentions the *archontes* alongside the elders, the scribes, and the chief priests. Similarly in Luke 23:13 "the chief priests and the *archontes*" are called together by Pilate, and 24:20 makes those two groups responsible for giving Jesus over to a judgment of death and for crucifying him.[31] The two difficulties mentioned at the end of the preceding paragraph in relation to John also apply here. Acts, written in the 80s or 90s, is contemporizing and using a general and imprecise term to communicate with readers who are not interested in the precise titles of the Jewish authorities of Jesus' time. Moreover, this term enables Acts to draw a parallel between those hostile to Peter and Paul and those hostile to Jesus. Overall in reference to the passion, for Luke-Acts the *archontes* are equivalent to components of the Sanhedrin (especially the scribes and elders) and are unremittingly hostile to Jesus. The generic use of the term gives an impression of powers who are against him.

---

[30]Could that be a reference to Joseph from Arimathea, whom Luke 23:50 describes as a *bouleutēs*, i.e., a member of the *boulē*, "council," presumably the Sanhedrin (§18, B2)?

[31]The *archontes* may be present under another designation in Luke 19:47 where, after Jesus has cleansed the Temple and taught there, an effort to destroy him is mounted by "the chief priests and the scribes . . . and the first men [*prōtoi*] of the people"—compare, immediately afterward, 20:1: "the chief priests and the scribes, with the elders." The *Testimonium Flavianum* (Josephus, *Ant.* 18.3.3; #64; see pp. 373–74 above) says that Jesus came before Pilate upon the "indictment of the first-ranking men [*prōtoi andres*] among us."

APPENDIX VI: THE SACRIFICE OF ISAAC AND THE PASSION

Outline:

A. Theories Relating the *Aqedah* to the Death of Jesus
B. Contributive Elements in the Developing Story of the Sacrifice of Isaac
   1. In the Abraham Story of Gen 22:1–19
   2. In Early Jewish Literature (before AD 100)
   3. In Later Literature (Targums, Midrashim, Mishna)
C. Proposed NT Parallels to the Isaac Story
   1. Outside the Passion Narratives
   2. In the Passion Narratives
Bibliography

Abraham's willingness to offer Isaac, his beloved son, as a sacrifice if God commanded it (Gen 22:1–19) was reflected upon in Judaism in a way that made Isaac the center of a greatly developed narrative and theology. The end-product of the development about the sacrifice of Isaac is referred to as the *Aqedah,* a designation derived from the root "to bind," reflecting the judgment that Isaac was bound even as the lamb used in the daily burnt offering (the *tāmîd*) was bound, as described in Mishna *Tamid* 4.1. P. R. Davies ("Passover" 59) depicts the *Aqedah* theme thus: "The Offering of Isaac ... is an actually accomplished sacrifice in which blood was shed, constituting a definitively expiatory or redemptive act for all Israel."[1] Obviously there are parallels between the redemptive sacrifice of Jesus and the *Aqedah* theology of the redemptive sacrifice of Isaac, but how did such parallels come about? Let us begin with a survey of proposals.[2]

---

[1]Swetnam (*Jesus* 18) objects to this description because implicitly it does not equate the term *Aqedah* with the Abraham/Isaac story of Gen 22 or even with some minor imaginative embellishments of the figure of Isaac in the story. I think, however, that precision here is very wise, for it helps to prevent reading later ideas and terminology back into an earlier period in the literature of which they are unattested.

[2]A helpful brief history of *Aqedah* theorizing is offered by Swetnam, *Jesus* 4–22.

A. *Theories Relating the* Aqedah *to the Death of Jesus*

A. Geiger is generally credited with having inaugurated the discussion[3] by his claim that the *Aqedah* embodied alien theology brought into Judaism from Syrian Christianity by Babylonian Jewish writers of the period after AD 200. After some decades I. Lévi[4] objected that *Aqedah* themes were found among Palestinian Jewish writers of the same period, that the theology was not alien, and that the basic outlook on Isaac's sacrifice existed much earlier. By mid-20th cent. the thesis that *Aqedah* theology predated Christianity was gaining numerous adherents. For many this meant that the evaluation of Jesus' death in the NT (and even his resurrection: Schoeps) was influenced by the Jewish evaluation of the sacrifice of Isaac. Spiegel (*Last* 116), however, thought that "the two traditions on the one bound [Isaac] and the one crucified [Jesus] seem to point rather to a common source in the ancient pagan world." Shortly after Spiegel's book Dahl ("Atonement") argued with great nuance that early Christian interpretations of Isaac and the Jewish *Aqedah* traditions were parallel but independent developments from Gen 22.[5] Meanwhile in the early 1960s both Le Déaut and Vermes had appealed to Palestinian targums on the Pentateuch[6] as evidence for the pre-Christian existence of *Aqedah* theology (a view supported also by McNamara), particularly as part of the Passover liturgy. *Aqedah* influence on the NT was advocated in varying degrees by Wood and Daly (a maximalist view). Yet an extremely serious challenge to such an early dating for the targums has been mounted by Fitzmyer—a challenge with which I personally agree. A different challenge to the earliness of the *Aqedah* tradition in general can be found in Daniélou, while P. R. Davies and Chilton have rejected the arguments drawn from the Passover liturgy reconstructed on the basis of the targums. Indeed, one may ask how much is known from any source about the details of Passover liturgy in the 1st cent. AD. In the light of such uncertainties the most helpful approach, which I shall follow below, is to be rigorously descriptive as to which documents contribute what information.

B. *Contributive Elements in the Developing Story of the Sacrifice of Isaac*

Unquestionably from Gen 22 to the full-blown *Aqedah* picture there was a development over centuries. One cannot reconstruct that development with

---

[3]*Jüdische Zeitschrift für Wissenschaft und Leben* 10 (1872), 166–71.

[4]REJ 64 (1912), 161–84. Both scholars associated the *Aqedah* with the New Year's liturgy.

[5]Still another possibility is that *Aqedah* theology was developed as a Jewish counterweight to the Christian theology of Jesus' sacrificial death (Geiger, Chilton, P. R. Davies).

[6]These are the expansive Aramaic renditions known as Neofiti, Pseudo-Jonathan, and the Fragmentary Targum.

certitude, but one can look at the Abraham/Isaac story in documents of different eras and notice diverse elements in the presentation.

1. ELEMENTS IN THE ABRAHAM STORY OF GEN 22:1–19

Before beginning to list the elements, one should note that this is emphatically an Abraham, not an Isaac, story. It praises Abraham's obedience to and trust in God. Isaac is seemingly a little boy, subject to what his father says and does, who has a minor role as an object of Abraham's actions. The following elements are pertinent:

#1.   Isaac is Abraham's uniquely beloved son (22:2,12,16: *yāḥîd, agapētos*).

#2.   Abraham was told by God, "Take along your son . . . and go to the land of Moriah." Abraham took along (*paralambanein*) two young men servants and his son Isaac (22:2–3).

#3.   On arriving, Abraham said to the young men servants: "Sit in this place [*kathisate autou*] with the donkey; I and the little boy shall go on farther; and having worshiped, we shall return to you" (22:5).

#4.   Abraham took the wood for the offering and laid it on Isaac his son (22:6).

#5.   Isaac addressed Abraham as "(My) Father" (22:7: *'ābî; pater*).

#6.   Abraham bound (*'qd*) Isaac and laid him on the wood (22:9).

#7.   An angel of the Lord called to Abraham and told him not to lay his hand on the boy (22:11–12).

#8.   Having offered a ram instead, Abraham returned to his young men servants (22:19); nothing is said of the return of Isaac.[7]

2. ELEMENTS IN EARLY JEWISH LITERATURE (BEFORE AD 100)[8]

Under this rubric I shall include deuterocanonical literature like Sir, Wis, and I Macc that certainly was written before the Christian era, along with the works of Josephus composed in the 1st cent. AD. Among the apocrypha *Jubilees* cannot be dated much after 150 BC, and *IV Macc* is probably to be dated just before AD 50. The greatest problem is the dating of the *Biblical Antiquities of (Pseudo-)Philo:* It was composed just before or after AD 70; nevertheless, on the assumption that ideas found in it circulated before the

---

[7]This silence led to semimystical speculations about the whereabouts of Isaac.

[8]I shall include several early Christian references to the Gen 22 story where they coincide with the views in Jewish literature. *I Clement* can narrowly be included within the time framework.

composition, I am including it in this section of Jewish works that might have influenced the NT.[9]

#9. Most of the references in the deuterocanonical literature (and the NT) are to a story about Abraham wherein he manifests his resoluteness and loyalty to God (Sir 44:20–21; Wis 10:5; I Macc 2:52; Heb 11:17–20; James 2:21). A reference to Isaac's virtue appears in *IV Macc* 16:20: "He did not shrink."

#10. *Jub.* 17:16–18; 18:9; 19:8 make this the most severe of the ten trials of Abraham engineered by Mastema (Satan). This picture is harmonious with the dualistic angelic theology of *Jub.* and may not have been widespread.

#11. Mount Moriah, the place of sacrifice, is identified with Mount Zion (*Jub.* 18:13; see II Chron 3:1), the Davidic site of the future Temple (Josephus, *Ant.* 1.13.2; #226).

#12. The time of the sacrifice is set at Passover in *Jub.* 17:15 with 18:3.[10]

#13. Isaac addresses Abraham as "Father" twice in *Jub.* 18:6.

#14. The age of Isaac is given as twenty-five in Josephus, *Ant.* 1.13.3; #227.[11]

#15. Isaac rushes willingly to the altar (Josephus, *Ant.* 1.13.4; #232) and endures being sacrificed for the sake of religion (*IV Macc* 13:12). In *Ps-Philo* 32:3 Isaac says, "Have I not been born into the world to be offered as a sacrifice to him who made me?" (also 40:2: The one being offered was ready). *I Clement* 31:3 reports: "Isaac with confidence, knowing what was to happen, gladly was led as a sacrifice."

#16. *Jub.* 18:9 reports the discussions in the heavenly councils that lead to the staying of Abraham's hand, and the Lord Himself speaks to Abraham to stop him (18:11).

#17. Although Isaac did not die on the altar, there is a passage in *Ps-Philo* 32:4 ("And when he had offered the son upon the altar and had bound his feet so as to kill him") that some like Vermes, Le Déaut, and Daly use in arguing that *Ps-Philo* treats the sacrifice as complete. Swetnam (*Jesus* 53–54), pointing out that the words of Isaac in *Ps-Philo* 32 are difficult to interpret, states that the language of 32:3 "seems calculated to suggest that the sacrifice was not complete." Yet "the author regards Isaac's non-consummated sacrifice as an expiation of sin."

#18. In *IV Macc* we see Isaac becoming a model for martyrs: "Nor did Isaac flinch when he saw his father's hand, armed with a sword, descending

---

[9]P. R. Davies and Chilton ("Aqedah" 522–28) contend that *Ps-Philo* is too late to have influenced the NT.

[10]Le Déaut (*Nuit* 260–61) claims that this connection with Passover was widespread early.

[11]In midrashic tradition the age is elevated to thirty-seven, based on rabbinic calculations derived from data in Gen.

upon him" (16:20). The willingness of the mother of the seven sons to have her children die for God is compared to Abraham's willingness concerning Isaac (14:20; 15:28).

3. ELEMENTS IN LATER LITERATURE (TARGUMS, MIDRASHIM, MISHNA)

The chief point of dispute here concerns the elements in the targums. Already in literature datable to the end of the 1st cent. AD some of the elements of *Aqedah* theology and narrative about the sacrifice of Isaac had made their appearance (e.g., ##14, 15, 17 above). Yet in the Palestinian targums on Genesis a much more developed picture of Isaac is presented, containing some elements found also in the early midrashim, the Mishna, and the *Ep. of Barnabas,* indisputably 2d-cent. works. As I mentioned above, some scholars (Daly, Le Déaut, McNamara, Vermes, etc.) would contend that here the targums preserve 1st.-cent. thought. Certainly, however, these targums were *written* after the 1st cent.,[12] and I judge it extremely problematic to build from them an argument of influence on the NT. More likely they show us how the *Aqedah* theology developed in the 2d and 3d cents. AD. Let me list some aspects of the Isaac story that appear in one or more Palestinian targums or (where specified) in other Jewish literature written after AD 100.

#19.   Isaac expresses fear in face of death.
#20.   Isaac himself requests that he be bound (enhancing the idea of *Aqedah* and strengthening the parallelism to the bound lamb of the daily burnt offering [*tāmîd*]).
#21.   Isaac looks up and sees the angels in heaven (and the *shekina* or glory of God). A voice in heaven explains the scene: There are two chosen individuals, i.e., Abraham sacrificing and Isaac sacrificed.[13]
#22.   The blood of Isaac is mentioned in Midrash *Mekilta* (*Pisha* 7, lines 79,81) and even the ashes of Isaac in TalBab *Taʿanit* 16a ("That [God] may remember for our sake the ashes of Isaac").
#23.   In the targum on Job (3:19) Isaac is identified as the "servant of Yahweh."[14]
#24.   In the targumic elements of the Passover liturgy the deliverance of Isaac and the deliverance of Israel from Egypt are related. In the 5th-cent. *Pesikta de-Rab Kahana* (Supp. 1.20) we read that because of the merit of Isaac who offered himself bound on the altar, God will quicken the dead.

---

[12]See NJBC 68:108–10; P. R. Davies and Chilton, "Aqedah" 542–45.

[13]In the Dura Europos synagogue painting the hand of God stops Abraham from slaying Isaac.

[14]Although few would date this targum earlier than the 4th cent. (and many would date it considerably later), scholars like Le Déaut, Vermes, and Wood think this was an early identification of Isaac. See Rosenberg, "Jesus."

#25.   *Ep. of Barnabas* 7:2 draws a direct parallel between the sacrifice of
        Isaac offered on the altar and the self-giving of Jesus on the cross. In
        his homily *On the Pasch* Melito makes two references to Isaac bound
        (59, 69) as foreshadowing the death of Jesus; and in fragments 9–10
        Melito points to several parallels: Both carried wood, both were led by
        a father—yet Isaac was released while Jesus suffered death.[15]

C. *Proposed NT Parallels to the Isaac Story*[16]

Clearly the later elements in the narrative and theology of Isaac (##19–24)
heighten the resemblance to the story of Jesus, and it is no wonder that specific comparisons (#25) began to be made in the 2d cent. I have mentioned
above that many scholars draw upon those later elements as background for
scenes in the NT.[17] Here, however, I shall confine my remarks to the Isaac
elements ##1–18 that plausibly are earlier than or contemporary with the NT
writings. First I shall point briefly to proposals for Isaac influence on NT
themes or writings outside the PN—if they are valid, they heighten the possibility of influence on the PN. The latter will be the concern in the second
section below.

1. PARALLELS OUTSIDE THE PASSION NARRATIVES

▪ *References to the sacrifice of Christ.* I Cor 5:7 states: "For Christ, our pasch(al
  lamb), has been sacrificed," and this has been seen as reflecting the sacrifice
  of Isaac which took place at Passover (#12), a sacrifice in which Isaac was
  bound (as a sacrificial lamb would have been). According to Rom 8:32 God
  "did not spare His own Son but rather gave him over for all of us."[18] In John
  3:16 we find: "God so loved the world that He gave the only Son."[19] This

---

[15]See R. Wilken, "Melito, the Jewish Community at Sardis, and the Sacrifice of Isaac," TS 37
(1976), 53–69.

[16]The designation "Isaac story" is by preference: The issue is not simply the influence of the
Abraham story in Gen 22 on the NT, nor am I thinking of the fully developed *Aqedah* (as defined at
the beginning of the APPENDIX), which in my judgment may not have existed in Judaism before the
2d–3d cents. AD.

[17]As an example, Stegner attempts to find a parallel between element #21 and the baptismal
scene where Jesus sees the heavens opened, as a voice from heaven explains what is happening. The
Servant motif of Isa 42:1 invoked in Mark 1:11 would then be comparable to #23.

[18]Dahl ("Atonement") emphasizes this verse along with Gal 3:13–14 (Christ hanged on a tree [in
the Isaac story "a ram caught in a thicket"], followed by a reference to the blessing of Abraham)
and Rom 3:25–26 (God put forward Christ as an expiation by his blood). A relation to the Isaac
story in such passages is subtle, to say the least.

[19]Originally this text probably did not refer to the death of Jesus but to the incarnation or God's
sending the Son into the world. Nevertheless, I John 4:10 can be looked on as a reinterpretation to
include the death: "God sent His only Son into the world . . . to be the expiation for our sins."

phrasing could have been influenced by the portrait of Abraham's generous willingness to sacrifice his beloved son (#1), especially if Isaac was looked on as an adult and willing victim who also exemplified obedience (##14–15). Yet we note that the parallels suggested are very much on the implicit level.

- *Influence on the Epistle to the Hebrews.* Swetnam (*Jesus* 86–129) has argued that a passage like Heb 11:17–19 shows Isaac influence.[20] True, Abraham is the principal figure who is invoked because of his readiness "to offer up his only son," so that one might think only of Gen 22. But for Swetnam the theme of testing (#10) and the reference to Abraham's figuratively receiving Isaac back from the dead are factors that point to an "unquestioned appearance of the Aqedah in Heb 11:17–19" (p. 129). On pp. 130–77 he argues for *Aqedah* background in Heb 2:5–18 with its references to the seed of Abraham (Isaac) and the hostile work of the devil (#10). He would invoke several other Heb passages as well; but, as one can see, the proposed allusions to the developed Isaac story are very subtle.

- *Influences on the Last Supper.*[21] In *Jubilees* and perhaps more widely before AD 100 the sacrifice of Isaac was imagined to have taken place at Passover (#12), and his blood becomes a theme in the midrashim. The Synoptics portray the Last Supper as a Passover meal, and in Mark 14:24 and Matt 26:28 Jesus specifies that his blood is "poured out for many." Had the sacrifice of Isaac at Passover already taken on an expiatory aspect and been associated with the liberation of Israel (as would become specific later: #24)? As mentioned above, scholars like P. R. Davies and Chilton have created real doubt about this.

The few examples given above illustrate how subtle are the claimed parallels between the NT and the developments of the Isaac story (beyond the Abraham story in Gen 22:1–19). If one does not allow an appeal to the existence in the 1st cent. AD of *Aqedah* motifs that are documented only in the targums and other later Jewish literature, there is no clear NT allusion outside the PN to developed Isaac theology and themes. Therefore, one must evaluate the proposed parallels in the PN on their own merit without much support from the rest of the NT.

2. PARALLELS IN THE PASSION NARRATIVES[22]

- In Matt 26:36 (but not in Mark 14:32), as Jesus enters Gethsemane, he says to the body of disciples, "Sit in this place [*kathisate autou*] until going away, I

[20]For a favorable evaluation of Swetnam's thesis, see R. Williamson, JTS NS 34 (1983), 609–12.

[21]In a wider sense the supper scene could be construed as part of the PN, but this commentary has treated a PN beginning after the Last Supper.

[22]Grassi ("*Abba*" 450–54) gives a helpful list of proposals from which I select some as worthy of attention. Some proposals are too farfetched (the Mount of Olives in Jesus' passion as parallel to Mount Moriah in #11); others are based on Isaac material that is not demonstrably as early as the NT

pray there"; and then he takes along (*paralambanein*) Peter and the two sons of Zebedee. Good linguistic parallels may be found in the Gen 22 story as exhibited in ##2–3 above. Yet notice that the parallel is more between Jesus and Abraham than between Jesus and Isaac.

- A motif in the Gethsemane scene is Jesus' warning to the disciples to watch and pray lest they enter into trial (*peirasmos:* Mark 14:38; Matt 26:41; Luke 22:40,46; also Heb 4:15, *peirazein*). One may compare this with the theme in *Jubilees* (#10) of the trials of Abraham engineered by Mastema (cf. John 16:11 about the passion as a judgment on the Prince of this world, and Luke 22:53 about a confrontation with the power of darkness). Once more the parallelism is between Jesus and Abraham.

- In Jesus' Gethsemane prayer (Mark 14:36; Matt 26:39; Luke 22:41) Jesus addresses God as "(My) Father" (see also the Johannine parallel in 12:27b–28). In Gen 22 Isaac addresses Abraham as "(My) Father" (#5) and that motif is increased in *Jubilees* (#13). It is hard to judge how significant this is since it would be natural for Isaac to speak thus to his father.[23]

- In (some mss. of) Luke 22:43 an angel from heaven strengthens Jesus in his prayer on the Mount of Olives; in Matt 26:53 Jesus says he could have called on the Father and been supplied with twelve legions of angels; in John 12:28b–29 the heavenly voice that speaks to Jesus is mistaken for an angel. In Gen 22 there is the intervention of an angel on behalf of Isaac (#7), and the developing story stresses the heavenly role (#16). Heavenly intervention, specifically angelic, is not uncommon in the OT and the Jewish apocrypha; and so positing here the specific influence of the Isaac story on the Gospel passages is imaginative, especially since Jesus is not spared as Isaac was.

- In John 18:11, as Jesus is arrested, he says, "The cup the Father has given me—am I not to drink it?" Previously he said (10:17–18): "I lay down my life . . . no one has taken it away from me; rather I lay it down of my own accord." Before Pilate (18:37) Jesus shows an awareness of his destiny: "The reason for which I have been born and for which I have come into the world is that I may bear witness to the truth." Some would find a parallel in Isaac's willingness to be sacrificed (#15), and a vocabulary parallel in his question "Have I not been born into the world to be offered as a sacrifice to him who made me?" In the PN, however, this attitude is peculiar to the Johannine Jesus, and almost as good a parallel to Isaac can be found in Heb 10:7 where in a psalm quotation Christ is imagined to have said, "Lo, I have come to do your will, O God."

- As Jesus goes out to Golgotha, John 19:17a reports: "And carrying the cross

---

(Jesus' being sorrowful unto death and asking not to drink the cup as parallel to Isaac's expression of fear in #19).

[23]Grassi ("*Abba*") would make a major point of this, but the real parallel would have to be in the later targumic tradition.

by himself, he came out." A patristic interpretation, already appearing in Melito (#25), would see a parallel here to Abraham's taking the wood for the offering and laying it on Isaac (#4). Once more the "parallel," which is not linguistic, is found only in John (since the Synoptics introduce Simon the Cyrenian) and is to Gen 22 without the later Isaac developments.

By way of overall summary I would judge that of the proposed parallels to Isaac in the PNs, those that have plausibility are the parallels to the Gen 22 account of Abraham and Isaac. There is very little that is plausibly related to the later Isaac developments and the *Aqedah*.

Bibliography for Appendix VI:
The Sacrifice of Isaac

This is a working bibliography to be supplemented by the exhaustive bibliography on the Isaac question in Swetnam's book listed below.

Chilton, B. D., "Isaac and the Second Night: a Consideration," *Biblica* 16 (1980), 78–88.

Dahl, N. A., "The Atonement—an Adequate Reward for the Akedah? (Ro 8:32)," in *Neotestamentica et Semitica,* eds. E. E. Ellis and M. Wilcox (Honor of M. Black; Edinburgh: Clark, 1969), 15–29.

Daly, R. J., "The Soteriological Significance of the Sacrifice of Isaac," CBQ 39 (1977), 45–75.

Daniélou, J., "La typologie d'Isaac dans le christianisme primitif," *Biblica* 28 (1947), 363–93.

Davies, P. R., "Martyrdom and Redemption: On the Development of Isaac Typology in the Early Church," in *Studia Patristica,* ed. E. A. Livingstone (8th International Conf. on Patristic Studies, 1979; Oxford: Pergamon, 1982), 2.652–58.

———, "Passover and the Dating of the Aqedah," JJS 30 (1979), 59–67.

———, and B. D. Chilton, "The Aqedah: A Revised Tradition History," CBQ 40 (1978), 514–46.

Grassi, J. A., "*Abba,* Father (Mark 14:36): Another Approach," JAAR 50 (1982), 449–58.

Hayward, C.T.R., "The Sacrifice of Isaac and Jewish Polemic against Christianity," CBQ 52 (1990), 292–306.

Le Déaut, R., "De nocte paschatis," VD 41 (1963), 189–95.

———, *La nuit pascale* (AnBib 22; Rome: PBI, 1963).

McNamara, M., *The New Testament and the Palestinian Targum to the Pentateuch* (AnBib 27a; 2d printing; Rome: PBI, 1978), 164–68.

Rosenberg, R. A., "Jesus, Isaac, and the 'Suffering Servant,'" JBL 84 (1965), 381–88.

Schoeps, H. J., "The Sacrifice of Isaac in Paul's Theology," JBL 65 (1946), 385–92.

Spiegel, S., *The Last Trial: On the Legends and Lore of . . . the Akedah* (New York: Pantheon, 1967).

Stadelmann, L.I.J., "O sacrifício de Isaac: Um texto clássico sobre o discernimento espiritual na Bíblia," *Perspectiva Teológica* 23 (1991), 317–32.

Stegner, W. R., "The Baptism of Jesus: A Story Modeled on the Binding of Isaac," *Bible Review* 1 (#3, Fall 1985), 35–45.

Swetnam, J., *Jesus and Isaac: A Study of the Epistle to the Hebrews in the Light of the Aqedah* (AnBib 94; Rome: PBI, 1981).

Vermes, G., *Scripture and Tradition in Judaism* (Leiden: Brill, 1961), 193–227.

Wood, J. E., "Isaac Typology in the New Testament," NTS 14 (1967–68), 583–89.

APPENDIX VII: THE OLD TESTAMENT BACKGROUND OF THE PASSION NARRATIVES

After some preparatory remarks the material will be divided thus:

A. Passion Parallels in the Old Testament in General
   1. The Pentateuch
   2. Historical Books
   3. Prophetical Books
   4. Wisdom or Sapiential Books
B. Passion Parallels in the Psalms
   1. Proposed Psalm Parallels (except Ps 22) for the Passion
   2. Ps 22 and the Passion
Bibliography

Already §1B introduced the theory that the PN arose not from the memory of what happened but simply from imaginative reflection on the OT, especially on passages describing the suffering of the just one at the hands of enemies who plot against him, mocking his trust in God. Although I offered reasons for rejecting such a radical approach (at least in regard to the main outline of the canonical PNs), it is impossible to deny that the OT background influenced heavily early Christian presentation of the passion, highlighting what should be recounted in order to expand the preaching outline into dramatic narratives. Moreover, in passion material which did not go through the crucible of common preaching or synagogue debate and in which popular imagination was allowed freer rein (e.g., the Matthean special material and *GPet*), OT influence was truly creative. This is why, for instance, in Matt 27:3–10 and Acts 1:16–25 we have two different stories of the death of Judas, each dramatized in imagery borrowed from the death of a wicked OT figure, respectively Ahithophel and Antiochus Epiphanes. As my commentary on the PN proceeded through the Gospels verse by verse, I pointed to OT background for individual episodes or expressions. In this APPENDIX, however, I shall survey the issue in OT sequence,[1] concentrating

---

[1]Moo, *Old Testament,* one of several writings offering a more detailed study, concentrates on particular themes (Suffering Servant, Zech 9–14, Lament Psalms, sacrificial imagery) and does not follow the OT sequence.

on the books that most influenced the PNs, and then turning particularly to the psalms and, indeed, to the most influential single work, Ps 22. This brief study should help to establish the extent to which early Christians looked on the passion as the working out of the will of God, foreshadowed in the sufferings of the innocent just of Israel.

By way of general introduction, it should be noted that the passion echoes the OT in different ways. Sometimes there is simply an allusion without any notification to the reader that Scripture is in mind. If a detected allusion is to an OT situation but uses none of the vocabulary of the OT description of the situation, we are not always certain that the NT writer intended the reference.[2] (That is one of the reasons why lists of OT passages that influenced the PNs disagree; my listing in what follows claims only to offer the parallels that I thought important.) Other times in the PNs OT vocabulary is unmistakably echoed; and indeed in a few instances the citation of the OT is made explicit through the use of a formula, e.g., "This happened in order that the Scripture (or words of the prophet) might be fulfilled. . . ."[3] For references to (sacred) writings or Scripture in the Mark/Matt PN,[4] see particularly Mark 14:27 (= Matt 26:31); and Mark 14:49 (cf. Matt 26:54,56). Outside these a fulfillment citation has been introduced into the Matthean special material in 27:9–10. Luke's only fulfillment citation is at the Last Supper in 22:37. In the Johannine PN[5] fulfillment of OT Scripture appears in 19:24,36–37 (see also 19:28), and fulfillment of Jesus' own word in 18:9,32.

To appreciate a broader influence of the OT on the way in which Christians understood Jesus' passion, other factors should be kept in mind. First, I am concentrating here on the *Gospel* PNs, but there are references to Jesus' death in most other NT books. Often these references have also been influenced by the OT, but not necessarily by the same passages that have influenced the Gospels. Second, we tend to think of the familiar written OT

---

[2]A judgment that the proposed reference is not farfetched is assisted if unambiguously elsewhere the respective OT situation served other early Christian writers. Even without that assistance Dillon ("Psalms" 431) thinks that the overall scriptural coloration of the PNs creates an atmosphere sympathetic to recognizing the likelihood of allusions.

[3]In statistics covering the whole Gospels, fulfillment citations are more frequent in Matt and John. Occasionally the idea that these things happened to fulfill the Scriptures confuses believers and supplies ammunition to skeptics. How can there be responsibility or guilt on the part of those who executed Jesus or of those for whose sins he died if it all had to happen? Such a question fails to recognize that biblical thought often does not distinguish between God's providence and predestination, so that whatever happens is presented as being willed by God. According to a more subtle understanding God did not will (= wish) the violent death of the Son, but foresaw it and turned it into something salvific for all.

[4]Earlier at the Last Supper, see Mark 14:21 (= Matt 26:24).

[5]At the Last Supper see 13:18 echoing Ps 41:10, probably cited implicitly in Mark 14:18. John 15:25 has fulfillment of a text contained "in their law" ("They hated me without cause"), which echoes Pss 69:5 and 35:19.

Scriptures of our Bibles. Yet we know that through a midrashic approach, the understanding of OT episodes among Jews in Jesus' time had gone beyond the written text. For instance, in BBM 194, 215–16 I showed that Matt's story of Herod and the birth of Jesus reflected not only the account in Exod 1:8–16 of how Pharaoh killed the male children to control the growth of the Hebrews in Egypt, but also developed features of that story known to us from Philo and Josephus, namely, that magi warned Pharaoh of the birth of a marvelous Hebrew male child who would save his people. Similarly there is the likelihood that NT writers drew for the passion on midrashic developments beyond the literal sense of the OT.[6]

For convenience' sake let me organize the survey according to standard OT groupings (Pentateuch, Historical Books, Prophetical Books, Wisdom Books), with the final subsections dedicated to the Psalms and Ps 22. In general, preference is given to the LXX form of OT passages.

A. *Passion Parallels in the Old Testament in General*

1. THE PENTATEUCH

Two Genesis stories were seen to offer parallels to the death of Jesus. The first was the testing of Abraham in Gen 22:1–14 where the patriarchal father showed himself obedient to God even when commanded to sacrifice Isaac, his beloved son. That story is probably in mind implicitly in passages like Rom 8:32, which describes God as not sparing "His own Son" but giving him for all, and I John 4:9–10, where God is said to have shown love for us in sending the Son as an expiating sacrifice.[7] If the midrashic elaboration of the Abraham story known as the *Aqedah* (i.e., the binding of Isaac) was already in circulation, the Gospel PNs may echo it in certain details; but each proposed example is debatable (see APPENDIX VI). The second influential story was the selling of Joseph into Egypt at the suggestion of Judah for twenty (thirty) pieces of silver (Gen 37:26–28) and Joseph's eventual salvation of his eleven brothers. This had parallels to the silver paid to Judas (= Judah) for giving Jesus over, the failure of the other eleven to help Jesus, and Jesus' postresurrectional reestablishment of them as his brothers.

Exod 12 describes the ritual of the eating of the Passover lamb and the sprinkling of its blood with hyssop on the doorposts of the Israelites to spare them when the angel slew the Egyptian firstborn. The Synoptic evangelists

---

[6] I shall regularly insist, however, that we must have evidence that such midrashic developments were known *in the 1st cent.;* appeal to later Jewish midrashim is methodologically weak.

[7] See APPENDIX VI, n. 19.

describe the Last Supper as a Passover meal. John calls Jesus the Lamb of God and has him sentenced at the noon hour when Passover lambs were killed in the Temple precincts; there is a sponge laden with vinegary wine that was put on hyssop to be offered to him, and a formula citation calling attention to his fulfilling Scripture by not having a bone fractured (similar to the lamb of Exod 12:46; Num 9:12).[8] Another symbol of Israel's exodus experience, the serpent lifted up in the desert to bring healing (Num 21:9; see Wis 16:5–7), is seen in John 3:14–15 as a foreshadowing of the Son of Man being lifted up in crucifixion so that believers may have abundant life.

2. HISTORICAL BOOKS[9]

Since Jesus was thought to be descended from David, indeed entitled "son of David," a parallel to the passion was found in the most desperate moment of David's life, as described in II Sam 15:13–37; 17:23. There, after his trusted friend and advisor Ahithophel (= Judas) had gone over to his enemy, David crossed the Kidron (see John 18:1) and went to the Ascent of Olives (see Mark 14:26 and par.) where he wept and prayed (Synoptic Mount-of-Olives scene). David arranged for his followers not to suffer his fate but to go back to Jerusalem and wait for a future reunion (see John 18:8b), while the unfaithful Ahithophel, seeing that his plan against David was unsuccessful, went home and hanged himself (see Matt 27:5b).

At the end of the OT historical period the dramatic Maccabean stories of martyrs (the aged Eleazar, the mother and the seven sons) who resisted the pagan king Antiochus Epiphanes (II Macc 6:18–7:42; *IV Macc* 5:1–18:23) have often been suggested as models for Jesus' refusal to acquiesce to Pilate's interrogation, especially as narrated in John 19:10–11 where Jesus disputes the governor's power over him (see II Macc 7:16). Yet the Gospel PNs are singularly lacking in important features of the Maccabean martyr stories, e.g., gruesome descriptions of the tortures, and defiant speeches calling down punishment on the ruler. The veneration of the tombs of the Maccabees (p. 1280 above) helps us to appreciate the possibility that Christians might have kept a memory of the tomb of Jesus and annually recalled the story of his death.

3. PROPHETICAL BOOKS

Isaiah comes first in the collection of the Latter (or writing) Prophets. Acts 8:32–33 has Philip explain to the Ethiopian eunuch that Isa 53:7–8

---

[8]See also I Cor 5:7 and I Pet 1:19 for the sacrifice or blood of Christ the lamb, and possibly Heb 9:14.

[9]Four of these are known in the Hebrew collection as the Former Prophets.

(sheep led to the slaughter) refers to Jesus. Accordingly many consider the Isaian Suffering Servant passages[10] a major source for Christian reflection on the passion of Jesus.[11] I Pet 2:22–24 reports that Jesus did no wrong, that there was no deceit in his mouth[12] (echoing Isa 53:9b), and that he gave himself up, bringing our sins to the cross (echoing Isa 53:10: the Servant giving his life as an offering for sin, and Isa 53:5: the Servant pierced for our offenses, crushed for our sins). The theme of Jesus being given over (*paradidonai*), which is a favorite in the PNs (p. 211 above), reflects the theme of the Servant being given up in Isa 53:6,12.[13] In Mark's account of the ministry (9:12) "Scripture" is quoted as saying that the Son of Man must suffer much and be despised, echoing Isa 53:3 where the Servant is spurned. Matt 8:17 specifies that Jesus was fulfilling the words of Isaiah (53:4) inasmuch as he took our infirmities and bore our ills. Despite this wide use of the Servant passages (especially the fourth song), evidence for the Servant theme in the PN proper is not extensive. The only direct citation (of Isa 53:12: "And with outlaws was he reckoned") is during the sword passage of the Lucan Last Supper (22:37). The idea that this Isaian passage was in mind in the descriptions of Jesus on the cross between two bandits/wrongdoers (Mark 15:27 and par.) is dubious because of the difference in vocabulary.[14] That same type of difference makes uncertain a connection between the description of the Servant in Isa 53:7 ("He does not open his mouth") and the silence of Jesus and his refusing to answer at the trials.[15] A clearer allusion to the Servant is found in the Jewish mockery of Jesus (Mark 14:65 and par.), for Isa 50:6–7 describes the Servant as having his cheeks slapped, and his face spit on.[16]

Jeremiah. Closer than the Maccabean martyr stories to the complex sur-

---

[10]Four Servant songs are usually detected (Isa 42:1–4; 49:1–7; 50:4–11; 52:13–53:12); yet we do not know the extent to which in NT times these passages were seen as interrelated and/or distinguishable from the rest of Isa.

[11]R. A. Guelich, "'The Beginning of the Gospel': Mark 1:1–15," BR 27 (1982), 5–15, and others would see massive Isaian influence on Mark's Gospel; for they understand 1:1–2a to mean that Mark is beginning *the gospel* of Jesus Christ *as written* (foretold) *by Isaiah* the prophet. On the other side of the ledger, Hooker's study of the passion in *Jesus* is skeptical of much provable influence of Isa in this area of the Gospels.

[12]See also I John 3:5: "In him there was no sin."

[13]*Paradidonai* for giving over (to enemies or death) also appears in Pss 27:12; 118:18; 119:121; 140:9. In the second of the three detailed Synoptic passion predictions (Table 13 in APPENDIX VIII), Mark 9:31 has the Son of Man "given over into the hands of men [*anthrōpoi*]"; the imagery of "the hand of" (sinners, etc.) is found in Pss 71:4; 97:10; 140:5.

[14]Isa 53:12 is cited in Mark 15:28, but that is a later copyist's addition, not a genuine Marcan text (pp. 933, 970 above).

[15](Mark 14:61 [= Matt 26:63]; Mark 15:5 [= Matt 27:12,14; John 19:9]; and Luke 23:9). Hooker (*Jesus* 89) is very strong in rejecting the influence of Isa on the accounts of the silence of Jesus.

[16]Outside the Servant songs, some have proposed as background for the crucifixion Isa 65:2: "I spread out my hands the whole day to a disobedient and contradictory people."

rounding the death of Jesus is the plot in Jer 26, including the prophet's warning against the Jerusalem Temple,[17] the assemblage of priests and prophets against him, the participation of "all the people," the warning that they would bring innocent blood on themselves, and the contention that he "deserved" death. I have suggested in §2 that the pattern of the Book of Jeremiah, with prophetic words and actions, and a narrative of the prophet's suffering and rejection, may have influenced the idea of writing a gospel about Jesus that would join these features. Part of that suggestion would have "the passion of Jeremiah" (including the later tradition of a violent death) influence the passion of Jesus. Worthy of notice is that the closest PN allusions to Jeremiah are in the Matthean special passion material (innocent blood, Judas' silver, the potter's field, "all the people"),[18] a distribution suggesting that on a popular level the analogy between Jesus and Jeremiah was strongly influential. If one may add Lamentations to the Jeremiah background for the passion, Lam 2:15 has all who pass along wag their heads at the afflicted daughter of Jerusalem, even as Mark 15:29; Matt 27:39 have the passersby wag their heads at the crucified Jesus. Lam 3:28–30 envisions that the one who waits for the Lord keeps silence when the yoke is laid on him and offers the cheek to the one who hits him.

Ezekiel 37, the vision of the revitalization of the dry bones (especially 37:12–13: "I will open your tombs, and I will bring you up out of your tombs, and I will lead you into the land of Israel"), is the background of other Matthean special material, namely, the poetic quatrain describing what happened when Jesus died: "The tombs were opened, and many bodies of the fallen-asleep holy ones were raised. . . . They entered into the holy city" (Matt 27:52–53). The influence of Ezekiel on this Matthean scene may be stronger if we use the later frescoes of Dura Europos as a guide to the popular understanding of Ezek 37, for there an earthquake rends the rocks, opening the tombs (Matt 27:51: "The earth was shaken, and the rocks were rent").

Daniel 7 is often seen as the background for the Gospel use of "Son of Man" for Jesus. Certainly as Jesus stands before the high priest in Mark 14:62 and par., his words ("You will see the Son of Man sitting at the right of the Power and coming with the clouds of heaven") echo a combination of Ps 110:1 ("sit at my right hand") and Dan 7:13 with its vision of "one like a son of man coming with the clouds of heaven."[19] The Danielic vision concerns a heavenly court where judgment is given to a son of man (= saints of

---

[17]The poetic form of this (Jer 7:11) is cited in Mark 11:17 and par.

[18]Jer 18:2; 19:1–2; 26:15–16. Outside that material see Jer 15:9 where an oracle of doom for Jerusalem warns "her sun is set in the middle hour of the day." In the Last Supper context one may compare the "new covenant" in the Lucan eucharistic formula (22:20) with Jer 31:31.

[19]See earlier allusions to this verse of Dan in Mark 8:38 and 13:26.

the Most High: 7:10,22), even as Jesus' Son-of-Man statement has the context of a court and judgment. The issue of blasphemy at the trial may echo the antiGod figure of Dan 7:8,20,25 who speaks arrogantly against the Most High. We saw above that Ezek 37 offered background for Matt's description of the phenomena surrounding the death of Jesus, but the raising of the bodies of the fallen-asleep saints may also reflect Dan 12:2: "And many of those who sleep in the dust of the earth shall be awakened, some to eternal life." The Sanhedrin trial of Jesus in Mark/Matt resembles the Susanna story in Dan 13 (elders, false witnesses).

Minor Prophets. Darkness over the whole earth from the sixth hour (noon) to the ninth hour (3 P.M.) in Mark 15:33 and par. is often seen as an allusion to the eschatological day of the Lord in Amos 8:9: "The sun shall set at midday, and the light shall be darkened on the earth in the daytime." (See also Zeph 1:15; Joel 2:2.) This darkness is part of what leads to the centurion's confession of Jesus as God's Son in Mark 15:39 and par.; and the next verse in Amos (8:10) states, "I will make them mourn as for an only son."

Zech 9–14 requires special attention (see Bruce, "Book"); for as a single OT passage, next to Ps 22, it offers the most extensive background for the passion. Indeed, if one begins the passion as I have done, after the Last Supper with Jesus proceeding across the Kidron to the Mount of Olives, his very first words (Mark 14:27; Matt 26:31) are a formal citation of Zech 13:7 about striking the shepherd and scattering the sheep. Jesus' entry into Jerusalem (Mark 11:1–10 and par.), seated on a colt and greeted by hosannas, echoes Zech 9:9. Zech 14:21 would have the house of the Lord purified of all merchants by the final day, even as Jesus purifies the Temple (Mark 11:15–19 and par.; especially John 2:16). Jesus' Last Supper statement identifying the wine with blood of the covenant seems to allude to Zech 9:11 ("the blood of my covenant with you"). Zech 11:12–13 sets the price of the shepherd at thirty pieces of silver which are thrown into the House of the Lord into the potter (see p. 642 above on Matt 27:3–10). John 19:34,37, when the soldier stabs the dead Jesus' side with a lance, recalls Zech 12:10 about looking on the one who has been pierced.[20]

4. WISDOM OR SAPIENTIAL BOOKS[21]

Prov 31:6–7 would give strong drink to those who are perishing and wine to those in bitter distress in order to make them forget their misery; it is often proposed as the background for Mark 15:23 and Matt 27:34 where as soon

---

[20]John 7:38 with its water flowing from within Jesus may echo Zech 14:8 that has the water flowing from Jerusalem.

[21]Those Wisdom Books found in the Hebrew Bible are often classified in or with "the Other Books (Writings)."

as Jesus arrives at Golgotha, even before he is crucified, he is offered wine. The Book of Wisdom (of Solomon), composed in Greek, probably in Alexandria ca. 100 BC, has a passage about the suffering just one that seems to be echoed in a remarkable way in the PNs.[22] Scoffers have been oppressing the just man (2:10ff.), angry at him because he professes to have knowledge of God and styles himself a child of God (2:13), and because by that very claim his life is not like that of other men (2:15). In 2:18 they cry out for a test to see whether the words of this man are true: "If the just man be the son of God, He will defend him, and deliver him from the hand of his foes." In tone the mockery of Jesus on the cross in the three Synoptics is close to this passage, especially the wording peculiar to Matt 27:43: "He has trusted in God. Let him be delivered if He wants him, for he said, 'I am Son of God.'" The equivalence in the Wisdom passage between "just one" and "son of God" throws light on the variant Gospel forms of the centurion's confession when Jesus dies: "Truly this (man) was God's Son" (Mark 15:39; Matt 27:54) and "Certainly this man was just" (Luke 23:47).[23]

B. *Passion Parallels in the Psalms, Especially Ps 22*

Psalms is *facile princeps* among OT books in supplying background for the PN. Rose ("Influence") is particularly helpful in detecting the many parallels I shall discuss below. Yet, as Homerski (Abstract) correctly points out, the psalm parallels are to secondary details that fill in the story (mostly to incidents involving what other people do to Jesus); and no psalm offers a parallel to the basic Gospel outline of Jesus' passion. Nor does it seem that in fleshing out the outline, early Christians did a verse-by-verse interpretation of any psalm (even Ps 22) similar to what appears in the Qumran pesharim on the psalms (McCaffrey, "Psalm" 73–74). Most psalms cited or alluded to in the PNs would be classified as Lamentations or Petitions centered on the sufferings of the innocent just, but Thanksgiving Psalms (34) and Royal Psalms (2; 110) also serve as passion background. Next to Ps 22, the psalms most indisputably in mind were 69[24] and 31, with Pss 42/43 having special

---

[22]This situation causes us to notice how early the knowledge of books that were never part of the Hebrew Bible entered into Christian reflection on the "Scriptures."

[23]The victory of the suffering just one is depicted in Wis 5:1–5, which offers a better general parallel to the victory of the risen Jesus than does the second part of Ps 22 (to be discussed below). A reasonable case can be made that the figure of the Isaian Suffering Servant influenced the picture in Wisdom.

[24]Before the PNs Ps 69:10 ("Zeal for your House consumes me") is used in the account of the cleansing of the Temple in John 2:17. Other psalm uses in passages preparatory to the passion would include Ps 118:22–23 as part of the warning Parable of the Tenants in the Vineyard (Mark 12:10–11 and par.); and Ps 118:26–27 alluding to the entry of Jesus to Jerusalem (Mark 11:7–11 and par.). See also n. 5 above for the Last Supper citations of Pss 41:10; 69:5, and perhaps 35:19.

influence on John.[25] Below I shall follow the numerical order of the psalms in citing passages[26] that have been proposed as offering background for the passion of Jesus. Sometimes the proposed allusion is very general and highly speculative; other times (where I use boldface type) the proposal has high possibility, probability, or certainty. Subsection 1 will treat all the psalms except Ps 22, which will be treated in subsection 2.

1. PROPOSED PSALM PARALLELS (EXCEPT PS 22) FOR THE PASSION

Ps 2:1–2 (LXX) reads, "Why did the Gentiles act arrogantly, and the people think of empty things? The kings of the earth came to take their stand, and the rulers gathered together [*synagein*] in the same place against the Lord and against His Messiah." It is cited in Acts 4:25–27 in reference to Herod (king) and Pilate (ruler), the Gentiles and the Israelites, gathering against Jesus the anointed servant of God. In the PN Luke alone (23:6–12) gives Herod a place alongside Pilate in the trial of Jesus. The verb "gather together," in reference to the assembling of Jesus' Jewish opponents against him, is found in Matt 26:3,57; 27:17,62; and Luke 22:66.

Ps 18:7, "From His holy sanctuary He heard my cry," may be echoed in Mark 15:37–38 and par., where Jesus' "loud cry" is followed by the divine rending of the sanctuary veil.

Pss 26:6 and 73:13 use the imagery of washing one's hands in innocence and serve as background for Matt 27:24, where Pilate washes his hands, saying, "I am innocent of the blood of this man."

Pss 27:12 and 35:11 have unjust (*adikoi*) witnesses rise up against the just one; cf. the false witnesses against Jesus in Mark 14:57,59; Matt 26:59–60.

Ps 31:6, "Into your hands I shall place my spirit," supplies Jesus' last words in Luke 23:46: "Father, into your hands I place my spirit." (The use of this psalm of the suffering just one should be compared to Jesus' last words in Mark/Matt; see 1* under Ps 22 below.) For Ps 31:12 see n. 51 below.

Ps 31:14 has: "While they were gathered together [*synagein*] against me, they took counsel [*bouleuein*] how to take my life."[27] After the gathering

---

[25]See the debate between Beutler and Freed. Beutler maintains that 42/43 served for John the function that 69 and 22 served for the Synoptics; Freed insists that passages where Beutler sees the influence of Pss 42/43 are freely composed with several different OT pericopes influencing the vocabulary and imagery.

[26](I remind readers of how psalm numbers and verses are cited; see p. xix in this volume.) Some may wonder about the order if I listed the more plausible psalm parallels (those to appear in boldface) in a sequence that followed the Gospel PN order of events or words that echo the psalms. Such a sequence would yield Ps 41:10; Ps 42:6; Ps 110:1; Ps 2:1–2; Ps 69:22; Ps 31:6; Ps 34:21; Ps 38:12. In no Gospel would the sequence of incidents with psalm parallels follow the numerical order of the psalms.

[27]See also Ps 71:10 for enemies taking counsel against the just one.

together against Jesus in Matt 26:3 (see Ps 2:1–2 above), the chief priest and the elders took counsel together (*symbouleuein*) to seize Jesus by stealth and kill him (Matt 26:4). See also the report in John 18:14 that Caiaphas "advised" or "counselled" (*symbouleuein*) that Jesus should die.

Ps 31:23 has the plea of the just one heard when he shouts out to the Lord; cf. Mark 15:37–38 and par.

Ps 34:21, where the Lord watches over the bones of the just so that not even one of them would be fractured, may be added to the description of the paschal lamb as another source of the Scripture cited in John 19:36, "His bone shall not be fractured."

Ps 35:21 has the enemies of the just one exclaiming "Aha"; cf. Mark 15:29. See under Ps 27:12 above for the use of Ps 35:11, and under n. 5 above for the Last-Supper use of Ps 35:19. See also n. 52 below.

Ps 38:12 has those who were close to the afflicted "standing from [*apo*] a distance" (see also Pss 88:9; 69:9). Mark 15:40–41 and Matt 27:55 have the women followers observing from a distance the death of Jesus on the cross; to these women Luke 23:49 adds "all those known to him."

Ps 39:10 has a suppliant who under chastisement was struck mute and did not open his mouth. This has been suggested as a parallel to the times when Jesus stayed silent and answered nothing.[28]

Ps 41:7 has an enemy coming to the just one, speaking without sincerity; cf. the behavior of Judas in Mark 14:45; Matt 26:49; and John 18:3.

Ps 41:10, describing the trusted friend who partook of the just man's bread and then raised his heel against him, appears in a fulfillment citation at the Last Supper in John 13:18 in reference to Judas. It may also underlie Mark 14:18 and par.[29]

Ps 42:2–3, "My soul has thirsted for the living God," is sometimes seen as the background for the words of the crucified Jesus in John 19:28, "I thirst" (but see Ps 22:16).

Ps 42:6 (see also 42:12), "Why are you very sorrowful, my soul, and why do you disturb [*syntarassein*] me?" is echoed by Jesus in Gethsemane in Mark 14:34; Matt 26:38 ("My soul is very sorrowful"[30]) and Ps 42:7, "My

---

[28]See n. 15 above. Some would also invoke the MT of Ps 38:14: "I have become like . . . a mute who opens not his mouth [LXX: a man who has no reproofs in his mouth]," but this is an even more uncertain parallel to Jesus' silence than Isa 53:7.

[29]In treating Ps 22, Fisher ("Betrayed" 27–36) discusses Ps 41, combining the Judas parallel with II Sam 15–17 (Ahithophel betrays David) discussed in §5. Ps 41:2 blesses the one who has regard for the lowly and the poor, something that Judas pretended to do in John 12:4–5.

[30]The words of Jesus continue "unto death," perhaps echoing Judg 16:16 (where Samuel's soul was vexed unto death) and particularly Sir 37:2: "Is it not a sorrow unto death when your companion or friend is turned enemy?"

soul is disturbed [*tarassein*]," is echoed in John 12:27 ("Now is my soul disturbed").[31] For Ps 42:11 see n. 51 below.

Ps 69:4 portrays the just one as weary from shouting out and his throat as parched or hoarse; see the reference to Jesus' loud death cry in Mark 15:34,37 and to his thirst in John 19:28. See n. 5 above for the Last-Supper use of Ps 69:5.

Ps 69:22, "And they gave for my bread gall, and for my thirst they gave me to drink vinegary wine [*oxos*]," is clearly echoed in Matt 27:34 and 48 where the crucified Jesus is given wine (*oinos*) mixed with gall and later vinegary wine. It is probably alluded to in Mark 15:36; Luke 23:36; and John 19:29 where Jesus is offered vinegary wine. Is the psalm also background for Mark 15:23 where Jesus is offered wine (*oinos*) mixed with myrrh?

Ps 109:25 makes the just one the subject of mockery to those who see him and wag their heads, even as the passersby blaspheme the crucified Jesus and wag their heads in Mark 15:29; Matt 27:39. However, this expression of scorn is common in the OT; see Lam 2:15; and especially Ps 22:8.

Ps 110:1, where the Lord God says "to my lord, 'Sit at my right,'" supplies the context for the Son of Man "sitting at the right of the Power" (Mark 14:62 and par.) in Jesus' warning to the high priest in the Synoptic account of the Jewish trial.

Ps 118:22 speaks of the stone that the builders rejected (*apodokimazein*), a passage used by Jesus in Mark 12:10 as a warning to the hostile audience of the parable of the tenants in the vineyard. In the first of the three detailed Synoptic passion predictions (Table 13 in APPENDIX VIII), Mark 8:31 and Luke 9:22 foresee that the Son of Man will be "rejected."[32]

Let us now turn to the psalm that offers the most parallels to the PNs.

2. Ps 22 AND THE PASSION

Tertullian (*Adv. Marcion* 3.19.5; CC 1.533) spoke of "the 21st [= Hebrew 22nd] psalm containing the whole of Christ's passion"; indeed it has been called simply *the* passion psalm. Let us begin with some general remarks about the structure, origin, and import of the psalm. As generally agreed, it

---

[31]The Johannine Jesus goes on (12:27) to ask, "And what should I say? Father, save me from this hour?" Ps 6:4–5 has: "My soul is greatly disturbed. . . . O Lord . . . save me for your mercy's sake." See also Hab 3:2 (LXX).

[32]Instead of *apodokimazein*, the citation of this psalm in Acts 4:11 uses *exouthenein*, a variant form of *exoudenein*, "to consider as nothing, disdain," which appears in Ps 22:7.

consists of two parts: an individual lament in 22:2–22[33] and a thanksgiving in 22:23–32 (with 22:28–32 sometimes designated as an eschatological hymn of praise). An "I" who is suffering speaks throughout the first part; but suddenly that "I" fades into the background in the second part, and the congregation praises the Lord. The Hebrew helps the transition, for v. 22 ends with "You have answered me" (absent from the LXX) that explains the change of tone.[34] Duhm and others have contended that two originally separate psalms were joined; but the majority of scholars (e.g., Gunkel, Kittel, Lagrange, Westermann) treat the psalm as a unity, with the possible exception of vv. 28–32.[35] The understanding is that the lamentation implicitly or explicitly contains a vow to render thanksgiving when the suppliant is heard (a hearing that is assured). In this particular case there is a recognition that the Lord has rescued the suppliant from extinction. Thus it is quite appropriate to have a lamentation coupled with a thanksgiving. (Those psalms where thanksgiving is virtually the whole message are fulfilling the vow of the lamentation.) An argument for unity is found in v. 25, which implies that someone has been afflicted and cried out to God, as did the "I" of the first part of Ps 22.

The title (22:1) attributing the psalm to David[36] and Jesus' applying 22:2 to himself (Mark 15:34; Matt 27:46) gave rise to the early Christian view that the psalm was a prophecy about the suffering Messiah.[37] Accordingly, as Salguero ("Quién" 28) points out, from Augustine to Aquinas a literal application of Ps 22 to the crucified Jesus was dominant. Justin (*Dialogue* 97.3–4) berated Trypho and the Jews for not seeing that Ps 22:17 had to be spoken of the crucified Christ since no other Jewish king had his hands and

---

[33]This may be subdivided into two subsections: 2–11 (direct address and lament to God) and 12–22 (description of the trouble and a plea to God); or into three subsections (e.g., Gese), 2–6, 7–12, 13–22, each involving a complaint (ascending in intensity and length) and an expression of prayerful confidence.

[34]However, as indicated by my italics, many scholars emend because of the abruptness of the clause ("Save me from the mouth of the lion, and from the horns of the wild ox [save] *my afflicted self*") or prefer another verbal meaning: "*make me triumph.*"

[35]Those who divide part one of the psalm into two subsections (n. 33 above) may see the second part divided into two subsections as well: 23–27 and 28–32. However, Gelin, Martin-Achard, and E. Podechard are among those who think vv. 28–32 had a different origin, reflected in its different theme (the kingship of Yahweh). E. Lipinski (*Biblica* 50 [1969], 153–68) sees it as a hymn from the 8th or 7th cents. BC.

[36]One can debate whether *ldwd* contains a *lamed auctoris* ("by David") or is designed to make the psalm royal: "for the Davidic king." R. B. Hays, "Christ Prays the Psalms: Paul's Use of an Early Christian Exegetical Convention," in *The Future of Christology,* eds. A. Malherbe and W. Meeks (L. E. Keck Festschrift; Minneapolis: Fortress, 1993), 122–36, contends that the tradition of reading the royal (Davidic) lament psalms as prefiguration of the Messiah was early enough to be prePauline.

[37]Aquila translated what is often thought to be a musical notation in the title of the psalm (22:1: *lmnṣḥ:* "for the leader") as "to the maker of victory" (so also Jerome); and the LXX has "to the end"—thus the messianism could be given an eschatological thrust. See Bornhäuser, *Death* 2.

feet pierced.[38] Indeed, the view of Theodore of Mopsuestia that the psalm was not a prophecy was disapproved at the Second (Fifth Ecumenical) Council of Constantinople and condemned by Pope Vigilius on May 14/24, 553 (PL 69.84ff.). Nevertheless, some continued to interpret typically or spiritually the figure described in the psalm rather than resorting to a theory of direct prophecy. One of the ancient factors supporting this thesis is the second clause of 22:2 in the LXX and Vulgate: "Far from my salvation are the words [i.e., recounting] of my sins"—the reference to "my sins," inapplicable to Jesus, could be understood if the figure in the psalm represented humanity. In later Jewish exegesis (Rashi) the psalmist's fate was identified with that of the Jewish people. Yet such collective interpretations are also open to objection, for the psalm is close to the laments of individuals, e.g., of Jeremiah. Senior ("Death Song" 1461) thinks that the psalm probably originated in the genuine personal experience of the anonymous psalmist, experience that eventually was looked on as appropriate to the just Israelite. Soggin ("Appunti" 109–13) contends that to do justice to both the royal-individual and the collective interpretations of the psalm we should think of the figure as the king-spokesman for the community, but a humiliated king as in Zech 9:9.[39]

To an extent the ancient disputes about direct prophetic application to Jesus are no longer pertinent.[40] Although some scholars think of the psalm being composed in the latter part of the monarchical period with heavy reorientation after 586 BC, the majority think of composition in the postexilic period—either dating rules out Davidic composition. Rather than fitting the psalm into the life of a historical OT individual like David who suffered the afflictions described, most would now think of a liturgical context. Schmid ("Mein Gott" 124) finds in the psalm the priestly religion of the postexilic period, where liturgically the individual believer's prayer is related to the community whose faith assures that God will answer. Stolz ("Psalm 22") speaks of a postexilic circle of righteous sufferers who endured great tribulation but remained firm in anticipating divine help. As for prophecy, we note

[38]*Dialogue* 98–106 is largely concerned with applying this psalm to Jesus' whole career, including his birth.

[39]Ps 22:10–11 with its suggestion that the psalmist who speaks was taken from the womb and set aside from birth may be compared with Ps 2:7 that involves the divine begetting of the king. Following Scandinavian interpreters, Soggin ("Appunti" 114–15) contends that the king and the Suffering Servant may have been joined in Jewish expectation, especially among the Anawim or poor ones.

[40]Yet as late as 1948 in Roman Catholicism, Feuillet ("Souffrance") was urging that Ps 22 is broadly messianic, as interpreted in a typical rather than a literal sense, so that the psalmist did not have to know about Christ ahead of time. In 1972 Lange ("Relationship" 610), arguing for a typological application, pointed out that among Missouri Synod Lutherans a literal prediction by David would still be the more common interpretation.

that in the MT of the psalm the suffering is expressed in the present tense, without reference to the future, and is not primarily a prediction. The figure whom the psalmist addresses as "My God" (22:2) is enthroned in the Jerusalem Temple receiving the praises of Israel (22:4) and in heaven anticipating the praises of the whole earth (22:28–30). A particular liturgical context that has been envisioned by many is the service of the *tôdâ*[41] involving the one whose prayer for deliverance has been answered. Going to the sanctuary, that person fulfilled the vow involved in the lamentation, and supplied a sacrificial meal for relatives and friends, singing the hymn of thanksgiving. The dating in a postexilic context makes it conceivable that Jeremiah's vocalization of his complaints to God may have had an effect on the formulation of this lamentation pattern.[42] The reference to the psalmist being taken from "my mother's" belly and womb (22:10–11) may be compared to Jer 1:5 (cf. 20:17–18) where the prophet has been set aside before coming from his mother's womb. The Ps 22 pattern of discouragement and confidence matches the tone of Jeremiah's soliloquies; and Martin-Achard ("Remarques" 82) points to the psalmist as a Jeremiah-like person with greater confidence who refuses to end his psalm on the note of Jer 20:14–18, cursing the day he was born. Parallels have also been detected between Ps 22 and the Suffering Servant songs of Deutero-Isaiah, with the mistreatment in Ps 22:7–9 comparable to that in Isa 50:6; 53:3.[43] The Servant pierced (MT *ḥll*) for our sins in Isa 53:5 may be compared to the psalmist who in the LXX of 22:17 speaks of the piercing of his hands and feet. (It has often been suggested that the Servant was patterned on Jeremiah, so that we may be comparing parallel literature, prophetic and liturgical, with the same antecedent.[44]) A joining of the Servant Song of Isa 53 and Ps 22:7–9 is attested at the end of the 1st cent. AD in *I Clement* 16.

[41]Advocacy of parts of this theory is associated with J. Begrich, ZAW 52 (1934), 81–92; it has been challenged by R. Kilian, BZ 12 (1968), 172–85, chiefly in reference to whether a priestly oracle of fulfillment is involved. In reference to Ps 22 and the PN the *tôdâ* background is accepted by Dillon, Gese, Mays, Reumann, etc. Specifically Senior ("Death" 1460) points to Lev 7:11ff. with its description of the peace offering.

[42]So Gelin, "Quatre" 31. Holladay ("Background") calls attention to persuasive parallels between Ps 22 and Jer, but thinks the prophet drew on the psalm.

[43]See Ruppert, *Leidende* 49–50; Feuillet, "Souffrance" 141–45. Although Worden ("My God" 12) thinks the psalmist modeled the portrait on the image of the Servant, an essential element of the Servant depiction is absent, namely, vicarious suffering. It should be noted that the description of the one buffeted and spat upon in Isa 50:6 leads into praise of God's help in 50:7ff. Similarly the portrait of the Servant as not crying out in Isa 42:2 is followed by a description of a divine vocation (seemingly from creation) to serve salvific purposes—a sequence not unlike Ps 22:7–11. Yet the Servant songs result in the vindication or raising up of the Servant while Ps 22 does not stress the personal vindication of the lamenter.

[44]Stuhlmueller ("Faith" 18) reports with favor the view of H.-J. Kraus: So many passages and converging traditions are echoed in Ps 22 that it may have been composed by many authors over a long period of time. However, it is more likely that an old psalm was revised through the centuries.

There is no evidence that Ps 22 was applied in preChristian Judaism to the expected Messiah,[45] despite the fact that the ending of the psalm gives a strong eschatological thrust to the sufferings of the depicted just one. Martin-Achard ("Remarques" 85) speaks of a hasid or holy one who is also an eschatological personage. Perhaps that context explains the interesting application of themes similar to those of Ps 22 in a Qumran thanksgiving hymn, 1QH 5:5–19.[46] In these hymns the speaker is often thought to be the community hero, the Righteous Teacher, vocalizing not only his own anguish but also the pain and faith of the community living in the last times. 1QH 5:10–11, "They have not opened their mouth against me," contains wording from Ps 22:14. 1QH 5:12–13, "For in the distress of my soul You have not abandoned me; You have heard my cry in the bitterness of my soul; and have received the clamor of my affliction in my groaning," may be compared with the sentiments of the psalmist who, after crying to God in 22:3,20–22, states in 22:25: "He has not spurned or abhorred the afflicted in his affliction, and He has not turned His face from him; but in his shouting out to Him, He has heard."[47] The continuation in 1QH 5:13, "You have delivered the soul of the afflicted," echoes the prayer of Ps 22:21, "Deliver my soul."

The background just cited helps us to understand the Christian application of the Ps 22 to the suffering Jesus[48] who was also looked on as the Suffering Servant and a Jeremiah-like figure. Using an example of a special (perhaps even regal) pious or just person,[49] the psalmist was vocalizing the thesis that the just who trust in God frequently suffer atrociously at the hands of adversaries, even to the point of feeling abandoned by God; yet finally God always vindicates the just. (This is an indirect refutation of another, more facile thesis that God will deliver favored ones from suffering—see the proposal of Jesus' opponents in Matt 27:43.) The fact that the psalmist does not

---

[45]A half-millennium after Jesus' time the *Midrash on Psalms* (Braude translation, 1.298ff.) shows a royal application of Ps 22 to King Hezekiah when threatened by Sennacherib, or to Queen Esther when the Jews were threatened by Haman.

[46]See Fisher, "Betrayed" 25–27; Lange, "Relationship" 611–13; Rupert, *Leidende* 114–33. Dillon ("Psalms" 435) sees in 1QH 3:19–36 an analogy of structure to Ps 22, except that the Qumran hymn has the order: thanksgiving, retrospective lament, and eschatological outlook.

[47]Note that in 1QH there is a parallel to the second, more positive part of the psalm, while in the Gospel PNs the clear parallels are all to the lamenting lines of the first part.

[48]Despite the strong likelihood that the psalm had a liturgical or cultic background, the parallels in the Qumran thanksgiving hymns suggest the possibility of a community applying the psalm to an individual even outside of Temple liturgy. As for Christian application to Jesus, whether the psalm was first applied to Jesus in a liturgical context, e.g., in a Christian *tôdâ* related to the eucharist, is debated.

[49]Mays ("Prayer" 329) contends: "Psalm 22 cannot be the prayer and praise of just any afflicted Israelite. Though we cannot know for certain for whom it was written and through what revisions it may have passed, in its present form the figure in the psalm shares in the corporate vocation of Israel and the messianic role of David."

pray for the punishment of these adversaries lent a special adaptability to Jesus, as did the eschatological ending in 22:28–32; for through this just sufferer all the ends of the earth, including the families of the Gentiles, are brought to worship the God of Israel. Since the early Christians would have thought the psalm was composed by David, that understanding also affected their application of the psalm to the Son of David. And, once the tradition was developed that the dying Jesus himself cited the opening line of the psalm (22:2 in Mark 15:34; Matt 27:46), further Christian use of the psalm for details of the crucifixion would have been predictable.

Let us now list allusions to Ps 22 that scholars have detected in the Gospel PNs.[50] The list follows the psalm order, indicating with boldface type allusions or citations that are more plausible or certain (for this distinction, see also Oswald, "Beziehungen" 56). The translation of the psalm reflects the LXX.

1* **Ps 22:2a:** "My God, my God, *receive me,* to what purpose have you forsaken me?" In having Jesus quote this, Matt 27:46 is slightly closer to the LXX wording than is Mark 15:34, but neither quotes the italicized phrase, which is also absent from the MT.

2* Ps 22:3, "My God, I have shouted . . . by night, and there is no rest for me," may be alluded to in the Synoptic pattern of darkness over the whole earth to the ninth hour when Jesus uttered a loud cry (Mark 15:33–34; Matt 27:45–46; Luke 23:44,46).

3* **Ps 22:7b,** "Reviled [*oneidizein*] by human beings and considered as nothing [*exouthenein*] by people," is plausibly alluded to in the mockery of Jesus on the cross where Mark 15:29,32b and Matt 27:39,44 have the passersby blaspheme him and the co-crucified "revile" him.[51] In Luke 23:11 Herod treats Jesus as nothing (= "with contempt"); see also n. 32 above.

4* **Ps 22:8a,** "All those observing me sneered at me," is probably alluded to in the Lucan form (23:35a) of the mockery of Jesus on the cross: "And the people were standing there observing. But there were also rulers sneering."[52]

5* **Ps 22:8b,** "They spoke with the lips; they wagged the head," is probably

[50]Ps 22 passages cited or alluded to elsewhere in the NT, outside the Gospels, include: *Ps 22:14* (enemies "like a roaring lion") in I Pet 5:8 ("devil a roaring lion"); *Ps 22:22* ("Save me from the mouth of the lion") in II Tim 4:17 ("I was delivered from the mouth of the lion"); *Ps 22:23* ("I will tell of Your name to my brothers; in the midst of the church [*ekklēsia*] I will hymn You") almost verbatim in Heb 2:12.

[51]Pss 31:12; 42:11; 102:9; and 119:22 refer to being reviled by enemies. Rom 15:3 cites Ps 69:10 on Christ being reviled.

[52]Mockery is described as "sneering" also in Ps 35:16.

alluded to in Mark 15:29; Matt 27:39 where those passing by are "wagging their heads."

6* **Ps 22:9,** "He has hoped in the Lord; let Him deliver him; let Him save him because He wants him," is partially echoed in the challenge to Jesus on the cross: "Save yourself" (Mark 15:30; Matt 27:40; Luke 23:39b). It is more fully echoed in Matt 27:43: "He has trusted in God. Let him be delivered if He wants him."

7* Ps 22:16b, "My tongue has stuck to my jaws," may be part of the background of John 19:28 where, in order that the Scripture be completed, Jesus says, "I thirst." (See also Pss 42:2–3; 69:4.)

8* Ps 22:17b, "A company of evildoers [*ponēroumenoi*] has encircled me," may lie behind depicting the crucified Jesus between two bandits (Mark 15:27; Matt 27:38; cf. John 19:18), especially in Luke 23:33: "They crucified him and the wrongdoers [*kakourgoi*], the one on the right, and the other on the left."

9* **Ps 22:17c,** "They have pierced[53] my hands and my feet," is probably echoed in the portrait of the crucified, *risen* Jesus in Luke 24:39, "See my hands and my feet" (cf. John 20:25,27: "the place of the nails . . . see my hands").

10* **Ps 22:19,** "They divided up my clothes among themselves, and for my clothing they threw lots," lies behind the description of the division of the crucified Jesus' clothes in all four Gospels,[54] and appears verbatim as a fulfillment citation in John 19:24.

11* Ps 22:25c, "And in my shouting [*kragein*] to Him, He heard me," may be alluded to in the Synoptic sequence where, when Jesus has expired with a loud cry (*phonē*), divine intervention takes place with the rending of the sanctuary veil (Mark 15:37–38; Matt 27:50–53; but cf. Luke 23:46,45b).

12* Ps 22:28b, "All the families of the nations shall worship before Him," may be remotely alluded to in the reaction of the (Gentile) centurion

---

[53]The MT has "*kā'ărî* [like a lion] my hands and my feet," which Aquila and Jerome read as "they bound," presumably interpreting the consonants as a form from *krh* (which should have yielded the form *kārû*, a verb which elsewhere is not attested in that meaning). The LXX uses *oryssein,* "to dig," drawing on an attested meaning of *krh* (but never in a figurative sense as here). Others, drawing on Akkadian parallels, suppose that *krh* can mean "to be short, shrivel." (See J.J.M. Roberts, VT 23 [1973], 247–52.) It is also possible to accept the MT text and understand a verb: "Like a lion (they maul) my hands and my feet."

[54]Presumably in their descriptions the evangelists are using the psalm language freely; and Robbins ("Reversed" 2.1176) shows how Mark has rephrased it in his own style. Yet Scheifler ("Salmo") has argued that some of the forms may represent use of a text different from that in the MT or LXX, e.g., Luke's participial "dividing his clothes" (23:34b) reflecting the targumic participial form over against the MT/LXX finite verb. One would need to have more proof that the targum was available in the 1st cent. and that Luke could read Aramaic.

confessing Jesus who had just died (Mark 15:39; Matt 27:54; Luke 23:47).

These twelve proposals for citations of or allusions to Ps 22 in the PNs have very uneven value. Nevertheless, what impressions emerge when we consider them? The order of the psalm verses does not correspond to the order of the parallels in any of the four Gospels.[55] Accordingly the sequence of the PN was scarcely created from this psalm.[56] Indeed, the parallels all refer to crucifixion episodes, not to anything earlier or later in the PN. This, then, should be called a crucifixion psalm rather than "the passion psalm," for there is no visible way that it created or heavily influenced other parts of the passion. Within the crucifixion narrative, the three areas of concentration are, to use the terminology of my sections in the commentary, the setting of the crucifixion (§40: 8*,9*,10*), the mocking of Jesus on the cross (§41: 3*,4*,5*,6*), and the death and its aftermath (§§42–44: 1*,2*,7*,11*,12*). In other words, given the historical tradition that Jesus died on a cross, *at most* this psalm caused Christians: (1) to concentrate on certain details, e.g., the presence of co-crucified wrongdoers, the pierced hands (and feet), the division of clothes; (2) to dramatize the mocking hostility shown to Jesus by those around the cross, challenging his claim to have God's help; and (3) to highlight the reversal in an abandoned death and subsequent victory.

Although all four Gospels use the psalm (10*, perhaps 8*), the respective usage is not the same. The widest use of Ps 22 is in Mark/Matt (1*,2*,3*,5*,6*,8*,10*,11*,12*), with Matt's use distinctively stronger only in 6*. Thus the formative effect of Ps 22 on the PN was already strong when the first Gospel was written (if not before). Some speak of the Marcan use as apologetic (e.g., McCaffrey, "Psalm" 82–83), presumably in arguments with Jews who rejected Jesus. However, (1) and (2) in my analysis in the preceding paragraph would not really serve that purpose; the chief citation (1*) is so despairing that it created problems for apologetics; and there is no known history of the psalm having messianic connotations that would make

[55]For instance, the pertinent passages Mark 15:24,27,29,30,32b,33–34,37–38,39 correspond to the Ps 22 passages listed as 10*,8*,3*,5*,6*,3*,2*,1*,11*,12*. Since 11* and 12* are very dubious, Robbins ("Reversed" 2.1179) may be correct that, in terms of numerical order, the echoes of Ps 22 in Mark begin with 22:19 (10*) and move backward to 22:2(1*). In my judgment the clearest Marcan uses of the psalm are of 22:19 in Mark 15:24 and of 22:2 in 15:34 (10* and 1*).

[56]Stadelmann ("Salmo") exercises extraordinary imagination in finding the outline of the whole of Mark 14–16 in Ps 22, so that the Synoptic PNs were structured on this psalm. Nor are Ps 22 parallels particularly helpful for theories of preMarcan sources. For example, in the thesis of two preMarcan sources proposed by Taylor (see APPENDIX IX), there would be Ps 22 parallels in each source:1*,3*,5*,6*,10*,12* in A; 2*,8* in B; and 11* in both.

it apologetically attractive.[57] Far more likely the earliest appeal to the psalm was to enable Christians to see the relationship between what happened and God's plan. The events around which the psalm parallels were clustered are not implausible factors in crucifixion, e.g., a number of condemned would be crucified at the same time, their possessions including their clothes would be divided among the executors, the crucified would be reviled. But through the psalm a bridge was created between the ordinary details of crucifixion and OT expression (Oswald, "Beziehungen" 63).

A special issue arises with respect to the Mark/Matt use of the psalm. With the exceptions of the dubious 11* and 12*, all the proposed parallels are from the first part of the psalm. Accordingly if the main purpose of citing the psalm (especially in 1*) was to call attention to the victory in the second part, the evangelists have taken an extraordinarily obscure route to signify this. I have already argued in the commentary against underplaying the strong sense of desolate isolation that the use of Ps 22:2 gives to the Marcan (and Matthean) Jesus; and indeed by reversing order and using the opening verse of the psalm (1*) at the end of the crucifixion as Jesus' last words, Mark (followed by Matt) puts the culminating emphasis on the most desperate lament in the psalm.[58] Yet a somewhat different question arises when we consider what *follows* the PN: Does the thanksgiving section of the psalm (where the lament has been heard) influence the Mark/Matt narrative of what happened after Jesus' death? Gese ("Psalm 22") is a major proponent of this thesis, and would even connect the psalm's influence on the resurrection narrative with the eucharist as a Christian *tôdâ* or thanksgiving meal. The allusions in 11* and 12*, which can be rated possible at most, lie within the PN following the death; but after the burial, in the *postresurrectional* Matthean sequence, possible but quite disputable parallels include *Ps 22:23,* "I will tell of Your name to my brothers," parallel to the instruction to the women in Matt 28:10, "Go, announce to my brothers that they should go to Galilee";[59] and *Ps 22:28,* "All the families of the nations will worship before Him," parallel to Matt 28:19, "Going, therefore, make disciples of all nations." (Note that there is no really parallel vocabulary in Mark to either of these proposed parallels in Matt; any attempt to make a parallel between Joseph from Arimathea and Ps 22:28 where all the ends of the earth turn to

[57]One can debate whether in 6* Matt introduces an apologetic tone stronger than that found in Mark, at least in the direction of polemic, by adding a clearer reference from Ps 22:9 to the mocking of Jesus *by the chief priests.*

[58]True, the 2d-cent. -AD Midrash Mekilta (*Shirata* 3) does cite Ps 22:2, "My God, my God, why have you forsaken me?" as an example of mercy, but it accompanies that citation with a justifying explanation from other passages invoking God.

[59]See also John 20:17, "Go to my brothers and say to them. . . ."

the Lord fails to recognize that Joseph is not presented as converted to Jesus in Mark.) Some have tried to find a reference to resurrection in the words of Ps 22:30 (an obscure verse) about those who go down to the dust bowing down before God; but these are clearly the proud groveling before God's rule and so the passage is not even a good parallel to Matt's emergence of the holy ones from the tombs (27:52). I am not overly convinced by all this. It is one thing to maintain that a very early understanding of the passion and its aftermath was that the suffering of Jesus led to the inbreaking of the eschatological kingdom—an understanding that one can find supported in Ps 22. It is another thing, however, to move beyond the lucidly clear influence of Ps 22 on the Mark/Matt narrative of the crucifixion to posit continued influence of the psalm on the Mark/Matt resurrection *narrative* where there is no clear allusion to Ps 22, especially since in that narrative the victory is embodied primarily in Jesus whereas the psalm does not speak of the victory of the one who uttered the lament but rather submerges the individual in the liturgical community.

A survey of the Lucan use of psalms in the PN (previous subsection) shows that Luke is not particularly close to Mark, and that is true with respect to Ps 22 as well. McCaffrey ("Psalm" 27) thinks Luke gives evidence of a separate tradition on this score, but the differences from Mark may simply reflect editorial option.[60] Certainly the rejection of 1* can be attributed to Lucan christology, and the rejection of the role of the passersby in 3* attributed to Luke's desire to portray Jews (the people) favorable to Jesus at the end of his life, matching those who greeted his birth. When it comes to the mockery of Jesus by the rulers, in 4* Luke can heighten the Marcan use of the psalm (5*). The agreement with Mark in 2*,6*,8*, and 10* concerns crucifixion details on which Luke had no specific sensitivity different from Mark's theology. The Lucan introduction of the Ps 22 reference found in 9* probably does not concern the crucifixion directly but reflects Luke's apologetic interest in the reality of the risen body.

The only clear Johannine use of the psalm is 10*, because 9*, 8*, and 7* are respectively only possible or remotely likely. If one posits John's dependence on Mark,[61] one has to imagine that the evangelist removed most of the Marcan psalm references (many of them in episodes about which there would be no special Johannine theological difference), but then heightened another (10*). It has even been argued that John substituted a different psalm as a major guiding factor in the PN (n. 25 above). All this constitutes a

---

[60]Oswald ("Beziehungen" 64) suggests that Luke may have been more interested in a martyrological presentation of the passion, different from that of Ps 22.

[61]John does not follow any of the peculiar uses of Ps 22 in Matt (6*) or in Luke (4*), with the possible exception of 9*.

peculiar modus operandi to say the least. Once more it is easier to posit that the Johannine tradition of the passion (or of the crucifixion) developed independently, at times with appeal to OT passages different from those that dominated the preMarcan and Marcan tradition.

Bibliography for Appendix VII:
The OT Background of the Passion Narratives

Many writings discuss the use of the OT in the NT; this bibliography is confined to discussions of the use of the OT in the Gospel PNs.

Basset, J.-C., "Le psaume 22 (LXX:21) et la croix chez les pères," RHPR 54 (1974), 383–89.

Beutler, J., "Psalm 42/43 im Johannesevangelium," NTS 25 (1978–79), 33–57.

Bligh, J., "Typology in the Passion Narratives: Daniel, Elijah, Melchizedek," HeyJ 6 (1965), 302–9.

Bruce, F. F., "The Book of Zechariah and the Passion Narrative," BJRL 43 (1960–61), 336–53.

Deissler, A., " 'Mein Gott, warum hast du mich verlassen . . . !' (Ps 22,2): Das Reden zu Gott und von Gott in den Psalmen—am Beispiel von Psalm 22," in *"Ich will euer Gott werden,"* eds. H. Merklein and E. Zenger (SBS 100; Stuttgart: KBW, 1981), 97–121.

Dillon, R. J., "The Psalms of the Suffering Just in the Accounts of Jesus' Passion," *Worship* 61 (1987), 430–40.

Feigel, F. K., *Der Einfluss des Weissagungsbeweises und anderer Motive auf die Leidensgeschichte* (Tübingen: Mohr, 1910).

Feuillet, A., "Souffrance et confiance en Dieu. Commentaire du psaume xxii," NRT 70 (1948), 137–49.

Fisher, L. R., "Betrayed by Friends, an Expository Study of Psalm 22," *Interpretation* 18 (1964), 20–38.

Flesseman-van Leer, E., "Die Interpretation der Passionsgeschichte vom Alten Testament aus," ZBTJ 79–96.

Freed, E. D., "Psalm 42/43 in John's Gospel," NTS 29 (1983), 62–73.

Gelin, A., "Les quatre lectures du Psaume xxii," BVC 1 (1953), 31–39.

Gese, H., "Psalm 22 und das Neue Testament. Der älteste Bericht vom Tode Jesu und die Enstehung des Herrenmahles," ZTK 65 (1968), 1–22. Eng. summary in TD 18 (1970), 237–43.

Guichard, D., "La reprise du Psaume 22 dans le récit de la mort de Jésus (Marc 15,21–41)," FV 87 (1988), 59–64.

Holladay, W. L., "The Background of Jeremiah's Self-Understanding: Moses, Samuel and Psalm 22," JBL 83 (1964), 153–64.

Homerski, J., Abstract of his Polish article on OT allusions in the PN, NTA 26 (1980–81), #452.

Hooker, M. D., *Jesus and the Servant: The Influence of the Servant Concept of Deutero-Isaiah in the New Testament* (London: SPCK, 1959), esp. 86–102.

Kee, H. C., "The Function of Scriptural Quotations and Allusions in Mark 11–16," in *Jesus und Paulus*, eds. E. E. Ellis and E. Grässer (W. G. Kümmel Festschrift; Göttingen: Vandenhoeck & Ruprecht, 1975), 165–88.

Kissane, E. J., " 'Foederunt manus meas et pedes meos,' " ITQ 19 (1952), 72–74.

Kleinknecht, K. T., *Der leidende Gerechtfertige. Die alttestamentlich-jüdische Tradition vom "leidende Gerechten" und ihre Rezeption bei Paulus* (WUNT 2/13; Tübingen: Mohr, 1984).

Lange, H. D., "The Relationship between Psalm 22 and the Passion Narrative," CTM 43 (1972), 610–21.

Lohse, E., "Die alttestamentlichen Bezüge im neutestamentlichen Zeugnis vom Tode Jesu Christi," ZBTJ 97–112.

McCaffrey, U. P., "Psalm quotations in the passion narratives of the Gospels," *Neotestamentica* 14 (1981), 73–89.

Martin-Achard, R., "Remarques sur le Psaume 22," VCaro 17 (1963), 78–87.

Mays, J. L., "Prayer and Christology: Psalm 22 as Perspective on the Passion," TToday 42 (1985), 322–31.

Moo, D. J., *The Old Testament in the Gospel Passion Narratives* (Sheffield: Almond, 1983).

Oswald, J., "Die Beziehungen zwischen Psalm 22 und den vormarkinischen Passionsbericht," ZKT 101 (1979), 53–66.

Reumann, J. H., "Psalm 22 at the Cross," *Interpretation* 28 (1974), 39–58.

Robbins, V. K., "The Reversed Contextualization of Psalm 22 in the Markan Crucifixion: A Socio-Rhetorical Analysis," FGN 2.1161–83.

Rose, A., "L'influence des psaumes sur les annonces et les récits de la Passion et de la Résurrection dans les Évangiles," in *Le Psautier,* ed. R. De Langhe (Orientalia et Biblica Lovaniensia 4; Louvain Univ., 1962), 297–356.

Ruppert, L., *Der leidende Gerechte* (Forschung zur Bibel 5; Würzburg: Echter, 1972).

———, *Jesus als der leidende Gerechte?* (SBS 59; Stuttgart: KBW, 1972).

Salguero, J., "¿Quién es el 'desamparado' des salmo 22?" CTom 84 (1957), 3–35.

Scheifler, J. R., "El Salmo 22 y la Crucifixión del Señor," EstBib 24 (1965), 5–83.

Schmid, H. H., " 'Mein Gott, mein Gott, warum has du mich verlassen?' Psalm 22 als Beispiel alttestamentlicher Rede von Krankheit und Tod," *Wort und Dienst* NS 11 (1971), 119–40.

Senior, D., "A Death Song," TBT 69 (1974), 1457–63 (on Ps 22 and Matt 27:46).

Soggin, J. A., "Appunti per l'esegesi cristiana della prima parte del Salmo 22," BeO 7 (1965), 105–16. Eng. form in his *Old Testament and Oriental Studies* (Biblica et Orientalia 29; Rome: PBI, 1975), 152–65.

Stadelmann, L.I.J., "O salmo 22(21) e a história de Paixão," *Perspectiva Teológica* 15 (1983), 193–221. Eng. abstract in *Internationale Zeitschriftenschau für Bibelwissenschaft und Grenzgebiete* 31 (1984–85), 128, #922.

Stolz, F., "Psalm 22: Alttestamentliches Reden vom Menschen und neutestamentliches Reden von Jesus," ZTK 77 (1980), 129–48.

Stuhlmueller, C., "Faith and Abandonment in the Psalms of Supplication," TLOTC 1–28, esp. 18–24 on Pss 22 and 69.

Suhl, A., *Die Funktion der alttestamentlichen Zitate und Anspielungen im Markusevangelium* (Gütersloh: Mohn, 1965), esp. 26–66 on the PN.

Vaccari, A., "Psalmus Christi patientis (Ps 22)," VD 20 (1940), 72–80, 97–104.

Worden, T., "My God, my God, why hast Thou forsaken me?" *Scripture* 6 (1953–54), 9–16.

Yubero, D., "La Pasión de Cristo . . . según los Profetas," CB 10 (1953), 73–76 (on Ps 22).

Zehrer, F., "Sinn und Problematik der Schriftverwendung in der Passion," TPQ 121 (1973), 18–25.

APPENDIX VIII: JESUS' PREDICTIONS OF HIS PASSION AND DEATH

The controversial "Jesus Seminar" took votes on the authenticity of Jesus' sayings in this manner: red = he undoubtedly said this or something very much like it; pink = probably he said something like this; gray = the ideas are his even though he did not say this; black = he did not say this; it represents later or different tradition.[1] In 1987 eleven Synoptic sayings wherein Jesus spoke about his future passion were all recommended to be voted black (Butts, "Passion" 107). In another set of votes the overwhelming majority voted that Jesus did not foretell his death in a way beyond the perceptive powers of one involved in dangerous times. A factor at the root of the issue was that most of the participants were unwilling to grant that Jesus spoke of his impending death by virtue of "super-ordinary" powers (Borg, "Jesus Seminar" 83–84). Obviously a great distance separates the mind-set of these interpreters from that of the evangelists. Having described a ministry where, acting with God's power, Jesus calmed the storm, multiplied loaves, turned water to wine, healed the sick, resuscitated the dead, made the blind see and the mute speak and the deaf hear, the evangelists surely thought that divine power enabled Jesus to foresee the future. Consequently in interpreting the place and development of Gospel passion predictions, an a priori rejection of extraordinary or miraculous foreknowledge is a handicap. This rejection also distorts the quest for history. Historicity should be determined not by what we think possible or likely, but by the antiquity and reliability of the evidence; and as far back as we can trace, Jesus was known and remembered as one who had extraordinary powers. In what follows, then, I shall proceed without assuming that "super-ordinary" knowledge of the future is impossible[2] and let the Gospel material itself guide judgments about how a tradition developed in which Jesus foretold his passion and death. The material will be divided thus:

[1] See R. W. Funk, *Forum* 2 (#1; 1986), 54–55.

[2] The Synoptic evangelists saw no contradiction between attributing to Jesus foreknowledge of what would necessarily happen and describing his prayer on the Mount of Olives asking to be delivered from what he had foreseen. The author of Hebrews saw no contradiction between having Christ say "I have come to do your will, O God" (10:7) and his having to learn "obedience from the things that he suffered" (5:8). On the theological issue of the compatibility of freedom with a foreknowledge of what is predestined, see Whitely, "Christ's."

A. Synoptic Predictions of the Passion and Violent Death of Jesus
   1. Less Precise or More Allusive Predictions
   2. The Three Detailed Predictions of the Passion and Death of the Son of Man
B. Johannine Predictions of the Passion and Death of Jesus
C. Comparison of John and the Synoptics and Conclusions
Bibliography

It should be noted that in dealing with Jesus' predictions of his passion, we are bordering on the larger issue of how Jesus understood his death. Schürmann (*Jesu* 5) lists a series of interesting questions under that issue, which it may be helpful to paraphrase. Could Jesus count on the serious possibility of a violent death? Was he prepared for it? (Bultmann raises the possibility of Jesus' virtual collapse when faced with the eventuality.) Did this danger affect the way he acted? Could Jesus reconcile such a death with his ministry? Would he have attributed a salvific value to such a death? Did he speak publicly (or at least before his disciples) of an oncoming violent death? Did he indicate the salvific meaning of his death on those occasions and/or at the Last Supper? This APPENDIX does not attempt to answer all those questions, but the issue we discuss has relevance to them.

A. *Synoptic Predictions of the Passion and Violent Death of Jesus*

To avoid making this subdivision unduly long it will be necessary to confine most of the discussion to the three famous detailed predictions of the fate of the Son of Man (Mark 8:31; 9:31; 10:33–34; and par.). Nevertheless, we must realize that those are not isolated anticipations of future violence; and so I shall list in Table 12 on the next page all the sayings of the Synoptic Jesus that might reasonably be considered predictions of a passion or crucifixion, and shall give a quick survey of the less precise or more allusive predictions before I turn to the special three (which are marked I, II, III in the table). Inevitably, in deciding which passages are predictions, commentators emerge with slightly different lists. A major difficulty is determining whether a highly allusive statement should be included. For instance, in Mark 8:34 (Matt 10:38; 16:24; Luke 9:23; 14:27) Jesus says, "If anyone wishes to follow after me, let him deny himself and take up his cross and follow me." While this statement would scarcely have been preserved if Jesus had not been crucified, the fact that the carrying of the cross is being urged on all followers (only a few of whom will actually be crucified) greatly weakens its role as a prediction of Jesus' precise fate. Despite a few

TABLE 12. SYNOPTIC GOSPEL PREDICTIONS
OF JESUS' PASSION AND VIOLENT DEATH

MARK		MATT		LUKE	
	2:20		9:15		5:35
I	8:31	I	16:21	I	9:22
	9:12		17:12b		(see 17:25)
II	9:31	II	17:22–23	II	9:44
					13:33
					17:25
III	10:33–34	III	20:18–19	III	18:31b–33
	10:38		20:22		(12:50)
	10:45		20:28		
	12:7–8		21:38–39		20:14–15
			26:2		
	14:8		26:12		
	14:21		26:24		22:22
	14:27–28		26:31–32		

possible disagreements of judgment, however, this table of predictions is broadly representative of those to be discussed seriously.[3]

1. LESS PRECISE OR MORE ALLUSIVE PREDICTIONS

(a) The four "predictions" beneath the heavy horizontal line in Table 12 are spoken in their Gospel sequence at the threshold of or within the PN itself. I shall comment on them in this paragraph, even though I prefer to confine the range of selection to the public ministry so that the *predictions* occur sufficiently *before* what happens in the storyline. Just before the chief priests and scribes assemble to seek a way to arrest Jesus (a search to which

---

[3]For instance, the table covers most of the passages treated in Taylor's full-length book on the predictions (*Jesus*) with the exception of the eucharistic words of Jesus that Taylor regards as predictions of his death.

Judas will respond), Matt 26:2 has Jesus tell his disciples: "You know that after two days the Passover is coming and the Son of Man is (to be) given over to be crucified." Despite the use of "the Son of Man," which is very characteristic of passion predictions, the formative background of this saying rules it out as a true prediction. Matt has simply taken the chronological notice in Mark 14:1, "The Passover and the Unleavened Bread was [to be] after two days" (see Luke 22:1; John 12:1), and placed it on the lips of Jesus as a theological reminder of the extent to which God had planned all that would happen. At Bethany, in the immediately following scene (Mark 14:8; Matt 26:12; cf. John 12:7) the woman is said by Jesus to have anointed his body for burial; but many would see this as a hindsight interpretation after death had occurred. Mark 14:21; Matt 26:24; Luke 22:22, in the context of Jesus' predicting that one of the Twelve would give him over, have him say, "The Son of Man goes as it is written of him [Luke: according to what was determined], but woe to that man by whom the Son of Man is given over." Many regard this taken by itself as a very old prediction or combination of predictions (especially if they can remove the reference to Scripture ["written"] as Luke has done). Nevertheless, in its present context when Judas has already struck the bargain with the chief priests, Jesus has more the air of knowing what has happened rather than what will happen. Finally, at the beginning of what I would consider the PN proper, as Jesus leaves the Supper and goes to the Mount of Olives, we find him predicting: "It is written, 'I will strike the shepherd, and the sheep (of the flock) will be scattered.' However, after my resurrection I shall go before you into Galilee" (Mark 14:27–28; Matt 26:31–32). This passage has already been discussed on pp. 130–33 above. Like the great passion predictions it contains a reference to the resurrection; but unlike other predictions, it is not phrased in terms of the Son of Man and explicitly cites Scripture. Let us now turn to passages from earlier in Jesus' ministry, which I have printed above the heavy horizontal line in Table 12.

(b) Mark 2:20; Matt 9:15; and Luke 5:35 stand out as being placed at the beginning—a placing harmonious with the Johannine presentation of a Jesus who knows from the start what is going to happen to him. The basic (Marcan) form is highly allusive: "The days will come when the bridegroom will be taken away from them, and they will fast on that day." The choice of the verb (a possible echo of Isa 53:8: "His life is taken away from the earth") and the mournful fasting to which the "taking away" leads to are thought by many to indicate an anticipation of a violent death. Nevertheless, if Jesus had died a nonviolent death, the saying could probably have been reconciled with that; and so I would not consider it, taken in isolation, a persuasive example of Jesus' precise foreknowledge of his death.

(c) Mark 9:12, "It is written of the Son of Man that he should suffer many things and be treated as nothing [*exoudenein*],"[4] follows both the first (I) detailed Marcan passion prediction (8:31) and a reference to the Son of Man rising from the dead (9:9). The abbreviated Matthean form (17:12b), "So also the Son of Man will suffer from [*hypo:* by] them," is in the same sequence. A similar statement in Luke 17:25 that the Son of Man "must suffer many things and be rejected by [*apo*] this generation" follows the second (II) specific Lucan passion prediction.[5] Although in their context these references to suffering clearly anticipate the whole passion and crucifixion, some would argue that in themselves they are not more specific than the OT descriptions of the just one maltreated by his enemies. In light of the Scripture to be discussed below under (2) it is worth noting that in Isa 53:3 *exoudenein* is used of the Servant of the Lord in the Greek of Aquila, Symmachus, and Theodotion. (See also APPENDIX VII, n. 32.)

(d) In Luke 13:33, after being told that Herod wants to kill him (13:31), Jesus says, "But it is necessary that today and tomorrow and the next day I go on, for it is not possible that a prophet perish outside Jerusalem." There is no doubt that this is a reference to a violent death at the hands of those who oppose prophets (as the next verse makes explicit). However, such a statement, taken by itself, could represent general inevitability rather than precise foreknowledge.

(e) Mark 10:38 is addressed to James and John (the parallel Matt 20:22 is addressed to their mother): "Are you able to drink the cup which I drink, or to be baptized with the baptism with which I am baptized?" (See Luke 12:50: "I have a baptism to be baptized with, and how I am distressed until it is finished.") That Jesus refers here to his violent death is clear from the fact that this follows the third (III) and most detailed passion prediction (Mark 10:33–34; Matt 20:18–19) and from the reuse of the cup imagery in all four Gospels as Jesus begins his passion (Mark 14:36 and par.). Once again, however, taken in isolation, it is very allusive; and, were Jesus' fate other, it could still have been used by Christians.

(f) Mark 10:45 (Matt 20:28), "The Son of Man also came not to be served but to serve, and to give his life as a ransom for many," comes a few verses later and so again is clarified by the context—the giving will take place on the cross. Yet taken by itself, if there had been no crucifixion, this statement of Jesus could probably have been understood as a more general reference

---

[4]This occurs within the context of a question. Note that Jesus is shown as maintaining that the suffering Son of Man is part of the scriptural record; there is no consciousness that this portrayal is an innovation.

[5]Luke 17:25 is secondary, perhaps influenced by Mark 9:12, but even more surely derivative from Luke 9:22 (I) that in turn is derivative from Mark 8:31 (I). See Fitzmyer, *Luke* 2.1165.

to the way he dedicated his life. Many scholars regard the "as a ransom for many" as secondary and a reflection of the description of the Servant in Isa 53:11–12 who suffered for many. Similar sayings with the serving motif in Luke 22:27 and John 13:16 do not have the ransom element.

(g) Mark 12:7–8 (Matt 21:38–39; Luke 20:14–15), contained in a parable, describes how the tenants killed and cast out (or cast out and killed) the beloved son of the man who planted the vineyard that they were renting. While there is no doubt that the evangelists understood Jesus to be referring to himself in the portrait of the son, had he been decisively rejected by the authorities in a way other than a death sentence, this portrayal would probably have been explained by commentators as simply parabolic exaggeration.

Evaluation. One way or another these statements point to death with suffering, sometimes in figurative OT or parabolic language. We have seen that none of them, taken singly, shows clear foreknowledge of a crucifixion of Jesus by the Romans. Yet considering them singly and in isolation does not do justice to their cumulative effect. If the passages from (b) to (g) are found in the public ministry, all except (b) occur in the latter part of the Gospel account of that period, namely, when antagonism toward Jesus had mounted. Such an arrangement may stem from a plan to show a progression from an acceptance of Jesus at the beginning to rejection at the end. Yet would a different historical sequence be truly plausible? Frequently enthusiasm for a challenging religious figure is stronger at the beginning of his proclamation, only to lessen as the disturbing quality of his message become clearer. Thus historically, as Jesus' career progressed, opposition to him may have increased; and he would have become increasingly pessimistic, anticipating the worst. If these sayings only vaguely or allusively predict the manner of Jesus' death, that is because their wording does *not* reflect exactly what happened in the passion of the respective Gospel. Accordingly it is not possible to dismiss them simply as retrojections of what happened. Other factors may lead scholars to judge some of them as formulations of the early church rather than as words of Jesus; but can one reasonably claim that all these predictive sayings phrased in such differing vocabulary and imagery are postJesus? Before we answer that question, we must discuss the most famous of the passion predictions.

2. THE THREE DETAILED PREDICTIONS OF THE PASSION AND DEATH OF THE SON OF MAN

There is wide variance in scholarly views about the origin of these predictions, as well summarized by Maartens ("Son" 85). Bultmann and Conzelmann regard them as creations of the Hellenistic church. Hahn, Tödt, Fuller,

TABLE 13. THE THREE DETAILED SYNOPTIC PREDICTIONS
OF THE PASSION OF THE SON OF MAN

I. First Passion Prediction		
Mark 8:31	**Matt 16:21**	**Luke 9:22**
That it is necessary for the Son of Man	That it is necessary for him (Jesus)	That it is necessary for the Son of Man
	to go away to Jerusalem	
to suffer many things	and to suffer many things	to suffer many things
and to be rejected		and to be rejected
by [*hypo*] the elders and the chief priests and the scribes	from [*apo*] the elders and chief priests and scribes	from/by [*apo*] the elders and chief priests and scribes
and to be killed	and to be killed	and to be killed
and after three days	and on the third day	and on the third day
to rise	to be raised	to be raised

II. Second Passion Prediction		
Mark 9:31	**Matt 17:22–23**	**Luke 9:44**
That the Son of Man	The Son of Man	For the Son of Man
is given over	is about to be given over	is about to be given over
into the hands of men;[6]	into the hands of men;	into the hands of men;
and they will kill him,	and they will kill him,	
and having been killed,		
after three days	on the third day	
he will rise	he will be raised	

and Hooker attribute them to the early Aramaic-speaking church of Palestine, with some of Fuller's argumentation pointing to the early 30s. Maartens himself (88–89) gathers arguments to show that in substance they may have

[6]The plural of *anthrōpos*, although it refers to human beings, is translated "men" here to catch the play on "the Son of Man [*anthrōpos*]."

TABLE 13. CONTINUED

III. Third Passion Prediction		
Mark 10:33–34	**Matt 20:18–19**	**Luke 18:31b–33**
And the Son of Man	And the Son of Man	4. And to the Son of Man[7]
will be given over	will be given over	1. will be completed
to the chief priests and the scribes;	to the chief priests and scribes;	2. all the things written 3. through the prophets;
and they will judge against him to [dative] death	and they will judge against him unto [*eis*] death	
and they will give him over	and they will give him over	for he will be given over
to the Gentiles	to the Gentiles	to the Gentiles
and they will mock him	to mock	and he will be mocked
		and he will be arrogantly mistreated;
and they will spit on him		and he will be spat on;
and they will scourge him	and to scourge	and having scourged (him)
and they will kill (him)	and to crucify	they will kill him
and after three days	and on the third day	and on the third day
he will rise	he will be raised	he will rise

come from the historical Jesus.[8] In what is, after all, a tangential issue to my commentary on the PNs, there is no way in which I can hope to present and evaluate the minute details of such discussions. In what follows I concentrate on what is useful for understanding the issues.

We must pay attention to the exact wording of the predictions in the three Synoptics (Table 13). In general, Marcan priority will explain the relationships among the Gospel variants, but there are some interesting points. Matt and Luke always prefer the set kerygmatic formula "raised [*egeirein*] on the third day" (I Cor 15:4), despite the fact that Mark has "rise [*anistanai*] after

[7]The Arabic numerals indicate the order of these phrases in Luke's Greek. The "to" of "to the Son of Man" may be governed by "completed" (and thus equivalent to "in") or by "written" (and thus equivalent to "about").

[8]In Casey's survey of literature on Jesus' use of "the Son of Man" (§22, n. 35), he raises the interesting but complicating possibility that Jesus may have made a genuine prediction of his suffering death into which Christians introduced a reference to "the Son of Man."

three days";[9] once again this illustrates the influence of oral tradition even when copying from a written Gospel. In II they also agree[10] in shifting from Mark's present tense, "is given," to the future with *mellei* ("is about to"—in different word order, however), presumably evidencing a mutual instinct to clarify what Mark means.[11] As in the PN proper, Luke evidences more freedom toward Mark than does Matt, omitting the second part of II and recasting the first part of III.[12]

The first issue is how many original predictions we are dealing with. Very few scholars are willing to maintain that on three different occasions the historical Jesus made these independent predictions. Many choose one of the predictions as more original and regard the other two as variants of it.[13] Jeremias (*New Testament* 281) would contend that the arrangement of three came because Mark took over three complexes of material, each of which by chance had a variant of the one basic prediction. This suggestion seems desperate. Perrin ("Towards" 20) argues that the three predictions are basic to the structure of Mark 8:22–10:52, and therefore that Mark composed them. Perrin can scarcely conceive of a situation (*Sitz*) for them other than the one Mark has given. Yet as we shall see, John too has three predictions about the lifting up in death of the Son of Man, and certainly John has found

---

[9]It may well be that "raised" and "rise" reflect variant translations into Greek from the same Aramaic verb form *yĕqûm*. Since Farmer has written an article on these predictions as proofs for his approach to the Synoptic problem which maintains that Mark drew upon Matt and Luke, let me note that I find here an argument entirely to the contrary. Matt and Luke are in agreement here and are using a well-established kerygmatic formula; yet Mark prefers a different reading. I cannot understand why Mark would not have followed them; I can understand why they would have corrected him.

[10]The agreement of Matt and Luke in I in using *apo* ("from") in place of Mark's *hypo* ("by") for the agents of rejection is not significant because respectively in different ways they are letting the verb "suffer" dominate the grammatical relationship. They also agree in disliking Mark's ponderous repetition of the definite article before "chief priests" and "scribes." Strangely Farmer ("Passion" 559) regards this easily accountable grammatical preference as definitive proof that Matt and Luke did not depend on Mark. Yet he has no problem in maintaining that Luke (who, he hypothesizes, drew from Matt and did not know Mark) omitted gratuitously Matt's "to go away to Jerusalem" and substituted "and to be rejected," a reading that later Mark as well preferred to Matt's more original phrase.

[11]The opposite thesis is more difficult: Why, if Mark used both Matt and Luke, does he disagree with them here in preferring the more obscure present in place of their common, clearer future?

[12]Whether one argues that Matt and Luke depend on Mark or (with Farmer) that Mark depends on Matt and Luke (and Luke knew Matt), the appearance of different verb forms in all three Gospels in III after "to the Gentiles" is a problem. Against Farmer, why would Mark have chosen the "*will* mock" and "*will* spit" verb forms that are found in neither Matt nor Luke? And, again against Farmer, why if Luke knew Matt but not Mark, did he add "spit" without any support from Matt and without internal support in his own account since in Luke no one ever spits at Jesus? In the more widely held thesis that Luke (and Matt) drew from Mark, the verbs "mock" and "spit" came to Luke from Mark.

[13]Lohmeyer contended that all three Marcan predictions stemmed from Luke 17:25, but most think the Lucan passage secondary. See n. 5 above.

a situation for them other than Mark's. Nevertheless, if one would posit that there was a preGospel pattern of three that Mark and John developed independently, that still leaves the problem of whether the three emerged from one prediction. Predictions II and III share the pattern of the Son of Man being "given over" while prediction I speaks of "suffering many things," and so it would not be unreasonable to think of two different sayings.[14] In either case, III as the most detailed prediction is regarded by many as a secondary creation, enlarged retrospectively in light of what happened in the PN. Mark 14:64 describes the chief priests and the scribes judging against Jesus; 15:15–20a has the Roman soldiers (Gentiles) flog (scourge), spit, mock, and crucify (kill) Jesus. Thus the distinctive additions of III over I and II may be echoes of the Marcan PN. Matt's form of III increases similarity to the PN by substituting "crucify" for "kill."[15]

If we concentrate on I and II, Strecker argues for I as more original; Fuller, Jeremias, Lindars, and Tödt argue for II. Certainly the vague agency in II ("by the hands of men") is less influenced by the PN than the agency of the elders, the chief priests, and the scribes in I. On the other hand, if II were more original, Mark seems not to have recognized that, or why would he have put it in the middle? The discussion is frightfully complicated and involves many factors, which it may be helpful to lay out before the readers.

(a) All three predictions include resurrection after three days or on the third day, so that many would refuse to discuss Jesus' anticipation of his death without treating his anticipation of his resurrection (Lindars, *Jesus* 62). According to the Gospel evidence Jesus was buried late on Friday afternoon and was raised before Sunday morning (or according to Matt 28:1 before the beginning of Sunday shortly after darkness on Saturday), and thus after little more than twenty-four hours in the tomb—not "after three days" and only broadly "on the third day." Above (p. 444) in reference to Jesus' prophecy about destroying the sanctuary and building it (or another) "within three days," I pointed out that this time span in its various wordings may mean no more than a short time, with precision being added or detected post factum. See also under A1d above the time span for Jesus' going on, namely, "today and tomorrow and the next day," in the prediction (Luke 13:33) that a prophet must not perish outside Jerusalem. As for "rise" or "be raised," one may

---

[14]Some who think of two basic sayings do not choose Mark 8:31 and 9:31; Fuller ("Son of Man Came" 47) looks to 14:21a "The Son of Man goes" and the 14:21b "The Son of Man is given over" (with the latter pattern reflected in 9:31). See under A1a above.

[15]Luke's III has its own problems: The Lucan PN does not have the Romans spit on or scourge Jesus, and so Luke has taken those features over from Mark in III without recognizing that his rearrangement of Mark's PN means that Jesus' prediction now remains unfulfilled (p. 858 above).

debate as to whether this is a post-factum vocalization of a more general prediction of victory over a hostile death.[16] A prediction of resurrection after three days or on the third day may be a rewording of Jesus' prediction that if he died a violent death at the hands of his enemies, he would quickly be vindicated.[17]

(b) Some would exclude all these statements because they have Jesus speaking of "the Son of Man"; and in their judgment he never used that term of himself. On pp. 506–15 above I explained the three types of "Son of Man sayings" found in the Gospels and various theories about them (including the unlikely thesis that in the future sayings Jesus was talking about someone other than himself).[18] I offered arguments for thinking that Jesus may well have expanded the symbolic portrait of "one like a son of man [human being]" whom God strengthens and makes victorious (Dan 7:13–14; Ps 80:18) so that it became "the Son of Man," the specific human figure through whom God manifests his eschatological triumph.[19] He would then have identified himself as this instrument in God's plan. In opening that possibility I moved against a very common presupposition that underlies this whole discussion, namely, the thesis that if a concept or pattern is traceable to such a scriptural background, it cannot have come from Jesus. The argument proceeds thus: We know that the early Christians understood and explained Jesus by appealing to biblical passages on which his career had thrown light (see the Lucan opening of III). Therefore any use of Scripture may have arisen in the early church, and we cannot safely attribute it to Jesus. I would argue that it is more unsafe to deny two factors that upset that argument.[20] First, there must have been continuity between Jesus and his earliest followers, many of whom had been with him in his lifetime. If he had no ideas on an issue that

[16]Even centrist scholars doubt that Jesus foretold literally his bodily resurrection on the third day. In the storyline of the four Gospels none of his disciples understood him to mean that, and all of them had some difficulty in comprehending when in fact he did rise by the third day. Their failure to understand is without doubt a theological motif but still suggests that in the tradition Jesus had not been lucidly clear on this point. The question has been asked whether in thinking about God's plan for future history, Jesus distinguished in any detail among parousia, resurrection, consummation, and building of the Temple sanctuary. Are these simply different ways of phrasing the one basic eschatological vision or foresight? Be that as it may, I do not agree with the suggestion (see Lindars, *Jesus* 73) that any or all of this could have been predicted without making Jesus central to what would happen: He is God's agent of the kingdom in this age and the age to come.

[17]So Black ("Son of Man" 7) who thinks that the oldest Son-of-Man stratum may have referred to suffering and vindication without reference to resurrection; he points out that John's three Son-of-Man sayings (that we have yet to discuss) come close to that.

[18]Marshall, "Son of Man," offers a balanced survey of views.

[19]I remind the reader that since "the Son of Man" appears almost exclusively on Jesus' lips, it is not easily attributed to the early church. Also it is not easy to deny that Jesus reflected on Dan 7 since that is one of the very few OT places where there is reference to God's kingdom.

[20]In other words, I do not accept the thesis that a minimalist principle like discontinuity is truly scientific (since sayings that get through that net can safely be attributed to Jesus); it guarantees atrocious distortion.

was essential to them, namely, how he fitted into the revealed plan of God, why did they move to thinking in that direction? "For the sake of apologetics" is an insufficient answer; they came to faith themselves before they argued with others. Second, no Jewish religious figure of Jesus' time could have ignored the Scriptures. A Jesus who never thought of himself in the light of the Scriptures becomes even more inconceivable now that we have a contemporary witness to the mentality of his time in the Dead Sea Scrolls, which portray an intense effort to relate the life of the group to the Law and the Prophets. Consequently I shall proceed with this discussion of Jesus' anticipation of his fate by accepting as fact that Jesus did use the Scriptures and by ignoring the a priori prejudice that while Dan 7 might have offered early Christians a base for developing an outlook on him in terms of the Son of Man, it could not have offered Jesus himself that base.

(c) Even some who admit that Jesus spoke of the Son of Man deny that he did this in relation to his suffering (one of the three types of "Son of Man sayings").[21] They contend that nothing in Dan 7 suggests that the one like a son of man would suffer. As Schaberg has so well pointed out,[22] that is not accurate. Dan 7:25 has one of the horns of the fourth beast oppress the holy ones of the Most High who are "given into his hands for a time, two times, and a half time" (3½ times) before the Most High will give them kingdom and dominion. Most scholars would identify these holy ones as the ones symbolized by "the one like a son of man" of 7:13–14 to whom the Ancient of Days will give kingdom and dominion. If Jesus recognized his own role in Dan 7:13–14, he might have used the phraseology of 7:25 to predict that he would be given over into the hands of men hostile to him and have to wait for a period of three days before he would be made victorious. It is worth noting that although in these predictions Jesus does not speak of his victory in terms of kingdom, Mark 14:25; Matt 26:29; and Luke 22:28–30 have him doing that at the Last Supper. In predictions I, II, and III he speaks of resurrection; and although above I noted that theme as possibly a post-factum explication, Schaberg ("Daniel" 209–12) points out that Dan 12:1–2 has a resurrection of the holy people of God. If Daniel could be the background from which the saying in Mark 9:31 (II) was shaped, was II in turn the saying from which I and III were formed; or is it likely that reflection on the Scriptures gave rise to those variant forms? Most scholars think that

[21]A factor in this judgment is the absence from Q of suffering-Son-of-Man sayings. Yet since Q does not have a PN, would it have been a logical vehicle for preserving predictions pertinent to the passion? Of the five Son-of-Man sayings that Lindars would accept as authentically from Jesus, three (Mark 9:31; 10:45; 14:21) involve suffering. Yet Lindars's thesis (*Jesus*) that "Son-of-Man" means "a man like me" makes little sense of 10:45 or 14:21 without major editing.

[22]She acknowledges ("Daniel" 213–14) that scattered ideas that she presents have been proposed by Best, Lindars, and Hooker; but certainly she has made the best synthesis.

the reference in III to the Son of Man being given over "to the Gentiles" is a retrojection from the PN, even though *ta ethnē* is not used for the Gentiles in any PN.[23] (Acts 4:25–27 refers to "Gentiles," and some would contend that Mark picked up the expression from early preaching: see under [d] below.) However, the horn of the fourth beast to whom the holy ones of the Most High (symbolized earlier by one like a son of man) are given over in Dan 7:25 is a Gentile ruler.

Also there is the likelihood that other Scripture passages have been combined with Daniel in formulating the predictions. A plausible candidate is the picture of the Suffering Servant in Isa 52:13–53:12. Taylor ("Origin") contends that use of Isaian Servant imagery belongs to early NT layers. In particular some have appealed to the targum on Isa 53:5 "given over [*msr*] for our iniquities" as a proof that Jesus might have spoken in Aramaic of the Son of Man being "given over" as in prediction II.[24] As for prediction I, the "spurned and held in no esteem" of Isa 53:3 is thought to have an echo in "be rejected," while "he carried [*sbl*] our sufferings" of Isa 53:4 may be background for "suffer many things." When one thinks of these passages as background, one is not necessarily positing that Jesus identified himself as the Servant. As we see in the Qumran hymns and in the Benedictus and Magnificat hymns, a main theme that has a primary OT analog often picks up images, phrases, and words from many other OT passages because the spokesperson (author) had a mind imbued with biblical background. Under A1f above we discussed sayings in which Jesus saw himself in a servant role, and so passages (including Isa 53) that spoke of a servant type could have shaped his thought. And indeed the Servant passage in Isa 50:4–11 may also have been part of the background. Most scholars look on the specific outrages predicted in III as retrojections from the actual PN accounts of what was done, e.g., that they would spit on Jesus and scourge him; but Isa 50:6 has the Servant say, "My back I gave to scourges . . . I did not turn my face from the shame of spitting."[25] What is interesting is that if Isaiah influenced any or all of I, II, and III, the atoning or soteriological aspect of the Isaian

[23]Luke 23:2 and John 18:35 use the singular *ethnos* for the Jewish people.

[24]The *paradidonai* of the Marcan Greek is found in the LXX of Isa 53:6,12. It is tempting to suggest that this verb, which appears in Dan 7:25, facilitated the association of Dan 7 and Isa 53; but that would have to be on the Greek level of Christian reflection, for the underlying Semitic verbs in Dan 7:25, Isa 53:6,12 (and in the targum of Isa 53:5) are not the same. Yet *4 Ezra* (13:32), a Jewish work written originally in Hebrew, associates the apocalyptic figure of the "man" (echoing "son of man" in Dan) with the "servant" of the Most High (echoing Isa), and so the connection between these figures may have been made on a preChristian level. In the passion predictions, as in the Isaian background pertaining to the servant, the one who gives over is God (not Judas).

[25]See pp. 577, 869 above for the possible influence of the Isaian text on the PN accounts of the abuse of Jesus, so that one has to deal with a triangular relationship involving the Isaian description, the predictions, and the PN accounts.

Suffering Servant's role so beloved of the early church (our infirmities, our sufferings, our sin, we were healed, guilt of us all) has *not* been taken over into those predictions. In that sense they could be looked on as less theologically developed than Mark 10:45 ("as a ransom for many"; see A1f above); or Rom 4:25 ("given over for our transgressions"); or Rom 8:32 ("God gave him over for [*hyper*] us all").[26] Besides Daniel and Isaiah, other passages, particularly from the psalms, have been suggested as formative background for the passion predictions, e.g., Ps 118:22 ("the stone the builders rejected") for the "rejected" of I.[27] The language "to give over" and "the hand of" (sinners, etc.) is found in the psalms as well (APPENDIX VII, n. 13).

(d) Other factors that underlie the discussion of passion predictions involve whether the language in which they are phrased appears in early Christian preaching and at which stage of that preaching. A radical principle is that if the vocabulary of a saying is found in the preaching (e.g., in the sermons of Acts, in Pauline kerygmatic phrases), it cannot safely be attributed to Jesus.[28] As above in dealing with the use of Scripture, I think such a principle guarantees deformity in understanding Jesus. If his disciples were responsible for the preaching, and if Paul mentions that he "received" some formulas (from the earliest Christians), would not considerable continuity between Jesus' phrasing and the formulas reflected in the preaching have been inevitable?[29] Acts 3:15 has Peter say that the men of Israel "killed" the author of life. Why do we have to think that "killed" in predictions I, II, and III is a retrojection of that language? If Jesus actually predicted that he would be killed, what more natural than that believers would have proclaimed that he was "killed" just as he said he would be?

The possibility (or likelihood) of linguistic continuity may be rejected

[26]Also Rom 5:8 ("while we were yet sinners, Christ died for [*hyper*] us"). *Hyper* language is not used in Isa 53, and Perrin ("Use" 208) would attribute it to the Greek stage of early Christian preaching.

[27]Fuller ("Son of Man Came" 48) stresses the psalm background. If we move to other Son-of-Man predictions, Perrin, working with Mark 14:62 ("You will see the Son of Man sitting at the right of the Power and coming with the clouds of heaven"), would see a creative combination of Dan 7:13–14; Ps 110:1; and Zech 12:10ff.

[28]A variant of the argument is found in Perrin ("Towards" 26–27). "After three days" is distinctly Marcan and would not go back to Jesus. Beyond the dubious adequacy of the base for this argument, see above on p. 56 about the issue of where Mark got his language.

[29]Perrin ("Towards" 28) rejects the *dei* ("it is necessary") of Mark 8:31 (I) as coming from Jesus since it reflects early Christian apologetic. I think a case can be made for not attributing to Jesus the vocabulary of apologetic since the context of Christian struggle with the synagogues would have been alien to Jesus' lifetime. But was "it is necessary" with relation to God's plan created (and not merely used) in apologetic debate? Or was it originally part of the inner Christian attempt to understand Jesus' career and (dare I suggest) even part of Jesus' attempt to understand the turns of his own life? The issue of the necessity of what is predicted, which is important because it lends an air of inevitability, is conveniently studied under the rubric of the usage of *dei*. That is probably too narrow a rubric, however; Mowery ("Divine") points out that *dei* is only one of six different ways in which Luke refers to divine intervention in the passion.

when the preaching formulas are phrased in a Greek that cannot be retro-verted into an Aramaic that Jesus could have spoken,[30] but that occurs rela-tively seldom. Jeremias, arguing for the originality of Mark 9:31 (II), draws heavily on his ability to reconstruct the underlying Aramaic.[31] However, one must be cautious on several scores. Septuagintal Greek influenced NT preachers and writers—a semitized Greek shaped by the Hebrew or Ara-maic original that was being translated. Therefore the wording of a saying of Jesus in a semitized Greek that can be translated back into Aramaic or Hebrew does not necessarily prove that an initial Semitic saying existed. Original composition in this semitized Greek remains a possibility. Jeremias points to an Aramaic play on words in II in *bar 'ĕnāšā' līdê bĕnê 'ĕnāšā'* ("the Son of *Man* into the hands of *men*"); but the play also exists in the Greek that Mark has given us: *huios anthrōpou . . . eis cheiras anthrōpōn.* "Given over into the hands of" is a Semitic expression, but it appears in the LXX. Much more solid is Fitzmyer's contention ("New Testament" 146–49) that "the Son of Man" is scarcely a believable creation in Greek and surely represents the Aramaic (not Hebrew) *br 'nš.*[32] Yet even when a plausible Ara-maic substratum can be reconstructed, one has not shown the genuineness of the saying; the early Christian followers of Jesus spoke Aramaic as well.

Before drawing any conclusions about whether Jesus made any of the pre-dictions attributed to him in the Synoptic tradition, let us look briefly at the contributions to the picture in John.

B. *Johannine Predictions of the Passion and Death of Jesus*

John will be treated more briefly than were the Synoptics, but even a brief treatment will seem meaningless to those who hold that the Fourth Gospel can tell us nothing about the historical Jesus. I began this APPENDIX with a reference to the Jesus Seminar; in 1991 the press reported that the voting majority in the seminar would not consider a single saying in John to be authentically from Jesus.

There are in John, as in the Synoptics (A1 above), allusive references to a violent death, although those I mention in this paragraph are not overly helpful for our purposes. In John 1:29 John the Baptist hails Jesus as "the

[30]On p. 439 above I pointed out the difficulty of retroverting into Aramaic the Greek adjectival phrases modifying "sanctuary" in the prediction of Mark 14:58, "I will destroy this sanctuary *made by hand,* and within three days another *not made by hand* I will build."

[31]Recognizing Aramaic substrata is not an exact science. Jeremias distrusts the *dei* ("it is neces-sary") of I as a later element, while Black ("Son of Man" 3) sees the construction that begins I as Semitic rather than Greek.

[32]I cite that form because, although they appear in later Aramaic, the forms *br nš* or *br nš'* are not found in the 1st cent. AD; nor is the meaning "I" for "Son of Man."

Lamb of God who takes away the sin of the world." I explained in APPENDIX II, B4, that within the Gospel this designation relates Jesus' death to the paschal lamb shedding its blood—a meaning derived from early Christian reflection on the fact that he died at Passover time (I Cor 5:7). Yet in BGJ 1.58–63 I pointed out that this is not necessarily the earliest meaning of the description of Jesus as a lamb, and that if the description went back to JBap, he could have been speaking of the victorious apocalyptic lamb or even of the Servant figure in Isa 53:7 who was "like a sheep that is led to the slaughter, and like a lamb before its shearers." For our purposes here, however, even though the Johannine Jesus accepts the designation tacitly, it is not part of *his* prediction of his fate. In John 2:19 "the Jews" are challenged by Jesus: "Destroy this sanctuary, and in three days I will raise it up"; and 2:21 tells us that the sanctuary was his own body. However, reading between the lines of 2:22 shows that the evangelist is giving a later interpretation of an enigmatic saying (pp. 449–52 above), which in any case is not a clear prediction but more a warning of what will happen if Jesus' adversaries proceed on their hostile course.

More important in the Johannine picture is that partway through the ministry (proportionately at the point where the Synoptics begin to have frequent allusive predictions of violent death, as seen in Table 12 above) there begins a series of attempts by "the Jews" and the authorities in Jerusalem to kill Jesus (5:18; 7:1,25; 8:37,40,59; 10:31; 11:8), culminating sometime before Passover in a meeting of the Sanhedrin that formally makes plans to have him killed (11:49–53). Many scholars recognize that John's picture of Jesus coming on several occasions to Jerusalem is more historical than the simplified Marcan outline of only one journey to Jerusalem, at the time of his death. (It is historically likely that on those occasions he encountered opposition.) In John, then, as Jesus' Jerusalem adversaries become more and more aggressive, the likelihood of a violent death at their hands is before Jesus constantly. When Jesus says in John 10:15, "For these sheep I lay down my life," in Johannine theology he is expressing his own sovereignty over his death (10:17–18—"no one has taken it [my life] away from me"); but on the level of the storyline the kind of death about which Jesus theologizes is inevitable. Similarly when Jesus associates with his burial the perfume that Mary puts on his feet (12:3,7), his comment reflects both inevitability and foreknowledge.

The most important element in the Johannine Jesus' predictions of his fate consists of three Son-of-Man sayings:[33]

---

[33]Many commentaries on John treat the Johannine Son-of-Man theme. See also R. Schnackenburg, "Der Menschensohn im Johannesevangelium," NTS 11 (1964–65), 123–37; S. Smalley, "The Johannine Son of Man Sayings," NTS 15 (1968–69), 278–301; J. Coppens, "Le Fils de l'homme

- "Just as Moses lifted up the serpent in the desert, so is it necessary that the Son of Man be lifted up" (3:14)
- "When you [Jews and Pharisees] lift up the Son of Man, then you will know that I AM" (8:28)
- "And I, when I am lifted up from the earth, shall draw all to myself" (12:32). The evangelist comments, "Now he was saying this, giving a sign by what type of death he was going to die" (12:33). This is followed by a hostile reaction of the hearers: "How can you say that it is necessary for the Son of Man to be lifted up?" (12:34)

That this "lifting up" involves death is clear from the interpretation which the evangelist supplies for the third saying. That the death involves hostile action by his opponents is implied in the second. That it involves crucifixion is strongly suggested in the first (he is to be elevated on a pole so that all can see) and is emphasized in the explanation of the third (the "type of death he was going to die").[34] Thus, these statements are *pre*dictions. Even though in the storyline the second and third are made after there have been attempts on Jesus' life, those attempts would lead one to anticipate stoning (8:59; 10:31; 11:8), not crucifixion. Moreover, the "lifting up" also and even primarily involves exaltation, for when it is done all will recognize that Jesus is of God ("know that I AM" in the second saying), and all will be drawn to believe in him and become one with him (the third).[35] As on the cross Jesus is lifted up physically from the ground, he is at the same time being lifted up symbolically to God and returning to his Father (see 17:11,13). In this area, too, John wants readers to see Jesus as truly predicting; for when he has been lifted up on the cross, Joseph from Arimathea and Nicodemus, who hitherto had been hesitant disciples, come forward publicly to give him an honorable burial, acting as representatives of the "all" whom Jesus has begun to draw to himself.

C. *Comparison of John and the Synoptics and Conclusions*

In my judgment the three Johannine predictions (referred to here as first, second, and third) are clearly related to the three Synoptic Son of Man passion predictions (I, II, III). All have the same "Son of Man" subject. (Note

---

dans l'évangile johannique," ETL 52 (1976), 28–81; F. J. Moloney, *The Johannine Son of Man* (2d ed.; Rome: Libreria Ateneo Salesiano, 1978).

[34]This is confirmed in the PN in 18:31–32 when it becomes clear that physically Pilate, not the Jews, must put Jesus to death (and thus he will die by the Roman penalty of crucifixion) "in order that there might be fulfilled the word of Jesus that he spoke signifying what type of death he was going to die."

[35]G. C. Nicholson, *Death as Departure* (SBLDS 63; Chico, CA: Scholars Press, 1983), 75–144, puts strongest emphasis on the exaltation factor.

that while Jesus says, "I" in the third, the audience has heard "Son of Man.") There is a *dei* ("it is necessary") in the first as there was in I.[36] While in Mark's I, II, and III there is a prediction of being killed, Matt's III turns that into a prediction of being crucified, even as John's third finds in "lifted up" the type of death he was going to die. The passive "given over" appears in the Synoptic II and III, whereas Synoptic I places greater emphasis on human agency ("rejected by"); John uses a passive form of "lift up" in his first and third, but emphasizes human agency in the second ("When *you* lift up"). All three Synoptic predictions involve Jesus' ultimate victory: to rise or be raised. All Johannine predictions involve his exaltation to God. In a way John's predictions are less developed than those of the Synoptics, for what will happen is expressed only symbolically ("lift up") without the Synoptic details. Yet the soteriological effect, absent from the three Synoptic predictions, is present in John's predictions: the "you will know" in the second; the "draw all to myself" in the third.[37]

Do these similarities make probable that John derived his three sayings from the Synoptic three? Did the fourth evangelist read Mark 8–10 and pick out I, II, and III and decide to recast them in totally symbolic phraseology and to scatter them throughout his Gospel? That seems farfetched. A more likely hypothesis in my judgment is that already on a preGospel level there was a collection of three sayings predicting the death and resurrection of the Son of Man, and that the Marcan and Johannine traditions and/or evangelists developed those sayings and used them independently.[38] If plausibly Dan 7 offered the basis for the idea that one like a son of man might be victimized by the representative of evil but made triumphant and exalted to the presence of the Ancient of Days, the Marcan form of the Son-of-Man predictions kept some of the Danielic vocabulary and imagery (given into the hands of the Gentile leader and [perhaps] resurrection) but omitted the exaltation of this son-of-man figure to God's throne. John's form, except for the derived title "Son of Man," has none of the Danielic imagery but has preserved the basic thrust of exaltation. We saw above the likelihood of an influence of the Isaian

---

[36]The people have heard a *dei* in the third as well even though Jesus did not say so. Are we to assume that in the Johannine storyline this audience remembers the first saying and is interpreting the third through the first? Is this evidence that these three predictions were once a unified block?

[37]Elsewhere in comparing John and the Synoptics, e.g., on the multiplication of the loaves, I find exactly the same phenomenon involving what one might deem to be earlier and later features. That works against the thesis of simple borrowing: A copyist would have to create new, earlier-style features as well as include or exclude later features.

[38]Létourneau ("Quatrième") shows how this development fits the respective theology of the two Gospels. In Mark, besides alerting the disciples about the future of Jesus, the three sayings with their concentration on suffering teach the disciples that if they wish to follow Jesus, they will have to share the same fate. In John the concentration in the three sayings on the lifting up of Jesus teaches the relationship between Jesus' exaltation and faith that brings salvation.

Suffering Servant passages on the Marcan predictions. Many think that John's *hypsoun* ("lift up") stems from Isa 52:13: "My servant shall be . . . lifted up and greatly exalted."[39] However, Schaberg ("Daniel" 218) notes that Dan 12:1 (LXX, not Theodotion) uses this verb for the lifting up of God's people in the last times. In n. 24 above I pointed out that on the Greek level a connection could be made between the LXX of Daniel and of Isaiah, both of which use the verb *paradidonai* that appears in the Synoptic passion predictions; similarly a connection can be made between the LXX of Daniel and Isaiah, both of which use the verb *hypsoun* that appears in the Johannine predictions.[40] It is this kind of scriptural reflection connecting passages (along with the respective theological thrusts of the evangelists[41]) that may have led from a common preGospel pattern of three predictions to what has emerged independently in Mark and John.

But why would both traditions have worked with Daniel and Isaiah? Was that proclivity already on the preGospel level, and if so did it go back to earlier Christians on a preGreek level or to Jesus himself? Related to that issue is the question raised earlier but left unsolved: Was there one basic prediction or several behind the three? Despite affirmations made with assurance in some scholarly treatments of the predictions, such queries ask for precision that I doubt even our modern methods of investigation are capable of supplying. Let me simply list general concluding observations that I find persuasive.

It is solid history that Jesus was associated with John the Baptist and that JBap was put to death by Herod (Antipas) because his preaching made him a dangerous figure. Somehow the beginning of Jesus' ministry of public preaching was tied in with the end of JBap's career. How could Jesus not have anticipated that his own career might bring him a similar violent fate?

It is quite plausible that Jesus vocalized this anticipation. A consideration of the three Synoptic and the three Johannine Son-of-Man predictions and of the more numerous allusive and less detailed predictions (Table 12 above) shows that foresight was attributed to Jesus widely and in very varied language. Only a small proportion of that language is clearly derivable from

[39]The LXX reads: "My servant . . . shall be lifted up and *glorified* exceedingly," and certainly the glorification of Jesus is a strong Johannine theme.

[40]There has been an attempt to trace John's *hypsoun* to a passive form of Aramaic *zqp,* which in Ezra 6:11 means "impale," and hence "crucify," and in later Aramaic (Syriac) means "raise, lift up." Thus, John would be playing on both meanings when he wrote in Greek of Jesus being lifted up on the cross. In one verb John would be summing up the type of formula Acts places in the apostolic speeches: You crucified him but God exalted him (see Acts 2:32,36; 5:30–31). One needs more proof that in 1st-cent. Aramaic the root *zqp* had both meanings and that John worked from an Aramaic base.

[41]See n. 17 above for Black's suggestion that the preGospel stratum may have been closer to John's final form than to that of Mark.

the Gospel PNs. Therefore, one should not facilely claim that the predictions are all retrojections from what the evangelists knew to have happened. Nor is it easy to see how all these formulations are reducible to one basic prediction. Thus I judge very unlikely the thesis that none of these sayings anticipating a violent death stems from Jesus. Clearly early Christian preachers enlarged and intensified the motif of Jesus' foreknowledge of the divine plan, but such massive creativity without some basis in Jesus himself is implausible. Nevertheless, since continuity from Jesus' own expressed predictions to those shaped by early Christian preaching would surely produce resemblances in motif and phrasing, it is very difficult to determine what form of which saying is or is not from Jesus.

Some of these many predictions echo OT descriptions of just ones who suffer and are persecuted by the wicked. Undoubtedly early Christians used Scripture to reflect on Jesus' death, but there is no serious reason to doubt that Jesus used Scripture as well to interpret his role in God's plan. After all, the kingdom of God is Danielic language. In particular, some activities of Jesus seem intentionally designed to evoke the prophets of old, like Elijah and Elisha;[42] and Jesus had to know that their careers in proclaiming God's word jeopardized their lives by attracting the hostility of rulers. Surely Jesus was aware that Jeremiah's denunciation of the Jerusalem authorities led to a plot against his life (Jer 26; 37–38). By this time in Jewish thought most of the prophets were thought to have been killed by hostile authorities (Luke 11:50–51; 13:33; see *The Lives of the Prophets*). In various journeys to Jerusalem during his ministry Jesus must have come more than once into conflict with the authorities there, and his knowledge of Scripture surely made him aware that a prophet's fate awaited him if he continued his challenging proclamations.[43] His scriptural reflections on his fate may well have oriented the more detailed scriptural reflections by his followers after his death. There is nothing implausible, then, in thinking that Jesus may have made use of Daniel and Isaiah in such reflections. Paradoxically, however, it may be impossible to determine precisely how much usage of these OT books attested in the NT did come from Jesus himself.

If Jesus anticipated a violent death at the hands of those who opposed him, if he spoke about this and phrased his anticipations in biblical language, how much detail might have entered into his description of his fate? On the one hand, only the three Synoptic predictions (I, II, III) offer detail; and so

---

[42]Healings, resuscitations, multiplication of loaves, exercising power over storms. (On not easily dismissing the miracles of Jesus, see NJBC 78:20; 81:96,103–9.) See the works in the SECTIONAL BIBLIOGRAPHY below by Davies, Downing, and Gnilka for the possibility that Jesus' seeing himself as martyr-prophet may supply the key to understanding Jesus' foreknowledge of his fate.

[43]Gnilka, *Jesu,* thinks this involved Jesus' having a salvific outlook on his death.

one may suspect that Jesus did not go into details in foretelling a violent outcome. Yet let me point out that a Jewish prophetic figure who knew the religious and political situation of the early 1st cent. AD could well have been somewhat detailed in his expectations. If Jesus expected trouble in Jerusalem, he would have known that the chief priests would be involved. The attested violence of the chief priests against the Samaritans, the Pharisees, and the Qumran Teacher, which was already history by Jesus' time, would clearly point in that direction. Josephus shows us the high priest involved with a Sanhedrin or council in his actions; and so the inclusion of elders and scribes in Jesus' generalizations about those opposed to him is not incredible. (Of course, we must take into account that a grouping like elders, chief priests, and scribes is, with variations, an established pattern of the PNs; but that does not mean that the grouping was unhistorical. If factually a Sanhedrin considered what to do with Jesus, that Sanhedrin would have consisted of various types of Jewish leaders.) Indeed, if Jesus was familiar with Jer 26; 37–38 and its lineup of priests, prophets, and princes who demanded the punishment and death of the prophet, he might well have included other hostile groups alongside the chief priests in anticipating those who would do him violence. Would he have envisioned Gentile (Roman) involvement? If he "went up" to Jerusalem only at feasts, he would know the likelihood (establishable from Josephus) that the Roman prefect would be in Jerusalem at the very moment that the chief priests might attempt to get rid of him. Josephus shows that on such occasions the Jewish authorities had to deal with the Roman governor, and Jesus' apocalyptic view of his proclamation of the kingdom might well envisage a hostile Gentile action. As for the mocking, spitting, and scourging predicted in III, OT descriptions of the persecution of the just guided the PN descriptions of the violence that was done to Jesus. If Jesus thought he would be made to suffer, how else would he have imagined his suffering except in this same OT language? Having made these observations, let me reiterate how seldom (sometimes only once) such detail is found in Jesus' statements about his destiny. This paragraph simply serves the purpose of reminding ourselves that a Jesus who would not have thought about any of these things would have been an oddity.

While a certain amount of foresight could have come to Jesus from reading the signs of the times, and more foresight from reflecting on what had happened to prophets and the just ones of God in the past, we do not do justice to a figure so God-imbued as Jesus if we overrationalize the source of his conviction that he would be rejected and die violently but emerge vindicated. Whatever reasoning went into his understanding of what would happen to him, he would surely attribute his conviction on this score to his status as the one whom God sent to proclaim the kingdom. I can understand, even though I do not agree with, the position of those who deny that Jesus had any such role in relation to God. I find more difficult the position of those who acknowledge that he had such a role but can imagine that he never spoke about where that path would lead him. The proclamation of the kingdom had to involve convictions about how that kingdom would come about; and for one who attached the inbreaking of the kingdom to his own activity, that would include convictions about his own fate[44]—convictions that he would trace to the God whose kingdom was being proclaimed.

I have just written about Jesus' "convictions" and "foresight"; previously I have written about "anticipation" and "expectation." Oberlinner, who has devoted a book to this question, would probably allow all these terms under his German heading *Todeserwartung;* but he insists that this does not necessarily amount to sure foreknowledge (*Todesgewissheit*). He thinks that Jesus expressed his expectation of a violent death, and so was not unprepared for it and neither were his disciples. Yet he was not certain of what would happen. He knew what might plausibly happen but had no absolutely fixed schema of the events. I see no way of determining the extent to which his relation to God in heaven moved Jesus beyond foresight to foreknowledge, and it may well be that he himself could not have answered that question. Subtlety does far more justice to the likelihoods than a negative vote that Jesus did not make (and perhaps could not have made) any of the predictions attributed to him.

Bibliography for Appendix VIII:
Jesus' Predictions of His Passion

Most books on NT christology have a section on these predictions, e.g., Fuller, Hahn, Tödt.

Bastin, M., *Jésus devant sa Passion* (LD 92; Paris: Cerf, 1976).

Black, M., "The 'Son of Man' Passion Sayings in the Gospel Tradition," ZNW 60 (1969), 1–8.

Borg, M. J., "The Jesus Seminar and the Passion Sayings," *Forum* 3 (#2; 1987), 81–95.

---

[44]As I pointed out at the beginning of this APPENDIX, it is another question how Jesus' own evaluation of his fate was related to the soteriological value attached to his death by the early Christians. They said that he died for all, for sins, as a sacrifice, by way of redemption or justification or salvation, etc. Did he think in any of those categories, or did he somehow relate his death to the coming of the kingdom (Mark 14:25)? There is an immense literature on the theological import of the death of Jesus (§1, n. 32); but it is worth noting that Léon-Dufour (*Face* 168–71) holds that it cannot be historically demonstrated that Jesus declared that he would die to save the world from sin—he left in God's hands that salvation. Segalla ("Gesù") judges the implications of that opinion too minimalist for an adequate christology.

Butts, J. R., "Passion Apologetic, the Chreia, and the Narrative," *Forum* 3 (#3; 1987), 96–127, esp. 107–11.

Davies, P. E., "Did Jesus Die as a Martyr Prophet?" BR 2 (1957), 19–30; 19 (1974), 34–47.

Downing, J., "Jesus and Martyrdom," JTS NS 14 (1963), 279–93.

Farmer, W. R., "The Passion Prediction Passages and the Synoptic Problem: a Test Case," NTS 36 (1990), 558–70.

Feuillet, A., "Les trois grandes prophéties de la Passion et de la Résurrection des évangiles synoptiques," RThom 67 (1967), 533–60; 68 (1968), 41–74.

Fitzmyer, J. A., "The New Testament Title 'Son of Man' Philologically Considered," FAWA 143–60.

Fuller, R. H., "The Son of Man Came to Serve, Not to Be Served," in *Ministering in a Servant Church,* ed. F. A. Eigo (Proceedings of the Theology Institute of Villanova Univ., 1978), 45–72.

———, "The Son of Man: a Reconsideration," in *The Living Text,* eds. D. E. Groh and R. Jewett (Honor of E. W. Saunders; Latham, MD: University of America, 1985), 207–17, esp. 211–13.

Gnilka, J., *Jesu ipsissima mors. Der Tod Jesu im Lichte seiner Martyriumsparänese* (Munich: Minerva, 1983).

Jeremias, J., *New Testament Theology* (London: SCM, 1971), esp. 276–99.

Kittel, G., "Jesu Worte über sein Sterben," *Deutsche Theologie* 3 (1936), 166–89.

Létourneau, P., "Le quatrième évangile et les prédictions de la passion dans les évangiles synoptiques," DJS 579–86.

Lindars, B., *Jesus Son of Man* (London: SPCK, 1983), esp. 65–84.

Marshall, I. H., "The Son Of Man in Contemporary Debate," EQ 42 (1970), 67–87.

Mouson, J., "De tribus praedictionibus Passionis apud Synopticos," *Collectanea Mechliniensia* 40 or 25 NS (1955), 709–14.

Oberlinner, L., *Todeserwartung und Todesgewissheit Jesu* (SBB 10; Stuttgart: KBW, 1980).

Perrin, N., "Towards an Interpretation of the Gospel of Mark," in *Christology and a Modern Pilgrimage,* ed. H. D. Betz (Claremont, CA, 1971), 1–78, esp. 14–28.

———, "The Use of *(para)didonai* in Connection with the Passion of Jesus in the New Testament," in *Der Ruf Jesu und die Antwort der Gemeinde,* ed. E. Lohse (J. Jeremias Festschrift; Göttingen: Vandenhoeck & Ruprecht, 1970), 204–12.

Pesch, R., "Die Passion des Menschensohnes. Eine Studie zu den Menschensohnworten der vormarkinischen Passionsgeschichte," in *Jesus und der Menschensohn,* eds. R. Pesch and R. Schnackenburg (A. Vögtle Festschrift; Freiburg: Herder, 1975), 166–95.

Schaberg, J., "Daniel 7,12 and the New Testament Passion-Resurrection Predictions," NTS 31 (1985), 208–22.

Schmithals, W., "Die Worte vom leidenden Menschensohn," in TCSCD 417–45.

Strecker, G., "The Passion- and Resurrection Predictions in Mark's Gospel," *Interpretation* 22 (1968), 421–42. German orig. in ZTK 64 (1967), 16–39.

Taylor, V., *Jesus and his Sacrifice: A Study of the Passion-sayings in the Gospels* (London: Macmillan, 1937).

————, "The Origin of the Markan Passion-sayings," *New Testament Essays* (London: Epworth, 1970), 60–71 (orig. article 1955).

Tödt, H. E., *The Son of Man in the Synoptic Tradition* (Philadelphia: Westminster, 1965), esp. 141–221.

Whiteley, D.E.H., "Christ's Foreknowledge of His Crucifixion," StEv I, 100–14.

Willaert, B., "La connexion littéraire entre la première prédiction de la passion et la confession de Pierre chez les Synoptiques," ETL 22 (1956), 24–35.

APPENDIX IX: THE QUESTION OF A PREMARCAN PASSION NARRATIVE*

By Marion L. Soards

Professor of New Testament Studies
Louisville Presbyterian Theological Seminary

In recent years much has been written on the sources of Mark's PN, reflecting a fundamental difference of opinion. On one side, there are scholars who maintain that Mark had a primitive source for the PN which he took over virtually intact; on the other side, there are scholars who argue that Mark created the PN using existing independent traditions and did not draw on a continuous earlier PN. The range of opinion is illustrated by the positions of the following scholars: E. Linnemann (*Studien*) employs *Redaktionsgeschichte* to arrive at the conclusion that the evangelist, Mark, was himself responsible for the connected form of the PN and that, at best, we may speak of various other traditions that the author has employed in constructing the PN. J. Ernst ("Passionserzählung") avers that I Cor 15:3–4 lays out the authentic track of the original PN: death → grave → resurrection. He concludes that in Mark 15:30b through 16:8 (minus redactional elements) we find this original PN track. R. Pesch (*Markus*) treats all the material between Mark 8:27 and 16:8 as the preMarcan PN, made up of thirty-nine story units which are easily organized into thirteen groups of three stories. W. Schmithals[1] argues that a single foundation document (*Grundschrift*) lies behind the entire Gospel and so the preMarcan PN should be regarded as a section of that earlier unified work.

Since scholarly opinion varies greatly on the dimensions of the preMarcan PN, it is necessary to establish the section to be considered in this APPENDIX.

---

* Note from R. E. Brown: The contents of this APPENDIX were published as an article in *Biblebhashyam* 11 (1985), 144–69. Prof. Soards has updated the study and kindly allowed me to edit it to the terse style of my commentary and to shorten it by eliminating bibliographical and other duplications. I submitted the final form to him for approval. For my appreciation of his work, see p. 75 above.

[1]*Das Evangelium nach Markus* (Ökumenischer Taschenbuchkommentar zum Neuen Testament 2; 2 vols.; Gütersloh: Mohn, 1979).

I shall treat the material in Mark from the arrest of Jesus in Gethsemane through his death and burial, namely, 14:32 to 15:47.[2] Four major sections comprise my treatment:

A. Annotated list of thirty-five scholars with a summary of the working method of each
B. Table 14 surveying the verses these scholars[3] attribute to the preMarcan PN(s)[4]
C. Methods/criteria for determining the shape (or nonexistence) of the pre-Marcan PN
   1. Parallels
   2. Internal Tensions
   3. Vocabulary and Style
   4. Theological Themes and Literary Motifs
   5. Conceptual Clusters
D. Conclusions from this survey: evaluation and implications for the origins of the PN

A. *Scholars and Works: An Annotated List*

The scholars discussed here will have their opinions surveyed in Section B (Table 14). After each author's name and the title of the pertinent work(s),[5] there is a description of the aim, method, and conclusions of the scholar's study.

The words "source" and "tradition" will appear throughout this study— words that are often used with ambiguity in writing on the Marcan PN. In this APPENDIX "source" designates a resource, oral or written, that existed in a basically fixed form prior to Mark drawing upon it. "Tradition" indicates a resource that was brief and probably not fixed in form prior to Mark's use of it. For example, if we consider the story of Peter's denial (§27 above:

---

[2]In this commentary Brown began with Mark 14:26, and so his introductory §5 (14:26–32) is not covered in Table 14 of my APPENDIX.

[3]From among the thirty-five, only Mohr is not included (for reasons to be explained). Outside the thirty-five, several outstanding writers on Mark are not included, e.g., J. Gnilka, E. Güttgemanns, M.-J. Lagrange, E. Linnemann, E. Lohmeyer, and J. Schniewind, not because their scholarship is not helpful, but because their approach and style made it impossible to present their conclusions in Table 14 devised for the present analysis. See also PMK, since some authors whose work is represented in Table 14 contributed to it. The positions they take in PMK do not vary from those given in the table.

[4]Also F. Neirynck ("Redactional" 144–62) helpfully gives in lists the redactional text of Mark as it is described by Gnilka, Pesch, and others.

[5]Abbreviated titles are used for works already cited in the bibliographies of the commentary, especially the part of the GENERAL BIBLIOGRAPHY dealing with Mark's PN (§3, Part 2).

with the narrative, i.e., those parts of the Marcan PN that are in tension with the materials around them (either by breaking the continuity of the immediate context or by disturbing the narrative sequence of the whole).

J. R. DONAHUE, *Are You*, holds that the PN is a Marcan creative formation, e.g., Mark composed the Sanhedrin trial scene and intercalated it into the account of Peter's denial. Donahue employs the tools of redaction criticism and composition criticism to argue that Mark used at least two diverse, independent preMarcan traditions in composing the *first* PN. One was an apologetic tradition based upon OT texts; the other was a historical tradition wherein Jesus was led away to the high priest. They have been combined in a thoroughgoing Marcan redaction to produce Mark 14:53a–65. Donahue utilizes observations related to language, style, structure, patterns, and theological themes and motifs to separate tradition from redaction.

D. DORMEYER, *Passion*, employs vocabulary statistics and style criticism, along with the detection of theological themes and motifs, to separate Mark 14:1–16:8 into three neat, distinct, separable layers. The first was an old martyr-story with a historical core. Later, this layer was popularized by the addition of dialogues and legendary expansions imitative of prophetic biographies. Finally, Mark added verses of parenetic material to this preMarcan core.

J. ERNST, "Passionserzählung," takes the primitive Christian confession of I Cor 15:3–4 as a starting point for knowledge about the passion of Jesus and lays out a track: death → grave → resurrection. He suggests that Mark 15:20b–16:8 contains the preMarcan core (PN) that follows this track. Ernst separates that core from the Marcan redactional elements by focusing on theological components and arguing from a stylistic and compositional perspective that certain narrative elements are secondary.

F. C. GRANT, *The Earliest Gospel* (New York: Abingdon-Cokesbury, 1943); and *The Gospels: Their Origin and Their Growth* (New York: Harper, 1957), works essentially as a form critic, focusing on the continuity of the whole PN and asking whether individual pericopes could or did have an independent existence outside the context of the PN. In both method and conclusions Grant's position is almost identical to Dibelius's. He holds that Mark took over in toto a preMarcan PN and expanded it by making additions. In addition to the verses indicated in Table 14, Grant contends that the preMarcan PN included 14:1–2, 10–11, 17–18a, 21–27, 29–31.

S. E. JOHNSON, *A Commentary on the Gospel According to St. Mark* (New York: Harper & Brothers, 1966), refers to the "considerable agreement" among scholars concerning the passages to be assigned to the preMarcan PN. He refers to the work of Grant and Dibelius and then lists the verses in

Mark which were part of the preMarcan PN: 14:1–2,10–11,17–18a,21–27,29–31,43–53a; 15:1–15,21–22,24a,25–27,29a,32b–37,39. Johnson suspects that this PN was read along with the OT in early Christian worship.

W. KELBER, KKS, works similarly to Donahue (see above). He finds "some glimmer of a preMarcan tradition" (p. 539); but by studying Mark 14:32–42 from the perspective of Marcan terms, vocabulary, motifs, structures, and theological concerns, Kelber concludes that "Mark is not merely the redactor, but to a high degree the creator and composer of the Gethsemane story" (p. 540).

E. KLOSTERMANN, *Das Markusevangelium* (4th ed.; Handbuch zum Neuen Testament 3; Tübingen: Mohr, 1950), claims to follow Bultmann in positing a preMarcan PN. He distinguishes the basic, continuous story of this preMarcan PN from expansions that are both "earlier already existing stories" and "newly arisen creations."

A. KOLENKOW, "Trial," analyzes Mark 15:1–20a, focusing on (1) material in the story for which Mark does not prepare the reader, and (2) the essential structure of the piece. Kolenkow's method and conclusions are similar to those of Kelber and Donahue in putting the emphasis on Mark's composition rather than on preMarcan sources.

K. G. KUHN, "Jesus," by studying the Gethsemane scene in light of theological themes and motifs, is able to distinguish two sources that were employed in the formation of Mark 14:32–42. One source was christological and spoke of the "hour." The other source was parenetic and spoke of "the cup."

W. L. LANE, *The Gospel according to Mark* (New International Commentary on the NT; Grand Rapids: Eerdmans, 1974), starts with the assumption of the early form critics that Mark had a primitive source that he took over virtually intact. Lane claims that Mark "chose to supplement it with parallel or complementary traditions and to orchestrate it for the development of certain themes" (p. 485). To determine how Mark did this, Lane employs parallel traditions from Paul and Acts and asks whether a particular pericope could have had an originally independent existence outside the PN.

X. LÉON-DUFOUR, "Passion," outlines in a general manner the opinions of several scholars concerning the contents of the preMarcan PN and then reports the work of Taylor in detail and with approval. He also refers to Buse, "St John . . . Marcan," which notes striking parallels between the Fourth Gospel and the B stratum (not the A) of the preMarcan PN as Taylor isolates it. It is therefore permissible to doubt that story A offers the primitive PN. Scrutinizing each canonical PN individually and comparatively, Léon-Dufour concludes that there is a degree of independence for each account, but that Matthew and Mark shared one common source while Luke and John shared a common tradition. Behind the four PNs grouped two-by-two, he discerns a primitive story, written or oral, that the evangelists would themselves have transformed through the incorporation of relevant oral traditions. Although Léon-Dufour does not offer a precise reconstruction, he defines the general boundaries of the "primitive story": Going out from the room where the Lord's Supper was taken, Jesus was arrested in the Garden of Olives; he was delivered by the high priest to Pilate; he was condemned to death and crucified. The story closed with the sepulcher and probably an appearance. So far as I can detect, it would have consisted of 14:3–9,22–25,32–42,47–52,54,65,66–72; 15:2,6–14,16–20,25,27,31–33,38,40–41,47.

R. H. LIGHTFOOT, *History and Interpretation in the Gospels* (New York: Harper, 1934), focuses on Mark 14:1–16:8 and works as a form critic to identify later development beyond the preMarcan PN. The critical criteria are similar to those used by Bultmann.

E. LOHSE, *History*, argues that Mark 10:33–34 presupposes a brief account of the passion. He works with the methods of form criticism (see Bultmann) to determine the original form of the preMarcan PN.

D. LÜHRMANN, *Markus*, follows the lead of J. Becker and T. A. Mohr in noticing striking and extensive similarities between the Marcan and the Johannine PNs. He insists one must account for these parallels since John's Gospel is otherwise literarily independent of the Synoptics and shows a different theological interpretation of the meaning of Jesus' passion. Lührmann concludes that some source necessarily lies behind the commonality; but in discerning the scope of this preGospel PN, one should recognize that rather than being slavishly bound to it, Mark incorporated it with integrity. Lührmann would attribute to it: 14:1,3–9,17–20,27,29–56,60–61a; 14:63–15:29a; 15:32b–38; 15:40–16:6,8a.

W. MOHN, "Gethsemane," uses the tools of redaction criticism (see Donahue and Kelber) to argue that an apocalyptic original (*Vorlage*) with an emphasis on "hour" and "sleep" lay behind the present Gethsemane scene.

T. A. MOHR, *Markus*, investigates the historical, traditional, and theological bases of the Marcan PN by careful comparison of the Marcan and Johannine PNs. He concludes that Mark employed a major source that had itself previously experienced a revision. Mohr's reconstruction of the source (subdividing verses as a, b, c and then further subdividing as aa, ab, ba, etc.) is so complex as to defy being charted in Section B below; and so his results are listed here, as he himself gives them: 14:1–2 (in part), 3,4,5a,6aa,8b, 7ac,9ac; 11:1aa (up to *Hierosolyma*), 8,9a (in part), 9b,10 (in part), 11ab,15abb,16,[19]; 14:18a (in part), 18ba,20b,21c,22–23,24 (without *tēs diathēkēs*), 25,32,33,34,35a,36 (without *ho patēr*), 37 (without bb), 38–39,40aba,42a,43 (in part), 45,46,47,50,51–52,53a,55–56,61b (without *palin* and probably with *kai* inserted), 62,63–64,65b; 15:1 (in part), 3,2,6,9,11,7,12 (without *hon legete*), 13,15 (without *boulomenos* through *poiēsai*), 16a*a*,16b,17,18 (in part), 19,20a (up to *autou*), 20b–22a,24,26–27,34a (without *tē enatē hōra*), 36a,37b,40, 42b,43,45b,46,47; 16:1,2,3, 4a,5,8a (up to *mnēmeiou*)—then followed an account of the appearance to Mary Magdalene similar to the account in John 20:11b–18.

M. MYLLYKOSKI, *Letzten Tage,* analyzes the Marcan PN at and beyond the level of individual words and phrases by focusing, above all, on the "narrative thread" (*Erzählfaden*) that unifies the different elements of the story. After careful and complementary readings of Mark and John (and the other Gospels), he contends that observable tensions and repetitions disturb the continuity of the narrative and point to a preMarcan PN. Myllykoski distinguishes between the oldest stratum of the PN and an enlarged PN that both Mark and John would have used as the basis of their own presentations. (Asterisks are explained on p. 1501 below.) The *oldest passion tradition* comprised (Mark) 11:11*,15c,27b*,28*; 14:58*; 14:1–2*,10–11*,17*,26*,43*,45*,46–47*,50,53a,61b*,62a,65ca*; 15:1*,3*,2*,15b,19a*,20b–22a,23–24a,27,26. The *enlarged passion source* (with material from the oldest passion tradition in brackets) contained 11:8–10* [11:11*,15c,27b*,28*; 14:58*;14:1–2*]; 14:3–8* [14:10–11*], 14:17–20*,27a,29–31*,33–36*,41–42*[14:43*,45*,46–47*,50,53a],14:54* [14:61a*,62a,65ca*], 14:66–72* [15:1*,3*,2*]; 15:6–15a* [15:15b], 15:16–18,19b [15:19a*,20b–22a,23–24a], 15:24b [15:27,26], 15:29a,30*,34*, 36a,37*,40*,42–46*; and John 20:1,11bβ,12 ... 19ac,20*,22–23. I am grateful to Dr. Myllykoski for supplying me with a copy of vol. 1 of his study and several ms. pages from vol. 2 that is still in production at this writing; he graciously cooperated in determining the precise contents of this descriptive paragraph.

D. E. NINEHAM, *The Gospel of St. Mark* (Pelican NT Commentaries; Baltimore: Penguin, 1963), refers frequently to the work of "scholars" (without much identification) in arguing toward the recovery of the preMarcan PN. Using form-critical methods, he asks whether a tradition is likely to be historical, i.e., could a tradition extend back to an eyewitness. He also employs a criterion that is similar to the redaction-critical analysis of theological concerns.

C. D. PEDDINGHAUS, *Entstehung,* argues that a preMarcan PN, originally inspired from Psalm 22, was later elaborated and finally became the text Mark drew from (*Vorlage*). The methods of study are largely those of form criticism with an awareness of the methods of redaction criticism.

R. PESCH, *Markus,* contending that Mark's commitment to earlier Jesus-material(s) has been underestimated in much contemporary study, maintains that Mark used extensive sources, i.e., at least seven blocks of preMarcan tradition. One of these was an extensive earlier PN, comprised of 8:27–33; 9:2–13,30–35; 10:1,32–34,46–52; 11:1–23,27–33; 12:1–12,35–37,41–44; 13:1–2; and 14:1–16:8. Since the scope of this PN material is broader than the span of verses summarized in Table 14, only the relevant portions of Pesch's proposed PN are shown on that chart.

E. J. PRYKE, *Redactional,* lists fourteen syntactical features as guidelines to Mark's own style. His discussion of "redactional verses" that scholars have identified allows him to classify the elements of the "redactional text of Mark" under nine headings, eight of which are applicable to redactional verses in the PN. Thus, Pryke isolates the traditional materials that Mark employed.

W. SCHENK, *Passionsbericht,* using vocabulary and style criticism and focusing on theological themes and motifs, isolates two sources that lay behind the Marcan PN. The first source (a Simon-tradition) was a simple story employing OT allusions to establish the innocence of Jesus. The second, an apocalyptic tradition, represented the theology advocated by Mark's opponents. Mark combined these with additional individual elements (*Einzelstücke*), coordinating the components under the rubrics of the suffering Jesus and of imitation by disciples.

L. SCHENKE, *Gekreuzigte,* with the help of literary criticism, focuses on theological themes in the PN. He isolates the earliest preMarcan concern: a Suffering-of-the-Just-One motif that presented Jesus' suffering and death as that of the Messiah. At a later preMarcan stage, material was worked from a polemically apologetic angle that made clear the sharp distinction between the Christian community and official Judaism.

G. SCHILLE, "Leiden," using the principles of form criticism, isolates a preMarcan PN that may be described as a cultically oriented traditions-collection in three parts: (1) a Maundy Thursday tradition, (2) a Good Friday tradition, and (3) a tomb-stories tradition. The overall scope of these collected traditions is 14:18–16:8 with the omission of 14:55–65.

W. SCHMITHALS, *Markus,* envisions a single unified writing (*Grundschrift*) that lay behind the entire Gospel and contained a PN. "The *Grundschrift* and the redactional reworking are relatively clearly separated from one another because in general with regard to his redaction of the *Grundschrift* Mark does not revise the *Grundschrift* but rather supplements and occasionally shortens or rearranges it" (p. 43).

G. SCHNEIDER, "Verhaftung" and "Gab," who does not posit a preMarcan PN, is most interested in the process of composition of the present Marcan text. He employs the methods of form and redaction criticism (see Bultmann and Donahue).

J. SCHREIBER, *Kreuzigungsbericht* and *Theologie,* employs language and style criticism, while taking note of OT citations and apocalyptic conceptions. He distinguishes two sources that lay behind the text of the Marcan PN (see Schenk).

E. SCHWEIZER, *Mark,* in suggesting the shape and substance of the preMarcan PN, takes seriously the parallels between Mark and John and employs the methods of form criticism.

R. SCROGGS, in KKS, claims that while Mark 15:20b–39 displays a complex history of transmission, Mark did not create this section. Indeed, Mark changed the tradition that he received very little. Scroggs suggests that style and vocabulary are "too uncertain" (p. 557) to be used as definitive methodological criteria. He uses the methods of form criticism and emphasizes the isolation and correlation of different conceptual clusters that are found in the text for the process of reconstructing the history of transmission.

V. TAYLOR, *Mark,* isolates two sources that lay behind the Marcan PN. Source A, called the Roman source, was a continuous, flowing narrative of summary character marked by realism. Source B, called the Semitic source, was made of short, self-contained bits full of possible semitisms that were intercalated into A. The criteria of form criticism are coupled with questions of style and vocabulary in Taylor's work.

B. *Table 14: Theories of Various Scholars about the Composition of the Marcan Passion Narrative*

Eight double-pages make up this table. The Marcan text is the literal translation that Brown made for this commentary. The symbols used are explained below. The absence of a symbol in reference to a particular verse usually indicates that the verse in question is considered to be redactional by the scholar whose opinion concerning the preMarcan PN is being given in symbols. Any exceptions to this principle were noted above in the description of the individual scholar's working methods.

SYMBOLS USED IN TABLE 14 COVERING MARK 14:32–15:47

A   identifies a verse as belonging to a/the preMarcan source or tradition that has been incorporated by Mark into the text of his PN.

B   identifies a verse as belonging to a second, independent preMarcan source or tradition, different from A, that has been incorporated by Mark into the text of his PN.

C   identifies a verse as belonging to a third, independent preMarcan source or tradition, different from A and B, that has been incorporated by Mark into the text of his PN.

$A^{1/2/3}$ indicates a verse from what was once an independent tradition that became a part of a later, unified, single source that in turn was incorporated by Mark into the text of his PN, e.g., see under Dormeyer, where after 15:27 A^1 means that he attributes v. 27 to a first preMarcan stage of tradition-history. Again, see under Peddinghaus, where after 15:27 A^2 means that he attributes v. 27 to a second preMarcan stage of tradition-history. B and C are sometimes subdivided also.

a/b/c/   following a symbol designates part of the verse to which the symbol refers, e.g., under Buckley, after 14:32 Aa and Bb mean that he attributes 32a to A and 32b to B.

*   following a symbol indicates that a word or words in the verse to which that symbol refers are likely redactional but that the preponderance of the verse is preMarcan.

?   following another symbol indicates that the author did not make a clear decision as to whether a verse was preMarcan or redactional.

[ ]   around a symbol indicate that an author considers a verse to be a secondary addition to the primary source that the symbol designates and that this secondary addition was made prior to Mark's incorporation of the source (primary and secondary addition) into the text of his PN.

—   area of the PN not treated by the respective author

Mark 14:32–42	Anderson	Buckley	Bultmann	Czerski	Dibelius	Donahue	Dormeyer	Ernst	Grant	Johnson	Kelber	Klostermann	Kolenkow	Kuhn
32And they come into the plot of land the name of which was Gethsemane; and he says to his disciples, "Sit here while I pray."	[B]	Aa Bb					Aa¹ Ab²				Aa		—	A
33And he takes along Peter, and James, and John with him, and he began to be greatly distraught and troubled.	[A]	Aa Bb											—	B
34And he says to them, "My soul is very sorrowful unto death. Remain here and keep on watching."	[A]	A									Ab?		—	B
35And having gone forward a little, he was falling on the earth and was praying that if it is possible, the hour might pass from him.	[B]	B					Aa²				A?		—	A
36And he was saying, "*Abba*, Father, all things are possible to you: Take away this cup from me. But not what I will but what you (will)."	[A]	A					A²				A?		—	B
37And he comes and finds them sleeping, and he says to Peter, "Simon, are you sleeping? Were you not strong enough to watch one hour?	[A]	B					Aa²						—	B
38Keep [pl.] on watching and praying lest you [pl.] enter into trial. Indeed the spirit is willing, but the flesh is weak."	[A]	B									A*		—	B
39And again having gone away, he prayed, saying the same word.		B											—	
40And again having come, he found them sleeping; for their eyes were very burdened, and they did not know what they should answer him.	[B]	A											—	A
41And he comes the third time and says to them, "Do you go on sleeping, then, and taking your rest? The money is paid; the hour has come; behold the Son of Man is given over into the hands of the sinners.	[Bb]	B					Ab²						—	A
42Get up; let us go; behold the one who gives me over has come near."		B											—	

Lane	Léon-Dufour	Lightfoot	Lohse	Lührmann	Mohn	Myllykoski	Nineham	Peddinghaus	Pesch	Pryke	Schenk	Schenke	Schille	Schmithals	Schneider	Schreiber	Schweizer	Scroggs	Taylor
A	A	A	A	A	A		[A]		A	Ab	A	Aa*1	A	A				—	B
A	A	A		A		B*	[A]		A		A B	Ab1	A					—	B
A	A	A	A	A		B*	[A]		A	A	A	A1	A	Ab				—	B
A	A	A	A	A	A	B*	[A]		A	A	A B	Aa1	A	A				—	B
A	A	A		A		B*	[A]		A	A	A	A1	A	A				—	B
A	A	A	A	A	Aa		[A]		A	A	A	A1	A	A				—	B
A	A	A		A			[A]		A		A	Ab1	A	A				—	B
A	A	A	[A]	A					A		A		A	A				—	B
A	A	A	[A]	A			[A]		A		A	Ab1 [Ac1]	A	A				—	B
A	A	A	Aa	A	Ab	B*	[A]		A		A B	Aa*1 [Ac*1]	A	A*				—	B
A	A	A		A		B*	[A]		A		A	A1	A					—	B

Mark 14:43–52	Anderson	Buckley	Bultmann	Czerski	Dibelius	Donahue	Dormeyer	Ernst	Grant	Johnson	Kelber	Klostermann	Kolenkow	Kuhn
[43]And immediately, while he was still speaking, there arrives Judas, one of the Twelve, and with him a crowd with swords and wooden clubs, from the chief priests and the scribes and the elders.	A	A	A	A	A		Ab[1]		A	A	—	A	—	—
[44]The one who was giving him over had given them a signal, saying, "Whomever I shall kiss, he is (the one). Seize him and lead him away securely."	A	B	A	A	A				A	A	—	A	—	—
[45]And having come, immediately having come up to him, he says, "Rabbi," and he kissed him warmly.	A	A	A	A	A		A[2]		A	A	—	A	—	—
[46]But they laid hands on him and seized him.	A	A	A	A	A		A[1]		A	A	—	A	—	—
[47]But a certain one of those standing by, having drawn the sword, hit at the servant of the high priest and took off his ear.		B	A		A		A[2]		A	A	—	A	—	—
[48]And in answer Jesus said to them, "As if against a bandit have you come out with swords and wooden clubs to take me?		A	A		A				A	A	—	A	—	—
[49]Day after day I was with you in the Temple teaching, and you did not seize me. However—let the Scriptures be fulfilled!"	Aa	A	A		A				A	A	—	A	—	—
[50]And having left him, they all fled.	A	A	A		A		A[1]		A	A	—	A	—	—
[51]And a certain young man was following with him, clothed with a linen cloth over his nakedness; and they seize him.			A		A		A[1]		A*	A	—	A	—	—
[52]But he, having left behind the linen cloth, fled naked.			A		A		A[1]		A*	A	—	A	—	—

Lane	Léon-Dufour	Lightfoot	Lohse	Lührmann	Mohn	Myllykoski	Nineham	Peddinghaus	Pesch	Pryke	Schenk	Schenke	Schille	Schmithals	Schneider	Schreiber	Schweizer	Scroggs	Taylor
A		A	A	A		A*	Ab	A^3	A		A	A*^{1}	A	A*	A		A	—	A
A		A	A	A			A	A^2	A	A	A B	A^1	A		A		A	—	A
A		A	A	A		A*	A	A^2	A	A	A	A^1	A		A		A	—	A
A		A	A	A		A*	A	A^2	A	A	A B	A^1	A	A	A		A	—	A
A	A	A	[A?]	A		A*	[A?]	A^2	A		A	A^1	A	[A]			A	—	B
A	A	A	A	A			[A?]	A^3	A		A		A	A			A	—	B
A	A	A	A	A			[A?]	A^3	A		A		A	A			A	—	B
A	A	A	A	A		A	A?	A^2	A		A B	A^1	A	A			A	—	B
	A	A	A	A			A	A^2	A		A		A	[A]			A	—	B
	A	A	A	A			A	A^2	A		A		A	[A]			A	—	B

Mark 14:53–65	Anderson	Buckley	Bultmann	Czerski	Dibelius	Donahue	Dormeyer	Ernst	Grant	Johnson	Kelber	Klostermann	Kolenkow	Kuhn
^{53}And they led Jesus away to the high priest, and there (now) come together all the chief priests, and the elders, and the scribes.	A	A	Aa	A	A	Aa	Aa^2		Aa	Aa	—	A	—	—
^{54}And Peter followed him from a distance until inside the court of the high priest, and he was seated together with the attendants and warming himself near the blazing flame.	B?	A			A	B	A^2		A		—		—	—
^{55}But the chief priests and the whole Sanhedrin were seeking testimony against Jesus in order to put him to death, and they were not finding (any).	A	B		A			A^1				—		—	—
^{56}For many were giving false testimony against him, and the testimonies were not consistent.	A	B		A		C	A^2				—		—	—
^{57}And some, having stood up, were giving false testimony against him, saying	A	A		A		C*					—		—	—
^{58}that "We have heard him saying that 'I will destroy this sanctuary made by hand, and within three days another not made by hand I will build.'"	A	A		A							—		—	—
^{59}And even so their testimony was not consistent.	A			A		C					—		—	—
^{60}And having stood up, the high priest in (their) midst questioned Jesus, saying, "Have you nothing at all to answer to what these are testifying against you?"	A	A		A		A					—		—	—
^{61}But he stayed silent and answered nothing at all. Again the high priest was questioning him and says to him, "Are you the Messiah, the Son of the Blessed?"	A	Aa Bb		A		Aa	Ab^2				—		—	—
^{62}But Jesus said, "I am, and you [pl.] will see the Son of Man sitting at the right of the Power and coming with the clouds of heaven."	A	B		A			Aa^2				—		—	—
^{63}But the high priest, having torn his garments, says, "What further need do we have of testifiers?	A	B		A			A^2				—		—	—
^{64}You have heard the blasphemy. What does it appear to you?" But they all judged against him as being guilty, punishable by death.	A	B		A			A^2				—		—	—
^{65}And some began to spit on him, and to cover his face and strike him and say to him, "Prophesy"; and the attendants got him with slaps.	A	A	A?	A		C	Ab^2				—	A?	—	—

Lane	Léon-Dufour	Lightfoot	Lohse	Lührmann	Mohn	Myllykoski	Nineham	Peddinghaus	Pesch	Pryke	Schenk	Schenke	Schille	Schmithals	Schneider	Schreiber	Schweizer	Scroggs	Taylor
A		A		A		Aa		Aa^2 Ab^3	A	Ab	A B	Aa^1	A	Aa	Aa		Aa	—	[A]
A	A	A		A		B*	A?	A^3	A	A	A		A	A			A	—	B
A			A	A					A	A	A	A^1					A?	—	[A]
A			A	A					A	A	A	A^1					A	—	[A]
A			A						A		B	A^2					Aa*	—	[A]
A			A						A		B	A^2					A	—	[A]
A			A						A			A^2						—	[A]
A			A	A					A	A	B	A^1					A	—	[A]
A			Aa			Ab*			A		A B	A^1			Ab		Aa	—	[A]
A						Aa			A	A	A	Aa^1 Ab^2			A			—	[A]
A			A	A					A	A	A	A^1			Aa		A	—	[A]
A			A	A					A	A	A	A^1			Aa		A?	—	[A]
A	A		A	A		Aca*			A		B	A^1					A	—	B

Mark 14:66–72	Anderson	Buckley	Bultmann	Czerski	Dibelius	Donahue	Dormeyer	Ernst	Grant	Johnson	Kelber	Klostermann	Kolenkow	Kuhn
66And Peter being below in the court, one of the servant women of the high priest comes;		B			A		Ab²				—		—	—
67and having seen Peter warming himself and having looked at him, she says to him, "You too were with the Nazarene, Jesus."	Bb	B			A		Ab²				—		—	—
68aBut he denied, saying, "I don't know nor understand what you are saying." 68bAnd he went outside into the forecourt [and a cock crowed].	B	Ba Ab			A		A²				—		—	—
69And the servant woman, having seen him, began again to say to the bystanders that "This is one of them."	B	A			A						—		—	—
70aBut again he was denying it. 70bAnd after a little, the bystanders again were saying to Peter, "Truly you are one of them, for indeed you are a Galilean."	B	A			A						—		—	—
71But he began to curse and swear that "I don't know this man of whom you speak."	B	A			A						—		—	—
72And immediately a second time a cock crowed; and Peter remembered the word as Jesus had spoken it to him, that "Before a cock crows twice, three times you will deny me." And having rushed out, he was weeping.		A			A		Ac²				—		—	—

Lane	Léon-Dufour	Lightfoot	Lohse	Lührmann	Mohn	Myllykoski	Nineham	Peddinghaus	Pesch	Pryke	Schenk	Schenke	Schille	Schmithals	Schneider	Schreiber	Schweizer	Scroggs	Taylor
A	A	A		A		B*	A	A^3	A	Ab	A		A	Ab			A	—	B
A	A	A		A		B*	A	A^3	A		A		A	A			A	—	B
A	A	A		A		B*	A	A^3	A		A		A	A			A	—	B
A	A	A		A		B*	A	A^3	A		A		A	A			A	—	B
A	A	A		A		B*	A	A^3	A	Ab	A		A	A			A	—	B
A	A	A		A		B*	A	A^3	A	Ab	A		A	A			A	—	B
A	A	A		A		B*	A	A^3	A		A		A	A			A	—	B

Mark 15:1–15	Anderson	Buckley	Bultmann	Czerski	Dibelius	Donahue	Dormeyer	Ernst	Grant	Johnson	Kelber	Klostermann	Kolenkow	Kuhn
[1]And immediately, early, having made their consultation, the chief priests with the elders and scribes and the whole Sanhedrin, having bound Jesus, took him away and gave him over to Pilate.			A		A		Ab[1]		A	A	—	A		—
[2]And Pilate questioned him, "Are you the King of the Jews?" But in answer he says to him, "You say (so)."	A	B		A	A		A[2]		A	A	—	A		—
[3]And the chief priests were accusing him of many things.	A	A	A	A	A		A[1]		A	A	—	A		—
[4]But Pilate tried to question him again, saying, "Do you answer nothing at all? Behold how much they have accused you of."	A	A	A	A	A				A	A	—	A		—
[5]But Jesus answered nothing further, so that Pilate was amazed.	Aa	A	A	A	A		A[1]		A	A	—	A		—
[6]But at a/the feast he used to release to them one prisoner whom they requested.	A	B			A		A[1]		A	A	—		A	—
[7]But there was someone called Barabbas imprisoned with the rioters, those who had done killing during the riot.	A	A			A		A[1]		A	A	—		A	—
[8]And the crowd, having come up, began to request (that he do so) as he used to do for them.	A	A			A				A	A	—		A	—
[9]But Pilate answered them, saying, "Do you will that I release to you 'the King of the Jews'?"	A	B			A		A[2]		A	A	—		A	—
[10]for he had knowledge that (it was) out of envy/zeal that the chief priests had given him over.	A	B			A		A[2]		A	A	—			—
[11]But the chief priests stirred up the crowd that he should rather release Barabbas to them.	A	B			A		A[1]		A	A	—			—
[12]But in answer again, Pilate kept saying to them, "What therefore shall I do with him whom you call 'the King of the Jews'?"	A	B			A				A	A	—			—
[13]But they shouted back, "Crucify him."	A	B			A				A	A	—		A	—
[14]But Pilate kept saying to them, "For what has he done that is bad?" But they shouted even more, "Crucify him."	A	B			A				A	A	—			—
[15]But Pilate, desiring to satisfy the crowd, released to them Barabbas; and he gave over Jesus, having had him flogged, in order that he be crucified.	A	A	Ab		A		A[1]		A	A	—	Ab	Ab	—

Lane	Léon-Dufour	Lightfoot	Lohse	Lührmann	Mohn	Myllykoski	Nineham	Peddinghaus	Pesch	Pryke	Schenk	Schenke	Schille	Schmithals	Schneider	Schreiber	Schweizer	Scroggs	Taylor
A		A		A		A*	A?	A^2	A	Ab	A B	A^{*1}	·	A*			Aa? Ab	—	A
A	A	A		A		A*	[A]	A^3	A		A	A^1	B				A	—	B
A		A		A		A*	A	A^3	A	A	B	A^1	B	A*			A	—	A
A		A		A			A	A^3	A	A		A^1	B	A			A	—	A
A		A		A			A	A^3	A	A	B	A^1	B	A*			A	—	A
A	A	A		A		B*	A	A^3	A	A		A^2	B	A*			A	—	B
A	A	A		A		B*	A	A^3	A		C	A^2	B	A			A	—	B
A	A	A		A		B*	A	A^3	A		C	A^2	B	A			A	—	B
A	A	A		A		B*	A	A^3	A	A		A^2	B	A			A	—	B
A	A	A		A		B*	A	A^3	A			A^2	B	A			A	—	B
A	A	A		A		B*	A	A^3	A	A	C	A^2	B	A*			A	—	B
A	A	A		A		B*	A	A^3	A		B	A^2	B				A	—	B
A	A	A		A		B*	A	A^3	A	Ab	B	A^2	B				A	—	B
A	A	A		A		B*	A	A^3	A	Aa	B	A^2	B				A	—	B
A		A		A		Ab Ba*	A	Aa^3 Ab^2	A	Aa Ab*	B C	Aa^2 $[Ab^{*1}]$	B	A			A	—	A

Mark 15:16–26	Anderson	Buckley	Bultmann	Czerski	Dibelius	Donahue	Dormeyer	Ernst	Grant	Johnson	Kelber	Klostermann	Kolenkow	Kuhn
[16] But the soldiers led him away inside the court, that is, the praetorium, and called together the whole cohort.	[A]	B		A			Aac²				—	A	A	—
[17] And they put purple on him; and having woven a thorny crown, they put it on him.	[A]	B		A			A²				—	A	A	—
[18] And they began to salute him, "Hail, King of the Jews."	[A]	B		A			A²				—	A	A	—
[19] And they were striking his head with a reed and spitting on him; and bending the knee, they worshiped him.	[A]	B		A			Ab²				—	A	A	—
[20a] When they had mocked him, they undressed him of the purple and dressed him with his own clothes. [20b] And they lead him out in order that they might crucify him;	[Aa] Ab	Ba	Ab	A			Aa² Ab¹	Ab			—	A	Aa	—
[21] and they compel a certain passerby, Simon the Cyrenian, coming in from the field, the father of Alexander and Rufus, to take up his [Jesus'] cross.	A		A	A	A		A¹	A	A	A	—	A		—
[22] And they bring him to the Golgotha place, which is interpreted Skull-Place;	A	B	A	A	A		Aa¹	A	A	A	—	A		—
[23] and they were giving him wine with myrrh, but he did not take it.	A		A	A	A		A¹	A	A?		—	A		—
[24] And they crucify him; and they divide up his clothes, throwing lots for them as to who should take what.	Aa Ab?	A	Aa	A	A		Aa¹	A	A?	Aa	—	Aa		—
[25] Now it was the third hour, and they crucified him.		B		Λ	A				A?	A	—	A		—
[26] And there was an inscription of the charge against him, inscribed "The King of the Jews."	A?			A	A		A¹	A	A	A	—	A		—

Lane	Léon-Dufour	Lightfoot	Lohse	Lührmann	Mohn	Myllykoski	Nineham	Peddinghaus	Pesch	Pryke	Schenk	Schenke	Schille	Schmithals	Schneider	Schreiber	Schweizer	Scroggs	Taylor
A	A	A	A	A		B	[A?]		A	Aa	A B	A^1	B				A	—	B
A	A	A	A	A		B	[A?]		A	A	A	A^1	B				A	—	B
A	A	A	A	A		B	[A?]		A		A	A^1	B				A	—	B
A	A	A	A	A		Aa* Bb	[A?]		A	A	A	A^1	B				Ab	—	B
A	A	A	A	A		Ab	[Aa?] Ab	Ab^2	A	Aa Ab*	A	A^1	B			Ab	A	Ab^1	B
		A	A	A		A	A	A^2	A	A	A	A^2	B	A		A	A	A^1	A
		A	A	A		Aa	A	A^2	A	Aa	A	A^1	B	A		Aa	A	A^1	A
A		A	A	A		A	A	A^3	A	A	A	A^1	B	A			A	A^1	A
		A	A	A		Aa Bb	Aa	A^2	A	A	A	A^1	B	A		A	Aa [Ab]	Aa^1 Ab^3	A
A	A	A		A				A^1	A		B	A^1	B			B	[A]	A^2	B
A		A	A	A		A		A^1	A		B	A^1	B			B	A	A^4?	A

Mark 15:27–39	Anderson	Buckley	Bultmann	Czerski	Dibelius	Donahue	Dormeyer	Ernst	Grant	Johnson	Kelber	Klostermann	Kolenkow	Kuhn
[27]And with him they crucify two bandits, one on the right and one on his left.		A	A?	A	A		A^1	A	A	A	—	A	—	—
[29]And those passing by were blaspheming him, wagging their heads and saying, "Aha, O one destroying the sanctuary and building it in three days,	A	A		A	A			A	Aa	Aa	—	A	—	—
[30]save yourself by having come down from the cross."	A	A		A	A			A			—	A	—	—
[31]Similarly also the chief priests, mocking him to one another with the scribes, were saying, "Others he saved; himself he cannot save.	A	B		A	A		Aa^1 Ab^2	A			—	A	—	—
[32]Let the Messiah, the King of Israel, come down now from the cross in order that we may see and believe." Even those who had been crucified together with him were reviling him.	A	Ba Ab		A	A		Aa^2 Ac^1	A	Ab	Ab	—	A	—	
[33]And the sixth hour having come, darkness came over the whole earth until the ninth hour.	B	B			A				A	A	—	A*?	—	—
[34]And at the ninth hour Jesus screamed with a loud cry, "*Elōi, Elōi, lama sabachthani?*" which is interpreted, "My God, my God, for what reason have you forsaken me?"	B	B		A	A		Aab^1		A	A	—	A*?	—	—
[35]And some of the bystanders, having heard, were saying, "Look, he is crying to Elijah."	B	B		A	A				A	A	—	A*?	—	—
[36]But someone, running, having filled a sponge with vinegary wine, having put it on a reed, was giving him to drink, saying, "Leave (be). Let us see if Elijah comes to take him down."	Aa Bb	B	Aa?	A	A				A	A	—	A*?	—	—
[37]But Jesus, having let go a loud cry, expired.	A		A?	A	A		A^1	A	A	A	—	A*?	—	—
[38]And the veil of the sanctuary was rent into two from top to bottom.	B				A		A^1				—	A*?	—	—
[39]But the centurion who had been standing there opposite him, having seen that he thus expired, said, "Truly this man was God's Son."		A		A	A				A	A	—	A*?	—	—

Lane	Léon-Dufour	Lightfoot	Lohse	Lührmann	Mohn	Myllykoski	Nineham	Peddinghaus	Pesch	Pryke	Schenk	Schenke	Schille	Schmithals	Schneider	Schreiber	Schweizer	Scroggs	Taylor
A	A	A	A	A		A	A	A^2	A		A	A^1	B	A		A	A		B
A		A	A	Aa		Ba		A^2	A		A B	Aa^1 Ab^2	B	A*		Ba	A	Aa^3	A
A		A	A			B*		A^2	A		B	A^2	B	A			A	A^3	A
A	A	A						Ac^3	A			Ab^1	B	A				Ab^3	B
A	A	A		Ab			Ab	Aab^3 Ac^2	A			A^1	B	A*		Bc	Ab	Aa^4	B
A	A	A		A				A^1	A		B	A^2	B			B	[A]	A^2	B
A		A	A	A		B*	A?	Aa^2 $Abcd^5$	A	Aa	B	Aa^1	B	A*		Ba	[A]	Aa^2 Abc^3	A
A		A	A	A		A?		A^2	A	A			B	A			A		A
A		A	A	A		Ba $Ab?$	Aa	Aa^2 Abc^3	A	Ab		Aa^1	B	A			A	Aa^3	A
A		A	A	A		B*	A	A^2	A	A	B	A^1	B	A		B	A	Aa^2	A
A	A	A		A				$A^{1/2}$	A	A	B	A^2	B			B	[A]		B
A	A					A?		A^2	A		B	A^1	B					$[A^2]$	A

Mark 15:40–47	Anderson	Buckley	Bultmann	Czerski	Dibelius	Donahue	Dormeyer	Ernst	Grant	Johnson	Kelber	Klostermann	Kolenkow	Kuhn
40But there were also women observing from a distance, and among them Mary Magdalene, and Mary mother of James the younger and of Joses, and Salome	A						A¹	A			—		—	—
41(who, when he was in Galilee, used to follow him and serve him), and many others who had come up with him to Jerusalem.	A							A			—		—	—
42And, it being already evening, since it was preparation day, that is, the day before Sabbath,		A					Ab¹	A			—		—	—
43Joseph from Arimathea having come (a respected council member who was also himself awaiting the kingdom of God), having taken courage, came in before Pilate and requested the body of Jesus.	[A]	A					Aac¹	A			—		—	—
44But Pilate was amazed that he had already died; and having called over the centurion, he questioned him if he was dead for some time.	[B?]	A						A			—		—	—
45And having come to know from the centurion, he granted the corpse to Joseph.	[B?]	A						A			—		—	—
46And having bought a linen cloth, having taken him down, with the linen cloth he tied up and put him away in a burial place that was hewn out of rock; and he rolled over a stone against the door of the tomb.	[A]	A					Aa¹	A			—		—	—
47But Mary Magdalene and Mary of Joses were observing where he was placed.	[A]	A						A			—		—	—

Lane	Léon-Dufour	Lightfoot	Lohse	Lührmann	Mohn	Myllykoski	Nineham	Peddinghaus	Pesch	Pryke	Schenk	Schenke	Schille	Schmithals	Schneider	Schreiber	Schweizer	Scroggs	Taylor
A	A	A	A	A		B*	A?		A	Ab			B	A			A	—	B
A	A	A	A	A			Aa?		A	A			B	A				—	B
A		A	A	A		B*	A		A			A^{*1}	C	Ab			[A]	—	A
		A	A	A		B*	A		A	Aa	C	A^1	C	A			[A]	—	A
		A	A	A		B*			A	A		A^1	C	A				—	A
		A	A	A		B*			A	A		A^1	C	A			[A]	—	A
A		A	A	A		B*			A	A	C	A^1	C	A			[A]	—	A
A	A	A	A	A					A	A	C	A^1	C	A			[A]	—	B

C. *Discussion of Methods and Criteria*

It is possible to classify the methods that scholars employ to determine the form and content of the sources or traditions that lie behind the Marcan PN in a number of ways; but I will do so under five headings as indicated in the outline at the beginning of the APPENDIX.

1. PARALLELS

Scholars focus on parallels between the Marcan PN and other writings in order to make comparisons of form, content, sequence, language, and style. Bultmann (BHST 275) finds parallels between Mark and John to be significant since these authors most likely wrote independently of one another. Ernst ("Passionserzählung" 171) studies the Marcan PN in relation to the primitive Christian confession of I Cor 15:3–4. Lane (*Mark* 485) compares Mark with bits of tradition found in Acts, I Cor, Gal, and I Tim. Lohse (*History* 15–16) contrasts both Mark 10:33–34 and the sermons in the first part of Acts with the Marcan PN. Schneider ("Gab" 27,35–38) compares parts of Luke's PN with segments of Mark's PN. Further, many scholars notice parallels between the Marcan PN and certain OT texts, especially from Psalms and Deutero-Isaiah.[6] Finally, still others treat the mishnaic tractate *Sanhedrin* like a parallel in discussing the trial sequence in Mark.[7]

Parallels between the Marcan PN and other NT works or traditions are used to reconstruct a simpler, more primitive form of the PN since it is assumed that traditions found only in the Marcan PN are secondary. OT materials enable scholars to see possible lines of influence and development leading to the PN. The mishnaic materials raise general questions about the historical plausibility of the Marcan PN.

Problems arise, however, in the application of this method of study. With regard to parallel materials found elsewhere in the NT, how valid is the assumption that only the common points shared by Mark and another NT tradition made up the earliest PN (e.g., Ernst)? While this method may help us to recover a simpler form of the PN, we must remember that nothing has been proved about the shape and substance of the specific PN presumably employed by Mark. The preMarcan PN may already have had a complex tradition history prior to its incorporation in the Marcan PN. As for OT par-

---

[6]E.g., Donahue (*Are You* 53–102) and Lohse (*History*).

[7]For a general history of the scholarly employment of the tractate *Sanhedrin* to criticize the Marcan PN, see Winter, *On the Trial,* esp. 23, n. 6. For a careful analysis of the problems, see Blinzler, *Trial* and *Prozess.* Among scholars whose opinions are registered in Table 14, see Grant, *Earliest* 177–78.

allels, it is difficult or impossible to determine how the lines of the earliest tradition were influenced by the OT texts that give theological color to the events portrayed (e.g., Dibelius). How does one know at which point in time the OT motif was worked into the passion tradition—before Mark or by Mark? Finally, because of the late date of the codification of the Mishna, the relevance of mishnaic texts is questionable. How can we know whether the procedure described in tractate *Sanhedrin* was actually practiced in the 1st cent.?

2. INTERNAL TENSIONS

There are within the text of the Marcan PN observable enigmas some-times used as signs of secondary expansions of original PN sources/tradi-tions. H. W. Anderson speaks of awkward connections between Mark 14:46,47,48,49a, and 49b.[8] Bultmann identifies 14:55–64 and 15:1 as doub-lets.[9] Dibelius (*Message* 145–46) describes the Gethsemane scene as a piece that breaks the flow of the larger, unified, continuous PN tradition. Kolen-kow claims that certain material stands out as preMarcan tradition because Mark has not prepared the reader for the information that he gives.[10] Schmit-hals (*Markus* 2.694) views 15:33,38, and 39 as Marcan developments be-cause these verses add a motif that is more thoroughly hellenized than is the basic narrative, e.g., the motif of the death of Jesus as the Son of God.

This method attempts to grapple with the unusual and/or difficult within the text and make sense of apparent problems. Operating similarly to textual criticism, this method prefers a simple explanation over a more elaborate one. But how valid is such an inherent bias toward simplicity and continuity? Inconsistencies that seem problematic to us apparently did not appear to be problems to the author who produced the final text that we have; and how can we be sure that so-called inconsistencies did not exist at an earlier pre-Marcan stage? In short, this method cannot distinguish between secondary elements that Mark has added and secondary elements that became part of the PN before it reached Mark.

[8]*Mark* 321–22. As a result of his analysis of the internal tensions found in Mark 14:43–52, Ander-son reasons that vv. 47, 48, and 49b were Marcan additions.

[9]BHST 276–77. From the identification of these pieces as doublets, Bultmann reasons "that indi-vidual stories constitute the main ingredient of the Passion story." The "detailed report" of Mark 14:55–64 splits the Peter tradition and is called "a secondary explanation of the brief statement in 15:1."

[10]"Trial" 551–53. An example of such information is the title "the King of the Jews." The implica-tion of this contention is that material for which Mark has prepared the reader is more likely to be attributed to Mark. Such reasoning is obviously questionable.

3. VOCABULARY AND STYLE

These criteria are employed in various ways by scholars. Many compare phrases and sentences in Mark with the usual Greek of the period, and thus would detect habitual patterns of Marcan grammar, syntax, and word choice. Bultmann (BHST 262–74) focuses simply on style, speaking of certain parts of the Marcan PN as editorial because of their secondary, explanatory character. On the other hand, by compiling a list of redactional characteristics from Mark's introductory and concluding statements, Donahue (*Are You* 53–102), Kelber (*KKS* 537–43), Kolenkow ("Trial" 550–56) and Pryke (*Redactional*) claim to distinguish between Marcan and nonMarcan elements in any given pericope. Mohn focuses on the words "hour" and "sleep" in distinguishing Marcan from preMarcan language. Taylor (*Mark* 649–64) uses the linguistic criteria of vividness and the presence of possible semitisms within a narrative to distinguish one preMarcan source from another.

When the criteria of vocabulary and style are used in conjunction with another criterion, they can provide helpful information for understanding the possible history of tradition. For instance, by contrasting the vocabulary of parallel traditions found in both the Marcan and Johannine PNs, the interpreter may cast light on the tradition(s) that lay behind these accounts. Further, an emphasis on style and vocabulary can help the interpreter to locate and focus attention on significant themes in the PN. Nevertheless, the use of style and vocabulary for distinguishing Marcan from preMarcan elements in the PN does not prove to be the definitive criterion that some critics would claim. Signs of Marcan style do not tell us whether Mark has created the narrative independently or simply retold in his own words a narrative he found in an earlier PN. Questionable results can be produced by isolating a part of a narrative by strictly linguistic methods.[11]

4. THEOLOGICAL THEMES AND LITERARY MOTIFS

Scholars have claimed that the presence of these in Mark's PN can be used as a guide to Mark's composition, either because they are characteristic of Mark's Gospel as a whole (and so presumably come from him) or are not (and so presumably come from elsewhere, namely a preMarcan PN).

Ernst ("Passionserzählung" 173–76) focuses on the titles of Christ, such as "Son of God" (14:61–62; 15:39), on the signs in nature (15:33,34,38),

---

[11]Scroggs's careful study (KKS 529–37) of the value of style and vocabulary for distinguishing Marcan and preMarcan traditions marshals statistical evidence against the claim that definitive criteria have been established whereby critics can make such distinctions using strictly linguistic methods.

and on the horarium (15:25,33–34) in the Marcan PN in order to distinguish Marcan from preMarcan elements. Kuhn ("Jesus") studies the Gethsemane scene and finds two themes that reveal two preMarcan sources: a christological source characterized by reference to Jesus' hour and a parenetic source that refers to the cup. Schille ("Leiden") distinguishes the days in the Marcan PN and speaks of a preMarcan source, consisting of three once-separate pieces that focused on Thursday, Friday, and the Tomb. Schreiber (*Theologie,* esp. 32–33), followed by Schenk (*Passionsbericht*), distinguishes two theological themes that enable him to posit two preMarcan sources: one apologetic, the other a statement on the death of Jesus from an OT/apocalyptic perspective.

The focus of this method is helpful in distinguishing primary from secondary literary elements. Nevertheless, there are problems. First, if a theme or motif appears only in the PN and not elsewhere in Mark, there is no guarantee that it is preMarcan. Possibly the only appropriate place for such a theme/motif to appear is in the context of the PN (e.g., "the King of the Jews"). If a theme or motif appears in both the PN and the remainder of the Gospel, we cannot automatically conclude that this element is originally Marcan. A theme/motif could have been present in the preMarcan PN and could have so significantly impressed Mark that he prepared the reader for this PN theme/motif in the sections of the Gospel prior to the PN. A particular theme could have been in both the Marcan PN and a source other than Mark; or indeed in the Marcan PN, in the rest of the Gospel, and in a source other than Mark. Having made this observation, we must recognize that we possess no tool for determining whether the theme/motif was employed first by the author of Mark or at an earlier stage in the history of the tradition.

5. CONCEPTUAL CLUSTERS

Scroggs (KKS 556–63) advocates the employment of conceptual clusters in the study of the Marcan PN. In studying 15:20b–39, he claims that the researcher is "left with the content of the language as his only clue," since "matters of style and word choice are too uncertain in such a brief narrative to use with any confidence" (p. 557). So Scroggs locates "materials in the story which cluster around certain conceptual frameworks [i.e., (a) the hours scheme, (b) Jesus as the righteous sufferer, (c) Jesus as the Messiah, (d) the references to Elijah, and (e) the references to the Temple sanctuary] which are different from, if not contradictory to, other conceptual frameworks." By separating these clusters (a through e above) from the basic narrative, he identifies 20b–24a as "a close-knit section" (p. 559) to which the conceptual clusters were later added. He speaks "only with the greatest caution, of certain stages through which the narrative passed, each stage contributing its own motif to the theological interpretation of the death of Jesus."

Thus, from distinguishing between both conceptual clusters and a kernel of narrative, this method allows the interpreter speculatively to describe the history of the tradition. The frank admission of the speculative nature of such reconstruction is in itself a strength, even if it means that certainty can never be achieved. Nevertheless, this method suffers from the weakness of not being able to distinguish Marcan from preMarcan phases in the growth of the tradition. Moreover, the interpreter who employs this method runs two risks: (1) the temptation to force parts of the tradition into clusters for which they are not totally suited, and (2) the possibility of ignoring certain elements of the tradition in reconstructing the history of the tradition because there is no convenient place to locate these pieces.[12]

D. *Conclusions*

Our survey of methods that scholars employ in determining the form and content of the sources or traditions that lie behind the Marcan PN produces several conclusions: (1) No single method allows us to distinguish Marcan from preMarcan elements in the PN, and so we should see the necessity of using as full a range of methods as possible. (2) Because there are strengths and weaknesses inherent in each of the methods that we employ, we should vary the method(s), allowing the text to suggest the most appropriate method(s) for study. (3) Since we recognize the danger that particular methods can produce particular and often predictable results, conclusions about the existence or nonexistence of a preMarcan PN need to be carefully nuanced.

It is not within the boundaries of this study to attempt a fresh critical reconstruction of the preMarcan PN. It may be asked, however, if such cautions about the limitations of the critical tools lead to a strictly negative conclusion with respect to our ability to know anything about the preMarcan PN. I think not.

Coming where it does in Mark's Gospel, the description of Judas at 14:43, "Judas, one of the Twelve," is striking. Is the reader in need of such information? No. Mark presents Judas two times (3:19; 14:10) prior to 14:43. As recently as at 14:10, Mark describes Judas Iscariot as *one of the Twelve.* While it may be accurate to describe Mark's style as sometimes redundant, it is not fair to say that Mark's Gospel is characterized by such almost needless

---

[12]In his reconstruction Scroggs never accounts for Mark 15:27.

repetition as occurs at 14:43.[13] The explanation that best accounts for the redundancy of 14:43 is that Mark is employing a source. Without the earlier parts of Mark's Gospel, the reader would need a piece of information concerning Judas such as 14:43. But what are we to conclude from the present repetitiousness? The description at 14:10 is probably Marcan redaction based in part on 14:43. When Mark introduces Judas to the reader, he does so in a list of the Twelve (3:14–19). At 3:19, when Mark mentions Judas, we learn (1) that Judas is "Judas Iscariot," and (2) that he is the one "who indeed gave him [Jesus] over." At 14:43, Judas is simply "Judas,"[14] and he is described as "one of the Twelve." Thus it is likely that when at 14:10 Mark describes "Judas Iscariot, (the) one of the Twelve," the name Judas Iscariot reflects 3:19 and the description "one of the Twelve" reflects 14:43. Both the form of the name and the description at 14:10 and the needless repetition of basically unnecessary information at 14:43 suggest that Mark is using a source for the latter.

What can be said about that source? (1) We cannot with absolute certainty know where the source began, but this would have been the first mention of Judas. (2) There would have been little use for a tradition that related only that Judas gave Jesus over. Therefore, the activity of Judas at this point demands that the story continue with an account of the arrest, condemnation, and execution of Jesus. Yet we cannot be absolutely certain about where Mark's source would have ended.

When we turn our attention to Mark's account of the arrest, condemnation, and execution of Jesus, we find a narrative with a complex history of traditions, as shown in the work of Bultmann and Scroggs. Nevertheless, the present Marcan PN (as we have studied it from 14:32–15:47) does not have extremely rough edges or obvious seams. Mark weaves whatever source he employs into his Gospel with skill, leaving only traces (e.g., 14:43) of the earlier existence of the source.

Our investigation brings us thus to a positive conclusion and a point of challenge. We may safely conclude that Mark uses a source in writing his PN. We know that source, however, only as incorporated in Mark. The greatest challenge that lies before us is not the separation of tradition from Mar-

[13]It may amuse readers that the argument I am using to show our ability to detect a preMarcan PN contradicts a point that Brown has made in his commentary (p. 246 above). He argues that the repetition of "one of the Twelve" is not redundant, for at the very moment of betrayal it emphasizes the heinousness of what is happening: It is one of Jesus' very own Twelve who gives him over. It may further amuse readers to know that since first drafting (1982) and subsequently revising for publication (1985) the work that now appears in this APPENDIX, I have become less than enthusiastic about this particular argument for a preMarcan PN source.

[14]The textual support for adding "Iscariot" is weak, and neither Matt nor Luke reads that name in Mark. The insertion is easily accounted for as a scribal modification that brings this reference to Judas into conformity with Mark's two previous references to him.

can redaction; for, as our earlier work shows, that task may finally be an impossible one. Rather, we must investigate the rich layers of traditions that come to us in the form of the Marcan PN. This conclusion does not mean that we may simply discard any notion of editorial activity. It demands, however, that a preoccupation with the data of that editorial work not be our first concern.[15]

---

[15]The position that I am taking is similar to that of Juel, *Messiah.*

INDEXES

BIBLIOGRAPHICAL INDEX OF AUTHORS

This is not an index of the discussions of authors' views; rather it lists the page on which readers can find the full title and data of a book or article that has been used in this commentary. Throughout the commentary most references are made by giving the author's last name and one or two significant words from the title, and this abbreviated title is included in the index to facilitate searching for the pertinent data (generally in one of the bibliographies). Where no title is included, the index supplies the page on which (in text or footnote) bibliographical data may be found for a work that has entered the discussion but is not included in the bibliographies because its primary focus is different from or less directly pertinent to the PN research of this commentary.

Family names beginning in *de, di, du* and in *van, von* are listed under *d* and *v* respectively. Those beginning in *Mc* are treated as if the prefix were *Mac*. Roman-numbered references in the index are keyed to the page-numbering in the abbreviation list at the front of Volume One. That list, repeated in the front of Volume Two, begins eight pages earlier than in Volume One. Generally these Roman-numbered references in the index can be found in Volume Two by subtracting eight from the indicated numeral (e.g., page xx is page xii in Volume Two). References to Arabic-numbered pages 1–878 are to be found in Volume One; those to pages 879–1524, in Volume Two.

INDEX OF SUBJECTS

A few authors are listed here, not for bibliographical purposes (see preceding index), but because there is a discussion of their views. References to pages 1–877 are to be found in Volume One; those to pages 878–1534, in Volume Two.

GOSPEL PASSAGE INDEX
CONSISTING OF TRANSLATIONS OF
THE FOUR PASSION NARRATIVES

(Indicating Principal Comments on Individual Passages)

In this commentary a very literal translation of the pertinent PN passages appears at the beginning of each section that comments on them. Since overall I have followed the Marcan order, occasionally I have treated Lucan or Johannine passages out of their own Gospel sequence. A sequential translation of each PN, therefore, facilitates finding individual passages. In the adjacent column I have created an index indicating where in this book the principal treatment of every passage in the PN may be found.

THE PASSION ACCORDING TO MARK
(Mark 14:26–15:47)

Translation	Index of Principal Comments

Prayer and Arrest in Gethsemane (14:26–52)

26And having sung a hymn/hymns, they went out to the Mount of Olives. 27And Jesus says to them that: "You will all be scandalized because it is written, 'I will strike the shepherd, and the sheep will be scattered.' 28However, after my resurrection I shall go before you into Galilee."

122
126

130

29But Peter said to him, "Even if all are scandalized, yet not I." 30And Jesus says to him, "Amen, I say to you that today, this very night, before a cock crows twice, three times you will deny me." 31But he was saying vehemently, "Even if it be necessary for me to die with you, I will not deny you." And they were all saying the same.

133
134

137

---

³²And they come into the plot of land the name of which   147
was Gethsemane; and he says to his disciples, "Sit here while
I pray." ³³And he takes along Peter, and James, and John with   151
him, and he began to be greatly distraught and troubled.
³⁴And he says to them, "My soul is very sorrowful unto   154
death. Remain here and keep on watching."

³⁵And having gone forward a little, he was falling on the   164
earth and was praying that if it is possible, the hour might   165
pass from him. ³⁶And he was saying, "*Abba,* Father, all   172
things are possible to you: Take away this cup from me. But   168
not what I will but what you (will)."   175

³⁷And he comes and finds them sleeping, and he says to   193
Peter, "Simon, are you sleeping? Were you not strong
enough to watch one hour? ³⁸Keep [pl.] on watching and   195
praying lest you [pl.] enter into trial. Indeed the spirit is will- 197
ing, but the flesh is weak."   198

³⁹And again having gone away, he prayed, saying the same   204
word. ⁴⁰And again having come, he found them sleeping; for
their eyes were very burdened, and they did not know what
they should answer him.

⁴¹And he comes the third time and says to them, "Do you   206
go on sleeping, then, and taking your rest? The money is   208,1379
paid; the hour has come; behold the Son of Man is given   209,210
over into the hands of the sinners. ⁴²Get up; let us go; behold 213
the one who gives me over has come near."

⁴³And immediately, while he was still speaking, there ar-   245
rives Judas, one of the Twelve, and with him a crowd with   246
swords and wooden clubs, from the chief priests and the
scribes and the elders. ⁴⁴The one who was giving him over
had given them a signal, saying, "Whomever I shall kiss, he
is (the one). Seize him and lead him away securely." ⁴⁵And   252
having come, immediately having come up to him, he says,   253
"Rabbi," and he kissed him warmly. ⁴⁶But they laid hands on
him and seized him.   263

⁴⁷But a certain one of those standing by, having drawn the   265
sword, hit at the servant of the high priest and took off his   272,271

Translation of Mark 14:48–64

ear. ⁴⁸And in answer Jesus said to them, "As if against a bandit have you come out with swords and wooden clubs to take	281
me? ⁴⁹Day after day I was with you in the Temple teaching,	284
and you did not seize me. However—let the Scriptures be	286
fulfilled!" ⁵⁰And having left him, they all fled.	287
⁵¹And a certain young man was following with him,	294–304

⁵¹And a certain young man was following with him, clothed with a linen cloth over his nakedness; and they seize him. ⁵²But he, having left behind the linen cloth, fled naked.

Jesus before the Jewish Authorities (14:53–15:1)

⁵³And they led Jesus away to the high priest, and there	400
(now) come together all the chief priests, and the elders, and	
the scribes. ⁵⁴And Peter followed him from a distance until	402
inside the court of the high priest, and he was seated together	
with the attendants and warming himself near the blazing	
flame.	
⁵⁵But the chief priests and the whole Sanhedrin were seek-	432
ing testimony against Jesus in order to put him to death, and	
they were not finding (any). ⁵⁶For many were giving false	433
testimony against him, and the testimonies were not consis-	
tent. ⁵⁷And some, having stood up, were giving false testi-	444,448
mony against him, saying ⁵⁸that "We have heard him saying	434
that 'I will destroy this sanctuary made by hand, and within	438
three days another not made by hand I will build.'" ⁵⁹And	
even so their testimony was not consistent.	445
⁶⁰And having stood up, the high priest in (their) midst	462
questioned Jesus, saying, "Have you nothing at all to answer	
to what these are testifying against you?" ⁶¹But he stayed	463
silent and answered nothing at all. Again the high priest was	465
questioning him and says to him, "Are you the Messiah, the	467
Son of the Blessed?" ⁶²But Jesus said, "I am, and you [pl.]	488
will see the Son of Man sitting at the right of the Power and	494
coming with the clouds of heaven." ⁶³But the high priest,	
having torn his garments, says, "What further need do we	517,519
have of testifiers? ⁶⁴You have heard the blasphemy. What	520

Translation of Mark 14:65–15:5	Index of Principal Comments

does it appear to you?" But they all judged against him as being guilty, punishable by death.

[527]

65And some began to spit on him, and to cover his face and strike him and say to him, "Prophesy"; and the attendants got him with slaps.

[573]

[576]

(PETER'S DENIALS) 66And Peter being below in the court, one of the servant women of the high priest comes; 67and having seen Peter warming himself and having looked at him, she says to him, "You too were with the Nazarene, Jesus." 68aBut he denied, saying, "I don't know nor understand what you are saying."

[593]

[595]

[599]

68bAnd he went outside into the forecourt [and a cock crowed]. 69And the servant woman, having seen him, began again to say to the bystanders that "This is one of them." 70aBut again he was denying it.

[600]

[602]

70bAnd after a little, the bystanders again were saying to Peter, "Truly you are one of them, for indeed you are a Galilean." 71But he began to curse and swear that "I don't know this man of whom you speak." 72And immediately a second time a cock crowed; and Peter remembered the word as Jesus had spoken it to him, that "Before a cock crows twice, three times you will deny me." And having rushed out, he was weeping.

[603]

[604]

[605]

[607,609]

15:1And immediately, early, having made their consultation, the chief priests with the elders and scribes and the whole Sanhedrin, having bound Jesus, took him away and gave him over to Pilate.

[627,629]

[634]

The Roman Trial (15:2–20a)

2And Pilate questioned him, "Are you the King of the Jews?" But in answer he says to him, "You say (so)." 3And the chief priests were accusing him of many things. 4But Pilate tried to question him again, saying, "Do you answer nothing at all? Behold how much they have accused you of." 5But Jesus answered nothing further, so that Pilate was amazed.

[729,732]

[733]

[734]

Jesus Crucified (15:20b–41)

should take what. [25]Now it was the third hour, and they cru-   958,960
cified him. [26]And there was an inscription of the charge
against him, inscribed "The King of the Jews." [27]And with   962
him they crucify two bandits, one on the right and one on   968
his left.*

[29]And those passing by were blaspheming him, wagging   985,986
their heads and saying, "Aha, O one destroying the sanctuary
and building it in three days, [30]save yourself by having come   994
down from the cross."

[31]Similarly also the chief priests, mocking him to one an-   990
other with the scribes, were saying, "Others he saved; himself he cannot save. [32]Let the Messiah, the King of Israel,   992
come down now from the cross in order that we may see
and believe."

Even those who had been crucified together with him   999
were reviling him.

[33]And the sixth hour having come, darkness came over the   1034
whole earth until the ninth hour. [34]And at the ninth hour Je-   1043
sus screamed with a loud cry, "*Elōi, Elōi, lama sabach-*   1051
thani?" which is interpreted, "My God, my God, for what   1054
reason have you forsaken me?" [35]And some of the bystanders, having heard, were saying, "Look, he is crying to Elijah."   1060
[36]But someone, running, having filled a sponge with vine-   1059
gary wine, having put it on a reed, was giving him to drink,   1063
saying, "Leave (be). Let us see if Elijah comes to take him
down." [37]But Jesus, having let go a loud cry, expired.   1078

[38]And the veil of the sanctuary was rent into two from top   1098
to bottom. [39]But the centurion who had been standing there   1143
opposite him, having seen that he thus expired, said, "Truly
this man was God's Son." [40]But there were also women ob-   1146
serving from a distance, and among them Mary Magdalene,   1152

---

*The Koine Greek tradition, the Latin, and the Syriac Peshitta add a v. 28: "And
the Scripture was fulfilled that says, 'And with outlaws was he reckoned.'" This is
the text from Isa 53:12 that Luke cites in 22:37. MTC 119 comments that Mark
very seldom expressly quotes the OT, and that if this verse were originally in Mark,
there is no reason for Matt or for scribes to have omitted it.

THE PASSION ACCORDING TO MATTHEW
(Matt 26:30–27:66)

the shepherd, and the sheep of the flock will be scattered.'
³²But after my resurrection I shall go before you into   130
Galilee."

³³But in answer Peter said to him, "If all are scandalized   133
in you, I will never be scandalized." ³⁴Jesus said to him,
"Amen, I say to you on this very night, before a cock crows, 134
three times you will deny me." ³⁵Peter says to him, "Even if 137
it be necessary for me to die with you, I will not deny you."
And so said all the disciples.

³⁶Then Jesus comes with them into the plot of land called   147
Gethsemane; and he says to the disciples, "Sit in this place
until, going away, I pray there." ³⁷And having taken along   151
Peter and the two sons of Zebedee, he began to be sorrowful
and troubled. ³⁸Then he says to them, "My soul is very sor- 154
rowful unto death. Remain here and keep on watching with
me."

³⁹And having gone forward a little, he fell on his face   164
praying and saying, "My Father, if it is possible, let this cup 171,168
pass from me. Nevertheless, not as I will but as you (will)." 175

⁴⁰And he comes to the disciples and finds them sleeping,   193
and he says to Peter, "So you [pl.] were not strong enough
to watch one hour with me. ⁴¹Keep [pl.] on watching and   195
praying lest you [pl.] enter into trial. Indeed the spirit is will- 197
ing, but the flesh is weak."   198

⁴²Again, a second time, having gone away, he prayed say-   204
ing, "My Father, if it is not possible for this to pass if I do
not drink it, let your will be done." ⁴³And having come again,
he found them sleeping, for their eyes were burdened.

⁴⁴And having left them, again having gone away, he   206
prayed a third time, saying the same word again. ⁴⁵Then he
comes to the disciples and says to them, "Do you go on
sleeping, then, and taking your rest? Behold the hour has   209
come near, and the Son of Man is given over into the hands   210
of sinners. ⁴⁶Get up; let us go; behold, there has come near 213
the one who gives me over."

⁴⁷And while he was still speaking, behold Judas, one of   245

the Twelve, came, and with him a numerous crowd with   246
swords and wooden clubs, from the chief priests and elders
of the people. ⁴⁸But the one who was giving him over gave   252
them a sign, saying, "Whomever I shall kiss, he is (the one).
Seize him." ⁴⁹And immediately having come up to Jesus, he   253
said, "Hail, Rabbi," and he kissed him warmly. ⁵⁰But Jesus
said to him, "Friend, that's what you are here for." Then, hav-   256,1385
ing come up, they laid hands on Jesus and seized him.   263

⁵¹And behold one of those with Jesus, having stretched   265
out his hand, drew out his sword; and having struck the ser-   272
vant of the high priest, he took off his ear. ⁵²Then Jesus says   271
to him, "Return your sword to its place, for all who take the   275
sword, by the sword will perish. ⁵³Do you think that I am not
able to call upon my Father, and He will at once supply me   276
with more than twelve legions of angels? ⁵⁴How then would   277
the Scriptures be fulfilled that it must happen thus?" ⁵⁵In that
hour Jesus said to the crowds, "As if against a bandit have   282
you come out with swords and wooden clubs to take me?
Day after day in the Temple I was sitting teaching, and you   284
did not seize me. ⁵⁶But this whole thing has happened in
order that the Scriptures of the prophets might be fulfilled."   286
Then all the disciples, having left him, fled.   289

Jesus before the Jewish Authorities (26:57–27:10)

⁵⁷And having seized Jesus, they led him away to Caiaphas   400
the high priest where the scribes and the elders were brought
together. ⁵⁸But Peter was following him from a distance until   402
the court(yard) of the high priest; and having entered inside,
he sat with the attendants to see the end.

⁵⁹But the chief priests and the whole Sanhedrin were   431
seeking false testimony against Jesus so that they might put   433
him to death. ⁶⁰And they did not find (any), although many
false testifiers came forward. But at last two, having come   435,444
forward, ⁶¹said, "This person stated, 'I am able to destroy the   435
sanctuary of God, and within three days I will build (it).'"   453–454
⁶²And having stood up, the high priest said to him, "Have   462

you nothing to answer to what these are testifying against   463
you?" 63But Jesus stayed silent. And the high priest said to
him, "I adjure you according to the living God that you say   465
to us if you are the Messiah, the Son of God." 64Jesus says to   470
him, "*You* have said it. Yet I say to you [pl.], 'From now you   488,489
will see the Son of Man sitting at the right of the Power and   494,500
coming on the clouds of heaven.'" 65Then the high priest   517
tore his clothes, saying, "He blasphemed. What further need   519
do we have of testifiers? Behold now you heard the blas-   520
phemy. 66What does it seem to you?" But in answer they
said, "He is guilty, to be punished by death."   527

    67Then they spat in his face and struck him. But there   577
were those who slapped him 68saying, "Prophesy for us,
Messiah, who is it that hit you?"

(PETER'S DENIALS) 69But Peter sat outside in the court   593
(yard); and one servant woman came up to him saying, "You   595
too were with Jesus the Galilean." 70But he denied before all,
saying, "I don't know what you are saying."   599

    71But after his having gone out into the entranceway, an-   600
other woman saw him and says to those there, "This one was
with Jesus the Nazorean." 72But again he denied with an oath
that "I don't know the man."

    73But after a little, those present, having come up, said to   603
Peter, "Truly you too, you are one of them, for indeed your
speech makes you obvious." 74Then he began to curse and
swear that "I don't know the man." And immediately a cock   605
crowed; 75and Peter remembered the word spoken by Jesus
that "Before a cock crows, three times you will deny me."
And having gone outside, he wept bitterly.   607–609

    27:1And when the early hour had come, all the chief priests   628
and the elders of the people took a decision against Jesus   632
that they should put him to death. 2And having bound him,
they led him away and gave him over to Pilate the governor.   634

(JUDAS' MONEY) 3Then Judas, the one who gave him   638
over, having seen that he [Jesus] was judged against, having changed with remorse, returned the thirty silver pieces

to the chief priests and elders, ⁴saying, "I sinned in having   640
given over innocent blood." But they said, "What is that
to us? You must see to it." ⁵And having cast the silver   642
pieces into the sanctuary, he departed; and having gone
away, he hanged himself.   643

⁶But having taken the silver pieces, the chief priests said,   644
"It is not permitted to throw these into the treasury since it
is the price for blood." ⁷Having taken a decision, they bought   645
with them the potter's field for a burial ground of strangers.
⁸Therefore that field has been called "Field of Blood" to
this day.

⁹Then there was fulfilled what was spoken through Jere-   647
miah the prophet saying, "And they took the thirty silver   648
pieces, the price of the one priced, whom the sons of Israel
priced. ¹⁰And they gave them for the potter's field, according
to what the Lord directed me."

The Roman Trial (27:11–31a)

¹¹But Jesus stood in front of the governor; and the gover-   729,735
nor questioned him, saying, "Are you the King of the Jews?"
But Jesus said, "You say (so)." ¹²And although he was being   736
accused by the chief priests and elders, he answered nothing.
¹³Then Pilate says to him, "Do you hear how much they are
testifying against you?" ¹⁴And he did not answer him, not to
even one word, so that the governor was greatly amazed.

¹⁵But at a/the feast the governor was accustomed to re-   794
lease to the crowd one prisoner whom they willed. ¹⁶But at
that time they had a notorious prisoner called [Jesus] Bar-   796,798
abbas. ¹⁷So when they had gathered together, Pilate said to   794
them, "Whom do you will that I release to you: [Jesus] Bar-   800
abbas or Jesus who is called Messiah?" ¹⁸For he was aware   801
that (it was) out of envy/zeal that they gave him over. ¹⁹But   802
while he was sitting on the judgment seat, his wife sent to   803
him, saying, "Let there be nothing between you and that just   806
man, for many things have I suffered today in a dream be-
cause of him." ²⁰But the chief priests and the elders per-   807

suaded the crowds that they should request Barabbas, but
Jesus they should destroy. [21]But in answer the governor said   809
to them, "Which of the two do you will that I should release
to you?" But they said, "Barabbas."

[22]Pilate says to them, "What therefore shall I do with Je-   825
sus called the Messiah?" All say, "Let him be crucified."   829
[23]But he said, "For what that is bad has he done?" But they
kept shouting even more, saying, "Let him be crucified."   831
[24]But Pilate, having seen that nothing was of use, but rather   833
a disturbance was taking place, having taken water, washed
off his hands before the crowd, saying, "I am innocent of the   834
blood of this man. You must see to it." [25]And in answer all   836
the people said, "His blood on us and on our children."   831,836
[26]Then he released to them Barabbas; but having had Jesus   849
flogged, he gave (him) over in order that he be crucified.   851,853

[27]Then the soldiers of the governor, taking Jesus into the   864
praetorium, gathered together the whole cohort against him.
[28]And having undressed him, they put a scarlet cloak around   865
him; [29]and having woven a crown of thorns, they put it on his
head and a reed into his right hand. And kneeling before him,   867
they mocked him, saying, "Hail, King of the Jews." [30]And   868
having spit at him, they took the reed and were striking at his
head. [31a]And when they had mocked him, they undressed him   869
of thecloak and dressed him with his own clothes.

Jesus Crucified (27:31b–56)

[31b]And they led him away to be crucified. [32]But coming   911
out, they found a Cyrenian man by the name of Simon; this   913
fellow they compelled to take up his [Jesus'] cross.

[33]And having come to a place called Golgotha, which is   936
called Skull-Place, [34]they gave him to drink wine mixed with   942
gall; and having tasted, he did not wish to drink. [35]But having
crucified him, they divided up his clothes, throwing lots.   945,952
[36]And having sat, they were keeping (guard over) him there.
[37]And they put up above his head the charge against him,   962
written "This is Jesus, the King of the Jews." [38]Then there

Index of
Principal
Comments

---

are crucified with him two bandits, one on the right, and one   968
on the left.

³⁹But those passing by were blaspheming him, wagging   985,986
their heads ⁴⁰and saying, "O one destroying the sanctuary
and in three days building it, save yourself, if you are Son of   988
God, and come down from the cross."

⁴¹Similarly also the chief priests, mocking him with the   990
scribes and elders, were saying, ⁴²"Others he saved; himself
he cannot save. He is the King of Israel—let him come down   992
from the cross, and we shall believe. ⁴³He has trusted in God.
Let him be delivered if He wants him, for he said, 'I am Son   994
of God.'"

⁴⁴In the same way even the bandits who were crucified   999
together with him were reviling him.

⁴⁵But from the sixth hour darkness came over all the earth   1036
until the ninth hour. ⁴⁶But about the ninth hour Jesus   1043
screamed out with a loud cry, saying, *"Ēli, Ēli, lema sabach-*   1051
thani?"—that is, "My God, my God, to what purpose have   1054
you forsaken me?" ⁴⁷But some of those standing there, having heard, were saying that "This fellow is crying to Elijah."   1060
⁴⁸And immediately one of them, running and taking a
sponge full of vinegary wine and having put it on a reed, was   1059
giving him to drink. ⁴⁹But the rest said, "Leave (be). Let us   1063
see if Elijah comes saving him." ⁵⁰But Jesus, again having
shouted with a loud cry, let go the spirit.   1078

⁵¹And behold, the veil of the sanctuary was rent from top   1098
to bottom into two. And the earth was shaken, and the rocks   1118
were rent, ⁵²and the tombs were opened, and many bodies of   1122–23
the fallen-asleep holy ones were raised. ⁵³And having come   1124
out from the tombs after his raising they entered into the   1129
holy city; and they were made visible to many. ⁵⁴But the cen-   1131–32
turion and those who with him were keeping (guard over)   1143
Jesus, having seen the (earth)shaking and these happenings,
feared exceedingly, saying, "Truly this was God's Son." ⁵⁵But   1146
there were there many women observing from a distance,   1152
such ones as had followed Jesus from Galilee, serving him,   1159

⁵⁶among whom was Mary Magdalene, and Mary mother of   1153
James and of Joseph, and the mother of the sons of Zebedee.

Burial of Jesus (27:57–66)

⁵⁷But it being evening, there came a rich man from Ari-   1223
mathea whose name was Joseph, who had also himself been
a disciple of Jesus. ⁵⁸This man, having come before Pilate,   1225
requested the body of Jesus. Then Pilate ordered (it) to be
given up. ⁵⁹And having taken the body, Joseph wrapped it up   1252
in a clean white linen cloth ⁶⁰and placed him in his new tomb   1253
which he had hewn in the rock; and having rolled a large
stone to the door of the tomb, he went away. ⁶¹But Mary   1254
Magdalene was there and the other Mary, sitting off opposite
the sepulcher.

⁶²But on the next day, which is after the preparation day,   1288
there gathered together the chief priests and the Pharisees   1289
before Pilate, ⁶³saying, "Lord, we remembered that that de-   1290
ceiver said when he was still living, 'After three days I am
(to be) raised.' ⁶⁴So order the sepulcher to be made secure   1291
until the third day, lest, having come, the disciples steal him
and say to the people, 'He was raised from the dead,' and
the last deception will be worse than the first." ⁶⁵Pilate said   1294
to them, "You (may) have a custodial guard. Go, make se-   1295
cure as you know how." ⁶⁶Having gone, they made the sepulcher secure with the custodial guard, having sealed the stone.   1296

THE PASSION ACCORDING TO LUKE
(Luke 22:39–23:56)

| | Index of Principal |
| Translation | Comments |

Prayer and Arrest on the Mount of Olives (22:39–53)

³⁹And having gone out, he proceeded according to his custom to the Mount of Olives; and the disciples too followed him. ⁴⁰And being at the place, he said to them, "Keep on praying not to enter into trial."

123–124

157

⁴¹And he drew away from them as if a stone's throw; and having knelt, he was praying, ⁴²saying, "Father, if you desire, take away this cup from me. Nevertheless, not my will but yours be done."

164

171

168,175

⁴³But an angel from heaven appeared to him, strengthening him. ⁴⁴And being in agony, he was praying more earnestly. And his sweat became as if drops of blood falling down to the earth.

179–190

188,189

184

⁴⁵And having stood up from prayer, having come to the disciples, he found them asleep from sorrow; ⁴⁶and he said to them, "Why do you sleep? Having stood up, keep on praying lest you enter into trial."

192

⁴⁷While he was still speaking, behold a crowd; and the man named Judas, one of the Twelve, was coming in front of them; and he came near Jesus to kiss him. ⁴⁸But Jesus said to him, "Judas, with a kiss do you give over the Son of Man?"

245,247

246

252

258

⁴⁹But those about him, having seen what would be, said, "Lord, shall we strike with the sword?" ⁵⁰And a certain one of them struck the servant of the high priest and took off his right ear. ⁵¹But in answer Jesus said, "Let that be enough!" And having touched the ear, he healed him. ⁵²But Jesus said to the chief priests and captains of the Temple and elders who were arrived against him, "As if against a bandit have you come out with swords and wooden clubs? ⁵³Even though day after day I was with you in the Temple, you did not

265

269

272,271

279

281

282,247

283

285

Translation of Luke 22:54–69	Index of Principal Comments

stretch out your hands against me; however, this is your hour and the power of darkness!"   291

Jesus before the Jewish Authorities (22:54–71)

⁵⁴ᵃBut having taken (him), they led and brought him into the house of the high priest.   400

(PETER'S DENIALS) ⁵⁴ᵇBut Peter was following at a distance.   402 ⁵⁵But when they had kindled a fire in the middle of   594 the court and had sat down together, Peter sat down in their midst. ⁵⁶But having seen him seated near the blazing flame   595 and having stared at him, a certain servant woman said, "This one too was with him." ⁵⁷But he denied, saying, "I   599 don't know him, Woman."

⁵⁸And after a short time another man, having seen him,   600 said, "You too are one of them." But Peter said, "Man, I am not."

⁵⁹And after about one hour had passed, a certain man was   603 insisting, saying, "In truth this one too was with him, for indeed he is a Galilean." ⁶⁰But Peter said, "Man, I don't know what you are saying." And at that moment while he was still speaking, a cock crowed. ⁶¹And the Lord, having turned,   605,608 looked at Peter; and Peter remembered the saying of the Lord as he had spoken it to him, that "Before a cock crows today, you will deny me three times." ⁶²And having gone out-   609 side, he wept bitterly.

⁶³And the men who were holding him were mocking him,   581 beating him; ⁶⁴and having covered him, they were questioning him saying, "Prophesy, who is it that hit you?" ⁶⁵And   583–584 blaspheming, they were saying many other things against him.

⁶⁶And as it became day, there was brought together the   430–431 assembly of the elders of the people, both chief priests and scribes; and they led him away to their Sanhedrin, ⁶⁷saying, "If you are the Messiah, say to us." But he said to them, "If   471,485 I shall say to you, you will never believe. ⁶⁸But if I shall ask   487 a question, you will never answer. ⁶⁹But from the present

there will be the Son of Man sitting at the right of the power	494,504
of God." ⁷⁰But they all said, "Are you then the Son of God?"	471
But he said to them, "You (yourselves) say that I am." ⁷¹But	488,492
they said, "What further need of testimony do we have? For	519
we ourselves have heard from his own mouth."	520,527

The Roman Trial (23:1–25)

²³:¹And the whole multitude of them, having stood up, led   634
him to Pilate. ²But they began to accuse him, saying, "We   736
have found this fellow misleading our nation, both forbid-   738
ding the giving of taxes to Caesar, and saying that he is Messiah king. ³But Pilate asked him, saying, "Are you the King   741,727
of the Jews?" But in answer, he said to him, "You say (so)."
⁴But Pilate said to the chief priests and the crowds, "I find   742
nothing guilty in this man." ⁵But they were insistent, saying
that "He stirs up the people, teaching through the whole of
Judea, having begun from Galilee even to here."   743

⁶But having heard (this), Pilate questioned whether this   760–786
man was a Galilean; ⁷and having ascertained that he was   761
from Herod's (sphere of) power, he sent him off to Herod   764
who was himself in Jerusalem in these days. ⁸Now Herod,   765,768
having seen Jesus, rejoiced greatly since for much time he
had been wishing to see him because of what he had heard
about him; indeed he was hoping to see some sign done by
him. ⁹Accordingly with much talking he tried to question   770
him; but Jesus answered nothing to him, ¹⁰even though the   772
chief priests and the scribes had been standing there insis-   771
tently accusing him. ¹¹But having treated him with contempt   773
and made a mockery, Herod with his troops, having clothed
him with a splendid garment, sent him back to Pilate. ¹²But   774
both Herod and Pilate on this same day became friends with   777
each other, for previously they were at enmity toward the
other.

¹³But Pilate, having called together the chief priests and   789
the rulers and the people, ¹⁴said to them, "You brought to me   791
this man as leading astray the people; and behold, having

investigated him in your presence, I have found nothing in   791
this man (making him) guilty of what you charged against
him. ¹⁵Neither did Herod, for he sent him back to us; and   791
behold there is nothing worthy of death that has been done   792–793
by him. ¹⁶Having chastised him (by whipping), therefore, I
shall let him go." ⁽¹⁷*⁾ ¹⁸But all together they shouted out,   807
saying, "Take this fellow but release to us Barabbas," ¹⁹who
was someone thrown into prison because of a certain riot   796
that had taken place in the city and (because of) killing.

    ²⁰But again Pilate cried out in addressing them, wishing   825
to release Jesus. ²¹But they kept crying out in return saying,
"Crucify, crucify him." ²²But he said to them a third time,   826
"For what that is bad has this fellow done? I have found
nothing in him (making him) guilty of death. Having chas-   852
tised him (by whipping), therefore, I shall release him."
²³But they were pressing with loud cries, demanding him to   830
be crucified; and their cries were getting stronger. ²⁴And Pi- 856
late made the judgment that their demand should be put into
effect; ²⁵so he released the one who had been thrown into   856,797
prison for riot and murder whom they had been demanding,
but Jesus he gave over to their will.   857

Jesus Crucified (23:26–49)

    ²⁶And as they led him away, having taken hold of Simon,   911
a certain Cyrenian coming in from the field, they put upon   913
him the cross to bring behind Jesus. ²⁷Now there was follow-   917–932
ing him [Jesus] a large multitude of the people and of   918
women who were beating themselves and lamenting for him.
²⁸But having turned to them, Jesus said, "Daughters of Jeru-   920
salem, do not weep for me. Rather for yourselves weep, and
for your children ²⁹because, behold, coming are days in   922
which they will say, 'Blessed are the barren, and the wombs

---

*In the Koine Greek mss. and the versions (OL, Vulgate, Peshitta) there is a v.
17 which is probably a scribal addition to make Luke correspond to Mark/Matt:
"But he had the obligation to release one person to them at a/the feast."

Index of
Principal
Comments

that have not borne, and the breasts that have not fed.' ³⁰Then   924
they will begin to say to the mountains, 'Fall on us,' and to
the hills, 'Cover us.' ³¹Because if in the green wood they   925
do such things, in the dry what will happen?" ³²But others
also were being led off, two wrongdoers, with him to be put   927
to death.

³³And when they came to the place named Skull, there   936
they crucified him and the wrongdoers, the one on the right,   945,968
the other on the left. ³⁴[But Jesus was saying, "Father, forgive   971
them, for they do not know what they are doing."] But divid-   952
ing his clothes, they threw lots.

³⁵And the people were standing there observing.   989

But there were also rulers sneering, saying, "Others he   990
saved; let him save himself, if this is the Messiah of God, the   992,994
chosen one."

³⁶Moreover, also the soldiers mocked, coming forward,   996
bringing forward to him vinegary wine, ³⁷and saying, "If you   997,1059
are the King of the Jews, save yourself." ³⁸For there was also
an inscription over him: "The King of the Jews, this (man)."   998,962

³⁹Moreover one of the hanged wrongdoers was blasphem-   999
ing him, "Are you not the Messiah? Save yourself and us."

⁴⁰But in answer the other, rebuking him, said, "Do you   1000–13
not even fear God? Because you are under the same condem-   1003
nation; ⁴¹and indeed we justly, for we are receiving what is
worthy of what we did, but he did nothing disorderly." ⁴²And   1005
he was saying, "Jesus, remember me whenever you come
into your kingdom." ⁴³And he said to him, "Amen, I say to   1008
you, this day with me you shall be in paradise."

⁴⁴And it was already about the sixth hour, and darkness   1038
came over the whole earth until the ninth hour, ⁴⁵the sun hav-   1039
ing been eclipsed. The veil of the sanctuary was rent in the   1043,1102
middle. ⁴⁶And having cried out with a loud cry, Jesus said,   1066
"Father, into your hands I place my spirit." But having said   1068
this, he expired.   1078

⁴⁷But the centurion, having seen this happening, was glo-   1160–73
rifying God, saying, "Certainly this man was just." ⁴⁸And all   1161

Translation of Luke 23:49–56	Index of Principal Comments

the crowds who were gathered together for the observation
of this, having observed these happenings, returned striking
their breasts. 49But all those known to him were standing
from a distance, and the women who were following him
from Galilee, seeing these things.

Burial of Jesus (23:50–56)

50And behold a man, Joseph by name, being a member of
the council, a good and just man—51he was not in agreement
with their decision and course of action—from Arimathea,
a city of the Jews, who was awaiting the kingdom of God.
52This man, having come before Pilate, requested the body
of Jesus. 53And having taken (it) down, he wrapped it up
with a linen cloth and placed him in a rock-hewn burial place
where no one was yet laid. 54And it was preparation day, and
Sabbath was dawning. 55But the women who had come up
with him out of Galilee, having followed after, looked at the
tomb and how his body was placed. 56aBut having returned,
they got spices and myrrh ready. 56bAnd then on the Sabbath
they rested according to the commandment.

Index of Principal Comments:
1167
1169
1226
1228
1229
1254
1256
1257
1287

THE PASSION ACCORDING TO JOHN
(John 18:1–19:42)

Translation	Index of Principal Comments

Arrest in the Garden across the Kidron (18:1–11)

1Having said these things, Jesus went out with his disciples across the Kidron valley where there was a garden into
which he entered with his disciples. 2But Judas too, the one
who was giving him over, knew this place because many

Index of Principal Comments:
122
149
245
246

---

times Jesus had come there together with his disciples. ³So
Judas, having taken the cohort and, from the chief priests   248
and the Pharisees, attendants, comes there with lanterns and   249–251
torches and weapons. ⁴So Jesus, having known all the things   259–262
to come upon him, came out and says to them, "Whom are
you seeking?" ⁵They answered him, "Jesus the Nazorean."
He says to them, "I am (he)." Now standing there with them   260
was also Judas, the one who was giving him over.

   ⁶So as Jesus said to them, "I am (he)," they went backward   261
and fell to the ground. ⁷So again he asked them, "Whom are
you seeking?" But they said, "Jesus the Nazorean." ⁸Jesus
answered, "I told you that I am (he). If therefore you are   289
seeking me, let these go away, ⁹in order that the word may   290
be fulfilled which says that 'those whom you have given me,
I have not lost one of them.'" ¹⁰So Simon Peter, having a   267
sword, pulled it out and hit at the servant of the high priest,   272
and cut off his right ear. (The name of the servant was   271
Malchus.) ¹¹So Jesus said to Peter, "Put the sword into the   278
scabbard. The cup the Father has given me—am I not to
drink it?"

Jesus before the High Priest (18:12–27)

   ¹²Thereupon the cohort and the tribune and the attendants   400,402
of the Jews took Jesus and bound him. ¹³And they led (him)
first to Annas, for he was father-in-law of Caiaphas who was   404–411
high priest that year. (¹⁴Now Caiaphas was the one who had
advised the Jews that "It is better that one man die for the
people.") ¹⁵But following Jesus was Simon Peter and another   589
disciple. But that disciple was known to the high priest, and
he entered together with Jesus into the court of the high   592
priest. ¹⁶But Peter was standing at the gate outside. Accord-   596
ingly the other disciple, the one known to the high priest,   597
came out and spoke to the gatekeeper and brought Peter in.
¹⁷And so the servant woman, the gatekeeper, says to Peter,
"Are you too one of the disciples of this man?" He says, "I   599
am not." ¹⁸But the servants and the attendants were standing

around, having made a charcoal fire because it was cold; and   595
they were warming themselves. But Peter too was with them,
standing and warming himself.

¹⁹Thereupon the high priest questioned Jesus about his   411
disciples and about his teaching. ²⁰Jesus answered him, "I   414
have spoken openly to the world. I always taught in a syna-   415,286
gogue and in the Temple, where all the Jews come together;
and in secret I spoke nothing. ²¹Why do you question me?   415
Question those who have heard what I spoke to them. Behold these know what I said."

²²But when he had said these things, one of the attendants   416
who was standing by gave Jesus a slap, saying, "In such a   416,585
way do you answer the high priest?" ²³Jesus answered him,
"If I have spoken badly, give testimony about what is bad. If   416
(I have spoken) well, why do you beat me?" ²⁴Thereupon
Annas sent him bound to Caiaphas the high priest.   405

²⁵But Simon Peter was standing there and warming him-   600
self. So they said to him, "Are you too one of his disciples?"
And he denied and said, "I am not."

²⁶One [masc.] of the servants of the high priest, being a   603
relative of him whose ear Peter had cut off, says, "Didn't I
see you in the garden with him?" ²⁷And so Peter denied
again, and immediately a cock crowed.   605

The Roman Trial (18:28–19:16a)

²⁸Then they lead Jesus from Caiaphas to the praetorium.   743–749
Now it was early. And they did not enter into the praetorium   744
lest they be defiled and in order that they might eat the Pass- 745
over (meal). ²⁹So Pilate went out to them and says, "What
accusation do you bring against this man?" ³⁰They answered   746
and said to him, "If this fellow were not doing what is bad,
we would not have given him over to you." ³¹So Pilate said
to them, "Take him yourselves, and according to your law
judge him." The Jews said to him, "It is not permitted us to   747
put anyone to death," ³²in order that there might be fulfilled

the word of Jesus that he spoke, signifying what kind of
death he was going to die.

³³So Pilate went again into the praetorium, and called Je- 749–753
sus and said to him, "Are you the King of the Jews?" ³⁴Jesus 749,727
answered, "Of yourself do you say this, or have others told
you this about me?" ³⁵Pilate answered, "Am I a Jew? Your
nation and the chief priests have given you over to me. What
have you done?" ³⁶Jesus answered, "My kingdom is not of 750
this world. If my kingdom were of this world, my attendants
would have struggled lest I be given over to the Jews. But as
it is, my kingdom is not from here." ³⁷So Pilate said to him,
"So then you are a king." Jesus answered, "You say that I am 751,727
a king. The reason for which I have been born and for which
I have come into the world is that I may bear witness to the
truth. Everyone who is of the truth hears my voice." ³⁸ᵃPilate
says to him, "What is truth?" 752

³⁸ᵇAnd having said this, again he went out to the Jews and 793
says to them, "I find no case at all against him. ³⁹You have a
custom that I release to you one person at Passover. So do 794
you desire that I release to you 'the King of the Jews'?" ⁴⁰So 800
they yelled back, "Not this fellow but Barabbas." But Barab- 807
bas was a bandit. 808,797

¹⁹:¹Then Pilate took Jesus and had him scourged. ²And the 827
soldiers, having woven a crown of thorns, put it on his head; 865
and they clothed him with a purple robe. ³And they were
coming up to him and saying, "Hail, O King of the Jews." 868
And they gave him slaps. 869

⁴And again Pilate went outside and says to them, "Look, 826–830
I lead him out to you so that you may know that I find no
case at all [against him]." ⁵Therefore, Jesus went outside
bearing the thorny crown and the purple robe; and he [Pilate]
says to them, "Behold the man." ⁶So when the chief priests 827
and the attendants saw him, they yelled out saying, "Crucify,
crucify." Pilate says to them, "Take him yourselves and cru- 829
cify, for I do not find a case against him." ⁷The Jews answered him, "We have a law, and according to the law he

ought to die, because he has made himself God's Son." ⁸So when Pilate heard this statement, he was more afraid.　830

⁹And he went back into the praetorium and says to Jesus,　840–849 "From where are you?" But Jesus did not give him an answer. ¹⁰So Pilate says, "Do you not speak to me? Do you not　841 know that I have power to release you and power to crucify you?" ¹¹Jesus answered, "You have no power over me at all　842 except what was given to you from above. Therefore the one who gave me over to you has the greater sin."

¹²From this Pilate was seeking to release him. But the　843 Jews yelled out saying, "If you release this fellow, you are not a friend of Caesar. Anyone who makes himself a king contradicts Caesar." ¹³Now Pilate, having heard these words,　844,1388 led Jesus outside and sat on the judgment seat in the place called Lithostrotos, but in Hebrew Gabbatha. ¹⁴Now it was　845 preparation day for Passover; it was the sixth hour. And he　846 says to the Jews, "Look, your king." ¹⁵So they yelled out,　848 "Take (him), take (him), crucify him." Pilate says to them, "Shall I crucify your king?" The chief priests answered, "We have no king but Caesar." ¹⁶ᵃSo then he gave him over to　849 them in order that he be crucified.　855

Jesus Crucified and Buried (19:16b–42)

¹⁶ᵇSo they took Jesus along; ¹⁷and carrying the cross by　911,916 himself, he came out to what is called the Place of the Skull,　936 which is called in Hebrew Golgotha, ¹⁸where they crucified　945 him and with him two others, here and there, but Jesus in　968 the middle.

¹⁹But Pilate also wrote a notice and put it on the cross.　962 Now it was written, "Jesus the Nazorean, the King of the　964–968 Jews." ²⁰So many of the Jews read this notice because the place where he was crucified was near the city, and it was written in Hebrew, Latin, and Greek. ²¹So the chief priests　966 of the Jews were saying to Pilate, "Do not write 'The King of the Jews,' but that that fellow said, 'I am King of the Jews.'" ²²Pilate answered, "What I have written, I have written."　967

Index of
Principal
Comments

---

²³So the soldiers, when they crucified Jesus, took his
clothes and made four parts, a part to each soldier; and (they   952
took) the tunic. Now the tunic was without seam, from the   955–958
top woven throughout. ²⁴So they said to one another, "Let us
not tear it, but let us gamble about it (to see) whose it is," in
order that the Scripture be fulfilled,   953

    They divided up my clothes among themselves,
    and for my clothing they threw lots.
So then the soldiers did these things.

²⁵But there was standing near the cross of Jesus his   1013–26
mother, and his mother's sister, Mary of Clopas, and Mary   1014
Magdalene. ²⁶So Jesus, having seen his mother and the dis-   1019
ciple whom he loved standing nearby, says to his mother,
"Woman, look: your son." ²⁷Then he says to the disciple,
"Look: your mother." And from that hour the disciple took   1023
her to his own.

²⁸After this, Jesus having known that already all was fin-   1069–78
ished, in order that the Scripture be completed, says, "I   1072
thirst." ²⁹A jar was there laden with vinegary wine. So, putting on hyssop a sponge laden with the vinegary wine, they   1074
brought it forward to his mouth. ³⁰So when he took the vine-   1077
gary wine, Jesus said, "It is finished"; and having bowed his   1078
head, he gave over the spirit.   1082

³¹Then the Jews, since it was preparation day, in order that   1173–88
the bodies might not remain on the cross on the Sabbath, for
that Sabbath was a great day, asked Pilate that their legs be   1175
broken and they be taken away. ³²So the soldiers came and   1176
broke the legs of the one and of the other who had been
crucified with him; ³³but having come to Jesus, when they
saw him already dead, they did not break his legs. ³⁴How-   1177
ever, one of the soldiers stabbed his side with a lance, and
immediately there came out blood and water. ³⁵And the one   1178
who has seen has borne witness, and true is his witness; and   1182
that one knows that he speaks what is true in order that you
too may believe. ³⁶For these things happened in order that   1184
the Scripture might be fulfilled: "Its (his) bone shall not be   1185

fractured." ³⁷And again another Scripture says, "They shall   1186
see whom they have pierced."

³⁸But after these things Joseph from Arimathea, being a   1230
disciple of Jesus but hidden because of fear of the Jews,   1231
asked Pilate that he might take away the body of Jesus, and
Pilate permitted (it). So he came and took away his body.   1258–70
³⁹But there came also Nicodemus, the one who had first   1259
come to him at night, bringing a mixture of myrrh and aloes,   1261
about a hundred pounds. ⁴⁰So they took the body of Jesus;   1260
and they bound it with cloths together with spices, as is the   1264
custom among the Jews for burying. ⁴¹But there was in the
place where he was crucified a garden, and in the garden a   1268
new tomb in which no one had ever yet been placed. ⁴²So
there, on account of the preparation day of the Jews, because
the tomb was near, they placed Jesus.